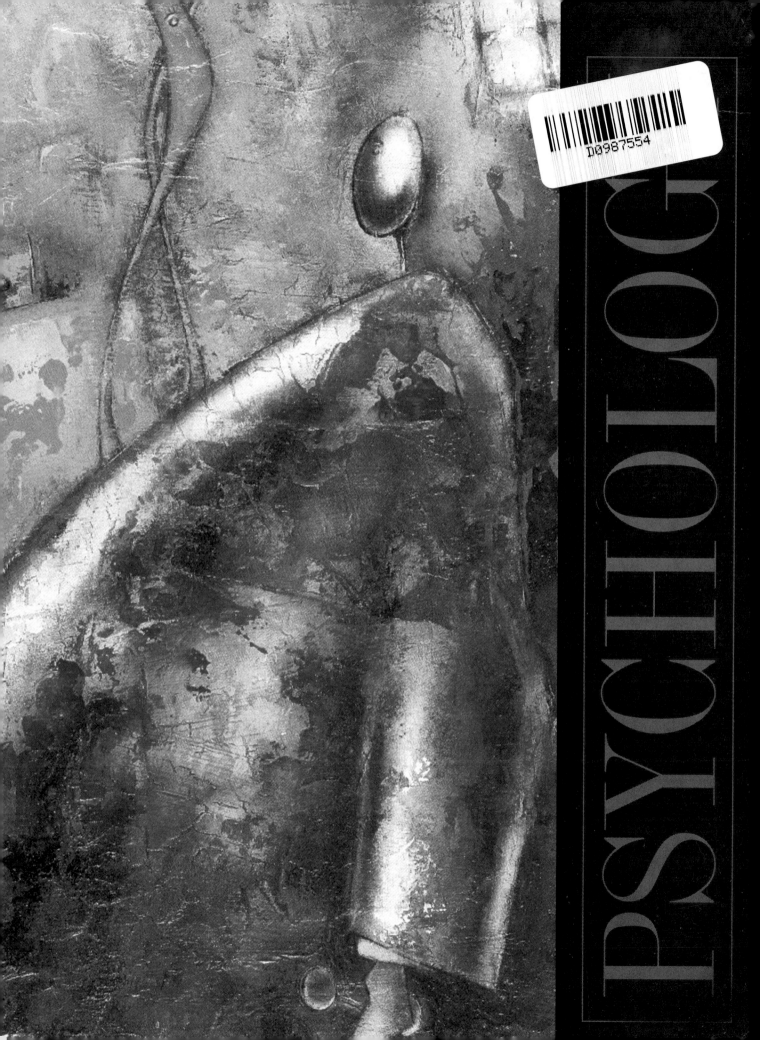

PSYCHOLOGY

third edition

PSYCHOLOGY

lester m. sdorow

lafayette college
beaver college

WCB Brown &
Benchmark
PUBLISHERS

Madison, Wisconsin · Dubuque, Iowa

Book Team

Executive Editor   *Michael Lange*
Production Editor   *Gloria G. Schiesl*
Designer   *Eric Engelby*
Art Editor   *Mary E. Powers*
Photo Editor   *Rose Deluhery*
Permissions Coordinator   *Karen L. Storlie*
Visuals/Design Freelance Specialist   *Mary L. Christianson*
Marketing Manager   *Steven Yetter*
Promotions Manager   *Mike Matera*
Production Manager   *Beth Kundert*

**WCB Brown &
Benchmark**

A Division of Wm. C. Brown Communications, Inc.

Executive Vice President/General Manager   *Thomas E. Doran*
Vice President/Editor in Chief   *Edgar J. Laube*
Vice President/Marketing and Sales Systems   *Eric Ziegler*
Vice President/Production   *Vickie Putman*
Director of Custom and Electronic Publishing   *Chris Rogers*
National Sales Manager   *Bob McLaughlin*

Wm. C. Brown Communications, Inc.

President and Chief Executive Officer   *G. Franklin Lewis*
Senior Vice President, Operations   *James H. Higby*
Corporate Senior Vice President and President of Manufacturing   *Roger Meyer*
Corporate Senior Vice President and Chief Financial Officer   *Robert Chesterman*

The credits section for this book begins on page C–1 and is
considered an extension of the copyright page.

Cover: "The Diceman" —illustration by Brad Gray

Copyedited by Wendy Nelson

In memory of my grandmother, Rose, who made it all possible.

BRIEF CONTENTS

6
CONSCIOUSNESS

7
LEARNING

8
MEMORY

9

THINKING AND LANGUAGE

10

INTELLIGENCE

11

MOTIVATION

12
EMOTION

13
PERSONALITY

14

PSYCHOLOGICAL DISORDERS

15

THERAPY

16
PSYCHOLOGY
AND HEALTH

17
SOCIAL BEHAVIOR

ANATOMY OF A CLASSIC RESEARCH STUDY

PREFACE

In regard to authors, it has been said that there is the book one intended to write, the book one thought one wrote, and the book one actually wrote. According to responses from users and reviewers of the first two editions of this book, the book I actually wrote was, indeed, the one I intended to write and thought I had written.

What was the book I intended to write? To accomplish all that I originally intended, the book would easily have been twice as long as it is now. A century ago, William James, disturbed at the length of his now-classic *Principles of Psychology*, gave his own stinging review of it. He called it, among other things, "a bloated tumescent mass." Though this comment may have been written during one of James's frequent bouts with depression, it indicates that, from psychology's inception as a separate discipline, authors of introductory psychology textbooks have been confronted with the need to convey a broad discipline to students in a book of reasonable length. Given that psychology has become an even broader discipline and has accumulated an enormous information base, I quickly discovered that I would somehow have to manipulate a kind of intellectual "Rubik's cube" of seven goals to avoid producing a bloated, tumescent mass (or what textbook reviewers often, perhaps euphemistically, refer to as an "encyclopedic" book). My goals could only be achieved by considering each goal in light of the others.

MY SEVEN GOALS

1. To Do Justice to the Breadth of Psychology

My students often express amazement at the breadth of psychology. One psychologist might devote a career to studying the relationship between brain activity and schizophrenia; another might devote a career to studying the social factors that promote human love. And while one member of a psychology department studies the perceptual abilities of newborn infants, another studies the language abilities of chimpanzees. Because of this breadth, I was forced to be selective in the topics, studies, and concepts that I included in the book. Nonetheless, I believe the book presents a fair, representative sampling of the discipline.

2. To Present Material in Sufficient, but not Excessive, Detail

Again compromise was in order. As a teacher and a student, I have disliked textbooks that go to extremes. At one extreme are textbooks that present many topics but only superficial coverage of them. At the other extreme are textbooks that present fewer topics but overwhelm the reader with details. Though my discussions of topics naturally vary somewhat in their extensiveness, I have provided enough information to assure student comprehension, while permitting coverage of a sufficient number of topics to assure a good representation of the entire discipline. The main exceptions to this approach are topics covered in greater depth in the "Thinking about Psychology" sections (discussed below) that end each chapter.

3. To Encourage Appreciation of the Research Process

A psychology textbook should provide students with more than theories and research findings. It should discuss "how we know" as well as "what we know." To give students enough background to appreciate the research process, I introduce, in chapter 2, psychology as a science, the methods of psychological research, and the statistical analysis of research data. The chapter includes a concrete example of the scientific method that shows how it relates to a classic study of interpersonal attraction. The chapter also includes data from a hypothetical health-psychology study and tells how to calculate descriptive statistics using that data.

In trying to help the student appreciate the research process, I have once again tried to strike a balance throughout the book by discussing research studies in moderate detail. For examples of this, turn to page 325 for the discussion of a study on naturalistic concepts in which nonartists formed concepts of artistic styles from paintings without being able to state the defining features that distinguish one style from another; or turn to page 583 and read the discussion of a study of the use of classical conditioning to suppress the immune system. The moderately detailed discussion of research studies contrasts with textbooks that present little more than research findings and with textbooks that describe research studies in overwhelming detail.

4. To Promote Critical Thinking

I believe that students should know scientific methodology, research findings, and how to critically evaluate what they read by relying on objective, rational evaluation of empirical evidence. Chapter 2 describes formal steps in thinking critically. Students will find that the ability to think critically benefits them in their daily lives when confronted with claims made by friends, relatives, politicians, advertisers, or anyone else. Almost every page of this book gives the student an opportunity to think about popular claims, provide alternative explanations for research findings, or think of possible implications of research findings. For an example of how I have integrated critical thinking in the text, turn to page 231 for a discussion of hypnosis as an altered state of consciousness. Most of the "Thinking about Psychology" sections also provide extended examples of critical thinking.

5. To Present Psychology in Context

An article in the June 1991 issue of the *American Psychologist,* dealing with psychology and the liberal arts curriculum, stressed that providing students with the historical context of psychology is an essential goal in undergraduate psychology education. Introductory psychology textbooks should not present psychology as though it developed in "ivory towers" divorced from a historical or personal context. Throughout this book, you will find many ways in which topics are given a historical grounding. For example, chapter 10 traces the nature-nurture debate regarding intelligence back to the work of Francis Galton and the flood of immigrants in the early twentieth century. And chapter 11 highlights changing values concerning sexuality by discussing the case of an article submitted to the *Journal of the American Medical Association* in 1899 but not published until 1983.

I have also taken care to show that psychology is a human endeavor, practiced by people with emotions as well as intellects, and that scientific progress depends on serendipity as well as cool calculation. For example, chapter 1 discusses William James's effort to have Harvard University grant the doctoral degree to Mary Whiton Calkins, who became an eminent psychologist, but who, as a woman, was denied the degree despite fulfilling the requirements for it. Chapter 3 tells how the first demonstration of the chemical basis of communication between nerve cells came to Otto Loewi in a dream. Chapter 7 explains why the name *Pavlov* rings a bell but the name *Twitmyer* does not. And chapter 10 describes how psychoanalyst Alfred Adler's concept of the inferiority complex may be rooted in his own sickly childhood.

6. To Present a Balanced and Scholarly View of Psychology

This is not a psychoanalytic book, a behavioristic book, a cognitive book, a humanistic book, or a biopsychological book. It is a bit of each, which reflects my belief that an introductory psychology textbook should introduce students to a variety of perspectives, rather than reflect the author's favored one. Over the decades, the perspectives have waxed and waned in their dominance. Students are introduced to the major psychological perspectives in chapter 1 and continue to encounter them throughout the book, most obviously in the chapters on personality, psychological disorders, and therapy.

For students to respect psychology as a science, the textbook they use must be scholarly. Though popular examples are sprinkled throughout this text, they are not used as substitutes for evidence provided by scientific research. A perusal of the reference list at the end of the text reveals that it is up-to-date in its coverage of research studies, yet does not slight classic studies. Of course, solving my intellectual "Rubik's cube" prevented me from including every important classic study or many other worthy "cutting edge" studies.

7. To Show the Relevance of Psychology to Everyday Life

I enjoy books that give me a sense of the author by providing "coloration" for the typically sober material that is presented. I believe that the examples I use in showing the relevance of psychology to everyday life provides this coloration. The examples come from virtually every area of life, including art, literature, history, biography, entertainment, sport, politics, and student life. Instead of showing the relevance of psychology by using the common practice of segregating it in "boxes," I have interwoven the examples into the body of the text. For example, page 221 provides research-based suggestions for overcoming insomnia, page 270 discusses how operant conditioning is used to train animals, and page 306 describes ways to improve one's memory and study habits.

SPECIAL FEATURES

Anatomy of a Research Study

New to this edition of the text is a unique examination of research methodology. Beginning with chapter 2, each chapter now features brief expositions of both a classic and a contemporary psychological research study. These "Anatomy of a Research Study" sections briefly highlight the rationale, methods, and results of featured studies in an accessible manner for beginning students. These studies are tied directly to the text discussion and emphasize both methodology and critical thinking. This new feature reinforces the focus on essential and ongoing issues of psychology that run throughout the book and is highlighted in the "Thinking about Psychology" sections that end each chapter.

Thinking about Psychology

In a senior seminar course I have taught over the years, entitled "Current Issues in Psychology," students read many journal articles and some popular articles on a host of controversial topics, which they then discuss or debate. Because of the success of this course—students enjoy sinking their teeth into controversial issues—I have adapted its rationale for this text in many of the topics covered in the "Thinking about Psychology" sections. To provide adequate discussion of each topic, I devote several pages to presenting the status of a particular issue or application.

Many of the topics in these sections illustrate how psychologists think critically about issues such as hemispheric specialization, parapsychology, unconscious influences, ape language, personality consistency, effectiveness of psychotherapy, and Type A behavior. Other "Thinking about Psychology" sections illustrate the connection of research to practical reality, as in the sections discussing biofeedback and motivation and sport. And some of the sections illustrate how scientific issues cannot always be divorced from ethics, values, and politics; these include the sections on the ethics of psychological research, the nature-nurture controversy in regard to intelligence, the study of sex differences, the insanity defense, and the effect of pornography on aggression.

Marginal Glossary

A marginal glossary eliminates the need to torture one's prose into the formal tone of a dictionary definition when introducing new concepts. Terms that are printed in boldface are defined in the margins. The marginal definitions are also collected in a page-referenced glossary at the end of the book, which provides a handy reference for students who encounter those terms in other chapters.

Illustrations

I selected or helped design all of the illustrations in this book. In doing so, I tried to make each of them serve a sound pedagogical purpose. Though the illustrations make the book aesthetically more appealing, they were chosen mainly because their visual presentations complement material discussed in the text.

Recommended Readings

I believe that the list of recommended readings at the end of each chapter is a unique feature of the book. The lists are extensive and are arranged according to the major headings of the chapters. Each list ends with biographical or autobiographical readings about contributors to psychology. The readings provide substantial material for students who are interested in learning more about particular topics or persons, or who would like a starting point for writing research papers.

Appendix A: Majoring in Psychology

The appendix "Majoring in Psychology" will prove useful for psychology majors interested in preparing for a career. It might also help other students decide whether or not to major in psychology.

Appendix B: Statistics

The appendix "Statistics" provides an extended discussion and examples of the use of statistics in describing and making inferences from research data.

Other Features

Each chapter begins with an *outline* to provide a skeleton on which to place the content of the chapter. Each chapter ends with a *summary* that captures the essential points made in the major sections of the chapter. Following the summary is an alphabetical list of *important concepts,* which were boldfaced in the text, and the page numbers on which they were discussed. This is followed by a list of *major contributors*, important figures who were discussed in the chapter. All of the textual citations are collected in a *reference section* at the end of the book. Also included are a *name index* and a *subject index*.

CHANGES IN THE THIRD EDITION

The responses of professors and students to the second edition indicated that I had accomplished my goals well enough that wholesale revisions in the organization or content of the book were unnecessary. After synthesizing comments from users and reviewers, I found that they considered the second edition scholarly and challenging, yet interesting and clearly written. They particularly appreciated its attention to the historical context of psychology. As many pundits have noted, "If it ain't broke, don't fix it." Nonetheless, I have made some important changes in the third edition.

First, the feature called "Anatomy of a Research Study" has been added. Second, the book has been updated to keep up with advances in the discipline. It contains hundreds of new references. Third, the treatment of many topics has been expanded, while the treatment of a few has been condensed. The most notable example of the latter is the combination of developmental psychology into one unified chapter. The net result is a third edition that is significantly shorter than the previous edition, making it more usable for a single term. Finally, the new edition also features greater emphasis on issues of human diversity. Expanded treatment of gender issues and cultural factors that influence behavior now runs throughout the entire text.

REQUEST FOR COMMENTS

Realizing that the ideal textbook might be approached, but never achieved, I would welcome your comments about the book and suggestions for improving it. Just as user comments improved the second edition, user comments will improve the third edition. Please send your correspondence to the following address:

Lester M. Sdorow
c/o Psychology Editor
Brown and Benchmark Publishers
25 Kessel Court
Madison, WI 53711

A SPECIAL NOTE TO THE STUDENT

Years ago, I was in the position you might be in right now—enrolled in my first psychology course. Serendipity played a part in my enrolling in it. I was an English major looking for an elective course to fit into my schedule. I had not even considered taking psychology—that is, until one day, while perusing the course listings, I heard a fellow student rave about how terrific his introductory psychology course was. Trusting his judgment, I enrolled in that course and, as they say, the rest is history.

I changed my major to psychology and have never regretted it—though I never lost my love for English. Of course, most students who take introductory psychology courses are not psychology majors, and most of them will never take another psychology course. In writing this textbook, I have kept the student in mind. The book reflects my attempt to include qualities I have preferred in the teachers I have had and the textbooks I have read. I have preferred teachers and textbooks that are well-organized, explain concepts clearly, provide interesting examples of concepts, and use visual aids. Thus, I believe you will find the book coherent; written in a clear, conversational tone; packed with interesting, concrete examples of all concepts; and easier to comprehend because of its judicious use of illustrations. I hope that psychology will appeal to you as an intellectual pursuit, if not a career choice.

This textbook has several features designed to make your task easier. Each chapter begins with an outline that indicates major topics and subtopics. Use the outlines to organize the information that you read and memorize. The boldfaced terms in each chapter are defined in the margins and collected together in a glossary at the end of the book. Mastering these terms is an important step in comprehending the material and studying for exams. All concepts introduced in the book are accompanied by concrete examples from research or everyday life. Thus, you are provided with more than abstract definitions. The illustrations complement the material in the text, as well as make your task more aesthetically pleasing. You might find the summary at the end of each chapter useful as either an overview of the chapter or as a quick way to recall the major points in the chapter. The lists of important concepts and major contributors at the end of each chapter are good study tools. And the lists of recommended readings provide you with sources of additional information on topics or persons you find interesting.

SUPPLEMENTARY MATERIALS

With Brown & Benchmark, I've tried to combine a student-oriented textbook with an integrated ancillary package designed to meet the unique needs of instructors and students. Our goal has been to create a package that is as enjoyable to teach with as it is to study from.

The **Instructor's Course Planner,** prepared by Steven A. Schneider of Pima Community College, provides separate teaching units for each major topic in the textbook. Learning objectives, lecture suggestions, film suggestions, and much more information is provided, along with an array of suggested classroom activities and handouts. The Instructor's Course Planner is also available on disk for IBM, Apple, or Macintosh computers.

The Course Planner can be arranged by chapter, along with an unbound copy of each text chapter, your own notes, the Course Success Guide, and the Transparency Sets, allowing you to keep all of your classroom materials organized and at your fingertips.

The **Test Item File,** which I personally compiled, has more than 2,000 multiple-choice items. This is meant to provide instructors with a large selection of consistently high-quality test items. I wrote many new items especially for the third edition of this text. Each item is keyed to the text and learning objectives and designated as factual, conceptual, or applied, using the first three levels of Benjamin Bloom's *Taxonomy of Educational Objectives.* Many of the items in this Test Item File were class-tested by my colleagues James Calhoun at the University of Georgia, Edwin Martin at the University of Kansas, and Frank Vattano at Colorado State University. With their help, I am able to provide a core of proven items as well as a selection of new items. Al Cohen, director of the Office of Testing and Evaluation Services at the University of Wisconsin–Madison, also provided valuable assistance in the development of this Test Item File.

Test Item File #2 was constructed by Richmond Johnson of Moravian College and contains an additional 2,500 multiple-choice items. A special feature of this test bank is the inclusion of over 800 items from the Course Success Guide, which are clearly identified for your use.

Test Item File #3 was constructed by Bradley Caskey of the University of Wisconsin–River Falls. Brad is an award-winning teacher and has worked extensively with the Educational Testing Service (ETS) as a writer of test items for the Advanced Placement Test for Psychology. This comprehensive test bank includes an additional 2,500 items, giving instructors who adopt this textbook a total of 7,000 multiple-choice items to choose from in creating their exams.

The questions in the Test Item Files are available on **MicroTest III,** a powerful but easy-to-use test-generating program by Chariot Software Group. MicroTest is available for DOS, Windows, and Macintosh. With MicroTest, instructors can easily select questions from the Test Item File and print tests and answer keys. Instructors can also customize questions, headings, and instructions; add or import their own questions; and print tests in a choice of printer-supported fonts. Contact your local Brown & Benchmark sales representative for more information.

The **Course Success Guide,** also by Richmond E. Johnson, provides students with friendly, practical advice for success in the introductory psychology course and beyond. This helpful manual offers, among its many learning activities, a guided review and four practice tests for each chapter.

The **Brown & Benchmark Reference Disk Set,** which I created, is available free to adopters. The disks include over 15,000 journal and book references arranged in files by introductory topics. The complete set of five disks is available in either 5.25- or 3.5-inch size.

The **Brown & Benchmark Introductory Psychology Transparency or Slide Set** includes approximately 150 full-color acetates or slides specifically designed for classroom use. A second set of 60 additional full-color transparencies or slides based upon selected visuals in *Psychology*, Third Edition, is also available to adopters.

A large selection of **videotapes** is also available to adopters, based upon the number of textbooks ordered directly from Brown & Benchmark by your bookstore.

The AIDS Booklet, Third Edition, by Frank D. Cox of Santa Barbara City College, is a brief but comprehensive introduction to the Acquired Immune Deficiency Syndrome, which is caused by HIV (Human Immunodeficiency Virus) and related viruses.

The Critical Thinker, written by Richard Mayer and Fiona Goodchild of the University of California, Santa Barbara, uses excerpts from introductory psychology textbooks to show students how to think critically about psychology. Either this or the AIDS booklet is available at no charge to first-year adopters of our textbook. Both can be purchased separately.

Our **Custom Publishing Service** also allows you to have your own notes, handouts, or other classroom materials printed and bound very inexpensively for your course use. Contact your Brown & Benchmark representative for details.

A **Customized Transparency Program** is available to adopters of *Psychology*, Third Edition, based on the number of textbooks ordered. Consult your Brown & Benchmark representative for ordering policies.

The Psychology Disk is a set of 10 interactive simulations of psychology experiments designed for student use. The disk can be used with IBM and compatible hardware. Your bookstore can order The Psychology Disk directly from Brown & Benchmark.

The Brown & Benchmark Human Development Interactive Videodisc Set contains a series of short (3–5 minute) segments designed to help you begin lectures or cover additional topics in the classroom. Consult your Brown & Benchmark sales representative for details.

The Brain Modules on Videodisc, created by WNET New York, Antenne 2 TV/France, the Annenberg/CPB Foundation, and Professor Frank J. Vattano of Colorado State University, is based upon the Peabody award-winning series "The Brain." Thirty segments, averaging 6 minutes each, vividly illustrate an array of psychology topics. Consult your Brown & Benchmark sales representative for details.

ACKNOWLEDGMENTS

In revising this book, I have continued to appreciate the pride and intrinsic interest of the editorial staff at Brown & Benchmark in producing textbooks of high quality. Michael Lange, psychology editor, has been a constant source of wisdom, creative insights, and emotional support. My developmental editor, Sheralee Connors, provided valuable sounding boards for my practical concerns and "author's rantings." Production editor Gloria Schiesl once again showed her remarkable ability to maintain a cordial demeanor while undergoing the stress of coordinating the many persons who contribute to the creation of a textbook. The beautiful appearance of the book also owes much to the diligence and expertise of book designer Eric Engelby, art editor Mary Swift, and photo editor Rose Deluhery. I would also like to thank permissions editor Karen Storlie, who again made my life easier by her conscientious performance of a tedious task.

A special thanks is owed those who contributed to the ancillaries that are available with this book. My longtime friend and mentor Rick Johnson contributed his 30 years of teaching experience in writing a truly distinctive study guide. My newer friend Steve Schneider has created a marvelous course planner. Rick Johnson and Brad Caskey also each created an excellent Test Item File.

Any of the good qualities of the textbook owe themselves in great measure to the many reviewers who read drafts of this text in part or in whole. I have valued, seriously considered, and even savored, each of their suggestions.

For their help with the third edition, I'd like to thank the following individuals:

Barbara L. Andersen, *Ohio State University*
Robert C. Beck, *Wake Forest University*
Virginia Wise Berninger, *University of Washington*
Fredda Blanchard-Fields, *Louisiana State University*
Laura Freberg, *California Polytechnic State University, San Luis Obispo*
Malcolm Grant, *Memorial University of Newfoundland*
Elaine Hatfield, *University of Hawaii*
Susan M. Heidenreich, *Loyola University, New Orleans*
Valerye A. Hunt, *University College of the Frazier Valley*
Mindy L. Kornhaber, *Harvard University*
Randy J. Larsen, *University of Michigan*
Mark R. Leary, *Wake Forest University*
Thomas Hardy Leahey, *Virginia Commonwealth University*
Paul A. Miller, *Arizona State University West*
Jodi A. Mindell, *St. Joseph's University*
David I. Mostofsky, *Boston University*
Tibor Palfai, *Syracuse University*
Cheryl L. Sisk, *Michigan State University*
Sara Rader Staats, *Ohio State University, Newark*
Benjamin Wallace, *Cleveland State University*

I'd also like to thank my colleagues who reviewed this text in its first and second editions:

Thomas R. Alley, *Clemson University*
Joseph Bilotta, *Vanderbilt University*
J. E. Boggs, *Purdue University*
John P. Broida, *University of Southern Maine*
J. S. Caldwell, *California State University, Chico*
James F. Calhoun, *University of Georgia*
J. B. Clement, *Dayton Beach Community College*
Kenneth Coffield, *University of Alabama*
Richard T. Comstock, *Monroe Community College*
Katherine Covell, *Brock University*
Patricia Crane, *San Antonio College*
Joseph Culkin, *Queensborough Community College*
Duane Cuthbertson, *Bryan College*
George M. Diekhoff, *Midwestern State University*
Paul Doerksen, *University of Saskatchewan*
Thomas Evans, *John Carroll University*
William F. Ford, *Bucks County Community College*
Laurel Furomoto, *Wellesley College*
Grace Galliano, *Kennesaw College*
William Glassman, *Ryerson Polytechnical Institute*
Richard Haude, *University of Akron*
Peter Hill, *Grove City College*
Morton Hoffman, *Metropolitan State College*
James E. Jans, *Concordia College*
James Johnson, *Illinois State University*
Richmond Johnson, *Moravian College*
Seth Kalichman, *Medical College of Wisconsin*
Cindy Kennedy, *University of Dayton*
Melvyn King, *SUNY-Cortland*
Daniel K. Lapsley, *Brandon University*

Fred Leavitt, *California State University, Hayward*
T. C. Lewandowski, *Delaware County Community College*
Inez Livingston, *Eastern Illinois College*
Karen Macrae, *University of South Carolina*
Leonard Mark, *Miami University*
Mark McCourt, *North Dakota State University*
Kevin Moore, *DePauw University*
James Mosely, *University of Calgary*
W. Stephen Royce, *University of Portland*
Ina Samuels, *University of Massachusetts*
Steven Schneider, *Pima Community College*
Thomas J. Schoeneman, *Lewis & Clark College*
R. Lance Shotland, *Pennsylvania State University*
Dale Simmons, *Oregon State University*
Gordon Timothy, *Ricks College*
Frank Vattano, *Colorado State University*
Wayne Viney, *Colorado State University*
Deborah Du Nann Winter, *Whitman College*

I also owe special thanks to my colleagues, students, friends, and family. My department chairpersons, Barbara Nodine of Beaver College and Susan Basow, Howard Gallup, and Ann McGillicuddy-Delisi of Lafayette College, have provided me with the opportunity to teach in two psychology departments that are dedicated to excellence in undergraduate psychology.

I have benefited from the continued support of my brother Eric and my sister-in-law Connie, my cousin Caryn Stark, and my friends Gregg Amore, Annette Benert, Jim Buchanan, Phil Curson, Joe Lambert, Aimee Morris and Charles Olson. Special thanks to Lino and Carla Fuentes, as well as Christine Biddington, who have provided me with friendship and great food at the Duck Soup Cafe in New Hope.

Of course, foremost in my mind are my parents. My father, Harvey, was more excited than anyone about my writing and fancied himself an informal editor. He inspired my desire to be excellent in whatever I do. My mother Millie, has been an everpresent source of emotional support and motherly advice.

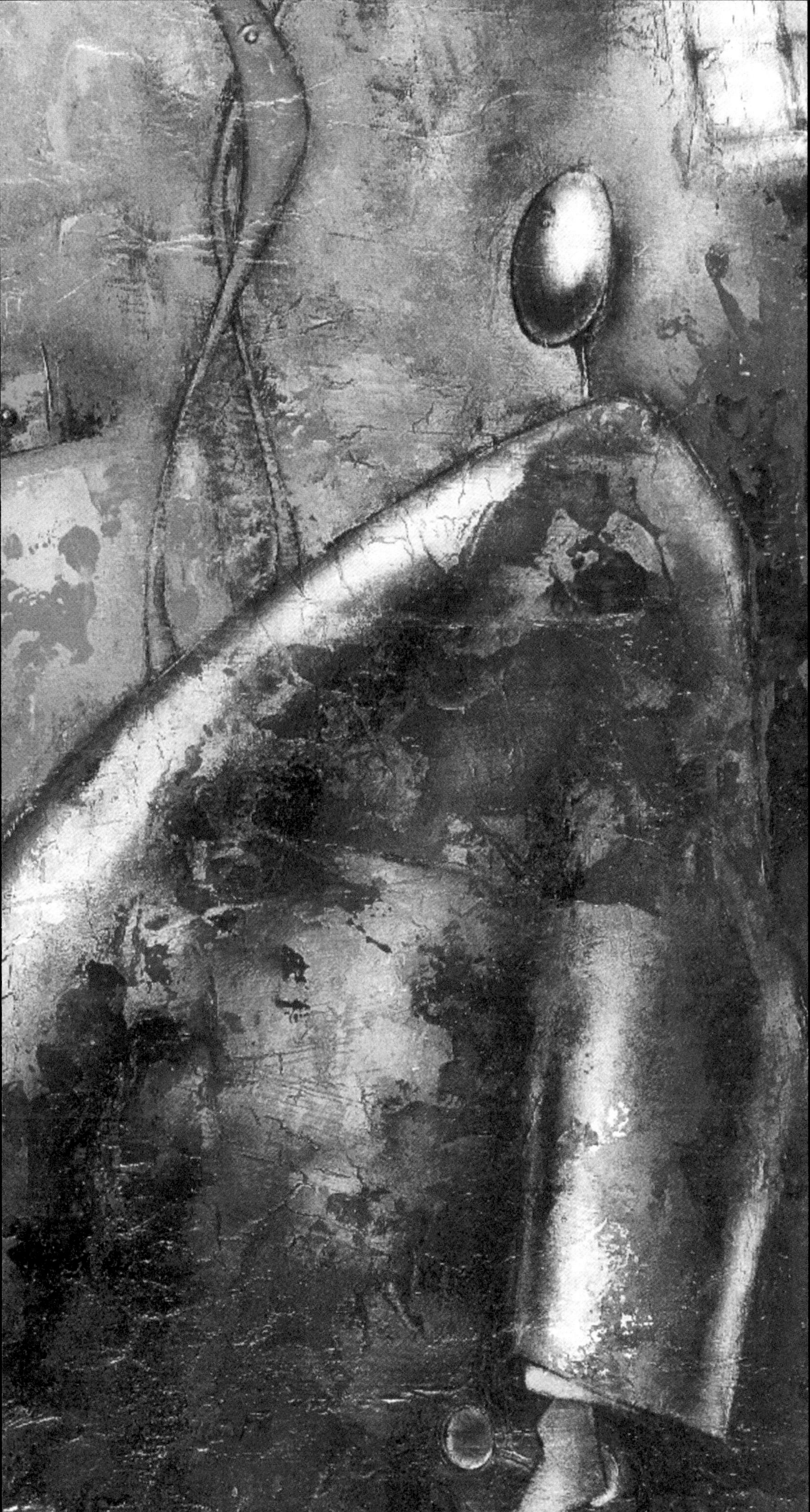

PSYCHOLOGY

Charles Olson
Recognition
1993

THE NATURE OF PSYCHOLOGY

Can brain damage be cured by the transplantation of brain tissue? Do children of working mothers suffer ill effects? Do eyewitnesses give accurate testimony? Can chimpanzees learn to use language? Do lie detectors really detect lies? Is there a heart-attack-prone personality? Does pornography incite violence against women? The science that seeks the answers to these—and thousands of other—diverse questions about human and animal behavior and mental processes is psychology.

But what is psychology? The word *psychology* was coined in the sixteenth century from the Greek terms *psyche,* meaning "soul," and *logos,* meaning "the study of a subject." Thus, the initial meaning of *psychology* was "the study of the soul" (La Pointe, 1970). This reflected the early interest of theologians in topics that are now considered the province of psychologists. Psychology has continued to be defined by its subject matter, which has changed over time. By the late nineteenth century, when psychology emerged as a science, it had become "the Science of Mental Life" (James, 1890/1981, Vol. 1, p. 15).

Beginning in the second decade of this century, many psychologists—believing that a true science can study only directly observable, measurable events—abandoned the study of the mind in favor of the study of overt behavior. This meant that most psychologists moved from studying mental experiences, such as thirst or anger, to studying their observable manifestations in overt behaviors, such as drinking or aggression. Consequently, by the 1920s psychology was commonly defined as "the scientific study of behavior." This definition was widely accepted until the 1960s, when there was a revival of interest in studying the mind. As a result, **psychology** is now more broadly defined as "the science of behavior and mental processes."

psychology
The science of behavior and mental processes.

What makes psychology a science? Psychology is a science because it relies on the *scientific method.* Sciences are "scientific" because they share a common method, not because they share a common subject matter. Physics, chemistry, biology, and psychology differ in what they study, yet each uses the scientific method in pursuit of common goals: description, prediction, control, and explanation. While a chemist might pursue these goals in studying the effects of toxic pollutants, a psychologist might pursue them in studying the behavior or mental experiences of a person suffering from severe depression. The scientific method and the goals of science are discussed in chapter 2.

THE HISTORY OF PSYCHOLOGY

Like any other science, psychology has evolved over time. It has been influenced by developments in other disciplines and by its social, cultural, and historical contexts. To appreciate the nature of psychology today, you must understand its origins. In reading about the history of psychology, or any science, you should avoid **presentism,** which sees the past in the context of present knowledge and beliefs, much in the way "Monday-morning quarterbacks" use second-guessing to evaluate the performance of their favorite teams. Presentism has the unfortunate effect of demeaning the efforts of some of the greatest minds in history by ridiculing claims that are obviously wrong when seen through hindsight. In contrast, **historicism** assumes that claims put forth by scientists must be considered in the context of the available knowledge, methods, and values of their times (Stocking, 1965). Keep this in mind when you read of some seemingly outrageous proclamation made by a historical contributor to psychology. Even geniuses work under practical constraints.

presentism
An approach to history that studies the past in the context of present beliefs and knowledge.

historicism
An approach to history that studies the past for its own sake, in the context of beliefs and knowledge that characterized the period being studied.

The Scientific Study of Behavior and Mental Processes
Psychologists from a variety of fields of psychology could provide insight into the behavior of expert skateboarders. A *biopsychology* researcher might study how their brains control their actions. A *learning* researcher might be interested in how they perfect their skills. A *motivation* researcher might explore the reasons why they choose to become competitive skateboarders. A *health psychologist* might assess the effects of skateboarding on their physical and psychological well-being. And a *social psychology* researcher might be interested in the effect of an audience on their performance.

The Roots of Psychology

Psychology's historical roots are in philosophy and science. When scientists of the late nineteenth century began to use the scientific method to study the mind, psychology became an independent scientific discipline. Though scientists and philosophers alike rely on systematic observation and formal reasoning as sources of knowledge, philosophers rely relatively more on reasoning. For example, a philosopher might use reasoning to argue whether we are ever truly altruistic (that is, completely unselfish) in helping other people, whereas a psychologist might approach this issue by studying the emotional and situational factors that determine whether one person will help another.

The Philosophical Roots of Psychology

The philosophical roots of psychology reach back to the philosophers of ancient Greece, most notably Plato (427–347 B.C.) and Aristotle (384–322 B.C.), who were especially interested in the origin of knowledge. Plato, who was renowned for both physical and mental prowess, excelling as both a soldier and an intellectual, was suspicious of the senses as a source of knowledge. He believed that our senses can deceive us, as in illusions like the apparent bending of a straight stick that is partly immersed in a pool of water. Plato also believed that human beings enter the world with inborn knowledge. He believed that reasoning gives us access to this knowledge, a philosophical approach called **rationalism.** Plato used reason to study a variety of psychological topics, including dreams, perception, and mental illness. Yet, when using reasoning to retrieve supposedly inborn knowledge, even Plato and other brilliant philosophers could be wrong. For example,

rationalism
The philosophical position that true knowledge comes through correct reasoning.

empicicism
The philosophical position that true knowledge comes through the senses.

Plato reasoned, incorrectly, that we see objects because they are illuminated by beams of light emanating from our eyes. Scientific findings about the nature of vision are discussed in chapter 5.

Though Aristotle accepted the importance of reasoning, he was more willing than Plato to accept sensory experience as a source of knowledge—a philosophical approach called **empiricism.** But Aristotle, like Plato, reached some false conclusions. For example, because the heart seemed more responsive than the brain during strong emotional experiences, he believed the heart was the site of mental processes. Aristotle contributed to psychology by being one of the first thinkers to speculate formally on psychological topics, as indicated by the titles of his works, including *On Dreams, On Sleep and Sleeplessness, On Memory and Reminiscence,* and *On the Senses and the Sensed.* Scientific research on each of these topics is described in upcoming chapters.

During the early Christian and medieval eras, answers to psychological questions were given more often by theologian philosophers than by secular philosophers like Plato or Aristotle. The dominant Western authority was Saint Augustine (354–430), who lived almost all of his life in what is now Algeria. As a young man, Augustine sowed his wild oats as a follower of Epicurean philosophy, which proclaimed, "Eat, drink, and be merry, for tomorrow we die." He pursued this lifestyle until he experienced a religious conversion. Augustine wrote of his views on memory, emotion, and motivation in the self-analysis he presented in his classic autobiographical *Confessions.* He anticipated Sigmund Freud in providing insight into the continual battle between our human reason and our animal passions, especially the power of the sex drive (Gay, 1986). Though Augustine used reason to study psychological processes, neither he nor his contemporaries used the scientific method to study them (Pratt, 1962).

During the Middle Ages, when the Christian West was guided largely by religious dogma, and those who dared to conduct empirical studies risked punishment, scientific investigations became almost solely the province of Islamic intellectuals. The most noteworthy of these was the Persian scientist and philosopher Abu Ibn Sina (980–1037), better known in the West as Avicenna, who kept alive the teachings of Aristotle (Afnan, 1958/1980). With the revival of Western intellectual activity in the late Middle Ages, scholars who had access to Arabic translations of the Greek philosophers rediscovered Aristotle. But most of these scholars limited their efforts to reconciling Aristotle's ideas and Christian teachings. One brave exception was the Franciscan friar Roger Bacon (c. 1214–c. 1294). Bacon was influenced by Arab scientists, who stressed the importance of gaining knowledge through the senses. As a consequence, Bacon urged philosophers to favor empiricism over authority, which made him run afoul of religious pundits (Lindberg, 1983).

With the coming of the Renaissance, which extended from the fourteenth through the sixteenth centuries, Western authorities relied less on theology and more on philosophy, once again, to provide answers to psychological questions. The spirit of the Renaissance inspired René Descartes (1596–1650), the great French philosopher-mathematician-scientist. Descartes had broad interests, including dancing, dueling, gambling, traveling, and inventing. Among his inventions were a wheelchair for disabled persons and a way to prevent hair from turning gray (Vrooman, 1970).

Descartes, the first of the modern rationalists, insisted that we should doubt everything that is not proved self-evident by our own reasoning. In fact, in his famous statement "I think, therefore I am," Descartes went to the extreme of using reasoning to prove to his own satisfaction that he existed. Descartes contributed to the modern intellectual outlook, which opposes blind acceptance of proclamations put forth by authorities, religious or otherwise. Church leaders felt so threatened by Descartes's challenge to their authority that his works were put on their list of banned books. Descartes's ideas regarding the relationship of mind and body are discussed in chapter 3.

Other intellectuals, though favoring empiricism instead of rationalism, joined Descartes in rejecting the authority of theologians to provide answers to scientific questions. Chief among these intellectuals was the English politician-philosopher-scientist

Sir Francis Bacon (1561–1626). Bacon (not related to Roger Bacon) was not only brilliant but a bit of a shady character—not above committing bribery, betraying his friends, and fawning on the powerful. This incited the poet Alexander Pope to call him "the wisest, brightest, and meanest of mankind" (Quinton, 1980).

Yet, in his role as an intellectual, Bacon inspired the modern scientific attitude that favors skepticism, systematic observation, and verification of claims by other observers (Hearnshaw, 1985). He was also a founder of applied science, which seeks practical applications of research findings. In support of this, Bacon asserted that "to be useless is to be worthless." Ironically, his interest in the application of scientific findings cost him his life. While studying the possible use of refrigeration to preserve food, he experimented by stuffing a chicken with snow—and caught a severe chill that contributed to a fatal case of pneumonia.

Following in Francis Bacon's empiricist footsteps was the English philosopher John Locke (1632–1704). According to Locke (borrowing from Aristotle), each of us is born a blank slate—or *tabula rasa*—on which are written the life experiences we acquire through our senses. While rationalists like Descartes believe that much of our knowledge is inborn, empiricists like Locke believe that knowledge is acquired solely through life experiences. This concern with the relative importance of heredity and life experiences is known as the *nature versus nurture* controversy. This issue, which is a recurring theme in psychological theory and research, appears in later chapters in discussions about a host of topics, including language, intelligence, personality, and psychological disorders.

A compromise between strict rationalism and strict empiricism was offered by the German philosopher Immanuel Kant (1724–1804). Kant was the ultimate "ivory tower" intellectual, never marrying and devoting his life to philosophical pursuits. He maintained a strict daily schedule, rising at 5 A.M., working for several hours, and eating lunch at 1 P.M. He was so renowned that fans from many countries visited his home city of Königsberg just to catch a glimpse of him having lunch. To avoid them (much as a celebrity would today), Kant repeatedly changed restaurants. Despite his international acclaim and offering the first academic course in physical geography, he never left his home province—and probably never saw an ocean or a mountain (Paulsen, 1899/1963).

Kant taught that knowledge is the product of inborn mental faculties that organize and interpret sensory input from the physical environment. For example, though the specific language you speak (whether English or other) depends on experience with your native tongue, your ability to speak any language depends on inborn brain mechanisms. If not, other animals that can hear speech and that have a vocal apparatus might develop a spoken language when exposed to one.

Despite studying psychological topics, Kant denied that psychology could be a science. He believed this because the mind is not tangible; it cannot be directly observed, measured, or manipulated. Moreover, its contents are in a constant state of flux. Because of this, according to Kant, the study of mind could never have objectivity—a prerequisite for any science.

The Scientific Roots of Psychology

By the nineteenth century, scientists were making progress in answering questions about the nature of psychological processes that philosophers were having difficulty with. As a consequence, intellectuals began to look more and more to science for guidance in the study of psychological topics. For example, in the mid nineteenth century, popular belief, based on reasoning, held that nerve impulses travel the length of a nerve as fast as electricity travels along a wire—that is, almost instantaneously. This claim was contradicted by research conducted by the German physiologist Hermann von Helmholtz (1821–1894), arguably the greatest scientist of the nineteenth century. Helmholtz also made important contributions to our knowledge of vision and hearing, including the ophthalmoscope, which is used to examine the inside of the eye. His contributions to the study of vision and hearing are described in chapter 5.

Francis Bacon (1561–1626)
"If a man will begin with certainties, he shall end in doubts; but if he will be content to begin with doubts, he shall end in certainties."

Immanuel Kant (1724–1804)
"Though all our knowledge begins with experience, it by no means follows that all arises out of experience. For on the contrary, it is quite possible that our empirical knowledge is a compound of that which we receive through impressions, and that which the faculty of cognition supplies from itself."

Hermann von Helmholtz (1821–1894)
"I have found that there is a measurable period of time during which the effect of a stimulus consisting of a momentary electrical current applied to the iliac plexus of a frog is transmitted to the calf muscles at the entrance of the crural nerve."

Paul Broca (1824–1880)
"From the observations (cases) I have collected, and from the large number I have read in the literature, I believe I am justified in advancing the view that the principal lawgiver of speech is to be found in the anterior lobes of the brain."

psychophysics
The study of the relationship between the physical characteristics of stimuli and the conscious psychological experiences they produce.

In studying nerve impulses, Helmholtz found that they took a measurable fraction of a second to travel along a nerve. He demonstrated this in experiments on animal and human subjects. In one experiment, he had human subjects press a button as soon as they felt a touch on the foot or thigh. A clock recorded their reaction time. Subjects reacted slower to a touch on the foot than to a touch on the thigh. Helmholtz attributed this difference in reaction time to the longer distance that nerve impulses must travel from the foot to the spinal cord and then on to the brain. This indicated that nerve impulses are not instantaneous.

Helmholtz's scientific contemporaries made important discoveries about brain functions. The leading brain researcher was the French physiologist Pierre Flourens (1794–1867), who studied the effects of damage to specific brain structures on animal behavior. For example, he found that damage to the cerebellum, a large structure protruding from the back of the brain, caused motor incoordination. His fellow Frenchman Paul Broca (1824–1880), a surgeon and anthropologist, conducted similar research on brain damage in human beings. He found that patients with damage to a region on the left side of the front of the brain lost their ability to speak.

Other nineteenth-century scientists were more interested in the scientific study of mental processes, apart from the brain structures that served them. The most notable of these scientists was the German mystic-physicist-philosopher Gustav Fechner (1801–1887). Fechner was critical of the pretensions of scientists and philosophers alike. In fact, under the pen name "Dr. Mises," he poked fun at them in satirical articles such as "The Comparative Anatomy of Angels" (Marshall, 1969).

In his research, Fechner used a technique called *psychophysics*, which had been invented by the German physiologist Ernst Weber (1795–1878). **Psychophysics** let Fechner quantify the relationship between physical stimulation and mental experience (Narens & Mausfeld, 1992). This accomplishment would have surprised his predecessor Immanuel Kant, who believed it was impossible to study the mind scientifically. Psychophysics considers questions such as, How much change in the intensity of a light is necessary for a person to experience a change in its brightness? and How much change in the intensity of a sound is necessary for a person to experience a change in its loudness? Psychophysics contributed to psychology's maturation from a child of philosophy and science to an independent discipline with its own subject matter, and it has had important applications during the past century. For example, the researchers who perfected television relied on psychophysics to determine the relationship between physical characteristics of the television picture and the viewer's mental experience of qualities such as color and brightness (Baldwin, 1954).

Psychologists of the late nineteenth century were also influenced by the theory of evolution, put forth by the English naturalist Charles Darwin (1809–1882). Darwin announced his theory in *The Origin of Species* (Darwin, 1859/1975), which described the results of research he conducted while studying the plants and animals he encountered during a 5-year voyage around the world on the H.M.S. Beagle. Though thinkers as far back as ancient Greece had proposed that existing animals had evolved from common ancestors, Darwin (along with fellow English naturalist Alfred Russell Wallace) was the first to propose a natural process that could account for it. According to Darwin, through natural selection physical characteristics that promote the survival of the individual are more likely to be passed on to offspring, because individuals with these characteristics are more likely to live long enough to reproduce.

Darwin's theory had its most immediate impact on psychology through the work of his cousin, the Englishman Francis Galton (1822–1911). Galton was an eminent scientist and a man of many interests. He explored Africa and drew some of the first maps of it; he studied meteorology and developed the concepts of highs, lows, and fronts; and he invented the practice of fingerprinting, which helped Scotland Yard solve crimes. In applying Darwin's theory of evolution, Galton argued that natural selection could account for the development of human abilities. Moreover, he claimed that individuals with the most highly developed abilities would be the most likely to survive. This led him to found the field of **differential psychology** (Buss, 1976), which studies variations among human beings in intellectual, personality, and physical characteristics. Galton's impact on the study of intelligence is discussed in chapter 10.

Differential psychology was introduced to America by the psychologist James McKeen Cattell (1860–1944), who studied with Galton. In 1890 Cattell coined the term *mental test,* which he used to describe various tests of vision, hearing, and physical skills that he administered to his students, first at the University of Pennsylvania and then at Columbia University. Cattell served as president of the American Psychological Association in 1895 and became the first psychologist to be elected to the National Academy of Sciences. But he fell into disrepute after being fired by Columbia University for opposing America's entrance into World War I (Poffenberger, 1947/1973). Banished from academia, Cattell started his own business, the Psychological Corporation, which to this day is active in the development of tests that assess abilities, intelligence, and personality. Thus, Cattell was a pioneer in the development of psychology as both a science and a profession (Garfield, 1992).

The Growth of Psychology

Cattell is considered to have been the first psychology professor in the world (that is, he was the first person to hold such a position independent of an academic philosophy or biology department). He was given that professorship barely a century ago, a fact that supports a remark made by Hermann Ebbinghaus (1850–1909), a pioneer in psychology: "Psychology has a long past, but only a short history" (Boring, 1950, p. ix). Ebbinghaus noted that though intellectuals have been interested in psychological topics since the era of ancient Greece, psychology did not become a separate discipline until the late nineteenth century.

Most psychologists attribute the founding of this new discipline to the German physiologist Wilhelm Wundt (1832–1920). Wundt's childhood did not foreshadow his future importance. He was at first a mediocre student and socially withdrawn; his sole friend was a mentally retarded boy who could barely speak. But Wundt persevered, became an excellent student, and served for 6 years as Hermann von Helmholtz's laboratory assistant. He even became more socially outgoing and participated in politics, the labor movement, and student rights demonstrations.

In 1874, in his landmark book *Principles of Physiological Psychology,* Wundt announced his intention to found a science of psychology. The use of the term *physiological* in the title of the book did not mean that physiological psychology was its sole topic. Instead, it referred to the application of the scientific method used by physiologists to the study of psychological processes.

In 1875 Wundt set up a laboratory at the University of Leipzig in a small room that had served as a dining hall for students. Wundt's request for a more impressive laboratory had been rejected by the school's administrators, who did not want to promote a science they believed would drive students crazy by encouraging them to scrutinize the contents of their minds (Hilgard, 1987). Beginning in 1879 Wundt's laboratory was the site of formal research conducted by many students who later became some of the most renowned European and North American psychologists, including James McKeen Cattell. Modern-day psychologists recognized Wundt's accomplishment by celebrating 1979 as psychology's centennial year.

Wundt was a prolific writer and wrote tens of thousands of pages, despite being partially blind and relying on his students to do his reading for him. Cattell, who was fond of Wundt, helped him obtain a typewriter (which was as revolutionary then as a personal computer was in the 1980s). The sometimes vicious nature of rivalries among psychologists at the time is epitomized in the reaction of an adversary who called the typewriter an "evil gift" because it permitted Wundt to write twice as much as he could without it (Bringmann & Tweney, 1980).

Gustav Fechner (1801–1887)
". . . body and mind parallel each other; changes in one correspond to changes in the other."

differential psychology
The field of psychology that studies individual differences in intellectual, personality, and physical characteristics.

James McKeen Cattell (1860–1944)
"In so far as experiment can be used in the study of mind, scientific progress is assured."

Wilhelm Wundt (1832–1920)
Wundt (*third from left*) is shown surrounded by colleagues in his laboratory at the University of Leipzig in 1912. Research conducted in the laboratory in 1879 marked the founding of experimental psychology.

The early growth of the new discipline was marked by the rise of competing approaches championed by charismatic leaders, who often were trained in both philosophy and science. These approaches were known as *schools* of psychology, and included *structuralism, functionalism, behaviorism, Gestalt psychology,* and *psychoanalysis.* The schools differed in three significant ways: (1) in their object of study (the conscious mind, the unconscious mind, or overt behavior); (2) in their goal of study (analyzing the contents of the mind, examining the functions of the mind, or observing the effect of the environment on behavior); and (3) in their method of study (having subjects report the contents of their minds, or observing overt behavior).

Structuralism

structuralism
The early school of psychology that sought to identify the components of the conscious mind.

The first school of psychology—**structuralism**—arose in the late nineteenth century. Structuralists were inspired by the efforts of biologists, chemists, and physicists to analyze matter and categorize it into cells, molecules, and atoms. Following the lead of these scientists, structuralists tried to analyze the mind into its component elements and discover how the elements interact.

Structuralism was named and popularized by Wundt's student Edward Titchener (1867–1927). Titchener, an Englishman, introduced structuralism to the United States after joining the faculty of Cornell University. He liked to play the role of the somber European scholar, maintaining a stern demeanor and wearing his academic gown to class. To study the mind, Titchener had his subjects use **analytic introspection,** a procedure aimed at analyzing complex mental experiences into what he believed were the three basic mental elements: images, feelings, and sensations (Hindeland, 1971). In a typical study using analytic introspection, Titchener would present a subject with a stimulus (for example, a sound) and then ask the subject to report the images, feelings, and sensations evoked by it. As you know from your own experience, stimuli such as paintings, musical passages, and familiar smells do evoke combinations of images, feelings, and sensations. But analytic introspection was a meticulous—and tedious—procedure. A subject might have to perform 10,000 introspections before being permitted to participate in a study. And even then, it might take 20 minutes to make a single introspective report in response to a stimulus that had been presented for a mere second or two (Lieberman, 1979).

analytic introspection
A research method in which highly trained subjects report the contents of their conscious mental experiences.

Among Titchener's contributions was research that analyzed tastes, which led to the discovery that even complex tastes are mixtures of the four basic tastes of sour, sweet, salty, and bitter (Webb, 1981). Despite Titchener's renown, structuralism became not only the first school of psychology to appear, but the first to disappear. This was caused, in part, by its being limited to the laboratory. In fact, Titchener frowned on psychologists who tried to apply the new science of psychology to everyday life (Krech, 1968), a practice more in keeping with the scientific approach of Francis Bacon than with that of his mentor Wilhelm Wundt.

But the demise of structuralism owed more to its reliance on introspection, which limited it to the study of conscious mental experience in relatively intelligent, verbally skillful, adult human beings. Psychologists also found introspection to be unreliable, because introspective reports in response to a particular stimulus by a given subject were inconsistent from one presentation of the stimulus to another. Similarly, introspective reports in response to the same stimulus were inconsistent from one subject to another. And, perhaps most important, the very act of introspecting changed the conscious experience that was being reported—a point that Kant had made many years earlier. For example, suppose that you are asked to report your mental experience while you are angry. The very act of observing your own anger might weaken it, making your verbal report of your anger experience inaccurate (Marx & Cronan-Hillix, 1987). Though the shortcomings of analytic introspection made it fade into oblivion, many psychologists today rely on the related research procedure of having their subjects give verbal reports of their mental processes (Ericsson & Crutcher, 1991).

Functionalism

The American school of psychology called **functionalism** arose chiefly as a response to structuralism. Functionalists criticized the structuralists for limiting themselves to analyzing the content of the mind. The functionalists preferred, instead, to study how the mind affects what people do. Whereas structuralists might study the mental components of tastes, functionalists might study how the ability to distinguish different tastes affects behavior. This reflected the influence of Darwin's theory of evolution, which stressed the role of inherited characteristics in helping the individual adapt to the environment. The functionalists assumed that the conscious mind evolved because it promoted the survival of individual human beings. Your conscious mind permits you to evaluate your current circumstances and select the best course of action to adapt to them (Rambo, 1980). Recall a time when you tasted food that had gone bad. You quickly spit it out, vividly demonstrating the functional value of the sense of taste.

The most prominent functionalist was the American psychologist and philosopher William James (1842–1910). In his lifelong pursuit of the meaning of life, James worked in a variety of intellectual disciplines. His initial interest in pursuing a career as an artist gave way to involvement in, in turn, medicine, physiology, psychology, parapsychology (see chapter 5), philosophy, and religion. James led a full life, filled with friends and travel. His handsome appearance, intellectual brilliance, and attractive personality contributed to his exceptional popularity. He was a favorite with students, because he treated them as equals, made sure to include examples from everyday life in his lectures, and was one of the first professors to use student course evaluations to help improve lectures. Yet even James could occasionally become as irascible as the next professor toward students, on one occasion complaining to his wife: "I'm interrupted every moment here by students, come to fight about their marks" (Bjork, 1988, p. 178).

In his approach to psychology, James viewed the mind as a stream, which, as in the case of a real stream, cannot be meaningfully broken down into discrete elements. Thus, he believed that the mind—or *stream of consciousness*—is not suited to the kind of analytic study favored by structuralists. This led to a rivalry with Wundt. In 1875, the same year that Wundt established his laboratory at Leipzig, James established a psychology laboratory at Harvard University. But, unlike Wundt, he used the laboratory for demonstrations, not for experiments. In fact, James was both uninterested in laboratory research and critical of psychologists who limited themselves to the study of narrow behaviors or mental experiences in the laboratory (Jacobson, 1979). James urged psychologists, instead, to study how people function in the world outside of the laboratory.

Though he conducted few experiments, James made several contributions to psychology. His classic two-volume textbook *The Principles of Psychology* (1890/1981) highlighted the interrelationship of philosophy, physiology, and psychology. But James, prone

Edward B. Titchener (1867–1927)
"Since all the sciences are concerned with the one world of human experience, it is natural that scientific method, to whatever aspect of experience it is applied, should be in principle the same."

functionalism
The early school of psychology that studied how the conscious mind helps the individual adapt to the environment.

William James (1842–1910)
"Consciousness, then, does not appear to itself chopped up in bits. Such words as *chain* or *train* do not describe it fitly as it presents itself in the first instance. It is nothing jointed; it flows. A *river* or a *stream* are the metaphors by which it is most naturally described. *In talking of it hereafter, let us call it the stream of thought, of consciousness, or of subjective life.*"

Hugo Münsterberg (1863–1916)
"The period of pure theoretical psychology is closed. I should neglect my duties if I were not to join and try to lead in the movement toward applied psychology."

Francis Sumner (1895–1954)
G. Stanley Hall, a leader of the functionalist movement, made one of his many contributions to psychology by sponsoring the graduate education of Francis Sumner. When he received his doctorate from Clark University in 1920, Sumner, a functionalist, became the first African American to receive a Ph.D. in psychology in the United States. Sumner went on to develop the undergraduate psychology program at Howard University, which has graduated more African Americans who have become psychologists than has any other school. Sumner was also one of the most prolific contributors to *Psychological Abstracts*, the basic library research tool for scholars and students of psychology. Proficient in several languages, he wrote almost 2,000 abstracts of articles written in English, French, Spanish, German, and Russian (Bayton, 1975).

to depression, was so distressed that it had taken him 12 years to write the book that he disdainfully called it "a loathsome, distended, tumefied, bloated dropsical mass" (Bjork, 1988, p. 180). Nonetheless, the book is so interesting, informative, and beautifully written that it is one of the few century-old psychology books that is still in print.

James also contributed a theory of emotion (discussed in chapter 12) that is still influential today. And his encouragement inspired his student Mary Whiton Calkins (1863–1930) to pursue a career in which she achieved prominence as the first great woman psychologist, despite being hampered by sex discrimination. Calkins's life and contributions to psychology are discussed in the section "Thinking about Psychology" that concludes this chapter.

As a group, the functionalists broadened the subjects used in psychological research by including animals and children, as well as people suffering from mental disorders. The functionalists also expanded the subject matter of psychology to include such topics as memory, thinking, and personality. And unlike the structuralists, who limited their research to the laboratory, the functionalists, in the tradition of Francis Bacon, applied their research to everyday life. The functionalist John Dewey (1859–1952) applied psychology to the improvement of educational practices. But the functionalist credited with founding the field of applied psychology was Hugo Münsterberg (1863–1916), who became a tragic figure in the history of psychology.

In 1892 William James, tiring of the demands of running the psychology laboratory at Harvard, hired Münsterberg, who had earned his Ph.D. under Wilhelm Wundt and become a renowned German psychologist, to take over the laboratory. Münsterberg quickly gained stature in America. In 1898 he became president of the American Psychological Association, in 1899 head of the Harvard philosophy and psychology department, and in 1907 president of the American Philosophical Association. During the first decade of this century, Münsterberg was second only to James in his fame as a psychologist. He had popularized psychology through his speeches and writings, and counted many eminent persons among his friends, including writer H. G. Wells, industrialist Andrew Carnegie, and President Theodore Roosevelt. Ironically, though he was hired to run the Harvard psychology laboratory, Münsterberg's main contributions were in his role as a founder of applied psychology. He conducted research and wrote books describing how psychology could be applied to law, industry, education, psychotherapy, and film criticism (Moskowitz, 1977).

Despite his prominence and contributions to applied psychology, Münsterberg became a forgotten figure (Landy, 1992). This was, in part, the result of his early ostracism from psychology. He had the misfortune of being a German national at a time when the deterioration of relations between America and Germany culminated in America's entrance into World War I. Despite this, Münsterberg continued to promote good relations between America and Germany. However, his adoring colleagues and public turned against him; some even accused him of being a German spy. When his Harvard associates proceeded to ostracize him, his emotional stress increased. This may have contributed to his death. While in the middle of a classroom lecture at Radcliffe College (Harvard's sister school), he collapsed, dead of a stroke. Münsterberg, arguably the leading psychologist of his day, was mourned by few and passed into obscurity (Hale, 1980).

Because Münsterberg and his fellow functionalists dared to move psychology out of the laboratory and into the everyday world, they felt the wrath of structuralists, such as Titchener, who insisted that psychology could be a science only if it remained in the laboratory. Titchener even held in contempt G. Stanley Hall (1844–1924), a leader of the functionalist school, for using unorthodox research methods, such as questionnaires, and unorthodox subjects, such as people with mental disorders (Goodwin, 1987). Despite Titchener's criticisms, most psychologists would applaud the functionalists for increasing the kinds of research methods, research subjects, and research settings used by psychologists.

Behaviorism

In 1913 a leading functionalist published an article entitled "Psychology as the Behaviorist Views It." The article included the following proclamation:

* * * Psychology as the behaviorist views it is a purely objective experimental branch of natural science. Its theoretical goal is the prediction and the control of behavior. Introspection forms no essential part of its methods, nor is the scientific value of its data dependent on the readiness with which they lend themselves to interpretation in terms of consciousness. (Watson, 1913, p. 158)

This bold statement by the American psychologist John B. Watson (1878–1958) heralded the advent of **behaviorism,** a school of psychology that dominated the discipline for half a century. Watson rejected the position shared by structuralists and functionalists that the mind is the proper object of study for psychology. He and other behaviorists were emphatic in their opposition to the study of mental experience. The eminent Russian physiologist and behaviorist Ivan Pavlov (1849–1936) even threatened to fire anyone in his laboratory who dared to use mental terminology (Fancher, 1990). You can read about Pavlov's contributions to psychology in chapter 7.

Before founding behavorism, Watson was educated in a functionalist graduate psychology program at the University of Chicago and became one of the leading animal psychologists of his day. Watson's rebellion against the study of the mind reflected a lifelong willingness to go against the status quo. During adolescence he engaged in delinquent behavior, and he even claimed that he had had to repeat his senior year at Furman University after ignoring a professor's threat that he would flunk any student who handed in his final exam backward.

To behaviorists like Watson and Pavlov, the proper subject matter for psychological research is observable behavior. Unlike mental experiences, this can be recorded and subjected to verification by other scientists. For example, some psychologists might study the mental experience of hunger, but behaviorists would prefer to study the observable behavior of eating. Though Watson denied that mental processes could cause behaviors, he did not deny the existence of the mind (Gray, 1980). Thus, he would not have denied that human beings have the mental experience called "hunger," but he would have denied that the mental experience of hunger *causes* eating. Instead, he would have favored explanations of eating that placed its causes in the body (such as low blood sugar) or in the environment (such as a tantalizing aroma) instead of in the mind (such as feeling famished).

Watson impressed his fellow psychologists enough to be elected president of the American Psychological Association in 1915. Behaviorism later became so popular that Edwin Boring, an early historian of psychology, wrote that "for a while in the 1920s it seemed as if all America had gone behaviorist" (Boring, 1950, p. 645). But in 1920, just as behaviorism was becoming influential, Watson dropped out of academic psychology. He had been forced to resign from his faculty position at Johns Hopkins University because of a scandalous divorce following another instance of his willingness to flout convention—an affair with his graduate student Rosalie Rayner, whom he married later that same year.

After leaving Johns Hopkins, Watson joined the J. Walter Thompson advertising agency in New York City. He began by going door to door selling Yuban coffee, and eventually rose to the position of vice president (Kreshel, 1990). Watson devised market research techniques, experiments to determine brand appeal, and sophisticated advertising campaigns. He was also an early champion of the use of sex to sell products. In one advertising campaign, he associated Pebeco toothpaste with romantic appeal (Buckley, 1982). From 1922 to 1926 Watson kept his hand in teaching by giving weekly lectures at the New School for Social Research in Greenwich Village (Buckley, 1989).

behaviorism
The early school of psychology that rejected the study of mental processes in favor of the study of overt behavior.

John B. Watson (1878–1958)
"Psychology . . . needs introspection as little as do the sciences of chemistry and physics."

Watson was an attractive and charismatic person who popularized his brand of psychology by giving speeches and writing books and articles. He placed great faith in the effect of environmental stimuli on the control of behavior, particularly children's behavior (Horowitz, 1992). His "stimulus-response" psychology placed him firmly in the empiricist tradition of John Locke and is best expressed in his famous pronouncement on child development:

> Give me a dozen healthy infants, well-formed, and my own specified world to bring them up in and I'll guarantee to take any one at random and train him to become any type of specialist I might select—doctor, lawyer, artist, merchant-chief and, yes, even beggarman and thief, regardless of his talents, penchants, tendencies, abilities, vocations, and race of his ancestors. (Watson, 1930, p. 104)

Apparently, no parents rushed to offer their infants to Watson to be trained as specialists. Nonetheless, Watson's views on child rearing became influential. Despite some of their excessive claims, behaviorists injected optimism into psychology by fostering the belief that human beings are minimally limited by heredity and easily changed by experience. In favoring nurture over nature, behaviorists assumed that people, regardless of their hereditary background, could improve themselves and their positions in life. Watson and his fellow behaviorists were more than willing to suggest ways to bring about such improvements. Watson even hoped to establish a utopian society based on behavioristic principles (Morawski, 1982). Sadly for Watson, after the death of his wife Rosalie in 1935 his life became far from utopian. He became a depressed recluse, living on a farm in Connecticut. Television actress Mariette Hartley, his granddaughter by his first marriage, recalled that her most vivid memory of her grandfather's later years was the smell of bourbon permeating his home (Buckley, 1989).

As for Watson's influence on psychology, behaviorism led to a decline in the study of mental processes. In fact, from 1930 to 1960 the term *mind* rarely appeared in psychological research articles (Mueller, 1979). But during the past three decades, the mind has returned as a legitimate object of study. The weakened influence of behaviorism is also shown by renewed respect for the constraints that heredity places on learning (a topic discussed in chapter 7).

Gestalt Psychology

The structuralists' attempt to analyze the mind into its component parts and the behaviorists' view of the human being as a passive responder to environmental stimuli were countered by the German psychologist Max Wertheimer (1880–1943), who founded the school of **Gestalt psychology.** Wertheimer used the word *gestalt*, meaning "form" or "shape," to underscore his belief that we perceive wholes rather than combinations of individual elements. A famous tenet of Gestalt psychology asserts that "the whole is different from the sum of its parts." Because of this basic assumption, Wertheimer ridiculed structuralism as "brick-and-mortar psychology" for its attempt to analyze mental experience into discrete elements.

The founding of Gestalt psychology can be traced to a vacation trip taken by Wertheimer in 1912. While aboard a train he daydreamed about the **phi phenomenon**—apparent motion in the absence of actual motion (as in a motion picture). At a stop Wertheimer left the train and bought a toy stroboscope, which, like a motion picture, produces the illusion of movement by rapidly presenting a series of pictures that are slightly different from one another. On returning to his laboratory at the University of Frankfurt, he continued studying the phi phenomenon by using a more sophisticated device called a *tachistoscope*, which flashes visual stimuli for a fraction of a second. Wertheimer had the tachistoscope flash two lines in succession, first a vertical one and then a horizontal one. When the interval between flashes was just right, a single line appeared to move from vertical to horizontal.

According to Wertheimer, the phi phenomenon shows that the mind does not respond passively to discrete stimuli, but instead organizes stimuli into coherent wholes.

Gestalt psychology
The early school of psychology that claimed that we perceive and think about wholes rather than simply about combinations of separate elements.

phi phenomenon
Apparent motion caused by the presentation of different stimuli in rapid succession.

Thus, perception is more than a series of individual sensations. This is in keeping with Immanuel Kant's notion of the mind as an active manipulator of environmental input. If the mind responded passively to discrete stimuli, in observing Wertheimer's demonstration you would first see the vertical line appear and disappear and then the horizontal line appear and disappear.

For another example of how the mind can create a whole different from the sum of its parts, consider a melody. A given melody, such as "Yankee Doodle Dandy," can be recognized regardless of whether it is sung, hummed, or whistled; whether it is played on a banjo or by a symphony orchestra; and whether it is played in any of a variety of keys. Thus, a melody is not simply the product of a series of particular sensations produced by a particular source. Instead, a melody depends on the mind's active processing of sensations that may be produced by a variety of sources. Gestalt psychology gave a new direction to psychology by stressing the active role of the mind in organizing sensations into meaningful perceptions.

Though founded by Wertheimer, Gestalt psychology was popularized by his colleagues Kurt Koffka (1886–1941), the most prolific and influential writer among the Gestaltists (Henle, 1987), and Wolfgang Kohler (1887–1967), who promoted Gestalt psychology as a natural science (Henle, 1993) and applied it to the study of problem solving. Koffka and Kohler introduced Gestalt psychology to the United States after fleeing Nazi Germany. Kohler, a Christian college professor, had provoked the Nazis by writing and speaking out against their oppression of his Jewish colleagues (Henle, 1978b). He became a respected psychologist and was elected president of the American Psychological Association in 1959. In his presidential address, Kohler (1959) urged Gestaltists and behaviorists to create a psychology that included the best aspects of both of their schools. As you will read later in this chapter, psychologists who favor the cognitive perspective have followed Kohler's advice.

Gestalt psychology also influenced the field of social psychology, mainly through the efforts of the German psychologist Kurt Lewin (1890–1947). After studying with Wertheimer, Koffka, and Kohler in Germany, he emigrated to the United States, where he taught at several universities. Lewin applied Gestalt concepts in his pioneering research on the effects of leadership styles, the principles of small-group behavior, and the best means of resolving social conflicts.

Psychoanalysis

Unlike Gestalt psychology and the other early schools of psychology, which originated in universities, **psychoanalysis** originated in medicine. Sigmund Freud (1856–1939), the founder of psychoanalysis, was an Austrian neurologist who considered himself "a conquistador of the mind" (Gay, 1988). His theory, which views the human being as first and foremost an animal, owes a debt to Darwin's theory of evolution. Psychoanalysis grew, in part, from Freud's attempts to treat patients suffering from physical symptoms, such as paralyzed legs, inability to speak, or loss of body sensations, that had no apparent physical causes. Based on his treatment of patients suffering from such symptoms of *conversion hysteria*, Freud concluded that the disorder was the result of unconscious psychological conflicts about sex caused by cultural prohibitions against sexual enjoyment. These conflicts were "converted" into the physical symptoms seen in conversion hysteria, which often provided the patient with an excuse to avoid engaging in the taboo behaviors.

Freud's case studies of patients led him to infer that unconscious conflicts, usually related to sex or aggression, were prime motivators of human behavior. Though Freud's recognition of the importance of unconscious motives was not new, he was the first person to include the unconscious mind in a formal psychological theory. Freud believed that all behavior—whether normal or abnormal—is influenced by psychological motives, often ones of which we are unaware. This belief is called **psychic determinism.** In his book *The Psychopathology of Everyday Life*, Freud (1901/1990) explained how even apparently unintentional behaviors could be explained by psychic determinism.

Max Wertheimer (1880–1943)
". . . the comprehension of whole-properties and whole-conditions must precede consideration of the real significance of parts."

psychoanalysis
The early school of psychology that emphasized the importance of unconscious causes of behavior.

psychic determinism
The Freudian assumption that all behaviors are influenced by unconscious motives.

Sigmund Freud (1856–1939)
Freud is shown here with a group of eminent psychologists during his only visit to the United States, in 1909, when he came to attend the famous Clark University psychology conference. (*Seated, left to right:* Freud, his host G. Stanley Hall, and Carl Jung. *Standing, left to right:* Abraham Brill, Ernest Jones, and Sandor Ferenczi.)

Psychic determinism explains misstatements, popularly known as "Freudian slips," like that of the radio announcer who began a bread commercial by saying, "For the breast in bed . . . I mean, for the best in bread. . . ." As one psychologist noted, the concept of psychic determinism meant that "the forgotten lunch engagement, the slip of the tongue, the barked shin could no longer be dismissed as accident" (Bruner, 1956, p. 465). In addition to shocking the public by claiming that human beings are motivated chiefly by unconscious—often sexual—motives (Rapp, 1988), Freud made the controversial claim that early childhood experiences were the most important factors in personality development. Freud believed that memories of early childhood experiences stored in the unconscious mind continue to affect behavior throughout life. According to Freud, these unconscious influences explain the irrationality of much human behavior and the origins of psychological disorders. Even John B. Watson, who professed disdain for anything to do with mental explanations of moods or behaviors, expressed grudging admiration for Freud's theory after finding himself unable to discover a reason for a debilitating period of emotional turmoil he experienced while pursuing his doctorate (Buckley, 1989).

Freudian psychoanalysis has been so extraordinarily influential that a 1981 survey of chairpersons of graduate psychology departments found that they considered Freud to be the most important figure in the history of psychology (Davis, Thomas, & Weaver, 1982). Nonetheless, psychoanalysis has been the target of severe attacks. Critics have pointed out that the unconscious mind can be too easily used to explain any behavior for which there is no obvious cause. William James had expressed this concern even before Freud's views had become widely known. James warned that the unconscious "is the sovereign means for believing whatever one likes in psychology and of turning what might become a science into a tumbling ground for whimsies" (James, 1890/1981, Vol. 1, p. 166).

Psychoanalysis has also been subjected to criticism for failing to provide adequate research evidence for its claims of the importance of sexual motives, unconscious processes, and early childhood experiences (Hobson, 1985). In fact, Freud never tested his theory experimentally. Instead, he based his theory on notes written hours after seeing patients, which made his conclusions subject to his own memory lapses and personal

| TABLE 1.1 | | Early Schools of Psychology | |

School	Object of Study	Goal of Study	Method of Study
Structuralism	Conscious experience	Analyzing the structure of the mind	Analytic introspection
Functionalism	Conscious experience	Studying the functions of the mind	Introspection and measures of performance
Behaviorism	Observable behavior	Controlling behavior	Observation and experimentation
Gestalt Psychology	Conscious experience	Demonstrating the holistic nature of the mind	Introspection and demonstrations
Psychoanalysis	Unconscious motivation	Understanding personality	Clinical case studies

biases. Moreover, Freud violated good scientific practice by generalizing to all people the results of his case studies of a handful of people with psychological disorders.

Despite these shortcomings, Freud's views have influenced the psychological study of topics as diverse as dreams, creativity, motivation, development, personality, and psychotherapy. Freud's views have also inspired the works of artists, writers, and film-makers, including Eugene O'Neill's play *Mourning Becomes Electra* (1931) and the classic science fiction film *Forbidden Planet* (1956). Freud's contributions to a variety of psychological topics are discussed in several other chapters. Table 1.1 summarizes the major characteristics of psychoanalysis and the other early schools of psychology.

Contemporary Psychological Perspectives

According to Thomas Kuhn (1970), an influential philosopher of science, as a science matures it develops a unifying **scientific paradigm,** or model, that determines its appropriate goals, methods, and subject matter. Though there are no longer separate schools of psychology, with charismatic leaders and loyal followers, psychology still lacks a unifying scientific paradigm to which most psychologists would subscribe. Instead, there are rival psychological perspectives: the *behavioral perspective*, the *psychoanalytic perspective*, the *humanistic perspective*, the *cognitive perspective*, and the *biopsychological perspective*.

scientific paradigm
A model that determines the appropriate goals, methods, and subject matter of a science.

The Behavioral Perspective

The **behavioral perspective** descended from behaviorism. The leading proponent of the behavioral perspective was the American psychologist B. F. Skinner (1904–1990). As a young man, Skinner pursued a career as a writer, and even spent 6 months living in Greenwich Village to soak up its creative Bohemian atmosphere. After discovering that he was not cut out to be a writer, and being excited by the writings of John B. Watson, he decided to become a psychologist (Keller, 1991). Though Skinner eventually became the most prominent psychologist in the world (Korn, Davis, & Davis, 1991), it took many years for him to achieve that standing. In fact, by the end of World War II, in 1945, his landmark book *The Behavior of Organisms* (which had been published in 1938) had sold only 80 copies.

Like John B. Watson, Skinner urged psychologists to ignore mental processes and to limit psychology to the study of observable behavior. Strict behaviorists still refuse to treat verbal reports of mental experiences as appropriate subject matter for psychological research. But in contrast to Watson, Skinner stressed the role of the consequences of behavior, rather than environmental stimuli, in controlling behavior. He noted that animals and people tend to repeat behaviors that are followed by positive consequences. Consider your performance in school. If your studying (a behavior) pays off with an A on an exam (a positive consequence), you will be more likely to study in the future. In Skinner's terms, your behavior has been "positively reinforced."

behavioral perspective
The psychological viewpoint, descended from behaviorism, that emphasizes the importance of studying environmental influences on overt behavior, yet in some cases permits the study of mental processes.

B. F. Skinner (1904–1990)
"I am a radical behaviorist simply in the sense that I find no place in the formulation for anything which is mental."

psychoanalytic perspective
The psychological viewpoint, descended from psychoanalysis, that places less emphasis on biological motives and more emphasis on the importance of interpersonal relationships.

Melanie Klein (1882–1960)
"The infant's emotional life, the early defenses built up under the stress of the conflict between love, hatred, and guilt, and the vicissitudes of the child's identifications—all these are topics which may well occupy analytical research for a long time to come"

humanistic perspective
The psychological viewpoint that holds that the proper subject matter of psychology is the individual's subjective experience of the world.

Skinner, like Watson, was a utopian. In 1948 Skinner published *Walden Two*, a still-popular book that describes an ideal society based on behavioral principles. In Skinner's utopia, society is run by benevolent behaviorists who control its citizens by providing positive reinforcement for desirable behaviors. The tiny community of Twin Oaks, Virginia, was founded on principles presented in *Walden Two*. Though there is still no behavioral utopia, the behavioral perspective has contributed to improvements in education, child rearing, industrial productivity, and therapy for psychological disorders; these are discussed in later chapters.

Despite Skinner's efforts, the influence of the behavioral perspective has waned in recent years in the face of growing dissatisfaction with the lack of attention that strict behaviorists give to mental processes. This has prompted some behaviorists to study the relationship between mental processes such as images or thoughts, which cannot be directly observed, and overt behavior, which can. These psychologists are called *cognitive behaviorists*; their most influential leader has been Albert Bandura. The views of Skinner and Bandura are discussed further in chapter 7.

The Psychoanalytic Perspective

Like the behavioral perspective, the **psychoanalytic perspective** is a descendant of an early school of psychology—psychoanalysis. The decline of Freudian psychoanalysis began when two of Freud's followers, Carl Jung (1875–1961) and Alfred Adler (1870–1937), developed psychoanalytic theories that contradicted important aspects of Freud's theory. Jung, Adler, and other so-called *neo-Freudians* placed less emphasis on the biological drives of sex and aggression and more emphasis on the importance of social relationships. Jung developed his own theory of personality, which included the concepts of the inner-directed *introvert* and the outer-directed *extravert*. Adler based his personality theory on his belief that each of us tends to overcompensate for natural childhood feelings of inferiority by striving for superiority, as in the case of daredevils who try to prove their fearlessness by engaging in reckless behaviors.

Other neo-Freudians also contributed to the psychoanalytic perspective. Anna Freud (1895–1982), Sigmund Freud's daughter, was a leader in the field of child psychoanalysis, as was her intellectual rival, Melanie Klein (1882–1960), who developed the technique of play therapy. Karen Horney (1895–1952) asserted that the most important factor in personality development is the way we choose to reduce the anxiety caused by the feeling of insecurity that we all experience as weak, dependent infants. Erich Fromm (1900–1980) put forth a similar theory, which explained how the human need for security accounts for the tendency toward social conformity, even to the extent of passively submitting to dictators. Harry Stack Sullivan (1892–1949) was a leader in the application of psychoanalytic techniques to the understanding and treatment of schizophrenia. And Erik Erikson has contributed a theory of development across the life span, with special emphasis on the crises that must be resolved at each stage of the life cycle. The views of the neo-Freudians are discussed in later chapters, most extensively in chapter 13.

Though the psychoanalytic perspective downplays the importance of biological drives, it accepts the importance of early childhood experiences and the unconscious mind. During the past two decades researchers have devised techniques—some of them ingenious—that permit the scientific study of unconscious mental processes. (You can read about research on the unconscious mind in chapter 6.) The success of these techniques supports the claim that "no psychological model that seeks to explain how human beings know, learn, or behave can ignore the concept of unconscious psychological processes" (Shevrin & Dickman, 1980, p. 432).

The Humanistic Perspective

Because it provided the first important alternative to the psychoanalytic and behavioral perspectives, the **humanistic perspective** is called the "third force" in psychology. It was founded in the 1950s by the American psychologists Abraham Maslow (1908–1970) and Carl Rogers (1902–1987) to promote the idea that human beings have free will and are not merely pawns in the hands of unconscious motives or environmental stimuli. Maslow, who served as president of the American Psychological Association in 1967, had begun as a behaviorist, but later rejected its narrow focus on observable behavior and the effects of the environment. He stressed the human being's natural tendency toward *self-actualization*, which was the term he applied to the attainment of all of one's potentials.

Maslow's views were echoed by Rogers. Both assumed that the subject matter of psychology should be the individual's unique subjective mental experience of the world. In doing so, they showed an intellectual kinship to William James. Humanistic psychology's assumption that human beings have free will and its emphasis on the study of subjective mental experience reveal its kinship with **existential psychology.** Existential psychologists base their approach on the belief that our psychological development depends on the way we choose to face the reality of our ultimate mortality and the realization that we are responsible for our own lives. Whereas one person might choose to face mortality by ignoring it, another person might face it by becoming religious, and still another person might face it by "living for today," spending every spare moment seeking pleasure.

Humanistic psychology has been a prime mover in the field of psychotherapy, most notably through the efforts of Carl Rogers (Gendlin, 1988). His *person-centered therapy*, one of the chief kinds of psychotherapy, is discussed in chapter 15. Though person-centered therapy has been the subject of extensive scientific research, other aspects of humanistic psychology, such as techniques that promote personal "growth experiences" and "consciousness raising," have been criticized for having little scientific support (Wertheimer, 1978). This lack of scientific rigor may have contributed to the relatively minor impact that humanistic psychology has had on academic psychology, a fact lamented by Rogers (1985) near the end of his life. Despite its scientific shortcomings, humanistic psychology has made a valuable contribution in promoting the study of positive aspects of human experience, including love, altruism, and healthy personality development. Moreover, many humanistic psychologists have become more willing to use experimentation to test their theories (Rychlak, 1988).

The Cognitive Perspective

Recent decades have witnessed a so-called cognitive revolution in psychology (Gardner, 1985), leading to the emergence of a **cognitive perspective.** The cognitive perspective combines aspects of Gestalt psychology and behavioral psychology. Like Gestalt psychologists, cognitive psychologists stress the active role of the mind in organizing perceptions, processing information, and interpreting experiences. And, like behavioral psychologists, cognitive psychologists stress the need for objective, well-controlled, laboratory studies. Thus, cognitive psychologists infer mental processes from observable responses, without relying on verbal reports alone. But, unlike strict behavioral psychologists, who claim that mental processes, such as thoughts, cannot affect behavior, many cognitive psychologists believe that mental processes can (O'Connor, 1981).

The cognitive perspective is illustrated in the work of the Swiss biologist-psychologist Jean Piaget (1896–1980), who put forth a cognitive-developmental theory of the child's mental development based on his interviews with children as they solved various problems. Piaget's research is discussed in chapter 4. The cognitive perspective has also been influenced by the computer revolution of the past three decades, which stimulated research on the human brain as an information processor. A leader in this field has been the Nobel-prize-winning psychologist Herbert Simon. Some cognitive psychologists use computer programs to create models of human thought processes; others use their knowledge of human thought processes to improve computer programs, like those for computer chess games.

As you will realize while reading upcoming chapters, the cognitive perspective pervades almost every field of psychology. For example, the cognitive psychologist George Kelly (1905–1967) put forth a theory that has been applied to the study of personality,

Abraham Maslow (1908–1970)
"I suppose it is tempting, if the only tool you have is a hammer [that is, the behaviorist's sole reliance on studying overt behavior], to treat everything as if it were a nail."

existential psychology
A form of humanistic psychology that emphasizes subjective mental experience and human free will.

cognitive perspective
The psychological viewpoint that favors the study of how the mind organizes perceptions, processes information, and interprets experiences.

Herbert Simon
"On the American side of the Atlantic Ocean, there was a great gap in research on human thinking from the time of William James almost down to World War II. . . . Cognitive processes . . . were hardly mentioned, and the word *mind* was reserved for philosophers, not to be uttered by respectable psychologists."

biopsychological perspective
The psychological viewpoint that stresses the importance of physiological factors in behavior and mental processes.

Roger Sperry (1913–1994)
"The new mentalist position of behavioral and cognitive science seems to hold promise, not only as a more valid paradigm for all science but also for all human belief."

psychological disorders, and psychotherapy. Kelly believed we are guided by cognitive structures, which he called *personal constructs* (see chapter 13). These are subjective expectations that we have for the behavior of other people.

The Biopsychological Perspective

Though the schools of psychology of the early twentieth century had their roots in nineteenth-century physiology, there was never a strictly biological school of psychology. In recent decades, growing interest in the biological basis of behavior and mental processes, combined with the development of sophisticated research equipment, has led to the emergence of a **biopsychological perspective.**

Biological psychologists are interested in studying the brain, the hormonal system, and the effects of heredity on psychological functions. Though most researchers in biological psychology rely on animals as subjects, some of their most important studies have used human subjects. For example, in the course of surgery on the brains of epilepsy victims to reduce their seizures, the Canadian neurosurgeon Wilder Penfield (1891–1976) mapped the brain by using weak electrical currents to stimulate points on its surface. He found that stimulation of particular points on one side of the brain caused movements of particular body parts on the opposite side.

In 1981 the American neuroscientist Roger Sperry was awarded a Nobel prize for his studies of epilepsy victims whose left and right brain hemispheres had been surgically separated to reduce their seizures. Sperry and his colleagues found that each hemisphere was superior to the other in performing particular psychological functions. Chapter 3 describes the research of Penfield, Sperry, and other contributors to biopsychology. Because of the increasing influence of the biopsychological perspective, psychology may be moving toward an even broader definition as "the science of behavior and mental processes, and the physiological processes underlying them."

Putting the Perspectives in Perspective

To appreciate the differences among the psychological perspectives, consider how each might explain your psychology professor's classroom behavior. Suppose that you find that your professor is an unusually "happy" person—smiling, cracking jokes, and complimenting students on their brilliant insights. A behavioral psychologist might assume that your professor is happy because she or he has received positive reinforcement, which might include students who remain alert and interested during lectures. A psychoanalytic psychologist might assume that your professor is happy because she or he has successfully expressed unconscious aggressive urges in socially acceptable ways, perhaps by playing racquetball or creating extremely difficult exams. A humanistic psychologist might assume that your professor is happy because she or he has a sense of self-actualization, having reached his or her potential as a friend, spouse, parent, artist, athlete, and psychology professor. A cognitive psychologist might assume that your professor is happy because she or he has an optimistic outlook on life, marked by positive thoughts about herself or himself, the world, and the future. And a biological psychologist might assume that your professor is happy because she or he has unusually high levels of brain chemicals associated with positive moods.

While reading the upcoming chapters, you should keep in mind that each psychological perspective is worthwhile and has something to add to our fund of knowledge. Just because a psychologist favors one perspective does not mean that she or he necessarily discounts the value of the other perspectives. In fact, many psychologists are eclectic—they accept aspects of several perspectives in guiding their own research or practice. A century ago, William James insisted that while seeking to unify psychology, psychologists should also revel in its diversity (Viney, 1989).

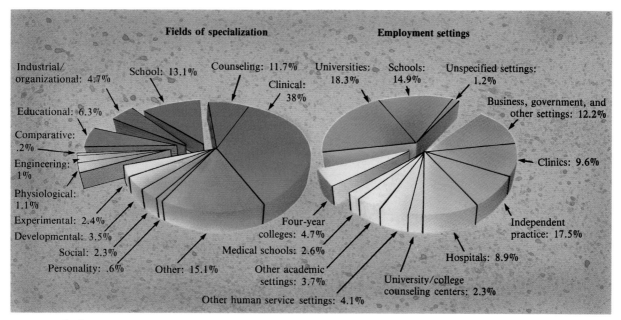

Fields of specialization

Industrial/organizational: 4.7%
School: 13.1%
Counseling: 11.7%
Clinical: 38%
Educational: 6.3%
Comparative: .2%
Engineering: 1%
Physiological: 1.1%
Experimental: 2.4%
Developmental: 3.5%
Social: 2.3%
Personality: .6%
Other: 15.1%

Employment settings

Universities: 18.3%
Schools: 14.9%
Unspecified settings: 1.2%
Business, government, and other settings: 12.2%
Clinics: 9.6%
Independent practice: 17.5%
Hospitals: 8.9%
University/college counseling centers: 2.3%
Four-year colleges: 4.7%
Medical schools: 2.6%
Other academic settings: 3.7%
Other human service settings: 4.1%

FIGURE 1.1

Fields of Specialization and Employment Settings of Psychologists
The pie graph on the left presents the percentage of psychologists working in major fields of specialization. The pie graph on the right presents the percentage of psychologists who work in particular employment settings (Stapp, Tucker, & VandenBos, 1985).

PSYCHOLOGY AS A PROFESSION

As psychology has evolved as a science, its fields of specialization have multiplied, and its educational and training requirements have become formalized. Today there are more than 100,000 psychologists in the United States (Stapp, Tucker, & VandenBos, 1985), working in a wide variety of fields in both academic and professional settings (illustrated in figure 1.1). Appendix A discusses the psychology major and ways of pursuing a career as a psychologist, whether academic or professional.

Academic Fields of Specialization

Most of the chapters in this book discuss academic fields of specialization in psychology, usually practiced by psychologists working at colleges or universities. In fact, as indicated in figure 1.1, colleges and universities are the main employment settings for psychologists. Because each field of psychology contains subfields, which, in turn, contain sub-subfields, a budding psychologist has hundreds of potential specialties from which to choose. For example, a psychologist specializing in the field of sensation and perception might be interested in the subfield of vision, with special interest in the sub-subfield of color vision.

Many academic psychologists prefer to conduct **basic research,** aimed at finding answers to psychological questions out of intellectual curiosity. Many others prefer to conduct **applied research,** aimed at using research findings to improve the quality of life or to solve practical problems. Keep in mind that basic research and applied research are not mutually exclusive. Many psychologists conduct both kinds of research, and findings from basic research can often be applied outside of the laboratory. For example, basic research on learned taste aversions in rats has led to applications in preventing cancer chemotherapy patients from becoming nauseated by food, which might make them stop eating and become emaciated.

basic research
Research aimed at finding answers to questions out of theoretical interest or intellectual curiosity.

applied research
Research aimed at improving the quality of life and solving practical problems.

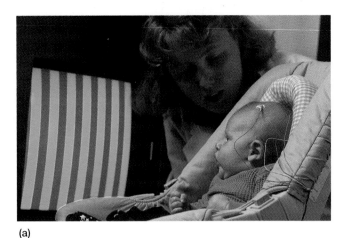
(a)

(b)

Psychological Research
Psychologists conduct research on human and animal subjects, such as measuring the brain's response to changing patterns of visual stimulation in infancy (*a*) and training dolphins to communicate with human beings (*b*).

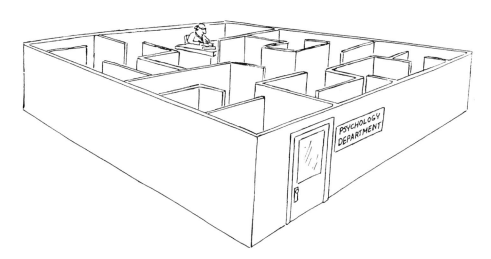

experimental psychology
The field primarily concerned with laboratory research on basic psychological processes, including perception, learning, memory, thinking, language, motivation, and emotion.

The largest field of academic specialization in psychology is **experimental psychology.** Experimental psychologists restrict themselves chiefly to laboratory research on basic psychological processes, including perception, learning, memory, thinking, language, motivation, and emotion. Though this field is called experimental psychology, it is not the only field that uses experiments. Psychologists in almost all fields of psychology use experiments in doing their research.

Consider some of the topics tackled by experimental psychologists that will be discussed in upcoming chapters. Chapter 5 describes how perception researchers determine whether human beings can identify others by their odor. Chapter 8 explains how memory researchers assess the effect of our moods on our ability to recall memories. And chapter 12 discusses how emotion researchers demonstrate the effect of facial expressions on emotional experiences.

biopsychology
The field that studies the relationship between physiological and psychological processes.

Psychologists in the field of **biopsychology** study the biological basis of behavior and mental processes. Chapter 3 discusses research by biopsychologists on the effects of natural opiates in the brain, the possibility of using tissue transplants to treat brain damage, and the differences in functioning between the left and right hemispheres of the brain. In chapter 6 you will learn of research by biopsychologists on the effects of psychoactive drugs on mind and behavior.

comparative psychology
The field that studies similarities and differences in the physiology, behaviors, and abilities of animals, including human beings.

The related field of **comparative psychology** studies similarities and differences in the physiology, behaviors, and abilities of animals, including human beings. Compara-

(a)

(b)

(c)

FIGURE 1.2

Emerging Fields of Professional Psychology
In recent years, several new fields of professional psychology have emerged. Professionals in the field of (a) *sport psychology* help amateur and professional athletes, such as slalom skiers, improve their performance. Practitioners of (b) *health psychology* contribute to the prevention of physical illness by promoting adherence to healthy behaviors, including regular aerobic exercise, such as rowing. And (c) *environmental psychology* applies research findings to improve the physical environment, as in designing neighborhoods to reduce noise, crowding, and other sources of stress.

tive psychologists study motives related to eating, drinking, aggression, courtship, mating, and parenting. Chapter 9 discusses how comparative psychologists even study whether apes can learn to use human language.

The field of **developmental psychology** is home to psychologists who study the factors responsible for physical, cognitive, and social changes across the life span. Chapter 4 presents research showing that learning can take place in the womb, that infants are born with better perceptual skills than is commonly believed, and that many sex differences might be smaller than commonly believed.

Personality psychology is concerned with differences in behavior among individuals. As noted in chapter 13, this field seeks answers to such questions as, Are our personalities determined more by nature or by nurture? and To what extent do people behave consistently from one situation to another? Personality psychologists also devise tests for assessing personality, such as the famous Rorschach "inkblot test."

Psychologists in the related field of **social psychology** study the effects people have on one another. In chapter 17 you will learn how social psychologists study the factors affecting interpersonal attraction, the problem of "groupthink" in making important decisions, and the reasons why people are often all too willing to follow orders to harm other human beings.

Professional Fields of Specialization

Professional psychologists commonly work in settings outside of college or university classrooms and laboratories. As indicated in Figure 1.1, two of the largest fields of professional psychology are **clinical psychology** and **counseling psychology,** which deal with the causes, prevention, diagnosis, and treatment of psychological disorders. Clinical psychology and counseling psychology are so similar that even practitioners of one or the other find it difficult to specify the features that distinguish one from the other. There is a tendency, however, for counseling psychologists to deal with problems of everyday living related to career planning, academic performance, and marriage and family. In contrast, clinical psychologists typically treat more severe disorders, including phobias, alcoholism, drug abuse, and severe depression. Chapter 15 discusses the various techniques used by clinical and counseling psychologists, as well as research concerning the important question, Is psychotherapy effective?

developmental psychology
The field that studies physical, cognitive, and psychosocial changes across the life span.

personality psychology
The field that focuses on factors accounting for the differences in behavior and enduring personal characteristics among individuals.

social psychology
The field that studies how people affect one another's thoughts, feelings, and behaviors.

clinical psychology
The field that applies psychological principles to the prevention, diagnosis, and treatment of psychological disorders.

counseling psychology
The field that applies psychological principles to help individuals deal with problems of daily living, generally less severe ones than those treated by clinical psychologists.

psychiatry
The field of medicine that diagnoses and treats psychological disorders by using medical or psychological forms of therapy.

school psychology
The field that applies psychological principles to improving the academic performance and social behavior of students in elementary, junior high, and high schools.

educational psychology
The field that applies psychological principles to improving curriculum, teaching methods, and administrative procedures.

industrial/organizational psychology
The field that applies psychological principles to improve productivity in businesses, industries, and government agencies.

engineering psychology
The field that applies psychological principles to the design of equipment and instruments.

forensic psychology
The field that applies psychological principles to improve the legal system, including the work of police and juries.

sport psychology
The field that applies psychological principles to help amateur and professional athletes improve their performance.

health psychology
The field that applies psychological principles to the prevention and treatment of physical illness.

environmental psychology
The field that applies psychological principles to improving the physical environment, including the design of buildings and the reduction of noise.

Clinical psychology and counseling psychology are distinctly different from the medical field of **psychiatry.** A psychiatrist is not a psychologist, but a physician who has served a residency in psychiatry, which takes a medical approach to the treatment of psychological disorders. Because psychiatrists are physicians, they may prescribe drugs or other biomedical treatments. Chapter 15 considers the various biomedical treatments, including drugs to treat schizophrenia, psychosurgery to calm agitated patients, and electroconvulsive therapy to relieve depression.

Psychology has other well-established professional fields. Psychologists who specialize in **school psychology** evaluate students for proper class placement, set up programs to improve student academic performance and school behavior, and provide counseling, often in cooperation with parents and teachers, to students who are having social or academic problems. School psychologists work in elementary schools, junior high schools, and high schools. The allied field of **educational psychology** tries to improve the educational process, including curriculum, teaching, and administration of academic programs. Educational psychologists are usually faculty members at colleges or universities.

Psychologists who practice **industrial/organizational psychology** work to increase productivity in businesses, industries, and government agencies. They do so by improving working conditions, methods for hiring and training employees, and management techniques of administrators.

Specialists in **engineering psychology** are experts in human factors, the aspects of human body structure, behavior, and mental processes that must be considered when designing equipment and instruments. An engineering psychologist might assist in the design of the instrument panel of an airplane, the warning system in a nuclear power plant, or the barriers erected at a railroad crossing.

Psychologists who practice **forensic psychology** participate in the legal system. They study the validity of eyewitness testimony, the jury deliberation process, and the best ways to select jurors. Some train police to handle domestic disputes, negotiate with hostage takers, and cope with job-related stress. Chapter 2 describes an experiment concerned with a timely forensic psychology issue: How accurate are police, bartenders, and ordinary people in detecting drunkenness in others? Figure 1.2 illustrates three emerging fields of professional psychology: **sport psychology, health psychology,** and **environmental psychology.**

THINKING ABOUT *Psychology*

WHAT ROLE DID WOMEN PLAY IN THE GROWTH OF PSYCHOLOGY?

Little more than a decade ago, Florence Denmark, then president of the American Psychological Association, remarked that "women have contributed a great deal to the growth and development of the discipline of psychology.... For the most part, however, women have been unrecognized, undervalued, and invisible in our recorded history" (Denmark, 1980, p. 1057). Since its founding a century ago, psychology has been more hospitable to women than has any other science, yet obstacles prevented some women from pursuing careers as psychologists, and those women who were pioneers in psychology have not been accorded the degree of recognition they deserve (Bohan, 1990).

EARLY OBSTACLES TO WOMEN IN PSYCHOLOGY

To appreciate the obstacles women faced in the early years of psychology, one must delve into the social and cultural factors that affected them. The chief factor that limited professional opportunities for women was the notion of "separate spheres" for men and women. The primary roles in a woman's sphere included being a good daughter, wife, and mother. In contrast, though a man was expected to be devoted to his family, his sphere included a variety of career choices, even the possibility of becoming a scientist. Women who pursued careers as scientists typically had to forsake (or at least postpone) marriage and parenthood, or faced customs and policies aimed at preventing them from leaving their sphere.

Some of the reasons given for keeping women within their sphere warned of dire consequences for the physical well-being of women who dared to venture into the man's sphere. G. Stanley Hall, an influential pioneer in psychology, claimed that there was an inverse relationship between the development of the female brain and the development of the female reproductive system. He insisted that a female who pursued education after puberty would suffer atrophy of her reproductive organs. He did not foresee the same fate for the reproductive organs of males who pursued education after puberty. Views like this, coupled with beliefs that women simply lacked the personal and intellectual abilities needed to profit from higher education, kept many women from entering the sciences, including psychology.

Moreover, women who wanted to pursue higher education were refused admission by many colleges and universities, were ineligible for financial aid, and were less likely to be offered faculty positions at prestigious universities after graduation. Women also were excluded from professional circles that helped scientists advance in their careers. For example, in 1904 Edward Titchener, appalled at what he believed was the American Psychological Association's movement toward applied psychology, established a psychological research society called The Experimentalists (Goodwin, 1985). Its bylaws excluded women, allegedly to permit men to engage in masculine activities, including smoking and "man talk." This blocked women psychologists from making the same useful professional connections as their male colleagues—that is, they were banned from what is known today as "networking."

The leading psychologist who opposed this exclusion was Christine Ladd-Franklin (1847–1930), who became known for her evolutionary theory of color vision (Furumoto, 1992), which is described in chapter 5. For more than two decades she acted as a gadfly, trying unsuccessfully to gain membership for women in the society. She even accused Titchener of hypocrisy for admitting males who were not true experimentalists while excluding women who were (Furumoto, 1988). No woman was admitted until 1929, two years after Titchener's death and a year before Ladd-Franklin's. The first woman member was Margaret Floy Washburn (1871–1939), the leading comparative psychologist of her day, author of the most widely used textbook on animal psychology, and a past president of the American Psychological Association (Goodman, 1980).

Despite the roadblocks faced by women, psychology has had a higher proportion of women members than has any other science. For example, in the 1920s, when less than 10 percent of other scientists were women, more than 20 percent of psychologists were women. And several women, including Ladd-Franklin and Washburn, became leaders in psychology. But how did women who left their sphere find ways to become pioneers in psychology and other sciences? Oftentimes, they had parents who supported education for women and would help them financially. The minority who married typically had supportive husbands. And many were championed by prominent male or female psychologists who helped them advance in their careers. To illustrate several of these factors and to appreciate the accomplishments of women pioneers in psychology, consider Mary Whiton Calkins (1863–1930), arguably the first great woman psychologist.

Florence Denmark
"The more we study women's history, the more we appreciate the power of society's norms and institutions to affect the development of psychology as well as the career paths of individual pychologists."

THE LIFE AND WORK OF
MARY WHITON CALKINS

In 1903 Calkins, along with Margaret Floy Washburn and Christine Ladd-Franklin, was listed in a ranking by James McKeen Cattell of the 50 most eminent American psychologists (O'Connell & Russo, 1990). As noted earlier, Calkins was one of William James's students. But, as pointed out by Laurel Furumoto (1980), who is an authority on Calkins, being a student of the most renowned psychologist of his time did not guarantee Calkins an easy path to a career as a psychologist.

Calkins, a resident of Newton, Massachusetts, was a descendant of the famous John and Priscilla Alden of Plymouth Colony. Her parents encouraged her to pursue a professional career. In 1885, after earning a bachelor's degree from Smith College, she became a Greek instructor at Wellesley College. In 1890 Wellesley's founder decided to introduce the new science of psychology to the school. Because there were too few psychologists to staff all the psychology departments sprouting up in North America, Calkins, an outstanding teacher, was asked to take graduate courses to prepare her to become Wellesley's first psychology professor.

Calkins sought admission to nearby Harvard University. Though Harvard did not let women enroll in its courses, her father, a respected minister, convinced Harvard's president to let her audit courses. Despite this initial good fortune, she suffered discrimination throughout her years at Harvard. In her autobiography, Calkins (1930) describes her first course, a seminar offered by William James, in which the other students—all males—withdrew. Given that James was a popular professor and that Harvard students had expressed alarm in the campus newspaper at the possible intrusion of women into their classes (Scarborough & Furumoto, 1987), one is left with the strong suspicion that they withdrew because they disapproved of her presence in the course.

As was her custom, instead of reacting angrily, Calkins converted a bad experience into a good one by reveling in her memories of the time she spent alone with the great William James in front of a library fireplace, discussing psychology and using his just-published *The Principles of Psychology* as the textbook. Imagine receiving private lessons in science from Albert Einstein, in acting from Meryl Streep, or in basketball from Michael Jordan and you might get a sense of her exhilaration.

Calkins also took courses with Edmund Clark Sanford, a leading psychologist, at Clark University. They collaborated on one of the earliest experimental studies of dreams, recounted in chapter 6, which produced findings that have held up remarkably well over the years. In 1891, with Sanford's and James's help, Calkins founded the psychology laboratory at Wellesley College, the first at a women's school. Sanford helped her select supplies and equipment, and James taught her how to dissect and store sheep brains (O'Connell & Russo, 1990). By 1895 Calkins had completed all the course work and the doctoral dissertation necessary for a Ph.D. in psychology. Her dissertation was based on research on memory she had carried out with Hugo Münsterberg. While conducting this research, she invented the paired-associates technique, which became one of the main tools of memory researchers. In 1895, several eminent members of the Harvard faculty, including William James and Hugo Münsterberg, gave Calkins the customary opportunity to defend her dissertation. James called her performance "the most brilliant examination for the Ph.D. that we have had at Harvard."

Münsterberg, her dissertation sponsor, petitioned the Harvard administration to grant her the Ph.D. she had earned. He noted that she was superior to all the male students and was one of the best college professors in America. His request was refused. In 1902 Calkins was offered a Ph.D. from Radcliffe College, Harvard's sister school. She

Laurel Furumoto
"Despite their presence in psychology's past, women psychologists have been a well-kept secret in the history of the discipline."

rejected it, insisting that she would not honor Harvard's discriminatory policy by accepting a degree from a school she had not attended. In 1927 several eminent Harvard alumni who had become leading psychologists petitioned the Harvard administration to finally grant Calkins the degree she had earned three decades earlier. Once again, the request was denied (Furumoto, 1980).

The lack of a doctorate did not deter Calkins from becoming a prominent psychologist. In 1905 she was elected the first woman president of the American Psychological Association. In her presidential speech, she defended her own theoretical creation, self psychology, and put it forth as an alternative to the competing schools of structuralism and functionalism. She urged psychologists to study the conscious mind, the environment (both physical and social), and the relationship between the conscious mind and the environment. She made self psychology the theme of her widely used introductory psychology textbook (Calkins, 1901).

Calkins also wrote the first article that criticized John B. Watson's call for a behaviorist approach to psychology (Calkins, 1913). She pointed out that ignoring the mind might be fine for the study of animals but was inadequate for the study of human beings. Unlike Watson, who viewed the human being as a passive responder to environmental stimuli, Calkins viewed the human being as active and purposive. Because of the recent cognitive trend in psychology and the reintroduction of the study of the mind, one historian of psychology has suggested that Calkins's relatively unknown self psychology was more prophetic of where psychology is now headed than was Watson's widely known behaviorist theory (Samelson, 1981). The recent increased attention to theories of the self (see chapter 13) is in keeping with the direction, if not necessarily the content, of her theory.

Calkins was beloved by her students and colleagues alike. They found her to be a warm, open-minded, and devoutly religious person. She also remained an active champion of women's rights (Furumoto, 1980). When her alma mater, Smith College, announced plans to institute a special curriculum that would prepare women for their sphere, she opposed it as being as illogical as offering completely separate diets for males and females. At a national suffrage convention in Baltimore, Calkins spoke out in favor of giving women the right to vote. She also pointed out that allegedly inborn intellectual and personality differences between males and females were more likely the products of sex-role training that begins in infancy and continues throughout life (Scarborough & Furumoto, 1987).

Calkins, like her mentor William James, developed an increasingly active interest in philosophy. In 1918, her fellow philosophers showed their respect for her by electing her president of the American Philosophical Association. In 1929, the year in which women were first admitted to Titchener's society of experimental psychologists, Calkins retired from Wellesley College to write and to care for her mother, only to die of cancer the following year. Though an outstanding psychologist in her day, she, like many other women psychologists, taught at a women's college that lacked a graduate program. This prevented her theory from being carried forth by graduate-student disciples in their own research, publications, and professional presentations—one of the ways in which psychologists build their reputations.

Calkins would be pleased that women are now at least as likely as men to pursue careers in psychology (Russo & Denmark, 1987). A perusal of upcoming chapters will show that women contributors to psychology are more recognized, valued, and visible today than they were when Mary Whiton Calkins fought the odds and became a pioneer in psychology.

Mary Whiton Calkins (1863–1930)
"I am more deeply convinced that psychology should be conceived as the science of the self, or person, as related to its environment, physical and social."

THE HISTORY OF PSYCHOLOGY

Psychology is the scientific study of behavior and mental processes. Psychology is a science because it relies on the scientific method; it differs from other sciences only in its subject matter. The roots of psychology are in philosophy and science. When nineteenth-century physiologists began to use the scientific method to study psychological processes, psychology emerged as an independent science. The commonly accepted founding date for psychology is 1879, when Wilhelm Wundt established the first formal psychology laboratory.

The late nineteenth century and early twentieth century were associated with the rise of schools of psychology, which differed in their approaches to the study of psychology. Structuralism, led by Edward Titchener, sought to analyze the mind into its component parts by studying conscious mental experience. Functionalism, led by William James, arose in opposition to structuralism and favored the study of how the conscious mind helps the individual adapt to the environment. Psychoanalysis, led by Sigmund Freud, was an outgrowth of medicine and studied the influence of unconscious sexual and aggressive motives on behavior. Behaviorism, led by John B. Watson, rejected the study of the mind in favor of the study of observable behavior, insisting that a science can study only observable, measurable events. And Gestalt psychology, led by Max Wertheimer, favored the study of mental processes and emphasized the active role of the mind in perceiving wholes rather than combinations of separate components.

To date, psychology has no unifying scientific paradigm. Instead, there are competing psychological perspectives. The psychoanalytic perspective, favored by neo-Freudians, downplays the influence of the biological motives of sex and aggression and stresses the influence of interpersonal relationships. The strict behavioral perspective, championed by B. F. Skinner, rejects the study of mental experiences in favor of the study of observable behavior. But cognitive behaviorists accept the study of mental experiences as long as they are carefully tied to observable behavior. The humanistic perspective, founded by Abraham Maslow and Carl Rogers, arose as a "third force" in opposition to both psychoanalysis and behaviorism. It favors the study of subjective mental experience and the belief that human beings are not merely puppets controlled by unconscious drives and environmental stimuli. The cognitive perspective, influenced by the work of Jean Piaget and Herbert Simon, views the brain as an active processor of information. The biopsychological perspective, exemplified by the work of Wilder Penfield and Roger Sperry, favors the study of the biological basis of behavior and mental experiences.

PSYCHOLOGY AS A PROFESSION

During its century of existence, psychology has seen the emergence of a wide variety of academic and professional fields of specialization. The academic fields of specialization are chiefly concerned with basic research, which aims to add to our fund of knowledge about behavior and mental processes. The major academic fields of specialization include experimental psychology, biopsychology, comparative psychology, developmental psychology, personality psychology, and social psychology. The professional fields of specialization are chiefly concerned with applied research, which tries to improve the quality of life. Among the major fields of professional psychology are clinical psychology, counseling psychology, school psychology, educational psychology, industrial/organizational psychology, engineering psychology, and forensic psychology. Emerging fields of professional psychology include sport psychology, health psychology, and environmental psychology.

THINKING ABOUT PSYCHOLOGY: WHAT ROLE DID WOMEN PLAY IN THE GROWTH OF PSYCHOLOGY?

Despite obstacles presented by laws and customs, women contributed to the growth of psychology. Several women psychologists managed to achieve eminence in the late nineteenth and early twentieth centuries. Perhaps the most noteworthy was Mary Whiton Calkins, who contributed to the study of dreams, memory, and personality, and who became the first woman to serve as president of the American Psychological Association.

IMPORTANT CONCEPTS

analytic introspection 10
applied research 21
basic research 21
behavioral perspective 17
behaviorism 13
biopsychological perspective 20
biopsychology 22
clinical psychology 23
cognitive perspective 19
comparative psychology 22
counseling psychology 23

developmental psychology 23
differential psychology 9
educational psychology 24
empiricism 6
engineering psychology 24
environmental psychology 24
existential psychology 19
experimental psychology 22
forensic psychology 24
functionalism 11
Gestalt psychology 14

health psychology 24
historicism 4
humanistic perspective 18
industrial/organizational
    psychology 24
personality psychology 23
phi phenomenon 14
presentism 4
psychiatry 24
psychic determinism 15
psychoanalysis 15

psychoanalytic perspective 18
psychology 4
psychophysics 8
rationalism 5
school psychology 24
scientific paradigm 17
social psychology 23
sport psychology 24
structuralism 10

Alfred Adler *18*
Aristotle *5*
Saint Augustine *6*
Avicenna *6*
Francis Bacon *7*
Roger Bacon *6*
Albert Bandura *18*
Paul Broca *8*
Mary Whiton Calkins *12, 26*
James McKeen Cattell *9*
Charles Darwin *8*
René Descartes *6*
Hermann Ebbinghaus *9*

Erik Erikson *18*
Gustav Fechner *8*
Pierre Flourens *8*
Anna Freud *18*
Sigmund Freud *15*
Erich Fromm *18*
Francis Galton *8*
G. Stanley Hall *12*
Hermann von Helmholtz *7*
Karen Horney *18*
William James *11*
Carl Jung *18*
Immanuel Kant *7*

George Kelly *19*
Melanie Klein *18*
Kurt Koffka *15*
Wolfgang Kohler *15*
Christine Ladd-Franklin *25, 26*
Kurt Lewin *15*
John Locke *7*
Abraham Maslow *18*
Hugo Münsterberg *12*
Ivan Pavlov *13*
Wilder Penfield *20*
Jean Piaget *19*
Plato *5*

Carl Rogers *19*
Herbert Simon *19*
B. F. Skinner *17*
Roger Sperry *20*
Harry Stack Sullivan *18*
Francis Sumner *12*
Edward Titchener *10*
Margaret Floy Washburn *25, 26*
John B. Watson *13*
Ernst Weber *8*
Max Wertheimer *14*
Wilhelm Wundt *9*

RECOMMENDED READINGS

FOR MORE ON THE HISTORY OF PSYCHOLOGY

General Historical Information

Benjamin, L. T., Jr. (1988). *A history of psychology: Original sources and contemporary research.* New York: McGraw-Hill.

Boring, E. G. (1950). *A history of experimental psychology (2nd ed.).* New York: Appleton-Century-Crofts.

Fancher, R. E. (1990). *Pioneers of psychology (2nd ed.).* New York: W. W. Norton.

Guthrie, R. V. (1976). *Even the rat was white: A historical view of psychology.* New York: Harper & Row.

Hilgard, E. R. (1987). *Psychology in America: A historical survey.* San Diego: Harcourt Brace Jovanovich.

Kessen, W., & Cahan, E. D. (1986). A century of psychology: From subject to object to agent. *American Scientist, 74,* 640–649.

Leahey, T. H. (1994). *A history of modern psychology (2nd ed.).* Englewood Cliffs, NJ: Prentice Hall.

Popplestone, J. A., & McPherson, M. W. (1994). *An illustrated history of modern psychology.* Dubuque, IA: Brown & Benchmark.

Viney, W. (1993). *A history of psychology: Ideas and context.* Boston: Allyn & Bacon.

Wright, M. J., & Myers, C. R. (1982). *History of academic psychology in Canada.* Toronto: Hogrefe.

The Roots of Psychology

Bowlby, P. J. (1989). *Evolution: The history of an idea.* Berkeley: University of California Press.

Clarke, E., & Jacyna, L. S. (1987). *Nineteenth-century origins of neuroscientific concepts.* Berkeley: University of California Press.

Cowan, R. S., & Rosenberg, C. (Eds.). (1985). *Sir Francis Galton and the study of heredity in the nineteenth century.* New York: Garland.

Darwin, C. (1859/1975). *The origin of species.* New York: W. W. Norton.

Field, G. (1974). *Plato and his contemporaries.* New York: Haskell.

Kemp, S. (1990). *Medieval psychology.* New York: Greenwood.

Robinson, D. N. (1989). *Aristotle's psychology.* New York: Columbia University Press.

The Growth of Psychology

Bringmann, W. G., & Tweney, R. D. (Eds.). (1980). *Wundt studies.* Toronto: Hogrefe.

Donnelly, M. E. (Ed.). (1992). *Reinterpreting the legacy of William James.* Washington, DC: American Psychological Association.

Evans, R. B., Sexton, V. S., & Cadwallader, T. C. (Eds.). (1992). *The American Psychological Association: A historical perspective.* Washington, DC: American Psychological Association.

Fine, R. (1987). *The development of Freud's thought.* Northvale, NJ: Aronson.

Kohler, W. (1947). *Gestalt psychology.* New York: New American Library.

Morawski, J. G. (Ed.). (1988). *The rise of experimentation in American psychology.* New Haven, CT: Yale University Press.

O'Donnell, J. M. (1985). *The origins of behaviorism: American psychology, 1870–1920.* New York: New York University Press.

Owens, D. A., & Wagner, M. (Eds.). (1992). *Progress in modern psychology: The legacy of American functionalism.* Westport, CT: Greenwood.

Contemporary Psychology

Berry, J. W., Poortinga, Y. A., Segall, M. H., & Dasen, P. R. (1992). *Cross-cultural psychology: Research and applications.* New York: Cambridge University Press.

Brislin, R. W. (1990). *Applied cross-cultural psychology.* Newbury Park, CA: Sage Publications.

Bronstein, P., & Quina, K. (Eds.). (1988). *Teaching a psychology of people: Resources for gender and sociocultural awareness.* Washington, DC: American Psychological Association.

Brown, D. E. (1991). *Human universals.* Philadelphia: Temple University Press.

Fisher, S., & Greenberg, R. P. (1985). *The scientific credibility of Freud's theories and therapy.* New York: Columbia University Press.

Gardner, H. (1985). *The mind's new science: A history of the cognitive revolution.* New York: Basic Books.

Gilgen, A. R. (1982). *American psychology since World War II: A profile of the discipline.* Westport, CT: Greenwood.

Klivington, K. (1989). *The science of mind.* Cambridge, MA: MIT.

Rychlak, J. F. (1988). *The psychology of rigorous humanism.* New York: New York University Press.

Schwartz, B., & Lacey, H. (1982). *Behaviorism, science, and human nature.* New York: W. W. Norton.

FOR MORE ON PSYCHOLOGY AS A PROFESSION

Fagan, T. K., & VandenBos, G. R. (Eds.). (1993). *Exploring applied psychology: Origins and critical analyses.* Washington, DC: American Psychological Association.

Gifford, R. (1991). *Applied psychology: Variety and opportunity.* Boston: Allyn & Bacon.

Stricker, G., Davis-Russell, E., Bourg, E., Duran, E., Hammond, W. R., McHolland, J., Polite, K., & Vaughn, B. E. (Eds.). (1990). *Toward ethnic diversification in psychology education and training.* Washington, DC: American Psychological Association.

FOR MORE ON CONTRIBU-
TIONS OF WOMEN TO THE
GROWTH OF PSYCHOLOGY

Bohan, J. S. (Ed.). (1992). *Re-placing women in psychology: Readings toward a more inclusive history*. Dubuque, IA: Kendall/Hunt.

O'Connell, A. N., & Russo, N. F. (1983). *Models of achievement: Reflections of eminent women in psychology* (Vol. 1). New York: Columbia University Press.

O'Connell, A. N., & Russo, N. F. (1988). *Models of achievement: Reflections of eminent women in psychology* (Vol. 2). Hillsdale, N.J.: Erlbaum.

O'Connell, A. N., & Russo, N. F. (Eds.). (1990). *Women in psychology: A bio-bibliographic sourcebook*. New York: Greenwood.

Russo, N. F., & Denmark, F. L. (1987). Contributions of women to psychology. *Annual Review of Psychology, 38*, 279–298.

Scarborough, E., & Furumoto, L. (1987). *Untold lives: The first generation of American women psychologists*. New York: Columbia University Press.

Wright, M. J. (1992). Women ground-breakers in Canadian psychology: World War II and its aftermath. *Canadian Psychology, 33*, 675–682.

FOR MORE ON CONTRIBU-TORS TO PSYCHOLOGY

Contributors to the Roots of Psychology

Philosophical Roots

Brown, P. (1967). *Augustine of Hippo*. Berkeley: University of California Press.

Cottingham, J. G. (1986). *Descartes*. New York: Basil Blackwell.

Cranston, M. (1979). *John Locke: A biography*. New York: Oxford University Press.

Easton, S. C. (1952). *Roger Bacon and his search for a universal science*. Westport, CT: Greenwood.

Goodman, L. E. (1992). *Avicenna*. New York: Routledge.

Quinton, A. (1981). *Francis Bacon*. New York: Oxford University Press.

Stuckenberg, J. H. (1882/1986). *The life of Immanuel Kant*. Lanham, MD: University Press of America.

Wilbur, J. B., & Allen, H. J. (Eds.). (1979). *The worlds of Plato and Aristotle*. Buffalo, NY: Prometheus.

Scientific Roots

Bowlby, J. (1991). *Charles Darwin: A new life*. New York: W. W. Norton.

Forrest, D. W. (1974). *Francis Galton: The life and work of a Victorian genius*. New York: Taplinger.

Köenigsberger, L. (1906). *Hermann von Helmholtz*. New York: Dover.

Schiller, F. (1979). *Paul Broca: Founder of French anthropology, explorer of the brain*. Berkeley: University of California Press.

Contributors to the Growth of Psychology

Structuralism

Rieber, R. W. (1980). *Wilhelm Wundt and the making of a scientific psychology*. New York: Plenum.

Functionalism

Dykhuizen, G. (1973). *The life and mind of John Dewey*. Carbondale: Southern Illinois University Press.

Hale, M., Jr. (1980). *Human science and social order: Hugo Münsterberg and the origins of applied psychology*. Philadelphia: Temple University Press.

Myers, G. E. (1986). *William James: His life and thought*. New York: Columbia University Press.

Ross, D. (1972). *G. Stanley Hall: The psychologist as prophet*. Chicago: University of Chicago Press.

Behaviorism

Babkin, B. P. (1975). *Pavlov: A biography*. Chicago: University of Chicago Press.

Buckley, K. W. (1989). *Mechanical man: John Broadus Watson and the beginnings of behaviorism*. New York: Guilford.

Gestalt Psychology

Harrower, M. (1984). *Kurt Koffka: An unwitting self-portrait*. Gainesville: University Presses of Florida.

Marrow, A. J. (1969). *The practical theorist: The life and work of Kurt Lewin*. New York: Basic Books.

Psychoanalysis

Gay, P. (1988). *Freud: A life for our time*. New York: W. W. Norton.

Rattner, J. (1983). *Alfred Adler*. New York: Frederick Ungar.

Stevens, A. (1990). *On Jung*. New York: Routledge.

Contributors to Contemporary Psychology

The Behavioral Perspective

Bjork, D. W. (1993). *B. F. Skinner: A life*. New York: Basic Books.

Evans, R. I. (1989). *Albert Bandura: The man and his ideas*. New York: Praeger.

The Psychoanalytic Perspective

Coles, R. (1970). *Erik Erikson: The growth of his work*. Boston: Atlantic/Little, Brown.

Grosskurth, P. (1986). *Melanie Klein: Her world and her work*. New York: Knopf.

Knapp, G. P. (1989). *The art of living: Erich Fromm's life and works*. New York: Peter Lang.

Perry, H. S. (1982). *Psychiatrist of America: The life of Harry Stack Sullivan*. Cambridge, MA: Harvard University Press.

Quinn, S. (1987). *A mind of her own: The life of Karen Horney*. New York: Summit.

Young-Bruehl, E. (1988). *Anna Freud*. New York: Summit.

The Humanistic Perspective

Hoffman, E. (1988). *The right to be human: A biography of Abraham Maslow*. Los Angeles: Tarcher.

Kirschenbaum, H. (1979). *On becoming Carl Rogers*. New York: Delacorte.

The Cognitive Perspective

Boden, M. A. (1980). *Jean Piaget*. New York: Viking Press.

Simon, H. A. (1991). *Models of my life*. New York: Basic Books.

The Biopsychological Perspective

Lewis, J. (1982). *Something hidden: A biography of Wilder Penfield*. New York: Doubleday.

CHAPTER 2

Vasily Kandinsky
Composition 8
July 1923

PSYCHOLOGY AS A SCIENCE

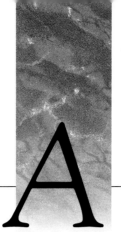

As noted in chapter 1, psychology is the science of behavior and mental processes. In discussing psychology as a science, this chapter will answer such questions as, Why do psychologists use the scientific method? What are the goals of psychological research? and How do psychologists employ the scientific method in their research? The answers to these questions will help you appreciate the scientific basis of the issues, theories, research findings, and practical applications presented throughout this book.

SOURCES OF KNOWLEDGE

Psychologists and other scientists favor the scientific method as their means of obtaining knowledge. To appreciate why they do, first consider everyday sources of knowledge.

Everyday Sources of Knowledge

Chapter 1 began with a list of questions pertinent to psychology. To find answers to them, you might rely on *common sense, appeal to authority, reasoning,* or *unsystematic observation.* The following discussion of these sources of knowledge will consider an issue regarding interpersonal attraction: Do "opposites attract"? Or do "birds of a feather flock together"?

Common Sense

When you rely on common sense, you assume that if most people share a belief, then it must be true. Common sense is sometimes correct, but it too often presents misleading versions of the "truth" (Fletcher, 1984). For example, in regard to interpersonal attraction, common sense can be used to support either the belief that opposites attract or the belief that birds of a feather flock together. In using common sense, you might declare, "Almost everyone I know agrees that opposites attract." A friend might then counter, "You're wrong; almost everyone I know agrees that birds of a feather flock together." The use of the scientific method to resolve the conflict between these two commonsense views of interpersonal attraction is described later in the chapter. The photograph of the student changing an answer to a multiple-choice exam presents another, perhaps surprising, example of the shortcomings of common sense.

Appeal to Authority

In seeking knowledge, you might also *appeal to authority*. But, as in the case of common sense, authorities can be wrong or contradict one another. Suppose that you wrote to advice columnists Dear Abby and Ann Landers, asking them to resolve your conflict about the nature of interpersonal attraction. Dear Abby might reply, "My experts tell me that opposites attract. So probably you'll marry (or have already married) someone very different from yourself." But Ann Landers might reply, instead, "My experts tell me that birds of a feather flock together. So probably you'll marry (or have already married) someone just like yourself."

Psychological authorities, too, may differ in their proclamations about a given issue. For example, two school psychologists might disagree about the best academic placement for mentally retarded children. One might favor placing them in special classes composed of mentally retarded students, and the other might favor placing them in regular classes, so-called *mainstreaming*. But the best solution to this problem comes from scientific research, which indicates that mentally retarded children benefit more

Sources of Knowledge
What accounts for interpersonal attraction? In seeking the answer to this question and the answers to all sorts of questions about human and animal behavior, each of us relies on common sense, authority, reasoning, and observation. But psychologists, as scientists, rely on the scientific method as the best source of knowledge.

Common Sense
Should you change your answers on multiple-choice tests? Student common sense would say no. You have probably heard the folk wisdom, "Don't change your answers on exams, because you'll be more likely to change a right answer to a wrong answer than a wrong answer to a right answer." You might be surprised that scientific research has consistently found that students are slightly more likely to change a wrong answer to a right answer than a right answer to a wrong answer (N. F. Skinner, 1983).

when placed in regular classes (Carlberg & Kavale, 1980). Authorities are more credible when their opinions are based on research findings.

Reasoning

Centuries ago, the inadequacy of the appeal to authority as a source of knowledge led René Descartes (1596–1650) to declare that "the first rule [is] never to accept anything as true unless I recognized it to be certainly and evidently such." As you might recall from chapter 1, Descartes, a rationalist, insisted that true knowledge comes through correct *reasoning*. In arguing about the interpersonal attraction issue, you might say, "I believe that opposites attract, because we find people who are different from us more interesting." In response, your friend might say, "I believe that birds of a feather flock together, because we get along better with people who share our values." But reasoning does not guarantee correct conclusions. Witness an instance of fallacious reasoning by, of all people, René Descartes: Descartes assumed that because thunder sounds like an avalanche, and because an avalanche is caused by snow sliding down a mountainside, then thunder must be caused by snow moving inside of clouds (Vrooman, 1970).

Despite the fallibility of reasoning, it is valuable to scientists as a tool in making predictions that they test in their research studies. Thus, psychologists will accept conclusions reached through reasoning when they are supported by scientific research (Bandura, 1978).

Unsystematic Observation

Long before Yogi Berra offered the profound insight that "you can observe a lot just by watchin'," John Locke (1632–1704), an empiricist, as mentioned in chapter 1, countered Descartes by insisting that true knowledge comes through *observation*—that is, through the senses:

* * * Let us suppose the mind to be, as we say, white paper, void of all characters, without any ideas; how comes it to be furnished? . . . To this I answer, in one word, from EXPERIENCE. In that all knowledge is founded, and from that it ultimately derives itself. (Locke, 1690/1956, p. 42)

In following Locke's suggestion to use observation as your source of knowledge, you might report, "After observing dozens of campus couples, I have found that opposites attract." Of course, your friend might report, "After observing dozens of campus couples, I have found that birds of a feather flock together." Because unsystematic observation like this depends on selective reporting and anecdotal reports unique to

René Descartes (1596–1650)
"I . . . have had many experiences that have gradually sapped the faith I had in the senses."

John Locke (1632–1704)
"No man's knowledge here can go beyond his experience."

particular observers, it is often an inaccurate source of knowledge. Nonetheless, it can spark initial interest in a topic, which will then lead to scientific research on it.

THE SCIENTIFIC METHOD

Because of the weaknesses of common sense, appeal to authority, reasoning, and unsystematic observation as sources of knowledge, scientists prefer the *scientific method*, which is based on certain assumptions and follows a formal series of steps.

Assumptions of Science

Albert Einstein was fond of saying, "God does not play dice with the universe." In using the scientific method, psychologists and other scientists share his assumption that there is *order* in the universe, meaning that there are lawful, rather than haphazard, relationships among events. In looking for these lawful relationships, scientists also share the assumption of **determinism,** which holds that every event has physical, potentially measurable, causes (Kimble, 1989). This rules out free will and supernatural influences as causes of behavior. B. F. Skinner (1971) championed determinism as the explanation for all behavior in his controversial book *Beyond Freedom and Dignity,* which denied free will.

Yet, as pointed out a century ago by William James, scientists might be committed to determinism in conducting their research, while being tempted to assume the existence of free will in their everyday lives (Immergluck, 1964). They might succumb to this temptation because, if carried to its logical extreme, the assumption of strict determinism would lead them to unpalatable conclusions—for example, that Mother Theresa does not deserve praise for her work with the poor and that Adolph Hitler did not deserve blame for his acts of genocide, because neither was free to choose otherwise. This also means that determinism is incompatible with the legal system, which assumes the existence of free will in order to hold criminals responsible for their actions (Viney, 1990). Despite centuries of philosophical debate, neither advocates of determinism nor advocates of free will have won the battle—a controversy that psychologists are no more likely than philosophers to resolve (Sappington, 1990).

Aside from assuming that the universe is an orderly place in which events—including behaviors—are governed by determinism, scientists today, like René Descartes before them, insist that open-minded **skepticism** is the best predisposition when judging the merits of any claim. Open-minded skepticism requires the maintenance of a delicate balance between cynicism and gullibility, which means neither rejecting claims outright nor accepting them uncritically. This skeptical attitude requires supportive evidence before accepting any claim.

But maintaining a balance between cynicism and gullibility can sometimes be difficult even for great psychologists. For example, because of William James's interest in topics such as spiritism and extrasensory perception, Margaret Floy Washburn, who was introduced in chapter 1 as a pioneer in psychology, accused him of being too open-minded. She believed he was so committed to tolerance of unpopular views that he sometimes found it impossible to reject claims even when they were based on flimsy evidence. This (perhaps excessive) open-mindedness might explain why James tried all sorts of quack cures for his failing heart in the last years of his life (Bjork, 1988).

Skepticism is especially important in psychology, because many psychological "truths" are tentative. They are subject to change as the result of subsequent research, in part because psychological research findings depend on the times and places in which the research takes place (Scarr, 1985). What is generally true of human behavior in one era or culture might be false in another era or culture. For example, sex differences in behavior in North America have changed dramatically over the past few decades, and sex differences in Western cultures might be unlike those in non-Western cultures.

Skepticism is valuable not only for scientists, but for all of us in our everyday lives. Skepticism is the basis of *critical thinking*—the systematic evaluation of claims.

determinism
The assumption that every event has physical, potentially measurable, causes.

skepticism
An attitude that doubts all claims not supported by solid research evidence.

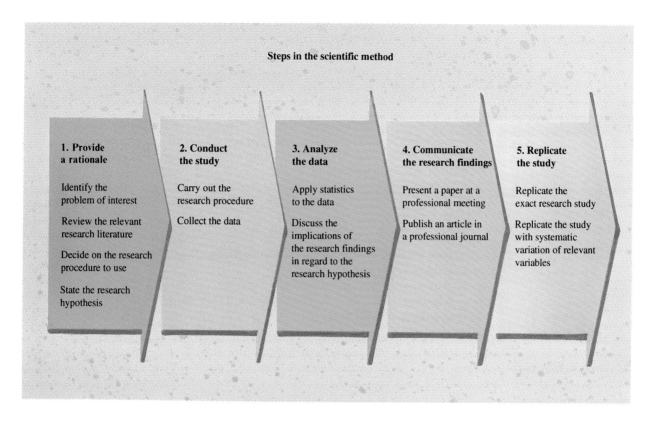

Steps in the scientific method

1. Provide a rationale

Identify the problem of interest

Review the relevant research literature

Decide on the research procedure to use

State the research hypothesis

2. Conduct the study

Carry out the research procedure

Collect the data

3. Analyze the data

Apply statistics to the data

Discuss the implications of the research findings in regard to the research hypothesis

4. Communicate the research findings

Present a paper at a professional meeting

Publish an article in a professional journal

5. Replicate the study

Replicate the exact research study

Replicate the study with systematic variation of relevant variables

FIGURE 2.1

The Scientific Method

The following steps in critical thinking will serve you well as you evaluate claims made in this book and in your everyday life. First, you should identify the claim being made. Ask yourself if the claim is based on empirical data (which would be subject to scientific evaluation) or on personal values or religious beliefs (which would be less subject to scientific evaluation). Second, examine the evidence in support of the claim. Is the evidence correct? If so, does it logically support the claim? Third, consider possible alternative explanations of the claim. Perhaps there is a better explanation than the one that has been presented.

Steps in Conducting Scientific Research

Because psychologists are skeptical about claims not supported by research findings, they employ the **scientific method** as their means of gaining knowledge. Though scientists vary in their approach to the scientific method (Danziger, 1990), ideally they follow a consistent series of steps (as shown in figure 2.1). The first step is to provide a *rationale* for the study. The scientist identifies the problem, reviews the relevant research literature, decides on the research method to use, and states the research **hypothesis.** A hypothesis (from the Greek word for "supposition") is a testable prediction about the relationship between two or more events or characteristics. The second step is to *conduct* the study. The scientist carries out the research procedure and collects data. The third step is to *analyze* the data, usually by using logical, mathematical techniques called **statistics,** and discuss the implications of the research findings. The fourth step is to *communicate* the research findings. The scientist presents papers at professional meetings and publishes articles in professional journals. In doing so, the scientist states the rationale for the research, the precise method that was used, the results of the research, and a discussion of the implications of the results. The fifth step, which is performed sometimes, is to replicate the study. **Replication** involves repeating the study, exactly or with

scientific method
A source of knowledge based on the assumption that knowledge comes from the objective, systematic observation and measurement of particular variables and the events they affect.

hypothesis
A testable prediction about the relationship between two or more events or characteristics.

statistics
Mathematical techniques used to summarize research data or to determine whether the data support the researcher's hypothesis.

replication
The repetition of a research study, usually with some alterations in its subjects, methods, or setting, to determine whether the principles derived from that study hold up under similar circumstances.

some variation. Successful replications of research studies strengthen confidence in their findings.

These steps were used by psychologist Donn Byrne, an authority on interpersonal attraction, and his colleagues (Byrne, Ervin, & Lamberth, 1970) in a classic research study on the issue of the moment: Do opposites attract? Or do birds of a feather flock together? In preparing his study, Byrne identified his problem of interest, reviewed the relevant research literature, decided on the research procedure, and stated his research hypothesis. In Byrne's study the problem concerned the relationship between interpersonal similarity and interpersonal attraction. After reviewing the psychological literature relevant to the problem, Byrne decided to conduct a *field experiment* in which male and female college students were studied in a real-life setting instead of in a laboratory. In fact, his study was a replication conducted to determine whether the results of previous laboratory studies on the effects of attitude similarity on social attraction would generalize to a field setting. Based on his review of the literature, Byrne hypothesized that (heterosexual) males and females with similar attitudes would be more likely to be attracted to each other.

Byrne had his subjects complete a 50-item questionnaire that assessed their attitudes as part of a computer-dating service. He told them that their responses would be used to pair them with an opposite-sex student who shared their attitudes. But the students were actually paired so that some partners were similar in attitudes and others were dissimilar. Their similarity on the questionnaire provided a concrete definition of "similarity." The 44 couples, selected from 420 volunteers, were then sent to the student union for a snack. After this 30-minute get-acquainted date, they were asked to rate their partners, which provided Byrne with his research data.

Byrne then analyzed the data. Like almost all researchers, he used statistics to summarize his data and to determine whether they supported his hypothesis. In this case, Byrne found that the data did support the hypothesis: Partners who had similar attitudes rated each other as more likable than did partners with dissimilar attitudes. Those with similar attitudes also stood closer to each other while speaking with the experimenter after the date. A follow-up lent further support. Partners who were similar in attitudes were more likely to recall each other's name, to have talked with each other since the date, and to desire to date each other again. Thus, in this study, the scientific method indicated that birds of a feather flock together rather than that opposites attract.

Byrne communicated his findings by publishing them in a professional journal. He might also have shared his findings by presenting them at a research conference. Even undergraduate psychology researchers can present the results of their research studies at undergraduate psychology research conferences held each spring throughout the United States. To further appreciate the scientific method and how it can contradict everyday sources of knowledge, consider the commonsense belief that we can identify a drunken person by simply observing his or her behavior.

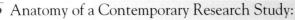

Anatomy of a Contemporary Research Study:
Is the Ability to Detect Drunkenness Simply a Matter of Common Sense?

Rationale

A New Jersey court in the landmark 1961 Zane decision stated, "Whether the man is sober or intoxicated is a matter of common observation not requiring special knowledge or skill" (Langenbucher & Nathan, 1983, p. 1071). This is an important assumption, because state laws in the United States, based on the commonsense assumption that drunkenness is easily detected, hold people, such as party hosts and tavern owners, legally responsible for the actions of people who become drunk at their homes or businesses. The ability to detect drunkenness was tested in a scientific study by alcohol researchers James Langenbucher and Peter Nathan (1983).

Undergraduate Psychology Research Conferences
The scientific commitment of psychology is evident at the undergraduate psychology research conferences held each spring throughout the United States. These conferences provide an opportunity for students to present their research and to attend presentations by other students.

The Detection of Drunkenness
Scientific research contradicts the commonsense belief that we can easily detect when someone is legally drunk.

Method

Langenbucher and Nathan had 12 bartenders, 49 social drinkers, and 30 police officers observe drinkers and judge whether they were legally drunk or sober. The drinkers in each case were two male and two female young adults. The drinkers consumed tonic water, moderate doses of vodka, or high doses of vodka. A breathalyzer assured that the desired blood-alcohol levels were achieved.

The bartenders observed their subjects being interviewed in a cocktail lounge. The social drinkers observed their subjects being interviewed in the Alcohol Behavior Research Laboratory at Rutgers University. And the police officers observed their subjects in a simulated nighttime roadside arrest in which they were given 3 minutes to determine whether the motorist they had pulled over was drunk or sober.

Results and Discussion

Langenbucher and Nathan used statistics to analyze their data. They found that the observers correctly judged the drinkers' level of intoxication only 25 percent of the time. Not a single legally drunk person was identified as such by a significant number of the observers. Of the 91 persons who served as judges, only 5 were consistently accurate—and each of them was a member of a New Jersey State Police special tactical unit for the apprehension of drunken drivers and had received more than 90 hours of training in the detection of drunkenness. The results implied that without special training even people with extensive experience in observing drinkers may be unable to determine whether a person is legally drunk or sober. The implication of these findings is that common sense is wrong in assuming that people with experience in observing drinkers can detect whether someone is drunk. We are even more confident in the findings of this study because they were replicated in a different experiment conducted by a different researcher, using different subjects, in a different research setting (Beatty, 1984). Perhaps bartenders and police officers should be given special training similar to that given the 5 police officers who performed well in the study.

GOALS OF SCIENTIFIC RESEARCH

In conducting their research, psychologists and other scientists share common goals. They pursue the goals of *description, prediction, control,* and *explanation.*

Description

To a scientist, *description* is the citing of the observable characteristics of an event, object, or individual. Thus, good observational skills are essential to psychologists (Boice, 1983). Consider *Type A behavior,* which has been implicated in cardiovascular disease. In describing the actions of people who display this behavior pattern, a psychologist would note that they tend to act in a hostile manner, work under chronic time pressure, and do several things at once. Psychologists, following in the intellectual tradition of

Francis Bacon (1561–1626), whose views are discussed in chapter 1, are *systematic* in what they describe. Instead of arbitrarily describing everything they observe, they describe only things that are relevant to their research problem. The need to be systematic in what you describe is expressed well in a statement about criminal investigations made by the fictional detective Sherlock Holmes to his friend Dr. Watson:

• • • A fool takes in all the lumber [facts] that he comes across, so that the knowledge which might be useful to him gets crowded out, or at best is jumbled up with a lot of other things. . . . It is of the highest importance, therefore, not to have useless facts elbowing out the useful ones. (Doyle, 1930)

In science, descriptions must be more than systematic; they must be precise. Precise descriptions are concrete, rather than abstract. This typically involves **measurement,** the use of numbers to represent events or characteristics. According to Francis Galton, "Until the phenomena of any branch of knowledge have been submitted to measurement . . . it cannot assume the status and dignity of a science" (Cowles, 1989, p. 2). Thus, describing a friend as "generous" would be acceptable in everyday conversation but would be too imprecise for scientific communication.

Scientists solve this problem by using **operational definitions** (Kimble, 1989), which define behaviors or qualities in terms of the procedures used to measure or produce them (as Donn Byrne did in defining *similarity* in his study of interpersonal attractiveness [Byrne, Ervin, & Lamberth, 1970]). You might operationally define *generous* as "donating more than 5 percent of one's salary to charity." A common operational definition of *drunk* is "a blood-alcohol level of at least 0.1 percent." And a psychologist might operationally define *Type A behavior* as "a score above 5 on the Framingham Type A Behavior Scale." Though operational definitions are desirable, psychologists sometimes find it difficult to agree on acceptable ones. For example, a recent journal article was devoted to a debate about how to best operationally define *psychological maltreatment* of children by parents (McGee & Wolfe, 1991).

Prediction

Psychologists are not content just to describe things. They also make predictions in the form of hypotheses about changes in behavior, mental experiences, or physiological processes. A hypothesis is usually derived from a **theory,** which is a set of statements that summarize and explain research findings and from which research hypotheses can be derived. For example, Sigmund Freud's theory of psychoanalysis integrates many observations he had made of the characteristics of people suffering from psychological disorders. Theories provide coherence to scientific research, making science more than the reporting of isolated facts (Kukla, 1989).

Because we cannot know all the factors that affect a person or an animal at a given time, psychologists are never certain about the predictions made in their research hypotheses (Manicas & Secord, 1983). In fact, it would be pointless to conduct a research study whose outcome was certain. Moreover, scientific predictions about human or animal behavior are more accurate in regard to people or animals in general than in regard to a specific person or animal. For example, your automobile insurance company can more accurately predict the percentage of people in your age group who will have an accident this year than it can predict whether you will have one. Likewise, though you might be correct in predicting that people who exhibit the Type A behavior pattern will be more likely to suffer heart attacks, you cannot predict with certainty whether a given Type A person will suffer a heart attack.

This situation is no different in the other sciences, which can make predictions only with varying degrees of probability of being correct (Hedges, 1987). Your physician might prescribe an antibiotic that, based on medical research, is usually effective in treating pneumonia, but she or he cannot guarantee that it will cure your pneumonia. Likewise, seismologists know that cities lying along geological faults are more likely to experience earthquakes, but they cannot accurately predict the day, or even the year,

measurement
The use of numbers to represent events or characteristics.

operational definition
The definition of behaviors or qualities in terms of the procedures used to measure them.

theory
An integrated set of statements that summarizes and explains research findings, and from which research hypotheses may be derived.

when Los Angeles will experience its next major earthquake. We owe modern recognition of the importance of such probabilistic prediction to the seventeenth-century Englishman John Graunt (1620–1674), who enjoyed calculating the probabilities of various events. In one case, he used probabilistic prediction to assure English citizens that they had only 1 chance in 1,500 of ending up as a "lunatick" in Bedlam, a notoriously inhumane insane asylum (which is discussed in chapter 15).

Control

Psychologists go beyond describing and predicting changes in behavior, mental experiences, and physiological processes. They also try to control them by manipulating factors that affect them. The notion of *control* is used in two ways (Cowles, 1989). First, as you will read in the upcoming discussion of methods of psychological research, control is an essential ingredient in the conduct of experiments. Second, psychologists try to apply their research findings to the control of behavior in everyday life. Thus, a behavior therapy program might help people with Type A behavior change their maladaptive habits, making them less hostile, less intent on working without letup, and more willing to do one thing at a time (Thurman, 1985).

Explanation

The ultimate goal of psychology is *explanation*—the discovery of the causes of overt behaviors, mental experiences, and physiological processes. We can *control* psychological events without necessarily being able to *explain* them. For example, psychiatrists can relieve severe depression by using electroconvulsive therapy, but we are not sure *why* it works.

A psychologist's favored perspective determines where she or he looks for explanations of psychological events. Psychologists who favor the cognitive, humanistic, or psychoanalytic perspective will look for causes in the mind. Psychologists who favor the behavioral perspective will look for causes in the environment. And psychologists who favor the biopsychological perspective will look for causes in the brain or hormonal system.

Consider possible explanations for a businesswoman's Type A behavior. A cognitive psychologist might explain that it is caused by her belief that she must be perfect and in control of every aspect of her life. A humanistic psychologist might explain that it is caused by feelings of inadequacy and the need to live up to standards that are not her own. A psychoanalytic psychologist might explain that it is caused by her unconscious desire to please her parents while repressing hostile feelings toward them. A behavioral psychologist might explain that it is caused by her taking on too many responsibilities and failing to delegate unimportant ones to other people. And a biopsychologist might explain that it is caused by an imbalance in brain chemicals that help regulate moods.

METHODS OF PSYCHOLOGICAL RESEARCH

Given that psychologists favor the scientific method as their primary source of knowledge, how do they use it in their research? And once they have collected their data, how do they make sense of it? As shown in figure 2.2, psychologists use research methods that permit them to describe, predict, control, or explain relationships among variables. *Descriptive research* pursues the goal of description, *correlational research* pursues the goal of prediction, and *experimental research* pursues the goals of control and explanation.

Descriptive Research

Descriptive research is descriptive because the researcher simply records what he or she has systematically observed. Descriptive research methods include *naturalistic observation, case studies, surveys, psychological testing,* and *archival research*.

descriptive research
Research that involves the recording of behaviors that have been observed systematically.

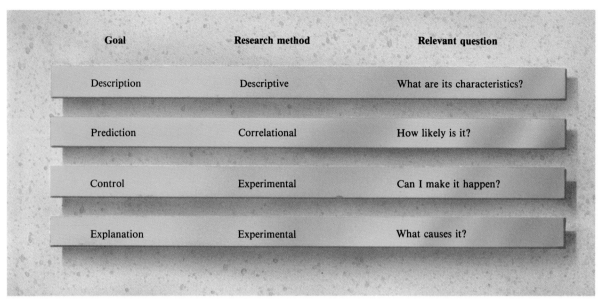

Goal	Research method	Relevant question
Description	Descriptive	What are its characteristics?
Prediction	Correlational	How likely is it?
Control	Experimental	Can I make it happen?
Explanation	Experimental	What causes it?

FIGURE 2.2

The Goals and Methods of Psychology

Naturalistic Observation

naturalistic observation
The recording of the behavior of subjects in their natural environments, with little or no intervention by the researcher.

In **naturalistic observation,** subjects are observed in their natural environment. Researchers who use naturalistic observation study topics as diverse as sex differences in flirtation (McCormick & Jones, 1989), behaviors of soldiers during combat (Williams, 1984), and subtle expressions of racial prejudice (Haskell, 1986–1987). To make sure that their observations represent natural behavior, observers refrain as much as possible from influencing the subjects they are observing. In other words, the observer remains *unobtrusive*. If you were studying the eating behavior of students in your school cafeteria, you would not announce your intention over the loudspeaker. Otherwise, your subjects might behave unnaturally. A person who normally gorged on cake, ice cream, and chocolate pudding for dessert might eat jello instead.

Suppose you wanted to use naturalistic observation to determine whether students read the assigned chapters in their textbooks. How might you do this unobtrusively? One researcher did so by sticking together selected pages of an introductory psychology book with a tiny dab of glue before any copies were sold to students. At the end of the semester, the books were collected and checked for broken seals. The results indicated that the students were more likely to read earlier assigned chapters than later ones, apparently indicating their increasing difficulty in keeping up with academic responsibilities as the semester progressed (Friedman & Wilson, 1975).

In some instances, researchers have devised especially clever unobtrusive ways of observing behavior in natural settings. In a study at Chicago's Museum of Science and Industry, curators determined the most popular exhibit by noting which floor tiles wore out the fastest. They found that the tiles at certain exhibits did not need to be replaced for years, while the tiles at the most popular exhibit—hatching chicks—had to be replaced every 6 weeks (Webb et al., 1966). Had the researchers, instead, walked from exhibit to exhibit carrying clipboards and recording the number of people at each exhibit, they might have increased the number at some, as visitors gathered around, and decreased it at others, as visitors tried to avoid them.

Naturalistic observation is also used in studying animal behavior. Some of the best-known studies employing naturalistic observation have been conducted by Jane Goodall, who has spent more than three decades observing chimpanzees in Gombe

Naturalistic Observation
Jane Goodall's naturalistic observations of chimpanzees in the wild have contributed to our understanding of their everyday habits, many of which had never been observed in zoos or laboratories.

National Park in Tanzania. To prevent new chimpanzees from acting unnaturally because of her presence, Goodall spends her initial observation periods letting them get used to her.

The study of animal behavior in the natural environment, as in Goodall's research, is called **ethology.** One of the advantages of an ethological approach is the potential discovery of behaviors not found in more artificial settings, such as zoos and laboratories. Goodall has reported observations of chimpanzee behavior that have not been made in zoos or laboratories, such as cannibalism, infanticide, and unprovoked killing of other chimpanzees (Goodall, 1990).

But researchers who use naturalistic observation, like those who use other research methods, must not be hasty in generalizing their findings. For example, naturalistic observation has found that short-term changes in the habitats of animals brought about by floods, droughts, or food shortages may temporarily alter the animals' normal behavior patterns (Lewin, 1986). And even the generalizability of Jane Goodall's observations must be qualified. The behavior of the Gombe chimpanzees differs from the behavior of chimpanzees in the Mahali Mountains of western Tanzania. For example, female Mahali chimpanzees hunt more often than do female Gombe chimpanzees (Takahata, Hasegawa, & Nishida, 1984).

Naturalistic observation is also limited by the possibility of unsystematic observation. What one person might notice, another might overlook. Moreover, naturalistic observation cannot determine the causes of the observed behavior, because there are simply too many factors at work in a natural setting. So, you could not determine why female chimpanzees hunt more in one part of Tanzania than in another. Is this caused by differences in prey, in climate, in topography, in another factor, or in some combination of factors? It would be impossible to tell just by using naturalistic observation.

ethology
The study of animal behavior in the natural environment.

Case Studies

Another descriptive research method is the **case study,** an in-depth study of a person typically conducted to gain knowledge about a particular psychological phenomenon, such as creative genius or suicidal depression. The researcher obtains as much relevant information as possible about a host of factors, including the person's thoughts, feelings, life experiences, and social relationships. The case study is often used in clinical studies of people suffering from psychological disorders. In fact, Sigmund Freud based his theory of psychoanalysis on data he obtained from clinical case studies.

case study
An in-depth study of an individual.

Drawing by Stevenson; © 1984 The New Yorker Magazine, Inc.

"What's even more astonishing is it coincides exactly with the World Series."

The Case Study
In the movie *Sybil*, Sally Field portrayed a young woman with sixteen different personalities. The movie was based on the case study of a woman who developed a multiple personality disorder, apparently as a consequence of extreme childhood abuse. This photograph shows Sybil (Field, *wearing glasses*) and her psychotherapist (as portrayed by Joanne Woodward).

More recently, a best-selling book and a television movie presented the case study of a woman called Sybil, who suffered from the rare psychological disorder known as *multiple personality*, in which the victim shifts from one distinct personality to another. Sybil had sixteen separate personalities, including males and females and adults and children. In seeking help for her disorder, Sybil attended 2,354 psychotherapy sessions, during which she and her psychiatrist discovered that her disorder was apparently the result of a childhood filled with physical and psychological torture inflicted by her mother.

Researchers use case studies to investigate a host of phenomena, both common and unusual. These include Alzheimer's disease, a brain disorder that causes deterioration of the intellect and personality (Kurz, Romero, & Lauter, 1990); anorexia nervosa, an eating disorder marked by self-starvation (Hamlett & Curry, 1990); and transsexualism, a condition associated with the feeling of being trapped in a body of the wrong sex (Kahn, 1990). The case study method is also useful in training therapists in the treatment of particular disorders and as a first step that might inspire experimental research on a particular psychological disorder (Trepper, 1990).

Because a person's behavior is affected by many variables, the case study method cannot determine the particular variables that caused the behavior being studied. Though it might seem reasonable to assume that Sybil's traumatic childhood experiences caused her to defend herself from intense emotional distress by developing multiple personalities, that assumption might be wrong. Other factors, unrelated to how she was treated by her mother, might have caused her disorder. It is even conceivable that Sybil's mother began torturing her only *after* discovering that she had multiple personalities.

Another shortcoming of the case study is that the results of a single case study, no matter how dramatic, cannot be generalized to all people. Even if Sybil's disorder was caused by traumatic childhood experiences, other people with multiple personalities might not have had traumatic childhoods. However, as you will learn in chapter 14,

Drawing by Chas. Addams; © 1982 The New Yorker Magazine, Inc.

"Would you say Attila is doing an excellent job, a good job, a fair job, or a poor job?"

other case studies also have shown that people with multiple personalities usually have had traumatic childhoods—making it more likely, but not certain, that a traumatic childhood is a cause of the disorder.

Surveys

When psychologists wish to collect information about behaviors, opinions, attitudes, life experiences, or personal characteristics of many people, they use the descriptive research method called the *survey*. A **survey** asks subjects a series of questions about the topic of interest, such as product preferences or political opinions. Surveys are commonly in the form of personal *interviews* or written *questionnaires*. The survey method was introduced by Francis Galton in 1861 when he used a questionnaire to gather opinions about weather from European meteorologists (Tankard, 1984). You have probably been asked to respond to several surveys in the past year, whether enclosed in the "You May Have Already Won!" offers that you receive in the mail or conducted by your student government association to get your views on dormitory visitation policies.

survey
A set of questions related to a particular topic of interest administered through an interview or questionnaire.

The prevalence of surveys—and the annoyance they induce—is not new. A century ago, William James (1890/1981) was so irritated by the seeming omnipresence of surveys that he called them "one of the pests of life." Today, the most ambitious of these "pests" is the United States Census, which is conducted every 10 years (most recently in 1990). Others you might be familiar with include the Gallup public opinion polls and Nielsen television ratings survey.

Good surveys use clearly worded questions that do not bias the respondent to answer in a particular way. But surveys are limited by the willingness of respondents to answer honestly and by social desirability—the desire to give appropriate responses. You can imagine the potential effect of social desirability on responses to surveys on delicate topics such as child abuse, academic cheating, or sexual practices.

Because of practical and financial constraints, surveys rarely include everyone of interest. Instead, researchers administer a survey to a **sample** of people who represent the target **population.** In conducting a survey at your school, you might interview a sample of 100 students. But, for the results of your survey to be generalizable to the entire student population at your school, your sample must be representative of the student

sample
A group of subjects selected from a population.
population
A group of individuals who share certain characteristics.

The Survey

Just as biased sampling affected the results of polls on voter preference during the 1936 presidential campaign, it did the same in 1948. The editor of the *Chicago Daily Tribune* had so much confidence in a Gallup poll that placed Thomas Dewey well ahead of Harry Truman that on the night of the election he published an edition proclaiming Dewey the winner. He was more than a little embarrassed when Truman won. The photograph shows Truman gleefully displaying the premature headline after learning that he had won. The Gallup poll was accused of making Dewey's supporters too confident, so that many failed to vote on election day, giving the election to Truman. Criticism that polls can have such an effect on voters has continued to this day.

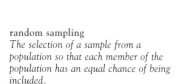

random sampling
The selection of a sample from a population so that each member of the population has an equal chance of being included.

body in age, sex, and any other relevant characteristics. This is best achieved by **random sampling,** which makes each member of the population equally likely to be included in the sample.

The need for a sample to be representative of its population was dramatically demonstrated in a poll conducted by the *Literary Digest* during the 1936 United States presidential election. The *Literary Digest* poll, based on millions of ballots, had accurately predicted each presidential election from 1916 through 1932. In 1936, based on that poll, the editors predicted that Alf Landon, the Republican candidate, would easily defeat Franklin Roosevelt, the Democratic candidate. Yet Roosevelt defeated Landon in a landslide.

But why was the poll wrong? Evidently, the subjects included in the survey were a *biased sample*, not representative of those who voted. Many of the subjects were selected from telephone directories or automobile registration lists during an era when telephones and automobiles were luxuries to many people. As a result, those who had telephones or automobiles tended to be wealthier than those who did not. Because Republican candidates attracted wealthier voters than did Democratic candidates, people who had telephones or automobiles were more likely to favor the Republican, Landon, than the Democrat, Roosevelt. The previous polls did not suffer from this bias because economic differences among voters did not significantly affect their party allegiances until the 1936 election. This was not the only occasion on which a presidential election poll was inaccurate. As vividly illustrated in the photograph of him holding aloft the newspaper that had declared his defeat, Harry Truman was elated to learn that another biased election poll had picked the wrong winner of the 1948 presidential race.

Psychological Testing

A widely used descriptive research method is the **psychological test,** which is a formal sample of a person's behavior, whether written or performed. There are many such tests, including tests of interests, attitudes, abilities, intelligence, and personality. As noted by Anne Anastasi (1985), an influential authority on psychological testing for the past few decades, a good test reflects important principles of test construction: *standardization, reliability,* and *validity.*

psychological test
A formal sample of a person's behavior, whether written or performed.

There are two kinds of **standardization.** The first kind assures that the test will be administered and scored in a consistent manner. In giving a test, all test administrators must use the same instructions, the same time limits, and the same scoring system. If they do not, a test taker's score might misrepresent her or his characteristics. The second kind of standardization establishes **norms,** which are the standards used to compare the scores of test takers. Without norms, a score on an intelligence test would be a meaningless number. Norms are established by giving the test to samples of hundreds or thousands of people who are representative of the people for whom the test is designed. If a test is to be used in North America, samples might include representative proportions of males and females; blacks and whites; lower-, middle-, and upper-class individuals; and city and country dwellers.

An adequate psychological test must be *reliable*. The **reliability** of a test is the degree to which it gives consistent results. Suppose you took an IQ test and scored 105 (average) one month, 62 (mentally retarded) the next month, and 138 (mentally gifted) the third month. Because your level of intelligence would not fluctuate that much in 3 months, you would argue that the test is unreliable.

One way to determine whether a test is reliable is to use the *test-retest method*, in which the same test is given to a group of people on two occasions. The greater the consistency of the scores on the tests from one occasion to the other, the higher the reliability of the test. Intelligence tests typically have high reliability, but personality tests typically have low to moderate reliability. The uses of intelligence testing and personality testing are discussed in chapters 10 and 13, respectively.

A reliable test would be useless if it were not also valid. **Validity** is the extent to which a test measures what it is supposed to measure. Good tests have *content validity*, meaning that the items they contain are a representative sample of what is being tested. A baking test in which all the questions referred to baking pies would not have content validity, because it would not include questions about other kinds of baking. Similarly, an introductory psychology test on this chapter that asked questions only about this section would not have content validity.

Another kind of validity, *predictive validity*, indicates that the test accurately predicts behavior related to what the test is supposed to measure. A test of mechanical ability with predictive validity would accurately predict who would perform better as an automobile mechanic. The behavior that is being predicted by a test, whether baking, automobile repair, or academic performance, is called a *criterion*.

A third kind of validity, *construct validity*, is the extent to which the test measures the supposed concept, or *construct*, it presumes to measure (Anastasi, 1986). Thus, people who score high on a test of verbal ability should perform better in reading, writing, and vocabulary than do people who score low on the test. This would provide evidence that the test is a valid measure of the construct "verbal ability."

Archival Research

The largest potential source of knowledge from descriptive research is **archival research,** which examines collections of letters, manuscripts, tape recordings, video recordings, or similar materials. Archives are valuable sources of historical information. Chiefly through the efforts of John Popplestone and Marion McPherson, the Archives of the History of American Psychology at the University of Akron, which is the main repository of records related to the growth of American psychology, has provided insight into the major issues, pioneers, and landmark events in the history of American psychology (Popplestone & McPherson, 1976).

The uses of archival research are virtually without limit. Does your signature have psychological implications? An archival study of signatures written in books and on library cards found that the size of the signature increased with the individual's status and self-esteem (Zweigenhaft, 1977). You could conduct a similar study by noting whether the signatures of famous people are larger than those of everyday people. What changes have there been in sex roles? An archival study found that the proportion of

Anne Anastasi
"The test user cannot properly evaluate a test without having some familiarity with the major steps in test construction and some knowledge of the psychometric features of tests, especially as they pertain to norms, reliability, and validity."

standardization
1. A procedure assuring that a test is administered and scored in a consistent manner. 2. A procedure for establishing test norms by giving a test to large samples of people who are representative of those for whom the test is designed.

norm
A score, based on the test performances of large numbers of subjects, that is used as a standard for assessing the performances of test takers.

reliability
The extent to which a test gives consistent results.

validity
The extent to which a test measures what it is supposed to measure.

archival research
The systematic examination of collections of letters, manuscripts, tape recordings, video recordings, or other materials.

Marion McPherson and John Popplestone
"The Archives of the History of American Psychology was established in 1965 at the University of Akron to promote research in the history of psychology by collecting, cataloguing, and preserving both unpublished documents and obsolete laboratory equipment."

correlational research
Research that studies the degree of relationship between two or more variables.

correlation
The degree of relationship between two or more variables.

variable
An event, behavior, or characteristic that has two or more values.

positive correlation
A correlation in which variables tend to change in the same direction.

negative correlation
A correlation between two variables in which the variables tend to change in opposite directions.

causation
The demonstration of an effect of one or more variables on another variable.

acknowledgments in psychology books and journal articles of help given by women increased from 1959 to 1979 (Moore, 1984). This indicates that women may have played a progressively greater role in psychology over that period.

Note that, as is true of all descriptive research, archival research does not permit definite causal statements about the findings. Based on the preceding archival studies, you cannot determine *why* high-status people had larger signatures or *why* women were mentioned more often in acknowledgments.

Archival research deals with a variety of other questions, including the following: How well does the Graduate Record Examination predict the academic performance of students (Boudreau et al., 1983)? Is there a home field *disadvantage* in deciding games of the baseball World Series (Baumeister & Steinhilber, 1984)? The answers to these questions, provided by archival research, are presented in upcoming chapters.

Correlational Research

When psychologists want to predict one variable from another, rather than simply describe something, they turn to **correlational research.** A **correlation** refers to the degree of relationship between two or more *variables.* A **variable** is an event, behavior, condition, or characteristic that has two or more values. Examples of possible variables include age, height, temperature, and intelligence. A **positive correlation** between two variables indicates that they tend to change in the same direction. That is, as the first increases, the second increases, and as the first decreases, the second decreases. A **negative correlation** between two variables indicates that they tend to change in opposite directions. For example, as age increases in adulthood, visual acuity decreases. Correlations range in magnitude from zero, meaning that there is no systematic relationship between the variables, to 1.00, meaning that there is a perfect relationship between them. Thus, a perfect positive correlation would be +1.00, and a perfect negative correlation would be −1.00.

Consider the relationship between obesity and exercise. The more people exercise, the less they tend to weigh. This indicates a negative correlation between exercise and body weight. As one increases, the other decreases. But it is essential to realize that when two variables are correlated, one can be used to *predict* the other, but it does not necessarily *cause* the other (Brigham, 1989). That is, *correlation* does not necessarily imply **causation.** Even though it is plausible that exercise causes lower body weight, it is also possible that the opposite is true: Lower body weight might cause people to exercise. Lighter people might exercise more because they find it less strenuous, less painful, and less embarrassing than do heavier people.

As another example, there is a positive correlation between educational level and the likelihood of developing a deadly form of skin cancer called malignant melanoma ("Melanoma Risk and Socio-Economic Class," 1983). This means that as educational level rises, the probability of getting the disease also rises. You would be correct in predicting that people who attend college will be more likely, later in life, to develop malignant melanoma than will people who never go beyond high school.

But does this mean that you should drop out of school today to avoid the disease? The answer is no, because the positive correlation between educational level and malignant melanoma does not necessarily mean that attending college causes the disease. Other variables common to people who attend college might cause them to develop the disease. Perhaps they increase their risk of malignant melanoma by exposing themselves to the sun more than do those who have only a high school education. College students might be more likely to spend spring breaks in Florida, find summer jobs at beach resorts, or go on Caribbean vacations after finding full-time jobs. Instead of dropping out of college to avoid the disease, students might be wiser to spend less time in the sun.

Psychologists are careful not to confuse causation and correlation. They are aware that if two variables are positively correlated, the first might cause the second, the second might cause the first, or another variable might cause both. For example,

Causation versus Correlation
People who exercise regularly tend to be thinner than those who do not. But does exercise cause thinness? Perhaps not. Thin people might simply be more likely to exercise than are fat people. So, a negative correlation between exercise and body weight does not imply that exercise causes weight loss. Only experimental research can determine whether there is such a causal relationship.

Type A behavior might cause cardiovascular disease, but the opposite is also possible: Cardiovascular disease might induce physiological changes that, in turn, cause Type A behavior. Moreover, another variable, such as an inherited predisposition, might cause both Type A behavior and cardiovascular disease.

Because of the difficulty in distinguishing causal relationships from mere correlational ones, correlational research has stimulated controversies in important areas of research. Does televised violence cause real-life aggression? A review of research on that question found a significant positive correlation between watching televised violence and exhibiting aggressive behavior. But this does not indicate that televised violence *causes* aggressive behavior (Freedman, 1984). Perhaps people who are aggressive for other reasons simply prefer to watch violent television programs.

Consider another controversial issue: Is intelligence best explained by heredity or by life experiences? A positive correlation has been established between intelligence and genetic similarity. Thus, identical twins are most similar in intelligence, ordinary siblings are moderately similar in intelligence, and unrelated people are least similar in intelligence. But does this positive correlation mean that heredity causes similarities in intelligence? Perhaps another variable, such as the degree of similarity in life experiences, causes the positive correlation between genetic closeness and intelligence. The continuing controversy over the causes of intelligence, which pits the intellectual descendants of René Descartes and Francis Galton (who would have favored the "nature" view) against those of John Locke and John B. Watson (who would have favored the "nurture" view), is discussed at length in chapter 10.

Experimental Research

The research methods discussed so far do not enable you to discover causal relationships between variables. Even when there is a large correlation between two variables, one cannot presume a causal relationship between them. To determine whether there is a causal relationship between two variables, one must use the **experimental method** (Miller, Chaplin, & Coombs, 1990).

Experimental Method

As in correlational research, the components of an experiment are called variables. Every experiment includes at least one *independent variable* and one *dependent variable*. The **independent variable** is manipulated by the experimenter, which means that she or

experimental method
Research that manipulates one or more variables, while controlling others, to determine the effects on one or more other variables.

independent variable
A variable manipulated by the experimenter to determine its effect on another, dependent, variable.

A variable showing the effect of the independent variable.

he determines its values before the experiment begins. The **dependent variable** shows any effects of the independent variable. In terms of cause-effect relationships, the independent variable would be the *cause* and changes in the dependent variable would be the *effect*. Thus, in a study of the effects of drinking on driving, the independent variable of alcohol intake would be the cause of changes in the dependent variable of steering accuracy.

The simplest experiment uses one independent variable with two values (an experimental condition and a control condition) and one dependent variable. A group of subjects, the **experimental group,** is exposed to the experimental condition, and a second group of subjects, the **control group,** is exposed to the control condition. The control condition is often simply the absence of the experimental condition. For example, the experimental condition might be exposure to a particular advertisement, and the control condition might be nonexposure to the advertisement. The dependent variable might be the number of sales of the advertised product. The control group provides a standard of comparison for the experimental group. A study in which only a single group is exposed to a single condition is called a *preexperimental design*. It is an inadequate design because it lacks a control group for comparison. If you failed to include a control group in the suggested experiment on the effects of advertising, you would be unable to determine whether the advertising accounted for changes in the volume of sales.

experimental group
The subjects in an experiment who are exposed to the experimental condition of interest.

control group
The subjects in an experiment who are not exposed to the experimental condition of interest.

To appreciate the nature of the experimental method, imagine you are a health psychologist interested in conducting an experiment on the effect of swimming on weight loss, which is illustrated in figure 2.3. The experimental group swims daily for 10 weeks, while the control group does not swim at all. As the experimenter, you would try to keep constant all other factors that might affect the two groups. By treating both groups the same except for the condition to which the experimental group is exposed, you would be able to conclude that any significant difference in weight loss between the experimental group and the control group was probably caused by the experimental group's swimming regularly. Without the use of a control group, you would have no standard of comparison and would be less secure in concluding that any changes in weight by members of the swimming group were caused by the swimming program.

In this experiment on exercise and weight loss, exercise is an independent variable with two values: swimming and no swimming. The experimenter is interested in the effect of the independent variable on the dependent variable. The dependent variable is weight loss, with many possible values: 2 pounds, 7 pounds, and so on.

As an experimenter, you would try to hold constant all factors other than the independent variable, so that the effects of those factors are not confused with the effect of the independent variable. In the exercise-and-weight-loss experiment, you would not want differences between the experimental group and the control group in diet, drugs, and other forms of exercise to cause changes in the dependent variable that you would mistakenly attribute to the independent variable.

In some cases, for practical or ethical reasons, experimenters cannot assign subjects to an experimental group and a control group. For example, if you wanted to determine the effects of parental loss on children's moral judgments, it would be unethical to conduct a true experiment, which would literally require taking some children away from their parents. In such cases, researchers turn to **quasi-experimental research** methods, which are used to study already-formed groups. In conducting a quasi-experimental study, you might compare the moral judgments of children who have already lost a parent to those of children who have not. But quasi-experimental research is not as good as experimental research in determining causality. One reason is that the dependent variable in a quasi experiment might be affected by initial differences between the subjects other than the difference being studied. Children who have lost a parent might differ from other children in ways other than just the loss of a parent. Figure 2.4 contrasts the experimental, preexperimental, and quasi-experimental research designs.

quasi-experimental research
The use of experimental research methods in situations in which the researcher might not be able to randomly assign subjects to the experimental and control conditions.

Quasi-experimental research methods are especially popular in the field of *program evaluation*, which evaluates programs in industry, government, education, adver-

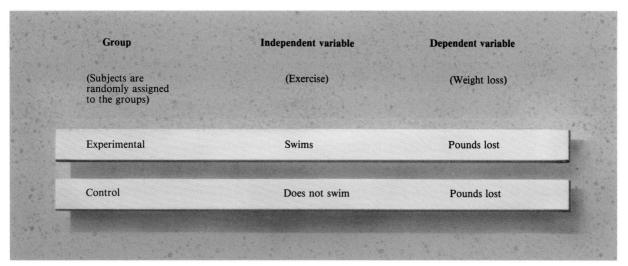

FIGURE 2.3

A Basic Experimental Research Design
Consider a two-group experiment on the effects of exercise on weight loss conducted by a health psychologist. The experimental group is exposed to a condition in which subjects swim daily for 10 weeks, while the equivalent control group is not. The groups are equivalent because the subjects have been randomly assigned to them. The experimenter would assume that a significant difference in weight loss between the two groups at the end of the 10 weeks was caused by the exposure of the experimental group to the swimming condition.

tising, and social services. For example, it has been used to compare turnover rates in salespersons who are promoted and those who are not (Johnston et al., 1993) and to determine the effects of different directional signs on the behavior of shoppers in department stores (Terry & Stanley, 1974).

Quasi experimentation is even useful in sports. A problem in major league baseball is deciding when to trade a player—during the season or between seasons. Because it would be impossible to use an experiment to study this problem (teams would not let researchers control when players would be traded), researchers used quasi experimentation to tackle this issue. The researchers compared the subsequent performance of baseball players who were traded during the season to that of baseball players who were traded between seasons. The independent variable was *trade* (in-season or off-season) and the dependent variable was *performance* (batting statistics). The results indicated that players traded during the season showed a greater improvement in performance than did those traded between seasons (Bateman, Karwan, & Kazee, 1983). To take advantage of this tendency, teams thinking of trading for a player would perhaps do well to trade for him during the season.

Internal Validity

An experimenter must do more than simply manipulate an independent variable and record changes on a dependent variable. The experimenter must also promote the **internal validity** of the experiment by *controlling* any extraneous factors whose effects on the dependent variable might be confused with those of the independent variable. Such extraneous factors are called **confounding variables,** because their effects are confused, or *confounded,* with those of the independent variable. A confounding variable might be associated with the procedures, subjects, or experimenters involved in an experiment.

In carrying out the procedure in the exercise-and-weight-loss experiment, you would not want any confounding variables to affect weight loss. You would want the subjects treated the same, except that those in the experimental group would swim daily over a 10-week period. But suppose that a locker-room attendant gave some of those in the swimming group amphetamines (so-called diet pills) after each exercise session.

internal validity
The extent to which changes in a dependent variable can be attributed to one or more independent variables rather than to a confounding variable.

confounding variable
A variable whose unwanted effect on the dependent variable might be confused with that of the independent variable.

FIGURE 2.4

Research Designs

Quasi-Experimental Research
Quasi-experimental research on baseball trades has found that players perform better when traded during the season rather than between seasons. As a recent example, Fred McGriff, traded from the San Diego Padres to the Atlanta Braves during the 1993 baseball season, helped his team come from ten games behind the San Francisco Giants to overtake them for first place.

Preexperimental research design

Subjects	All subjects are assigned to the same group.
Preassessment	All subjects are measured on the dependent variable.
Condition	All subjects are exposed to the same condition of interest.
Postassessment	1. All subjects are measured on the dependent variable.
	2. Changes from the preassessment to the postassessment are determined.
Weakness	Lack of control group makes it impossible to determine whether changes from preassessment to postassessment were caused by the condition of interest or, instead, by some other factor.

Experimental research design

Subjects	Half the subjects are randomly assigned to an experimental group and half to a control group.
Preassessment	All subjects are measured on the dependent variable.
Condition	The experimental group is exposed to the condition of interest and the control group is not exposed to it.
Postassessment	1. All subjects are measured on the dependent variable.
	2. Changes from the preassessment to the postassessment are determined.
	3. Experimental group changes are compared to control group changes.
Strengths	1. Control group provides standard of comparison for the experimental group.
	2. Random assignment of subjects equates experimental group and control group.

Quasi-experimental research design

Subjects	Half the subjects are in an experimental group and half in a control group.
Preassessment	All subjects are measured on the dependent variable.
Condition	Experimental group subjects have been exposed to the condition of interest in their everyday lives and control group subjects have not been exposed to it.
Postassessment	1. All subjects are measured on the dependent variable.
	2. Changes from the preassessment to the postassessment are determined.
	3. Experimental group changes are compared to control group changes.
Weakness	Lack of random assignment of subjects makes it possible that initial differences between the experimental group subjects and the control group subjects on factors other than the condition of interest cause subsequent differences in experimental group changes compared to control group changes.

If, at the end of the study, the experimental group showed greater weight loss than did the control group, the results might be attributable not to differences in exercising, but to a confounding variable—differences in drug use.

As an example of the importance of controlling potential confounding procedural variables, consider what happened when the Pepsi-Cola company conducted one of its "Pepsi Challenge" taste tests, an example of consumer psychology ("Coke-Pepsi Slugfest," 1976). Coca-Cola drinkers were asked to taste each of two unidentified cola drinks and state their preference. The drinks were Coca-Cola and Pepsi-Cola. The brand of cola was the independent variable, and the preference was the dependent variable. To keep the subjects from knowing which cola they were tasting, they were given Pepsi-Cola in a cup labeled M and Coca-Cola in a cup labeled Q. To the delight of Pepsi-Cola stockholders, most of the subjects preferred Pepsi-Cola.

The Pepsi-Cola company proudly—and loudly—advertised this as evidence that even Coca-Cola drinkers preferred Pepsi-Cola. But, knowing the pitfalls of experimentation, the Coca-Cola company replicated the experiment, this time filling both cups with Coca-Cola. Most of the subjects still preferred the cola in the cup labeled M. Evidently, the Pepsi Challenge had not demonstrated that Coca-Cola drinkers preferred Pepsi-Cola. It had demonstrated only that Coca-Cola drinkers preferred the letter M to the letter Q. The effect of the letters on the dependent variable (the taste preference) had been confounded with that of the independent variable (the kind of cola).

If you were asked to design a Coke-Pepsi challenge, how would you control the effect of the letter of the cup? Pause to think about this question before reading on. One way to control it would be to use cups without letters. Of course, the experimenter would have to keep track of which cup contained Coke and which contained Pepsi. A second way to control the effect of the letter would be to label each of the colas M on half of the taste trials and Q on the other half. Thus, two ways to control potential confounding procedural variables are to eliminate them or to assure that they affect all conditions equally.

Experimenters must likewise control potential confounding subject variables that might produce effects that would be confused with those of the independent variable. Suppose that in the exercise-and-weight-loss experiment the subjects in the experimental group initially differed from the subjects in the control group on several variables, including health status, eating habits, and exercise practices. These differences might affect weight loss during the course of the study, giving the false impression that exercise (the independent variable) caused a significant difference in weight loss (the dependent variable) between the two groups.

Experimenters increase the chance that the experimental group and the control group will be initially equivalent on as many subject variables as possible by relying on *random assignment* of subjects to groups. In **random assignment,** subjects are as likely to be assigned to one group as to another. Given a sufficiently large number of subjects, random assignment will make the two groups initially equivalent on many, though not necessarily all, subject variables.

After randomly assigning subjects to the experimental group and the control group, you would still have to control other subject variables. One of the most important of these is **subject bias,** the tendency of people who know they are participants in a study to behave differently than they normally do. As in the case of naturalistic observation, you might choose to be unobtrusive, exposing people to the experimental condition without their being aware of it. If this were impossible, you might choose to misinform the subjects about the true purpose of the study. This might prevent those in the exercise group from changing their eating habits in an effort to lose as much weight as possible. (The ethical issues involved in using deception are discussed later in the chapter.)

Experimenters must control not only potential confounding variables associated with the research procedure or the research subjects, but potential confounding variables associated with themselves. *Experimenter effects* on dependent variables may be caused by the experimenter's personal qualities, actions, and treatment of data.

random assignment
The assignment of subjects to experimental and control conditions so that each subject is as likely to be assigned to one condition as to another.

subject bias
The tendency of people who know they are subjects in a study to behave in a way other than they normally would.

Experimenter effects have been studied most extensively by Robert Rosenthal and his colleagues, who have demonstrated them in many studies since the early 1960s (Harris & Rosenthal, 1985). Rosenthal has found that the experimenter's personal qualities—including sex, attire, and attractiveness—can affect subjects' behavior (Barnes & Rosenthal, 1985).

Also of concern is the effect of the experimenter's actions on subjects' behavior, as in the **experimenter bias effect.** This occurs when the experimenter's expectancy about the outcome of a study affects the results through her or his unintentional actions. The tendency of subjects to behave in accordance with experimenter expectancy is called *self-fulfilling prophecy*. Actions that might promote self-fulfilling prophecy include, among others, facial expressions (perhaps smiling at subjects in one group and frowning at those in another), mannerisms (perhaps shaking hands with subjects in one group but not with those in another), or tone of voice (perhaps speaking in an animated voice to subjects in one group and speaking in a monotone voice to those in another).

In a widely publicized study of self-fulfilling prophecy, Rosenthal found that elementary school teachers' expectancies for the performance of their students affected how well the children performed. Students whose teachers were led to believe they were fast learners performed better than students whose teachers were led to believe they were slow learners. Yet the students did not differ in their initial ability (Rosenthal & Jacobson, 1968). This became known as the *Pygmalion effect*, after the story in which an uneducated woman improves herself because of the faith her mentor has in her. The Pygmalion effect can also occur between parents and children, employers and workers, and therapists and patients. In a recent study, Rosenthal found that even the expectancies of nurses and personal aides toward the likelihood of physical rehabilitation of residents of a nursing home may affect the residents' emotional and physical well-being (Learman et al., 1990). The following classic research study demonstrated that experimenter expectancies can even affect the behavior of animals.

Anatomy of a Classic Research Study:
Can Experimenter Expectancies Affect the Behavior of Laboratory Rats?

Rationale
Robert Rosenthal noted that, in the early twentieth century, Ivan Pavlov had found that each succeeding generation of his animal subjects learned tasks faster than the preceding one. At first he presumed this supported the (since-discredited) notion of the inheritance of acquired characteristics. But he came to believe that the animals' improvement was caused by changes in the way in which his experimenters treated them. Rosenthal decided to determine whether experimenter expectancies could likewise affect the performance of laboratory animals.

Method
Rosenthal and his colleague Kermit Fode (Rosenthal & Fode, 1963) had 12 students act as experimenters in a study of maze learning in rats. While 6 of the students were told that their rats were specially bred to be "maze bright," the other 6 were told that their rats were specially bred to be "maze dull." In reality, the rats did not differ in their inborn maze-learning potential. Each student was given 5 albino rats to run in a T-shaped maze, with one horizontal arm of the maze painted white and the other painted gray. The rats received a food reward whenever they ran into the gray arm. The arms were interchanged on various trials so that the rats had to learn to respond to the color gray rather than the direction left or right. The students ran the rats 10 times a day for 5 days and recorded how long it took them to reach the food.

Results and Discussion
As shown in figure 2.5, the results indicated the apparent influence of experimenter expectancy: On the average, the "maze-bright" rats ran faster than the "maze-dull" rats. Because there was no evidence of cheating or misrecording of data by the students, the researchers attributed the results to experimenter expectancy. The students' expectancies apparently influenced the manner in which they trained or handled the rats, somehow leading the rats to perform in accordance with the expectancies. For

experimenter bias effect
The tendency of experimenters to let their expectancies alter the way they treat their subjects.

Robert Rosenthal
"Recent experiments have shown that an investigator's expectation can . . . come to serve as a self-fulfilling prophecy."

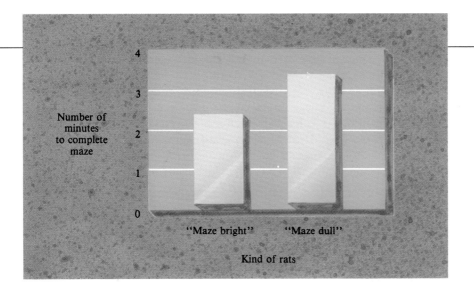

FIGURE 2.5

Experimenter Bias
The graph shows the results of the Rosenthal and Fode (1963) experiment, which found that allegedly maze-bright rats ran mazes faster than allegedly maze-dull rats.

example, those who trained "maze-bright" rats reported handling them more, and more gently, than did those who trained "maze-dull" rats. Confidence in the experimenter expectancy effect with animal subjects was supported in a replication by a different researcher, using different rats, and involving a different task (Elkins, 1987). This indicates that those responsible for handling animals during an experiment should, if possible, be kept unaware of any presumed differences among the animals.

Experimenter effects involve not only the personal qualities and actions of researchers, but also unintentional biases in the treatment of data in nonexperimental research. Such biased treatment of data was a problem long before Rosenthal began his formal research in the 1960s. A nineteenth-century physician named S. G. Morton, who believed in inherited differences in intelligence between the races, assumed that brain size indicates intelligence level. In pursuing his interests through archival research, he accumulated the world's largest collection of human skulls—more than a thousand. By measuring the sizes of the skulls, he concluded that whites had larger brains than did blacks or American Indians, supporting his claim that whites were more intelligent.

But a reexamination of data left in his personal archives found that he was selective (presumably based on a personal bias of which he was unaware) in choosing which skulls to measure and in his interpretation of the measurements. In each case he erred in a direction that supported his bias in favor of whites (Gould, 1978). Researchers can avoid measurement bias like this by using, when feasible, electronic data recording, whether in studies of human beings (Uliano & Carey, 1984) or in studies of animals (Sanberg et al., 1984). By the way, the relationship between brain size and intelligence is still hotly debated between those whose data show a positive correlation (Rushton, 1990b) and those who find that the data show no such relationship (Cain & Vanderwolf, 1990).

How might experimenter bias affect the results of the exercise-and-weight-loss study? The experimenter might act more friendly and encouraging toward the subjects in the experimental group, perhaps motivating them to swim more vigorously than they would have otherwise, thereby leading to greater weight loss in that group. Subjects with a higher need for social approval would be especially susceptible to experimenter expectancy effects like this (Hazelrigg, Cooper, & Strathman, 1991). One way to control experimenter bias would be to have those who interact with the subjects be unaware of the research hypothesis, eliminating the influence of the experimenter's expectancies on the subjects' performance.

At times both subject bias and experimenter bias might become confounding variables. This may prompt experimenters to use the **double-blind technique,** in which neither the experimenter nor the subjects know the conditions to which the subjects have been

double-blind technique
A procedure that controls experimenter bias and subject bias by preventing experimenters and subjects from knowing which subjects have been assigned to particular conditions.

assigned. The double-blind technique was used in a study of the effects of alcohol on interest in erotic or violent slides. One group of subjects were told they would be drinking vodka and a second group were told they would be drinking tonic. In reality, half of the subjects in each group were given vodka and half were given tonic (which tastes like an alcoholic beverage to many people). To assure the "blindness" of this procedure, research assistants who did not interact with the subjects poured the drinks and recorded which subjects received vodka and which received tonic.

The results indicated that alcohol expectancy, rather than alcohol intake, affected the length of time spent viewing the erotic or violent slides: Subjects who believed they had ingested alcohol but who had actually ingested tonic viewed the slides longer than did those who believed they had ingested tonic but who had actually ingested alcohol. Subjects who believed they had ingested alcohol reported more sexual arousal in response to the erotic slides than did subjects who believed they had ingested tonic, regardless of what they had actually ingested. An important conclusion to draw from this study is that our reactions to alcohol may depend less on the alcohol and more on the sexual and aggressive effects we have learned to expect from it (George & Marlatt, 1986).

External Validity

Though experimenters are chiefly concerned with matters of internal validity, they are also concerned with matters of **external validity**—the extent to which they can generalize their research findings to other subjects, settings, and procedures. In regard to external validity, an experimenter might ask, "Will the findings of my exercise-and-weight-loss experiment with students here at Grimley College hold true for different people swimming in pools other than the one at the Grimley Physical Fitness Center?" The experimenter might also ask, "Would people who are more obese than those in my study benefit as much from swimming?" and "Would other forms of aerobic exercise, such as rowing, running, bicycling, or cross-country skiing, have the same effect as swimming did in my study?"

Because psychology relies heavily on college students as subjects, external validity is an important consideration in psychological research (Sears, 1986). This reliance on undergraduates as subjects runs counter to research practices in the late nineteenth and early twentieth centuries, when experimenters typically used themselves and their colleagues as subjects. The widespread use of undergraduates did not become well established until the 1930s (Danziger, 1990).

Another problem affecting external validity is the use of volunteer subjects. Those who volunteer to take part in a given experiment might differ from those who refuse, possibly limiting the generalizability of the research findings. In a study on volunteer subjects, female and male undergraduates were given the choice of volunteering for either a study in which they would take a personality test or a study in which they would report their responses to sexual films. The results indicated that, in comparison to those who volunteered to take the personality test, males and females who volunteered for the sexual experiment were more sexually experienced. This indicates that those who participate in sexual experiments might not be representative of people in general, limiting the confidence with which sex researchers can generalize their findings (Saunders et al., 1985).

Of course, differences between volunteers and nonvolunteers do not automatically mean that the results lack external validity. The best way to determine whether the results of research studies do, in fact, have external validity is to replicate them. Replication also enables researchers to determine whether the results of laboratory studies will generalize to the real world. Most replications are approximate; they rarely use the same setting, subjects, or procedures. For example, confidence in the Pygmalion effect was strengthened when it was replicated by different researchers, using different teachers, with different students, in a different school (Meichenbaum, Bowers, & Ross, 1969). The ideal would be to replicate studies systematically several times, varying one

external validity
The extent to which the results of a research study can be generalized to other people, animals, or settings.

aspect of the study each time (Hendrick, 1990). Thus, you would be more confident in your ability to generalize the findings of the exercise-and-weight-loss experiment if people of varying degrees of obesity, performing any of a variety of aerobic exercises, in any of a variety of settings, succeeded in losing weight.

Now that you have been introduced to the descriptive, correlational, and experimental methods of research, you should be able to recognize them as you read about research studies described in later chapters. As you read particular studies, try to determine which kind of method was used, as well as its possible strengths and weaknesses—most notably, any potential confounding variables. You are now ready to learn how psychologists analyze the data generated by their research methods.

STATISTICAL ANALYSIS OF RESEARCH DATA

How would you make sense out of the data generated by the exercise-and-weight-loss experiment? In analyzing the data, you would have to do more than simply state that Jane Rogers lost 2 pounds, Steve White gained 1 pound, Sally Jones lost 8 pounds, and so on. You would have to identify overall patterns in the data and whether the data support the research hypothesis that inspired the experiment. As mentioned earlier, to make sense out of their data, psychologists rely on statistics. The word *statistics* was originally used to refer to the practice of recording quantitative political and economic information about European nation-states (Cowles, 1989).

Over the past few decades, the use of statistics to analyze research data has become more and more prevalent in articles published in psychology journals (Parker, 1990). Psychologists use *descriptive statistics* to summarize data, *correlational statistics* to determine relationships between variables, and *inferential statistics* to test their research hypotheses. Appendix B presents an expanded discussion of statistics and their calculation.

Descriptive Statistics

You would summarize your data by using **descriptive statistics,** which summarize research data, and include *measures of central tendency* and *measures of variability*. A **measure of central tendency** is a single number used to represent a set of scores. The measures of central tendency include the *mode*, the *median*, and the *mean*. Psychological research uses the mode least often, the median somewhat more often, and the mean most often.

The **mode** is the most frequent score in a set of scores. As shown in table 2.1, in the exercise-and-weight-loss experiment the mode for the experimental group is 6 pounds and the mode for the control group is 2 pounds. The **median** is the middle score in a set of scores that have been arranged in numerical order. Thus, in the exercise-and-weight-loss experiment the median score for each group is the eighth score. The median for the experimental group is 11 pounds and the median for the control group is 3 pounds. You are most familiar with the **mean,** which is the *arithmetic average* of a set of scores. You use the mean when you calculate your exam average, batting average, or gas mileage average. In the exercise-and-weight-loss experiment, the mean for the experimental group is 11.07 pounds and the mean for the control group is 4.20 pounds.

One of the problems in the use of measures of central tendency is that they can be used selectively to create misleading impressions. Suppose you had the following psychology exam scores: 23, 23, 67, 68, 69, 70, 91. The mode (the most frequent score) would be 23, the median (the middle score) would be 68, and the mean (the average score) would be 58.7. In this case, you would prefer the median as representative of your performance. But what if you had the following scores: 23, 67, 68, 69, 70, 91, 91? The mode would be 91, the median would be 69, and the mean would be 68.43. In that case, you would prefer the mode as representative of your performance.

Product advertisers, government agencies, and political parties are also prone to this selective use of measures of central tendency, as well as other statistics, to support their claims. But the use of statistics to mislead is not new. Its prevalence in the

descriptive statistics
Statistics that summarize research data.

measure of central tendency
A statistic that represents the "typical" score in a set of scores.

mode
The score that occurs most frequently in a set of scores.

median
The middle score in a set of scores that have been ordered from lowest to highest.

mean
The arithmetic average of a set of scores.

TABLE 2.1 Descriptive Statistics from a Hypothetical Experiment on the Effect of Exercise on Weight Loss

Experimental Group ("swim")				Control Group ("no swim")			
Subject	Loss	d (deviation from mean)	d²	Subject	Loss	d (deviation from mean)	d²
1	9	−2.07	4.28	1	2	−2.2	4.84
2	21	9.93	98.60	2	11	6.8	46.24
3	6	−5.07	25.70	3	2	−2.2	4.84
4	6	−5.07	25.70	4	5	.8	.64
5	15	3.93	15.44	5	8	3.8	14.44
6	12	.93	.86	6	0	−4.2	17.64
7	2	−9.07	82.26	7	2	−2.2	4.84
8	13	1.93	3.72	8	7	2.8	7.84
9	18	6.93	48.02	9	2	−2.2	4.84
10	17	5.93	35.16	10	4	− .2	.04
11	5	−6.07	36.84	11	3	−1.2	1.44
12	6	−5.07	25.70	12	0	−4.2	17.64
13	11	− .07	.00	13	1	−3.2	10.24
14	15	3.93	15.44	14	12	7.8	60.84
15	10	−1.07	1.14	15	4	− .2	.04
	Sum = 166		Sum = 418.86		Sum = 63		Sum = 196.40

Mode = 6 lb
Median = 11 lb
Mean = 166/15 = 11.07 lb
Range = 21 − 2 = 19 lb

$$\text{Variance} = \frac{\text{sum of } d^2}{\text{\# of subjects}} = \frac{418.86}{15} = 27.92 \text{ lb}$$

Standard deviation = $\sqrt{27.92}$ = 5.28 lb

Mode = 2 lb
Median = 3 lb
Mean = 63/15 = 4.20 lb
Range = 12 − 0 = 12 lb

$$\text{Variance} = \frac{\text{sum of } d^2}{\text{\# of subjects}} = \frac{196.40}{15} = 13.09 \text{ lb}$$

Standard deviation = $\sqrt{13.09}$ = 3.62 lb

nineteenth century prompted British Prime Minister Benjamin Disraeli to declare, "There are three kinds of lies: lies, damned lies, and statistics." Even a basic understanding of statistics will make you less likely to be fooled by claims based on their selective use.

To represent a distribution of scores, psychologists do more than report a measure of central tendency. They also report a **measure of variability,** which describes the degree of dispersion of the scores. Do the scores tend to bunch together, or are they scattered? Commonly used measures of variability include the *range* and the *standard deviation.* The **range** is the difference between the highest and the lowest score in a set of scores. In table 2.1 the range of the experimental group is 21 − 2 = 19 pounds, and the range of the control group is 12 − 0 = 12 pounds. But the range can be misleading, because one extreme score can create a false impression. Suppose that a friend reports that the range of weight loss in his group is 37 pounds, with the largest loss being 40 pounds and the smallest loss 3 pounds. You might conclude that there was a great deal of variability in the distribution of scores. But what if he then reported that only one subject lost 40 pounds and none of the others lost more than 5 pounds? Obviously, the variability of scores would be much less than you had presumed.

Because of their need to employ more meaningful measures of variability than the range, psychologists prefer to use the standard deviation. The **standard deviation** represents the degree of dispersion of scores around their mean and is the square root of a measure of variability called the *variance.* Table 2.1 shows that the standard deviation of the experimental group is 5.28 pounds, while the standard deviation of the control group is 3.62 pounds. Thus, the distribution of scores in the experimental group has a larger mean and standard deviation than does the distribution of scores in the control group.

Correlational Statistics

If you were interested in predicting one set of scores from another, you would use a *measure of correlation.* The concept of correlation was put forth in 1888 by Francis

measure of variability
A statistic describing the degree of dispersion in a set of scores.

range
A statistic representing the difference between the highest and lowest scores in a set of scores.

standard deviation
A statistic representing the degree of dispersion of a set of scores around their mean.

Galton, who wanted a way to represent the relationship between parents and offspring on factors, such as intelligence, presumed to be affected by heredity. The mean and standard deviation are useful in describing individual sets of scores; a statistic called the **coefficient of correlation** is useful in quantifying the degree of association between two or more sets of scores. The coefficient of correlation was devised by the English mathematician Karl Pearson (1857–1926) and is often called *Pearson's r*. As you learned earlier, a correlation can be positive or negative, and can range from zero to +1.00 or –1.00. In a *positive correlation* between two sets of scores, relatively high scores on one set are associated with relatively high scores on the other, and relatively low scores on one set are associated with relatively low scores on the other. For example, there is a positive correlation between height and weight and between high school and college grade point averages.

In a *negative correlation* between two sets of scores, relatively high scores on one set are associated with relatively low scores on the other. For example, there is a negative correlation between driving speed and gas mileage and between age and hours of nightly sleep. A *zero correlation* indicates that there is no relationship between one set of scores and another. You would find an approximately zero correlation between the intelligence levels of two groups of randomly selected strangers. The types of correlations are illustrated graphically in figure 2.6.

The higher the correlation between two variables, the more the scores on one variable will be predictive of scores on the other. For example, suppose you found a correlation of –.83 between the number of hours people swim each week and their average body weight. This relatively large correlation would make you fairly confident in predicting that as the number of hours of swimming increases, the average body weight decreases. If, instead, you found a relatively small correlation of –.17, you would have less confidence in making that prediction.

Inferential Statistics

In the exercise-and-weight-loss experiment, the experimental group lost more weight than did the control group. But is the difference in weight loss between the two groups large enough for you to conclude with confidence that exercise was responsible for the difference? In other words, would you be willing to bet that if the experiment were repeated over and over, you would obtain similar results? Perhaps the difference happened by chance—that is, because of a host of random factors other than swimming. To determine whether the independent variable, rather than chance factors, caused the changes in the dependent variable, psychologists use **inferential statistics.** By permitting psychologists to determine the causes of events, inferential statistics help them achieve the goals of control and explanation. Inferential statistics are "inferential" because they enable experimenters to make inferences from the sample of subjects used in their experiment to the population of individuals they represent.

If there is a low probability that the difference between groups on the dependent variable is attributable to chance (that is, to random factors), the difference is **statistically significant** and is attributed to the independent variable. The concept of statistical significance was put forth by the English mathematician Ronald Fisher (1890–1962) when he sought a way to test a noblewoman's claim that she could tell whether tea or milk had been added to her cup first (Tankard, 1984). Though he never carried out the demonstration, he proposed presenting her with a series of cups in which tea was sometimes added first and milk was sometimes added first. He assumed that if she could report the correct order at a much greater than chance level, her claim would be verified. To rule out simple lucky guessing, she would have to be correct significantly more than 50 percent of the time—the chance level of guessing between two events.

In the exercise-and-weight-loss experiment, you would expect that chance factors would account for some changes in the weights of subjects in both groups during the course of the study. For the difference in average weight loss between the two groups to be statistically significant, it would have to be significantly larger than would be expected by chance alone. Psychologists usually accept a difference as statistically

coefficient of correlation
A statistic that assesses the degree of association between two or more variables.

Karl Pearson (1857–1936)
"Statistics in one form or another are fundamental in nearly every branch of science in precisely the same manner as mathematics are fundamental in astronomy and physics."

inferential statistics
Statistics used to determine whether changes in a dependent variable are caused by an independent variable.

statistical significance
A low probability (usually less than 5 percent) that the results of a research study are due to chance factors rather than to the independent variable.

FIGURE 2.6

Correlations
In a *positive correlation*, scores on the measures increase and decrease together. An example is the relationship between SAT verbal scores and college grade point average (GPA). In a *negative correlation*, scores on one measure increase as scores on the other measure decrease. An example is the relationship between age and nightly sleep. In a *zero correlation*, scores on one measure are unrelated to scores on the other. An example is the relationship between the number of times people brush their teeth each day and the number of houseplants they have.

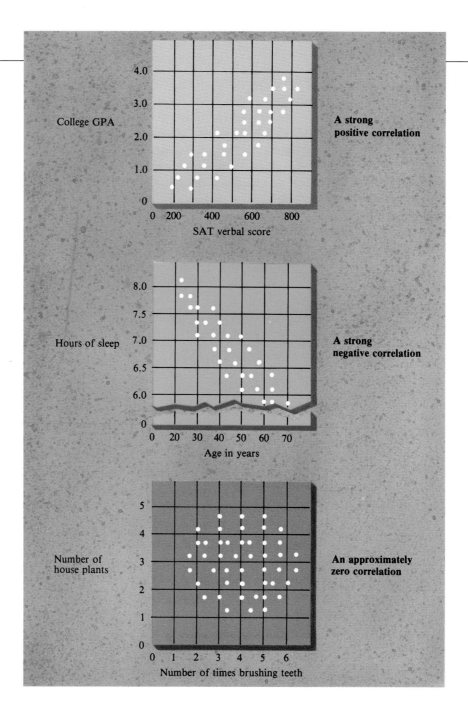

significant when there is less than a 5 percent (5 in 100) probability that the difference is the product of chance factors.

One of the main inferential statistics, the *t test*, is used to determine whether there is a significant difference between the scores of two groups. The *t* test was invented by statistician and brewmaster William Sealy Gosset (1876–1937) to maintain quality control in the brewing and storage of Guinness stout, the popular dark, bitter beer. The beverage is still produced by Arthur Guinness, Son and Company, which shows its continued interest in statistics by publishing the *Guinness Book of World Records*. Gosset compared pairs of batches of stout that had been treated differently in regard to factors such as ingredients, brewing temperature, or storage temperature. He analyzed the data using what became known as Student's *t* test. It was given this name because the brewery refused to permit its employees to publish anything that might reflect poorly on the company, leading Gosset to take the pseudonym "Student." The first use of the *t* test in psychological research was in a paper published by Gosset in 1925 that found that one sleep medication was better than another in the treatment of insomnia.

Another important inferential statistic, the *analysis of variance*, enables researchers to compare two or more groups. The analysis of variance is also called the *F* test, after Ronald Fisher (1890–1962), who devised it in his research aimed at the improvement of agricultural productivity through the varying of various factors, including manure. In fact, the first use of the analysis of variance in a published study was in a 1923 article entitled "The Manuarial Response of Different Potato Varieties."

As you read the research studies discussed in later chapters, keep in mind that virtually all were analyzed by descriptive statistics, correlational statistics, or inferential statistics. You should also note that statistical significance does not necessarily imply practical significance. For example, a variety of relaxation techniques have been used in treating high blood pressure. Though studies have found that some of these techniques can induce statistically significant decreases in blood pressure, those decreases might not be of practical significance. In other words, they might not be large enough to be considered clinically important.

THINKING ABOUT *Psychology*

WHAT ARE THE ETHICS OF PSYCHOLOGICAL RESEARCH?

Psychologists must be as concerned with the ethical treatment of their data and subjects as they are with the quality of their research methods and statistical analyses. A serious ethical violation in the treatment of data is falsification. During the past few decades there have been several notorious cases in which medical, biological, or psychological researchers have been accused of falsifying their data. Chapter 10 discusses the most prominent case in psychology, in which Sir Cyril Burt, an eminent psychologist, was so intent on demonstrating that intelligence depends on heredity that he misrepresented his research findings. Though occasional lapses in the ethical treatment of data have provoked controversy, there has been even greater controversy over the ethical treatment of research subjects, both human and animal.

ETHICAL TREATMENT OF HUMAN SUBJECTS

The first code of ethics for the treatment of human subjects in psychological research was developed in 1953, partly in response to the Nuremberg war crimes trials following World War II (Reese & Fremouw, 1984). The trials disclosed the cruel medical experiments performed by Nazi physicians on prisoners of war and concentration camp inmates. Today, the United States government requires institutions that receive federal research grants to establish committees that review research proposals to assure the ethical treatment of human subjects.

The American Psychological Association's code of ethics contains specific requirements for the treatment of human subjects. First, the researcher must inform potential subjects of all aspects of the research procedure that might influence their decision to participate. Second, potential subjects must not be forced to participate in a research study. This becomes an issue when psychology departments offer extra-credit points for student participation in subject pools (Lindsay & Holden, 1987). Of concern is whether students, desiring a good grade, find the offer of extra-credit points a coercive influence on their willingness to participate. One study found that students generally do not feel coerced by extra credit (Leak, 1981). Third, subjects must be permitted to withdraw from the study at any time. Because those who remain in studies might differ from those who drop out, the loss of subjects can adversely affect the generalizability of research findings to target populations (Trice & Ogden, 1987). Fourth, the researcher must protect the subjects from physical harm and mental distress. Again, the use of deception might violate this provision by inducing mental distress. Fifth, if a subject does experience harm or distress, the researcher must try to alleviate it. But some critics argue that it is impossible to routinely determine whether attempts to relieve distress produce long-lasting benefits (Norris, 1978). Sixth, information gained from subjects must be kept confidential. This becomes a major issue in research on sensitive topics, such as AIDS, because laws might force researchers to reveal data that their subjects presumed were confidential (Melton & Grey, 1988).

Despite their code of ethics, psychologists sometimes confront ethical dilemmas in their treatment of human subjects, as in the use of deception to reduce subject bias. Psychologists might fail to inform people that they are subjects in a study or might misinform subjects about the true nature of a study. This is of concern, in part, because it violates the ethical norm of informed consent. Recall that the computer-dating study (Byrne, Ervin, & Lamberth, 1970) used deception by falsely claiming that all participants would be matched with partners who shared their attitudes. Today, for this to be considered ethical, the researcher would have to demonstrate to a research review committee that the experiment could not be conducted without the use of deception and that its potential findings are important enough to justify the use of deception. Moreover, at the completion of the study, the subjects would have to be debriefed. In **debriefing** subjects, the researcher explains the reasons for the deception and tries to relieve any distress that might have been experienced. Try to think of a way in which the computer-dating study could have tested its hypothesis without using deception.

As you can now appreciate, researchers' personal values affect how they interpret and apply ethical principles to their research (Kimmel, 1991). Diana Baumrind (1985), a critic of deceptive research, argues that not even the positive findings of studies that use deception outweigh the distress of subjects who learn that they have been fooled or the resulting distrust of psychological researchers that such studies might promote. Baumrind's belief that procedures to remove the negative effects of deceptive research can be ineffective might be shared by students and by faculty members who are not involved in deceptive research (Lindsay & Adair, 1990). But arguments against deceptive research have been countered by psychologists who argue that it would be unethical *not* to conduct deceptive studies that might produce important findings (Christensen, 1988).

While some psychologists argue about the use of deception, others try to settle the debate over deceptive research by using the results of empirical research. In one study, undergraduates who had been subjects in deceptive experiments rated their experience as more positive than did those who had participated in nondeceptive ones. Moreover, those in deceptive experiments did not rate psychologists as less trustworthy. Any negative emotional effects reported by subjects seemed to be relieved by debriefing. The researchers concluded that debriefing eliminates any negative effects of deception, perhaps because the subjects learn the importance of the research study (Smith & Richardson, 1983).

But this interpretation of the findings has been criticized. You might wish to pause now and see if you can think of an alternative explanation of why subjects in deceptive experiments responded more positively. One possibility is that the procedures used in deceptive experiments are more interesting and enjoyable than those used in nondeceptive ones (Rubin, 1985). Remembering that psychology, as a science, resolves issues through empirical research instead of through argument alone, how might you conduct a study

debriefing
A procedure, after the completion of a research study, that informs subjects of the purpose of the study and aims to remove any physical or psychological distress caused by participation.

Diana Baumrind
"Deceptive practices do not succeed in accomplishing the scientific objectives that are used to justify such deception any better than methods that do not require deception."

to determine whether this assumption is correct? One way would be to conduct experiments whose procedures have been rated as equally interesting, and use deception in only half of them. If the subjects still rate the deceptive experiments more positively, then the results would support Smith and Richardson (1983). If the subjects rate the deceptive experiments less positively, then the results would support Rubin (1985).

ETHICAL TREATMENT OF ANIMAL SUBJECTS

At the 1986 Annual Meeting of the American Psychological Association in Washington, D.C., animal rights advocates picketed in the streets and disrupted talks, including one by the prominent psychologist Neal Miller, a defender of the use of animals in psychological research. The present conflict between animal rights advocates and psychologists who study animals is not new. In the early twentieth century, animal rights advocates attacked the work of leading psychologists, including John B. Watson and G. Stanley Hall. In 1925, in part to blunt these attacks, the American Psychological Association's Committee on Precautions in Animal Experimentation established a code of regulations for the use of animals in research (Dewsbury, 1990).

Many *animal rights* advocates oppose all laboratory research using animals, regardless of its scientific merit or practical benefits. A survey of demonstrators at an animal rights march in Washington, D.C., in 1990 found that almost 80 percent of animal rights advocates valued animal life at least as much as human life, and 85 percent wanted to eliminate all animal research (Plous, 1991). Animal rights advocates go beyond *animal welfare* advocates, who would permit laboratory research on animals as long as the animals are given humane care and when the potential benefits of the research outweigh any pain and distress caused to the animals. Bernard Rollin, an ethicist who has tried to resolve the ethical conflict between animal researchers and animal rights advocates, would permit animal research but urges that, when in ethical doubt, experimenters should err in favor of the animal (Bekoff et al., 1992).

The American Psychological Association's current ethical standards for the treatment of animals are closer to those of animal welfare advocates than to those of animal rights advocates. The standards require that animals be treated with respect, housed in clean cages, and given adequate food and water. Researchers must also subject their animal subjects to as little pain and distress as possible; when it is necessary to kill the animals, researchers must do so in a humane, painless way. Moreover, all institutions that receive research grants from the U.S. government must have committees that judge

Bernard Rollin
"Methodologies must be devised which maximize the respect for individual animals studied in the research process."

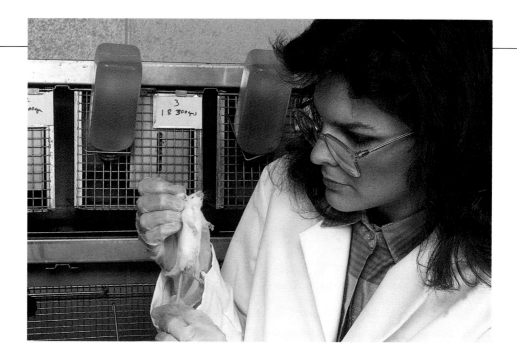

Animal Research
Those who favor animal research note the medical and psychological benefits it produces for human beings and, in some cases, animals.

whether research proposals for experiments using animal subjects meet ethical standards (Holden, 1987a). The Canadian government likewise regulates the treatment of research animals in universities, government laboratories, and commercial institutions (Rowsell, 1988).

But with so many human beings available, why would psychologists be interested in studying animals? First, some psychologists are simply intrigued by animal behavior and wish to learn more about it. To learn about the process of echolocation of prey, you would have to study animals like bats rather than college students. Second, it is easier to control potential confounding variables that might affect the behavior of an animal. You would be less likely to worry about subject bias effects, for instance, when studying pigeons. Third, developmental changes across the life span can be studied more efficiently in animals. If you were interested in the effects of the complexity of the early childhood environment on memory in old age, you might take 70 years to complete an experiment using human subjects, but only 3 years to complete an experiment using rats.

Fourth, research on animals can generate hypotheses that are then tested using human subjects. B. F. Skinner's research on learning in rats and pigeons stimulated research on learning in human beings. Fifth, research on animals can benefit animals themselves. For example, as described in chapter 7, psychologists have developed techniques to make coyotes feel nauseated by the taste of sheep; perhaps these can someday be used to protect sheep from coyotes, and coyotes from angry sheep ranchers. Sixth, because of an assumption that animals do not have the same moral rights as human beings (Baldwin, 1993), certain procedures that are not ethically permissible with human subjects are ethically permissible under current standards with animal subjects. Thus, if you wanted to conduct an experiment in which you studied the effects of surgically removing a particular brain structure, you would be limited to the use of animals as subjects.

But these reasons have not convinced animal rights advocates of the merits of psychological research on animals. Animal rights advocates argue that the benefits of laboratory research that submits animals to painful procedures do not outweigh the suffering they induce (Bowd, 1990). During the past decade some animal rights advocates have even vandalized animal research laboratories and stolen animals from their laboratory cages. The vast majority of advocates, however, have been content to lobby for stronger laws limiting animal research or to picket meetings of animal researchers.

Prior to the meeting at which he was harassed, Neal Miller (1985) had pointed out that for every dog and cat used in laboratory research, 10,000 are abandoned by their owners, and that, in contrast, few psychology experiments inflict pain or distress on animals. He urged animal rights advocates to spend more time helping the millions of abandoned pets that are killed in pounds, starve to death, or die after being struck by motor vehicles.

Miller (1985) has also cited ways in which animal research contributes to human welfare. Findings from animal research have contributed to progress in the treatment of pain; the development of behavior therapy for phobias; the rehabilitation of victims of neuromuscular disorders, such as Parkinson's disease; the understanding of neurological disorders associated with aging, such as Alzheimer's disease; and the development of drugs for treating anxiety, depression, and schizophrenia. Nonetheless, Miller's critics accuse him of exaggerating the benefits of animal research (Kelly, 1986).

While reasonable people may disagree about the ethical limits of psychological research on animals, the attention given to such research might be out of proportion to its extent and to the pain and distress it causes. Only 5 percent of psychologists conduct research with animals. Of their animal subjects, 95 percent are mice, rats, and birds; less than 1 percent are dogs, cats, monkeys, and chimpanzees—the kinds of animals to which people feel the greatest kinship (Gallup & Suarez, 1985). Moreover, few psychological studies on animals inflict pain or distress (Coile & Miller, 1984). And, despite the special attention that psychological research receives from animal rights advocates, a government report praised the American Psychological Association's ethical standards for the care and use of animals in research as superior to those of any other science (Fisher, 1986). No responsible psychologist would condone a cavalier disregard for the pain and suffering of laboratory animals. Nonetheless, it seems that animal rights advocates have been more effective than animal researchers in influencing the public and lawmakers (Johnson & Morris, 1987).

SUMMARY

SOURCES OF KNOWLEDGE

Psychologists prefer the scientific method to other sources of knowledge, which include common sense, appeal to authority, reasoning, and unsystematic observation. The scientific method is based on the assumptions of order, determinism, and skepticism. In using the scientific method to perform a research study, a psychologist first provides a rationale for the study, then conducts the study, analyzes the resulting data, and, finally, communicates the results to other researchers. Psychologists may try to replicate research studies.

GOALS OF SCIENTIFIC RESEARCH

In conducting research, psychologists pursue the goals of description, prediction, control, and explanation. Scientific descriptions are systematic and rely on operational definitions. Scientific predictions are probabilistic, not certain. Scientists exert control over events by manipulating the factors that cause them. And scientific explanations state the causes of events.

METHODS OF PSYCHOLOGICAL RESEARCH

Psychologists use descriptive, correlational, and experimental research methods. Descriptive research methods pursue the goal of description through naturalistic observation, case studies, surveys, psychological testing, and archival research. Correlational research pursues the goal of prediction by uncovering relationships between variables. In using correlational research, psychologists avoid confusing correlation with causation. Experimental research pursues the goals of control and explanation by manipulating an indepen-

dent variable and measuring its effect on a dependent variable. In quasi-experimental research, the researcher cannot randomly assign subjects to the experimental group and control group and therefore must use groups that have already been formed.

Experimenters promote internal validity by controlling confounding variables whose effects might be confused with those of the independent variable. These variables might be associated with the experimental procedure itself, the subjects of the experiment, or the experimenter. Random assignment of subjects is used to make the experimental group and control group equivalent before exposing them to the independent variable. Experimenters must also control for subject bias and experimenter bias. Another concern of experimenters is external validity: whether their results are generalizable from their subjects and settings to other subjects and settings. Experimenters rely on replication to determine whether their research has external validity.

STATISTICAL ANALYSIS OF RESEARCH DATA

Psychologists make sense of their data by using mathematical techniques called statistics. They use descriptive statistics to summarize data, correlational statistics to determine relationships between variables, and inferential statistics to test their experimental hypotheses. Descriptive statistics include measures of central tendency (including the mode, median, and mean) and measures of variability (including the range and standard deviation). Correlational statistics let researchers use the values of one variable to predict the values of another. And inferential statistics examine whether numerical differences between experimental and control groups are statistically significant. Statistical significance does not necessarily indicate practical significance.

THINKING ABOUT PSYCHOLOGY: WHAT ARE THE ETHICS OF PSYCHOLOGICAL RESEARCH?

American and Canadian psychologists have ethical codes for the treatment of human subjects and animal subjects. In research using human subjects, researchers must obtain informed consent, not force anyone to participate, let subjects withdraw at any time, protect subjects from physical harm and mental distress, alleviate any inadvertent harm or distress, and keep information obtained from the subjects confidential. The use of deception in research has been an especially controversial issue.

The use of animals in research has also been controversial. Many animal rights supporters oppose all research on animals, whereas animal welfare supporters approve of research on animals as long as the animals are treated humanely and the potential benefits of the research outweigh any pain and distress caused to the animals. Though only 5 percent of the members of the American Psychological Association conduct research on animals, most psychologists support the use of animals in research because of the benefits of such research to both human beings and animals. Moreover, few psychologists treat their research animals in a less than humane way.

IMPORTANT CONCEPTS

archival research 47
case study 48
causation 48
coefficient of correlation 59
confounding variable 51
control group 50
correlation 48
correlational research 48
debriefing 62
dependent variable 50
descriptive research 41
descriptive statistics 57
determinism 36
double-blind technique 55

ethology 43
experimental group 50
experimental method 49
experimenter bias effect 54
external validity 56
hypothesis 37
independent variable 49
inferential statistics 59
internal validity 51
mean 57
measure of central tendency 57
measure of variability 58
measurement 40
median 57

mode 57
naturalistic observation 42
negative correlation 48
norm 47
operational definition 40
population 45
positive correlation 48
psychological test 46
quasi-experimental research 50
random assignment 53
random sampling 46
range 58
reliability 47
replication 37

sample 45
scientific method 37
skepticism 36
standardization 47
standard deviation 58
statistical significance 59
statistics 37
subject bias 53
survey 45
theory 40
validity 47
variable 48

MAJOR CONTRIBUTORS

Anne Anastasi 46
Francis Bacon 40
Diana Baumrind 62
René Descartes 35

Ronald Fisher 59
Jane Goodall 42
William Sealy Gosset 60

William James 36, 45
John Locke 35
Neal Miller 6

Karl Pearson 59
Bernard Rollin 63
Robert Rosenthal 54

RECOMMENDED READINGS

FOR GENERAL WORKS ON PSYCHOLOGY AS A SCIENCE
Brannigan, G. G., & Merrens, M. R. (Eds.). (1993). The undaunted psychologist: Adventures in research. New York: McGraw-Hill.
Burnham, J. C. (1987). How superstition won and science lost: Popularizing science and health in the United States. New Brunswick, NJ: Rutgers University Press.
Danziger, K. (1990). Constructing the subject: Historical origins of psychological research. New York: Cambridge University Press.

Leahey, T. H., & Leahey, G. E. (1983). Psychology's occult doubles: Psychology and the problem of pseudoscience. Chicago: Nelson-Hall.
Leavitt, F. (1991). Research methods for behavioral scientists. Dubuque, IA: Wm. C. Brown.
Robinson, D. N. (1985). Philosophy of psychology. New York: Columbia University Press.
Siegel, M. H., & Zeigler, H. P. (Eds.). (1976). Psychological research: The inside story. New York: Harper & Row.

Stanovich, K. E. (1992). How to think straight about psychology (3rd ed.). New York: Harper Collins.

FOR MORE ON SOURCES OF KNOWLEDGE
Boice, R. (1983). Observational skills. Psychological Bulletin, 93, 3–29.
Hager, M. (1982). The myth of objectivity. American Psychologist, 37, 576–579.
Sappington, A. A. (1990). Recent psychological approaches to the free will versus determinism issue. Psychological Bulletin, 108, 19–29.

Siegfried, J. (Ed.). (1993). The status of common sense in psychology. Norwood, NJ: Ablex.

FOR MORE ON THE GOALS OF SCIENTIFIC RESEARCH
Cummins, R. (1983). The nature of psychological explanation. Cambridge, MA: MIT Press.
Rogers, T. B. (1989). Operationism in psychology: A discussion of contextual antecedents and an historical interpretation of its longevity. Journal of the History of the Behavioral Sciences, 25, 139–153.

Runyan, W. M. (1981). Why did Van Gogh cut off his ear?: The problem of alternative explanations in psychobiography. *Journal of Personality and Social Psychology, 40*, 1070–1077.

White, P. A. (1990). Ideas about causation in philosophy and psychology. *Psychological Bulletin, 108*, 3–18.

FOR MORE ON METHODS OF PSYCHOLOGICAL RESEARCH

Anastasi, A. (1985). Psychological testing: Basic concepts and common misconceptions. In A. M. Rogers & C. J. Scheirer (Eds.), G. *Stanley Hall Lecture Series*, Vol. 5, pp. 87–120. Washington, D.C.: American Psychological Association.

Balance, W. D. (1975). Frustrations and joys of archival research. *Journal of the History of the Behavioral Sciences, 11*, 37–40.

Brislin, R. W., Lonner, W. J., & Thorndike, R. M. (1973). *Cross-cultural research methods*. New York: Wiley.

Bromley, D. B. (1986). *The case-study method in psychology and related disciplines*. New York: Wiley.

Campbell, D. T., & Stanley, J. C. (1966). *Experimental and quasi-experimental designs for research*. Boston: Houghton Mifflin.

Converse, J. M. (1987). *Survey research in the United States: Roots and emergence, 1890–1960*. Berkeley: University of California Press.

Danziger, K. (1985). The origins of the psychological experiment as a social institution. *American Psychologist, 40*, 133–140.

Goodall, J. (1986). *The chimpanzees of Gombe: Patterns of behavior*. Cambridge, MA: Belknap/Harvard.

Kenny, D. A. (1979). *Correlation and causality*. New York: Wiley.

Lonner, W. J., & Berry, J. W. (1986). *Field methods in cross-cultural research*. Newbury Park, CA: Sage Publications.

Shadish, W. R., Cook, T. D., & Leviton, L. C. (1990). *Foundations of program evaluation*. Newbury Park, CA: Sage Publications.

Thorndike, R. M., & Lohman, D. F. (1990). *A century of ability testing*. Chicago: Riverside.

Triandis, H. C., & Berry, J. W.. (Eds.). (1980). *Handbook of cross-cultural psychology: Vol 2. Methodology*. Boston: Allyn & Bacon.

FOR MORE ON INTERNAL AND EXTERNAL VALIDITY

Berkowitz, L., & Donnerstein, E. (1982). External validity is more than skin deep: Some answers to criticisms of laboratory experiments. *American Psychologist, 37*, 245–257.

Boring, E. G. (1954). The nature and history of experimental control. *American Journal of Psychology, 67*, 573–589.

Mook, D. G. (1983). In defense of external validity. *American Psychologist, 38*, 379–387.

Neuliep, J. W. (Ed.). (1991). *Replication research in the social sciences*. Newbury Park, CA: Sage Publications.

Orne, M. T. (1991). *On the social psychology of the psychological experiment: With particular reference to demand characteristics and their implications*. New York: Irvington.

Rosenthal, R. (1976). *Experimenter effects in behavioral research*. New York: Irvington.

Rosenthal, R., & Jacobson, L. (1968). *Pygmalion in the classroom*. New York: Holt, Rinehart & Winston.

Webb, E. J., Campbell, D. T., Schwartz, R. D., & Sechrest, L. (1966). *Unobtrusive measures: Nonreactive research in the social sciences*. Chicago: Rand McNally.

FOR MORE ON THE STATISTICAL ANALYSIS OF DATA

Cowles, M. (1989). *Statistics in psychology: An historical perspective*. Hillsdale, NJ: Erlbaum.

Holmes, C. B. (1990). *The honest truth about lying with statistics*. Springfield, IL: Charles C Thomas.

Huff, D. (1954/1982). *How to lie with statistics*. New York: W. W. Norton.

Spence, J. T., Cotton, J. W., Underwood, B. J., & Duncan, C. P. (1990). *Elementary statistics* (5th ed.). Englewood Cliffs, NJ: Prentice Hall.

FOR MORE ON THE ETHICS OF PSYCHOLOGICAL RESEARCH

American Psychological Association. (1993). *American Psychological Association ethics code*. Washington, DC: Author.

Baumrind, D. (1985). Research using intentional deception: Ethical issues revisited. *American Psychologist, 40*, 165–174.

Christensen, L. (1988). Deception in psychological research: When is its use justified? *Personality and Social Psychology Bulletin, 14*, 664–675.

Dewsbury, D. A. (1990). Early interaction between animal psychologists and animal activists and the founding of the APA Committee on Precautions in Animal Experimentation without animal rights influence. *American Psychologist, 45*, 315–327.

Fox, M. A. (1986). *The case for animal experimentation: An evolutionary and ethical perspective*. Berkeley: University of California Press.

Kohn, A. (1987). *False prophets: Fraud, error and misdemeanor in science and medicine*. New York: Basil Blackwell.

Miller, N. E. (1985). The value of behavioral research on animals. *American Psychologist, 40*, 423–440.

Regan, T. (1983). *The case for animal rights*. Berkeley: University of California Press.

Rollin, B. E. (1985). The moral status of research animals in psychology. *American Psychologist, 40*, 920–926.

Rollin, B. E. (1989). *The unheeded cry: Animal consciousness, animal pain, and science*. New York: Oxford University Press.

Ulrich, R. E. (1991). Animal rights, animal wrongs, and the question of balance. *Psychological Science, 2*, 197–201.

FOR MORE ON CONTRIBUTORS TO PSYCHOLOGY AS A SCIENCE

Anastasi, A. (1980). Anne Anastasi. In G. Lindzey (Ed.), *A history of psychology in autobiography* Vol. 4 (pp. 1–37). San Francisco: W. H. Freeman.

Cottingham, J. G. (1986). *Descartes*. New York: Basil Blackwell.

Cranston, M. (1979). *John Locke: A biography*. New York: Oxford University Press.

Goodall, J. (1990). *Through a window: My thirty years with the chimpanzees of Gombe*. Boston: Houghton Mifflin.

Myers, G. E. (1986). *William James: His life and thought*. New Haven, CT: Yale University Press.

Quinton, A. (1981). *Francis Bacon*. New York: Oxford University Press.

Tankard, J. W., Jr. (1984). *The statistical pioneers*. Cambridge, MA: Schenkman.

Georgia O'Keeffe
Radiator Building-Night
New York 1927

BIOPSYCHOLOGICAL PROCESSES

As you read this page, your eyes inform your brain about what you are reading. At the same time, your brain interprets the meaning of that information and stores some of it in your memory. When you reach the end of the right-hand page, your brain will direct your hand to turn to the next one. But how do your eyes inform your brain about what you are reading? How does your brain interpret and store the information it receives? And how does your brain direct the movements of your hand? The answers to these questions are provided by the field of biological psychology, or **biopsychology** (Davis et al., 1988), which studies the relationship between biological processes (such as brain activity) and psychological functions (such as memory).

Interest in biopsychology is not new. A century ago, Sigmund Freud predicted that researchers would eventually discover the physiological processes underlying his theory of psychoanalysis (Sulloway, 1979). At about the same time, William James (1890/1981), in his classic psychology textbook, *The Principles of Psychology*, stressed the close association between biology and psychology. In fact, James declared, "I have felt most acutely the difficulties of understanding either the brain without the mind or the mind without the brain" (Bjork, 1988, p. 107). Freud and James were influenced by Charles Darwin's (1859/1975) theory of evolution, which holds that individuals who are biologically well adapted to their environment are more likely to survive, reproduce, and, as a result, pass on their physical characteristics to succeeding generations.

Thus, the human brain has evolved into its present form because it helped human beings in thousands of earlier generations adapt successfully to their environment and survive long enough to pass on their genes. Because of its remarkable flexibility in helping us adapt to different circumstances, the brain that helped ancient people survive without automobiles, grocery stores, or electric lights helps people today survive in the arctic, outer space, and New York City.

THE NERVOUS SYSTEM

The brain is part of the **nervous system,** the chief means of communication within the body. The nervous system is composed of **neurons,** cells that are specialized for the transmission and reception of information. The term *neuron* was coined by the German anatomist Wilhelm Waldeyer (1836–1921). As illustrated in figure 3.1, the two divisions of the nervous system are the *central nervous system* and the *peripheral nervous system*. The **central nervous system** contains the **brain** and the **spinal cord.** The **peripheral nervous system** contains the **nerves,** which provide a means of communication between the central nervous system and the sensory organs, skeletal muscles, and internal bodily organs.

The peripheral nervous system contains the *somatic nervous system* and the *autonomic nervous system*. The **somatic nervous system** includes *sensory nerves,* which send messages from the sensory organs to the central nervous system, and *motor nerves,* which send messages from the central nervous system to the skeletal muscles. The **autonomic nervous system** controls automatic, involuntary processes, such as sweating, heart contractions, and intestinal activity, through the action of its two subdivisions: the *sympathetic nervous system* and the *parasympathetic nervous system*. The **sympathetic nervous system** arouses the body to prepare it for action, and the **parasympathetic nervous system** calms the body to conserve its energy.

Imagine that you are playing a tennis match. Your sympathetic nervous system speeds up your heart rate to pump more blood to your muscles, makes your liver release

biopsychology
The field that studies the relationship between physiological and psychological processes.

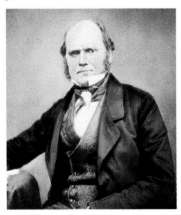

Charles Darwin (1809–1882)
"I have called this principle, by which each slight variation, if useful, is preserved, by the term Natural Selection."

nervous system
The chief means of communication in the body, which transmits messages along neurons.

neuron
A cell specialized for the transmission of information in the nervous system.

central nervous system
The division of the nervous system consisting of the brain and the spinal cord.

brain
The portion of the central nervous system that is located in the skull and plays important roles in sensation, movement, and information processing.

spinal cord
The portion of the central nervous system that is located in the spine and plays a role in body reflexes and in communicating information between the brain and the peripheral nervous system.

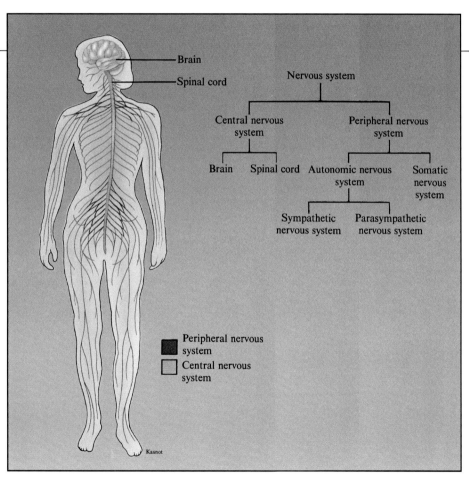

FIGURE 3.1

The Organization of the Nervous System
The nervous system comprises the brain, spinal cord, and nerves.

peripheral nervous system
The division of the nervous system, composed of the nerves, that conveys sensory information to the central nervous system and motor commands from the central nervous system to the skeletal muscles and internal organs.

nerve
A bundle of axons that conveys information to or from the central nervous system.

somatic nervous system
The division of the peripheral nervous system that sends messages from the sensory organs to the central nervous system and messages from the central nervous system to the skeletal muscles.

autonomic nervous system
The division of the peripheral nervous system that controls automatic, involuntary physiological processes.

sympathetic nervous system
The division of the autonomic nervous system that arouses the body to prepare it for action.

parasympathetic nervous system
The division of the autonomic nervous system that calms the body and serves maintenance functions.

sugar into your bloodstream for quick energy, and induces sweating to keep you from overheating. As you cool down after the match, your parasympathetic nervous system slows your heart rate and constricts the blood vessels in your muscles to divert blood for use by your internal organs. Chapter 12 describes the role of the autonomic nervous system in emotional responses, and chapter 16 explains how chronic activation of the sympathetic nervous system can contribute to the development of stress-related diseases. To appreciate how the autonomic nervous system and all other parts of the nervous system carry out their functions, you must first understand the workings of the neuron.

THE NEURON

You are able to read this page because **sensory neurons** are relaying input from your eyes to your brain. You will be able to turn the page because **motor neurons** from your spinal cord are sending commands from your brain to the muscles of your hand. *Sensory neurons* send messages to the brain or spinal cord. *Motor neurons* send messages to the glands, the cardiac muscle, and the skeletal muscles, as well as to the smooth muscles of the arteries, small intestine, and other internal organs.

The nervous system contains ten times more *glial cells* than neurons. **Glial cells** provide a physical support structure for the neurons (*glial* comes from the Greek word for "glue"). Glial cells also supply neurons with nutrients, remove neuronal metabolic waste, and help regenerate damaged neurons in the peripheral nervous system. Research indicates that glial cells may even facilitate the transmission of messages by neurons (Cornell-Bell et al., 1990).

To appreciate the role of neurons in communication within the nervous system, consider the functions of the *spinal cord*, the long, tubelike structure that is enclosed in the protective spinal column and extends from the brain to the tip of the spine. Neurons in the spinal cord convey sensory messages from the body to the brain and motor messages from the brain to the body. The sensory and motor functions of the spinal cord were suspected as long ago as the second century, when the Greek physician Galen noted that victims of spinal cord injuries suffered limb paralysis or loss of bodily sensations. You might know people who have injured their spinal cords in diving or automobile accidents, causing them to lose the ability to move their limbs or feel bodily sensations below the point of the injury.

In 1730 the English scientist Stephen Hales demonstrated that the spinal cord also plays a role in limb reflexes. Hales decapitated a frog (to eliminate any input from the brain) and then pinched one of its legs. The leg reflexively pulled away. He concluded that the pinch had sent a signal to the spinal cord, which, in turn, sent a signal to the leg, eliciting its withdrawal. We now know that this limb-withdrawal **reflex** involves, as shown in figure 3.2, sensory neurons that convey signals from the site of stimulation to the spinal cord, where they transmit their signals to **interneurons** in the spinal cord. The interneurons then send signals to motor neurons, which stimulate flexor muscles to contract and pull the limb away from the source of stimulation.

The fact that the limb-withdrawal reflex does not require input from the brain is advantageous. Suppose that the reflex did require that signals be sent to the brain and that the brain then send signals down the spinal cord to make the limb withdraw. It would take a fraction of a second longer for you to pull your hand away from a hot pan or your foot away from a misplaced thumbtack—making you more susceptible to injury. Of course, a split second after you withdraw your limb from a hot pan or your foot from a thumbtack, your brain receives input from neurons in the spinal cord that causes you to say "Ouch!" (or something even more colorful).

To understand how neurons communicate information, you should first become familiar with the structure of the neuron. Figure 3.3 contains a drawing of a neuron showing its major structures, and a photograph of neurons, taken with a microscope. The **soma** (or *cell body*) contains the nucleus, which directs the neuron to act as a nerve

sensory neuron
A neuron that sends messages from sensory receptors to the central nervous system.

motor neuron
A neuron that sends messages from the central nervous system to smooth muscles, cardiac muscle, or skeletal muscles.

glial cell
A kind of cell that provides a physical support structure for the neurons, supplies them with nutrition, removes neuronal metabolic waste materials, facilitates the transmission of messages by neurons, and helps regenerate damaged neurons in the peripheral nervous system.

reflex
An automatic, involuntary motor response to sensory stimulation.

interneuron
A neuron that conveys messages between neurons in the brain or spinal cord.

soma
The cell body, which serves as the neuron's control center.

Bypassing the Spinal Cord
This person lost the ability to use her legs after suffering spinal cord damage. She is shown learning to walk with the aid of a computer that sends bursts of electricity to stimulate her leg muscles in a coordinated manner.

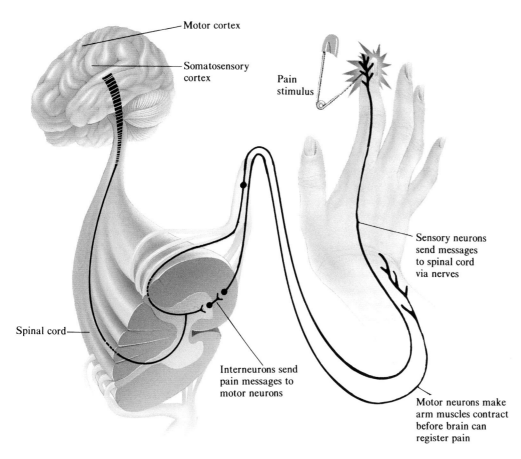

Motor cortex

Somatosensory cortex

Pain stimulus

Spinal cord

Sensory neurons send messages to spinal cord via nerves

Interneurons send pain messages to motor neurons

Motor neurons make arm muscles contract before brain can register pain

FIGURE 3.2

The Limb-Withdrawal Reflex
When your hand touches an object that stimulates pain receptors in the skin, sensory neurons convey this information to interneurons in the spinal cord, which send signals along motor neurons that make certain muscles contract and pull your hand away.

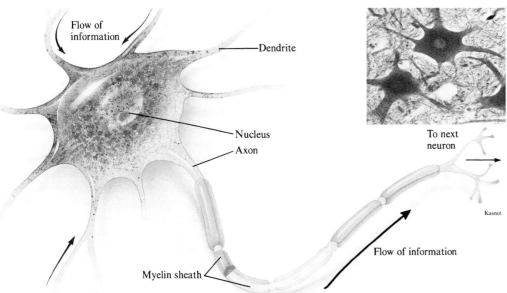

Flow of information

Dendrite

Nucleus

Axon

Myelin sheath

To next neuron

Kasnot

Flow of information

FIGURE 3.3

The Neuron
Both the drawing and the photograph show the structure of the motor neuron. Neurons have dendrites that receive signals from other neurons or sensory receptors, a cell body that controls cellular functions, and an axon that conveys signals to skeletal muscles, internal organs, or other neurons.

cell rather than as a fat cell, a muscle cell, or any other kind of cell. The **dendrites** (from the Greek word for "tree") are short, branching fibers that receive neural impulses. The dendrites are covered by bumps called *dendritic spines*, which provide more surface area for the reception of neural impulses from other neurons (Koch & Poggio, 1983). The **axon** is a single fiber that sends neural impulses. Axons range from a tiny fraction of an inch (as in the brain) to more than 3 feet in length (as in the legs of a 7-foot-tall basketball player). Just as bundles of wires form telephone cables, bundles of axons form

dendrites
The branchlike structures of the neuron that receive neural impulses.

axon
The relatively long fiber of the neuron that conducts neural impulses.

the nerves of the peripheral nervous system. A nerve can contain motor neurons or sensory neurons, or both.

The Neural Impulse

How does the neuron convey information? It took centuries of investigation by some of the most brilliant minds in the history of science to find the answer. Before the neuron was discovered in the nineteenth century, scientists were limited to studying the functions of nerves. In doing so, they typically were influenced by their other research interests.

In the seventeenth century, René Descartes (1596–1650) was intrigued by moving statues in the royal gardens of King Louis XIII, which were controlled hydraulically by fluid-filled tubes. This led Descartes to speculate that the body is controlled in a similar way by fluids, which he called *vital spirits*, flowing through the nerves. He assumed that our limbs move when vital spirits expand the muscles that control them. Descartes even built his own hydraulic statue, which he took along to study on an ocean voyage. But the ship's captain, seeing the statue moving about on deck, accused it of being the work of the devil and threw it overboard—cutting short the research side of Descartes's vacation (Wilson, 1967).

Decades later, the English physicist Isaac Newton (1642–1727) provided an alternative view based on his research on the nature of vibrating strings, like those of guitars or violins. Newton believed that information is conveyed in the nervous system by the vibration of nerves (Gregory, 1987). The more frequent the nerve vibrations, the faster or stronger would be limb movements or sensory experiences. Though Descartes's and Newton's views were shown by later research to be wrong, they stimulated interest in discovering the means by which nerves conduct impulses.

In 1786 the Italian physicist Luigi Galvani (1737–1798) gave demonstrations hinting that the nerve impulse is electrical in nature. Galvani found that by touching the leg of a freshly killed frog with two different metals, such as iron and brass, he could create an electric current that made the leg twitch. He believed he had discovered the basic life force—electricity. Some of Galvani's followers, who hoped to use electricity to raise the dead, obtained the fresh corpses of hanged criminals and stimulated them with electricity. To the disappointment of these would-be resurrectors, they failed to induce more than the flailing of limbs (Hassett, 1978). Another of Galvani's contemporaries, Mary Shelley, later used lightning, a powerful form of electricity, to revive the dead in her classic novel, *Frankenstein*.

Though Galvani and his colleagues failed to demonstrate that electricity was the basic life force, they put scientists on the right track toward understanding how neural impulses are conveyed in the nervous system. But it took almost two more centuries of research before scientists identified the exact mechanisms. We now know that neuronal activity, whether involved in hearing a doorbell, throwing a softball, or recalling a childhood memory, depends on electrical-chemical processes, beginning with the *resting potential*.

Resting Potential

In 1952, English scientists Alan Hodgkin and Andrew Huxley, using techniques that let them study individual neurons, discovered the electrical-chemical nature of the processes that underlie **axonal conduction,** the transmission of a *neural impulse* along the length of the axon. Hodgkin and Huxley found that in its inactive state, the neuron maintains an electrical **resting potential,** produced by differences between the *intracellular fluid* inside of the neuron and the *extracellular fluid* outside of the neuron. These fluids contain *ions*, which are positively or negatively charged molecules. In regard to the resting potential, the main positive ions are *sodium* and *potassium*, and the main negative ions are *proteins* and *chloride*.

The *neuronal membrane*, which separates the intracellular fluid from the extracellular fluid, is *selectively permeable* to ions. This means that some ions pass back and forth

axonal conduction
The transmission of a neural impulse along the length of an axon.

resting potential
The electrical charge of a neuron when it is not firing a neural impulse.

Chapter Three

through tiny *ion channels* in the membrane more easily than do others. Because ions with like charges repel each other and ions with opposite charges attract each other, you might assume that the extracellular fluid and intracellular fluid would end up with the same relative concentrations of positive ions and negative ions. But, because of several complex processes, the intracellular fluid ends up with an excess of negative ions and the extracellular fluid ends up with an excess of positive ions. This makes the inside of the resting neuron negative relative to the outside, so the membrane is said to be *polarized*, just like a battery. For example, at rest the inside of a motor neuron has a charge of −70 millivolts relative to its outside. (A millivolt is 0.001 volt.)

Action Potential

When a neuron is stimulated sufficiently by other neurons or by a sensory organ, it stops "resting." The neuronal membrane becomes more permeable to positively charged sodium ions, which, attracted by the negative ions inside, rush into the neuron. This makes the inside of the neuron less electrically negative relative to the outside, a process called *depolarization*. As sodium continues to rush into the neuron, and the inside becomes less and less negative, the neuron reaches its *firing threshold* (about −60 millivolts in the case of a motor neuron) and an *action potential* occurs at the point where the axon leaves the cell body.

An **action potential** is a change in the electrical charge across the axonal membrane, with the inside of the membrane becoming more electrically positive than the outside and reaching a charge of +40 millivolts. Once an action potential has occurred, that point on the axonal membrane immediately restores its resting potential through a process called *repolarization*. During repolarization, the ions are actively transported across the axonal membrane by chemical "pumps" and returned to their original distributions. This restores the resting potential. Figure 3.4 illustrates the changes that occur during depolarization and repolarization.

If an axon fails to depolarize enough to reach its firing threshold, no neural impulse occurs—not even a weak one. If you have ever been under general anesthesia, you became unconscious because you were given a drug that prevented the axons in your brain that are responsible for the maintenance of consciousness from depolarizing enough to fire off action potentials (Nicoll & Madison, 1982). When an axon reaches its firing threshold and an action potential occurs, a neural impulse travels the entire length of the axon at full strength, as sodium ions rush in at each successive point along the axon. This is known as the **all-or-none law.** It is analogous to firing a gun: If you do not pull

action potential
A series of changes in the electrical charge across the axonal membrane that occurs after the axon has reached its firing threshold.

all-or-none law
The principle that once a neuron reaches its firing threshold, a neural impulse travels at full strength along the entire length of its axon.

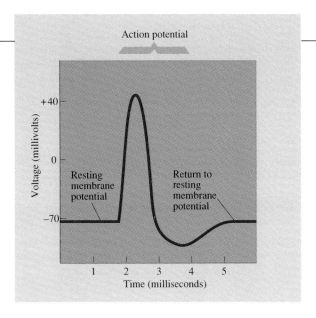

FIGURE 3.4

The Action Potential
During an action potential, the inside of the axon becomes electrically positive relative to the outside, but quickly returns to its normal resting state, with the inside again electrically negative relative to the outside.

the trigger hard enough, nothing happens; but if you do pull the trigger hard enough, the gun fires and a bullet travels down the entire length of its barrel.

Thus, when a neuron reaches its firing threshold, a neural impulse travels along its axon, as each point on the axonal membrane depolarizes (producing an action potential) and then repolarizes (restoring its resting potential). This process of depolarization–repolarization is so rapid that an axon may conduct up to 1,000 neural impulses a second. The loudness of sounds you hear, the strength of your muscle contractions, and the level of arousal of your brain all depend on the number of neurons involved in those processes and the rate at which they conduct neural impulses.

The speed at which the action potential travels along the axon varies from less than 1 meter per second in certain neurons to more than 100 meters per second in others. The speed depends on several factors, most notably whether sheaths of a white fatty substance called **myelin** (which is produced by glial cells) are wrapped around the axon. At frequent intervals along myelinated axons, tiny areas are nonmyelinated. These are called *nodes of Ranvier*, after the French anatomist Louis Antoine Ranvier, who first identified them in 1871. In myelinated axons, such as those forming much of the brain and spinal cord, as well as the motor nerves that control our muscles, the action potential jumps from node to node, instead of traveling from point to point along the entire axon. This explains why myelinated axons conduct neural impulses faster than nonmyelinated axons.

If you were to look at a freshly dissected brain, you would find that the inside appeared mostly white and the outside appeared mostly gray, because the inside contains many more myelinated axons. You would be safe in concluding that the brain's *white matter* conveyed information faster than its *gray matter*. Some neurological disorders are associated with abnormal myelin conditions. In the disease *multiple sclerosis*, portions of the myelin sheaths in neurons of the brain and spinal cord are destroyed, causing muscle weakness, sensory disturbances, memory loss, and cognitive deterioration as a result of the disruption of normal axonal conduction (Devins & Seland, 1987).

To summarize, a neuron maintains a *resting potential* during which its inside is electrically negative relative to its outside. Stimulation of the neuron makes positive sodium ions rush in and *depolarize* the neuron (that is, make the inside less negative relative to the outside). If the neuron depolarizes enough, it reaches its *firing threshold* and an *action potential* occurs. During the action potential, the inside of the neuron becomes electrically positive relative to the outside. Because of the *all-or-none law*, a *neural impulse* is conducted along the entire length of the axon at full strength. Axons covered by a *myelin sheath* conduct impulses faster than other axons. After an action potential has occurred, the axon *repolarizes* and restores its resting potential.

Synaptic Transmission

If all the neuron did was conduct a series of neural impulses along its axon, we would have an interesting, but useless, phenomenon. The reason why we can see a movie, feel a mosquito bite, think about yesterday, or ride a bicycle is because neurons can communicate with one another by the process of **synaptic transmission,** communication across gaps between neurons.

The Synapse

The question of how neurons communicate with one another provoked a heated debate in the late nineteenth century. The Italian anatomist Camillo Golgi (1843–1926) led the majority of researchers, who argued that neurons were connected to one another in a network. His rival, the Spanish anatomist Santiago Ramón y Cajal (1852–1934), led the minority, including Sigmund Freud, who argued that neurons were separate from one another (Koppe, 1983). Ramón y Cajal won the debate by using a microscopic technique (ironically, invented by Golgi) to show that neurons do not form a network (Ramón y Cajal, 1937/1966).

myelin
A white fatty substance that forms sheaths around certain axons and increases the speed of neural impulses.

Santiago Ramón y Cajal (1852–1934)
"For all those who are fascinated by the bewitchment of the infinitely small, there wait in the bosom of the living being millions of palpitating cells which, for the surrender of their secret, and with it the halo of fame, demand only a clear and persistent intelligence to contemplate, admire, and understand them."

synaptic transmission
The conveying of a neural impulse between a neuron and another neuron or a gland, muscle, or sensory organ.

For their efforts, in 1906 Golgi and Ramón y Cajal shared the Nobel Prize for Physiology and Medicine. In 1897 the English physiologist Charles Sherrington (1857–1952) coined the term **synapse** (from the Greek word for "junction") to refer to the gaps that exist between neurons. You should note that synapses also exist between neurons and glands, between neurons and muscles, and between neurons and sensory organs.

As is usually the case with scientific discoveries, the observation that neurons were separated by synapses led to still another question. How could neurons communicate with one another across these gaps? At first, some scientists assumed that the neural impulse simply jumped across the synapse, just as sparks jump across the gap in a spark plug. But the correct answer came in 1921—in a dream.

The dreamer was Otto Loewi, an Austrian physiologist who had been searching without success for the mechanism of synaptic transmission. Loewi awoke from his dream and carried out the experiment it suggested. He removed the beating heart of a freshly killed frog, along with the portion of the *vagus nerve* attached to it, and placed it in a solution of saltwater. By electrically stimulating the vagus nerve, he made the heart beat slower. He then put another beating heart in the same solution. Though he had not stimulated its vagus nerve, the second heart also began to beat slower. If you had made this discovery, what would you have concluded? Loewi concluded, correctly, that stimulation of the vagus nerve of the first heart had released a chemical into the solution. It was this chemical, which he later identified as *acetylcholine*, that slowed the beating of both hearts.

Neurotransmitters

Acetylcholine is one of a group of chemicals called **neurotransmitters,** which transmit neural impulses across synapses. Neurotransmitters are stored in round packets called *synaptic vesicles* in the intracellular fluid of bumps called *synaptic knobs* that project from the end branches of axons.

The discovery of the chemical nature of synaptic transmission led to the question of how chemicals facilitate this transmission. Subsequent research revealed the processes involved, which are illustrated in figure 3.5. First, when a neural impulse reaches the end of an axon, it induces a chemical reaction that makes some synaptic vesicles release neurotransmitter molecules into the synapse. Second, the molecules diffuse across the synapse and reach the dendrites of another neuron. Third, the molecules attach to tiny areas on the dendrites called *receptor sites*. Fourth, the molecules interact with the receptor sites to excite the neuron; this slightly depolarizes the neuron by permitting sodium ions to enter it. But for a neuron to depolarize enough to reach its firing threshold, it must be excited by neurotransmitters released by many other neurons. To further complicate the process, a neuron can also be affected by neurotransmitters that inhibit it from depolarizing. Thus, a neuron will fire an action potential only when the combined effects of *excitatory neurotransmitters* sufficiently exceed the combined effects of *inhibitory neurotransmitters*. Fifth, neurotransmitters do not remain attached to the receptor sites, continuing to affect them indefinitely. Instead, after the neurotransmitters have done their job, they are either broken down by chemicals called *enzymes* or taken back into the neurons that had released them—in a process called *re-uptake*.

Of the neurotransmitters, acetylcholine is the best understood. In the peripheral nervous system, it is the neurotransmitter at synapses between the neurons of the parasympathetic nervous system and the organs they control, such as the heart. Acetylcholine also is the neurotransmitter at synapses between motor neurons and muscle fibers, where it stimulates muscle contractions. *Curare*, a poison that Amazon Indians put on the darts they shoot from their blowguns, paralyzes muscles by preventing acetylcholine from attaching to receptor sites on muscle fibers. The resulting paralysis of muscles, including the breathing muscles, causes death by suffocation.

In the brain, acetylcholine helps regulate memory processes. The actions of acetylcholine in the brain can be impaired by drugs or disease. For example, chemicals in

synapse
The junction between a neuron and another neuron, a gland, a muscle, or a sensory organ.

Otto Loewi (1873–1961)
"I got up immediately, went to the laboratory, made the experiment on the frog's heart . . . , and at five o'clock the chemical transmission of nervous impulses was conclusively proved."

neurotransmitters
Chemicals secreted by neurons that provide the means of synaptic transmission.

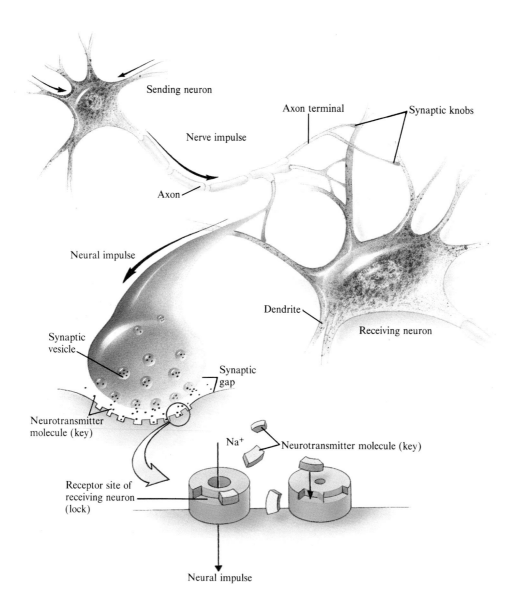

Sending neuron

Nerve impulse

Axon terminal

Synaptic knobs

Axon

Neural impulse

Dendrite

Receiving neuron

Synaptic vesicle

Synaptic gap

Neurotransmitter molecule (key)

Na⁺

Neurotransmitter molecule (key)

Receptor site of receiving neuron (lock)

Neural impulse

FIGURE 3.5

Synaptic Transmission between Neurons
When a neural impulse reaches the end of an axon, it stimulates synaptic vesicles to release neurotransmitter molecules into the synapse. The molecules diffuse across the synapse and interact with receptor sites on another neuron, causing sodium ions to leak into that neuron. The molecules then disengage from the receptor sites and are broken down by enzymes or taken back into the axon.

Alzheimer's disease
A brain disorder characterized by difficulty in forming new memories and by general mental deterioration.

marijuana disrupt acetylcholine synapses involved in memory processes, so people who smoke it might have difficulty forming memories (Miller & Branconnier, 1983). **Alzheimer's disease,** a brain disorder common in late adulthood, is associated with the destruction of acetylcholine neurons in the brain. As a result, Alzheimer's victims gradually lose their ability to form new memories. Alzheimer's disease is also associated with a marked intellectual decline and severe personality deterioration (Kopelman, 1986).

Since the discovery of acetylcholine, dozens of other neurotransmitters have been identified. Your ability to perform smooth voluntary movements depends on brain neurons that secrete the inhibitory neurotransmitter *dopamine. Parkinson's disease,* which is marked by movement disorders, is caused by the destruction of dopamine neurons in the

brain. Dopamine in the brain is also implicated in the rewarding effects of eating and other pleasurable activities (Wise & Rompre, 1989). And elevated levels of dopamine are found in schizophrenia. Drugs that block dopamine activity alleviate some of the symptoms of schizophrenia (Carlsson, 1988).

Our moods vary with the level of the neurotransmitter *norepinephrine* in the brain, with a low level being associated with depression. Many antidepressant drugs work by increasing norepinephrine levels in the brain. Norepinephrine also induces eating. For example, when norepinephrine is infused into their brains, rats eat more, apparently because the norepinephrine stimulates neurons in a region of the brain that induces hunger (Leibowitz, 1988).

When you fall asleep, you owe it to activity in brain neurons that release the inhibitory neurotransmitter *serotonin*. Administration of *tryptophan*, the dietary amino acid from which serotonin is synthesized in the brain, has helped insomniacs fall asleep faster (Schneider-Helmert & Spinweber, 1986). Like norepinephrine, serotonin is implicated in depression. In fact, people who become so depressed that they try suicide often have unusually low levels of serotonin (Ricci & Wellman, 1990).

Some amino acids, such as tryptophan, serve as precursors of neurotransmitters; other amino acids serve as neurotransmitters. The main inhibitory amino acid neurotransmitter is *gamma aminobutyric acid* (or GABA). GABA induces muscle relaxation and inhibits anxiety. Tranquilizers, such as Valium, relieve anxiety by promoting the action of GABA (Breier & Paul, 1990). *Glycine*, another important inhibitory amino acid neurotransmitter, helps regulate memory formation. Drugs that block glycine activity disrupt memory formation (Handelmann et al., 1989). As discussed in chapter 7, the main excitatory amino acid neurotransmitter, *glutamate*, may play a positive role in the formation of memories (Cotman, Monaghan, & Ganong, 1988). Glutamate might also be the means by which lead poisoning damages children's brains. Lead inhibits the activity of an enzyme that deactivates glutamate. The resulting high levels of glutamate overexcite brain neurons, leading to their destruction (Engle & Volpe, 1990).

Another class of neurotransmitters comprises small proteins called *neuropeptides*. The excitatory neuropeptide *substance P* has sparked interest because of its apparent role in the transmission of pain impulses in the spinal cord (Mamberg & Yaksh, 1992). During the past few years, neuropeptides called **endorphins** have generated much research and publicity because of their possible roles in relieving pain and inducing feelings of euphoria.

endorphins
Neurotransmitters that play a role in pleasure, pain relief, and other functions.

Anatomy of a Classic Research Study:
Does the Brain Contain Its Own Opiate Receptors?

Rationale
The endorphin story began in 1973, when Candace Pert and Solomon Snyder of Johns Hopkins University discovered opiate receptors in the brains of animals (Pert & Snyder, 1973). Opiates are pain-relieving drugs (or narcotics)—including morphine, codeine, and heroin—derived from the opium poppy. Snyder and Pert became interested in conducting their research after finding hints in previous research studies by other scientists that animals might have opiate receptors.

Method
Pert and Snyder removed the brains of mice, rats, and guinea pigs. Samples of brain tissue were then treated with radioactive morphine and with naloxone, a chemical similar in structure to morphine that blocks morphine's effects. A special device detected whether the morphine and naloxone had attached to receptors in the brain tissue.

Results and Discussion
Pert and Snyder found that the chemicals had bound to specific receptors. If you had been a member of Pert and Snyder's research team, what would you have inferred from this observation? Pert and Snyder inferred that the brain must manufacture its own opiatelike chemicals. If it did not, then why had it evolved its own opiate receptors?—hardly in anticipation of the availability of opiates such as morphine, codeine, and heroin. This inspired the search for opiatelike chemicals in the brain. The search bore fruit in Scotland when Hans Kosterlitz and his colleagues found an opiatelike chemical in brain tissue taken from animals (Hughes et al., 1975). They called this chemical enkephalin *(from Greek terms meaning "in the head"). Enkephalin and similar chemicals discovered in the brain were later dubbed "endogenous morphine" (meaning "morphine from within"). This was then abbreviated into the now-popular term* endorphin.

Candace Pert
"Our brains probably have natural counterparts for just about any drug you could name."

Once researchers had located the receptor sites for the endorphins and had isolated endorphins themselves, they then wondered, Why has the brain evolved its own source of opiatelike neurotransmitters? With several research teams hot on its trail, the answer was not long in coming. Researchers found that endorphins have an inhibitory effect on synapses that transmit pain impulses, perhaps by blocking substance P release. Evidently, endorphins evolved, at least in part, because they provided pain relief. Perhaps the first animals blessed with endorphins were better able to function in the face of pain caused by diseases or injuries, making them more likely to survive long enough to reproduce and pass this physical trait on to successive generations (Levinthal, 1988).

Evidence supporting this speculation has come from human and animal experiments. In one experiment, researchers first recorded how long mice would allow their tails to be exposed to radiant heat from a lightbulb before the pain made them flick their tails away from it. Those mice were then paired with more aggressive mice, who attacked and defeated them. The losers' tolerance for the radiant heat was then tested again. The results showed that the length of time the defeated mice would permit their tails to be heated had increased. But when the defeated mice were given naloxone, which (as mentioned earlier) blocks the effects of morphine, they flicked away their tails as quickly as they had done before being defeated. The researchers concluded that the naloxone had blocked the pain-relieving effects of the endorphins (Miczek, Thompson, & Shuster, 1982).

Endorphin secretion is stimulated by sources of stress as varied as feeling pain, giving birth, or exercising vigorously (Cohen, Pickar, & DuBois, 1983). Perhaps athletes who continue playing despite painful injuries do so because their injuries stimulate increased endorphin activity, thereby relieving their pain. Endorphins might reduce the pain of giving birth, because pregnant women secrete increasing amounts of endorphins as labor approaches (Arehart-Treichel, 1981). There is also evidence that endorphins might be responsible for the feelings of euphoria we experience in trance states or states of ecstasy (Henry, 1982), including the "exercise high" experienced by many people who run, swim, or bicycle (Droste et al., 1991).

THE ENDOCRINE SYSTEM

Neurotransmitters are not the only chemical messengers. There are also **hormones,** which are chemicals secreted by glands in the **endocrine system.** The endocrine glands secrete hormones into the bloodstream, which transports them to their sites of action. This contrasts with *exocrine glands*, such as the sweat glands and salivary glands, which secrete their chemicals onto the body surface or into body cavities. Endocrine secretions have many behavioral effects, but exocrine secretions have few. The behavioral effects of exocrine secretions called *pheromones* are discussed in chapter 5.

Components of the Endocrine System

Figure 3.6 illustrates the locations of the major endocrine glands. The **pituitary gland,** an endocrine gland protruding from underneath the brain, regulates many of the other endocrine glands by secreting hormones that affect their activity. This is why the pituitary is known as the "master gland." The pituitary gland, in turn, is regulated by the brain structure called the *hypothalamus*, whose other functions are discussed later in this chapter. Feedback from circulating hormones stimulates the hypothalamus to signal the pituitary gland to increase or decrease their secretion.

Hormones

Table 3.1 lists the major hormones and their functions. Hormones can act directly on body tissues, serve as neurotransmitters, or modulate the effects of neurotransmitters.

Pituitary Hormones

Pituitary hormones are secreted by the *posterior pituitary gland* (the rear portion of the gland) and the *anterior pituitary gland* (the front portion of the gland). The posterior pituitary hormone *vasopressin* acts on kidney tissue to promote the retention of water. Vasopressin also enhances memory processes by stimulating acetylcholine activity in the brain (Faiman, de Erausquin, & Baratti, 1988).

Oxytocin, another posterior pituitary hormone, stimulates contractions of the uterus during labor and secretion of milk during nursing. In rodents, oxytocin has direct effects on sexuality and mothering. For example, oxytocin facilitates mating behavior in female rats (Schumacher et al., 1990) and prevents infanticide by female mice (McCarthy, 1990).

The anterior pituitary gland secretes more kinds of hormones than does the posterior pituitary gland. *Growth hormone* stimulates the physical development of bones and muscles. A child who secretes too much growth hormone may develop *giantism*, marked by excessive growth of the bones. A child who secretes insufficient growth hormone may develop *dwarfism*, marked by stunted growth. Giantism and dwarfism do not impair normal intellectual development.

Thyroid-stimulating hormone promotes the secretion of hormones by the **thyroid gland.** Thyroid hormones, most notably *thyroxin*, are needed for normal metabolism,

The Runner's High
The euphoric "exercise high" experienced by long-distance runners might be caused by the release of endorphins in the brain.

hormones
Chemicals, secreted by endocrine glands, that play a role in a variety of functions, including synaptic transmission.

endocrine system
Glands that secrete hormones into the bloodstream.

pituitary gland
An endocrine gland that regulates many of the other endocrine glands by secreting hormones that affect those glands.

thyroid gland
An endocrine gland that secretes hormones needed for normal metabolism, physical growth, and brain development.

FIGURE 3.6

The Endocrine System
Hormones secreted by the endocrine glands affect metabolism, behavior, and mental processes.

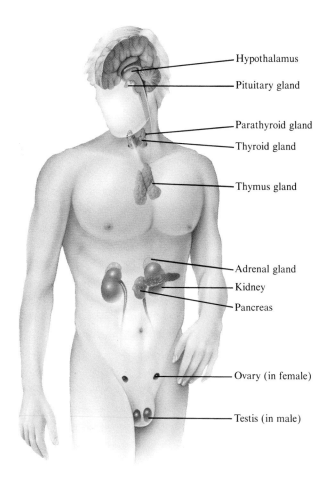

- Hypothalamus
- Pituitary gland
- Parathyroid gland
- Thyroid gland
- Thymus gland
- Adrenal gland
- Kidney
- Pancreas
- Ovary (in female)
- Testis (in male)

Growth Hormone
Hormonal imbalances can have extreme effects. For example, (*a*) a lack of growth hormone may produce a dwarf, such as the late actor Herve Villechaize, who starred as "Tattoo" on the television show "Fantasy Island." (*b*) An excess of growth hormone may produce a giant, such as the late wrestler Andre the Giant.

(a)

(b)

testes
The male gonads, which secrete hormones that regulate the development of the male reproductive system and secondary sex characteristics.

ovaries
The female gonads, which secrete hormones that regulate the development of the female reproductive system and secondary sex characteristics.

physical growth, and brain development (Dussault & Ruel, 1987). A lack of thyroid hormones in children causes *cretinism*, which is marked by stunted growth and mental retardation.

The anterior pituitary gland also secretes *gonadotropic hormones*, which stimulate the secretion of sex hormones by the *gonads*, the sex glands. The **testes,** the male gonads, secrete *testosterone*, which regulates the development of the male reproductive system and secondary sex characteristics. The **ovaries,** the female gonads, secrete *estrogens*, which regulate the development of the female reproductive system and secondary sex characteristics. The ovarian hormone *progesterone* regulates changes in the uterus that maintain pregnancy. The effects of sex hormones are also discussed in chapters 4 and 11.

TABLE 3.1	Functions of the Major Hormones	
Gland	**Hormone**	**Function**
Hypothalamus	Releasing hormones	The hypothalamus is a brain structure that regulates the release of pituitary hormones
Pituitary		
Anterior (front lobe)	Adrenocorticotropic hormone (ACTH)	Stimulates hormone secretion by the adrenal cortex
	Gonadotropic hormones	Regulate the gonads (testes and ovaries)
	Growth hormone	Stimulates growth
	Prolactin	Stimulates milk production in nursing women
	Thyroid-stimulating hormone	Stimulates hormone secretion by the thyroid gland
Posterior (rear lobe)	Vasopressin	Promotes water retention by the kidneys, and plays a role in the formation of memories
	Oxytocin	Stimulates contractions of the uterus during labor and secretion of milk during nursing
Adrenal		
Cortex (outer layer)	Aldosterone	Regulates excretion of sodium and potassium
	Cortisol	Regulates metabolism and response to stress
Medulla (inner layer)	Epinephrine and norepinephrine	Contribute to physiological arousal associated with activation of the sympathetic nervous system
Gonads		
Testes	Testosterone	Regulates development of the male reproductive system, secondary sex characteristics, and sex drive
Ovaries	Estrogens	Regulate development of the female reproductive system and secondary sex characteristics
	Progesterone	Regulates changes in the uterus to maintain pregnancy
Kidneys	Renin	Regulates aldosterone secretion and blood pressure
Pancreas	Insulin	Decreases blood sugar
	Glucagon	Increases blood sugar
Thyroid	Thyroxin	Regulates metabolism and growth
Pineal	Melatonin	Regulates arousal and biological rhythms

The anterior pituitary hormone *prolactin* stimulates milk production in nursing women. Because an elevated prolactin level is associated with both infertility and psychological stress, prolactin might also be implicated in stress-related infertility. This indicates that women who are highly anxious about their inability to become pregnant might enter a vicious cycle in which their anxiety increases the level of prolactin, which in turn makes them less likely to conceive (Edelmann & Golombok, 1989).

adrenal glands
Endocrine glands that secrete hormones that regulate the excretion of minerals and the body's response to stress.

Still another hormone secreted by the anterior pituitary gland is *adrenocorticotropic hormone* (or *ACTH*), which stimulates the secretion of hormones by the *adrenal cortex*, the outer layer of the **adrenal glands,** which lie on the kidneys. The adrenal cortical hormone *aldosterone* regulates the excretion of sodium and potassium, which contribute to proper neural functioning. The adrenal cortical hormone *cortisol* helps the body respond to stress by stimulating the liver to release sugar.

Other Hormones

In response to stimulation by the sympathetic nervous system, the *adrenal medulla*, the inner core of the adrenal gland, secretes *epinephrine* and *norepinephrine*, which function as both hormones and neurotransmitters. Epinephrine increases heart rate. It also promotes the storage and retrieval of memories (Stone, Rudd, & Gold, 1990). As noted earlier, norepinephrine acts as the neurotransmitter at synapses in the sympathetic nervous system, thereby arousing the body to take action. Because, in their roles as hormones, epinephrine and norepinephrine are long-acting, you may have noticed that your feelings of physical arousal, whether caused by an attractive person or a harrowing drive in a winter storm, last for a while even after the source of the arousal is gone.

pancreas
An endocrine gland that secretes hormones that regulate the level of blood sugar.

The **pancreas** secretes *insulin*, which reduces blood sugar by actively transporting it into body cells. By reducing blood sugar, insulin evokes hunger. In fact, the mere sight of food can induce hunger by stimulating the release of insulin (Rodin, 1985). Fast-food chains take advantage of this by presenting television commercials with food that looks tantalizing. Insufficient insulin can cause *diabetes mellitus*, marked by a failure to provide sugar to body cells and a resulting deterioration of body tissues.

pineal gland
An endocrine gland that secretes a hormone that has a general tranquilizing effect on the body and that helps regulate biological rhythms.

The **pineal gland,** a tiny structure at the center of the brain, secretes the hormone *melatonin*, which has a general tranquilizing effect on many physiological processes. Because of its inhibitory effect on brain arousal, caused by stimulation of GABA activity (Niles & Peace, 1990), melatonin has been used to treat insomnia. In a double-blind study, insomniacs given melatonin fell asleep faster and maintained sleep better than did insomniacs given a placebo (Waldhauser, Saletu, & Trinchard-Lugan, 1990). Melatonin also helps regulate *biological rhythms* (discussed in chapter 6), making it potentially beneficial in treating time-related problems caused by jet lag or shift work (Cassone, 1990).

THE BRAIN

"Tell me, where is fancy bred, in the heart or in the head?" (*The Merchant of Venice*, act 3, scene 2). The answer to this question from Shakespeare's play might be obvious to you. You know that your brain, and not your heart, is your feeling organ—the site of your mind. But you have the advantage of centuries of research, which have made the role of the brain in all psychological processes obvious even to nonscientists. Of course, the cultural influence of early beliefs may linger. Just imagine the response of a person who received a gift of Valentine's Day candy in a box that was brain-shaped instead of heart-shaped.

The ancient Egyptians associated the mind with the heart and discounted the importance of the apparently inactive brain. In fact, when the pharoah Tutankhamen ("King Tut") was mummified to prepare him for the afterlife, his heart and other bodily organs were carefully preserved, but his brain was discarded. The Greek philosopher Aristotle (384–322 B.C.) also believed that the heart was the site of the mind, because when the heart stops, mental activity stops (Laver, 1972). But the Greek physician-philosopher Hippocrates (460–377 B.C.), based on his observations of the effects of brain damage, did locate the mind in the brain:

> ● ● ● Some people say that the heart is the organ with which we think and that it feels pain and anxiety. But it is not so. Men ought to know that from the brain and from the brain alone arise our pleasures, joys, laughter, and tears. (Penfield, 1975, p. 7)

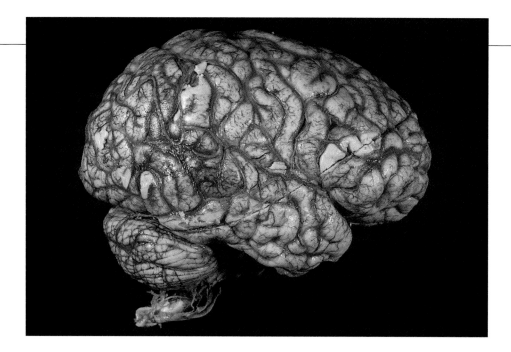

Does this mean that Hippocrates was brilliant and Aristotle foolish? On the contrary, each used the tools available to him—observation and reason—to come to logical, intelligent conclusions. Had subsequent research supported Aristotle's position, we would credit him with the foresight that we now credit to Hippocrates. As noted in chapter 1, we should avoid *presentism* in evaluating the past.

Functions of the Brain

The human brain's appearance does not hint at its complexity. Holding it in your hands, you might not be impressed by either its 3-pound weight or its walnutlike surface. You might be more impressed to learn that it contains billions of neurons (Goodman & Bastiani, 1984). And you might be astounded to learn that a given brain neuron may communicate with thousands of others, leading to a virtually infinite number of pathways for messages to follow in the brain.

As you read this section, you will find that much of what we know about the brain comes from studies of the effects of brain damage, electrical stimulation of the brain, recording of the electricity produced by brain activity, and computer scanning of the brain. As an example, consider the **electroencephalograph** (**EEG**), which records the pattern of electrical activity produced by neuronal activity in the brain. The EEG has a peculiar history, going back to a day at the turn of the century when an Austrian scientist named Hans Berger fell off a horse and narrowly escaped serious injury. That evening he received a telegram informing him that his sister felt he was in danger.

The telegram inspired Berger to investigate the possible association between *mental telepathy* (the alleged, though scientifically unverified, ability of one mind to communicate with another by extrasensory means) and electrical activity from the brain. In 1924, after years of experimenting on animals and his son Klaus, Berger succeeded in perfecting a procedure for recording electrical activity in the brain. He attached small metal disks called *electrodes* to Klaus's scalp and connected them with wires to a device that recorded changes in the patterns of electrical activity in his brain. Figure 3.7 illustrates a modern EEG device, which is a descendant of the device used by Berger.

Though Berger failed to find physiological evidence in support of mental telepathy, he identified two distinct rhythms of electrical activity. He called the relatively slow rhythm associated with a relaxed mental state the *alpha rhythm* and the relatively

electroencephalograph (EEG)
A device used to record patterns of electrical activity produced by neuronal activity in the brain.

FIGURE 3.7

The Electroencephalograph (EEG)
The EEG records patterns of electrical activity from the brain. The fast beta brain-wave pattern is associated with the alert, active mental state you might be in while taking an exam. The slower alpha brain-wave pattern is associated with the relaxed, unfocused mental state you might be in just after you lie down to go to sleep.

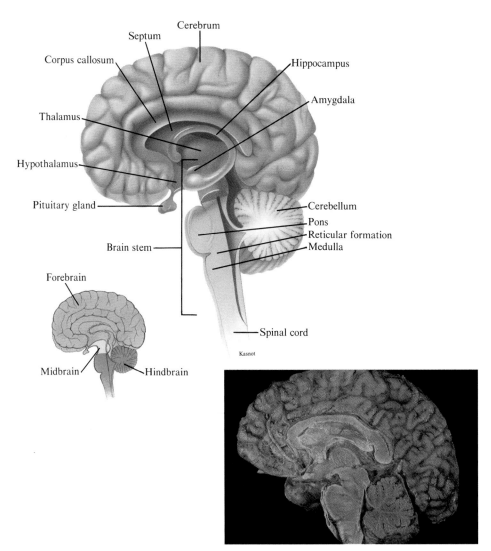

FIGURE 3.8

The Structure of the Human Brain
The structures of the hindbrain, midbrain, and forebrain serve a variety of life-support, sensorimotor, and cognitive functions.

fast rhythm associated with an alert, active mental state the *beta rhythm*. Berger also used the EEG to provide the first demonstration of the stimulating effect of cocaine on brain activity. He found that cocaine increased the beta rhythm in EEG recordings (Herning, 1985). The EEG and other devices have permitted scientists to unlock many of the brain's secrets. Figure 3.8 illustrates the major structures of the *hindbrain, midbrain,* and *forebrain.*

Functions of the Hindbrain

Your ability to survive from moment to moment depends on your hindbrain, which is located at the base of the brain. Of all the hindbrain structures, the most crucial to your survival is the **medulla oblongata** (or, simply, the *medulla*), which connects the brain and spinal cord. At this moment your medulla is regulating your breathing, heart rate, and blood pressure. Because the medulla controls so many vital functions, damage to it can be fatal, as in the 1968 assassination of presidential candidate Robert Kennedy, who was shot through the medulla. When called upon, your medulla also stimulates coughing, vomiting, or swallowing. By inducing vomiting, for example, the medulla prevents people who drink too much alcohol too fast from poisoning themselves.

medulla oblongata
A hindbrain structure that regulates breathing, heart rate, blood pressure, and other life functions.

Just above the medulla lies the bulbous structure called the **pons.** As explained in chapter 6, the pons regulates the sleep-wake cycle through its effect on consciousness. Sleep disorders are sometimes associated with abnormal activity in the pons (Culebras & Moore, 1989). And if you have ever been the unfortunate recipient of a blow to the head that knocked you out, your loss of consciousness was caused by the blow's effect on your pons (Hayes et al., 1984).

The pons (which means "bridge" in Latin) connects the **cerebellum** (meaning "little brain") to the rest of the brain. The cerebellum enables the eyes to move smoothly as they track a moving object (Lisberger, Morris, & Tychsen, 1987). The cerebellum also controls the timing of well-learned sequences of movements that are too rapid to be controlled consciously, as in running a sprint, singing a song, or playing the piano. As you know from your own experience, conscious efforts to control normally automatic sequences of movements such as these can disrupt them. A pianist who thinks of each key he or she is striking while playing a well-practiced piece would be unable to maintain proper timing.

Passing from the hindbrain through the midbrain and into the forebrain is the **reticular formation,** a diffuse network of neurons that helps regulate vigilance and brain arousal. The role of the reticular formation in maintaining vigilance is shown by the "cocktail party phenomenon," in which you can be engrossed in a conversation but still notice when someone elsewhere in the room says something of significance to you, such as your name. Thus, the reticular formation acts as a filter, letting you attend to an important stimulus while ignoring irrelevant ones.

Experimental evidence supporting the role of the reticular formation in brain arousal came from a study by Giuseppe Moruzzi and Horace W. Magoun in which they awakened sleeping cats by electrically stimulating the reticular formation (Moruzzi & Magoun, 1949). Destruction of the reticular formation by drug overdoses can induce a permanent coma, as in the widely publicized case of Karen Ann Quinlan, who lived in a coma for years before her parents won the right to remove her from a respirator.

As you can see, the structures of the hindbrain let you carry out some of the most basic life functions. Your hindbrain is responsible for your ability to maintain your vital processes, to follow a sleep-wake cycle, to move effectively, to maintain your vigilance, to selectively attend to stimuli, and to adjust your level of brain arousal.

Functions of the Midbrain

The *midbrain* is a relatively small region in mammal brains (though it is relatively large in bird, reptile, and amphibian brains). Forming the roof of the midbrain is a structure called the **tectum,** which mediates adaptive, reflexive responses to visual and auditory stimuli. For example, your startle response to a sudden noise is mediated by the tectum (Parham & Willott, 1990). To appreciate the adaptive function of the tectum, suppose that a hidden prankster throws a snowball at your head. By responding to input from your eyes, the tectum would detect the snowball and prompt you to duck your head before you even realized that the object was a snowball. Damage to the tectum can prevent such defensive responses to potential dangers (Stehouwer, 1987).

The tectum also helps identify stimuli, even enabling bats to find insects to eat. The bat's sonar system emits sound waves that strike flying insects, creating echoes that differ according to their wingbeat patterns. The tectum helps the bat identify the insect by analyzing the distinctive pattern of echoes it produces (Pollak, Wenstrup, & Fuzessey, 1986).

The graceful movements of gymnasts, ballet dancers, and trapeze artists depend on the midbrain structure called the **substantia nigra,** which acts in conjunction with other brain structures to promote smooth voluntary body movements. Less-dramatic abilities, such as writing and walking, that require smooth movements also rely on the substantia nigra. Many older adults who suffer from **Parkinson's disease,** caused by degeneration of dopamine neurons in the substantia nigra, have difficulty performing even these simple acts. Victims of Parkinson's disease might also have a blank facial expression, walk with

pons
A hindbrain structure that regulates the sleep-wake cycle.

cerebellum
A hindbrain structure that controls the timing of well-learned movements.

reticular formation
A diffuse network of neurons, extending from the hindbrain through the midbrain and into the forebrain, that helps maintain vigilance and an optimal level of brain arousal.

tectum
A midbrain structure that mediates reflexive responses to visual and auditory stimuli.

substantia nigra
A midbrain structure that promotes smooth voluntary body movements.

Parkinson's disease
A degenerative disease of the dopamine pathway from the substantia nigra, which causes marked disturbances in motor behavior.

a shuffling gait, and exhibit hand tremors when simply holding a cup of coffee. They also may have marked difficulty in initiating movements (Lang et al., 1990). Because Parkinson's symptoms are caused by a dopamine deficit, the treatment of choice is administration of the drug *L-dopa*, which is converted into dopamine in the brain.

Functions of the Forebrain

Above the hindbrain and midbrain is the *forebrain*, which serves the "higher functions" of thinking, learning, memory, emotion, and personality. The forebrain helps you adapt to changes in the environment by integrating information from your senses and your memory. Some of the evidence supporting the importance of the forebrain in emotion and personality has come from case studies of people with damage to it, such as Phineas Gage. On a fall day in 1848, Gage, the 25-year-old foreman of a Vermont railroad crew laying track, was clearing away rocks. While he was using an iron tamping rod to pack a gunpowder charge into a boulder, a spark ignited the gunpowder. The resulting explosion hurled the rod into Gage's left cheek, through his forebrain, and out the top of his skull.

Miraculously, Gage survived, recuperated, and lived 12 more years, with little apparent change in his intellectual abilities. But there were dramatic changes in his personality and emotionality. Instead of remaining the friendly, popular, hardworking man he had been before the accident, he became an ornery, disliked, irresponsible bully. Gage's friends believed he had changed so radically that "he was no longer Gage" (Blakemore, 1977, p. 4).

This case study implies that the forebrain structures damaged by the tamping rod might be important in emotion and personality. But, as explained in chapter 2, it is impossible to determine causality from a case study. Perhaps Gage's emotional and personality changes were caused not by the brain damage itself, but instead by Gage's psychological response to his traumatic accident or by changes in how other people responded to him. Nonetheless, the forebrain's importance in emotion and personality has been supported by experimental research. Disorders of the frontal lobes are often, as in Gage's case, associated with antisocial behavior, including criminality (Kandel & Freed, 1989).

Among the major structures of the forebrain are the **basal ganglia,** which work in conjunction with the substantia nigra of the midbrain to aid in the smooth execution of movements (Marsden, 1982). Located at the center of the forebrain is the egg-shaped **thalamus.** (The portion of the brain extending from the medulla through the thalamus is called the *brainstem.*) The thalamus functions as a sensory relay station, sending taste, bodily, visual, and auditory sensations on to other areas of the brain for further processing. The visual information from this page is being relayed by your thalamus to areas of your brain that process vision. The one sense whose information is not relayed through

basal ganglia
A set of forebrain structures that promote smooth voluntary movements.

thalamus
A forebrain structure that acts as a sensory relay station for taste, body, visual, and auditory sensations.

Phineas Gage's Skull and the Tamping Rod That Pierced His Forebrain

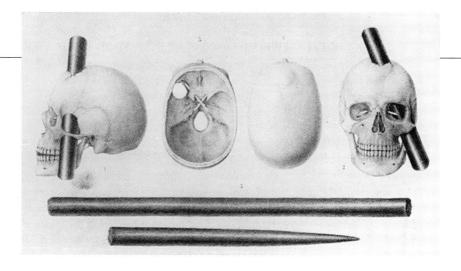

the thalamus is smell. Sensory information from smell receptors in the nose goes directly to areas of the brain that process smells.

Surrounding the thalamus is a group of forebrain structures that compose the **limbic system.** (The word *limbic* comes from the Latin for "border.") These structures were given this collective name by Paul Broca (a major nineteenth-century brain researcher introduced in chapter 1) because they form a border between the cerebral hemispheres (Schiller, 1979). The limbic system interacts with other brain structures to promote the survival of the individual and, as a result, the continuation of the species. The components of the limbic system include the *hypothalamus,* the *septum,* the *amygdala,* and the *hippocampus.*

Just below the thalamus, on the underside of the forebrain, lies the **hypothalamus** (in Greek the prefix *hypo-* means "below"), a structure that is important to a host of functions. The hypothalamus helps regulate eating, drinking, emotion, sexual behavior, and body temperature. It exerts its influence by regulating the secretion of hormones by the pituitary gland and by signals sent along neurons to bodily organs controlled by the autonomic nervous system.

The importance of the hypothalamus in emotionality was discovered by accident. Psychologists James Olds and Peter Milner (1954) of McGill University in Montreal inserted fine wire electrodes into the brains of rats to study the effects of electrical stimulation of the reticular formation. They had already trained the rats to press a lever to obtain food rewards. When a wired rat now pressed the lever, it obtained mild electrical stimulation of its brain. To the experimenters' surprise, the rats, even when hungry or thirsty, ignored food and water in favor of pressing the lever—sometimes thousands of times an hour, until they dropped from exhaustion up to 24 hours later (Olds, 1956). Olds and Milner examined brain tissue from the rats and discovered that they had mistakenly inserted the electrodes near the hypothalamus, and not into the reticular formation. Olds and Milner concluded that they had discovered a "pleasure center" in that region. Subsequent research studies have shown that the hypothalamus is but one structure in an interconnected group of brain structures that induce feelings of pleasure when stimulated.

The **amygdala** of the limbic system continuously evaluates information from the immediate environment, thereby eliciting appropriate emotional responses (Henke, 1988). If you saw a pit bull dog running toward you, your amygdala would help you quickly decide whether the dog was vicious, friendly, or simply roaming around. Depending on your evaluation of the situation, you might feel happy and pet the dog, feel afraid and jump on top of your desk, or feel relief and go back to studying. In the late 1930s, Heinrich Klüver and Paul Bucy (1937) found that lesions of the amygdala in monkeys led to "psychic blindness," an inability to evaluate environmental stimuli properly. The monkeys indiscriminately examined objects by mouth, tried to mate with members of other species, and acted fearless when confronted by a snake.

In 1966 the amygdala was implicated in the notorious Texas tower massacre (Holmes, 1986), in which a young man named Charles Whitman shot randomly at people on the campus of the University of Texas, killing 16 and wounding 31. He shot most of his victims from the roof of the main administration building before dying in a shoot-out with police. In a diary found after his death, Whitman complained of overwhelming homicidal impulses. An autopsy of his brain discovered that he had a tumor of the amygdala. Were police, physicians, and reporters right in attributing his murderous rampage to this tumor? Possibly, though once again you must be careful not to confuse correlation with causation. Perhaps the presence of the tumor and Whitman's rampage were purely coincidental.

While your amygdala helps you evaluate information from your environment, the limbic system structure that is most important in helping you form memories of that information (including what you are now reading) is the **hippocampus** (Barnes, 1987). Much of what we know about the hippocampus comes from case studies of people who have suffered damage to it. The most famous study is of a man known as H. M. (Scoville

limbic system
A group of forebrain structures that promote the survival of the individual and, as a result, the continuation of the species by their influence on emotion, motivation, and memory.

hypothalamus
A forebrain structure that helps to regulate aspects of motivation and emotion, including eating, drinking, sexual behavior, body temperature, and stress responses, through its effects on the pituitary gland and the autonomic nervous system.

amygdala
A limbic system structure that evaluates information from the immediate environment, contributing to feelings of fear, anger, or relief.

hippocampus
A limbic system structure that contributes to the formation of memories.

The Amygdala and Violence
A tumor of the amygdala may have motivated Charles Whitman to go on a shooting rampage at the University of Texas, killing 16 people and wounding 31.

& Milner, 1957), whose hippocampus was surgically removed in 1953 to relieve his uncontrollable epileptic seizures. Since the surgery, H. M. has formed few new memories, though he can recall events that occurred before his surgery. You can read more about the implications of his case in regard to memory in chapter 7.

Damage to the hippocampus has been implicated in the memory loss associated with Alzheimer's disease. Victims of this disease suffer from degeneration of the neurons

REPRINTED COURTESY
OMNI MAGAZINE © 1986.

"It's times like this that our larger brains seem curiously unimportant"

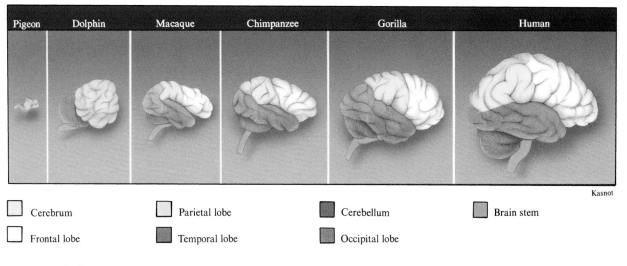

| Pigeon | Dolphin | Macaque | Chimpanzee | Gorilla | Human |

Kasnot

☐ Cerebrum   ☐ Parietal lobe   ■ Cerebellum   ☐ Brain stem

☐ Frontal lobe   ■ Temporal lobe   ■ Occipital lobe

FIGURE 3.9

The Evolution of the Brain
Animals that are more cognitively complex have evolved brains that are larger in proportion to their body sizes. Their cerebral cortex is also larger in proportion to the size of their other brain structures, which creates a more convoluted brain surface.

that serve as pathways between the hippocampus and other brain areas. Because Alzheimer's disease is marked by the inability to form new memories, a victim might be able to recall her third birthday party but not what she ate for breakfast this morning. Alzheimer's disease is also associated with personality deterioration, including delusions and mood disturbances (Cummings & Victoroff, 1990).

Covering most of the brain is the crowning achievement of brain evolution—the **cerebral cortex** of the forebrain. Cortex means "bark" in Latin. And just as the bark is the outer layer of the tree, the cerebral cortex is the thin, 3-millimeter-thick outer layer of the uppermost portion of the forebrain called the *cerebrum*. The cerebral cortex of human beings and other mammals has evolved folds called *convolutions*, which, as shown in figure 3.9, give it the appearance of kneaded dough. The convolutions permit more cerebral cortex to fit inside the skull. This is necessary because evolution has assigned so many complex brain functions to the mammalian cerebral cortex that the brain has,

cerebral cortex
The outer covering of the forebrain.

FIGURE 3.10

The Lobes of the Brain
The cerebral cortex covering each cerebral hemisphere is divided into four lobes: the frontal lobe, the temporal lobe, the parietal lobe, and the occipital lobe.

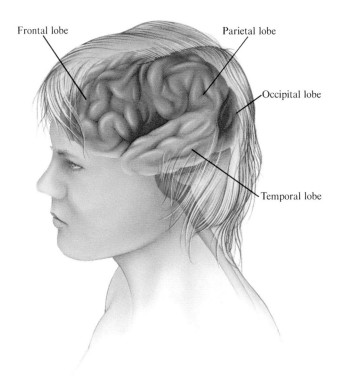

cerebral hemispheres
The left and right halves of the cerebrum.

primary cortical areas
Regions of the cerebral cortex that serve motor or sensory functions.

association areas
Regions of the cerebral cortex that integrate information from the primary cortical areas and other brain areas.

frontal lobe
A lobe of the cerebral cortex responsible for motor control and higher mental processes.

motor cortex
The area of the frontal lobes that controls specific voluntary body movements.

in a sense, outgrown the skull in which it resides. If the cerebral cortex were smooth instead of convoluted, the human brain would have to be enormous to permit the same amount of surface area. The brain would be encased in a skull so large that it would give us the appearance of creatures from science fiction movies.

The cerebrum is divided into left and right halves called the **cerebral hemispheres.** Figure 3.10 shows that the cerebral cortex covering each hemisphere is divided into four regions, which are called *lobes*: the *frontal lobe*, the *temporal lobe*, the *parietal lobe*, and the *occipital lobe*. The lobes have **primary cortical areas** that serve motor or sensory functions. The lobes also have **association areas** that integrate information from the primary cortical areas and other brain areas in activities such as speaking, problem solving, and recognizing objects. The unusually large association areas of the human cerebral cortex provide more area for processing of information. This contributes to the greater flexibility of human beings in adapting to diverse circumstances (Killackey, 1990).

With the layout of the cerebral cortex in mind, you are ready to begin a tour of its lobes. Your tour begins in 1870, when the German physicians Gustav Fritsch and Eduard Hitzig (1870/1960) published their findings that electrical stimulation of a strip of cerebral cortex along the rear border of the right or left **frontal lobe** of a dog induces limb movements on the opposite side of the body. This is known as *contralateral control*. The area they stimulated is called the **motor cortex.** They were probably the first to demonstrate conclusively that specific sites on the cerebral cortex control specific body movements (Breathnach, 1992).

Figure 3.11 presents a "map" of the motor cortex of the frontal lobe, represented by a *motor homunculus* (*homunculus* is from the Latin terms meaning "small human"). Each area of the motor cortex controls a particular contralateral body movement. Certain sites on the motor cortex even show activity in anticipation of arm movements in particular directions (Alexander & Crutcher, 1990). Note that the motor homunculus is upside down, with the head represented at the bottom and the feet represented at the top. You might also be struck by the disproportionate sizes of the body parts on the motor homunculus—each body part is represented in proportion to the precision of its movements, not in proportion to its actual size. Because your fingers move with great precision in manipulating objects, the region of the motor cortex devoted to your fingers is

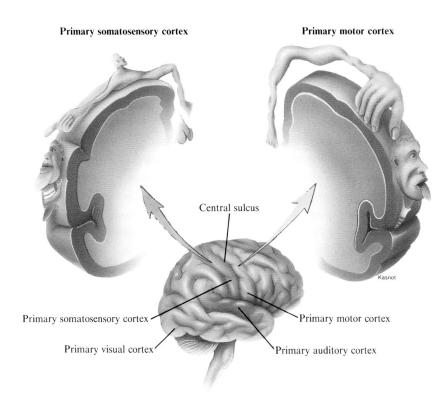

Primary somatosensory cortex

Primary motor cortex

Central sulcus

Kasnot

Primary somatosensory cortex

Primary motor cortex

Primary visual cortex

Primary auditory cortex

FIGURE 3.11

The Motor Cortex and the Somatosensory Cortex
Both the motor cortex and the somatosensory cortex form distorted, upside-down maps of the contralateral side of the body.

disproportionately large relative to the regions devoted to body parts that move with less precision, such as your arms.

The primary cortical areas of the frontal lobes control movements; the primary cortical areas of the other lobes process sensory information. You will notice in figure 3.11 that the primary cortical area of the **parietal lobes** runs parallel to the motor cortex of the frontal lobes. This area is called the **somatosensory cortex,** because it processes information related to bodily senses such as pain, touch, and temperature. As in the case of the motor cortex, the somatosensory cortex forms a distorted, upside-down homunculus of the body and receives input from the opposite side of the body. Each body part is represented on the *sensory homunculus* in proportion to its sensory precision rather than its size. This is why the region devoted to your highly sensitive lips is disproportionately large relative to the region devoted to your less sensitive back.

How do we know that a motor homunculus and a sensory homunculus exist on the cerebral cortex? We know because of research conducted by neurosurgeon Wilder Penfield (1891–1976), of the Montreal Neurological Institute, in the course of brain surgery to remove defective tissue causing epileptic seizures. World War I almost ended Penfield's life before he had a chance to make his major contributions to brain research. After being badly wounded when a German U-boat blew up a passenger ship he was on, Penfield believed God let him survive to serve an important purpose. He found his purpose in the relief of human suffering as a neurosurgeon. Of his many contributions, his most important was the "Montreal procedure" for surgically removing scar tissue that caused epilepsy. In using the procedure, he made the first use of Hans Berger's EEG, by comparing brain activity before and after surgery to see if it had been successful in abolishing the abnormal brain activity that had triggered the patient's seizures.

In using the Montreal procedure, Penfield made an incision through the scalp, pulled the scalp away from the skull, sawed through a portion of the skull, and removed a large flap of bone—exposing the cerebral cortex. His patients required only a local anesthetic at the site of the scalp and skull incisions, because incisions in the brain itself do not cause pain. This let the patients remain awake during surgery and converse with him.

parietal lobe
A lobe of the cerebral cortex responsible for processing body sensations and perceiving spatial relations.

somatosensory cortex
The area of the parietal lobes that processes information from sensory receptors in the skin.

Wilder Penfield (1891–1976)
"The mind remains, still, a mystery that science has not solved."

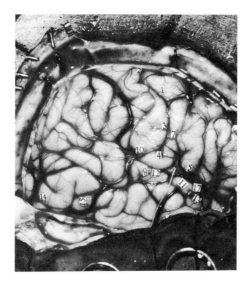

Penfield then administered a weak electrical current to the exposed cerebral cortex. He did so for two reasons. First, he wanted to induce an *aura* that would indicate the site that triggered the patient's seizures. An aura is a sensation (such as an unusual odor) that precedes a seizure. Second, he wanted to avoid cutting through parts of the cerebral cortex that serve important functions.

Penfield found that stimulation of a point on the right frontal lobe might make the left forefinger rise, and that stimulation of a point on the left parietal lobe might make the patient report a tingling feeling in the right foot. After stimulating points across the entire cerebral cortex of many patients, Penfield found that the regions governing movement and bodily sensations formed the distorted upside-down maps of the body shown in figure 3.11. His discovery has been verified by research on animals as well as human beings. For example, stimulation of points on the cerebral cortex of baboons produces similar distorted "maps" of the body (Waters et al., 1990).

temporal lobe
A lobe of the cerebral cortex responsible for processing hearing.

auditory cortex
The area of the temporal lobes that processes sounds.

The **temporal lobes** have their own primary cortical area, the **auditory cortex.** The auditory cortex of each lobe receives input from both ears, but more so from the contralateral ear (Geffen & Quinn, 1984). Particular regions of the auditory cortex are responsible for processing sounds of particular frequencies. When you listen to a symphony, certain areas of the auditory cortex respond more to the low-pitched sound of a tuba, while other areas respond more to the high-pitched sound of a flute.

occipital lobe
A lobe of the cerebral cortex responsible for processing vision.

visual cortex
The area of the occipital lobes that processes visual input.

At the back of the brain are the **occipital lobes,** which contain the **visual cortex.** This region integrates input from your eyes. Because of the nature of the pathways from your eyes to your visual cortex, visual input from objects in your *right visual field* is processed in your left occipital lobe, and visual input from objects in your *left visual field* is processed in your right occipital lobe. Damage to a portion of an occipital lobe produces a blind spot in the contralateral visual field.

As stated earlier, our knowledge of the functions of the cerebral cortex and other brain areas comes primarily from studies of brain damage, electrical stimulation of the brain, and EEG recordings of brain activity. In recent years, researchers have added a new tool, the brain scan. Perhaps the most important kind of brain scan to psychologists is **positron-emission tomography (PET)**, which lets them measure ongoing activity in

positron-emission tomography (PET)
A brain-scanning technique that produces color-coded pictures showing the relative activity of different brain areas.

particular regions of the brain. In using the PET scan, researchers inject radioactive glucose (a type of sugar) into a subject. Because neurons use glucose as a source of energy, the most active region of the brain takes up the most radioactive glucose. The amount of radiation emitted by each region is measured by a donut-shaped device that encircles the head. This information is analyzed by a computer, which generates color-coded

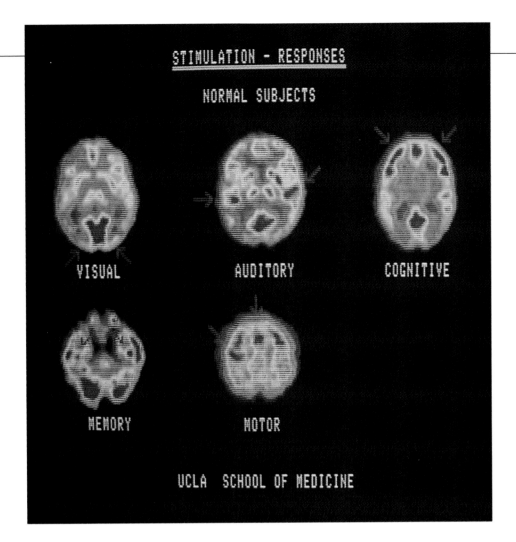

STIMULATION - RESPONSES

NORMAL SUBJECTS

VISUAL   AUDITORY   COGNITIVE

MEMORY   MOTOR

UCLA SCHOOL OF MEDICINE

FIGURE 3.12

The PET Scan
The red areas of these PET scans reveal the regions of the brain that have absorbed the most glucose, indicating that they are the most active regions during the performance of particular tasks (Phelps & Mazziotta, 1985).

pictures that show the relative degree of activity in different brain regions. As illustrated in figure 3.12, PET scans are useful in revealing the precise patterns of brain activity during the performance of motor, sensory, and cognitive tasks (Phelps & Mazziotta, 1985).

Two other brain-scanning techniques, which are useful for displaying brain structures but not ongoing brain activity, are **computed tomography (CT)** and **magnetic resonance imaging (MRI)**. The CT scan takes many X rays of the brain from a variety of orientations around it. Detectors then record how much radiation has passed through the different regions of the brain. A computer uses this information to compose a picture of the brain. The MRI scan exposes the brain to a powerful magnetic field, and the hydrogen atoms in the brain align themselves along the magnetic field. A radio signal then disrupts the alignment. When the radio signal is turned off, the atoms align themselves again. A computer analyzes these changes, which differ from one region of the brain to another, to compose an even more detailed picture of the brain than does the CT scan. CT and MRI scans have been useful in detecting structural abnormalities. For example, degeneration of brain neurons in living victims of Alzheimer's disease has been verified by CT scans (DeCarli et al., 1990) and MRI scans (Jernigan et al., 1991).

In reading about the brain, you might have gotten the impression that each area functions independently of the others. That is far from the truth. Consider the association areas that compose most of the cerebral cortex. These areas combine information

computed tomography (CT)
A brain-scanning technique that relies on X rays to construct computer-generated images of the brain or body.

magnetic resonance imaging (MRI)
A brain-scanning technique that relies on strong magnetic fields to construct computer-generated images of the brain or body.

from other areas of the brain. For example, the association areas of the frontal lobes integrate information involved in thinking, planning, and problem solving. Damage to the frontal lobes causes emotional apathy, inability to change problem-solving strategies, and inadequate monitoring of one's social behavior (Stuss & Benson, 1984). This indicates that the association areas of the frontal lobes are especially important in helping us adapt our emotions and behavior to diverse situations.

The integration of different brain areas underlies many psychological functions. Even your ability to recognize faces depends on the interaction of association areas running along the underside of the occipital, parietal, and temporal lobes. Electrical recordings from this region of the brains of sheep and monkeys show that it becomes more active when they are shown the faces of people or animals. For example, certain neurons in the visual cortex of sheep respond to the faces of sheep, others to the faces of sheepdogs, and still others to the faces of human beings (Kendrick & Baldwin, 1987).

People who have suffered damage to this region exhibit **prosopagnosia,** the inability to recognize faces (Sergent & Signoret, 1992). Imagine a child with prosopagnosia. She might fail to recognize her father's face, yet still recognize his voice. Every time they met, he would have to speak so that she could identify him (Young & Ellis, 1989). Why do you suppose we have evolved cortical association areas devoted to such a narrow function? Perhaps we have done so because the ability to recognize friend from foe has important survival value for us.

To gain more appreciation for the way in which cortical association areas interact, consider the process of speech, one of the most distinctly human abilities. Speech depends on the interaction of the association cortex of the frontal and temporal lobes. In most left-handed people and almost all right-handed people, the left cerebral hemisphere is superior to the right in processing speech. The speech center of the frontal lobe, **Broca's area,** is named for its discoverer, the French surgeon and anthropologist Paul Broca (1824–1880). In 1861 Broca treated a 51-year-old man named Leborgne, who was given the nickname "Tan" because he had a severe speech disorder that made *tan* the only syllable he could pronounce clearly. After Tan died of an infection, Broca performed an autopsy and found damage to a small area of the left frontal lobe of his brain. Broca concluded that this area controls speech. Tan's speech disorder is now called *Broca's aphasia*. (The word *aphasia* comes from the Greek word for "speechlessness.")

Though Broca was the first to formalize the relationship between a specific brain site and speech production, he was not the first to note that damage to the left hemisphere was associated with speech disruption. The relationship was noted as long ago as ancient Egypt (Sondhaus & Finger, 1988). Broca's observation was also confirmed in later autopsies of the brains of people who had speech disorders similar to Tan's. CT scans have also verified that damage to Broca's area in living people is, indeed, associated with Broca's aphasia (Breathnach, 1989).

What is the nature of Broca's aphasia? Though its victims retain the ability to comprehend speech, they speak in a telegraphic style that can be comprehended only by listeners who pay careful attention. To illustrate this, when one victim of Broca's aphasia was asked about a family dental appointment, he said, "Monday . . . Dad and Dick . . . Wednesday nine o'clock . . . doctors and teeth" (Geschwind, 1979, p. 186). The speaker expressed the important thoughts but failed to express the connections between them. Nonetheless, you probably got the gist of the statement.

Speech also depends on a region of the temporal lobe cortex called **Wernicke's area,** named for the German physician Karl Wernicke. In contrast to Broca's area, which controls the production of speech, Wernicke's area controls the meaningfulness of speech. In 1874, Wernicke reported that patients with damage to the rear margin of the left temporal lobe spoke fluently but had difficulty comprehending speech and made little or no sense to even the most attentive listener. This became known as *Wernicke's aphasia*.

Consider the following statement by a victim of Wernicke's aphasia that describes a picture of two boys stealing cookies behind a woman's back: "Mother is away here working her work to get her better, but when she's looking the two boys looking in the

prosopagnosia
The inability to recognize faces, which is typically caused by damage to the occipital lobes.

Broca's area
The area of the frontal lobe responsible for the production of speech.

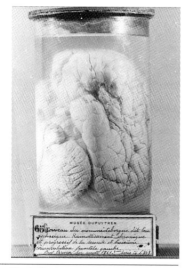

Tan's Brain
Tan's brain, preserved for more than a century, shows the damage to Broca's area in the left forebrain that destroyed his ability to speak.

Wernicke's area
The area of the temporal lobe responsible for the comprehension of speech.

CHAPTER THREE

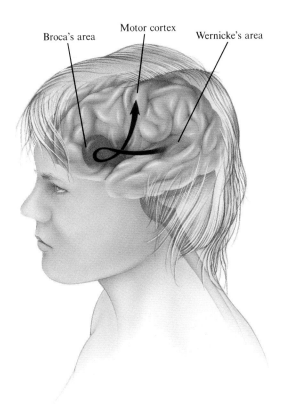

Broca's area   Motor cortex   Wernicke's area

FIGURE 3.13

Speech and the Brain
Wernicke's area, Broca's area,
and the motor cortex interact in
producing speech.

other part. She's working another time" (Geschwind, 1979, p. 186). The statement sounds more grammatical than the telegraphic speech of the victim of Broca's aphasia, but it is impossible to comprehend—it is virtually meaningless.

The consensus among researchers is that, as diagrammed in figure 3.13, speech production requires the interaction of Wernicke's area, Broca's area, and the motor cortex (Geschwind, 1979). Wernicke's area selects the words that will convey your meaning and communicates them to Broca's area. Broca's area then selects the muscle movements to express those words and communicates them to the region of the motor cortex that controls the speech muscles. Finally, the motor cortex communicates these directions through motor nerves to the appropriate muscles, and you speak the intended words. As you can see, speaking phrases as simple as *let's go out for pizza* involves the interaction of several areas of your brain.

Localization of Brain Functions

The extent to which psychological functions can be localized in particular areas of the brain has been a controversial issue for the past two centuries. The controversy began when the Viennese physician-anatomist Franz Joseph Gall (1758–1828) proclaimed that particular regions of the cerebral cortex control particular psychological functions. Gall's interest in the localization of psychological functions began in his childhood, when he observed that classmates with superior memory ability had protruding eyes. From that limited sample, Gall mistakenly inferred that memory is localized in the cerebral cortex located just behind the eyes. He assumed that the thicker the cerebral cortex in that region, the better the memory and the more the eyeballs would be pushed out of their sockets.

Gall devised a system for associating the bumps and depressions of the skull with intellectual abilities and personality traits. He assumed, incorrectly, that the bumps and depressions of the skull reflected the amount of brain tissue lying under them. And as he did in the case of memory, Gall often jumped to conclusions based on single cases. For example, he identified the "combativeness" area of the brain from bumps on the head of a drunken, quarrelsome companion.

FIGURE 3.14

Phrenology
Phrenologists such as Gall and Spurzheim developed maps of the head indicating the supposed functions of areas of the brain underlying particular places on the skull.

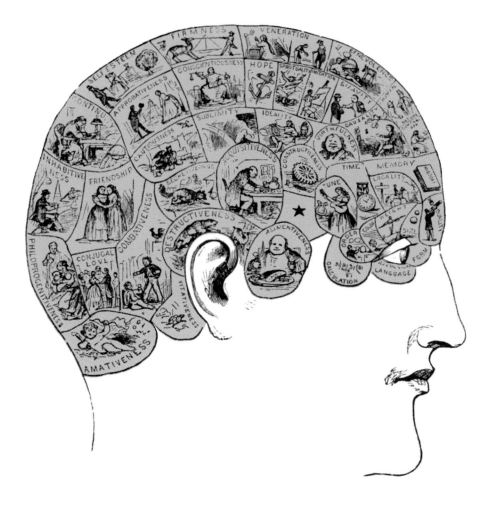

phrenology
A discredited technique for determining intellectual abilities and personality traits by examining the bumps and depressions of the skull.

Gall's student Johann Spurzheim popularized the system as **phrenology** (Greek for "science of the mind"). The term *phrenology* had first been used by the American psychiatrist Benjamin Rush to refer to the study of mental abilities. When Gall and Spurzheim combined that practice with the practice of *craniology* (the study of the skull), phrenology was born (Noel & Carlson, 1970). Figure 3.14 presents a typical phrenological map of the skull.

Gall and Spurzheim gave demonstrations of phrenology throughout Europe (McCoy, 1985), but they and their followers failed to provide adequate scientific support for their claims. On one occasion, prior to a demonstration of phrenology on the preserved brain of a genius, a practical joker replaced that brain with the brain of a mentally retarded person. Despite this exchange, the phrenologist proceeded to praise the intellectual qualities of the brain (Fancher, 1979). You might recognize this as an instance of experimenter bias, discussed in chapter 2.

During the height of its popularity in the nineteenth century, phrenology impressed members of the intellectual elite, including Walt Whitman, Charles Darwin, and Edgar Allen Poe. Phrenology even lasted into this century. One twentieth-century device, the psychograph, automatically measured the size and shape of the skull and translated those measurements into phrenological evaluations of the person's psychological traits. During the early 1930s, it was promoted as a means of vocational guidance for those who were unemployed as a result of the Great Depression. But it soon became strictly an entertainment device that fell into oblivion soon after its demonstration at the 1933 Chicago World's Fair (Risse, 1976). Though phrenology had its scientific shortcomings, even Paul Broca recognized that it had initiated interest in the localization of brain functions (Schiller, 1979).

The decline of phrenology in the early nineteenth century was accompanied by research suggesting that psychological functions require the interaction of different areas of the brain. This position was championed by the French physiologist Pierre Flourens (1794–1867) and later by the American psychologist Karl Lashley (1890–1958). Lashley based his belief on experiments in which he trained rats to run mazes to find food and then destroyed specific areas of their cerebral cortex. He found that the destruction of any given area had only a slight effect on their performance. Lashley (1950) concluded that psychological processes, particularly memory, are not localized in specific areas of the brain but require the interaction of diverse areas. More-recent experiments on rats support Lashley's position that memory requires the interaction of diverse areas of the brain (Meyer, Gurklis, & Cloud, 1985).

Today, many biopsychologists would favor a position between Gall's and Lashley's, viewing the brain as a collection of structures that interact flexibly with one another, according to the demands of the situation. Thus, each psychological function requires the interaction of several brain areas but can be disrupted by damage to one or more of them (Kaas, 1987). The interaction of Wernicke's area, Broca's area, and the motor cortex in the production of speech supports this position.

Plasticity of the Brain

The human brain is remarkable in its ability to learn from experience and to promote adaptive behavior. In doing so, the brain shows **plasticity**—that is, it is not completely "hardwired" at birth. Plasticity is shown by the elimination of excess neurons (Kolb, 1989) and synaptic connections (Huttenlocher, 1990) in childhood and the formation of new synaptic connections throughout life.

plasticity
The ability of the brain to alter its neuronal pathways.

The biggest challenge to the plasticity of the brain is brain damage, whether caused by a stroke, a disease, or a blow to the head. Natural processes in response to brain damage promote a limited degree of recovery. More recently, a technique formerly relegated to science fiction—brain tissue transplantation—has shown promise as a means of encouraging greater recovery from brain damage.

Recovery of Functions after Brain Damage

Brain damage can produce devastating effects, including paralysis, sensory loss, memory disruption, and personality deterioration. But what are the chances of recovering from such damage? It depends on the kind of animal whose brain has been damaged. Though certain species of fish and amphibians recover from brain damage by regenerating damaged axons, mammals, including human beings, do not. Human beings can regenerate damaged axons only in the peripheral nervous system. Glial cells in the peripheral nervous system form tunnels that guide the regrowth of damaged axons. In contrast, glial cells in the brain and spinal cord simply remove dead neurons and may actually impede regeneration by forming scar tissue. Human beings and other mammals depend on factors other than the regeneration of neurons for the recovery of lost brain and spinal cord functions.

In human beings and other primates, perhaps the most important factor in the recovery of functions that have been lost because of brain damage is the ability of intact brain areas to take over the functions of damaged ones (Bach-y-Rita, 1990). In one experiment, researchers surgically destroyed portions of the somatosensory cortex of monkeys. They found that the somatosensory cortical "map" representing those portions gradually shifted to intact adjacent areas of the parietal lobes, restoring the ability to experience bodily sensations (Fox, 1984). Through *collateral sprouting* (illustrated in figure 3.15), branches from the axons of nearby healthy neurons grow into the pathways normally occupied by the axons of the damaged neurons. The healthy neurons then take over the functions of the damaged ones. The younger the individual, the more likely this is to occur.

Because of *equipotentiality*, more than one area of the brain might be able to control a given function. When the area controlling a function is damaged, another area

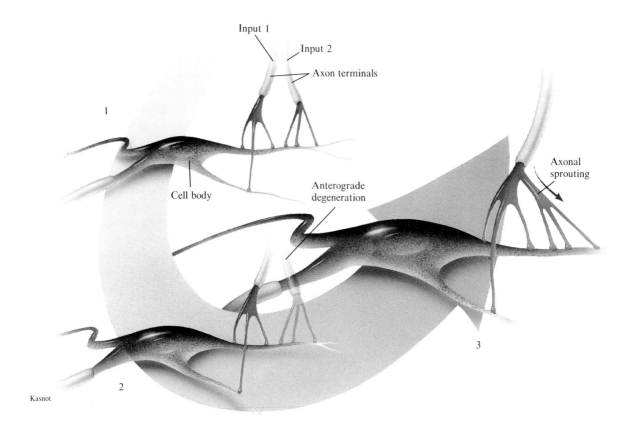

Input 1
Input 2
Axon terminals
1
Cell body
Anterograde
degeneration
Axonal
sprouting
3
2
Kasnot

FIGURE 3.15

Collateral Sprouting
When an axon dies and its connections to the dendrites of other neurons degenerate, adjacent axons may sprout branches that form synapses with the vacated sites.

might gradually take over for it (Nonneman & Corwin, 1981). This is shown by the amazing recovery of some children who have had a *hemispherectomy* (the surgical removal of an entire cerebral hemisphere), usually because of uncontrollable epilepsy. In some cases, the remaining hemisphere takes over the functions of the missing hemisphere. Though such children typically experience some sensory and motor deficits, they may function well intellectually and even go on to succeed in college. That children have greater recuperative powers than adults do after damage to a cerebral hemisphere was noted more than a century ago by Paul Broca (Schiller, 1979). This degree of recovery does not occur in adolescents or adults who have had a hemispherectomy, because their brains have less plasticity than do young brains (Ogden, 1989).

Neural Transplantation

Though plasticity may restore some lost functions, most people who have suffered brain damage do not recover completely. This has led to research on possible ways to repair damaged brains, including attempts to administer chemicals that promote the growth of axons (Kromer, 1987) or to stimulate the same processes that permit axons of the peripheral nerves to regenerate (Liuzzi & Lasek, 1987). The most widely publicized, and controversial, way has been to use **neural grafting**—the transplantation of healthy tissue into damaged brains (Kimble, 1990).

Though Mary Shelley's vision of transplanting whole brains is still a topic better suited for science fiction, scientists have been studying the use of brain tissue transplants

neural grafting
The transplantation of brain tissue or, in some cases, adrenal gland tissue into a brain to restore functions lost because of brain damage.

to treat Parkinson's disease. In an early study, researchers destroyed neurons in the substantia nigra of rats, inducing movement disturbances like those seen in victims of Parkinson's disease. The researchers then transplanted tissue from the substantia nigra of healthy fetal rats into the brains of the brain-damaged rats. After several weeks, the recipients showed a reduction in their symptoms, indicating that the transplanted tissue may have taken over the lost functions of the damaged tissue (Perlow et al., 1979).

More-recent studies have reported a variety of successful applications of neural grafting in animals. Epileptic seizures that have been experimentally induced by surgically created brain damage in rats have been reduced by the transplantation of inhibitory GABA neurons from fetal rat brains (Fine, Meldrum, & Patel, 1990). Even the spinal cord can benefit from tissue transplants. In a study of rats whose spinal cords had been surgically lesioned to cause hindlimb paralysis, grafts of fetal spinal cord cells reduced the severity of their paralysis (Bernstein & Goldberg, 1989). Thus, neural transplants show promise in treating damage to the central nervous system of animals. Researcher Jacqueline Sagen and her colleagues have even conducted studies using neural grafts of endorphin-producing adrenal medulla tissue into the brains (Hama & Sagen, 1993) or spinal cords (Sagen, Pappas, & Perlow, 1986) of animals to help relieve pain.

But how do neural transplants achieve their beneficial effects? They appear to do so by secreting neurotransmitters that the damaged region lacks (Becker, Curran, & Freed, 1990), by forming new neural circuits to replace damaged ones (Gash & Sladek, 1984), or by secreting substances that promote neural regeneration (Lescaudron & Stein, 1990). Before becoming too optimistic about neural transplants, you should realize that many attempts at them have failed (Swenson et al., 1989). And even "successful" transplants might not have the intended effects—the new secretion of neurotransmitters or the new neural circuits can disrupt existing pathways, creating even more functional deterioration (Amemori et al., 1989).

Given the success of some experiments on fetal neural transplants in animals, it is natural to consider the possibility of using such transplants in human beings, perhaps even to treat Alzheimer's disease (Dunnett, 1991). Some studies in which fetal brain tissue has been transplanted to human victims of brain damage have produced significant, long-lasting restoration of lost functions. For example, researchers in Sweden have reported success in reducing symptoms of Parkinson's disease by using fetal cell transplants (Lindvall et al., 1990). In the future, if such neural grafts are perfected, brain damage caused by strokes, tumors, diseases, or accidents might be treated by brain tissue transplants.

As you might imagine, this possibility has already sparked controversy about where we would get tissue to transplant. From animals? From aborted fetuses? From terminally ill patients? Ethicists are already dealing with this issue. In regard to fetal tissue, one set of guidelines that has been offered is to use only dead fetuses, to keep abortion and transplantation decisions separate, and to ban the buying and selling of fetal tissue (Mahowald, 1989). As noted in chapter 2, scientists must confront ethical, as well as technical, issues in conducting their research.

Because initial efforts to transplant human fetal brain tissue into the brains of victims of Parkinson's disease have met with both technical and ethical problems, researchers have turned to transplanting cells from the brain-damaged person's adrenal glands into his or her own brain. Cells from the adrenal medulla produce dopamine, the neurotransmitter lacking in the brains of victims of Parkinson's disease. In 1982, researchers in Sweden reported disappointing results following the first such adrenal transplants. But 5 years later, researchers in Mexico City announced the first successful use of adrenal transplants.

Jacqueline Sagen
"The ability to successfully transplant neural tissues into the adult central nervous system (CNS) has opened up the exciting possibility for repair of damaged neuronal circuitry."

Can Neural Transplants Repair Brain Damage?

Rationale

Ignacio Madrazo and his colleagues (1987) observed that symptoms of Parkinson's disease in animals had been relieved by grafting tissue from the adrenal medulla into the brain and that Swedish researchers had technical, though not therapeutic, success with grafts from the adrenal medulla of Parkinson's patients. Madrazo decided to replicate the Swedish study.

Method

The subjects were a 35-year-old man and a 39-year-old man, both with Parkinson's disease. Both received neural grafts of tissue taken from their own adrenal medullas and transplanted into their brains.

Results and Discussion

Over the next few months, both patients showed marked reduction of their symptoms. They had fewer hand tremors, their facial expressions became more normal, they were able to speak more clearly, and they were able to use their limbs with greater facility. Madrazo attributed the success to the release of dopamine by the neural grafts. Unfortunately, subsequent replications of this study with patients elsewhere failed to produce such dramatic improvements (Lewin, 1988). Though neural grafts have yet to demonstrate their everyday practical worth, researchers may be on the verge of breakthroughs that will restore functions that have been lost as the result of brain or spinal cord damage.

THINKING ABOUT *Psychology*

DO THE CEREBRAL HEMISPHERES SERVE DIFFERENT FUNCTIONS?

During the past few years, you may have noted popular reports in the media alleging that the cerebral hemispheres control different psychological functions, leading to the notion of "left-brained" and "right-brained" people. Though most researchers would not assign complete responsibility for any psychological function to just one hemisphere, they have reached agreement on some of the psychological functions for which each hemisphere is primarily responsible (Hellige, 1990). The left hemisphere is *somewhat* superior at performing verbal, sequential, analytical, rational, and mathematical functions, and the right hemisphere is *somewhat* superior at performing nonverbal, spatial, holistic, emotional, and creative functions (Springer & Deutsch, 1989).

In a sense, the left hemisphere would be better at giving directions to a driver by speaking, and the right hemisphere would be better at giving directions by drawing a map. But be careful not to overstate the differences in functions between the hemispheres. Each hemisphere might make unique contributions, but both hemispheres are involved in virtually all psychological processes. For example, mental images are created by activity in both the left and the right hemispheres. Research indicates that the left hemisphere retrieves stored memories of the parts of objects and the right hemisphere arranges the parts into whole images (Kosslyn, 1988). Music perception provides another example of how both hemispheres contribute to particular psychological processes. Damage to the right hemisphere, particularly the right temporal lobe, is associated with poor

PEANUTS *reprinted by permission of* UFS, Inc.

performance on tasks that require the perception of unfamiliar melodies. Damage to the left hemisphere, in contrast, produces difficulty in perceiving familiar melodies (Zatorre, 1984).

An obvious way in which the cerebral hemispheres differ is in their contralateral control of the hands, with most human beings showing a hand preference. Even lower animals—including rats, cats, and monkeys—show consistent paw preferences, at least when reaching for food. Because about 90 percent of human beings are right-handed (Hardyck & Petrinovich, 1977) and the manufactured environment is built for righties, lefties have some difficulties functioning in the everyday world. For example, lefties have difficulty operating control panels designed for righties, especially under stressful conditions that can cause confusion, as in airplane cockpits. Because of this, human-factors engineers must consider left-handed people when designing control consoles (Garonzik, 1989).

Given that each hemisphere is, to a certain extent, superior at particular tasks, how do psychologists identify the functions of the cerebral hemispheres? They do so by studying the intact brain, the damaged brain, and the split brain.

EVIDENCE FROM THE INTACT BRAIN

Psychologists interested in hemispheric specialization have devised several methods for studying the intact brain. One of the chief methods has subjects perform tasks while an EEG records the electrical activity of their cerebral hemispheres. Studies have found that people produce greater electrical activity in the left hemisphere while performing verbal tasks, such as solving verbal analogy problems, and greater electrical activity in the right hemisphere while performing spatial tasks, such as mentally rotating geometric forms (Loring & Sheer, 1984).

A more recent approach to studying hemispheric specialization in the intact brain uses the PET scan to create color-coded pictures of the relative activity in regions of the left hemisphere and right hemisphere. Figure 3.16 shows the results of one such study. Another approach, the **Wada test,** studies human subjects in whom a hemisphere has been anesthetized in the course of brain surgery to correct a neurological defect (Loring et al., 1991). This is done by injecting an anesthetic into the carotid artery serving either

Wada test
A technique in which a cerebral hemisphere is anesthetized to assess hemispheric specialization.

FIGURE 3.16

The PET Scan and Hemispheric Specialization
The red areas of these PET scans show that the left hemisphere is more active when we listen to speech and the right hemisphere is more active when we listen to music (Phelps & Mazziotta, 1985).

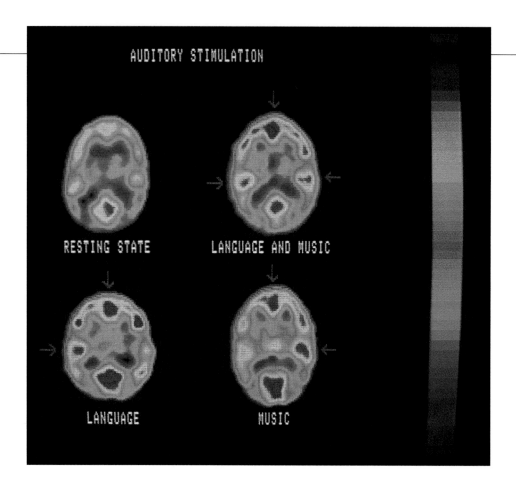

neglect syndrome
A disorder, caused by damage to a parietal lobe, in which the individual acts as though the side of her or his world opposite from the damaged lobe does not exist.

the left or the right hemisphere. As you might expect, anesthetization of the left hemisphere, but only rarely of the right hemisphere, induces temporary aphasia. The Wada test has found that many psychological functions depend on both hemispheres. For example, the ability to sing familiar songs is disrupted when either the left or the right hemisphere is anesthetized (Zatorre, 1984).

EVIDENCE FROM THE DAMAGED BRAIN

Case studies of people who have suffered damage to one cerebral hemisphere, often as the result of a stroke, are the oldest sources of evidence on hemispheric specialization. As noted earlier, in the 1860s Paul Broca found that damage to the left hemisphere was associated with the disruption of speech. In the 1880s, the English neurologist John Hughlings Jackson found that damage to the right hemisphere was associated with the disruption of spatial perception, which underlies the ability to read books, draw pictures, or put together puzzles (Levy, 1985).

A profound example of the role of the right hemisphere in spatial perception is the **neglect syndrome,** a disorder caused by damage to the right parietal cortex. A victim of this disorder acts as though the left side of her or his world does not exist (Posner et al., 1987). A man with this syndrome might shave the right side of his face, but not the left, and might eat the pork chop on the right side of his plate but not the potatoes on the left. The neglect syndrome is even associated with the failure to notice odors presented to the left nostril, while noticing odors presented to the right (Bellas et al., 1988). Figure 3.17 shows self-portraits painted by an artist who exhibited the neglect syndrome. Though the neglect syndrome is usually found after right parietal lobe damage, it is sometimes found in people who have suffered left parietal lobe damage; these people show neglect for objects in the right half of their spatial world (Dronkers & Knight, 1989).

FIGURE 3.17

The Neglect Syndrome
These self-portraits painted by the German artist Anton Raderscheidt were painted over a period of time following a stroke that damaged the cortex of his right parietal lobe. As his brain recovered, his attention to the left side of his world returned (Wurtz, Goldberg, & Robinson, 1982).

EVIDENCE FROM THE SPLIT BRAIN

Studies of damaged brains and intact brains have provided most of the evidence regarding cerebral hemispheric specialization, but the most fascinating approach has been **split-brain research.** This involves people whose hemispheres have been surgically separated from each other. Though split-brain research is only a few decades old, the idea was entertained in 1860 by Gustav Fechner, who was introduced in chapter 1 as a founder of psychology. Fechner claimed that if a person survived the surgical separation of the cerebral hemispheres, he or she would have two separate minds in one head (Springer & Deutsch, 1993). Decades later English psychologist William McDougall argued that such an operation would not divide the mind, which he considered indivisible. McDougall even volunteered to test Fechner's claim by having his own cerebral hemispheres surgically separated if he ever became incurably ill.

Though McDougall never had split-brain surgery, it was performed on patients in the early 1960s, when neurosurgeons Joseph Bogen and Phillip Vogel severed the **corpus callosum** of epileptic patients to reduce seizure activity that had not responded to drug

split-brain research
Research on hemispheric specialization that studies individuals in whom the corpus callosum has been severed.

corpus callosum
A thick bundle of axons that provides a means of communication between the cerebral hemispheres, which is severed in so-called split-brain surgery.

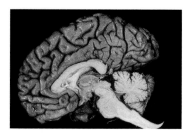

FIGURE 3.18

Split-Brain Surgery
Severing the corpus callosum
disconnects the cerebral hemispheres
from each other. Note that in "split-
brain" surgery, the entire brain is not
split. That would cut through the
hindbrain structures that control vital
functions, causing immediate death.

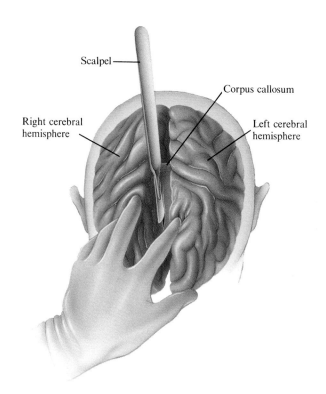

treatments. As illustrated in figure 3.18, the corpus callosum is a thick bundle of axons
that provides the means of communication between the cerebral hemispheres. Split-
brain surgery works by preventing seizure activity in one hemisphere from spreading to
the other. Split-brain patients behave normally in their everyday lives, but special testing procedures have revealed an astonishing state of affairs: Their left and right hemispheres can no longer communicate with each other. Each acts independently of the
other.

During the past three decades, biopsychologist Roger Sperry (1982), of the California Institute of Technology, and his colleagues, including Jerre Levy and Michael
Gazzaniga, have been at the forefront of split-brain research. You may recall from chapter 1 that Sperry won a Nobel prize in 1981 for this and other neuroscience research. In
a typical study of a split-brain patient, information is presented to one hemisphere and
the subject is asked to give a response that depends more on one hemisphere than on
the other. In one study, a split-brain patient performed a block-design task in which he
had to arrange multicolored blocks so that their upper sides formed a pattern that matched
the pattern printed on a card in front of him. This is illustrated in figure 3.19. When the
subject performed with his left hand, he did well, but when he performed with his right
hand, he did poorly. Can you figure out why that happened?

Because the left hand is controlled by the right hemisphere, which is superior in
perceiving spatial relationships, such as those in designs, he performed well with his left
hand. And because the right hand is controlled by the left hemisphere, which is inferior
in perceiving spatial relationships, he performed poorly with his right hand—even though
he was right-handed. At times, when his right hand was having a hard time completing
the design, his left hand would sneak up on it and try to help. This led to a bizarre battle
for control of the blocks—as if each hand belonged to a different person (Gazzaniga,
1967).

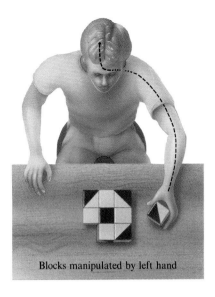
Blocks manipulated by left hand

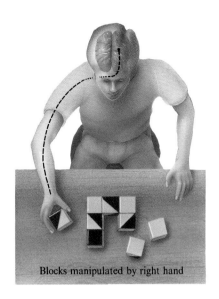
Blocks manipulated by right hand

Pattern to copy

Pattern to copy

FIGURE 3.19

A Split-Brain Study
Gazzaniga (1967) had a split-brain patient arrange multicolored blocks to match a design printed on a card in front of him. The patient's left hand performed better than his right, because the left hand is controlled by the right hemisphere, which is superior at perceiving spatial relationships. You would be able to perform a block-design task equally well with either your right or your left hand, because your intact corpus callosum would let information from your spatially superior right hemisphere help your left hemisphere control your right hand.

Despite such dramatic findings, Jerre Levy believes that researchers, particularly Gazzaniga, have exaggerated the extent to which each hemisphere regulates particular psychological processes. Gazzaniga (1983) insists that complex cognitive ability is almost entirely a function of the left hemisphere; Levy (1983) counters that the right hemisphere also makes important contributions to such ability. Levy believes that both hemispheres are extensively involved in verbal and spatial functions and in the analytic and holistic processing of information. Levy views the left hemisphere as analytic for spatial tasks and the right hemisphere as holistic for spatial tasks—thus, as you look at an object, your left hemisphere would process details of the object, while your right hemisphere would process the object as a whole.

Levy (1985) also views the right hemisphere as analytic for verbal tasks and the left hemisphere as holistic for verbal tasks. Thus, as you read, your right hemisphere might process individual letters, while your left hemisphere might process whole syllables. Levy's position has been supported by research that found the left hemisphere more active during analytic spatial perception and the right hemisphere more active during holistic spatial perception (Barchas & Perlaki, 1986). As always, only additional scientific research will resolve the Levy-Gazzaniga debate, which, you might note, is an example of the continual controversy over the degree to which psychological functions are localized in particular areas of the brain.

Aside from questions about the degree to which each cerebral hemisphere is involved in specific psychological functions, how should we interpret the findings of split-brain research? Roger Sperry supports Fechner's prediction, made more than a century ago, by claiming, "Everything we have seen so far indicates that the surgery has left these people with two separate minds, that is, two separate spheres of consciousness" (Springer

Jerre Levy
"Although the right hemisphere is nonlinguistic (except in unusual or pathological cases), the evidence is overpowering that it is active, responsive, highly intelligent, thinking, conscious, and fully human with respect to its cognitive depth and complexity."

& Deutsch, 1989, p. 322). But other psychologists side with William McDougall in denying that severing the corpus callosum literally divides one mind into two (Robinson, 1982).

Recent research on the split brain indicates, however, that the hemispheres can maintain separate streams of consciousness. One study found that the hemispheres in split-brain patients have independent attentional systems. In fact, when performing a task that requires the scanning of displays in the right and left visual fields, split-brain patients perform faster than those with intact brains, indicating that each hemisphere attends on its own (Luck et al., 1989).

Beyond the question of whether split-brain patients have one mind or two is the question, What is the mind? Descartes favored a position called *dualism*, which views the mind as an immaterial substance, separate from the material brain. He believed that the pineal gland, located at the center of the brain, was the site where the mind and brain interact. Other philosophers have favored a position called *monism*, viewing the mind and brain as a single material, or immaterial, substance. Most monists believe that the mind and brain are both matter, with the mind dependent on brain activity for its existence. Roger Sperry favors that view, and claims that the mind arises from brain activity:

> • • • I don't see any way for consciousness to emerge or be generated apart from a functioning brain. Everything indicates that the human mind and consciousness are inseparable attributes. (Baskin, 1983, p. 98)

In contrast, Wilder Penfield, the great brain mapper, favored a position closer to that of Descartes, though he did not implicate the pineal gland. Penfield claimed that the mind is not dependent on the brain for its existence (a view that he used to support his religious belief that the mind survives death):

> • • • For my own part, after years of striving to explain the mind on the basis of brain action alone, I have come to the conclusion that it is simpler (and far easier to be logical) if one adopts the hypothesis that our being does consist of two fundamental elements. (Penfield, 1975, p. 80)

Though psychologists have used the scientific method to determine the mental functions of the brain, they have made little progress in determining whether the mind exists apart from the brain—one of the ultimate philosophical issues. The relationship between the mind and the brain is discussed further in chapter 6.

▶▶▶ ▶

SUMMARY

THE NERVOUS SYSTEM

The field of biopsychology studies the relationships between physiological processes and psychological functions. The nervous system is composed of cells called neurons and serves as the main means of communication within the body. The nervous system is divided into the central nervous system, which comprises the brain and the spinal cord, and the peripheral nervous system, which comprises the nerves of the somatic nervous system and the autonomic nervous system. The autonomic nervous system is subdivided into the sympathetic nervous system, which arouses the body, and the parasympathetic nervous system, which conserves energy.

THE NEURON

The nervous system carries information along sensory neurons, motor neurons, and interneurons, as in the limb-withdrawal reflex mediated by the spinal cord. The neuron generally receives signals through its dendrites and sends signals along its axon.

The neuron maintains a resting potential during which it is electrically negative on the inside relative to its outside, as a result of a higher concentration of negative ions inside. Sufficient stimulation of the neuron causes it to depolarize (become less electrically negative) and reach its firing threshold. This produces an action potential, which causes a neural impulse to travel along the entire length of the axon.

The neural impulses stimulate the release of neurotransmitter molecules into the synapse. The molecules cross the synapse and attach to receptor sites on glands, muscles, or other neurons. These molecules exert either an excitatory or an inhibitory influence. In recent years, the neurotransmitters known as endorphins have inspired research because of their role in pain relief and euphoria.

THE ENDOCRINE SYSTEM

Hormones, secreted into the bloodstream by endocrine glands, also serve as a means of communication within the body. Hormones participate in functions as diverse as sexual development and responses to stress. Most endocrine glands are regulated by hormones secreted by the pituitary gland, which, in turn, is regulated by the hypothalamus.

THE BRAIN

The functions of the brain have been revealed by studies of the effects of brain damage, electrical stimulation of the brain, recording of the electricity produced by brain activity, and computer scanning of the brain. The brain is divided into the hindbrain (including the medulla, pons, and cerebellum), the midbrain (including the tectum and the substantia nigra), and the forebrain (including the basal ganglia, the thalamus, the limbic system, and the cerebral cortex). The medulla regulates vital functions, such as breathing; the pons regulates arousal and attention; and the cerebellum controls the timing of well-learned sequences of movements. Extending up from the hindbrain, through the midbrain, and into the forebrain is the reticular formation, which regulates brain arousal and helps maintain vigilance. The tectum mediates visual and auditory reflexes, and the substantia nigra promotes smooth movements.

The hypothalamus regulates the pituitary gland, as well as emotion and motives such as eating, drinking, and sex. The thalamus relays sensory information (except smell) to various regions of the brain for further processing. Within the limbic system, the amygdala continuously evaluates the immediate environment for potential threats, and the hippocampus processes information into memories.

The cerebral cortex covers the brain and is divided into the frontal, temporal, parietal, and occipital lobes. Well-defined areas of the lobes regulate movements and process sensory information. But most areas of the cerebral cortex—the association areas—are devoted to integrating information from different brain areas, such as those devoted to speech. In the past decade, positron-emission tomography (the PET scan) has contributed to our understanding of the functions of different areas of the brain. Researchers have historically disagreed about the extent to which particular psychological functions are localized in particular areas of the brain.

Neurons in the central nervous system do not regenerate. Recovery of functions after brain damage demonstrates the brain's plasticity through the ability of undamaged areas to take over the functions of damaged ones. An exciting, and controversial, topic of research is the possibility of using neural grafts to restore brain functions in people who have suffered brain damage.

THINKING ABOUT PSYCHOLOGY: DO THE CEREBRAL HEMISPHERES SERVE DIFFERENT FUNCTIONS?

Each cerebral hemisphere has psychological functions at which it excels, though both hemispheres influence virtually all functions. Studies of the degree of activity in each hemisphere, of the effects of damage to one hemisphere, and of people whose hemispheres have been surgically disconnected show that the left hemisphere is typically superior at verbal tasks and the right hemisphere is typically superior at spatial tasks. Researchers argue whether people with "split brains" literally have two separate minds.

IMPORTANT CONCEPTS

action potential 75
adrenal glands 84
all-or-none law 75
Alzheimer's disease 78
amygdala 89
association areas 92
auditory cortex 94
autonomic nervous system 70
axon 73
axonal conduction 74
basal ganglia 88
biopsychology 70
brain 70
Broca's area 96
central nervous system 70
cerebellum 87
cerebral cortex 91
cerebral hemispheres 92
computed tomography (CT) 95
corpus callosum 105
dendrites 73

electroencephalograph (EEG) 85
endocrine system 81
endorphins 80
frontal lobe 92
glial cell 72
hippocampus 89
hormones 81
hypothalamus 89
interneuron 72
limbic system 89
magnetic resonance imaging (MRI) 95
medulla oblongata 86
motor cortex 92
motor neuron 72
myelin 76
neglect syndrome 104
nerve 70
nervous system 70
neural grafting 100

neuron 70
neurotransmitters 77
occipital lobe 94
ovaries 82
pancreas 84
parasympathetic nervous system 70
parietal lobe 93
Parkinson's disease 87
peripheral nervous system 70
phrenology 98
pineal gland 84
pituitary gland 81
plasticity 99
pons 87
positron-emission tomography (PET) 94
primary cortical areas 92
prosopagnosia 96
reflex 72
resting potential 74

reticular formation 87
sensory neuron 72
soma 72
somatic nervous system 70
somatosensory cortex 93
spinal cord 70
split-brain research 105
substantia nigra 87
sympathetic nervous system 70
synapse 77
synaptic transmission 76
tectum 87
temporal lobe 94
testes 82
thalamus 88
thyroid gland 81
visual cortex 94
Wada test 103
Wernicke's area 96

MAJOR CONTRIBUTORS

Hans Berger 85
Paul Broca 96
Charles Darwin 70
René Descartes 74
Gustav Fritsch and Eduard
Hitzig 92

Franz Joseph Gall and Johann
Spurzheim 97, 98
Michael Gazzaniga 106
Alan Hodgkin and Andrew
Huxley 74
Karl Lashley 99

Jerre Levy 106
Otto Loewi 77
James Olds and Peter Milner 89
Wilder Penfield 93
Candace Pert and Solomon
Snyder 80

Santiago Ramón y Cajal 76
Jacqueline Sagen 101
Roger Sperry 106
Karl Wernicke 96

RECOMMENDED READINGS

FOR GENERAL WORKS ON BIOPSYCHOLOGY

Brazier, M. A. B. (1984). *A history of neurophysiology in the 17th and 18th centuries*. New York: Raven Press.

Brazier, M. A. B. (1988). *A history of neurophysiology in the 19th century*. New York: Raven Press.

Clarke, E., & Jacyna, L. S. (1987). *Nineteenth-century origins of neuroscientific concepts*. Berkeley: University of California Press.

Darwin, C. (1859/1975). *The origin of species*. New York: W. W. Norton.

Levinthal, C. F. (1990). *Introduction to physiological psychology*. (3rd ed.). Englewood Cliffs, NJ: Prentice Hall.

Neuberger, M. (1981). *The historical development of experimental brain and spinal cord physiology before Flourens*. Baltimore: The Johns Hopkins University Press.

FOR MORE ON THE NEURON AND NEUROTRANSMITTERS

Aidley, D. J. (1990). *The physiology of excitable cells*. New York: Cambridge University Press.

Ascher, P., Choi, D. W., & Christen, Y. (Eds.). (1991). *Glutamate, cell death, and memory*. New York: Springer-Verlag.

Chafetz, M. D. (1989). *Nutrition and neurotransmitters: The nutrient basis of behavior*. Englewood Cliffs, NJ: Prentice Hall.

Coyle, J. T., Price, D. L., & DeLong, M. R. (1983). Alzheimer's disease: A disorder of cortical cholinergic innervation. *Science, 219,* 1184–1190.

Gottlieb, D. I. (1988, February). GABAergic neurons. *Scientific American*, pp. 82–89.

Idzikowski, C., & Cowen, P. J. (Eds.). (1991). *Serotonin, sleep, and mental disorder*. New York: Taylor & Francis.

Kim, S. U. (Ed.). (1989). *Myelinization and demyelinization*. New York: Plenum.

Koob, G. F., Sandman, C. A., & Strand, F. L. (Eds.). (1990). *A decade of neuropeptides*. New York: New York Academy of Sciences.

Koppe, S. (1983). The psychology of the neuron: Freud, Cajal, and Golgi. *Scandinavian Journal of Psychology, 24,* 1–12.

Leeman, S. E. (Ed.). (1992). *Substance P and related peptides*. New York: New York Academy of Sciences.

Levinthal, C. F. (1988). *Messengers of paradise: Opiates and the brain*. New York: Anchor/Doubleday.

Mason, S. T. (1984). *Catecholamines and behaviour*. New York: Cambridge University Press.

Ottersen, O. P., & Storm-Mathisen, J. (Eds.). (1990). *Glycine neurotransmission*. New York: Wiley.

Panksepp, J. (1986). The neurochemistry of behavior. *Annual Review of Psychology, 37,* 77–107.

Rodgers, R. J., & Cooper, S. J. (Eds.). (1988). *Endorphins, opiates, and behavioral processes*. New York: Wiley.

Shepherd, G. M. (1991). *Foundations of the neuron doctrine*. New York: Oxford University Press.

Snyder, S. H. (1989). *Brainstorming: The science and politics of opiate research*. Cambridge, MA: Harvard University Press.

Steriade, M., & Biesold, D. (Eds.). (1991). *Brain cholinergic systems*. New York: Oxford University Press.

Willner, P., & Scheel-Kruger, J. (Eds.). (1991). *The mesolimbic dopamine system*. New York: Wiley.

Wise, R. A., & Rompre, P. P. (1989). Brain dopamine and reward. *Annual Review of Psychology, 90,* 191–225.

FOR MORE ON HORMONES

Bliss, M. (1984). *The discovery of insulin*. Chicago: University of Chicago Press.

Donovan, B. T. (1985). *Hormones and human behavior*. New York: Cambridge University Press.

Imura, H. (1985). *The pituitary gland*. New York: Raven Press.

James, V. H. (1992). *The adrenal gland*. New York: Raven Press.

McNabb, F. M. (1992). *Thyroid hormones*. Englewood Cliffs, NJ: Prentice Hall.

Muller-Hermelink, H. K. (Ed.). (1986). *The human thymus*. New York: Springer-Verlag.

Reiter, R. J. (1984). *The pineal gland*. New York: Raven Press.

Yesalis, C. E. (Ed.). (1993). *Anabolic steroids in sport and exercise*. Champaign, IL: Human Kinetics.

FOR MORE ON THE BRAIN

Aggletone, J. P. (1992). *The amygdala*. New York: Wiley.

Andreasen, N. C. (Ed.). (1989). *Brain imaging: Applications in psychiatry*. Washington, DC: American Psychiatric Press.

Bloom, F. E., Lazerson, A., & Hofstadter, L. (1988). *Brain, mind, and behavior*. New York: W. H. Freeman.

Cohen, N. J., & Eichenbaum, H. (1993). *Memory, amnesia, and the hippocampal system*. Cambridge, MA: MIT Press.

Corsi, P. (Ed.). (1991). *The enchanted loom: Chapters in the history of neuroscience*. New York: Oxford University Press.

Doane, B. K., & Livingston, K. E. (1986). *The limbic system: Functional organization and clinical disorders*. New York: Raven Press.

Finger, S. (1993). *Origins of neuroscience: A history of brain function*. New York: Oxford University Press.

Franks, A. J. (Ed.). (1992). *Function and dysfunction in the basal ganglia*. New York: Pergamon.

Hobson, J. A., & Brazier, M. A. (Eds.). (1979). *The reticular formation revisited*. New York: Raven Press.

Jones, E. G. (1985). *The thalamus*. New York: Plenum.

Klemm, W. R., & Vertes, R. P. (Eds.). (1990). *Brainstem mechanisms of behavior*. New York: Wiley.

Llinas, R., & Sotelo, C. (Eds.). (1992). *The cerebellum revisited*. New York: Springer-Verlag.

Peters, A., & Rockland, K. S. (Eds.). (1993). *Cerebral cortex*. New York: Plenum.

Reichlin, S. (Ed.). (1978). *The hypothalamus*. New York: Raven Press.

Sacks, O. (1985). *The man who mistook his wife for a hat and other clinical tales*. New York: Summit.

Stern, M. B. (1971). *Heads and headlines: The phrenological Fowlers*. Norman: University of Oklahoma Press.

Stuss, D. T., & Benson, D. F. (1986). *The frontal lobes*. New York: Raven Press.

Young, R. M. (1990). *Mind, brain, and adaptation in the nineteenth century: Cerebral localization and its biological context from Gall to Ferrier*. New York: Oxford University Press.

FOR MORE ON THE PLASTICITY OF THE BRAIN

Aoki, C., & Siekevitz, P. (1988, December). Plasticity in brain development. *Scientific American*, pp. 56–64.

Azmitia, E. C., & Bjorklund, A. (Eds.). (1987). *Cell and tissue transplantation into the adult brain*. New York: New York Academy of Sciences.

Byrne, J. H., & Berry, W. O. (Ed.). (1989). *Neural models of plasticity*. San Diego: Academic Press.

Cotman, C. W., & Nieto-Sampedro, M. (1982). Brain function, synapse renewal, and plasticity. *Annual Review of Psychology, 33*, 371–401.

Dunnett, S. B., & Bjorklund, A. (Eds.). (1992). *Neural transplantation: A practical approach*. New York: Oxford University Press.

Fine, A. (1986, August). Transplantation in the central nervous system. *Scientific American*, pp. 52–58B.

Finger, S., LeVere, T. E., Almli, C. R., & Stein, D. G. (1988). *Brain injury and recovery: Theoretical and controversial issues*. New York: Plenum.

Kimble, D. P. (1990). Functional effects of neural grafting in the mammalian central nervous system. *Psychological Bulletin, 108*, 462–479.

Kolb, B. (1989). Brain development, plasticity, and behavior. *American Psychologist, 44*, 1203–1212.

Lindvall, O. (Ed.). (1993). *Restoration of brain function by tissue transplantation*. New York: Springer-Verlag.

Marshall, J. F. (1984). Brain function: Neural adaptations and recovery from injury. *Annual Review of Psychology, 35*, 277–308.

FOR MORE ON HEMISPHERIC SPECIALIZATION

Beaton, A. (1985). *Left side, right side: A review of laterality research*. New Haven, CT: Yale University Press.

Benson, D. F., & Zaidel, E. (Eds.). (1985). *The dual brain: Hemispheric specialization in humans*. New York: Guilford.

Coren, S. (1992). *The left-hander syndrome: The causes and consequences of left-handedness*. New York: Free Press.

Gazzaniga, M. S. (1967, August). The split brain in man. *Scientific American*, pp. 24–29.

Geschwind, N., & Galaburda, A. M. (1986). *Cerebral lateralization: Biological mechanisms, associations, and pathology*. Cambridge, MA: MIT Press.

Hahn, W. K. (1987). Cerebral lateralization of function: From infancy through childhood. *Psychological Bulletin, 101*, 376–382.

Hellige, J. B. (1990). Hemispheric asymmetry. *Annual Review of Psychology, 41*, 55–80.

Kitterle, F. L. (Ed.). (1991). *Cerebral laterality: Theory and research*. Hillsdale, NJ: Erlbaum.

Levy, J. (1985, May). Right brain, left brain: Fact and fiction. *Psychology Today*, pp. 38–39.

Loring, D. W., Meador, K. J., Lee, G. P., & King, D. W. (Eds.). (1991). *Amobarbital effects and lateralized brain function: The Wada test*. New York: Springer-Verlag.

McManus, I. C., & Bryden, M. P. (1991). Geschwind's theory of cerebral lateralization: Developing a formal, causal model. *Psychological Bulletin, 110*, 237–254.

Molfese, D. L., & Segalowitz, S. J. (Eds.). (1988). *Brain lateralization in children*. New York: Guilford.

Poizner, H., Klima, E., & Bellugi, U. (1987). *What the hands reveal about the brain*. Cambridge, MA: MIT Press.

Quen, J. M. (Ed.). (1986). *Split minds/split brains: Historical and current perspectives*. New York: New York University Press.

Sperry, R. (1982). Some effects of disconnecting the cerebral hemispheres. *Science, 217*, 1223–1226.

Springer, S. P., & Deutsch, G. (1993). *Left brain, right brain* (4th ed.). New York: W. H. Freeman.

FOR MORE ON THE RELATIONSHIP BETWEEN MIND AND BRAIN

Fodor, J. A. (1981, January). The mind-body problem. *Scientific American*, pp. 114–123.

Penfield, W. (1975). *The mystery of the mind*. Princeton, NJ: Princeton University Press.

Pribram, K. H. (1986). The cognitive revolution and mind/brain issues. *American Psychologist, 41*, 507–520.

Sperry, R. W. (1988). Psychology's mentalist paradigm and the religion/science tension. *American Psychologist, 43*, 607–613.

FOR MORE ON CONTRIBUTORS TO THE STUDY OF BIOPSYCHOLOGY

Goldberg, J. R. (1984, July). The creative mind: Jerre Levy. *Science Digest*, pp. 46–47, 90–92.

Hooper, J. (1982, February). Interview: Candace Pert. *Omni*, pp. 62–65, 110–112.

Koenigsberger, L. (1906/1965). *Hermann von Helmholtz*. New York: Dover.

Loewi, O. (1960). An autobiographic sketch. *Perspectives in Biology and Medicine, 4*, 3–25.

Lewis, J. (1982). *Something hidden: A biography of Wilder Penfield*. New York: Doubleday.

Olmsted, J. M., Cohen, I. B., & Fulton, J. F. (1944/1981). *Francois Magendie*. Salem, NH: Ayer.

Ramón y Cajal, S. (1937/1989). *Recollections of my life*. Cambridge, MA: MIT Press.

Schiller, F. (1979). *Paul Broca: Founder of French anthropology, explorer of the brain*. Berkeley: University of California Press.

CHAPTER 4

Edward Potthast
Children at Shore
1919

HUMAN DEVELOPMENT

developmental psychology
The field that studies physical, cognitive, and psychosocial changes across the life span.

maturation
The sequential unfolding of inherited predispositions in physical and motor development.

G. Stanley Hall (1844–1924)
"There is really no clue by which we can thread our way through all the mazes of culture and the distractions of modern life save by knowing the true nature and needs of childhood and adolescence."

*E*ach of us changes markedly across the life span. You are not the same today as you were in infancy or will be in old age. The field of **developmental psychology** studies the physical, perceptual, cognitive, and psychosocial changes that take place across the life span. Developmental psychologists, and this chapter, address questions such as the following: Are adopted children more similar to their adoptive parents or to their biological parents? Can we form memories before we are born? Is day care harmful to children? Are there significant psychological sex differences? Is adolescence necessarily a period of emotional turmoil? Do parents suffer from an "empty nest syndrome" after their last child has left home? What accounts for the development of our moral judgment?

THE NATURE OF DEVELOPMENTAL PSYCHOLOGY

Though opinions about the nature of human development can be found in the writings of ancient Greek philosophers, the scientific study of human development did not begin until the 1870s. That decade saw the appearance of the "baby biography," usually written by a parent, which described the physical, perceptual, cognitive, and psychosocial development of an infant. One of the first baby biographies was written by Charles Darwin (1877/1977) about the early development of his son. The German physiologist Wilhelm Preyer (1882/1973) wrote a more influential baby biography, *The Mind of the Child,* describing the development of his son's motor skills, language ability, and emotional reactions from birth to 3 years. In seeking to explain infant development, Preyer recognized that heredity provides the infant with certain abilities at birth, but he assumed that further development depends solely on learning (Berndt & Zigler, 1985). Though infant development depends chiefly on learning, much of it is guided by physical **maturation**—the sequential unfolding of inherited predispositions (as in the progression from crawling to standing to walking).

The 1890s saw the beginning of research on child development after infancy (White, 1990), most notably at Clark University by G. Stanley Hall (1844–1924). Hall, recognized as the founder of *child psychology,* applied research findings to the improvement of education and child rearing. Until the 1950s the study of human development was considered synonymous with child psychology. During that decade, psychologists began to study human development across the whole life span. The issue of the relative influence of heredity and environment on human development is one of the main concerns of developmental psychologists today, as it was a century ago.

The Influence of Heredity and Environment

To what extent are you the product of your heredity, and to what extent are you the product of your environment? This issue of "nature versus nurture" has been with us since the era of ancient Greece, when Plato championed nature and Aristotle championed nurture. Plato believed we are born with some knowledge; Aristotle believed that at birth our mind is a blank slate (or *tabula rasa*) and that life experiences provide us with knowledge. As noted in chapter 1, this argument remained intense even centuries later, with followers of René Descartes (1596–1650) favoring nature and followers of John Locke (1632–1704) favoring nurture.

The argument became even more heated after Charles Darwin (1859/1975) put forth his theory of evolution in the mid nineteenth century. Darwin noted that animals and human beings vary in their physical traits. Given the competition for resources (including food and water) and the need to foil predators (by defeating them or escaping from them), animals and human beings with physical traits best adapted to these purposes would be the most likely to survive long enough to produce offspring, who would also have those traits. As long as particular physical traits provide a survival advantage, those traits will have a greater likelihood of showing up in succeeding generations. Darwin called this process *natural selection*. Followers of Darwin favored the nature side of the nature-nurture controversy, insisting that evolution has provided us with inherited physical and psychological traits that, over several million years, increased our ancestors' chances of survival (Vidal, Buscaglia, & Voneche, 1983).

Behavioral Genetics

As noted in chapter 1, the main proponent of the dominance of nature over nurture was Francis Galton, Darwin's cousin. He was so intrigued by the implications of evolution for human development that he abandoned his interests in geography and meteorology to study the importance of individual differences (Rabinowitz, 1984). He reasoned that if physical traits exist today because they helped our ancestors survive long enough to pass on those traits, then people who are superior on those traits would be the fittest to reproduce. Through his writings and lectures, Galton popularized the phrase *nature versus nurture* (Teigen, 1984).

Galton's book *Hereditary Genius* (1869) reveals his bias in favor of nature over nurture. The book traced the family trees of 1,000 reputed geniuses, all males, from 300 families. Given his estimate that genius occurs in only 1 in 4,000 men, Galton concluded, reasonably enough, that genius runs in families. He did not immediately attribute this to heredity, being well aware that environmental similarity goes hand in hand with hereditary similarity. Siblings share not only common hereditary backgrounds, but common rearing environments. Thus, heredity and environment are confounded variables. As explained in chapter 2, this means that the effect of one variable might be confused with the effect of the other. So, without more information, we have no more right to attribute sibling similarities to their common heredity than to attribute them to their common environment.

Galton, after considering the available evidence, concluded that genius is, in fact, produced by nature and not by nurture. One of the pieces of evidence he used to support this conclusion was the fact that the United States did not produce proportionately more geniuses than did Great Britain—despite the more widespread availability of education in the United States. Because the superior educational environment of the United States failed to produce more geniuses, Galton concluded that heredity, rather than life experiences, accounted for cases of superior intellectual development (Schlesinger, 1985). Those who favored the nurture side of the nature-nurture controversy had their own supporters, including Hermann von Helmholtz, perhaps the greatest scientist of the nineteenth century (Koenigsberger, 1906/1965).

The hereditarian bias of early psychology weakened with the rise of behaviorism in the 1920s. Behaviorists urged psychologists to downplay the importance of heredity and to stress the role of life experiences. The waning of behaviorism since the 1960s has been accompanied by renewed interest in the hereditary basis of human behavior. This has stimulated the growth of **behavioral genetics,** which studies how heredity and life experiences interact in affecting development. Research in behavioral genetics has found evidence of a hereditary basis for characteristics as diverse as obesity (Epstein & Cluess, 1986), intelligence (Horn, 1983), criminality (Mednick, Gabrielli, & Hutchings, 1984), schizophrenia (McGue, Gottesman, & Rao, 1986), and religious values (Waller et al., 1990).

To appreciate behavioral genetics, you should have at least a basic understanding of genetics itself. The science of genetics can be traced to 1866, when the Austrian monk and amateur botanist Gregor Mendel published a paper that described the principles governing the inheritance of physical traits in pea plants. These traits included

behavioral genetics
The study of the relationship between heredity and behavior.

"Not guilty by reason of genetic determinism, Your Honor."

their size, color, and skin characteristics. Mendel's work was overlooked until the turn of the century, when several scientists independently rediscovered it.

Today we know more about the principles of heredity, and the basic physical mechanisms as well. The cells of the human body contain 23 pairs of *chromosomes*, which are long strands of *deoxyribonucleic acid (DNA)* molecules. (Unlike the other body cells, the egg cell and sperm cell each contain 23 single chromosomes.) DNA molecules are ribbonlike structures composed of segments called *genes*, which direct the synthesis of *ribonucleic acid (RNA)*. RNA, in turn, directs the synthesis of proteins, which are responsible for the structure and functioning of our tissues and organs.

Though our genes direct our development, their effects on our behavior are indirect—there are, for example, no "motorcycle daredevil genes." Instead, physiological factors, such as hormones, neurotransmitters, and brain structures, are influenced by genes. These factors, in turn, make people somewhat more likely to engage in particular behaviors. Perhaps people destined to become motorcycle daredevils inherit a less physiologically reactive nervous system, making them experience less anxiety in dangerous situations. As you will learn in chapter 11, research findings support this view.

Our outward appearance and behavior may not indicate our exact genetic inheritance. In recognition of this, scientists distinguish between our *genotype* and our *phenotype*. Your **genotype** is your genetic inheritance. Your **phenotype** is the overt expression of your inheritance in your appearance or behavior. Your eye color is determined by the interaction of a gene inherited from your mother and a gene inherited from your father. The brown-eye gene is *dominant*, and the blue-eye gene is *recessive*. Dominant genes take precedence over recessive genes. Traits carried by recessive genes show up in phenotypes only when recessive genes occur together. If you are blue-eyed, your genotype includes two blue-eye genes (both recessive). If you have brown eyes, your genotype may include two brown-eye genes (both dominant) or one brown-eye gene (dominant) and one blue-eye gene (recessive).

In contrast to simple traits like eye color, most characteristics are governed by more than one pair of genes. This means that they are *polygenic*. With rare exceptions,

genotype
An individual's genetic inheritance.

phenotype
The overt expression of an individual's genetic inheritance, which may also show the influence of the environment.

Drawing by Lorenz; © 1983 The New Yorker Magazine, Inc.

"In extenuation, Your Honor, I would like to suggest to the court that my client was inadequately parented."

this is especially true of genetic influences on human abilities and behaviors. Your athletic, academic, and social skills depend on the interaction of many genes, as well as your life experience. For example, your muscularity (your phenotype) depends on both your genetic endowment (your genotype) and your dietary and exercise habits (your life experience).

To appreciate research studies that try to determine the relative contributions of heredity and environment to human development, you should understand the concept of heritability. **Heritability** refers to the proportion of variability in a trait across a population. For example, human beings differ in their intelligence (as measured by IQ tests). To what extent is this variability caused by heredity, and to what extent is it caused by experience? Heritability values range from 0.0 to 1.0. If heritability accounted for none of the variability in intelligence, it would have a value of 0.0. If heritability accounted for all of the variability in intelligence, it would have a value of 1.0. In reality, estimates of heritability for all psychological characteristics fall above 0.0 and below 1.0. Based on recent research studies, the heritability of intelligence, as measured by IQ tests, is estimated to be between .50 (Chipuer, Rovine, & Plomin, 1990) and .70 (Bouchard et al., 1990). This indicates that the variability in intelligence is strongly, but not solely, influenced by heredity. Environmental factors also account for much of the variability.

heritability
The extent to which variability in a characteristic within a group can be attributed to heredity.

Studies of Relatives

Research procedures that assess the relative contributions of nature and nurture to human development involve the study of relatives. These include family studies and adoption studies. *Family studies* investigate similarities between relatives with varying degrees of genetic similarity. These studies consistently find that the closer the genetic relationship (that is, the more genes that are shared) between relatives, the more alike they tend to be on a variety of traits. Though it is tempting to attribute this to their degree of genetic similarity, an alternative explanation is possible. As discussed earlier, degree of genetic similarity and similarity of family environment go hand in hand, making it impossible to determine from family studies alone whether similarities between family members are more attributable to nature or to nurture.

Robert Plomin
"The evidence from behavioral genetics research indicates that nongenetic factors are at least as important as genetic factors."

The best kind of family study is the *twin study,* which compares identical (or *monozygotic*) twins to fraternal (or *dizygotic*) twins. Identical twins, because they come from the same fertilized egg, have the same genetic inheritance. Fraternal twins, because they come from different fertilized eggs, do not—they merely have the same degree of genetic similarity as ordinary siblings. Moreover, twins, whether identical or fraternal, are born at about the same time and share similar environments. Because research has found that identical twins reared in similar environments are more psychologically similar than fraternal twins reared in similar environments, it is reasonable to attribute the greater similarity of identical twins to heredity. Nonetheless, there is an alternative, environmental explanation. Perhaps identical twins become more psychologically similar because they are reared more alike than fraternal twins are. Identical twins are often dressed alike, confused with each other, and treated as though they were indistinguishable (Hoffman, 1991).

Superior to family studies are *adoption studies,* which measure the correlation in particular traits between adopted children and their biological parents and between those same adopted children and their adoptive parents. Research has consistently found that adoptees are more similar to their biological parents than to their adoptive parents. An ongoing adoption study conducted at the University of Colorado by Robert Plomin and his colleagues has found that the intelligence of adoptees is positively correlated with that of their biological parents but bears little relationship to that of their adoptive parents (Plomin, Loehlin, & DeFries, 1985). Adoption studies also have found that adoptees are more similar to their biological parents than to their adoptive parents in body fat (Price & Gottesman, 1991), vocational interests (Lykken et al., 1993), and religious values (Waller et al., 1990). These findings indicate that the genes that adoptees inherit from their biological parents affect their development more than does the environment they are provided with by their adoptive parents.

Yet the environment cannot be ruled out as an explanation for the greater similarity between adoptees and their biological parents. As explained later in this chapter, prenatal experiences can affect the development of children. Perhaps adoptees are more like their biological parents, not because they share the same genes, but because the adoptees spent their prenatal months in their biological mother's womb, making them subject to their mother's drug habits, nutritional intake, or other environmental influences. Moreover, experiences with their biological parents in early infancy, before adoptees are adopted, may affect their development, making them more similar to their biological parents.

Possibly the best procedure is to study *identical twins reared apart.* Research on a variety of traits consistently finds higher positive correlations between identical twins reared apart than between fraternal twins reared together. This provides strong evidence in favor of the nature side of the debate. A widely publicized ongoing study of identical twins who were separated in infancy and reunited later in life is being conducted at the University of Minnesota. As discussed in chapter 13, the study has found some uncanny similarities in the habits, abilities, and physiological responses of the reunited twins (Bouchard et al., 1990), yet even the results of studies of identical twins reared apart might be attributable to selective reporting of similarities (Wyatt et al., 1984). Thus, no kind of study is flawless in demonstrating the superiority of heredity over environment in guiding development.

Regardless of the influence of heredity on development, experience is also important. For example, a Swedish study of identical twins reared apart and assessed in late adulthood found that their personality similarity depended on the interaction between heredity and environment (Bergeman et al., 1988). Thus, heredity might have provided you with the intellectual potential to become a Nobel prize winner, but without adequate academic experiences you might not perform well enough even to graduate from college.

Research Methods in Developmental Psychology

Though developmental psychologists often use the same research methods as other psychologists (including, as just discussed, the use of correlational methods in assessing intellectual and personality similarities between relatives), they also rely on methods that are unique to developmental psychology. These include *longitudinal research, cross-sectional research,* and *cohort-sequential research,* which enable researchers to study age-related changes in their subjects.

Longitudinal Research

Longitudinal research follows the same group of subjects over a period of time, typically ranging from months to years. The researcher looks for changes on particular characteristics, such as language, personality, intelligence, or perceptual ability. Suppose you wanted to study changes in the social maturity of college students. If you chose to use a longitudinal design, you might assess the social maturity of an incoming class of freshmen and then note changes in their social maturity during their 4 years in college. Some of the earliest longitudinal studies were conducted by Arnold Gesell (1880–1961) at the Yale Clinic for Child Development from 1911 to 1961. His work contributed to our knowledge of motor, language, and emotional development, as well as other aspects of development throughout infancy and childhood.

Longitudinal research has been used to study a variety of topics, including personal characteristics that promote outstanding creative achievement (Torrance, 1993), effects of part-time employment on adolescents' school performance and social behavior (Steinberg, Fegley, & Dornbusch, 1993), and factors associated with a risk of divorce in newlywed couples (Kurdek, 1993). Chapter 10 discusses perhaps the most ambitious example of longitudinal research of all: Lewis Terman's Genetic Studies of Genius. Terman began his study of childhood geniuses in the 1920s—and his subjects have been studied across their life spans, provoking interest by researchers even in the 1990s (Pyryt, 1993).

Though longitudinal research has the advantage of permitting us to study individuals as they change across their life spans, it has major weaknesses. First, the typical longitudinal study takes months, years, or (as in the case of Terman's study) decades to complete. This requires ongoing financial support and continued commitment by researchers—neither of which can be guaranteed. Second, the longer the study lasts, the more likely it is that subjects will drop out—they might refuse to continue or might move away or even die. If those who drop out differ in important ways from those who remain, the results of the research may be less generalizable to the population of interest. For example, a 14-year longitudinal study of changes in adult intelligence found that those who dropped out had scored lower on intelligence tests than did those who remained. This made it unwise to generalize the study's findings to all adults (Schaie, Labouvie, & Barrett, 1973).

Cross-Sectional Research

The weaknesses of longitudinal research do not characterize **cross-sectional research,** which compares groups of subjects of different ages at the same time. Each of the age groups is called a **cohort.** If you chose to use a cross-sectional design to study changes in social maturity, you might compare the current social maturity of four cohorts: freshmen, sophomores, juniors, and seniors. One example of cross-sectional research is a study that followed different cohorts of children from 9 to 36 months old and found systematic changes in the sequence of arm motions they used in reaching for objects (Kawai, 1991).

The main weakness of cross-sectional research is that it can produce misleading findings if a cohort in the study is affected by circumstances unique to that cohort. Thus, cross-sectional studies can identify differences between cohorts of different ages, but

longitudinal research
A research design in which the same group of subjects is tested or observed repeatedly over a period of time.

Arnold Gesell (1880–1961)
"The protection of mental health, beginning in infancy, should be primarily based on a science of normal human growth, and only secondarily on psychopathology."

cross-sectional research
A research design in which groups of subjects of different ages are compared at the same point in time.

cohort
A group of people of the same age.

those differences might not hold true if cohorts of those ages were observed during another era. Suppose that you conduct a cross-sectional study and find that older adults are more prejudiced against minorities than are younger adults. Does this mean that we become more prejudiced with age? Not necessarily. Perhaps, instead, the cohort of older adults was raised at a time when prejudice was more acceptable than it is today. Members of the cohort might simply have retained attitudes they developed in their youth.

Cohort-Sequential Research

One way to deal with the shortcomings of longitudinal and cross-sectional research is to use **cohort-sequential research,** which begins as a cross-sectional study by comparing different cohorts and then follows the cohorts longitudinally. A cohort-sequential research design was employed in a study of alcohol use in old age. Healthy cohorts ranging in age from 60 to 86 years old were first compared cross-sectionally. The results showed a decline in the percentage of drinkers with age. The cohorts were then followed longitudinally for 7 years. The results remained the same, making it more likely that the decline in drinking with age was related to age rather than to life experiences peculiar to different cohorts (Adams et al., 1990).

Longitudinal research, cross-sectional research, and, to a lesser extent, cohort-sequential research are staples of developmental research across the life span. Modern technology permits developmental psychologists to study ongoing developmental processes even before birth, during the prenatal period.

PRENATAL DEVELOPMENT

You, Julius Caesar, Oprah Winfrey, and anyone else who has ever lived began as a single cell. The formation of that cell begins the *prenatal period*, which lasts about 9 months and is divided into the *germinal stage*, the *embryonic stage*, and the *fetal stage*. Figure 4.1 presents several illustrations of prenatal development.

The Germinal Stage

The **germinal stage** begins with conception, which occurs when a *sperm* from the male unites with an egg (or *ovum*) from the female in one of her two *fallopian tubes*, forming a one-celled *zygote*. The zygote contains 23 pairs of chromosomes, one member of each pair coming from the ovum and the other coming from the sperm. The chromosomes, in turn, contain genes that govern the development of the individual. The zygote begins a trip down the fallopian tube, during which it is transformed into a larger, multicelled ball by repeated cell divisions. By the end of the second week, this ball attaches to the wall of the uterus. This marks the beginning of the embryonic stage.

The Embryonic Stage

The **embryonic stage** lasts from the end of the second week through the eighth week of prenatal development. The embryo, nourished by nutrients that cross the *placenta*, increases in size and begins to develop specialized organs, including the eyes, heart, and brain. What accounts for this rapid, complex process? The development and location of body organs is regulated by genes, which determine the kinds of cells that will develop and also direct the actions of *cell-adhesion molecules*. These molecules direct the movement of cells and determine which cells will adhere to one another, thereby determining the size, shape, and location of organs in the embryo (Edelman, 1984). By the end of the embryonic stage, development has progressed to the point at which the heart is beating and the approximately one-inch-long embryo has facial features, limbs, fingers, and toes.

But what determines whether an embryo becomes a male or a female? The answer lies in the 23rd pair of chromosomes, the sex chromosomes, which are designated X or Y. Embryos that inherit two X chromosomes are genetic females, and embryos that inherit one X and one Y chromosome are genetic males. Near the end of the embryonic period, the primitive gonads of male embryos secrete the hormone *testosterone*, which

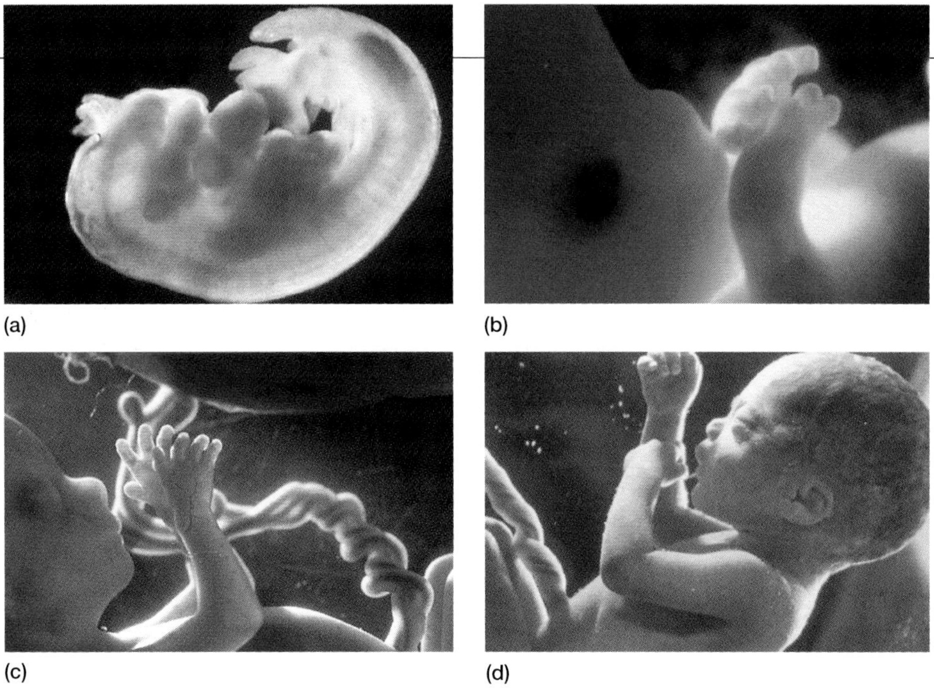

(a)

(b)

(c)

(d)

FIGURE 4.1
Prenatal Development
Prenatal development is marked by rapid growth and differentation of structures. (*a*) At 4 weeks, the embryo is about 0.2 inches long, has a recognizable head, arm buds, leg buds, and a heart that has begun beating. (*b*) At 8 weeks—the end of the embryonic stage—the embryo has features that make it recognizable as distinctly human, including a nose, a mouth, eyes, ears, hands, fingers, feet, and toes. This marks the beginning of the fetal stage. (*c*) At sixteen weeks, the fetus is about 7 inches long and makes movements that can be detected by the mother. The remainder of the fetal stage involves extremely rapid growth. (*d*) At 9 months the fetus is fully formed and ready to be born.

stimulates the development of male sexual organs. If testosterone is not secreted, the newborn male's external genitals will look feminine. In contrast, the secretion of excessive amounts of testosterone in female embryos leads to the development of masculine-looking external genitals. This phenomenon was discovered in 1865 by an Italian anatomist who autopsied a man who lacked testes, only to find that in addition to a penis the man had ovaries, a uterus, and a vagina. The "man" was actually a genetic female whose adrenal glands (located on the kidneys, and normally a minor source of sex hormones) had secreted an excessive amount of testosterone during prenatal development, causing her clitoris to enlarge into a penislike organ (J. A. Miller, 1984).

The Fetal Stage

The presence of a distinctly human appearance marks the beginning of the **fetal stage,** which lasts from the beginning of the third month until birth. By the fourth prenatal month, pregnant women report movement by the fetus. And by the seventh month all of the major organs are functional, which means that an infant born even 2 or 3 months prematurely has a chance of surviving. The final 3 months of prenatal development are associated with most of the increase in the size of the fetus. Premature infants tend to be smaller and less physically and cognitively mature than full-term infants. For example, when an object approaches the eyes of a premature infant, the infant might not exhibit normal defensive blinking (Pettersen, Yonas, & Fisch, 1980).

Though prenatal development usually produces a normal infant, in some cases genetic defects produce distinctive physical and psychological syndromes. For example, the chromosomal disorder called *Down syndrome* (discussed in chapter 10) is associated with mental retardation and abnormal physical development. Other sources of prenatal defects are **teratogens,** which are noxious substances or other factors that can disrupt prenatal development and prevent the individual from reaching her or his inherited potential. (The word *teratogen* was coined from Greek terms meaning "that which produces a monster.") One potential teratogen is the X ray. Prenatal exposure to X rays may disrupt the migration of brain cells to their intended targets, leading to mental retardation (Schull, Norton, & Jensh, 1990).

Most teratogens affect prenatal development by first crossing the placenta. For example, a potent teratogen is the German measles (rubella) virus, which can cause

fetal stage
The prenatal period that lasts from the end of the eighth week through birth.

teratogen
A noxious substance, such as a virus or drug, that can cause prenatal defects.

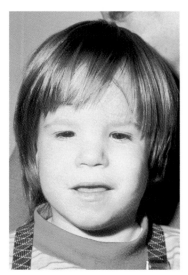

FIGURE 4.2

Fetal Alcohol Syndrome
Prenatal exposure to alcohol may produce fetal alcohol syndrome, which is marked by mental retardation and facial deformities.

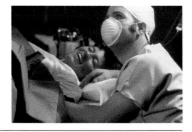

Natural Childbirth
The recognition that in modern society the once natural act of childbirth had become a technological, medical procedure has led to interest in returning to a more personal, natural approach to childbirth. A popular method was introduced in 1951 by a French obstetrician named Lamaze. The *Lamaze method* includes attendance at childbirth classes during the last few months of pregnancy. The parents learn about the physical changes that occur during gestation and what to expect during labor and delivery. The parents are instructed in how to control pain through special breathing techniques, muscular relaxation, and mental distraction. The father also serves as a labor coach to the mother during delivery. The effectiveness of natural childbirth methods such as the Lamaze method in reducing pain and improving maternal attitudes toward childbirth has not been adequately assessed. Evidence of its positive effects has generally come from anecdotal reports, rather than from controlled experiments (Wideman & Singer, 1984).

defects of the eyes, ears, and heart—particularly during the first 3 months of prenatal development. Many popular drugs, both legal and illegal, can cross the placenta and cause abnormal physical and psychological development. These drugs include cocaine (Sobrian et al., 1990), nicotine (Gusella & Fried, 1984), and marijuana (Fried & Watkinson, 1990). Pregnant women who drink alcohol may afflict their offspring with **fetal alcohol syndrome**. The hallmarks of the disorder are facial deformities and mental retardation. Figure 4.2 shows a child who suffers from fetal alcohol syndrome. There is also evidence that women who ingest even small amounts of alcohol during pregnancy may produce offspring who fail to reach their intellectual potential (Streissguth, Randels, & Smith, 1991). Perhaps the wisest course of action is for expectant mothers to refrain from all alcohol (and other drug) consumption.

Though researchers who study prenatal development tend to be most interested in the physical development of the fetus, clever research studies have revealed that, near the end of pregnancy, the fetus may have surprisingly sophisticated cognitive abilities, including the ability to hear sounds and form memories of them.

Anatomy of a Contemporary Research Study:
Can We Form Memories Before We Are Born?

Rationale
Anthony DeCasper and Melanie Spence found that previous research studies had demonstrated that environmental sounds can penetrate a pregnant woman's abdomen and reach her developing child. They decided to investigate whether newborn infants could recall their own mother's voice, which the infants presumably heard while in the womb (DeCasper & Spence, 1986).

Method
DeCasper and Spence had pregnant women read a story (such as Dr. Seuss's The Cat in the Hat) out loud, twice a day, during the last 6 weeks of pregnancy. Each woman also tape-recorded herself reading the story she read out loud to the fetus, as well as two other stories that she did not read out loud to the fetus. After the women had given birth, their newborn infants were given electronic nipples that controlled the playing of the tape recordings made by their mothers. The infants, by sucking on the nipple in one of two particular patterns, could turn on either the recording of their mother reading the story she had read during pregnancy or a recording of a story she had not read during pregnancy. A control group of newborn infants whose mothers had read none of the stories to them before birth, but who did tape-record themselves reading the three stories, was also given access to the electronic nipple.

Results and Discussion
The infants whose mothers read to them prenatally showed a preference for the story they had heard prenatally. In contrast, infants in the control group showed no preference for a particular story. This indicated that the infants whose mothers had read to them prenatally had formed memories that enabled them to recognize the sound qualities (such as the rhythm) of the story they had heard. Thus, it can be inferred that infants are born with the ability to form memories, however rudimentary.

INFANT AND CHILD DEVELOPMENT

Childhood extends from birth until puberty and begins with **infancy,** a period of rapid physical, cognitive, and psychosocial development, extending from birth to age 2 years. During the past century, childhood has been recognized as a distinct period of the life span that is qualitatively different from adulthood. Today many developmental psychologists devote themselves to studying the changes in physical development (including growth and motor skills), perceptual development (including vision, hearing, and other senses), cognitive development (including thinking, language, and intelligence), and psychosocial development (including emotions, personality, and social relations) that occur during childhood.

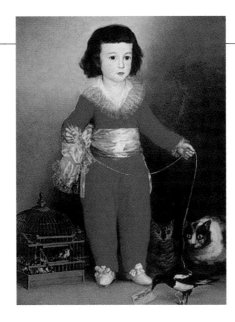

Childhood as a Modern Invention Childhood has been a privileged period of life only since the late nineteenth century. Until then children were treated as smaller, less-experienced versions of adults, with no special needs or rights.

Physical Development

Newborn infants exhibit reflexes that promote their survival, such as blinking to protect their eyes from an approaching object, coughing to dislodge food from their throat, or rooting for a nipple when their lips or cheeks are touched. Through maturation and learning, the infant quickly develops motor skills that go beyond mere reflexes. The typical infant is crawling by 6 months and walking by 13 months. Though infant motor development follows a consistent sequence, the timing of motor milestones varies somewhat from one infant to another. Figure 4.3 depicts the major motor milestones.

Infancy is also a period of rapid brain development, during which many connections between brain cells are formed and many others are eliminated (Huttenlocher, 1990). Though these changes are governed by maturation, they may also be affected by experience.

Research studies by Marian Diamond and her colleagues over the past few decades have demonstrated that life experience can affect brain development (Diamond, 1988). This finding was replicated in a more recent study that determined the effect of enriched and impoverished environments on the brain development of rats (Camel, Withers, & Greenough, 1986). A group of infant rats spent 30 days in an enriched environment and another group spent 30 days in an impoverished environment. In the enriched environment, the rats were housed together in two large, toy-filled cages, one containing water and one containing food, which were attached to the opposite ends of a maze. The pattern of pathways and dead ends through the maze was changed daily. In the impoverished environment, the rats were housed individually in small, empty cages.

Microscopic examination of the brains of the rats found that those exposed to the enriched environment had longer and more numerous dendrites (see chapter 3) on their brain neurons than did those exposed to the impoverished environment. The increased size and number of dendrites would provide the rats exposed to the enriched environment with more synaptic connections among their brain neurons. Studies such as these, which demonstrate the importance of experience in the development of the brain, have inspired attempts to improve the cognitive abilities of mentally retarded children. This is done through programs that provide them with enriched environments offering high levels of sensory, motor, and cognitive stimulation (Rosenzweig, 1984). The effectiveness of these programs remains to be determined.

fetal alcohol syndrome
A disorder, marked by physical defects and mental retardation, that can afflict the offspring of women who drink alcohol during pregnancy.

childhood
The period that extends from birth until the onset of puberty.

infancy
The period that extends from birth through 2 years of age.

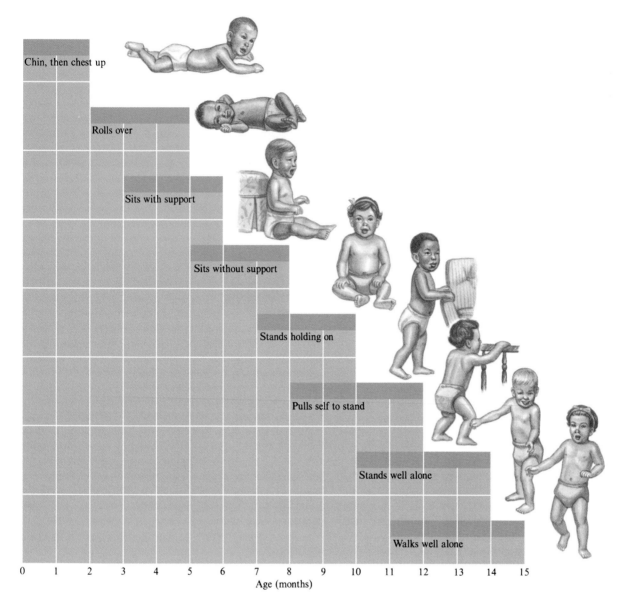

Chin, then chest up

Rolls over

Sits with support

Sits without support

Stands holding on

Pulls self to stand

Stands well alone

Walks well alone

0   1   2   3   4   5   6   7   8   9   10   11   12   13   14   15

Age (months)

FIGURE **4.3**

Motor Milestones
Infancy is a period of rapid motor development. The infant begins with a set of motor reflexes and, over the course of little more than a year, develops the ability to manipulate objects and move independently through the environment. The ages at which normal children reach motor milestones vary somewhat from child to child, but the sequence of motor milestones does not.

After infancy, the child's growth rate slows, and most children grow two or three inches a year until puberty. The child's motor coordination also improves. Children learn to perform more-sophisticated motor tasks, such as using scissors, tying their shoes, riding bicycles, and playing sports. The development of motor skills even affects the development of cognitive skills. For example, children's ability to express themselves through language depends on the development of motor abilities that permit them to speak and to write. With special training, children may develop motor skills even earlier than you might assume. In an experiment on the development of swimming ability, children between the ages of 2 and 5 years old were divided into an experimental group that received training in swimming and a control group that did not. After 8 months, those who had received training in swimming performed better on a variety of swimming tasks than did those who had not (Erbaugh, 1986).

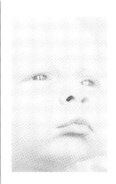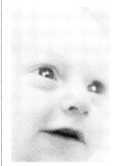

FIGURE **4.4**

Abilities of Newborn Infants
Newborn infants not only see better than has been traditionally assumed, they can also imitate facial expressions of surprise, sadness, and happiness.

Perceptual Development

A century ago, in describing what he believed was the chaotic mental world of the newborn infant, William James (1890/1981, vol. 1, p. 462) claimed, "The baby, assailed by eyes, ears, nose, skin, and entrails at once, feels it all as one great blooming, buzzing confusion." But subsequent research has shown that newborn infants have more highly developed sensory, perceptual, and cognitive abilities than James believed. For example, though newborns cannot focus on distant objects, they can focus on objects less than a foot away—the typical distance of the face of an adult who might be holding them (Aslin & Smith, 1988).

One of the earliest ongoing research programs devoted to perceptual, as well as cognitive, development in infants began in the late 1920s at the Institute of Child Welfare in California under the direction of Nancy Bayley (Bayley, 1933). Since then, ingenious studies have permitted researchers to infer what infants perceive by recording changes in their eye movements, head movements, body movements, sucking behavior, or physiological responses (such as changes in heart rate or brain-wave patterns). For example, infant preferences can be determined by recording which targets they look at longer or by presenting them with a stimulus, waiting for them to *habituate* to it (that is, stop noticing it), and then changing the stimulus. If they notice the change, they will show alterations in physiological activity, such as a decrease in heart rate.

Studies using these techniques have found that infants have remarkably well-developed sensory abilities. For example, Tiffany Field has demonstrated that, as shown in figure 4.4, infants less than 2 days old can imitate sad, happy, and surprised facial expressions (Field et al., 1982). Figure 4.5 describes the use of the "visual cliff" by Eleanor Gibson and Richard Walk in testing infant depth perception, the topic of the following study.

Tiffany Field
"We now have evidence for both the discrimination and imitation of facial expressions at an even younger age, shortly after birth."

Anatomy of a Classic Research Study:

When Do Infants Develop Depth Perception?

Rationale

One of the most important perceptual abilities is depth perception. It lets us tell how far away objects are from us, preventing us from bumping into them and providing us with time to escape from potentially dangerous ones. But how early can infants perceive depth? This was the subject of a classic study by Gibson and Walk (1960).

Method

Gibson and Walk used a "visual cliff" made from a piece of thick, transparent glass set about four feet off the ground. Just under the "shallow side" was a red and white checkerboard pattern. The same

FIGURE 4.5

The Visual Cliff
Eleanor Gibson and Richard Walk (1960) developed the *visual cliff* to test infant depth perception. The visual cliff consists of a thick sheet of glass placed on a table: The "shallow" end of the visual cliff has a checkerboard surface just below the glass. The "deep" end of the visual cliff has a checkerboard surface a few feet below the glass. An infant who has reached the crawling stage will crawl from the center of the table across the shallow end, but not across the deep end, to reach his or her mother. This indicates that by 6 months infants can perceive depth. Of course, this does not preclude the possibility that they can perceive depth even before they can crawl.

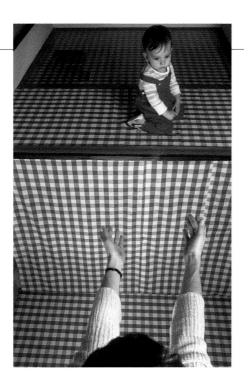 

pattern was placed at floor level under the "deep side." The sides were separated by a one-foot-wide wooden board. The subjects were 36 infants, aged 6 to 14 months. The infants were placed, one at a time, on the wooden board. The infants' mothers called to them, first from one side and then from the other.

Results and Discussion

When placed on the board, 9 of the infants refused to budge. The other 27 crawled onto the shallow side toward their mothers. But only 3 of the 27 crawled onto the deep side. The remaining ones instead cried or crawled away from it. This indicated that the infants could perceive the depth of the two sides—and fear the deep side. It also demonstrated that depth perception is present by 6 months of age. Replications of the study using a variety of animals found that depth perception develops by the time the animal begins moving about on its own—as early as the first day after birth, for chicks and goats. This is adaptive, because failure to perceive depth while moving about might prove harmful. More-recent research on human infants, using decreases in heart rate as a sign that they notice changes in depth, indicates that rudimentary depth perception is present in infants as young as 4 months (Aslin & Smith, 1988).

Infants also have good auditory abilities, including the ability to localize sounds. Between the ages of 8 and 28 weeks, infants can localize sounds that shift in location by only a few degrees, as indicated by head turns or eye movements in response to the shifts (Morrongiello, Fenwick, & Chance, 1990). Newborn infants also prefer high-pitched sounds, which may account for the popularity of "baby talk," high-pitched speech that evokes positive responses from infants (Grieser & Kuhl, 1988).

Infants can even match the emotional tone of sounds to the emotional tone of facial expressions. In one study, 7-month-old infants were shown a sad face and a happy face. At the same time, they were presented with tones that either increased or decreased in pitch. When presented with a descending tone, they looked longer at a sad face than a happy face, as if they were equating the lower tones with a sad mood and the higher tones with a happy mood (Phillips et al., 1990). As the preceding studies attest, the infant is perceptually more sophisticated than William James presumed.

Cognitive Development

Infancy is also a time of rapid cognitive development. Jean Piaget (1896–1980), a Swiss biologist and psychologist, put forth the most influential theory of cognitive develop-

TABLE 4.1

Stage	Description	Age Range
Sensorimotor	The infant progresses from reflexive, instinctual action at birth to the beginning of symbolic thought. The infant constructs an understanding of the world by coordinating sensory experiences with physical actions.	Birth–2 years
Preoperational	The child begins to represent the world with words and images; these words and images reflect increased symbolic thinking and go beyond the connection of sensory information and physical action.	2–7 years
Concrete Operational	The child now can reason logically about concrete events and can mentally reverse information.	7–11 years
Formal Operational	The adolescent reasons in more abstract, idealistic, and logical ways.	11–15 years

TABLE 4.1   Piaget's Stages of Cognitive Development

From John W. Santrock, *Children*, 2d ed. Copyright © 1990 Wm. C. Brown Communications, Inc., Dubuque, Iowa. All Rights Reserved. Reprinted by permission.

ment. As shown in table 4.1, Piaget (1952) proposed that children pass through four increasingly sophisticated cognitive stages of development. According to Piaget, a child is more than an ignorant adult; the child's way of thinking is qualitatively different from the adult's. Though Piaget assumed that complete passage through one stage is a prerequisite for success in the next one, research suggests that children can achieve characteristics of later stages without completely passing through earlier ones (Berninger, 1988). The issue of whether human development is continuous (gradual and quantitative) or discontinuous (in stages and qualitative) remains unresolved (Fischer & Silvern, 1985). The stages put forth by Piaget are the *sensorimotor stage, preoperational stage, concrete operational stage*, and *formal operational stage*. Cross-cultural research indicates that children tend to pass through these stages in the same order, though the timing varies (Segall et al., 1990).

Sensorimotor Stage

Piaget called infancy the **sensorimotor stage,** during which the child learns to coordinate sensory experiences and motor behaviors. Infants learn to interact with the world by sucking, grasping, crawling, and walking. In little more than a year, they change from reflexive, physically immature individuals into purposeful, locomoting, language-using individuals. By the age of 9 months, for example, sensorimotor coordination becomes sophisticated enough for the infant to grasp a moving object by aiming her or his reach somewhat ahead of the object instead of where the object appears to be at that moment (Hofsten, 1983).

Motor development involves not only learning effective movements, but learning to eliminate excessive movements (Lazarus & Todor, 1987). Thus, the infant, who might at first clumsily fling her whole body at an object that is her target will gradually refine her movements to reach out and gently grasp the desired object. The ability to manipulate objects contributes to the developing infant's sense of mastery and competence (MacTurk et al., 1987).

Piaget claimed that experiences with the environment help the infant form **schemas,** which are mental models incorporating the characteristics of persons, objects, events, procedures, or situations. This means that infants do more than simply gather information about the world. Their experiences actively change the way in which they think about the world. Schemas permit infants to adapt their behaviors to changes in the environment. But what makes schemas persist or change? They do so as the result of the interplay between **assimilation** and **accommodation,** terms that were introduced in the 1890s by the American child psychologist James Mark Baldwin and later employed by Piaget.

We *assimilate* when we fit information into our existing schemas and *accommodate* when we revise our schemas to fit new information. Consider the schema "food." You

sensorimotor stage
The Piagetian stage, from birth through the second year, during which the infant learns to coordinate sensory experiences and motor behavior.

Jean Piaget (1896–1980)
"As the child's thought evolves, assimilation and accommodation are differentiated and become increasingly complementary."

schema
A mental model incorporating the characteristics of particular persons, objects, events, or situations.

assimilation
The cognitive process that interprets new information in light of existing schemas.

accommodation
The cognitive process that revises existing schemas to incorporate new information.

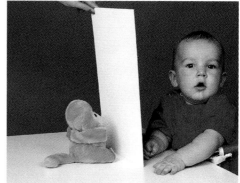

FIGURE 4.6

Object Permanence
After young infants see an object being hidden from view, they act as though it no longer exists. This indicates that they lack the concept of *object permanence*—the realization that an object that is no longer in view may still exist.

object permanence
The realization that objects exist even when they are no longer visible.

have probably observed the indiscriminate way in which young infants place objects of all kinds in their mouths. By tasting and chewing on the different objects, infants learn which are edible and which are not. For example, an infant learns early in life to assimilate milk into the schema "food." But an infant who later drinks milk that has gone sour will accommodate by revising the schema to exclude sour-tasting milk.

Young infants, prior to 6 months old, share an important schema in which they assume that the removal of an object from sight means that the object no longer exists. If an object is hidden by a piece of cloth, for example, the young infant will not look for it, even after watching the object being hidden. As illustrated in figure 4.6, to the young infant, out of sight truly means out of mind. As infants gain experience with the coming and going of objects in the environment, they accommodate and develop the schema of **object permanence**—the realization that objects not in view may still exist. At 8 months infants might look for an object that has been removed, but only at the site where they last saw it. But researchers have questioned Piaget's explanation that young infants fail to search for hidden objects because they lack a schema for object permanence. Perhaps, instead, they simply forget the location of an object that has been hidden from view (Bjork & Cummings, 1984).

After the age of 8 months, most infants demonstrate their appreciation of object permanence by searching at other places for an object they have seen being hidden from view. At this point in their development they can retain a mental image of a physical object even after it has been removed from their sight, and they realize that the object might be elsewhere. This also signifies the beginning of *representational thought*—the use of symbols to stand for physical objects. But Piaget may have placed the development of object permanence too late, because infants as young as 3 or 4 months may show an appreciation of it (Baillargeon & DeVos, 1991).

Preoperational Stage

preoperational stage
The Piagetian stage, extending from 2 to 7 years of age, during which the child's use of language becomes more sophisticated but the child has difficulty with the logical mental manipulation of information.

According to Piaget, when the child reaches the age of 2 years and leaves infancy, the sensorimotor stage gives way to the **preoperational stage,** which lasts until about age 7. The stage is called preoperational because the child cannot perform what Piaget called *operations*—mental manipulations of reality. For example, before about the age of 5 the early preoperational child cannot perform mental addition or subtraction of objects. During the preoperational stage, however, the child improves in the use of language, including a rapid growth in vocabulary and a more sophisticated use of grammar. Thus mental development sets the stage for language development. Unlike the sensorimotor-stage child, the preoperational-stage child is not limited to thinking about objects that are physically present.

FIGURE **4.7**

Conservation
During the concrete operational stage, the child develops an appreciation of conservation. The child comes to realize that changing the form of something does not change its amount—for instance, that the containers pictured here can hold the same amount of liquid. In a classic demonstration used by Piaget, a child is shown a tall, narrow container and a short, wide container that can hold equal amounts of a liquid. When the liquid in the short container is poured into the empty tall container, the preoperational child will perceive the tall container as holding more liquid than did the short container. In contrast, the concrete operational child realizes that the tall container now holds the same amount of liquid as did the short container.

During the preoperational stage the child also exhibits what Piaget called **egocentrism,** the inability to perceive reality from the perspective of another person. Egocentrism declines between 4 and 6 years of age (Ruffman & Olson, 1989). Children display egocentrism when they draw a picture of their family but fail to include themselves in the drawing. You should note that, contrary to popular belief, children who play hide-and-seek by covering their eyes with their hands are not so egocentric that they assume other people cannot see them. Though children who cover their eyes may say that other people cannot see them, they actually mean that other people cannot see their face. They are aware that other people can still see their body (Flavell, Shipstead, & Croft, 1980). Even older children may be somewhat egocentric. In some capital criminal cases, lawyers might gain a reduced sentence for a child defendant if they can convince the jury that the child had not progressed beyond egocentrism and therefore was unaware of the effect of the criminal act on the victim (Ellison, 1987).

egocentrism
The inability to perceive physical reality from the perspective of another person.

Concrete Operational Stage

At about the age of 7, the child enters what Piaget calls the **concrete operational stage,** which lasts until about the age of 12. The child learns to reason logically but is at first limited to reasoning about physical things. For example, when you first learned to do arithmetic problems, you were unable to perform mental calculations. Instead, until perhaps the age of 8, you counted by using your fingers or other objects. An important kind of reasoning ability that develops during this stage is the ability to make **transitive inferences**—the application of previously learned relationships to infer new relationships. For example, suppose that a child is told that John is taller than Paul, and that Paul is taller than James. A child who can make transitive inferences will correctly conclude that John is taller than James. Though Piaget claimed that the ability to make transitive inferences develops by age 8, research has shown that children as young as 4, when given age-appropriate tasks, can make them (Pears & Bryant, 1990).

By the age of 8, the child in the concrete operational stage also develops what Piaget called **conservation**—the realization that changing the form of a substance or the arrangement of a set of objects does not change the amount. Suppose that a child is shown two balls of clay of equal size. One ball is then rolled out into a snake, and the child is asked if either piece of clay has more clay. The child who has not achieved conservation will reply either that the snake has more clay because it is longer or, less likely, that the ball has more clay because it is fatter. Figure 4.7 shows a classic means of testing whether a child has developed the schema of conservation. The effect of

concrete operational stage
The Piagetian stage, extending from 7 to 12 years of age, during which the child learns to reason logically about objects that are physically present.

transitive inference
The application of previously learned relationships to infer new relationships.

conservation
The realization that changing the form of a substance does not change its amount.

TABLE 4.2	Erikson's Stages of Psychosocial Development	
Age	Conflict	Successful Resolution
First Year	Trust vs. mistrust	The infant develops a sense of security.
Second Year	Autonomy vs. shame and doubt	The infant achieves a sense of independence.
3–5 Years	Initiative vs. guilt	The child finds a balance between spontaneity and restraint.
6 Years–Puberty	Industry vs. inferiority	The child attains a sense of self-confidence.
Adolescence	Identity vs. role confusion	The adolescent experiences a unified sense of self.
Young Adulthood	Intimacy vs. isolation	The adult forms close personal relationships.
Middle Adulthood	Generativity vs. stagnation	The adult promotes the well-being of others.
Late Adulthood	Integrity vs. despair	The adult enjoys a sense of satisfaction by reflecting on a life well lived.

Adapted from *Childhood and Society*, Second Edition, by Erik H. Erikson, by permission of W. W. Norton and Company, Inc. Copyright 1950, © 1963 by W.W. Norton and Company, Inc. Copyright renewed 1978, 1991 by Erik H. Erikson.

experience on the timing of conservation was demonstrated in a study of children in a Mexican village whose parents were pottery makers. The children who normally helped their parents in making pottery learned conservation (at least of mass) earlier than other children did (Price-Williams, Gordon, & Ramirez, 1969). In early adolescence, the concrete operational stage may give way to the formal operational stage, which is discussed in the section of this chapter on adolescent development.

Psychosocial Development

Just as Piaget believed that the child passes through stages of cognitive development, psychoanalyst Erik Erikson (1902–1994) believed that the child passes through stages of psychosocial development. Erikson believed that, across the life span, we go through 8 distinct stages. Each stage is marked by a conflict that must be overcome, as described in table 4.2. Research has supported Erikson's belief that we pass through the stages sequentially—though people differ in the ages at which they pass through them (Vaillant & Milofsky, 1980). Erikson was one of the first researchers to consider cultural differences in psychosocial development, having studied children in Sioux, Yurok, and other Native American cultures (Coles, 1970).

Early Social-Emotional Development

Erikson found that the major conflict of the first year of infancy is **trust versus mistrust.** As observed by later researchers, one of the most important factors in helping the infant develop trust is **social attachment,** a strong emotional bond between an infant and a caregiver that develops during the first year. John Bowlby (1988), favoring an evolutionary viewpoint, suggested that infants have evolved an inborn need for attachment because their survival depends on adult caregivers. Thus, infants seek to evoke responses from adults through crying, cooing, smiling, and clinging. Similarly, Sigmund Freud assumed that an infant becomes attached to his or her mother for a functional reason—she provides nourishment through nursing.

Freud's assumption was contradicted by research conducted by Harry Harlow and his colleagues on social attachment in rhesus monkeys. Harlow separated infant monkeys from their parents and peers and raised them for 6 months with two "surrogate mothers." The surrogates were wire monkeys with wooden heads. One surrogate was covered with terry cloth and the other was left bare. Harlow found that the monkeys preferred to cling to the cloth-covered surrogate, even though milk was available only from a bottle attached to the bare-wire surrogate (see figure. 4.8). Harlow concluded

trust versus mistrust
Erikson's developmental stage in which success is achieved by having a secure social attachment with a caregiver.

social attachment
A strong emotional relationship between an infant and a caregiver.

Harry Harlow
"We now know that the development of attachment during the first year of infancy is important to a person's self-concept and ability to interact successfully with others."

FIGURE 4.8

Social Attachment
Harry Harlow found that infant
monkeys became more attached to a
terry-cloth-covered wire surrogate
mother than to a bare-wire surrogate
mother. Even when fed only from a
nipple protruding from the bare-wire
surrogate mother, the infant monkeys
preferred to cling to the terry-cloth-
covered surrogate mother. Harlow
concluded that social attachment
might depend more on physical
contact than on the provision of
nourishment (Harlow & Zimmerman,
1959).

that physical contact is a more important factor than nourishment in promoting infant
attachment to the mother (Harlow & Zimmerman, 1959).

Harlow's findings inspired interest in the possible role of attachment in human
psychosocial development. Of course, today's ethical standards would prevent the replication of Harlow's experiment with human infants (and perhaps even with infant
monkeys). Much of what we know about attachment in human infants comes from
research by Mary Ainsworth (1993) and her colleagues on the mother-infant relationship. In Western cultures, mothers are more nurturant than fathers in providing for their
children's physical needs, while fathers are more likely than mothers to play with their
children (Bronstein, 1984). Thus, the mother is more likely to be the primary caregiver.

In assessing the mother's influence on the child, Ainsworth makes a distinction
between *securely attached* and *insecurely attached* infants. The securely attached infant
seeks physical contact with the mother, yet, despite mildly protesting, freely leaves her
to play and explore, using the mother as a secure base. In contrast, the insecurely attached infant clings to the mother, acts either apathetic or highly anxious when separated from her, and is either unresponsive or angry when reunited with her. An infant
whose mother is more sensitive, accepting, and affectionate will become more securely
attached (Goldsmith & Alansky, 1987). Infants who are securely attached are, in turn,
more likely to become sociable children (LaFreniere & Sroufe, 1985).

Just as infants show remarkable perceptual and cognitive sophistication, they also
show surprising emotional and social sophistication. Infants are capable of expressing
three of the basic emotions: fear, surprise, and happiness. In one experiment, infants
between 10 and 12 months old were tested in two situations designed to elicit fear (the
visual cliff and the approach of a stranger), two designed to elicit surprise (the switching
of a toy and the vanishing of an object), or two designed to elicit happiness (a collapsing
toy and a game of peek-a-boo). Judges blind to the conditions were asked to assess the
infants' emotions based on their facial expressions and behaviors. The judgments of
emotions matched what would be expected from each condition, supporting the notion
that infants can experience these basic emotions (Hiatt, Campos, & Emde, 1980).

One factor in early social relations is baby talk directed at the infant. An experiment on infants aged 18 to 30 weeks found that they were more attentive to a video
recording of people delivering infant-directed talk than to one of adult-directed talk.

Mary Ainsworth
"Gaining an understanding of
attachment over the whole life span
will enrich psychologists' knowledge
of human nature."

"I find there's a lot of pressure to be good."

This was replicated in an experiment with groups of infants aged 4 to 5 months or 7 to 9 months. But perhaps the infants were responding to the facial features of the speakers and not to their voices. This possibility led to a third experiment, in which adult facial features were held constant. The infants still attended more to the infant-directed talk, indicating that it was the voices, not the faces, that made the difference. When undergraduates were asked to rate the appeal of the infants, they found infants who listened to infant-directed talk more appealing in appearance. This suggests that infant-directed talk may serve to promote infant responses that make them more likely, in turn, to evoke positive emotional responses from potential caretakers (Werker & McLeod, 1989).

According to Erikson, during the second year the child experiences a conflict involving **autonomy versus shame and doubt.** The child explores the physical environment, begins to learn self-care skills, such as feeding, and tries out budding motor and language abilities. In doing so, the child develops a greater sense of independence from her or his parents. This may account for the popular notion of the "terrible twos," when the child enjoys behaving in a contrary manner and saying no to any request. Parents who stifle efforts at reasonable independence or criticize the child's awkward efforts will promote feelings of shame and doubt.

At 3 years of age, the child enters the stage that involves the conflict Erikson calls **initiative versus guilt.** The child shows initiative in play, social relations, and exploration of the environment. The child also learns to control his or her impulses, feeling guilt for actions that go beyond limits set by parents. So, at this stage, parents might

autonomy versus shame and doubt
Erikson's developmental stage in which success is achieved by gaining a degree of independence from one's parents.

initiative versus guilt
Erikson's developmental stage in which success is achieved by behaving in a spontaneous but socially appropriate way.

permit their child to rummage through drawers but not to throw clothing around the bedroom. Thus, while the stage of autonomy versus shame and doubt deals with the development of abilities, the stage of initiative versus guilt deals with the development of a sense of right and wrong.

At the age of 6, and continuing until about the age of 12, Erikson observed, the child faces the conflict of **industry versus inferiority.** The industrious child who achieves successes during this stage is more likely to feel competent. This is important, because children who feel academically and socially competent are happier than other children (Blechman et al., 1985). A child who develops a sense of inferiority may lose interest in academics, avoid social interactions, or fail to participate in sports.

industry versus inferiority
Erikson's developmental stage in which success is achieved by developing a sense of competency.

Child-Rearing Practices

One of the most important factors in psychosocial development is the approach that parents take to child rearing, particularly their use of discipline. Psychologist Diana Baumrind discusses three kinds of parenting: permissive, authoritarian, and authoritative. *Permissive* parents set few rules and rarely punish misbehavior. Permissiveness is undesirable, because children will be less likely to adopt positive standards of behavior. At the other extreme, *authoritarian* parents set strict rules and rely on punishment. They respond to questioning of their rules by saying, "Because I say so!"

Authoritarian parents may also resort to physical discipline, which can mushroom into child abuse. Aside from the potential for injury to the child, child abuse is associated with lasting emotional effects on the target of the abuse. Abused children have poorer self-esteem and are more socially withdrawn (Kaufman & Cicchetti, 1989), they tend to be more aggressive and less empathetic toward children in distress (Main & George, 1985), and they are more likely to become juvenile delinquents (Bowers, 1990).

Of great concern is the vicious cycle in which abused children become abusive parents. For example, children who are victims of sex abuse are more likely to become sex abusers themselves (Vander Mey, 1988). However, though most child abusers were abused as children, only 30 percent of abused children become abusers—a far cry from claims that being an abused child automatically makes one a future child abuser (Kaufman & Zigler, 1987). So, if you were unfortunate enough to have suffered child abuse, you may very well be able to break the vicious cycle.

Given that permissive parenting and authoritarian parenting are undesirable, Baumrind has found that the best approach is **authoritative parenting** (Baumrind, 1983). Authoritative parents tend to be warm and loving, yet insist that their children behave appropriately. They encourage independence within well-defined limits, show a willingness to explain the reasons for their rules, and permit their children to express verbal disagreement with them. By maintaining a delicate balance between freedom and control, authoritative parents help their children internalize standards of behavior.

authoritative parenting
An effective style of parenting, in which the parent is warm and loving, yet sets well-defined limits that he or she enforces in an appropriate manner.

Children who have authoritative parents are more likely to become socially competent, independent, and responsible. They are less likely to use drugs (Baumrind, 1991) and more likely to perform better in school (Steinberg et al., 1992) and to show better social adjustment (Durbin et al., 1993). But, as cautioned in chapter 2, be wary of concluding that parenting style causes these effects. Remember that only experimental, not correlational, research permits statements about causality. Perhaps the direction of causality is the opposite of what one would assume. For example, good performance in school might promote authoritative parenting.

Effects of Day Care

Another important, and controversial, factor in child rearing is day care. Until recently, widely available day care was found only in countries in which mothers traditionally worked outside the home, such as China, Israel, and the former Soviet Union. The recent increase in the number of women who work outside the home in the United States has led to a rise in the number of preschool children who spend their weekdays in day-care centers. The number of children placed in day care will increase during the

Day Care
Research indicates that children enrolled in high-quality day care programs do not suffer ill effects. But high-quality day care is not yet available for all parents who need it for their children.

1990s, when about 75 percent of women with school-age children will be working outside the home (Silverstein, 1991). Children's emotional well-being and cognitive development are affected less by the absence of their parents during the day than by the quality of day care they receive (Etaugh, 1980).

Yet the jury is still out on the effects of day care on infants. Today, the mothers of more than half the infants in the United States work outside of the home. Research findings are contradictory in regard to the effects of day care on infants. On the negative side are studies finding that infant day care of more than 20 hours a week in the first year of life is associated with insecure attachment during infancy and greater noncompliance and aggressiveness in early childhood (Belsky, 1988) and that children who enter day care before age 2 later perform more poorly in high school than do children who enter day care after age 2 (Ispa, Thornburg, & Gray, 1990). On the positive side are studies finding that children in day care do not become insecurely attached (Burchinal et al., 1992) and that they later do well in school and act less aggressively than other children do (Field, 1991). These contradictory findings reflect the complex nature of the issue, which involves numerous variables, including the characteristics of the infants, their parents, their caretakers, and their day-care settings. Because many working parents have no choice but to place their infants in day care, it is reassuring to know that research indicates that day care, so long as it is of high quality, is probably not harmful (Lamb & Sternberg, 1990).

While many preschool children spend their days in day-care centers, many school-age children live as so-called latchkey children. When these children return home from school, they care for themselves until a parent returns home from work. Extreme concern about the possible negative psychosocial effects of being a latchkey child may be unwarranted. For example, there appear to be no differences in the academic performance (Messer, Wuensch, & Diamond, 1989), social adjustment (Rodman, Pratto, & Nelson, 1985), or behavior problems (Lovko & Ullman, 1989) of latchkey children and children who have a parent at home.

But the *physical* well-being of latchkey children might be at risk. Most of these children lack essential knowledge of how to fix meals or how to protect themselves from fires, accidents, or strangers when home alone (Peterson, 1989). As evidence of this, consider a study involving naturalistic observation of latchkey children attending kindergarten through the third grade. The study assessed the children's responses to a phone call and an attempted package delivery when home alone. The children typically failed

(a)

(b)

Child's Play
Young children gradually shift from
(a)parallel play to (b)interactive play.

to respond to the phone call in a safe way, which would have included stating that their parent could not come to the phone, taking a message, and refusing to give their name. Worse yet, they all responded to the mock package delivery by opening the door and taking the package, sometimes even announcing they were home alone (Kraizer et al., 1990).

Influence of Parental Relationships

Children are also affected by the quality of their parents' marital relationship. Children exposed to parental discord suffer greater emotional distress (Grych & Fincham, 1990). In some cases marital discord leads to divorce. Because about half of all marriages in the United States end in divorce, many children spend at least part of their childhood primarily with one parent. Research on the effects of divorce on children has produced inconsistent findings. One study found that younger children are affected more adversely than older children are and that divorce has more negative effects on boys than on girls (Lowery & Settle, 1985). A national survey of more than 1,000 children found—based on reports by parents, teachers, and children—that children of divorce tend to suffer more emotional distress, to perform worse in school, and to have poorer peer relations. As in the preceding study, these negative effects applied more strongly to young children, but, in contrast to the preceding study, the negative effects applied more strongly to girls than to boys (Allison & Furstenberg, 1989).

Because divorce involves so many variables, including the age and economic status of the parents, the age of the children, the custody arrangements, and a host of other factors, different combinations of these variables can have different effects on the children. The effects of each combination remain to be determined. It should be noted, however, that children from divorced families have a greater sense of well-being than do children from intact families with intense parental conflict (Amato & Keith, 1991).

Interaction with Peers

Children are affected by their relationships with friends and siblings as well as those with parents. Few children develop friendships before the age of 3, and 95 percent of childhood friendships are between members of the same sex (Hartup, 1989). Boys and girls differ in the kinds of relationships they have with their peers. Girls tend to have fewer, but more intimate, friendships than do boys (Berndt & Hoyle, 1985). Adequate peer relationships are important, because children with poor peer relationships are at risk for academic and social problems. A study of kindergarten students found that those who made more classroom friends during the first 2 months of school developed more positive perceptions of school and did better academically (Buhrmester, 1990).

Peer relationships in childhood involve play. An early study (Parten, 1932) found that the interactive play of children gradually increased between 2 and 4 years of age, but that throughout this period children engaged mainly in parallel play, as when two children play separately from each other with pails and shovels in a sandbox. The results of this study have been replicated. For example, a longitudinal study of children from

16 to 32 months old found a shift from parallel play to interactive play (Eckerman, Davis, & Didow, 1989).

Among our most important peers are our siblings. Sibling birth order is a factor in social development, with firstborn children usually being less socially popular than later-born. This might occur because the firstborn interacts more with adults than with siblings, compared to the later-born, who interact extensively with both parents and siblings. As a consequence, the later-born may be more likely to develop social skills that are well-suited for interacting with peers (Baskett, 1984). As for the only child, the popular belief that she or he suffers because of the absence of siblings is unfounded. For example, an only child is usually superior to all except firstborn children and children from two-child families in intelligence and academic achievement (Falbo & Polit, 1986).

Gender-Role Development

gender roles
The behaviors that are considered appropriate for females or males in a given culture.

One of the most important aspects of psychosocial development in childhood is the development of **gender roles,** which are behavior patterns that are considered appropriate for males or females in a given culture. Gender roles vary across cultures and over time. During the nineteenth century, as the United States moved from being an agricultural country to being an industrial country, the concept of "separate spheres" arose. In the male sphere, men began to play the "good provider" role, and in the female sphere women began to play the "homemaker" role. No longer did the typical husband and wife work together on the family farm or in the family business. Instead, the husband went off to work, while the wife took care of the home and children. Because the family's income depended on the husband's job, his role increased in stature relative to the wife's (Bernard, 1981).

What factors account for the development and maintenance of gender roles? The first formal theory of gender-role development was put forth by Sigmund Freud. He assumed that the resolution of what he called the Oedipus conflict (discussed in chapter 13) at age 5 or 6 led the child to adopt the gender of the same-sex parent. The Oedipus conflict begins with the child's sexual attraction to the opposite-sex parent. According to Freud, because the child fears punishment for desiring the opposite-sex parent, the child comes to identify with the same-sex parent. But studies of children show that gender identity develops even in children who live in one-parent households. Because of the lack of research support for Freud's theory, most researchers favor more-recent theories of gender-role development.

social-learning theory
A theory of gender-role development that assumes that people learn social behaviors mainly through observation and mental processing of information.

Social-learning theory stresses the importance of observational learning, rewards, and punishment. Thus, social-learning theorists assume that the child learns gender-relevant behaviors by observing gender-role models and by being rewarded for appropriate, and punished for inappropriate, gender-role behavior. This process of gender typing begins on the very day of birth. In one study, new parents were interviewed within 24 hours of the birth of their first child. Though there are no observable differences in the physical appearance of male and female newborns whose genitals are covered, parents were more likely to describe newborn daughters as cuter, weaker, and less coordinated than newborn sons (Rubin, Provenzano, & Luria, 1974). But an influential review of research on sex differences by Eleanor Maccoby found that parents reported that they did not treat their sons and daughters differently (Maccoby & Jacklin, 1974). Of course, parents might believe they treat their daughters and sons the same, while actually treating them differently. A more recent review, however, supported Maccoby by finding that gender-role development seems, at best, weakly related to differences in how parents treat their sons and daughters (Lytton & Romney, 1991).

Eleanor Maccoby
"Socialization pressures, whether by parents or others, do not by any means tell the whole story of the origins of sex differences."

Traditional gender roles can also be perpetuated by the presence of women and men in stereotypic gender-role positions. For example, as long as women are more likely to be homemakers and men are more likely to be workers outside the home, children will be more likely to view these as appropriate gender-related behaviors. Moreover, educational approaches to changing gender roles will have less impact than the increased presence of males and females in nontraditional gender roles (Eagly, 1984). When it comes to gender roles, "Do as I do" may be more powerful than "Do as I say."

Gender Roles
According to social-learning theory, children learn gender-role behaviors by being rewarded for performing those behaviors and by observing adults, particularly parents, engaging in them.

An alternative to the social learning theory of gender-role development is Lawrence Kohlberg's (1927–1987) **cognitive-developmental theory,** which is based on Piaget's theory of cognitive development. According to Kohlberg (1966a), the child must first understand the concept of male and female genders before adopting behaviors that are gender related. He found that this occurs at about the age of 3, though children might have an inconsistent appreciation of gender until age 6 or 7. Children with the best-developed sense of gender will be the most likely to act in accordance with gender roles. This view was supported in a study of children aged 21 to 40 months old, in which those who could discriminate between males and females were more likely to prefer same-sex peers and to show gender-related differences in their aggressiveness, with the boys acting more aggressively than the girls (Fagot, Leinbach, & Hagan, 1986). But there is also evidence that contradicts Kohlberg's theory of gender-role development. For example, even children with a low level of gender awareness imitate same-sex models in preference to opposite-sex models. This provides stronger support for the social-learning theory of gender-role development (Bussey & Bandura, 1984).

cognitive-developmental theory
A theory of gender-role development that assumes the child must first understand the concept of gender before adopting behaviors that are gender related.

As a compromise between social-learning theory and cognitive-developmental theory, Sandra Bem (1981) put forth a **gender-schema theory,** which combines aspects of both. She believes that the process by which gender identity develops is best explained by cognitive-developmental theory, but that the adoption of specific behaviors that are appropriate to the female and male genders is best explained by social-learning theory. Bem's theory holds that social learning leads the child to adopt specific gender-related behaviors that are integrated into a gender schema, which then leads the child to perform behaviors that are consistent with that schema. In essence, the child assimilates and accommodates culture-specific information into the schemas of "male" and "female."

gender-schema theory
A theory of gender-role development that combines aspects of social learning theory and cognitive-developmental theory.

Sex Differences

In the nineteenth century, scientific interest in sex differences was stimulated by Darwin's theory of evolution and promoted by Francis Galton, whose views on sex differences were influenced by sexist Victorian attitudes (A. R. Buss, 1976). Galton assumed that females and males evolved physical and psychological differences that help them function in particular roles, and he insisted that they should remain in those roles (Shields, 1975). Today, the study of sex differences is both a political and a scientific issue. Researchers concerned with this controversy are often advocates who believe either that

Sex Differences
The similarity in gross motor skills
between boys and girls makes it
possible for them to participate
together in sports.

there are significant, perhaps inborn, sex differences or that there are only minor sex differences, most likely the products of cultural upbringing. This brings into question the objectivity of researchers in the area of sex differences even more than in less emotionally charged areas (Wittig, 1985).

Researchers concerned with sex differences are particularly concerned with cognitive differences and psychosocial differences. In studying cognitive differences between females and males, researchers have concentrated on differences in verbal, spatial, and mathematical abilities. The first major review of cognitive sex differences was published by Eleanor Maccoby and Carol Jacklin (1974), two decades ago. They reported that females were superior in verbal abilities and males were superior in spatial and mathematical abilities. Females tend to be superior to males in verbal abilities such as speaking, spelling, vocabulary, and reading comprehension. Yet, contrary to the popular stereotype, men are more talkative than women (Hyde & Linn, 1988). Though research has tended to find that men are superior on spatial tasks, such as rotating mental images of objects, the adequacy of this research has been questioned by researchers who are not convinced by such findings, because the differences are generally small and inconsistent (Caplan, MacPherson, & Tobin, 1985).

Perhaps the most strongly established cognitive sex difference is that males, on the average, perform better than females on standardized mathematics tests. A national talent search by Camilla Benbow and Julian Stanley (1983) found that among seventh- and eighth-graders who took the mathematics subtest of the Scholastic Aptitude Test (SAT), males performed better. Among those scoring higher than 700 (out of 800), males outnumbered females by a ratio of 13 to 1. Could this be attributable to males' having more experience in mathematics? Benbow and Stanley say no, having found little difference in the number of mathematics courses taken by females and males. And because they found no other life experiences that could explain their findings, Benbow and Stanley concluded that heredity was probably the basis for this difference. Some researchers agree with their conclusion (Thomas, 1993).

But their conclusion has provoked controversy. Critics argue that the sex differences in mathematical abilities reported by Benbow and Stanley may be attributable to mathematically gifted girls' having been less willing to take part in the study, to girls' having less experience in activities associated with mathematics beyond classes in mathematics, and to cultural norms that teach girls that mathematics is a pursuit more appropriate for boys (Tomizuka & Tobias, 1981). Also, boys do not perform better than girls on all measures of mathematical ability. Though boys receive higher scores on mathematics achievement tests, girls receive higher grades in mathematics courses (Kimball, 1989).

If cognitive sex differences exist, what might account for them? One possibility would be brain differences. But efforts to associate specific cognitive differences with differences in brain structures have produced mixed results. A decade ago researchers who examined the brains of deceased men and women created a stir when they reported that a portion of the corpus callosum called the splenium was larger in women than in men (DeLacoste-Utamsing & Holloway, 1982). As explained in chapter 3, the corpus callosum provides a means of communication between the left and right hemispheres of the brain. In discussing the results of their study, the researchers concluded that the larger female splenium might explain why females seem to make more equal use of the cognitive abilities associated with the two cerebral hemispheres. But a replication of this study, which used magnetic resonance imaging to examine the brains of living people, found no sex differences in the size of the splenium. Moreover, the relationship, if any, between the size of the splenium and its role in hemispheric communication is unknown (Byrne, Bleier, & Houston, 1988).

The possibility that cognitive sex differences are caused more by social and cultural factors than by biological factors is supported by studies that have found a narrowing of cognitive sex differences between males and females during the past 20 years. The recent cultural trend to provide female and male children with similar treatment might explain this (Jacklin, 1989). Even Benbow (1988) agrees that environmental, as well as hereditary, factors play an important role in cognitive abilities such as mathematics.

Researchers also study sex differences in social behavior. For example, popular belief holds that females are more socially empathetic than males are. But this apparent difference depends on how empathy is measured. When asked to report on their level of empathy, females score higher than males. But when empathy is measured by physiological arousal or overt behavior, sex differences disappear. Evidently, social expectations that females will be more emotionally sensitive than males create differences in their subjective feelings but not in their actual behavior (Eisenberg & Lennon, 1983).

Just as females are reputed to be more empathetic than males, males are reputed to be more aggressive than females. Males are more physically aggressive than females are, as in fighting, sports, or crime. But Alice Eagly has found that males are only slightly more verbally aggressive (Eagly & Steffen, 1986). Males are also reputed to be more dominant in social situations. But sex differences in social dominance may reflect differences in social status, rather than sex differences. For example, Eagly has found that men may be more influential, and women more influenceable, because men are more likely than women to hold high-status positions (Eagly, 1984).

Evidence supporting the biological basis of sex differences in social behavior implicates hormonal factors. For example, masculine females tend to have higher levels of testosterone and perceive themselves as more self-directed, more action oriented, and less socially caring than other females (Baucom, Besch, & Callahan, 1985). Yet despite studies that provide evidence supporting a biological basis for sex differences in social behavior, life experiences appear to be more important in accounting for them (Deaux, 1985).

Camilla Benbow and Julian Stanley
"By age 13 years a large sex difference in mathematical reasoning ability exists and . . . is especially pronounced at the high end of the distribution where males outnumber females 13 to 1."

After two decades of extensive research, no sex differences have emerged that are large enough to predict with confidence how particular males and females will behave (Deaux, 1985). This means that decisions concerning the suitability of a given female or male for a specific academic or vocational position should not be influenced by assumptions concerning sex differences in cognitive or social behavior. Even if, on the average, there are sex differences, males and females are still more similar than they are different.

The relatively few demonstrated sex differences and the decrease in the size of sex differences over the past few decades have led psychologist Roy Baumeister (1988) to argue that we should no longer study them. Why study differences that are too few or too small to have practical significance? And why study sex differences when reports of even small differences might support discrimination against one sex or the other? This view was countered by psychologist Sandra Scarr (1988), who believes that objective scientific research on sex differences should continue, even if it might discover differences that we would prefer did not exist. We could then decide whether it would be desirable to try to reduce those differences.

ADOLESCENT DEVELOPMENT

social clock
The major events that typically occur at certain times in the typical life cycle in a given culture.

Change marks the entire life span, though it is more dramatic at certain stages than at others. Keep in mind that biological factors, social factors, and cultural factors all affect development across adolescence and adulthood. These factors vary in their influence during particular periods. Biological factors have more obvious influence during adolescence and late adulthood than during early and middle adulthood. Social factors exert their greatest influence through the **social clock,** which includes major events that occur at certain times in the typical life cycle in a given culture. In Western cultures, for example, major milestones of the social clock include graduation from high school, leaving home, finding a job, getting married, having a child, and retiring from work.

Cultural and historical factors can have different effects on different cohorts. Depending on your cohort, your adolescent and adult experiences may differ from those of other cohorts. Consider an 18-year-old college freshman. College freshmen in the late 1960s and early 1970s were influenced by the turmoil of the divisive Vietnam War, the cynicism generated by the Watergate scandal, the "psychedelic" style and music of the Beatles and Jimi Hendrix, and television programs such as "All in the Family," which broached the formerly taboo topics of racism, sexism, and sexuality.

Today's traditional-age college freshmen, whose adolescence spanned the late 1980s and early 1990s, experienced the militarily successful Persian Gulf War, the demolition of the Berlin wall and the downfall of communism, the commercially oriented music of Madonna and M. C. Hammer, and television programs such as "The Cosby Show," which portray blacks in a more positive light than programs traditionally did. Thus, as you read, keep in mind that while common biological factors and social clocks may make generations somewhat similar in their development, cultural and historical factors that are unique to particular cohorts can make them somewhat different from cohorts that precede or succeed them.

Adolescence is unknown in many nonindustrialized countries. Instead, adulthood begins with the onset of puberty and is commonly celebrated with traditional rites of passage. With the advent of universal free education and child labor laws in Western countries, children, who otherwise would have entered the adult work world by the time they reached puberty, entered a period of life during which they developed an adult body yet maintained a childlike dependence on parents. Formal study of this transitional period between childhood and adulthood, known as **adolescence,** began with the work of G. Stanley Hall (1904) at the beginning of this century (Proefrock, 1981). But adolescence became a major field of study only in the past few decades. In fact, the *Annual Review of Psychology* did not include a review of research on adolescence until 1988— its 39th volume (Petersen, 1988).

adolescence
The transition period lasting from the onset of puberty to the beginning of adulthood.

(a)

(b)

(c)

Cohort Experiences
Exposure to important cultural, political, or historical factors that are unique to particular cohorts may make those cohorts different from cohorts that precede or succeed them. Consider (a) how college students of the late 1950s and early 1960s were influenced by Elvis Presley and the Cuban missle crisis; (b) how college students of the late 1960s and early 1970s were influenced by Jimi Hendrix and the Vietnam War; and (c) how college students of the late 1980s and early 1990s were influenced by Madonna and the Persian Gulf War.

Physical Development

Recall your own adolescence. What you may recall most vividly are the rapid physical changes associated with **puberty** (from the Latin word for "adulthood"). As illustrated in figure 4.9, puberty is marked by a rapid increase in height; girls show a growth spurt between the ages of 10 and 12, and boys show a spurt between the ages of 12 and 14. The physical changes of puberty also include the maturation of primary and secondary sex characteristics. Primary sex characteristics are hormone-induced physical changes that enable us to engage in sexual reproduction. These changes include growth of the vagina, uterus, and ovaries in females and growth of the penis and testes in males. Secondary sex characteristics are stimulated by sex hormones, but are unrelated to the act of sexual reproduction. Pubertal males develop facial hair, deeper voices, and larger muscles. Pubertal females develop wider hips, larger breasts, and more-rounded physiques, caused in part by increased deposits of fat.

These physical changes are triggered by a spurt in the secretion of the female sex hormone estrogen between ages 10 and 11 and the male sex hormone testosterone between ages 12 and 13. Boys have their first semen ejaculation between the ages of 13 and 15, typically while asleep. Girls exhibit earlier physical maturation than boys and experience **menarche,** their first menstrual period, between the ages of 11 and 13. Old medical records indicate that the age of menarche has declined over the centuries. In the ancient Greek and medieval eras, menarche occurred at about age 14. The age increased

puberty
The period of rapid physical change that occurs during adolescence, including the development of the ability to reproduce sexually.

menarche
The beginning of menstruation, usually occurring between the ages of 11 and 13.

FIGURE 4.9

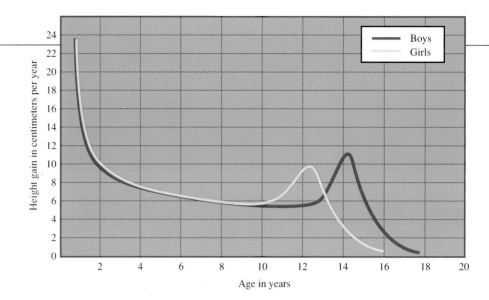

The Adolescent Growth Spurt
The onset of puberty is associated with a rapid increase in height. Note that the growth spurt of females occurs earlier than that of males.

somewhat during the nineteenth century and then decreased during the twentieth century (Diers, 1974). Today, menarche occurs, on the average, at age 12½ (Paikoff & Brooks-Gunn, 1991). This decline in the age of menarche is attributable to improved health and nutrition.

Though the dramatic physical changes of puberty are caused by hormonal changes, adolescent mood swings are not necessarily the by-products of hormones run wild. Hormone fluctuations affect the adolescent's moods, but life events have a greater effect (Brooks-Gunn & Warren, 1989). Of course, the physical changes of puberty, including acne, rapid growth, and genital maturation, can, in themselves, produce emotional distress. This is especially true if the adolescent is unprepared for them or is made to feel self-conscious by peers or parents. Males find it difficult enough to deal with scruffy facial hair, unwanted penile erections, and voices that crack, without being made more anxious about those changes. Females, likewise, find it difficult enough to discover suddenly that they have enlarged breasts, experience monthly menstrual flow, and tower several inches above many of their male peers. Adolescents who know what physical changes to expect find puberty less distressing than do those who are not informed; for example, girls who are told about menarche in advance find it a less stressful event (Rierdan & Koff, 1990).

The great variability in the onset of puberty creates a situation in which adolescents in the same classroom or peer group may look like a mixture of children and young adults. Early maturation and late maturation have different effects on males and females. Mary Cover Jones (1965), who was one of John B. Watson's students, found that boys who matured early had better self-images and peer relationships than those who matured late. Early-maturing boys are also more likely to become leaders and to excel in sports (Petersen, 1988). For girls, early maturation, with its increase in fat deposits, is associated with the development of a chunky physique, leading many adolescent girls to be dissatisfied with their bodies and leaving them more prone to the onset of eating disorders (which are discussed in chapter 11). Because early-maturing girls look older than their age peers, they tend to date earlier and to engage in sexual relations earlier (Phinney et al., 1990).

Cognitive Development

Adolescent cognitive development is less dramatic, with no obvious surge in mental development to match the surge in physical development. According to Piaget's theory, at about 12 years of age, some, but not all, adolescents pass from the concrete operational

Puberty
Because adolescents enter puberty at different ages, groups of young adolescents include individuals who vary greatly in height and physical maturity. As a consequence, a typical junior high school class might appear to include a wider age range than it actually does.

stage to the **formal operational stage.** A person who reaches this stage is able to reason about abstract, not just concrete, situations. The adolescent who has reached the formal operational stage can apply abstract principles and make predictions about hypothetical situations. In essence, formal operational thought has much in common with scientific thinking, which solves problems by starting with what is known, making hypotheses about what is not known, and then systematically testing the hypotheses. In contrast, an adolescent still in the concrete operational stage would rely more on blind trial and error than on a formal approach to problem solving.

To appreciate this, imagine that you are given four chemicals and are then asked to produce a purple liquid by mixing them—but it is left up to you to discover the proper mixture. People at the concrete operational level would approach this task in an unsystematic manner, hoping that through trial and error they would hit upon the correct combination of chemicals. In contrast, people at the formal operational level would approach it systematically, perhaps by mixing each possible combination of two of the chemicals, then each possible combination of three, and finally all four.

High school and college students who have reached the stage of formal operations perform better in school (Mwamwenda, 1993). Whether a student performs well in science courses, in particular, may depend on her or his stage of cognitive development. A study of adolescent students found that those in transition between the concrete operational stage and the formal operational stage showed better understanding of abstract concepts presented in a physics textbook than did those still in the concrete operational stage (Renner et al., 1990). In another study, researchers observed the performances of high school science students as they tried to predict the effects of independent variables on dependent variables related to water pollution. Those at the formal operational stage were more accurate in their predictions (Lavoie & Good, 1988).

Psychosocial Development

Erik Erikson noted that psychosocial development continues through adolescence into adulthood and old age. Perhaps the most important psychosocial tasks of adolescence are the formation of a personal identity and the development of healthy relationships with peers and parents.

formal operational stage
The Piagetian stage, beginning at about age 12, marked by the ability to use abstract reasoning and to solve problems by testing hypotheses.

Erik Erikson (1902–1994)
"If ever an identity crisis was central and long drawn out in somebody's life it was so in mine."

identity versus role confusion
Erikson's developmental stage in which success is achieved by establishing a sense of personal identity.

Identity Achievement

According to Erikson (1963), the most important task of adolescence is to resolve the conflict of **identity versus role confusion.** The adolescent develops a sense of identity by adopting his or her own set of values and social behaviors—often to the displeasure of parents. Erikson believes this is a normal part of finding answers to questions related to one's identity, such as, What do I believe is important? and What are my goals in life?

Erikson's emphasis on the importance of the identity crisis may reflect, in no small part, his own life history. He was the offspring of a Jewish mother and a Danish Christian father, who abandoned his wife while she was pregnant with Erik. His mother then married a Jewish physician, and Erik was raised as a Jew and adopted his new father's surname, making him Erik Homburger. Erik, uncomfortable among Jews and gentiles alike, sought to find himself by traveling in European artistic and intellectual circles, as many did in the 1920s. He even had a showing of his paintings in Munich. Eventually he met Sigmund Freud's daughter, Anna, who was an influential psychoanalyst in her own right, and was analyzed by her in a room in Freud's home. In 1933, after being trained as a psychoanalyst by Anna, Erikson decided to pursue a career in the United States and changed his name to Erik Homburger Erikson. His long, rich life has been a testament to his success in finding his identity as a husband, writer, teacher, and psychoanalyst.

To appreciate the task that confronts the adolescent in developing an identity, consider the challenge of having to adjust simultaneously to a new body, a new mind, and a new social world. The adolescent body is larger and sexually mature. The adolescent mind can question the nature of reality and argue about abstract concepts regarding ethical, political, and religious beliefs. The social world of the adolescent requires achieving a balance between childlike dependence and adultlike independence. This also manifests itself in the conflict between parental and peer influences. Children's values mirror their parents', but adolescents' values oscillate between those of their parents and those of their peers. The adolescent moves from a world guided by parental wishes to a world in which she or he is confronted by a host of choices regarding sex, drugs, friends, schoolwork, and other things. Erikson's theory of adolescence has received support from studies showing that, in fact, adolescents typically move from a state of role confusion to a state of identity achievement (Constantinople, 1969).

Psychologist Carol Gilligan (1982) believes that Erikson's theory applies more to males than to females. She points out that Erikson based his theory on studies of males, who might place a greater premium on the development of self-sufficiency than do females, who might place a greater premium on intimate relationships in which there is mutual caring. Thus, an adolescent female who fails to develop an independent identity at the same time as her male age peers might unfairly be considered abnormal. Once again, this demonstrates the importance of considering the cultural context of theoretical positions. For example, the Inuit people of Canada see personal identity as inseparable from the physical, animal, and social environments. The Inuits would find it maladaptive if members of their culture formed more individualistic, Western-style identities (Stairs, 1992).

Social Relationships

Because the adolescent is dependent on parents while seeking an independent identity, adolescence has traditionally been considered a period of conflict between parents and children, or what G. Stanley Hall called a period of "storm and stress." Parents might be shocked by their child's preferences in dress, music, and vocabulary. Adolescents, in trying out various styles and values, are influenced by the cohort to which they belong. Thus, adolescent males shocked their parents by wearing pompadours in the 1950s, shoulder-length hair in the 1970s, and sculptured hairdos in the 1990s.

Despite the normal conflicts between parental values and adolescent behaviors, most adolescents have positive relations with their parents. A major survey of 20,000 adolescents from 1962 to 1982 found little evidence of widespread insecurity, conflicts with parents, or antisocial behavior, though a sizable minority did have a turbulent adolescence (Offer & Sabshin, 1984). Overall, adolescence is a time of slightly increased parent-child conflict (Paikoff & Brooks-Gunn, 1991). Some adolescents adopt negative identities that promote antisocial, or even delinquent, behaviors; this is more common in adolescents whose parents set few rules, fail to discipline them, and fail to supervise their behavior (Loeber & Dishion, 1983).

As was eloquently and painfully noted by Saint Augustine 1,500 years ago, the onset of puberty is associated with an important biologically based psychosocial conflict between the powerful urge to engage in sexual relations and societal values against premarital sex. The proportion of American adolescents engaging in sex increased steadily from the 1930s, when less than 10 percent had premarital sex, to today, when most older adolescents engage in it. But the sexes differ in their sexual liberality. Adolescent males are more willing to engage in casual sex, while adolescent females are more likely to consider sex to be part of a more intimate relationship (Hendrick et al., 1985).

Though American and European adolescents have similar levels of sexual activity, there are more unwanted pregnancies among Americans. This is attributable in part to the greater ignorance and recklessness of American youths in the use of contraception. This begins from the very first sexual experience, when most American adolescents do not use contraceptives (Brooks-Gunn & Furstenberg, 1989). Another factor is the adolescent's level of cognitive development. Adolescents who have reached the formal operational stage are more likely to make effective use of contraceptives than are those who are still in the concrete operational stage (Gordon, 1990). Promiscuity and unprotected sex increase the risks of sexually transmitted diseases such as herpes, syphilis, and AIDS. Moreover, irresponsible sexual activity in America leads to thousands of abortions, many fatherless offspring, and inadequate care for resulting offspring (Brooks-Gunn & Furstenberg, 1989).

Adolescence is also a period associated with widespread use of psychoactive drugs, including alcohol, nicotine, marijuana, and cocaine. Today alcohol is the main drug of choice among American adolescents, with more than two-thirds of high school seniors using it regularly (Newcomb & Bentler, 1989). Peer-group drug use is the strongest factor in the promotion of adolescent drug use (Swaim et al., 1989). A study of college students found that those experiencing stressful life events over which they felt a lack of control were more likely to resort to alcohol or other drugs to relieve their emotional distress (Newcomb & Harlow, 1986). Fortunately, despite the risks associated with sexual irresponsibility and drug and alcohol abuse, most adolescents survive the trials and tribulations of adolescence and enter adulthood relatively unscathed.

ADULT DEVELOPMENT

In Western cultures, **adulthood** begins when adolescents become independent of their parents and assume responsibility for themselves. No single age automatically signifies the onset of adulthood. The ages at which a person can legally vote, drive, drink, marry, or assume several other adult responsibilities vary. Interest in adult development, which accelerated in the 1950s after being inspired by Erikson's theory of life-span

adulthood
The period beginning when the individual assumes responsibility for her or his own life.

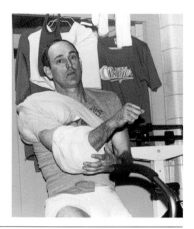

An Ageless Wonder
Nolan Ryan, who pitched his seventh
no-hitter at the age of 44, ices down
his elbow and goes through his usual
postgame workout—riding an exercise
cycle for half an hour.

development (Levinson, 1986), brought an increased realization that physical, cognitive, and psychosocial changes take place across the entire life span.

Physical Development

Adults reach their physical peak in their late twenties, and then begin a slow physical decline that does not accelerate appreciably until old age. Most athletes peak in their twenties, as is shown by the ages at which world-class athletes achieve their best performances (Schulz & Curnow, 1988). Beginning in the twenties, the basal metabolic rate (the rate at which the body burns calories when at rest) also decreases, accounting in part for the tendency to gain weight in adulthood. This makes it especially important for adults to pay attention to diet and exercise, which can also counter the tendency to experience lung, heart, and muscle deterioration in early and middle adulthood. A prime example of this is Kareem Abdul Jabbar, who, by meticulous attention to maintaining a healthy diet and a state of physical fitness, played 20 years of professional basketball.

Aging also brings sexual changes. As men age, they produce fewer and fewer sperm, yet they can still father children into old age. But they might have increasing difficulty achieving penile erections (Doyle, 1989). By the time women reach their late forties, many have experienced *menopause*—the cessation of their menstrual cycle. This is associated with a reduction in estrogen secretion, cessation of ovulation, and, consequently, the inability to become pregnant. The reduction in estrogen may cause sweating, hot flashes, and brittle bones, as well as atrophy of the vagina, uterus, and mammary glands (Greendale & Judd, 1993). Menopause signals an end to the childbearing years, but it does not signal an end to sexuality. Postmenopausal women can still have fulfilling sex lives.

Marked changes in physical abilities usually do not occur until late adulthood. The older adult exhibits deterioration in heart output, lung capacity, reaction time, muscular strength, and motor coordination (Maranto, 1984). Older adults tend to become farsighted, as evidenced by an increasing tendency to hold books and newspapers at arm's length. Old age also brings a decline in hearing, particularly of high-pitched sounds. This may force some older adults to ask others to repeat what they have just said. Eventually, no matter how well we take care of our bodies, all of us reach the ultimate physical change—death. Though the upper limit of the human life span seems to be about 120 years, few people live to even 100. But why is death inevitable? Death seems to be genetically programmed into our cells by limiting their ability to repair or reproduce themselves (Hayflick, 1980).

Research indicates that aging can be slowed by the reduction of daily caloric intake, which prevents the buildup of certain metabolic by-products that promote aging. In a study on the effects of caloric intake, rats kept on a low-calorie diet failed to show the normal age-related decline in learning and spatial memory, as measured by the performance of aged rats in a water maze. Evidently, their brains aged less than those of comparable rats on a higher-calorie diet (Pitsikas et al., 1990).

In human beings, even the mere act of continuing to work is associated with slower aging. In a study supporting this, elderly people who continued to work or who retired but participated in regular physical activities showed a constant level of cerebral blood flow over a 4-year period. In contrast, elderly people who retired and did not participate in regular physical activities showed a significant decline in cerebral blood flow. Those who continued to work also scored better on cognitive tests than did the inactive retirees (Rogers, Meyer, & Mortel, 1990). There is even evidence that individuals who engage in complex activities can generate new synapses in the brain, partly countering some of the negative effects of aging (Black, Isaacs, & Greenough, 1991). Thus, while physical aging is inevitable, people who maintain an active lifestyle may exhibit a slower rate of aging. Note that these results do not conclusively demonstrate that activity *causes* a slowing of the effects of aging. Perhaps, instead, people who age more slowly are more likely to stay active. Again we're faced with the conundrum of causation versus correlation.

(a)

(b)

(c)

Aging and Physical Well-Being
These people show that proper diet and exercise can help us maintain our physical well-being as we age: (*a*) By following a strict dietary and exercise routine, 41-year-old Gregg Amore won the 1988 "Mr. North America" bodybuilding championship in the over-35 age class. He did so while caring for his family, running a farm, and serving as director of counseling at Allentown College. (*b*) Even people in their eighties, such as marathon runner Ruth Rothfarb, can compete in athletics. (*c*) And downhill skiing, too, can be enjoyed by the elderly, including these two men in their seventies.

fluid intelligence
The form of intelligence that reflects reasoning ability, memory capacity, and speed of information processing.

crystallized intelligence
The form of intelligence that reflects knowledge acquired through schooling and in everyday life.

Cognitive Development

One of the most controversial issues in developmental psychology is the pattern of adult cognitive development, particularly intellectual development. Early studies of this showed that we experience a steady decline in intelligence across adulthood. But this apparent decline is found more often in cross-sectional studies than in longitudinal studies. Longitudinal studies have found that a marked decline in intelligence does not begin until about age 60. This indicates that the decline in intelligence across adulthood found in cross-sectional studies might be a cohort effect (perhaps due to differences in early educational experiences) rather than an aging effect (Schaie & Hertzog, 1983). Moreover, the intellectual decline in old age does not encompass all facets of intelligence. Instead, it holds for fluid intelligence but not for crystallized intelligence (Wang & Kaufman, 1993). **Fluid intelligence** reflects the ability to reason and to process information; **crystallized intelligence** reflects the ability to gain and retain knowledge.

But what accounts for the decline in fluid intelligence in old age? The Seattle Longitudinal Study of 1,620 adults between 22 and 91 years old conducted by Warner Schaie (1989) found that the speed of information processing slows in old age. The slowing of information processing is especially detrimental to short-term memory (Salthouse, 1991), which is the stage of memory that involves the conscious, purposeful manipulation of information. Thus, short-term memory enables us to perform functions such as mental arithmetic or deciding whether two objects are the same.

K. Warner Schaie
"Those who wish to maintain a high level of intellectual functioning in old age must maintain flexible behavior and attitudes, remain involved in a broad spectrum of intellectually stimulating activities, and practice their problem-solving abilities."

Back to School
The myth that rapid intellectual decline is a normal aspect of aging is countered by the increasing numbers of older adults beginning their undergraduate careers. The older students who might now be in your classes were rare only a decade ago.

intimacy versus isolation
Erikson's developmental stage in which success is achieved by establishing a relationship with a strong sense of emotional attachment and personal commitment.

Older adults do more poorly than adolescents and young adults on cognitive tasks. One factor that explains why is that they have been out of school for many years. This was the finding of a quasi-experimental study that compared the recall ability of college students of traditional age, their peers not attending college, and older people not attending college. The average age of the younger groups was 22, and the average age of the older group was 69. The three groups were equal in their level of intelligence.

The results showed that the recall ability of the college group was better than that of the other two groups. But there was no difference in the performance of the groups of older persons and younger persons who were not attending college. This indicates that it might be the failure to use one's memory, rather than simply brain deterioration accompanying aging, that accounts for the inferior performance of the elderly on tests of recall. When it comes to the maintenance of cognitive abilities, the adage "Use it or lose it" might have some validity (Ratner et al., 1987).

Psychosocial Development

Social development continues through early, middle, and late adulthood. Keeping in mind that these divisions are somewhat arbitrary, we'll say that early adulthood extends from age 20 to age 40, middle adulthood from age 40 to age 65, and late adulthood from age 65 on. The similarities exhibited by people within these periods are related to the common social experiences of the "social clock." In recent decades, the typical ages at which some of these experiences occur have varied more than in the past. A graduate student might live at home until his late twenties, a woman working toward her medical degree might postpone marriage until her early thirties, and a two-career couple might not have their first child until they are in their late thirties. Of course, events that are unique to each person's life can also play a role in psychosocial development. Chance encounters in our lives, for example, contribute to our unique development (Bandura, 1982a). You might reflect on chance encounters that influenced your choice of an academic major or that helped you meet your current boyfriend, girlfriend, husband, or wife.

Early Adulthood

Though Sigmund Freud paid little attention to adult development, he did note that normal adulthood is marked by the ability to love and to work. Erik Erikson agreed that the capacity for love is an important aspect of early adulthood, and he claimed that the first major task of adulthood is facing the conflict of **intimacy versus isolation.** Intimate relationships involve a strong sense of emotional attachment and personal commitment. A study of college women supported Erikson's belief that the development of the capacity for intimacy depends on the successful formation of a psychosocial identity in adolescence. Women who were capable of a high degree of intimacy felt more secure and confident as separate individuals and responded with less distress to separations from persons to whom they were attached (Levitz-Jones & Orlofsky, 1985).

About 95 percent of young adults eventually experience the intimate relationship of marriage. A survey of childless adults aged 20 to 30 who had never been married found that women were more motivated to marry than were men. Men and women were similar in their ratings of the benefits and drawbacks of marriage. But while men were especially concerned with future career considerations, women were equally concerned with career and family considerations (Inglis & Greenglass, 1989).

What characteristics do adults look for in potential spouses? As you might expect, both women and men tend to seek spouses who are kind, loyal, honest, considerate, intelligent, affectionate, and interesting. But men tend to be more concerned than women with the potential spouse's physical attractiveness, and women tend to be more concerned than men with the potential spouse's earning capacity (Buss & Barnes, 1986). These preferences might reflect cultural norms that differentially affect male and female marital expectations.

Marital Happiness
The willingness of couples to discuss problems promotes marital happiness.

What determines whether a marriage will succeed? An important factor is similarity—in age, religion, attitudes, ethnicity, personality, intelligence, and educational level (O'Leary & Smith, 1991). Another important factor in marital happiness is the willingness to discuss marital issues. Active discussion of issues produces more-effective problem solving than does avoidance of them (Miller et al., 1986). Erikson found that openness is an important component of intimacy. This is especially true in marriage. Spouses who have successfully resolved the intimacy-versus-isolation conflict show an enhanced ability to maintain their marriages, in part because they are more willing to engage in self-disclosure (Prager, 1989). As will be discussed in chapter 17, people who mutually disclose their values, feelings, and experiences tend to have more successful relationships.

Unfortunately, for many couples marital happiness is elusive. One of the hallmarks of an unhappy marriage is the tendency of the spouses to consistently offer negative explanations for their spouse's behavior (Bradbury & Fincham, 1990). In the United States, about half of first marriages are so unhappy that they end in divorce. In fact, the United States has the highest divorce rate of any industrialized country (O'Leary & Smith, 1991).

For most couples, parenthood is a major component of marriage. Raising children can be one of the greatest rewards in life, but it can also be one of life's greatest stresses. Because women still tend to be the primary caregiver, their parental responsibilities tend to be especially stressful. But mothers who receive emotional support from their husbands show less distress in regard to parenting (Levitt, Weber, & Clark, 1986). Overall, parenthood brings a modest decline in marital happiness, caused, in part, by having less time for recreation and more conflict with one's spouse (Belsky & Pensky, 1988). Of course, some couples remain childless. They are not necessarily unhappy. In fact, especially if they are voluntarily childless, they may be more happy than couples with children (Bell & Eisenberg, 1985).

Middle Adulthood

In 1850 few Americans lived beyond what we now call early adulthood. The average life span was only 40 years (Shneidman, 1989). But improved nutrition, sanitation, and health care have almost doubled that life span. What was the end of the life span more than a century ago is today simply the beginning of middle adulthood. Daniel Levinson

FIGURE 4.10

Age and Achievement
Outstanding creative and leadership
achievements peak in the late thirties
and early forties (Simonton, 1988).

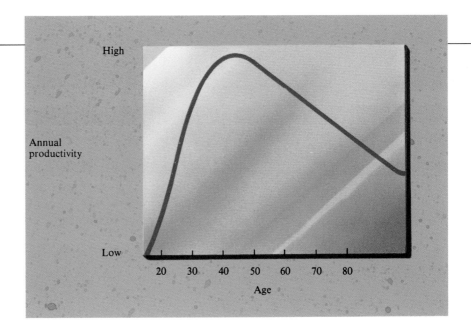

generativity versus stagnation
*Erikson's developmental stage in which
success is achieved by becoming less self-
absorbed and more concerned with the
well-being of others.*

(1978) found that during the transition to middle adulthood, men commonly experience a midlife crisis, in which they realize that the "dream" they had pursued in regard
to their life goals will not be achieved, or, even if achieved, will seem transient in the
face of the inevitability of death. This need to resolve the contradiction between the
pursuit of one's life dream and the realization of one's mortality is an aspect of Levinson's
theory that shows a kinship with existential views of human development. Other studies
indicate, however, that the midlife crisis is less intense than Levinson found in his
research (Fagan & Ayers, 1982). Moreover, the life dreams of women tend to be more
complex than the life dreams of men, because men typically focus on their careers while
women may focus on marriage and children, as well as their careers (Roberts & Newton,
1987).

According to Erik Erikson, the main task of middle adulthood is the resolution of
the conflict of **generativity versus stagnation.** Those who achieve generativity become
less self-absorbed and more concerned about being a productive worker, spouse, and
parent. They are also more satisfied with their lives (McAdams, de St. Aubin, & Logan,
1993). One way of achieving generativity is to serve as a mentor for a younger person,
as your college professors may do for many of their students. This lets mentors realize
their life dreams vicariously and know that their dreams will continue even after their
own deaths (Barnett, 1984). In regard to the life dream, as illustrated in figure 4.10, the
transition between early and middle adulthood, from the late thirties to the early forties,
is a time when leaders and creative people tend to make their most outstanding contributions to their fields (Simonton, 1988).

Experiences as parents during early adulthood lay the groundwork for the achievement of generativity in middle adulthood (Snarey et al., 1987). Middle adulthood also
brings transitions affected by one's parental status. Couples who have children must
eventually face the day when their last child leaves home. You might be surprised to
learn that parents become more distressed and experience more marital unhappiness
after their first child leaves home than after their last child leaves home. In fact, after
the last child has left home, parents tend to be relieved and experience improved marital
relations (Harris, Ellicott, & Holmes, 1986). Perhaps the notion of an "empty nest
syndrome" (after the last child has left home) should be replaced by the notion of a
"partly-empty nest syndrome" (after the first child has left home). Moreover, a growing
trend in Canada and the United States is the "crowded nest," caused by the return home
of young adults who find it personally or financially impossible to live on their own
(Schnaiberg & Goldenberg, 1989).

(a)

(b)

Late Adulthood

Now that more people are living into their seventies and beyond, developmental psychologists have become more interested in studying late adulthood. In 1900 only one person in thirty was over 65. By 1970, one person in nine was over 65, and, by 2020, one person in five will be over 65 (Eisdorfer, 1983). Though this increase in the elderly population will bring new concerns about physical well-being in old age, it will also bring new concerns about psychosocial development in old age. Erikson claimed that the main psychosocial task of late adulthood is to resolve the crisis of **integrity versus despair.** A sense of integrity results from reflecting back on a meaningful life through a successful "life review." In fact, Erikson claimed that pleasurable reminiscing is essential to satisfactory adjustment in old age. This was supported by a study of institutionalized war veterans. Those who frequently reminisced scored higher on a questionnaire that measured their level of ego integrity (Boylin, Gordon, & Nehrke, 1976). And old age is not necessarily a time of physical decay, cognitive deterioration, and social isolation. For many, it is a time of physical activity, continued education, and rewarding social relations (Whitbourne & Hulicka, 1990).

Eventually, many adults must confront one of the greatest psychosocial challenges of old age—the death of a spouse. Bereaved spouses are more likely to suffer depression, illness, or death during the period immediately following the death of their spouse than are their peers with living spouses. This increased morbidity and mortality may stem

integrity versus despair
Erikson's developmental stage in which success is achieved by reflecting back on a meaningful life.

Cicely Saunders
"I . . . started to work at St. Joseph's hospice in 1958 and introduced new ways of pain relief and attention to detail of patients' needs, but we have always dated the beginning of the movement to 1967, when St. Christopher's was opened. That has proved to be the catalyst for the movement as a whole."

hospice movement
The movement to provide care for the terminally ill in settings that are as close as possible to everyday life, and that emphasizes the need to reduce pain and suffering.

from the loss of the emotional and practical support previously provided by the now-deceased spouse. Widowers are usually more devastated than widows, apparently because widows receive greater social support, particularly from their friends (Stroebe & Stroebe, 1983).

Though, as Benjamin Franklin observed in 1789, "in this world nothing's certain but death and taxes," we can at least improve the way in which we confront death. In old age, successful resolution of the crisis of ego integrity versus despair is associated with less fear of death (Goebel & Boeck, 1987). Prior to the twentieth century, death was accepted as a public part of life. People died at home, surrounded and comforted by loved ones. Today, people commonly die alone, in pain, in hospital rooms, attached to life-support systems.

One of the most promising developments in our approach to death and dying is the **hospice movement,** founded in 1958 by the British physician Cicely Saunders, who was disturbed by her colleagues' inability to respond sensitively to dying patients and their families. The hospice movement was introduced to the United States in 1963 in a lecture Saunders gave at Yale Medical School (Saunders, personal communication, March 23, 1992). Hospice provides comprehensive care for the dying patient in a hospital, residential, or home setting, and differs in several ways from the traditional twentieth-century approach to dying (Hayslip & Leon, 1993).

What are the psychological experiences of the dying? The person who has sparked interest in studying the experiences of dying persons is the Swiss psychiatrist Elisabeth Kübler-Ross (1969), beginning in the late 1960s. She saw death and suffering as a young adult as she traveled through France and Poland to help victims of World War II and later when she worked as a physician in the United States (Gill, 1980). Based on her observations of dying patients, she identified five stages experienced by terminally ill patients: denial, anger, bargaining, depression, and acceptance. At first, the patients deny their medical diagnoses, then become angry at their plight, bargain with God to let them live, suffer depression at the thought of dying, and finally come to accept their impending death. Kübler-Ross, however, has found that not all terminally ill patients go through all the stages or go through them in the same order (Kübler-Ross, 1974). Though flawed by subjective interpretations and unsystematic recording of patients' reactions to terminal illness, her research has inspired others to study the psychology of dying (Corr, 1993).

THINKING ABOUT *Psychology*

WHAT IS THE BASIS OF MORAL DEVELOPMENT?

An often-overlooked aspect of life-span development is moral development. According to Sigmund Freud, moral values arise from the resolution of the Oedipus conflict at the age of 5 or 6. During the Oedipus conflict, the child begins with an attraction to the parent of the opposite sex and, out of fear of punishment, identifies with the same-sex parent and adopts that parent's moral teachings. There is little research support for Freud's view of moral development (Hunt, 1979). Today, the most influential theory of moral development is Lawrence Kohlberg's (1981) *cognitive-developmental theory.*

(a)

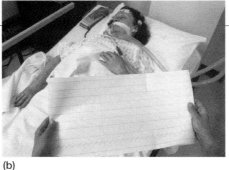

(b)

KOHLBERG'S THEORY OF MORAL DEVELOPMENT

Kohlberg's theory, formulated in the 1960s, is based on Piaget's (1932) proposal that a person's level of moral development depends on his or her level of cognitive development. Piaget found that children, in making moral judgments, are at first more concerned with the consequences of actions. Thus, a young child might insist that accidentally breaking ten dishes is morally worse than purposely breaking one dish. As children become more cognitively sophisticated, they base their moral judgments more on a person's intentions than on the consequences of the person's behavior.

Kohlberg assumed that as individuals become more cognitively sophisticated, they reach more-complex levels of moral reasoning. Research findings indicate that adequate cognitive development is, indeed, a prerequisite for each level of moral reasoning (Walker, 1986).

Kohlberg, agreeing with Piaget, developed a stage theory of moral development based on the individual's level of moral reasoning. Kohlberg determined the individual's level of moral reasoning by presenting a series of stories, each of which includes a moral dilemma. The person must suggest a resolution of the dilemma and give reasons for choosing that resolution. The person's stage of moral development depends not on the resolution, but instead on the reasons given for that resolution. Your moral reasoning in resolving the following dilemma proposed by Kohlberg would reveal your level of moral development:

> ● ● ● In Europe, a woman was near death from a very bad disease, a special kind of cancer. There was one drug that the doctors thought might save her. It was a form of radium that a druggist in the same town had recently discovered. The drug was expensive to make, but the druggist was charging 10 times what the drug cost him to make. He paid 200 dollars for the radium and charged two thousand dollars for a small dose of the drug. The sick woman's husband, Heinz, went to everyone he knew to borrow the money, but he could get together only about one thousand dollars, which was half of what it cost. He told the druggist that his wife was dying and asked him to sell it cheaper or let him pay later. But the druggist said, "No, I discovered the drug, and I am going to make money from it." So Heinz got desperate and broke into the man's store to steal the drug for his wife. (Kohlberg, 1981, p. 12)

The levels of moral development represented by particular responses to this dilemma are presented in table 4.3. Kohlberg has identified three levels: the *preconventional*, the *conventional*, and the *postconventional*. Each level contains two stages, making a total of six stages of moral development. As Piaget noted, as we progress to higher levels of moral reasoning, we become more concerned with the actor's motives than with the consequences of the actor's actions. This was supported by a study of moral judgments about aggressive behavior, which found that high school and college students at higher stages of moral reasoning were more concerned with the aggressor's motivation than were students at lower stages (Berkowitz et al., 1986).

TABLE 4.3   Kohlberg's Theory of Moral Development

Levels	Stages	Moral Reasoning in Response to the Heinz Dilemma	
		In Favor of Heinz's Stealing the Drug	*Against Heinz's Stealing the Drug*
I. **Preconventional Level: Motivated by Self-Interest**	**Stage 1** *Punishment and obedience orientation:* Motivation to avoid punishment	"If you let your wife die, you will get in trouble."	"You shouldn't steal the drug because you'll be caught and sent to jail if you do."
	Stage 2 *Instrumental relativist orientation:* Motivation to obtain rewards	"It wouldn't bother you much to serve a little jail term, if you have your wife when you get out."	"He may not get much of a jail term if he steals the drug, but his wife will probably die before he gets out, so it won't do him much good."
II. **Conventional Level: Motivated by Conventional Laws and Values**	**Stage 3** *Good boy–nice girl orientation:* Motivation to gain approval and to avoid disapproval	"No one will think you're bad if you steal the drug, but your family will think you're an inhuman husband if you don't."	"It isn't just the druggist who will think you're a criminal, everyone else will too."
	Stage 4 *Society-maintaining orientation:* Motivation to fulfill one's duty and to avoid feelings of guilt	"If you have any sense of honor, you won't let your wife die because you're afraid to do the only thing that will save her."	"You'll always feel guilty for your dishonesty and lawbreaking."
III. **Postconventional Level: Motivated by Abstract Moral Principles**	**Stage 5** *Social-contract orientation:* Motivation to follow rational, mutually agreed-upon principles and maintain the respect of others	"If you let your wife die, it would be out of fear, not out of reasoning it out."	"You would lose your standing and respect in the community and break the law."
	Stage 6 *Universal ethical principle orientation:* Motivation to uphold one's own ethical principles and avoid self-condemnation	"If you don't steal the drug, . . . you would have lived up to the outside rule of the law but you wouldn't have lived up to your own standards of conscience."	"If you stole the drug, . . . you'd condemn yourself because you wouldn't have lived up to your own conscience and standards of honesty."

preconventional level
In Kohlberg's theory, the level of moral reasoning characterized by concern with the consequences that behavior has to oneself.

conventional level
In Kohlberg's theory, the level of moral reasoning characterized by concern with upholding laws and conventional values and by favoring obedience to authority.

postconventional level
In Kohlberg's theory, the level of moral reasoning characterized by concern with obeying mutually agreed upon laws and by the need to uphold human dignity.

People at the **preconventional level** of moral reasoning, usually children, are mainly concerned with the consequences of moral behavior to themselves. In stage 1, the child has a *punishment and obedience orientation*, in which moral behavior serves to avoid punishment. In stage 2, the child has an *instrumental relativist orientation*, in which moral behavior serves to get rewards or favors in return, as in "You scratch my back and I'll scratch yours."

People at the **conventional level** of moral reasoning, usually reached in late childhood or early adolescence, uphold conventional laws and values by favoring obedience to parents and authority figures. Kohlberg calls stage 3 the *good boy–nice girl orientation*, because the child assumes that moral behavior is desirable because it gains social approval, especially from parents. Kohlberg calls stage 4 the *society-maintaining orientation*, in which the adolescent views moral behavior as a way to do one's duty, show respect for authority, and maintain the social order.

At the end of adolescence, some of those who reach Piaget's formal operational stage of cognitive development also reach the **postconventional level** of morality. At this level of moral reasoning, people make moral judgments based on ethical principles that may conflict with self-interest or with the maintenance of social order. In stage 5, the *social-contract orientation*, the person assumes that adherence to laws is in the long-

(a)

(b)

term best interest of society but that unjust laws might have to be violated. The U.S. Constitution is based on this view. Stage 6, the highest stage of moral reasoning, is called the *universal ethical principle orientation*. The few people at this stage assume that moral reasoning must uphold human dignity and their conscience—even if that brings them into conflict with their society's laws or values. Thus, an abolitionist who helped runaway slaves flee to Canada in the nineteenth century would be acting at this highest level of moral reasoning.

CRITICISMS OF KOHLBERG'S THEORY

Kohlberg's theory has received mixed support from research studies. Children do appear to proceed through the stages he described in the order he described (Walker, 1989). And a study of adolescents on an Israeli kibbutz found that, as predicted by Kohlberg's theory, their stages of moral development were related to their stages of cognitive development (Snarey, Reimer, & Kohlberg, 1985). But Kohlberg's theory has been criticized on several grounds. First, the theory explains moral reasoning, not moral action. A person's moral actions might not reflect her or his moral reasoning. Yet some research supports a positive relationship between moral reasoning and moral actions. One study found that people at higher stages of moral reasoning tend to behave more honestly and more altruistically (Blasi, 1980).

Lawrence Kohlberg (1926–1986)
"In the study of moral behavior, it is essential to determine the actor's interpretation of the situation and the behavior since the moral quality of the behavior is itself determined by that interpretation."

A second criticism is that the situation, not just the person's level of moral reasoning, plays a role in moral decision making and moral actions. This was demonstrated in a study of male college students who performed a task in which their goal was to keep a stylus above a light moving in a triangular pattern—a tedious, difficult task. When provided with a strong enough temptation, even those at higher stages of moral reasoning succumbed to cheating (Malinowski & Smith, 1985).

Other critics insist that Kohlberg's theory might not be generalizable beyond individualistic Western cultures. This criticism has been countered by Kohlberg and his colleagues. They found that when people in other cultures are interviewed in their own languages, using moral dilemmas based on situations that are familiar to them, Kohlberg's theory holds up well. In other cultures, the stages of moral reasoning unfold in the order claimed by Kohlberg, though postconventional moral reasoning is not found in all cultures (Snarey, Reimer, & Kohlberg, 1985).

Still another criticism of Kohlberg's theory is that it is biased in favor of a male view of morality. The main proponent of this criticism has been Carol Gilligan (1982). She points out that Kohlberg's theory was based on research on male subjects, and she claims that Kohlberg's theory favors the view that morality is concerned with legalistic justice (an allegedly masculine orientation) rather than with social care (an allegedly feminine orientation). Gilligan believes that women's moral reasoning is colored by their desire to relieve distress, while men's moral reasoning is colored by their desire to uphold laws. The results of a recent study supported Gilligan's claim that males and females differ in their notions of morality. As Gilligan would have predicted, females

Carol Gilligan
"Just as the conventions that shape women's moral judgment differ from those that apply to men, so also women's definitions of the moral domain diverge from that derived from studies of men."

tended to have a care orientation and males tended to have a justice orientation. In addition, the more feminine the male, the more likely he was to favor a care orientation (Ford & Lowery, 1986).

Another study, based on a controversial and widely publicized legal case of the 1980s, lends mixed support to Gilligan's position. Undergraduates were asked what they would have decided in the notorious "Baby M" case, in which Mary Beth Whitehead, a surrogate mother, fought over custody with William Stern, the baby's biological father, whose sperm had been used to impregnate Whitehead. The subjects were asked to give the reasons for their decisions. The results indicated that 82 percent of the responses reflected a justice orientation and only 18 percent reflected a care orientation. But, as predicted by Gilligan's viewpoint, more females (23 percent) than males (13 percent) showed a care orientation (Hendrixson, 1989). Despite some research support for Gilligan's position, there does not appear to be a moral chasm between males and females. A major published review of the research literature found that there are no overall, consistent sex differences in moral reasoning (Walker, 1984).

SUMMARY

THE NATURE OF DEVELOPMENTAL PSYCHOLOGY

Developmental psychology is the field that studies the physical, perceptual, cognitive, and psychosocial changes that take place across the life span. The field began a century ago with the publication of baby biographies, which gave detailed descriptions of the development of individual infants. An overriding issue in developmental psychology is the relative influence of nature and nurture. The nature view was championed by scientists influenced by Darwin's theory of evolution, including his cousin Francis Galton. The nurture view was championed by followers of behaviorism, founded by John B. Watson. Today, psychologists in the field of behavioral genetics try to determine the extent to which heredity affects human development. The main source of evidence pertinent to this is research on similarities between relatives and research on the effects of enriched environments. Research on relatives includes studies of families, twins, adoptees, and identical twins reared apart. Animals reared in enriched environments show superior development. Research designs typical of developmental psychology include longitudinal research, cross-sectional research, and cohort-sequential research.

PRENATAL PERIOD

The prenatal period is divided into the germinal, embryonic, and fetal stages. Cell-adhesion molecules direct the size, shape, and location of organs in the embryo. Teratogens can impair prenatal development. Women who drink alcohol, a teratogen, during pregnancy might have offspring who suffer from fetal alcohol syndrome. During the third trimester, the fetus can respond to sounds and can even form memories of distinctive patterns of sounds it has heard.

INFANCY AND CHILDHOOD

Childhood extends from birth until puberty. The first 2 years of childhood are called infancy. Motor development follows a consistent sequence, though the timing of motor milestones varies somewhat among infants. Jean Piaget found that children pass through distinct cognitive stages of development. During the sensorimotor stage, the infant learns to coordinate sensory experiences and motor

behavior, and forms schemas that represent aspects of the world. The preoperational stage is marked by egocentrism. In the concrete operational stage, the child learns to make transitive inferences and to appreciate conservation.

Erik Erikson put forth an influential theory of psychosocial development. He believed that the life span consists of eight distinct stages, each associated with a crisis that must be overcome. An important factor in infant development is social attachment, a strong emotional tie to a caregiver. Permissive and authoritarian child-rearing practices are less effective than authoritative ones. Children who receive high-quality day care do not appear to suffer ill effects from being separated from their parents, though this might not be true of infants. Latchkey children do not appear to suffer psychological damage from being home alone, though they might be at risk of physical harm because of their inability to respond properly to emergencies or strangers. Research on the effects of divorce on children has produced inconsistent results, with some studies finding no effects, others finding negative effects, and still others finding positive effects. Though the causes of male and female gender development are still unclear, social learning theory, cognitive-developmental theory, and gender-schema theory try to explain it.

Research on sex differences has found no consistent differences in male and female brains. Girls and boys differ little in their gross motor abilities until puberty, when boys begin to outperform girls. Females tend to have better verbal abilities, while males tend to have better spatial and mathematical abilities. Males also tend to be more physically aggressive than females. Research on sex differences is controversial, because of fears that its findings might be used to promote and legitimate discrimination. Sex differences are based on group averages and are so small that they should not be used to make decisions about individuals.

ADOLESCENCE

Adolescence is a transitional period between childhood and adulthood that begins with puberty. In regard to physical development, the adolescent experiences the maturation of primary and secondary sex characteristics. In regard to cognitive development, some adolescents enter Piaget's formal operational stage, meaning that they can engage in abstract, hypothetical reasoning. And, in regard to psychosocial development, adolescence is a time of identity formation, an important stage in Erik Erikson's theory of development. The adolescent also becomes more and more influenced by peer values, especially in regard to fashions, sexuality, and drug use.

ADULTHOOD

Adulthood begins when adolescents become independent from their parents. In regard to physical development, adults reach their physical peak in their late twenties, at which point they begin a gradual decline that does not accelerate appreciably until old age. Middle-aged women experience menopause, which, contrary to popular belief, is rarely a traumatic event. In regard to cognitive development, though aging brings some slowing of cognitive processes, people who continue to be mentally active show less cognitive decline than do their peers who do not stay active.

In regard to social development, Erik Erikson saw the main task of early adulthood as the establishment of intimacy, typically between a husband and wife. About 95 percent of adults marry, but half of today's marriages will end in divorce. The most successful marriages are those in which the spouses discuss, rather than avoid, marital issues. Erikson saw the main task of middle adulthood as the establishment of a sense of generativity, which is promoted by parenting. After the last child leaves home, parents typically improve their emotional and marital well-being. Erikson saw the final stage of life as ideally promoting a sense of integrity in reflecting on a life well lived. Eventually, all people must face their own mortality. The hospice movement, founded by Cicely Saunders, has promoted more humane, personal, and homelike care for the dying patient. Elisabeth Kübler-Ross stimulated interest in the study of death and dying. She found that dying people typically go through the stages of denial, anger, bargaining, depression, and acceptance.

THINKING ABOUT PSYCHOLOGY: WHAT IS THE BASIS OF MORAL DEVELOPMENT?

The most influential theory of moral development has been Lawrence Kohlberg's cognitive-developmental theory, which is based on Piaget's belief that a person's level of moral development depends on his or her level of cognitive development. Kohlberg proposes that we pass through preconventional, conventional, and postconventional levels of moral development. Carol Gilligan argues that Kohlberg's theory is biased toward a masculine view of morality. Research has provided mixed support for Kohlberg's theory.

IMPORTANT CONCEPTS

accommodation 127
adolescence 140
adulthood 145
assimilation 127
authoritative parenting 133
autonomy versus shame and doubt 132
behavioral genetics 115
childhood 122
cognitive-developmental theory 137
cohort 119
cohort-sequential research 120
concrete operational stage 129

conservation 129
conventional level 154
cross-sectional research 119
crystallized intelligence 147
developmental psychology 114
egocentrism 129
embryonic stage 120
fetal alcohol syndrome 122
fetal stage 121
fluid intelligence 147
formal operational stage 143
gender roles 136
gender-schema theory 137
generativity versus stagnation 150

genotype 116
germinal stage 120
heritability 117
hospice movement 152
identity versus role confusion 144
industry versus inferiority 133
infancy 122
initiative versus guilt 132
integrity versus despair 151
intimacy versus isolation 148
longitudinal research 119
maturation 114
menarche 141
object permanence 128

phenotype 116
postconventional level 154
preconventional level 154
preoperational stage 128
puberty 141
schema 127
sensorimotor stage 127
social attachment 130
social clock 140
social learning theory 136
teratogen 121
transitive inference 129
trust versus mistrust 130

MAJOR CONTRIBUTORS

Mary Ainsworth 131
Diana Baumrind 133
Camilla Benbow and Julian Stanley 138,139
John Bowlby 130
Charles Darwin 114
Marian Diamond 123

Alice Eagly 139
Erik Erikson 130,132,144
Tiffany Field 125
Sigmund Freud 130
Francis Galton 115
Arnold Gesell 119

Carol Gilligan 144,155–156
G. Stanley Hall 114
Harry Harlow 130
Lawrence Kohlberg 137,153–155
Elisabeth Kübler-Ross 152
Daniel Levinson 149

Eleanor Maccoby 136
Gregor Mendel 115
Jean Piaget 126–130
Robert Plomin 118
Cicely Saunders 152
K. Warner Schaie 147

FOR GENERAL WORKS ON DEVELOPMENTAL PSYCHOLOGY

Lerner, R. M. (Ed.). (1983). *Developmental psychology: Historical and philosophical perspectives.* Hillsdale, NJ: Erlbaum.

Nsamenang, A. B. (1992). *Human development in cultural context: A third world perspective.* Newbury Park, CA: Sage Publications.

Santrock, J. W. (1992). *Life-span development* (4th ed.). Dubuque, IA: Wm. C. Brown.

FOR MORE ON HEREDITY AND ENVIRONMENT

Bouchard, T. J., Jr., Lykken, D. T., McGue, M., Segal, N. L., & Tellegen, A. (1990). Sources of human psychological differences: The Minnesota Study of Twins Reared Apart. *Science, 250,* 223–228.

Caudill, E. (1989). *Darwinism in the press: The evolution of an idea.* Hillsdale, NI: Erlbaum.

Cravens, H. (1988). *The triumph of evolution: The heredity-environment controversy: 1900–1941.* Baltimore: The Johns Hopkins University Press.

Diamond, M. (1988). *Enriching heredity: The impact of the environment on the anatomy of the brain.* New York: Free Press.

Dunn, J., & Plomin, R. (1990). *Separate lives: Why siblings are so different.* New York: Basic Books.

Kevles, D. J. (1985). *In the name of eugenics: Genetics and the uses of human heredity.* New York: Knopf.

Neubauer, P. (1990). *Nature's thumbprint: The role of genetics in human development.* Boston: Addison-Wesley.

Plomin, R., & DeFries, J. C. (1985). *Origins of individual differences in infancy: The Colorado Adoption Project.* Orlando, FL: Academic Press.

Plomin, R., DeFries, J. C., & McClearn, G. E. (1990). *Behavioral genetics: A primer.* New York: W. H. Freeman.

Smith, J. D. (1988). *Psychological profiles of conjoined twins: Heredity, environment, and identity.* Westport, CT: Praeger.

FOR MORE ON RESEARCH METHODS IN DEVELOPMENTAL PSYCHOLOGY

Menard, S. (1991). *Longitudinal research.* Newbury Park, CA: Sage Publications.

Miller, S. A. (1987). *Developmental research methods.* Englewood Cliffs, NJ: Prentice Hall.

Young, C. H., Savola, K. L., & Phelps, E. (1991). *Inventory of longitudinal studies in the social sciences.* Newbury Park, CA: Sage Publications.

FOR MORE ON THE PRENATAL PERIOD

Abel, E. L. (1989). *Behavioral teratogenesis and behavioral mutagenesis.* New York: Plenum.

Abel, E. L. (1990). *Fetal alcohol syndrome.* New York: Basil Blackwell.

Fedor-Freybergh, P. G., & Vogel, M. L. (Eds.). (1988). *Prenatal and perinatal psychology and medicine.* Pearl River, NY: Parthenon.

FOR MORE ON INFANCY

Bower, T. G. R. (1989). *The rational infant: Learning in infancy.* New York: W. H. Freeman.

Bowlby, J. (1988). *A secure base: Parent-child attachment and healthy human development.* New York: Basic Books.

Fein, G. G., & Fox, N. (1990). *Infant day care.* Norwood, NJ: Ablex.

Harlow, C. M. (Ed.). (1986). *From learning to love: The selected papers of H. F. Harlow.* New York: Praeger.

Lamb, M. E., Thompson, R. A., Gardner, W., & Charnov, E. L. (1985). *Infant-mother attachment: The origins and developmental significance of individual differences in strange situation behavior.* Hillsdale, NJ: Erlbaum.

Maurer, D., & Maurer, C. (1989). *The world of the newborn.* New York: Basic Books.

Preyer, W. (1890/1973). *The mind of the child.* Salem, NH: Ayer.

Snow, C. W. (1989). *Infant development.* Englewood Cliffs, NJ: Prentice Hall.

Stern, D. N. (1990). *Diary of a baby.* New York: Basic Books.

Yonas, A. (Ed.). (1987). *Perceptual development in infancy.* Hillsdale, NJ: Erlbaum.

FOR MORE ON CHILDHOOD

Ainslie, R. C. (1985). *The psychology of twinship.* Lincoln: University of Nebraska Press.

Aries, P. (1962). *Centuries of childhood: A social history of family life.* New York: Knopf.

Bank, S. P., & Kahn, M. D. (1982). *The sibling bond.* New York: Basic Books.

Brodzinsky, D. M., & Schechter, M. D. (Eds.). (1990). *The psychology of adoption.* New York: Oxford University Press.

Clarke-Stewart, A. (1993). *Daycare* (2nd ed.). Cambridge, MA: Harvard University Press.

Ernst, C., & Angst, J. (1985). *Birth order: Its influence on personality.* New York: Springer-Verlag.

Erwin, P. (1993). *Friendship and peer relations in children.* New York: Wiley.

Gallahue, D. L., & Ozmun, J. (1994). *Understanding motor development: Infants, children, adolescents, adults.* Madison, WI: Brown & Benchmark.

Gesell, A. (1939/1974). *Biographies of child development.* Salem, NH: Ayer.

Grusec, J. E., & Lytton, H. (1993). *Social development.* New York: Springer-Verlag.

Hall, G. S. (1904/1976). *Youth: Its education, regimen, and hygiene.* Salem, NH: Ayer.

Hetherington, E. M., & Arasteh, J. D. (Eds.). (1988). *Impact of divorce, single parenting, and stepparenting on children.* Hillsdale, NJ: Erlbaum.

Lamb, M. E., Sternberg, K. J., Hwang, C.-P., & Broberg, A. G. (Eds.). (1992). *Child care in context: Cross-cultural perspectives.* Hillsdale, NJ: Erlbaum.

Nance, R. D. (1970). G. Stanley Hall and John B. Watson as child psychologists. *Journal of the History of the Behavioral Sciences, 6,* 303–316.

Rosser, R. A. (1993). *Cognitive development: Psychological and biological perspectives.* Boston: Allyn & Bacon.

Santrock, J. W., & Yussen, S. R. (1994). *Child development* (6th ed.). Madison, WI: Brown & Benchmark.

Wagner, D. A., & Stevenson, H. W. (Eds.). (1982). *Cultural perspectives on child development.* San Francisco: Freeman.

Watson, J. B. (1928/1972). *Psychological care of the infant and child.* Salem, NH: Ayer.

FOR MORE ON JEAN PIAGET'S THEORY OF COGNITIVE DEVELOPMENT

Ault, R. L. (1983). *Children's cognitive development: Piaget's theory and the process approach.* New York: Oxford University Press.

Bringuier, J.-C. (1980). *Conversations with Jean Piaget.* Chicago: University of Chicago Press.

Chapman, M. (1988). *Constructive evolution: Origins and development of Piaget's thought.* New York: Cambridge University Press.

Dasen, P. R. (Ed.). (1977). *Piagetian psychology: Cross-cultural contributions.* New York: Gardner Press.

Evans, R. I. (1981). *Dialogue with Jean Piaget.* New York: Greenwood.

Modgil, S., & Modgil, C. (Eds.). (1982). *Jean Piaget: Consensus and controversy.* New York: Praeger.

Phillips, J. L., Jr. (1981). *Piaget's theory: A primer.* New York: W. H. Freeman.

Piaget, J. (1929). *The child's conception of the world.* London: Routledge & Kegan Paul.

FOR MORE ON ERIK ERIKSON'S THEORY OF PSYCHOSOCIAL DEVELOPMENT

Erikson, E. H. (1963). *Childhood and society.* New York: W. W. Norton.

Evans, R. I. (1967). *Dialogue with Erik Erikson.* New York: Harper & Row.

Gross, F. L., Jr. (1986). *Introducing Erik Erikson: An invitation to his thinking.* Lanham, MD: University Press of America.

FOR MORE ON GENDER-ROLE DEVELOPMENT

Basow, S. A. (1992). *Gender stereotypes and roles* (3rd ed.). Monterey, CA: Brooks/Cole.

Doyle, J. A. (1989). *The male experience* (2nd ed.). Dubuque, IA: Wm. C. Brown.

Doyle, J. A., & Paludi, M. (1991). *Sex and gender* (2nd ed.). Dubuque, IA: Wm. C. Brown.

Gilligan, C. (1982). *In a different voice: Psychological theory and women's development.* Cambridge, MA: Harvard University Press.

Gilmore, D. D. (1990). *Manhood in the making: Cultural concepts of masculinity.* New Haven, CT: Yale University Press.

Hyde, J. S. (1991). *Half the human experience.* Lexington, MA: D. C. Heath.

FOR MORE ON SEX DIFFERENCES

Eagly, A. H. (1987). *Sex differences in social behavior: A social-role interpretation.* Hillsdale, NJ: Erlbaum.

Halpern, D. F. (1986). *Sex differences in cognitive abilities.* Hillsdale, NJ: Erlbaum.

Hyde, J. S., & Linn, M. C. (Eds.). (1986). *The psychology of gender: Advances through meta-analysis.* Baltimore: The Johns Hopkins University Press.

Maccoby, E. E., & Jacklin, C. N. (1974). *Psychology of sex differences* (2 vols.). Stanford, CA: Stanford University Press.

FOR MORE ON ADOLESCENT DEVELOPMENT

Erikson, E. (1963). *Identity: Youth and crisis.* New York: W. W. Norton.

Golub, S. (1992). *Periods: From menarche to menopause.* Newbury Park: Sage Publications.

Hall, G. S. (1905/1979). *Adolescence.* Salem, NH: Ayer.

Hynes, A. (1989). *Puberty.* New York: St. Martin's Press.

Masserman, J. H., & Uribe, V. M. (1990). *Adolescent sexuality.* Springfield, IL: Charles C Thomas.

Petersen, A. C. (1988). Adolescent development. *Annual Review of Psychology, 39,* 583–607.

Santrock, J. W. (1993). *Adolescence: An introduction* (5th ed.). Dubuque, IA: Brown & Benchmark.

FOR MORE ON ADULT DEVELOPMENT

Cate, R. M., & Lloyd, S. A. (1992). *Courtship.* Newbury Park, CA: Sage Publications.

Colman, L. L., & Colman, A. D. (1990). *Pregnancy: The psychological experience.* New York: Farrar, Straus & Giroux.

Fincham, F. D. (Ed.). (1990). *The psychology of marriage.* New York: Guilford.

Lamb, M. E. (1986). *The father's role.* New York: Wiley.

Levinson, D. (1978). *The seasons of a man's life.* New York: Knopf.

McCrae, R. R., & Costa, P. T., Jr. (1990). *Personality in adulthood.* New York: Guilford.

Mercer, R. T., Nichols, E. G., & Doyle, G. C. (1989). *Transitions in a woman's life.* New York: Springer.

Price, S. J., & McKenry, P. C. (1988). *Divorce.* Newbury Park, CA: Sage Publications.

Rybash, J., Roodin, P., & Santrock, J. (1991). *Adult development and aging* (2nd ed.). Dubuque, IA: Wm. C. Brown.

FOR MORE ON AGING

Alzheimer, A. (1987). *The early story of Alzheimer's disease: Translation of the historical papers.* New York: Raven Press.

Aries, P. (1974). *Western attitudes toward death: From the Middle Ages to the present.* Baltimore: The Johns Hopkins University Press.

Belsky, J. K. (1990). *Psychology of aging.* Monterey, CA: Brooks/Cole.

Blackmore, S. (1993). *Dying to live: Near-death experiences.* Buffalo, NY: Prometheus.

Glenner, G. G., & Wurtman, R. J. (Eds.). (1987). *Advancing frontiers in Alzheimer's disease research.* Austin: University of Texas Press.

Hampton, J. K. (1991). *The biology of human aging.* Dubuque, IA: Wm. C. Brown.

Hayslip, B., Jr., & Leon, J. (1992). *Hospice care.* Newbury Park, CA: Sage Publications.

Kastenbaum, R. (1992). *The psychology of death.* New York: Springer.

Kübler-Ross, E. (1969). *On death and dying.* New York: Macmillan.

Saunders, C. (1990). *St. Christopher's in celebration: Twenty-one years at Britain's first modern hospice.* North Pomfret, VT: Trafalgar Square.

Wurtman, R. J. (1985, January). Alzheimer's disease. *Scientific American,* pp. 62–66, 71–74.

FOR MORE ON MORAL DEVELOPMENT

Gilligan, C., Ward, J. V., & Taylor, J. M. (1988). *Mapping the moral domain: A contribution of women's thinking to psychological theory and education.* Cambridge, MA: Harvard University Press.

Kohlberg, L. (1981). *Essays on moral development: Vol. 1. The philosophy of moral development.* San Francisco: Harper & Row.

Kohlberg, L. (1984). *Essays on moral development: Vol. 2. The psychology of moral development.* San Francisco: Harper & Row.

Kurtines, W. M., & Gewirtz, J. (Eds.). (1991). *Handbook of moral behavior and development: Vol. 1. Theory.* Hillsdale, NJ: Erlbaum.

Kurtines, W. M., & Gewirtz, J. (Eds.). (1991). *Handbook of moral behavior and development: Vol. 2. Research.* Hillsdale, NJ: Erlbaum.

Kurtines, W. M., & Gewirtz, J. (Eds.). (1991). *Handbook of moral behavior and development: Vol. 3. Application.* Hillsdale, NJ: Erlbaum.

Modgil, S., & Modgil, C. (Eds.). (1986). *Lawrence Kohlberg: Consensus and controversy.* Bristol, PA: Hemisphere.

Piaget, J. (1932). *The moral judgment of the child.* New York: Harcourt, Brace & World.

Schrader, D. E. (Ed.). (1990). *The legacy of Lawrence Kohlberg.* San Francisco: Jossey-Bass.

FOR MORE ON CONTRIBUTORS TO THE STUDY OF HUMAN DEVELOPMENT

Ames, L. B. (1989). *Arnold Gesell: Themes of his work.* New York: Human Sciences Press.

Boden, M. A. (1980). *Jean Piaget.* New York: Viking Press.

Coles, R. (1970). *Erik Erikson: The growth of his work.* Boston: Atlantic/Little, Brown.

Du Boulay, S. (1984). *Cicely Saunders: Founder of the modern hospice movement.* Albuquerque: Amaryllis Press.

Forrest, D. W. (1974). *Francis Galton: The life and work of a Victorian genius.* New York: Taplinger.

Gill, D. (1980). *Quest: The life of Elisabeth Kübler-Ross.* New York: Harper & Row.

Ross, D. (1972). *G. Stanley Hall: The psychologist as prophet.* Chicago: University of Chicago Press.

Grant Wood
Fall Plowing
1931

SENSATION AND PERCEPTION

elen Keller (1880–1968), though deaf and blind from infancy, lived a rich, fulfilling life by using her other senses. She became an inspirational figure, finding success as a writer, a lecturer, and an educator. Nonetheless, without vision and hearing she was at greater risk of injury or death, and cut off from many experiences that would have added to her joy in life. To understand how the senses operate in protecting and enriching our lives requires a knowledge of *sensory processes*.

SENSORY PROCESSES

As we discussed in chapter 1, because sensory processes are so important to our functioning in everyday life, the first scientific studies by psychologists were concerned with them. Today psychologists distinguish between *sensation* and *perception* (Bloomquist, 1985). The starting point for both processes is a *stimulus* (plural, *stimuli*), a form of energy (such as light waves or sound waves) that can affect sensory organs (such as the eyes or the ears). **Sensation** is the process that detects stimuli from one's body or environment. **Perception** is the process that organizes sensations into meaningful patterns. Visual sensation lets you detect the black marks on this page; visual perception lets you organize the black marks into letters and words. To appreciate the difference between sensation and perception, try to identify the picture in figure 5.1. Most people cannot identify it, because they *sense* the light and dark marks on the page but fail to *perceive* a meaningful pattern.

For a real-life example of the difference between sensation and perception, consider a case study presented by neurologist Oliver Sacks (1985). One of his patients, a music professor he called "Dr. P.," suffered from brain damage that caused him to develop *prosopagnosia* (see chapter 3), the inability to recognize faces. Dr. P. could recognize his students by the sounds of their voices, but he could not recognize them by sight. His disorder was so severe that he sometimes patted fire hydrants, thinking they were children's heads. He would even grab his wife's head, mistaking it for a hat. Yet he was not nearsighted—he could easily see a pin on the floor. Thus, he had visual *sensations* of people's facial features, but he could not organize them into recognizable faces (visual *perceptions*).

Sensation depends on specialized cells called **sensory receptors**, which detect stimuli and convert their energy into neural impulses. This process is called **sensory transduction**. Receptors serve our visual, auditory, smell, taste, skin, and body senses. But some animals have receptors that serve unusual senses. Sharks have receptors that detect the weak electrical fields that emanate from the fish on which they prey (Kalmun, 1982). Whales and dolphins navigate by using receptors that sense variations in Earth's magnetic field; disruption of their magnetic sense might account for some of the periodic strandings of whales and dolphins on beaches (Weisburd, 1984).

Sensory Thresholds

How intense must a sound be for you to detect it? How much change in light intensity must occur for you to notice it? Questions like these are the subject matter of **psychophysics**, the study of the relationship between the physical characteristics of stimuli and the corresponding psychological responses to them. Psychophysics was developed more than a century ago by the German scientists Ernst Weber (1795–1878) and Gustav Fechner (1801–1887). Fechner, after the publication of his classic *Elements of Psychophysics* in

Helen Keller (1880–1968)
Because she was deaf and blind, Helen Keller relied on her senses of touch and smell to perceive the world. She used her fingers to read Braille well enough to earn a college degree, and she used her nose to recognize people by their scent.

sensation
The process that detects stimuli from the body or surroundings.

perception
The process that organizes sensations into meaningful patterns.

sensory receptors
Specialized cells that detect stimuli and convert their energy into neural impulses.

sensory transduction
The process by which sensory receptors convert stimuli into neural impulses.

psychophysics
The study of the relationship between the physical characteristics of stimuli and the conscious psychological experiences they produce.

FIGURE 5.1

Sensation and Perception
Do you see anything in this picture?
Though *sensation* lets you see the
pattern of light and dark in the
picture, *perception* lets you organize
what you sense into a meaningful
pattern—a cow looking at you.

1860, devoted the rest of his life to studying the relationship between physical stimulation and mental experiences (D. J. Murray, 1990).

Absolute Threshold

The minimum amount of stimulation that a person can detect is called the **absolute threshold**, or *limen*. For example, a cup of coffee would require a certain amount of sugar before you could detect a sweet taste. Because the absolute threshold for a particular sensory experience varies, psychologists operationally define the absolute threshold as the minimum level of stimulation that can be detected 50 percent of the time when a stimulus is presented over and over. Thus, if you were presented with a low-intensity sound 30 times and you detected it 15 times, that level of intensity would be your absolute threshold for that stimulus. Figure 5.2 shows the absolute thresholds for several everyday sensations.

absolute threshold
The minimum amount of stimulation that an individual can detect through a given sense.

The absolute threshold is also affected by factors other than the intensity of the stimulus. Because of this, researchers have devised **signal-detection theory**, which assumes that the detection of a stimulus depends on both its intensity and the physical and psychological state of the individual. One of the most important psychological factors is the *response bias*—how ready the person is to report the presence of a particular stimulus. Imagine that you are walking down a street at night. Your predisposition to detect a sound would depend, in part, on your estimate of the probability of being mugged, so you would be more likely to perceive the sound of footsteps in a neighborhood you believe to be dangerous than in a neighborhood you believe to be safe.

signal-detection theory
The theory holding that the detection of a stimulus depends on both the intensity of the stimulus and the physical and psychological state of the individual.

Signal-detection researchers study four kinds of reports that a subject might make in response to a stimulus. A *hit* is a correct report of the presence of a target stimulus. A *miss* is a failure to report the presence of a target stimulus that is, in fact, present. A *false alarm* is a report of the presence of a target stimulus that is not, in fact, present. And a *correct rejection* is a correct report of the absence of a target stimulus. Consider these four kinds of reports in regard to walking down a dark street at night. A signal-detection hit would be perceiving footsteps when they actually occur. A miss would be failing to perceive footsteps when they actually occur. A false alarm would be perceiving footsteps when they do not occur. And a correct rejection would be failing to perceive footsteps when they do not occur.

Signal-detection theory has important applications to crucial tasks, such as detecting aircraft blips on radar screens and identifying bombs put through airport X-ray machines. Even pain researchers use signal-detection theory to determine the effects of treatments. For example, some procedures for measuring the effectiveness of treatments

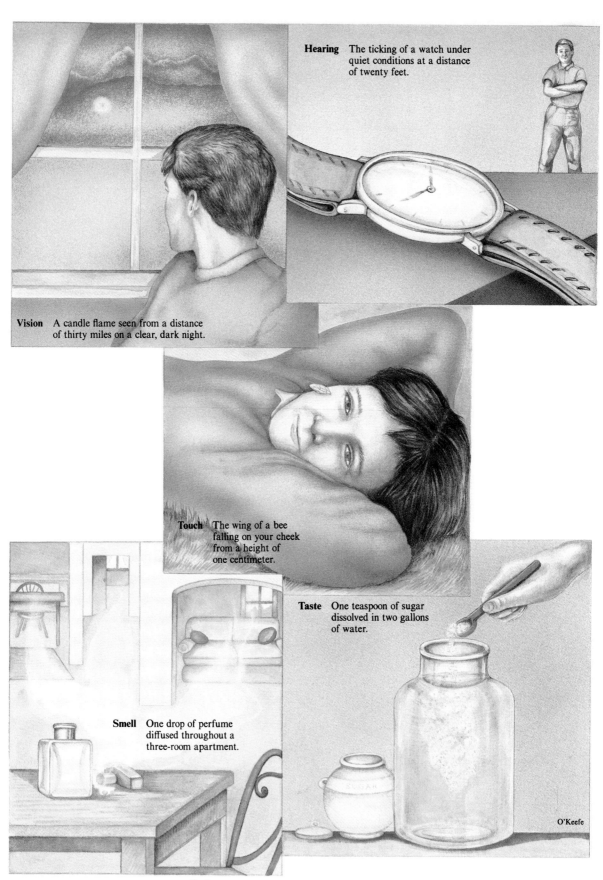

Hearing The ticking of a watch under quiet conditions at a distance of twenty feet.

Vision A candle flame seen from a distance of thirty miles on a clear, dark night.

Touch The wing of a bee falling on your cheek from a height of one centimeter.

Taste One teaspoon of sugar dissolved in two gallons of water.

Smell One drop of perfume diffused throughout a three-room apartment.

O'Keefe

FIGURE 5.2

Absolute Thresholds
These absolute thresholds illustrate the remarkable sensitivity of our senses (Galanter, 1962).

to relieve pain may affect a person's *response bias* more than they affect his or her *sensitivity* to pain (Lloyd & Appel, 1976). This might lead to the mistaken belief that a new pain medication is effective when, in reality, it is not. The proper application of signal-detection theory might prevent that from happening.

Difference Threshold

In addition to detecting the presence of a stimulus, we must be able to detect changes in the intensity of a stimulus. The minimum amount of change in stimulation that can be detected is called the **difference threshold**. For example, a cup of coffee would require a certain amount of additional sugar before you could detect an increase in its sweetness. Similarly, you would have to increase or decrease the intensity of the sound from your compact-disc player a certain amount before you could detect a change in its volume. Like the absolute threshold, the difference threshold for a particular sensory experience varies from person to person and from occasion to occasion. Therefore, psychologists formally define the difference threshold as the minimum change in stimulation that can be detected 50 percent of the time by a given person.

Weber and Fechner referred to the difference threshold as the **just noticeable difference** (jnd). They found that the amount of change in intensity of stimulation needed to produce a jnd is a constant fraction of the original stimulus. This became known as **Weber's law**. For example, because the jnd for weight is about 2 percent, if you held a 50-ounce weight you would notice a change only if there was at least a 1-ounce change in it. But a person holding a 100-ounce weight would require the addition or subtraction of at least 2 ounces to notice a change. Research findings indicate that Weber's law holds better for stimuli of moderate intensity than for stimuli of extremely low or high intensity.

Sensory Adaptation

Given that each of your senses is constantly bombarded by stimulation, why do you notice only certain stimuli? One reason is that if a stimulus remains constant in intensity, you will gradually stop noticing it. For example, after diving into a swimming pool, you might shiver. Yet a few minutes later you might invite someone to join you, saying, "The water's fine." On entering a friend's dormitory room, you might be struck by the repugnant stench of month-old garbage. Yet a few minutes later you might not notice the odor at all. This tendency of our sensory receptors to have decreasing responsiveness to an unchanging stimulus is called **sensory adaptation**.

Sensory adaptation lets us detect potentially important changes in our environment while ignoring unchanging aspects of it. For example, when vibrations repeatedly stimulate your skin, you stop noticing them (Hollins, Delemos, & Goble, 1991). Thus, if you were having a bumpy train ride that made your seat vibrate against your bottom, you would initially notice the vibrations, but it would serve little purpose for you to continue noticing them. Likewise, once you have determined that the swimming pool water is cold or that your friend's room smells, it would serve little purpose to continue noticing those stimuli—especially when more important changes might be taking place elsewhere in your surroundings. Of course, you will not adapt completely to extremely intense sensations, such as severe pain or freezing cold. This is adaptive, because to ignore such stimuli might be harmful or even fatal.

VISION

Because of our reliance on vision, psychologists have conducted more research on it than on all the other senses combined. **Vision** lets us sense objects by the light reflected from them into our eyes. *Light* is the common name for the **visible spectrum**, a narrow band of energy within the *electromagnetic spectrum* (depicted in figure 5.3). The *wavelength* of light corresponds to its *hue*, the perceptual quality that we call color. The wavelength is the distance between two wave peaks, measured in *nanometers* (billionths of a meter).

difference threshold
The minimum amount of change in stimulation that can be detected.

just noticeable difference (jnd)
Weber and Fechner's term for the difference threshold.

Weber's law
The principle that the amount of change in stimulation needed to produce a just noticeable difference is a constant proportion of the original stimulus.

sensory adaptation
The tendency of the sensory receptors to respond less and less to a constant stimulus.

vision
The sense that detects objects by the light reflected from them into the eyes.

visible spectrum
The portion of the electromagnetic spectrum that we commonly call light.

Light varies in wavelength from 380 nanometers to 760 nanometers. A light composed of short wavelengths of light appears violet; a light composed of long wavelengths appears red.

Though human beings have visual receptors that sense only the visible spectrum, certain animals have visual receptors that detect other forms of electromagnetic energy. Some birds and insects have visual receptors that are sensitive to the relatively short wavelengths of *ultraviolet* light (Chen, Collins, & Goldsmith, 1984), which affects human beings chiefly by causing sunburn. Rattlesnakes have receptors located in pits below their eyes that are sensitive to the relatively long wavelengths of *infrared* light, which conveys heat. This lets rattlesnakes hunt at night by detecting the heat emitted by nearby prey (Newman & Hartline, 1982).

Returning to the visible spectrum, the height, or *amplitude*, of light waves determines the perceived *brightness* of a light. When you use a dimmer switch to adjust the brightness of a lightbulb, you change the amplitude of the light waves emitted by the bulb, thereby changing the brightness of the light you see. The *purity* of a light's wavelengths determines its *saturation*, or vividness. The narrower the range of wavelengths, the more saturated the light. A highly saturated red light, for example, would seem "redder" than a less saturated red light.

The Visual System

Vision depends on the interaction of the eyes and the brain. The eyes sense light reflected from objects and convey this information to the brain, where visual perception takes place. But what accounts for this? In the sixth century B.C., the Greek mathematician Pythagoras put forth the "emanation hypothesis," which states that vision depends on the illumination of objects by light beams from the eyes. But if this were so, why would we be blind in the dark? Plato came to the rescue by simply stating that the light beams cannot penetrate darkness. Plato's student Aristotle discounted the emanation hypothesis because he did not believe that eyes have the power to send beams to distant objects, such as the moon and stars. Much later, the Arab scientist Alhazen (ca. 965–1039) countered the emanation theory by proposing that light beams come from the objects we see rather than from the eyes (Riggs, 1985). Now consider what modern research has discovered about the functions of the eyes.

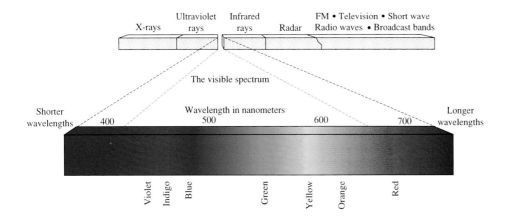

FIGURE 5.3

The Visible Spectrum
The human eye is sensitive to only a narrow slice of the electromagnetic spectrum. This visible spectrum appears in rainbows, when sunlight is broken into its component colors as it passes through raindrops in the atmosphere.

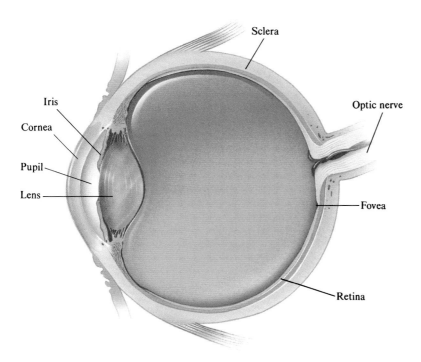

FIGURE 5.4

The Human Eye

The Eye

The *eye* (pictured in figure 5.4) is a fluid-filled sphere. The "white" of your eye is a tough membrane called the **sclera,** which maintains the shape of the eye and protects it from injury. At the front of the sclera is the round, transparent **cornea,** which focuses light into the eye. Are you blue-eyed? brown-eyed? green-eyed? Your eye color is determined by the color of your **iris,** a donut-shaped band of muscles behind the cornea. (Iris was the ancient Greek goddess of the rainbow.) At the center of the iris is an opening called the **pupil.** The iris controls the amount of light that enters the eye by regulating the size of the pupil, dilating it to let in more light and constricting it to let in less. Your pupils dilate when you enter a dimly lit room and constrict when you go outside into sunlight.

You can demonstrate the pupillary response to light by first noting the size of your pupils in your bathroom mirror. Next turn out the light for 30 seconds. Then turn on the light and look in the mirror. Notice how much larger your pupils have become and how quickly they constrict in response to the light.

The size of the pupil is also affected by a variety of psychological factors. When we are psychologically aroused, as when we exert mental effort on a task, the sympathetic nervous system makes our pupils dilate (Beatty, 1982). Because pupil dilation is

sclera
The tough, white outer membrane of the eye.

cornea
The round, transparent area in the front of the sclera that allows light to enter the eye.

iris
The donut-shaped band of muscles behind the cornea that gives the eye its color and controls the size of the pupil.

pupil
The opening at the center of the iris that controls how much light enters the eye.

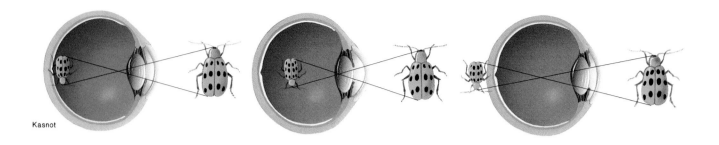

Normal vision
(a)

Myopia
(b)

Hyperopia
(c)

FIGURE 5.5

Visual Acuity
In normal vision, the lens focuses images on the retina. In myopia, the lens focuses images in front of the retina. In hyperopia, the lens focuses images at a point that would fall behind the retina.

a sign of arousal, psychotherapists have used it to monitor the effectiveness of therapy for snake phobia (that is, an intense fear of snakes that interferes with everyday functioning). Changes in pupil size are used to confirm participants' subjective reports of their level of anxiety. As the participants' anxiety decreases, their pupils dilate less when they look at a snake (Sturgeon, Cooper, & Howell, 1989).

The size of our pupils varies not only with our level of anxiety but with our level of interest in a particular stimulus. Merchants in some cultures have traditionally made use of this fact by observing changes in a customer's pupils while bargaining over merchandise. A merchant will ask a higher price for an item that evokes the greatest pupil dilation in a customer (Hess, 1975). Some consumer psychologists have even turned to *pupillometry* to measure the appeal of certain products. Pupillometry uses sophisticated equipment to measure changes in pupil size. But the assumption that the things we find the most *attention-grabbing* are necessarily the things we find the most *appealing* has not received consistent research support (Mudd, Conway, & Schindler, 1990). So, checking the pupils of a potential customer for your used car will not be the best way to set the price.

Regardless of the psychological phenomena associated with the pupil, its primary function is to regulate the amount of light that enters the eye. After passing through the pupil, light is focused by the **lens** onto the **retina**, the light-sensitive inner membrane of the eye. Tiny ciliary muscles connected to the lens control **accommodation**, the process by which the lens increases its curvature to focus light from close objects or decreases its curvature to focus light from distant objects. This was demonstrated in 1801 by the English physicist Thomas Young (1773–1829). Prior to that, the accepted scientific wisdom was that accommodation depended on changes in the shape of the cornea or eyeball (Riggs, 1985).

Disruption of normal accommodation has important effects. One of the reasons why it is dangerous to drink and drive is that alcohol impairs accommodation, causing blurred vision (Miller, Pigion, & Martin, 1985). As we age, the lens loses its elasticity, making it less able to accommodate when focusing on near objects (Fukuda, Kanada, & Saito, 1990). Many adults discover this in their early forties, when they find themselves holding books and newspapers at arm's length to focus the print more clearly on their retinas. This is correctable by the use of reading glasses.

Many people, whether young or old, have conditions that make them unable to focus clear images on the retina. The two most common conditions are illustrated in figure 5.5. In **myopia**, or *nearsightedness*, the lens focuses images of near objects on the retina, but focuses images of far objects at a point in front of the retina. In **hyperopia**,

lens
The transparent structure behind the pupil that focuses light onto the retina.

retina
The light-sensitive inner membrane of the eye that contains the receptor cells for vision.

accommodation
The process by which the thickness of the lens in the eye changes to focus images of objects located at different distances from the eye.

myopia
Visual nearsightedness, which is caused by an elongated eyeball.

hyperopia
Visual farsightedness, which is caused by a shortened eyeball.

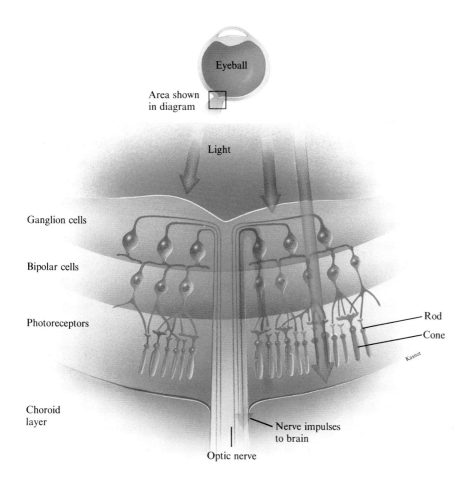

Eyeball

Area shown
in diagram

Light

Ganglion cells

Bipolar cells

Photoreceptors

——Rod

——Cone

Kasnot

Choroid
layer

Nerve impulses
to brain

Optic nerve

FIGURE 5.6

The Cells of the Retina
Light must first pass through layers of
ganglion cells and bipolar cells before
striking the rods and cones. Neural
impulses from the rods and cones are
transmitted to the bipolar cells,
which, in turn, transmit neural
impulses to the ganglion cells. The
axons of the ganglion cells form the
optic nerves, which transmit neural
impulses to the brain.

or *farsightedness*, the lens focuses images of far objects on the retina, but focuses images
of near objects at a point that would fall behind the retina. Both of these conditions are
easily corrected with prescription eyeglasses or contact lenses that make images focus on
the retina.

Today we know that the image cast on the retina is upside down. In the fifteenth
century, Leonardo da Vinci (1452–1519) had rejected this possibility, because he could
not explain how the brain saw a right-side-up world from an upside-down image. So he
assumed that the image was refracted twice in the eye, first inverting and then reverting,
making it appear right side up on the retina (Riggs, 1985). In the early seventeenth
century, René Descartes (1596–1650) went a step further by studying the question
empirically. He scraped the back of a cow eyeball until it was thin enough to be transparent and found that images of scenes focused on the retina were, contrary to da Vinci's
belief, upside down. But why, then, do we not see the world upside down? The neural
pathways in the brain simply "flip" the image to make it appear right side up.

It took centuries for scientists to discover how the retinal image is transmitted to
the brain. As shown in figure 5.6, the retina contains cells called *photoreceptors*, which
respond when stimulated by light. The photoreceptors were first identified in the nineteenth century by scientist Heinrich Müller (1820–1864), with the use of a microscope
(Riggs, 1985). There are two kinds of photoreceptors, **rods** and **cones**, whose names

rods
*Receptor cells of the retina that play an
important role in night vision and
peripheral vision.*

cones
*Receptor cells of the retina that play an
important role in daylight vision and color
vision.*

optic nerve
The nerve formed from the axons of ganglion cells that carries visual impulses from the retina to the brain.

reflect their shapes. Each eye has about 120 million rods and about 6 million cones. The rods and cones stimulate *bipolar cells,* which in turn stimulate *ganglion cells.* The axons of the ganglion cells form the **optic nerves,** which convey visual information to the brain.

While the rods are especially important in night vision and peripheral vision, the cones are especially important in color vision and detailed vision. Rod vision and cone vision depend on different pathways in the brain (Shapley, 1990). The rods are more prevalent in the periphery of the retina, and the cones are more prevalent in the center. You can demonstrate this for yourself by taking small pieces of colored paper and selecting one without looking at it. Hold it beside your head, and slowly move it forward while staring straight ahead. Because your peripheral vision depends on your rods and your color vision depends on your cones, you will notice the paper before you can identify its color.

fovea
A small area at the center of the retina that contains only cones and provides the most acute vision.

A small area in the center of the retina, the **fovea,** contains only cones. One reason why people differ in their visual acuity is that they vary in the number of cones in their fovea (Curcio et al., 1987). Because the fovea provides our most acute vision, we try to focus images on it when we want to see fine details. As you read this sentence, words focused on your cone-rich fovea look clear. Meanwhile, words focused on the cone-poor area around your fovea look blurred. One reason foveal vision is more acute is that each cone transmits neural impulses to one bipolar cell. This means that the exact retinal site of input from a given rod is communicated along the visual pathway. In contrast, neural impulses from an average of fifty rods are sent to a given bipolar cell (Cicerone & Hayhoe, 1990). Thus, the exact retinal site of stimulation of a given rod is lost. But in dim light the many rods sending their output to a given bipolar cell help make rod vision more sensitive than cone vision.

smooth pursuit movements
Eye movements that track objects.

To keep objects focused on the fovea, we use two kinds of eye movements: *smooth pursuit movements* and *saccadic movements.* **Smooth pursuit movements** help our eyes track moving objects. One of the dangers of drinking and driving is that alcohol disrupts smooth pursuit movements (Burns & Moskowitz, 1989–1990). The following study illustrates how scientists study these movements.

Anatomy of a Contemporary Research Study:
Can Batters Really Keep Their Eyes on the Ball?

Rationale
Professional athletes make faster smooth pursuit movements with their eyes than amateurs do (Harbin, Durst, & Harbin, 1989). This is important because, for example, a professional baseball batter might have to track a baseball thrown by a pitcher at more than 90 miles an hour from a distance of only 60 feet. Ted Williams, arguably the greatest hitter in the history of baseball, called hitting a baseball the most difficult single task in any sport. Given this, is there any scientific support for the commonsense suggestion to batters, "Keep your eye on the ball"? Let's look at a study by Terry Bahill and Tom LaRitz (1984), of the University of Arizona, in which they sought the answer to this question.

Method
Bahill and LaRitz rigged a device that propelled a ball toward home plate along a string at up to 100 miles an hour on a consistent path. A photoelectric device recorded the batter's eye movements as he tracked the ball. Several professional baseball players took part in the study.

Results and Discussion
Eye-movement recordings indicated that the batters were able to track the ball until it was about 5 feet from home plate. Over the last few feet they could not keep the ball focused on their foveae—it simply traveled too fast over those last few degrees of visual arc. Thus, the commonsense advice to keep your eye on the ball is well intentioned, but it is impossible to follow the ball's movement all the way from the pitcher's hand to home plate. The reason some hitters, including Ted Williams, claim that they can see the ball strike the bat is that, based on their extensive experience in batting, their brains automatically calculate both the speed and the trajectory of the ball. This allows them to anticipate the point in space where the bat will meet the ball, and make a final eye movement to the exact point at which the bat will meet the ball.

Keep Your Eye on the Ball?
A commonsense piece of advice given to baseball batters is to "keep your eye on the ball" as the ball travels all the way from the pitcher's hand until it hits the bat. Scientific research indicates that this might be impossible.

"You have a choice of three courses. You could increase speed somewhat and retain your comprehension, you could increase speed considerably and reduce comprehension, or you could increase speed tremendously and eliminate comprehension completely."

As you scan a scene, such as this page, your eyes make continuous darting movements. These **saccadic movements** bring new portions of scenes into focus on your foveae. After each saccadic movement, the eyes fixate on a target for about a quarter of a second (Rayner et al., 1983). We pick up visual information only during these fixations. Golfers who are excellent putters make more-efficient use of saccadic movements while putting than do those who are poor putters (Vickers, 1992).

saccadic movements
Continuous small darting movements of the eyes that bring new portions of scenes into focus on the foveae.

The time needed to make saccadic movements and to extract information during fixations limits the fastest readers to a maximum of 1,000 words a minute—a phenomenal rate. Yet some "speed-reading" programs claim that they can increase your reading speed to 10,000 words a minute. How do they do so? By teaching you to skim what you read. Though skimming increases the rate at which you turn pages, it also hurts your comprehension of what you read (Homa, 1983).

The retinal images of the words you read, or of any object on which your eyes are focused, are coded as neural impulses sent to the brain along the optic nerves. In the seventeenth century, the French scientist Edmé Mariotte demonstrated the existence of the *blind spot*, the point at which the optic nerve leaves the eye (Riggs, 1985). He placed a small disk on a screen, closed one eye, stared at the disk, and moved his head until the image of the disk disappeared. It disappeared when it fell on the blind spot. The blind spot is "blind" because it contains no rods or cones. To repeat Mariotte's demonstration, follow the procedure suggested in figure 5.7.

The Brain

Figure 5.8 traces the path of neural impulses from the eyeballs into the brain. Descartes believed, wrongly, that each eye sent an image to its own hemisphere of the brain, which then relayed it to the pineal gland, where the two images were combined into one. We now know that the optic nerves travel under the frontal lobes of the brain and meet at a point called the **optic chiasm**. (*Chiasm* comes from the Greek word for X.) At the optic chiasm in human beings, axons from the half of each optic nerve toward the nose cross to the opposite side of the brain. Axons from the half of each optic nerve nearer the ears travel to the same side of the brain as they began on. As shown in the drawing in figure 5.9, Isaac Newton hypothesized, and he was perhaps the first to do so, that visual information traveled along these pathways to reach the brain (Riggs, 1985). Some axons of the optic nerves go to the *tectum* (see chapter 3) of the midbrain, which controls vision reflexes like blinking. Most axons of the optic nerves go to the *thalamus* (see chapter 3), which transmits visual information to the **visual cortex** of the *occipital lobes*. Retinal

optic chiasm
The point under the frontal lobes at which some axons from each of the optic nerves cross over to the opposite side of the brain.

visual cortex
The area of the occipital lobes that processes visual input.

FIGURE 5.7

Finding Your Blind Spot
Because your retina has no rods or cones at the point where the optic nerve leaves the eye, your retina is "blind" at that spot. To find your blind spot, hold this book at arm's length, close your right eye, and focus your left eye on the black dot. Move the book slowly toward you. When the book is about a foot away, the image of the ladybug should disappear. It disappears when it becomes focused on your blind spot. You do not normally notice your blind spot because your eyes see different views of the same scene, your eyes are constantly focusing on different parts of the scene, and your brain fills in missing details of the scene.

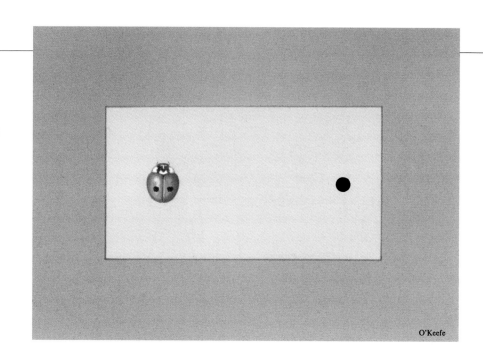

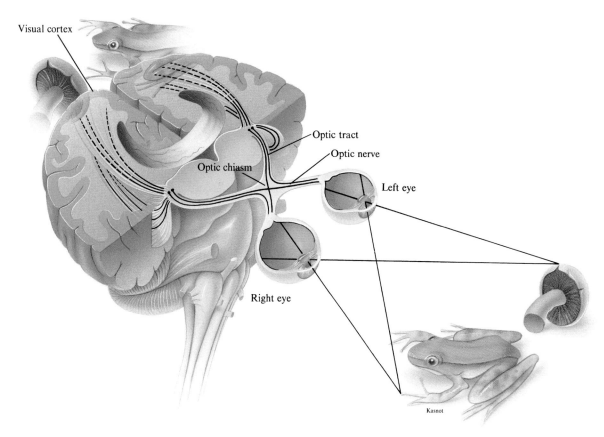

FIGURE 5.8

The Visual Pathway
Images of objects in the right visual field are focused on the left side of each retina, and images of objects in the left visual field are focused on the right side of each retina. This information is conveyed along the optic nerves to the optic chiasm and then on to the thalamus. The thalamus then relays the information to the visual cortex of the occipital lobes. Note that images of objects in the right visual field are processed by the left occipital lobe and images of objects in the left visual field are processed by the right occipital lobe.

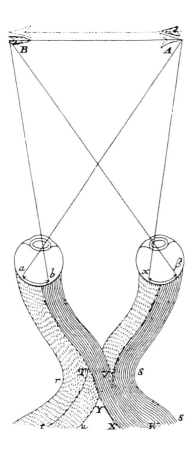

FIGURE 5.9

Newton's Drawing of the Visual
Pathways
Sir Isaac Newton had good knowledge
of the visual pathways of the brain.

information about objects in the right visual field is processed in the left occipital lobe, and retinal information about objects in the left visual field is processed in the right occipital lobe. The visual cortex integrates visual information about objects, including their shape, color, distance, and movement (Livingstone & Hubel, 1988).

Because the visual cortex is covered by a "map" with a point-by-point representation of the retinas, people who have gone blind because of damage to their eyes or optic nerves may someday have their vision restored by devices that directly stimulate the visual cortex. Researchers have invented an electronic system that consists of a video camera connected to a microprocessor, which in turn is connected to a matrix of sixty-four electrodes attached to the visual cortex. Stimulation of these electrodes produces a pattern of spots of light called *phosphenes* that can be used to represent the outlines of objects seen by the camera. In initial demonstrations, blind people who used the device recognized common objects, including letters (Dobelle et al., 1976). Perhaps more sophisticated devices will one day permit blind people to use vision to read textbooks, paint pictures, and drive automobiles.

Visual Sensation

People with normal vision can see because of processes taking place in their retinas. Visual sensations depend on chemicals called **photopigments**. Rod vision depends on the photopigment *rhodopsin*, and cone vision depends on three kinds of photopigments called *iodopsin*. Until the late nineteenth century, when the role of photopigments was first discovered, prominent scientists, including Thomas Young, claimed that vision depended on light rays striking the retina, making the optic nerves vibrate (Riggs, 1985). Note how much that explanation owed to Isaac Newton's hypothesis about nerve function, discussed in chapter 3.

Today we know that when light strikes the rods or cones it breaks down their photopigments. The breakdown of photopigments begins the process by which neural

photopigments
Chemicals, including rhodopsin and iodopsin, that enable the rods and cones to generate neural impulses.

FIGURE 5.10

Dark Adaptation
When you enter a dark room, your photoreceptors adapt by becoming more sensitive to light. The cones reach their maximum sensitivity in about 10 minutes, and the rods reach their maximum sensitivity in about 30 minutes. Though the cones adapt to the dark faster than the rods do, the rods become more sensitive than the cones. This means that the absolute threshold of the rods becomes much lower than that of the cones.

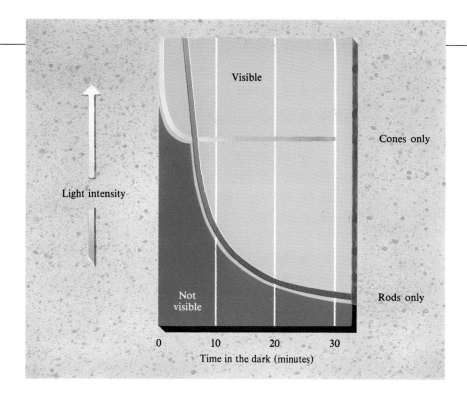

impulses are eventually sent along the auditory nerves to the brain. After being broken down by light, the photopigments are resynthesized—more rapidly in dim light than in bright light. The cones function better than the rods in normal light, but the rods function better than the cones in dim light. Because of this, in normal light we try to focus fine details on the fovea. But if you were to look directly at a star in the night sky, you would be unable to see it because it would be focused on the fovea. To see the star, you would have to turn your head slightly, thereby focusing the star on the rod-rich periphery of the retina. The photoreceptors are also important in the processes of *dark adaptation* and *color vision*.

Dark Adaptation

When you enter a darkened movie theater, you have difficulty finding a seat because your photoreceptors have been bleached of their photopigments by the light in the lobby. But your eyes adapt by increasing their rate of synthesis of iodopsin and rhodopsin, gradually increasing your ability to see the seats and people in the theater. The cones reach their maximum sensitivity after about 10 minutes of dim light. But your rods continue to adapt to the dim light, reaching their maximum sensitivity in about 30 minutes. So, you owe your ability to see in dim light to your rods. Figure 5.10 illustrates the changes that take place during **dark adaptation**, the process by which the eyes become more sensitive to light. Impaired dark adaptation, which accompanies aging, has been implicated in the disproportionate number of night driving accidents that involve older adults (Mortimer & Fell, 1989).

The preceding discussion explains why motorists should dim their high beams when approaching oncoming traffic and why passengers should not turn on the dome light to read maps. High beams shining into the eyes or dome lights illuminating the inside of the vehicle bleach the rods, impairing the driver's ability to the see objects that might be ahead. You should also note that the cones are most sensitive to the longer wavelengths of the visible spectrum (which produce the experience of red), and the rods are most sensitive to the medium wavelengths (which produce the experience of green). This explains why at dusk (when we shift from cone vision to rod vision) a red jacket looks dull while a patch of green grass looks vibrant.

dark adaptation
The process by which the eyes become more sensitive to light when under low illumination.

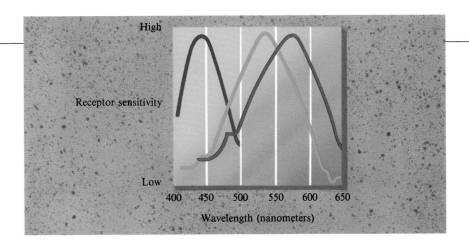

FIGURE 5.11

Relative Sensitivity of the Cones
Each of the three kinds of cones (blue, green, and red) responds to a wide range of wavelengths of light. But each is maximally sensitive to particular wavelengths. The blue cones are maximally sensitive to short wavelengths, the green cones to medium wavelengths, and the red cones to long wavelengths. According to the trichromatic theory, the perceived color of a light depends on the relative amount of activity in each of the three kinds of cones.

Color Vision

Color enhances the quality of our lives, as manifested by our concern with the colors of our clothes, furnishings, and automobiles. Primates such as apes, monkeys, and human beings have good color vision. Most other mammals, including dogs, cats, and cows, have little or no color vision. They lack a sufficient number of cones. Most birds and fish have good color vision. But fish that live in the dark depths of the ocean lack color vision, which would be useless to them because cones function well only in bright light (Levine & MacNichol, 1982).

What processes account for color vision? One answer was offered in 1802 when British physicist Thomas Young presented the **trichromatic theory** of color vision, which was championed in the 1850s by German scientist Hermann von Helmholtz (1821–1894). Helmholtz has been called "the last universal scientist," because he was a physicist, physiologist, and psychologist. His classic three-volume work on vision, the *Treatise on Physiological Optics* (Helmholtz, 1866/1962), exemplifies his scientific breadth; it tackles the physics, physiology, and psychology of vision. Helmholtz even invented the *ophthalmoscope*, which is still used today by physicians for examining the inside of the eye. Young and Helmholtz found that red, green, and blue lights could be mixed into any color, leading them to conclude that the input of three receptors was pooled by the brain. Today the trichromatic theory is also called the *Young-Helmholtz theory*. It assumes that the retina has three kinds of receptors (which we now know are cones) that are maximally sensitive to red, green, or blue light.

A century after Helmholtz put forth his theory, George Wald (1964) provided evidence for it in research that earned him a Nobel prize. Wald found that some cones responded maximally to red light, others to green light, and still others to blue light (see figure 5.11). The colors we experience depend on the relative degree of stimulation of the cones. Figure 5.12 illustrates the principles of mixing colored lights and mixing colored pigments, which differ from each other. Mixing colored lights is an *additive* process: Wavelengths added together stimulate more cones. Mixing red light and green light produces yellow. Mixing pigments is a *subtractive* process: Pigments mixed together absorb more wavelengths than does a single pigment. Mixing blue paint and yellow paint subtracts those colors and leaves green to be reflected into the eyes.

In the 1870s, the German physiologist Ewald Hering (1834–1918) proposed an alternative explanation of color vision, the **opponent-process theory**. He did so, in part, to explain the phenomenon of **afterimages**—images that persist after the removal of a visual stimulus. If you stare at a red or blue surface for a minute and then stare at a white surface, you will see an afterimage that is the complementary color. For example, staring at red will produce a green afterimage, and staring at blue will produce a yellow afterimage. You can experience an afterimage by following the instructions in figure 5.13.

The opponent-process theory assumes that there are *red-green, blue-yellow,* and *black-white* opponent processes (with the black-white opponent process determining the

A Green Fire Truck?
Because the rods are more sensitive to the green region of the visible spectrum than to the red region, green objects look brighter in dim light than do red objects. So, though red fire trucks look bright in the daylight, they look grayish in dim light. This has led some fire departments to increase the evening visibility of their trucks by painting them a yellowish green color.

Are Bulls Infuriated by Red Capes?
Because bulls are color blind, the red cape waved by matadors is used only for dramatic effect—a bull will charge a cape of any color.

trichromatic theory
The theory that color vision depends on the relative degree of stimulation of red, green, and blue receptors.

opponent-process theory
The theory that color vision depends on red-green, blue-yellow, and black-white opponent processes in the brain.

afterimage
A visual image that persists after the removal of a stimulus.

FIGURE 5.12

Color Mixing
In additive mixing, lights of different colors are combined. As you can see, (*a*) mixing red, green, and blue lights of equal intensity yields white. In subtractive mixing, pigments of different colors are combined. Because each color absorbs certain wavelengths of light, (*b*) mixing red, yellow, and blue pigments of equal intensity yields black.

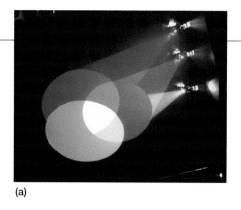

(a)

(b)

FIGURE 5.13

Color Afterimages
Stare at the dot in the center of the flag for at least 30 seconds. Then stare at a sheet of white paper. You should see an afterimage of the American flag with its normal red, white, and blue colors. These colors are complementary to those of the green, black, and yellow flag. Such complementary afterimages support the opponent-process theory of color vision.

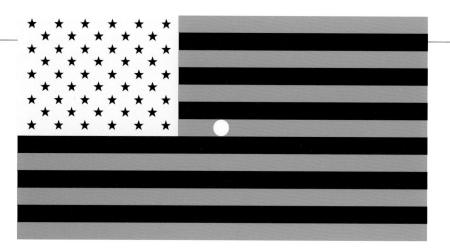

color blindness
The inability to distinguish between certain colors, most often red and green.

lightness or darkness of what we see). Stimulation of one process inhibits its opponent. When stimulation stops, the inhibition is removed and the complementary color is seen as a brief afterimage. This explains why staring at red leads to a green afterimage and staring at blue leads to a yellow afterimage, and why we cannot perceive reddish greens or bluish yellows. Complementary colors cannot be experienced simultaneously because each inhibits the other.

Psychologist Russell de Valois and his colleagues (1966) provided evidence that supports the opponent-process theory. For example, certain ganglion cells in the retina and certain cells in the thalamus send impulses when the cones that send them input are stimulated by red and stop sending impulses when the cones that send them input are stimulated by the complementary color of green. Other ganglion cells and cells in the thalamus send impulses when the cones that send them input are stimulated by green and stop sending impulses when the cones that send them input are stimulated by red. There is stronger evidence for red-green and blue-yellow opponent processes than for a black-white opponent process (Sokolov & Izmailov, 1988).

The opponent-process theory also explains another phenomenon that the trichromatic theory cannot explain by itself: **color blindness**. People with normal color vision are *trichromats*—they have three kinds of iodopsin (red, blue, and green). Most color-blind people are *dichromats*—they lack one kind of iodopsin (Cicerone & Nerger, 1989). The most common form of color blindness is the inability to distinguish between red and green. People with red-green color blindness have cones with blue iodopsin, but their red and green cones have the same iodopsin, usually green. Because many people suffer from red-green color blindness, traffic lights always have the red light on top so that color-blind people will know when to stop and when to go. See if you can pass the item from a color-blindness test in figure 5.14.

Sunday Afternoon on the Island of La Grande Jatte
The late-nineteenth-century postimpressonist French painter Georges Seurat used a technique called pointillism, which involves painting with tiny dots of paint instead of brush strokes. By placing dots of complementary colors next to each other, Seurat made his colors more vibrant. When viewed from a distance, the dots become indistinct and even create hues that are mixtures of the complementary colors.

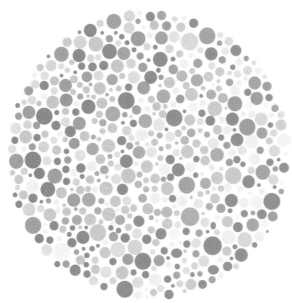

FIGURE **5.14**

Testing for Color Blindness
A person with red-green color blindness might fail to see the number in this pattern. A complete test of color blindness would present a series of patterns like this one.

This has been reproduced from Ishihara's Tests for Colour Blindness published by Kanehara & Co., Ltd., Tokyo, Japan, but tests for color blindness cannot be conducted with this material. For accurate testing, the original plates should be used.

Christine Ladd-Franklin (1847–1930)
"The color sense is now in the third stage of its evolution. In the first stage the only elements were white and black; the second stage added yellow and blue; and the third stage, red and green."

Because color blindness is a recessive trait carried on the X chromosome, males are more likely than females to be color blind. This means that a male who inherits the trait on his single X chromosome will be color blind. In contrast, a female must inherit the trait on *both* of her X chromosomes to be color blind (Mollon, 1982). Few dichromats have blue-yellow color blindness. And even fewer people are *monochromats*—completely color blind.

Christine Ladd-Franklin (1847–1930), introduced in chapter 1, believed color blindness revealed the influence of evolution. She reasoned that red-green color blindness occurs most often because red-green color vision evolved more recently than blue-yellow, making red-green color vision more fragile (Ladd-Franklin, 1929). But how does color blindness support the opponent-process theory? It does so because, though dichromats cannot distinguish between the complementary colors of red and green or blue and yellow, they never fail to distinguish between red and blue, red and yellow, green and blue, or green and yellow.

James J. Gibson (1904–1979)
"Eyes evolved so as to see the world, not a picture. Since this became clear to me I have tried to give up any use whatever of the term 'retinal image'. The assumption that there is a picture on the retina has led to all sorts of unnecessary and insoluble problems, problems for psychology, art, and optics. . . . I now assume that perception does not depend on sensory impressions at all, but instead only on the pickup of stimulus information."

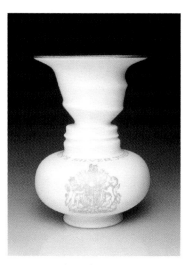

FIGURE **5.15**

Figure-Ground Perception
As you view this picture you will note that it seems to reverse. At one moment you see a vase, and at the next you see the profiles of two faces. What you see depends on what you perceive as figure and what you perceive as ground.

figure-ground perception
The distinguishing of an object (the figure) from its surroundings (the ground).

feature-detector theory
The view that we construct our perceptions from neurons of the brain that are sensitive to specific features of stimuli.

Today the trichromatic theory and the opponent-process theory are combined in explaining color vision this way (Boynton, 1988): Impulses from the red, green, and blue cones of the retina are sent to the opponent-process ganglion cells and then further integrated in the thalamus and visual cortex.

Visual Perception

Visual sensations provide the raw materials that are organized into meaningful patterns by *visual perception*. Do we have to learn through experience to convert sensations into accurate perceptions? This is the basic assumption of the *constructionist theory* of Hermann von Helmholtz. Or, instead, does visual perception depend mainly on inborn mechanisms that automatically convert sensations into perceptions of stimuli? This is the basic assumption of the *ecological theory* of James J. Gibson (1904–1979). According to Gibson (1979), evolution has endowed us with brain mechanisms that create perceptions directly from information provided by the sense organs, without the need for experience to help us interpret the information. Recent research, discussed in chapter 4, on the sophisticated inborn perceptual abilities of newborn infants supports Gibson's theory. Nonetheless, perception researchers have traditionally believed that we "construct" our perceptions based on what Helmholtz called *unconscious inferences* that we make from our sensations (Cutting, 1987). These inferences are based on our experience with objects in the physical environment.

Form Perception

To perceive *forms* (meaningful shapes or patterns) we must distinguish a *figure* (an object) from its *ground* (its surroundings). Gestalt psychologist Edgar Rubin (1886–1951) called this **figure-ground perception**. For example, the words on this page are figures against the ground of the white paper. Gestalt psychologists stress that form perception is an active, rather than a passive, process. Your expectancies might affect what you see in an ambiguous figure, for instance (Davis, Schiffman, & Greis-Bousquet, 1990). If you were first shown pictures of pottery, you would be more likely to perceive a vase if you were then shown figure 5.15; if you were first shown pictures of faces, you would be more likely to perceive two profiles. The idea that our expectations impose themselves on sensations to form perceptions (so-called *top-down processing*) runs counter to the idea that we construct our perceptions by mechanically combining sensations (so-called *bottom-up* processing).

Gestalt psychologists, including Max Wertheimer, Kurt Koffka, and Wolfgang Kohler, were the first to study the formal principles that govern form perception. The principle of *proximity* states that stimuli that are close together tend to be perceived as parts of the same form. The principle of *closure* states that we tend to fill in gaps in forms that we perceive. The principle of *similarity* states that stimuli that are similar to one another tend to be perceived as parts of the same form. The principle of *continuity* states that we tend to group stimuli into forms that follow continuous lines or patterns. Three of these principles are illustrated in figure 5.16.

According to Gestalt psychologists, forms are perceived as wholes, rather than as combinations of component features. This might prompt you to recall the famous Gestalt saying, mentioned in chapter 1, that "the whole is different from the sum of its parts." Thus, in figure 5.17 you see an image of an elephant rather than a bunch of black marks. Though some research findings support the Gestalt position that forms are perceived holistically (Navon, 1974), other research findings suggest that forms can be perceived through the analysis of their features (Oden, 1984).

Consider the letter A. Do we perceive it holistically as a single shape, or analytically as a combination of lines of various lengths and angles? Gestalt psychologists would assume that we perceive it holistically. But the **feature-detector theory** of David Hubel and Torsten Wiesel (1979) assumes that we construct it from its component lines and angles. Hubel and Wiesel base their theory on studies in which they implanted microelectrodes into single cells of the visual cortex of cats and then presented them

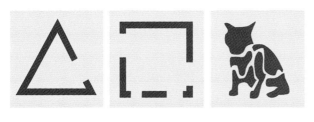

(a)

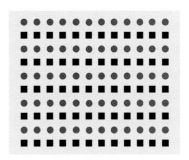

FIGURE **5.16**

Gestalt Principles of Form Perception
These patterns illustrate the roles of (*a*) closure, (*b*) proximity, and (*c*) similarity in form perception.

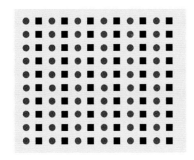

(b)

(c)

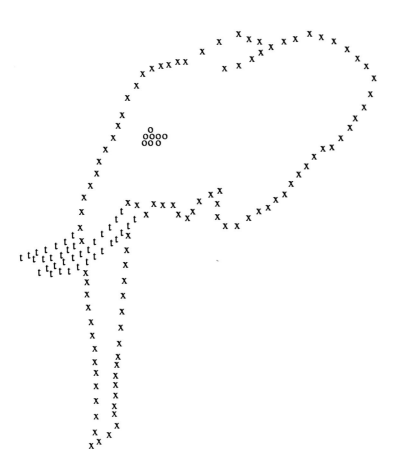

FIGURE **5.17**

The Whole Is Different from the Sum of Its Parts
According to Gestalt psychologists, you see a picture of an elephant instead of a random grouping of marks because your brain imposes organization on what it perceives. Your perception of the elephant depends on each of the Gestalt principles of similarity, proximity, closure, and continuity. As discussed later in this chapter, your perception of the elephant also depends on your prior experience. A person from a culture unfamiliar with elephants might fail to perceive the marks as a meaningful form.

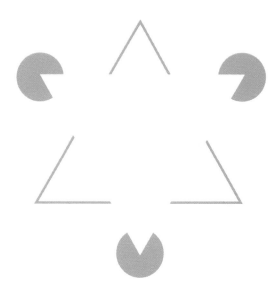

FIGURE 5.18

Illusory Contours
Seeing a complete triangle when only its corners exist is an example of the Gestalt principle of closure. Feature-detector cells in the visual cortex respond to such illusory contours as if they were real. This supports the Gestalt position that the brain imposes organization on stimuli.

FIGURE 5.19

Spatial Frequency Analysis
Squint your eyes and focus on the photo on the right. It will look more like the one on the left. Squinting filters out certain high spatial frequencies, leaving lower ones.

David Hubel and Torsten Wiesel
Hubel and Wiesel are shown celebrating the Nobel prize they won for their research on visual feature detectors in the brain.

illusory contours
The perception of edges that do not actually exist, as though they were the outlines of real objects.

spatial frequency filter theory
The theory that visual perception depends on the detection and analysis of variations in patterns of light and dark.

depth perception
The perception of the relative distance of objects.

binocular cues
Depth perception cues that require input from the two eyes.

with lines of various sizes, orientations, and locations. Certain cells responded to specific features of images on the retina, such as a line of a certain length, a line at a certain angle, or a line in a particular location. Hubel and Wiesel concluded that we construct our visual perceptions from activity in such *feature-detector cells*. For their efforts, Hubel and Wiesel won a Nobel prize in 1981.

Some feature-detector cells in the visual cortex respond to remarkably specific combinations of features. As noted in chapter 3, different cells in the visual cortex of sheep respond to the faces of sheep, sheepdogs, or human beings (Kendrick & Baldwin, 1987). Feature-detector cells in the visual cortex even provide an anatomical basis for the **illusory contours** shown in figure 5.18, responding to nonexistent contours as if they were the edges of real objects (von der Heydt, Peterhans, & Baumgartner, 1984).

An alternative to the feature-detector theory of pattern perception is the **spatial frequency filter theory**. It holds that perception depends not on constructing figures from lines, curves, and angles, but rather on the detection and analysis of variations in patterns of light and dark (de Valois & de Valois, 1980). Highly detailed figures will have narrow (high-frequency) bands of light and dark; less-detailed figures will have wider (low-frequency) bands of light and dark. These variations in light and dark bands are called *spatial frequencies* and are illustrated in figure 5.19. Certain neurons in the visual cortex respond to patterns with wide bands and others respond to patterns with narrow bands (Foley, 1988).

Depth Perception

If we lived in a two-dimensional world, form perception would be sufficient. Because we live in a three-dimensional world, we have evolved **depth perception**—the ability to judge the distance of objects. Consider the importance of depth perception to aircraft pilots. In a study conducted by the U.S. Coast Guard, helicopter pilots tried to obtain four target altitudes between 25 and 200 feet without the use of an altimeter. They either ascended from the ground or descended from 500 feet, over both land and water. The pilots tended to be inaccurate, especially when descending. You can imagine the danger this would pose when landing a helicopter or maneuvering it above objects (Ungs & Sangal, 1990).

Given that images on the retina (such as the image of a helicopter landing pad) are two-dimensional, how can we perceive depth? That is, how can we determine the distance of an object (the *distal stimulus*) from the pattern of stimulation on our retinas (the *proximal stimulus*)? Researchers in the tradition of Helmholtz's constructionist theory maintain that depth perception depends on the use of *binocular cues* and *monocular cues*. The two kinds of **binocular cues** require the interaction of both eyes. One binocular cue is *retinal disparity*, the degree of difference between the images of an object that are focused on the two retinas. The closer the object, the greater the retinal disparity. To demonstrate retinal disparity for yourself, point a forefinger vertically between your eyes. Look at the finger with one eye closed. Then look at it with the other closed. You will notice that the background shifts as you view the scene with different eyes. This demonstrates that the two eyes provide different views of the same stimulus. The "Viewmaster" device you might have used as a child creates the impression of visual depth by presenting slightly different images to the eyes at the same time—mimicking retinal disparity. Retinal disparity is greater when an object is near you than when it is farther away from you. Certain cells in the visual cortex detect the degree of retinal disparity, which the brain uses to estimate the distance of an object focused on the retinas (DeAngelis, Ohzawa, & Freeman, 1991).

The second binocular cue to depth is *convergence*, the degree to which the eyes turn inward to focus on an object. As you can confirm for yourself, the closer the object, the greater the convergence of the eyes. Hold a forefinger vertically in front of your face and move it toward your nose. You should notice an increase in ocular muscle tension as your finger approaches your nose. Neurons in the cerebral cortex translate the amount of muscle tension into an estimate of the distance of your finger (Takagi et al., 1992). Convergence is associated with important everyday activities. For example, drinking alcohol impairs depth perception by disrupting the normal convergence of the eyes (Stapleton, Guthrie, & Linnoila, 1986), and using a computer terminal for hours induces eye fatigue caused by continuous convergence (Tyrrell & Leibowitz, 1990).

Binocular cues require two eyes, whereas **monocular cues** require only one. This means that even people who have lost sight in one eye may still have good depth perception. One monocular cue is *accommodation*, which, as explained earlier, is the change in the shape of the lens that lets you focus the image of an object on the retina. Neurons in the tectum assume that the greater the accommodation of the lens, the closer the object (Judge & Cumming, 1986). But prolonged accommodation can alter your depth perception. For example, if you stare at a near object for a long time and then look at a more distant object, the more distant object will look farther away than it is. This is attributable to the brain's overcompensation for the continuous accommodation of the lens while it was focused on the near object (Fisher & Ciuffreda, 1989).

A second monocular cue is *motion parallax*, the tendency to perceive ourselves as passing objects faster when they are closer to us than when they are farther away. You will notice this when you drive on a rural road. You perceive yourself passing nearby telephone poles faster than you are passing a distant farmhouse. Animal research indicates that particular brain cells might respond to motion parallax. For example, the cat's brain has cells whose firing rate varies with the degree of motion parallax (Mandl, 1985).

The remaining monocular cues are called *pictorial cues* because artists use them to create depth in their drawings and paintings. Figure 5.20 depicts several pictorial cues. Leonardo da Vinci formalized pictorial cues 500 years ago in teaching his art students how to use them to make their paintings look more realistic (Haber, 1980). He noted that an object that overlaps another object will appear closer, a cue called *interposition*. Because your psychology professor overlaps the blackboard, you know that she or he is closer to you than the blackboard is. Comparing the *relative size* of objects also provides a cue to their distance. If two people are about the same height and one casts a smaller image on your retina, you will perceive that person as farther away.

You probably have noticed that parallel objects, such as railroad tracks, seem to get closer together as they get farther away (and farther apart as they get closer). This pictorial cue, *linear perspective*, may even have practical applications. During World War II, naval aviation cadets flying at night sometimes crashed into airplanes ahead of them, apparently because of a failure to judge the distance of those planes. The problem was solved by taking advantage of linear perspective. The traditional single taillight was replaced by two taillights set a standard distance apart. As a result, when pilots noticed that the taillights of an airplane appeared to move farther apart, they realized that they were getting closer to it (Fiske, Conley, & Goldberg, 1987).

monocular cues
Depth perception cues that require input from only one eye.

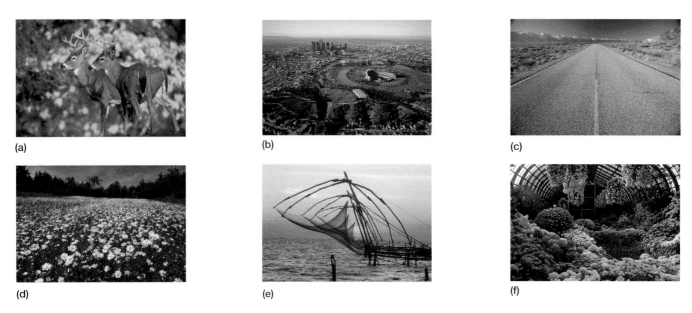

(a) (b) (c)

(d) (e) (f)

FIGURE 5.20

Pictorial Cues to Depth
Artists make use of pictorial cues to portray depth in their drawings and paintings. These cues include (*a*) interposition, (*b*) aerial perspective, (*c*) linear perspective (*d*) texture gradient (*e*) elevation, and (*f*) shading patterns.

An object's *elevation* provides another cue to its distance. Objects that are higher in your visual field seem to be farther away. If you paint a picture, you can create depth by placing more-distant objects higher on the canvas. *Shading patterns* provide cues to distance because areas that are in shadow tend to recede, while areas that are in light tend to stand out. Painters use shading to make balls, balloons, and oranges appear round. *Aerial perspective* depends on the clarity of objects. Closer objects seem clearer than more distant ones. A distant mountain will look hazier than a near one.

The final monocular cue, the *texture gradient*, affects depth perception because the nearer an object, the more details we can make out, and the farther an object, the fewer details we can make out. When you look across a field, you can see every blade of grass near you, but only an expanse of green far away from you. Even 7-month-old infants respond to the texture-gradient cue. When presented with drawings that use the texture gradient to make some objects appear to be in the foreground and others in the background, infants will reach for an object in the foreground (Arterberry, Yonas, & Benson, 1989).

Perceptual Constancies

The image of a given object focused on your retina may vary in size, shape, and brightness. Yet, because of *perceptual constancy*, you will continue to perceive the object as stable in size, shape, and brightness. This is adaptive, because it provides you with a more visually stable world, making it easier for you to function in it. The size of the object on your retina does not, by itself, tell you how far away it is. As an object gets farther away from you, it produces a smaller image on your retina. If you know the actual size of an object, **size constancy** makes you interpret a change in its retinal size as a change in its distance rather than as a change in its size. When you see a car a block away, it does not seem smaller than one that is half a block away, even though the more distant car produces a smaller image on your retina. Size constancy can be disrupted by alcohol. In one study, young adults drank alcohol and were then asked to estimate the size of an object. They tended to underestimate its size. Disruption of size constancy might be one way that alcohol intoxication promotes automobile accidents (Farrimond, 1990).

Shape constancy assures that an object of known shape will appear to maintain its normal shape regardless of the angle from which you view it. Close this book and hold

size constancy
The perceptual process that makes an object appear to remain the same size despite changes in the size of the image it casts on the retina.

shape constancy
The perceptual process that makes an object appear to maintain its normal shape regardless of the angle from which it is viewed.

it at various orientations relative to your line of sight. Unless you look directly at the cover when it is on a plane perpendicular to your line of vision, it will never cast a rectangular image on your retinas, yet you will continue to perceive it as rectangular. Shape constancy occurs because your brain compensates for the slant of an object relative to your line of sight (Wallach & Marshall, 1986).

Though the amount of light reflected from a given object can vary, we perceive the object as having a constant brightness. This is called **brightness constancy**. A white shirt appears equally bright in dim light or bright light, and a black shirt appears equally dull in dim light or bright light. But brightness constancy is relative to other objects. If you look at a white shirt in dim light in the presence of nonwhite objects in the same light, it will maintain its brightness. But if you look at the white shirt by itself, perhaps by viewing a large area of it through a hollow tube, it will appear dull in dim light and brighter in sunlight.

Visual Illusions

In Edgar Allen Poe's story "The Sphinx," a man looks out his window and is horrified by what he perceives to be a monstrous animal on a distant mountain. He learns only later that the "monster" was actually an insect on his window. Because he perceived the animal as far away, he assumed it was relatively large. And because he never had seen such a creature, he assumed that it was a monster. This shows how the misapplication of a visual cue, in this case perceived size constancy, can produce a **visual illusion** (Gregory, 1991). Visual illusions provide clues to the processes involved in normal visual perception (Gordon & Earle, 1992).

For example, from ancient times to modern times, people have been mystified by the **moon illusion**, illustrated in figure 5.21, in which the moon appears larger when it is at the horizon than when it is overhead. This is an illusion because the moon is the same distance from us at the horizon as when it is overhead. Thus, the retinal image it produces is the same size when it is at the horizon as when it is overhead. The earliest explanation of the moon illusion was put forth by the Greek astronomer Ptolemy in the second century. His explanation, based on the principle of size constancy, is called the *apparent-distance hypothesis* (Kaufman & Rock, 1962). Ptolemy assumed that we perceive the sky as a flattened dome, with the sky at the horizon appearing farther away than it does overhead. Because the image of the moon on the retina is the same size whether the moon is overhead or at the horizon, the brain assumes that the moon must be larger at the apparently more-distant location—the horizon. But modern research has found that, contrary to the apparent-distance hypothesis, the sky looks *farther away* overhead than at the horizon. So, if the apparent-distance hypothesis were correct, the moon would appear *larger* overhead than it does at the horizon (Baird & Wagner, 1982).

Another theory, based on the angle at which our eyes view the moon, was favored by psychologist Edwin Boring (1943). To demonstrate his theory, Boring had subjects view the horizon moon and the overhead moon from strange positions, including lying on their backs with their heads draped over a handy log. This made the horizon moon shrink in apparent size, but not nearly enough to explain the illusion (Kaufman & Rock, 1962). Bemused by this seeming scientific wackiness, the poet Helen Bevington wrote "Academic Moon," which first appeared in *The New Yorker* magazine:

> *I have been walking under the sky in the moonlight*
> *With a professor. And am pleased to say*
> *The moon was luminous and high and profitable.*
> *Moonlit was the professor. Clear as day,*
> *He had read, of late, how extraordinary moons are*
> *Upside down. Aloft in the night sky*
> *One drifted upright, in the usual fashion.*
> *But the professor, glad to verify*
> *Hypothesis of truth, when he is able—*
> *Even, it seems, to set the moon askew—*
> *Proposed that we reverse our own perspective.*
> *And, on the whole, it was a lovelier view.*

FIGURE **5.21**

The Moon Illusion
Psychologists have put forth several theories to explain why the moon looks larger when it is at the horizon than when it is high up in the sky.

brightness constancy
The perceptual process that makes an object maintain a particular level of brightness despite changes in the amount of light reflected from it.

visual illusion
A misperception of physical reality usually caused by the misapplication of visual cues.

moon illusion
The misperception that the moon is larger when it is at the horizon than when it is overhead.

Big Foot?
Size perception is affected by our interpretation of objects. If we presume that here former U.S. president George Bush was photographed from behind a sunbather's foot, we would see the foot as normal size. If, instead, we presume that he is jogging past a sculpture of a foot (which he is), we would see the foot as huge.

REPRINTED COURTESY OMNI MAGAZINE © 1988.

"It's a hell of a lot more impressive from a distance!"

Of white circumference—smaller now, he fancied,
A tidier sphere. This last I could not tell
From so oblique an angle. I only remember
Enjoying the occasion very well. (Riggs, 1985, pp. 292–293)

An alternative explanation of the moon illusion, the *relative-size hypothesis,* attributes the illusion to the difference in the amount of space that surrounds the moon overhead and at the horizon (Restle, 1970). This hypothesis was first put forth by the thirteenth-century scientist-philosopher Roger Bacon (ca. 1220–1292), who assumed that intervening objects between the observer and the horizon moon made the horizon look farther away than the overhead sky. As a result, again based on size constancy, the horizon moon would look larger (Ross & Ross, 1976).

(a)

(b)

FIGURE 5.22

The Ames Room
(*a*) The "giant" children on the right are actually shorter than the "tiny" adult on the left. (*b*) The floor plan of the Ames room shows that the persons on the left are farther away than the ones on the right, and the floor-to-ceiling height is greater on the left than on the right. The window on the left is also larger than the one on the right. This makes each of the persons seem like they are standing the same distance away from the viewer in a rectangular room. The illusion occurs because the persons on the right fill more of the space between the floor and the ceiling and because we assume that when two objects are the same distance away, the object that produces a smaller image on our retinas is, in fact, smaller.

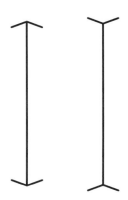

FIGURE 5.23

The Müller-Lyer Illusion
Perhaps the most widely studied illusion was developed a century ago by Franz Müller-Lyer. Note that the vertical line on the right appears longer than the one on the left. If you take a ruler and measure the lines, you will find they are equal in length. Though no explanation has achieved universal acceptance (Mack et al., 1985), a favored one relies on size constancy and the resemblance of the figure on the right to the inside corner of a room and the resemblance of the figure on the left to the outside corner of a building. Given that the lines project images of equal length onto the retina, the line that appears farther away will be perceived as longer. Because an inside corner of a room appears farther away than an outside corner of a building, the line on the right appears farther and, therefore, longer than the line on the left (Gillam, 1980).

Despite hundreds of studies of the moon illusion, researchers have yet to agree on the best explanation of it, though a modified version of the relative-size hypothesis might turn out to be the best candidate (Baird, Wagner, & Fuld, 1990). To further complicate matters, the moon illusion is even present in drawings. The moon appears larger when drawn at the horizon than when drawn with exactly the same diameter high in the sky (Coren & Aks, 1990). Figures 5.22 and 5.23 depict other visual illusions that have stimulated research studies.

Experience and Perception

As you have just read, visual perception depends on the interaction of the eyes and the brain. But it also depends on life experiences. Even the visual pathways themselves can be altered by specific experiences, as demonstrated by studies of *sensory restriction*.

Anatomy of a Classic Research Study:
Can Early Experience Affect the Development of the Visual Pathways?

Rationale

As we discussed earlier, David Hubel and Torsten Wiesel found that feature detectors in the visual cortex respond to lines of particular orientations. Other researchers (Hirsch & Spinelli, 1970) reared kittens with one eye exposed to vertical stripes and the other eye exposed to horizontal stripes. When the kittens later were exposed to lines of either orientation with one eye, certain feature-detector neurons in their visual cortexes responded only to lines of the orientation to which that eye had been exposed. But what would occur if kittens were reared in an environment that exposed both eyes to either only vertical or only horizontal stripes? This was the question addressed in a study by Colin Blakemore and Graham Cooper (1970) of Cambridge University in England.

Method

Blakemore and Cooper reared kittens from the age of 2 weeks to the age of 5 months in darkness, except for 5 hours a day in a lighted, large cylinder with walls covered by either vertical or horizontal black and white stripes. Because the kittens also wore large saucer-shaped collars, they could not even see their own legs or bodies. This prevented their being exposed to lines other than the vertical or horizontal stripes.

Results and Discussion

After 5 months the kittens' vision was tested under normal lighting by waving a rod in front of them, sometimes vertically and sometimes horizontally. Kittens that had been exposed to vertical lines swatted at the vertical rod but not at the horizontal rod. And kittens that had been exposed to horizontal lines swatted at the horizontal rod but not at the vertical rod. Recordings of the activity in certain neurons in the visual cortex showed that particular neurons acted as feature detectors by responding to either vertical or horizontal lines, depending on the stripes to which the kittens had been exposed during the previous 5 months (Blakemore & Cooper, 1970). More-recent research indicates that neurons in the visual cortex that are responsive to lines of different orientations are present at birth. But in an individual who is not exposed to lines of a particular orientation, the neurons responsive to that orientation will degenerate (Swindale, 1982).

Another source of evidence for the effect of experience on perception comes from studies of people blind from birth who have gained their sense of vision years later. The German physiologist Max von Senden (1932-1960) reviewed all the studies of people who had been born blind because of lens cataracts and who gained their vision after surgical removal of the cataracts. He found that the newly sighted were immediately able to distinguish colors and to separate figure from ground, but had difficulty recognizing objects they had learned to identify by touch. They did, however, show gradual improvement in visual object recognition (Dember & Bagwell, 1985).

Visual perception can also be influenced by life experiences related to one's culture (Akande, 1991). This was confirmed by the anthropologist Colin Turnbull (1961), who studied the Bambuti Pygmies of central Africa. Turnbull drove one of the Pygmies, Kenge, who lived in a dense forest, to an open plain. Looking across the plain at a herd of grazing buffalo, Kenge asked Turnbull to tell him what kind of insect they were. Turnbull responded by driving Kenge toward the herd. As the image of the "insects" got bigger and bigger on his retinas, Kenge accused Turnbull of witchcraft for turning the insects into buffaloes. Because he had never experienced large objects at a distance, Kenge had a limited appreciation of size constancy. To him the tiny images on his retinas could only be insects. Because of his understandable failure to apply size constancy

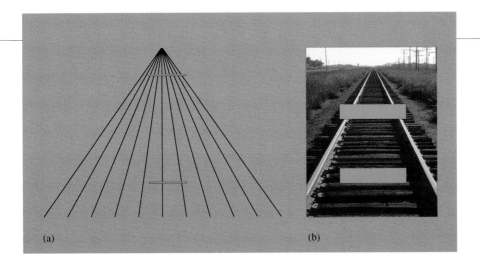

FIGURE **5.24**

The Ponzo Illusion
(*a*)The two horizontal lines are actually the same length. (*b*) Likewise, the two bars are the same length.

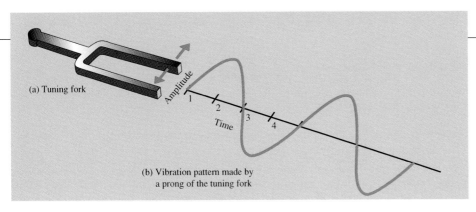

FIGURE **5.25**

Sound Waves
Vibrations from objects that produce sounds cause successive compression and expansion of the air around them. Sound waves vary in their amplitude and frequency. Most sounds are not pure but instead are produced by sound waves with different amplitudes and frequencies.

appropriately, Kenge mistook the distant buffalo for a nearby insect (as opposed to the man in Poe's short story, who mistook the nearby insect for a distant monster).

To gain even more appreciation for the influence of cultural experience on visual perception, consider the *Ponzo illusion*, illustrated in figure 5.24. As with most illusions, the Ponzo illusion is caused by the misapplication of perceptual cues. As you read earlier, linear perspective is a cue to depth. Because the train tracks appear to come together in the distance, the horizontal bar higher in the figure appears farther away than the one lower in the figure. If you measure the bars, you will find that they are actually equal in length. Yet, because both bars produce images of equal length on your retinas, the bar that appears farther away seems to be longer. Experiences with monocular cues to depth, such as linear perspective, affect responses to the Ponzo illusion. Rural Ugandan villagers, who have little experience with monocular cues in two-dimensional stimuli, are less susceptible to the Ponzo illusion than are Ugandan college students, who have more experience with such cues in art, photographs, and motion pictures (Leibowitz & Pick, 1972).

HEARING

Like the sense of vision, the sense of hearing (or **audition**) helps us function by informing us about objects at a distance from us. Unlike vision, audition informs us about objects we cannot see because they are behind us, hidden by darkness, or blocked by another object. Sound is produced by vibrations carried by air, water, or other mediums. Because sound requires a medium through which to travel, it cannot travel in a vacuum. (Of course, this has not prevented the *Star Trek* and *Star Wars* movies from enhancing their dramatic effects by including the sounds of massive explosions and roaring rocket engines in the vacuum of outer space.) As shown in figure 5.25, sound vibrations create

audition
The sense of hearing.

FIGURE 5.26

The Human Ear

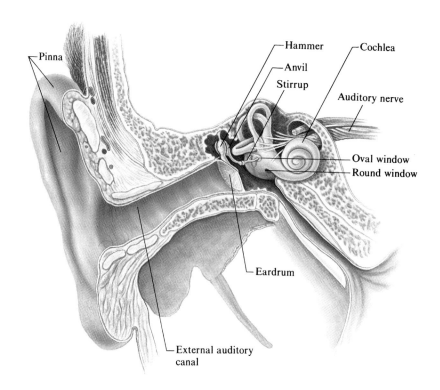

a successive bunching and spreading of molecules in the sound medium. A *sound wave* is composed of a series of these bunching-spreading cycles. The height of a sound wave is its *amplitude*, and the number of sound-wave cycles that pass a given point in a second is its *frequency*. Sound frequency is measured in *hertz (Hz)*, named for the nineteenth-century German physicist Heinrich Hertz. A 60-Hz sound would have a frequency of 60 cycles a second.

The Auditory System

Sound waves are sensed and perceived by the *auditory system*, which begins at the ear. The structure of the ear is illustrated in figure 5.26. The ear is divided into an outer ear, a middle ear, and an inner ear. The *outer ear* includes the *pinna*, the oddly shaped flap of skin and cartilage that we commonly called the "ear." Though the pinna plays a small role in human hearing, some animals, such as deer, have large, movable pinnas that help them detect and locate faint sounds. Sound waves gathered by the pinna pass through the *external auditory canal* and reach the **tympanic membrane**, better known as the *eardrum*. Sound waves make the eardrum vibrate, and our hearing is responsive to even the slightest movement of the eardrum. If our hearing were any more acute, we would hear the air molecules that are constantly bouncing against the eardrum (von Békésy, 1957).

The eardrum separates the outer ear from the *middle ear*. Vibrations of the eardrum are conveyed to the bones, or *ossicles*, of the middle ear. The ossicles are three tiny bones connected to one another by ligaments. The Latin names of the ossicles reflect their shapes: the *malleus* (hammer), the *incus* (anvil), and the *stapes* (stirrup). Infections of the middle ear must be taken seriously; in children they can produce hearing losses that adversely affect language ability and intellectual development (Roberts & Schuele, 1990).

Connecting the middle ear to the back of the throat are the *eustachian tubes*, which permit air to enter the middle ear to equalize air pressure on both sides of the eardrum. You may become painfully aware of this function during airplane descents, when the pressure increases on the outside of the eardrum relative to the inside. Chewing gum can help open the eustachian tubes and equalize the pressure. You may also have noticed that infants begin crying during airplane descents; they are feeling painful pressure changes

tympanic membrane
The eardrum; a membrane separating the outer and middle ears that vibrates in response to sound waves that strike it.

Chapter Five

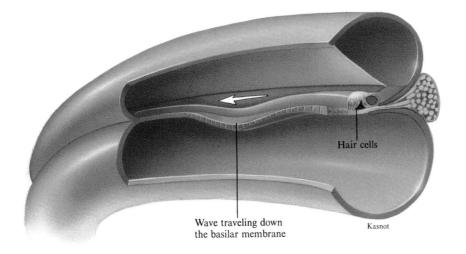

FIGURE 5.27

The Cochlea
Waves traveling through a fluid-filled chamber that runs the length of the cochlea set in motion the basilar membrane. This causes bending of hair cells that cover the basilar membrane.

Hair cells

Wave traveling down the basilar membrane

Kasnot

The Pinna
This girl is experiencing the amplification of sounds that large pinnas provide to animals such as deer.

in their ears. One way to prevent this is to bottle-feed them during the descent. This helps to force air through the eustachian tube into the middle ear. In a study of infants' reactions to airplane landings, crying was displayed by only 29 percent of those who were being bottle-fed but 78 percent of those who were not (Byers, 1986).

Vibrations of the stapes are conveyed to the *oval window* of the *inner ear*. The oval window is a membrane in the wall of a spiral structure called the **cochlea** (from a Greek word meaning "snail"). Vibrations of the oval window send waves through a fluid-filled chamber that runs the length of the cochlea (see figure 5.27). These waves set in motion the **basilar membrane**, which also runs the length of the cochlea. The movement of the basilar membrane causes bending of *hair cells* that protrude from it. The bending triggers impulses that travel along the axons of the neurons that form the **auditory nerve**. Auditory impulses eventually reach the thalamus, where some processing takes place (Edeline & Weinberger, 1991). Input to the thalamus is then relayed to the **auditory cortex** of the temporal lobes of the brain, the ultimate site of sound perception.

cochlea
The spiral, fluid-filled structure of the inner ear that contains the receptor cells for hearing.

basilar membrane
A membrane running the length of the cochlea that contains the auditory receptor (hair) cells.

auditory nerve
The nerve that conducts impulses from the cochlea to the brain.

auditory cortex
The area of the temporal lobes that processes sounds.

Auditory Perception

How do vibrations conveyed to the basilar membrane (the proximal stimulus) create a complex auditory experience regarding their source (the distal stimulus)? Your ability to perceive voices, music, and sounds of all kinds depends on *pitch perception*, *loudness perception*, *timbre perception*, and *sound localization*.

Pitch Perception

The frequency of a sound is the main determinant of its perceived *pitch*, whether the low-pitched sounds of a tuba or the high-pitched sounds of a flute. When you use the tone control on a radio, stereo, or television, you alter the frequency of the sound waves produced by the vibration of the speakers. This, in turn, alters the pitch of the sound. People with so-called absolute pitch can identify specific musical notes when they hear them (Miyazaki, 1990). Human beings and other animals vary in the range of frequencies they can hear. Human beings hear sounds that range from 20 Hz to 20,000 Hz. Because elephants can hear sounds only up to 10,000 Hz, they cannot hear higher-pitched sounds that human beings can hear. Dogs, in turn, can hear sounds up to about 45,000 Hz (Heffner, 1983). Because dog whistles produce sounds between 20,000 and 45,000 Hz, they are audible to dogs but not to human beings.

What accounts for **pitch perception**? In 1863 Hermann von Helmholtz put forth the **place theory**, which assumes that particular points on the basilar membrane vibrate maximally in response to sound waves of particular frequencies. Georg von Békésy (1899–1972), a Hungarian scientist, won a Nobel prize in 1961 for his research on the place theory. He took the cochleas from the ears of guinea pigs and human cadavers, stimulated the oval window, and, using a microscope, noted the response of the basilar membrane through a hole cut in the cochlea. He found that as the frequency of the stimulus increased, the point of maximal vibration produced by the traveling wave on the basilar membrane moved closer to the oval window. And as the frequency of the stimulus decreased, the point of maximal vibration moved farther from the oval window (von Békésy, 1957). The place theory is also supported by the high-frequency hearing loss that tends to accompany aging; this loss is associated with the destruction of hair cells near the oval window (McFadden & Wightman, 1983).

But the place theory fails to explain pitch perception much below 1,000 Hz, because such low-frequency sound waves do not make the basilar membrane vibrate maximally at any particular point. Instead, the entire basilar membrane vibrates equally. Because of this limitation, perception of sounds below 1,000 Hz is explained best by a theory first put forth by the English physicist Ernest Rutherford (1861–1937) in 1886. His **frequency theory** assumes that the basilar membrane vibrates as a whole in direct proportion to the frequency of the sound waves striking the eardrum. The neurons of the auditory nerve will, in turn, fire at the same frequency as the vibrations of the basilar membrane. But because neurons can fire only up to 1,000 times a second, the frequency theory holds only for sounds below 1,000 Hz.

Still another theory, the **volley theory** of psychologist Ernest Wever (Wever & Bray, 1937), explains pitch perception between 1,000 Hz and 5,000 Hz. The volley theory assumes that sound waves in this range induce certain groups of auditory neurons to fire in volleys. Though no single neuron can fire at more than 1,000 Hz, the brain might interpret the firing of volleys of particular auditory neurons as representing sound waves of particular frequencies up to 5,000 Hz (Zwislocki, 1981). For example, the pitch of a sound wave of 4,000 Hz might be coded by a particular group of five neurons, each firing at 800 Hz. Though there is some overlap among the theories, the frequency theory best explains the perception of low-pitched sounds, the place theory best explains the perception of high-pitched sounds, and the volley theory best explains the perception of medium-pitched sounds.

Georg von Békésy (1899–1972)
"[The ear] is so sensitive that it can almost hear the random rain of air molecules bouncing against the eardrum. Yet in spite of its extraordinary sensitivity, the ear can withstand the pounding of sound waves strong enough to set the body vibrating."

pitch perception
The subjective experience of the highness or lowness of a sound, which corresponds most closely to the frequency of the sound waves that compose it.

place theory
The theory of pitch perception that assumes that hair cells at particular points on the basilar membrane are maximally responsive to sound waves of particular frequencies.

frequency theory
The theory of pitch perception that assumes that the basilar membrane vibrates as a whole in direct proportion to the frequency of the sound waves striking the eardrum.

volley theory
The theory of pitch perception that assumes that sound waves of particular frequencies induce auditory neurons to fire in volleys, with one volley following another.

TABLE 5.1		Sound Levels (Decibels)
Harmful to Hearing		
	140	Jet engine (25 m distance)
	130	Jet takeoff (100 m away)
		Threshold of pain
	120	Propeller aircraft
Risk Hearing Loss		
	110	Live rock band
	100	Jackhammer/pneumatic chipper
	90	Heavy-duty truck
		Los Angeles, third-floor apartment next to freeway
		Average street traffic
Very Noisy		
	80	Harlem, second-floor apartment
Urban		
	70	Private car
		Boston row house on major avenue
		Business office
		Watts—8 miles from touch down at major airport
	60	Conversational speech or old residential area in L.A.
Suburban and Small Town		
	50	San Diego—wooded residential area
	40	California tomato field
		Soft music from radio
	30	Quiet whisper
	20	Quiet urban dwelling
	10	Rustle of leaf
	0	Threshold of hearing

Reprinted with permission from *Science News*, the weekly newsmagazine of science. Copyright 1982 by Science Service, Inc.

Because the decibel scale is a logarithmic measure of sound intensity, values don't add in the usual way: a 60 = dB sound played atop another 60 = dB sound corresponds to 63 = dB noise. And a 10 = dB difference means one sound is 10 times louder than the other, so that the ratio between 140 dB and 0 dB is roughly 100 trillion to 1. Readings for cities represent levels actually measured by EPA and expressed as a day-night average.

Loudness Perception

Sounds vary in intensity, or *loudness*, as well as pitch. The loudness of a sound depends mainly on the amplitude of its sound waves. When you use the volume control on a radio, stereo, or television, you alter the amplitude of the sound waves leaving the speakers. **Loudness perception** depends on both the number and the firing thresholds of hair cells on the basilar membrane that are stimulated. Hair cells with higher firing thresholds require more-intense stimulation. As a result, the firing of hair cells with higher firing thresholds increases the perceived loudness of a sound.

loudness perception
The subjective experience of the intensity of a sound, which corresponds most closely to the amplitude of the sound waves composing it.

The unit of sound intensity is the *decibel (dB)*. The decibel is one-tenth of a bel, a unit named for Alexander Graham Bell, who invented the telephone. The faintest detectable sound has an absolute threshold of 0 dB. For each change of 10 decibels, the perceived loudness doubles. Thus, a 70-decibel sound is twice as loud as a 60-decibel sound. Table 5.1 presents the decibel levels of some everyday sounds. Exposure to high-decibel sounds promotes hearing loss. Chronic exposure to loud sounds first destroys hair cells nearest the oval window, which respond to high-frequency sound waves. Loud sounds are so prevalent in most American communities that even infants show some destruction of their hair cells (Schneider, Trehub, & Bull, 1980). The loss of hair cells continues throughout childhood and into adulthood, as we are repeatedly exposed to loud music, vehicles, and machinery. A study of a sample of audience members at a rock-music concert found that they all displayed a hearing loss immediately after the concert.

Rocking His Way to Deafness
As rock musicians reach middle age and beyond, many will experience hearing loss induced by decades of exposure to loud music.

conduction deafness
Hearing loss usually caused by blockage of the auditory canal, damage to the eardrum, or deterioration of the ossicles of the middle ear.

nerve deafness
Hearing loss caused by damage to the hair cells of the basilar membrane or the axons of the auditory nerve.

timbre
The subjective experience that identifies a particular sound and corresponds most closely to the mixture of sound waves composing it.

Three days later, most of them still showed a hearing loss (Danenberg, Loos-Cosgrove, & LoVerde, 1987). Elderly North Americans, after a lifetime of exposure to loud sounds, tend to have poor high-frequency hearing. In contrast, the typical 90-year-old in certain rural African tribes, whose surroundings only occasionally produce loud sounds, has better hearing than the typical 30-year-old North American (Raloff, 1982).

In extreme cases, individuals can lose more than their high-frequency hearing. They can become deaf. In **conduction deafness**, there is a mechanical problem in the outer or middle ear that interferes with hearing. The auditory canal might be filled with wax, the eardrum might be punctured, or the ossicles might be fused and inflexible. Conduction deafness caused by deterioration of the ossicles can be treated by surgical replacement with plastic ossicles. Conduction deafness is more often overcome by hearing aids, which amplify sound waves that enter the ear.

In **nerve deafness**, a problem of the inner ear, the basilar membrane, the auditory nerve, or the auditory cortex is damaged. Victims typically lose the ability to perceive sounds of certain frequencies. Nerve deafness responds poorly to surgery or hearing aids. But *cochlear implants* (pictured in figure 5.28), which provide electronic stimulation of the basilar membrane, promise to restore at least rudimentary hearing in people with nerve deafness. Some recipients of cochlear implants hear well enough to perceive simple speech (Tyler et al., 1992).

Timbre Perception

Sounds vary in *timbre*, as well as in pitch and loudness. **Timbre** is the quality of a sound, which reflects a particular mixture of sound waves. Middle C on the piano has a frequency of 256 Hz, but it has a distinctive timbre because of overtones of varying frequencies. Timbre lets us identify the source of a sound, whether a voice, a musical instrument, or even—to the chagrin of students—a fingernail scratching across a chalkboard. The timbre of that spine-chilling sound is similar to that of the warning cry of macaque monkeys. Perhaps our squeamish response to it reflects an inborn vestigial response inherited from our common distant ancestors who used it to signal the presence of predators (Halpern, Blake, & Hillerbrand, 1986).

Timbre lets us not only identify musical instruments, but evaluate their relative quality. Because musical notes of the same frequency differ in timbre when played on different instruments, no two instruments produce exactly the same sounds. Two instruments playing the same note would also produce different mixtures of accompanying

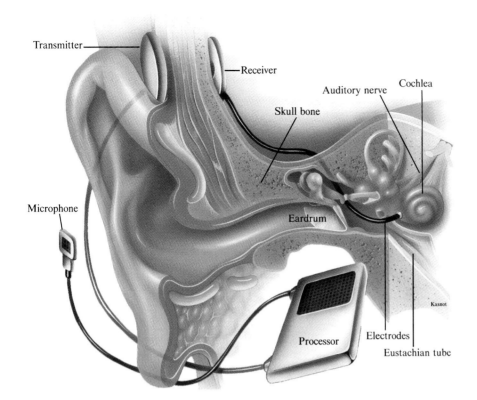

Transmitter

Receiver

Auditory nerve

Cochlea

Skull bone

Microphone

Eardrum

Kasnot

Processor

Electrodes

Eustachian tube

FIGURE 5.28

The Bionic Ear
Cochlear implants involve electrodes attached to different points along the basilar membrane. A microphone worn behind the ear picks up sounds and transmits them to a microprocessor. The microprocessor then analyzes the sounds into their component frequencies and sends impulses through the electrodes to stimulate the places on the basilar membrane that respond to those frequencies (Loeb, 1985).

sound waves. This helps you to tell a violin from a guitar and a cheap violin from an expensive one (Hutchins, 1981).

Sound Localization

We need to localize sounds, as well as identify them. Human beings have an impressive ability to localize sounds, whether of voices at a crowded party or of instruments in a symphony orchestra. But some animals have even more impressive **sound localization** ability. A barn owl can capture a mouse in the dark simply by following the faint sounds produced by its movements (Knudsen, 1981). We are aided in localizing sounds by having two ears. Sounds that come from points other than those equidistant between our two ears reach one ear slightly before they reach the other. Such sounds are also slightly more intense at the ear closer to the sound source, because the head blocks some of the sound waves as they move from one side of the head to the other. The auditory cortex has cells that respond to these differences in intensity and arrival time, permitting the brain to determine the location of a sound (Phillips & Brugge, 1985). Even sounds that come from points equidistant between our ears can be located, because the irregular shape of the pinna alters sounds differently, depending on the direction from which they enter the ear (Middlebrooks & Green, 1991).

sound localization
The process by which the individual determines the location of a sound.

CHEMICAL SENSES

In front of the Monell Chemical Senses Center in Philadelphia stands a 6-foot-tall statue of a face with a nose and a mouth, but with no eyes or ears. This statue symbolizes the senses that are studied by Monell scientists—the *chemical senses* of smell and taste.

Smell

Helen Keller identified her friends by smelling them and could even tell whether a person had recently been in a kitchen, garden, or hospital room by his or her odor (Ecenbarger, 1987). Even newborn infants can identify their caregivers by their distinctive odors (Schaal, 1988). Though most of us do not rely on smell to that extent, the

The Monell Chemical Senses Center

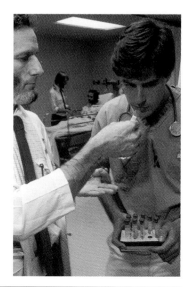

Smell and Medical Diagnosis
Dr. Lewis Goldfrank, chief of emergency medicine at New York City's Bellevue Hospital, trains his staff to recognize the odors of poisons and diseases that might be given off by incoming patients.

Smell and Marketing
Manufacturers of household products realize that our purchasing decisions are often influenced by our sense of smell.

olfaction
The sense of smell, which detects molecules carried in the air.

stereochemical theory
The theory of olfaction and gustation that assumes that receptors are stimulated by molecules of particular sizes and shapes.

sense of smell (or **olfaction**) is important to all of us. It warns us of dangers, such as fire, deadly gases, or spoiled food, and lets us enjoy the pleasant odors of food, nature, and other people. Our moods may be altered by concentrations of odors in room air that are so weak we are unaware of them (Lorig et al., 1990).

North Americans find odors so important that they spend millions of dollars on perfumes, colognes, and deodorants to make themselves more socially appealing. There might even be a "sweet smell of success," at least as perceived by women. This was demonstrated in a study in which female job interviewers gave higher ratings to male and female job applicants who wore fragrances. In contrast, male interviewers gave lower ratings to applicants who wore fragrances (Baron, 1983).

What accounts for our ability to smell odors? In part because of the practical difficulty of gaining access to the olfactory pathways, we have relatively limited knowledge of how olfactory anatomy affects the detection, recognition, and discrimination of odors (Eslinger, Damasio, & Van Hoesen, 1982). We do know that molecules carried in inhaled air stimulate smell receptor cells on the olfactory epithelium high up in the nasal passages (see figure 5.29). Isaac Newton had rejected the possibility that odors were caused by a minute bit of an object wafting into the nostrils. He concluded this because a piece of musk that he kept on his desk as an air freshener failed to decrease in weight over a period of decades. He had no way of knowing that even a few molecules of an object can evoke an odor. As for the physical site of smell receptors, though Aristotle had proposed the correct view that it was in the olfactory epithelium, the second-century physician Galen claimed that smell receptors were located in the ventricles, which are fluid-filled spaces in the brain. Galen's view of olfaction was accepted by most scientists until the past century (Bartoshuk, Cain, & Pfaffman, 1985).

Today, research findings indicate that molecules that reach the olfactory epithelium alter the resting potential and firing frequency of receptor cells, stimulating some and inhibiting others. Distinctive patterns in the firing of receptor cells evoke particular odors. Neural impulses from the receptor cells travel along the short *olfactory nerves* to the frontal lobes of the brain. Smell is the only sense that is not first processed in the thalamus before being relayed to other olfactory centers in the brain. The *limbic system*, an important emotional center of the brain discussed in chapter 3, receives many neural connections from the olfactory nerves. This might account for the powerful emotional effects of certain odors that evoke vivid memories of important events, places, or persons (Schab, 1991). Said Rudyard Kipling, "Smells are surer than sounds or sights to make your heart-strings crack" (Gibbons, 1986, p. 324).

Though researchers have not reached agreement on a set of basic odors, a common system of categorizing odors recognizes seven: *ethereal* (e.g., dry-cleaning fluid), *camphoraceous* (e.g., mothballs), *musky* (e.g., musk cologne), *floral* (e.g., roses), *pepperminty* (e.g., peppermint candy), *pungent* (e.g., vinegar), and *putrid* (e.g., rotten eggs). According to this system, all other odors are mixtures of these basic odors. Those who favor the **stereochemical theory** of smell believe that smell receptors responsive to particular odors are sensitive to molecules of specific sizes, shapes, or electrical charges (Amoore, 1963). But there is no consistent relationship between the size or shape of molecules and the odors they induce. For example, substances with similar molecular structures may produce different odors, and substances with different molecular structures may produce similar odors (Richardson & Zucco, 1989).

Our sense of smell has a remarkably low absolute threshold; we can detect minute amounts of chemicals diffused in the air. For example, a smell survey by *National Geographic* magazine needed less than an ounce of a particular odorous chemical to include a sample of it with 11 million copies of the survey (Gibbons, 1986). Our ability to identify familiar odors was highlighted in a study of college students who showered themselves, put on fresh T-shirts, and then used no soap, deodorant, or perfume for 24 hours. The subjects then sniffed the shirts, one at a time, through an opening in a bag. Of the 29 subjects, 22 correctly identified their own shirts (Russell, 1976).

Though smell is important to human beings, it is more important to many other animals. For example, salmon have an amazing ability to travel hundreds of miles to

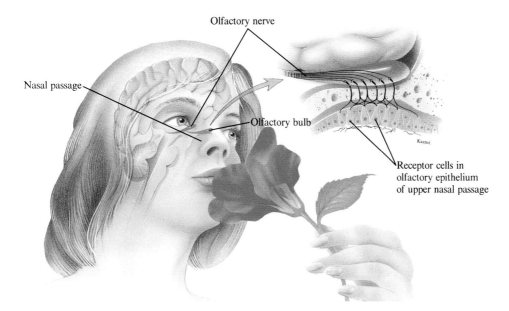

Olfactory nerve

Nasal passage

Olfactory bulb

Receptor cells in
olfactory epithelium
of upper nasal passage

Kasnot

FIGURE 5.29

The Olfactory Pathway
Molecules from the flower are inhaled
and reach receptor cells high up in
the nasal passages. This stimulates the
olfactory nerves, which send impulses
to brain regions that process the sense
of smell.

their home streams to spawn, following the familiar odors of the soil and plants on the banks of the waterways that mark the correct route home (Gibbons, 1986). Researchers have been especially interested in the effects of secretions called **pheromones** on the sexual behavior of animals. For example, aphrodisin, a vaginal pheromone released by female hamsters and inhaled by males, stimulates copulation (Singer & Macrides, 1990). Some fragrance manufacturers have added animal sex pheromones to perfumes and colognes, hoping to sell them as human aphrodisiacs. But before you run out to purchase a pheromone fragrance, you should note that research findings on the effects of sex pheromones on human beings have been inconclusive. In one study, males and females exposed to animal sex pheromones rated photographs of females as more attractive than did subjects not exposed to them (Maugh, 1982a), but a replication of that study, using photographs of males, found no such effect (Filsinger et al., 1984).

pheromones
Odorous chemicals secreted by an animal that affect the behavior of other animals.

Taste

Our other chemical sense, taste (or **gustation**), protects us from harm by preventing us from ingesting poisons and enhances our enjoyment of life by letting us savor food and beverages. Taste depends on thousands of **taste buds,** which line the grooves between bumps called *papillae* on the surface of the tongue. The taste buds contain receptor cells that send neural impulses when stimulated by molecules dissolved in saliva. Taste sensitivity varies with the number of taste buds. One study compared the taste sensitivity of a group of subjects who had almost twice as many taste buds as a second group of subjects. When presented with different taste stimuli, the group with more taste buds reported more-intense tastes (Miller & Reedy, 1990). Taste buds die and are replaced every few days, so the taste buds that are destroyed when you burn your tongue with hot food or drink are quickly replaced. But because replacement of taste buds slows with age, elderly people may find food less flavorful than they did earlier in life (Cowart, 1981).

gustation
The sense of taste, which detects molecules dissolved in the saliva.

taste buds
Structures lining the grooves of the tongue that contain the taste receptor cells.

There is more agreement among researchers about the basic tastes than about the basic odors. In the eleventh century, the Arab scientist Avicenna proposed that there were four basic tastes: sweet, sour, salty, and bitter. In 1891 Hjalmar Ohrwall provided support for Avicenna's proposal. Ohrwall tested the sensitivity of the papillae by applying a variety of chemicals, one at a time, to different papillae. Some papillae responded to one taste and some to more than one. But, overall, he found that particular papillae were maximally sensitive to sweet, sour, salty, or bitter substances (Bartoshuk, Cain, & Pfaffman, 1985). Figure 5.30 shows that different areas of the tongue are most sensitive to sweet and salty, the sides are most sensitive to sour and salty, and the back is most sensitive to bitter. All other tastes are combinations of these basic tastes and depend on the pattern of stimulation of the taste receptors (Rogers, 1985).

FIGURE 5.30

The Basic Tastes
All regions of the tongue are sensitive to each of the four basic tastes, but certain regions are more sensitive to particular ones. (*a*) Sweet receptors line the tip of the tongue; (*b*) sour receptors line the sides; (*c*) salty receptors line the tip and sides; and (*d*) bitter receptors line the back.

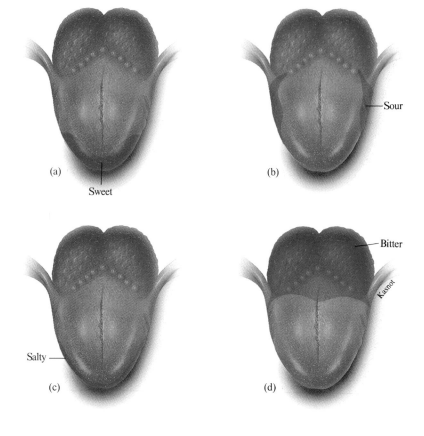

(a) Sweet

(b) Sour

(c) Salty

(d) Bitter / Kasnot

The Art of Wine Tasting
Professional wine tasters rely on both their sense of smell and their sense of taste to determine the flavor characteristics of the wines they evaluate.

skin senses
The senses of touch, temperature, and pain.

As in the case of smell, gustation depends, in part, on the shape and size of molecules that stimulate the taste receptors. Taste researchers use this knowledge when they develop artificial sweeteners. Taste receptors in different areas of the tongue are maximally sensitive to molecules of particular shapes. This stereochemical theory of taste, analogous to the one for smell, was anticipated by the Epicurean poet Lucretius in the first century B.C.:

> Simple tis to see that whatsoever
> Can touch the senses pleasingly are made
> Of smooth and rounded elements, whilst those
> Which seem the bitter and the sharp, are held
> Entwined by elements more crook'd, and so
> Are wont to tear their way into our senses
> And rend our body as they enter in. (Ziporyn, 1982, p. 277)

Do not confuse taste with *flavor*, which is more complex. While taste depends on sensations from the mouth, flavor relies on both taste and smell. If you closed your eyes and held your nose, you would have trouble telling the difference between a piece of apple and a piece of potato placed in your mouth. Because smell is especially important for flavor, you might find that when you have a head cold that interferes with your ability to smell, food lacks flavor. In fact, people who lose their sense of smell because of disease (a condition known as *anosmia*) find food less appealing (Ferris & Duffy, 1989). And one of the reasons that elderly people may show less interest in food is a decline in their ability to detect and identify odors (Stevens, 1989).

SKIN SENSES

We rely on our **skin senses** of touch, temperature, and pain to identify objects, communicate feelings, and protect us from injury. Though there are a variety of receptors that produce skin sensations, there is no simple one-to-one relationship between specific kinds of receptors and specific skin senses. For example, there is only one kind of receptor in the cornea, but it is sensitive to touch, temperature, and pain. The pattern of stimulation of receptors, not the specific kind of receptor, determines skin sensations. Neural impulses from the skin receptors reach the thalamus, which relays them to the **somatosensory cortex** of the brain. As discussed in chapter 3, this is a strip of cerebral cortex on the parietal lobe that processes sensory information from the skin.

Touch

Your sense of *touch* lets you identify objects rapidly and accurately even when you cannot see them, as when you find your house key while fumbling with a key chain in the dark. Touch is also important in our social attachments, whether between lovers or between parent and child. Touch sensitivity depends on the concentration of receptors; the most sensitive areas of the skin include the lips, face, tongue, hands, and genitals. The more sensitive the area of skin (such as the lips or fingertips), the larger its representation on the somatosensory cortex. The sense of touch is so precise that it can be used as a substitute for vision. In 1824 a blind Frenchman named Louis Braille invented the Braille system for reading and writing, which uses patterns of raised dots to represent letters. The Braille concept has been extended to provide a substitute for vision, as shown in figure 5.31. The blind person wears a camera on special eyeglasses and a special computer-controlled electronic vest covered with a grid of tiny Teflon cones. Outlines of images provided by the camera are impressed onto the skin by vibrations of the cones. People who have used the device have been able to identify familiar objects (Hechinger, 1981).

Temperature

In 1927, psychologist Karl Dallenbach "mapped" the temperature receptors of the skin. He drew a grid on the skin and touched each square in the grid alternately with a warm probe and a cold probe. He found that each spot was sensitive to warm or cold, but not both. More-recent research supports this, having found receptors that respond to cold objects and others that respond to warm ones (Sumino & Dubner, 1981). But what of receptors for sensing *hot* objects? Hot objects stimulate both the cold receptors and the warm receptors. The brain interprets this as hot. Figure 5.32 shows how cold and warm sensations can combine to induce hot sensations.

Since Dallenbach's early study, scientists have discovered that temperature receptors detect *changes* in temperature: Cold receptors detect decreases in skin temperature, and warm receptors detect increases (Darian-Smith, 1982). Unless the skin is extremely hot or cold, which would induce pain sensations, the temperature receptors adapt, as when you enter a bathtub filled with hot water. At first you feel uncomfortably hot, but your skin quickly adapts to it and you eventually stop noticing it.

In the late seventeenth century, John Locke gave a demonstration of how temperature sensations depend on the detection of changes in skin temperature. To repeat Locke's demonstration, take three bowls and fill one with cold water, one with hot water, and one with lukewarm water. Place one hand in the cold water and the other in the hot water. Keep your hands submerged for a minute to allow temperature adaptation to occur. Then place both hands in the lukewarm water. The water will feel hot to the hand that had been in cold water and cold to the hand that had been in hot water. Thus, the temperature receptors would be responding to the change in temperature, not to the actual temperature of the lukewarm water.

Pain

The sense of *pain* protects us from injury or even death. People born without a sense of pain, or who lose it through nerve injuries, may harm themselves without realizing it. Because intense acute pain or moderate chronic pain can be extremely distressing, many researchers are studying the factors that cause pain and possible ways of relieving it.

FIGURE 5.31

Tactile Sensory Replacement
This man is "seeing" with his skin. Images provided by the video camera on his eyeglasses are impressed onto his skin by tiny vibrating Teflon cones. People who have used this device have been able to identify objects with distinctive shapes (Hechinger, 1981).

FIGURE 5.32

Paradoxical Hot
If cold water circulates through one coil and warm water through the other, a person grasping the coils will feel a hot sensation and quickly let go. This demonstrates that hot sensations are produced by the combined stimulation of receptors responsive to cold and receptors responsive to warmth.

somatosensory cortex
The area of the parietal lobes that processes information from sensory receptors in the skin.

Ronald Melzack
"Research and observation indicate that a gate-control theory of pain is a better way of understanding pain and approaches to blocking pain."

gate-control theory
The theory that pain impulses can be blocked by the closing of a neuronal gate in the spinal cord.

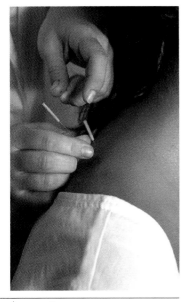

Acupuncture
Acupuncture appears to achieve its pain-relieving effects by stimulating the release of endorphins.

placebo
An inactive substance that may induce some of the effects of the drug for which it has been substituted.

acupuncture
A pain-relieving technique that relies on the insertion of fine needles into various sites on the body.

Pain Factors

An injury or intense stimulation of sensory receptors induces pain. So, bright lights, loud noises, hot spices, and excessive pressure, as well as cuts, burns, and bruises, are painful. The main pain receptors are *free nerve endings* in the skin. Two kinds of neuronal fibers transmit pain impulses: *A-delta fibers* carry sharp or pricking pain, and *C fibers* carry dull or burning pain. One substance implicated in pain is *bradykinin*, a chemical that accumulates at the site of an injury. Aspirin relieves pain in part by inhibiting the release of bradykinin (Inoki et al., 1978).

Many pain receptor neurons transmit pain impulses by releasing the neurotransmitter *substance P* from their axons. For example, the intensity of arthritis pain varies with the amount of substance P released by neurons that convey pain impulses from the joints (Levine et al., 1984). People with a rare medical disorder that reduces their sensitivity to pain have unusually low levels of substance P at synapses that transmit neural impulses from pain receptors (Pearson, Brandeis, & Cuello, 1982).

The most influential theory of pain is the **gate-control theory** formulated by psychologist Ronald Melzack and biologist Patrick Wall (1965). The theory assumes that pain impulses from the limbs or body pass through a part of the spinal cord called the *substantia gelatinosa*, which provides a "gate" for pain impulses. Stimulation of neurons that convey touch sensations "closes" the gate, preventing input from neurons that convey pain sensations. This might explain why rubbing a shin that you have banged against a table will relieve the pain. The closing of the pain gate is stimulated by the secretion of *endorphins*, which (as described in chapter 3) are the brain's natural opiates. Endorphins might close the gate by inhibiting the secretion of substance P (Ruda, 1982).

The pain gate is also affected by neural impulses that originate in the brain (Dubner & Bennett, 1983). This might explain why anxiety, relaxation, and other psychological factors can affect pain perception. For example, it may explain the so-called Anzio effect, in which wounded soldiers returning from the fierce World War II battle for control of Anzio, Italy, needed less morphine than did civilians with similar wounds. Perhaps because the soldiers interpreted their wounds as tickets away from the battlefield, they experienced their pain as less intense (Wallis, 1984). Their pain might have been reduced by neural impulses sent from the brain to the substantia gelatinosa, closing the pain gate. The Anzio effect also shows that the *reinterpretation* of pain can reduce its intensity (Devine & Spanos, 1990).

Pain Relief

Chronic pain afflicts millions of Americans. Back pain alone torments about 80 percent at some time in their lives (Dolce & Raczynski, 1985). The pain of cancer, surgery, injuries, headaches, and backaches makes pain control an important topic of research in both medicine and psychology. The most popular approach to the relief of severe pain relies on drugs such as morphine, which affects endorphin receptors in the brain. Even **placebo** "sugar pills," which are supposedly inactive substances that are substituted for pain-relieving drugs, can relieve pain. Placebos work by stimulating the release of endorphins. Patients with chronic pain who respond to placebos produce higher levels of endorphins than do those who fail to respond (Lipman et al., 1990).

Other techniques that do not rely on drugs or placebos also relieve pain by stimulating the release of endorphins. For example, the technique of **acupuncture**, popular in China for thousands of years, relies on the insertion of fine needles into various sites on the body. Naloxone, a drug that blocks the effects of opiates, reverses the analgesic effects of acupuncture. This provides evidence for the role of endorphins in acupuncture (Takeshige, 1985).

A similar, more modern technique for pain relief relies on **transcutaneous electrical nerve stimulation (TENS)**, which involves electrical stimulation of sites on the body. TENS has proved effective in relieving many kinds of pain, including dental pain (Schwolow, Wilckens, & Roth, 1988), facial pain (Crockett et al., 1986), and headache pain (Solomon & Guglielmo, 1985). As in the case of placebos and acupuncture, TENS relieves pain by stimulating the release of endorphins (Mayer, 1983).

Still another technique, hypnosis, has proved effective in relieving pain as varied as that experienced by burn victims (Weir, 1990) and women in labor (Werner, Schauble, & Knudson, 1982). But, unlike other pain-relieving techniques, hypnosis does not appear to work by stimulating the release of endorphins. We know this because the pain-relieving effects of hypnosis are not blocked by naloxone. In one study, pain was induced by electrical stimulation of tooth roots. Even when given naloxone, hypnotized subjects still experienced pain relief (Joubert & Van Os, 1989).

Pain victims can also control their pain by using distracting thoughts or distracting stimuli to provide pain relief (Williams & Kinney, 1991). You may find it helpful to distract yourself from pain by watching television, listening to music, or imagining pleasant scenes. For this reason, many dentists have music playing as they work on their patients (though the kind of music might induce more distress than it relieves). In a study of adult dental patients, subjects exposed to music during dental procedures experienced less pain and emotional distress than did control subjects who were not exposed to it (Anderson, Baron, & Logan, 1991). But distraction works best for mild, rather than intense, pain. Moreover, a combination of techniques is often most effective in pain relief. For example, in prepared-childbirth classes, pregnant women learn to reduce their pain by relaxing their muscles, breathing deeply, and distracting themselves by imagining pleasant scenes (McCaul & Malott, 1984).

BODY SENSES

While your skin senses let you judge the state of your skin, your *body senses* tell you the position of your limbs and help you maintain your equilibrium. The body senses—the *kinesthetic sense* and the *vestibular sense*—are often taken for granted and have inspired less research than have the other senses. But they are important in everyday functioning.

The Kinesthetic Sense

The **kinesthetic sense** informs you of the position of your joints, the tension in your muscles, and the movement of your arms and legs. This information is provided by special receptors in your joints, muscles, and tendons. Even with your eyes closed, you can sense the location of your limbs as they move about. Kinesthetic receptors in your muscles let you judge the force as well as the path of your limb movements (Jones, 1986).

If your leg has ever "fallen asleep" (depriving you of kinesthetic sensations) and collapsed on you when you stood up, you realize that the kinesthetic sense helps you maintain enough tension in your legs to stand erect. Your kinesthetic sense also protects you from injury. If you are holding an object that is too heavy, kinesthetic receptors signal you to put it down to prevent injury to your muscles and tendons.

Imagine losing your kinesthetic sense permanently, as happened to a woman described in a case study by Oliver Sacks (1985). This robust, athletic young woman, named Christina, developed a rare inflammatory condition that affected only her kinesthetic neurons. She lost all feedback from her body, making it impossible for her to sit, stand, or walk. Her body became as floppy as a rag doll, and she reported feeling like a disembodied mind. She was able to compensate only slightly by using her sense of vision to regulate her body posture and movements. Thus, our kinesthetic sense, which we usually take for granted, plays an important role in our everyday functioning.

The Vestibular Sense

While the kinesthetic sense informs you of the state of your body parts, your **vestibular sense**, which depends on organs in the inner ear, informs you of your position in space, helping you maintain your balance and orientation. The **otolith organs** detect horizontal or vertical linear movement of the head and help you orient yourself in regard to gravity. The other vestibular organs are the **semicircular canals,** which are three fluid-

transcutaneous electrical nerve stimulation (TENS)
The use of electrical stimulation of sites on the body to provide pain relief, apparently by stimulating the release of endorphins.

The Body Senses
The kinesthetic sense and the vestibular sense provide gymnasts, as well as dancers, athletes, and other performers, with exquisite control over their body movements.

kinesthetic sense
The sense that provides information about the position of the joints, the degree of tension in the muscles, and the movement of the arms and legs.

vestibular sense
The sense that provides information about one's position in space and helps in the maintenance of balance.

otolith organs
The vestibular organs that detect horizontal or vertical linear movement of the head.

semicircular canals
The curved vestibular organs of the inner ear that detect movements of the head in any direction.

FIGURE 5.33

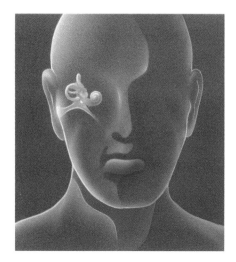

The Semicircular Canals
When your head moves, fluid movement in the semicircular canals stimulates hair cells that send neural impulses to the brain.

filled tubes oriented in different planes. Their location is indicated in figure 5.33. When your head moves in a given direction, the jellylike fluid in the semicircular canal oriented in that direction at first lags behind the movement of the walls of the canal. This makes hair cells protruding into the fluid bend in the direction opposite to the direction of head movement. The bending of hair cells triggers neural impulses that are relayed to your *cerebellum*, to help you maintain your equilibrium.

Your semicircular canals also let you keep your eyes fixed on a target even when you are rotating your head. This is aided by the *vestibulo-ocular reflex*, which compensates for rotary head movements by moving the eyes a proportionate degree in the opposite direction. A baseball outfielder tracking a fly ball benefits from this reflex. A person with damage to the semicircular canals will suffer not only impaired balance but disruption of the vestibulo-ocular reflex (Smith & Curthoys, 1989).

Though the vestibular sense helps you maintain your equilibrium, it can also induce motion sickness, including carsickness, airsickness, and seasickness. In fact, the word *nauseous* comes from the Greek word for "seasick." The sixth-century B.C. philosopher Anacharsis suffered from seasickness so severe that he divided human beings into three categories: the living, the dead, and the seasick. Seasickness has plagued such eminent people as Julius Caesar, Charles Darwin, and Admiral Horatio Nelson. Lawrence of Arabia even had bouts of motion sickness in the middle of the desert—when riding a camel (Swain, 1984). Fortunately, repeated exposure to situations that induce motion sickness tends to produce tolerance. A study of paratroopers found that two-thirds had motion sickness on their first jump, but only one-quarter had it on their fifth jump (Antunano & Hernandez, 1989). Moreover, motion sickness is reduced by a sense of control—which might explain why we are less likely to develop motion sickness when we are driving an automobile than when we are passengers in one (Rolnick & Lubow, 1991).

The mechanisms that underlie motion sickness are still debated, but an influential view holds that motion sickness is induced by conflict between visual and vestibular sensations (Lackner & DiZio, 1991). Suppose you are in a windowless cabin aboard a ship in a rough sea. Your eyes tell you that you are stationary in relationship to one aspect of your environment—your cabin. Yet your vestibular sense tells you that you are moving in relationship to another aspect of your environment—the ocean. But this does not explain *why* conflict between visual and vestibular sensations induces nausea. One hypothesis is that the motion-induced disruption of the normal association between visual and vestibular sensations is similar to that produced by toxins, such as those in spoiled food, that induce nausea (Treisman, 1977).

Drugs that inhibit neural activity in the semicircular canals can reduce motion sickness (Oosterveld, 1987). One of the earliest drug treatments for motion sickness was devised by a Canadian research team led by Wilder Penfield during World War II (Lewis,

1981). As described in chapter 3, Penfield is better known for "mapping" the cerebral cortex. In his research on motion sickness, Penfield and his colleagues rode various rides at an amusement park near Montreal until they discovered the kind of motion that best simulated that of a ship at sea. He then built a machine that reproduced this motion. Finally, after testing a variety of drugs, he found one that inhibited the motion sickness sometimes induced by the machine. This discovery helped prevent nausea in sailors on ships and soldiers in landing craft.

Motion sickness can also be reduced by psychological means. Consider sailors below deck. While their vestibular sense tells them that their ship is rolling back and forth, their visual sense tells them that it is not. This can induce nausea. Would providing a means of convincing the eyes that the ship was rolling reduce their nausea? The results of an experiment indicate that the answer is yes. Sailors were tested while performing a series of tasks in a tilting room under each of three conditions. In one condition, the room's window was covered. In the second condition, it was uncovered. In the third condition, the window was covered and an artificial horizon was projected on the wall with a laser beam. The results showed that the subjects felt significantly less nausea and performed better in the second and third conditions. Thus, the provision of a means of reducing the discrepancy between visual and vestibular input may reduce seasickness in sailors who work below deck (Rolnick & Bles, 1989).

THINKING ABOUT *Psychology*

WHY DO PSYCHOLOGISTS DISCOUNT ESP?

As you have just read, perception depends on the stimulation of sensory receptors by various kinds of energy. But you have certainly heard claims that support the possibility of perception independent of sensory receptors, so-called **extrasensory perception (ESP)**. The field that studies ESP and related phenomena is called **parapsychology** (*para* means "besides"). The name indicates its failure to gain widespread acceptance within mainstream psychology. Parapsychological abilities are typically called *paranormal*.

Despite scientific skepticism about paranormal abilities, a survey found that more than 99 percent of college students believed in at least one paranormal ability and that more than 65 percent claimed a personal experience with at least one (Messer & Griggs, 1989). Public belief in paranormal abilities was exemplified in a 1986 lawsuit in which a Philadelphia woman who made a living as a psychic sued a hospital, insisting that a CT scan of her head made her lose her ESP abilities. A jury, impressed by the testimony of police officers who claimed that she had helped them solve crimes by using ESP, awarded her $988,000 for the loss of her livelihood (Tulsky, 1986). (The jury's decision was later overturned on appeal.) Given such widespread public acceptance of paranormal abilities, why do most psychologists discount it? Before learning some answers to that question, consider several of the paranormal abilities studied by parapsychologists.

extrasensory perception (ESP)
The ability to perceive events without the use of sensory receptors.

parapsychology
The study of extrasensory perception, psychokinesis, and related phenomena.

ALLEGED PARANORMAL ABILITIES

Two decades ago, members of the rock group the Grateful Dead had their audiences at a series of six concerts in Port Chester, New York, try to transmit mental images of slides to a person asleep in a dream laboratory miles away at Maimonides Hospital in Brooklyn.

mental telepathy
The ability to perceive the thoughts of others without any sensory contact with them.

clairvoyance
The ability to perceive objects or events without any sensory contact with them.

precognition
The ability to perceive events in the future.

deja vu
The feeling that one has experienced a present experience sometime in the past.

psychokinesis (PK)
The ability to control objects with the mind alone.

When the sleeper awoke he described the content of his dreams. Independent judges rated his dream reports as more similar to the content of the slides than were the dream reports of another person who had not been designated to receive the images (Ullman, Krippner, & Vaughan, 1973). This was reported as a successful demonstration of **mental telepathy**, the alleged ability to perceive the thoughts of others.

A more recent study of dream telepathy had a "sender" advertise in a national newspaper that he would send a dream telepathy image between midnight and 10 A.M. on a specified night. Different images were sent every 2 hours. More than five hundred readers sent dream reports and the times they "received" the images. Judges blind to the target sequence decided whether the reports matched the pictures. Unlike the results of the Grateful Dead demonstration, their assessments provided no support for dream telepathy—the reports did not match the images that were sent (Hearne, 1989).

Related to mental telepathy is **clairvoyance**, the alleged ability to perceive objects or events without any sensory contact with them. You might be considered clairvoyant if you could identify all of the objects in your psychology professor's desk drawer without looking in it. Many colleges host "psychic" entertainers, such as "the Amazing Kreskin," who impress their audiences by giving demonstrations such as "reading" the serial number of a dollar bill in an audience member's wallet.

Mental telepathy and clairvoyance deal with the present, whereas **precognition** is the alleged ability to perceive events in the future. Psychics like Jean Dixon make careers of writing tabloid newspaper columns in which they predict events of personal or national interest. Do not confuse precognition with **deja vu**, an uncanny feeling that you have experienced a present situation in the past and that you can anticipate what will happen in the next few moments. There is no widely accepted explanation of deja vu (Sno, Schalken, & de Jonghe, 1992).

Closely allied with ESP is **psychokinesis (PK)**, the alleged ability to control objects with the mind alone. Our use of "body English" to affect the movements of dice, roulette wheels, baseballs, golf balls, or bowling balls reflects a superstitious belief in PK. Perhaps you have seen a televised performance by psychic Uri Geller, who gives demonstrations in which he apparently bends spoons, fixes watches, or takes photographs by using mental power alone.

PROBLEMS WITH PARANORMAL RESEARCH

Parapsychology has attracted many prominent supporters. Mark Twain, William James, and G. Stanley Hall were members of the Society for Psychical Research, with James serving a term as president and Hall a term as vice president. But credit for making parapsychology a legitimate area of scientific research to some scientists goes to J. B. Rhine (1895–1980) of Duke University, who began a program of experimentation on paranormal phenomena in the 1930s (Mauskopf & McVaugh, 1981). Several leading British universities have also lent credibility to parapsychology by sponsoring paranormal research. Edinburgh University in Scotland even set up the first faculty chair in parapsychology with a $750,000 grant from the estate of author Arthur Koestler (Dickson, 1984).

"Never mind that—can you bend the spoon?"

Despite the popular acceptance of parapsychology, most psychologists remain skeptical. One reason is that many supposed instances of paranormal phenomena turn out to be the result of poorly controlled demonstrations. In a case reported by the magician James "The Amazing" Randi, a woman claimed that she could influence fish by PK. Every time she put her hand against one side of an aquarium, the fish swam to the opposite side. Randi responded, "She calls it psychic; I call it frightened fish." He suggested that she put dark paper over a side of the aquarium and test her ability on that side. After trying Randi's suggestion and finding that the fish no longer swam to the opposite side, she exclaimed, "It's marvelous! The power doesn't penetrate brown paper!" (Morris, 1980, p. 106).

Supporters of parapsychology might also too readily accept chance events as evidence of paranormal phenomena (Diaconis, 1978). For example, at some time you probably have decided to call a friend, picked up the phone, and found your friend already on the other end of the line. Does this mean that mental telepathy made you call each other at the same time? Not necessarily. Perhaps you and your friend call each other often and at about the same time of the day, so on occasion you might call each other at exactly the same moment by mere coincidence.

Another blow against the credibility of parapsychology is that some impressive demonstrations have later been found to involve fraud. In a widely publicized case, the noted psychic Tamara Rand claimed to have predicted the 1981 assassination attempt on U.S. President Ronald Reagan in a videotape made before the attempt and later shown on the "Today" show. This was considered evidence of precognition—until James Randi discovered that she had made the videotape *after* the assassination attempt ("A Psychic Watergate," 1981).

Magic tricks are also often passed off as paranormal phenomena. G. Stanley Hall, after finding little evidence in support of paranormal phenomena, used his outstanding skill as a magician to debunk some alleged psychics by exposing their trickery (Ross, 1972). James Randi, following in the tradition of Hall, sponsored an elaborate hoax that demonstrated the inability of parapsychology researchers to detect magic tricks. In 1979 James McDonnell, chairman of the board of the McDonnell-Douglas corporation, gave $500,000 to Washington University in St. Louis to establish a parapsychology research laboratory. A respected physics professor took charge of the project and invited alleged psychics to be tested there. Randi sent two magicians, aged 17 and 18, to be tested as "psychics." After demonstrating their PK "abilities" during 120 hours of testing over a 3-year period, the two were proclaimed the only subjects with PK ability.

J. B. Rhine (1895–1980)
"Good evidence of parapsychological ability is not only more difficult to obtain than that of the whole range of sensorimotor exchange; it is also harder to accept. Therefore, it requires more security in the way of test conditions, perhaps the most of any field."

James "The Amazing" Randi and
His Two Proteges

But both had relied on magic—in some instances, beginner's-level magic. For example, they demonstrated PK by moving a clock across a table by using an ultrathin thread held between their thumbs. Because of demonstrations such as this, Randi has urged parapsychologists to permit magicians to observe their research so that magic tricks are not mistaken for paranormal phenomena ("Psychic Abscam," 1983). Since 1965 Randi has an ongoing offer of $10,000 to anyone who can demonstrate a true paranormal ability under well-controlled conditions. No one has yet earned the reward.

Parapsychologists defend their research by insisting that critics often reject positive findings by *assuming* that they are impossible and therefore must be caused by some other factor, such as poor controls, magic tricks, or outright fraud (Child, 1985). Moreover, parapsychologists argue, paranormal abilities might be so subtle that they require highly motivated subjects to demonstrate them. For example, believers in paranormal abilities perform better on paranormal tests than do nonbelievers (Schmeidler, 1985).

But even many parapsychologists agree that, from a scientific standpoint, the main weakness of research studies on paranormal abilities is the difficulty in replicating them. As discussed in chapter 2, scientists discredit events that cannot be replicated under similar conditions. Yet some parapsychologists insist that positive research findings related to paranormal phenomena have been replicated more often than critics of parapsychology will acknowledge (Honorton & Ferrari, 1989).

A final criticism of parapsychology is that there is no satisfactory explanation of paranormal phenomena. Their acceptance might require the discovery of one or more new forms of energy. But attempts to detect any unusual form of energy radiating from people with supposed paranormal abilities have failed (Balanovski & Taylor, 1978). Parapsychologists point out, however, that failure to know the cause of something does not mean that the phenomenon does not exist (Rockwell, 1979). They remind psychologists to be skeptical rather than cynical, because many phenomena that are now scientifically acceptable were once considered impossible and unworthy of study. For example, scientists used to ridicule reports of stones falling from the sky and refused to investigate them. In 1807, after hearing of a report by two Yale University professors of a stone shower in Connecticut, President Thomas Jefferson, a scientist himself, said, "Gentlemen, I would rather believe that those two Yankee professors would lie than to believe that stones fell from heaven" (Diaconis, 1978). Today, even young children know that such stones are meteorites and that they, indeed, fall from the sky. Nonetheless, because alleged paranormal abilities are so unusual, inexplicable, and difficult to demonstrate reliably, even open-minded psychologists will continue to discount them unless they receive more-compelling evidence (Hoppe, 1988).

SUMMARY

SENSORY PROCESSES

Sensation is the process that detects stimuli from one's body or environment. Perception is the process that organizes sensations into meaningful patterns. Psychophysics is the study of the relationships between the physical characteristics of stimuli and the conscious psychological experiences they produce. The minimum amount of stimulation that can be detected is called the absolute threshold. According to signal-detection theory, the detection of a stimulus depends on both its intensity and the physiological and psychological state of the receiver. The minimum amount of change in stimulation that can be detected is called the differential threshold. Weber's law states that the amount of change in stimulation needed to produce a just noticeable difference is a constant proportion of the original stimulus. The tendency of our sensory receptors

to be increasingly less responsive to an unchanging stimulus is called sensory adaptation.

VISION

Vision lets us sense objects by the light reflected from them into our eyes. Light is focused by the lens onto the rods and cones of the retina. Visual input is transmitted by the optic nerves to the brain, ultimately reaching the visual cortex. During dark adaptation the rods and cones become more sensitive to light, with the rods becoming significantly more sensitive than the cones. The trichromatic theory of color vision considers the interaction of red, green, and blue cones. In contrast, the opponent-process theory assumes that color vision depends on activity in red-green, blue-yellow, and black-white ganglion cells and cells in the thalamus. Color blindness is usually caused by an inherited lack of a cone pigment. The most common kind of color blindness is red-green.

Form perception depends on distinguishing figure from ground. In studying form perception, Gestalt psychologists identified the principles of proximity, similarity, closure, and continuity. Whereas Gestalt psychologists claim that we perceive objects as wholes, other theories claim that we construct objects from their component parts. This is supported by research showing that the visual cortex has feature-detector cells that respond to specific features of objects.

Depth perception lets us determine how far away objects are from us. Binocular cues to depth require the interaction of both eyes. The two main binocular cues are convergence of the eyes and retinal disparity. Monocular cues to depth require only one eye. The monocular cues include accommodation, motion parallax, and various pictorial cues (interposition, relative size, linear perspective, elevation, shading, patterns, aerial perspective, and texture gradient).

Experience in viewing objects contributes to size constancy, shape constancy, and brightness constancy. The misapplication of depth perception cues and perceptual constancies can contribute to visual illusions. Sensory experience and cultural background both affect visual perception.

HEARING

The sense of hearing (audition) detects sound waves produced by the vibration of objects. Sound waves cause the tympanic membrane to vibrate. The ossicles of the middle ear convey the vibrations to the oval window of the cochlea, which causes waves to travel through fluid within the cochlea. The waves make hair cells on the basilar membrane bend, sending neural impulses along the auditory nerve. Sounds are ultimately processed by the auditory cortex of the temporal lobes.

The frequency of a sound determines its pitch. Pitch perception is explained by the place theory, frequency theory, and volley theory. The intensity of a sound determines its loudness. People may suffer from conduction deafness or nerve deafness. The mixture of sound waves determines a sound's quality, or timbre. Sound localization depends on differences in a sound's arrival time and intensity at the two ears.

CHEMICAL SENSES

The chemical senses of smell and taste detect chemicals in the air we breathe or the substances we ingest. The sense of smell (olfaction) depends on receptor cells on the nasal membrane that respond to particular chemicals. Odorous secretions called pheromones affect the sexual behavior of animals. The sense of taste (gustation) depends on receptor cells on the taste buds of the tongue that respond to particular chemicals. The basic tastes are sweet, salty, sour, and bitter.

SKIN SENSES

Skin senses depend on receptors that send neural impulses to the somatosensory cortex. Touch sensitivity depends on the concentration of receptors in the skin. Though we have separate receptors for cold and warm temperatures, we depend on the simultaneous stimulation of cold and warm receptors to produce hot sensations. Pain depends on both physical and psychological factors. According to the gate-control theory of pain, stimulation of touch neurons closes a spinal "gate," which inhibits neural impulses underlying pain from traveling up the spinal cord. Pain-relieving techniques such as placebos, acupuncture, and transcutaneous nerve stimulation relieve pain by stimulating the release of endorphins. Hypnosis appears to relieve pain by distracting the hypnotized person.

BODY SENSES

Your body senses make you aware of the position of your limbs and help you maintain your equilibrium. The kinesthetic sense informs you of the position of your joints, the tension in your muscles, and the movement of your arms and legs. The vestibular sense informs you of your position in space, helping you maintain your equilibrium. The vestibular organs comprise the otolith organs and the semicircular canals.

THINKING ABOUT PSYCHOLOGY: WHY DO PSYCHOLOGISTS DISCOUNT ESP?

Most members of the lay public accept the existence of paranormal phenomena such as extrasensory perception and psychokinesis; most psychologists do not. Psychologists are skeptical because research in parapsychology has been marked by sloppy procedures, acceptance of coincidences as positive evidence, fraudulent reports, use of magic tricks, failure to replicate studies, and inability to explain paranormal phenomena. Supporters of parapsychology claim that their research has been subjected to unfair criticism.

IMPORTANT CONCEPTS

▶▶▶ MAJOR CONTRIBUTORS

▶▶▶ RECOMMENDED READINGS

FOR GENERAL WORKS ON
SENSATION AND PERCEPTION
Ackerman, D. (1990). A natural
   history of the senses. New York:
   Random House.
Boring, E. G. (1942). Sensation and
   perception in the history of
   experimental psychology. New
   York: Appleton-Century-Crofts.
Coren, S., Ward, L. M., & Ennis, J.
   (1989). Sensation and perception.
   (4th ed.). San Diego: Harcourt
   Brace Jovanovich.
Dember, W. N. (1990). William
   James on sensation and
   perception. Psychological
   Science, 1, 163–166.
Hamlyn, D. W. (1961). Sensation
   and perception: A history of the
   philosophy of perception. London:
   Routledge & Kegan Paul.
Keller, H. (1970). The story of my
   life. New York: Airmont.
Yost, W. A., Popper, A. N., & Fay,
   R. R. (Eds.). (1993). Human
   psychophysics. New York:
   Springer-Verlag.

FOR MORE ON VISION

The Eye
Chekaluk, E., & Llewellyn, K.
   (Eds.). (1992). The role of eye
   movements in perceptual
   processes. New York: Elsevier.
Dawson, H. (1990). Physiology of the
   eye. New York: Pergamon.
Dowling, J. E. (1987). The retina:
   An approachable part of the brain.
   Cambridge, MA: Belknap/
   Harvard University Press.

Janisse, M. P. (1977). Pupillometry:
   The psychology of the pupillary
   response. New York: Halsted.
Mazzolini, R. G. (1980). The iris in
   18th-century physiology. Bern,
   Switzerland: Huber.

Color Vision
Boynton, R. M. (1988). Color
   vision. Annual Review of
   Psychology, 39, 69–100.
Fletcher, R., & Voke, J. (1985).
   Defective color vision. New York:
   Taylor & Francis.
Wasserman, G. S. (1978). Color
   vision: An historical introduction.
   New York: Wiley.

Visual Perception
Bruce, V., & Green, P. (1990).
   Visual perception. Hillsdale, NJ:
   Erlbaum.
Cutting, J. E. (1987). Perception
   with an eye for motion.
   Cambridge, MA: MIT Press.
Gibson, J. J. (1979). The ecological
   approach to visual perception.
   Boston: Houghton Mifflin.
Glickstein, M. (1988, September).
   The discovery of the visual
   cortex. Scientific American, pp.
   118–127.
Gordon, I. E. (1991). Theories of
   visual perception. New York:
   Wiley.
Haber, R. N. (1980). How we
   perceive depth from flat
   pictures. American Scientist, 69,
   370–380.

Hatfield, G. (1990). The natural and
   the normative: Theories of spatial
   perception from Kant to
   Helmholtz. Cambridge, MA:
   MIT Press.
Hoffman, H. S. (1989). Vision and
   the art of drawing. Englewood
   Cliffs, NJ: Prentice Hall.
Hubel, D. H. (1988). Eye, brain,
   and vision. New York: W. H.
   Freeman.
Kubovy, M. (1986). The psychology
   of perspective and Renaissance art.
   New York: Cambridge
   University Press.
Lombardo, T. J. (1987). The
   reciprocity of perceiver and
   environment: The evolution of
   James J. Gibson's ecological
   psychology. Hillsdale, NJ:
   Erlbaum.
Pastore, N. (1971). Selective history
   of theories of visual perception:
   1650–1950. New York: Oxford
   University Press.
Van Hoorn, W. (1972). As images
   unwind: Ancient and modern
   theories of visual perception.
   Amsterdam: University Press of
   Amsterdam.

Visual Illusions
Block, J. R., & Yuker, H. E. (1989).
   Can you believe your eyes? Over
   250 illusions and other visual
   oddities. New York: Gardner
   Press.
Hershenson, M. (Ed.). (1989). The
   moon illusion. Hillsdale, NJ:
   Erlbaum.

Livingstone, M. S. (1988, January).
   Art, illusion, and the visual
   system. Scientific American, pp.
   78–85.
Petry, S., & Meyer, G. (Eds.).
   (1987). The perception of illusory
   contours. New York: Springer-
   Verlag.
Shepard, R. N. (1990). Mind sights:
   Original visual illusions,
   ambiguities, and other anomalies.
   New York: W. H. Freeman.

FOR MORE ON HEARING
Aitkin, L. M. (1990). The auditory
   cortex. New York: Routledge.
Blauert, J. (1983). Spatial hearing:
   The psychophysics of human
   sound localization. Cambridge,
   MA: MIT Press.
Miller, J. M., & Spelman, F. A.
   (Eds.). (1990). Cochlear
   implants: Models of the electrically
   stimulated ear. New York:
   Springer-Verlag.
Moore, B. C. J. (1989). An
   introduction to the psychology of
   hearing. (3rd ed.). London:
   Academic Press.
Paul, P. V., & Jackson, D. W.
   (1992). Toward a psychology of
   deafness: Theoretical and
   empirical perspectives. Boston:
   Allyn & Bacon.
Sloboda, J. A. (1985). The musical
   mind: The cognitive psychology of
   music. New York: Oxford
   University Press.
Wilson, J. P., & Kemp, D. T.
   (Eds.). (1989). Cochlear
   mechanisms. New York: Plenum.

FOR MORE ON THE CHEMICAL SENSES

Smell

Agosta, W. C. (1992). *Chemical communication: The language of pheromones*. New York: W. H. Freeman.

Engen, T. (1982). *The perception of odors*. New York: Academic Press.

Gibbons, B. (1986). The intimate sense of smell. *National Geographic, 170*, 324–361.

Rindisbacher, H. J. (1992). *The smell of books: A cultural-historical study of olfactory perception in literature*. Ann Arbor: University of Michigan Press.

Tagaki, S. (1988). *Human olfaction: From art to science*. Irvington, NY: Columbia University Press.

Van Toller, S., & Dodd, G. H. (Eds.). (1988). *Perfumery: The psychology and biology of fragrance*. London: Chapman & Hall.

Taste

Bolles, R. C. (Ed.). (1991). *The hedonism of taste*. Hillsdale, NJ: Erlbaum.

Cowart, B. J. (1981). Development of taste perception in humans: Sensitivity and preference through the life span. *Psychological Bulletin, 90*, 43–73.

FOR MORE ON THE SKIN SENSES

Touch

Barnard, K. E., & Brazelton, T. B. (Eds.). (1990). *Touch: The foundation of experience*. Madison, CT: International Universities Press.

Heller, M., & Schiff, W. (Eds.). (1991). *The psychology of touch*. Hillsdale, NJ: Erlbaum.

Katz, D. (1989). *The world of touch*. Hillsdale, NJ: Erlbaum.

Pain

McGrath, P. A. (1990). *Pain in children: Nature, assessment, and treatment*. New York: Guilford.

Miller, T. W. (Ed.). (1990). *Chronic pain* (2 vols.). Madison, CT: International Universities Press.

Ottoson, D., & Lundeberg, T. (1988). *Pain treatment by transcutaneous electrical nerve stimulation*. New York: Springer-Verlag.

Stux, G., & Pomeranz, B. (1993). *Basics of acupuncture* (2nd ed.). New York: Springer-Verlag.

Wall, P. D., & Melzack, R. (Eds.). (1994). *Textbook of pain* (3rd ed.). Edinburgh, Scotland: Churchill Livingstone.

FOR MORE ON THE BODY SENSES

Hudspeth, A. J. (1983, January). The hair cells of the inner ear. *Scientific American*, pp. 54–64.

Parker, D. E. (1980, November). The vestibular apparatus. *Scientific American*, pp. 118–135.

Swain, R. B. (1984, August). Message from a heaving deck. *Discover*, pp. 60–64.

FOR MORE ON PARAPSYCHOLOGY

Alcock, J. E. (1989). *Science and supernature: A critical appraisal of parapsychology*. Buffalo, NY: Prometheus.

James, W. (1986). *Essays in psychical research*. Cambridge, MA: Harvard University Press.

Morris, S. (1980, April). Interview: James Randi. *Omni*, pp. 76–78, 104–108.

Neppe, V. M. (1983). *The psychology of deja vu: Have I been here before?* Portland, OR: International Specialized Book Services.

Randi, J. (1982). *Flim-flam: Psychics, ESP, unicorns, and other delusions*. Buffalo, NY: Prometheus.

Wolman, B. B., Dale, L. A., Schmeidler, G. R., & Ullman, M. (Eds.). (1985). *Handbook of parapsychology*. New York: Van Nostrand Reinhold.

FOR MORE ON CONTRIBUTORS TO THE STUDY OF SENSATION AND PERCEPTION

Cadwallader, T. C., & Cadwallader, J. V. (1990). Christine Ladd-Franklin. In A. N. O'Connell & N. F. Russo (Eds.), *Women in psychology* (pp. 220–229). Westport, CT: Greenwood.

Cranston, M. (1979). *John Locke: A biography*. New York: Oxford University Press.

Koenigsberger, L. (1906/1965). *Hermann von Helmholtz*. New York: Dover.

Myers, G. E. (1986). *William James: His life and thought*. New Haven, CT: Yale University Press.

Randi, J. (1991). *James Randi: Psychic investigator*. London: Boxtree.

Rao, K. R. (Ed.). (1982). *J. B. Rhine: On the frontiers of science*. Jefferson, NC: McFarland.

Reed, E. S. (1988). *James J. Gibson and the psychology of perception*. New Haven, CT: Yale University Press.

CHAPTER 6

Henri Rousseau
The Sleeping Gypsy
1897

CONSCIOUSNESS

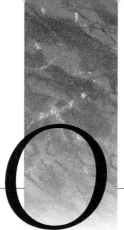

On January 21, 1959, a New York disc jockey named Peter Tripp began a radiothon to raise money for the March of Dimes fight against polio. He stayed awake for 200 hours, each night broadcasting his show from an army recruiting booth in Times Square, but as the days passed he developed symptoms of psychological disturbance. After 4 days he experienced hallucinations, seeing a rabbit run across the booth and flames shooting out of a drawer in his hotel room. On the sixth day he began taking stimulant drugs to stay awake. And on the final day he displayed delusional thinking, even insisting that his physician was coming to prepare him for burial. After his ordeal, Tripp slept 13 hours and returned to his normal state of psychological well-being (Segal & Luce, 1966).

Did Tripp's experience demonstrate that we need to sleep to maintain healthy psychological functioning? Possibly—but possibly not. First, his experiences were those of a single subject. Perhaps his reactions to sleep deprivation were unique. Second, the delusions he displayed near the end of his ordeal might have been caused by the stimulant drug he took to stay awake rather than by his lack of sleep. As you will read about in this chapter, our knowledge of the effects of sleep deprivation and the effects of stimulant drugs comes from research by psychologists and other scientists interested in the study of *consciousness*.

Two Hundred Hours without Sleep
Peter Tripp experienced emotional, perceptual, and cognitive disturbances during his 200-hour radiothon.

consciousness
The awareness of one's own mental activity, including thoughts, feelings, and sensations.

THE NATURE OF CONSCIOUSNESS

What is consciousness? In 1690 John Locke wrote that "consciousness is the perception of what passes in a man's own mind" (Locke, 1690/1959, p. 138). Today psychologists share a similar view of **consciousness,** defining it as the awareness of one's own mental activity, including thoughts, feelings, and sensations. Two hundred years after Locke, William James (1890/1981) pointed out that consciousness is personal, selective, continuous, and changing. Consider your own consciousness. It is *personal* because you feel that it belongs to you—you do not share it with anyone else. Consciousness is *selective* because you can attend to certain things while ignoring other things—right now you can shift your attention to a nearby voice, the first word in the next sentence, or the feel of this book against your fingers. Consciousness is *continuous* because its contents blend into one another—the mind cannot be broken down into meaningful segments. And consciousness is *changing* because its contents are in a constant state of flux—normally, you cannot focus on one thing for more than a few seconds without other thoughts, feelings, or sensations drifting through your mind.

Because consciousness is both continuous and changing, James likened it to a stream. Your favorite fishing stream remains the same stream even though the water where you are fishing is continuously being replaced by new water. You might recognize this view of the mind in the works of James Joyce and other "stream of consciousness" writers, who portray the seemingly random thoughts, feelings, and sensations that pass through the consciousness of their characters from moment to moment. Even as you read this paragraph, you might notice irrelevant thoughts, feelings, and sensations passing through your own mind. Some may grab your attention, while others may quickly fade away. If you were to write them down as they occurred, a person reading what you had written might think you were confused or even that you were mentally ill. The disjointed nature of stream-of-consciousness writing makes it hard to follow without knowing the context of the story. You can appreciate this by trying to make sense of the opening passage from James Joyce's *A Portrait of the Artist as a Young Man:*

Once upon a time and a very good time it was there was a moocow coming down along the road and this moocow that was coming down along the road met a nicens little boy named baby tuckoo . . . .

His father told him that story: his father looked at him through a glass: he had a hairy face.

He was baby tuckoo. The moocow came down the road where Betty Byrne lived: she sold lemon platt.

O, the wild rose blossoms

On the little green place.

He sang that song. That was his song.

O, the green wothe botheth.

When you wet the bed first it is warm then it gets cold. His mother put on the oilsheet. That had the queer smell.

His mother had a nicer smell than his father. She played on the piano the sailor's hornpipe for him to dance. (Joyce, 1916/1967, p. 171)

As a functionalist, William James believed that consciousness is an evolutionary development that enhances our ability to adapt to the environment. James declared, "It seems reasonable to suppose that, unless consciousness served some useful purpose, it would not have been superadded to life" (quoted in Rieber, 1980, p. 205). Today many psychologists agree with James's view and note that consciousness provides us with a mental representation of the world that permits us to try out courses of action in our mind before acting on them (Yates, 1985). This makes us more reflective and more flexible in adapting to the world, thereby reducing our tendency to engage in aimless, reckless, or impulsive behavior.

One of the ways in which we manipulate mental representations of the world is through **daydreaming,** a state of consciousness in which we voluntarily shift our attention from mental experiences stimulated by external stimuli to mental experiences generated by the brain. A clever study by psychologist Eric Klinger found that college students devote several hours a day to daydreaming. Each student was given a pocket alarm to carry all day for several days. The alarm beeped at random times during the day, but on the average beeped every 40 minutes. Whenever the students heard their alarms, they reported their mental activity. The results showed that the students spent one-third of their waking hours daydreaming (Bartusiak, 1980). This leads to the remarkable conclusion that college students spend more than half of each 24-hour day either asleep or daydreaming. As a student, even Wilhelm Wundt, the founder of psychology, spent much of his waking day lost in daydreams (Rieber, 1980).

Given that daydreaming occupies so much of our time, what functions might it serve? Surveys by Jerome Singer (1975), a leading researcher on daydreaming, have found that, as William James would have stressed, daydreaming lets us mentally rehearse alternative courses of action. A second reason why we daydream is to keep mentally aroused while in situations that provide inadequate external stimulation—as any student who has sat through a dull lecture knows all too well. A third reason people daydream is to solve problems. Mark Twain, Edgar Allen Poe, and Robert Louis Stevenson wrote stories inspired by daydreams. And the chemist Friedrich Kekulé, during the drowsy *hypnagogic* state that we enter just before falling asleep, discovered the ringlike structure of the benzene molecule in a daydream of a snake biting its own tail (Schachter, 1976). In the seventeenth century, René Descartes made use of the hypnagogic state by habitually awakening each morning and allowing his mind to wander as he meditated on intellectual problems (Vrooman, 1970). A fourth reason to daydream is the pleasure it brings us, as when we daydream about sex (Purifoy, Grodsky, & Giambra, 1992). The pleasurable nature of daydreaming was recognized by the seventeenth-century English writer John Dryden in his poem *Rival Ladies:*

I strongly wish for what I faintly hope:
Like the daydreams of melancholy men,
I think and think on things impossible,
Yet love to wander in the golden maze.

daydreaming
A state of consciousness that involves shifting attention from external stimuli to self-generated thoughts and images.

Eric Klinger
"Daydreams are so much a part of you that what you experience in them affects what you do in the real world."

Daydreaming
Students may spend one-third of class time daydreaming. One of the functions of daydreaming is to escape from boring situations.

The Cocktail Party Phenomenon
At a cocktail party, the selectivity of attention lets you listen to one conversation out of the many taking place.

attention
The process by which the individual focuses awareness on certain contents of consciousness while ignoring others.

Today researchers are especially interested in another of the aspects of consciousness identified by James: its *selectivity*. We refer to the selectivity of consciousness as **attention,** which functions like a tuner to make us notice certain stimuli. What determines whether we will attend to a given stimulus? Some factors are related to the perceiver, and others are related to the stimulus itself. The perceiver's *motivation* and *expectation* are important. A hungry person is more likely to attend to the odors emanating from a bakery, and a student who expects to see a friend in the student center is more likely to notice her in a crowd of hundreds of students. Among the many stimulus factors that affect attention are whether the stimulus is important, moving, changing, or novel. We tend to notice stimuli that are personally *important*. A baby's cry might be an important stimulus to a parent, attracting his or her attention even when other adults fail to notice it. Our attention is also drawn to stimuli that are *moving*. While driving down a busy street, you are more likely to notice a car crossing your path than one parked at the curb. A *change* in stimulation is likely to attract our attention. When watching television, you are more likely to pay attention to a commercial that is much louder or quieter than the program it interrupts. And we are more likely to notice stimuli that are *novel*— that is, unusual or unexpected. This principle has even been used to reduce speeding. A small town in Georgia once set its speed limit at 19 miles per hour, based on the assumption that a limit that was not a multiple of five would be so unusual that it would grab motorists' attention.

From the 1920s to the 1950s, in the heyday of behaviorism, there was little research on attention. The renewed interest in studying attention as an aspect of consciousness led Wilse Webb, a noted consciousness researcher, to proclaim: "I suspect that the angels in heaven will sigh with relief and students nod with approval when consciousness and attention are once again discussed together" (Webb, 1981, p. 140). In the 1950s, scientific research on attention was inspired in part by concerns about the ability of air traffic controllers to attend to relevant pilot voices and to ignore irrelevant ones while directing takeoffs and landings. Research on attention was also inspired by the "cocktail party phenomenon," in which you might be engrossed in one conversation at a party, yet notice that your name has been mentioned in another conversation (Moray, 1959).

The selectivity of attention was demonstrated in a study in which subjects watched a television screen on which two videotapes were shown simultaneously (Neisser & Becklen, 1975). One videotape portrayed two people playing a hand-slapping game, and the other portrayed three people bouncing and throwing a basketball. The subjects were told to watch one of the games and to press a response key whenever a particular action occurred. Those watching the hand game had to respond whenever the participants slapped hands with each other. Those watching the ball game had to respond whenever the ball was thrown. The results showed that the subjects made few errors. But when they were asked to watch both games simultaneously, using their right hand to respond to one game and their left hand to respond to the other, their performances deteriorated and they made significantly more errors than when they attended to just one of the games. This study indicated that the chief advantage of attention—its enabling us to focus on a single aspect of our environment—is also a weakness. You realize this when you try to read and watch television at the same time. You must continually shift your attention between the two, which interferes with your ability to do either well.

Though William James pointed out the importance of attention and other aspects of consciousness, he insisted that consciousness exists as pure mental experience; that is, consciousness is a process, not a substance (James, 1904). James viewed the study of consciousness as the main goal of psychology. About a decade after James proclaimed that consciousness was not an entity, yet worth studying as a process, John B. Watson published his classic 1913 article proclaiming the behaviorist position. He argued that consciousness, being unobservable, could not be studied scientifically. Watson insisted

Drawing by Frascino; © 1983 The New Yorker Magazine, Inc.

"If you ask me, all three of us are in different states of awareness."

that "the time seems to have come when psychology must discard all references to consciousness" (Watson, 1913, p. 163).

As you read in chapter 1, the behaviorist position dominated psychology from the 1920s to the 1960s, a period when relatively few psychologists studied consciousness (Webb, 1981). But the 1960s brought renewed interest in the study of consciousness as a result of a growing interest in Eastern mysticism, the widespread use of psychoactive drugs, and the development of devices that could record physiological changes accompanying states of consciousness associated with sleep, hypnosis, meditation, and psychoactive drugs. The current interest in studying altered states of consciousness reflects James's observation that "our normal waking consciousness, rational consciousness as we call it, is but one special type of consciousness, whilst all about it, parted from it by the filmiest of screens, there lie potential forms of consciousness entirely different" (James, 1902/1992, p. 388). Perhaps the most obvious of these is *sleep*.

SLEEP AND DREAMS

We spend about one-third of each day in the altered state of consciousness called *sleep*. The daily sleep-wake cycle is the most obvious of our **circadian rhythms,** which are 24-hour cycles of psychological and physiological changes. The word *circadian* is derived from the Latin *circa*, meaning "about," and *dies*, meaning "a day." Our circadian rhythm of body temperature parallels our circadian rhythm of brain arousal, with most people beginning the day at low points on both and rising on them through the day. College roommates who are out of phase with each other in their circadian rhythms are more likely to express dissatisfaction with their relationship than are roommates who are in phase with each other (Watts, 1982). A student who is a "morning person"—already warmed up and chipper at 7 A.M.—might find it difficult to socialize with a roommate who can barely crawl out of bed at that time.

What governs our circadian rhythms? One factor is the **pineal gland,** an endocrine gland in the center of the brain that secretes the hormone *melatonin*. Melatonin secretion varies with light levels, decreasing in daylight and increasing in darkness. Sleepiness increases as the secretion of melatonin increases. This has led researchers to investigate the possible use of melatonin as a treatment for insomnia. In a study of chronic

circadian rhythms
Twenty-four-hour cycles of psychological and physiological changes, most notably the sleep-wake cycle.

pineal gland
An endocrine gland that secretes a hormone that has a general tranquilizing effect on the body and that helps regulate biological rhythms.

FIGURE 6.1

The Extended Sleep-Wake Cycle
When subjects are kept isolated from cues related to the normal day-night cycle, they gradually adopt a 25-hour cycle. They then go to sleep 1 hour later each day.

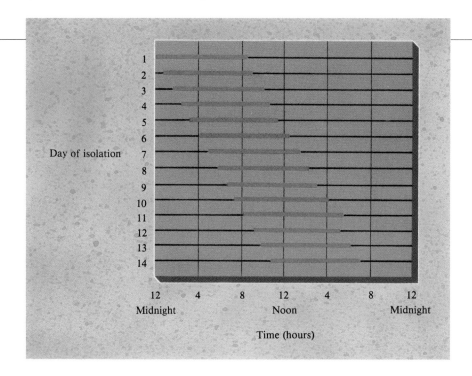

Day of isolation

Time (hours)

phase advance
Shortening the sleep-wake cycle, as occurs when traveling from west to east.

phase delay
Lengthening the sleep-wake cycle, as occurs when traveling from east to west.

insomniacs, the subjects received a dose of either melatonin or a placebo at 10 P.M. every day for 14 days. Those who received melatonin reported better sleep and more alertness during the day than did those who received the placebo (MacFarlane et al., 1991). Human circadian rhythms, though affected by light, continue even in total darkness. This occurs because of a region of the hypothalamus called the *suprachiasmatic nucleus*, which maintains circadian rhythms even in the absence of light (Gillette, 1986).

When subjects are cut off from cues related to the day-night cycle, perhaps by having them live in a cave or in a windowless room for several weeks, a curious thing happens. For unknown reasons their sleep-wake cycle changes from 24 hours to 25 hours in length (as shown in figure 6.1). This might explain why "jet lag" is more severe when we fly west to east than when we fly east to west. Consider a professional baseball player. Eastbound travel shortens his sleep-wake cycle (**phase advance**), countering its natural tendency to lengthen. In contrast, westbound travel lengthens his sleep-wake cycle (**phase delay**), which agrees with its natural tendency to lengthen. So, phase advance requires more adjustment by the athlete. The symptoms of jet lag, caused by a disruption of the normal sleep-wake cycle, include daytime sleepiness, nighttime insomnia, depressed mood, and lack of motivation (Davis, 1988).

The one-quarter of American workers on rotating shifts, including nurses, police officers, and factory workers, also find their sleep-wake cycles disrupted. This can be dangerous, because it can cause workers to become less alert or even fall asleep on the job (Akerstedt, 1988). Given the natural tendency of the sleep-wake cycle to increase in length, workers on rotating shifts respond better to phase delay than to phase advance. This was demonstrated in a study of industrial workers. Those on a phase-delay schedule moved from the night shift (12 midnight to 8 A.M.) to the day shift (8 A.M. to 4 P.M.) to the swing shift (4 P.M. to 12 midnight). Those on a phase-advance schedule moved in the opposite direction, from the night shift to the swing shift to the day shift. The results showed that workers on a phase-delay schedule had better health, greater satisfaction, higher productivity, and lower turnover (Czeisler, Moore-Ede, & Coleman, 1982). You can imagine the importance of research on the effects of circadian rhythms on workers who serve crucial functions, such as members of airplane flight crews (Gander et al., 1993).

Patterns of Sleep

Intellectual interest in sleep can be traced back to ancient Greece. According to Aristotle and Hippocrates, sleep is caused by the cooling of the blood, and waking is caused by its warming. Other than literary works, little was written about sleep until the nineteenth century, when physiologists and psychologists became interested in it. One of the first books to summarize the emerging field of sleep research, *Sleep: Its Physiology, Pathology, Hygiene, and Psychology*, by the French scientist Marie de Manaceine, was published in 1899. De Manaceine was also one of the first scientists to conduct systematic experiments on sleep. Despite research interest in sleep, until the 1960s it was not an important part of mainstream psychology, as evidenced by its coverage in introductory psychology textbooks. In 1960, four popular introductory psychology textbooks made no mention of sleep, and the most extensive coverage in any introductory textbook was two pages. In 1980, in contrast, all introductory psychology textbooks included coverage of sleep, ranging from three to seventeen pages (Webb, 1985).

Though psychologists are interested in studying the effects of changes in the sleep-wake cycle, they are especially interested in studying sleep itself. Imagine that you are a subject in a sleep study. You would first sleep a night or two in a sleep laboratory to get accustomed to the novel surroundings. You would then sleep several nights in the laboratory while special devices recorded changes in your brain waves, eye movements, heart rate, blood pressure, body temperature, breathing rate, muscle tension, and respiration rate.

The physiological recordings would reveal that you do not simply drift into deep sleep, stay there all night, and suddenly awaken in the morning. Instead, they would reveal that you pass through repeated sleep cycles, marked by variations in your depth of sleep, as defined by particular brain-wave patterns. Figure 6.2 illustrates these patterns, which were first identified in the 1930s (Loomis, Harvey, & Hobart, 1937). As you lie in bed with your eyes closed, an EEG recording would show that your brain-wave pattern changes from primarily high-frequency *beta waves*, which mark an alert mental state, to a higher proportion of lower-frequency *alpha waves*, which mark a relaxed, introspective mental state. As you drift off to sleep, you would exhibit slow, rolling eye movements and your brain-wave pattern would show a higher proportion of *theta waves*, which have a lower frequency than alpha waves. You would also exhibit a decrease in other signs of arousal, including heart rate, breathing rate, muscle tension, and respiration rate.

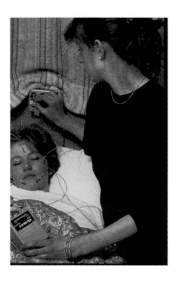

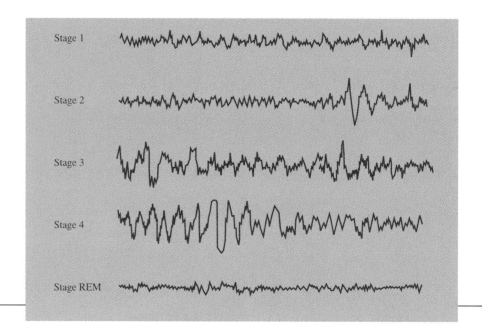

FIGURE 6.2

The Stages of Sleep
Studies of subjects in sleep laboratories have found that the stages of sleep are associated with distinctive patterns of brain-wave activity. As we drift into deeper stages of sleep, our brain waves decrease in frequency and increase in amplitude. When we are in REM sleep, our brain-wave patterns are similar to those in the waking state.

REM sleep
The stage of sleep associated with rapid eye movements, an active brain-wave pattern, and vivid dreams.

NREM sleep
The stages of sleep not associated with rapid eye movements and marked by relatively little dreaming.

The cessation of the rolling eye movements would signify the onset of sleep (Ogilvie et al., 1988). This initial light stage of sleep is called *stage 1*. After 5 to 10 minutes in stage 1, you would enter the slightly deeper *stage 2*, associated with periodic bursts of higher-frequency brain waves known as *sleep spindles*. After 10 to 20 minutes in stage 2, you would enter *stage 3*, marked by the appearance of extremely low-frequency *delta waves*. When at least 50 percent of your brain waves are delta waves, you would be in *stage 4*, the deepest stage of sleep. After remaining in stages 3 and 4 for 30 to 40 minutes, you would drift up through stages 3, 2, and 1 until, about 90 minutes after falling asleep, you would reach the *rapid eye movement stage*, better known as **REM sleep.**

REM sleep gets its name from the darting eye movements that characterize it. You have probably seen these movements under the eyelids of sleeping people—or even a sleeping pet dog or cat. Because stages 1, 2, 3, and 4 are not characterized by darting eye movements, they are collectively called *non-REM*, or **NREM sleep.** NREM sleep is characterized by slow brain waves, deep breathing, regular heart rate, and lower blood pressure. After an initial 10-minute period of REM sleep, you would again drift down into NREM sleep, eventually reaching stage 4. Each complete cycle of NREM-REM sleep takes an average of 90 minutes, meaning that you pass through four or five cycles in a typical night's sleep. Adults normally spend about 25 percent of the night in REM sleep, 5 percent in stage 1, 50 percent in stage 2, and 20 percent in stages 3 and 4. As shown in figure 6.3, the first half of your night's sleep has relatively more NREM sleep than does the second half, whereas the second half has relatively more REM sleep than does the first half. You might not even reach stages 3 and 4 during the second half of the night.

While you are in REM sleep, your heart rate, respiration rate, and brain-wave frequency increase, making you appear to be awake. But you also experience flaccid paralysis of your limbs, making it impossible for you to shift your position in bed. Because you would be physiologically aroused, yet immobile and difficult to awaken, REM sleep is also called *paradoxical sleep*. And because we are paralyzed during REM sleep, sleepwalking (or *somnambulism*) occurs only during NREM sleep. Sleepwalking is more common in children than in adults (Berlin & Qayyum, 1986). Despite warnings to the contrary, sleepwalkers may be awakened without fear of physically or psychologically harming them. But the habitual sleepwalker should be protected from injury by keeping doors and windows locked (Vela-Bueno, Soldatos, & Julius, 1987). In rare cases, a sleepwalker might become violent. This can lead to a legal dilemma: Is a sleepwalker respon-

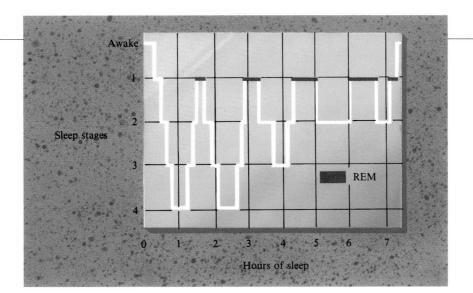

FIGURE 6.3

A Typical Night's Sleep
During a typical night's sleep we pass
through cycles that involve stages of
NREM sleep and the stage of REM
sleep. Note that we obtain our deepest
sleep during the first half of the night
and that the periods of REM sleep
become longer with each successive
cycle (Cartwright, 1978).

sible for an assault committed while sleepwalking? In England, some defendants who
have killed a person while sleepwalking have been acquitted of murder charges after
claiming the defense of "insane automatism" (Howard & D'Orban, 1987).

Another characteristic of REM sleep is erection of the penis or clitoris. Arousal
of the sex organs during REM sleep occurs spontaneously and is not always indicative
of a sexual dream. Sleep clinics use REM erections to determine whether men who are
unable to have erections while awake are suffering from a physical or a psychological
disorder. If a man has erections while in REM sleep, his problem is psychological, not
physical.

REM sleep *is*, however, associated with dreaming. We know this because of research conducted in the early 1950s by Eugene Aserinsky and Nathaniel Kleitman (1953)
of the University of Chicago. When they awakened sleepers exhibiting rapid eye movements, the sleepers usually reported that they had been dreaming. In contrast, people
awakened during NREM sleep rarely report that they had been dreaming. Instead, they
might report that they were merely thinking (Webb, 1985). Because the longest REM
period occurs during the last sleep cycle of the night, you can often find yourself in the
middle of a dream when your alarm clock wakes you in the morning. You might be
tempted to infer that rapid eye movements reflect the scanning of dream scenes, but
Aserinsky and his colleagues (1985) have found that they do not— so if you were dreaming about, say, a tennis match, your rapid eye movements would not have been following
the ball's flight.

Duration of Sleep

Human beings are moderately long sleepers, with young adults averaging 8 hours of sleep
a day. In contrast, some animals, such as elephants, sleep as little as 2 hours a day, while
other animals, such as bats, sleep as much as 20 hours a day. Efforts to wean human
subjects from sleep indicate that it cannot be reduced much below 4 hours without
inducing extreme drowsiness and mood alterations (Webb, 1985). Figure 6.4 indicates
that our need for sleep varies across the life span. Infants typically sleep 16 hours a day;
elderly people typically sleep 6 hours a day. Of course, you might need to sleep more or
less than other people your age. This variability in normal sleep duration among people
of the same age appears to have a hereditary basis (Heath et al., 1990).

Regardless of how much sleep they may need, North American adults habitually
get less than their normal quota of sleep. They may stay awake to watch television, do
schoolwork, or perform other activities. You might go to bed when you want to (perhaps
after watching the late movie) and awaken when you have to (perhaps in time for an

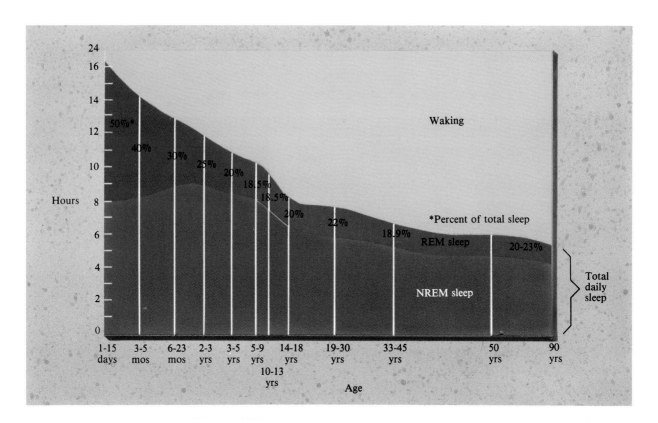

FIGURE **6.4**

Sleep across the Life Span
Our amount of daily sleep declines across the life span, decreasing rapidly in infancy and childhood and more gradually in adulthood. The proportion of time spent in REM sleep also declines across the life span.

From H. P. Roffwarg, et al., "Ontogenetic Development of the Human Sleep-Dream Cycle" in Science, *152:608, 29 April 1966. Copyright 1966 by the AAAS. Revised since publication. Reprinted by permission of the publisher and the author.*

8 A.M. class), making you chronically sleep deprived. This was supported by a study showing that, indeed, when given the chance, young adults sleep longer than their everyday lives permit (Webb & Agnew, 1975). Difficulty in getting a good night's sleep has been increasing among college students. A survey of college students conducted in 1992 found that they reported sleeping less and being less satisfied with their sleep than did a survey of college students conducted in 1978 (Hicks, Johnson, & Pellegrini, 1992). Fortunately, if we fail to get our nightly quota of sleep during the week (a common problem for college students), we will regain our optimal level of alertness after a single night's normal sleep on the weekend (Carskadon & Dement, 1981).

Many people try to overcome the effects of abbreviated nighttime sleep by taking daytime naps. Students and business executives alike value their "power naps." No claim for the benefits of napping has been more extreme than that made by the eccentric surrealist painter Salvador Dalí. Dalí would put a tin plate on the floor, sit on a chair, loosely hold a spoon over the plate, and quickly fall asleep. As you would expect, as soon as he fell asleep, the spoon would slip from his grasp and hit the plate, immediately waking him. Dalí claimed that he was refreshed by these extraordinarily brief periods of sleep (Dement, 1976). Though Dalí's claim might be exaggerated, normal naps can be beneficial. In one study, workers who took a 2.3-hour nap before working on an assembly-line task on a night shift improved in their level of alertness and their performance on the task (Schweitzer, Muehlback, & Walsh, 1992).

Despite the fatigue-inducing effect of sleep loss, in some cases intentional sleep reduction can relieve depression. Deprivation of REM-sleep, in particular, can elevate

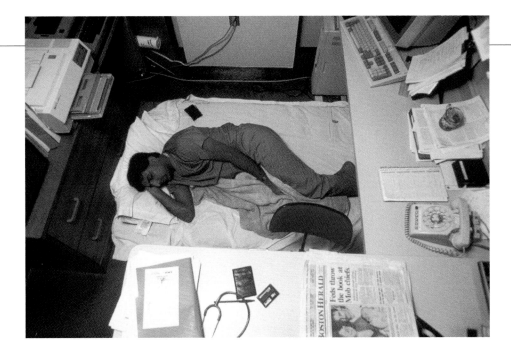

the mood of depressed people. Though the reason for this effect is unclear, it might be due to increases in neurotransmitters, such as serotonin and norepinephrine, that elevate moods (Wu & Bunney, 1990).

Functions of Sleep

Assuming that you live to be 75, you will have spent about 25 years asleep. Are you wasting one-third of your life, or does sleep serve important functions for you? If sleep serves no function, why do we benefit from naps and why do we eventually succumb to sleep no matter how hard we try to stay awake? Among the many hypothesized functions of sleep, three are most prominent: sleep as restorative, sleep as adaptive inactivity, and sleep as an aid to memory.

Sleep As Restorative

The most commonsense view of sleep holds that it restores the body and the mind after the wear and tear imposed by waking activities. Sleep may remove metabolic waste products, replenish brain neurotransmitters, and repair body tissues. One way of testing whether sleep is restorative is to observe the effects of sleep deprivation. In the case of Peter Tripp, sleep deprivation led to hallucinations and delusional thinking, which disappeared after a single night's sleep. In a similar case in 1964, Randy Gardner, a 17-year-old San Diego high school student, stayed awake 264 hours to get his name in the *Guinness Book of World Records* (his record has since been broken). He experienced less-severe disturbances than Tripp did, including some fatigue, irritability, and perceptual distortions. On his eleventh day without sleep, Gardner beat William Dement, a prominent sleep researcher, one hundred consecutive times at a pinball game. After 15 hours of sleep, Gardner awoke—restored both physically and mentally (Gulevich, Dement, & Johnson, 1966).

More-formal research has provided evidence of the detrimental effects of sleep loss and the restorative effects of sleep. In one study, subjects who stayed awake for 60 hours experienced mood disturbances and difficulty performing cognitive tasks, including mental arithmetic (Angus, Heslegrave, & Myles, 1985). Chronic sleep deprivation is one of the major stressors of medical residents, who might be asked to make life-and-death decisions and perform delicate procedures after being awake for 24 hours or more (Spurgeon & Harrington, 1989). Even performance in everyday activities, such as driving, is

Wilse Webb

"Natural sleep is when you go to bed when you're sleepy and wake up when you're rested. But the modern system of sleeping is to go to bed when you want to and get up when you have to."

adversely affected by sleep deprivation. In fact, one of the most common causes of automobile accidents is a lack of alertness caused by sleepiness (Roth & Roehrs, 1988).

Another source of evidence for the restorative function of sleep is research on the effects of vigorous physical activity on sleep. Sleep, especially deep sleep, increases in length on the nights after vigorous exercise (Vein et al., 1991). A study of runners who participated in a 57-mile ultramarathon race found that they had a significant increase in sleep, particularly stage 3 and stage 4, on the first two nights after the race (Shapiro et al., 1981). Despite circumstantial evidence that sleep has a restorative function, we still do not know exactly *what* sleep restores.

Sleep As Adaptive Inactivity

An alternative view, championed by sleep researcher Wilse Webb (1975), is that sleep evolved because it protected the sleeper from harm. Our prehistoric ancestors who slept at night were less likely to gain the attention of hungry nocturnal predators. The limb paralysis accompanying REM sleep might have evolved because it prevented cave dwellers from acting out their dreams, when they might have bumped into trees, fallen off cliffs, or provided dinner for saber-toothed tigers. Evidence for this protective function of REM sleep comes from studies showing that destruction of a portion of the pons that normally induces REM paralysis in cats produces stalking and attacking movements during sleep, as though they are acting out their dreams (Morrison, 1983).

Another reason to believe that sleep may be a period of adaptive inactivity is that it conserves energy. Evidence supportive of this view comes from studies of the food-finding habits of different species. Because the normal duration of sleep for a given species is negatively correlated with how long it takes members of that species to find their daily food, perhaps animals stay awake only long enough to eat sufficient food to meet their energy needs. Animals might have evolved sleep to conserve energy the remainder of the time. Thus, the typical young adult's need for about 8 hours of sleep might mean that our prehistoric ancestors needed about 16 hours to find their daily food (Cohen, 1979).

Sleep As an Aid to Memory

Sleep can help to consolidate long-term memories. When subjects learn new material and are then deprived of sleep, particularly REM sleep, their memory for the material is impaired as compared to subjects who are not deprived (Li et al., 1991). Consider a study in which undergraduates were awakened periodically to deprive them of equal amounts of either REM sleep or stage 4 sleep. The next day they were asked to recall a story they had read the day before. Subjects who had been deprived of REM sleep showed poorer recall than subjects who had been deprived of stage 4 sleep (Tilley & Empson, 1978).

Memory for material learned during the day improves as the length of REM sleep increases. In one study, undergraduates learned Morse code just before bedtime on three consecutive nights. After awakening, they were given a Morse code test. The results revealed a positive correlation between the length of REM sleep and their performance (Mandai et al., 1989). In another study, competitors in a marathon 146-hour tennis match slept 4 or 5 hours less than normal per night. Physiological recordings indicated that they continued to get their normal NREM sleep, but at the cost of a decrease in their REM sleep. They also showed poorer memory after the match, perhaps because of their decrease in REM sleep (Edinger et al., 1990).

Sleep Disorders

You might take sleep for granted, but many people do not. They suffer from sleep disorders such as *insomnia, sleep apnea,* or *narcolepsy.*

Insomnia

Millions of Americans suffer from **insomnia,** which is chronic difficulty in either falling asleep (sleep-onset insomnia) or staying asleep all night (sleep-maintenance insomnia). Some people with sleep-maintenance insomnia awaken repeatedly during the night. Other people with sleep-maintenance insomnia experience *early-morning awakening*—they sleep through most of the night, only to awaken 2 or 3 hours earlier than they wish to. Many insomniacs resort to sedatives, so-called sleeping pills, to fall asleep. But sleeping pills interfere with the sleep cycle (for instance, they decrease REM sleep), eventually lose their effectiveness, and cause harmful side effects (including drug dependence). Thus, alternative ways of treating insomnia are preferable.

The shortcomings of drug-induced sleep have led scientists to search for a natural chemical treatment for insomnia. In 1913, French scientist Henri Pieron found that transfusions of cerebrospinal fluid from sleepy dogs induced sleep in alert dogs. More recently, scientists isolated a sleep-inducing chemical from human urine. When infused into the brains of rabbits, the chemical, called factor S, causes them to fall sleep. But factor S, composed of several amino acids, is difficult to study—it takes 4.5 tons of urine to isolate one dose (Maugh, 1982b). A more practical approach to sleep induction is to use L-tryptophan. This amino acid is a precursor of the neurotransmitter serotonin, which promotes the onset of sleep. Subjects who receive doses of L-tryptophan do, in fact, fall asleep faster (Spring, Chiodo, & Bowen, 1987).

Instead of turning to drugs or sleep-inducing chemicals, individuals can devise behavioral techniques for obtaining a good night's sleep. For example, when attending foreign meetings, British prime minister Winston Churchill insisted on a room with two beds. During the night, when the sheets on the bed he was in got too wrinkled, he moved to the other bed (Segal & Luce, 1966). Psychologists have developed effective treatments for insomnia that rely on neither drugs nor peculiar sleeping habits. If you suffer from insomnia, you should reduce your presleep arousal by avoiding exercise and caffeine products too close to bedtime. You might also use *paradoxical intention,* in which you try to stay awake while lying in bed. This might, paradoxically, induce sleep by preventing fruitless, anxiety-inducing efforts to fall asleep (Katz, 1984). Another technique, *stimulus control,* requires arranging your bedtime situation to promote sleep. First, go to bed only when you feel sleepy. Second, to assure that you associate lying in bed with sleep and not with being awake, do not eat, read, watch television, or listen to music while lying in bed. Third, if you toss and turn, get out of bed and return only when you are sleepy. Finally, avoid napping. If you nap during the day, you might not feel sleepy enough to fall asleep at your desired bedtime (Ladouceur & Gros-Louis, 1986).

Sleep Apnea

Some people, usually men, experience a form of sleep-maintenance insomnia called **sleep apnea.** When sleep apnea victims fall asleep, they stop breathing. After about 10 to 60 seconds, the person awakens enough to breathe for several minutes and then falls asleep again. This cycle can occur hundreds of times a night, leading the person to complain of chronic daytime sleepiness. Some cases of sleep apnea are caused by a failure of the respiratory centers of the brain to maintain normal breathing. These cases might respond to drug therapy (Mendelson, Maczaj, & Holt, 1991). Other cases of sleep apnea can be caused by collapse of the pharnyx, which is more common in obese people, as in the "Pickwickian syndrome" found in obese men whose necks can constrict their windpipes while they are asleep. The syndrome is named for *The Pickwick Papers,* a novel by Charles Dickens in which an obese servant-boy has trouble staying awake during the day (Hall, 1986). In cases of sleep apnea caused by constriction of the breathing passage, the victim can wear a mask attached to a device that provides constant air pressure in the windpipe, which makes it resist collapsing—a procedure called *continuous*

insomnia
Chronic difficulty in either falling asleep or staying asleep.

Insomnia
If you suffer from sleep-onset insomnia, you should try to refrain from activities such as eating, reading, or watching television while you are in bed. This will help you associate lying in bed with sleep, rather than with being awake and active.

sleep apnea
A condition in which a person awakens repeatedly in order to breathe.

positive airway pressure (Montplaisir et al., 1992). In extreme cases, a surgeon may provide sleep apnea victims with a breathing tube inserted through a hole cut through the neck into the windpipe.

Narcolepsy

narcolepsy
A condition in which an awake person suffers from repeated, sudden, and irresistible REM sleep attacks.

If you suffered from **narcolepsy,** you would experience sudden and irresistible daytime sleep attacks in which you immediately fell into REM sleep for several seconds or several minutes. Because of its association with REM sleep, narcolepsy is usually accompanied by *cataplexy,* a loss of muscle tone that causes the victim to collapse to the ground. Narcolepsy usually begins in adolescence and lasts a lifetime. About two-thirds of those with narcolepsy will fall asleep while driving (Aldrich, 1992). Because narcoleptic attacks are instigated by strong emotions, victims try to maintain a bland emotional life, avoiding both laughing and crying. Their fear of maintaining a normal emotional life often contributes to their feelings of depression, which can lead to suicide. Though there seems to be a hereditary predisposition in those who develop narcolepsy, its exact cause is unknown. Victims may benefit from naps (Mullington & Broughton, 1993) or from stimulants (Mitler, Hajdukovic, & Erman, 1993).

Dreams

dream
A storylike sequence of visual images, usually occurring during REM sleep.

The most dramatic aspect of sleep is the **dream,** a storylike sequence of visual images that commonly evoke strong emotions. Actions that would be impossible in real life can seem perfectly normal in dreams. In a dream, you might find it reasonable to hold a conversation with a dinosaur or to leap across the Grand Canyon. But what are the major characteristics of dreams? This was the question addressed in a study conducted a century ago by Mary Whiton Calkins (1893).

Anatomy of a Classic Research Study:
What Is the Nature of Dreams?

Rationale

Though Sigmund Freud is famous for making the analysis of dreams an important part of psychoanalysis, beginning with the publication of The Interpretation of Dreams in 1900, he was not the first person to study them formally. An article published by Mary Whiton Calkins in 1893 described a dream study she conducted with her colleague Edmund Clark Sanford. The study is noteworthy because it was referred to by Freud in his book and its findings have held up well. It also shows the transition in late-nineteenth-century psychology from philosophical speculation about psychological topics, such as dreams, to empirical research on them.

Method

Calkins recorded her own dreams for 55 nights, and Sanford recorded his for 46 nights. They used alarm clocks to wake themselves up at varying times during the night in order to jot down any dreams they had been having.

Results and Discussion

As you will realize when reading the remainder of this section on dreams, Calkins observed dream characteristics that later research—often having the advantage of more-sophisticated equipment than an alarm clock—has confirmed. Among her findings were the following:

1. We dream every night. On several nights, Calkins believed she had not dreamt—only to find that she had written down several during the night. Ironically, Hugo Münsterberg, who supervised Calkins's doctoral dissertation research on memory, claimed that he never dreamed (Hale, 1980). She hypothesized that we forget our dreams because of a lack of congruity between the dreaming and waking states of consciousness. This finding anticipated interest in state-dependent memory, which has inspired research studies only in the past few decades and is discussed in chapter 8.

2. *We have about four dreams a night.* Calkins recorded 205 dreams on 55 nights, and Sanford 170 on 46 nights. This agrees with modern research indicating that we have four or five REM periods on a typical night.

3. *As the night progresses, we are more likely to be dreaming.* Calkins found that most dreams occurred during the second half of the night. This agrees with later research findings, obtained with physiological recording equipment, that successive REM periods increase in length across the night.

4. *Most dreams are mundane and refer to recent life events.* We do not realize that dreams are usually mundane because we tend to recall only the most dramatic ones.

5. *Dreams may incorporate external stimuli.* In one of her dreams Calkins found herself struggling to crawl from an elevator through a tiny opening into an eighth-floor apartment. She awoke to find herself in a cramped position with a heavy blanket over her face.

6. *What Calkins called "real thinking" occurs during sleep.* This finding anticipated research findings that NREM sleep is marked by ordinary thinking, as opposed to the fantastic images and events common to dreaming.

7. *We can reason while dreaming and even, to an extent, control our dreams.* This finding anticipated research on lucid dreaming, a serious topic of research only in the past decade.

8. *Dreams can disguise their true meaning.* Calkins reported a "romance dream" that included such disguised material. This finding anticipated Freud's belief that dreams can use symbols to represent their true—often sexual—meaning.

9. *Dream plots are not condensed into an instant.* Calkins noted that this contradicted the view of an influential French researcher named Maury, who claimed that we can have a complex dream in a few seconds. In support of this, he related the case of a man who dreamt he was arrested during the French Reign of Terror, put on trial, and beheaded by a guillotine, only to awaken and find that part of his bed had fallen on his chest. Maury claimed that the dream took place in the brief interval between the instant the man was struck and his awakening.

The Content of Dreams

Human beings have long been intrigued by dreams; references to the content of dreams are found on Babylonian clay tablets dating from 5000 B.C. As just described, Mary Whiton Calkins (1893) found that we tend to dream about mundane personal matters, usually involving familiar people and places. This finding was supported by the research of Calvin Hall (1966), who analyzed the content of thousands of dreams reported by his subjects. A more recent study likewise found that about half of our dreams include material about waking events of the preceding day (Botman & Crovitz, 1989–1990). Hall also found that the sex of characters in our dreams is affected by the sex of the dreamer—females dream about males and females equally, but males dream about males about 65 percent of the time. Hall (1984) reported that this finding held up across cultures.

The content of some dreams is frightening. These **nightmares** tend to occur when we are in emotional distress (Berquier & Ashton, 1992). Consider the apparent effect on nightmares of the major earthquake that struck the San Francisco Bay area of California in 1989: After the earthquake, a study of almost a hundred San Francisco Bay–area college students found they had twice as many nightmares as an equivalent group of subjects in Tucson, Arizona. And while 40 percent of the San Francisco subjects had nightmares about earthquakes, only 5 percent of the Tucson subjects had them (Wood et al., 1992).

Do not confuse nightmares, which occur during REM sleep, with **night terrors,** which occur during NREM sleep stages 3 and 4. Night terrors are especially common in childhood and may reflect a genetic predisposition (Carlson, White, & Turkat, 1982).

nightmare
A frightening REM dream.

night terror
A frightening NREM experience, common in childhood, in which the individual may suddenly sit up, let out a bloodcurdling scream, speak incoherently, and quickly fall back to sleep, yet usually fails to recall it on awakening.

The Nightmare
The Nightmare, painted by Henry Fuseli (1741–1825), depicts the fearsome imagery of the typical nightmare.

lucid dreaming
The ability to be aware that one is dreaming and to direct one's dreams.

The child experiencing a night terror will suddenly sit up in bed, let out a bloodcurdling scream, speak incoherently, and quickly fall back to sleep. Because the child does not recall the night terror, it is more disturbing to the family members who are rudely awakened by its effect on the child.

As noted by Mary Whiton Calkins, the content of dreams can be affected by immediate environmental stimuli. This was portrayed by Herman Melville in his novel *Moby Dick* in describing the effect of Captain Ahab's peg leg on the dreams of his ship's sailors. Melville wrote, "To his weary mates, seeking repose within six inches of his ivory heel, such would have been the reverberating crack and din of that bony step that their dreams would have been of the crunching teeth of sharks." Perhaps you have found yourself dreaming of an ice cream truck ringing its bell, only to awaken suddenly and discover that your dream had been stimulated by the ringing of your telephone.

Such anecdotal reports of the incorporation of stimuli into dreams have inspired laboratory research. In a recent study, subjects were either touched or not touched on their legs while they were in REM sleep. On awakening, those who had been touched during REM sleep reported more dreams in which they were touched on their legs (Nielsen, 1993). In another study, undergraduates were presented with an odor after entering REM sleep. After 1 minute they were awakened and asked to report their dreams. About 20 percent of the dreams incorporated the odor (Trotter, Dallas, & Verdone, 1988). In still another study, researchers sprayed sleepers with a water mist when they were in REM sleep; some of the subjects, on being awakened, reported dreams with watery themes, such as a leaky roof or being caught in the rain. Nonetheless, external stimuli only sometimes have such effects (Dement & Wolpert, 1958).

Mary Whiton Calkins also noted that we might be able to control our ongoing dreams. Some members of the Senoi tribe of Malaya make a practice of teaching their children to control the content of their ongoing dreams, even converting nightmares into enjoyable dreams. Their society is reportedly known for social cooperation, lack of violence, and a strong interrelationship between dreams and waking life. Dreams are discussed and interpreted publicly, and individuals are encouraged to confront the feelings revealed in their dreams (Herod & Smith, 1982). The Senoi approach has been used successfully to improve the enjoyment of dreams by American college students. In one study, subjects who participated in a 15-week program to practice Senoi strategies experienced more pleasurable dreams during the program and the ensuing 6 months than did subjects who had only read about dreams and kept daily dream diaries (Doyle, 1984). **Lucid dreaming** (LaBerge, 1985), in which the dreamer is conscious of dreaming and may even direct the dream, is a Western approach that has much in common with the Senoi approach. Individuals can be taught to dream lucidly (Zadra, Donderi, & Pihl, 1992), and lucid dreamers report an enhanced sense of well-being (Wolpin et al., 1992).

The Functions of Dreaming

REM sleep—dream sleep—is important. Subjects who have been deprived of sleep, and then are allowed to sleep as long as they like, show an increase in REM sleep (Dement, 1960). This is known as the *REM-rebound effect* and indicates that dream sleep serves certain functions, which are as yet unclear. Because some people who suffer from schizophrenia show a weaker REM-rebound effect (Keshaven, Reynolds, & Kupfer, 1990), the schizophrenic state might serve some of the same functions as dreaming, making REM-rebound less necessary for them.

But what are the functions of dreams? People have pondered this question for thousands of years. The ancient Hebrews, Egyptians, and Greeks believed that dreams brought prophecies from God or the gods, as in the dream of Pharaoh interpreted by Joseph in the Old Testament and in dreams described in Homer's *Iliad* and *Odyssey*. But Aristotle, who at first accepted the divine origin of dreams, later rejected this belief, claiming that apparent prophetic dreams are mere coincidences—instances in which causation is confused with correlation.

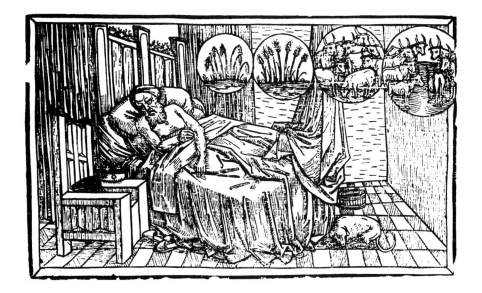

The Dream As Prophecy
Belief in the predictive nature of dreams has been common throughout history. This woodcut from the Lubeck Bible of 1494 illustrates Pharaoh's famous dream, which Joseph interpreted as portending 7 years of abundance, then famine.

Perhaps the most common view of the function of dreaming holds that dreams serve as wish fulfillments. The great fourteenth-century poet Chaucer expressed this view in his poem *The Parliament of Fowls*, in which knights dream of fighting and lovers dream of their romantic partners. Centuries later, Sigmund Freud (1900/1990) provided the first formal view of dreaming as wish fulfillment in his classic book *The Interpretation of Dreams*. The book received generally positive reviews from readers and reviewers (Kanzer, 1988), yet, to his disappointment, sold only 351 copies in its first 6 years after publication (Webb, 1985). Freud claimed that dreams serve as safe outlets for unconscious sexual or aggressive impulses that we cannot act on while we are awake because of cultural prohibitions. Freud distinguished between a dream's **manifest content,** which is the verbally reported dream, and its **latent content,** which is the dream's true meaning.

But how can we uncover a dream's true meaning? According to Freud, a dream's manifest content consists of symbols that disguise its latent sexual or aggressive content. This prevents us from being awakened by our dreams, as we would be if we dreamed directly about emotionally charged sexual or aggressive material. Thus, in our dreams, trees, rifles, or skyscrapers might act as phallic symbols that represent unconscious sexual impulses. A dream about planting a tree might provide a means of releasing sexual energy. The manifest content of a dream reported by a subject is translated into its latent content during the process of psychoanalysis, which is discussed in chapter 15.

The failure of psychoanalysts to provide convincing research support for dreaming as a form of disguised wish fulfillment (Fisher & Greenberg, 1985) led researchers to study other possible functions of dreams. One of these is problem solving. You may recall reading in chapter 3 how Otto Loewi discovered the chemical nature of synaptic transmission after carrying out an experiment that came to him in a dream. In an earlier case, the nineteenth-century inventor Elias Howe felt frustrated by his inability to determine where to put the hole in the needle of the sewing machine he was perfecting. The answer came to him in a dream in which savages were chasing him with spears. He noticed that each spear had a hole in its tip. This inspired Howe to put a hole in the tip of the sewing machine needle. Even athletes have solved problems in their dreams. Jack Nicklaus, perhaps the greatest golfer ever, reported that he took 10 strokes off his golf game by gripping his clubs in a manner suggested in a dream (Shepard, 1984).

Anecdotal reports such as these led Rosalind Cartwright (1978), a leading dream researcher, to conduct formal studies of the possible problem-solving function of dreaming. By studying dreams that occur in each of the REM periods across a night's sleep, she concluded that dreamers are concerned with finding possible solutions to personal

manifest content
Sigmund Freud's term for the verbally reported dream.

latent content
Sigmund Freud's term for the true, though disguised, meaning of a dream.

Rosalind Cartwright
"The dreams of a night have meaning which is characteristic of the individual and responsive to his or her particular waking situation."

activation-synthesis theory
The theory that dreams are the by-products of the mind's attempt to make sense of the spontaneous changes in physiological activity generated by the pons during REM sleep.

hypnosis
An induced state of consciousness in which one person responds to suggestions by another person for alterations in perception, thinking, and behavior.

problems. Dreams that occur early in the night present the problem and later dreams examine possible solutions. Cartwright's theory of dreams is relevant to the life of René Descartes, who reported that a series of three dreams he had one night when he was a young adult influenced the intellectual direction of his life. His first dream presented the problem, and the next two considered potential solutions (Vrooman, 1970). In a recent study, Cartwright (1991) found that dreaming can help men and women deal with the stress of divorce. Those who dreamed about their relationship with their spouse while they were going through a divorce became less depressed and better adjusted to single life a year later.

In another study demonstrating the possible ability of dreams to help us deal with emotional problems (Lauer et al., 1987), subjects were shown either a neutral film about the behavior of dolphins and chimpanzees or a disturbing film depicting distressing situations, including the massacre of a group of Native Americans and the deplorable living conditions in a juvenile prison. The next night, subjects who had viewed the disturbing film were more likely to incorporate content from the film into their early dreams and to experience a high degree of personal participation and intense anxiety or aggression. But their later dreams were more likely to be emotionally neutral or positive. This provided evidence that dreaming may help us adjust to disturbing events from the preceding day.

Most dream theorists believe that dreaming serves psychological functions, such as wish fulfillment or problem solving; others view it as just a by-product of brain activity. This belief was anticipated by pre-twentieth-century intellectuals such as the philosopher Gottfried Wilhelm Leibniz and the physiologist David Hartley (Lavie & Hobson, 1986). According to the **activation-synthesis theory** of J. Allan Hobson and Robert McCarley (1977), dreams are the by-products of the forebrain's attempt to make sense of the spontaneous changes in physiological activity generated by the pons during REM sleep. For example, a dream in which you are being chased but cannot run away might reflect the mind's attempt to explain the inability of signals from the motor areas of the brain to stimulate limb movements during the limb paralysis that accompanies REM sleep. Moreover, the strong emotion that we experience in such dreams might be a product of the activation of the limbic system that occurs during REM sleep. The inability of the forebrain to make sense of some patterns of spontaneous brain activity might explain why our night dreams tend to be more bizarre than our daydreams (Williams et al., 1992).

The activation-synthesis theory has been criticized by those who claim that it cannot explain how we can have personally meaningful dreams that are obviously more than the by-products of spontaneous brain activity. That is, the mind's interpretation of the brain activity presumably reveals something about the personality and experiences of the dreamer (Parisi, 1987). But the activation-synthesis theory does *not* completely discount the influence of one's personality on one's dreams. It simply assumes that dreams are generated by brain activity, not by unconscious wishes or personal problems. Such psychological factors come into play only *after* the onset of random brain activity (Hobson, 1988). Despite a century of research, no dream theory has clearly demonstrated its superiority in explaining the functions of dreams. One of the difficulties in dream research is that the same dream can be explained as wish fulfillment, as problem solving, or as the by-product of spontaneous brain activity. This possibility is illustrated in figure 6.5.

HYPNOSIS

While sleep is a naturally occurring state of consciousness, **hypnosis** is an induced state of consciousness in which one person responds to suggestions by another person for alterations in perception, thinking, and behavior. The ancient Egyptians and Greeks had healing temples, where they practiced hypnosislike techniques to treat physical disorders (Hilgard, 1987). Modern hypnosis originated in the work of the Viennese

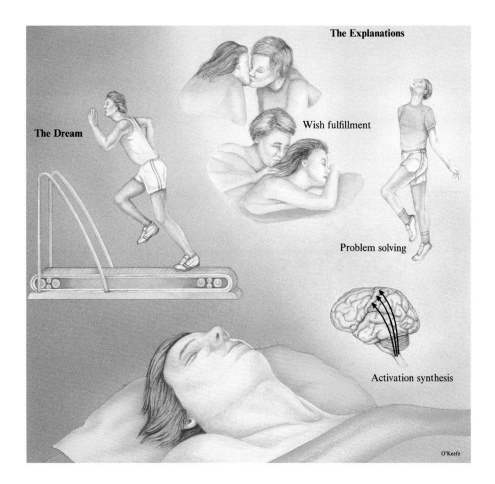

FIGURE 6.5

One Dream, Three Explanations
The Dream: The dreamer dreams that
he is running in place and can neither
move from that spot nor stop running.
The Explanations:

1. *Wish Fulfillment*—The manifest
content (the dream as reported) would
be translated into its latent content
(its true meaning). The dream might
reflect the conflict between the
dreamer's wish for sex (the desire to
move from the spot) and guilt feelings
about that wish (the desire to stop
running).
2. *Problem Solving*—The dreamer
has been concerned with recent
excessive weight gain, but has been
unable to decide on the best course of
action for losing weight. Perhaps the
dream is directing him to take up
aerobic exercise.
3. *Activation Synthesis*—During
REM sleep, the pons generates neural
impulses that activate random regions
of the cerebral cortex. Perhaps it has
activated the region of the motor
cortex that controls leg and arm
movements. Because his limbs are
paralyzed during REM sleep, the
dreamer might synthesize the cortical
arousal and limb paralysis into a
dream about running in place without
being able to move or stop.

physician Anton Mesmer (1734–1815), who claimed that he could cure illnesses by transmitting a form of energy he called *animal magnetism* to his patients, a process that became known as *mesmerism*.

In the late eighteenth century, Mesmer became the rage of Paris, impressing audiences with his demonstrations of mesmerism. In a typical demonstration, wealthy patients would gather in a luxurious room with thick carpeting, mirrored walls, subdued lighting, and soft music. Mesmer, wearing a flowing purple robe, would direct them to sit around a large oak tub called a *baquet*, which he had filled with mesmerized water, ground glass, and metal filings. The patients were mesmerized by holding onto metal rods protruding from the water and then responding to Mesmer's suggestions to enter a trance state in which they would feel their physical symptoms disappear (Ellenberger, 1970). Today we still use the word *mesmerized* to describe a person in a trancelike state during an activity and *animal magnetism* to describe a person who has a charismatic personality.

Mesmer's flamboyance and extravagant claims, as well as the professional jealousy of physicians, provoked King Louis XVI to appoint a commission to investigate mesmerism. In 1784 the commission, headed by Benjamin Franklin and including Antoine Lavoisier (the founder of modern chemistry) and J. I. Guillotin (the inventor of the infamous decapitation device, the guillotine), completed its investigation and concluded that there was no evidence of animal magnetism. The commission found that the effects of mesmerism were attributable to the power of suggestion and the subjects' active imagination. Mesmer, discredited, moved to Switzerland, where he lived out his life in obscurity.

In 1842 the English surgeon James Braid (1795–1860), who used mesmerism in his practice, concluded that it induced a sleeplike state. He renamed mesmerism *hypnotism*, from Hypnos, the Greek god of sleep. In the late nineteenth century, Sigmund Freud used hypnosis to help his patients gain insight into psychological problems that contributed to their physical symptoms. But Freud abandoned the use of hypnosis after devising what he found to be a more effective technique, psychoanalysis. Despite Freud's rejection of hypnosis, it has been widely used during the past century.

Hypnotic Induction

How do hypnotists induce a hypnotic state? The process depends less on the skill of the hypnotist than on the susceptibility of the subject. People vary in their degree of susceptibility; highly hypnotizable people have more-active fantasy lives and a capacity for absorption in what they are doing, whether reading a book, playing a sport, listening to music, or holding a conversation (Lynn & Rhue, 1988). Children, with their rich fantasy lives, are more susceptible to hypnosis than are adults (Chapman, Elkins, & Carter, 1982). Our susceptibility to hypnosis can be improved by training (Gorassini et al., 1991).

Psychologists have developed tests of hypnotizability, including the Stanford Hypnotic Susceptibility Scale (Weitzenhoffer & Hilgard, 1962) and the Harvard Group Scale of Hypnotic Susceptibility (Shor & Orne, 1962). These tests determine the extent to which subjects will comply with hypnotic suggestions after an abbreviated hypnotic induction. A simple suggestion, to indicate some susceptibility, might direct you to hold your hands in front of you and move them apart, while a more difficult suggestion, to indicate high susceptibility, might direct you to produce handwriting similar to that of a child. Most people are moderately susceptible; perhaps 10 percent of us are easily hypnotized and 10 percent are not susceptible at all (Hilgard, 1982). Regardless of their susceptibility, people cannot be hypnotized against their will.

The aim of hypnotic induction is to create a relaxed, passive, highly focused state of mind. During hypnotic induction the hypnotist might have you focus your eyes on a spot on the ceiling. The hypnotist might then suggest that you notice your eyelids closing, feet warming, muscles relaxing, and respiration slowing—events that would

take place even without hypnotic suggestions. You would gradually relinquish more and more control of your perceptions, thoughts, and behaviors to the hypnotist. But what effects can hypnosis produce?

Effects of Hypnosis

Many extreme claims for the amazing physical effects of hypnosis have been discredited by experimental research. Perhaps you have heard the claim that hypnotized people who are given the suggestion that their hand has touched a red-hot poker will develop a blister—a claim first made two centuries ago (Gauld, 1990). Experiments have shown that such hypnotic suggestions can, at best, merely promote warming of the skin by increasing the flow of blood to it (Spanos, McNeil, & Stam, 1982). Nonetheless, research has demonstrated a variety of impressive perceptual, cognitive, and behavioral effects of hypnosis.

Perceptual Effects

Stage hypnotists commonly use hypnosis to induce alterations in perception, such as convincing subjects that a vial of water is actually ammonia—these subjects will jerk their heads away after smelling it. But the most important perceptual effect of hypnosis is in pain relief. In the mid nineteenth century, the Scottish surgeon James Esdaile (1808–1859) used hypnosis to induce anesthesia in more than three hundred patients undergoing surgery for the removal of limbs, tumors, or cataracts (Ellenberger, 1970). Research has supported the effectiveness of hypnotically induced pain relief. For example, though hypnosis cannot promote healing of burn wounds, it has been successful in relieving the excruciating pain they induce (Patterson et al., 1992). As mentioned in chapter 5, hypnosis works by distracting people from their pain (Farthing, Venturino, & Brown, 1984).

Cognitive Effects

In 1976, 26 elementary school children and their bus driver were kidnapped in Chowchilla, California, and imprisoned in a buried tractor trailer. The bus driver and two of the children dug their way out and got help. The driver, Frank Ray, had seen the license plate number of the kidnappers' van but was unable to recall it. After being hypnotized and told to imagine himself watching the kidnapping unfold on television, he was able

hypermnesia
The hypnotic enhancement of recall.

to recall all but one of the digits of the number. This enabled the police to track down the kidnappers (M. C. Smith, 1983).

The Chowchilla case was a widely publicized example of one of the chief cognitive applications of hypnosis, **hypermnesia**—the enhancement of recall. Though many studies have demonstrated that hypnosis can enhance recall (Relinger, 1984), other studies have found that hypnosis can actually create "pseudomemories" (Sheehan, Green, & Truesdale, 1988). Moreover, hypnotized witnesses feel more confident about the memories they recall under hypnosis—regardless of their accuracy (Weekes et al., 1988). In one study, 27 subjects were hypnotized and then given the suggestion that they had been awakened by a loud noise one night during the preceding week. Later, after leaving the hypnotized state, 13 of the subjects claimed that the suggested event had actually occurred. Even after being informed of the hypnotic suggestion, 6 subjects still insisted that they had been awakened by the noise (Laurence & Perry, 1983). This indicates the potential danger of hypnotically enhanced eyewitness testimony, particularly when one considers that juries are more impressed by confident eyewitnesses (Sheehan & Tilden, 1983) and hypnotized eyewitnesses (Wagstaff, Vella, & Perfect, 1992). Yet the U.S. Supreme Court has opposed legislation that would eliminate hypnosis-induced hypermnesia in the courtroom, recommending instead that the admissibility of such testimony be determined on a trial-by-trial basis (Watkins, 1989).

Behavioral Effects

posthypnotic suggestions
Suggestions directing subjects to carry out particular behaviors or to have particular experiences after leaving hypnosis.

Hypnosis is effective in treating psychological and physical disorders. For example, hypnosis has helped people overcome their phobias (McGuinness, 1984) and recuperate after surgery (Blankfield, 1991). Hypnosis therapists make use of **posthypnotic suggestions**, which are suggestions for subjects to carry out certain behaviors in response to particular stimuli after leaving hypnosis. In one study, posthypnotic suggestions helped collegiate fencers reduce their performance anxiety (Wojcikiewicz & Orlick, 1987). Posthypnotic suggestions are more effective when they include suggestions for *posthypnotic amnesia,* which prevents subjects from being aware that they have been given a posthypnotic suggestion (Van Denburg & Kurtz, 1989).

Though hypnosis can help some people, what of its possible harmful effects? A century ago debate raged about whether hypnosis could be used to induce criminal or antisocial behavior (Liegois, 1899). Decades later Martin Orne and Frederick Evans (1965) demonstrated that hypnotized subjects could be induced to commit dangerous acts. Their study included a group of hypnotized subjects and a group of subjects who simulated being hypnotized. When instructed to do so, subjects in *both* groups plunged their hands into what they were told was nitric acid, threw the acid in another person's face, and handled a venomous snake. (Of course, the experimenters protected the participants from harm in each situation.) Because both groups engaged in dangerous acts, the influence of the research setting, rather than the influence of hypnosis, might have accounted for the results. Perhaps the subjects assumed that no one would be hurt. This remarkable willingness of people to obey even dangerous orders from legitimate authorities is discussed in chapter 17. Despite the possibility that under special circumstances hypnotized subjects might be induced to commit harmful acts, hypnosis generally poses no risks other than those involved in any therapeutic or experimental situation (Brentar & Lynn, 1989).

Some of the effects of stage hypnosis might also have less to do with hypnosis than with the setting in which they occur. For example, you may have seen a stage hypnotist direct a hypnotized audience volunteer to remain as rigid as a plank while lying extended between two chairs. But highly motivated, nonhypnotized persons can also perform this "human plank" trick. Even the willingness of hypnotized subjects to obey suggestions to engage in bizarre behaviors, such as acting like a chicken, might be more attributable to the theatrical "anything goes" atmosphere of stage hypnosis than to the effect of hypnosis itself (Meeker & Barber, 1971). You will appreciate this if you have ever watched contestants on television game shows engage in wacky antics—without even being hypnotized.

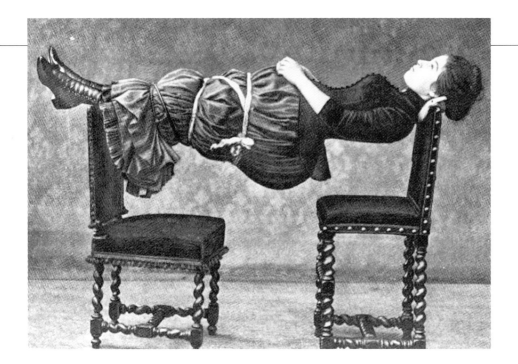

Stage Hypnosis
The "human plank" feat has long been a staple of stage hypnosis. But it can be performed by a motivated nonhypnotized person who places her or his calves on one chair and head and shoulders on the other.

The Nature of Hypnosis

In the late 1800s practitioners of hypnosis, most notably in France, disagreed whether hypnosis induced an altered, or *trance*, state of consciousness. One group, led by the eminent Paris neurologist Jean-Martin Charcot, argued that hypnosis induces an altered state of **dissociation,** in which parts of the mind become separated from one another and form independent streams of consciousness. This is similar to the practice of many long-distance runners, who use dissociation to divorce their conscious minds from possibly distressing bodily sensations while still remaining consciously aware of the racecourse ahead of them (Masters, 1992). In hypnotic dissociation, one stream remains under voluntary control, and the other is controlled by the hypnotist. Another group, led by the French country doctor Auguste Ambroise Liebeault, argued that hypnosis merely induces a state of heightened suggestibility (Ellenberger, 1970). This debate lingers on today; some researchers view hypnosis as an altered state of consciousness, and others view it as a normal state of waking consciousness.

dissociation
A state in which the mind is split into two or more independent streams of consciousness.

Hypnosis As an Altered State

Today, the main theory of hypnosis as an altered state is the **neodissociation theory,** a descendant of Charcot's concept of dissociation. This theory originated in a classroom demonstration of hypnotically induced deafness by Ernest Hilgard, who directed a hypnotized blind student to raise an index finger if he heard a sound. When blocks were banged near his head, the student did not even flinch. But when asked if some part of his mind had actually heard the noise, his finger rose. Hilgard calls this part of the mind the **hidden observer** (Hilgard, 1978).

neodissociation theory
The theory that hypnosis induces a dissociated state of consciousness.

Hilgard has used the concept of the hidden observer to explain hypnotically induced pain relief. He relies on the *cold pressor test*, in which a subject submerges an arm in ice water and is asked every few seconds to estimate her or his degree of pain. Though hypnotized subjects who are told that they will feel less pain report that they feel little or no pain, the hidden observer, when asked, reports that it has experienced intense pain (Hilgard, 1973). Hilgard noted that this phenomenon had been reported almost a century earlier by William James, who observed a hypnotized man who reported no pain when stuck in one hand by a pin. To James's surprise, the man's other hand wrote that a separate part of his mind had experienced the pain. James attributed this "automatic writing" to the dissociation of a part the man's mind from the rest of his mind.

hidden observer
Ernest Hilgard's term for the part of the hypnotized person's consciousness that is not under the control of the hypnotist.

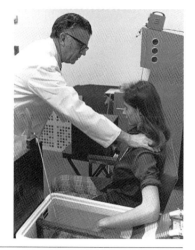

The Hidden Observer
Ernest Hilgard uses the cold pressor test to evaluate the ability of hypnosis to prevent the pain that normally accompanies having an arm immersed in ice water. Though the subject might report little or no pain, the "hidden observer" might report severe pain. The results of the study by Spanos and Hewitt (1980) indicate that the "hidden observer" is not an objective observer but, instead, will report whatever it has been told to expect.

Nicholas Spanos
"Hypnotic subjects are . . . actively engaged in interpreting the communications they receive and in presenting themselves in a manner that is congruent with their interpretations and with the social impression they wish to convey."

age regression
A hypnotic state in which the individual apparently behaves as she or he did as a child.

Hypnosis As a Normal State

Dissociation has not gone unchallenged as an explanation for hypnotic effects. The most prominent critics of hypnosis as an altered state are Theodore Barber, Nicholas Spanos, and Martin Orne, who insist that hypnotically induced effects are only responses to personal factors, such as the subject's motivation, and situational factors, such as the hypnotist's wording of suggestions. By arranging the right combination of factors, the hypnotist increases the likelihood that the subject will comply with hypnotic suggestions. Consider the following experiment, by Nicholas Spanos and Erin Hewitt (1980) of Carleton University in Ottawa, in which the hidden observer was made to give contradictory reports, depending on the hypnotist's suggestions.

Anatomy of a Contemporary Research Study:
Is There a "Hidden Observer" in Hypnotized People?

Rationale
As just discussed, Ernest Hilgard has conducted research that he believes indicates the presence of a hidden observer in hypnotized subjects that is separate from conscious awareness but still aware of what the person experiences. Thus, a person who is given suggestions for hypnotic analgesia will report less pain than the hidden observer reports. But is this the result of the dissociation of the subject's consciousness or of, instead, the subject's willingness to comply with a hypnotic suggestion? The possibility that a supposedly hidden part of consciousness might report a different experience simply because of hypnotic suggestions was first noted by William James's colleague Boris Sidis. This possibility was the inspiration for the present experiment.

Method
The experiment used undergraduate subjects who scored high on a hypnotizability scale and were then given suggestions for hypnotic analgesia. Two groups of subjects were given contradictory suggestions. One group was told that the hypnotized part of their minds would have little awareness of the pain, while a hidden part would be more aware of the actual intensity of the pain. Another group was told that the hypnotized part of their minds would have little awareness of the pain, while a hidden part would be even less aware of the pain. The subjects were asked to place a forearm in ice water, which induces pain. They were told to have the hypnotized parts of their minds state their level of pain on a scale from 0 to 20 every 5 seconds. They did so for 60 seconds. They also were told to hold a forearm in ice water while having their "hidden self" report their level of pain (from 0 to 20) by tapping out a simple code on a response key every 5 seconds. They also did this for 60 seconds.

Results and Discussion
When asked to report the intensity of the pain, the hidden observer reported what the subjects had been led to expect. It experienced more pain than the hypnotized part when told it would be more aware and less pain when told it would be less aware. The results are shown in figure 6.6. Thus, the hidden observer might simply be a result of the subject's willingness to act as though he or she has experienced suggested hypnotic effects. Spanos has found that this is not a case of faking, but probably reflects the well-established ability of subjects to distract themselves from their pain. Moreover, the hidden observer never appears spontaneously—it appears only when explicitly asked to. This study, as well as others by Spanos, indicates that the hidden observer is a product not of dissociation of consciousness, but instead of the subject's willingness to play a role suggested by the hypnotist.

Evidence for hypnosis as a form of role playing has also come from studies of hypnotic **age regression,** in which hypnotized subjects are told to return to childhood. A hypnotized adult might use baby talk or play with an imaginary teddy bear. But a review of research on hypnotic age regression found that subjects do not adopt the true mental, behavioral, and physiological characteristics of children; they just act as though they are children (Nash, 1987). In a classic study, Martin Orne (1951) hypnotized college students and suggested that they regress back to their sixth birthday party. He then asked them to describe the people and activities at the party, which they did in great detail. When Orne asked the subjects' parents to describe the same birthday party,

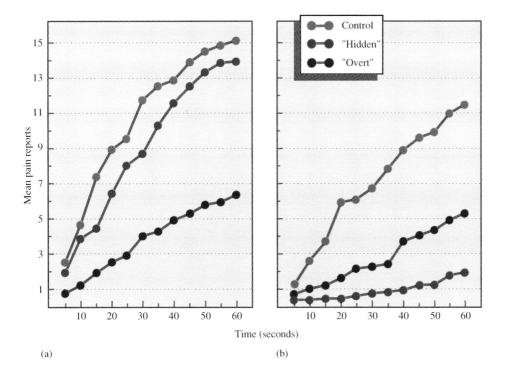

(a)   (b)

Time (seconds)

FIGURE 6.6

Pain Reports by the Hidden Observer
These two graphs show that the "hidden observer" might merely be the product of hypnotic suggestion, rather than an objective perceiver of reality. When told that it will be more aware, the "hidden observer" reports more pain (*a*). When told that it will be less aware, the "hidden observer" reports less pain (*b*).

he found that many of the subjects' "memories" had been fabrications. They reported people and events they *presumed* would have been at their own sixth birthday party. There was no evidence that they actually reexperienced their sixth birthday party.

Such challenges to hypnosis as an altered state of consciousness have not gone unmet. Especially strong evidence in favor of hypnosis as an altered state comes from experiments in which hypnotized subjects experience physiological changes in response to hypnotic suggestions. In one study, hypnotized subjects were given the suggestion that their view of an image on a television screen was blocked by a box. The pattern of electrical activity recorded from their occipital lobes (the site of visual processing in the brain) was similar to what would occur if their view had been blocked by a real box. This indicated that the hypnotic suggestion affected highly specific visual processing in the brain (Spiegel et al., 1985), which is difficult to attribute to mere suggestibility.

Neither side in the debate about the nature of hypnosis has provided sufficient evidence to discount the other side completely. As noted by William James a century ago, both trance and nontrance theorists may be correct: Hypnosis might be a dissociated state of consciousness that can be shaped by the social context and hypnotic suggestions (Kihlstrom & McConkey, 1990).

MEDITATION

Meditation is a procedure that uses mental exercises to achieve a tranquil, highly focused state of consciousness. Traditionally, meditation has been a religious practice aimed at reaching a mystical union with God or the universe. All major religions, including Buddhism, Christianity, Hinduism, Islam, Judaism, and Taoism, have centuries-old formal meditative practices. In the past two decades meditation has also gained popularity as a means of promoting physical and psychological well-being by reducing stress and inducing relaxation.

Common Meditative Practices

The popular forms of meditation share techniques aimed at producing physical relaxation and mental concentration. If you decided to meditate, you would seek a peaceful setting, maintain a comfortable seated position, focus on a sound, image, or object, and

Meditation
Through meditation, athletes can reduce their mental and physical arousal to help alleviate their precompetitive anxiety.

meditation
A procedure that uses mental exercises to achieve a highly focused state of consciousness.

FIGURE 6.7

The Relaxation Response
Oxygen consumption (blue line) and carbon dioxide elimination (black line) decrease during transcendental meditation. Both of these physiological changes are signs of relaxation.

From "The Physiology of Meditation" by R. K. Wallace and H. Benson. Copyright © 1972 by Scientific American, Inc. All rights reserved.

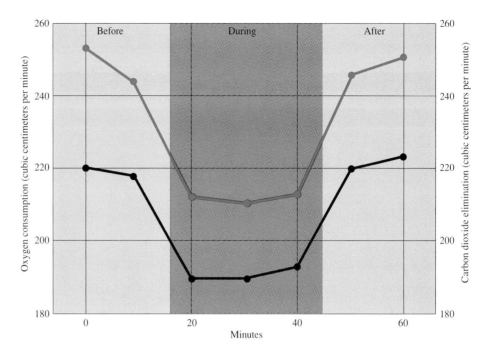

transcendental meditation (TM)
A form of meditation in which the individual relaxes and repeats a sound called a mantra for two 20-minute periods a day.

relaxation response
A variation of transcendental meditation in which the individual may repeat a sound other than a mantra.

calmly withdraw your attention from any intruding images, feelings, or sensations. Though some forms of meditation promote emptying the mind of all content, most are concentrative and involve focusing on one thing.

Meditation was popularized in the West in the late 1960s by Maharishi Mahesh Yogi, an Indian guru, through the influence of his most famous disciples, the Beatles. They promoted a Westernized form of meditation called **transcendental meditation (TM)**. In TM, you concentrate on repeating a sound called a *mantra* (a Sanskrit word such as *Om*) for two 20-minute periods a day. The alternation of *Om* and silence is presumed to represent fulfillment. In the early 1970s, cardiologist Herbert Benson introduced the **relaxation response,** a form of meditation that is identical to TM except that the meditator may mentally repeat a sound other than a mantra, such as the number one or a favorite brief prayer.

Effects of Meditation

Benson has promoted meditation as a technique that induces a unique state of physical and mental relaxation by increasing alpha brain waves and decreasing heart rate, respiration rate, oxygen consumption, and carbon dioxide expiration (Wallace & Benson, 1972). (The effects of meditation on physiological arousal are presented in figure 6.7.) Benson's claim that meditation induces a unique physiological state was challenged by David Holmes (1984), whose review of research on meditation indicated no difference in physiological arousal between subjects who meditated and subjects who merely rested. For example, an early study found that meditators and people who merely rested did not differ in the level of stress hormones in their blood—a good indicator of arousal level (Michaels, Huber, & McCann, 1976). Benson responded to Holmes by pointing to studies that did show unique effects of meditation on arousal (Benson & Friedman, 1985). One study contradicted Holmes by showing that meditators achieved a lower state of physiological arousal than did people who simply relaxed with their eyes closed—though the study did not find meditation superior to other relaxation techniques (Delmonte, 1984).

Whether or not meditation induces a unique physiological or psychological state, it is an effective means of stress reduction. The relaxation response has even proved successful in preparing patients for surgery. In a study of cardiac surgery patients, the experimental group practiced the relaxation response before and after surgery, while the control group did not. After surgery, the experimental group had less anger, lower anxiety, and fewer heart-rhythm irregularities than did the control group (Leserman et al., 1989). Of course, not all people will benefit to the same extent from practicing the relaxation response (Huber & Gramer, 1990).

PSYCHOACTIVE DRUGS

Normal waking consciousness can also be altered by **psychoactive drugs,** chemicals that induce changes in mood, thinking, perception, and behavior by affecting neuronal activity. Human beings seem drawn to psychoactive drugs. Many people drink beer to reduce social anxiety, take barbiturates to fall asleep, use narcotics to feel euphoric, drink coffee to get going in the morning, or smoke marijuana to enrich their perception of music.

The effects of psychoactive drugs depend on more than just their dosage and physiological effects, including the user's experience with them, the user's expectations about their effects, and the setting in which they are taken. All psychoactive drugs can cause *psychological dependence*—an intense desire to achieve the intoxicated state induced by the drug. Most psychoactive drugs also can cause *physical dependence (or addiction)*. This means that after people use the drug for a period of time they develop a physiological need for the drug. As people use physically addicting drugs, they develop *tolerance*—a decrease in physiological responsiveness to the drug. As a result, they require increasingly higher doses to achieve the desired effect. If an addicted person stops taking the drug, she or he will experience *craving* and *withdrawal symptoms* (Poulos & Cappell, 1991). The pattern and severity of withdrawal symptoms is specific to the kind of drug to which the person is addicted. Common withdrawal symptoms include chills, headache, fatigue, nausea, insomnia, depression, convulsions, and irritability. As shown in figure 6.8, the psychoactive drugs can be divided into three general categories: *depressants*, *stimulants*, and *hallucinogens*.

Depressants

Depressants reduce arousal by inhibiting activity in the central nervous system. Chapter 15 discusses two kinds of depressant drugs that are used in treating psychological disorders: *antianxiety drugs* (so-called tranquilizers), which are used to relieve anxiety, and *antipsychotic drugs* (so-called major tranquilizers), which are used to alleviate the symptoms of schizophrenia. This section discusses several other kinds of depressants: *alcohol, barbiturates, inhalants,* and *opiates*.

Alcohol

Ethyl alcohol, an addictive drug, has been used—and abused—for thousands of years. Even the ancient Romans had to pass laws against drunk driving—of chariots (Whitlock, 1987). Today, in the United States a person with a blood alcohol level of 0.10 percent is considered legally drunk. Canadian provinces are even stricter, setting the limit at 0.08 percent. Drunk drivers (whether they drive chariots or automobiles) are dangerous because they suffer from perceptual distortions, motor incoordination, and impaired judgment. Alcohol may work by facilitating the actions of the neurotransmitter GABA, which inhibits neuronal transmission in the brain. An experimental drug that blocks alcohol from stimulating the GABA receptor holds promise as a tool for treating alcoholism (Kolata, 1986).

Given that the typical person metabolizes about one ounce of alcohol an hour, a person who drinks faster than that will become intoxicated. Men metabolize alcohol more efficiently than women do, so women can become intoxicated on less alcohol than would make men intoxicated (Frezza et al., 1990). A full stomach slows the rate at which alcohol enters the bloodstream, so it is desirable to eat a meal before drinking alcohol.

Alcohol reduces activity in brain centers that normally inhibit social behaviors such as sex, aggression, or even helpfulness (Steele, Critchlow, & Liu, 1985). Inebriated people might even leave larger tips in restaurants (Lynn, 1988). You have probably seen

psychoactive drugs
Chemicals that induce changes in mood, thinking, perception, and behavior by affecting neuronal activity in the brain.

depressants
Psychoactive drugs that inhibit activity in the central nervous system.

ethyl alcohol
A depressant found in beverages and commonly used to reduce social inhibitions.

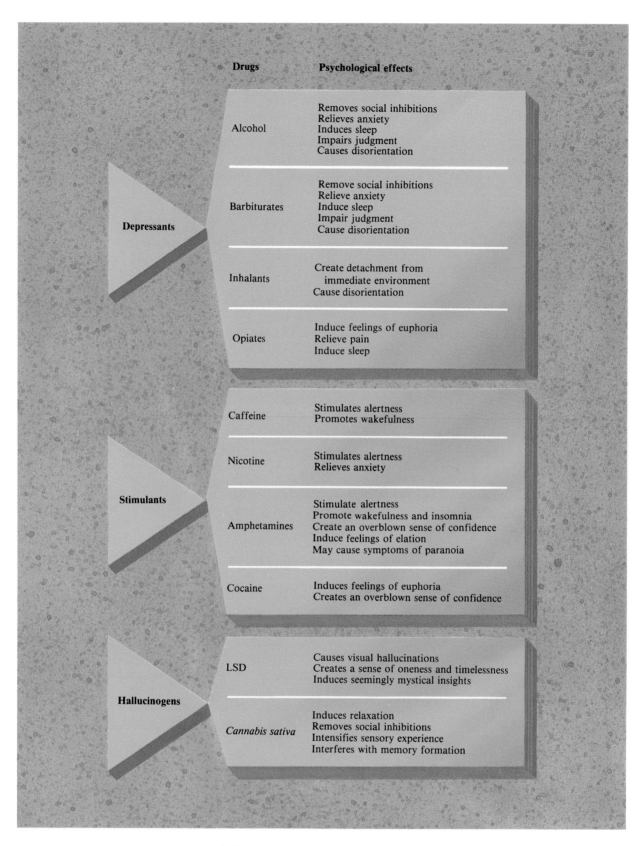

FIGURE 6.8

Psychoactive Drugs

proper people become sexually indiscriminate, meek people become verbally abusive or physically aggressive, and shy people become the life of the party after a few drinks. Moreover, because we are aware of alcohol's reputation for removing social inhibitions, we might use it as an excuse for engaging in socially questionable behaviors, such as casual sex (Hull & Bond, 1986). We can then blame our behavior on the alcohol, lessening our guilt and embarrassment.

Barbiturates

The **barbiturates** are derived from barbituric acid. Because barbiturates produce effects similar to those of alcohol (including their ability to produce addiction), they have been called "solid alcohol." Like alcohol, they work by facilitating the actions of GABA (Yu & Ho, 1990). The barbiturate Seconal, which acts quickly to induce drowsiness, is used as a sleeping pill. The barbiturate Pentothal is used as a general anesthetic in surgery. Because mild doses of Pentothal induce a drunken, uninhibited state in which the intoxicated person is more willing to reveal private thoughts and feelings, it is popularly known as "truth serum," though it does not guarantee that the information revealed will be true. A commonly abused relative of the barbiturates, which has similar effects, is methaqualone (Quaalude).

barbiturates
Depressants used to induce sleep or anesthesia.

Inhalants

One of the oldest means of inducing an altered state of consciousness is the use of **inhalants,** addictive drugs (including ether, chloroform, and nitrous oxide) that are ingested by inhaling their vapors. Inhalants have become popular with young drug abusers (Pollard, 1990), who commonly inhale fumes from plastic glue, aerosol sprays, or other household products that produce intoxicating fumes. Inhalants typically work like alcohol, first releasing inhibitions and then producing sedation and sleep (Miller & Gold, 1990). Greek legend holds that the Oracle at Delphi offered prophecies under the intoxicating influence of natural chemical vapors emitted by the ground.

inhalants
Depressants that are inhaled to induce altered states of consciousness.

In the nineteenth century, the consciousness-altering effects of inhalants appealed to many artists, writers, and intellectuals. William James (1882) used *nitrous oxide* to induce an altered state of consciousness in which he hoped to gain philosophical insights into the meaning of life. Peter Mark Roget, famous for his thesaurus, was also fond of nitrous oxide. We can only speculate on how many synonyms came to Roget in an intoxicated state (Brecher, 1972). You might be familiar with nitrous oxide as "whipits" or "laughing gas," which dentists use to induce a dreamy state of anesthesia. Nitrous oxide may produce its pain-relieving effects by either inducing the release of endorphins or directly stimulating endorphin receptors (Gilman, 1986). The pleasure-inducing effects of nitrous oxide were demonstrated in a study in which subjects inhaled either nitrous oxide or a placebo. The subjects were "blind" (see chapter 2) to their drug condition. Those who inhaled nitrous oxide reported a significantly more pleasurable state of intoxication than did those who inhaled the placebo (Dohrn et al., 1993).

opiates
Depressant drugs, derived from opium, used to relieve pain or to induce a euphoric state of consciousness.

Opiates

The opium poppy is the source of **opiates,** which include opium, morphine, heroin, and codeine. The opiates have been prized since ancient times for their ability to relieve pain and to induce euphoria. Sumerian clay tablets from about 4000 B.C. refer to the opium poppy as "the plant of joy" (Whitlock, 1987). The nineteenth century earned the title of "dope fiend's paradise" because opiates were cheap, legal, and widely available (Brecher, 1972). Some nineteenth-century artists and writers used opiates to induce altered states of consciousness. Samuel Taylor Coleridge wrote his famous poem "Kubla Khan" under the influence of opium.

Many nineteenth-century persons also relied on opiates for pain relief. Physicians and druggists prescribed a beverage called *laudanum*, a mixture of opium and alcohol, as a "magic elixir" for many physical and psychological problems. Laudanum relieved pain and made the person oblivious to her or his problems, but it did not cure any of them. Because a large enough dose of laudanum can be fatal, it was commonly used to commit suicide in nineteenth-century England (Clarke, 1985).

In the early 1860s, physicians used *morphine*, the main active ingredient in opium, to ease the pain of wounded soldiers in the American Civil War. Morphine was named after Morpheus, the Greek god of dreams, because it induces a state of blissful oblivion. In 1898 scientists used opium to derive a more potent drug—*heroin*. Heroin was named after the Greek god Hero, because it was welcomed as a cure for morphine addiction. But physicians soon found that heroin had no curative effect. It simply replaced morphine addiction with heroin addiction. By the early twentieth century, so many Americans had become addicted to opiates that in 1914 Congress passed the Harrison Narcotic Act banning their nonmedical use. Today, morphine, codeine, and the synthetic opiate Demerol are routinely prescribed to relieve severe pain. The euphoric and pain-relieving effects of the opiates are caused by their binding to endorphin receptors, which act to block pain impulses and stimulate the brain's pleasure centers (Levinthal, 1988).

Stimulants

Whereas depressant drugs reduce arousal, stimulant drugs increase it. **Stimulants** include *caffeine, nicotine, amphetamines, cocaine,* and *antidepressants*. Antidepressants, which are used to treat severe depression, are discussed in chapter 15.

stimulants
Psychoactive drugs that increase central nervous system activity.

Caffeine

caffeine
A stimulant used to increase mental alertness.

Few North Americans go a day without ingesting the addictive drug **caffeine,** which is found in a variety of products, including coffee, tea, soft drinks, chocolate, cold pills, diet pills, and stimulant tablets. The mind-altering effects of caffeine have made it a popular drug for centuries. Chocolate, for example, was considered a gift from the gods by the Aztecs of Mexico, who drank cocoa during their religious rituals. In eighteenth-century Europe, artists, writers, and philosophers gathered at coffeehouses to share their ideas under the stimulating effects of caffeine. In the late nineteenth century, Americans' use of coffee accelerated after the introduction of the first commercial mix of coffee beans at a Nashville hotel called Maxwell House (Ray, 1983).

Today caffeine is a popular means of maintaining mental alertness, apparently by increasing the release of the excitatory neurotransmitter glutamate (Silinsky, 1989). But it is important to note that the belief that a cup of coffee will help a drunken person sober up enough to drive home is a folk tale (Fudin & Nicastro, 1988). And caffeine's ability to enhance mental arousal can make it difficult to fall asleep. Excessive use of caffeine can lead to *caffeinism,* marked by agitation, insomnia, and intense anxiety. College students who suffer from caffeinism display poor academic performance. But it is unclear whether caffeinism causes poor academic performance or academically deficient students tend to ingest large amounts of caffeine (Gilliland & Andress, 1981). Once again, the need to distinguish between causation and correlation is apparent. Caffeine withdrawal is marked by headaches and drowsiness (Hughes et al., 1991).

Caffeine and Nicotine
To stay alert while studying, students may drink coffee or smoke cigarettes. But excessive caffeine ingestion can cause caffeinism, a condition associated with poor academic performance. And smoking can cause serious illness, including cancer and cardiovascular disease.

Nicotine

nicotine
A stimulant used to regulate physical and mental arousal.

"If you can't send money, send tobacco," read a 1776 appeal from General George Washington (Ray, 1983). Washington's troops actually craved **nicotine,** a powerful addictive drug contained in tobacco. Nicotine works by stimulating certain acetylcholine receptors, which may increase the efficiency of information processing in the brain (Warburton & Wesnes, 1984), a point not lost on students who smoke. Because nicotine's early effects are those of a stimulant and its later effects are those of a depressant, smokers adjust their intake of nicotine to achieve a desired level of arousal. In one study, 10 male smokers performed mental arithmetic under competitive pressure during one session and under noncompetitive pressure during another session. In each session, half of the subjects smoked real cigarettes and half smoked placebo cigarettes (which contained no nicotine). The smokers ingested more nicotine when under competitive pressure than when under noncompetitive pressure. Smoking produced greater reductions in reported anxiety levels in the competitive pressure condition than in the noncompetitive pressure condition. This reduction in anxiety was not a placebo effect, because it held only when the subjects smoked real cigarettes (Pomerleau & Pomerleau, 1987).

Amphetamines

amphetamines
Stimulants used to maintain alertness and wakefulness.

The **amphetamines**—including Benzedrine, Dexedrine, and Methedrine—are addictive synthetic stimulant drugs that are popularly known as "speed" and are more powerful than caffeine and nicotine. They exert their effects by stimulating the release of dopamine and norepinephrine and inhibiting their re-uptake by the neurons that secrete them. Because amphetamines dilate the breathing passages, Benzedrine, the first amphetamine, was initially prescribed for the treatment of asthma. In the 1930s truck drivers discovered that amphetamines would keep them alert during long hauls, letting them drive for many hours without sleeping. During World War II, soldiers used amphetamines to relieve fatigue, and for several decades college students have used amphetamines to stay awake while cramming for final exams. Because amphetamines also suppress appetite and increase the basal metabolic rate, they are commonly used as diet pills. But chronic users can also experience "amphetamine psychosis," marked by extreme suspiciousness and, sometimes, violent responses to imagined threats (Kokkinidis & Anisman, 1980). These, incidentally, are also symptoms of paranoid schizophrenia, a severe psychological disorder discussed in chapter 14.

cocaine
A stimulant used to induce mental alertness and euphoria.

Cocaine and Coca-Cola
This late-nineteenth-century advertisement indicates that Coca-Cola was a popular stimulant, that was also cheap, legal, and easily obtained.

hallucinogens
Psychoactive drugs that induce extreme alterations in consciousness, including visual hallucinations, a sense of timelessness, and feelings of depersonalization.

Cocaine

During the 1980s **cocaine,** a chemical extracted from the coca leaf, became the stimulant drug of choice for those who desired the brief but intense feeling of self-confidence and exhilaration that it induces. Cocaine acts by preventing the re-uptake of dopamine and norepinephrine by the neurons that secrete them (Gawin, 1991). Users snort cocaine in powdered form, smoke it in crystal form ("crack"), or inject it in solution form. But cocaine was popular long before the 1980s. People of the Andes have used it for more than a thousand years to induce euphoric feelings and to combat fatigue.

Cocaine may have reached the height of its popularity in the late nineteenth century. German troops used it to relieve fatigue. Sir Arthur Conan Doyle made his fictional character Sherlock Holmes a cocaine user. And Robert Louis Stevenson relied on cocaine to stay alert while taking just 6 days to write two drafts of *The Strange Case of Dr. Jekyll and Mr. Hyde.* Cocaine also joined opium as a popular ingredient in the patent medicines that were sold as cure-alls. In 1886 an Atlanta druggist named John Pemberton contributed to cocaine's popularity by introducing a stimulant soft drink that contained both caffeine and cocaine, which he named Coca-Cola. Even John B. Watson, the founder of behaviorism, relied on this concoction to keep himself alert:

> In my senior year at Furman University, I was the only man who passed the final Greek exam. I did it only because I went to my room at two o'clock the afternoon before the exam, took with me one quart of Coca-Cola syrup, and sat in my chair and crammed until time for the exam the next day. (Watson, 1961, p. 272)

Unfortunately, cocaine causes harmful side effects, as discovered by Sigmund Freud, who used it himself. In the 1880s, Freud praised cocaine as a wonder drug for combatting depression, inducing local anesthesia, relieving asthmatic symptoms, and curing opiate addiction. But Freud stopped using and prescribing cocaine after discovering its ability to cause addiction, paranoia, and hallucinations (Freud, 1974). In the early twentieth century, the dangers of cocaine use also led to its removal as an ingredient in Coca-Cola.

Hallucinogens

The **hallucinogens** induce extreme alterations in consciousness. Users may experience visual hallucinations, a sense of timelessness, and feelings of depersonalization. It has been difficult to determine whether adverse personality changes are caused mainly by the powerful effects of the drugs or by the tendency of people with psychological instability to use them (Strassman, 1984). The hallucinogens can induce psychological dependence, but there is little evidence that they can induce physical dependence. Among the most commonly used hallucinogens are *psilocybin, mescaline, LSD,* and *cannabis sativa.*

Psilocybin

Some cultures have relied on hallucinogens to induce mystical states of consciousness. The natives of Central America, including the Mayans, used a "magic mushroom" containing the hallucinogen *psilocybin* in their religious rituals and to inspire their works of art (McGuire, 1982). The drug has also been popular in North America. A survey of more than 1,500 college students found that of the 17 percent who reported using hallucinogens, more than 85 percent reported using psilocybin—and more than 50 percent reported using *only* psilocybin (Thompson et al., 1985). Apparently, the hallucinogenic mushroom may be the drug of choice for those who use only one psychoactive drug.

Mescaline

For many centuries Native Americans in the Southwest have used the peyote cactus, which contains the hallucinogen *mescaline,* in their religious rituals. Mescaline acts by blocking serotonin receptors (Wing, Tapson, & Geyer, 1990). Its hallucinogenic effects are described in Aldous Huxley's *The Doors of Perception* (1954). In the late nineteenth and early twentieth centuries, the Winnebago Indians of Nebraska practiced the peyote religion, but frowned on alcohol use (Hill, 1990). This illustrates how the notion of

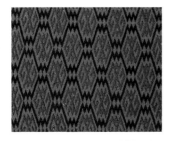

Hallucinogens
The geometric designs in these weavings by the Huichol Indians of Mexico were inspired by visual hallucinations induced by the ingestion of peyote, a cactus that contains the hallucinogen mescaline. LSD and other powerful hallucinogens can induce similar effects.

which drugs are licit or illicit varies from one culture to another. Pending the outcome of court decisions, members of the Native American Church still use peyote in their religious ceremonies.

LSD

On April 19, 1943, Albert Hofmann, director of research for the Sandoz drug company in Switzerland, accidentally ingested a microscopic amount of the chemical lysergic acid diethylamide (**LSD**). He surmised that he absorbed it through his skin. He reported that he felt as though he was losing his mind: "in a twilight state with my eyes closed . . . I found a continuous stream of fantastic images of extraordinary vividness and intensive kaleidoscopic colours" (Julien, 1981, p. 151). Hofmann found it a horrifying experience. Interest in LSD among nonscientists was sparked by a 1959 article in *Look* magazine in which actor Cary Grant claimed that it helped him overcome emotional problems. LSD was popularized in the 1960s as "acid" by Ken Kesey, author of *One Flew Over the Cuckoo's Nest* (Hilgard, 1987). Also during the 1960s, Timothy Leary, a former Harvard University psychologist, urged young people to take LSD and "turn on, tune in, and drop out." Because many people in the 1960s and 1970s used LSD recklessly, Hofmann (1983) called his autobiography *LSD: My Problem Child*.

Hofmann had first isolated LSD in 1938 from a fungus called ergot, which is found on damp rye grain. Ingestion of ergot from tainted rye grain might account for periodic outbreaks of *ergotism*, in which residents of an entire town can experience unexpected hallucinations and, understandably, become terrified and panic. Ergotism is also called "St. Anthony's fire," because St. Anthony is the patron saint of its victims, who have traditionally been treated by the Order of St. Anthony. The last major outbreak of ergotism was in the Soviet Union in the 1920s (Hofmann, 1983).

LSD, like mescaline, seems to exert its effects by affecting brain receptors for serotonin, stimulating some kinds and inhibiting other kinds (Pierce & Peroutka, 1990). A dose of LSD induces a "trip" that lasts up to 12 hours. The trip includes visual hallucinations, such as shifting patterns of colors, changes in the shapes of objects, and distortions in the sizes of body parts. Even **synesthesia** is possible. This phenomenon occurs when stimulation of sensory receptors triggers sensory experiences that characterize another sense (Cytowic, 1989). Thus, someone on an LSD trip while listening to music might report seeing the notes as different colors. Users of LSD may also report a sense of timelessness, a feeling of oneness with the universe, and, at times, mystical insights into the meaning of life.

The effects of LSD are so powerful that users may experience a "bad trip," in which the alteration in their consciousness is so disturbing that it induces feelings of panic. People with unstable personalities, who are not told what to expect, and who are in stressful circumstances, are more likely to have a "bad trip" (McWilliams & Tuttle, 1973). Hoffman, appalled by the indiscriminate use of LSD and the psychological harm it might do, has questioned whether the human mind should be subjected to such extreme alteration. After all, the brain evolved to help us function by letting us perceive reality in a particular way, unaffected by hallucinogens like LSD (Hofmann, 1983).

LSD
A hallucinogen derived from a fungus that grows on rye grain.

Albert Hofmann
"Now, little by little I could begin to enjoy the unprecedented colors and plays of shapes that persisted behind my closed eyes. Kaleidoscopic, fantastic images surged in on me, alternating, variegated, opening and then closing themselves in circles and spirals, exploding in colored fountains, rearranging and hybridizing themselves in constant flux."

synesthesia
The process in which an individual experiences sensations in one sensory modality that are characteristic of another.

Cannabis Sativa

The most widely used hallucinogenic drug is tetrahydrocannabinol (THC), a constituent of the hemp plant, **cannabis sativa.** The fibers of the hemp plant have traditionally been used in rope making; hemp has also been popular for two of its other products: *marijuana* and the more potent *hashish,* which many people smoke to induce an altered state of consciousness. Marijuana is a combination of the crushed stems, leaves, and flowers of the plant, and hashish is its dried resin. Marijuana and hashish exert their effects by stimulating THC receptors in the brain (Herkenhahn et al., 1991).

Marijuana has been used for thousands of years as a painkiller; the earliest reference to that use is in a Chinese herbal medicine book from 2737 B.C. (Julien, 1981). In the nineteenth century, marijuana was a popular remedy for the pain of headaches, toothaches, and stomachaches. Today most marijuana smokers use it for its mind-altering effects, which are related to its concentration of THC. Moderately potent marijuana makes time seem to pass more slowly and induces rich sensory experiences, in which music seems fuller and colors seem more vivid. Highly potent marijuana induces visual hallucinations, in which objects may appear to change their size and shape.

In 1937, after centuries of unregulated use, marijuana was outlawed in the United States because of claims that it induced bouts of wild sexual and aggressive behavior. Contrary to its popularity as an alleged aphrodisiac, marijuana at best causes disinhibition of the sex drive, which itself might be a placebo effect caused merely by its reputation as an aphrodisiac (Powell & Fuller, 1983). Allegations that link the hemp plant to aggressive behavior date back to at least the thirteenth century, when the explorer Marco Polo reported that hashish-smoking members of a Muslim sect murdered their leader's political enemies (Iyer, 1986).

Though the word *assassin* may have been derived from the word *hashish,* it is unlikely that hashish provoked these murders, because THC does not promote aggression. This was demonstrated in a study in which subjects were given low, moderate, or high doses of THC (Myerscough & Taylor, 1985). Those given moderate or high doses became less aggressive on a competitive reaction-time task than did those given low doses, indicating that THC does not promote aggression and, instead, might actually inhibit it. But this is not to say that marijuana use is desirable. It would be unwise to drive or to operate machinery while under the influence of marijuana—or any other psychoactive drug. Marijuana impairs coordination, visual tracking, and vigilance on the road (Moskowitz, 1985). And marijuana impairs memory as the result of THC's effect on neurons that process memories (Miller & Branconnier, 1983). The adverse effects on memory can last for weeks (Deahl, 1991). This finding should be of special concern to students who combine their studies with marijuana smoking.

THINKING ABOUT *Psychology*

ARE WE AFFECTED BY UNCONSCIOUS INFLUENCES?

In the late eighteenth century, the philosopher Gottfried Wilhelm Leibniz proposed the existence of unconscious thoughts, which he called "petites perceptions." In the late nineteenth century, William James (1890/1981), in his classic psychology textbook,

FIGURE **6.9**

Dichotic Listening
In studies of dichotic listening, the subject repeats a message presented to one ear while a different message is presented to the other ear.

included a section entitled "Can States of Mind Be Unconscious?" which presented ten arguments answering yes and ten answering no. Today the extent to which we are affected by unconscious influences still provokes animated debate. But the notion of the unconscious involves any of three different concepts: (1) *perception without awareness*, the unconscious perception of stimuli that exceed our normal absolute threshold but that fall outside our focus of attention; (2) *subliminal perception*, the unconscious perception of stimuli that are too weak to exceed the absolute threshold for detection; and (3) the *Freudian unconscious*, a region of the mind containing thoughts and feelings that influence us without our being aware of it.

PERCEPTION WITHOUT AWARENESS

There is substantial evidence that we can be affected by by stimuli that are above the normal absolute threshold but to which we are not attending at the time (as in the case of readers who read the word *by* earlier in this sentence but failed to notice that the word appeared twice in succession). At the turn of the century, the existence of such **perception without awareness** (Merikle, 1992) led some psychologists to assume that suggestions given to people while they sleep might help children study harder or adults quit smoking (Jones, 1900). But subsequent research failed to support such sleep learning (or *hypnopedia*). Any learning that does take place occurs during brief awakenings (Aarons, 1976)—so if you decide to study for your next psychology exam by playing an audiotape of class lectures while you are asleep, you will be more likely to disrupt your sleep than to learn significant amounts of material. Though there is little support for the concept of sleep learning, there is ample evidence supporting the formation of memories of sounds around us while we are under surgical anesthesia (Sebel, Bonke, & Winograd, 1993).

Research on attention, the aspect of consciousness that William James called "selectivity," also has demonstrated the existence of perception without awareness. Consider research on *dichotic listening,* in which the subject, wearing headphones, repeats—or "shadows"—a message being presented to one ear while another message is being presented to the other ear (Egeth, 1992). This is illustrated in figure 6.9. By shadowing one message, the subject is prevented from attending to the other one. Though the subject cannot recall the unattended message, she or he might recall certain qualities of it, such as whether it was spoken by a male voice or by a female voice. This demonstrates that

perception without awareness
The unconscious perception of stimuli that normally exceed the absolute threshold but fall outside our focus of attention.

Controlled Processing and Automatic Processing
When we learn a new task, we depend on controlled processing, which makes us focus our attention on each aspect of the task. With experience we depend less on controlled processing and more on automatic processing. Eventually, we may be able to perform the task while focusing our attention on other activities.

controlled processing
Information processing that involves conscious awareness and mental effort, and that interferes with the performance of other ongoing activities.

automatic processing
Information processing that requires less conscious awareness and mental effort, and that does not interfere with the performance of other ongoing activities.

subliminal perception
The unconscious perception of stimuli that are too weak to exceed the absolute threshold for detection.

our brain can process incoming stimuli that exceed the normal absolute threshold even when we do not consciously attend to them (Cherry, 1953).

Evidence of this also comes from studies of people with brain damage. Consider the case of a woman who suffered from the *neglect syndrome* (discussed in chapter 3), in which damage to the right parietal cortex makes the victim ignore stimuli in the left visual field. The woman was presented with two drawings of a house. One drawing, a burning house, was presented in the left visual field. The other drawing, an intact house, was presented in the right visual field. When asked to compare the drawings, the subject repeatedly reported that they were identical. Yet when asked which house she would prefer to live in, she reliably chose the intact house. This indicated that she could, at an unconscious level, distinguish between the two drawings (Marshall & Halligan, 1988).

The phenomenon of perception without awareness also occurs in cases of *prosopagnosia,* which is caused by damage to a particular region of the cerebral cortex. As described in chapter 3, prosopagnosia is marked by the inability to recognize familiar faces. In one study, two women with prosopagnosia were shown photographs of strangers, friends, and relatives while their galvanic skin response (a measure of arousal based on changes in the electrical activity of the skin) was recorded. Though the women were unable to name their friends and relatives from the photographs, they gave larger galvanic skin responses to those photographs than to the photographs of strangers. This indicated that intact visual pathways in the brain had distinguished between the faces without the women's conscious awareness of it (Tranel & Damasio, 1985).

Of course "awareness" is usually not an all-or-none phenomenon. For example, there is a continuum between *controlled processing* and *automatic processing* of information (Schneider & Shiffrin, 1977). At one extreme, when we focus our attention on one target, we use **controlled processing,** which involves more conscious awareness and mental effort, and interferes with the performance of other activities. At the other extreme, when we do one thing while focusing our attention on another, we use **automatic processing,** which requires less conscious awareness and mental effort and does not interfere with the performance of other activities. As we practice a task, we need to devote less and less attention to it because we move from controlled processing to automatic processing (Kihlstrom, 1987).

Think back to when you were first learning to write in script. You depended on controlled processing, which required you to focus your complete attention on forming each letter. Today, after years of practice in writing, you make use of automatic processing. This lets you write notes in class while focusing your attention on the teacher's words rather than on the movements of your pen. The transition from conscious, controlled processing to unconscious, automatic processing holds for numerous behaviors. Even Michael Jordan had to use controlled processing when he learned to play basketball, focusing his attention on dribbling the basketball and little else. In his championship years with the Chicago Bulls, he relied on automatic processing, because dribbling no longer required his attention.

SUBLIMINAL PERCEPTION

Research on **subliminal perception** investigates whether subjects can unconsciously perceive stimuli that do not exceed the absolute threshold. Subliminal presentation of emotionally charged words, such as *syphilis,* induces a significant increase in galvanic skin response as compared with neutral words, such as *carpet* (Kotze & Moller, 1990). In a study that demonstrated the emotional impact of subliminal stimulation, a device called a *tachistoscope* was used to flash slides of strangers to subjects too briefly (only a tiny fraction of a second) to exceed the absolute threshold. Because previous research had shown that we prefer stimuli with which we are familiar, the experimenters predicted that if subliminal perception exists, the subjects would later express more positive feelings toward people whose photographs had been presented subliminally. This was, in fact, what occurred (Bornstein, Leone, & Galley, 1987).

Subliminal Perception
In the 1960s certain songs by Bob
Dylan and the Beatles supposedly
contained subliminal messages.
Opponents of rock music even warn
that "Stairway to Heaven" by Led
Zeppelin contains satanic subliminal
messages that can be detected if the
song is played backward. But virtually
any song will have combinations of
sounds that, when played backward,
could be interpreted as satanic, sexual,
or violent lyrics—especially if you are
told what to listen for.

In another experiment, college students were shown slides of a novel cartoon character paired with subliminal slides of faces that expressed joy or disgust. When later asked to identify cartoon characters, the subjects performed faster if the cartoon characters they had viewed had been paired with faces consistent with their own emotional expressions. In a second part of the experiment, undergraduates were asked to form impressions of cartoon characters that were paired with subliminal presentations of faces expressing joy, disgust, or a neutral expression. Those who were exposed to the disgust condition mentioned more negative traits as descriptive of the cartoon than did subjects who were exposed to the joy condition (Niedenthal, 1990). Evidence from such studies indicates that stimulation of our photoreceptors can affect brain pathways involved in the recognition of objects, without the information's reaching consciousness. Moreover, messages that are presented subliminally might not have the same effects when presented above the absolute threshold (Bornstein & D'Agostino, 1990).

Given that we may be able to perceive subliminal stimuli and that we prefer stimuli with which we are familiar, could manufacturers make us like their products more by repeatedly presenting us subliminal messages about them? This is the heart of a controversy that has lasted since the late 1950s: Can subliminal advertising make people buy particular products? The controversy began after a marketing firm repeatedly flashed the words *Eat Popcorn* and *Drink Coca-Cola* during movies shown at a theater in Fort Lee, New Jersey. Though those watching the movies could not detect the advertisements, after several weeks, popcorn sales had increased 50 percent and Coke sales had increased 18 percent (McConnell, Cutter, & McNeil, 1958). Marketing executives expressed glee at this potential boon to advertising, but the public feared that subliminal perception could be used as a means of totalitarian mind control. However, psychologists pointed out that the uncontrolled conditions of the study made it impossible to determine the actual reason for the increase in sales. Perhaps sales increased because better movies, hotter weather, or more appealing counter displays attracted more customers during the period when subliminal advertising was used.

More recently, parents of teenagers have expressed concerns about the alleged subliminal messages in rock music recordings, such as Led Zeppelin's "Stairway to Heaven," that supposedly can be heard clearly when the recording is played backward. Despite the lack of evidence that such messages exist, fear that they might cause crime, satanism, and sexual promiscuity led California and other states to pass laws requiring warnings

"I worry about the subliminal message."

on recordings that contained subliminal messages. Yet even if recordings (or movies) contain subliminal messages, there is no evidence that listeners will *obey* them like zombies any more than they will obey messages of which they are aware (Vokey & Read, 1985). Nonetheless, because studies have shown that subliminal stimuli can have emotional, attitudinal, or behavioral effects, some researchers warn that subliminal messages might, in fact, have potential use as tools for spreading political propaganda (Bornstein, 1989).

But what of the popular subliminal self-help audiotapes that supposedly help you to do everything from increase your grades to decrease your weight? They, too, have been evaluated scientifically. In a study of university students, one group listened to sounds of ocean waves that masked subliminal messages promoting good study habits. A second group listened to a placebo audiotape of ocean waves with no subliminal messages. And a control group listened to neither. At the end of the study, the groups did not differ in their final-exam grades or in their grade point averages (Russell, Rowe, & Smouse, 1991). Studies like this one indicate that you would be wise to spend less money on self-help tapes and more time on studying.

THE FREUDIAN UNCONSCIOUS

During the 1988 National League playoffs between the New York Mets and the Los Angeles Dodgers, relief pitcher Brian Holton of the Dodgers became so nervous that he could not grip the baseball. Suddenly, he found himself singing the lyrics to a folk song, "You take the high road and I'll take the low road." This surprised him, because he

FIGURE 6.10

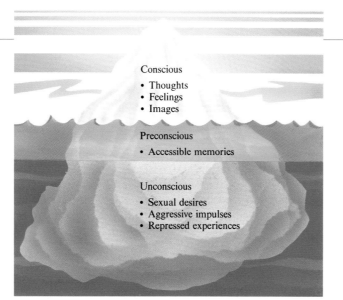

Conscious
• Thoughts
• Feelings
• Images

Preconscious
• Accessible memories

Unconscious
• Sexual desires
• Aggressive impulses
• Repressed experiences

Levels of Consciousness
According to Sigmund Freud, there are three levels of consciousness. The conscious level contains thoughts, images, and feelings of which we are aware. The preconscious level contains memories that we can retrieve at will. And the unconscious level contains repressed motives and memories that would evoke intense feelings of anxiety if we became aware of them.

believed he had never heard the song. Yet, for some reason, singing it relaxed him enough to enable him to grip the baseball. When he told his mother about this mysterious behavior, she informed him that his father had comforted him by singing the song to him when he was a young child.

Anecdotal reports such as this are used by psychoanalytic theorists to support the influence of the Freudian unconscious, which was anticipated centuries earlier by René Descartes and Leibniz, both of whom claimed that childhood experiences stored in the brain can continue to affect us without our awareness of them. In the late nineteenth century, the notion of such unconscious influences became the core of Sigmund Freud's psychoanalytic theory.

Freud divided consciousness into three levels: the *conscious*, the *preconscious*, and the *unconscious* (see figure 6.10). As had William James, Freud viewed the **conscious mind** as the awareness of fleeting images, feelings, and sensations. The **preconscious mind** contains memories of which we are unaware at the moment, but of which we can become aware at will. And the **unconscious mind** contains repressed feelings and memories of which we are unaware. Through what Freud called *psychic determinism*, discussed in chapter 1, the unconscious mind affects our behavior. Freud's notion of unconscious motivation is exemplified by slips of the tongue, or "Freudian slips," in which we replace intended words with sexual or aggressive ones.

Until recently, the Freudian unconscious was considered impossible to study scientifically because evidence of its existence came solely from anecdotal or clinical reports and because it seemed impossible to ever study something that could not be directly observed. But more-sophisticated techniques, though they do not necessarily convince all psychologists of the existence of the Freudian unconscious, at least make it subject to scientific research. One technique, developed by Lloyd Silverman, is called **subliminal psychodynamic activation** and is based on the assumption that emotionally charged subliminal messages will alter the recipient's moods and behaviors by stimulating unconscious fantasies (Weinberger & Silverman, 1990).

Silverman claimed that unconscious "oneness fantasies" (which express emotional union with one's mother) relieve anxiety and enhance task performance (Silverman & Lachmann, 1985). For example, a study of adults found that subjects exposed to the subliminal presentation of the printed phrase *Mommy and I are one* performed better on a motor task than did subjects exposed to the neutral phrase *People are walking* (Gustafson & Kallmen, 1990). But some studies have failed to find any effects of subliminal

conscious mind
The level of consciousness that includes the mental experiences that we are aware of at a given moment.

preconscious mind
The level of consciousness that contains feelings and memories that we are unaware of at the moment but can become aware of at will.

unconscious mind
The level of consciousness that contains thoughts, feelings, and memories that influence us without our awareness and that we cannot become aware of at will.

subliminal psychodynamic activation
The use of subliminal messages to stimulate unconscious fantasies.

"Good morning, beheaded—uh, I mean beloved."

psychodynamic activation. One study failed to find any difference in the effects of the subliminal messages "Beating Dad is okay" or "Beating Dad is wrong," or a neutral stimulus (anagrams) on the performance of males on a dart-throwing task (Kothera, Fudin, & Nicastro, 1990). Overall, the results of studies of subliminal psychodynamic activation indicate that it produces small, though statistically significant, effects on moods and behaviors (Hardaway, 1990).

A relatively recent topic of research somewhat related to the Freudian unconscious is *implicit memory* (Bornstein, 1993). **Implicit memory** refers to the process by which a past event or information stored in memory can influence a person's present behavior without the person's conscious recollection of it. This contrasts with **explicit memory,** the intentional recall of a past event or information that we are consciously aware of (Schachter, Chiu, & Ochsner, 1993). The Freudian unconscious can be viewed as the region of the mind that contains implicit memories that we have repressed because they are distressing to us.

Based on the foregoing discussion of unconscious influences, you should now realize that solid scientific evidence indicates that we can be affected by stimuli of which we are unaware. Some of the more-extreme claims for unconscious influences on our moods and behaviors, however, have tainted an otherwise legitimate topic for psychological research.

implicit memory
The process by which a past event or information stored in memory can influence our present behavior without our conscious recollection of the event or information.

explicit memory
The process by which we intentionally recall past events or information that we are consciously aware of.

SUMMARY

THE NATURE OF CONSCIOUSNESS

Consciousness is the awareness of one's own mental activity. William James noted that consciousness is personal, selective, continuous, and changing. Consciousness permits us to manipulate mental representations of the world, as in daydreaming. We daydream to rehearse courses of action, to maintain mental arousal, to solve problems, and to experience pleasure.

SLEEP AND DREAMS

The sleep-wake cycle follows a circadian rhythm. The pineal gland, which responds to changes in light, and the suprachiasmatic nucleus help regulate circadian rhythms. The depth of sleep is defined by characteristic brain-wave patterns. REM sleep is associated with

dreaming. Our nightly sleep duration and the percentage of time we spend in REM sleep decrease across the life span. The functions of sleep are still unclear. One theory views sleep as restorative. A second theory views it as adaptive inactivity, either because it protects us from danger when we are most vulnerable or because it conserves energy. A third theory views it as an aid to memory consolidation. The major sleep disorders include insomnia, sleep apnea, and narcolepsy.

The most dramatic aspect of sleep is the dream. Though we might fail to recall our dreams, everyone dreams. Most dreams deal with familiar people and situations. REM sleep can be disturbed by nightmares; NREM sleep can be disturbed by night terrors. In some cases we might incorporate stimuli from the immediate environment into our dreams. The major theories of dreaming view it as wish fulfillment, as problem solving, or as a by-product of spontaneous brain activity.

HYPNOSIS

Hypnosis is a state in which one person responds to suggestions by another person for alterations in perception, thinking, and behavior. Hypnosis had its origin in mesmerism, a technique promoted by Anton Mesmer to restore the balance of what he called animal magnetism. Hypnotic induction aims at the creation of a relaxed, passive, highly focused state of mind. Hypnosis is useful in treating pain. Though hypnosis can enhance memory, it might also make subjects more confident about inaccurate memories. Under certain conditions, hypnotized people—like nonhypnotized people—might obey suggestions to perform dangerous acts. The effects of stage hypnosis may have as much to do with the theatrical atmosphere as with being hypnotized. Researchers debate whether hypnosis is an altered state of consciousness or merely role playing. Ernest Hilgard has put forth the concept of the "hidden observer" to support his neodissociation theory of hypnosis as an altered state, which has been countered by Nicholas Spanos.

MEDITATION

Meditation is a procedure that uses mental exercises to achieve a highly focused state of consciousness. Transcendental meditation and the relaxation response are popular forms of meditation aimed at inducing mental and physical relaxation. As in the case of hypnosis, researchers debate whether meditation produces a unique physiological state.

PSYCHOACTIVE DRUGS

Psychoactive drugs induce changes in mood, thinking, perception, and behavior by affecting neuronal activity. Depressant drugs reduce arousal by inhibiting activity in the central nervous system.

The main depressants are alcohol, barbiturates, inhalants, and opiates. Stimulant drugs, which increase arousal, include caffeine, nicotine, amphetamines, and cocaine. Hallucinogens induce extreme alterations in consciousness, including hallucinations, a sense of timelessness, and feelings of depersonalization. The main hallucinogens are psilocybin, mescaline, LSD, and cannabis sativa (marijuana and hashish).

THINKING ABOUT PSYCHOLOGY: ARE WE AFFECTED BY UNCONSCIOUS INFLUENCES?

The answer to the question whether we are affected by unconscious influences depends on the concept of "unconscious" that is being used. Perception without awareness is the unconscious perception of stimuli that exceed the absolute threshold but fall outside our focus of attention. We may experience perception without awareness whenever we use automatic, rather than controlled, processing of information. Subliminal perception is the unconscious perception of stimuli that are too weak to exceed the absolute threshold for detection. Research has shown that we can be influenced by subliminal stimuli but has not supported fears that we might obey subliminal messages like zombies. The Freudian unconscious is a portion of the mind containing thoughts and feelings that influence us without our awareness. Because the Freudian unconscious deals with unobservable phenomena, it has proven difficult to study it scientifically. Subliminal psychodynamic activation provides one means of doing so.

IMPORTANT CONCEPTS

RECOMMENDED READINGS

FOR GENERAL WORKS ON CONSCIOUSNESS

Nature of Consciousness

Farthing, G. W., Jr. (1991). *Psychology of consciousness*. Englewood Cliffs, NJ: Prentice Hall.

Hilgard, E. (1980). Consciousness in contemporary psychology. *Annual Review of Psychology, 31,* 1–26.

Jaynes, J. (1976). *The origin of consciousness in the breakdown of the bicameral mind*. Boston: Houghton Mifflin.

Wallace, B., & Fisher, L. E. (1991). *Consciousness and behavior* (3rd ed.). Newton, MA: Allyn & Bacon.

Daydreaming

Klinger, E. (1990). *Daydreaming: Using waking fantasy and imagery for self-knowledge and creativity*. Los Angeles: Tarcher.

Mavromatis, A. (1990). *Hypnagogia: The unique state of consciousness between wakefulness and sleep*. New York: Routledge.

Singer, J. L. (1975). *The inner world of daydreaming*. New York: Harper & Row.

Watkins, M. M. (1976). *Waking dreams*. New York: Harper Colophon.

Attention

Kinchla, R. A. (1992). Attention. *Annual Review of Psychology, 43,* 671–742.

LaBerge, D. L. (1990). Attention. *Psychological Science, 1,* 156–162.

Pillsbury, W. (1908/1973). *Attention*. Salem, NH: Ayer.

Underwood, G. (Ed.). (1994). *The psychology of attention* (2 vols.). New York: New York University Press.

FOR MORE ON SLEEP AND DREAMS

Biological Rhythms

Davis, J. O. (1988). Strategies for managing athlete's jet lag. *Sport Psychologist, 2,* 154–160.

Montplaisir, J., & Godbout, R. (Eds.). (1990). *Sleep and biological rhythms*. New York: Oxford University Press.

Webb, W. B. (1982). *Biological rhythms, sleep, and performance*. New York: Wiley.

Sleep Processes

Arkin, A. M. (1981). *Sleep-talking: Psychology and psychophysiology*. Hillsdale, NJ: Erlbaum.

Ellman, S. J., & Antrobus, J. S. (Eds.). (1991). *The mind in sleep*. New York: Wiley.

Horne, J. (1988). *Why we sleep: The functions of sleep in humans and other mammals*. New York: Oxford University Press.

Kleitman, N. (1939/1963). *Sleep and wakefulness*. Chicago: University of Chicago Press.

Stampi, C. (Ed.). (1992). *Why we nap*. New York: Birkhauser.

Webb, W. B. (1992). *Sleep: The gentle tyrant*. Boston: Anker.

Sleep Disorders

Coleman, R. M. (1986). *Wide awake at 3:00 a.m.: By choice or by chance?* New York: W. H., Freeman.

Corr, C., Fuller, H., Barnickol, C. A., & Corr, D. (Eds.). (1991). *Sudden infant death syndrome*. New York: Springer.

Goswami, M., Crabtree, J., Pollak, C. P., Cohen, F. L., Thorpy, M. J., Kavey, N. B., & Kutscher, A. H. (Eds.). (1992). *Psychosocial aspects of narcolepsy*. Binghamton, NY: Haworth.

Guilleminault, C., & Partinen, M. (1990). *Obstructive sleep apnea syndrome: Clinical research and treatment*. New York: Raven Press.

Morin, C. M. (1993). *Insomnia: Psychological assessment and management*. New York: Guilford.

Williams, R. L., Moore, C. A., & Karacan, I. (Eds.). (1988). *Sleep disorders: Diagnosis and treatment*. New York: Wiley.

Dreams

Calkins, M. (1893). Statistics of dreams. *American Journal of Psychology, 5,* 311–343.

Cartwright, R. D. (1977). *Night life: Explorations in dreaming*. Englewood Cliffs, NJ: Prentice Hall.

Domhoff, G. W. (1985). *The mystique of dreams: A search for utopia through Senoi dream theory*. Berkeley: University of California Press.

Foulkes, D. (1982). *Children's dreams: Longitudinal studies*. New York: Wiley.

Freud, S. (1900/1990). *The interpretation of dreams*. New York: Basic Books.

Hartmann, E. (1984). *The nightmare: The psychology and biology of terrifying dreams*. New York: Basic Books.

Hobson, J. A. (1988). *The dreaming brain*. New York: Basic Books.

LaBerge, S., & Rheingold, H. (1990). *Exploring the world of lucid dreaming*. New York: Ballantine.

Lavie, P., & Hobson, J. A. (1986). The origin of dreams: Anticipation of modern theories in the philosophy and physiology of the eighteenth and nineteenth centuries. *Psychological Bulletin, 100,* 229–240.

Moffitt, A., Kramer, M., & Hoffman, R. (Eds.). (1993). *The functions of dreaming*. Albany: State University of New York Press.

Tedlock, B. (Ed.). (1987). *Dreaming: Anthropological and psychological interpretations*. New York: Cambridge University Press.

Wolff, W. (1952/1972). *The dream, mirror of conscience: A history of dream interpretation from 2000 b.c. and a new theory of dream synthesis*. New York: Greenwood.

FOR MORE ON HYPNOSIS

Baker, R. A. (1990). *They call it hypnosis*. Buffalo, NY: Prometheus.

Bowers, K. S. (1983). *Hypnosis for the seriously curious*. New York: W. W. Norton.

Hilgard, E. (1986). *Divided consciousness*. New York: Wiley.

Lynn, S. J., & Rhue, J. W. (Eds.). (1991). *Theories of hypnosis: Current models and perspectives*. New York: Guilford.

Mesmer, F. A. (1980). *Mesmerism: A translation of the original medical and scientific writings of F.A. Mesmer, M.D.* (G. J. Bloch, Ed.). Los Altos, CA: Kaufmann.

Spanos, N. P., & Chaves, J. F. (Eds.). (1989). *Hypnosis: The cognitive-behavioral perspective*. Buffalo, NY: Prometheus.

Tinterow, M. M. (1970). *Foundations of hypnosis: From Mesmer to Freud*. Springfield, IL: Charles C Thomas.

Zilbergeld, B., Edelstein, M. G., & Araoz, D. L. (1986). *Hypnosis: Questions and answers*. New York: W. W. Norton.

FOR MORE ON MEDITATION

Benson, H., & Proctor, W. (1984). *Beyond the relaxation response*. New York: Times Books.

Borysenko, J. (1987). *Minding the body, mending the mind*. Boston: Addison-Wesley.

Holmes, D. S. (1984). Meditation and somatic arousal reduction: A review of the experimental evidence. *American Psychologist, 34,* 1–10.

Shapiro, D. H., Jr., & Walsh, R. N. (Eds.). (1984). *Meditation: Classic and contemporary perspectives*. Hawthorne, NY: Aldine de Gruyter.

West, M. A. (Ed.). (1987). *The psychology of meditation*. New York: Oxford University Press.

FOR MORE ON PSYCHOACTIVE DRUGS

General

Carroll, C. R. (1993). *Drugs in modern society* (3rd ed.). Dubuque, IA: Wm. C. Brown.

Morgan, H. W. (1982). *Drugs in America: A social history, 1800–1980.* Syracuse, NY: Syracuse University Press.

Schivelbusch, W. (1992). *Tastes of paradise: A social history of spices, stimulants, and intoxicants.* New York: Pantheon.

Siegel, R. K. (1989). *Intoxication.* New York: Dutton.

Depressants

Critchlow, B. (1986). The powers of John Barleycorn: Beliefs about the effects of alcohol on social behavior. *American Psychologist, 41,* 751–764.

Glowa, J. B. (1992). *Inhalants: The toxic fumes.* New York: Chelsea House.

James, W. (1882). Subjective effects of nitrous oxide. *Mind, 7,* 186–208.

Levinthal, C. F. (1988). *Messengers of paradise: Opiates and the brain.* New York: Anchor Press/ Doubleday.

Stimulants

Freud, S. (1974). *Cocaine papers* (R. Byck, Ed.). New York: Stonehill.

Gilbert, R. (1992). *Caffeine: The most popular stimulant.* New York: Chelsea House.

Lippiello, P. M. (Ed.). (1992). *The biology of nicotine: Current research issues.* New York: Raven Press.

Lukas, S. E. (1992). *Amphetamines: Danger in the fast lane.* New York: Chelsea House.

Weiss, R. D., Mirin, S. M., & Bartel, R. L. (1993). *Cocaine* (2nd ed.). Washington, DC: American Psychiatric Press.

Hallucinogens

De Rios, M. D. (1991). *Hallucinogens: Cross-cultural perspectives.* Garden City, NY: Avery.

Furst, P. E. (1992). *Mushrooms: Psychedelic fungi.* New York: Chelsea House.

Gold, M. S. (1989). *Marijuana.* New York: Plenum.

Stevens, J. (1987). *Storming heaven: LSD and the American dream.* New York: Atlantic Monthly Press.

Stewart, O. C. (1987). *Peyote religion: A history.* Norman: University of Oklahoma Press.

FOR MORE ON UNCONSCIOUS INFLUENCES

General

Bowers, K. S., & Meichenbaum, D. (Eds.). (1984). *The unconscious reconsidered.* New York: Wiley.

Dixon, N. (1981). *Preconscious processing.* New York: Wiley.

Fuller, R. (1986). *Americans and the unconscious.* New York: Oxford University Press.

Kelly, W. L. (1991). *Psychology of the unconscious.* Buffalo, NY: Prometheus.

Perception without Awareness

Bornstein, R. F., & Pittman, T. S. (Eds.). (1992). *Perception without awareness: Cognitive, clinical, and social perspectives.* New York: Guilford.

Graf, P., & Masson, M. E. (Eds.). (1993). *Implicit memory: New directions in cognition, development, and neuropsychology.* Hillsdale, NJ: Erlbaum.

Langer, E. J. (1989). *Mindfulness.* Reading, MA: Addison-Wesley.

Sebel, P., Bonke, B., & Winograd, E. (1993). *Memory and awareness in anesthesia.* Englewood Cliffs, NJ: Prentice Hall.

Shiffrin, R. M., & Schneider, W. (1984). Automatic and controlled processing revisited. *Psychological Review, 91,* 269–276.

Weiskrantz, L. (1986). *Blindsight: A case study and implications.* New York: Oxford University Press.

Subliminal Perception

McConnell, J. V., Cutler, R. L., & McNeil, E. B. (1958). Subliminal stimulation: An overview. *American Psychologist, 13,* 229–242.

Vokey, J. R., & Read, J. D. (1985). Subliminal messages: Between the devil and the media. *American Psychologist, 40,* 1231–1239.

Freudian Unconscious

Balay, J., & Shevrin, H. (1988). The subliminal psychodynamic activation model: A critical review. *American Psychologist, 43,* 161–174.

Ellenberger, H. F. (1970). *The discovery of the unconscious.* New York: Basic Books.

Whyte, L. L. (1978). *The unconscious before Freud.* New York: St. Martin's Press.

FOR MORE ON CONTRIBUTORS TO THE STUDY OF CONSCIOUSNESS

Buranelli, V. (1975). *The wizard from Vienna: Franz Anton Mesmer.* New York: Coward, McCann, & Geohegan.

Calkins, M. W. (1930). Mary Whiton Calkins. In C. Murchison (Ed.), *A history of psychology in autobiography* (Vol. 1, pp. 31–62). Worchester, MA: Clark University Press.

Gay, P. (1988). *Freud: A life for our time.* New York: W. W. Norton.

Hofmann, A. (1983). *LSD: My problem child: Reflections on sacred drugs, mysticism, and science.* Los Angeles: Tarcher.

Leary, T. (1990). *Flashbacks: A personal and cultural history of an era.* Los Angeles: Tarcher.

Myers, G. E. (1986). *William James: His life and thought.* New Haven, CT: Yale University Press.

Henry O. Tanner
The Banjo Lesson
1893

LEARNING

learning
A relatively permanent change in knowledge or behavior resulting from experience.

ying your shoes, writing in script, riding a bicycle, performing mental arithmetic, and going out on a date are all activities that at first seemed difficult to you. Yet today you probably perform each of them easily. This indicates the importance of **learning,** which is a relatively permanent change in knowledge or behavior that results from experience. What you learn is *relatively* permanent; it can be changed by future experience.

This chapter will answer questions about the role of learning in a variety of areas, including these: How can children learn to stop bedwetting? How can learning explain drug overdoses? How can children receiving cancer chemotherapy learn to maintain their appetites? How do animal trainers apply learning principles in their work? How can learning account for compulsive gambling? How might depression depend on learning? How can we learn to exert greater control over our own physiological processes?

Do not confuse learning with reflexes, instincts, or maturation. A *reflex* is an inborn, involuntary response to a specific kind of stimulus, such as reflexively withdrawing your hand after touching a hot pot. An *instinct* is an inborn complex behavior found in members of a species (such as nest building in birds). And *maturation* is the sequential unfolding of inherited predispositions (such as walking in human infants). Moreover, learning is more flexible, enabling us to adapt to different circumstances.

Psychologists began the scientific study of learning in the late nineteenth century. In keeping with Charles Darwin's theory of evolution, they viewed learning as a means of adapting to the environment. Because Darwin stressed the continuity between animals and human beings, psychologists began studying learning in animals, hoping to identify principles they might also apply to human learning. As you will read, many of the principles of learning do, indeed, apply to both animals and people.

Psychologists have identified three kinds of learning. *Classical conditioning* considers the learning of associations between stimuli and responses. *Operant conditioning* considers the learning of associations between behaviors and their consequences. *Cognitive learning* considers learning through the mental manipulation of information.

CLASSICAL CONDITIONING

Classical conditioning grew out of a tradition that can be traced back to Aristotle, who believed that learning depended on *contiguity*—the occurrence of events close together in time and space (such as lightning and thunder). British philosophers of the seventeenth and eighteenth centuries, most notably John Locke and David Hume, became known as *associationists* because they agreed with Aristotle's view that learning depends on associating contiguous events with one another.

In the early twentieth century, the research of Ivan Pavlov (1849–1936) stimulated worldwide scientific interest in the study of associative learning. Pavlov, a Russian physiologist, won a Nobel prize in 1904 for his research on digestion in dogs. During the Russian Revolution, Pavlov, a giant among Russian scientists, was offered extra food rations. But, being feisty and dedicated to maintaining his research program, he refused to accept any unless he also received food for his dogs (Bolles, 1979).

In his research on digestion, Pavlov would place meat powder on a dog's tongue, which stimulated reflexive salivation. As shown in figure 7.1, he collected the saliva from a tube attached to one of the dog's salivary glands. He found that after repeated presentations of the meat powder, the dog would salivate in response to *stimuli* (that is, environmental events) associated with the meat powder. A dog would salivate at the

FIGURE 7.1

Pavlov's Research Apparatus
In studying the digestive process, Ivan Pavlov presented a dog with meat powder and collected saliva through a tube inserted into one of the dog's salivary glands. The amount of salivation was recorded by having a stylus write on a rotating drum. Pavlov found that dogs salivated to stimuli associated with the presentation of food, such as the mere sight of the laboratory assistant who brought the food.

Ivan Pavlov (1849–1936)
Pavlov is shown here in his laboratory, flanked by his assistants and one of his dogs.

sight of its food dish, the sight of the laboratory assistant who brought the food, or the sound of the assistant's footsteps. At first Pavlov was distressed by this phenomenon, which he called "psychic reflexes" or "conditional responses," because he could no longer control the onset of salivation by his dogs. But he eventually became so intrigued by the phenomenon that he devoted the rest of his career to studying it.

Pavlov was not alone in discovering this phenomenon. At the annual meeting of the American Psychological Association in 1904, the same year that Pavlov received his Nobel prize, E. B. Twitmyer, an American graduate student at the University of Pennsylvania, reported the results of a study on the "knee jerk" reflex. As you may know from your last physical examination, when a physician strikes you with a rubber hammer on your patellar tendon just below your bent knee, your lower leg reflexively extends. In his study, Twitmyer rang a bell as a warning that the hammer was about to strike. After repeated trials in which the sound of the bell preceded the hammer strike, the sound of the bell alone caused extension of the lower leg. But, to his disappointment, Twitmyer's presentation was met with indifference. In fact, William James, who chaired Twitmyer's session, was so bored (or hungry) that he adjourned the session for lunch—without providing the customary opportunity for discussion (Coon, 1982). North American psychologists began to take note of this kind of learning after John B. Watson described Pavlov's research in his presidential address at the annual meeting of the American Psychological Association in 1914. Because of Pavlov's extensive early research on "conditional responses," the phenomenon earned the name of *classical conditioning.*

Principles of Classical Conditioning

As Pavlov first noted, in **classical conditioning** a stimulus comes to elicit (that is, bring about) a response (either an overt behavior or a physiological change) that it does not normally elicit. But how does this occur?

Acquisition of the Conditioned Response

To demonstrate classical conditioning, you must first identify a stimulus that already elicits a reflexive response. The stimulus is called an **unconditioned stimulus (UCS)** and the response is called an **unconditioned response (UCR).** You then present several trials in which the UCS is preceded by a *neutral stimulus*—a stimulus that does not normally elicit the UCR. After one or more pairings of the neutral stimulus and the UCS, the neutral stimulus itself elicits the UCR. At that point the neutral stimulus has become a **conditioned stimulus (CS)**, and the response to it is called a **conditioned response (CR).**

Pavlov used the UCS of meat powder to elicit the UCR of salivation (figure 7.2). He then used a tone as the neutral stimulus. After several trials in which the tone preceded the meat powder, the tone itself became a CS that elicited the CR of salivation. In **higher-order conditioning,** a neutral stimulus may become a CS after being paired with an existing CS. In this case, the existing CS functions like a UCS. If the neutral stimulus precedes the existing CS, it elicits a CR similar to that elicited by the existing CS. This explains how neutral stimuli that have not been paired with a biological UCS such as food can gain control over our behavior. Higher-order conditioning might explain why music in commercials (such as those advertising fast-food restaurants) can affect our attitudes toward the products presented in the commercials (Blair & Shimp, 1992).

Of course, a tone is but one of many potential conditioned stimuli. Among the most important conditioned stimuli are words. In a clever classroom demonstration of this, a college professor used the word *Pavlov* as a neutral stimulus (Cogan & Cogan, 1984). Student subjects said "Pavlov" just before lemonade powder was placed on their tongues. The UCS of lemonade powder naturally elicited the UCR of salivation. After repeated pairings of *Pavlov* and the lemonade powder, *Pavlov* became a CS that elicited the CR of salivation. Classical conditioning may account, in part, for the power of words to elicit emotional responses. Perhaps the mere mention of the name of someone with whom you have a romantic relationship makes your heart "flutter."

Even bedwetting, or *nocturnal enuresis,* in childhood can be controlled by classical conditioning. An effective technique, devised half a century ago (Mowrer & Mowrer, 1938), uses an electrified mattress pad that consists of a cloth sheet sandwiched between two thin metal sheets. The upper metal sheet contains tiny holes. When a drop of urine penetrates that sheet and soaks through the cloth sheet, the moisture completes an electrical circuit between the two metal sheets. This sets off a battery-powered alarm, which wakes the child, who then goes to the toilet. The alarm serves as a UCS, which elicits awakening as a UCR. After repeated trials, bladder tension, which precedes the alarm, becomes a CS, which then elicits awakening as a CR. The child eventually responds to bladder tension by going to the toilet, instead of urinating in bed.

What factors affect classical conditioning? In general, the greater the intensity of the UCS and the greater the number of pairings of the CS and the UCS, the greater will be the strength of conditioning. The time interval between the CS and the UCS also affects acquisition of the CR. In *delayed conditioning,* the CS is presented first and remains at least until the onset of the UCS. An interval of about one second between the CS and the UCS is often optimal in delayed conditioning (Rescorla and Holland, 1982), though it varies with the kind of CR. In delayed conditioning using Pavlov's procedure, the tone is presented first and remains on at least until the meat powder is placed on the dog's tongue. Thus, the CS and UCS overlap. In *trace conditioning,* the CS is presented first and ends before the onset of the UCS. This requires that a memory trace of the CS be retained until the onset of the UCS. In trace conditioning using Pavlov's procedure,

classical conditioning
A form of learning in which a neutral stimulus comes to elicit a response after being associated with a stimulus that already elicits that response.

unconditioned stimulus (UCS)
In classical conditioning, a stimulus that automatically elicits a particular unconditioned response.

unconditioned response (UCR)
In classical conditioning, an unlearned, automatic response to a particular unconditioned stimulus.

conditioned stimulus (CS)
In classical conditioning, a neutral stimulus that comes to elicit a particular conditioned response after being paired with a particular unconditioned stimulus that already elicits that response.

conditioned response (CR)
In classical conditioning, the learned response given to a particular conditioned stimulus.

higher-order conditioning
In classical conditioning, the establishment of a conditioned response to a neutral stimulus that has been paired with an existing conditioned stimulus.

Classical Conditioning and Advertising
Advertisers know that they can make products more appealing to consumers by pairing them with sexual stimuli.

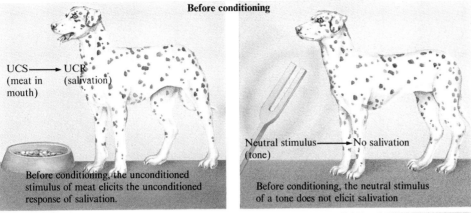

Before conditioning

UCS ⟶ UCR
(meat in   (salivation)
mouth)

Before conditioning, the unconditioned stimulus of meat elicits the unconditioned response of salivation.

Neutral stimulus ⟶ No salivation
(tone)

Before conditioning, the neutral stimulus of a tone does not elicit salivation

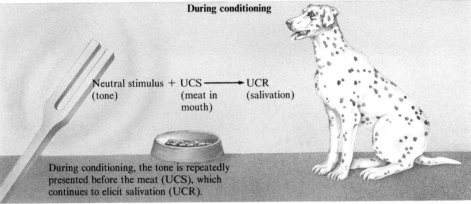

During conditioning

Neutral stimulus + UCS ⟶ UCR
(tone)   (meat in   (salivation)
                mouth)

During conditioning, the tone is repeatedly presented before the meat (UCS), which continues to elicit salivation (UCR).

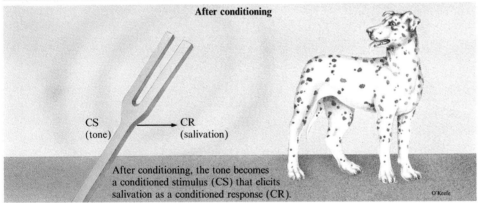

After conditioning

CS ⟶ CR
(tone)   (salivation)

After conditioning, the tone becomes a conditioned stimulus (CS) that elicits salivation as a conditioned response (CR).

O'Keefe

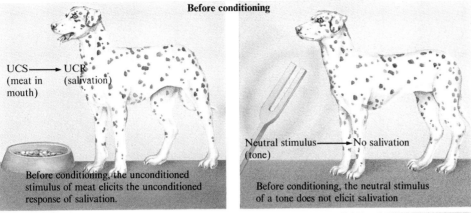

FIGURE 7.2

Classical Conditioning
Before conditioning, the unconditioned stimulus of meat elicits the unconditioned response of salivation, and the neutral stimulus of a tone does not elicit salivation. During conditioning, the tone is repeatedly presented before the meat (UCS), which continues to elicit salivation (UCR). After conditioning, the tone becomes a conditioned stimulus (CS) that elicits salivation as a conditioned response (CR).

the tone is presented and then turned off just before the meat powder is placed on the dog's tongue. In *simultaneous conditioning*, the CS and UCS begin together. In simultaneous conditioning using Pavlov's procedure, the tone and the meat powder are presented together. And in *backward conditioning,* the onset of the UCS *precedes* the onset of the CS. In backward conditioning using Pavlov's procedure, the meat powder is presented first, followed immediately by the tone. In general, delayed conditioning produces strong conditioning, trace conditioning produces moderately strong conditioning, and simultaneous conditioning produces weak conditioning. Backward conditioning is the least effective, though it is sometimes used successfully (Spetch, Wilkie, & Pinel, 1981).

Stimulus Generalization and Stimulus Discrimination

In classical conditioning, the CR may occur in response to stimuli that are similar to the CS. This is called **stimulus generalization.** For example, a dog conditioned to salivate to a dinner bell (a CS) might also salivate to a doorbell, a telephone bell, or an ice-cream

stimulus generalization
In classical conditioning, giving a conditioned response to stimuli similar to the conditioned stimulus.

FIGURE 7.3

Processes in Classical Conditioning
In classical conditioning, the pairing of the CS and the UCS leads to acquisition of the CR. When the CS is then presented without the UCS, the CR gradually disappears. After extinction and following a rest period, spontaneous recovery of the CR occurs. But extinction takes place again, even more rapidly than the first time.

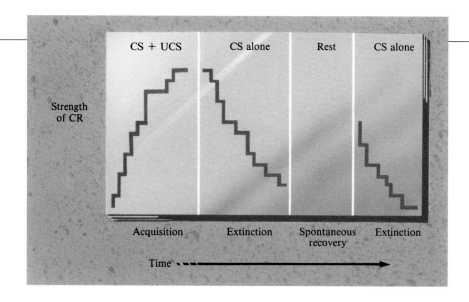

stimulus discrimination
In classical conditioning, giving a conditioned response to the conditioned stimulus but not to stimuli similar to it.

extinction
In classical conditioning, the gradual disappearance of the conditioned response when the conditioned stimulus is repeatedly presented without being paired with the unconditioned stimulus.

spontaneous recovery
In classical conditioning, the reappearance after a period of time of a conditioned response that has been subjected to extinction.

truck bell. But the dog might eventually salivate only in response to the dinner bell. This would be an instance of **stimulus discrimination,** in which the person or animal responds to the CS but not to stimuli that are similar to the CS. This would occur if the dog learns that the other bells are not followed by food.

Extinction and Spontaneous Recovery

In Pavlov's procedure, will a dog conditioned to salivate in response to a dinner bell do so forever? Not necessarily. If a CS is repeatedly presented without presenting the UCS, the CR will diminish and eventually stop occurring. This process is called **extinction.** A dog that has learned to salivate to a dinner bell (the CS) will eventually stop doing so unless presentations of the dinner bell are periodically followed by presentations of food (the UCS).

But extinction only inhibits the CR, it does not eliminate it (Bouton & Swartzentruber, 1991). In fact, after a CR has been subjected to extinction, it can reappear later if the CS is reintroduced. For example, suppose you produce extinction of the CR of salivation by no longer presenting the dog with food after ringing the dinner bell. If you rang the dinner bell a few days later, the dog would again respond by salivating. This process, by which a CR that has been subjected to extinction will again be elicited by a CS, is called **spontaneous recovery.** In spontaneous recovery, however, the CR is weaker and extinguishes faster than it did originally. Thus, after spontaneous recovery the dog's salivation to the dinner bell will be weaker and subject to faster extinction than it was originally. Figure 7.3 illustrates the acquisition, extinction, and spontaneous recovery of a classically conditioned response.

Applications of Classical Conditioning

In his 1932 novel *Brave New World*, Aldous Huxley warned of a future in which classical conditioning would be used to mold people into narrow social roles. In the novel, classical conditioning is used to make children who have been assigned to become workers repulsed by any interests other than work. This is achieved by giving them electric shocks (the UCS) in the presence of forbidden objects, such as books or flowers (the CS). Despite such fears of the diabolical use of classical conditioning, it has, in reality, been applied in less ominous, and often beneficial, ways. For example, chapter 16 describes how the immune system can be enhanced or impaired by classical conditioning (Kusnecov, King, & Husband, 1989). Classical conditioning has also been used to explain phobias, drug dependence, and taste aversions.

Explaining Phobias

Three hundred years ago, John Locke (1690/1956) observed that children who had been punished in school for misbehaving became fearful of their books and other stimuli associated with school. Today we might say that these children had been classically conditioned to develop school phobias. A *phobia* is an unrealistic or exaggerated fear, which was the subject of a classic study by John B. Watson.

Anatomy of a Classic Research Study:
Can Classical Conditioning Explain Phobias?

Rationale

The most famous study of a classically conditioned phobia was conducted by John B. Watson and his graduate student (and, later, wife) Rosalie Rayner (Watson & Rayner, 1920). Their subject was an 11-month-old boy, Albert B., later to become famous as "Little Albert," who enjoyed playing with animals, including tame white rats. Watson and Rayner hoped to provide scientific evidence that emotional responses could be learned by conditioning. This would provide an alternative to Freudian ideas of phobias as symbolic manifestations of unconscious conflicts that arise from early childhood sexual conflicts.

Method

In the study, Albert sat on a mattress. On several trials, just as Albert touched a white rat, Watson made a loud noise behind Albert's head by banging a steel bar with a hammer.

Results and Discussion

Albert responded to the noise (the UCS) with fear (the UCR). He jumped violently, fell forward, and buried his face in the mattress. After seven pairings of the rat and the noise (twice on the first day and five times a week later), Albert responded to the rat (the CS) with fear (the CR) by crying and showing distress in response to it. When tested later, Albert showed stimulus generalization. He responded fearfully to other furlike objects, including a dog, a rabbit, cotton wool, and a sealskin fur coat. Two months later he even showed fear of a Santa Claus mask. He had not shown fear of any of these objects at 9 months. Watson and Rayner hypothesized that pleasurable stimulation paired with a feared object would reduce Albert's phobia. But Albert left before they had the opportunity to try that technique. As discussed in chapter 15, Watson's student Mary Cover Jones (1924) used it a few years later to relieve a child's animal phobia.

Current ethical standards of psychological research (described in chapter 2) would prevent the experimental induction of phobias in children. Even Watson and Rayner noted the ethical pitfalls of their study, but downplayed them by stating that Albert was chosen because he was emotionally stable and that he would develop similar fears in everyday life. Attempts to locate Little Albert to determine the long-lasting effects of his experience have failed (Harris, 1979).

Though this study was done so haphazardly that it is not a convincing demonstration of a classically conditioned phobia, it led to sounder research studies demonstrating that phobias can, indeed, be learned through classical conditioning. It also contributed to the development of behavior therapy, which is discussed in chapter 15.

Little Albert
John B. Watson and Rosalie Rayner trained Little Albert to fear white rats. Through stimulus generalization, he also came to fear similar-looking objects.

Courtesy of Professor Benjamin Harris.

Explaining Drug Dependence

Classical conditioning might even explain dependence on psychoactive drugs. When a psychoactive drug (the UCS) such as heroin is administered, it produces characteristic physiological effects (the UCR). With continued use, higher and higher doses of the drug are required to produce the same physiological effects. This is known as *tolerance*, which may be, in part, the product of classical conditioning (Baker & Tiffany, 1985). Stimuli associated with the administration of certain drugs act as conditioned stimuli that elicit conditioned physiological responses *opposite* to those of the drug. For example, though heroin induces respiratory depression, stimuli associated with its

Conditioned Taste Aversion
A coyote that has been conditioned to be repulsed by the taste of sheep might no longer kill sheep.

conditioned taste aversion
A taste aversion induced by pairing a taste with gastrointestinal distress.

John Garcia
"Immediate reinforcement is simply not necessary for learning when illness is the reinforcer."

administration induce respiratory excitation. Why would stimuli associated with drug taking elicit effects opposite to those of the drug itself? Perhaps it is an adaptive, compensatory mechanism that prevents the physiological response to the drug from becoming too extreme.

Consider heroin addiction. Tolerance to heroin might occur because stimuli associated with its administration, such as hypodermic needles and particular settings, can act as conditioned stimuli to counter the physiological effects produced by the drug. This may explain why heroin addicts sometimes die of respiratory failure after injecting themselves with their normal dose of heroin in a setting different from that in which they normally administer the drug. By doing so they remove the conditioned stimuli that elicit conditioned physiological responses that normally counter the unconditioned physiological responses elicited by the drug. As a consequence, tolerance is reduced. This means that the unconditioned physiological responses, particularly respiratory depression, to a normal dose might be stronger than usual—in some cases strong enough to cause a fatal reaction (Siegel et al., 1982).

Explaining Taste Aversions

Have you ever eaten a meal, by coincidence developed a stomach virus several hours later, become nauseated, and later found yourself repulsed by something you had eaten at the meal? If so, you have experienced the phenomenon of a **conditioned taste aversion,** the classical conditioning of an aversion to a taste that has been associated with a noxious stimulus. Research on conditioned taste aversion was prompted by the need to determine the effects of atomic radiation, subsequent to the extensive atomic bomb testing of the 1950s. One of the leading researchers on conditioned taste aversion has been John Garcia. Garcia and his colleagues exposed rats to radiation in special cages. He found that the rats failed to drink water in the radiation cages, yet drank normally in their own cages. They continued to refrain from drinking in the radiation cages even when they were no longer exposed to radiation in them. Garcia concluded that the plastic water bottles lent a distinctive taste to the water in the radiation cages, which created a conditioned taste aversion after being paired with radiation-induced nausea. Because the water bottles in the rats' own cages were made of glass, the rats did not associate the taste of water from them with nausea (Garcia et al., 1956).

Garcia has also developed useful applications of conditioned taste aversion. In a clever application of this phenomenon, coyotes have been discouraged from killing sheep (Gustavson et al., 1974). Lithium chloride, a drug that causes gastrointestinal distress, is first injected into sheep carcasses. If a coyote eats this tainted meat, it becomes dizzy and nauseated, associates these sensations with eating sheep, and consequently refrains from killing them. This technique may provide a happy compromise between ranchers who want to kill coyotes and conservationists who want to save them. Unfortunately, in some cases it might merely inhibit predators from eating, rather than from killing, their prey (Timberlake & Melcer, 1988). Moreover, sheep ranchers have been reluctant to use the technique, preferring instead to eradicate the coyotes (Reese, 1986). Thus, a procedure that is scientifically feasible might not be practical.

In responding to Garcia's finding that a taste aversion could be learned even when the taste preceded feelings of nausea by hours, psychologists were at first shocked by this apparent violation of contiguity in classical conditioning. How could the taste of food be associated with nausea that occurs hours later? (Tastes do not linger long enough for that to be an explanation.) In part because Garcia's findings violated the principle of contiguity, editors of research journals refused to publish his studies, claiming that his findings were impossible (Garcia, 1981). Through the persistence of Garcia and his colleagues, who replicated his findings, conditioned taste aversion with a long interval between the stimulus and response is now an accepted psychological phenomenon. This

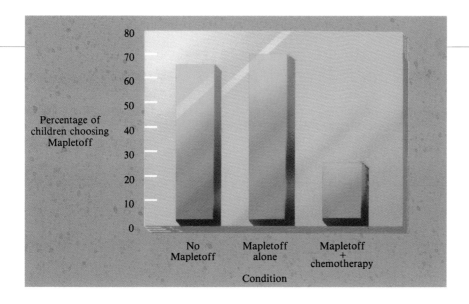

FIGURE 7.4

Chemotherapy and Conditioned Taste Aversion
Ilene Bernstein (1978) found that children undergoing cancer chemotherapy developed conditioned taste aversions to a novel flavor of ice cream (Mapletoff) eaten on the same days as they underwent treatment. The children may have developed the aversion to the flavor because it became associated with the nausea induced by the therapy. As the graph shows, when later given the choice of eating Mapletoff or playing a game, children who had eaten Mapletoff on the days when they received therapy were less likely to choose Mapletoff than were children who had never eaten it or who had eaten it on days when they did not receive therapy.

will remind you that scientists should maintain an attitude of skepticism, not cynicism. Of course, being human, psychologists, like all scientists, can succumb to their own biases in evaluating findings that contradict their cherished beliefs.

Had Garcia been less persistent, we might have been denied a potentially useful tool for combating the nausea-induced loss of appetite experienced by people undergoing cancer chemotherapy. Their loss of appetite makes them eat less and lose weight, weakening them and impairing their ability to fight the disease.

Anatomy of a Contemporary Research Study:
Can Classical Conditioning Improve the Appetites of Children Receiving Cancer Chemotherapy?

Rationale
Ilene Bernstein (1991), of the University of Washington, has conducted a program of research on taste aversion in chemotherapy patients. In one study, Bernstein (1978) determined whether children receiving chemotherapy would associate a novel taste with the nausea induced by chemotherapy.

Method
Bernstein assigned children receiving chemotherapy to one of three groups. One group ate "Mapletoff" ice cream, which has a novel maple-walnut flavor, before each chemotherapy session. The second group ate Mapletoff on days when they did not receive chemotherapy. And the third group never ate Mapletoff. Two to 4 weeks later the children were given the choice of eating Mapletoff or playing with a game. Later, at an average of 10 weeks after the first session, the children were given the chance to select Mapletoff or another novel-tasting ice cream.

Results and Discussion
As illustrated in figure 7.4, the results indicated that, when given the option of playing with a game, 67 percent of the children who never ate Mapletoff and 73 percent of the children who ate it only on days when they did not receive chemotherapy chose Mapletoff. In contrast, only 21 percent of the children who ate Mapletoff on days they received chemotherapy chose Mapletoff. When given the option of choosing Mapletoff or another novel ice cream flavor, only 25 percent of those in the Mapletoff-plus-chemotherapy group chose Mapletoff, while 50 percent of the Mapletoff-only group and 66 percent of the no-Mapletoff group chose it. Thus, the subjects exposed to Mapletoff and chemotherapy developed a taste aversion to Mapletoff. Based on these findings, and on findings that taste aversion is stronger in response to novel-tasting foods than to familiar-tasting foods (Kimble, 1981), perhaps cancer patients

Ilene Bernstein
"The demonstration of taste aversions in children receiving chemotherapy treatments may prove to be of importance to physicians who administer treatments which induce nausea and vomiting."

should be given a novel-tasting food before receiving chemotherapy. This might lead them to experience taste aversion in response only to the novel "scapegoat" food instead of to familiar foods, thereby helping them maintain their appetite for familiar, nutritious foods. Bernstein has, in fact, accomplished this with children receiving chemotherapy by using candies with unusual flavors (such as coconut) as "scapegoats" (Broberg & Bernstein, 1987).

Biological Constraints on Classical Conditioning

According to Ivan Pavlov (1928, p. 88), "Every imaginable phenomenon of the outer world affecting a specific receptive surface of the body may be converted into a conditioned stimulus." Until the past two decades, learning theorists agreed with Pavlov's proclamation. They assumed that any stimulus paired with an unconditioned stimulus could become a conditioned stimulus. But we now know that there are inherited biological constraints on the ease with which particular stimuli can be associated with particular responses (Kimble, 1981). This was demonstrated in an early study that tried to replicate Watson and Rayner's study on conditioned fear by using an opera glass instead of a white rat. The opera glass did not become a fear-inducing conditioned stimulus after being paired with an unconditioned stimulus that induced fear (Valentine, 1930). Chapter 14 presents research on phobia preparedness in human beings, which presumes that human beings are biologically predisposed to learn to fear objects and situations, such as snakes or heights, that threatened our evolutionary ancestors (McNally, 1987).

Biological constraints on classical conditioning were more recently demonstrated in a study of classically conditioned taste aversion in which two groups of rats were presented with a CS consisting of three components: saccharin-flavored water, a flash of light, and a clicking sound (Garcia & Koelling, 1966). For one group the CS was followed by a strong electric shock (the UCS) that induced pain (the UCR). For another group the CS was followed by X rays (the UCS) that induced nausea and dizziness (the UCR). The results indicated that the rats that had been hurt by the electric shock developed an aversion to the light and the click but not to the saccharin-flavored water. In contrast, the rats that had been made to feel ill developed an aversion to the saccharin-flavored water but not to the light and the click. This indicates that rats have a tendency, apparently inborn, to associate nausea and dizziness with tastes, but not with sights and sounds, and to associate pain with sights and sounds, but not with tastes. Thus, not all stimuli and responses are equally associable.

OPERANT CONDITIONING

In the late 1890s, while Russian physiologists were studying the relationship between stimuli and responses, an American psychologist named Edward Thorndike (1874–1949) was studying the relationship between actions and their consequences. While pursuing a doctoral degree at Harvard University, Thorndike studied learning in chicks by rewarding them with food for successfully negotiating a maze constructed of books. After his landlady objected to Thorndike's raising the chicks in his bedroom, William James, one of his professors, agreed to raise the chicks in his basement—much to the delight of the James children (Thorndike, 1961).

But, distraught after being rejected by a woman (whom he later married), Thorndike left Harvard and completed his studies at Columbia University. At Columbia he conducted research using cats in so-called puzzle boxes, which were constructed from Heinz wooden shipping crates. In a typical puzzle box study, Thorndike (1898) put a hungry cat in the box and a piece of fish outside of it. A sliding latch kept the door to the box closed. The cat could escape by stepping on a pedal that released the latch. At first the cat performed ineffective actions, such as biting the wooden slats or trying to squeeze between them. Eventually the cat accidentally performed the correct action, thereby releasing the latch, opening the door, and gaining access to the fish. Thorndike repeated

Edward Thorndike (1874–1949)
"When a certain connection [between a behavior and a consequence] has been followed by a satisfier the connection lasts longer than it does when it has been followed by an annoyer."

Puzzle Boxes
Edward Thorndike, working under a limited budget, used Heinz shipping crates to create puzzle boxes for conditioning his cats.

this for several trials and found that as the trials progressed the cat took less and less time to escape, eventually escaping as soon as it was placed in the box.

The results of his puzzle box studies led Thorndike to develop the **law of effect,** which states that a behavior followed by a "satisfying" state of affairs is strengthened and a behavior followed by an "annoying" state of affairs is weakened. In the puzzle box experiments, behaviors that let the cat reach the fish were strengthened and behaviors that kept the cat in the box were weakened. Because Thorndike studied the process by which behaviors are instrumental in bringing about certain consequences, the process became known as **instrumental conditioning.**

Principles of Operant Conditioning

Thorndike's work inspired B. F. Skinner (1904–1990), perhaps the best-known psychologist of the past few decades. Skinner called instrumental conditioning **operant conditioning,** because animals and people learn to "operate" on the environment to produce desired consequences, instead of just responding reflexively to stimuli (Iversen, 1992). Following in Thorndike's footsteps, Skinner used boxes, now known as **Skinner boxes,** to study learning in animals. Skinner devoted his career to studying the different kinds of relationships between behaviors and their consequences, which he called **behavioral contingencies.** Figure 7.5 summarizes the differences between the behavioral contingencies of *positive reinforcement, negative reinforcement, extinction,* and *punishment.*

Positive Reinforcement

Two centuries ago, while leading a fort-building expedition, Benjamin Franklin increased the likelihood of attendance at daily prayer meetings by withholding his men's rations of rum until they had prayed (Knapp & Shodahl, 1974). This showed his appreciation of the power of *reinforcement.* A *reinforcer* is a consequence of a behavior that *increases* the likelihood that the behavior will occur again. In **positive reinforcement** a behavior (for example, praying) that is followed by the *presentation* of a desirable stimulus (for example, rum) becomes more likely to occur in the future. Skinner called the desirable stimulus a *positive reinforcer.* You are certainly aware of the effect of positive reinforcement in your own life. For example, if you find that studying hard for exams earns you high grades, you will be more likely to study hard for exams in the future.

A handy approach to determining what will be an effective positive reinforcer is provided by the **Premack principle,** named for its discoverer, David Premack (1965). Premack pointed out that a behavior that has a higher probability of occurrence can be used as a positive reinforcer for a behavior that has a lower probability. Benjamin Franklin relied on this principle when he used the higher-probability behavior of drinking rum

law of effect
Edward Thorndike's principle that a behavior followed by a satisfying state of affairs is strengthened and a behavior followed by an annoying state of affairs is weakened.

instrumental conditioning
A form of learning in which a behavior becomes more or less probable, depending on its consequences.

operant conditioning
B. F. Skinner's term for instrumental conditioning.

Skinner box
An enclosure that contains a bar or key that can be pressed to obtain food or water, which is used to study operant conditioning in rats, pigeons, or other small animals.

behavioral contingencies
Relationships between behaviors and their consequences, such as positive reinforcement, negative reinforcement, extinction, and punishment.

positive reinforcement
In operant conditioning, an increase in the probability of a behavior that is followed by a desirable stimulus.

Premack principle
The principle that a more probable behavior can be used as a reinforcer for a less probable one.

FIGURE 7.5

Behavioral Contingencies

Contingency	Behavioral consequence	Probability of behavior	Example
Positive reinforcement	Brings about something desirable	Increases	You study for an exam and receive an A, which makes you more likely to study in the future.
Negative reinforcement	Removes something undesirable	Increases	You go to the dentist to have a cavity filled. This eliminates your toothache, which makes you more likely to visit the dentist in the future when you have a toothache.
Extinction	Fails to bring about something desirable	Decreases	You say hello to a person who repeatedly fails to greet you in return. This leads you to stop saying hello.
Punishment	Brings about something undesirable	Decreases	You overeat at a party and suffer from a severe upset stomach. In the future you become less likely to overeat.

The Skinner Box
The computer-controlled stainless steel and Plexiglas Skinner box is a far cry from Thorndike's puzzle box. Rats learn to obtain food by pressing a bar, and pigeons learn to obtain food by pecking a lighted disc.

primary reinforcer
In operant conditioning, an unlearned reinforcer, which satisfied a biological need such as air, food, or water.

secondary reinforcer
In operant conditioning, a neutral stimulus that becomes reinforcing after being associated with a primary reinforcer.

discriminative stimulus
In operant conditioning, a stimulus that indicates the likelihood that a particular response will be reinforced.

to reinforce the lower-probability behavior of praying. The Premack principle has even been used to improve the performance of restaurant employees (Welsh, Bernstein, & Luthans, 1992). Parents, too, use the Premack principle with their children when they make television a positive reinforcer for the completion of homework. Keep in mind that, according to the Premack principle, something that is reinforcing to one person might not be to another (Timberlake & Farmer-Dougan, 1991). Eating jello might be a positive reinforcer to you, yet repugnant to your friend.

In general, positive reinforcement is strengthened by increasing the magnitude of the reinforcer, decreasing the interval between the behavior and the reinforcer, and increasing the number of pairings of the behavior and the reinforcer. There are two classes of positive reinforcers. A **primary reinforcer** is biological and unlearned, such as oxygen, food, water, and sleep. In contrast, a **secondary reinforcer** (also known as a *conditioned reinforcer*) is learned and becomes reinforcing by being associated with a primary reinforcer. This was demonstrated in a classic study in which chimpanzees could obtain grapes by inserting tokens into a vending machine (Wolfe, 1936). After using tokens to obtain treats from the "chimp-o-mat," the chimps would steal tokens and hoard them. The tokens had become secondary reinforcers. Among the most powerful secondary reinforcers to human beings are praise, money, and success.

Why do behaviors that have been positively reinforced not occur continually? One reason is that behavior is controlled by discriminative stimuli, a process that Skinner calls *stimulus control*. A **discriminative stimulus** informs an individual when a behavior is likely to be reinforced. You would be silly to dial a telephone number if you did not first hear a dial tone, which acts as a discriminative stimulus to signal you that dialing might result in positive reinforcement—reaching the person whom you are calling.

A second reason that reinforced behaviors do not occur continually is the individual's relative degree of *satiation* in regard to the reinforcer. Reinforcement is more effective when the individual has been deprived of the reinforcer. In contrast, reinforcement is

Source: B. F. Skinner, "A Case History in Scientific Method" in American Psychologist, 11:221–233, 1956.

"Boy have I got this guy conditioned! Every time I press the bar down he drops in a piece of food."

ineffective when the individual has been satiated by having free access to the reinforcer. So, water is more reinforcing to a thirsty person and praise is more reinforcing to a person who is rarely praised.

Shaping and Chaining Positive reinforcement is useful in increasing the likelihood of behaviors that are already in an individual's repertoire. But how can we use positive reinforcement to promote behaviors that rarely or never occur? Consider the trained dolphins you have seen jump through hoops held high above the water. How do they learn to perform such a behavior, which is not a part of their natural repertoire? You cannot reinforce a behavior until it occurs. If the trainer waited until the dolphin jumped through a hoop held above the water, she or he might wait forever; dolphins do not naturally jump through hoops held above the water.

Animal trainers rely on a technique called **shaping** to train rats, dolphins, and other animals to perform actions that they would rarely or never perform naturally. In shaping, the individual is reinforced for *successive approximations* of the target behavior and eventually reinforced for the target behavior itself. A dolphin trainer might begin by giving a dolphin a fish for turning toward a hoop held underwater and then, successively, for moving toward the hoop, for coming near the hoop, and for swimming through the hoop. The trainer would then gradually raise the hoop and continue to reward the dolphin for swimming through it. Eventually the trainer would reward the dolphin for swimming through the hoop when it was held partly out of the water, then for jumping through the hoop when it was held slightly above the water, and, finally, for jumping through the hoop when it was held several feet above the water. Figure 7.6 shows that animal behavior, such as diving for food, can be shaped by nature, not just by human beings (Galef, 1980).

Shaping is not limited to animals. It is also useful in training people to perform behaviors that are not part of their behavioral repertoires. The successful application of what we now call shaping was reported as long ago as the seventh century, when it was used in England to help a mute person learn to speak (Cliffe, 1991). In a more recent application, shaping was used to train a child with Down syndrome to jump over a hurdle in preparation for the Special Olympics (Cameron & Cappello, 1993). Students can even use shaping to influence the behavior of their teachers. In one demonstration, a college professor asked her psychology students to shape her behavior during the semester (Chrisler, 1988). They were not to tell her what behavior was being shaped or what positive reinforcers were being used. As positive reinforcers, the students used nodding, smiling, eye contact, note taking, and class participation. The students successfully conditioned her to write more often on the chalkboard, to increase eye contact

shaping
An operant conditioning procedure that involves the positive reinforcement of successive approximations of an initially improbable behavior to eventually bring about that behavior.

FIGURE 7.6

Natural Shaping
Shaping occurs naturally in the wild. This may explain why wild rats living next to the Po River in Italy will dive to the river bottom to get shellfish to eat, while similar wild rats living next to other rivers will not. The Po River experiences radical changes in depth. (*a*) At times the rats living next to the Po can scamper across exposed areas of its bed to get shellfish. (*b*) As the water rises, the rats wade across the river and submerge their heads to get shellfish. (*c*) Eventually, when the water becomes deeper, they swim across the river and dive to get shellfish. Thus, the natural changes in the depth of the water shape the rats' behavior by reinforcing the rats with shellfish for successive approximations of diving (Galef, 1980).

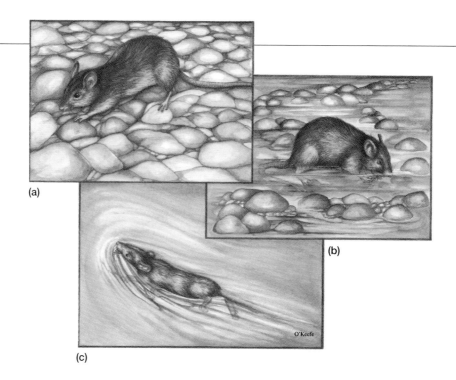

(a)

(b)

(c)

O'Keefe

chaining
An operant conditioning procedure used to establish a desired sequence of behaviors by positively reinforcing each behavior in the sequence.

with all members of the class, to move about the classroom more frequently, and to give more examples from her personal life experiences to illustrate concepts.

What if you wish to teach an individual to perform a *series* of behaviors, rather than single behaviors? You might use **chaining,** which involves the reinforcement of each behavior in a series of behaviors. In *forward chaining,* a sequence of actions is taught by reinforcing the first action in the chain and then working forward, each time adding a behavioral segment to the chain, until the individual performs all of the segments in sequence. Forward chaining has been successful in areas as diverse as teaching the use of a musical keyboard (Ash & Holding, 1990) and training mentally retarded people to make their beds (McWilliams, Nietupski, & Hamre-Nietupski, 1990).

In *backward chaining,* a sequence of actions is taught by reinforcing the final action in the chain and then working backward until the individual performs all of the segments in sequence. For example, a father could use chaining to teach his child to put on a shirt. The father would begin by putting the shirt on the child, leaving only the top button open. He would then work backward, first reinforcing the child for buttoning the top button, then for buttoning the top two buttons, and so on, until the child could perform the sequence of actions necessary for putting on a shirt. Even flight training programs for pilots are more successful when they have trainees practice individual segments of a chain of actions they are to learn and combine them together through backward chaining (Wightman & Lintern, 1984). Figure 7.7 shows Barnabus, a rat trained to perform a sequence of actions by backward chaining.

Schedules of Reinforcement   Once an individual has been operantly conditioned to perform a behavior, the performance of the behavior is influenced by its *schedule of reinforcement.* In a **continuous schedule of reinforcement,** every instance of a desired behavior is reinforced. A rat in a Skinner box that receives a pellet of food each time it presses a bar is on a continuous schedule of reinforcement. Similarly, candy vending machines put you on a continuous schedule of reinforcement. Each time that you insert the correct change, you receive a package of candy. If you do not receive the candy, you

continuous schedule of reinforcement
A schedule of reinforcement that provides reinforcement for each instance of a desired response.

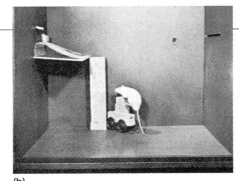

(a)   (b)

(c)   (d)

FIGURE 7.7

The Rat Olympics
Chaining has been used to train animals to perform amazing sequences of actions. Some psychology professors have even instituted so-called Rat Olympics, in which students compete in training rats to perform the longest sequence of actions (Solomon & Morse, 1981). Here, a rat has learned to obtain food by (a) pushing a cart to reach a stand, (b) climbing onto the cart, (c) jumping up to the top of the stand, and (d) running up a ramp. Note, however, that the rat learned this chain of behaviors backward, first learning to run up the ramp and finally learning to push the cart.

might pound on the machine, but you would, at best, insert coins only one more time. This illustrates another characteristic of continuous schedules of reinforcement—they are subject to rapid *extinction* when reinforcement stops.

In **partial schedules of reinforcement** (also known as *intermittent schedules*), reinforcement is given for only some instances of a desired behavior. Because partial schedules produce less-predictable reinforcement, they are more resistant to extinction than are continuous schedules. Skinner (1956) discovered partial schedules by accident when he ran short of food pellets and decided not to reinforce each response. Partial schedules are further divided into ratio schedules and interval schedules. In a *ratio schedule of reinforcement*, reinforcement is provided after the individual makes a certain number of desired responses. There are two kinds of ratio schedules: *fixed* and *variable*. A **fixed-ratio schedule** provides reinforcement after a specific number of desired responses. A rat in a Skinner box might be reinforced with a pellet of food after every five bar presses. Suppose that a garment worker is paid with a voucher after every three shirts sewn. That person, too, would be on a fixed-ratio schedule. Fixed-ratio schedules produce high, steady response rates, with a slight pause in responding after each reinforcement.

Unlike a fixed-ratio schedule, a **variable-ratio schedule** provides reinforcement after an unpredictable number of desired responses. The number of responses required will vary around an average. For example, a rat in a Skinner box might be reinforced with a food pellet after an average of 7 bar presses, with the number required varying each time—perhaps 5 presses one time, 10 presses a second time, and 6 presses a third time. People playing the slot machines in Atlantic City are on a variable-ratio schedule, because they cannot predict how many times they will have to play before they win. Even the archer fish, which hunts insects by spitting water at them as they fly by, continues to hunt that way (despite missing many times) because it is on a variable-ratio schedule of reinforcement (Goldstein & Hall, 1990).

Variable-ratio schedules produce high, steady rates of responding, which are more resistant to extinction than are those produced by any other schedule of reinforcement. In fact, by using a variable-ratio schedule of reinforcement, Skinner conditioned pigeons to peck a lighted disk up to 10,000 times to obtain a single pellet of food. This also

partial schedule of reinforcement
A schedule of reinforcement that reinforces some, but not all, instances of a desired response.

fixed-ratio schedule of reinforcement
A partial schedule of reinforcement that provides reinforcement after a set number of desired responses.

variable-ratio schedule of reinforcement
A partial schedule of reinforcement that provides reinforcement after varying, unpredictable numbers of desired responses.

Gambling and Schedules of Reinforcement

Gamblers are on variable-ratio schedules of reinforcement, which makes their gambling highly resistant to extinction. This is one of the reasons why compulsive gambling is so difficult to treat. People playing poker, betting on horses, or playing slot machines do not know when they will win, but they do know that they sometimes will. Pool hustlers take advantage of the resistance to extinction of variable-ratio schedules. By letting lesser players win periodically, pool hustlers encourage them to keep playing—and to keep losing several games for each one that they win.

fixed-interval schedule of reinforcement
A partial schedule of reinforcement that provides reinforcement for the first desired response made after a set length of time.

variable-interval schedule of reinforcement
A partial schedule of reinforcement that provides reinforcement for the first desired response made after varying, unpredictable lengths of time.

Fixed-Interval Schedules of Reinforcement

If you receive your mail at the same time every day, say at exactly 11 A.M., you are on a fixed-interval schedule of reinforcement. You would be reinforced the first time you checked your mailbox after 11 A.M., but you would not be reinforced if you checked it before 11 A.M.

negative reinforcement
In operant conditioning, an increase in the probability of a behavior that is followed by the removal of an aversive stimulus.

explains why compulsive gamblers find it so difficult to quit—they know they will eventually receive positive reinforcement, though they do not know when.

While ratio schedules of reinforcement provide reinforcement after a certain number of desired responses, *interval schedules of reinforcement* provide reinforcement for the first desired response after a period of time. As in the case of ratio schedules, there are two kinds of interval schedules: fixed and variable. A **fixed-interval schedule** reinforces the first desired response after a set period of time. For example, a rat in a Skinner box might be reinforced with a food pellet for its first bar press after intervals of 30 seconds. Bar presses given during the intervals would not be reinforced.

A fixed-interval schedule produces a drop in responses immediately after a reinforcement and a gradual increase in responses as the time for the next reinforcement approaches. Suppose that you have a biology exam every 3 weeks. You would study before each exam to obtain a good grade—a positive reinforcer. But you would probably stop studying biology immediately after each exam and not begin studying it again until a few days before the next exam.

A **variable-interval schedule** of reinforcement provides reinforcement for the first desired response made after varying periods of time, which vary around an average. For example, a rat might be reinforced for its first bar press after 19 seconds, then after 37 seconds, then after 4 seconds, and so on, with the interval averaging 20 seconds. When you are fishing, you are on a variable-interval schedule of reinforcement, because you cannot predict how long you will have to wait until a fish bites. Variable-interval schedules produce relatively slow, steady rates of responding, highly resistant to extinction. An individual may continue to fish even if the fish are few and far between. And teachers who give periodic surprise quizzes make use of variable-interval schedules to promote more-consistent studying by their students.

Ratio schedules produce faster response rates than do interval schedules, because the number of responses, not the length of time, determines the onset of reinforcement. Variable schedules produce steadier response rates than do fixed schedules, because the individual does not know when reinforcement will occur.

Negative Reinforcement

In **negative reinforcement** a behavior that brings about the *removal* of an *aversive* stimulus becomes more likely to occur in the future. Note that both positive and negative reinforcement *increase* the likelihood of a behavior. Consider the *negative reinforcer* known as the boring lecture. Because daydreaming lets you escape from boring lectures, you are likely to daydream whenever you find yourself listening to one. This form of negative reinforcement is called **escape learning**—learning to *end* something aversive.

Of course your class might be so boring that you stop attending it. This is a form of negative reinforcement called **avoidance learning**—learning to *prevent* something aversive. For example, dormitory students at some schools quickly learn to scamper out of the shower when they hear a toilet being flushed to avoid being scalded when cold water is diverted to the toilet (Reese, 1986). But if negative reinforcement involves engaging in a behavior that *removes* an aversive stimulus, how could avoidance learning (which only *prevents* an aversive stimulus) be a form of negative reinforcement? That is, what is the aversive stimulus that is being removed? Evidently, what is being removed is an *internal* aversive stimulus—the emotional distress caused by your anticipation of the aversive event, such as a boring class or a scalding shower. Thus, in escape learning the aversive stimulus itself is removed, while in avoidance learning the emotional distress caused by anticipation of that stimulus is removed (Mowrer, 1947).

Extinction and Spontaneous Recovery

As in classical conditioning, behaviors learned through operant conditioning are subject to **extinction.** Skinner discovered extinction by accident. In one of his early studies, he conditioned a rat in a Skinner box to press a bar to obtain pellets of food from a dispenser. On one occasion he found that the pellet dispenser had become jammed, preventing the release of pellets. Skinner noted that the rat continued to press the bar, though at a diminishing rate, until it finally stopped pressing at all. Extinction might occur when a student who raises her hand is no longer called on to answer questions. Because she is no longer being positively reinforced for raising her hand, she would eventually stop doing so.

Also, as with classical conditioning, a behavior that has been subjected to extinction can show **spontaneous recovery**—it can reappear after a period of time. This might have a functional advantage. For example, suppose that wild animals that visit a certain water hole normally obtain positive reinforcement by finding water there. If they visit the water hole on several successive occasions and find that it has dried up, their behavior will undergo extinction; they will stop visiting the water hole. But after a period of time, the animals might exhibit spontaneous recovery, again visiting the water hole—in case it had become refilled with water.

Punishment

Still another way of reducing the probability of behaviors is **punishment,** in which the consequence of a behavior decreases its likelihood. Do not confuse punishment with negative reinforcement. Negative reinforcement is "negative" because it involves the removal of an aversive stimulus; it does not involve punishment. Negative reinforcement *increases* the probability of a behavior by *removing* something undesirable as a consequence of that behavior; punishment *decreases* the probability of a behavior by *presenting* something undesirable as a consequence of that behavior. For example, a driver who gets a speeding ticket—an example of punishment—is less likely to speed in the future.

Though punishment can be an effective means of reducing undesirable behaviors, it is often ineffective. Consider some effective and ineffective ways of using punishment to discipline children (Walters & Grusec, 1977). First, punishment for misbehavior should be immediate so that the child will associate the punishment with the misbehavior. A mother or father should not resort to threats of "wait until your father [mother] gets home," which might separate the misbehavior and punishment by hours. Second, punishment should be strong enough to stop the undesirable behavior but not excessive. You might punish a child for throwing clothes about his room by having him clean the room, but you would be using excessive punishment if you had him clean every room in the house. Punishment that is excessive induces resentment aimed at the person who administers the punishment.

Third, punishment should be consistent. If parents truly want to reduce a child's misbehavior, they must punish the child each time it occurs. Otherwise the child learns only that her or his parents are unpredictable and that the misbehavior sometimes leads solely to positive reinforcement. Fourth, punishment should be aimed at the misbehavior, not at the child. Children who are told that they, rather than their behavior, are "bad" may lose self-esteem. For example, a child who is repeatedly called "stupid" for making mistakes while playing softball might feel incompetent and lose interest in softball and other sports. Fifth, punishing undesirable behavior merely suppresses the behavior and tells the child what *not to do*. To make sure that the child learns what *to do*, positive reinforcement of desirable behavior must be given.

One of the main controversies concerning punishment is the use of physical punishment. Children imitate parental models. If they observe that their parents rely on physical punishment, they may rely on it in dealing with their friends, siblings, and, eventually, their own children. Moreover, as noted in chapter 4, child abuse is a major problem in the United States, in part because parents may rely on physical punishment rather than positive reinforcement and nonphysical forms of punishment.

Applications of Operant Conditioning

B. F. Skinner (1986) claimed that many of our everyday problems could be solved by more-widespread use of operant conditioning. As one example, consider the problem of injuries and deaths caused by automobile accidents. As shown in figure 7.8, operant conditioning is effective in teaching children to use seat belts, thereby reducing their

Punishment
Behavior (such as touching a hot stove) that produces negative consequences (such as pain) will become less likely in the future.

FIGURE 7.8

Positive Reinforcement and Seat-Belt Use
Positive reinforcement (reward) is commonly used to promote adaptive behaviors. These graphs show the successful use of pizza, bumper stickers, and coloring books as positive reinforcers for seat-belt use by students at two elementary schools. Note that seat-belt use was higher during the reward phase.

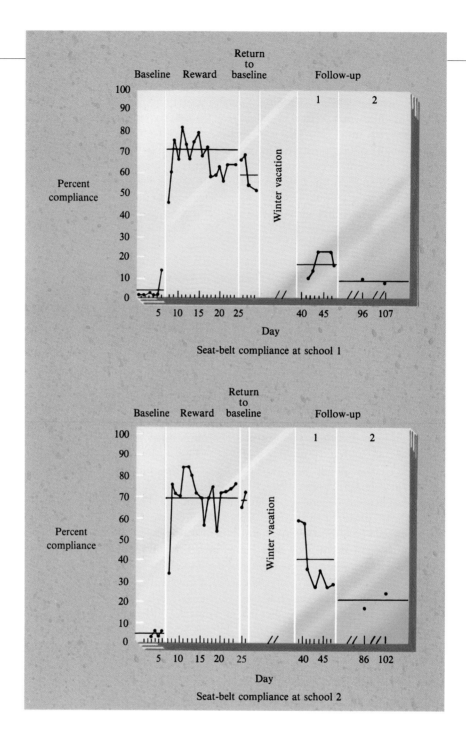

risk of injury (Roberts & Fanurik, 1986). Now consider several other ways in which operant conditioning has been applied to everyday life.

Animal Training

Skinner and some of his colleagues have been pioneers in the use of shaping and chaining to train animals to perform behaviors that are not part of their normal repertoire. Perhaps Skinner's most noteworthy feat in animal training occurred during World War II in "Project Pigeon." This was a secret project in which Skinner (1960) trained pigeons to guide missiles toward enemy ships by pecking at an image of the target ship shown on a display to obtain food pellets. Though this guidance system proved feasible, it was never used in combat.

More recently, pigeons have been trained to serve as air-sea rescue spotters in the Coast Guard's "Project Sea Hunt" (Stark, 1981). The pigeons are reinforced with food pellets for responding to red, orange, or yellow objects—the common colors of flotation devices. Three pigeons are placed in a compartment under a search plane so that they look out of windows oriented in different directions. When a pigeon spots an object floating in the sea, it pecks a key, which sounds a buzzer and flashes a light in the cockpit. Pigeons are superior to human spotters, because they have the ability to focus over a wider area and to scan the sea for longer periods of time without becoming fatigued.

In another beneficial application of operant conditioning, psychologists have trained capuchin monkeys to serve as aides to physically disabled people (Mack, 1981). These monkeys act as extensions of the disabled person—bringing drinks, turning pages in books, changing television channels, and performing a host of other services. The person directs the monkey by using an optical pointer that focuses a beam of light on a desired object.

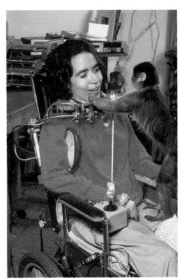

Child Rearing

In 1945 Skinner shocked the public when he published the article "Baby in a Box" in *Ladies Home Journal*, which described how he and his wife had reared their infant daughter in an enclosure called an *air crib*. The air crib filtered and controlled the temperature of the infant's air supply. Instead of diapers, it used a roll of paper that permitted sections to be placed under the baby and discarded when dirty. The parents could even pull down a shade over the front window of the air crib when the baby was ready to go to sleep. Skinner claimed the air crib was a more convenient way to rear infants and allowed more time for social interaction with them. Critics disagreed with Skinner, claiming that his treatment of his daughter was dehumanizing. Over the past few decades, rumors have claimed that Skinner's daughter's experience with the air crib eventually led her to sue her father, to become insane, or to commit suicide. In reality, she had a happy childhood and has pursued a successful career as an artist (Langone, 1983).

The air crib provoked fears of impersonal child rearing, and it was never widely used. Skinner had tried, unsuccessfully, to market the air crib under the clever brand name *Heir Conditioner*. But operant conditioning has proved useful in child rearing. For example, teachers have promoted toothbrushing by positively reinforcing children for having clean teeth by posting their names on the classroom wall (Swain, Allard, & Holborn, 1982). And parents have used extinction to eliminate their child's tantrums

The Air Crib
B. F. Skinner and his wife, Grace, are shown with their daughter Deborah, who spent her infancy in a sophisticated version of the air crib.

token economy
An operant conditioning procedure that uses tokens as positive reinforcers in programs designed to promote desirable behaviors, with the tokens later used to purchase desired items or privileges.

programmed instruction
A step-by-step approach, based on operant conditioning, in which the learner proceeds at his or her own pace through more and more difficult material and receives immediate knowledge of the results of each response.

computer-assisted instruction
The use of computers to provide programmed instruction.

(Williams, 1959). When parents ignore the tantrums, rather than giving in to the child's demand for toys, candy, or attention, the tantrums eventually stop.

Educational Improvement

Teachers have likewise used positive reinforcement to improve their students' classroom performance. For example, verbal praise has been used to increase participation in classroom discussions (Smith et al., 1982), and positive reinforcement in the form of *token economies* has been used to promote desirable classroom behaviors (Swiezy, Matson, & Box, 1992). In a **token economy** teachers use tokens to reward students for appropriate conduct and academic performance. The students then use the tokens to purchase items such as toys or privileges such as extra recess time.

Token economies have been used to decrease television watching by children (Wolfe, Mendes, & Factor, 1984), increase reading by students (Brown, Fuqua, & Otts, 1986), and improve social skills in mentally retarded adults (Sandford, Elzinga, & Grainger, 1987). Even mine-safety education has been improved by token economies. In one study, trading stamps were used as tokens at two open-pit mines. The workers earned stamps for working without lost-time injuries, for being in work groups in which no worker had lost-time injuries, for not being involved in equipment-damaging accidents, for making safety suggestions that were adopted, and for behavior that prevented an injury or accident. The workers lost stamps if they or others in their group were injured, caused equipment damage, or failed to report accidents or injuries. The token economy produced large reductions in the number of days lost from work because of injuries, the number of lost-time injuries, and the costs of accidents and injuries. The reduction in costs far exceeded the expense of operating the token economy. Improvements were maintained for several years after the end of the program (Fox, Hopkins, & Anger, 1987).

Perhaps the most distinctive contribution that operant conditioning has made to education has been **programmed instruction,** which had its origin in the invention of the *teaching machine* by Sidney Pressey of Ohio State University in the 1920s. His machines provided immediate knowledge of results and a piece of candy for correct answers (Benjamin, 1988). But credit for developing programmed instruction is generally given to B. F. Skinner for his invention of a teaching machine that takes the student through a series of questions related to a particular subject, gradually moving the student from simple to more complex questions. After the student answers a question, the correct answer is revealed.

The teaching machine failed to catch on in the 1950s and 1960s because of fears that it would be dehumanizing, that it could only teach certain narrow subjects, and that teachers would lose their jobs. Nonetheless, Skinner (1984) insisted that programmed instruction has several advantages over traditional approaches to education. Programmed instruction provides immediate feedback of results (positive reinforcement for correct answers and only mild punishment for incorrect answers), eliminates the need for anxiety-inducing exams, and permits the student to go at her or his own pace. Skinner claimed that if schools adopted programmed instruction, students would learn twice as much in the same amount of time.

Today's use of **computer-assisted instruction** (Skinner, 1989) in our schools is a descendant of Skinner's programmed instruction. Computer programs take the student through a graded series of items at the student's own pace. The programs even branch off to provide extra help on items that the student finds difficult to master. Though teaching machines and computers have not replaced teachers, they have added another teaching tool to the classroom. Computer-assisted instruction has proved useful with students, whether preschool (Clements, 1987), adult (Rachal, 1984), physically disabled (Lieber & Semmel, 1985), mentally retarded (Niemiec & Walberg, 1987), or intellectually gifted (Dover, 1983).

Computer-Assisted Instruction
Students may benefit from computer-assisted instruction because it permits them to go at their own pace, receive immediate feedback on their progress, and, in some cases, obtain remedial help in areas of weakness.

Understanding and Treating Psychological Disorders

Operant conditioning has enhanced our understanding of psychological disorders, particularly depression. As you will read in chapter 14, the concept of **learned helplessness** has gained influence as an explanation for depression through the work of Martin Seligman. In his original research, dogs restrained in harnesses were exposed to electric shocks. One group of dogs could turn off the shock by pressing a switch with their noses. A second group could not. The dogs were then tested in a shuttle box, which consisted of two compartments separated by an easily hurdled divider. A warning tone was sounded, followed a few seconds later by an electric shock. Dogs in the first group escaped by jumping over the divider into the other compartment. In contrast, dogs in the second group whimpered but did not try to escape (Seligman & Maier, 1967).

learned helplessness
A feeling of futility caused by the belief that one has little or no control over events in one's life, which might make one stop trying and develop feelings of depression.

Though replications of various versions of this study have produced inconsistent support for learned helplessness in animals (Klosterhalfen & Klosterhalfen, 1983) and human beings (Winefield, 1982), the possibility that learned helplessness is a factor in depression has inspired hundreds of studies. Depressed people feel that they have less control over obtaining positive reinforcers and avoiding punishments. As a consequence, they are less likely to try to change their life situations—which further contributes to their feelings of depression. You may have seen this in students who study many hours but still do poorly; they may become depressed, stop studying, and even drop out of school.

Operant conditioning has also been used to change abnormal behaviors. This is known as *behavior modification*. For example, token economies have been useful in training mental hospital patients to care for themselves (Woods, Higson, & Tannahill, 1984). Residents are trained to dress themselves, to use toilets, to brush their teeth, and to eat with utensils. They use the tokens to purchase merchandise or special privileges. Chapter 15 describes other applications of behavior modification in the treatment of psychological disorders.

Biological Constraints on Operant Conditioning

Around the turn of the century, Edward Thorndike put forth the concept of *belongingness* to explain why he found it easier to train cats to escape from his puzzle boxes by stepping on a pedal than by scratching themselves. Thorndike observed that animals seemed to inherit tendencies to associate the performance of certain behaviors with certain consequences. Cats are more predisposed to escape by performing actions that affect the environment, such as stepping on a pedal, than by performing actions that affect their bodies, such as scratching themselves.

Thorndike's observation had little influence on his contemporaries, and it was not until the 1950s that psychologists rediscovered what he had observed. The psychologists who first made this rediscovery were Keller and Marian Breland, former students of B. F. Skinner who became renowned animal trainers. Since its founding in 1947, their Animal Behavior Enterprises in Hot Springs, Arkansas, has trained animals to perform in zoos, fairs, movies, circuses, museums, amusement parks, department stores, and television commercials.

Despite their success in training animals, the Brelands were distressed by the tendency of some animals to "misbehave" (Breland & Breland, 1961). Their misbehavior was actually a reversion to behaviors characteristic of their species, which the Brelands called **instinctive drift.** For example, they used operant conditioning to train a chicken to hit a baseball by pulling a string to swing a miniature bat and then run to first base for food. Sometimes, instead, the chicken chased after the ball and pecked at it. This "misbehavior" of animals has distressed animal trainers, but it demonstrates that animals tend to revert back to *species-specific behaviors* even when being reinforced for other behaviors.

After considering instinctive drift and related problems in operant conditioning, psychologist Martin Seligman (1970) concluded that there is a continuum of **behavioral preparedness** for certain behaviors. Behavioral preparedness has been demonstrated in many studies. For example, a hamster learns to dig more easily than to wash its face to obtain positive reinforcement (Shettleworth & Juergensen, 1980). The continuum of behavioral preparedness ranges from *prepared* to *unprepared* to *contraprepared.* Behaviors for which members of a species are *prepared* have survival value for them and are easily learned by members of that species. Behaviors for which members of a species are *unprepared* have no survival value for them and are difficult to learn by members of that species. And behaviors for which members of a species are *contraprepared* have no survival value for them and are impossible to learn by members of that species. For example, human beings are prepared, chimpanzees are unprepared, and dogs are contraprepared to use language. Human beings can learn to speak, read, write, and use sign language. Chimpanzees can learn to use sign language. And dogs cannot learn any of these language skills.

COGNITIVE LEARNING

Both classical conditioning and operant conditioning have traditionally been explained by the principle of contiguity—the mere association of events in time and space. Contiguity has been used to explain the association of a conditioned stimulus and an unconditioned stimulus in classical conditioning and the association of a behavior and its consequence in operant conditioning. Over the past few decades, the associationistic explanation of learning has been criticized for viewing human and animal learners as passive reactors to "external carrots, whips, and the stimuli associated with them" (Boneau, 1974, p. 308). These critics, influenced by the "cognitive revolution" in psychology, favor the study of cognitive factors in classical conditioning and operant conditioning, as well as the study of learning by observation, which had routinely been ignored by learning researchers.

Cognitive Factors in Associative Learning

As discussed earlier, the traditional view of classical conditioning and operant conditioning is that they are explained by contiguity alone. But evidence has accumulated that mere contiguity of a neutral stimulus and an unconditioned stimulus is insufficient

instinctive drift
The reversion of animals to behaviors characteristic of their species even when being reinforced for performing other behaviors.

behavioral preparedness
The degree to which members of a species are innately prepared to learn particular behaviors.

to produce classical conditioning, and mere contiguity of a behavior and a consequence is insufficient to produce operant conditioning. This evidence has led to cognitive interpretations of associative learning, as in the case of operant conditioning. For example, secondary reinforcers have traditionally been thought to gain their reinforcing ability through mere *contiguity* with primary reinforcers. Cognitive theorists believe, instead, that secondary reinforcers gain their ability to reinforce behaviors because they have reliably *predicted* the occurrence of primary reinforcers (Rose & Fantino, 1978).

Suppose that you are using dog biscuits as positive reinforcers to train your dog to "shake hands." Just before giving your dog a biscuit, you might offer praise by saying "Good dog!" If you did so every time that your dog shook hands, the words "Good dog!" might become a secondary reinforcer. The traditional view of operant conditioning would claim that the praise became a secondary reinforcer by its mere *contiguity* with food. In contrast, the cognitive view would claim that the praise became a secondary reinforcer because it had become a good *predictor* of the food reward.

Psychologists have also provided cognitive explanations of classical conditioning that rule out mere contiguity as a sufficient explanation. The most influential of these explanations states that classical conditioning will occur only when the conditioned stimulus permits the individual to predict reliably the occurrence of the unconditioned stimulus. The better the conditioned stimulus is as a predictor, the stronger will be the conditioning. This means that conditioning involves learning relations, or contingencies, among events in the environment (Rescorla, 1988).

This was demonstrated by Robert Rescorla (1968), who favors a cognitive explanation of conditioning. In one experiment, he paired a buzzer (the neutral stimulus) with an electric shock (a UCS), which he administered to rats. All of the rats received the same number of pairings of the buzzer and the electric shock. But some of the rats were given additional shocks not preceded by a buzzer. According to the traditional contiguity-based explanation of classical conditioning, because the buzzer and the electric shock had been paired an equal number of times for all of the rats, the buzzer should have become an equally strong CS, eliciting a CR, for all of them. Yet those for whom the buzzer always preceded the electric shock showed stronger conditioning.

Rescorla would, instead, explain this cognitively. The rats who always received an electric shock after the buzzer developed a stronger *expectancy* that the buzzer would be followed by an electric shock than did the rats who sometimes did and sometimes did not receive an electric shock after the buzzer. Consider this explanation in regard to Pavlov's studies of salivation in dogs. The dog learns that a tone is followed by meat powder. The more consistently the tone precedes the meat powder, the more predictable will be the relationship and, as a consequence, the stronger will be the conditioning.

Another source of evidence that supports the cognitive explanation of classical conditioning is the phenomenon of **blocking,** in which a neutral stimulus paired with a CS that already elicits a CR will fail to become a CS itself (Kamin, 1969). Blocking is illustrated in figure 7.9. Suppose that you have conditioned a dog to salivate to the sound of a bell by repeatedly presenting the bell before presenting meat powder. If you then repeatedly paired a light with the bell before presenting the meat powder, the principle of contiguity would make you expect that the light, too, would gain the ability to elicit salivation. But it will not. Instead, the CS (the bell) "blocks" the neutral stimulus (the light) from becoming a conditioned stimulus. What accounts for blocking? According to one cognitive interpretation, blocking occurs because the neutral stimulus (the light) adds nothing to the predictability of the UCS (the meat powder). The CS (the bell) already predicts the occurrence of the UCS.

Still another source of evidence against a strictly contiguity-based view of classical conditioning comes from research on conditioned taste aversion. As you learned earlier, individuals who suffer gastrointestinal illness hours after eating novel food might avoid that food in the future. This contradicts the notion that events must be contiguous for us to learn to associate those events with each other.

Robert Rescorla
"Simple contiguity of CS and UCS fails to capture the relation required to produce an association."

blocking
The process by which a neutral stimulus paired with a conditioned stimulus that already elicits a conditioned response fails to become a conditioned stimulus.

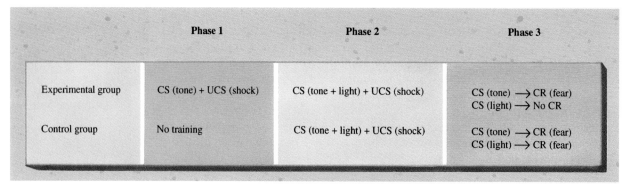

	Phase 1	Phase 2	Phase 3
Experimental group	CS (tone) + UCS (shock)	CS (tone + light) + UCS (shock)	CS (tone) → CR (fear) CS (light) → No CR
Control group	No training	CS (tone + light) + UCS (shock)	CS (tone) → CR (fear) CS (light) → CR (fear)

FIGURE 7.9

Blocking
In this example, in phase 1, rats in the experimental group are presented with a tone (the CS) immediately followed by an electric shock (the UCS), while rats in the control group receive neither stimulus. In phase 2, both groups are exposed to a tone and a light, followed by a shock. In phase 3, both groups show fear (the CR) in response to the tone, but only the control group shows fear in response to the light. Because the tone already served as a reliable predictor of the shock for the experimental group, the tone blocked the light from becoming a CS for the rats in that group.

Latent Learning

The "cognitive revolution" in psychology has also produced a trend in recent decades to view learning less in terms of changes in overt behavior, as in classical or operant conditioning, and more in terms of the acquisition of knowledge (Greeno, 1980). This means that learning can occur without revealing itself in observable behavior. For example, suppose that after studying many hours and mastering the material for a psychology exam, you fail the exam. Should your professor conclude that you had not learned the material? Not necessarily. Perhaps you failed the exam because the questions were ambiguous or because you were so anxious that your mind "went blank." Your performance on the exam did not reflect how well you had learned the material.

The first psychologist to stress the distinction between learning and performance was Edward Tolman (1932), who pointed out that learning can occur without reinforcement of overt actions, a process that he called **latent learning.** In latent learning, learning is not immediately revealed in performance but is revealed later when reinforcement is provided for performance. In a classic study, Tolman had three groups of rats run individually through a maze once a day for 10 days. One group received food as a reward for reaching the end of the maze and the other two groups did not. The rewarded rats quickly learned to run through the maze with few wrong turns, while the unrewarded rats did not. Beginning on the 11th day one of the groups of unrewarded rats was also rewarded with food for reaching the end of the maze. As shown in figure 7.10, the next day that group ran the maze as efficiently as the previously rewarded group did, while the remaining, still unrewarded group continued to perform poorly. This demonstrated latent learning. The rats that were not rewarded until the 11th day had learned the route to the end of the maze, but they revealed this learning only when rewarded for doing so (Tolman & Honzik, 1930).

More-recent research has provided additional support for latent learning. In one study, rats given an opportunity to observe a water maze before swimming through it for a food reward performed better than did rats who were not given such an opportunity (Keith & McVety, 1988). This provided evidence that rats can form what Tolman called "cognitive maps"—mental representations of physical reality. But they use their cognitive maps only when reinforced for doing so. Nonetheless, some researchers have found that in similar latent-learning experiments rats might be guided in their swimming not by cognitive maps, but instead by visual cues in their environment (Whishaw, 1991).

Observational Learning

In the 1960s, research on latent learning stimulated interest in **observational learning,** in which an individual learns a behavior by watching others (models) perform it. Observational learning is important to both animals and human beings in a variety of

latent learning
Learning that occurs without the reinforcement of overt behavior.

Edward Tolman (1886–1959)
"Our system . . . concerns mental processes as functional variables intervening between stimuli, initiating physiological states, and the general heredity and past training of the organism, on the one hand, and final resulting responses on the other."

observational learning
Learning a behavior by observing the consequences that others receive for performing it.

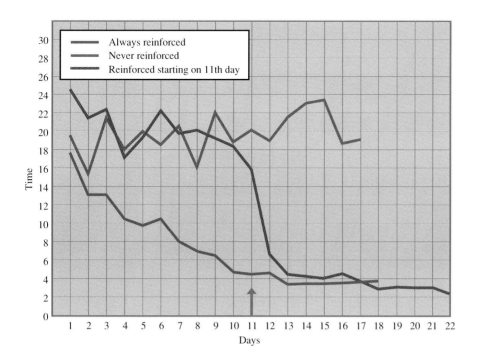

FIGURE 7.10

Latent Learning
Rats are capable of latent learning, in which they learn through experience, but they do not reveal this learning in overt behavior until they are reinforced for doing so. As the graph illustrates, in the Tolman and Honzik (1930) study, rats that merely explored a maze once a day for 10 days were given a food reward for reaching the end of the maze on the 11th day. On succeeding days they performed as well as rats that had been rewarded on the first 10 days, while other rats that had never been rewarded continued to perform poorly.

situations, and from early in life. A rat that observes other rats eating foods will be more likely to eat those foods (Galef, 1986), infant rats that observe older rats opening pine cones will learn to do so themselves (Aisner & Turkel, 1992), and rats that observe other rats pushing a joystick in a particular direction to get food will be more likely to push it in that direction themselves (Heyes, Dawson, & Nokes, 1992). In human beings, personnel development (Mayer & Russell, 1987), proper eating etiquette (Vanden Pol et al., 1981), and alcohol drinking habits (Collins & Marlatt, 1981) are some of the many behaviors affected by observation of models.

Observational learning is central to Albert Bandura's **social-learning theory,** which assumes that social behavior is learned chiefly through observation and the mental processing of information. What accounts for observational learning? Bandura (1986) has identified four factors: first, you must pay *attention* to the model's actions; second, you must *remember* the model's actions; third, you must have the *ability* to produce the actions; and fourth, you must be *motivated* to perform the actions. Consider a gymnast learning to perform a flying dismount from the uneven bars. She might learn to perform this feat by first paying attention to a gymnast who can already perform it. To be able to try the feat later, the learner would have to remember what the model did. But to perform the feat the learner must have the strength to swing from the bars. Assuming that she paid attention to the model, remembered what the model did, and had the strength to perform the movement, she still might be motivated only to perform the feat in important competitions.

Observational learning can promote undesirable, as well as desirable, behavior. For example, we can develop phobias vicariously through observing other people who exhibit them (Rachman, 1991). Even monkeys can develop fears through observing other monkeys (Mineka & Cook, 1993). In a study that found support for the concept of preparedness in the development of phobias through observation, rhesus monkeys watched videotapes of model monkeys showing fear of presumably fear-relevant stimuli (toy snakes or a toy crocodile) or presumably fear-irrelevant stimuli (flowers or a toy rabbit). The monkeys developed fears of the fear-relevant, but not the fear-irrelevant, stimuli (Cook & Mineka, 1989). Perhaps they are prepared by evolution to do so.

In an early study of observational learning, Bandura (1965) demonstrated the influence of such learning on the aggressiveness of children. Three groups of preschool children watched a film of an adult punching and verbally abusing a blow-up Bobo doll. Each group saw a different version of the film. In the first version the model was rewarded with candy, soda, and praise by another adult. In the second version the other adult scolded and spanked the model. And in the third version there were no

social-learning theory
A theory of gender-role development that assumes that people learn social behaviors mainly through observation and mental processing of information.

Albert Bandura
"Most human behavior is learned observationally through modeling."

FIGURE 7.11

Observational Learning
Children who observe aggressive behavior being positively reinforced are more likely to engage in it themselves (Bandura, 1965).

consequences to the model. The children then played individually in a room with a Bobo doll and other toys (see figure 7.11). Those who had seen the model being rewarded for being aggressive were more aggressive in their play than were those who had seen the other two versions of the film. This demonstrated that operant conditioning can occur vicariously, simply through observing others receiving positive reinforcement for engaging in the target behavior.

Studies such as this have contributed to concerns about the effects of movies and television on viewers, particularly on children. This concern may be well founded, because children who watch violent programs tend to be more aggressive, while children who watch altruistic programs such as "Mister Rogers' Neighborhood" tend to engage in more positive social behaviors (Huston, Watkins, & Kunkel, 1989). Chapter 17 discusses research on the effects of television on children.

THINKING ABOUT *Psychology*

IS BIOFEEDBACK AN EFFECTIVE MEANS FOR LEARNING SELF-REGULATION OF PHYSIOLOGICAL RESPONSES?

One day, more than two decades ago, the eminent learning researcher Neal Miller stood in front of a mirror trying to teach himself to wiggle one ear. By watching his ear in the mirror, he eventually was able to make it wiggle (Jonas, 1972). The mirror provided Miller with visual *feedback* of his ear's movement. This convinced him that people might learn to control physiological responses that are not normally subject to voluntary control if they were provided with feedback of those responses. Since the 1960s Miller and other psychologists have developed a technique called *biofeedback* to help people learn to control normally involuntary responses such as brain waves, blood pressure, and intestinal contractions.

THE NATURE OF BIOFEEDBACK

Biofeedback is a form of operant conditioning that enables an individual to learn to control a normally involuntary physiological response or to gain better control of a normally voluntary physiological response when provided with visual or auditory feedback of the state of that response. The feedback acts as a positive reinforcer for changes in the desired direction. How is this accomplished? The first step is to detect changes in electrical activity that reflect changes in the physiological response of interest. This is done by sensors, usually *electrodes*, attached to the body. The second step is to amplify the changes in electrical activity so that they can be recorded and used to generate a feedback signal. The third step is to present the subject with feedback indicating the state of the physiological response. The feedback might be provided by a light that changes in brightness as heart rate changes, a tone that changes in pitch as muscle tension changes, or any of a host of other visual or auditory stimuli that vary with changes in the target physiological response.

biofeedback
A form of operant conditioning that enables an individual either to learn to control a normally involuntary physiological process or to gain better control of a normally voluntary one when provided with visual or auditory feedback of the state of that process.

HISTORICAL BACKGROUND

Though the term *biofeedback* was not coined until 1969, the ability to gain extraordinary self-control of physiological responses was known long before then. For centuries Indian yogis have demonstrated the ability to gain control over involuntary responses, such as heart rate, that are regulated by the autonomic nervous system. Perhaps the first study of what we now call biofeedback occurred in 1885 when a Russian researcher reported the case of a patient who could control his heart rate when permitted to observe an ongoing recording of it (Tarchanoff, 1885). But until the 1960s few researchers conducted studies of learned control of normally involuntary physiological responses, in part because influential psychologists such as B. F. Skinner considered it impossible.

Nonetheless, some researchers were undaunted by this pessimistic outlook and continued research on voluntary self-control of physiological responses. Their research bore fruit in the early 1960s with reports of the successful use of physiological feedback in training subjects to control their heart rate (Shearn, 1962) and imperceptible muscle twitches in their hands (Basmajian, 1963). Biofeedback was popularized in the late 1960s by reports of subjects who learned to control their alpha brain-wave patterns (Kamiya, 1969), which, as described in chapter 6, are associated with a relaxed state of mind. But biofeedback did not become scientifically credible to many psychologists until Neal Miller reported success in training rats to gain voluntary control over physiological responses normally controlled solely by the autonomic nervous system. In his studies, Miller used electrical stimulation of the brain's reward centers (positive reinforcement) or, in some cases, escape or avoidance of shock (negative reinforcement) to train rats to increase or decrease their heart rate, intestinal contractions, urine formation, or blood pressure. Because Miller was an eminent, hard-nosed researcher, serious scientists became more willing to accept the legitimacy of biofeedback. Ironically, for unknown reasons, attempts at replicating his rat studies have generally failed (Dworkin & Miller, 1986).

Biofeedback
People provided with feedback on physiological processes may gain some control over normally involuntary ones, such as heart rate, or improved control over normally voluntary ones, such as muscle tension.

APPLICATIONS OF BIOFEEDBACK

Disappointment at the failure to replicate Miller's rat studies and of biofeedback to fulfill early promises to induce mystical states of consciousness led to skepticism about its merits. But even though biofeedback has not proved to be an unqualified success, it has not proved to be a failure. Hundreds of studies have demonstrated the effectiveness of biofeedback in helping people learn to control a variety of physiological responses. Clinical applications have included reducing hyperactivity by training children to regulate

Neal Miller
"The biofeedback and behavioral medicine techniques already available are preventing unnecessary suffering, correcting disabling conditions, and helping people regain control of their lives."

their own brain waves (Lubar, 1991), promoting relaxation by training anxious people to breathe more regularly (Clark & Hirschmanm 1990), and even improving visual acuity by training nearsighted people to control accommodation by the lenses of their eyes (Gilmartin, Gray, & Winn, 1991).

One of biofeedback's main uses has been in training people to gain better control of their skeletal muscles. Though we normally exert excellent control over our muscles, at times we might want to exert greater control over them. For example, auditory biofeedback has been used to train blind people to adopt more normal-looking facial expressions (Webb, 1977). In some cases, we want to reduce our level of muscle tension. Biofeedback has helped pregnant women remain relaxed during labor (Gregg, 1983), gymnasts relax their hip muscles (Wilson & Bird, 1981), violin players relieve excess tension in their hands (LeVine & Irvine, 1984), and victims of muscle tension headaches gain relief by relaxing their neck and forehead muscles (Hart & Cichanski, 1981). In other cases, we might want to increase our level of muscle tension. This is particularly true in physical rehabilitation (Basmajian, 1988). For example, muscle tension biofeedback has been used to restore control of foot movements in stroke victims (Santee, Keister, & Kleinman, 1980), use of thigh muscles in patients after total knee-joint replacement (Beckham et al., 1991), and use of facial muscles after surgery that reconnected the nerves serving those muscles (Nahai & Brown, 1983). Biofeedback has also been used to prevent carpal tunnel syndrome by warning typists when their wrists are in improper positions (Thomas et al., 1993).

Biofeedback has even been used to help increase muscle strength. In one study bodybuilders were randomly divided into two groups. Both groups worked out on a Cybex leg extension machine three times a week for five weeks. One group received visual and auditory biofeedback while using the machine, while the other group did not. At the end of the training period, the legs of those who had received biofeedback were stronger than the legs of those who had exercised without it. Those who received biofeedback benefited from continuous monitoring of their degree of exertion, which apparently served to increase their motivation to exert greater effort (Croce, 1986).

EVALUATING BIOFEEDBACK RESEARCH

Though biofeedback is widely used by psychologists and health professionals, it is not a panacea. In fact, there is controversy about its effectiveness and practicality. To demonstrate the effectiveness of biofeedback, one must show that learned self-regulation of physiological responses is caused by the feedback and not by extraneous factors (Roberts, 1985). For example, early biofeedback studies showed that feedback of alpha brain waves could increase them and induce a state of relaxation. But replications of those early studies showed that the effects were caused by the subjects' sitting quietly with their eyes closed. The brain-wave feedback added nothing (Plotkin, 1979).

Moreover, because biofeedback involves the use of sophisticated, scientifically impressive devices, it has the potential to create powerful placebo effects (Furedy, 1987). To control for such effects, researchers provide some subjects with *noncontingent feedback*, which is recorded feedback of the physiological activity of another subject. If the subjects who receive true feedback and the subjects who receive noncontingent feedback show equal improvement in self-regulation of a physiological response, then the improvement would be considered a placebo effect. But noncontingent feedback might be an inadequate control, because some subjects may realize that the feedback is not accurately reflecting changes in the physiological response. This is most likely true in studies that provide feedback of changes in muscle tension, which is more easily detected without biofeedback than are changes in brain waves, heart rate, or blood pressure (Burnette & Adams, 1987).

Even when the results of a biofeedback study can be attributed to the feedback, the technique might still not be of practical use. Why is this so? First, the typical biofeedback device costs hundreds or even thousands of dollars. Thus, clinicians must decide whether the benefits of biofeedback justify its cost, especially when other equally effective, less expensive treatments are available. For example, simple training in relaxation, requiring no costly apparatus, may be as useful as biofeedback-assisted relaxation (Kluger, Jamner, & Tursky, 1985). Yet, overall, treatment programs that include biofeedback have proven cost-effective in enhancing the quality of life and in reducing physician visits, medication use, medical care costs, hospital stays, rehospitalization, and mortality (Schneider, 1987).

Second, laboratory experiments on biofeedback can produce results that are statistically significant (a concept discussed in chapter 2) and merit being reported but that are too small to be of practical use in clinical settings (Steiner & Dince, 1981); for example, biofeedback might produce a *statistically significant* reduction in blood pressure in hypertensive persons that may be too small to be *clinically meaningful*. Third, biofeedback training in a clinician's office may produce results that do not last much beyond the training sessions. Fortunately, subjects who continue to practice what they have learned in biofeedback therapy sessions will be more likely to retain the benefits (Libo & Arnold, 1983). One way to promote the generalization of benefits from clinical training sessions to everyday life is to use portable biofeedback devices (Harrison, Gavin, & Isaac, 1988).

Finally, the results of laboratory studies might not be applicable to the clinical setting. For example, an important factor in any treatment program is an empathetic relationship between the therapist and the client (Duckro, 1991), which would usually not exist between an experimenter and a subject. In addition, unlike experimenters, therapists rarely, if ever, rely solely on a biofeedback device in treating disorders. The therapist who uses biofeedback typically achieves success by combining biofeedback with other therapeutic approaches. Thus, biofeedback does not achieve its clinical effects by itself, as an antibiotic might do in curing a bacterial infection (Green & Shellenberger, 1986).

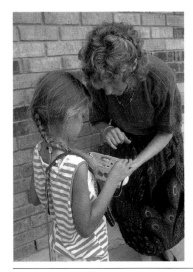

Transfer of Biofeedback Training
Portable, battery-operated biofeedback devices can help people transfer the physiological self-control they learn in the clinical setting to everyday life.

SUMMARY

CLASSICAL CONDITIONING

Learning is a relatively permanent change in knowledge or behavior resulting from experience. As demonstrated by Ivan Pavlov in the kind of learning called classical conditioning, a stimulus (the conditioned stimulus) comes to elicit a response (the conditioned response) that it would not normally elicit. It does so by being paired with a stimulus (the unconditioned stimulus) that already elicits that response (the unconditioned response).

In stimulus generalization, the conditioned response occurs in response to stimuli that are similar to the conditioned stimulus. And in stimulus discrimination, the conditioned response occurs only in response to the conditioned stimulus. If the conditioned stimulus is repeatedly presented without the unconditioned stimulus, the conditioned response diminishes and eventually stops. This is called extinction. But after a period of time the conditioned stimulus again elicits the conditioned response. This is called spontaneous recovery.

Classical conditioning has been applied in many ways, including in advertising and in explaining phobias, drug dependence, and learned taste aversions. In the past two decades, research has shown that in classical conditioning there are biological constraints on the ease with which particular stimuli can be associated with particular responses.

OPERANT CONDITIONING

While classical conditioning concerns the relationship between stimuli and responses, operant conditioning concerns the relationship between behaviors and consequences. B. F. Skinner identified four behavioral contingencies to describe the relationship between behaviors and consequences: positive reinforcement, negative reinforcement, extinction, and punishment. In shaping, positive reinforcement is used to increase the likelihood of a behavior that is not in an individual's repertoire. In chaining, positive reinforcement is used to teach an individual to perform a series of behaviors.

In operant conditioning, behavior is affected by schedules of reinforcement. In a continuous schedule, every instance of a desired behavior is reinforced. In partial schedules, reinforcement is not given for every instance. Partial schedules include ratio schedules, which provide reinforcement after a certain number of responses, and interval schedules, which provide reinforcement for the first desired response after a certain interval of time.

In negative reinforcement, a behavior followed by the removal of an aversive stimulus becomes more likely to occur in the future. Negative reinforcement is implicated in avoidance learning and escape learning. When a behavior is no longer followed by reinforcement, it is subject to extinction. But after a period of time the behavior reappears—only to be subject to even faster extinction it is still not reinforced. In punishment, an aversive consequence of a behavior decreases the likelihood of the behavior. To be effective, punishment should be immediate, firm, consistent, aimed at the misbehavior rather than the individual, and coupled with reinforcement of desirable behavior.

Operant conditioning has even more diverse applications than does classical conditioning; these include animal training, child rearing, educational improvement, understanding psychological disorders, and treating psychological disorders. Like classical conditioning, operant conditioning is subject to biological constraints, because members of particular species are more evolutionarily prepared to perform certain behaviors than to perform others.

COGNITIVE LEARNING

Cognitive psychologists have shown that contiguity is not sufficient to explain learning. Mere contiguity of a neutral stimulus and an unconditioned stimulus is insufficient to produce classical conditioning, and mere contiguity of a behavior and a consequence is insufficient to produce operant conditioning. Instead, for learning to occur, active cognitive assessment of the relationship between stimuli or the relationship between behaviors and consequences is essential. In latent learning, learning is revealed in overt behavior only when reinforcement is provided for that behavior. Albert

Bandura's social-learning theory considers how individuals learn through observing the behavior of others.

THINKING ABOUT PSYCHOLOGY: IS BIOFEEDBACK AN EFFECTIVE MEANS FOR LEARNING SELF-REGULATION OF PHYSIOLOGICAL RESPONSES?

Biofeedback is a form of operant conditioning that enables an individual to learn to control a normally involuntary physiological response or to gain better control of a normally voluntary physiological response when provided with visual or auditory feedback of the state of that response. Biofeedback gained scientific credibility through the research of Neal Miller. One of the most successful applications of biofeedback has been in the self-control of skeletal muscle activity, particularly in physical rehabilitation. To demonstrate the effectiveness of biofeedback, researchers must show that learned self-regulation of physiological responses is caused by the feedback and not by other factors, such as placebo effects. Its effects must be of practical, as well as statistical, significance. For biofeedback to be of practical value, its benefits must justify its cost. Moreover, the effects of biofeedback must transfer from the clinical setting to the everyday world for it to be useful in treating disorders.

IMPORTANT CONCEPTS

MAJOR CONTRIBUTORS

RECOMMENDED READINGS

FOR GENERAL WORKS ON LEARNING
Bower, G. H., & Hilgard, E. R. (1981). *Theories of learning* (5th ed.). Englewood Cliffs, NJ: Prentice Hall.

Brislin, R. W., Bochner, S., & Lonner, W. J. (Eds.). (1975). *Cross-cultural perspectives in learning*. New York: Halsted Press.

Domjan, M., & Burkhard-Ebin, B. (1992). *The principles of learning and behavior* (3rd ed.). Monterey, CA: Brooks/Cole.

Malone, J. C. (1991). *Theories of learning: A historical approach*. Belmont, CA: Wadsworth.

FOR MORE ON CLASSICAL CONDITIONING

Bechterev, V. M. (1932/1973). *General principles of human reflexology*. Salem, NH: Ayer.

Braveman, N. S., & Bronstein, P. (Eds.). (1985). *Experimental assessments and clinical applications of conditioned food aversions*. New York: New York Academy of Sciences.

Davey, G. (1987). *Cognitive processes and Pavlovian conditioning in humans*. New York: Wiley.

Gormezano, I., Prokasy, W. F., & Thompson, R. F. (Eds.). (1987). *Classical conditioning*. Hillsdale, NJ: Erlbaum.

Gustavson, C. R., & Garcia, J. (1974, August). Aversive conditioning: Pulling a gag on the wily coyote. *Psychology Today*, pp. 68–72.

Harris, B. (1979). Whatever happened to Little Albert? *American Psychologist, 34*, 151–160.

Klein, S. B., & Mowrer, R. R. (1989). *Pavlovian conditioning and the status of traditional learning theory*. Hillsdale, NJ: Erlbaum.

Pavlov, I. P. (1927/1960). *Conditioned reflexes*. Mineola, NY: Dover.

Rescorla, R. A. (1988). Pavlovian conditioning: It's not what you think it is. *American Psychologist, 43*, 151–160.

Siegel, S., Hinson, R., Krank, M. D., & McCully, J. (1982). Heroin "overdose" death: Contribution of drug-associated environmental cues. *Science, 216*, 436–437.

Watson, J. B., & Rayner, R. (1920). Conditioned emotional reactions. *Journal of Experimental Psychology, 3*, 1–14.

FOR MORE ON OPERANT CONDITIONING

Axelrod, S., & Apsche, J. (Eds.). (1983). *The effects of punishment on human behavior*. San Diego: Academic Press.

Benjamin, L. T., Jr. (1988). A history of teaching machines. *American Psychologist, 43*, 703–712.

Catania, A., & Harnad, S. (Eds.). (1988). *The selection of behavior: The operant behaviorism of B. F. Skinner*. New York: Columbia University Press.

Kazdin, A. E. (1977). *The token economy: A review and evaluation*. New York: Plenum.

Kinkade, K. (1973). *A Walden Two experiment: The first five years of Twin Oaks Community*. New York: Morrow.

Peterson, C., Maier, S. F., & Seligman, M.E. P. (1993). *Learned helplessness: A theory for the age of personal control*. New York: Oxford University Press.

Skinner, B. F. (1938). *The behavior of organisms*. New York: Appleton-Century-Crofts.

Skinner, B. F. (1948). *Walden two*. New York: Macmillan.

Thorndike, E. L. (1931/1970). *Human learning*. Cambridge, MA: MIT Press.

Tunick, M. (1992). *Punishment: Theory and practice*. Berkeley: University of California Press.

FOR MORE ON BIOLOGICAL CONSTRAINTS ON LEARNING

Breland, K., & Breland, M. (1961). The misbehavior of organisms. *American Psychologist, 16*, 681–684.

Domjan, M., & Galef, B. G. (1983). Biological constraints on instrumental and classical conditioning: Retrospect and prospect. *Animal Learning and Behavior, 11*, 151–161.

Kimble, G. A. (1981). Biological and cognitive constraints on learning. In L. T. Benjamin, Jr. (Ed.), *The G. Stanley Hall lecture series* (Vol. 1, pp. 7–60). Washington, DC: American Psychological Association.

Klein, S. B., & Mowrer, R. R. (1989). *Instrumental conditioning theory and the impact of biological constraints on learning*. Hillsdale, NJ: Erlbaum.

FOR MORE ON COGNITIVE LEARNING

Amsel, A. (1988). *Behaviorism, neobehaviorism, and cognitivism in learning theory: Historical and contemporary perspectives*. Hillsdale, NJ: Erlbaum.

Bandura, A. (1986). *Social foundations of thought and action: A social cognitive theory*. Englewood Cliffs, NJ: Prentice Hall.

Miller, N. E., & Dollard, J. (1962/1979). *Social learning and imitation*. Westport, CT: Greenwood.

Tolman, E. C. (1932). *Purposive behavior in animals and man*. New York: Appleton-Century-Crofts.

FOR MORE ON BIOFEEDBACK

Basmajian, J. V. (1988). Research foundations of EMG biofeedback in rehabilitation. *Biofeedback and Self-Regulation, 13*, 275–298.

Basmajian, J. V. (1989). *Biofeedback: Principles and practice for clinicians* (3rd ed.). Baltimore: Williams & Wilkins.

Hatch, J. P., Fisher, J. G., & Rugh, J. D. (Eds.). (1987). *Biofeedback: Studies in clinical efficacy*. New York: Plenum.

Sandweiss, J. H., & Wolf, S. L. (Eds.). (1985). *Biofeedback and sports science*. New York: Plenum.

Schneider, C. J. (1989). A brief history of biofeedback. *Biofeedback, 17*, 4–7.

FOR MORE ON CONTRIBUTORS TO THE STUDY OF LEARNING

Bjork, D. W. (1993). *B. F. Skinner: A life*. New York: Basic Books.

Buckley, K. W. (1989). *Mechanical man: John Broadus Watson and the beginnings of behaviorism*. New York: Guilford.

Evans, R. I. (1989). *Albert Bandura: The man and his ideas—a dialogue*. New York: Praeger.

Gray, J. A. (1979). *Ivan Pavlov*. New York: Viking Press.

Joncich, G. (1968). *The sane positivist: A biography of Edward L. Thorndike*. Middletown, CT: Wesleyan University Press.

Sechenov, I. M. (1935/1973). *I. M. Sechenov: Biographical sketch and essays*. Salem, NH: Ayer.

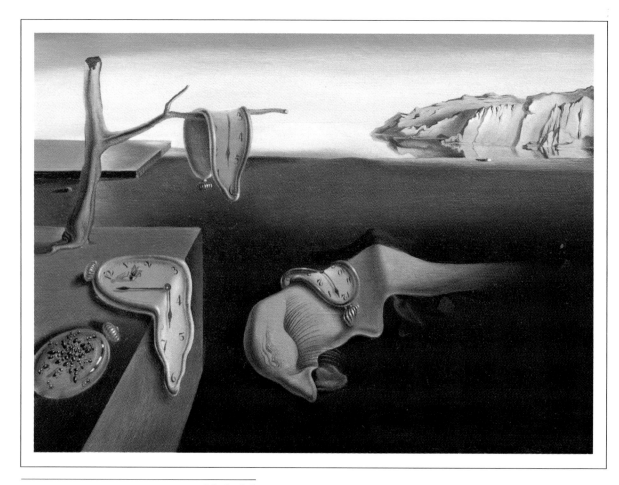

Salvador Dalí
The Persistence of Memory
1931

MEMORY

flashbulb memory
A vivid, long-lasting memory of a surprising, important, emotionally arousing event.

I n 1898 a survey of 179 middle-aged and elderly adults asked, "Do you recall where you were when you heard that Lincoln was shot?" Of those surveyed, 127 recalled where they were and what they were doing at that moment on April 14, 1865 (Colegrove, 1899). Such vivid, long-lasting memories of surprising, important, emotionally arousing events are called **flashbulb memories** (Brown & Kulik, 1977). People with flashbulb memories of an event may recall who told them about it, where they were, what they were doing, how they felt about it, and even trivial things that occurred shortly afterward. You might have a flashbulb memory from January 28, 1986, of the space shuttle *Challenger* exploding shortly after takeoff, which was shown live on television. Older students might have a flashbulb memory from November 22, 1963, when they heard that President John F. Kennedy had been assassinated. You also might have flashbulb memories of personally momentous events, such as your first kiss or your first day in college. Some women even have flashbulb memories of menarche, their first menstrual period. In keeping with the nature of flashbulb memories, the more surprised they were by menarche, the more detailed is their recollection of it (Pillemer et al., 1987).

What accounts for flashbulb memories? The answer is unclear. Some psychologists believe they are the product of a special brain mechanism (Schmidt & Bohannon, 1988) that evolved because it assures that we remember important experiences. Other psychologists disagree, claiming instead that normal memory processes, such as thinking more often and more elaborately about an experience, can explain the phenomenon (McCloskey, Wible, & Cohen, 1988).

One psychology professor took advantage of a coincidence to test the notion of flashbulb memories. On January 16, 1991, as part of a demonstration regarding flashbulb memories, he had students try to form a vivid memory of an ordinary event. On the same day, as shown on CNN, warplanes attacked Baghdad, beginning the Persian Gulf War. The students completed questionnaires about their memories for the classroom event and the beginning of the war. They completed them again in April 1991 and January 1992. The accuracy of the students' memories for the two events did not differ significantly. Their level of confidence in their memories, however, did. They were significantly more confident about their memories of the onset of the Persian Gulf War. These results indicate that flashbulb memories might seem special, not because of a special mechanism, but because of the undue confidence we place in them (Weaver, 1993).

memory
The process by which information is acquired, stored in the brain, and later retrieved.

The exact nature of flashbulb memories will be discovered by research on **memory,** the process by which we acquire, store, and later retrieve information (H. C. Ellis, 1987). Memory serves several functions. First, as William James noted a century ago, memory provides our consciousness with its continuity. Later in this chapter you will read about a man called "H. M." who suffers from brain damage that has impaired his ability to maintain this continuity of consciousness. Second, memory enables us to adapt to situations by letting us call on skills and information gained from our relevant past experiences. Your abilities to drive a car, to perform well on an exam, and to serve as a witness at a trial all depend on memory. Third, memory enriches our emotional lives. Your memory lets you reexperience moments from your past, whether poignant (such as a lost love) or uplifting (such as a family gathering).

In studying memory, psychologists consider several major "how" questions: How are memories formed? How are memories stored? How are memories retrieved? How are brain anatomy and brain chemistry related to memories? How dependable is memory? This chapter provides some answers to these questions.

Flashbulb Memories
Memory researchers are searching for explanations of flashbulb memories of momentous events.

INFORMATION PROCESSING AND MEMORY

During the past three decades, memory research has been driven by the "cognitive revolution" in psychology, which views the mind as an information processor. This is reflected in the most influential model of memory, developed by Richard Shiffrin and Richard Atkinson (1969). Their model assumes that memory involves the processing of information in three successive stages: *sensory memory*, *short-term memory*, and *long-term memory*. **Sensory memory** stores, in *sensory registers*, exact replicas of stimuli impinging on each of the senses. Sensory memories last for a brief period—from less than 1 second (in the case of visual sensory memory) to as long as 4 seconds or more (in the case of auditory sensory memory). This is adaptive, because it lets us hold information long enough to attend to it for further processing. When you attend to information in sensory memory, it is transferred to **short-term memory,** which stores it for about 20 seconds unless you maintain it through mental rehearsal—as when you repeat a phone number to yourself long enough to dial it. Information transferred from short-term memory into **long-term memory** is durable—it can be stored for a lifetime. You can appreciate this by stopping to recall some early childhood memories. Your ability to recall memories indicates that information can also move from long-term memory into short-term memory. The distinction between short-term memory and long-term memory is not new. William James (1890/1981) alluded to it a century ago when he distinguished between *primary memory* and *secondary memory*.

The handling of information at each memory stage has been compared to information processing by a computer, which involves encoding, storage, and retrieval. **Encoding** is the conversion of information into a form that can be stored in memory. When you strike the keys on a computer keyboard, your actions are translated into a code that the computer understands. Similarly, information in your memory is stored in codes that your brain can process. **Storage** is the retention of information in memory. Personal computers typically store information on diskettes. In human and animal memory, information is stored in the brain. **Retrieval** is the recovery of information from memory. When you strike certain keys, you provide the computer with cues that make it recall

sensory memory
The stage of memory that briefly, for at most a few seconds, stores exact replicas of sensations.

short-term memory
The stage of memory that can store a few items of unrehearsed information for up to about 20 seconds.

long-term memory
The stage of memory that can store a virtually unlimited amount of information relatively permanently.

encoding
The conversion of information into a form that can be stored in memory.

storage
The retention of information in memory.

retrieval
The recovery of information from memory.

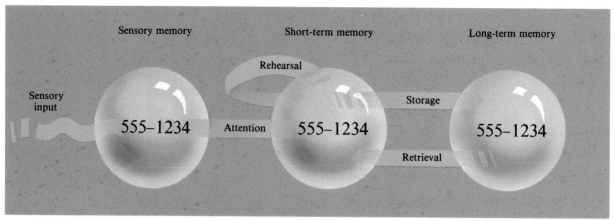

FIGURE **8.1**

Memory Processes
The information-processing model of memory assumes that information (such as a phone number) passes from sensory memory to short-term memory to long-term memory. Information may also pass from long-term memory to short-term memory. Each of the stages involves information encoding, storage, and retrieval.

forgetting
The failure to retrieve information from memory.

information-processing model
The view that the processing of memories involves encoding, storage, and retrieval.

the information you desire. Similarly, we often rely on cues to retrieve memories that have been stored in the brain. We are also subject to **forgetting**—the failure to retrieve information from memory. This is analogous to the erasing of information on a diskette. Figure 8.1 summarizes this **information-processing model** of memory. Though some psychologists question the existence of separate information-processing systems for sensory memory, short-term memory, and long-term memory, there is strong evidence in support of them (Cowan, 1988).

SENSORY MEMORY

Think back to the last movie you saw. It was really a series of frames, each containing a picture slightly different from the one before it. So why did you see smooth motion instead of a rapidly presented series of individual pictures? You did because of your *visual sensory memory*, which stores images for a fraction of a second. Visual sensory memory is called **iconic memory;** an image stored in it is called an *icon* (from the Greek word for "image"). The movie projector presented the frames at a rate that made each successive frame appear just before the previous one left your iconic memory, making the successive images blend together and create the impression of smooth motion. You have probably been at a movie when the projector suddenly presented the frames too rapidly, producing a blur on the screen (and hooting and hollering from the audience). You perceived a blur because the successive images overlapped too much in your iconic memory.

iconic memory
Visual sensory memory, which lasts up to about a second.

To experience iconic memory, close your eyes for 1 minute. Near the end of the minute, hold your hand about 12 inches from your eyes. Then blink once and keep your eyes closed. You should see an image of your hand that fades away within a second (H. C. Ellis, 1987). But how much of the information that stimulates our visual receptors is stored in iconic memory?

Sensory Memory
If you walked through Times Square in New York City, your senses would be bombarded by sights, sounds, and smells. An enormous amount of this stimulation would be stored in your sensory memory. But at any given moment you would be consciously aware of only a tiny portion of the stored information. This selectivity of attention prevents your consciousness from being overwhelmed by sensations.

Anatomy of a Classic Research Study:
Do We Form Sensory Memories of All the Information That Stimulates Our Sensory Receptors?

Rationale

Though we have a sensory register for each of our senses, most research on sensory memory has been concerned with iconic memory. The classic experiment on this was carried out by a Harvard University doctoral student named George Sperling (1960). Sperling used an ingenious procedure to test the traditional wisdom that sensory memory stores only a small amount of the information that stimulates our sensory receptors.

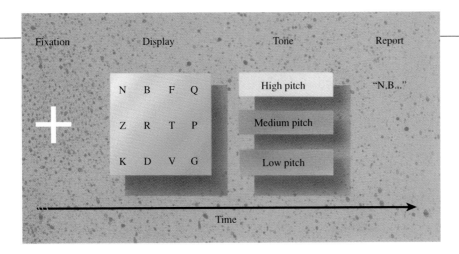

FIGURE 8.2

Testing Sensory Memory
In Sperling's (1960) study of sensory memory, the subject fixated on a cross on a projection screen. A display of letters was then flashed briefly on the screen. This was repeated with many different displays. At varying times after a display had been flashed, a tone signaled the subject to report the letters in a particular row. This enabled Sperling to determine how many of the letters were stored in sensory memory. By delaying the tone for longer and longer intervals, Sperling was also able to determine how quickly images in sensory memory fade.

Method

Sperling's procedure is illustrated in figure 8.2. The subjects, tested individually, stared at a screen as Sperling projected sets of 12 letters, arranged in three rows of 4, onto it. Each presentation lasted for only 0.05 second—a mere flash. Sperling then asked the subjects to report as many of the letters as possible. He found that the subjects could accurately report an average of only 4 or 5. The subjects claimed, however, that they had briefly retained an image of the 12 letters, but by the time they had reported a few of them the remaining ones had faded away.

Rather than dismiss these claims, Sperling decided to test them experimentally by using a variation of this task. Instead of using whole report (asking the subjects to report as many of the 12 letters as possible), he used partial report (asking the subjects to report as many of the 4 letters as possible from a designated row). The task again included displays of 12 letters arranged in three rows of 4. But this time, at the instant the visual display was terminated, a tone was sounded. The pitch of the tone signaled the subject to report the letters in a particular row: a high tone for the top row, a medium tone for the middle row, and a low tone for the bottom row.

Results and Discussion

When subjects gave partial reports, they accurately reported an average of 3.3 of the 4 letters in a designated row. Because the subjects did not know which row would be designated until after the display was terminated, the results indicated that, on the average, 9.9 of the 12 letters were stored in iconic memory. Sperling concluded that virtually all of the information from visual receptors is stored as an image in iconic memory, but, as his subjects had claimed, the image fades rapidly.

This inspired Sperling to seek the answer to another question: How fast does the information in iconic memory fade? He found the answer by repeating his partial-report procedure, but he delayed the tone that signaled the subject to give a partial report. He varied the period of delay from 0.1 second to 1.0 second. As the delay lengthened, the subject's ability to recall letters in a designated row declined more and more. Sperling found that when the delay reached 1.0 second, the number of letters that could be recalled was about the same as when a whole report was used. Subsequent research has found that the typical duration of iconic memory is closer to 0.3 seconds than to 1.0 second (Loftus, Duncan, & Gehrig, 1992), with more-intense visual stimulation evoking a longer-lasting image (Long & Beaton, 1982).

Auditory sensory memory serves a purpose analogous to that of visual sensory memory, blending together successive pieces of auditory information. Auditory sensory memory is called **echoic memory,** because sounds linger in it. Echoic memory stores information longer than iconic memory does, normally holding sounds for 3 or 4 seconds, but perhaps as long as 20 seconds (Cowan, 1984). The greater persistence of information in echoic memory lets you perceive speech by blending together successive spoken sounds that you hear (Ardila, Montanes, & Gempeler, 1986). If echoic memory storage were as brief as iconic memory storage, speech might sound like a staccato series of separate sounds instead of words and phrases.

George Sperling
"The fact that observers commonly assert that they can *see* more than they can *report* suggests that memory sets a limit on a process that is otherwise rich in available information."

echoic memory
Auditory sensory memory, which lasts up to 4 or more seconds.

You become aware of your echoic memory when someone says something to you that you do not become aware of until a few seconds after it was said. Suppose that while you are enthralled by a television movie a friend asks, "Where did you put the can opener?" After a delay of a few seconds you might say, "What? . . . Oh, it's in the second drawer to the left of the sink." Researchers have recently identified a precise region in the primary auditory cortex that processes echoic memories (Lu, Williamson, & Kaufman, 1992).

We also have *tactile sensory memory*, which lasts between 1 and 2 seconds and permits the integration of a series of touch sensations (Craig & Evans, 1987). This allows us to identify objects that we can touch but cannot see.

Based on Sperling's study, and subsequent research, we know that sensory memory can store virtually all the information provided by our sensory receptors and that this information fades rapidly (though the fade rates vary among the senses). Nonetheless, we can retain information that is in sensory memory by attending to it and transferring it into short-term memory.

SHORT-TERM MEMORY

When you pay attention to information in your sensory memory or information retrieved from your long-term memory, the information enters your short-term memory. Because you are paying attention to this sentence, it has entered your short-term memory. In contrast, other information in your sensory memory, such as the feeling of this book against your hands, will not enter your short-term memory until your attention is directed to it. And note that you are able to comprehend the words in this sentence because you have retrieved their meanings from your long-term memory. Because we use short-term memory to think about information provided by either sensory memory or long-term memory, it is also called *working memory*. Working memory becomes less efficient in old age, perhaps accounting for some of the decline in memory suffered by the elderly (Salthouse, 1990).

To appreciate the nature of working memory, you might compare it to a baker's table. Just as you can use the table to mix ingredients, you can use working memory to process information on which you focus your attention. And just as you can get ingredients to use on the table from a cupboard or from a grocery store, you can transfer information into your working memory from either your long-term memory or your sensory memory. Moreover, just as you can move ingredients from the table to a cupboard, you can transfer information from your working memory to your long-term memory.

Information transferred into short-term memory is represented by one of three codes (H. C. Ellis, 1987): a visual code (images), an acoustic code (sounds), or a semantic code (meanings). But we usually encode information as sounds—even when the information is visual. This was demonstrated in a study in which subjects were shown a series of 6 letters and immediately tried to recall them. The subjects' errors showed that they more often confused letters that sounded alike (for example, T and C) than letters that looked alike (for example, Q and O). This indicated that the letters, though presented visually, had been encoded according to their sounds (Conrad, 1962).

In comparison to sensory memory or long-term memory, short-term memory has a relatively small storage capacity. You can demonstrate this for yourself by performing this exercise: Read the following numerals one at a time, and then (without looking at them) write them down in order on a sheet of paper—6, 3, 9, 1, 4, 6, 5. Next, read the following numerals one at a time and write them down from memory—5, 8, 1, 3, 9, 2, 8, 6, 3, 1, 7. If you have average short-term memory storage capacity, you were probably able to recall the 7 numbers in the first set but not the 11 numbers in the second set.

The normal limit of 7 items in short-term memory was the theme of a famous article by psychologist George Miller (1956) entitled "The Magical Number Seven, Plus or Minus Two." Miller noted that short-term memory has, on the average, a capacity of 7 "chunks" of information, with a range of 5 to 9 chunks—though some researchers have found that the normal range is greater than that (Smith, 1992). Hermann Ebbinghaus, the founder of scientific memory research, had noted the magic number 7 in the late nineteenth century (Postman, 1985). A *chunk* is a meaningful unit of information, such as a date, a word, or an abbreviation. For example, to a college student familiar with American culture, a list that includes the meaningful chunks *CBS*, *NFL*, and *FBI* would be easier to recall than a list that includes the meaningless combinations of letters *JOL*, *APS*, and *CWE*. The ability to chunk individual items of information can increase the amount of information stored in short-term memory. For example, after a 5-second look at the positions of pieces on a chessboard, expert chess players are significantly better than novice chess players at reproducing the positions of the pieces. This reflects experts' greater ability to chunk chess pieces into familiar configurations (Chase & Simon, 1973). Thus, though chess experts do not store more memory chunks in their short-term memory than novices do, their memory chunks contain more information.

Given that about 7 chunks is the typical amount of information in short-term memory, how long will it remain stored? Without *maintenance rehearsal* (that is, without repeating the information to ourselves), we can store information in short-term memory for no more than about 20 seconds. But if we use maintenance rehearsal, we can store it in short-term memory indefinitely. You could use maintenance rehearsal to remember the items on a short grocery list long enough to select each of them at the store.

Early evidence that unrehearsed information in short-term memory lasts no longer than 20 seconds came from a study conducted by Lloyd and Margaret Peterson (1959) in which they orally presented *trigrams* that consisted of three consonants (for example, VRG) to their subjects. Their procedure is presented in figure 8.3. To distract the subjects and prevent them from engaging in maintenance rehearsal of the trigrams, immediately after a trigram was presented a light signaled the subject to count backward from a 3-digit number by threes (for example, "657, 654, 651, . . ."). Following an interval that varied from 3 seconds to 18 seconds, a light signaled that the subject was to recall the trigram. The longer the interval, the less likely the subjects were to recall the trigram. And when the interval was 18 seconds, the subjects could rarely recall the trigram. Thus, the results indicated that unrehearsed information normally remains in short-term memory for no longer than about 20 seconds.

Information stored in short-term memory is lost by *decay* (the mere fading of information over time) and by *displacement* by new information (Reitman, 1974). The displacement of information from short-term memory was demonstrated in a study in which subjects called a telephone operator for a long-distance number. They showed poorer recall of the number if the operator said "Have a nice day" after giving them the number than if the operator did not. Evidently the cheery message displaced the phone number from short-term memory (Schilling & Weaver, 1983).

LONG-TERM MEMORY

As mentioned earlier, information moves back and forth between short-term memory and long-term memory. When functioning at its best, long-term memory can store an enormous amount of information with great accuracy. For example, in the early twentieth century, Hebrew scholars from Poland were able to recall the entire contents of the thousands of pages in the twelve-volume *Babylonian Talmud*, a Hebrew holy book. In fact, when a pin was pushed through the pages of a volume, a scholar could recall each of the words pierced by the pin (Stratton, 1917).

Some people have another unusual memory ability called *eidetic imagery*, better known as "photographic memory" (the word *eidetic* comes from the Greek term for "seen form"). People with eidetic imagery can retain visual images so vivid that they can recall tiny details of the object several minutes after seeing it. Eidetic imagery is more common among children; it declines throughout childhood, and few adults have the ability (Kuzendorf, 1989). Though eidetic imagery might be associated with unusually long-lasting iconic memory, its causes are unknown. No cognitive, emotional, or physiological characteristics of the individual have been identified that explain it (Haber, 1979).

Lloyd Peterson and Margaret Peterson
"Forgetting was found to progress at differential rates dependent on the amount of controlled rehearsal of the stimulus."

FIGURE 8.3

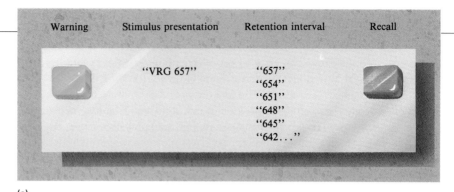

The Duration of Short-Term Memory
Peterson and Peterson (1959) demonstrated that the information in short-term memory lasts no more than 20 seconds. (*a*) A warning light signaled that a trial was to begin. The subject then heard a three-letter trigram and a three-digit number. To prevent rehearsal of the trigram, the subject counted backward by threes from the number. After a period of 3 to 18 seconds, a light signaled the subject to recall the trigram. (*b*) The longer the delay between presentation and recall of the trigram, the less likely the subject was to recall it accurately.

(a)

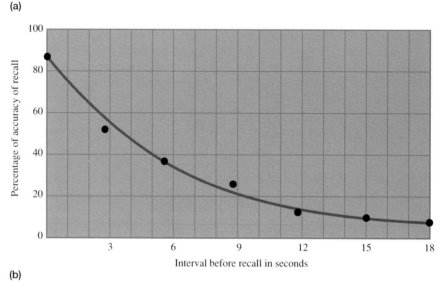

(b)

Normal information processing in long-term memory has been compared to the workings of a library. Information in a library is *encoded* in materials such as books or magazines, *stored* on shelves in a systematic way, *retrieved* by using cues given by on-line catalogs, and *forgotten* when it is misplaced or its computer record is erased. Similarly, information in long-term memory is encoded in several ways, stored in an organized manner, retrieved by using cues, and forgotten due to a failure to store it adequately or to use appropriate retrieval cues.

Encoding

William James (1890/1981, vol. 1, p. 646) noted, "A curious peculiarity of our memory is that things are impressed better by active than by passive repetition." To appreciate James's claim, take a moment to draw the face side of a United States penny from memory. Next, look at the drawings of pennies in figure 8.4. Which one is accurate? Even if you have handled thousands of pennies over the years and realize that the front of a penny has a date and a profile of Abraham Lincoln, you probably were unable to draw every detail. And even when presented with several drawings to choose from, you might still have chosen the wrong one. If you had difficulty, you are not alone. A study of adult Americans found that few could draw a penny from memory, and less than half could recognize the correct drawing of one (Nickerson & Adams, 1979).

What accounts for our failure to remember an image that is a common part of everyday life? The answer depends in part on the distinction between *maintenance rehearsal* and *elaborative rehearsal*. In using **maintenance rehearsal,** we simply hold information in short-term memory without trying to transfer it into long-term memory, as when we remember a phone number just long enough to dial it. In **elaborative rehearsal,** we actively organize information and integrate it with information already stored in

maintenance rehearsal
Repeating information to oneself to keep it in short-term memory.

elaborative rehearsal
Actively organizing new information to make it more meaningful, and integrating it with information already stored in long-term memory.

long-term memory, as when studying material from this chapter for an exam. Though maintenance rehearsal can encode some information (such as the main features of a penny) into long-term memory (Wixted, 1991), elaborative rehearsal encodes more information (such as the exact arrangement of the features of a penny) into long-term memory (Greene, 1987). Consider the common "next-in-line effect," in which a person who begins to speak forgets what another speaker has just said. Research findings indicate that this is caused by the tendency to use maintenance rehearsal, instead of elaborative rehearsal, of what the preceding speaker has said (Bond, Pitre, & Van Leeuwen, 1991).

You can experience the benefits of elaborative rehearsal when you are confronted by new concepts in a textbook. If you try to understand a concept by integrating it with information already in your long-term memory, you will be more likely to encode the concept firmly into your long-term memory. For example, when the concept "flashbulb memory" was introduced earlier in this chapter, you would have been more likely to encode it into long-term memory if it provoked you to think about your own flashbulb memories. Elaborative rehearsal also has important practical benefits. In one study, sixth-graders who were taught cardiopulmonary resuscitation showed better retention of what they learned if they used elaborative rather than maintenance rehearsal (Rivera-Tovar & Jones, 1990).

The superior encoding of information through elaborative rehearsal supports the **levels of processing theory** of Fergus Craik and Robert Lockhart (1972). They believe that the level, or "depth," at which we process information determines how well it is encoded and, as a result, how well it is stored in long-term memory (Lockhart & Craik, 1990). When you process information at a shallow level, you attend to its superficial, sensory qualities—as when you use maintenance rehearsal of a telephone number. In contrast, when you process information at a deep level, you attend to its meaning—as when you use elaborative rehearsal of textbook material. Similarly, if you merely listen to the sound of a popular song over and over on the radio—a relatively shallow level of processing—you might recall the melody but not the lyrics. But if you listen to the lyrics and think about their meaning (perhaps even connecting them to personally significant events)—a deeper level of processing—you might recall both the words and the melody.

In a study that supported the levels of processing theory, researchers induced subjects to process words at different levels by asking them different kinds of questions about each word just before it was flashed on a screen for a fifth of a second (Craik & Tulving, 1975). Imagine that you are replicating the study, and one of the words is *bread*. You could induce a shallow, *visual* level of encoding by asking how the word *looks*—for instance, "Is the word written in capital letters?" You could induce a somewhat deeper, *acoustic* level of encoding by asking how the word *sounds*—"Does the word rhyme with *head?*" And you could induce a much deeper, *semantic* level of encoding by asking a question related to what the word *means*—"Does the word fit in the sentence *The boy used the _____ to make a sandwich?*" After repeating this with several words, you would present the subject with a list of words and ask him or her to identify which of the words had been presented before. Craik and Tulving (1975) found that the deeper the level at which a word had been encoded, the more likely it was to be correctly identified (see figure 8.5). Thus, the deeper the level at which information is encoded, the better it will be remembered.

Storage

According to influential memory researcher Endel Tulving (1985), we store information in two kinds of long-term memory: **Procedural memory** includes memories of how to perform behaviors, such as making an omelette or using a word processor; **declarative memory** includes memories of facts. Declarative memory and procedural memory are also referred to, respectively, as explicit memory and implicit memory (Schachter, 1992), which are discussed in chapter 6 in regard to the unconscious mind. Tulving subdivides declarative memory into *semantic memory* and *episodic memory*. **Semantic memory**

levels of processing theory
The theory that the "depth" at which we process information determines how well it is encoded, stored, and retrieved.

procedural memory
The long-term memory system that contains memories of how to perform particular actions or skills.

declarative memory
The long-term memory system that contains memories of facts.

semantic memory
The subsystem of declarative memory that contains general information about the world.

FIGURE 8.4

Can You Identify the Real Penny?

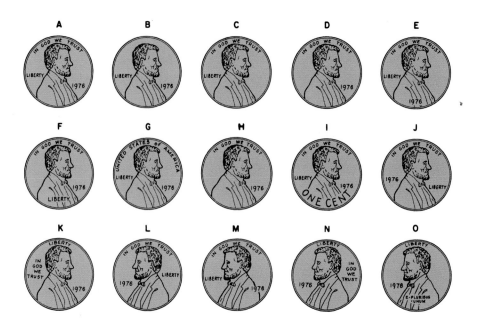

Endel Tulving
"Semantic memory is concerned with the retention and use of general . . . knowledge independent of personal time and space; episodic memory, with the storage and retrieval of information based on particular . . . experiences located in personal time and space."

episodic memory
The subsystem of declarative memory that contains memories of personal experiences tied to particular times and places.

includes memories of general knowledge, such as the definition of an omelette or the components of a word processor. **Episodic memory** includes memories of personal experiences tied to particular times and places, such as the last time you made an omelette or used a word processor.

Some memory researchers believe that the brain evolved different memory systems for storing these different kinds of memory (Squire, 1992). The main line of evidence in support of multiple memory systems in human beings comes from studies of people with brain damage, who may exhibit amnesia in one kind of memory while the other kinds remain intact. For example, one study (Ewert et al., 1989) found that victims of brain damage caused by head injuries may be able to learn new motor tasks (procedural memory) while being unable to recall written information (semantic memory) or recent events (episodic memory). In a case study, a man with a head injury that caused brain damage resulting in memory loss showed progressive recovery of his professional (semantic) memories but not his personal (episodic) memories (Tulving et al., 1988). In another case study (Schachter, 1983), a victim of Alzheimer's disease, a degenerative brain disorder marked by severe memory impairment, was able to play golf (procedural memory) and had good knowledge of the game (semantic memory) but could not find his tee shots (episodic memory). Nonetheless, some theorists believe that the selective loss of procedural, semantic, or episodic memories does not necessarily mean that we have separate memory systems (Horner, 1990). The question that memory researchers must answer is, Do different brain systems serve the different kinds of memory or does a single brain system serve all of them?

Regardless of how many memory systems we have, long-term memories must be stored in a systematic way. Unlike short-term memory, in which a few unorganized items of information can be stored and retrieved efficiently, long-term memory requires that millions of pieces of information be stored in an organized, rather than arbitrary, manner. Otherwise, you might spend years searching your memory until you retrieved the one you wanted, just as you might spend years searching the Library of Congress for William James's *The Principles of Psychology* if its books were shelved randomly. The better we are at organizing our memories, the better is our recall (Bjorklund & Buchanan, 1989). For example, a study of a waiter who could take twenty complete full-course dinner orders without writing them down found that he did so by quickly categorizing the items into meaningful groupings. When he was prevented from doing so, he was unable to recall all of the orders (Ericsson & Polson, 1988).

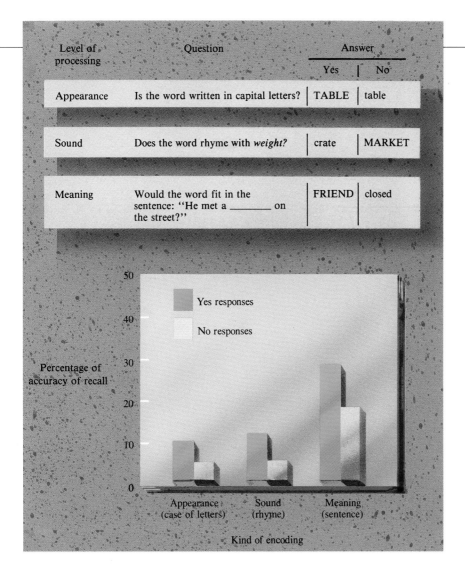

FIGURE **8.5**

Depth of Processing
Craik and Tulving (1975) found that the greater the depth of processing of words, the better will be memory for them. Encoding words according to their meaning produced better recognition of them than did encoding them according to their sound or appearance.

Semantic Network Theory

A theory that explains how semantic information is meaningfully organized in long-term memory is the **semantic network theory,** which assumes that semantic memories are stored as nodes interconnected by links. A *node* is a concept such as "pencil," "green," "uncle," or "cold," and a *link* is a connection between two concepts. Related nodes have stronger links between them. The retrieval of a node from memory stimulates activation of related nodes, so-called *spreading activation* (Collins & Loftus, 1975). Figure 8.6 presents an example of a semantic network.

Even young children organize memories into semantic networks. For example, preschool children who enjoy playing with toy dinosaurs and listening to their parents read to them about dinosaurs may organize their knowledge of dinosaurs into semantic networks (Chi & Koeske, 1983). The dinosaurs would be represented as nodes (for example, "Brontosaurus" or "Tyrannosaurus Rex") and their relationships would be represented by links. The retrieval of a dinosaur's name from memory would activate nodes with which it is linked. So, retrieval of *Brontosaurus* would be more likely to activate nodes that contain the names of other plant-eating dinosaurs than those that contain the names of meat-eating dinosaurs, such as *Tyrannosaurus Rex.*

semantic network theory
The theory that memories are stored as nodes interconnected by links that represent their relationships.

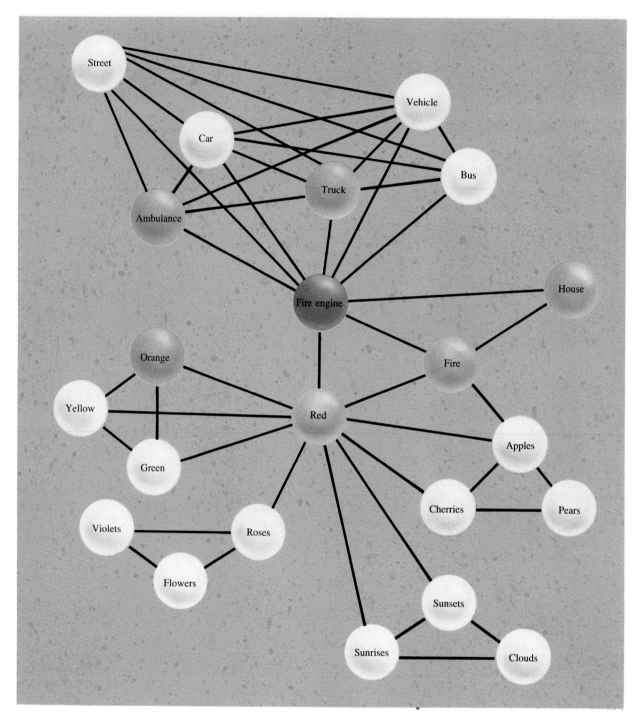

FIGURE 8.6

A Semantic Network
According to Collins and Loftus (1975), our long-term memories are organized into semantic networks in which concepts are interconnected by links. The shorter the link between two concepts, the stronger the association between them. After a retrieval cue has activated a concept, related concepts will also be activated and retrieved from long-term memory.

Schema Theory

An alternative to the semantic network theory of memory organization is the **schema theory,** which is used to explain both episodic memory and semantic memory. The schema theory was put forth decades ago by the English psychologist Frederick Bartlett (1932), who found that long-term memories are stored as parts of schemas. A *schema* is a cognitive structure that organizes knowledge about an event or an object and that affects the encoding, storage, and retrieval of information related to it (Alba & Hasher,

schema theory
The theory that long-term memories are stored as parts of schemas, which are cognitive structures that organize knowledge about events or objects.

1983). Examples of schemas include "birthday party," "class clown," and "Caribbean vacation." In a classic study, Bartlett had British college students read a Native American folktale called "The War of the Ghosts," which told about a warrior fighting ghosts, and later write the story from memory. He found that the subjects recalled the theme of the story but added, eliminated, or changed details to fit their own story schemas. For example, the subjects added a moral, left out an event, or altered an aspect (such as changing a canoe to a boat).

The gist of Bartlett's findings was replicated in a study in which college students read a brief biographical passage about either a famous person (Adolf Hitler or Helen Keller) or a fictitious person. Each student's ability to recognize individual sentences that had or had not been included in the original passages was tested one week later. Passages with a famous character yielded more false positive errors—that is, recognition of sentences that were not in the original passage but that could be plausibly associated with the famous person. Thus, knowledge of the topic of a passage affected subsequent memory for it through a constructive process influenced by the schema for Adolf Hitler or Helen Keller (Sulin & Dooling, 1974).

Retrieval

> * * * In short, we may search in our memory for forgotten ideas, just as we rummage our
> house for a lost object. In both cases we visit what seems to us the probable *neighbor-*
> *hood* of that which we miss. We turn over the things under which, or within which, or
> alongside which, it may possibly be; and if it lies near them, it soon comes to view. But
> these matters, in the case of a mental object sought, are nothing but its *associatives.*
> (James, 1890/1981, vol. 1, p. 615)

The semantic network theory of memory agrees with William James's statement that the retrieval of memories from long-term memory begins by searching a particular region of memory and then tracing the associations among nodes (memories) in that region, rather than by haphazardly searching through information stored in long-term memory. This is analogous to looking for a book in a library. You would use the on-line catalog to give you a retrieval cue (a book number) to help you locate the book you want. Similarly, when you are given a memory retrieval cue, the relevant stored memories are activated, which in turn activate memories with which they are linked (Anderson, 1983). There is some research support for the belief that information is stored in semantic networks organized in hierarchies from general to specific; these would promote efficient memory retrieval by searching along links in the hierarchies (Rapp & Caramazza, 1989).

To illustrate retrieval from a semantic network, suppose that you were given the cue "sensory memory." If your semantic network were well organized, the cue might activate nodes for "Sperling," "iconic," and "partial report." But if your semantic network were less well organized, the cue might also activate nodes for "amnesia," "chunks," or "Alzheimer's." And if your semantic network were poorly organized, the cue might activate nodes completely unrelated to sensory memory, such as "hallucination," "sensory deprivation," or "extrasensory perception."

In contrast to semantic network theory, schema theory assumes that when we retrieve memories we may alter them to make them consistent with our schemas. An example of the schematic nature of memory retrieval, taken from testimony about the 1972 Watergate burglary that led to the resignation of President Richard Nixon, was provided by the eminent memory researcher Ulric Neisser (1981). Neisser described how a schema influenced the testimony of John Dean, former legal counsel to President Nixon, before the Senate Watergate Investigating Committee in 1973. Dean began his opening testimony with a 245-page statement in which he recalled the details of dozens of meetings that he had attended over a period of several years. Dean's apparently phenomenal recall of minute details prompted Senator Daniel Inouye of Hawaii to ask skeptically, "Have you always had a facility for recalling the details of conversations which took place many months ago?" (Neisser, 1981, p. 1).

Ulric Neisser
"Constructive recall is the rule, literal recall is the exception."

constructive recall
The distortion of memories by adding, dropping, or changing details to fit a schema.

The Schematic Nature of Schemes
Comparisons between John Dean's testimony before the Senate Watergate Investigating Committee about meetings with President Nixon in the White House and secret tape recordings of those meetings made by Nixon showed that many of the details of Dean's testimony were inaccurate. Nonetheless, the gist of his testimony was correct. The inaccurate details may have been products of a schema: his knowledge that a burglary had occurred and that Nixon and other officials had tried to cover it up.

serial-position effect
The superiority of immediate recall for items at the beginning and end of a list.

Neisser found that Inouye's skepticism was well founded. In comparing Dean's testimony with tape recordings (secretly made by Nixon) of those conversations, Neisser found that Dean's recall of their themes was accurate, but his recall of many of the details was inaccurate. Neisser took this as evidence for Dean's reliance on a schema to retrieve memories. The schema reflected Dean's knowledge that there had been a cover-up of the Watergate break-in. Neisser used this to support his conclusion that, in recalling real-life events, "constructive recall is the rule, literal recall is the exception" (Neisser, 1984, p. 33).

What Neisser called **constructive recall** is the distortion of memories by adding or changing details to fit a schema. Schemas can even adversely affect the ability of scientists and undergraduates to remember the content of classic research studies they have read (Vicente & Brewer, 1993). But neither the schema theory nor the semantic network theory has yet emerged as the best explanation of the storage and retrieval of long-term memories. Perhaps a complete explanation will require both.

Forgetting

According to William James (1890/1981, vol. 1, p. 640), "if we remembered everything, we should on most occasions be as ill off as if we remembered nothing." James believed that forgetting is adaptive because it rids us of useless information that might impair our recall of useful information. But as you are sometimes painfully aware of when taking exams, even useful information that has been stored in memory is not always retrievable. We refer to this inability to retrieve previously stored information as *forgetting*.

The first formal research on forgetting was conducted by the German psychologist Hermann Ebbinghaus (1885/1913). Ebbinghaus (1850–1909) made a purposeful decision to do for the study of memory what Gustav Fechner had done for the study of sensation—subject it to the scientific method (Postman, 1985). Ebbinghaus studied memory by repeating lists of items over and over until he could recall them in order perfectly. The items he used were called *nonsense syllables* (consisting of a vowel between two consonants, such as VEM) because they were not real words. He used nonsense syllables instead of words because he wanted a "pure" measure of memory, unaffected by prior associations with real words. Despite this effort, he discovered that even nonsense syllables varied in their meaningfulness, depending on how similar they were to words or parts of words.

Ebbinghaus found that immediate recall is worse for items in the middle of a list than for those at the beginning and end of a list (see figure 8.7). His finding was replicated in the 1890s by Mary Whiton Calkins (Madigan & O'Hara, 1992). This differential forgetting is called the **serial-position effect.** The better memory for items at the beginning of a list is called the *primacy effect*, and the better memory for items at the end of a list is called the *recency effect*. Thus, in memorizing a list of terms from this chapter, you would find it harder to memorize terms from the middle of the list than terms from the beginning or end of the list. Even rats trained to learn, in order, items placed in an eight-arm radial maze show recall of the items in keeping with the serial position effect, including primacy and recency effects (Bolhuis & Van Kampen, 1988).

What accounts for the serial-position effect? The primacy effect seems to occur because the items at the beginning of a list are subjected to more rehearsal as a learner memorizes the list, firmly placing those items in long-term memory. And the recency effect seems to occur because items at the end of the list remain readily accessible in short-term memory. In contrast, items in the middle of the list are neither firmly placed in long-term memory nor readily accessible in short-term memory. Note that this explanation supports Shiffrin and Atkinson's distinction between short-term memory and long-term memory. But the explanation has not received universal support. For example, one study found that the primacy effect occurs even when subjects are prevented from rehearsing items at the beginning of a list that is to be recalled (Wright et al., 1990).

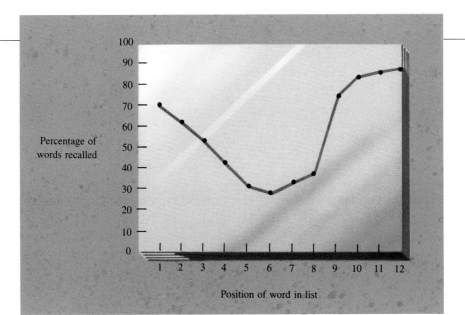

FIGURE 8.7

The Serial-Position Effect
This is a typical serial-position curve, showing that items in the middle of a list are the most difficult to recall.

Before Ebbinghaus's work, knowledge of memory was based on common sense, anecdotal reports, and reasoning, with little supporting empirical evidence. Ebbinghaus moved memory from the philosophical realm into the psychological realm, making it subject to scientific research.

Ebbinghaus also introduced the **method of savings,** which is commonly called *relearning,* as a way to assess memory. In using the method of savings, Ebbinghaus memorized items in a list until he could recall them perfectly, noting how many trials he needed to achieve perfect recall. After varying intervals, during which he naturally forgot some of the items, Ebbinghaus again memorized the list until he could recall it perfectly. The delay varied from 20 minutes to 31 days. He found that it took him fewer trials to relearn a list than to learn it originally. He called the difference between the number of original trials and the number of relearning trials *savings,* because he relearned the material more quickly the second time. The phenomenon of savings demonstrates that even when we cannot recall information, much of it still remains stored in memory, even though it is inaccessible to recall. If it were not still stored, we would take just as long to relearn material as we took to learn it originally.

When you study for a cumulative final exam, you experience savings. Suppose that your psychology course lasts 15 weeks and you study your notes and readings for 6 hours a week to perform at an A level on exams given during the semester. You will have studied for a total of 90 hours. If you then studied for a cumulative final exam, you would not have to study for 90 hours to memorize the material to your original level of mastery. In fact, you would have to study for only a few hours to master the material again. Savings occurs because relearning improves the retrieval of information stored in memory (MacLeod, 1988).

Relearning is one method of testing memory; other methods also test recognition, recall, and implicit memory. A *recognition test* measures your ability to identify information that you have been exposed to previously. Recognition tests you might encounter in college include matching, true–false, and multiple-choice exams. A *recall test* measures your ability to remember information without the information being presented to you. Recall tests you might encounter in college include essay and fill-in-the-blanks exams. Unlike tests of relearning, recognition, and recall, which are *explicit-memory tests* (because they test memories of information that we are aware of having been exposed to previously), an *implicit-memory test* tests our memory of information that we are unaware of having been exposed to previously—but that can still influence our behavior. For

method of savings
The assessment of memory by comparing the number of trials needed to memorize a given amount of information and the number of trials needed to memorize it again at a later time.

Hermann Ebbinghaus (1850–1909)
"Physical states of every kind, sensations, feelings, ideas, which at one time were present and then disappeared from consciousness, have not absolutely ceased to exist. Although an inward glance may not find them, they are not absolutely denied and annulled, but continue to live in a certain way, retained, as one says, in memory."

FIGURE 8.8

The Forgetting Curve
The graph at the top presents the results of a study by Ebbinghaus on memory for nonsense syllables. The graph at the bottom presents the results of a study on memory for Spanish words. Both graphs show that forgetting is initially rapid and then levels off.

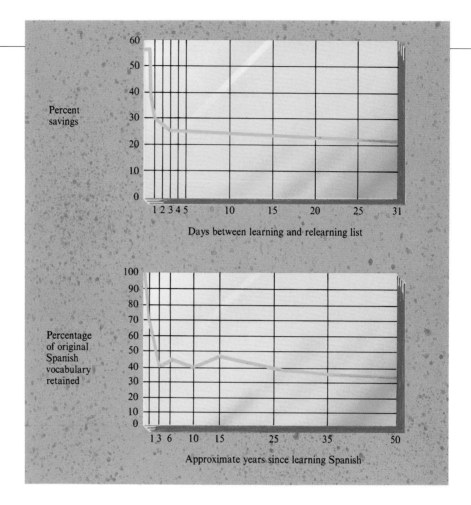

example, suppose you are exposed in passing to a list of words that includes *telegraph*. Later, despite having no recollection of having seen the word, you would be more likely to take the word fragment *tele-* and form the word *telegraph* than if you had not been exposed to that word earlier.

Ebbinghaus also found that, once we have mastered a list of items, forgetting is initially rapid and then slows. This phenomenon has been replicated many times (Wixted & Ebbesen, 1991). So, if you memorized a list of terms from this chapter for an exam, you would do most of your forgetting in the first few days after the exam. But in keeping with the concept of levels of processing, meaningless nonsense syllables are initially forgotten more rapidly than is meaningful material, such as psychology terms. Ebbinghaus's **forgetting curve,** which shows rapid initial forgetting followed by less and less forgetting over time, even holds for material learned decades before, as demonstrated in a study of the retention of Spanish words learned in high school by groups of subjects ranging from recent graduates to those who had graduated 50 years earlier. Though some of the subjects had not spoken Spanish in 50 years, they showed surprisingly good retention of some words. Figure 8.8 indicates that forgetting is rapid during the first 3 years after high school, then remains relatively unchanged. This indicates that after a certain amount of time, memories that have not been forgotten may become permanently held, in "permastore" (Bahrick, 1984).

Decay Theory

Plato, anticipating the **decay theory,** likened memory to an imprint made on a block of soft wax: Just as soft-wax imprints disappear over time, memories fade over time. But decay theory has received little research support, and a classic study provided evidence against it. John Jenkins and Karl Dallenbach (1924) had subjects memorize a list of

forgetting curve
A graph showing that forgetting is initially rapid and then slows.

decay theory
The theory that forgetting occurs because memories naturally fade over time.

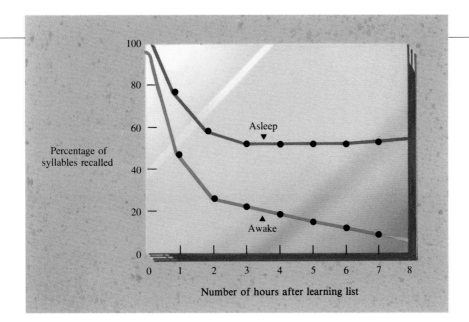

FIGURE 8.9

Percentage of syllables recalled

Asleep

Awake

Number of hours after learning list

Interference and Recall
Jenkins and Dallenbach (1924) found that when subjects learned a list of nonsense syllables and then slept, they forgot less than when they stayed awake.

10 nonsense syllables and then either stay awake or immediately go to sleep for 1, 2, 4, or 8 hours. At the end of each period, the subjects tried to recall the nonsense syllables. The researchers wondered whether sleep would prevent waking activities from interfering with the memories.

The graph in figure 8.9 shows that the subjects had better recall if they slept than if they remained awake. Though there was some memory loss during sleep, providing modest support for decay theory, if decay theory were an adequate explanation of forgetting, the subjects should have shown the same level of recall whether they remained awake or slept. Jenkins and Dallenbach concluded that the subjects forgot more if they remained awake because experiences they had while awake interfered with their memories of the nonsense syllables. In contrast, the subjects had forgotten less after sleeping because they had few experiences while asleep that could interfere with their memories for the nonsense syllables.

Interference Theory

Since Jenkins and Dallenbach's classic study contradicting decay theory, psychologists have come to favor *interference* as a better explanation of forgetting. **Interference theory** assumes that forgetting results from particular memories' interfering with the retrieval of other memories. In **proactive interference,** old memories interfere with new memories (if you move to a new home, for instance, your memory of your old phone number might interfere with your ability to recall your new one). In **retroactive interference,** new memories interfere with old ones (your memory of your new phone number might interfere with your memory of your old one).

You have certainly experienced both kinds of interference when taking an exam. Material you have studied for other courses sometimes interferes with your memories of the material on the exam. And interference is stronger when the materials are similar. Thus, biology material will interfere more than computer science material with your recall of psychology material. Because of the great amount of material you learn during a semester, proactive interference may be a particularly strong influence on your later exam performance (Dempster, 1985).

Motivation Theory

One day Eileen Franklin-Lipsker looked into her daughter's eyes and was overcome by a horrible memory. Twenty years earlier, as a young child, she had witnessed her father sexually assault and bludgeon to death her 8-year-old friend Susan Nason. Eileen's

interference theory
The theory that forgetting results from some memories' interfering with the ability to remember other memories.

proactive interference
The process by which old memories interfere with the ability to remember new memories.

retroactive interference
The process by which new memories interfere with the ability to remember old memories.

Motivated Forgetting

According to Sigmund Freud, a person (such as the man in this photograph, whose heroic effort to save a friend from a fire was futile) may forget a traumatic event by repressing its memory to the unconscious mind.

repression

The process by which emotionally threatening experiences are banished from the conscious mind to the unconscious mind.

father warned her that he would kill her if she told anyone about his crime. She was so emotionally overwhelmed that she forgot the event for two decades—until the look in her daughter's eyes evoked the same feelings she had when looking into the eyes of Susan as she was being attacked. Eileen also recalled the general area where her father had buried Susan's body, and she took the police to it. They found Susan's remains, and in 1990 Eileen's father was convicted of murder (MacLean, 1993).

Sigmund Freud might have explained Eileen's amnesia as an instance of motivated forgetting. Freud (1901/1965) claimed that we can forget experiences through **repression,** the process by which emotionally threatening experiences, such as witnessing a murder, are banished to the unconscious mind. Though research findings tend to contradict Freudian repression as an explanation of forgetting (Holmes, 1974), some evidence suggests that we are more motivated to forget emotionally upsetting experiences than other kinds of experiences.

In an experiment that possibly demonstrated motivated forgetting, subjects were shown one of two versions of a training film for bank tellers that depicted a simulated bank robbery. In one version, a shot fired by the robbers at pursuers hit a boy in the face. The boy fell to the ground, bleeding profusely. In the other version, instead of showing the boy being shot, the bank manager was shown talking about the robbery. When asked to recall details of the robbery, subjects who had seen the violent version had poorer recall of the details of the crime than did subjects who had seen the nonviolent version. One possible explanation is that the content of the violent version motivated subjects to forget what they had seen (Loftus & Burns, 1982). However, in some cases memory of traumatic events will be superior to memory of ordinary events (Christianson & Loftus, 1987).

At times we might be motivated to distort our recall of past events in ways that make the events more consistent with our current circumstances, much as schemas influence our recall of earlier experiences. This possibility was investigated in an experiment in which college students were randomly assigned to a study skills group or to a control group that was put on a waiting list (Conway & Ross, 1984). All subjects began by doing a self-evaluation of their study skills. Three weeks later, the subjects were asked to recall their initial self-evaluations. Members of the study skills group recalled their evaluations as worse than they had initially reported, but members of the control group recalled theirs accurately. Members of the study skills group also reported greater improvement in their study skills, and expected better final grades than did those in the control group. But the actual grades of the two groups did not differ. Six months later, members of the study skills group overestimated their academic performance for the period when the program was conducted. The distorted memories of the study skills group might have reflected their desire to have their participation pay off.

Cue-Dependence Theory

Because the retrieval of long-term memories depends on adequate retrieval cues, forgetting can sometimes be explained by the failure to have or to use them. For example, odors that we associate with an event can aid our recall of it (Smith, Standing, & de Man, 1992). This is known as *cue-dependence theory.* At times we might fail to find an adequate cue to activate the relevant portion of a semantic memory network. Consider the **tip-of-the-tongue phenomenon,** in which you cannot quite recall a familiar word—though you feel that you know it. As he did with many psychological phenomena, William James (1890/1981) noted this one a century ago. As a demonstration, you might induce a tip-of-the-tongue experience by trying to recall the seven dwarfs. You may fail to recall one or two of them, yet feel that you know them (Miserandino, 1991). The tip-of-the tongue phenomenon is universal, increases with age, and occurs about once a week for the typical person (Brown, 1991).

A study of the tip-of-the-tongue phenomenon presented college students with the faces of fifty celebrities and asked them to recall their names. The results indicated that the students searched for the names by using cues associated with the celebrities. The students tried to recall their professions, where they usually performed, and the last time they had seen them. Characteristics of the names also served as cues for recalling them. These cues included the first letters of the names, the first letters of similar-sounding names, and the number of syllables in the names (Yarmey, 1973). This study supports the concept of **encoding specificity,** which states that recall will be best when cues that were associated with the encoding of a memory are also present during attempts at retrieving the memory (Tulving & Thomson, 1973).

In an unusual experiment on encoding specificity, scuba divers memorized lists of words while underwater or on a beach, and then tried to recall the words while either in the same location or in the other location (Godden & Baddeley, 1975). The subjects communicated with the experimenter through a special intercom system. The results, illustrated in figure 8.10, indicated that when the subjects memorized and recalled the words in different locations, they recalled about 30 percent fewer than when they memorized and recalled the words in the same location. This tendency for recall to be best when the environmental context present during the encoding of a memory is also present during attempts at retrieving it is known as **context-dependent memory.** The findings of the study even have practical implications. Instructions given to scuba divers should be given underwater, as well as on dry land, and if divers are making observations about what they see underwater, they should record them there and not wait until they get on dry land (Baddeley, 1982).

The effect of environmental context on recall is not lost on theater directors, who hold dress rehearsals in full costume amid the scenery that will be used during actual performances. Similarly, even your academic performance can be affected by environmental cues. Half a century ago a study found that college students performed worse when their exams were given in classrooms other than their normal ones (Abernethy, 1940). Perhaps you have noticed this when you have taken a final exam in a strange room. If you find yourself in that situation, you might improve your performance by mentally reinstating the environmental context in which you learned the material (Smith, 1984).

There is controversy among memory researchers about whether the environmental context is important when *recall* is required, but not when *recognition* is required. This means that your performance on an essay exam might be impaired if you took an exam

tip-of-the-tongue phenomenon
The inability to recall information that one knows has been stored in long-term memory.

encoding specificity
The principle that recall will be best when cues that were associated with the encoding of a memory are also present during attempts at retrieving it.

context-dependent memory
The tendency for recall to be best when the environmental context present during the encoding of a memory is also present during attempts at retrieving it.

FIGURE 8.10

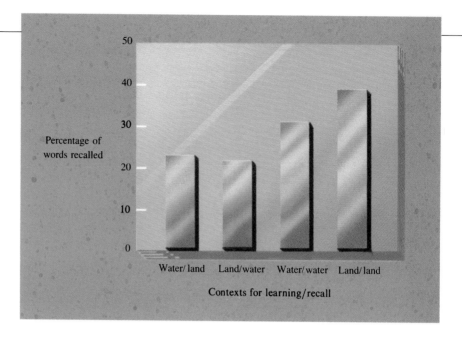

Context-Dependent Memory
Godden and Baddeley (1975) found that words learned underwater were best recalled underwater and that words learned on land were best recalled on land.

state-dependent memory
The tendency for recall to be best when one's emotional or physiological state is the same during the recall of a memory as it was during the encoding of that memory.

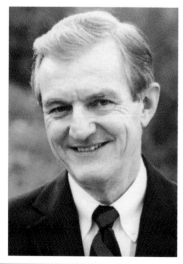

Gordon Bower
"People recall an event better if they somehow reinstate during recall the original emotion they experienced during learning."

in a strange room, but your performance on a multiple-choice test would not. Perhaps tasks that require recognition include enough retrieval cues of their own, making environmental retrieval cues relatively less important (Eich, 1980). But some research indicates that even recognition memory is affected by environmental context. In one study, undergraduates were presented, in a particular room, with lists of words to remember and were then asked to recognize the words in the same or a different room. The results supported context-dependent memory; recognition was best when memorization and recognition took place in the same room (Smith, 1985).

Our recall of memories depends not only on cues from the external environment but also on cues from our internal states. The effect on recall of the similarity between a person's internal state during encoding and during retrieval is called **state-dependent memory.** For example, memories encoded while the person is in a psychoactive drug-induced state will be recalled better when the person is in that state. A variety of drugs induce state-dependent memory. These include alcohol (Lowe, 1982), nicotine (Peters & McGee, 1982), Valium (Roy-Byrne et al., 1987), nitrous oxide (Mewaldt et al., 1988), and the Parkinson's disease drug L-dopa (Huber et al., 1989).

In a government-sponsored study on the possible state-dependent effects of marijuana (Eich et al., 1975), one group of subjects memorized a list of words after smoking marijuana, and a second group memorized the same list after smoking a placebo that tasted like marijuana. The subjects were "blind"; that is, they did not know whether they were smoking marijuana or a placebo. Four hours later, half of each group smoked either marijuana or a placebo and then tried to recall the words they had memorized. Recall was better either when subjects smoked the placebo on both occasions or when they smoked marijuana on both occasions than when they smoked marijuana on one occasion and the placebo on the other. You should *not* conclude that marijuana smoking improves memory. As noted in chapter 6, marijuana actually impairs memory. And, indeed, in this study the group that smoked the placebo on both occasions performed *better* than the groups that smoked marijuana on either occasion or both occasions.

Our internal states also reflect our moods, which can play a role in a form of state-dependent memory called *mood-dependent memory*, in which our recall of information that has been encoded in a particular mood will be best when we are in that mood again (Bower, 1981). The mood appears to act as a cue for the retrieval of memories. Thus, if you have an experience while you are in an angry mood, you might be more likely to recall details of that experience when you are again in an angry mood.

Closely related to mood-dependent memory is *mood-congruent memory*, which is the tendency to recall memories that are consistent with one's current mood. This effect was observed in a study in which moods were induced by having subjects smell either a pleasant odor (almond extract) or an unpleasant odor (the chemical pyridine). The subjects were then asked to recall past experiences. Those in the pleasant odor condition recalled a higher percentage of happy memories than did those in the unpleasant odor condition (Ehrlichman & Halpern, 1988).

Though mood-dependent memory has been demonstrated in a number of studies, Gordon Bower, the psychologist who was the first to study it formally, has had difficulty replicating his early research (Bower & Mayer, 1989). Moreover, there is stronger research support for mood-congruent memory than for mood-dependent memory (Blaney, 1986). Chapter 14 discusses how mood-congruent memory might account for the self-perpetuating nature of depression, as the depressed person recalls more depressing memories, and the depressing memories in turn maintain the depression (Matt, Vazquez, & Campbell, 1992). As you can see, the field of memory research is diverse, fascinating, and filled with promising applications to everyday life. One important application is the improvement of memory.

Mood-Dependent Memory
The current moods of these family members can influence the kinds of memories the photographs evoke. We tend to recall memories that are congruent with our current mood.

IMPROVING YOUR MEMORY

A century ago William James (1890/1981) criticized those who claimed that memory ability could be improved by practice. To James, memory was a fixed, inherited ability and not subject to improvement. He concluded this after finding that practice in memorizing did not decrease the time it took him and other subjects to memorize poetry or other kinds of literature. Regardless of the extent to which memory ability is inherited, we can certainly make better use of the ability we have by improving our study habits and by using *mnemonic devices*.

Study Habits

Given two students with equal memory ability, the one with better study habits will probably perform better in school. To practice good study habits, you would begin by setting up a schedule in which you would do the bulk of your studying when you are most alert and most motivated—whether in the early morning, late afternoon, or some other time. You should also study in a quiet, comfortable place, free of distractions. If you study in a dormitory lounge with students milling around and holding conversations, you might find yourself distracted from the information being processed in your short-term memory, making it more difficult for you to transfer the information efficiently into your long-term memory.

SQ3R method
A study technique in which the student surveys, questions, reads, recites, and reviews course material.

As for particular study techniques, you might consider using the **SQ3R method** (Robinson, 1970). SQ3R stands for Survey, Question, Read, Recite, and Review. This method has proved helpful to students in college (Martin, 1985) and elementary school (Darch, Carnine, & Kameenui, 1986). It requires elaborative rehearsal, in which you process information at a relatively deep level. This is distinct from rote memorization, in which you process information at a relatively shallow level. If you have ever found yourself studying for hours, yet doing poorly on exams, it might be the consequence of failing to use elaborative rehearsal. For example, in one study students used either rote memory, writing down unfamiliar terms and their definitions, or elaborative rehearsal, writing down how the words might or might not describe them. One week later, students who had used elaborative rehearsal recalled significantly more definitions than did students who had used rote memory (Flannagan & Blick, 1989).

Suppose that you decide to use the SQ3R method to study the final two sections of this chapter. You would follow several steps. First, *survey* the main headings and subheadings to create an organized framework in which to fit the information you are studying. Second, as you survey the sections, ask yourself *questions* to be answered when you read them. For example, you might ask yourself, What is the physiological basis of memory? or Is eyewitness testimony accurate? Third, *read* the material carefully, trying to answer your questions as you move through each section. In memorizing new terms, you might find it especially helpful to say them out loud. A study found that subjects who read terms out loud remembered more of them than did subjects who read them silently, wrote them down, or heard them spoken by someone else (Gathercole & Conway, 1988). Fourth, after reading a section, *recite* information from it to see whether you understand it. Do not proceed to the next section until you understand the one you are studying. Fifth, periodically (perhaps every few days) *review* the information in the entire chapter by quizzing yourself on it and then rereading anything you fail to recall. Asking questions of yourself as you read can increase elaborative rehearsal and the depth of processing, thereby improving your memory for the material (Andre, 1979). You will also find yourself experiencing savings; each time you review the material, it will take you less time to reach the same level of mastery. This would indicate that you are gaining greater command of the material.

overlearning
Studying material beyond the point of initial mastery.

You might also wish to apply other principles to improve your studying. First, take advantage of **overlearning** by studying the material until you feel you know all of it—and then going over it several more times. Research findings indicate that overlearning significantly improves the retention of material that has been memorized (Driskell, Willis, & Cooper, 1992). Overlearning works by making you less likely to forget material you have studied and more confident that you know it (Nelson et al., 1982), perhaps improving your exam performance by making you less anxious. The power of overlearning is revealed by the amazing ability people show for recognizing the names and faces of their high school classmates decades after graduation. This is attributable to their having overlearned the names and faces during their years together in school (Bahrick, Bahrick, & Wittlinger, 1975).

distributed practice
Spreading out the memorization of information or the learning of a motor skill over several sessions.

massed practice
Cramming the memorization of information or the learning of a motor skill into one session.

Second, use **distributed practice** instead of **massed practice.** The advantage of distributed practice over massed practice is especially important in studying academic material (Dempster & Farris, 1990). If you devote 5 hours to studying this chapter, you

Overlearning
In learning a script or a song, actors do not merely memorize it until they recall it perfectly once. Instead, they overlearn it by making sure that they can recall it perfectly several times. This aids their recall of the lines and improves their confidence, thereby improving their performance.

would be better off studying for 1 hour on five different occasions than studying for 5 hours on one occasion. You may recognize this as a suggestion to avoid "cramming" for exams. Note how the following explanation by William James for the negative effects of cramming anticipated recent research into the effects of elaborative rehearsal, overlearning, environmental cues, and semantic networks on memory:

> • • • The reason why *cramming* is such a bad mode of study is now made clear. . . . Things learned thus in a few hours, on one occasion, for one purpose, cannot possibly have formed many associations with other things in the mind. . . . Speedy oblivion is the almost inevitable fate of all that is committed to memory in this simple way. . . . Whereas on the contrary, the same information taken in gradually, day after day, recurring in different contexts, considered in various relations, associated with other external incidents, and repeatedly reflected on, grow into a fabric, lie open to so many paths of approach, that they remain permanent possessions. (James, 1890/1981, Vol. 1, pp. 623–624)

Even novice word processors can benefit from distributed practice, as in a study of students in a word-processing seminar. The students were assigned to groups that received either a single 60-minute session or a 60-minute session broken into two segments by a 10-minute break. The students were tested on their speed and accuracy immediately after the training and 1 week later. The group that had received distributed practice performed significantly faster and more accurately on both occasions. The results indicate that those who teach word processing might be wise to divide long sessions into shorter ones (Bouzid & Crawshaw, 1987).

Mnemonic Devices

About 2,500 years ago the Greek poet Simonides stepped outside of the banquet hall where he was to recite a poem in honor of a Roman nobleman. While Simonides was outside, the hall collapsed, killing all the guests and maiming them beyond recognition. Yet, by recalling where each guest had been sitting, Simonides was able to identify each of them. He called this the **method of loci** (*loci* means "place" in Latin), which he recommended to orators because paper and pens were too expensive to waste on writing routine speeches (Bower, 1970). The method of loci is useful for memorizing lists of items. You might memorize concrete terms from this chapter by associating them with places and landmarks on your campus, and then retrieving them while taking a mental walk across it. Figure 8.11 provides an example of the method of loci, which has even proved helpful in training older adults to improve their memory for grocery lists (Anschutz et al., 1985).

method of loci
A mnemonic device in which items to be recalled are associated with landmarks in a familiar place and then recalled during a mental walk from one landmark to another.

FIGURE 8.11

The Method of Loci
In using the method of loci to recall a shopping list, you would pair each item on the list with a familiar place. You would then take a mental tour, retrieving items as you go.

mnemonic devices
Techniques for organizing information to be memorized to make it easier to remember.

acronym
A mnemonic device that involves forming a term from the first letters of a series of words that are to be recalled.

pegword method
A mnemonic device that involves associating items to be recalled with objects that rhyme with the numbers 1, 2, 3, and so on, to make the items easier to recall.

link method
A mnemonic device that involves connecting, in sequence, images of items to be memorized, to make them easier to recall.

The method of loci is one of several **mnemonic devices,** which are techniques for organizing information and providing memory cues to make it easier to recall. These devices are named after Mnemosyne, the Greek goddess of memory. You are familiar with certain mnemonic devices, such as *acronyms*. An **acronym** is a term formed from the first letters of a series of words. Examples of acronyms include *USA, NFL,* and even *SQ3R.* Acronyms have proved useful to medical students, helping them learn lists of concepts, such as the symptoms that are associated with certain diseases (Wilding et al., 1986).

You are also familiar with the use of rhymes as mnemonic devices, as in "*I before e except after c*" and "Thirty days has September. . . ." Though rhymes are useful mnemonic devices, they can sometimes impair memory. In one study, children who listened to stories presented in prose had better recall of them than did children who listened to the stories presented in verse. Evidently, the children who listened to verse processed the stories at a shallow level, as sounds, while the children who listened to prose processed the stories at a deeper level, in terms of their meaning (Hayes, Chemelski, & Palmer, 1982).

A mnemonic device that relies on both imagery and rhyming is the **pegword method,** which begins with memorizing a list of concrete nouns that rhyme with the numbers *1, 2, 3, 4, 5, 6,* and so on. For the pegword method to work well, the image of the pegword object and the image of the object to be recalled should interact, rather than just be paired with each other (Wollen, Weber, & Lowry, 1972). Suppose that you wanted to remember the grocery list presented in figure 8.12. You might imagine, among other things, sugar being poured from a shoe, bees in a hive brushing their teeth, and a hen drinking from a soda bottle. To recall an item, you would simply imagine the pegword that is paired with a particular number, which would act as a cue for retrieving the image of the object that interacted with that pegword. Thus, if you imagined a shoe, you would automatically retrieve an image of sugar being poured from it.

Still another mnemonic device that makes use of imagery is the **link method,** which takes images of the items to be memorized and connects them in sequence. One version of the link method is the *narrative method,* in which unrelated items are connected to one another in a story. Figure 8.13 presents an example of the narrative method. In a study that showed its effectiveness, two groups of subjects memorized twelve lists of 10 nouns. One group used the narrative method to memorize the nouns; the other

CHAPTER EIGHT

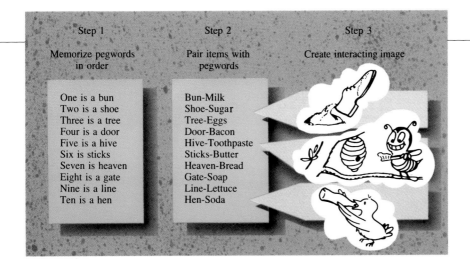

FIGURE 8.12

The Pegword Method
The pegword method can be used to recall a grocery list. Each grocery item is paired with a pegword. Thus, the retrieval of a pegword will cue the retrieval of the associated grocery item.

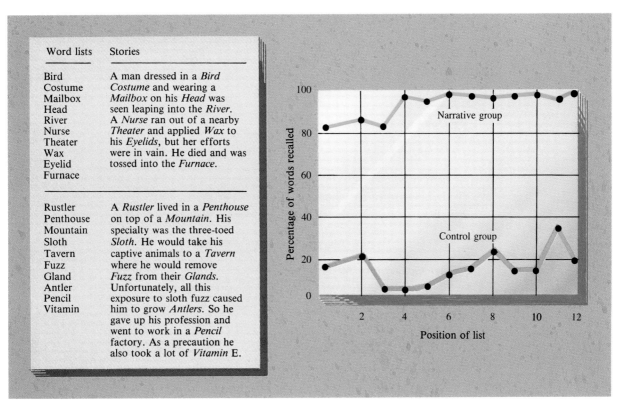

FIGURE 8.13

The Narrative Method
In using the narrative method to recall a list of words, you would create a story using each of the words. The graph shows the superior recall of subjects who used the narrative method in a study by Bower and Clark (1969).

group used ordinary mental rehearsal. Both groups showed nearly perfect immediate recall. But when later asked to recall all of the lists, the narrative group recalled an average of 93 percent of the words, while the mental rehearsal group recalled an average of only 13 percent (Bower & Clark, 1969). More-recent research has replicated this finding (Hill, Allen, & McWhorter, 1991).

Ironically, despite the usefulness of mnemonic devices, a survey of college professors found that memory researchers were no more likely than other professors to use formal mnemonic devices. Instead, memory researchers and other professors alike recommended that memory be improved by writing things down, by organizing material to

"When you're young, it comes naturally, but when you get a little older, you have to rely on mnemonics."

be learned, or by rehearsing material to be remembered (Park, Smith, & Cavanaugh, 1990). Like physicians who smoke, memory researchers can forget to practice what they preach.

THE BIOPSYCHOLOGY OF MEMORY

Though study habits and mnemonic devices depend on overt behavior and mental processes, they ultimately work by affecting the encoding, storage, and retrieval of memories in the brain. Today, research on the neuroanatomy and neurochemistry of memory is revealing more and more about its biological bases.

The Anatomy of Memory

During the first half of this century, psychologist Karl Lashley carried out an ambitious program of research aimed at finding the sites where individual memories are stored in the brain. As mentioned in chapter 3, Lashley trained rats to run through mazes to obtain food rewards. He then destroyed small areas of their cerebral cortex and noted whether this made a difference in their maze performance. To Lashley's dismay, no matter what area he destroyed, the rats still negotiated the mazes, showing at most a slight decrement in performance. Lashley concluded that he had failed in his lifelong search for the *memory trace*—or **engram**—which he had assumed was the basis of individual memories (Lashley, 1950).

But many scientists remained undaunted by Lashley's pessimistic conclusion and continued to search for the engram. This persistence paid off decades later when a team of researchers located the site of a specific engram in the cerebellum, a brain structure (discussed in chapter 3) that plays a role in both memory and the maintenance of equilibrium. The researchers classically conditioned rabbits to blink their eyes in response to a tone. Presentations of the tone (the conditioned stimulus) were repeatedly followed by puffs of air (the unconditioned stimulus) directed at the rabbit's eyes, which elicited blinking (the unconditioned response). Eventually, the tone itself elicited blinking (the

Karl Lashley (1890–1958)
"I sometimes feel, in reviewing the evidence on the localization of the memory trace, that the necessary conclusion is that learning just is not possible."

engram
A memory trace in the brain.

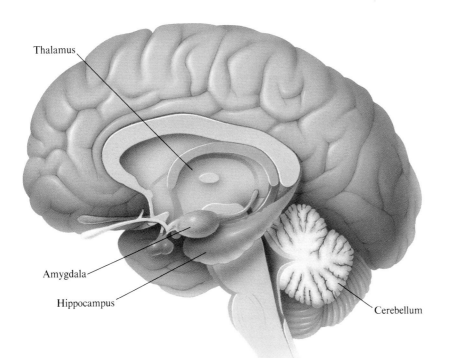

Thalamus

Amygdala

Hippocampus

Cerebellum

Kasnot

FIGURE 8.14

Anatomy of Memory
The brain contains no memory center.
Instead, memory depends on the
integration of activity in several areas
of the brain, including the thalamus,
the amygdala, the cerebellum, and,
especially, the hippocampus.

conditioned response). After conditioning, the researchers found that electrical stimulation of a tiny site in the cerebellum of the rabbit elicited the conditioned eye blink,
while destruction of the site eliminated it. Thus, they had succeeded in locating an
engram for a classically conditioned memory (Krupa, Thompson, & Thompson, 1993).

Advances in our knowledge of the cellular basis of memory also have come from
studies of the sea snail *Aplysia*. This creature has relatively few neurons, making it a
simpler subject of study than animals with complex brains. Researchers have identified
a neuronal engram formed when an *Aplysia* is classically conditioned to withdraw its
gills in response to the movement of water (Kandel & Schwartz, 1982). This (the unconditioned response) occurs after several trials in which the movement of the water
(the conditioned stimulus) has preceded an electric shock (the unconditioned stimulus)
that automatically elicits gill withdrawal (the unconditioned response).

As for human memory, in 1894 Sigmund Freud and Santiago Ramón y Cajal independently speculated that learning produces changes in the efficiency of synaptic
connections between neurons, and that these changes might be the basis of memory
formation. Recent research shows that memory might, indeed, depend on the facilitation of neural impulses across synapses in the brain. The most widely studied phenomenon related to the facilitation of neural impulses is *long-term potentiation,* in which
synaptic transmission of impulses is made more efficient by brief electrical stimulation
of specific neural pathways. This is viewed as a possible basis for long-term memory,
because long-term potentiation induced by specific experiences might strengthen synaptic connections in specific pathways (Bliss, 1990).

Researchers who study long-term potentiation are particularly interested in the
hippocampus, which lies deep within the temporal lobes. Figure 8.14 illustrates the
location of the hippocampus and other brain structures important in memory, including
the thalamus, the amygdala, and the cerebellum. Long-term potentiation in the hippocampus apparently is required for the storage of new memories, but is required for only
a limited period of time after a learning experience. Evidence for this comes from animal
studies in which the hippocampus is purposely damaged at varying times after learning.
The longer the delay before hippocampal damage, the less effect it has on the storage
of the new memories (Zola-Morgan & Squire, 1990). Evidence for the importance of the

Brenda Milner
"We have chosen to report these findings in full, partly for their theoretical significance, and partly as a warning to others of the risk to memory involved in bilateral surgical lesions of the hippocampal region."

Larry Squire
"Studies of human amnesia and studies of an animal model of human amnesia in the monkey have identified the anatomical components of the brain system for memory in the medial temporal lobe and . . . this neural system consists of the hippocampus and adjacent anatomically related cortex."

hippocampus in the formation of long-term memories comes from research on Alzheimer's disease, which is marked by degeneration of neural pathways from the hippocampus (Brady & Mufson, 1990). Victims of Alzheimer's disease find it progressively more difficult to form new long-term memories.

The most celebrated single source of evidence for the role of the hippocampus in memory comes from the case study of a man known as "H. M.," who has been studied since the 1950s by Brenda Milner of the Montreal Neurological Institute (Scoville & Milner, 1957). H. M. has formed few new declarative memories since undergoing brain surgery in 1953, when he was 27 years old. The surgery, performed to relieve uncontrollable epileptic seizures, removed almost all of his hippocampus. As a result, H. M. developed anterograde amnesia, the inability to form new long-term declarative memories (that is, memories of facts and events). Because he cannot recall events after 1953, he feels that each moment of his life is like waking from a dream, as short-term memories continually enter his consciousness and then fade away. H. M. can recall memories from before 1953, but because of his inability to convert short-term memories into long-term memories, H. M. will read the same magazine over and over, without realizing that he has read it before. He will meet the same person on repeated occasions, yet have to be reintroduced each time. Though H. M. cannot form new declarative memories, he can form new procedural memories (that is, memories of how to perform tasks). For example, he has learned to play tennis since his surgery and has retained that procedural memory—even though he does not recall having taken lessons (Herbert, 1983b).

The case of H. M. supports research findings by neuroscientist Larry Squire and his colleagues that the hippocampus is important in the formation of declarative memories but not of procedural memories. In one study, subjects suffering from the same form of anterograde amnesia as H. M. were trained to read words in a mirror. Though this is a difficult task, they were able to do so and improved in their performance over a 3-day period. Despite having the ability to form new procedural memories, the subjects also revealed an inability to form new declarative memories—they failed to recall having ever learned the task (Cohen & Squire, 1980). This indicates that procedural memories depend on still-unidentified brain structures other than the hippocampus. One candidate is the cerebellum.

The Chemistry of Memory

In 1959 James McConnell and his colleagues stunned the scientific world by reporting the results of an unusual experiment (McConnell, Jacobson, & Kimble, 1959). They had classically conditioned flatworms to contract their bodies in response to a light by repeatedly pairing presentations of the light with mild electric shocks. They then cut the flatworms in half. Because flatworms can regenerate themselves, both halves grew into whole flatworms. They were then retrained to contract in response to a light. As expected, the flatworms that had regenerated from the head (brain) ends showed memory savings—they took fewer trials to learn to respond to the light than had the original flatworms, which provided evidence that prior learning had been retained by the brain end. But, to the researchers' surprise, the flatworms that had regenerated from the tail ends learned to respond to the light as fast as those that had regenerated from the brain ends. This indicated that the memory of the classically conditioned response may have been encoded chemically and transported to the tail ends.

These findings led to a series of even more unusual experiments by a variety of researchers, which seemed to demonstrate that memories could be transferred from one animal to another. In one study, rats were trained to run to a lighted compartment instead of to a dark compartment (which they would normally favor) by shocking them whenever they entered the dark compartment. When extracts from the brains of these rats were injected into mice, the mice spent less time in the dark compartment than they normally would. The researchers later isolated the proteinlike substance apparently responsible for this effect, which they called *scotophobin,* meaning "fear of the dark" (Unger, Desiderio, & Parr, 1972).

As you might assume, the results of successful memory transfer studies created controversy, leading 23 researchers to write a letter to the influential journal *Science* in which they reported their failure to produce memory transfer in 18 studies in seven laboratories ("Memory Transfer," 1966). Failure to replicate memory transfer studies became the main reason to reject those that found positive results. But a few years later a published review of the research literature concluded that hundreds of studies of flatworms, goldfish, chickens, mice, rats, and hamsters had demonstrated the transfer of memories (Smith, 1974). Yet because of the failure of other researchers to replicate those studies and to identify a physiological basis for the chemical transfer of memories, interest in the study of memory transfer has waned. Perhaps interest has declined, in part, because the very notion of memory transfer seems better suited to science fiction than to science. As discussed in chapter 2, scientists in all disciplines, including biology, chemistry, and physics, tend to avoid topics that appear to violate accepted scientific paradigms that define what is conceivable.

In contrast to the conflict generated by research on the chemical transfer of memories, there is no controversy about whether neurotransmitters play a role in memory, because memory processing requires the chemical transmission of neural impulses from one neuron to another. But the exact relationship between neurotransmitter activity and memory has only recently begun to reveal itself. The major neurotransmitter that is most strongly implicated in memory processes is *acetylcholine*. Acetylcholine might be more important in the formation of declarative memories than in the formation of procedural memories. This was implied by the results of a study in which one group of young adult subjects received a drug that blocked the effects of acetylcholine, while another group received a placebo (Nissen, Knopman, & Schachter, 1987). Those who received the active drug showed a reduced ability to recall and recognize stimuli presented previously (declarative memory) but no reduction in their ability to perform a reaction-time task they had learned previously (procedural memory).

The most striking evidence of the role of acetylcholine in memory comes from studies of victims of Alzheimer's disease. Autopsies of victims of Alzheimer's disease show degeneration of acetylcholine neurons that connect the hippocampus to other brain areas. In fact, when normal subjects are given drugs that inhibit the activity of acetylcholine neurons, they show memory losses similar to those seen in victims of Alzheimer's disease (McKinney & Richelson, 1984).

It would seem logical that treatments aimed at elevating brain levels of acetylcholine would improve the ability of Alzheimer's victims to form new memories. One approach has been to administer *choline*—the dietary substance from which acetylcholine is synthesized and that is found in milk and eggs. Unfortunately, administration of high doses of choline has not been effective in improving the memory of Alzheimer's victims (Bartus et al., 1982). Evidently the degeneration of acetylcholine neurons prevents the additional choline from having a beneficial effect, just as adding gasoline to the empty tank of a car with no spark plugs would not make it more likely to start.

Perhaps the most exciting area of current research on the chemical basis of memory concerns N-methyl-D-aspartate (NMDA) receptors (Bliss & Collingridge, 1993). NMDA is an amino acid that, when injected into an animal, binds to specific receptors in the hippocampus and enhances the efficiency of synaptic transmission along specific neural pathways. Consider a study in which rats learned to respond to a conditioned stimulus that had been paired with an unconditioned stimulus. A drug that blocked NMDA receptors prevented the formation of a conditioned response, but only if it was given during conditioning trials. If it was given after them, it had no effect. This supports the role of NMDA receptors in the acquisition, but not the performance, of a conditioned response (Kim et al., 1991). Additional support for the role of NMDA receptors in long-term memory comes from research on Alzheimer's disease. In the brains of victims of the disease, the number of NMDA receptors is greatly reduced and neural degeneration occurs in pathways rich in NMDA receptors (Maragos et al., 1987).

Alzheimer's Disease
Because victims of Alzheimer's disease suffer severe memory impairment, they may benefit from a "prosthetic environment." Strategically placed signs enable this woman to locate her personal belongings.

Still another topic of research interest regarding the chemical basis of memory is the effect of blood sugar, glucose. There is a positive correlation between blood glucose levels and memory performance. For example, studies indicate that college students' performance on memory tasks is positively correlated with their levels of blood glucose (Benton & Sargent, 1992). Dietary supplements of glucose may improve memory in the elderly. In one study, older adults (aged 60 to 81 years) received doses of either glucose or saccharin before or after memorizing a brief prose passage. Their recall of the passage was tested 24 hours later. Those who had ingested glucose, before or after memorizing the passage, showed significantly better recall than did those who had ingested saccharin. Evidently, the glucose enhanced the storage of the prose passages in memory (Manning, Parsons, & Gold, 1992). Glucose supplements also can temporarily improve the memory of victims of Alzheimer's disease (Craft, Zallen, & Baker, 1992). But how does glucose improve memory? One way is by increasing the synthesis of acetylcholine in the hippocampus (Messier et al., 1990). Nonetheless, students should not conclude that it would be wise to ingest massive amounts of glucose. On the contrary, the greatest enhancement of memory is produced by moderate doses of glucose (Parsons & Gold, 1992).

As you can see, research on the physiology of memory cannot be divorced from the psychology of memory. And physiological research promises to discover ways of improving memory. This would be a boon both to people with intact brains and to people with damaged brains.

THINKING ABOUT *Psychology*

SHOULD WE TRUST EYEWITNESS TESTIMONY?

In August 1979, Father Bernard Pagano went on trial for a series of armed robberies. Seven eyewitnesses had identified him as the so-called gentleman bandit, a polite man who had robbed several convenience stores in Wilmington, Delaware. Father Pagano was arrested after several people who knew him told the police that he resembled published drawings of the bandit. Seven eyewitnesses, who were shown photographs in which Father Pagano wore his clerical collar, identified him as the robber. They might have been influenced by previous police reports that indicated that the perpetrator might have been a clergyman. Fortunately for Father Pagano, while he was on trial, another man, Ronald Clouser, confessed to the crimes (Rodgers, 1982).

As shown in figure 8.15, there was little resemblance between Father Pagano and Ronald Clouser. The possibility of convicting innocent people or of exonerating guilty people based on inaccurate *eyewitness testimony* has led psychologists to study the factors that affect eyewitness memories. This concern is not new. Hugo Münsterberg (1908), a pioneer in the study of psychology and the law, warned us to consider the imperfections of human memory when evaluating the accuracy of eyewitness testimony. And, around the turn of the century, Alfred Binet, who gained fame for developing the first IQ test, championed the scientific study of eyewitness testimony. He introduced the *picture-description test*, which required subjects to examine a picture of a scene and, after varying lengths of time, to recall as much as possible about the picture or to answer questions about it posed by an interrogator. Binet found that eyewitness testimony usually

FIGURE 8.15

Eyewitness Testimony
Eyewitnesses mistakenly identified Father Bernard Pagano (*left*) as the perpetrator of a series of convenience store robberies actually committed by Ronald Clouser (*right*).

included inaccuracies and that testimony under questioning was less accurate than spontaneous testimony (Postman, 1985).

During the past two decades, psychologists have conducted numerous studies of the factors that affect the accuracy of eyewitness testimony. Research on eyewitness memories shows that they are not like mental tape recordings that record and play back exactly. Instead, eyewitness recollections are reconstructive, somewhat altering the events that they represent.

CHARACTERISTICS OF THE EYEWITNESS

Many studies have investigated the relationship between eyewitness testimony and the characteristics of the eyewitness. One of the main issues regarding the characteristics of the eyewitness is whether the testimony of children is trustworthy—an issue that has concerned psychologists since the early twentieth century (Ceci & Brock, 1993). Studies have found that children tend to be less accurate than adults in their eyewitness accounts of crimes, in part because they are more suggestible—that is, they are more susceptible to leading questions. This was first demonstrated at the beginning of the century by the German psychologist William Stern (Bringmann et al., 1989). Concerns about children as eyewitnesses have been supported by research indicating that misleading information about events can distort children's memories of those events. In an experiment that tested this assumption, children aged 3 to 12 years listened to a story about a girl who had a *stomachache* after eating *eggs* too fast. When asked questions about the story, the children answered correctly almost all of the time. But when asked if they remembered the story of a little girl who got a *headache* because she ate her *cereal* too fast, the children typically responded that they had. The effect of misleading questions was greater on the younger children than on the older ones (Ceci, Ross, & Toglia, 1987). Of course, especially because of the prevalence of child abuse, courts must achieve a delicate balance between believing children's testimony and being skeptical of it. Fortunately, children can give accurate testimony, provided that they are not given leading questions and that the questions are worded so that they can understand them (Brooks & Siegel, 1991).

As mentioned in the discussion of hypnotically enhanced memory in chapter 7, because jurors attribute greater accuracy to the testimony of confident eyewitnesses, another important factor in eyewitness testimony is how confident eyewitnesses are about their memories. In the 1972 case of *Neil v. Biggers*, the United States Supreme Court even ruled that one of the criteria that juries should use in judging the accuracy of an eyewitness's testimony is the degree of confidence expressed by the eyewitness. But this ruling might be misguided, because eyewitnesses' level of confidence is generally unrelated to the accuracy of their testimony (Wells & Lindsay, 1985). As a consequence, it may be unwise for jurors to assume that a confident eyewitness is necessarily an accurate eyewitness.

QUESTIONING THE EYEWITNESS

Aside from the characteristics of the eyewitness, one of the main factors regarding eyewitness testimony is the wording of questions. This has been demonstrated in a series of experiments by Elizabeth Loftus, of the University of Washington, and her colleagues. The following study is one of the most influential of her experiments on eyewitness testimony.

Anatomy of a Contemporary Research Study:
Can Leading Questions Influence Eyewitness Testimony?

Rationale

Judges and lawyers are taught to beware of leading questions, which can affect the testimony of eyewitnesses. Nonetheless, clever lawyers use subtle wording to influence testimony. The present study by Elizabeth Loftus and John Palmer (1974) examined the effect of leading questions regarding eyewitness accounts of an automobile accident.

Method

Forty-five undergraduate subjects viewed one of seven driver-education films of two-car automobile accidents lasting 5 to 30 seconds. Some subjects were asked, "About how fast were the cars going when they smashed into each other?" Other subjects were asked a similar question, with the word smashed *replaced by* contacted, hit, bumped, *or* collided. *In a similar version of the experiment, 150 other undergraduate subjects likewise viewed films of two-car automobile accidents. Subjects in one group were asked, "About how fast were the cars going when they smashed into each other?" and subjects in a second group were asked, "About how fast were the cars going when they hit each other?" A week later, the subjects were asked, "Did you see any broken glass?" To avoid sensitizing the subjects to its purpose, the question was embedded in a list of 10 questions. In reality, there was no broken glass at the accident scene.*

Results and Discussion

As shown in figure 8.16, the subjects' estimates of the speed of the cars in the first part of the study were influenced by the severity of the word used in the question. The average estimates for contacted, hit, bumped, collided, *and* smashed *were, respectively, 31.8, 34.0, 38.1, 39.3, and 40.8 miles per hour. In the second part of the study, though there had been no broken glass, subjects in both groups recalled seeing some. But subjects who had been given the question containing the word* smashed *were significantly more likely to report having seen broken glass than were subjects who had been given the question containing the word* hit.

Loftus's findings have been replicated in other studies. In one study, college students were shown a videotaped mock crime. One week later they read a passage that described the crime. The passage contained leading, misleading, or control (no supplemental) information. When asked to recall the crime they had witnessed, the subjects placed more confidence in the biased information presented by the experimenter than in their own memories (Ryan & Geiselman, 1991).

Studies such as these demonstrate that the memories of eyewitnesses can be reconstructions, instead of exact replicas, of the events witnessed. Eyewitness memories can be altered by inaccurate information introduced during questioning (Loftus, 1982). This also supports the practice of barring leading questions in courtroom proceedings. Though leading questions can affect the recall of eyewitnesses, recent research indicates that eyewitnesses might be less susceptible to leading questions than had been suggested by earlier research (Kohnken & Maass, 1988).

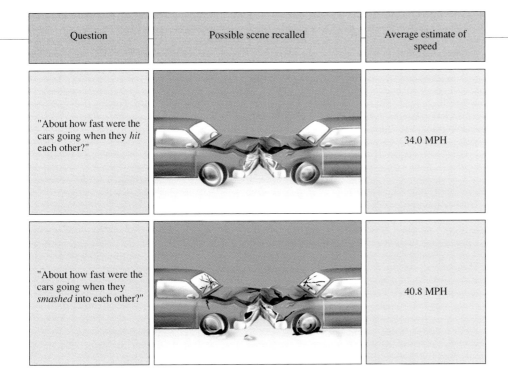

Question	Possible scene recalled	Average estimate of speed
"About how fast were the cars going when they *hit* each other?"		34.0 MPH
"About how fast were the cars going when they *smashed* into each other?"		40.8 MPH

FIGURE 8.16

Leading Questions
The wording of questions can influence the recall of eyewitnesses. As demonstrated in an experiment by Loftus and Palmer (1974), subjects who witnessed a collision between two cars gave different estimates of their speed, depending on the wording of the questions they were asked. The wording may have altered the scenes they recalled.

Eyewitness memory can be improved by relatively simple procedures. One procedure, based on the principle of encoding specificity, improves recall by mentally reinstating the physical setting of the event. In one study, store clerks were asked to identify a previously encountered customer from an array of photographs. The original context was reinstated by providing physical cues from the encounter and by instructing the clerk to mentally recall events that led up to the customer's purchase. As discussed earlier, mentally reinstating the context in which you learned something can improve your recall of it. In this study, the reinstatement of the original context led to a significant increase in the accuracy of identifications (Krafka & Penrod, 1985).

We can also prevent misleading information from influencing the memories of eyewitnesses by warning them about that possibility. This was the finding of a study in which subjects were warned just prior to the presentation of misleading information about a simulated crime. The subjects viewed slides of a wallet being snatched from a woman's purse and then read descriptions of the crime. Subjects who had been given warnings showed greater resistance to misleading information in the descriptions (Greene, Flynn, & Loftus, 1982). But some psychologists argue that informing jurors of the unreliability of eyewitness testimony might make already skeptical jurors too skeptical, perhaps leading to the exoneration of guilty persons (McCloskey & Egeth, 1983).

Regardless of the exact extent to which eyewitness testimony can be influenced by misleading information and the reasons for that influence, Elizabeth Loftus believes that eyewitness testimony is, in fact, too easily affected by such information. She expressed this in a statement that was a takeoff on John B. Watson's claim (quoted in chapter 1) regarding his ability to condition infants to become any kind of person one desired. Loftus remarked:

> • • • Give us a dozen healthy memories, well-informed, and our own specified world to handle them in. And we'll guarantee to take any at random and train it to become any type of memory that we might select—hammer, screwdriver, wrench, stop sign, yield sign, Indian chief—regardless of its origin or the brain that holds it. (Loftus & Hoffman, 1989, p. 103)

Elizabeth Loftus
"One reason most of us, as jurors, place so much faith in eyewitness testimony is that we are unaware of how many factors influence its accuracy."

INFORMATION PROCESSING AND MEMORY

Memory research has been influenced by the cognitive revolution in psychology. The most widely accepted model of memory assumes that memory processing involves the stages of sensory memory, short-term memory, and long-term memory. At each stage the processing of memories involves encoding, storage, retrieval, and forgetting.

SENSORY MEMORY

Stimulation of sensory receptors produces sensory memories. Visual sensory memory is called iconic memory, and auditory sensory memory is called echoic memory. George Sperling found that iconic memory contains more information than had been commonly believed and that almost all of it fades within a second.

SHORT-TERM MEMORY

Short-term memory is called working memory, because we use it to manipulate information provided by either sensory memory or long-term memory. We tend to encode information in short-term memory as sounds. We can store an average of seven chunks of information in short-term memory without rehearsal. Memories in short-term memory last about 20 seconds without rehearsal. Forgetting in short-term memory is caused by decay and displacement of information.

LONG-TERM MEMORY

Memories stored in long-term memory are relatively permanent. Elaborative rehearsal of information in short-term memory is more likely to produce long-term memories than is maintenance rehearsal. The levels of processing theory assume that information processed at deeper levels will be more firmly stored in long-term memory. Researchers distinguish between procedural, semantic, and episodic memories. Semantic network theory assumes that memories are stored as nodes interconnected by links. Schema theory assumes that memories are stored as cognitive structures that affect the encoding, storage, and retrieval of information related to them.

Hermann Ebbinghaus began the formal study of memory by employing the method of savings. He also identified the serial-position effect and the forgetting curve. The main theories of forgetting include decay theory, interference theory, motivation theory, and cue-dependence theory. The main versions of cue-dependence theory are context-dependent memory and state-dependent memory.

IMPROVING YOUR MEMORY

You can improve your memory by improving your study habits and by using mnemonic devices. A useful study technique is the SQ3R method, in which you survey, question, read, recite, and review. Overlearning and distributed practice are also useful techniques. Mnemonic devices are memory aids that organize material to make it easier to recall. The main mnemonic devices include acronyms, the method of loci, the pegword method, and the link method.

THE BIOPSYCHOLOGY OF MEMORY

Although Karl Lashley failed in his search for the engram, researchers have discovered some of the anatomical and chemical bases of memory. The hippocampus plays an important role in converting short-term memories into long-term memories. Research on NMDA receptors promises to contribute to our understanding of the physiological bases of memory. Neurotransmitters, particularly acetylcholine, play crucial roles in memory formation. Even blood glucose can facilitate memory formation.

THINKING ABOUT PSYCHOLOGY: SHOULD WE TRUST EYEWITNESS TESTIMONY?

Research by Elizabeth Loftus and her colleagues has shown that eyewitness testimony often can be inaccurate. One important finding is that eyewitnesses' confidence in their memories is not a good indicator of their accuracy. Another important finding is that leading questions can alter the recall of memories by eyewitnesses.

IMPORTANT CONCEPTS

acronym 308
constructive recall 298
context-dependent memory 303
decay theory 300
declarative memory 293
distributed practice 306
echoic memory 289
elaborative rehearsal 292
encoding 287
encoding specificity 303
engram 310
episodic memory 294

flashbulb memory 286
forgetting 288
forgetting curve 300
iconic memory 288
information-processing
  model 288
interference theory 301
levels of processing theory 293
link method 308
long-term memory 287
maintenance rehearsal 292
massed practice 306

memory 286
method of loci 307
method of savings 299
mnemonic device 308
overlearning 306
pegword method 308
proactive interference 301
procedural memory 293
repression 302
retrieval 287
retroactive interference 301
schema theory 296

semantic memory 293
semantic network theory 295
sensory memory 287
serial-position effect 298
short-term memory 287
SQ3R method 306
state-dependent memory 304
storage 287
tip-of-the-tongue
  phenomenon 303

MAJOR CONTRIBUTORS

RECOMMENDED READINGS

FOR GENERAL WORKS ON MEMORY

Baddeley, A. (1990). *Human memory: An ecological approach.* Needham Heights, MA: Allyn & Bacon.

Butler, T. (Ed.). (1989). *Memory: History, culture, and the mind.* Cambridge, MA: Basil Blackwell.

Cohen, G. (1989). *Memory in the real world.* Hillsdale, NJ: Erlbaum.

Ebbinghaus, H. (1885/1964). *Memory: A contribution to experimental psychology.* New York: Dover.

Hermann, D. J. & Chaffin, R. (Eds.). (1988). *Memory in historical perspective: The literature before Ebbinghaus.* New York: Springer-Verlag.

Loftus, E. (1980). *Memory.* Reading, MA: Addison-Wesley.

Neisser, U. (1982). *Memory observed: Remembering in natural contexts.* San Francisco: Freeman.

Neisser, U., & Winograd, E. (Eds.). (1988). *Remembering reconsidered: Ecological and traditional approaches to the study of memory.* New York: Cambridge University Press.

Schachter, D. L. (1982). *Stranger behind the engram: Theories of memory and the psychology of science.* Hillsdale, NJ: Erlbaum.

FOR MORE ON SENSORY MEMORY

Cowan, N. (1984). On short and long auditory stores. *Psychological Bulletin, 96,* 341–370.

Long, G. M. (1980). Iconic memory: A review and critique of the study of short-term visual storage. *Psychological Bulletin, 88,* 785–820.

Sperling, G. (1960). The information available in brief visual presentations. *Psychological Monographs, 74* (No. 498).

FOR MORE ON SHORT-TERM MEMORY

Baddeley, A. (1986). *Working memory.* New York: Oxford University Press.

Deutsch, D., & Deutsch, J. A. (Eds.). (1975). *Short-term memory.* San Diego: Academic Press.

Vallar, G., & Shallice, T. (Eds.). (1990). *Neuropsychological impairments of short-term memory.* New York: Cambridge University Press.

FOR MORE ON LONG-TERM MEMORY

Bartlett, F. C. (1932). *Remembering: A study in experimental and social psychology.* Cambridge, England: Cambridge University Press.

Brown, A. S. (1991). A review of the tip-of-the-tongue experience. *Psychological Bulletin, 109,* 204–223.

Freud, S. (1901/1965). *Psychopathology of everyday life.* New York: W. W. Norton.

Graf, P., & Masson, M. E. J. (1993). *Implicit memory: New directions in cognition, development, and neuropsychology.* Hillsdale, NJ: Erlbaum.

Holmes, D. S. (1974). Investigation of repression: Differential recall of material experimentally or naturally associated with ego threat. *Psychological Bulletin, 81,* 632–653.

Kuiken, D. (Ed.). (1991). *Mood and memory: Theory, research, and applications.* Newbury Park, CA: Sage Publications.

Luria, A. R. (1968). *The mind of a mnemonist.* New York: Basic Books.

Roediger, H. L., III, & Craik, F. I. M. (Eds.). (1989). *Varieties of memory and consciousness: Essays in honour of Endel Tulving.* Hillsdale, NJ: Erlbaum.

Ross, B. M. (1992) *Recovering the personal past: The conceptual background of autobiographical memory.* New York: Oxford University Press.

Schachter, D. L., & Tulving, E. (Eds.). (1994). *Memory systems.* Cambridge, MA: MIT Press.

Tulving, E. (1983). *Elements of episodic memory.* New York: Oxford University Press.

Winograd, E., & Neisser, U. (Eds.). (1992). *Affect and accuracy in recall: Studies of "flashbulb"* memories. New York: Cambridge University Press.

FOR MORE ON IMPROVING YOUR MEMORY

Baddeley, A. D. (1982). *Your memory: A user's guide.* New York: Macmillan.

Fogler, J., & Stern, L. (1994). *Teaching memory improvement to adults.* Baltimore: The Johns Hopkins University Press.

Herrmann, D. J., Weingartner, H., Searleman, A., & McEvoy, C. (Eds.). (1992). *Memory improvement: Implications for memory theory.* New York: Springer-Verlag.

Higbee, K. (1988). *Your memory: How it works and how to improve it.* (2nd ed.). New York: Paragon House.

Scruggs, T., & Mastropieri, M. (1990). *Teaching students ways to remember: Strategies for learning mnemonically.* Cambridge, MA: Brookline Books.

FOR MORE ON THE BIOPSYCHOLOGY OF MEMORY

Alkon, D. L. (1992). *Memory's voice: Deciphering the mind-brain code.* New York: Harper Collins.

Baudry, M., & Davis, J. L. (Eds.). (1994). *Long-term potentiation (2 vols.).* Cambridge, MA: MIT Press.

Cohen. N. J. & Eichenbaum, H. (1993). *Memory, amnesia, and the hippocampal system.* Cambridge, MA: MIT Press.

Mayes, A. R. (1988). *Human organic memory disorders.* New York: Cambridge University Press.

Mishkin, M., & Appenzeller, T. (1987, June). The anatomy of memory. *Scientific American,* pp. 80–99.

Squire, L. R., Weinberger, N. M., Lynch, G., & McGaugh, J. L. (Eds.). (1991). *Memory: Organization and locus of change.* New York: Oxford University.

Watkins, J. C., & Collingbridge, G. L. (Eds.). (1990). *The NMDA receptor.* New York: Oxford University Press.

FOR MORE ON EYE-WITNESS TESTIMONY

Ceci, S. J., Ross, D. F., & Toglia, M. P., (Eds.). (1989). *Perspectives on children's testimony.* New York: Springer-Verlag.

Doris, J. (Ed.). (1991). *The suggestibility of children's recollections: Implications for eyewitness testimony.* Washington, DC: American Psychological Association.

Goodman, G. S., & Bottoms, B. L. (Eds.). (1992). *Child victims, child witnesses: Understanding and improving testimony.* New York: Guilford.

Loftus, E. F. (1980). *Eyewitness testimony.* Cambridge, MA: Harvard University Press.

MacLean, H. N. (1993). *Once upon a time: A true story of memory, murder, and the law.* New York: HarperCollins.

Münsterberg, H. (1927). *On the witness stand.* New York: AMS Press.

Ross, D. F., Read, J. D., & Toglia, M. P. (Eds.). (1994). *Adult eyewitness testimony: Current trends and developments.* New York: Cambridge University Press.

Wells, G. L., & Loftus, E. A. (Eds.). (1984). *Eyewitness testimony: Psychological perspectives.* New York: Cambridge University Press.

Yarmey, A. D. (1979). *The psychology of eyewitness testimony.* New York: Free Press.

FOR MORE ON CONTRIBUTORS TO THE STUDY OF MEMORY

Allport, S. (1986). *Explorers of the black box: The search for the cellular basis of memory.* New York: W. W. Norton.

Loftus, E. F., & Ketcham, K. (1991). *Witness for the defense.* New York: St. Martin's Press.

Postman, L. (1968). Hermann Ebbinghaus. *American Psychologist, 23,* 149–157.

Suzuki Harunobu
A Young Woman in a Summer Shower
1765

THINKING AND LANGUAGE

everal years ago, an argument raged in the *Sporting News* about whether professional wrestling is an example of the *concept* "sport." During the past two decades, researchers have found that, contrary to common sense, people who are rewarded for their *creativity* may become less creative. In the near future, research in *artificial intelligence* may develop computer programs that will, finally, defeat world chess champions. And at this moment chimpanzees are communicating through *sign language* that they learned from other chimpanzees.

Each of these topics, which are discussed later in this chapter, falls within the domain of *cognitive psychology*—perhaps the most influential field of psychology in recent years. In fact, the 1950s and 1960s saw a "cognitive revolution" in which strict behaviorism was countered by increased concern with the study of both the mind and behavior (Gardner, 1985). This was inspired by an explosion of interest in the study of cognitive development, language acquisition, and computer science. **Cognitive psychology** combines William James's concern with mental processes and John B. Watson's concern with observable behavior (Massaro, 1991). Cognitive psychologists accomplish this by using techniques that permit them to infer mental processes from overt actions.

Thinking and language are different, yet interrelated, cognitive activities. Chapter 8 described the cognitive activity of memory, which permits you to store and retrieve information. Like memory, thinking and language help you profit from experience and adapt to your environment. Your ability to think and to use language will enable you to comprehend the information conveyed in this chapter and to apply some of it, perhaps, in your everyday life. After using your thinking and language abilities in reading this chapter, you will have stored, in your memory, information bearing on questions like these: How do we form concepts? What is the nature of creativity? Are there practical uses for artificial intelligence? How do children develop language? Can apes use language?

cognitive psychology
The psychological viewpoint that favors the study of how the mind organizes perceptions, processes information, and interprets experiences.

thinking
The mental manipulation of words and images, as in concept formation, problem solving, and decision making.

THINKING

Forming concepts. Solving problems. Being creative. Making decisions. Each of these processes depends on **thinking,** which is the purposeful mental manipulation of words and images. Yet, in 1925, John B. Watson, the founder of behaviorism, claimed that thinking is not a mental activity. Instead, he insisted that it was no more than subvocal speech—activity of the speech muscles that is too subtle to produce audible sounds. Margaret Floy Washburn (1916), Watson's contemporary, made a similar claim in her motor theory of thinking. There is an intuitive appeal to this claim, because you may sometimes find yourself engaging in subvocal speech—perhaps even while reading this chapter. Moreover, physiological recordings of activity in the speech muscles have shown that some people do subvocalize while thinking (McGuigan, 1970).

But this does not necessarily support Watson's claim that subvocal speech *is* thinking. Convincing evidence against Watson's claim came from a study in which a physician, Scott Smith, had himself paralyzed for half an hour by the drug curare (Smith et al., 1947). He did so to assess its possible use in the induction of general anesthesia. Because (as explained in chapter 3) curare paralyzes the skeletal muscles, including the breathing muscles, Smith was put on a respirator. After the curare wore off, he was able to report conversations that had taken place while he had been paralyzed. Because Smith was able to think and form memories while his speech muscles were paralyzed, this showed that thinking does not depend on subvocal speech.

Margaret Floy Washburn (1871–1939)
"The whole of inner life is correlated with and dependent upon bodily movement."

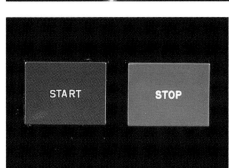

(a)   (b)

Most behaviorists did not equate thinking with subvocal speech, but they agreed with Watson's position that mental processes were not the proper object of study for psychologists. By the 1960s, though, dissatisfaction with the inability of strict behaviorism to explain memory, thinking, and certain other psychological processes contributed to the cognitive revolution. This reintroduced the study of mental processes, or "cognition," to psychology (Pribram, 1985). One of the basic cognitive processes is concept formation.

Concept Formation

If a biology teacher asked you to hold a snake, you would be more willing to hold a nonpoisonous snake than a poisonous snake. Similarly, you might be willing to eat a nonpoisonous mushroom but not a poisonous mushroom. Your actions would show that you understood the concepts "poisonous" and "nonpoisonous." A **concept** represents a category of objects, events, qualities, or relations whose members share certain features. For instance, poisonous objects share the ability to make you ill or kill you if you ingest them. During your life you have formed thousands of concepts, which provide the raw materials for your cognitive processes. Concepts enable us to respond to events appropriately and to store our memories in a more organized way (Corter & Gluck, 1992).

concept
A category of objects, events, qualities, or relations that share certain features.

Logical Concepts

How do we form concepts? Consider the case of a **logical concept,** which is formed by identifying the specific features possessed by all things that the concept applies to. "Great Lakes state" is a logical concept. Each of its members has the features of being a state and bordering one or more of the Great Lakes. The book of Leviticus in the Old Testament provides two of the oldest examples of logical concepts. Leviticus distinguishes between "clean" animals, which may be eaten, and "unclean" animals, which may not. As one example, "clean" sea animals have fins and scales, while "unclean" sea animals do not. This means that bass and trout are "clean" animals, while clams and lobsters are "unclean" animals (Murphy & Medin, 1985).

Logical concepts like those found in Leviticus, which refer to "real-life" concepts, have typically not been the kinds studied in the laboratory. Instead, laboratory studies

logical concept
A concept formed by identifying the specific features possessed by all things that the concept applies to.

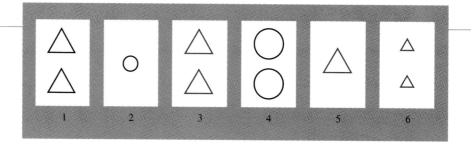

FIGURE 9.1

Concept Formation
Laboratory studies of the formation of logical concepts present subjects with a series of examples varying on specific features. The subject's task is to identify the features that compose the concept. The figures in this example can vary in size (small or large), shape (circle or triangle), color (black or magenta), or number (one or two). Given that the odd-numbered cards are members of the concept and the even-numbered cards are not, see how quickly you can identify the concept. (The answer appears at the bottom of this page.)

natural concept
A concept, typically formed through everyday experience, whose members possess some, but not all, of a common set of features.

prototype
The best representative of a concept.

Answer to question in figure 9.1: large triangles.

have generally used logical concepts created by the researcher. The use of logical concepts lets the researcher exert more-precise control over the definitions of particular concepts. An experiment on the formation of a logical concept might present subjects with a series of symbols varying in size, shape, and color. The subject's task is to discover the features that define the concept. For example, a symbol might have to be large, square, and blue to be considered an example of the particular concept. Subjects determine the features of the concept by testing hypotheses about its possible defining features on successive examples that are labeled as either positive or negative examples of it. A positive example would include the defining features of the concept (in this case, large, square, and blue), while a negative example would lack at least one of the defining features (for example, large, square, and red). Try to identify the concept presented in figure 9.1.

Natural Concepts

Is baseball a sport? How about table tennis? fishing? shuffleboard? golf? backgammon? bridge? roller derby? You have an intuitive sense of how "sportlike" each of these activities is. "Sport" is an example of a **natural concept,** a concept formed through everyday experience rather than by testing hypotheses about particular features that are common to all members of the concept. We might be unable to identify the defining features of natural concepts such as "sport." That is, natural concepts have "fuzzy borders." Such concepts include "truth" (Strichartz & Burton, 1990), "emotion" (Russell, 1991), "personality" (Broughton, 1990), and "romantic jealousy" (Sharpsteen, 1993). Even Saint Augustine, in the fifth century, noted that a natural concept can have fuzzy borders when he remarked, "I know what 'time' is until someone asks me" (Chadwick, 1986, p. 70).

The difficulty in defining natural concepts led psychologist Eleanor Rosch (1975) to propose that they are related to prototypes. A **prototype** is considered to be the best representative of a concept. According to Rosch, the more similarity between an example and a prototype, the more likely we are to consider the example to be a member of the concept represented by the prototype. A robin is a better prototype of a bird than is a penguin. Both have wings and feathers and hatch from eggs, but only the robin can fly.

In regard to the concept "sport," baseball is more prototypical than golf, which, in turn, is more prototypical than backgammon. The "fuzziness" of natural concepts can lead to arguments about whether a particular example is a member of a given concept (Medin, 1989). This was evident in 1988 in a series of letters to the editor of the *Sporting News* either supporting or opposing its coverage of Wrestlemania, the Indianapolis 500, and the World Chess Championship. Supporters considered these to be examples of the concept "sport"; opponents did not. Figure 9.2 illustrates how instances of a concept vary in how prototypical they are.

Subsequent research has indicated that we do form concepts by creating prototypes of the relevant objects, events, qualities, or relations (Nosofsky, 1991). In regard to the concept "love," one experiment found that love is better understood from the prototype perspective than from the logical concept perspective. Maternal love was considered most prototypical of "love," with romantic love, love of work, self-love, and

(a)   (b)   (c)

FIGURE 9.2

Prototypes
A prototype is the best representative of a concept. Which do you believe is the more prototypical
(a) dog? (b) tree? (c) airplane?

infatuation less so (Fehr & Russell, 1991). Reliance on prototypes can also have practical benefits. Medical students learn to diagnose medical disorders better when given
prototypes of the disorders than when given an array of specific instances of them (Bordage,
1987).

Influenced by the work of Rosch, psychologists have become more interested in
conducting laboratory studies of natural concept formation—the formation of concepts
without logically testing hypotheses about their defining features. Consider the following study of the identification of artistic styles (Hartley & Homa, 1981). Subjects who
were naive about artistic styles were shown works by the painters Manet, Renoir, and
Matisse. Later, the subjects were shown more paintings by these artists and by other
artists, without being told the identity of the artists. After viewing the second set of
paintings, the subjects accurately matched particular paintings with the styles of the
artists whose works they had seen in the first set of paintings. The subjects used the first
set to form concepts representing the styles of the three artists: a "Manet," a "Renoir,"
and a "Matisse." This could not be explained as an example of logical concept formation,
because the subjects were unable to identify a set of features that distinguished a Manet
from a Renoir from a Matisse. By reflecting for a moment, you may be able to conjure
up natural concepts for which you, too, cannot identify a set of defining features.

Problem Solving

One of the most important uses of concepts is in **problem solving,** the thought process
that enables us to overcome obstacles to reach goals. Suppose that your car will not start.
In looking for a solution to your problem, you might follow a series of steps commonly
used in solving problems (Kramer & Bayern, 1984). First, you identify the problem: My
car won't start. Second, you gather information relevant to the problem: Am I out of gas?
Is my battery dead? Are my ignition wires wet? Third, you try out a solution: I'm not out
of gas, so I'll dry off the wires. Finally, you evaluate the result: The car started, so the
wires were, indeed, wet. If the solution fails to work, you might try a different one:

problem solving
*The thought process by which an
individual overcomes obstacles to reach a
goal.*

(a)　　　　　　　(b)　　　　　　　(c)

Artistic Styles as Natural Concepts
We may be able to recognize an artistic style without necessarily being able to specify the characteristics that distinguish it from other styles. Thus, the concepts (*a*) "a Manet," (*b*) "a Renoir," and (*c*) "a Matisse" are natural concepts rather than logical concepts.

Drying off the wires didn't work, so I'll try a jump start. Problem solving commonly involves one of several strategies, including trial and error, insight, algorithms, and heuristics.

Trial and Error

A common strategy for solving problems is **trial and error,** which involves trying one possible solution after another until one works. Ivan Pavlov, though best known for his research on classical conditioning, was one of the first scientists to stress the importance of trial and error (Windholz, 1992). Even the lowly *E. coli* bacterium navigates by trial and error (Marken & Powers, 1989). For an example of trial and error in human problem solving, imagine that your psychology professor asks you to get a stopwatch from a laboratory and gives you a ring with 10 keys on it. Suppose that on reaching the laboratory you realize that you don't know which key opens the door to the laboratory. You would immediately identify the problem: finding the correct key. After assessing your situation you would probably decide to use trial and error to solve the problem. You would try one key after another until you found one that opened the door.

Though trial and error is often effective, it is not always efficient. For example, a study of novice computer programmers found that the slower learners relied too much on trial and error (Green & Gilhooly, 1990). If your professor gave you a ring with 50 keys on it, you might find it more efficient to return and ask your professor to identify the correct key rather than waste time trying one key after another. Even worse, imagine learning how to use a word processor by trying various combinations of keystrokes until you hit upon the correct ones to perform desired functions. It might take you several months, or years, to complete even a brief term paper.

Insight

In the third century B.C., the Greek physicist Archimedes was asked to solve a problem: Was King Hiero's new crown made of pure gold, or had the goldsmith cheated him by mixing cheap metals with the gold? Archimedes discovered a way to solve this problem when he noticed that if he sat in his bathtub the water level rose. After shouting "Eureka!" he decided to submerge the crown in water, measure the volume of water it displaced, and compare that volume to the volume displaced by an equal weight of pure gold. Archimedes found that the crown was, indeed, pure gold. To make this discovery, he relied on **insight,** an approach to problem solving that depends on mental manipulation of information rather than on overt trial and error.

Insight is also characterized by an "Aha!" experience—the sudden realization of the solution to a problem—as found in research by Janet Metcalfe. In a typical experiment, every 10 seconds Metcalfe asks subjects working on either insight problems or noninsight problems (such as algebra) how "warm" they feel—that is, how close they feel they are to the correct solution. She has found that those working on insight problems are less accurate, indicating that solutions to noninsight problems are incremental and predictable, whereas solutions to insight problems are sudden and unpredictable (Metcalfe & Wiebe, 1987). Nonetheless, her interpretations of her research findings have been countered by Robert Weisberg (1992), who claims that insight is a fiction—what we call insight may seem sudden and unpredictable, but it is the product of the gradual accumulation of knowledge as one works on a problem.

Can animals use insight to solve problems? The classic study of insight in animals was conducted by Gestalt psychologist Wolfgang Kohler (1887–1967) on the island of Tenerife in the Canary Islands during World War I. Kohler (1925) presented a chimpanzee named Sultan with bananas hanging from the top of his cage, well out of his reach (see figure 9.3). But his cage also contained several crates. After trying fruitlessly to reach the bananas by jumping, Sultan suddenly hit upon the solution. He piled the crates on top of one another, quickly climbed to the top, and grabbed a banana—just as the shaky structure came tumbling down.

The assumption that Sultan displayed insight was challenged more than a half century later by several behaviorists (Epstein et al., 1984). In a tongue-in-cheek study analogous to the one involving Sultan, they used food rewards to train a pigeon to first perform the separate acts of moving a tiny box to a specific location, standing on the box, and pecking a plastic, miniature banana. When later confronted with the banana hanging out of reach from the top of its cage, the pigeon at first seemed confused but then suddenly moved the box under the banana, climbed on the box, and pecked at the banana to get a food reward. The steps are illustrated in figure 9.4. According to the researchers, if a pigeon can perform supposedly insightful behavior, then perhaps insight in animals—and even in people—is no more than the chaining together of previously rewarded behaviors.

Algorithms

If you use the formula *length times width,* you will obtain the area of a rectangle. A mathematical formula is an example of a problem-solving strategy called an algorithm. An **algorithm** is a rule that, when followed step by step, assures that the solution to a problem will be found. The notion of the algorithm is an offshoot of research in computer science by cognitive psychologists Allen Newell and Herbert Simon (1972). Many computer programs rely on algorithms to process information.

But, like trial and error, an algorithm can be an inefficient means of finding the solution to a problem. To appreciate this, imagine that you are in the middle of a chess game. An algorithm for finding your best move would require tracing all possible sequences of moves from the current position. Because there is an average of 35 different moves that can be made in any single position in the middle of a chess game, you would need literally millions of years to find the best move by tracing all possible sequences of moves. Even using an algorithm to follow all possible sequences of just the next 3 moves

insight
An approach to problem solving that depends on mental manipulation of information rather than overt trial and error, and produces sudden solutions to problems.

Wolfgang Kohler (1887–1967)
"Association theorists know and recognize what one calls insight in man. . . . The only thing that follows for animal behavior is that, where it has an intelligent character, they will treat it in the same way; but not at all that the animal lacks that which is usually called insight in man."

algorithm
A problem-solving rule or procedure that, when followed step by step, assures that a correct solution will be found.

FIGURE 9.3

Insight in Apes
Kohler (1925) demonstrated that chimpanzees can use insight to solve problems. The chimpanzee Sultan found a way to reach bananas hanging out of reach without engaging in mere trial-and-error behavior.

FIGURE 9.4

Insight in a Pigeon?
This pigeon was trained to perform the separate actions of pushing a box to a designated location and climbing on the box to peck a plastic banana. When presented with the box and the banana in separate locations, the pigeon pushed the box under the banana, climbed on the box, and pecked the banana. This showed that an apparent instance of insight might be no more than performing a chain of previously learned behaviors.

Heuristics
If you had unlimited time, you could put together a 1,500-piece jigsaw puzzle by taking a piece and trying one piece after another until you found one that fit that piece. You would continue in a similar manner until you completed the puzzle. But you would perform more efficiently if you relied on heuristics. One heuristic might be, "Separate the pieces into piles of similar colors." A second might be, "Find the corner pieces first." And a third might be, "Complete the edges of the puzzle before proceeding to the center."

in the middle of a chess game would require the analysis of an average of 1.8 billion moves (Waltz, 1982). Because a formal chess match has a typical time limit of 5 hours, even world champions do not rely on algorithms. Instead, they rely on problem-solving strategies called heuristics.

Heuristics

A **heuristic** is a general principle, or "rule of thumb," that guides problem solving. Unlike an algorithm, a heuristic does not guarantee the discovery of a solution. But a heuristic can be more efficient, because it rules out many useless alternatives before they are even attempted. A chess player might rely on heuristics, such as trying to control the center of the board or trading weaker pieces for stronger ones.

Impediments to Problem Solving

Before reading on, try to solve the six problems presented in figure 9.5, in which you must use three jars to measure out exact amounts of water. If you are like most subjects, you could easily solve the first five problems but ran into difficulty with the sixth. In an early study using the water-jar problem, the subjects quickly realized that the solution to the first problem was to fill jar B, pour enough water from it to fill jar A, and then pour enough water from jar B to fill jar C twice. This left the desired amount in jar B. The subjects then found that the same strategy worked for each of the next four problems. But when they reached the sixth problem, two-thirds of them were unable to solve it. Those who failed to solve it had developed a strategy that was effective in solving previous examples but made the simple solution to problem 6 difficult to discover. In contrast, of subjects who were asked to solve only the sixth problem, few had difficulty

FIGURE 9.5

Given jars of the following sizes			Obtain the amount
A	B	C	
21	127	3	100
14	163	25	99
18	43	10	5
9	42	6	21
20	59	4	31
14	36	8	6

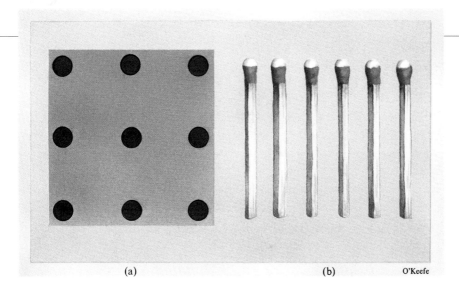

(a) (b) O'Keefe

FIGURE 9.6

Problem Solving
Test your problem-solving ability on these two brain teasers. (*a*) Connect the nine dots by drawing four straight lines without lifting your pencil. (*b*) Use the six matches to form four equilateral triangles. The solutions are given in figure 9.7. Did a mental set affect your performance on either problem?

discovering the simple solution: fill jar A and pour enough water from it to fill jar C, leaving the desired amount in jar A (Luchins, 1946).

This study demonstrated that we sometimes are hindered by a **mental set**, a problem-solving strategy that has succeeded in the past but that can interfere with solving a problem that requires a new strategy. In one study, expert computer programmers and novice computer programmers were given a programming problem that could be solved by using a simple programming strategy that is more often used by novices. The results showed that the novices were more likely to solve the problem, because the experts tried to use a more sophisticated, but ineffective, strategy that they had adopted during their careers as computer programmers. In other words, the experts had developed a mental set that blinded them to the simpler solution (Adelson, 1984).

How can you overcome a mental set? One way is to make assumptions opposite to those you normally make. This approach might have helped the expert computer programmers who were unable to solve the problem that the novices were able to solve. See if you can overcome mental sets by solving the problems in figure 9.6. Solutions to the problems appear in figure 9.7.

Besides mental sets, a second way in which past experience can impede our ability to solve problems is through **functional fixedness,** the inability to realize that a problem can be solved by using a familiar object in an unusual way. The term *functional fixedness*

heuristic
A general principle or "rule of thumb" that guides problem solving, though it does not guarantee a correct solution.

mental set
A tendency to use a particular problem-solving strategy that has succeeded in the past but that may interfere with solving a problem requiring a new strategy.

functional fixedness
The inability to realize that a problem can be solved by using a familiar object in an unusual way.

FIGURE 9.7

Solutions to the Nine-Dot and Six-Matchsticks Problems

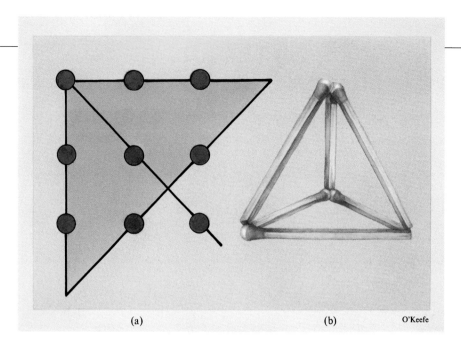

(a)   (b)   O'Keefe

FIGURE 9.8

Functional Fixedness
Maier (1931) asked subjects to tie two strings together even though they were too far apart to grasp at the same time. Functional fixedness interfered with finding some of the possible solutions, one of which is illustrated in Figure 9.9.

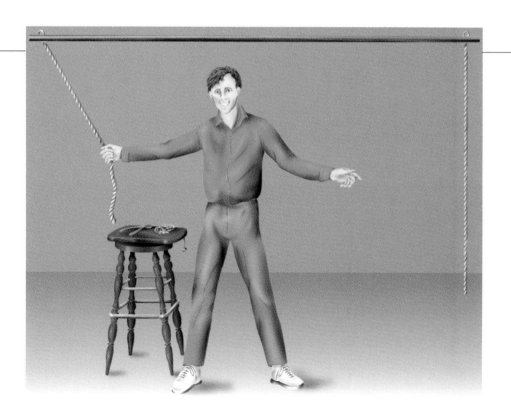

was coined by Gestalt psychologist Karl Duncker (1903–1940), who was a leader in the study of insight learning (Hilgard, 1987). The role of functional fixedness in problem solving was demonstrated in a classic study (Maier, 1931) in which each subject was asked to perform the simple task of tying together two long strings hanging from a ceiling. The problem was that the two strings were too far apart for the subject to grasp them both at the same time. As shown in figure 9.8, the room contained a variety of objects, including a table, a chair, an extension cord, and a pair of pliers.

Subjects were given 10 minutes to solve the problem. Each time the subject identified a solution, the experimenter said, "Now do it a different way." One solution was to tie the extension cord to one string, grasp the other string, pull the strings toward one another, and then tie them together. The solution that the experimenter was interested in is illustrated in figure 9.9. Subjects who discovered that solution tied the pliers to one of the strings and started it swinging like a pendulum. They then grabbed the other string, walked toward the swinging pliers, and tied the two strings together (Maier, 1931). To discover that solution, the subjects had to realize that the pliers could be used as a weight and not solely as a tool. Only 39.3 percent of the subjects discovered this solution on their own. More subjects discovered it when the experimenter provided a hint by subtly setting one of the strings in motion.

As with mental sets, functional fixedness can be overcome. One of the best ways is to change or ignore the names of familiar objects. In a study that used this technique, subjects were given a bulb, some wire, a switch, a wrench, and batteries. The subjects were told to create a circuit that would light the bulb, even though they had too little wire to complete the circuit. The solution was to use the wrench to complete it. Subjects who were told to use nonsense names such as "jod" to refer to the wrench were more likely to solve the problem than were subjects who called the wrench a "wrench" (Glucksberg & Danks, 1968). By using nonsense words to refer to the wrench, the subjects were less likely to think of it as only a mechanical tool.

Creativity

In 1950, in his final address as president of the American Psychological Association, creativity researcher J. P. Guilford expressed disappointment that of the more than 100,000 psychological studies published up until then, fewer than 200 dealt with creativity. Since Guilford's address, and influenced by the cognitive revolution, there has been a striking increase in the number of scientific studies of creativity (Barron & Harrington, 1981).

But what is creativity? Like other natural concepts, creativity cannot be defined by a specific set of features—that is, it has "fuzzy borders." We may be able to distinguish between creative and noncreative accomplishments without being able to identify exactly what makes one example creative and another noncreative. Psychologists generally define **creativity** as a form of problem solving characterized by finding solutions that are novel, as well as useful or socially valued (Mumford & Gustafson, 1988), whether artistic, scientific, or practical.

Novelty is not sufficient to demonstrate creativity (Epstein, 1991). Said the French mathematician Henri Poincaré (1948, p. 16), "To create consists precisely in not making useless combinations and in making those which are useful and which are only a small minority. Invention is discernment, choice." Thus, if you gave a monkey a canvas, a paintbrush, and a pallet of paint, it might produce novel paintings, but they would not be considered examples of creativity.

Characteristics of Creative People

What characteristics are associated with creativity? Though creative people tend to have above-average intelligence, you do not have to be an intellectual genius to be highly creative (Nicholls, 1972). For example, a study of undergraduates found that their scores on a test of intelligence and a test of creative thinking correlated .24, indicating a positive, but small, relationship between the two (Rushton, 1990a). Creative people also tend to prefer novelty, favor complexity, and make independent judgments (Barron & Harrington, 1981). Moreover, they are able to combine different kinds of thinking, being superior at combining verbal thinking with visual thinking (Kershner & Ledger, 1985) and reality-oriented thinking with imaginative thinking (Suler, 1980).

J. P. Guilford
"The subject of creative abilities had intrigued me since graduate-student days, when I realized that intelligence tests had little in them that would be likely to assess creative talent."

creativity
A form of problem solving that generates novel, socially valued solutions to problems.

FIGURE 9.9

One Solution to the Maier String
Problem

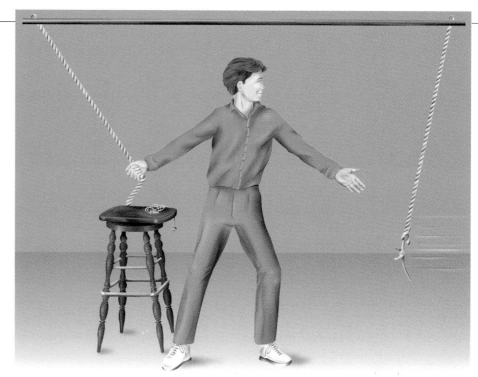

*REPRINTED COURTESY OMNI
MAGAZINE* ©1989.

"I paint what I see."

A Picasso of Pachydermia?
This elephant produces "original"
paintings. But are they examples of
creativity?

Anatomy of a Contemporary Research Study:
Can Rewarding Creative Behavior Inhibit Creativity?

Rationale
According to creativity researcher Teresa Amabile (1989), creative people are more motivated by their intrinsic interest in creative tasks than by extrinsic factors, such as fame, money, or approval. In fact, when people are presented with extrinsic reasons for performing intrinsically interesting creative tasks, they may lose their motivation to perform them. The present study by Amabile (1985) provided further evidence of this.

Method
Subjects were recruited through advertisements asking for writers to participate in a study of people's reasons for writing. Most of the respondents were undergraduate or graduate students in English or creative writing. All of the subjects were asked to write two brief poems on designated themes (the first on snow, and the second on laughter). Each subject was assigned to one of three groups. After the subjects wrote the first poem, one group completed a questionnaire that focused on intrinsic reasons for writing, such as the opportunity for self-expression, while a second group completed a questionnaire that focused on extrinsic reasons for writing, such as gaining public recognition. The third group served as a control group and was exposed to neither the intrinsic questionnaire nor the extrinsic questionnaire. Twelve experienced poets judged the creativity of the poems on a 40-point scale.

Results and Discussion
When the first poems were judged for their creativity, the three groups did not differ. However, when the second poems were judged for their creativity, the poems written by the group exposed to the questionnaire that focused on extrinsic reasons for writing were judged less creative than those written by the other two groups; the intrinsic-reasons group and the control group showed no change in creativity from the first poem to the second, but the extrinsic-reasons group showed a significant decrease. Thus, though concentrating on intrinsic reasons for creative writing did not improve creativity, concentrating on extrinsic reasons for creativity impaired it. Even the mere expectation of having one's performance evaluated will hamper creativity (Amabile, Goldfarb, & Brackfield, 1990). These findings agree with the experience of the noted American poet Sylvia Plath, who believed that her persistent writer's block was caused by her excessive concern about an extrinsic reason for writing— the recognition of her work by publishers, critics, and the public. Perhaps, given students who enjoy writing, teachers should avoid pointing out the extrinsic advantages of it, such as obtaining a better job or getting accepted into graduate school. Chapter 11 discusses theories that explain the negative effects of extrinsic motivation.

Teresa Amabile
"Intrinsic motivation is conducive to creativity, while extrinsic motivation is detrimental."

Creativity and Divergent Thinking

How many ways can you use a brick? If you could think of only such uses as "to build a house" or "to build a fireplace," you would exhibit convergent thinking. According to Guilford, **convergent thinking** focuses on finding conventional "correct" solutions to problems. If you also thought of less conventional "correct" uses for a brick, such as "to prop open a door," "to save water by putting it in a toilet tank," or "to break a window to enter your home after losing your house key," you would exhibit divergent thinking. **Divergent thinking,** a hallmark of creativity (Guilford, 1984), involves freely considering a variety of potential solutions to artistic, literary, scientific, or practical problems. The importance of divergent thinking in creativity was noted as long ago as the mid eighteenth century (Puccio, 1991).

Overemphasis on convergent thinking can impair divergent thinking and, as a result, inhibit creativity (Reddy & Reddy, 1983). One way of inducing divergent thinking is brainstorming, in which thinkers are encouraged to conjure up as many solutions as possible to a problem, though there is no guarantee that the many solutions produced by brainstorming will be superior to those produced by more-focused attempts at problem solving (Buyer, 1988).

To further appreciate the notion of divergent thinking, consider the Remote Associates Test developed by Sarnoff Mednick (1962), which presents subjects with

convergent thinking
The cognitive process that focuses on finding conventional solutions to problems.

divergent thinking
The cognitive process by which an individual freely considers a variety of potential solutions to artistic, literary, scientific, or practical problems.

FIGURE 9.10

The Remote Associates Test
Items like these are included in the Remote Associates Test (Mednick, 1962). For each of the items, find a word that is associated with all three of the given words.

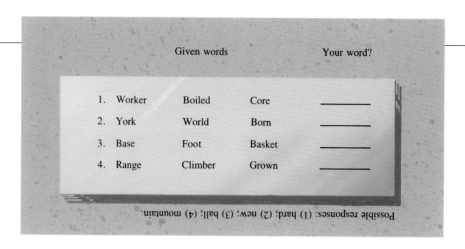

	Given words			Your word?
1.	Worker	Boiled	Core	_____
2.	York	World	Born	_____
3.	Base	Foot	Basket	_____
4.	Range	Climber	Grown	_____

Possible responses: (1) hard; (2) new; (3) ball; (4) mountain.

sets of three apparently unrelated words. For each set, the subjects are asked to find a fourth word that is related to the other three. To do so, they must use divergent thinking. For example, what word would you choose to associate with the words *piano, record,* and *baseball?* The word *player* would be one possibility. Try testing your ability to find remote associates for the items in figure 9.10. Though Mednick believes that the ability to form diverse associations is indicative of creative thinking, the Remote Associates Test is not a good predictor of creative behavior (Ochse & Van Lill, 1990).

Divergent thinking can be cultivated. It is promoted by parents who raise their children to be open to a wide variety of experiences (Harrington, Block, & Block, 1987). Even adults can learn to use divergent thinking. This idea is not lost on industrial leaders, who have their employees attend seminars so they can learn to think more creatively by engaging in divergent thinking (Basadur, Wakabayashi, & Takai, 1992). Divergent thinking is also promoted by positive emotional states. When you are angry, anxious, or depressed, you are more likely to engage in convergent thinking. Thus, teachers who evoke positive emotions in their students, and managers who evoke positive emotions in their employees, may encourage creative academic or vocational problem solving (Isen, Daubman, & Nowicki, 1987). Divergent thinking can also be impaired by a loss of sleep and the resulting feeling of fatigue (Horne, 1988), so individuals who must find a creative solution to a problem should make sure to get enough rest.

Decision Making

Each of our days is filled with decisions. They may be minor, such as deciding whether to take along a raincoat when leaving home, or major, such as deciding which college to attend. **Decision making** is a form of problem solving in which we try to make the best choice from among alternative courses of action to produce a desired outcome. In making decisions, we weigh two factors: utility and probability. Utility is the value we assign to a given outcome, and probability is our estimate of the likelihood that a given alternative will lead to a given outcome. Though we normally prefer outcomes of both high utility and high probability, we may make exceptions. Consider the decision to purchase state lottery tickets. Though a positive outcome has a low probability, that outcome has high utility (the potential to win millions of dollars), which makes purchasing a ticket an attractive decision to many people. Utility and probability influence decisions as diverse as those in gambling (Lopes, 1981), industrial purchases of computers (Joag, Mowen, & Gentry, 1990), and physicians' use of particular diagnostic tests (Moroff, 1986).

Though decision making seems like a simple matter of rationally calculating the utility and probability of particular outcomes, studies in the 1970s found that decision making is also subject to biases that can keep us from making objective decisions. Biases

Sarnoff Mednick
"All creative thinking . . . consists of the forming of mutually distant associative elements into new combinations which are useful and meet specified, or unforeseen requirements."

decision making
A form of problem solving in which one tries to make the best choice from among alternative judgments or courses of action.

in decision making have been studied most extensively by cognitive psychologists Amos Tversky and Daniel Kahneman, who have found that our decision making is often biased by our reliance on heuristics (Kahneman, 1991).

Heuristics and Decision Making

In using the **representativeness heuristic**, we assume that characteristics of a small sample are representative of its population (Kahneman & Tversky, 1973). For example, we use the representativeness heuristic when we eat at a fast-food restaurant and assume that other restaurants in the restaurant chain will be that good (or bad). Because a sample might not accurately represent its population, the use of the representativeness heuristic does not guarantee that our decisions will be correct ones. This is especially important when we are asked to make decisions while we are under emotional stress, which makes us more likely to rely on the representativeness heuristic (Shaham, Singer, & Schaeffer, 1992).

Consider a study of the effect of the representativeness heuristic in regard to the "hot hand" in basketball, in which a player makes several baskets in a row (Gilovich, Vallone, & Tversky, 1985). The study was prompted by a survey, which found that fans and players tend to believe that during a basketball game the chance of making a basket is greater following a made basket than following a miss. The researchers analyzed shooting records of the Boston Celtics and the Philadelphia 76ers. The results indicated that the chance of making a basket after a made basket was no greater than the chance following a miss. Apparently, fans and players alike incorrectly assume that brief runs of successful shooting are representative of a more general tendency to shoot well. The representativeness heuristic guides decisions as varied as choosing a lottery ticket number (Holtgraves & Skeel, 1992), buying or selling stocks on the stock market (Andreassen, 1988), and judging how entertaining a movie will be based on a brief description (Glass & Waterman, 1988).

To appreciate another kind of heuristic, answer the following question: In English, is the letter *k* more likely to be the first letter or the third letter of a word? Though the letter *k* is more likely to be the third letter, most people decide that it is more likely to be the first. This is explained by what Tversky and Kahneman (1973) call the **availability heuristic**, which is the tendency to estimate the probability of an event by how easily relevant instances of it come to mind. The more easily an instance comes to mind, the more probable we assume the event will be. But the ease with which instances come to mind might not reflect their actual probability. Instead, instances may come to mind because they are vivid, recent, or important. Thus, because it is easier to recall words that begin with *k*, such as *kick* or *kiss*, than words that have *k* as their third letter, such as *make* or *hike*, we conclude that more words have *k* as their first letter than as their third letter.

The practical effect of the availability heuristic was shown in a study in which subjects estimated the prevalence of cheating by welfare recipients. Subjects who first read a vivid case of welfare cheating overestimated its prevalence (Hamill et al., 1980). This reflects our tendency to respond to rare but vivid news reports of instances of welfare recipients living in luxurious comfort by overestimating the likelihood of welfare cheating. In fact, when we lack the information required for making an objective judgment, the availability of even a single instance of an event can make us overestimate the probability of other occurrences of that event (Lewicki, 1985). This holds true when judging the likelihood of product failures (Folkes, 1988), the success of organ transplants (McCauley et al., 1985), the effects of school desegregation (Billings & Schaalman, 1980), and the likelihood of a person's getting AIDS (Triplet, 1992).

Framing Effects

Consider the following statements: "Dr. Jones fails 10 percent of his students" and "Dr. Jones passes 90 percent of his students." Though both statements report the same reality, you might be more inclined to enroll in Dr. Jones's course after hearing the second

Amos Tversky and Daniel Kahneman
"Most people are . . . very sensitive to the difference between certainty and high probability and relatively insensitive to intermediate gradations of probability."

representativeness heuristic
In decision making, the assumption that characteristics of a small sample are representative of its population.

availability heuristic
In decision making, the tendency to estimate the probability of an event by how easily relevant instances of it come to mind.

The Availability Heuristic
Though flying in an airplane is much safer than driving in a car, vivid media reports of infrequent airplane crashes, such as this Delta Airlines crash at Dallas–Fort Worth Airport in 1985, might make us decide that flying is more dangerous than driving.

comment than you would be after hearing the first. This is an example of what Kahneman and Tversky call **framing effects,** biases introduced in the decision-making process by presenting a situation in a particular manner. Judges, lawyers, and prosecutors are aware of the framing effect in the form of "leading questions," which can unfairly influence jury decisions.

Framing effects also influence our everyday decisions. In one study (Levin, Schnittjer, & Thee, 1988), undergraduates rated the incidence of cheating at their school higher when told that "65 percent of students had cheated at some time in their college career" than when told that "35 percent of the students had never cheated." The undergraduates were also more likely to rate a medical treatment as more effective, and were more apt to recommend it to others, when they were told it had a "50 percent success rate" than when told it had a "50 percent failure rate." A similar study found that undergraduates rated meat more highly when it was labeled "75 percent lean" than when it was labeled "25 percent fat" (Levin & Gaeth, 1988). Note that in each study both statements present the same fact and differ only in how they frame the information.

To further appreciate the framing effect, consider the following study by Kahneman and Tversky (1982), in which people were asked one of the following two questions: "If you lost a pair of tickets to a Broadway play for which you paid $40, would you purchase two more?" or "If you lost $40 on your way to purchase tickets at the box office, would you still purchase tickets?" Though in each case the subject would be $40 poorer, more subjects answered yes to the second question. Thus, the way in which the questions were framed, not the amount of money the subjects would lose, influenced their decision. Their subjective evaluation was more important than the objective situation.

Artificial Intelligence

Almost 200 years ago a Hungarian inventor named Wolfgang von Kempelen toured Europe with the Maezel Chess Automaton, a chess-playing machine. The Automaton defeated almost all the people who dared play against it. Among its admirers was the noted American author Edgar Allen Poe, who wrote an essay speculating—incorrectly—on how it worked. After years of defeating one challenger after another, the Automaton's mechanism was finally revealed. Inside it was a legless Polish army officer named Worouski, who was a master chess player ("Program Power," 1981).

During the past three decades, computer scientists have developed computer programs that can play chess—instead of resorting to hiding an expert chess player inside of a computer. Computer chess programs are the offshoot of studies in **artificial intelligence (AI)**, a field founded by Nobel prize winner Herbert Simon, which integrates computer science and cognitive psychology. Those who study AI try to simulate or improve on human thinking by using computer programs. For example, computer scientists have developed a program that answers political questions as though it were either a politically liberal or a politically conservative person (Abelson, 1981).

Many AI researchers are interested in developing computer programs, so-called **expert systems,** that display expertise in specific domains of knowledge. Computer chess programs have led the way in these efforts—and have contributed to the development of cognitive psychology itself (Charness, 1992). The first computer chess programs were developed in the 1950s at Los Alamos Laboratory in New Mexico and improved steadily during the next two decades until they finally began defeating expert chess players. To date, they have not defeated a world-class player in a multiple-game match.

In 1978 David Levy, the chess champion of Scotland, got a scare when a computer chess program defeated him in the fourth game of a six-game chess match. Levy had made a $2,500 bet that no chess program could defeat him in a match. But Levy won or drew the other five games, and renewed his bet (Ehara, 1980). Despite his victory, Levy and world chess champions appear doomed to eventual defeat by computer chess programs. An ominous sign occurred in 1979 at a backgammon match in Monte Carlo, when a computer program defeated the world backgammon champion, Luigi Villa of Italy. This was the first time a computer program had defeated a human world champion in an intellectual game ("Teaching a Machine the Shades of Gray," 1981).

The computer chess program that finally defeats a world chess champion, might be a descendant of the program Belle. In 1981, at the Virginia Open Chess Tournament, Belle took fourth place in competition against master chess players ("Program Power," 1981). The only rating above master is grand master, the level achieved by the best chess players in the world. While other computer chess programs relied on algorithms—searching for all possible sequences of moves, several moves deep—to find the best move in a given position, Belle took a more sophisticated, human approach by using heuristics. Though Belle could follow potential sequences of moves four moves deep, it did not follow each sequence to its conclusion. Instead, Belle stopped following a sequence as soon as it proved inferior to another that had already been identified. This made Belle perform faster and examine more potentially effective moves in a given time span than did other computer chess programs (Peterson, 1983). Today, expert computer programs appear to be on the verge of defeating even world champion chess players (Hsu et al., 1990).

Though computer chess programs are the best known of expert systems, computer scientists have developed a variety of other systems. Among these expert systems, Mycin has helped physicians diagnose infectious diseases, Prospector has helped mining companies decide where to dig for minerals, and Dipmeter has helped analyze geological data from oil-well drillings (Davis, 1986). Expert systems can also help in the treatment of psychological disorders. The program Blue Box helps select the best kind of therapy for depressed people (Gingerich, 1990), and the program Sexpert helps in the assessment and treatment of sexual dysfunctions (Binik, Westbury, & Servan-Schreiber, 1989). Expert systems are helpful because, in narrow domains of knowledge, they can analyze data more quickly and more objectively than can human experts.

Despite the speed and objectivity with which computers process certain kinds of information, they will not process information in many everyday situations as efficiently as human beings until there are computer programs that function more like the human brain. Most computer programs perform decision-making processes chiefly serially, meaning that they perform one step at a time. In contrast, the human brain performs decision-making processes both serially and in parallel.

When information is processed in parallel, several decision-making steps occur simultaneously and are then integrated. As a consequence, the human brain can perform many kinds of thinking better than the fastest computers can. For example, AI scientists developed a cart that uses a computerized artificial vision system to find its way around obstacles. Human beings, who use both **serial processing** and **parallel**

A Computer Chess Champion?
World chess champion Gary Kasparov is shown with Deep Thought, a computer that, because of its powerful chess program, is capable of defeating all but (at least for now) the most outstanding chess players—such as Kasparov.

serial processing
The processing of information one step at a time.

parallel processing
The processing of different information simultaneously.

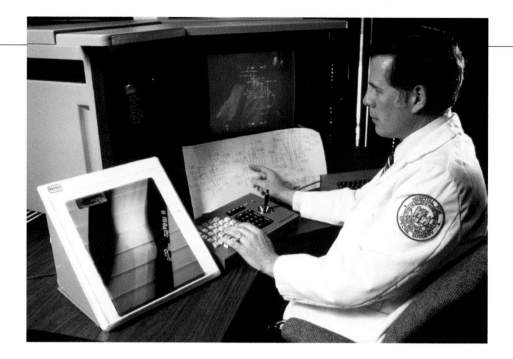

processing of the size, shape, color, brightness, location, and movement of objects can quickly find their way around obstacles. In contrast, the cart must stop after moving 3 feet so that its computer program can spend 15 minutes using serial processing just to determine its next movement (Waldrop, 1984a). Even human perception of color and form occurs in parallel before being integrated into a single perception of an object (Mordkoff, Yantis, & Egeth, 1990). So, for a computerized cart to recognize and rapidly negotiate its way around objects will require a computer program that includes some parallel processing. And it is unlikely that any computer program will defeat human world chess champions until AI researchers develop advanced chess programs that use both serial and parallel processing (Kurzweil, 1985).

LANGUAGE

Arguing about politics. Reading a newspaper. Using sign language. Each of these is made possible by **language**, a formal system of communication involving symbols—whether spoken, written, or gestured—and rules for combining them. In using language, we rely on spoken symbols to communicate through speech, written symbols to communicate through writing, and gestured symbols to communicate through sign language. We use language to communicate with other people, to store and retrieve memories, and to plan for the future.

But what makes a form of communication "language"? The world's several thousand languages share three characteristics: semanticity, generativity, and displacement. **Semanticity** is the conveying of the thoughts of the communicator in a meaningful way to those who understand the language. For example, you know that *anti-* at the beginning of a word means being against something and *-ed* at the end of a word means past action. As discussed in chapter 14, schizophrenics' language often lacks semanticity; it may be meaningless to other people.

Generativity is the combining of language symbols in novel ways, without being limited to a fixed number of combinations. In fact, each day you say or write sentences that might have never been said or written by anyone before. This generativity of language accounts for baby talk, rap music, Brooklynese, and the works of Shakespeare.

Displacement is the use of language to refer to objects and events that are not present. The objects and events may be in another place or in the past or future. Thus,

language
A formal system of communication involving symbols—whether spoken, written, or gestured—and rules for combining them.

semanticity
The characteristic of language marked by the use of symbols to convey thoughts in a meaningful way.

generativity
The characteristic of language marked by the ability to combine words in novel, meaningful ways.

displacement
The characteristic of language marked by the ability to refer to objects and events that are not present.

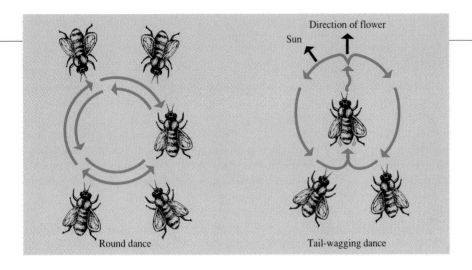

Round dance   Tail-wagging dance

you can talk about someone in China, your fifth birthday party, or who will win the World Series next year.

Language is only one form of communication. Many animals, ourselves included, can communicate without using language. For instance, a pet dog can indicate when it is hungry by pacing around its food dish, or indicate when it wants to go out by scratching at the door. But is the dog using language? No, because the only characteristic of language that the dog is displaying is semanticity. Dogs do not exhibit generativity or displacement in their communications.

Other animals also communicate without using true language. As illustrated in figure 9.11, a bee can communicate the location of nectar-containing flowers to residents of its hive. When a bee returns to its hive after finding nectar less than 50 yards away, it performs a "circle dance" on the wall of the hive. If the nectar is farther away, the bee does a "waggle dance," moving in a figure-eight pattern. The angle of the straight line in the figure-eight pattern relative to the sun indicates the direction of the nectar, and the duration of the dance indicates the distance of the nectar—the longer the duration, the farther away it is (von Frisch, 1974). But these dances are merely a form of communication, not language. They have semanticity and displacement, but they lack generativity—they are not used to indicate anything other than the location of nectar.

Consider also how monkeys use different alarm calls to signal the presence of particular kinds of predators. In one study, researchers presented monkeys with tape recordings of alarm calls that signified the presence of an eagle, a boa constrictor, or a leopard. The monkeys responded to eagle alarms by looking up, to boa constrictor alarms by looking down, and to leopard alarms by climbing up into trees (Seyfarth, Cheney, & Marler, 1980). Though monkeys use alarm calls to communicate, they do not use true language. Their calls have semanticity because they communicate the presence of a particular kind of predator, but they lack generativity and displacement. Monkeys neither combine their calls in novel ways nor use them to refer to animals that are not present.

In contrast to dogs, bees, and monkeys, human beings use true language. Without language, we would be severely limited in our ability to communicate with one another. You would not even be reading this book; books would not exist. Even the Old Testament book of Genesis recognizes the importance of language. In the story of the Tower of Babel, God punishes human beings for their pride by having them speak different languages—restricting their ability to communicate and engage in cooperative projects, such as building a tower to heaven.

The Structure of Language

English and all other languages have structures governed by rules known as **grammar.** The components of grammar include phonology, syntax, and semantics.

Phonology

All spoken languages are composed of **phonemes**—the basic sounds of a language. The study of phonemes is called **phonology.** Languages use as few as 20 and as many as 80 phonemes. English contains about 40—the number varies with the dialect. Each phoneme is represented by either a letter (such as the *o* sound in *go*) or a combination of letters (such as the *sh* sound in *should*). Words are combinations of phonemes, and each language permits only certain combinations. A native speaker of English would realize that the combination of phonemes in *cogerite* forms an acceptable word in English even though there is no such word. That person would also realize that the combination of phonemes in *klputng* does not form an acceptable word in English.

One language might not include all the phonemes found in another language, and people learning to speak a foreign language may have more difficulty pronouncing the phonemes in the foreign language that are not in their native language. For example, even after extensive conversational practice, native speakers of Japanese who learn English as adults have great difficulty in distinguishing between *r* sounds, as in *rock*, and *l* sounds, as in *lock* (Strange & Dittmann, 1984).

Because children who learn a foreign language have less difficulty pronouncing phonemes not found in their native language, there may be a critical period in childhood after which unused phonemes can no longer be pronounced correctly. Nonetheless, with special training even adults who learn a new language can improve their ability to pronounce unfamiliar phonemes. For example, if you say "the" and "theta," you will notice that there is a subtle difference between the *th* sounds. This distinction is not made by those whose native language is French. Difficulty in perceiving differences between phonemes in a foreign language is accompanied by difficulty in correctly pronouncing those phonemes. But French-speaking Canadians enrolled in a special language training program quickly learned to distinguish between the *th* sounds in words such as *the* and *theta* (Jamieson & Morosan, 1986).

Individual phonemes and combinations of phonemes form **morphemes,** the smallest meaningful units of language. Words are composed of one or more morphemes. For example, the word *book* is composed of a single morpheme. In contrast, the word *books* is composed of two morphemes: *book*, which refers to an object, and *-s*, which indicates the plural of a word. Among the common morphemes that affect the meaning of words is the *-ing* suffix, which indicates ongoing action. Note that the 40 or so phonemes in English build more than 100,000 morphemes, which in turn build almost 500,000 words. Using these words, we can create a virtually infinite number of sentences. This shows that one of the outstanding characteristics of language is, indeed, its generativity.

Syntax

In addition to rules that govern the acceptable combinations of sounds in words, languages have **syntax**—rules that govern the acceptable arrangement of words in phrases and sentences. Because you know English syntax, you would say "She ate the ice cream"

grammar
The set of rules that governs the proper use and combination of language symbols.

phoneme
The smallest unit of sound in a language.

phonology
The study of the sounds that compose languages.

morpheme
The smallest meaningful unit of language.

syntax
The rules that govern the acceptable arrangement of words in phrases and sentences.

CHAPTER NINE

but not "She the ice cream ate" (though poets do have a "license" to violate normal syntax). And syntax varies from one language to another. The English sentence *John hit Bill* would be translated into its Japanese equivalent as *John Bill hit*. This is because the normal order of the verb and the object in Japanese is the opposite of their normal order in English (Gliedman, 1983). As for adjectives, in English they usually precede the nouns they modify, while in Spanish, adjectives usually follow the nouns they modify. The English phrase *the red book* would be *el libro rojo* in Spanish. Therefore, a Spanish-speaking person learning English might say "the book red," while an English-speaking person learning Spanish might say "el rojo libro."

Semantics

Not only must words be arranged appropriately in phrases and sentences, they must be meaningful. The study of how language conveys meaning is called **semantics**. Psycholinguist Noam Chomsky has been intrigued by our ability to convey the same meaning through different phrases and sentences. Consider the sentences *The boy fed the horse* and *The horse was fed by the boy*. Both express the same meaning but use different syntax. Moreover, if either sentence were spoken in English, Chinese, or Swahili, its meaning would be the same.

To explain this ability to express the same meaning using different phrases or different languages, Chomsky distinguishes between a language's deep structure and its surface structure. The **deep structure** is the underlying meaning of a statement; the **surface structure** is the word arrangements that express the underlying meaning. Chomsky calls the rules by which languages generate surface structures from deep structures and deep structures from surface structures **transformational grammar.** In terms of transformational grammar, language comprehension involves transforming the surface structure, which is the verbal message, into its deep structure, which is its meaning. Thus, the sentences *The boy fed the horse* and *The horse was fed by the boy* are transformed into the same meaning.

The meaning of a statement depends not only on its words and their arrangement but on the social context in which the statement is made. The branch of semantics that is concerned with the relationship between language and its social context is called **pragmatics**. To appreciate the relationship between language and its social context, consider the following statement made by a student about an upcoming meal in the cafeteria: "I can't wait to have dinner tonight." If spoken in an enthusiastic voice during Thanksgiving week, the statement might mean that the student expects to enjoy a delicious turkey dinner. Yet, if spoken in a sarcastic voice during a normal school week, the same statement might mean that the student expects to be confronted by the cafeteria's notorious "mystery meat."

Consider the following embarrassing incident recounted by Elisabeth Kübler-Ross, the prominent death-and-dying researcher introduced in chapter 4. She was reared in Switzerland but lived most of her adult life in the United States. "Last evening I spent 10 minutes trying to understand what a nurse was talking about when she invited me to attend a baby shower! Why should I want to look at a bathroom constructed for infants?" (Gill, 1980, p. 201). The incident is an example of the importance of a fund of cultural and other knowledge as a basis for language pragmatics (Reeder & Shapiro, 1993).

The importance of pragmatics is also exemplified by the difficulty scientists have had in developing computer programs that comprehend speech (Levinson & Liberman, 1981). A program capable of comprehending speech would have to consider characteristics of the message, the speaker, and the situation. The difficulty in employing pragmatics in developing computer programs that can comprehend speech is illustrated in the following conversation (Gorman, 1985, p. 65) between a news reporter (R) and a computer "therapist" called Eliza (E):

R: Row, row, row your boat

E: What about your own boat?

semantics
The study of how language conveys meaning.

deep structure
The underlying meaning of a statement.

surface structure
The word arrangements used to express thoughts.

transformational grammar
The rules by which languages generate surface structures from deep structures, and deep structures from surface structures.

pragmatics
The relationship between language and its social context.

Transformational Grammar
Though the messages on this sign differ in their surface structure, with one in English and one in French, they communicate the same message—that is, they have the same deep structure.

R: Gently down the stream

E: Why do you say that?

R: Merrily, merrily, merrily, merrily

E: I am not sure I understand you fully

R: Life is but a dream

E: What does the dream suggest to you?

The Acquisition of Language

What accounts for a child's ability to progress from a crying, gurgling infant to a talkative 3-year-old? The process of language acquisition seems to be universal, with infants in all cultures acquiring language in similar ways as they pass through distinct stages (Rice, 1989). Though the timing of the stages may vary among infants, the order does not.

Stages in Language Acquisition

For the first few months after birth, infants are limited to communicating vocally through cooing, gurgling, and crying, which they use to indicate that they are content, happy, distressed, hungry, or in pain. Between 4 and 6 months of age infants enter the babbling stage. When infants babble they repeat sequences of phonemes, such as *ba-ba-ba*. Infants in all cultures begin babbling at about the same age and produce the same range of phonemes, including some that are not part of their parents' language (Roug, Landberg, & Lundberg, 1989). Even deaf infants begin babbling at the same age as infants who can hear, though their babbling is different from that of hearing infants (Oller & Eilers, 1988). The universality of the onset and initial content of babbling indicates that it is a product of the maturation of an inborn predisposition, rather than a product of experience. Nonetheless, by the age of 9 months, infants begin to show the influence of experience, as they limit their babbling to the phonemes of their family's language.

When infants are about 1 year old, they begin to say their first words. Their earliest words typically refer to objects that interest them. Thus, common early words include *dada, milk,* and *doggie*. In using words, older infants exhibit **overextension**, applying words too broadly (Behrend, 1988). Consider an infant who refers to her cat as "kitty." If she also refers to dogs, cows, horses, and other four-legged animals as "kitty," she would be exhibiting overextension. In contrast, if she refers to her cat, but to no other cats, as "kitty," she would be exhibiting **underextension**—applying words too narrowly (Caplan & Barr, 1989). As infants gain experience with objects and language, they rapidly learn to apply their words to the appropriate objects.

After learning to say single words, infants begin using them in **holophrastic speech**, which is the use of single words to represent whole phrases or sentences. For example, an infant might say "car" on one occasion to indicate that the family car has pulled into the driveway, and on another occasion to indicate that he would like to go for a ride. Between the ages of 18 and 24 months, infants go beyond holophrastic speech by speaking two-word phrases, typically including a noun and a verb in a consistent order. The infant is now showing a rudimentary appreciation of proper syntax, as in "Baby drink" or "Mommy go." Because, in the two-word stage, infants rely on nouns and verbs and leave out other parts of speech (such as articles and prepositions), their utterances are called **telegraphic speech.** As you know, to save time and money, telegrams leave out connecting parts of speech yet still communicate meaningful messages.

Until they are about 2 years old, infants use words to refer only to objects that are located in their immediate environment. At about age 2, children begin speaking sentences that include other parts of speech in addition to nouns and verbs. They also begin to exhibit displacement, as when a 2-year-old asks, "Grandma come tomorrow?" After age 2, children show a rapid increase in their vocabulary and in the length and complex-

overextension
The tendency to apply a word to more objects or actions than it actually represents.

underextension
The tendency to apply a word to fewer objects or actions than it actually represents.

holophrastic speech
The use of single words to represent whole phrases or sentences.

telegraphic speech
Speech marked by reliance on nouns and verbs, while omitting other parts of speech, including articles and prepositions.

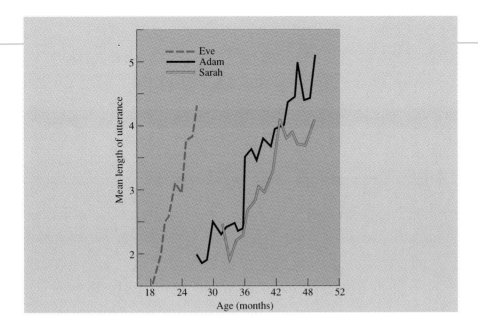

FIGURE 9.12

Mean Length of Utterance
Roger Brown (1973) used the mean length of utterance to assess the language maturity of children. The graph shows changes in the mean length of utterance for three children.

ity of their sentences. Psychologist Roger Brown (1973) invented a unit of measurement, the **mean length of utterance (MLU)**, to assess a child's level of language maturation. The MLU is calculated by taking samples of a child's statements and finding their average length in morphemes. Figure 9.12 shows that the MLU increases rapidly in early childhood, though there is some variability from one child to another. The MLU is a better predictor of overall language ability at younger ages than in later childhood (Scarborough et al., 1991).

The increased sophistication that young children show in their use of language is partly attributable to their application of language rules, which they learn from listening to the speech of those around them. From the day of their birth, infants are exposed to sophisticated language. In fact, studies have found that, contrary to popular impressions, staff members in hospital nurseries do not rely solely on baby talk and soothing sounds when speaking to newborn infants. Instead, staff members spend much of the time speaking to the infants with normal, though perhaps simple, phrases and sentences (Rheingold & Adams, 1980).

The language rules that children learn are strongly influenced by their mothers' speech (Hoff-Ginsberg, 1986). But English has many exceptions to grammatical rules, which might explain the phenomenon of **overregularization**—the application of grammatical rules without making necessary exceptions (Marcus et al., 1992). At first, children using the past tense will, correctly, say words such as *did, went,* and *brought,* which violate the *-ed* rule for forming the past tense. They learn these specific words by hearing the speech of older children and adults. But as children learn the *-ed* rule, they say words such as *doed, goed,* or *bringed.* Later, when they realize that grammatical rules have exceptions, they learn not to apply the *-ed* rule to irregular verbs, and again say *did, went,* and *brought* (Kolata, 1987).

How do we know that infants learn rules, rather than a series of specific instances of correct grammar? One source of evidence is a study by Jean Berko (1958), who reasoned that if children use correct grammar when confronted with words they have never heard, then they must be relying on rules, not rote memory. To test her assumption, Berko developed the "Wugs test," which included drawings of imaginary creatures called "wugs." Berko found that children would, indeed, apply grammatical rules to novel words. For example, when shown a picture identified as a "wug" and then a picture with two of them, infants completed the statement "There are two _____" with the word *wugs.* This indicates that they have learned to use the *-s* ending to indicate the plural.

mean length of utterance (MLU)
The average length of spoken statements, used as a measure of language development in children.

Jean Berko Gleason
"Theorists of language have been at odds with one another for the last quarter century over questions having to do with the nature of language and the possible prerequisites of its development."

overregularization
The application of a grammatical rule without making necessary exceptions to it.

The Wild Boy of Aveyron
Francois Truffaut's movie *The Wild Child* portrayed the case of Victor, the so-called Wild Boy of Aveyron. After living for years in the woods without human contact, Victor failed to develop normal language despite intensive efforts to teach him. This provided evidence that there might be a critical period for language development that ends before adolescence. The photo shows Victor learning to identify common objects.

Is There a Critical Period for Language Acquisition?

In 1800 a boy who appeared to be about 12 years old emerged from a forest near Aveyron, France, apparently having survived for many years without human contact (Shattuck, 1980). The boy, named Victor by physician Jean Itard, became known as the "Wild Boy of Aveyron." Though Itard made an intensive effort to teach him French, Victor only learned to say "lait" (milk). Similar reports have provided evidence of a **critical period** for language acquisition that extends from infancy to adolescence, during which language learning is optimal (Hurford, 1991). If people are not exposed to a language until after childhood, they might never become proficient in speaking it. The critical period also seems to affect the acquisition of sign language (Mayberry & Eichen, 1991) and second languages (Johnson & Newport, 1989).

A more recent and well-documented case described a girl named Genie, who had been raised in isolation. In 1970, 13-year-old Genie was discovered by welfare workers in a room in which her father had kept her restrained in a harness and isolated from social contact—and language—since infancy. He communicated with her by barking and growling, and beat her whenever she made a sound. By 1981, more than a decade after being returned to society and undergoing intensive language training, Genie had acquired only a rudimentary ability to speak telegraphically and failed to use proper syntax. Like Victor, Genie may have been past her critical period for language acquisition when she returned to society (Pines, 1981).

Though the cases of Victor and Genie support the view that there is a critical period for language acquisition, you may recall from chapter 2 that it is unwise to generalize too freely from case studies. For example, some children who have lived for years in social isolation, such as Kaspar Hauser, who was discovered in Nuremberg, Germany, in 1828 at age 17, have been able to learn language after reaching adolescence (Simon, 1979). Perhaps other factors could account for the findings in the cases of Victor and

critical period
A period in childhood when experience with language produces optimal language acquisition.

Genie. For example, suppose that Victor and Genie were born with brain disorders that interfered with their ability to acquire language. Even if they had been reared from birth in normal family settings, they might still have failed to acquire mature language.

Perhaps a stronger line of research on critical periods is one concerned with adults who learn second languages. Second languages become progressively more difficult to learn as we get older. Support for this came from a study in which older Korean and Chinese immigrants to the United States found it more difficult to learn English than did their younger fellow immigrants—even though the groups were intellectually equal (Johnson & Newport, 1989). Nonetheless, this finding must be viewed with caution in light of the many other factors that could account for differences in the ease with which younger and older immigrants learn a new language.

Theories of Language Acquisition

In the thirteenth century Frederick II, emperor of the Holy Roman Empire, reportedly tested the popular belief that even if infants were not exposed to language, they would eventually begin speaking a recognizable classical language, such as Greek, Latin, or Hebrew. Frederick ordered that several newborn infants be raised without any exposure to speech. But the infants died of illnesses before reaching childhood, bringing the study to a premature halt (Pines, 1981). Though current ethical standards would prevent such a study today, language researchers still debate this question: Is language acquired solely through learning, or is it strongly influenced by the maturation of an inherited predisposition to develop language? Those who favor the learning position assume that if it were possible to raise two infants together with no exposure to language, they would not develop true language. In contrast, those who favor the view that language emerges from an inherited predisposition assume that the two infants might develop a rudimentary form of language marked by semanticity, generativity, and displacement. According to this position, learning normally determines only which language an infant will speak, whether English, French, or Navajo.

B. F. Skinner (1957) claimed that language is acquired solely through learning, chiefly through the positive reinforcement of appropriate speech. For example, a 1-year-old child might learn to say "milk" because her parents give her milk and praise her when she says "milk." Similarly, a 2-year-old child named Jane might be given a cookie and praise for saying "Give Jane cookie" but not for saying "Jane cookie give." As you can see, Skinner assumed that vocabulary and grammar are learned through positive reinforcement. In a study supportive of Skinner's position, two groups of infants between 2 and 7 months old were positively reinforced for producing different phonemes. The infants were reinforced by smiles, *tsk* sounds, and light stroking of the abdomen. One group was reinforced for making vowel sounds, while the other group was reinforced for making consonant sounds. The infants responded by increasing their production of the phonemes that were reinforced. This study showed that positive reinforcement can affect language acquisition (Routh, 1969). Of course, it does not indicate that language is acquired *solely* through learning.

Albert Bandura (1977), the influential cognitive-behavioral psychologist, stresses the role of observational learning in language acquisition. He assumes that children develop language primarily by imitating the vocabulary and grammatical constructions used by their parents and others in their everyday lives. In a study that supported his position, adults replied to statements made by 2-year-old children by purposely using slightly more-complex syntax than they normally would. After 2 months, the children had developed more-complex syntax than did children who had not been exposed to the adult models (Nelson, 1977). Additional support for the effect of modeling comes from findings that 2-year-olds whose parents read to them acquire language more rapidly than do 2-year-olds whose parents do not (Whitehurst et al., 1988). Yet we cannot discount the possibility that other differences between the two groups of parents produce this effect.

The assumption that language is acquired solely through learning has been challenged by the linguist Noam Chomsky (1986) and his followers. Chomsky insists that infants are born with the predisposition to develop language. He believes they inherit a language acquisition device—a brain mechanism that makes them sensitive to phonemes, syntax, and semantics. In analyzing the interactions of parents and children, Chomsky has found that children progress through similar stages and learn their native languages without formal parental instruction. Children say things that adults never say, and their parents do not positively reinforce proper grammar (or correct improper grammar) in any consistent manner. Modeling, too, cannot explain all language learning, because observations of children show that they vary greatly in the extent to which they imitate what their parents say (Snow, 1981).

What evidence is there to support Chomsky's position? One source of evidence is the universality in the basic design features of language and the stages of language acquisition (Miller, 1990), which indicates that the tendency to develop language is inborn. Studies of deaf children support Chomsky's position. One study observed deaf children who were neither rewarded for using sign language nor exposed to a model who used it. Nonetheless, the children spontaneously developed their own gestural system, in which they communicated by using signs with the characteristics of true language (Goldin-Meadow & Mylander, 1983).

Despite the evidence favoring language as innate and contradicting learning as an explanation for language acquisition, research has provided some support for the learning position (Stemmer, 1990). One study tested the claim made by those who favor Chomsky's position that adults typically ignore children's speech errors and fail to correct their ungrammatical statements. The study found that language acquisition does depend on feedback provided by adults who correct specific instances of improper grammar. Adults do so by repeating a child's grammatically incorrect statements in grammatically correct form or by asking the child to clarify his or her statements (Bohannon & Stanowicz, 1988).

It seems that the positions of Chomsky, Skinner, and Bandura must be integrated to explain how language is acquired. We appear to be born with a predisposition to develop language, which provides us with an innate sensitivity to grammar. But we may learn our specific language, including formal aspects of its grammar, mainly through operant conditioning and observational learning.

The Relationship between Language and Thinking

In his novel *1984*, George Orwell (1949) envisioned a totalitarian government that controlled its citizens' thoughts by controlling their language. By adding, removing, or redefining words, the government used *Newspeak* to ensure that citizens would not think rebellious thoughts against their leader, "Big Brother." For example, in Newspeak the word *joycamp* was added to refer to a forced labor camp. And the word *free* was redefined to refer only to statements about physical reality, such as *the dog is free from lice*, rather than to statements relating to political freedom. Even democratic government officials will, at times, resort to euphemisms reminiscent of Newspeak. For example, to reduce public outrage about deceptive government practices, American officials coined the word *misinformation* to replace the word *lying*.

The Linguistic Relativity Hypothesis

Orwell's view of the influence of language on thought was shared by the linguist-anthropologist Benjamin Lee Whorf (1897–1941), who expressed it in his **linguistic relativity hypothesis,** which assumes that our perception of the world is determined by the particular language we speak. Whorf (1956) pointed out that the Eskimo language has several words for snow (such as words that distinguish between falling snow and fallen snow), while the English language has only one. According to the linguistic relativity hypothesis, the variety of words in the Eskimo language causes people who speak it to perceive differences in snow that people who speak English do not.

Critics argue that, on the contrary, thinking determines language. Perhaps the greater importance of snow in Eskimo culture led them to coin several words for snow,

Modeling Language
The modeling of language by parents is an important factor in the acquisition of a particular language by the child.

Noam Chomsky
"We should expect heredity to play a major role in language because there is really no other way to account for the fact that children learn to speak in the first place."

linguistic relativity hypothesis
The assumption that one's perception of the world is molded by one's language.

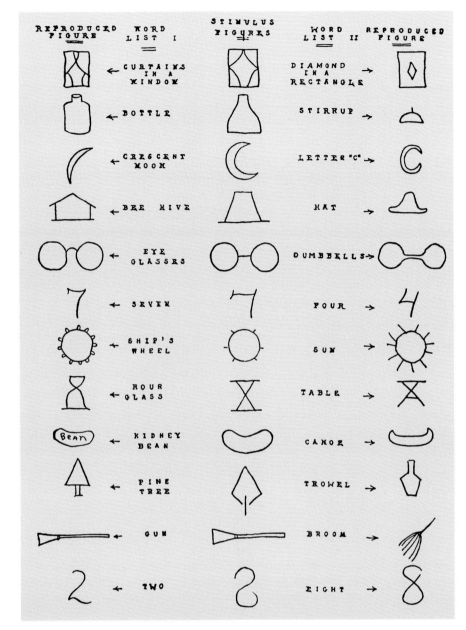

FIGURE 9.13

The Effect of Labels on Recall
Subjects were shown the pictures in the middle column with one of two different labels. When later asked to draw what they had seen, the subjects drew pictures that were consistent with the labels, not with the pictures (Carmichael, Hogan, & Walter, 1932). This indicates that language can affect how we think about the world, even though it might not affect how we perceive the world.

George Orwell (1903–1950)
"Newspeak was designed not to extend but to *diminish* the range of thought, and this purpose was indirectly assisted by cutting the choice of words down to a minimum."

The Linguistic Relativity Hypothesis
According to Whorf's linguistic relativity hypothesis, a forest ranger who has learned the names of many kinds of trees would, as a consequence, perceive more differences between trees than would people who know the names of few trees.

each referring to a different kind. Moreover, English-speaking people to whom snow is important, such as avid skiers, use different adjectives to describe different kinds of snow. Their ability to distinguish between crusty, powdery, and granular snow indicates that even English-speaking people can perceive wide variations in the quality of snow. Moreover, the number of words for snow in the Eskimo language may have been exaggerated in the early reports that influenced Whorf and other linguistic relativity theorists (Pullum, 1991).

What does formal research have to say about the linguistic relativity hypothesis? In an early study bearing on Whorf's hypothesis (Carmichael, Hogan, & Walter, 1932), subjects were presented with ambiguous drawings of objects that were given either of two labels. As shown in figure 9.13, when later asked to draw the objects, the subjects

"Love it! 'People of smoke' instead of 'Smokers.'"

drew pictures that looked more like the object that had been named than like the object they had seen. This supported Whorf's hypothesis, at least in that language appeared to influence the objects that the subjects recalled. Another topic of interest related to Whorf's hypothesis is the possible influence of language on the perception of colors.

Anatomy of a Classic Research Study:
Does Language Influence Our Perception of Colors?

Rationale

Eleanor Rosch conducted a study to test whether language influences the perception of colors. She hypothesized that if the linguistic relativity hypothesis were correct, people who speak a language that has many color words would perceive colors differently than would people who speak a language with few color words.

Method

Rosch visited the Dani people of New Guinea, who live in a Stone Age culture. She found that the Dani language has two basic color words: mili for dark, cool colors, and mola for light, warm colors. In contrast, English has eleven basic color words: black, white, red, green, yellow, blue, brown, purple, pink, orange, and gray. To describe these colors, the Dani use relatively long phrases. Rosch wondered whether these differences in language would be associated with differences in the perception of colors. She decided to test this by using "focal" colors, which are considered the best representatives of each of the colors (for example, "fire-engine red" for red), and nonfocal colors.

Method

The subjects, Dani and American, were given a series of trials on which they were first shown a colored plastic chip for 5 seconds. After another 30 seconds, they were asked to select the chip from among 160 colored chips.

Results and Discussion

Both the English-speaking subjects and the Dani subjects performed better when the chip to be recalled was a focal color than when it was a nonfocal color. This contradicted Whorf's hypothesis, because the results indicated that though the Dani use only two color names, they are as capable as English-speaking people of perceiving all the focal colors in the English language. Perhaps we are physiologically prepared to perceive these focal colors, regardless of whether our language takes special note of them.

Linguistic Relativity and Sexist Language

Though language does not *determine* how we think about the world, it might *influence* how we think about the world (Hoffman, Lau, & Johnson, 1986). This is the basis of the current concern about the traditional use of masculine pronouns, such as *his* and *him*, to refer to persons when no sexual identification is intended. Critics of this practice point out that it makes people think that such statements refer primarily to males (Hyde, 1984). Perhaps repeated exposure to such use of the male pronoun to refer to both males and females promotes the belief that certain sex-neutral activities are more suitable for males than for females.

This assumption has been supported by empirical research. Undergraduates in one study were more likely to assume that the antecedent to the supposedly neutral pronoun *he* was a male (Hamilton, 1988). In another study, students read sentences and described images that came to mind. When subjects read sentences with the pronoun *he*, they reported a disproportionate number of male images (Gastil, 1990). Because our use of language can affect the way we think about gender roles, as well as other aspects of everyday life, the linguistic relativity hypothesis may have some merit, as long as it is used to recognize that though language influences thinking, it does not determine it (Hunt & Agnoli, 1991).

THINKING ABOUT *Psychology*

CAN APES USE LANGUAGE?

In the early seventeenth century, the philosopher René Descartes argued that language was the critical feature that distinguished human beings from other animals. Interest in teaching animals cognitive skills, such as language, that normally are associated with human beings was stimulated by the case of "Clever Hans," a horse who impressed onlookers by solving arithmetic problems in Germany in the early twentieth century. Hans was trained to count out the answers to arithmetic problems by tapping one of his hooves until he reached the correct answer. He counted anything present, including persons, hats, or umbrellas. But a psychologist named Oskar Pfungst showed that Hans stopped counting when he noticed tiny movements of his questioner's head, which cued the initiation and termination of counting. When the questioner knew the answer, Hans was correct almost all of the time. But when the questioner did not know the answer, Hans was wrong all of the time. So, Hans may have been clever, but he had no idea how to perform arithmetic (Davis & Memmott, 1982).

Clever Hans
An audience watches Clever Hans perform arithmetic calculations in Berlin in 1904.

As interest in teaching animals to perform arithmetic waned, interest in teaching them language grew. As you read at the beginning of the chapter, animals as diverse as bees, dogs, and monkeys can communicate in limited, stereotyped ways. But they do not use true language, which is characterized by semanticity, generativity, and displacement. Research on language learning in dolphins (Herman, Morrel-Samuels, & Pack, 1990) and sea lions (Gisiner & Schusterman, 1992) is promising, but has yet to provide conclusive findings. A much larger body of research supports the possibility that there might be at least one kind of nonhuman animal capable of acquiring true language—the ape.

STUDIES OF LANGUAGE IN APES

More than 50 years ago, Winthrop and Luella Kellogg (1933) published a book about their experiences raising a chimpanzee named Gua with their infant son, Donald. Even after being exposed to speech as a member of the family, Gua could not speak a single

Washoe
Allen and Beatrix Gardner taught Washoe to use American sign language. Here Washoe is signing "sweet" in response to a lollipop.

Nim Chimpsky
According to Herbert Terrace, even his own chimpanzee, Nim Chimpsky, uses sign language only in response to cues from his trainers. The photo shows Nim learning the sign for "drink."

Koko
While most ape-language researchers have used chimpanzees as subjects, Francine Patterson has taught sign language to the gorilla Koko. Here Koko is signing "love" in response to her pet kitten, All Ball.

word. Another couple, Cathy and Keith Hayes (Hayes, 1951), had only slightly better results with Viki, a chimpanzee they, too, raised as a member of their family. Despite their intensive efforts over a period of several years, Viki learned to say only four words: *mama, papa, cup,* and *up.* The Hayeses concluded that the vocal anatomy of apes is not designed for producing speech.

In 1925 the primatologist Robert Yerkes, wondering whether apes have lots to say but no way of saying it, suggested teaching them to use sign language instead of speech. His suggestion was not carried out until 1966, when Allen and Beatrix Gardner (1969) of the University of Nevada began teaching American Sign Language (ASL) to a 1-year-old chimpanzee named Washoe. They raised Washoe in a trailer next to their house. To encourage her to use ASL, they never spoke in her presence—instead, they signed to each other and Washoe using simple words about various objects and everyday events. They also asked Washoe simple questions, praised her correct utterances, and tried to comply with her requests, just as parents do with young children. After 4 years of training, Washoe had a repertoire of 132 signs, which she used to name objects and to describe qualities of objects. The Gardners later replicated their work with four other apes, teaching each to use sign language (Gardner, 1992).

Washoe also displayed the ability to generalize her signs to refer to similar things. For example, she used the sign for *open* to refer to doors on a car, a house, and a refrigerator. Washoe even seemed to show an important characteristic of true language—generativity. On seeing a swan for the first time, Washoe made the sign for *water bird.* And, in a chimpanzee colony in Washington State, Washoe taught ASL to a young chimpanzee named Loulis, whom she had "adopted" (Cunningham, 1985). After 5 years, Loulis had acquired a vocabulary of more than 50 ASL signs, which he could have learned only from Washoe and other chimpanzees, since all human signing was forbidden when Loulis was present (Gardner, 1992).

During the past two decades several other apes have been taught to use sign language or other forms of language. Ann and David Premack taught a laboratory chimpanzee named Sarah to use plastic chips of different shapes and colors to represent words (Premack, 1971). Sarah learned to answer questions by arranging the chips in different orders on a board to form sentences. Duane Rumbaugh taught a chimpanzee named Lana to use a computer to create sentences by pressing large keys marked by lexigrams—geometric shapes representing particular words (Rumbaugh, Gill, & von Glasersfeld, 1973). Lana formed sentences by pressing keys in a particular order. Lana's language was called "Yerkish" in honor of Robert Yerkes. When Lana made grammatically correct requests, she was rewarded with food, toys, music, or other things she enjoyed.

CONTROVERSY ABOUT APE-LANGUAGE RESEARCH

Have Washoe, Sarah, and Lana learned to use true language? Do they exhibit semanticity, generativity, and displacement? That is, can they communicate meaningfully, create novel combinations of signs, and refer to objects that are not present? Columbia University psychologist Herbert Terrace, who once held that apes use language, says no (Terrace et al., 1979). Terrace taught a chimpanzee named Nim Chimpsky to use sign language. (Nim was named after Noam Chomsky, who believes that apes cannot learn true language.) After 5 years of training, Nim had mastered 125 signs. At first, Terrace assumed that Nim had learned true language. But after analyzing videotapes of conversations with Nim and videotapes of other apes that had been taught sign language, he concluded that Nim and the other apes did not display true language.

On what did Terrace base his conclusion? He found that apes merely learned to make signs, arrange forms, or press computer keys in a certain order to obtain rewards. In other words, their use of language was no different from that of a pigeon that learns to peck a sequence of keys to get food rewards. No researcher would claim that the pigeon is using language. So, the ability of an ape to produce a string of words does not

Austin and Sherman
Duane Rumbaugh and Sue Savage-Rumbaugh have trained two chimpanzees, Austin and Sherman, to use computer keyboards to communicate with each other. Here Sherman responds to Austin's request for bread by obtaining a piece of bread from a tray and handing it to him.

Duane Rumbaugh and Sue Savage-Rumbaugh
"Pygmy chimpanzees may employ a sort of primitive language in the wild."

Kanzi
To date, Kanzi is the ape who has shown the most sophisticated use of language. Here he is using Yerkish, a language consisting of geometric symbols.

indicate that the ape has learned to produce a sentence. Terrace also claims that the apparent generativity of ape language might be a misinterpretation of their actions. For example, Washoe's apparent reference to a swan as a "water bird" might have been a reference to two separate things—water and a bird.

As additional evidence against ape language, Terrace claims that many instances of allegedly spontaneous signing by chimpanzees are actually responses to subtle cues from trainers. Terrace found that Nim communicated primarily in response to prompting by his trainer or by imitating signs recently made by his trainer. Thus, he did not use language in an original or spontaneous way, and his signs were simply gestures prompted by cues from his trainer that produced consequences he desired—a kind of operant conditioning (Terrace, 1985).

Terrace's attack has not gone unchallenged. Francine Patterson taught a gorilla named Koko to use more than 300 signs ("Ape Language," 1981). Koko even displays generativity, as in referring to a zebra as a "white tiger." Patterson criticizes Terrace for basing his conclusions on his work with Nim and on isolated frames he has examined from films of other apes using ASL. She claims that Nim's inadequate use of language may stem from his being confused by having sixty different trainers, which could account for Nim's failure to use sign language in a spontaneous way. In contrast, Patterson reported that Koko had only one primary trainer and used signs more spontaneously than did Nim. For example, Koko responded to a velvet hat by signing "that soft" (Patterson, Patterson, & Brentari, 1987).

In recent years, the strongest evidence in support of ape language comes from studies by Duane Rumbaugh and Sue Savage-Rumbaugh of Georgia State University and the Yerkes Language Research Center. They trained two chimpanzees, Austin and Sherman, to communicate through Yerkish, the language used earlier by Lana. Austin and Sherman use language in a more sophisticated way than previous chimpanzees. In one study, Austin, Sherman, and Lana were taught to categorize three objects (an

"Remember, don't talk sex, politics, or religion."

orange, a beancake, and a slice of bread) as "edible" and three objects (a key, a stick, and a pile of coins) as "inedible." When given other objects, Austin and Sherman, but not Lana, were able to categorize them as edible or inedible. Perhaps Lana could not learn this task because she had been trained to use language to associate labels with specific objects rather than to understand the concepts to which the labels referred (Savage-Rumbaugh et al., 1980).

Even when housed in different rooms, Austin and Sherman can request objects from each other. This was demonstrated by giving one of the chimpanzees a box from which he could obtain food or drink only by using a tool located in the other chimpanzee's room. The chimpanzee in the room with the food indicated the tool he needed by striking a particular series of keys on a computer keyboard. The chimpanzee in the room with the tools responded by passing that tool to the other chimpanzee (Marx, 1980).

More recently, Sue Savage-Rumbaugh and her colleagues (1986) described their work with two pygmy chimpanzees, Kanzi and Mulika, who have achieved language ability superior to that of previous apes. Kanzi learned Yerkish spontaneously by observing people and other chimpanzees pressing appropriate symbols on a keyboard (Savage-Rumbaugh, 1990). He can also identify symbols referred to in human speech. Previous apes depended on their particular language system to comprehend human communications. Kanzi can even form requests in which other individuals are either the agent or the recipient of action. Previously, apes such as Nim made spontaneous requests only in which they were the targets of a suggested action. Moreover, Kanzi shows displacement, using lexigrams to refer to things that are not present (Savage-Rumbaugh, 1987).

Perhaps future studies using pygmy chimpanzees will succeed where others have failed in demonstrating convincingly that apes are capable of using true language. But even if apes can use true language, no ape has gone beyond the language level of a 3-year-old child. Is that the upper limit of ape language ability, or is it just the upper limit using current training methods? Research during the next decade may provide the answer. We do know that apes are capable of more-complex communication than simply grunting to convey crude emotional states.

THINKING

Thinking is the purposeful mental manipulation of words and images. Thinking depends on concepts, which are categories of objects, events, qualities, or relations whose members share certain features. A logical concept is formed by identifying specific features possessed by all members of the concept. A natural concept is formed through everyday experiences and has "fuzzy borders." The best representative of a concept is called a prototype.

One of the most important uses of concepts is in problem solving, the thought process that enables us to overcome obstacles to reach goals. A basic method of solving problems is trial and error, which involves trying one possible solution after another until finding one that works. The problem-solving strategy called insight depends on the mental manipulation of information. An algorithm is a rule that, when followed step by step, assures that the solution to a problem will be found. A heuristic is a general principle that guides problem solving but does not guarantee the discovery of a solution. A mental set is a problem-solving strategy that has succeeded in the past but that can interfere with solving a problem that requires a new strategy. Our past experience can also impede problem solving through functional fixedness, the inability to realize that a problem can be solved by using a familiar object in an unusual way.

Creativity is a form of problem solving characterized by novel solutions that are also useful or socially valued. Creative people tend to have above-average intelligence and are able to integrate different kinds of thinking. Creative people are more motivated by intrinsic interest in creative tasks than by extrinsic factors. Creativity also depends on divergent thinking, in which a person freely considers a variety of potential solutions to a problem.

In decision making we try to make the best choice from among alternative courses of action. Our decisions are influenced by the factors of utility and probability. In using the representativeness heuristic, we assume that characteristics of a small sample are representative of its population. In using the availability heuristic, we estimate the probability of an event by how easily relevant instances of it come to mind. We are also subject to framing effects, which are biases introduced in the decision-making process by presenting a situation in a certain manner.

Artificial intelligence is a field that integrates computer science and cognitive psychology to try to simulate or improve on human thinking by using computer programs. Computer programs called expert systems display expertise in specific domains of knowledge. Computer scientists are trying to develop programs that use parallel information processing, as well as serial information processing.

LANGUAGE

True language is characterized by semanticity, generativity, and displacement. The rules of a language are its grammar. Phonemes are the basic sounds of a language, and morphemes are its smallest meaningful units. A language's syntax includes rules governing the acceptable arrangement of words and phrases. Semantics is the study of how language conveys meaning. Noam Chomsky calls the underlying meaning of a statement its deep structure and the words themselves its surface structure. We translate between the two structures by using transformational grammar. The branch of semantics concerned with the relationship between language and its social context is called pragmatics.

Infants in all cultures progress through similar stages of language development. They begin babbling between 4 and 6 months of age and say their first words when they are about 1 year old. At first they use holophrastic speech, in which single words represent whole phrases or sentences. Between the ages of 18 and 24 months, infants begin speaking two-word sentences and use telegraphic speech. As infants learn their language's grammar, they may engage in overregularization, in which they apply grammatical rules without making necessary exceptions. There might be a critical period for language acquisition, extending from infancy to adolescence. B. F. Skinner and Albert Bandura believe that language is acquired solely through learning, while Chomsky believes we have an innate predisposition to develop language.

Benjamin Lee Whorf's linguistic relativity hypothesis assumes that our view of the world is determined by the particular language we speak. But research has shown that though language can influence thinking, it does not determine it.

THINKING ABOUT PSYCHOLOGY: CAN APES USE LANGUAGE?

Researchers have taught apes to communicate by using sign language, form boards, and computers. The most well known of these apes include the gorilla Koko and the chimpanzees Washoe, Sarah, and Lana. Herbert Terrace, the trainer of Nim Chimpsky, claims that apes have not learned true language; instead, they have learned to give responses that lead to rewards, just as pigeons learn to peck at keys to obtain food. Francine Patterson, Duane Rumbaugh, and Sue Savage-Rumbaugh have countered by providing evidence that the apes have, indeed, learned true language characterized by semanticity, generativity, and displacement.

IMPORTANT CONCEPTS

MAJOR CONTRIBUTORS

RECOMMENDED READINGS

FOR MORE ON COGNITION

Altarriba, J. (Ed.). (1993).
  Cognition and culture: A cross-cultural approach to psychology.
  New York: Elsevier.
Baars, B. J. (1986). *The cognitive revolution in psychology.* New York: Guilford.
Ellis, H. C., & Hunt, R. R. (1993). *Foundations of cognitive psychology* (5th ed.). Madison, WI: Brown & Benchmark.
Gardner, H. (1985). *The mind's new science: A history of the cognitive revolution.* New York: Basic Books.
Mayer, R. E. (1990). *The promise of cognitive psychology.* Lanham, MD: University Press of America.
Posner, M. I. (Ed.). (1989). *Foundations of cognitive science.* Cambridge, MA: MIT Press.
Topping, D. M., Crowell, D. C., & Kobayashi, V. N. (eds.). (1989). *Thinking across cultures.* Hillsdale, NJ: Earlbaum.
Varela, F., Thompson, E., & Rosch, E. (1991). *The embodied mind: Cognitive science and human experience.* Cambridge, MA: MIT Press.
Washburn, M. F. (1916/1973). *Movement and mental imagery.* New York: Arno Press.

FOR MORE ON CONCEPT FORMATION

Bolton, N. (1977). *Concept formation.* New York: Pergamon.
Harnad, S. (1990). *Categorical perception.* New York: Cambridge University Press.

Lakoff, G. (1987). *Women, fire, and dangerous things.* Chicago: University of Chicago Press.
Markman, E. (1989). *Categorization and naming in children.* Cambridge, MA: MIT Press.
Neisser, U. (Ed.). (1987). *Concepts and conceptual development.* New York: Cambridge University Press.
Rosch, E., & Lloyd, B. L. (Eds.). (1978). *Cognition and categorization.* Hillsdale, NJ: Erlbaum.
Smith, E. E., & Medin, D. L. (1981). *Categories and concepts.* Cambridge, MA: Harvard University Press.
Taylor, J. R. (1989). *Linguistic categorization: Prototypes in linguistic theory.* New York: Oxford University Press.
Tsohatsidis, S. (1990). *Meanings and prototypes: Studies in linguistic categorization.* New York: Routledge.

FOR MORE ON PROBLEM SOLVING

Bransford, J. D., & Stein, B. S. (1993). *The ideal problem solver: A guide to improving thinking, learning, and creativity.* New York: W. H. Freeman.
Holding, D. H. (1985). *The psychology of chess skill.* Hillsdale, NJ: Erlbaum.
Kohler, W. (1925/1976). *The mentality of apes.* New York: Liveright.
Levine, M. (1988). *Effective problem solving.* Englewood Cliffs, NJ: Prentice Hall.

Mayer, R. E. (1991). *Thinking, problem solving, and cognition* (2nd ed.). New York: W. H. Freeman.
Wertheimer, M. (1959/1978). *Productive thinking.* Westport, CT: Greenwood.

FOR MORE ON CREATIVITY

Abra, J. (1988). *Assaulting Parnassus: Theoretical views of creativity.* Lanham, MD: University Press of America.
Amabile, T. M. (1983). *The social psychology of creativity.* New York: Springer-Verlag.
Arieti, S. (1976). *Creativity: The magic synthesis.* New York: Basic Books.
Baer, J. (1993). *Creativity and divergent thinking: A task-specific approach.* Hillsdale, NJ: Erlbaum.
Boden, M. (1991). *The creative mind: Myths and mechanisms.* New York: Basic Books.
Finke, R. A., Ward, T. B., & Smith, S. M. (1992). *Creative cognition: Theory, research, and applications.* Cambridge, MA: MIT Press.
Freeman, M. (1993). *Finding the muse: A socio-psychological inquiry into the conditions of artistic creativity.* New York: Cambridge University Press.
Gardner, H. (1982). *Art, mind, and brain: A cognitive approach to creativity.* New York: Basic Books.
Ghiselin, B. (1952). *The creative process.* New York: New American Library.

Glover, J. A. (Ed.). (1989). *Handbook of creativity: Assessments, research, and theory.* New York: Plenum.
Koestler, A. (1990). *The act of creation.* New York: Penguin.
May, R. (1975). *The courage to create.* New York: W. W. Norton.
Runco, M. A. (1991). *Divergent thinking.* Norwood, NJ: Ablex.
Runco, M. A., & Albert, R. S. (Eds.). (1990). *Theories of creativity.* Newbury Park, CA: Sage Publications.
Weber, R. J. (1992). *Forks, phonographs, and hot air balloons: A field guide to inventive thinking.* New York: Oxford University Press.
Weisberg, R. W. (1993). *Creativity: Beyond the myth of genius.* New York: W. H. Freeman.

FOR MORE ON DECISION MAKING

Bell, D. F., Raiffa, H., & Tversky, A. (1988). *Decision making: Descriptive, normative, and prescriptive interactions.* New York: Cambridge University Press.
Gilovich, T. (1993). *How we know what isn't so: The fallibility of human reason in everyday life.* New York: Free Press.
Kahnemann, D., Skovic, P., & Tversky, A. (Eds.). (1982). *Judgment under uncertainty: Heuristics and biases.* New York: Cambridge University Press.

Kahneman, D., & Tversky, A. (1982, January). The psychology of preferences. *Scientific American,* pp. 160–173.

Kahneman, D., & Tversky, A. (1984). Choices, values, and frames. *American Psychologist, 39,* 341–350.

Nisbett, R., & Ross, L. (1985). *Human inference: Strategies and shortcomings of social judgment.* Englewood Cliffs, NJ: Prentice Hall.

Plous, S. (1993). *The psychology of judgment and decision making.* New York: McGraw-Hill.

Rachlin, H. (1989). *Judgment, decision, and choice.* New York: W. H. Freeman.

Yates, J. F. (1990). *Judgment and decision making.* Englewood Cliffs, NJ: Prentice Hall.

FOR MORE ON ARTIFICIAL INTELLIGENCE

Berry, D., & Hart, A. (Eds.). (1990). *Expert systems: Human issues.* Cambridge, MA: MIT Press.

Boden, M. A. (1989). *Artificial intelligence in psychology.* Cambridge, MA: MIT Press.

Crevier, D. (1993). *AI: The tumultuous history of the search for artificial intelligence.* New York: Basic Books.

Haugeland, J. (1985). *Artificial intelligence: The very idea.* Cambridge, MA: MIT Press.

Kurzweil, R. (1985). What is artificial intelligence anyway? *American Scientist, 73,* 258–264.

Kurzweil, R. (1990). *The age of intelligent machines.* Cambridge, MA: MIT Press.

Levy, D. N. (Ed.). *Computer chess compendium.* New York: Springer-Verlag.

McCorduck, P. (1979). *Machines who think: A personal inquiry into the history and prospects of artificial intelligence.* San Francisco: W. H. Freeman.

Pratt, V. (1987). *Thinking machines: The emergence of artificial intelligence.* New York: Basil Blackwell.

Wagman, M. (1993). *Cognitive psychology and artificial intelligence: Theory and research in cognitive science.* Westport, CT: Greenwood.

Waldrop, M. M. (1987). *Man-made minds: The promise of artificial intelligence.* New York: Walker.

FOR MORE ON LANGUAGE

Blumenthal, A. L. (1980). *Language and psychology: Historical aspects of psycholinguistics.* Huntington, NY: Krieger.

Carroll, D. W. (1994). *Psychology of language* (2nd ed.). Monterey, CA: Brooks/Cole.

Gleason, J. B., & Rattner, N. B. (Eds.). (1993). *Psycholinguistics.* San Diego: Harcourt Brace Jovanovich.

FOR MORE ON LANGUAGE ACQUISITION

Botha, R. P. (1989). *Challenging Chomsky.* Cambridge, MA: Basil Blackwell.

Brown, R. (1973). *A first language: The early stages.* Cambridge, MA: Harvard University Press.

Chomsky, N. (1966/1991). *Review* of Verbal Behavior *by B. F. Skinner.* New York: Irvington.

Chomsky, N. (1985). *Knowledge of language: Its nature, origin, and use.* New York: Praeger.

Curtiss, S. (1977). *Genie: A psycholinguistic study of a modern-day "wild child."* New York: Academic Press.

Green, G. M., Norman, D., & Ortony, A. (Eds.). (1988). *Pragmatics and natural language understanding.* Hillsdale, NJ: Erlbaum.

Ingram, D. (1989). *First language acquisition.* New York: Cambridge University Press.

Marcus, G. F., Pinker, S., Ullman, M., Hollander, M., Rosen, T. J., & Xu, F. (1992). *Overregularization in language acquisition.* Chicago: University of Chicago Press.

Scovel, T. (1988). *A time to speak: A psycholinguistic examination of the critical period for language acquisition.* Boston: Heinle & Heinle.

Skinner, B. F. (1957). *Verbal behavior.* Englewood Cliffs, NJ: Prentice Hall.

FOR MORE ON THINKING AND LANGUAGE

Berlin, B., & Kay, P. (1989). *Basic color terms: Their universality and evolution.* Berkeley: University of California Press.

Bloom, A. (1981). *The linguistic shaping of thought: A study in the impact of language on thinking in China and the West.* Hillsdale, NJ: Erlbaum.

Hoosain, R. (1991). *Psycholinguistic implications for linguistic relativity: A case study of Chinese.* Hillsdale, NJ: Erlbaum.

Lucy, J. A. (1992). *Language diversity and thought: A reformulation of the linguistic relativity hypothesis.* New York: Cambridge University Press.

Pullum, G. K. (1991). *The great Eskimo vocabulary hoax, and other irreverent essays on the study of language.* Chicago: University of Chicago Press.

Schultz, E. A. (1991). *Dialogue at the margins: Whorf, Bakhtin, and linguistic relativity.* Madison: University of Wisconsin Press.

Whorf, B. L. (1956). *Language, thought, and reality: Selected writings of Benjamin Lee Whorf* (J. B. Carroll, Ed.). Cambridge, MA: MIT Press.

FOR MORE ON APE LANGUAGE

Fernald, D. (1984). *The Hans legacy: A story of science.* Hillsdale, NJ: Erlbaum.

Gardner, R. A., Gardner, B. T., & Van Cantfort, T. E. (Eds.). (1989). *Teaching sign language to chimpanzees.* Albany, NY: State University of New York Press.

Hayes, C. (1951). *The ape in our house.* New York: Harper & Row.

Kellogg, W. N., & Kellogg, L. A. (1933). *The ape and the child.* New York: McGraw-Hill.

Parker, S. T., & Gibson, K. R. (1990). *"Language" and intelligence in monkeys and apes.* New York: Cambridge University Press.

Patterson, F., & Linden, E. (1981). *The education of Koko.* New York: Holt, Rinehart & Winston.

Premack, D. (1986). *Gavagai! The future history of the ape language controversy.* Cambridge, MA: MIT Press.

Premack, D., & Premack, A. J. (1983). *The mind of an ape.* New York: W. W. Norton.

Savage-Rumbaugh, E. S. (1986). *Ape language: From conditioned response to symbol.* New York: Columbia University Press.

Savage-Rumbaugh, E. S., Murphy, J., Sevcik, R. A., Brakke, K. E., Williams, S. L., & Rumbaugh, D. (1993). *Language comprehension in ape and child.* Chicago: University of Chicago Press.

Sebeok, T. A., & Rosenthal, R. (Eds.). (1981). *The Clever Hans phenomenon: Communication with horses, whales, apes, and people.* New York: New York Academy of Science.

Sebeok, T. A., & Umiker-Sebeok, J. (Eds.). (1980). *Speaking of apes: A critical anthology of two-way communication with man.* New York: Plenum.

Terrace, H. S. (1986). *Nim: A chimpanzee who learned sign language.* Irvington, NY: Columbia University Press.

FOR MORE ON CONTRIBUTORS TO THE STUDY OF THINKING AND LANGUAGE

Bjork, D. W. (1993). *B. F. Skinner: A life.* New York: Basic Books.

Bruner, J. (1983). *In search of mind: Essays in autobiography.* New York: Harper & Row.

Haley, M. C., & Lunsford, R. F. (1993). *Noam Chomsky.* New York: Macmillan.

Kessel, F. S. (Ed.). (1987). *The development of language and language researchers: Essays in honor of Roger Brown.* Hillsdale, NJ: Erikson.

Ley, R. (1990). *A whisper of espionage: Wolfgang Kohler and the apes of Tenerife.* Garden City, NY: Avery.

Simon, H. A. (1991). *Models of my life.* New York: Basic Books.

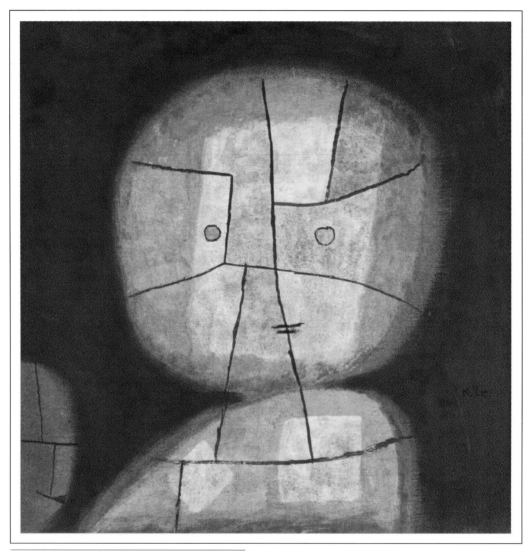

Paul Klee
Bust of a Child
1933

INTELLIGENCE

In the 1988 movie *Rainman*, which won an Academy Award for best picture, Dustin Hoffman played an autistic man who could perform amazing mental feats, such as recalling the telephone number of anyone in the telephone book. Hoffman portrayed a so-called idiot savant (French for "learned fool"). Idiot savants are now called *autistic savants* to avoid the negative connotation of the word *idiot*. An autistic savant is an autistic person (a person suffering from a disorder that impairs one's ability to communicate and to relate to others socially) with below-average intelligence but with an outstanding ability, typically in art, music, memory, or calculating. This phenomenon was first noted in 1751 in an article in a German magazine that described the case of an uneducated farmhand who had an extraordinary memory (Foerstl, 1989).

In a more recent case, an autistic savant could give the day of the week for any date in the twentieth century (Hurst & Mulhall, 1988). He had spent many hours memorizing the day of the week of each date, just as Dustin Hoffman's character spent many hours memorizing the telephone book. Because autistic people tend to be socially aloof and persistent at tasks, they can spend the many hours needed to memorize large amounts of material, such as calendar dates (Howe & Smith, 1988). Their feats are similar to the ability of some children to memorize statistics from the backs of hundreds of baseball cards and then recall any statistic for any player. In some cases, instead of memorizing thousands of calendar dates, autistic savants discover the rules of calendar construction and use them to calculate the day of the week for specific dates (O'Connor & Hermelin, 1992).

An autistic savant who memorizes enormous amounts of material is displaying intelligence. You certainly recognize intelligent behavior when you see it: someone getting an A on a calculus exam, or writing a great symphony, or discovering a cure for a disease. Recognizing intelligent behavior, though, is easier than defining intelligence itself. The word *intelligence* comes from the Latin word meaning "to understand," but intelligence is a broader concept than that. Finding a universally acceptable definition of intelligence is difficult because intelligence is a natural concept. As discussed in chapter 9, natural concepts have "fuzzy borders"—they are not easily defined by a distinct set of features.

Almost four decades ago David Wechsler (1958), a leading intelligence researcher, put forth an influential definition of intelligence. He called **intelligence** the global capacity to act purposefully, to think rationally, and to deal effectively with the environment. In other words, intelligence reflects how well we *function*. This definition is in the spirit of the first American school of psychology, functionalism (discussed in chapter 1), which stressed the importance of adaptive functioning in everyday life. And, indeed, intelligent people tend to function better. For example, a study of the children of criminals found that the higher the children scored on intelligence tests, the less likely they were to become criminals themselves. Apparently, those with a higher level of intelligence perform better in school, become less alienated, and use their educational success as a means to a socially acceptable career (Kandel et al., 1988).

INTELLIGENCE TESTING

Modern interest in the study of intelligence began with the development of tests of mental abilities, which include achievement tests, aptitude tests, and intelligence tests. An **achievement test** assesses knowledge of a particular subject. For decades, New York

The Savant Syndrome
Tom Cruise and Dustin Hoffman are shown in a scene from *Rainman*, in which Hoffman portrays an autistic savant.

David Wechsler (1896–1981)
"Intelligence, operationally defined, is the aggregate or global capacity of the individual to act purposefully, to think rationally, and to deal effectively with his environment."

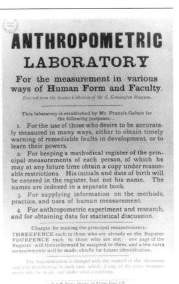

State has required students to pass the Regents Exams, which are achievement tests designed to measure students' knowledge of major academic areas such as English, history, and mathematics. An **aptitude test** predicts your potential to benefit from instruction in a particular academic or vocational setting. Of course, an aptitude test is, in part, an achievement test—your performance on it depends on previous experience with the material covered by the test. Aptitude tests are commonly used to screen job applicants and college applicants. For example, a wire-bending aptitude test is a good predictor of the performance of dental students on dental procedures (Kao et al., 1990). In applying to colleges, you may have submitted the results of your performance on either the Scholastic Aptitude Test (SAT), now called the Scholastic Assessment Test, or the American College Test (ACT). These scores help admissions committees determine whether applicants have the potential to succeed in college. An **intelligence test,** the main topic of this section, is a kind of aptitude test that assesses overall mental ability.

The History of Intelligence Testing

Though some psychologists question the strength of the evidence (Bowman, 1989), the use of tests of mental abilities has been traced back to 2200 B.C., when the Chinese appear to have used them to select talented individuals to serve as civil servants (Fox, 1981). But ability testing did not become the subject of scientific study until a century ago, when the English scientist Sir Francis Galton (1822–1911) set up his Anthropometric Laboratory at the 1884 International Health Exhibition in London.

Francis Galton and Anthropometry

The word *anthropometric* means "human measurement." More than 9,000 visitors to Galton's laboratory paid to be measured on a variety of physical characteristics, including head size, grip strength, visual acuity, and reaction time to sounds (Johnson et al., 1985). Galton was inspired by his cousin Charles Darwin's theory of evolution. According to Darwin, individuals who are the most physically well adapted to their environment are the most likely to survive long enough to produce offspring, who would be likely to also have those physical characteristics. Galton similarly assumed that people

Francis Galton (1822–1911)
"Social hindrances cannot impede men of high ability from being eminent . . . [and] social advantages are incompetent to give that status to a man of moderate ability."

intelligence
The global capacity to act purposefully, to think rationally, and to deal effectively with the environment.

achievement test
A test that measures knowledge of a particular subject.

aptitude test
A test designed to predict a person's potential to benefit from instruction in a particular academic or vocational setting.

intelligence test
A test that assesses overall mental ability.

with superior physical abilities, especially sensory and motor abilities, are better adapted for survival. He viewed such people as more intelligent than those with average or inferior physical abilities.

Galton's interest in studying physical differences reflected his interest in studying all sorts of individual differences, including the relative beauty of women from different countries. (In a possible instance of experimenter bias, Galton found that the women of England, his home country, were the most beautiful.) His research on individual differences established the field of **differential psychology,** which is concerned with the study of cognitive and behavioral differences among individuals. Galton's anthropometric method was introduced to the United States by James McKeen Cattell (1860–1944), who administered Galton's tests—which Cattell called *mental tests*—to American students (Cattell, 1890).

But anthropometry proved fruitless as a way of measuring general intelligence, because many anthropometric measurements, such as grip strength, proved to have little or no relationship to mental measures of intelligence, such as reasoning ability. Recent research, however, has demonstrated a positive correlation between mental measurements and physical measures such as reaction time. For example, a study of elementary school children found that their reaction time was related to intelligence test scores: Higher test scores were associated with faster reaction times (Lynn & Wilson, 1990). One explanation for this relationship is that intelligence might depend, in part, on the speed of neural impulse conduction (Barrett, Daum, & Eysenck, 1990). Perhaps one can, indeed, be "quick-witted."

Alfred Binet, Theodore Simon, and the IQ Test

The first formal test of general intelligence—the *Binet-Simon Scale*—appeared in 1905. It grew out of an 1881 French law that required all children to attend school even if they could not profit from a standard curriculum (Levine, 1976). This led the French minister of public education to ask psychologist Alfred Binet (1857–1911) to develop a test to identify children who required special classes for slow learners.

Binet collaborated with psychiatrist Theodore Simon (1873–1961) to develop a test that could assess children's ability to perform in school. Binet and Simon began by administering many questions related to language, reasoning, and arithmetic to elementary school children of all ages. Some of the items had been developed by other eminent psychologists, including Hugo Münsterberg and Hermann Ebbinghaus (whose other contributions to psychology are discussed in earlier chapters). Binet and Simon eliminated questions that tended to be answered the same by children of all ages. Questions that were answered correctly by more and more children at each successive age were retained and became the Binet-Simon Scale.

The test was administered to children who needed to be placed in school. Each student was assigned a *mental age*, based on the number of test items she or he passed—the greater the number of items passed, the higher the mental age. A student with a mental age significantly below his or her chronological age was considered a candidate for placement in a class for slow learners. Binet urged that his test be used solely for class placement. He disagreed with those who claimed that the test measured a child's inherited level of intelligence or that a child's level of intelligence could not be improved by education.

The Binet-Simon Scale proved useful, but the mental age, at times, proved misleading. Suppose that a 10-year-old child had a mental age of 8 and a 6-year-old child had a mental age of 4. Both would be two years below their chronological ages, but the 6-year-old would be proportionately farther behind her or his age peers than the 10-year-old would be. This problem was solved by the German psychologist William Stern (1871–1938), who recommended using the ratio of mental age to chronological age to determine a child's level of intelligence (Kreppner, 1992). A 10-year-old with a mental age of 8 has a ratio of 8/10 = 0.80, and a 6-year-old with a mental age of 4 has a ratio of 4/6 = 0.67. This indicates that the 6-year-old is relatively farther behind his or her age

differential psychology
The field of psychology that studies individual differences in intellectual, personality, and physical characteristics.

Alfred Binet (1857–1911)
"It will be seen that a profound knowledge of the normal intellectual development of the child would not only be of great interest but useful in formulating a course of instruction really adapted to their aptitudes."

The Army Tests
During World War I, more than 1.7 million recruits took either the verbal Army Alpha Test (*left*) or the nonverbal Army Beta Test (*right*).

peers. Stern eliminated the decimal point by multiplying the ratio by 100. Thus, 0.80 becomes 80, and 0.67 becomes 67. The formula (mental age/chronological age) × 100 became known as the **intelligence quotient**—or **IQ.** As you can see, a child whose mental and chronological ages are the same has an IQ of 100, and a child who has a higher mental than chronological age has an IQ above 100.

Mental Testing in America

The Binet-Simon Scale was translated into English and first used in the United States by the American psychologist Henry Goddard (1866–1957) in New Jersey at the Vineland Training School for Feebleminded Girls and Boys. A revised version of the Binet-Simon Scale, more suitable for children reared in American culture, was published in 1916 by Stanford University psychologist Lewis Terman (1877–1956). The American version became known as the *Stanford-Binet Intelligence Scale,* which is still used today. Ironically, the Binet-Simon Scale was neither widely used nor widely known in France until after the Stanford-Binet had become popular in America (Schneider, 1992). Terman also redesigned the Stanford-Binet to make it suitable for testing both children and adults. (The test was revised in 1937, 1960, 1972, and 1986.)

Because the Stanford-Binet is given individually and can take an hour or more to administer, it is not suitable for testing large groups of people in a brief period of time. This became a problem during World War I, when the United States Army sought a way to assess the intelligence of large groups of recruits. The army wanted to reject recruits who did not have the intelligence to perform well and to identify recruits who would be good officer candidates. The solution to this problem was provided by Terman and his student A. A. Otis. They developed two group tests of intelligence—the *Army Alpha Test* and the *Army Beta Test.* The Army Alpha Test was given in writing to those who could read English, and the Army Beta Test was given orally to those who could not read English. The tests, reflecting their functionalist heritage, viewed intelligence as the ability to adapt to the environment (von Mayrhauser, 1989). Descendants of these group intelligence tests include the *Otis-Lennon Mental Abilities Tests* and the *Armed Forces Qualification Test.*

After World War I the Stanford-Binet became the most widely used intelligence test. But the ratio IQ devised by Stern, which was adequate for representing the intelligence of children, proved inadequate for representing the intelligence of adults. Because growth in mental age slows markedly after childhood, the use of the ratio IQ led to the absurdity of people with average or above-average intelligence becoming below average simply because their chronological age increased. For example, consider a 15-year-old girl with a mental age of 20. She would have an IQ of (20/15) × 100 = 133. This would put her in the mentally gifted range (that is, above 130). Suppose that at age 40 she had retained the mental age of 20. She would then have an IQ of (20/40) × 100 = 50. This would put her well within the mentally retarded range (that is, below 70). Yet she might be a successful lawyer, physician, or professor.

This inadequacy of the ratio IQ was overcome by David Wechsler (1896–1981). He replaced Stern's ratio IQ with a *deviation IQ,* which compares a person's intelligence test score with the mean score of his or her age peers. Those who perform at exactly the

intelligence quotient (IQ)
1. Originally, the ratio of mental age to chronological age; that is, MA/CA ×100.
2. Today, the score on an intelligence test, calculated by comparing a person's performance to norms for her or his age group.

mean of their age peers receive an IQ of 100; those who perform above the mean of their age peers receive an IQ above 100; and those who perform below the mean of their age peers receive an IQ below 100.

In 1939 Wechsler developed his own intelligence test. While working as chief psychologist at Bellevue Hospital in New York City, he sought a way to assess the intelligence of those with low verbal ability among the psychiatric patients he encountered there. Because the Stanford-Binet stressed verbal ability, it was not suitable for that purpose. This led Wechsler to develop an intelligence test that tested nonverbal, as well as verbal, ability, which he called the *Wechsler-Bellevue Intelligence Scale*.

Wechsler later developed versions of his test for use with different age groups, beginning with the *Wechsler Intelligence Scale for Children (WISC)*, for ages 6 to 16; followed by the *Wechsler Adult Intelligence Scale (WAIS)*, for ages from late adolescence through adulthood; and concluding with the *Wechsler Preschool and Primary Scale of Intelligence (WPPSI)*, for ages 4 to 6 1/2. The Wechsler scales have been revised periodically, leading to their current acronyms, *WISC-R, WAIS-R,* and *WPPSI-R*. Each of the Wechsler intelligence scales contains 11 subtests that measure different aspects of verbal and nonverbal intelligence. The test taker receives a verbal IQ, a performance (that is, nonverbal) IQ, and an overall IQ. Research has supported the division of intelligence, as measured by the Wechsler scales, into general intelligence, verbal intelligence, and performance intelligence (LoBello & Gulgoz, 1991).

Issues in Intelligence Testing

Chapter 2 noted that formal tests must be standardized, reliable, and valid. *Standardization* refers to both the establishment of performance norms on a test and uniformity in how the test is administered and scored. When an intelligence test is standardized, the mean performance of the standardization group for each age range is given a score of 100, with a standard deviation of 15. As mentioned in chapter 2, the standard deviation is a measure of how variable a group of scores are around their mean. Figure 10.1 shows that IQ scores fall along a *normal curve*. For the Wechsler scales, this means that about 68 percent of test takers will score between 85 and 115, and about 95 percent will score between 70 and 130. Average intelligence falls between 85 and 115. IQs below 70 fall in the mentally retarded range, and IQs above 130 fall in the mentally gifted range.

The Reliability of Intelligence Tests

You would have confidence in an intelligence test only if it were reliable. As discussed in chapter 2, the *reliability* of a test is the degree to which it gives consistent results. Suppose you took an IQ test and scored 102 (average) one month, 53 (mentally

FIGURE 10.1

The Normal Distribution of IQ Test Scores

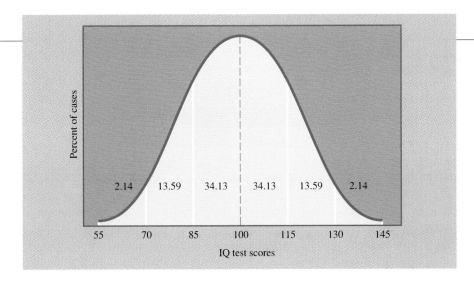

retarded) the next month, and 146 (mentally gifted) the third month. Because your level of intelligence normally would not fluctuate that much in 3 months, you would argue that the test is unreliable. Because the test-retest reliability correlations for the Stanford-Binet and Wechsler scales are at least .90 (out of a maximum of 1.00), the tests are reliable.

Though standardized IQ tests are reliable in the short run, an individual's IQ score may change over a period of years. The Berkeley Growth Study, conducted at the University of California at Berkeley, contradicted the once-popular belief that intelligence does not change during childhood. The study found that mental ability increases steadily until adolescence, slows down, and then levels off at about the age of 20 (Bayley, 1955). The nature of intellectual change later in life is discussed in chapter 4.

The Validity of Intelligence Tests

A reliable test is not necessarily a valid one. A test's *validity* (discussed in chapter 2) depends on whether the test measures what it is supposed to measure. *Predictive validity* is especially important. Consider the SAT's ability to predict school performance. A published review of research on the SAT reported that the SAT correlates .41 with the criterion of first-year college grade point average. This means that the SAT is a moderately good predictor. But high school grade point average, which correlates .52 with first-year college grade point average, is an even better predictor. Moreover, the combination of the SAT and high school grade point average is a still better predictor, correlating .58 with first-year college grade point average (Linn, 1982).

Claims that students with access to SAT preparation courses have an unfair advantage over others may be unfounded. Such courses produce modest gains. An increase of just 20 to 30 points on the verbal and mathematics subtests would require hours of study almost equivalent to full-time schooling (Messick & Jungeblut, 1981). Of course, because this is based on averages, some students might benefit from extra preparation.

The Stanford-Binet and Wechsler scales correlate between .40 and .75 with school performance, depending on the aspect of school performance being measured (Aiken, 1982). These moderately high correlations indicate that the tests are good, but far from perfect, predictors of school performance. Because the correlations are less than a perfect 1.00, factors other than those measured by the SAT or IQ tests also contribute to school performance. This has made the fairness of intelligence tests one of the most controversial issues in contemporary psychology.

Critics argue that IQ tests and other tests of mental ability might be unfair to minority groups, most notably blacks, in the United States. American blacks score an average of 10 to 15 IQ points lower than American whites on IQ tests (Mackenzie,

1984). Critics of IQ testing allege that because blacks are less likely to have the same cultural and educational experiences as whites, they tend, on the average, to perform more poorly on IQ tests that assume cultural and educational experiences common to whites (Miller-Jones, 1989).

But does this mean that IQ tests are *biased* against blacks? The issue of the validity of IQ tests for blacks reached the courts in the 1970s. In 1979 Judge Robert Peckham of the federal district court in San Francisco ruled that without court approval California schools could no longer use IQ tests to place black schoolchildren in classes. His ruling came in the case of *Larry P. v. Wilson Riles* (Riles was the California superintendent of education), which was brought on behalf of six black children in San Francisco who had been placed in classes for the educable mentally retarded (that is, those with mild mental retardation). After hearing 10,000 pages of testimony from experts and advocates on both sides of the issue, Peckham ruled that the use of IQ tests violated the civil rights of black children, because a proportionately greater number of black children than white children were being placed in classes for the mentally retarded. His decision convinced school districts in several other states to abandon the use of IQ tests for determining the school placement of black children (Taylor, 1990).

But Peckham's decision was also met by arguments that IQ tests are not biased against blacks, because the tests have good predictive validity—they accurately predict the performance of both black children and white children in elementary school classes. The differences in IQ scores between black children and white children might reflect the greater likelihood of black children's being reared in socially disadvantaged circumstances that do not provide them with the opportunity to gain experiences that are important in doing well on IQ tests and in school (Lambert, 1981). A committee of scholars from several academic fields reported to the National Academy of Science that standardized tests are accurate predictors of school and job performance for all groups and therefore are not biased against any particular group ("NAS Calls Tests Fair but Limited," 1982).

Nonetheless, the issue has become as political as it is scientific. On the one side are those, such as Judge Peckham, who believe that biased tests of mental abilities are being used to perpetuate discrimination against blacks by placing black children in slower classes and by preventing black adults from obtaining desirable jobs. Peckham and his supporters favor outlawing the use of such tests. On the other side are those who believe that blaming IQ tests for revealing the negative consequences of discrimination and deprived upbringings is like killing the messenger who brings bad news. They would favor changing the conditions that contribute to the poorer average IQ test performance of blacks and other minority groups (Elliott, 1988).

One possible solution presents a compromise: Use tests that are not affected by the test taker's cultural background. But efforts to develop "culture-free" tests, in the 1940s (Cattell, 1940), and "culture-fair" tests, in the 1950s (Davis & Eels, 1953), produced disappointing results. These tests presented test takers with items that emphasized perceptual and spatial abilities, rather than verbal abilities, and avoided the use of items that would presume an extensive background in a particular culture. Figure 10.2 presents an example of the Raven Progressive Matrices, a nonverbal intelligence test that some have favored over the Stanford-Binet or Wechsler scales (Basu, 1982). But, just like on traditional intelligence tests, people of higher socioeconomic status perform better on these nonverbal tests than do people of lower socioeconomic status (Jensen, 1980). Even the Cattell Culture Fair Intelligence Test, which was designed to reduce cultural bias in testing, might contain culturally biased items, as indicated in a study of Indian, American, and Nigerian adolescents who took the test (Nenty, 1986).

Imagine how Alfred Binet would have reacted to the controversy that has arisen over the use of standardized tests, considering that he saw testing as an objective means of assessing students' abilities. In fact, despite the shortcomings of standardized tests, no alternative is as unbiased in assessing individuals without regard to irrelevant characteristics such as sex, race, or ethnic background (Reilly & Chao, 1982). As Richard Weinberg, a leading intelligence researcher, has noted:

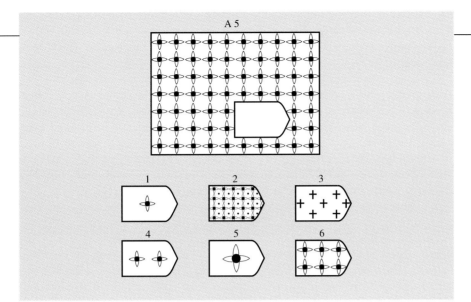

FIGURE 10.2

Raven Progressive Matrices Test
In this "culture-fair" test, the person is presented with a series of matrices and must complete each by selecting the appropriate symbol from an accompanying group of symbols.

* * * In the light of the effectiveness of current IQ tests to predict school performance, it is ironic that tests have been outlawed for the very purpose for which they were designed—to prevent subjective judgment and prejudice from being the basis for assigning students to special classes or denying them certain privileges. (Weinberg, 1989, p. 100)

EXTREMES OF INTELLIGENCE

Another controversial issue regarding intelligence is the classification and education of people who fall at either extreme of the range of intelligence. As you learned earlier, 95 percent of the population score between 70 and 130 on IQ tests. Of the remaining 5 percent, half score below 70 and half score above 130. Those who score below 70 fall in the mentally retarded range, and those who score above 130 fall in the mentally gifted range—though the classification of a person as mentally retarded or mentally gifted is not based on IQ scores alone.

Mental Retardation

Depending on the criteria used to define **mental retardation,** from slightly more than 3 million to almost 7 million Americans are mentally retarded. The estimate varies because the person's level of adaptive behavior, and not just his or her level of intelligence, needs to be assessed before he or she is classified as mentally retarded. In fact, the current trend in classification is to rely more on the person's everyday functioning and less on his or her IQ score (Haywood, Meyers, & Switzky, 1982).

mental retardation
Intellectual deficiency marked by an IQ below 70 and difficulties performing in everyday life.

Classification of Mental Retardation

We have come a long way in our use of terms to classify the mentally retarded. In the early twentieth century, the mentally retarded were placed in one of three categories, each referring to an increasing degree of mental retardation: moron (from a Greek word meaning "foolish"), imbecile (from a Latin word meaning "weak-minded"), and idiot (from a Greek word meaning "ignorant"). Fortunately, these terms are no longer used by professionals, but, as you are well aware, they have become common terms of disparagement in everyday language.

To be classified as mentally retarded, a person must have an IQ below 70 and, beginning in childhood, difficulties performing in everyday life (Landesman & Ramey, 1989)—including difficulties in self-care (such as eating and dressing), schoolwork (such as reading and arithmetic), and social relationships (such as conversing and developing friendships). Moreover, before a person can be classified as mentally retarded, alternative causes of the person's low IQ score and performance difficulties must be ruled out. These alternative causes include physical illness, impairment of vision or hearing, and coming from a family of people who are not native speakers of the language in which the IQ test was administered.

Today, there are four categories of mental retardation (American Psychiatric Association, 1987). Persons with IQs of 50 to 70 have *mild retardation* and comprise 85 percent of the mentally retarded. They are able to care for themselves, reach a sixth-grade level of education, hold responsible jobs, be married, and serve as adequate parents. Those with IQs of 35 to 49 have *moderate retardation* and comprise 10 percent of the mentally retarded. They may be trained to care for themselves, reach a second-grade level of education, and hold menial jobs, often in sheltered workshops. But they have difficulty maintaining social relationships and they rarely marry.

Those with IQs between 20 and 34 have *severe retardation* and comprise 3 to 4 percent of the mentally retarded. They can learn rudimentary language and work skills but may be unable to care for themselves, benefit from schooling, hold jobs, or maintain normal social relationships. And those with IQs below 20 have *profound retardation* and comprise 1 to 2 percent of the mentally retarded. They have so few skills that they may spend their lives in institutions that provide them with no more than custodial care.

Causes of Mental Retardation

In 1912 Henry Goddard traced the descendants of a Revolutionary War soldier whom he called Martin Kallikak. The soldier produced two lines of descendants. One line arose from his affair with a mentally retarded tavern maid. The other line arose from his marriage to a respectable woman of normal intelligence. Goddard found that the descendants of the tavern maid included many derelicts, prostitutes, and mentally retarded people. In contrast, the descendants of his wife included few such people.

The differences between the two lines of descendants account for Goddard's use of the name *Kallikak*. The name is a combination of the Greek words *kalos* (meaning "good") and *kakos* (meaning "bad"). Goddard concluded that the descendants of the soldier's wife inherited the tendency to be moral and intelligent, while the descendants of the tavern maid inherited the tendency to be immoral and mentally retarded. He discounted the effects of the markedly different sociocultural environments into which the children in each branch of the family were born as the probable causes of the differences.

Controversy has arisen about retouched photographs of the Kallikaks that Goddard (1912) included in a book he wrote. Critics claimed that Goddard (perhaps to show the dire effects of inferior genes) retouched the photographs to make the family members look more mentally retarded and unappealing (Smith, 1988). Others claim that this is much ado about nothing. They insist that Goddard probably retouched the photographs for aesthetic reasons—perhaps to bring out indistinct facial features (Fancher, 1987). This controversy even inspired an empirical study in which adult subjects rated the photographs of the Kallikaks. The subjects generally rated the Kallikaks as kind and very bright (Glenn & Ellis, 1988). Thus, even if Goddard intended to make them look more ominous, his attempt was not successful.

cultural-familial retardation
Mental retardation apparently caused by social or cultural deprivation.

Today research findings indicate that about 75 percent of cases of mental retardation are caused, not by heredity, but by sociocultural deprivation, so-called **cultural-familial retardation** (Scott & Carran, 1987). In fact, almost all mildly retarded persons come from such backgrounds. Their families might fail to provide them with adequate intellectual stimulation, such as discussing current events with them, encouraging them to read, helping them with homework, and taking them on trips to zoos, museums, and other educational settings. They are also more likely to attend inferior schools, to suffer from malnutrition, and to lack adequate medical care—each of which can impair intellectual growth.

Though most cases of mental retardation are caused by sociocultural deprivation, many cases are caused by brain damage. Pregnant women who ingest drugs can cause brain damage in their offspring. For example, women who drink alcohol while pregnant

(a)

(b)

Down Syndrome
People with Down syndrome can live rewarding lives, both personally and professionally. (a) John Mark Stallings provides emotional support for his father, Gene, the head football coach for the University of Alabama. (b) Actor Chris Burke starred in the successful television series "Life Goes On."

may give birth to children who suffer from *fetal alcohol syndrome*, marked by physical deformities and mental retardation (Graham-Clay, 1983). Pregnant women who have certain diseases, such as *rubella* (German measles) during the first trimester, also have a greater risk of giving birth to mentally retarded offspring. Women who are infected with the genital *herpes* virus have about a 10 percent chance of producing mentally retarded offspring (Eichhorn, 1982). Women who suffer from severe *malnutrition* while pregnant can produce infants who are mentally retarded because of a reduction in the number of their brain cells (Read, 1982). Prenatal exposure to X rays can impair the normal migration of brain cells, increasing the possibility of mental retardation (Schull, Norton, & Jensh, 1990). And a newborn infant who fails to breathe for several minutes after birth will experience *hypoxia*, a lack of oxygen to the brain and the most common cause of perinatal brain damage (Towbin, 1978). Hypoxia can cause **cerebral palsy**, a form of brain damage characterized by movement disorders and often—but not always—accompanied by mental retardation.

Mental retardation is also caused by genetic defects, such as defects that cause abnormal metabolism, which in turn can lead to brain damage, as in the case of **phenylketonuria (PKU).** PKU is caused by an inherited lack of the enzyme required to metabolize the amino acid *phenylalanine*, which is found in milk and other common foods. This eventually causes brain damage, which leads to mental retardation by the age of 3. Fortunately, routine screening of newborns in the United States and other countries can detect PKU early enough to protect infants from brain damage by putting them on a diet that eliminates almost all of their intake of phenylalanine. This dietary restriction might be necessary throughout adolescence (Clarke et al., 1987).

Some cases of mental retardation are caused by genetic defects that cause abnormal development during gestation, as in the case of **Down syndrome.** This disorder is named for the English physician Langdon Down, who identified it in 1866. Human beings normally have 23 pairs of chromosomes, with one member of each pair coming from each parent. A person with Down syndrome has an extra, third chromosome on the 21st pair. The extra chromosome can come from either the mother's egg or the father's sperm. The chances of having a child with Down syndrome increase with age, being more common in middle-aged parents than in younger ones.

Children with Down syndrome are usually moderately retarded and exhibit distinctive physical characteristics. These include small ears and hands; short necks, feet, and fingers; protruding tongues; and a fold over the eyes, giving them an almond-shaped, Asian appearance. Because of this, Down syndrome was originally called "Mongolism."

cerebral palsy
A movement disorder caused by brain damage and that is sometimes accompanied by mental retardation.

phenylketonuria (PKU)
A hereditary enzyme deficiency that, if left untreated in the infant, causes mental retardation.

Down syndrome
A form of mental retardation, associated with certain physical deformities, that is caused by an extra, third chromosome on the 21st pair.

TABLE 10.1	A Step-by-Step Approach for Training Mentally Retarded People to Shower Themselves

Task-Analyzed Steps of Showering

1.	Acquire washcloth	15.	Wash left leg and foot
2.	Turn on the water	16.	Wash right leg and foot
3.	Adjust temperature	17.	Wash back
4.	Get wet, then turn water off	18.	Wash buttocks
5.	Wash hair	19.	Rinse off soap
6.	Lather cloth	20.	Wring out cloth
7.	Wash face, ears, and neck	21.	Properly dispose of cloth
8.	Wash shoulders	22.	Get a towel
9.	Wash left arm	23.	Dry hair
10.	Wash under left arm	24.	Dry face, ears, and neck
11.	Wash right arm	25.	Dry remainder of body
12.	Wash under right arm	26.	Put towel in hamper
13.	Wash chest and stomach	27.	Apply deodorant
14.	Wash genitals		

Reprinted from *Behavior Research and Therapy*, 19: 399–405. J. L. Matson, T. M. DiLorenzo, and K. Esvelt-Dawson. "Independence Training as a Method of Enhancing Self-Help Skills Acquisition of the Mentally Retarded," pages 399–405. Copyright 1981, with kind permission from Elsevier Science Ltd, The Boulevard, Langford Lane, Kidlington OXS IGB, UK.

The Special Olympics
Mentally retarded people have the opportunity to demonstrate their athletic abilities at the Special Olympics.

This reflected the nineteenth-century Western belief that victims of the disorder failed to develop beyond what was then presumed by Westerners to be the more primitive physical and intellectual level of Asians, such as Mongolians (Gould, 1981).

Education of the Mentally Retarded

Over the centuries, the mentally retarded have been treated as everything from children of God, who brought good luck, to subhumans, who were locked up as dangerous (Wolfensberger, 1972). Today psychologists interested in the mentally retarded stress their potential to benefit from education and training. One reason why mentally retarded people do not perform as well as other people is that they fail to use effective methods of information processing. For example, when mentally retarded people are given a series of words or pictures to remember, they tend not to rehearse the items or group them into chunks—techniques that are commonly used by people who are not mentally retarded (Campione & Brown, 1979). As explained in chapter 8, memory is enhanced by the rehearsal and chunking of information.

Today mildly retarded persons are called "educable," and moderately retarded persons are called "trainable." From the 1950s to the 1970s, the educable mentally retarded were placed in special classes in which they received teaching tailored to their level of ability. But in the 1970s, dissatisfaction with the results of this approach led to *mainstreaming*, which places mentally retarded children in as many normal classes as possible and encourages them to participate in activities with nonretarded children. To promote mainstreaming in America, the Education for All Handicapped Children Act of 1975 mandated that retarded children be given instruction in the most normal academic setting that is feasible for them (Sussan, 1990).

Mentally retarded persons have educational needs that are not limited to academic subjects. They may also need training in self-care skills (including eating, toileting, hygiene, dressing, and grooming); home management skills (including home maintenance, clothing care, food preparation, and home safety); consumer skills (including telephone use, money management, and shopping); and community mobility skills (including pedestrian safety and use of public transportation). Behavior modification has been especially useful in training the mentally retarded in self-care. For example, as presented in table 10.1, behavior modification has been used successfully in training mentally retarded people to shower themselves (Matson, DiLorenzo, & Esveldt-Dawson, 1981).

A movement that has paralleled mainstreaming is *normalization*, the transfer of mentally retarded individuals from large institutional settings into community settings so that they can live more normal lives. Given adequate support services, even severely and profoundly retarded people can progress in settings other than large, custodial institutions (Landesman & Butterfield, 1987).

Mental Giftedness

Interest in the study of mental retardation has been accompanied by interest, though less extensive interest, in the study of **mental giftedness.** Sir Francis Galton (1869) began the study of the mentally gifted—or "geniuses"—in the late nineteenth century. Lewis Terman, introduced earlier, considered Galton to be mentally gifted. Terman based his assessment on Galton's early accomplishments, including his ability to recite the alphabet when he was 18 months old and read classical literature when he was 5 years old (Terman, 1917). Today the mentally gifted are considered those with IQs above 130 and with exceptionally high scores on achievement tests in specific subjects, such as mathematics (Fox, 1981).

The special needs of the mentally gifted have traditionally received less attention than those of the mentally retarded (Reis, 1989). Perhaps the most well-known organization dedicated to meeting the needs of the mentally gifted is Mensa (Serebriakoff, 1985), which limits its membership to those who score in the top 2 percent on a standardized intelligence test. One of the reasons for the traditional lack of interest in the mentally gifted was the belief in "early ripe, early rot." This belief assumed that children who are intellectually precocious are doomed to become academic, vocational, and social failures.

The classic case study in support of this viewpoint was that of William James Sidis. He was named in honor of William James, a colleague of his father, Boris, at Harvard University. Sidis was a mathematically gifted boy who enrolled at Harvard in 1909 at the age of 11 and received national publicity a year later when he gave a talk on higher mathematics to the Harvard Mathematical Club. But constant pressure from his father to excel and the glare of publicity eventually led Sidis to retreat from the world. In his early twenties, Sidis left the faculty position he had taken at Rice Institute in Houston and spent the rest of his life working at menial jobs. Years later, in 1937, James Thurber, writing under a pen name in the *New Yorker*, published a sarcastic article about Sidis entitled "April Fool" (Sidis was born on April 1). Thurber wrote that Sidis was a failure, living in a single room in a rundown section of Boston, which Thurber used as evidence of the dire consequences of being too intelligent at too young an age. Sidis sued the *New Yorker* for libel and won a modest settlement shortly before dying—in obscurity—in 1944 (Wallace, 1986).

Terman's Genetic Studies of Genius

Contrary to the case of William James Sidis, mentally gifted children do not tend to become failures. In fact, they tend to be more successful in every area of life and show better adjustment and less emotional disturbance than other people do (Grossberg & Cornell, 1988). This was demonstrated in perhaps the most famous longitudinal study ever conducted, Lewis Terman's Genetic Studies of Genius, which still inspires interest today—more than 70 years after it began (Cravens, 1992).

Anatomy of a Classic Research Study:
What Is the Fate of Childhood Geniuses?

Rationale
Terman began his study in 1921, and it has continued ever since—even after his death. He hoped to counter the commonsense belief that being too intelligent too early led to later failure.

Method
Terman used the Stanford-Binet Intelligence Scale to identify California children with IQs above 135. He found 1,528 such children between the ages of 8 and 12. Their average IQ was 150. Reports on Terman's gifted children have appeared every decade or two since 1921. After Terman's death in 1956, the study was continued by Robert and Pauline Sears of Stanford University.

A Group Home
Mentally retarded people may live in supervised group homes, instead of in large institutions. They learn to develop the skills of self-reliance, including preparing their own meals.

mental giftedness
Intellectual superiority marked by an IQ above 130 and exceptionally high scores on achievement tests in specific subjects, such as mathematics.

William James Sidis (1867–1944)
"He died alone, obscure, and destitute, and he left a troublesome legacy best termed the 'Sidis Fallacy'—that talent like his rarely matures or becomes productive" (Montour, 1977, p. 265).

The Mentally Gifted
Children who are mentally gifted, like those who are mentally retarded, benefit from special educational programs to help them develop their abilities.

Lewis Terman (1877–1956)
"Children of IQ 140 or higher are, in general, appreciably superior to unselected children in physique, health, and social adjustment; markedly superior in moral attitudes as measured either by character tests or trait ratings; and vastly superior in their mastery of school subjects."

Results and Discussion

The Study of Genius has shown that mentally gifted children tend to become socially, physically, vocationally, and academically superior adults. They are healthier and more likely to attend college, to have professional careers, and to have happy marriages. The 1972 report on Terman's subjects, then at an average age of 62, found that they were generally satisfied with life, combining successful careers with rewarding family lives (Sears, 1977).

Of course, Terman's study is not without certain weaknesses. Perhaps the subjects' awareness of being in such an important study affected how they performed in life—a kind of self-fulfilling prophecy. Also, could socioeconomic status, and not solely intelligence, have been a contributing factor? A follow-up study of samples of men from the original study found that men who maintained better health, had more stable marriages, and pursued more lucrative careers were less likely to come from families in which there was divorce, alcoholism, or other major family problems (Oden, 1968). Evidently, even for geniuses, the family environment influences their success in life.

The Study of Mathematically Precocious Youth

Perhaps the best-known recent study of mentally gifted children is the longitudinal *Study of Mathematically Precocious Youth* conducted by Camilla Benbow and Julian Stanley (1983) at Johns Hopkins University. They provided special programs for young adolescents who scored above 700 (out of a maximum of 800) on the mathematics subtest of the SAT. The programs offered intensive summer courses in science and mathematics, accelerated courses at universities, and counseling for parents to help them meet the academic and emotional needs of their gifted children. A 10-year follow-up found that subjects in the study had many outstanding educational achievements (Benbow, Arjmand, & Walberg, 1991). Moreover, there is no evidence that these gifted children are prone to the personal and social problems that plagued William James Sidis. In fact, a program such as this might have helped him pursue a rewarding career as a mathematician instead of fading into obscurity.

THEORIES OF INTELLIGENCE

Is intelligence a general characteristic that affects all facets of behavior, or are there different kinds of intelligence, each affecting a specific facet of behavior? Today intelligence researchers tend to assume that there are several kinds of intelligence (Sternberg & Wagner, 1993). Consider, for example, a study of men who spent much of their recreational time at racetracks betting on horse races. The results indicated that the men's ability to handicap races accurately was unrelated to their scores on a test of general intelligence. This indicated that handicapping horse races taps a specific kind of mental ability (Ceci & Liker, 1986).

Factor-Analytic Theories of Intelligence

At about the same time as Alfred Binet was developing his intelligence test, the British psychologist Charles Spearman (1863–1945) was developing a theory of intelligence. He considered it a general ability that underlies a variety of behaviors.

Spearman's Theory of General Intelligence

In 1927, after more than two decades of research, Spearman published his conclusions about the nature of intelligence. He used a statistical technique called **factor analysis,** which determines the degree of correlation between performances on various tasks. If performances on certain tasks have a high positive correlation, then they are presumed to reflect the influence of a particular underlying factor. For example, if performances on a vocabulary test, a reading test, and a writing test correlate highly, they might reveal the influence of a "verbal ability" factor.

factor analysis
A statistical technique that determines the degree of correlation between performances on various tasks to determine the extent to which they reflect particular underlying characteristics, which are known as factors.

In using factor analysis, Spearman first gave a large group of people a variety of mental tasks. He found that scores on the tasks had high positive correlations with one another. This meant that subjects tended to score high *or* moderate *or* low on all the tests. This led Spearman to conclude that performance on all of the tasks depended on the operation of a single underlying factor. He called this "g"—a general intelligence factor.

But because the correlations between the tasks were less than a perfect 1.00, Spearman concluded that performance on each task also depended, to a lesser extent, on its own specific factor, which he called "s." For example, Spearman explained that scores on vocabulary tests and arithmetic tests tended to have a high positive correlation with each other because vocabulary ability and arithmetic ability are both influenced by a general intelligence factor. But because scores on vocabulary tests and arithmetic tests are not perfectly correlated, each ability must also depend on its own intelligence factor. Nonetheless, Spearman believed that the general intelligence factor was more important than any specific intelligence factor in governing a given ability. The existence of the "g" factor has received some research support. It appears to reflect the ability to be precise and flexible in manipulating information in one's short-term memory (Larson & Saccuzzo, 1989).

Thurstone's Theory of Primary Mental Abilities

Like Spearman, Louis Thurstone (1887–1955) used factor analysis to determine the nature of intelligence. But, unlike Spearman, Thurstone (1938) concluded that there was no general intelligence factor. Instead, based on a battery of tests that he gave to college students, he identified seven factors, which he called *primary mental abilities*: reasoning, word fluency, perceptual speed, verbal comprehension, spatial visualization, numerical calculation, and associative memory.

Though scores on tests measuring these abilities had moderately high positive correlations with one another, they did not correlate highly enough for Thurstone to assume the existence of a general underlying intelligence factor. Suppose that you took tests to assess your abilities in reasoning, verbal comprehension, and numerical calculation. Thurstone would insist that your performance on any single test would reflect, not the influence of a general intelligence factor, but instead the influence of a specific intelligence factor related to the particular ability assessed by that test.

Guilford's Theory of the Structure of the Intellect

Like Thurstone, J. P. Guilford (1897–1987) rejected the notion of a general intelligence factor (Guilford, 1959). He did so because of the unevenness he observed in children's abilities. As shown in figure 10.3, instead of the mere 7 factors in Thurstone's theory,

FIGURE 10.3

The Structure of the Intellect
Guilford identified 120 factors
underlying intelligence, based on the
interaction of five kinds of operations,
four kinds of contents, and six kinds
of products.

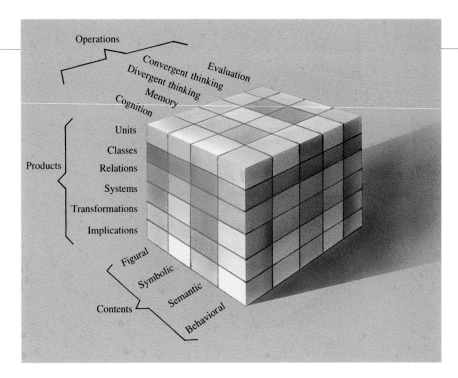

Raymond Cattell
"Two major forms of intelligence
emerge out of development and
acculturation: fluid and crystallized."

fluid intelligence
*The form of intelligence that reflects
reasoning ability, memory capacity, and
speed of information processing.*

crystallized intelligence
*The form of intelligence that reflects
knowledge acquired through schooling and
in everyday life.*

Guilford identified 120 factors through the use of factor analysis. Each of these factors represents the interaction among dimensions that Guilford called *operations* (thought processes, such as memory), *contents* (information that a person is thinking about, such as symbols), and *products* (results of thinking about the information, such as implications). By the end of his life, Guilford (1985) had increased the number of factors to 150. Of course, given so many factors, it is unlikely that researchers will ever determine the merits of all of them. Before his death, Guilford hoped to help students improve themselves on the specific factors that composed intelligence (Comrey, Michael, & Fruchter, 1988).

Horn and Cattell's Two-Factor Theory of Intelligence

A recent theory of intelligence based on factor analysis was developed by John Horn and Raymond Cattell (1966), who identified two intelligence factors. **Fluid intelligence** reflects thinking ability, memory capacity, and speed of information processing. Horn and Cattell believe that fluid intelligence is largely inherited, is affected little by training, and declines in late adulthood. The decline of fluid intelligence across adulthood has been supported by other researchers, as well (Wang & Kaufman, 1993). In contrast, **crystallized intelligence** reflects the acquisition of skills and knowledge through schooling and everyday experience. Horn and Cattell believe that crystallized intelligence increases or remains the same in late adulthood. Changes in fluid intelligence and crystallized intelligence across the life span are illustrated in figure 10.4. Special educational programs can enhance fluid and, especially, crystallized intelligence (Stankov & Chen, 1988).

After reviewing arguments for the existence of fluid and crystallized intelligence, Guilford (1980) insisted that Horn and Cattell had failed to demonstrate the existence of these two factors. It remains for psychologists to determine which, if any, of the factor-analytic theories of intelligence is the best. Perhaps a more telling criticism of factor-analytic theories of intelligence is that they assume that intelligence reflects primarily those cognitive abilities needed to perform in school. A more encompassing theory of intelligence would consider a broader range of abilities (Frederiksen, 1986). Theories proposed by Robert Sternberg and Howard Gardner have done so.

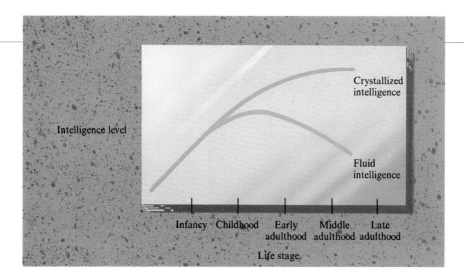

FIGURE 10.4

Life-Span Changes in Intelligence
While fluid intelligence tends to decline in old age, crystallized intelligence tends to increase (Horn & Donaldson, 1976).

Robert Sternberg
"The triarchic theory is an attempt to account for, in a single theory, what in the past has been accounted for by multiple theories often perceived to be in conflict with each other."

triarchic theory of intelligence
Robert Sternberg's theory of intelligence, which assumes that there are three main kinds of intelligence: componential, experiential, and contextual.

The Triarchic Theory of Intelligence

As a child, Robert Sternberg performed poorly on IQ tests and suffered from severe test anxiety, yet he later earned a Ph.D. and became a leading researcher in cognitive psychology. This contributed to his belief that intelligence comprises more than the abilities measured by traditional intelligence tests (Trotter, 1986). To determine the views of laypersons on the nature of intelligence, Sternberg and his colleagues (1981) surveyed people reading in a college library, entering a supermarket, or waiting for a train. They were asked to list what they believed were the main characteristics of intelligent people. The results showed that the respondents assumed that intelligent people had good verbal skills, good problem-solving abilities, and good social judgment.

During the past decade, Sternberg (1984) has developed a **triarchic theory of intelligence,** which claims that intelligence comprises three kinds of abilities similar to those reported by the people in his earlier survey. He bases his theory on his observations of how people process information. *Componential intelligence* is similar to the kind of intelligence considered by traditional theories of intelligence. It primarily reflects our information-processing ability, which helps in academic performance. *Experiential intelligence* is the ability to combine different experiences in insightful ways to solve novel problems. It reflects creativity, as exhibited by an artist, composer, or scientist. According to Sternberg, creative geniuses, such as Leonardo da Vinci and Albert Einstein, have especially high levels of experiential intelligence. *Contextual intelligence* is the ability to function in practical, everyday social situations. It reflects "street smarts," as in negotiating the price of a new car. Of course, many situations require the use of all three kinds of intelligence.

The triarchic theory recognizes that we must be able to function in settings other than school. Moreover, we might excel in one kind of intelligence without excelling in the other two. Sternberg believes that each of the three kinds of intelligence can be improved by special training, and he is developing ways of testing and improving each (Okagaki & Sternberg, 1993). Though Sternberg's theory goes beyond traditional theories by considering creative intelligence and practical intelligence, as well as academic intelligence, more research is needed to determine its merits.

The Theory of Multiple Intelligences

While Sternberg bases his theory on his study of information processing, Gardner (1983) bases his **theory of multiple intelligences** on his belief that the brain has evolved separate systems for different adaptive abilities that he calls "intelligences." According to Gardner, there are seven types of intelligence, each of which is developed to a different

theory of multiple intelligences
Howard Gardner's theory of intelligence, which assumes that the brain has evolved separate systems for seven kinds of intelligence.

The Theory of Multiple Intelligences
Howard Gardner believes that we have evolved seven kinds of intelligence, which are developed to different extents in each of us. Former Texas Congresswoman Barbara Jordan's excellent speaking ability exemplifies linguistic intelligence. Basketball star Michael Jordan's superb athletic ability exemplifies bodily-kinesthetic intelligence. Rock musician Neil Young's proficiency in singing, playing, and composing music exemplifies musical intelligence. And physicist Stephen Hawking has used his outstanding logical-mathematical intelligence to contribute to our knowledge of the cosmos—despite being disabled by amyotrophic lateral sclerosis (Lou Gehrig's disease).

Howard Gardner
"There is pervasive evidence for the existence of several *relatively autonomous* human intellectual competences, abbreviated . . . as 'human intelligences'."

extent in each of us: linguistic, logical-mathematical, spatial, musical, bodily-kinesthetic, intrapersonal, and interpersonal. Gardner assumes that certain brain structures and pathways underly these intelligences and that brain damage interferes with one or more of the intelligences. For example, damage to speech centers interferes with linguistic intelligence, and damage to the cerebellum interferes with bodily-kinesthetic intelligence.

Several of Gardner's kinds of intelligence are assessed by traditional intelligence tests. *Linguistic intelligence* is the ability to communicate through language. If you are good at reading textbooks, writing term papers, and presenting oral reports, you would be high in linguistic intelligence. A person with high *logical-mathematical intelligence* would be good at analyzing arguments and solving mathematical problems. And a person with high *spatial intelligence*, such as a skilled architect or carpenter, would be good at perceiving and arranging objects in the environment.

The remaining kinds of intelligence are assessed little, if at all, by traditional intelligence tests. *Musical intelligence* is the ability to analyze, compose, or perform music. A person with good *bodily-kinesthetic intelligence* would be able to move effectively, as in dancing or playing sports, or to manipulate objects effectively, as in using tools or driving a car. If you have high *intrapersonal intelligence*, you know yourself well and understand what motivates your behavior. For example, emotionally depressed people high in intrapersonal intelligence might be more likely to find ways to relieve their depression. And if you have high *interpersonal intelligence*, you function well in social situations because you are able to understand the needs of other people and to predict their behavior.

As you have certainly observed in your own life, a person might excel in one or more of Gardner's intelligences while being average or below average in others. In extreme cases, we have the autistic savant who excels in painting but cannot read, the child prodigy who excels in mathematics but cannot dance, the student who excels in

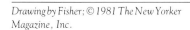

Drawing by Fisher; © 1981 The New Yorker Magazine, Inc.

"... and give me good abstract-reasoning ability, interpersonal skills, cultural perspective, linguistic comprehension, and a high sociodynamic potential."

science but has no friends, and the athlete who excels in sports but cannot write a coherent sentence. Of course, you may have also encountered the so-called Renaissance person, who excels in several of Gardner's intelligences.

According to Gardner, our ability to succeed in life depends on the degree to which we develop the kinds of intelligence that are needed to function well in our culture. For example, for most people in the United States, success depends more on linguistic intelligence than on musical intelligence. Success in a culture that relies on hunting skills would put a greater premium on spatial intelligence and bodily-kinesthetic intelligence. Gardner's theory is so new that it has yet to generate sufficient research to determine its merits. But it is potentially superior to traditional theories of intelligence in its attention to the kinds of abilities needed to function in both academic and non-academic settings. Gardner has begun applying his theory to enhancing the intellectual development of children (Krechevsky & Gardner, 1990).

THINKING ABOUT *Psychology*

DOES INTELLIGENCE DEPEND MORE ON NATURE OR ON NURTURE?

In 1951 the movie *Bedtime for Bonzo*, starring Ronald Reagan and a chimpanzee named Bonzo, comically questioned whether a chimpanzee reared in a human household would become more intelligent than the typical chimpanzee. And in the 1983 movie *Trading Places*, two upper-class men argued about whether our social positions are determined more by heredity or by environment. They agreed to settle their argument by manipulating a rich white man and a poor black man into trading homes (a mansion versus the street), vocations (big business versus begging), and financial status (wealth versus poverty). Both movies illustrate the popular concern with the issue of *nature versus nurture*.

Nature versus Nurture
Even Hollywood movies, such as
Bedtime for Bonzo, have dealt with the
issue of nature versus nurture.

eugenics
*The practice of encouraging supposedly
superior people to reproduce, while
preventing supposedly inferior people
from reproducing.*

The phrase *nature versus nurture* was popularized in the 1870s by Sir Francis Galton
(Fancher, 1984). As a follower of his cousin Charles Darwin, he assumed that intelligence was inherited. Galton (1869) concluded this after finding that eminent men had
a higher proportion of eminent relatives than did other men. This led Galton to champion **eugenics** (Rabinowitz, 1984), the practice of encouraging supposedly superior people
to reproduce, while preventing supposedly inferior people from reproducing. Galton's
views also influenced the attitudes of psychologists toward immigrants in the early twentieth
century.

EARLY STUDIES OF IMMIGRANTS

In 1912 Henry Goddard (1866–1957) became director of testing the intelligence of
immigrants arriving at Ellis Island in New York Harbor. Goddard (1917) made the
astonishing claim that 79 percent of Italians, 80 percent of Hungarians, 83 percent of
Jews, and 87 percent of Russians scored in the "feebleminded" range, which today we
would call mildly retarded. Even after later reevaluating his data, he claimed that an
average of "only" 40 percent of these groups were feebleminded (Gelb, 1986). Goddard,
following in the footsteps of Galton, concluded that these ethnic groups were, by nature,
intellectually inferior.

You probably realize that Goddard discounted possible environmental causes for
the poor test performance of immigrants. He failed to consider a lack of education, a long
ocean voyage below deck, and anxiety created by the testing situation as causes of their
poor performance. Moreover, even though the tests were translated into the immigrants'
native languages, the translations were often inadequate. Despite the shortcomings of
the tests, low test scores were used as the basis for having many supposedly "feebleminded" immigrants deported. This was ironic, because at the 1915 meeting of the
American Psychological Association in Chicago a critic of Goddard's program of intelligence testing reported that the native-born mayor of Chicago had taken an IQ test and
had scored in the feebleminded range (Gould, 1981).

Further support for Goddard's position was provided by the army's intelligence
testing program during World War I, which was headed by Robert Yerkes (1876–1956).
One of Yerkes's colleagues, Carl Brigham (1923), published the results of the testing
program. He found that immigrants scored lower on the IQ tests than did American-

born whites. Brigham attributed these differences in IQ scores to differences in heredity. The U.S. Congress passed the Immigration Act of 1924, which restricted immigration from eastern and southern Europe. There is disagreement between those who believe Brigham's findings influenced passage of the act (McPherson, 1985) and those who believe that they did not (Snyderman & Herrnstein, 1983).

Regardless, in 1930 Brigham stated that he had been wrong in assuming that the poorer performance of immigrants was attributable to heredity. He noted that in their everyday lives, immigrants—living in their original cultures—might not have had the opportunity to encounter much of the material in the army IQ tests. To appreciate this, consider the following multiple-choice items from the Army Alpha Test: "Crisco is a: patent medicine, disinfectant, toothpaste, food product [the correct answer];" and "Christy Mathewson is famous as a(n): writer, artist, baseball player [the correct answer], comedian" (Gould, 1981). Similarly, the poorer performance of blacks on IQ tests was attributed to sociocultural deprivation caused by segregation (Rury, 1988).

RESEARCH ON THE INFLUENCE OF HEREDITY AND ENVIRONMENT

After three decades of relative indifference to it, the issue of nature versus nurture reemerged in the 1960s when President Lyndon Johnson began *Project Head Start*, which provides preschool children from deprived socioeconomic backgrounds with enrichment programs to promote their intellectual development. Head Start was stimulated in part by the finding that blacks scored lower than whites on IQ tests. Those who supported Head Start attributed this difference to the poorer socioeconomic conditions in which black children were more likely to be reared.

But in 1969 an article by psychologist Arthur Jensen questioned whether programs such as Head Start could significantly boost the intellectual level of deprived children. Jensen's doubts were based on the notion of **heritability,** the extent to which the variability in a characteristic within a group can be attributed to heredity. Jensen claimed that intelligence has a heritability of .80, which would mean that 80 percent of the

heritability
The extent to which variability in a characteristic within a group can be attributed to heredity.

The Nurturing of Intelligence
Children from (a) higher socioeconomic classes will be more likely than children from (b) lower socioeconomic classes to receive the intellectual enrichment they need to reach their intellectual potential.

(a)

(b)

variability in intelligence among the members of a group can be explained by heredity. This led him to conclude that the IQ gap between white and black children was mainly attributable to heredity. But he was accused of making an unwarranted inference. Just because intelligence may have high heritability *within* a group does not mean that IQ differences *between* groups, such as blacks and whites, are caused by heredity. Moreover, research has found that the heritability of intelligence is closer to .50 than to .80 (Plomin & Rende, 1991). Jensen's article led to accusations that he was a racist and to demonstrations against him when he spoke on college campuses, illustrating the tension between academic freedom and social sensitivity.

In the tradition of eugenics, one of Jensen's chief supporters, William Shockley (1972), urged that the federal government pay Americans with below-average IQ scores (who would be disproportionately black) to undergo sterilization. He recommended paying them $1,000 for each point by which their IQ scores were less than 100. Though Shockley was not a psychologist or even a social scientist, he gained media attention because he had won a 1956 Nobel prize for inventing the transistor. Shockley and several other Nobel prize winners have even deposited their sperm in a "sperm bank" in California for use by women of superior intelligence who wish to produce highly intelligent offspring ("Superkids?", 1980).

A vigorous response to those who claimed that intelligence is chiefly the product of heredity came from Leon Kamin (1974). Kamin discovered that important data supporting the hereditary basis of intelligence had been falsified. Sir Cyril Burt (1883–1971), a British psychologist, had reported findings from three studies showing that the positive correlation in IQ scores between identical twins reared apart was higher than the correlation in IQ of fraternal twins reared together. Because identical twins reared apart have the same genes but different environments, yet had a higher correlation in intelligence than did fraternal twins reared together, the data supported the greater influence of heredity on intelligence.

In each of his studies, published in 1943, 1955, and 1966, Burt reported that the correlation in intelligence between identical twins reared apart was .771. But, as Kamin observed, the odds against finding the same correlation to three decimal places in three different studies are so high as to defy belief. Burt's findings were literally too good to be true. Even Burt's official biographer, who began as an admirer and who believed that Burt had not falsified his data, grudgingly concluded that the data were indeed fraudulent (Hearnshaw, 1979). This has not prevented others from coming to Burt's defense (Fletcher, 1990). Ironically, less than a decade after Kamin's critique of Burt's research the Minnesota Study of Twins Reared Apart found that identical twins reared apart had a correlation of .710 in their intelligence—not very different from what Burt had reported (Lykken, 1982).

FAMILY STUDIES OF INTELLIGENCE

Though the publicity generated by the discovery of Burt's deception struck a blow against the hereditary view of intelligence, other researchers have conducted legitimate family studies of intelligence. As shown in figure 10.5, the closer the genetic relationship

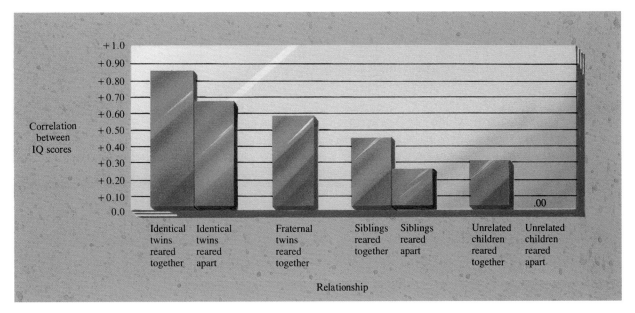

FIGURE 10.5

Heredity versus Environment
The correlation in IQ between relatives increases as their hereditary or environmental similarity increases.

between relatives, the more similar they are in intelligence (Bouchard & McGue, 1981). But the closer the genetic relationship between relatives, the more likely they also are to share similar environments. Consequently, the size of the correlation in intelligence between relatives of varying degrees of genetic similarity is, by itself, inadequate to determine whether this similarity is caused primarily by hereditary factors or by environmental factors.

Perhaps the higher correlation in intelligence between identical twins reared together than between fraternal twins reared together might be attributable to the more-similar treatment received by identical twins. But research findings have provided strong evidence against this interpretation. When identical twins are mistakenly reared as fraternal twins they become as similar in intelligence as identical twins who are reared as identical twins. Moreover, fraternal twins who are mistakenly reared as identical twins become no more similar in intelligence than do fraternal twins reared as fraternal twins (Scarr & Carter-Saltzman, 1979). These findings indicate that the similarity in intelligence between twins is determined more by their genetic similarity than by their environmental similarity.

To separate the effects of heredity and environment, researchers have turned to adoption studies. Some of these studies compare the correlation in intelligence between adopted children and their adoptive parents to the correlation in intelligence between adopted children and their biological parents. A published review of adoption studies found that the positive correlation in intelligence between adoptees and their biological parents is larger than the positive correlation between adoptees and their adoptive parents (Turkheimer, 1991). This provides evidence for the genetic basis of intelligence; the genes inherited from the natural parents appear to exert a stronger influence on adoptees than does the environment provided by their adoptive parents (Bouchard & McGue, 1981). Both the Colorado Adoption Project (Coon et al., 1990) and the Texas Adoption Project (Loehlin, Horn, & Willerman, 1989) have provided strong support for a hereditary component in intelligence. The influence of heredity on the variability in intelligence among children *increases* from infancy through childhood. For example, the Colorado Adoption Study has found that the heritability of intelligence is only .09 at age 1 but .36 at age 7 (Fulker, DeFries, & Plomin, 1988). This means that as children spend more years in their home environment, the environment—counter to what common sense would predict—*decreases* in its influence on the variability in intelligence.

Nonetheless, adoption studies have also provided some support for the effect of the environment on intelligence. Consider the following study sponsored by the University of Minnesota.

Anatomy of a Contemporary Research Study:
What Is the Effect of Adoption on the Intellectual Development of Adopted Children?

Rationale

If nature dominates nurture, then children from lower socioeconomic classes who are adopted by parents from higher socioeconomic classes should show little or no gain in IQ when compared to equivalent children who remain with their biological parents. This possibility was tested by Sandra Scarr and Richard Weinberg (1976) in the Minnesota Adoption Study.

Method

The study included black children who had been adopted by white Minnesota couples of higher socioeconomic status than the children's biological parents.

Results and Discussion

The study found that the children who had been adopted had an average IQ of 110. This indicated that the environment had a strong effect on their intelligence, because the adoptees scored about 20 points higher than the average IQ of comparable black children reared by their biological parents. These findings indicate that nurture, as well as nature, is important in intellectual development, because children adopted into higher socioeconomic-status families have IQs that are higher than those of their biological parents but lower than those of their adoptive parents (Weinberg, Scarr, & Waldman, 1992).

A study of adopted children in France found that these results also held for white children. The subjects of the study were 32 children who had been abandoned at birth by their lower-socioeconomic-class parents and adopted at an average age of 4 months by white professionals. When compared with their siblings who were reared by their biological parents, the adoptees scored an average of 14 points higher in intelligence and were less likely to be left back in school (Schiff et al., 1982).

A more recent study in France included 87 adolescents given up at birth and adopted before 3 years of age into different socioeconomic classes. The results showed a significant negative correlation of .37 between the social class of the adoptive fathers and the likelihood of repeating a grade in school. This means that as the socioeconomic class of the adoptive fathers increased, the likelihood of an adoptee's having to repeat a grade decreased. This supported the importance of the environment in determining intellectual performance (Duyme, 1988). Based on their review of adoption studies, Scarr and Weinberg (1983) concluded that intelligence is influenced by both heredity and environment, with neither dominating the other. But other researchers have found that adopted children reared in families of higher socioeconomic status than their biological families show a smaller enhancement of their intelligence than has been reported by other researchers (Locurto, 1990).

Support for the influence of the environment comes from family configuration studies. A survey of 400,000 19-year-old men in the Netherlands found that the larger their families and the later they were in the birth order, the less intelligent they tended to be (Belmont & Marolla, 1973). This finding has been explained by Robert Zajonc's (1986) **confluence model**, which assumes that each child is born into an intellectual environment that depends on the intelligence level of his or her parents and siblings. The greater the number of children and the smaller the average interval between births, the lower will be what Zajonc calls the *average intellectual environment* into which a child is born. One of the reasons for this drop may be the inevitable reduction in the attention parents give to each of their children after the birth of a child (Gibbs, Teti, & Bond, 1987).

In a bold gesture, Zajonc (1976) used the confluence model to predict that the decline in SAT scores that had begun in 1963 would stop in 1980 and then begin to rise. Zajonc based his prediction on the fact that high school students who took the SAT

confluence model
The view that each child is born into an intellectual environment that is dependent on the intelligence levels of her or his parents and siblings, with the number of children and the interval between births affecting the intelligence of each successive child.

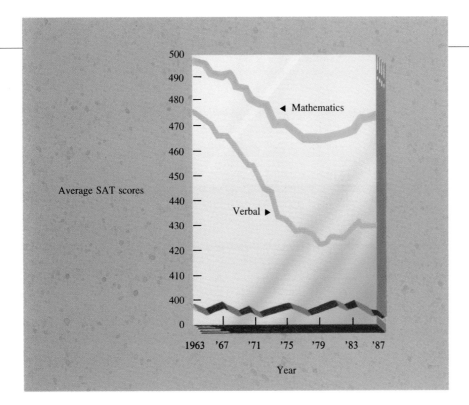

FIGURE 10.6

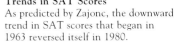

Trends in SAT Scores
As predicted by Zajonc, the downward trend in SAT scores that began in 1963 reversed itself in 1980.

between 1963 and 1980 had been born into increasingly larger families during the post–World War II baby boom. But after 1980, high school students who would take the SAT would come from smaller and smaller families. Zajonc's prediction was supported: As figure 10.6 indicates, SAT scores continued to decline until 1980 and then began to rise. Of course, the decline could have a host of other explanations, including greater numbers of academically poor students taking the test (Astin & Garber, 1982).

Though Zajonc (1993) continues to present evidence supporting the confluence model, other researchers present evidence contradicting it (Barbut, 1993). For example, data from a study by the National Institutes of Health, which included 47,000 women and their 53,000 children, failed to find a relationship between the intelligence of the children and the average interval between the births in their families (Brackbill & Nichols, 1982). Moreover, the confluence model has demonstrated, at best, a *correlational*, rather than a *causal*, relationship between family configuration and intelligence. Perhaps other unidentified factors account for the relationship (Rodgers, 1988).

Robert Zajonc
"The greater the number of children and the shorter the intervals between successive births, the less mature, on the average, is the intellectual milieu for each child."

Intellectual Enrichment Programs

Further support for the influence of the environment on intelligence comes from the finding that the difference in white and black performance on the SAT narrowed between 1976 and 1983 (Jones, 1984). Moreover, the difference in IQ test scores between black and white children is declining, possibly because black children have gained access to better educational and economic resources (Vincent, 1991). Access to enrichment programs such as Project Head Start might also play a role. Socioeconomically deprived children who attend Project Head Start show an average gain of 10 points in their IQ scores (Zigler et al., 1982) and make greater gains in their cognitive abilities, compared to those not in such programs. This contradicts Jensen's (1969) prediction that Head Start would have no significant effect on intellectual growth. Unfortunately, the gains achieved by children in preschool enrichment programs may decline over the first few years of grade school (Locurto, 1991). This might indicate the need to continue enrichment programs beyond the preschool years.

Project Head Start
Intellectual enrichment programs, such as Project Head Start, provide a stimulating preschool environment that better prepares children for success in elementary school.

Preschool enrichment programs other than Head Start can also have beneficial effects, as shown in a study of disadvantaged black children who attended Head Start, other preschool, or no preschool programs. Those in the Head Start and preschool programs showed greater improvement in several intellectual abilities than did those who did not attend either kind of program. This could not be attributed to initial differences in intellectual abilities, because the children were statistically matched on various relevant characteristics (Lee et al., 1990).

Other countries have also found that intellectual enrichment programs can be beneficial. Possibly the most ambitious of all enrichment programs took place from 1979 to 1983 in Venezuela, under its minister of state for the development of intelligence (Gonzalez, 1989). The program provided good prenatal care and infant nutrition, as well as sensory stimulation of preschoolers and special training in cognitive skills. New mothers watched videocassettes on proper child rearing while in their hospital rooms, schoolchildren attended "learning to think" classes, and television commercials promoted the need to develop the minds of Venezuelan children (Walsh, 1981). The more than 400 Venezuelan seventh-graders who participated in a program to teach thinking skills (such as reasoning, problem solving, and decision making) achieved better academic performance than did comparable control students who had not participated (Herrnstein et al., 1986).

Even more evidence of the influence of the environment on intelligence comes from the finding that IQ scores have increased from 5 to 25 points in fourteen nations during the past 30 years, apparently because of better nutrition, education, and health care (Flynn, 1987). And both Galton and Goddard would be surprised to find that today the Japanese, whom they considered intellectually inferior, score significantly higher than Americans on IQ tests that have been standardized on Americans. Japanese children score about 10 points higher than American children (Lynn, 1982). The Japanese increase in IQ scores parallels that country's increased emphasis on education, with children going to school more hours, attending school more days, and studying more hours than American children do.

Even the academic achievements of Asian Americans surpass those of white and black Americans. What might account for this? Stanley Sue, a cross-cultural psychologist, insists that it is wrong to attribute these achievements to either an inborn intellectual superiority or a culture that places a high value on education. Instead, Sue looks to simple adaptive behavior. Because Asian Americans have had cultural and discriminatory barriers to their upward mobility in careers (such as sports, politics, entertainment, and corporate leadership) that place less emphasis on education, they have sought to pursue careers that provide fewer barriers. These more accessible alternatives (such as science, mathematics, and engineering) typically place a premium on academic excellence (Sue & Okazaki, 1990). Sue's explanation remains to be tested.

Some psychologists have suggested that it might not be in our best interest to study the relative importance of nature and nurture in intellectual development (Sarason, 1984). To do so might discover little of scientific import, while providing apparent scientific support for discrimination against racial or ethnic minorities. Instead of examining the relative importance of nature versus nurture, it might be better to do what Anne Anastasi (1958), an authority on psychological testing, suggested more than three decades ago: determine *how* both achieve their effects (Turkheimer, 1991). The current trend to view intelligence as comprising a variety of abilities and as being improvable by proper education may change the focus of research from trying to determine whether particular groups are naturally more intelligent than other groups to trying to discover ways of helping all people approach their intellectual potential.

SUMMARY

INTELLIGENCE TESTING

Intelligence is the global capacity to act purposefully, to think rationally, and to deal effectively with the environment. An achievement test assesses knowledge of a particular subject, an aptitude test predicts the potential to benefit from instruction in a particular academic or vocational setting, and an intelligence test is a kind of aptitude test that assesses overall mental ability.

Sir Francis Galton began the study of mental abilities in the late nineteenth century and founded the field of differential psychology. The first formal test of general intelligence was the Binet-Simon Scale, which was developed to help place children in school classes. The American version of the test became known as the Stanford-Binet Intelligence Scale. Today that test and the Wechsler Intelligence Scales are the most popular intelligence tests.

Tests must be standardized so that they are administered in a uniform manner and so that test scores can be compared with norms. A test must also be reliable, giving consistent results over time. And a test must be valid, meaning that it measures what it is supposed to measure.

Controversy has arisen over whether intelligence testing is fair to minority groups, particularly blacks. Those who oppose intelligence testing claim that because blacks, on the average, score lower on them than whites do, the tests are biased against blacks. Those who support their use claim that the tests accurately predict the academic performance of both blacks and whites, and attribute the differences in performance to the deprived backgrounds that are more common among black children. Attempts to develop tests that are not affected by the test taker's cultural background have failed.

EXTREMES OF INTELLIGENCE

To be classified as mentally retarded, a person must have an IQ below 70 and, beginning in childhood, difficulties performing in everyday life. The four categories of mental retardation are mild retardation, moderate retardation, severe retardation, and profound retardation. Though most cases of mental retardation are caused by cultural-familial factors, some are caused by brain damage. Most mentally retarded people can benefit from education and training programs.

To be classified as mentally gifted, a person must have an IQ above 130 and demonstrate unusual ability in at least one area, such as art, music, or mathematics. Lewis Terman's Genetic Studies of Genius have demonstrated that mentally gifted children tend to become successful in their academic, social, physical, and vocational lives. Benbow and Stanley's Study of Mathematically Precocious Youth identifies children with outstanding mathematical ability, provides them with special programs, and counsels their parents about how to help them reach their potential.

THEORIES OF INTELLIGENCE

Theories of intelligence have traditionally depended on factor analysis, a statistical technique for determining the abilities that underlie intelligence. The theories differ in the extent to which they view intelligence as a general factor or a combination of different factors. The most recent factor-analytic theory distinguishes between fluid intelligence and crystallized intelligence.

Robert Sternberg's triarchic theory of intelligence is based on his research on information processing. The theory distinguishes between componential (academic) intelligence, experiential (creative) intelligence, and contextual (practical) intelligence. Sternberg also believes that people can be taught to process information more effectively, thereby increasing their level of intelligence.

Howard Gardner's theory of multiple intelligences is a biopsychological theory, which assumes that the brain has evolved separate systems for different adaptive abilities that he calls "intelligences": linguistic, logical-mathematical, spatial, musical, bodily-kinesthetic, intrapersonal, and interpersonal intelligences. All of us vary in the degree to which we have developed each of these kinds of intelligence.

THINKING ABOUT PSYCHOLOGY: DOES INTELLIGENCE DEPEND MORE ON NATURE OR ON NURTURE?

One of the most controversial issues in psychology has been the extent to which intelligence is a product of heredity or environment. Early studies of immigrants concluded that many were "feeble-minded." The examiners attributed this to hereditary factors rather than a host of cultural and environmental factors that actually accounted for that finding. Arthur Jensen created a stir by claiming that heredity is a much more powerful determinant of intelligence than is environment. Studies of twins, adopted children, family configuration effects, and enrichment programs indicate that neither heredity nor environment is a significantly more important determinant of intelligence. Moreover, there is no widely accepted evidence that differences in intelligence between particular racial or ethnic groups are caused by heredity.

IMPORTANT CONCEPTS

achievement test 358
aptitude test 359
cerebral palsy 367
confluence model 380
crystallized intelligence 372
cultural-familial retardation 366

differential psychology 360
Down syndrome 367
eugenics 376
factor analysis 371
fluid intelligence 372
heritability 377

intelligence 358
intelligence quotient (IQ) 361
intelligence test 359
mental giftedness 369
mental retardation 365

phenylketonuria (PKU) 367
theory of multiple
     intelligences 373
triarchic theory of
     intelligence 373

MAJOR CONTRIBUTORS

RECOMMENDED READINGS

FOR GENERAL WORKS ON INTELLIGENCE

Binet, A., & Simon, T. (1916/1973). *The development of intelligence in children*. Salem, NH: Ayer.

Ceci, S. J. (1990). *On intelligence . . . more or less*. Englewood Cliffs, NJ: Prentice Hall.

Irvine, S. H., & Berry, J. W. (Eds.). (1988). *Human abilities in cultural context*. New York: Cambridge University Press.

Jenkins, J. J., & Paterson, D. G. (Eds.). (1961). *Studies in individual differences: The search for intelligence*. New York: Appleton-Century-Crofts.

Scarr, S. (1984). Intelligence: What an introductory psychology student might want to know. In A. M. Rogers & C. J. Scheirer (Eds.), *The G. Stanley Hall Lecture Series* (Vol. 4, pp. 59–99). Washington, DC: American Psychological Association.

Sternberg, R. J. (1986). *Intelligence applied: Understanding and increasing your intellectual skills*. New York: Harcourt Brace Jovanovich.

Wolman, B. B. (Ed.). (1985). *Handbook of intelligence: Theories, measurement, and applications*. New York: Wiley.

FOR MORE ON INTELLIGENCE TESTING

Aiken, L. R. (1987). *Assessment of intellectual functioning*. Needham Heights, MA: Allyn & Bacon.

Anastasi, A. (1988). *Psychological testing*. New York: Macmillan.

Chapman, P. D. (1988). *Schools as sorters: Lewis M. Terman, applied psychology, and the intelligence testing movement, 1890–1930*. New York: New York University Press.

Crouse, J., & Trusheim, D. (1988). *The case against the SAT*. Chicago: University of Chicago Press.

Elliott, R. (1987). *Litigating intelligence: IQ tests, special education, and social science in the courtroom*. New York: Greenwood.

Frank, G. (1983). *The Wechsler enterprise: An assessment of the development, structure and use of the Wechsler tests of intelligence*. New York: Pergamon.

Irvine, S. H., & Berry, J. W. (Eds.). (1986). *Human abilities in cultural context*. New York: Cambridge University Press.

Jensen, A. R. (1980). *Bias in mental testing*. New York: Free Press.

Reynolds, C. R., & Brown, R. T. (Eds.). (1984). *Perspectives on bias in mental testing*. New York: Plenum.

Thorndike, R. M., & Lohman, D. F. (1990). *A century of ability testing*. Chicago: Riverside.

FOR MORE ON MENTAL RETARDATION

Beirne-Smith, M., Patton, J. R., & Ittenbach, R. (1994). *Mental retardation*. New York: Macmillan.

Dolce, L. (1994). *Mental retardation*. New York: Chelsea House.

Hodapp, R. M., Burack, J. A., & Zigler, E. (Eds.). (1990). *Issues in the developmental approach to mental retardation*. New York: Cambridge University Press.

Matson, J. L., & Mulick, J. A. (Eds.). (1990). *Handbook of mental retardation*. New York: Pergamon.

Miller, L. K. (1989). *Musical savants*. Hillsdale, NJ: Erlbaum.

Patterson, D. (1987, August). The causes of Down syndrome. *Scientific American*, pp. 52–60.

Smith, S. B. (1983). *The great mental calculators: The psychology, methods, and lives of calculating prodigies, past and present*. New York: Columbia University Press.

Zigler, E., & Hodapp, R. M. (1986). *Understanding mental retardation.* New York: Cambridge University Press.

FOR MORE ON MENTAL GIFTEDNESS

Albert, R. S. (1990). *Genius and eminence.* New York: Pergamon.

Feldman, D. H. (1986). *Nature's gambit: Child prodigies and the development of human potential.* New York: Basic Books.

Horowitz, F. D., & O'Brien, M. (Eds.). (1985). *The gifted and talented: Developmental perspectives.* Washington, DC: American Psychological Association.

Howe, M. J. (1990). *The psychology of exceptional abilities.* New York: Basil Blackwell.

Howe, M. J. (1989). *Fragments of genius: Investigations of the strange feats of mentally retarded idiot savants.* New York: Routledge.

Murray, P. (Ed.). (1989). *Genius: The history of an idea.* New York: Basil Blackwell.

Seagoe, M. V. (1975). *Terman and the gifted.* Los Altos, CA: Kaufmann.

Serebriakoff, V. (1985). *Mensa: The society for the highly intelligent.* New York: Stein & Day.

Shurkin, J. N. (1992). *Terman's kids: The groundbreaking study of how the gifted grow up.* Boston: Little, Brown.

Storfer, M. D. (1990). *Intelligence and giftedness: The contributions of heredity and early environments.* San Francisco: Jossey-Bass.

Subotnik, K. A., & Arnold, K. D. (Eds.). (1993). *Beyond Terman: Contemporary longitudinal studies of giftedness and talent.* Norwood, NJ: Ablex.

Terman, L. M. (1926). *Genetic studies of genius: Mental and physical traits of a thousand gifted children.* Stanford, CA: Stanford University Press.

Treffert, D. A. (1989). *Extraordinary people: Understanding "idiot savants."* New York: Harper & Row.

Trent, J. W. (1994). *Inventing the feebleminded: A history of mental retardation in the United States, 1840–1990.* Berkeley: University of California Press.

Wallace, A. (1986). *The prodigy.* New York: Dutton.

FOR MORE ON THEORIES OF INTELLIGENCE

Cattell, R. B. (1987). *Intelligence: Its structure, growth, and action.* New York: Elsevier.

Gardner, H. (1983). *Frames of mind: The theory of multiple intelligences.* New York: Basic Books.

Gardner, H. (1993). *Multiple intelligences: The theory in practice.* New York: Basic Books.

Spearman, C. (1923/1973). *The nature of "intelligence" and the principles of cognition.* New York: Arno Press.

Sternberg, R. J. (1984). *Beyond IQ: A triarchic theory of intelligence.* New York: Cambridge University Press.

Thurstone, L. L. (1924/1973). *The nature of intelligence.* Westport, CT: Greenwood.

FOR MORE ON NATURE VERSUS NURTURE

Eysenck, H. J., & Kamin, L. (1981). *The intelligence controversy.* New York: Wiley.

Fletcher, R. (1990). *The Cyril Burt scandal: Case for the defense.* New York: Macmillan.

Galton, F. (1869/1972). *Hereditary genius: An inquiry into its laws and consequences.* Magnolia, MA: Peter Smith.

Goddard, H. H. (1931/1973). *The Kallikak family: A study in the heredity of feeble-mindedness.* Salem, NH: Ayer.

Gould, S. J. (1981). *The mismeasure of man.* New York: W. W. Norton.

Joynson, R. B. (1989). *The Burt affair.* New York: Routledge.

Modgil, S., & Modgil, C. (Eds.). (1987). *Arthur Jensen: Consensus and controversy.* New York: Hemisphere.

Spitz, H. H. (1986). *The raising of intelligence: A selected history of attempts to raise retarded intelligence.* Hillsdale, NJ: Erlbaum.

Zigler, E., & Valentine, J. (Eds.). (1979). *Project Head Start: A legacy of the war on poverty.* New York: Free Press.

FOR MORE ON CONTRIBUTORS TO THE STUDY OF INTELLIGENCE

Anastasi, A. (1980). Anne Anastasi. In G. Lindzey (Ed.), *A history of psychology in autobiography* (Vol. 7, pp. 1–37). San Francisco: Freeman.

Fancher, R. E. (1985). *The intelligence men: Makers of the IQ controversy.* New York: W. W. Norton.

Forrest, D. W. (1974). *Francis Galton: The life and work of a Victorian genius.* New York: Taplinger.

Hearnshaw, L. S. (1979). *Cyril Burt: Psychologist.* Ithaca, NY: Cornell University Press.

Minton, H. L. (1988). *Lewis M. Terman: Pioneer in psychological testing.* New York: New York University Press.

Wolf, T. H. (1973). *Alfred Binet.* Chicago: University of Chicago Press.

CHAPTER 11

Romare Beardon
Saxaphone Solo
1987

MOTIVATION

motivation
The psychological processes that arouse, direct, and maintain behavior toward a goal.

Motivation
Why did Bill Irwin, a blind man, risk hiking the entire Appalachian Trail, which extends from Maine to Georgia? Psychologists rely on the concept of motivation to explain this and other behavior.

William McDougall (1871–1938)
"The human mind has certain innate or inherited tendencies which are the essential springs or motive powers of all thought and action."

instinct
A relatively complex, inherited behavior pattern characteristic of a species.

I n 1972, survivors of an airplane crash in a frigid, isolated region of the Andes mountains of Chile turned to cannibalism, eating the flesh of dead passengers to stay alive (Read, 1974). At the 1988 Olympic Games in Korea, left-handed pitcher Jim Abbott led the United States to a gold medal in baseball, even fielding well, despite being born without a right hand. Why would civilized people eat human flesh? Why would a one-handed person pursue a baseball career when even excellent two-handed athletes often fail?

To explain extraordinary behaviors such as these, as well as everyday behaviors, psychologists employ the concept of **motivation,** which refers to the psychological processes that arouse, direct, and maintain behavior toward a goal. The Andes survivors were motivated by hunger, which aroused them to find food, directed them to eat human flesh, and maintained their cannibalism until they were rescued. Jim Abbott was motivated by his need for achievement, which aroused him to excel as a pitcher, directed him to learn how to play baseball with one hand, and maintained his participation despite periodic failures.

Because we cannot directly observe people's motivation, we must infer it from their behavior. We might infer that a person who drinks a quart of water is motivated by a strong thirst and that a person who becomes dictator of a country is motivated by a strong need for power. The concept of motivation is also useful in explaining fluctuations in behavior over time (Atkinson, 1981). If yesterday morning you ate three stacks of pancakes but this morning you ate only a piece of toast, your friends would not attribute your change in behavior to a change in your personality. Instead, they would attribute it to a change in your degree of hunger—your motivation.

SOURCES OF MOTIVATION

What are the main sources of motivation? In seeking answers to this question, psychologists have implicated *heredity, drives,* and *incentives.*

Heredity

In the early twentieth century, many psychologists, influenced by Charles Darwin's theory of evolution and led by William McDougall (1871–1938), attributed human and animal motivation to inherited *instincts.* An **instinct** is a complex, inherited (that is, unlearned) behavior pattern characteristic of a species. Instincts are at work when birds build nests, spiders weave webs, and salmon swim upstream to their spawning grounds. But what of human instincts? McDougall (1908) claimed that human beings are guided by a variety of instincts, including instincts for "pugnacity," "curiosity," and "gregariousness." As discussed in chapter 13, McDougall's contemporary, Sigmund Freud, based his theory of personality on instincts that motivate sex and aggression. And William James (1890/1981) claimed that human beings are motivated by more instincts than any other animal.

In the 1920s, psychologists, influenced by behaviorist John B. Watson, rejected instincts as factors in human motivation. One reason why instinct theorists lost scientific credibility was that they had attempted to explain almost all human behavior as instinctive, in some cases compiling lists of thousands of alleged human instincts (Cofer, 1985). Taking this to its extreme, you might say that people paint because of an "aesthetic instinct," play sports because of a "competitive instinct," and pray because of a "religious instinct." Perhaps you are reading this book because of your "psychocuriosity instinct."

A second reason why instinct theorists fell out of favor was their failure to *explain* the behaviors they labeled as instinctive. Consider the following hypothetical dialogue about an alleged "parenting instinct":

Why do parents take care of their children?

Because they have a parenting instinct.

But how do you know parents have a parenting instinct?

Because they take care of their children.

Such circular reasoning neither explains why parents take care of their children nor provides evidence of a parenting instinct. Each of the assertions is simply used to support the other.

Though instinct theory, as applied to human beings, has fallen into disfavor, some scientists believe that human social behavior does, in fact, have a genetic basis. The chief proponents of this belief work in the field of **sociobiology,** founded by Edward O. Wilson in the 1970s, which studies the hereditary basis of human and animal social behavior (Wilson, 1975).

But sociobiology has been criticized for overestimating the role of heredity in human social behavior. Critics fear that acceptance of sociobiology would lend support to the status quo, making us less inclined to change what many people believe has been "ordained by God or nature," such as differences in the social status of men and women, blacks and whites, and rich and poor. Nonetheless, research on topics such as personality (see chapter 13) lends support to some sociobiological notions.

Edward O. Wilson
"The hypothalamus and the limbic system are engineered to perpetuate DNA."

sociobiology
The study of the hereditary basis of human and animal social behavior.

Drives

Following the decline of the instinct theory of human motivation, the **drive-reduction theory** of Clark Hull (1884–1952) dominated psychology from the 1940s to the 1950s (Webster & Coleman, 1992). According to Hull (1943), a **need** caused by physiological deprivation, such as a lack of food or water, induces a state of tension called a **drive,** which motivates the individual to reduce it. The thirst drive motivates drinking, the hunger drive motivates eating, and the sex drive motivates sexual relations.

Drive reduction aims at the restoration of **homeostasis,** a steady state of physiological equilibrium. Consider your thirst drive. When your body loses water, as when you perspire, receptor cells in your *hypothalamus* (see chapter 3) respond and make you feel thirsty. Thirst arouses you, signaling you that your body lacks water, and directs you to drink. By drinking, you reduce your thirst and restore homeostasis—your body's normal water level. However, though we are undoubtedly motivated to reduce drives such as thirst, hunger, and sex, drive reduction cannot explain all human motivation. In some cases we perform behaviors that do not reduce physiological drives, as in Jim Abbott's participation in baseball. His behavior shows that we are sometimes motivated by *incentives*.

drive-reduction theory
The theory that behavior is motivated by the need to reduce drives such as sex or hunger.

need
A motivated state caused by physiological deprivation, such as a lack of food or water.

drive
A state of psychological tension induced by a need.

homeostasis
A steady state of physiological equilibrium.

Clark Hull (1884–1952)
"The incentive is that substance or
commodity in the environment which
satisfies a need, that is, which reduces
a drive."

Incentives

While a drive is an internal state of tension that "pushes" you toward a goal, an **incentive** is an external stimulus that "pulls" you toward a goal. Through experience, we learn that certain stimuli (such as a puppy) are desirable and should be approached, making them *positive* incentives. We also learn that other stimuli (such as elevator music) are undesirable and should be avoided, making them *negative* incentives. Thus, we are pulled toward positive incentives and away from negative ones.

Incentives are often associated with drives. For example, your thirst drive motivates you to replenish your body's water, but incentives determine what you choose to drink. You could satisfy your thirst by drinking, say, water, lemonade, apple juice, or cherry soda. Your thirst would push you to drink, but your favorite flavor would pull you toward a particular beverage. As with all incentives, your favorite flavor would partly depend on learning, which in this case would depend on your past experience with a variety of flavors. In the case of the Andes survivors, a strong hunger drive made them respond to a weak incentive, human flesh. The opposite may occur in your everyday life. Despite feeling little hunger, you might be motivated to eat in response to a strong incentive, such as an ice cream sundae.

Maslow's Hierarchy of Needs

If forced to make a choice, would you prefer enough food to eat or straight A's in school? Would you prefer to have a home or close friends? In each case, though both options are appealing, you would probably choose the first; this shows that some motives have priority over others. The fact that we have such preferences led the humanistic psychologist Abraham Maslow (1970) to develop a **hierarchy of needs,** depicted in figure 11.1, which ranks important needs by their priority. Maslow used the term *need* to refer to both physiological and psychological motives. According to Maslow you must first satisfy your basic *physiological* needs, such as your needs for food and water, before becoming motivated to meet your higher needs for *safety* and *security,* and so on up the hierarchy from the need for *belongingness and love,* through the need for *esteem,* and ultimately to the needs for *self-actualization* (achievement of all your potentials) and *transcendence* (spiritual fulfillment). According to Maslow, because few people satisfy all their lower needs, few reach these latter two levels. Nonetheless, success in meeting lower-level needs in the hierarchy is positively associated with psychological well-being (Lester, 1990). Though Maslow died before conducting much research on people who had reached transcendence, he did study the lives of people he considered self-actualized, including Abraham Lincoln and Eleanor Roosevelt. The characteristics of self-actualized people are listed in chapter 13. Though research has supported the existence of the needs included in Maslow's hierarchy, it has shown that we do not necessarily pass through the levels of the hierarchy in a fixed sequence (Goebel & Brown, 1981). Thus, parents will ignore their own safety and run into a burning building to save their children, and martyrs such as Mahatma Gandhi will starve themselves for the sake of others.

To appreciate the hierarchy of needs, consider a study conducted during World War II on conscientious objectors (people who refused to perform military service out of a sense of moral conviction). The purpose of the study was to understand the effects of starvation on the many refugees, prisoners of war, and concentration camp inmates who suffered from it. The subjects volunteered to eat half their normal amount of food for 6 months. During that period they lost weight, lacked energy, and became apathetic. They also became obsessed by food—daydreaming about it, collecting cookbooks, and talking for hours about recipes. Moreover, as Maslow would have predicted, they lost interest in their higher social need for belongingness and love in favor of their lower physiological need for food, even preferring pictures of food to pictures of their girlfriends (Keys et al., 1950). Now consider the biological motives of *hunger, sex,* and *arousal,* and the social motive of *achievement.*

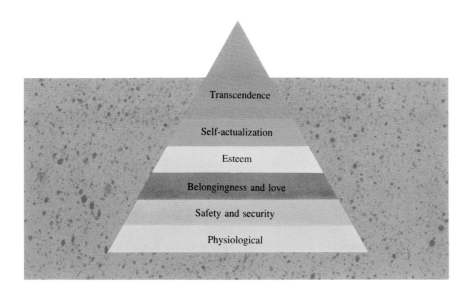

FIGURE 11.1

Maslow's Hierarchy of Needs
Abraham Maslow assumed that our
needs are arranged in a hierarchy,
with our most powerful needs at the
bottom. We will be weakly motivated
by higher needs until our lower needs
are met.

THE HUNGER MOTIVE

The World War II study on the effects of semistarvation showed the power of the *hunger* motive, which impels you to eat to satisfy your body's need for nutrients. If you have just eaten, food might be the last thing on your mind. But if you have not eaten for a few days—or even for a few hours—food might be the *only* thing on your mind.

Factors Regulating Hunger

What accounts for the waxing and waning of hunger? Hunger is regulated by factors in the body, the brain, and the environment.

Factors in the Body

The main bodily mechanisms that regulate hunger involve the mouth, the stomach, the small intestine, the liver, and the pancreas. Taste receptors in the mouth play a role in hunger by sending taste sensations to the brain, informing it of the nutrient content of the food being tasted (M.G. Miller, 1984). Your brain favors the tastes of foods that contain nutrients you may lack. If you lack protein, you may find yourself craving a steak. If you lack sugar, you may find yourself craving starchy foods such as bread.

Though sensations from your mouth affect hunger, they are not its sole source. This was demonstrated when American physician William Beaumont reported the case study of Alexis St. Martin, a Canadian fur trapper who survived a gunshot wound that tore a hole through his abdomen into his stomach that was too large to sew closed (Beaumont, 1833/1988). St. Martin was able to regulate his intake of food even when he was fed through the hole, bypassing his mouth.

But how does the stomach affect hunger? In 1912, physiologist Walter Cannon and his assistant Arthur Washburn set out to answer that question. As illustrated in figure 11.2, Washburn swallowed a balloon, which inflated in his stomach. The balloon was connected by a tube to a device that recorded stomach contractions by measuring changes they caused in the air pressure inside the balloon. Whenever Washburn felt a hunger pang, he pressed a key, producing a mark next to the recording of his stomach contractions. The recordings revealed that Washburn's hunger pangs were associated with stomach contractions, prompting Cannon and Washburn (1912) to conclude that stomach contractions cause hunger.

Might they have interpreted their findings another way? Perhaps the opposite was true; Washburn's hunger might have caused the stomach contractions. Or, given that

FIGURE 11.2

Cannon's Study of Hunger Pangs
Walter Cannon studied the relationship between stomach contractions and hunger pangs by using the device shown in this drawing. The subject pressed a key whenever he felt a hunger pang. A rotating drum recorded both the hunger pangs and the stomach contractions (Cannon & Washburn, 1912).

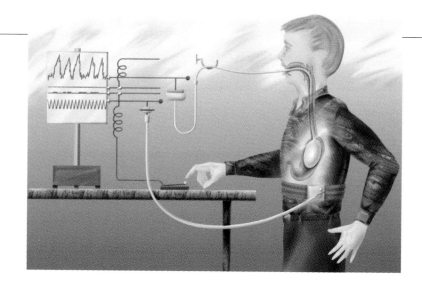

Insulin and Hunger
The mere sight of rich, delicious food can stimulate your pancreas to secrete insulin, making you more hungry and, as a consequence, more likely to eat the food.

we now know that stomach contractions occur when the stomach contains food, perhaps the balloon itself caused Washburn's stomach contractions, which he misinterpreted as a sign of hunger. Moreover, later research revealed that hunger sensations are not entirely dependent on the stomach; even people whose stomachs have been removed because of cancer or severe ulcers can experience hunger (Ingelfinger, 1944).

Though the stomach is not necessary for the regulation of hunger, it normally plays an important role. Receptor cells in the stomach detect the amount of food it contains. After gorging yourself on a Thanksgiving dinner, you may become all too aware of the stretch receptors in your stomach that respond to the presence of food (Stricker & McCann, 1985). These receptors inform the brain of the amount of food in the stomach by sending neural impulses along the *vagus nerve* to the brain, reducing your level of hunger.

Food stored in the stomach eventually reaches the small intestine, the main site of digestion, where it stimulates the small intestine to secrete the hormone *cholecystokinin,* which in turn stimulates the vagus nerve to send neural impulses to the brain, reducing your level of hunger (Gosnell & Hsiao, 1984). In a double-blind study, adult males received daily oral doses of either a placebo or a drug that blocks the effects of cholecystokinin on intestinal receptors. Subjects who received the drug reported greater hunger than did subjects who received the placebo, providing evidence that cholecystokinin does, indeed, reduce hunger (Wolkowitz et al., 1990).

Another organ that regulates hunger is the liver, which stores glucose (a sugar) as *glycogen. Glucose receptors* in the liver send neural impulses along the vagus nerve to the brain, informing it of changes in the level of blood sugar. A low level of blood sugar makes you feel hungry; a high level makes you feel satiated (Tordoff, Novin, & Russek, 1982).

Of special importance in the regulation of hunger is the hormone *insulin,* which is secreted by the pancreas. Insulin helps blood sugar enter body cells for use in metabolism, promotes conversion of glucose to fat, and induces feelings of hunger. In fact, hunger depends more on increased levels of insulin than on decreased levels of blood sugar. We know this from studies in which the level of blood sugar has been held constant by a continuous infusion of glucose while insulin levels are permitted to rise. Subjects in those studies reported increased levels of hunger (Rodin, 1985).

Factors in the Brain

Signals from the body regulate hunger by their effects on the brain. In 1902 Viennese physician Alfred Frohlich reported that patients with tumors of the pituitary gland (see chapter 3) often became obese. Frohlich concluded that the pituitary gland regulates

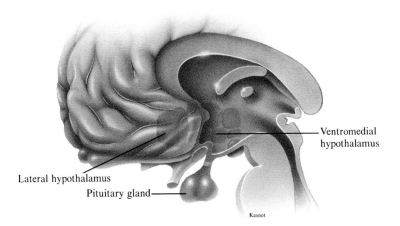

FIGURE 11.3

The Hypothalamus and Hunger
The lateral hypothalamus and ventromedial hypothalamus play important roles in regulating hunger.

Ventromedial hypothalamus

Lateral hypothalamus

Pituitary gland

Kasnot

hunger. But later research found that, in reality, the tumors influenced hunger by affecting the *hypothalamus*, which, as shown in figure 11.3, lies just above the pituitary gland. The neurotransmitter norepinephrine promotes eating by stimulating receptors in the hypothalamus (Towell, Muscat, & Willner, 1989).

Two areas of the hypothalamus are especially important in the regulation of hunger. Electrical stimulation of the *ventromedial hypothalamus* (VMH), an area at the lower middle of the hypothalamus, inhibits eating, and its destruction induces eating. In the 1940s, researchers demonstrated that rats whose VMH had been destroyed would eat until they became grossly obese and would then eat enough to maintain their new, higher level of weight (Hetherington & Ranson, 1942).

While the VMH has been implicated in reducing hunger, the *lateral hypothalamus* (LH), comprising areas on both sides of the hypothalamus, has been implicated in increasing it. Research findings indicate that one way in which cholecystokinin inhibits hunger is by enhancing neuronal activity in the LH and suppressing it in the VMH (Shiraishi, 1990). Electrical stimulation of the LH promotes eating, while its destruction inhibits eating. Rats whose LH has been destroyed will stop eating and starve to death even in the presence of food. Only force-feeding will keep them alive long enough for them to recover their appetite (Anand & Brobeck, 1951). Though early experiments led to the conclusion that the LH acts as our "hunger center" and the VMH acts as our "satiety center," later experiments have shown that these sites are merely important components in the brain's complex system for regulating hunger and eating (Stricker & Verbalis, 1987). There is no simple "on-off" switch for eating.

But how does damage to the hypothalamus affect hunger? It does so, in part, by altering the body's **set point;** that is, its normal weight. Damage to the LH lowers the set point, reducing hunger and making the animal eat less to maintain a lower body weight. In contrast, damage to the VMH raises the set point, increasing hunger and making the animal eat more to maintain a higher body weight (Keesey & Powley, 1986). While signals from the body regulate changes in hunger from meal to meal, the set point regulates changes in hunger over months or years.

Factors in the Environment

Hunger, especially in human beings, is regulated by external, as well as internal, factors. Food can act as an incentive to make you feel hungry. The taste, smell, sight, sound, and texture of food can pull you toward it. Have you ever been watching television, with no appreciable feeling of hunger, only to become hungry after viewing a commercial showing an enticing array of fast-food donuts? Or perhaps you have felt full after a multicourse dinner and insisted that you could not eat another bite, only to have someone coax you into eating a luscious chocolate dessert. But how can the mere sight of food induce

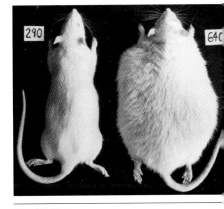

The VMH Rat
Destruction of the ventromedial hypothalamus induces overeating and gross obesity. A rat whose ventromedial hypothalamus has been destroyed may eat until it becomes three times its normal weight.

set point
A specific body weight that the brain tries to maintain through the regulation of diet, activity, and metabolism.

"Let's just go in and see what happens."

feelings of hunger? One way is by increasing the level of insulin in your blood. In fact, even daydreaming about food can stimulate your pancreas to release insulin, making you hungry and possibly sending you on a hunt for cake, candy, or ice cream (Rodin, 1985).

Obesity

obesity
A body weight more than 20 percent above the norm for one's height and build.

basal metabolic rate
The rate at which the body burns calories just to keep itself alive.

Obesity is defined as a body weight more than 20 percent above the norm for one's height and build. Given the many factors that regulate hunger and eating, why do some people become obese? An important factor in obesity is the body's set point, which reflects the amount of fat stored in the body. Though fat cells can increase in number and can increase or decrease in size, they cannot decrease in number. Once you have fat cells, they are yours forever. This means that obese people can lose weight only by shrinking the size of their fat cells. Because this induces constant hunger, it is difficult to maintain weight loss for an extended period of time (Kolata, 1985).

Another important factor in obesity is the **basal metabolic rate,** the rate at which the body burns calories just to keep itself alive. The basal metabolic rate uses 65 to 75 percent of the calories that your body ingests (Shah & Jeffery, 1991). This might explain why one of your friends can habitually ingest a milkshake, two hamburgers, and a large order of french fries, yet remain thin, while another gains weight by habitually ingesting a diet cola, a hamburger without a bun, and a few french fries. Your first friend might have a basal metabolic rate high enough to burn a large number of calories; your second friend might have a basal metabolic rate too low to burn even a modest number of calories, which forces the body to store much of the ingested food as fat. One way that aerobic exercise promotes weight loss is by elevating the rate at which the body burns calories (Davis et al., 1992).

Your body alters its basal metabolic rate to defend its set point, increasing the rate if you eat too much and decreasing the rate if you eat too little. But what determines the set point? Thinness and obesity run in families, and some researchers have found a genetic basis for this tendency (de Castro, 1993). The role of heredity in obesity has been supported by studies of identical twins. Identical twins who have been reared together show a correlation of .75 in their amount of body fat. Even when identical twins have been reared apart, they show only a slightly lower correlation in their amount of body fat (Price & Gottesman, 1991). Evidence that heredity helps determine the set point was also provided by archival research on Danish adoption records. The results, illustrated in figure 11.4, revealed a strong relationship between the weights of adoptees and the weights of their biological parents, but no relationship between the weights of

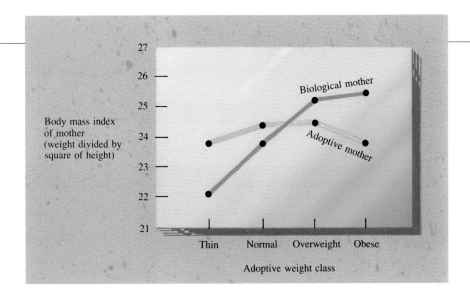

FIGURE 11.4

Heredity and Obesity
Data from Danish adoption records indicate that there is a positive relationship between the weight of adopted children and that of their biological parents, but no relationship between the weight of adopted children and that of their adoptive parents. The graph illustrates the relationship between adoptees and their biological and adoptive mothers. The relationship also holds true for adoptees and their biological and adoptive fathers (Stunkard et al., 1986).

adoptees and those of their adoptive parents. This indicates that heredity plays a more important role in obesity than do habits learned from the family in which one is reared (Stunkard, Stinnett, & Smoller, 1986). A major published review of research on the role of nature and nurture in obesity supported this conclusion, because it found that one's amount of body fat depends significantly more on one's genes than on one's life experiences (Grilo & Pogue-Geile, 1991).

The set point also seems to be affected by early nutrition, as shown by the results of an archival study of 300,000 men who, years earlier, had been exposed to a famine in Holland during World War II. The famine followed a German embargo on food entering Holland as punishment for Dutch resistance to Nazi occupation. Men who had been exposed to the famine during a critical period of development, which encompassed the third trimester of gestation and the first month after birth, were less likely to become obese than were men who had been exposed to the famine at other times during their early development (Ravelli, Stein, & Susser, 1976). The men exposed to the famine during the critical period may have developed lower set points than did the other men. Even the results of the study of Danish adoptees (Stunkard, Stinnett, & Smoller, 1986) might be explained by prenatal nutrition rather than by heredity. Perhaps adopted offspring are more similar in body weight to their biological mothers, not because they share their genes, but because they spent their prenatal period in their wombs, where they were subject to environmental influences, such as nutrients provided by their mothers. These prenatal influences might affect their later body weight (Bonds & Crosby, 1986).

Some researchers have also linked obesity to differences in responsiveness to external food cues. Because a series of studies in the 1960s indicated that obese people feel hungrier and eat more in the presence of external food cues, Stanley Schachter (1971) concluded that obese people are more responsive to those cues. Subsequent studies have provided some support for this belief. One study found that, unlike nonobese people, who find additional food less tasty after they have eaten a high-calorie meal, obese people find food just as tasty after a high-calorie meal. Perhaps one reason why obese people eat more than other people do is that food continues to taste good to them even after they are full (Gilbert & Hagen, 1980). In another study, which used naturalistic observation, researchers observed people eating in a diner. When a waitress provided an appetizing description of a dessert, obese people were more likely to order it than when she did not. Nonobese people were unaffected by her description of the dessert (Herman, Olmsted, & Polivy, 1983).

Though studies like these support the belief that obese people are more responsive to food cues, the "externality" of obese people does not seem to *cause* their obesity.

Judith Rodin
"Almost any overweight person can lose weight; few can keep it off."

Instead, their obesity might cause their externality. Why? Many obese people are constantly dieting, so they might be in a chronic state of hunger, making them more responsive to food cues. Moreover, obesity researcher Judith Rodin (1981) has found that obese people may have chronically high levels of insulin, making them hungrier and, as a result, more responsive to food cues. This gives the false impression that obese people become obese because they are more external than nonobese people.

Still another external factor, stressful situations, can induce hunger and, in some cases, overeating (Levitan & Ronan, 1988). You may have suspected this when observing the voracious appetites that some students exhibit during final-exams week. Under stressful conditions, which can induce negative emotions such as anger, boredom, depression, and loneliness, obese people are more likely than nonobese people to overeat (Ganley, 1989).

But how does stress induce overeating? One possibility is by stimulating the brain to secrete *endorphins*. As discussed in chapters 3 and 5, endorphins are neurotransmitters that relieve pain. Another of their effects is to stimulate eating. In one study, pigs that were given doses of endorphins began to eat more. When the pigs were given naloxone, a drug that blocks the effect of endorphins, they ate less—even when they had been deprived of food (Baldwin, de la Riva, & Ebenezer, 1990). In a similar study with human subjects, those given doses of naloxone consumed less food than they normally did (Mitchell et al., 1986). Because endorphin levels increase when we are under stress, they might contribute to stress-related overeating (Morley & Levine, 1980). Perhaps obese people eat more under stress than do nonobese people because stress induces greater increases in their endorphin levels.

As you can see, hunger is associated with many factors, some of which contribute to obesity. Chapter 16 describes the effects of obesity on health and the approaches used to help obese people lose weight.

Eating Disorders

What do you think of your body? As revealed by the following study, your answer may depend, in part, on whether you are a female or a male.

● Anatomy of a Contemporary Research Study:
How Satisfied Are Males and Females with Their Bodies?

Rationale
Some researchers believe that eating disorders, which are more common in females, can be promoted by distorted body images. This inspired researchers April Fallon and Paul Rozin (1985) to examine the issue empirically.

Method
College students were presented with a set of nine figure drawings that ranged from very thin to very heavy. The subjects were asked to indicate which figures were closest to their current physique, their ideal physique, and the physique they felt was most attractive to the opposite sex.

Results and Discussion
As shown in figure 11.5, for men, the current, the ideal, and the most attractive physiques were almost identical. For women, the current physique was heavier than the most attractive, and the most attractive was heavier than the ideal. The women also thought men liked women thinner than the men actually reported. Moreover, women tended to be less satisfied with their own physiques than men were with their own physiques. This tendency to have a negative body image might put more pressure on women to lose weight. Perhaps this contributes to the greater tendency of women to develop eating disorders marked by excessive concern with weight control, most notably anorexia nervosa *and* bulimia nervosa. *People who disparage their own bodies for being fat, whether or not it is objectively true that they are fat, are more likely to develop eating disorders (Hsu & Sobkiewicz, 1991).*

The ideal that women should be thin permeates our culture, including product advertisements and personal advertisements. A study of magazines popular among young adults found that women's

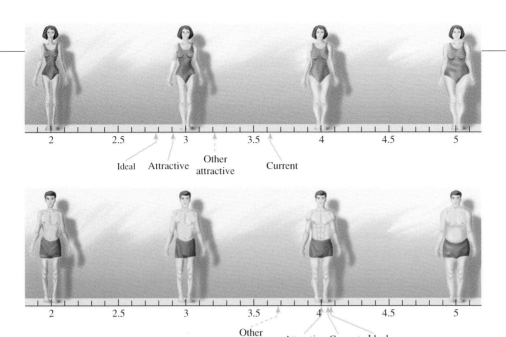

Ideal　Attractive　Other attractive　Current

Other attractive　Attractive Current Ideal

FIGURE 11.5

Sex Differences in Body Images
Fallon and Rozin (1985) found that for men (lower illustration) their self-perceived physique ("Current"), the physique they believed was ideal ("Ideal"), and the physique they believed was most attractive to women ("Attractive"), were almost identical. The physique they believed women preferred ("Attractive") was heavier than the one women actually preferred ("Other Attractive"). In contrast, for women (upper illustration), their self-perceived physique ("Current") was heavier than the physique they believed was ideal ("Ideal") and the physique they believed was most attractive to men ("Attractive"). Moreover, the physique they believed men preferred ("Attractive") was thinner than the one men actually preferred ("Other Attractive").

magazines contained 10.5 times more articles and advertisements promoting weight loss than did men's magazines (Andersen & DiDomenico, 1992). A study of personal advertisements, which are used to find romantic partners, found that men tended to seek thin women and women tended to describe themselves as thin—indicating that women's thinness was an important criterion of attractiveness (Andersen et al., 1993).

Anorexia Nervosa

In 1983 the popular singer Karen Carpenter died of heart failure caused by starvation—despite having access to all the food she could want. She suffered from **anorexia nervosa,** a sometimes fatal disorder in which the victim is so desperate to lose weight that he or she goes on a starvation diet and becomes emaciated. As in the case of Karen Carpenter, people who die from anorexia nervosa usually succumb to cardiac disorders caused by electrolyte abnormalities (Sharp & Freeman, 1993). Anorexia nervosa is more common in young women; perhaps 15 percent of cases occur in males (Bemis, 1978). Victims view themselves as fat, even when they are objectively thin, and they are preoccupied with food—talking about it, cooking it, and urging others to eat it.

The causes of anorexia nervosa are unclear. Possible causes include a malfunctioning hypothalamus (Gold et al., 1980), excessive secretion of cholecystokinin (Philipp et al., 1991), a conflict concerning social maturation (Strober & Humphrey, 1987), and a reaction to the tendency to accumulate unwanted body fat during puberty (Attie & Brooks-Gunn, 1989). In regard to conflict about social maturation, the victims' upbringing might provide them with high achievement standards, yet they might feel inadequate to meet the demands of puberty, college, or marriage. Some women victims even become physically childlike; they stop menstruating and lose their mature physiques. Treatment of severe anorexia nervosa commonly begins with the provision of nourishment through intravenous feeding or feeding through a nasogastric tube. Therapists then try to promote more-adaptive ways of thinking about food (Mitchell & Eckert, 1987).

Bulimia Nervosa

In a related, more common disorder, **bulimia nervosa,** people go on repeated eating binges in which they might ingest thousands of calories at a time. They might eat a half gallon of ice cream, a two-pound box of chocolates, a loaf of French bread, and other high-carbohydrate foods. Nonetheless, they maintain normal weight by ridding themselves

Karen Carpenter
Popular singer Karen Carpenter died from cardiac complications of anorexia nervosa.

anorexia nervosa
An eating disorder marked by self-starvation.

bulimia nervosa
An eating disorder marked by bingeing and purging.

of the food by self-induced vomiting. People with bulimia nervosa think obsessively about food and fear becoming obese. As in the case of anorexia nervosa, most victims of bulimia nervosa are young women; about 10 to 15 percent of victims are males (Carlat & Camargo, 1991). The repeated bouts of vomiting can lead to medical problems, such as dehydration, tooth decay, or ulceration of the esophagus.

The causes of bulimia nervosa are unclear. There is evidence that people with bulimia nervosa have a genetic predisposition to develop the disorder (Hsu, Chester, & Santhouse, 1990). One possible cause is a low level of the neurotransmitter serotonin, which is associated with depression (Goldbloom & Garfinkel, 1990). Binge eating of carbohydrates might elevate mood by increasing serotonin levels in the brain. This hypothesis is supported by research showing that antidepressant drugs that increase serotonin levels are useful in treating bulimia nervosa. In one study, bulimic women were given fluoxetine (Prozac), an antidepressant that inhibits the re-uptake of serotonin by the neurons that secrete it. While on the drug, the subjects snacked less frequently and ate less at each meal. Moreover, the drug inhibited binge eating (Wilcox, 1990). Even inadequate secretion of cholecystokinin may be involved in bulimia nervosa. Bulimic patients secrete less of the hormone after meals than do other people (Geracioti & Liddle, 1988).

Factors other than brain chemistry also play a role in bulimia nervosa. People who pursue activities that emphasize weight control are more likely to develop the disorder. For example, males with bulimia nervosa are often dancers, jockeys, or collegiate wrestlers (Striegel-Moore, Silberstein, & Rodin, 1986). Victims of bulimia nervosa tend to come from families that fail to support social independence and emotional expression (Johnson & Flach, 1985). And victims of bulimia nervosa may be *restrained eaters*, people who are continually concerned with controlling their desire for food (Heatherton, Polivy, & Herman, 1990). Our culture has made restrained eating especially common among women, because constant dieting has become a normal eating pattern for many of them.

How does restrained eating explain bingeing? When restrained eaters eat a "taboo" food, such as ice cream, they might say to themselves, "I've blown my diet, so I might as well keep eating." In contrast, nonrestrained eaters do not share this all-or-nothing belief. They can ingest a rich food, such as a milkshake, without going on an eating binge (Weber, Klesges, & Klesges, 1988). Restrained eaters might also be less attuned to their internal hunger cues. In one study, restrained and unrestrained eaters were given a placebo that they were told was a vitamin pill. The subjects were told either nothing about how the "vitamin" would affect them or that it would make them feel hungry or full. The results indicated that restrained eaters followed the placebo message. They ate more when given the "hungry" instructions and less when given the "full" instructions. Unrestrained eaters did just the opposite, eating less ice cream under the "hungry" instructions and more under the "full" instructions. Perhaps restrained eaters are underresponsive to internal hunger cues and overresponsive to external cues (Heatherton, Polivy, & Herman, 1989).

What is the treatment for bulimia? One approach has victims attend therapy sessions in which they receive psychotherapy and learn to eat without vomiting (Leitenberg et al., 1988). Group therapy and individual therapy are equally effective in treating bulimia, with abstinence from bingeing and purging achieved in about 40 percent of those who seek therapy (Cox & Merkel, 1989).

THE SEX MOTIVE

Every February, newsstands sell about 2 million copies of a special issue of *Sports Illustrated*, instead of the 100,000 copies they normally sell. The magazine isn't selling 20 times its normal number of copies because the special issue contains fascinating articles about celebrated athletes. As you probably know, the issue is popular because it contains photographs of beautiful women in skimpy bathing suits. This demonstrates both the power of the sex *drive* and the *incentive* value of sexual stimuli. Though some individuals, such as religious celibates, can live long lives without engaging in sexual intercourse, the

Sex as a Drive and an Incentive
Would *Sports Illustrated* have as much success with a "baseball uniform issue" as it has with its "swimsuit issue"?

survival of the species requires that many individuals engage in it. Had sexual intercourse not evolved into an extremely pleasurable behavior, we would have no inclination to seek it. But what factors account for the power of the sex motive?

Physiological Factors

Important physiological factors in sexual motivation are sex hormones secreted by the **gonads,** the sex glands. The secretion of sex hormones is controlled by hormones secreted by the pituitary gland, which in turn is controlled by the hypothalamus. Sex hormones direct sexual development as well as sexual behavior. Their influence on sexual development is discussed in chapter 4.

gonads
The male and female sex glands, the testes and the ovaries.

Though hormones exert a direct effect on human sexual development, they are less-influential motivators of sexual behavior in humans than they are in animals. Research indicates that testosterone motivates both male and female sexual behavior (though females secrete less than males do) and that estrogen contributes little to the sexual motivation of either females or males. Human males or females who, for medical reasons, have been castrated before puberty typically show a weak sex drive as adults. In contrast, castration after puberty typically produces only a slight reduction in the human sex drive (Feder, 1984).

Psychological Factors

Many sex researchers study psychological factors in human sexuality. Among the most important of these are sociocultural factors.

Sociocultural Factors

Sex hormones are the main motivators of animal sexual behavior, but human sexual behavior depends more on sociocultural factors. Because in most animals sexual motivation is rigidly controlled by hormones, members of a given species will vary little in their sexual behaviors. In contrast, because human sexual motivation is influenced more by sociocultural factors, we vary greatly in our sexual behavior. For example, breast caressing is a prelude to sexual intercourse among the Marquesan islanders of the Pacific but not among the Sirionian Indians of Bolivia. And though the Pukapukan children of Polynesia are allowed to masturbate in public, the Cuna children of Panama are whipped if caught masturbating even in private (Klein, 1982). In extreme cases, human beings may engage in **paraphilias,** which are ways of obtaining sexual gratification that violate cultural norms concerned with proper sexual objects and practices (Levine, Risen, & Althof, 1990). Several paraphilias are described in table 11.1.

paraphilia
A way of obtaining sexual gratification that violates legal or cultural norms concerning proper sex objects and sexual practices.

TABLE 11.1	Paraphilias

Fetishism

A person with a *fetish* gains sexual gratification from inanimate objects such as shoes or panties. In an especially bizarre case, a man obtained brassieres by claiming to be an agent of the Environmental Protection Agency and convincing women to remove their brassieres so that he could administer a "breathing test" to determine whether a local atomic power plant had affected breathing capacities (Duke & Nowicki, 1986).

Transvestitism

A *transvestite* gains sexual gratification from dressing in opposite-sex clothing. Because women in American culture have greater freedom to wear male clothing, almost all transvestites are males. Some transvestites work as female impersonators.

Voyeurism

A *voyeur* gains sexual gratification primarily from watching people who are naked or engaged in sex. According to a popular legend, in A.D. 1057 Lady Godiva rode naked through Coventry, England. Her husband, the Lord of Coventry, had decreed that everyone stay indoors and keep their shutters closed. But Tom, the town tailor, peeked at her and was punished for his voyeuristic act, contributing the name *Peeping Tom* to our language.

Sadomasochism

A *sadomasochist* gains sexual pleasure from giving and receiving pain. In the eighteenth century, the Marquis de Sade, a French nobleman, described the sexual pleasure he obtained from brutalizing women. Thus, a *sadist* gains sexual gratification from inflicting humiliation and pain. In the nineteenth century, Leopold Sacher-Masoch, an Austrian author, wrote novels about men who experienced sexual pleasure from submitting to physical abuse by women. Thus, a *masochist* gains sexual gratification from being forced to submit to bondage, beatings, and humiliation.

The World's Longest Kiss
Kissing is unknown in some cultures, but it is common in others. This photograph shows a Chicago couple entering the Guinness Book of World Records by kissing for 17 days, 9 hours. (Of course, in this case the couple was more motivated by their need for achievement than by their desire for romance.)

In Western cultures, acceptable sexual behavior has varied over time. The ancient Greeks viewed bisexuality as normal and masturbation as a desirable way for youths to relieve their sexual tensions. In contrast, most Americans and Europeans of the Victorian era in the nineteenth century believed that all sexual activity should be avoided except when aimed at procreation. The Victorian emphasis on sexual denial led John Harvey Kellogg to invent what he claimed was a nutritional "cure" for masturbation—cornflakes (Money, 1986).

The liberalization of attitudes toward sexual behavior in Western industrialized countries during the twentieth century was shown in 1983 when the *Journal of the American Medical Association* published an article on human sexuality. This would not be noteworthy except that the article had been submitted for publication in 1899—near the end of the Victorian era. The article, based on a paper presentation by gynecologist Denslow Lewis (1899/1983) at the annual meeting of the American Medical Association, concerned female sexuality. Lewis described the female sexual response, the need for sex education, the importance of sex for marital compatibility, and techniques for overcoming sexual problems. Lewis even made the radical (for his time) suggestion that wives be encouraged to enjoy sex as much as their husbands did. At the time, the editor of the journal refused to publish the paper, which a prominent physician called "filth" and another editor feared would bring charges of sending obscene material through the mail (Hollender, 1983).

Kinsey's Surveys of Human Sexual Behavior

Denslow Lewis's critics would have been even more upset by research in human sexuality that has taken place in the past few decades, beginning with the post–World War II research of Alfred Kinsey. Kinsey, a biologist at Indiana University, found that he was unable to answer his students' questions about human sexual behavior because of a lack of relevant information. This inspired him to conduct surveys to gather information on the sexual behavior of men (Kinsey, Pomeroy, & Martin, 1948) and women (Kinsey et al., 1953).

Kinsey and his colleagues obtained their data from interviews with thousands of men and women and published their findings in two best-selling books. The books (which contained statistics but no pictures) shocked the public, because Kinsey reported that masturbation, oral sex, premarital sex, extramarital sex, homosexuality, and other sexual behaviors were more prevalent than commonly believed. Among the many findings were that most of the men and almost half of the women engaged in premarital sexual intercourse and most of the women and almost all of the men masturbated.

Scientists warned that care should be taken in generalizing Kinsey's findings to all Americans, because his sample was not representative of the American population—the sample included primarily white, well-educated Easterners and Midwesterners who were willing to be interviewed about their sexual behavior. Moreover, what is true of people in one generation might not be true of those in another. For example, from the 1950s to the 1980s, premarital sex in the United States increased. Several factors might account for this (Beeghley & Sellers, 1986): Casual sex had been portrayed in a positive light in the media; more effective and more easily obtained forms of contraception made pregnancy less of a risk; modern medicine had reduced the fear of common venereal diseases, such as syphillis and gonorrhea; the "double standard" that prohibited females from being as sexually active as males had weakened; and laws and social norms had become less restrictive in regard to sexual relations between consenting persons. In the 1980s, however, premarital sexual activity with multiple partners tapered off, due to increased fears about incurable venereal diseases, including AIDS and genital herpes (Gerrard, 1987). The transmission and prevention of AIDS are discussed in chapter 16.

In regard to Kinsey's findings, changes in sexual behavior indicate that norms of sexual conduct do, indeed, depend on the time period when they are studied. A survey of almost 4,000 women found that, compared to Kinsey's subjects, they reported earlier onset of intercourse, less likelihood of having a fiancé or husband as their first sexual partner, a higher number of sexual partners, a broader range of sexual behaviors, and greater use of contraceptive methods (Wyatt, Peters, & Guthrie, 1988). Oral sex has also increased among males and females since Kinsey's early surveys, with adolescent females engaging in oral sex more than intercourse, and adolescent males engaging in intercourse more than oral sex (Newcomer & Udry, 1985).

Despite the easing of the "double standard," males and females differ in their sexuality. Surveys of subjects in 1963, 1971, and 1978 found that sexual conduct among college students became more liberal, primarily because of changes in female, rather than male, behavior (Sherwin & Corbett, 1985). In regard to the decision to lose one's virginity, females place a greater premium on an intimate relationship than do males (Christopher & Cate, 1985). A survey of almost 2,000 men and almost 3,000 women found that males and females even differ in their sexual fantasies—males favoring fantasies of voyeurism and group sex, and females favoring fantasies of committed partners and romantic settings (Wilson, 1987). Males and females also differ in what they perceive as sexually provocative behavior. Males are more likely to perceive friendly behavior by females as sexually flirtatious (Saal, Johnson, & Weber, 1989). A survey of 472 male and 323 female college students found that they were equally likely to engage in sexual intercourse (67 percent of males and 68 percent of females), and 27 percent of the women reported that they had experienced date rape (Miller & Marshall, 1987). In another survey, involving 507 male and 486 female undergraduates, more women had experienced unwanted sexual activity, but more men had experienced unwanted sexual intercourse. This was attributed to peer pressure and the desire to "prove" oneself to other males (Muehlenhard & Cook, 1988).

Masters and Johnson's Research on the Human Sexual Response Cycle

The shocked response to Kinsey's surveys was mild compared to that generated in the 1960s by the research of William Masters and Virginia Johnson. Unlike Kinsey, Masters and Johnson were not content with just asking people about their sexual motivation and behavior. Instead, they studied ongoing sexual behavior and recorded physiological changes that accompanied it in hundreds of males and females. To study the female sexual response, they even invented a transparent plastic "penis" through which they could photograph vaginal changes during sexual arousal.

Based on their study of more than 10,000 orgasms experienced by more than 300 men and 300 women, Masters and Johnson (1966) identified four phases in the **sexual response cycle**. Figure 11.6 shows the four phases that take place in this cycle: excitement, plateau, orgasm, and resolution. During the *excitement phase*, mental or physical

Alfred Kinsey (1894–1956)
"The present study was undertaken because the senior author's students were bringing him, as a college teacher of biology, questions on matters of sex. . . . They had found it more difficult to obtain strictly factual information which was not biased by moral, philosophic, or social interpretations."

sexual response cycle
During sexual activity, the phases of excitement, plateau, orgasm, and resolution.

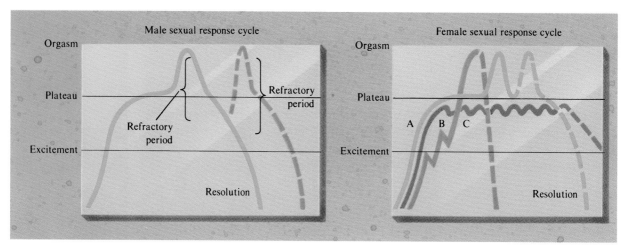

FIGURE 11.6

The Human Sexual Response Cycle
Masters and Johnson found that males and females have sexual response cycles comprising four phases: excitement, plateau, orgasm, and resolution. After reaching orgasm, males cannot achieve another orgasm until they have passed through a refractory period. In contrast, pattern A shows that females may experience more than one orgasm during a single cycle. Pattern B shows a cycle during which a female has reached the plateau stage without proceeding to orgasm. Pattern C shows a cycle during which a female has reached orgasm quickly. Males, too, may experience pattern B and pattern C.

stimulation causes sexual arousal. In males the penis becomes erect as it becomes engorged with blood. In females the nipples become erect, the vagina becomes lubricated, and the clitoris protrudes as it, too, becomes engorged with blood. During the *plateau phase*, heart rate, blood pressure, muscle tension, and breathing rate increase. In males the erection becomes firmer and the testes are drawn closer to the body to prepare for ejaculation. Drops of seminal fluid, possibly containing sperm (and capable of causing pregnancy), may appear at the tip of the penis. In females the body flushes, lubrication increases, the clitoris retracts, and the breasts swell (making the nipples seem to shrink).

The excitement and plateau phases compose the period of sexual foreplay. Males and females differ in the importance they assign to this. A survey of young adults found that women chose foreplay as more important than either intercourse or afterplay, while men chose intercourse as most important. Women also preferred to spend more time on foreplay and afterplay than did men. Women reported more than men did that they enjoyed the verbal and physical affection of sexual behavior (Denney, Field, & Quadagno, 1984).

During the *orgasm phase*, heart rate and breathing rate reach their peak, males ejaculate *semen* (a fluid containing sperm), and both males and females experience intensely pleasurable sensations induced by rhythmic muscle contractions. When females and males are asked to write subjective descriptions of their orgasms, readers cannot distinguish between male and female descriptions (Vance & Wagner, 1976). This indicates that female and male experiences during orgasm are similar.

The pleasure induced by orgasm might be caused by the actions of endorphins in the brain. In a study in which male rats were conditioned to associate orgasm with a particular site, they showed less preference for that site after ejaculating when they had been given naloxone, which blocks the effect of endorphins. Apparently, naloxone prevented ejaculation from being rewarding to the rats. Perhaps compulsive sexual behavior in human beings is maintained by the stimulation of endorphin receptors in the brain (Agmo & Berenfeld, 1990).

Women find that stimulation of the clitoris is the most efficient way to achieve an orgasm; stimulation of the front wall inside of the vagina may also lead to orgasm (Alzate, 1985). Using a special recording device, researchers in a study of young adults found that female orgasms induced by masturbation lasted an average of 16.7 seconds, with a range from 7.5 to 25 seconds (Geer & Quartaaro, 1976).

Research on heterosexual intercourse shows that the timing of the orgasm is also important to sexual satisfaction. A survey of 709 women found that those who experienced orgasm after their partners had experienced it felt less sexually satisfied (Darling, Davidson, & Cox, 1991). This is especially problematic for some women because during sexual intercourse young adult males tend to reach orgasm in just 2 to 3 minutes (Levitt, 1983).

Following the orgasm phase, the person enters the *resolution phase*, as blood leaves the genitals and sexual arousal lessens. This is associated with a *refractory period*, lasting from minutes to hours, during which the person cannot achieve orgasm. For some women, however, continued sexual stimulation may induce multiple orgasms.

Sexual Dysfunctions

After Masters and Johnson had identified the normal phases of the human sexual response cycle, they became interested in studying **sexual dysfunctions,** which are chronic problems at phases in the sexual response cycle. Marital happiness is associated with sexual satisfaction; and male sexual dysfunctions create more discord than do female dysfunctions (Rust, Golombok, & Collier, 1988). Sex therapists treat dysfunctions through a combination of sex education, communication training, homework assignments, and discussion of nonsexual issues that pertain to the couple's personal relationship (Kilmann et al., 1986).

Male Sexual Dysfunctions

Among the most common male sexual dysfunctions are erectile dysfunction, premature ejaculation, and retarded ejaculation. About 4 to 9 percent of males suffer from an *erectile dysfunction*—failing either to attain an erection or to maintain it through the arousal phase (Spector & Carey, 1990). Erectile dysfunction is sometimes a symptom of diabetes mellitus. A male who exhibits *premature ejaculation* will reach the orgasm phase too fast for his female partner to be sexually satisfied. About one-third of all males experience premature ejaculation (Spector & Carey, 1990). Premature ejaculators reach orgasm at lower levels of sexual arousal and have longer periods of abstinence from intercourse (Spiess, Geer, & O'Donohue, 1984). In contrast, males who have *retarded ejaculation* cannot achieve orgasm despite being sexually excited. This dysfunction afflicts about 4 to 10 percent of all males (Spector & Carey, 1990).

Female Sexual Dysfunctions

Among women, the most common sexual dysfunctions include orgasmic dysfunction, dyspareunia, and vaginismus. A woman experiencing *orgasmic dysfunction*, present in 5 to 10 percent of women (Spector & Carey, 1990), is unable to reach the orgasm phase. Women who are not orgasmic tend to have difficulty discussing sexual activities that stimulate the clitoris, more negative attitudes toward masturbation, and greater sexual guilt (Kelly, Strassberg, & Kircher, 1990). Women who suffer from *dyspareunia* experience pain during or after sexual intercourse (Brashear & Munsick, 1991). Those with *vaginismus* have difficulty engaging in sexual intercourse because of muscle spasms around the opening of the vagina (Hawton & Catalan, 1990).

Sex Therapy

Based on their research findings, Masters and Johnson (1970) concluded that the psychological causes of sexual dysfunctions are usually sexual guilt, sexual ignorance, or anxiety about sexual performance. A common factor in sexual dysfunction is focusing one's attention on how one is performing instead of on erotic feelings (Barlow, 1986). In treating sexual dysfunctions, Masters and Johnson first have their clients examined by a physician to rule out any physical causes, such as drugs, diabetes, or hormonal imbalances. They then counsel their clients to help them overcome their sexual guilt, educate them about sexual anatomy, sexual motivation, and sexual behavior, and teach them specific ways of reducing performance anxiety. Of course, none of these procedures is of much use unless the clients are sexually attracted to each other.

sexual dysfunction
A chronic problem at one or more phases of the sexual response cycle.

Masters and Johnson
"Aside from obvious anatomic variants, men and women are homogenous in their physiological responses to sexual stimuli."

sensate focusing
A sex therapy technique that at first involves nongenital caressing and gradually progresses to sexual intercourse.

The main technique in Masters and Johnson's sex therapy is **sensate focusing,** in which the partners first participate in nongenital caressing, later proceed to genital stimulation, and finally engage in sexual intercourse. The partners are urged to concentrate on their pleasurable feelings instead of striving for erections and orgasms. They are also instructed to tell each other what kinds of stimulation they enjoy and what kinds they do not enjoy.

Masters and Johnson also teach their clients other techniques, when they are appropriate. In treating premature ejaculation, they may have the man's partner repeatedly stimulate his penis just to the point before orgasm to teach him to gain control over its timing. This is the treatment of choice in cases of premature ejaculation (St. Lawrence & Madakasira, 1992). They may have a woman with an orgasmic dysfunction practice masturbating to orgasm as a step toward reaching orgasm during sexual intercourse, a more difficult feat. One study found that women who received therapy for orgasmic dysfunction significantly increased their likelihood of having an orgasm during sexual intercourse. They went from having orgasms on 9.5 percent of the occasions before therapy to having orgasms on 36.9 percent of the occasions after therapy (Milan, Kilmann, & Boland, 1988).

Masters and Johnson (1970) reported that more than two-thirds of their clients showed improvement. But they were criticized for not operationally defining what they meant by "improvement" and for failing to conduct follow-up studies of their clients to determine whether the positive effects of therapy were long-lasting. They were also criticized for being more concerned with the importance of sex as a physical act than with its importance as an intimate emotional relationship (Pryde, 1989).

Nonetheless, studies of sex therapy by many other therapists have provided convincing evidence of its effectiveness (LoPiccolo & Stock, 1986). A follow-up study of 140 couples who had participated in sex therapy found that, when they were assessed 1 to 6 years after therapy, success was achieved with at least one partner in 75 percent of the cases. Though relapses were common, coping strategies learned in sex therapy helped many couples overcome their relapses (Hawton et al., 1986). A survey of 289 members of the American Association of Sex Educators, Counselors, and Therapists found that a difference in sexual desire between partners was the most common problem they saw. Success rates for sex therapy were highest for premature ejaculation, orgasmic dysfunction, and desire disparities. Erectile dysfunction had the lowest success rate (Kilmann et al., 1986). During the past few decades, Masters and Johnson have also joined with other sex researchers in studying the factors that account for **gender identity** and **sexual orientation.**

Gender Identity

gender identity
A person's self-perceived sex.

sexual orientation
One's sexual attraction toward members of either one's own sex or the opposite sex.

In 1953 Christine Jorgensen shocked the world by announcing that "she" was a man who had undergone surgery and hormone treatments to look more like a woman. Though this procedure had been performed since the 1930s, Jorgensen's case was the first widely publicized instance of **transsexualism,** a disorder of *gender identity* in which a person who is physically a male or female feels psychologically like a member of the opposite sex. The extent to which heredity, hormonal imbalances, or childhood experiences contribute to transsexualism is unknown. Transsexuals may undergo surgery to change the appearance of their sex organs. This is accompanied by hormonal treatments to eliminate physical characteristics of the original sex and to produce those of the other sex (Asscheman & Gooren, 1992). Though two-thirds of all transsexuals express satisfaction with the results of sex-change surgery, many suffer serious emotional distress, develop psychological disorders, or even attempt suicide. Females who become males achieve slightly better psychological adjustment than do males who become females (Abramowitz, 1986). Success depends to a great extent on how well the surgery creates genitals that resemble those of the other sex (Lundstrom, Pauly, & Walinder, 1984). As for sexual performance, the capacity to achieve orgasms tends to increase in female-to-male transsexuals and to decrease in male-to-female transsexuals (Lief & Hubschman, 1993).

transsexualism
A condition in which a genetic male or female has the gender identity of the opposite sex.

(a)   (b)

Transsexualism
(*a*) Physician and tennis player
Richard Raskin felt like a female
trapped in a male body. This led him
to undergo surgery and hormone
treatments to make him look more like
a woman. (*b*) He then created
controversy by briefly pursuing a career
on the women's tennis tour under the
new name of Renee Richards.

Sexual Orientation

Transsexualism should not be confused with **homosexuality,** a *sexual orientation* that is
marked by a preference for sexual relations with members of one's own sex. Unlike the
transsexual, the homosexual does not feel trapped in the body of the wrong sex. Male
homosexuals are called *gays*, and female homosexuals are called *lesbians*, after the island
of Lesbos, on which the Greek poet Sappho (ca. 620 B.C.–ca. 565 B.C.) ran a school for
women. Sappho killed herself after a student failed to return her love. Today, attitudes
toward homosexuality vary both among and within cultures. In 1973, in keeping
with evidence that homosexuality is not associated with any psychological disorders
and the increasingly liberal attitudes toward homosexuality in the United States, the
American Psychiatric Association voted to eliminate homosexuality from its list of
mental disorders.

homosexuality
*A consistent preference for sexual
relations with members of one's own sex.*

Given that our reproductive anatomy and cultural norms favor heterosexuality,
why are an estimated 1 percent of women and 4 percent of men homosexual (Ellis &
Ames, 1987)? Theories of homosexuality abound, and none has gained universal acceptance. Physiological theories of homosexuality implicate hereditary and physiological
factors. Homosexuality runs in families—homosexuals have more homosexual siblings
than do heterosexuals (Pillard, Poumadere, & Carretta, 1981). Identical twins are more
likely to be both homosexual than are fraternal twins, but the extent to which this
difference is due to shared genetic or shared environmental influences is unclear (Bailey
et al., 1993). Stronger support for the hereditary basis of homosexuality comes from
research showing that identical twins (who have the same genes) adopted as infants by
different families have a higher likelihood of both becoming homosexuals than do ordinary siblings reared together in the same family (Eckert et al., 1986). A recent study
of 40 families in which there were two homosexual brothers indicated that 26 of the
sibling pairs (64 percent) shared a genetic marker on the X chromosome, the sex chromosome inherited from their mother (Hamer et al., 1993).

Support for the physiological basis of homosexuality comes from research showing
that the administration of estrogen produces a physiological response in homosexual
men that is intermediate between that produced in heterosexual men and that produced
in heterosexual women (Gladue, Green, & Hellman, 1984). Females exposed to excessively high levels of male sex hormones prenatally are more likely to develop a homosexual orientation (Meyer-Bahlburg, 1990–1991). Homosexuality is also associated with
hormonal activity during a critical period between the second and the fifth month after
conception that differs from that of heterosexuals. This might affect the development

(a)

(b)

(c)

(d)

Sexual Orientation
Research indicates that your sexual orientation is the outcome of the interaction of biological, psychological, and social factors. While this interaction leads most persons to develop a heterosexual orientation, many persons—such as (a) author Willa Cather, (b) author Oscar Wilde, (c) tennis star Martina Navratilova, and (d) U.S. Representative Barney Frank—develop a homosexual orientation.

of the hypothalamus, which helps regulate sexual orientation, in a way that predisposes some people toward a homosexual orientation (Ellis & Ames, 1987). Autopsies on the brains of homosexual men and heterosexual men have found that an area of the hypothalamus called the suprachiasmatic nucleus is almost twice as large in homosexual men as in heterosexual men. But it is unclear whether this contributes to the development of homosexuality or, instead, is a consequence of a homosexual lifestyle (Swaab & Hofman, 1990).

But what of possible social factors that might account for sexual orientation? The traditional view favored the Freudian notion that homosexuality is caused by a dominant, overly affectionate mother and an aloof, unemotional father. Though some homosexuals have such backgrounds, others do not. In fact, there is no evidence that any particular pattern of childhood experiences alone causes a person to become a homosexual (Bell, Weinberg, & Hammersmith, 1981). A controversial learning theory of homosexuality holds that our sexual orientation, whether heterosexual or homosexual, depends on the sex of the children with whom we are socializing when our sex drive first emerges (Storms, 1981). Reports by homosexuals indicate that their sex drive typically emerges 2 to 3 years before that of heterosexuals, at a time when they are more likely to be socializing exclusively with same-sex peers. Because of this, they might attach their sexual feelings to those children. In contrast, the sex drive of most children emerges later, at a time when they are more likely to be socializing with members of both sexes. This makes them more likely to attach their sex drive to the culturally more approved opposite sex.

Despite numerous studies on the origins of sexual orientation, none has identified any physiological or social factor that, by itself, explains why one person develops a heterosexual orientation and another develops a homosexual orientation. As suggested by Alfred Kinsey 50 years ago, it might even be mistaken to view homosexuality and heterosexuality as mutually exclusive categories. This was the finding of a study in which homosexual men and heterosexual men rated their degree of homosexuality-heterosexuality and the size of their penile erections was measured while they watched brief movie clips of nude men and nude women. The men's self-ratings and penile responses showed a positive correlation. As you might expect, the more homosexual their rating, the greater their penile response to nude males; and the more heterosexual their rating, the greater their penile response to nude females. Yet both the homosexual men and the heterosexual men tended to respond at least somewhat both to nude males and to nude females (McConaghy & Blaszcynski, 1991).

According to John Money (1987), a leading sex researcher, sexual orientation is affected by physiological, psychological, and sociocultural factors, the relative influence of which varies. Money points, as an example, to the Sambia tribe of New Guinea, in which males between the ages of 9 and 19 are encouraged to follow a homosexual orientation to become more manly. At age 19 the males marry and switch to a heterosexual orientation. Thus, a complete explanation of human sexual orientation will probably have to be a biopsychosocial one (Friedman & Downey, 1993).

THE AROUSAL MOTIVE

Though the hunger motive and sex motive seem to dominate North American culture, human beings are also influenced by another biological motive, the **arousal motive.** *Arousal* is the general level of physiological activation of the brain and body. As noted in chapter 3, the reticular formation regulates brain arousal, and the autonomic nervous system and endocrine system regulate body arousal. In 1908 researchers reported that animals performed tasks best at moderate levels of stimulation, and that the more complex the task, the lower the level of optimal stimulation (Yerkes & Dodson, 1908). Later researchers, led by Donald Hebb (1955) of McGill University in Montreal, showed that human beings perform best at a moderate level of arousal, with performance deteriorating under excessively high or low arousal levels. This relationship between arousal and performance, represented by an inverted U-shaped curve (illustrated in figure 11.7), became known as the **Yerkes-Dodson law,** after the researchers who had conducted the earlier animal study.

Hebb found that optimal arousal is higher for simple tasks than for complex tasks. For example, the optimal level of arousal for doing a simple addition problem would be higher than for a complex geometry problem. Hebb also found that optimal arousal is higher for well-learned tasks than for novel tasks. Your optimal level of arousal for reading is higher now than it was when you were first learning to read. Perhaps, when you are bored by studying, you find that playing music in the background helps you raise your level of brain arousal enough for you to maintain your concentration (Patton, Routh, & Stinard, 1986).

But how does arousal level affect performance? According to Hebb, it lets us concentrate and attend to tasks, such as exams. If you are underaroused, your mind might wander to irrelevant details, like when you make careless errors on exams, such as darkening the letter C when you meant to darken the letter B. But if you are overaroused, your focus of attention might become too narrow, reducing your ability to shift to other details that might help you solve a problem, as when you find yourself so anxious that you stare at a particular exam question for several minutes. Overarousal impairs performance in part by interfering with the retrieval of information in short-term memory (Anderson, Revelle, & Lynch, 1989).

Research findings support the notion that there is an optimal level of arousal. In a study of arithmetic performance in third- and fourth-graders under time pressure, low-anxious children performed better than did moderately anxious or high-anxious children (Plass & Hill, 1986). How could the concept of optimal arousal explain these findings? Assume that before performing arithmetic the low-anxious children began *below* their optimal level of arousal, the moderately anxious children began at their optimal level, and the high-anxious children began *above* their optimal level. The additional arousal induced by the arithmetic task may have boosted the arousal of the low-anxious children *to* their optimal level and the arousal of the moderately anxious children *above* their optimal level, while the high-anxious children may have been boosted even further above their optimal level.

Moreover, for any given task there is no single optimal level of arousal; the optimal level varies from person to person (Ebbeck & Weiss, 1988). So, an outstanding math student would have a higher optimal level of arousal for performing arithmetic than would a poor math student. As a consequence, the outstanding math student might have to "psych up" before an exam, and the poor math student might have to relax—each in an effort to reach an optimal arousal level.

John Money
"On the issue of the determinants of sexual orientation as homosexual, bisexual, or heterosexual, the only scholarly position is to allow that prenatal and postnatal determinants are not mutually exclusive."

arousal motive
The motive to maintain an optimal level of physiological activation.

Yerkes-Dodson law
The principle that the relationship between arousal and performance is best represented by an inverted U-shaped curve.

FIGURE 11.7

The Yerkes-Dodson Law
The graph depicts the relationship between arousal level and task performance. Note that the best performance occurs at a moderate level of arousal. Performance declines when arousal is below or above that level. Note that the optimal level of arousal is lower for complex tasks than for simple tasks.

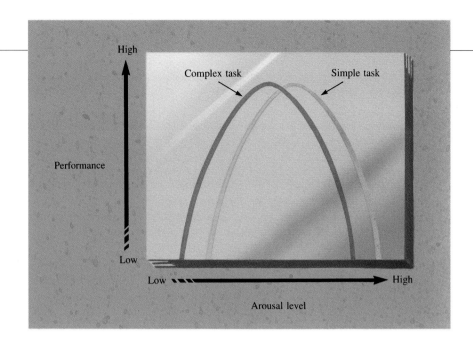

Sensory Deprivation

Though people differ in the amount of arousal they prefer, we require at least a minimal amount for our brains to function properly. Anecdotal reports from Arctic explorers, shipwrecked sailors, and prisoners in solitary confinement made early psychologists aware that human beings require sensory stimulation for proper perceptual, cognitive, and emotional functioning. Today, selection processes for members of Arctic research teams consider who will function best during the *sensory deprivation* that accompanies long periods of isolation (Rothblum, 1990).

• Anatomy of a Contemporary Research Study:
What Are the Effects of Prolonged Sensory Deprivation?

Rationale

sensory deprivation
The prolonged withdrawal of normal levels of external stimulation.

Sensory deprivation is the prolonged withdrawal of normal levels of external stimulation. When people are subjected to sensory deprivation, they may experience delusions, hallucinations, and emotional arousal caused by the brain's attempt to restore its optimal level of arousal. The experimental study of sensory deprivation began in the early 1950s when the Defense Research Board of Canada asked Donald Hebb to find ways of countering the "brainwashing" techniques that the Chinese communists used on prisoners during the Korean War. During brainwashing, prisoners were deprived of social and physical stimulation. This became so unpleasant that it motivated them to cooperate with their captors just to receive more stimulation (Hebb, 1958).

Method

Hebb and his colleagues conducted studies of sensory deprivation in which each subject was confined to a bed in a soundproof room with only the monotonous hum of a fan and an air conditioner. A typical room is illustrated in figure 11.8. The subjects wore translucent goggles to reduce visual sensations and cotton gloves and cardboard tubes over their arms to reduce touch sensations. They were permitted to leave the bed only to eat or to use the toilet. They stayed in the room for as many days as they could tolerate.

Results and Discussion

After many hours of sensory deprivation, some subjects experienced hallucinations, emotional instability, and intellectual deterioration. Though the students who served as volunteers for the study were paid

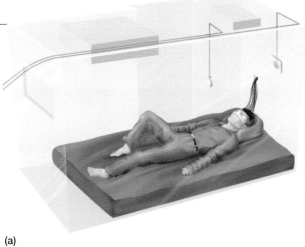

(a)

(b)

FIGURE 11.8

Restricted Environmental Stimulation
(*a*) The sensory deprivation room was used in Canadian studies in the 1950s. (*b*) The flotation tank has been used in more recent studies.

(*a*) *Adapted from The Pathology of Boredom by W. Heron. Copyright © 1957 by Scientific American, Inc. All rights reserved.*

$20 a day (a large amount at the time) for participating, most quit within 48 hours. They found the lack of sensory stimulation so aversive that they preferred to forego the monetary incentive in favor of sensory stimulation (Bexton, Heron, & Scott, 1954).

Research on sensory deprivation demonstrates that inadequate external stimulation might motivate us to seek external stimulation or to generate our own stimulation through alterations in brain activity. This is especially true of people who perform monotonous tasks in relative isolation, such as those who conduct research in the Arctic, drive long-distance trucking hauls, or live for extended periods in outer space. And, as you are certainly aware, even college students seek external stimulation to combat boring classes and dull campus life (Weinstein & Almaguer, 1987).

A form of sensory deprivation called flotation *restricted environmental stimulation (REST)*, developed by Peter Suedfeld, has been effective in reducing arousal without causing hallucinations, distress, or cognitive impairment (Suedfeld & Coren, 1989). In flotation REST, subjects float in a dark, soundproof tank filled with warm salt water. Flotation REST has proved successful in eliminating the use of drugs, such as nicotine (Suedfeld, 1990), that are taken to reduce anxiety. In one study, college students who were heavy social drinkers were assigned either to an experimental group that practiced flotation REST or to a control group that did not. After 2 weeks, the experimental group showed a significant decrease in alcohol intake. This was sustained at a follow-up 6 months after the treatment ended. In contrast, the control group showed an increase in alcohol intake (Cooper, Adams, & Scott, 1988).

Flotation REST has been applied successfully in a variety of other ways, particularly in situations that call for a reduction in arousal. These applications include the relief of chronic tension headache (Wallabaum et al., 1991), the reduction of high blood pressure (McGrady et al., 1987), the promotion of hypnotic susceptibility (Barabasz & Barabasz, 1989), and the enhancement of scientific creativity (Suedfeld, Metcalfe, & Bluck, 1987).

Sensation Seeking

Would you prefer to ride a roller coaster or lie on a beach? Would you prefer to attend a lively party or have a quiet conversation? Your preferences would depend in part on your degree of **sensation seeking,** which is your motivation to seek sensory stimulation. People high in sensation seeking prefer activities that increase their arousal levels; those low in sensation seeking prefer activities that decrease their arousal (Zuckerman, Buchsbaum, & Murphy, 1980). High sensation seekers respond to novel stimuli with greater physiological arousal than do low sensation seekers, who exhibit no change, or even a decrease, in arousal in response to novel stimuli (Zuckerman, 1990).

Peter Suedfeld
"Flotation REST is a relative newcomer to the repertoire of stimulus-reducing environments. However, its dramatic ability to induce deep relaxation, both physiologically and psychologically, has made it an instant focus of attention."

Marvin Zuckerman
"Differences between psychophysiological responses of high and low sensation seekers are . . . reflective of different evolved biological strategies for processing novel or intense stimulation."

sensation seeking
The extent to which an individual seeks sensory stimulation.

Sensation Seeking
These two groups of people may differ
markedly in their degree of sensation
seeking.

The concept of sensation seeking might have important practical applications. Consider the potentially dangerous practice of high-speed police pursuits. Police officers who score high on the Sensation Seeking Scale are significantly more likely to engage in such pursuits—endangering themselves and innocent motorists and pedestrians. Perhaps a police officer's score on the scale might be considered when training officers and implementing pursuit policies (Homant, Kennedy, & Howton, 1993).

THE ACHIEVEMENT MOTIVE

Human beings are motivated by social, as well as physiological, needs. Interest in studying social motivation was stimulated in the 1930s and 1940s by the work of Henry Murray (1938), who identified a variety of important social motives, including dominance, achievement, and affiliation. Since Murray's pioneering research, psychologists, led by David McClelland and John Atkinson, have been especially interested in studying the **achievement motive,** which is the desire for mastery, excellence, and accomplishment.

achievement motive
The desire for mastery, excellence, and accomplishment.

In the context of Maslow's hierarchy of needs, the need for achievement would be associated with one of the higher levels, the need for esteem. This means that the need for achievement would be stronger in cultures, such as Canada and the United States, in which most people have satisfied their lower needs. But even in the United States the relative importance of the need for achievement has changed over time. Figure 11.9 shows the results of a survey of children's readers published between 1800 and 1950, which found that the number of achievement themes in the readers increased until about 1890 and then decreased through 1950. This was accompanied by a parallel change in the number of patents issued, indicating that changes in a country's achievement motivation may affect its practical achievements (DeCharms & Moeller, 1962). Nonetheless, it is not certain from the data that changes in achievement motivation *caused*

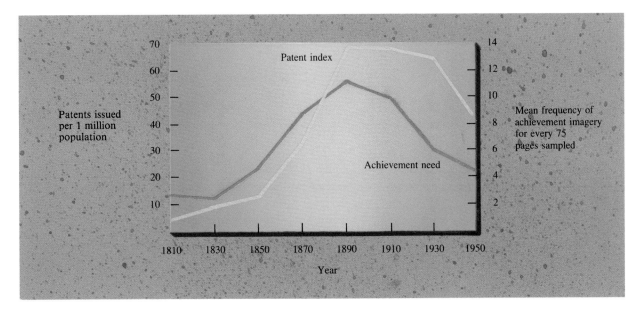

FIGURE 11.9

Achievement Themes and the Patent Index
Between 1800 and 1950, there was a strong positive correlation between the number of achievement themes in children's readers and the number of patents issued by the U.S. Patent Office (DeCharms & Moeller, 1962).

changes in practical achievements. You will once again recall that a positive correlation between two variables does not necessarily mean that changes in one *cause* changes in the other. Of course, it does not preclude the possibility of a causal relationship, either.

Changes in the achievement motive over time also differ for males and females. From the late 1950s to the late 1970s, American men showed no change in their achievement motivation, whereas American women showed a marked increase. This has been attributed to the women's movement of the past few decades, which made it more acceptable for women to pursue personal achievement outside of traditional women's domains, such as homemaking (Veroff et al., 1980).

Need for Achievement

Henry Murray (1938) referred to the achievement motive as the *need for achievement,* which reveals itself in efforts to meet high standards of performance or to compete successfully against other people. How do psychologists measure the need for achievement? The most common means has been the *Thematic Apperception Test* (TAT), developed by Murray and his colleague Christiana Morgan in the 1930s to assess social motivation (Morgan & Murray, 1935). The TAT is based on the assumption that our fantasies reveal our motives. The test consists of a series of drawings of people in ambiguous situations; an example is shown in figure 11.10. The subject is asked to tell what is happening in the picture, what led up to it, how the people feel, and how the situation turns out. The responses are scored for any themes that run through them. Individuals with a high need for achievement will tell stories in which people overcome obstacles, work hard to reach goals, and accomplish great things.

What do we know about people who score high on the need for achievement? Research shows that they persist at tasks in the face of difficulties, delay gratification in the pursuit of long-term goals, and achieve greater success than people with a low need for achievement. They also select moderately difficult challenges, neither so easy that they guarantee success nor so difficult that they guarantee failure (McClelland, 1985). Even psychologists with a high need for achievement become more successful, at least as measured by the recognition accorded their research by fellow psychologists. The

**Henry Murray (1893–1988)
Christiana Morgan (1897–1967)**
"The strength of a need as a consistently ready reaction system of personality is measured by noting the frequency of its occurrence under given conditions."

FIGURE 11.10

The Thematic Apperception Test
What is happening in this picture? What led up to it? How does the person feel? How will it turn out? Your responses to several ambiguous pictures like this might contain themes revealing the strength of your need for achievement.

incentive value
The perceived rewards that accompany success in a particular area.

expectancy
In achievement situations, the perceived probability of success in a particular area.

fear of failure
The motivation to avoid achievement situations that might bring failure.

David McClelland
". . . achievement motivation training is very cost effective for improving small business performance. . . ."

published research of psychologists with a high need for achievement is cited more often in articles written by other psychologists (Helmreich et al., 1980).

The need for achievement varies with the achievement situation. People with a high need for achievement rarely seek success in more than a few areas of life. So, your achievement behavior depends on more than just the strength of your general need for achievement. Your achievement behavior also depends on **incentive value,** the perceived rewards that accompany success in a particular area, and **expectancy,** the perceived probability of success in a particular area (McClelland, 1985). Still another factor that affects your achievement behavior is what John Atkinson labeled the **fear of failure,** the motivation to avoid situations that might bring failure (Atkinson & Litwin, 1960).

Consider these factors in regard to your achievement behavior in a psychology course. If you are high in achievement motivation, if you find that a good grade in the course has high incentive value for you, and if you expect that studying hard is likely to result in a good grade, you are more likely to work hard in the course. Yet if you are high in achievement motivation but do not value a high grade in psychology (perhaps because it is only an elective course) or believe that you have little chance of success in the course (perhaps because the professor is a notoriously hard grader), you might not work as hard. But what of your fear of failure? If you had a strong fear of failure, you might work harder to avoid doing poorly and being subjected to criticism from your parents. Or if your fear of failure overcame you, you might choose to take the course pass-fail.

Research has also shown that the need for achievement can interact with arousal to determine a person's performance. As you read earlier, we all perform best at our optimal level of arousal for a given task. In an arousing situation, such as giving a speech to a class, a student with a low need for achievement might perform well because the situation raises the student to her optimal level of arousal. In the same situation, a student with a high need for achievement, already at an optimal level of arousal, might perform poorly because the situation raises the student beyond his optimal level (Humphreys & Revelle, 1984).

(a)

(b)

(c)

(d)

Achievement Motivation
The need for achievement is demonstrated in the lives of persons who reach the top of their fields, including (a) the late Andy Warhol, who championed Pop art; (b) Toni Morrison, who won a Nobel prize for her writing; (c) Julia Child, who became a famous television chef; and (d) General Colin Powell, who served as head of the U.S. army.

Goal Setting

Suppose that you are high in the need for achievement in academics, sports, or some other area. How should you seek to fulfill that need? Hundreds of studies, including McClelland's study of Indian businessmen, have demonstrated the importance of **goal setting.** Goals increase motivation and improve performance by providing incentives. Your goals focus your attention, increase your effort, maintain your persistence, and encourage you to develop strategies for reaching them. Goal setting has been especially useful in business and industry in stimulating productivity (Nordstrom, Lorenzi, & Hall, 1990). *Management by objectives,* in which employees participate in setting goals, has been especially effective. Of 70 studies included in a review of research on the effectiveness of management by objectives, 68 found that it increased productivity (Rodgers & Hunter, 1991).

But how should you set your goals? Research findings by Edwin Locke and his colleagues provide several suggestions (Locke & Latham, 1985). Specific, challenging goals (such as "I will increase my studying by one hour a night") produce better performance than do no goals, vague goals (such as "I will increase the time I spend studying"), easy goals (such as "I will increase my studying by 10 minutes a week"), or mere encouragement to do your best. Feedback on your progress toward a goal (such as keeping a record of how much time you spend studying) will help you reach that goal. And a goal that you set yourself will motivate you more than a goal imposed on you (as when a parent forces a child to stay home and study every day after school).

Another effective technique is to use short-term goals to help you reach long-term ones. This was demonstrated in a program aimed at improving children's arithmetic performance. Children who were given short-term goals did better in arithmetic than did those given long-term goals (Bandura & Schunk, 1981). Suppose you have the long-term goal of owning your own business. You would be wise to have shorter-term goals also. These might include finding a summer job in your field of interest, earning a bachelor's degree, and gaining an entry-level position after graduation.

Intrinsic Motivation

If you have ever written a term paper just to obtain a grade, you can appreciate William James's distress at having to complete his now-classic 1890 textbook for an extrinsic reason. According to Edward Thorndike (1961, p. 267), "James wrote the *Principles* with

goal setting
The establishment of a particular level of performance to achieve in the future.

Edwin Locke
"Goals affect performance by affecting effort, persistence, and direction of attention, and by motivating strategy development."

wailing and gnashing of teeth to fulfill a contract with a publishing firm." Though James enjoyed writing, he did not enjoy writing for money. He was not unusual, because research has shown that receiving extrinsic rewards for performing intrinsically rewarding activities can make those activities less rewarding and reduce the motivation to perform them.

Intrinsic motivation is the desire to perform a task for its own sake. In contrast, **extrinsic motivation** is the desire to perform a task to gain external rewards, such as praise, grades, or money. For example, you might take a psychology course because you find it interesting (an intrinsic reason) or because it is a graduation requirement (an extrinsic reason).

Until the 1970s, most psychologists agreed with B. F. Skinner that rewards will increase the probability of behavior or, at worst, have no effect on it. But then research began to show otherwise. In one of the first experiments on intrinsic motivation, children were given a period of time during which they could draw. Some of them were then given a certificate as a reward for having drawn. When given a subsequent chance to draw, students who had been rewarded for drawing spent less time at it than did students who had not been rewarded (Lepper, Greene, & Nisbett, 1973). Fortunately, children who have been trained to stress intrinsic reasons for engaging in creative activities are somewhat immunized against the negative effects of extrinsic rewards (Hennessey & Zbikowski, 1993).

Later studies have also supported the benefits of intrinsic motivation and the detrimental effects of extrinsic motivation. Children who are given external rewards for playing with toys later play less with those toys (Margolis & Mynatt, 1986). High school students who are intrinsically interested in intellectual pursuits perform better in their courses (Lloyd & Barenblatt, 1984). Among elementary school students, high achievers tend to be more intrinsically motivated and low achievers more extrinsically motivated (Diaz Soto, 1989). And employees governed by extrinsic rewards, such as fringe benefits, are less motivated than are employees governed by intrinsic rewards, such as control over their own work schedule (Notz, 1975). Even the sense of moral obligation can be undermined by extrinsic rewards. This was the outcome of a study in which students who were paid for tape-recording a text for a blind student showed a reduced sense of moral obligation in comparison with those who were not paid for doing so (Kunda & Schwartz, 1983).

Given the everyday observation that extrinsic rewards can increase achievement motivation, especially in people who initially have little or no motivation in a particular area, why do extrinsic rewards sometimes decrease achievement motivation? Two theories provide possible answers. **Overjustification theory** assumes that an extrinsic reward decreases intrinsic motivation when a person attributes his or her performance to the extrinsic reward. The children who were rewarded for drawing might have attributed their behavior to the reward rather than to their interest in drawing. Overjustification occurs when there is high intrinsic interest and the reward is perceived as more than adequate justification for performing the act. In a study of first- and second-graders, children played with an interesting or uninteresting toy and were rewarded or not rewarded. Rewards reduced the motivation to play with the interesting, but not the uninteresting, toy (Newman & Layton, 1984).

An alternative theory, **cognitive-evaluation theory,** put forth by Edward Deci, holds that a reward perceived as providing *information* about a person's competence in an activity will increase her or his intrinsic motivation to perform that activity (Deci, Nezlek, & Sheinman, 1981). But a reward perceived as an attempt to *control* a person's behavior will decrease his or her intrinsic motivation to perform that activity. Consider a student whose teacher rewards her for doing well in drawing. If the student believes that the reward is being used to provide information about her competence, her intrinsic motivation to perform that activity may increase. But if she believes that the reward is being used to control her behavior (perhaps to make her spend more time drawing), her intrinsic motivation to perform may decrease. There is strong research support for this theory (Rummel & Feinberg, 1988). So, when you reward people for performing

intrinsic motivation
The desire to perform a behavior for its own sake.

extrinsic motivation
The desire to perform a behavior to obtain an external reward, such as praise, grades, or money.

Edward Deci
"When the controlling aspect of a reward is more salient, it will decrease one's intrinsic motivation. . . . When the informational aspect is more salient (and when the information is positive), it will increase one's intrinsic motivation by initiating the change in perceived competence."

overjustification theory
The theory that an extrinsic reward will decrease intrinsic motivation when a person attributes her or his performance to that reward.

cognitive-evaluation theory
The theory that a person's intrinsic motivation will increase when a reward is perceived as a source of information but will decrease when a reward is perceived as an attempt to exert control.

activities that they find intrinsically motivating, you must be careful to use rewards as information rather than as controls.

You should now have a better appreciation of the influence of motivation, particularly the hunger, sex, arousal, and achievement motives, in your everyday life. To appreciate how motivation affects behavior in an area of life that is important to many people, consider the role of motivation in sport.

THINKING ABOUT *Psychology*

WHAT IS THE RELATIONSHIP BETWEEN MOTIVATION AND SPORT?

Just before the turn of the century, Indiana University psychologist Norman Triplett (1898) observed that bicyclists rode faster when competing against other bicyclists than when competing against time. Given the popularity of instinct theories near the turn of the century, you would probably not be surprised that he attributed this performance to stimulation of the "competitive instinct," which supposedly released stored energy and increased the bicyclist's level of arousal. This was perhaps the first study in **sport psychology,** the field that studies the relationship between psychological factors and sport performance. If you watched the most recent summer or winter Olympics, you probably saw reports about elite athletes who used the services of sport psychologists to help motivate them to perform up to their capabilities. In studying motivation in sport, researchers are especially interested in the arousal motive and the achievement motive.

sport psychology
The field that applies psychological principles to help amateur and professional athletes improve their performance.

THE AROUSAL MOTIVE AND SPORT

Your arousal motive, particularly your degree of sensation seeking, influences your choice of sports. People high in sensation seeking prefer more-exciting, more-dangerous sports than do people low in sensation seeking. People who participate in a highly stimulating sport, such as hang gliding or auto racing, score higher on the Sensation Seeking Scale (Zuckerman, 1979) than do those who participate in the less stimulating sport of intercollegiate bowling (Straub, 1982). Similarly, rugby players score higher on the Sensation Seeking Scale than do marathon runners (Potgieter & Bisschoff, 1990). Participants in whitewater canoeing and kayaking score significantly above average on the Sensation Seeking Scale, and their scores on the scale are negatively correlated with their level of anxiety. This means that the higher the score in sensation seeking, the lower their level of anxiety (Campbell, Tyrrell, & Zingaro, 1993).

If you have ever played a competitive sport, you know what it is to "choke"—to be so anxious that you perform below your normal level of ability. Choking occurs when your anxiety makes you attend to the normally automatic movements involved in playing a sport. If you consciously attend to those movements, they will be disrupted (Baumeister, 1984). Consider foul shooting in basketball. If you attend to each movement of your arm and hand as you shoot foul shots, you will disrupt the smooth sequence of movements that foul shooting requires. Athletes at an optimal level of arousal are less likely to be undermotivated or to choke, as shown in a study of women collegiate basketball players. Those with a moderate level of pregame anxiety performed better than did those with a low or high level (Sonstroem & Bernardo, 1982).

(a)   (b)   (c)

Arousal and Athletic Performance
The optimal level of arousal will vary from one sport to another—the more delicate the task, the lower the level of optimal arousal. Thus, (a) professional golfer Nancy Lopez will putt better at a low level of arousal; (b) track star Carl Lewis will jump farther at a more moderate level of arousal; and (c) champion sumo wrestler Konishiki will be better able to push his opponents out of the ring when he is at a high level of arousal.

The Yerkes-Dodson law might explain why some athletes perform better during practice than during competition. For example, if you play intramural softball, you might be at your optimal level of arousal during practice, a relatively unstressful situation, but rise above your optimal level during a game, a relatively stressful situation. Similarly, the Yerkes-Dodson law may also explain why some athletes perform better during competition than during practice. In that case, you might be below your optimal level of arousal during practice but rise up to your optimal level during a game.

A good coach will realize which of her or his athletes must be psyched up and which must be calmed down to achieve an optimal level of arousal during competition. There is no single optimal level of arousal. Each athlete has his or her own optimal level for a given sport (Raglin & Turner, 1993). Thus, Knute Rockne–like "win one for the Gipper" pep talks might hurt the performance of moderately or highly aroused athletes. Yet such pep talks can be good for athletes who are too relaxed before competition, especially in aggressive sports such as football or weight lifting.

As mentioned earlier, the optimal level of arousal is lower for complex tasks than for simple tasks. This is also true in sports (Gardner, 1986). Your optimal level of arousal while hitting a golf ball (a relatively complex task) would be lower than your optimal level while playing shuffleboard (a relatively simple task). Moreover, the more skillful the athlete, the higher will be her or his optimal level of arousal. The golfer who makes a putt on the eighteenth green to win the U.S. Open might be so skillful that he has a higher optimal level of arousal than does the golfer who "chokes" in the same situation. This also means that when teaching beginners to play golf, to ride a bicycle, or to serve a volleyball, you should try to keep their arousal levels from becoming too high. To achieve this, beginners should refrain from competition and not practice while being watched by people other than the coach or instructor.

One technique for achieving optimal arousal in athletes is flotation REST. In a study of intercollegiate tennis players, subjects practiced visual imagery alone or combined with flotation REST. Those who practiced both visual imagery and flotation REST showed improved first-serve accuracy, while those who used visual imagery alone did not (McAleney, Barabasz, & Barabasz, 1990). In a study of the effects of flotation REST on recreational basketball performance, college students who practiced flotation REST reported greater confidence and performed better than control subjects who did not practice it (Suedfeld & Bruno, 1990). Flotation REST also improves the performance of dart players (Suedfeld, Collier, & Hartnett, 1993), and rifle shooters (Barabasz, Barabasz, & Bauman, 1993), and varsity collegiate basketball players (Wagaman, Barabasz, & Barabasz, 1991).

Researchers have become more refined in studying the relationship between arousal and performance by distinguishing between mental and physical arousal. A study of competitive swimmers found an inverted-U relationship between *physical* arousal and swimming speed, as predicted by the Yerkes-Dodson law. That is, subjects who had

PLAY IT A BIT TO THE RIGHT... NOT TOO FAST... DON'T BABY, IT, EITHER...

AND DON'T CHOKE!

DIK BROWNE 2-10

Reprinted with special permission of King Features Syndicate.

moderate physical arousal swam faster than those who had either low or high physical arousal. But the study failed to find such a relationship between *mental* arousal and swimming speed. Instead, the lower the swimmers' self-reported mental arousal, the faster they swam (Burton, 1988).

THE ACHIEVEMENT MOTIVE AND SPORT

On June 4, 1986, six weeks after setting the collegiate record for the 10,000-meter run, Kathy Ormsby, running among the leaders, veered off the track midway through the final race at the NCAA championships in Indianapolis. She left the stadium, ran to the nearby White River Bridge, and leaped 50 feet to the river bank. The fall broke her back, damaged her spinal cord, and paralyzed her from the waist down. Besides excelling at running, Ormsby had been her high school's valedictorian (with an average of 99 percent out of 100), was a premedical student at North Carolina State University, and was dedicated to living up to the strict standards of behavior required by her religious beliefs. As one of her teachers said, "If a human being can be perfect, I would say that Kathy was perfect" (Dwyer, 1986, p. 8-A). Ormsby was certainly high in her need for achievement.

Ormsby had been overcome periodically by anxiety strong enough to force her to drop out of races. Her friends and coaches believed she succumbed to what they called "her will to succeed." Though her high need for achievement certainly motivated her to compete, she apparently succumbed to her fear of failure, finding it more and more difficult to motivate herself to compete against other elite athletes. Kathy Ormsby's tragic story shows that the achievement motive can be a powerful force in athletic competition, as it is in other areas of life.

Athletes with a high need for achievement are motivated to seek competition that provides a fair test of their abilities. Early evidence for this came from a study in which college students played a game of ringtoss. Those with a high need for achievement were more likely to stand at an intermediate distance from the peg, while those with a low need for achievement were more likely to stand either close to the peg or far from it (Atkinson & Litwin, 1960). Similarly, if you were high in your need for achievement in tennis, you would probably choose to play someone of your own ability. Neither playing a 5-year-old child nor playing Gabriela Sabatini would be a fair test of your ability. In contrast, a person low in the need for achievement or high in the fear of failure might prefer to play either someone who barely knows how to grip a racket, which would assure success, or a professional tennis player, which would assure that losing would be attributable to the professional opponent's excellence rather than to personal incompetence.

One way in which superior athletes make competition against lesser athletes more motivating is by giving themselves a handicap, making the competition a moderate challenge, rather than a guaranteed success (Nicholls, 1984). If you are an excellent table tennis player, you might provide a more moderate challenge for yourself by giving

Kathy Ormsby

Achievement Motivation and Sport
Being physically disabled does not necessarily reduce one's motivation to achieve. Despite being born without a right hand, Jim Abbott has become a successful pitcher. He led the United States to a gold medal in baseball in the 1988 Olympic Games and now excels as a major league pitcher for the New York Yankees.

FIGURE 11.11

Goal Setting and Hockey Performance

These graphs show the superiority of goal setting in improving the performance of the University of Notre Dame hockey team by increasing body checking. The *mean hit rate* is the average number of body checks per minute on ice. In regard to interventions, *Bsin* refers to a body-checking baseline period, *Fbk* refers to a body-checking performance feedback, *Goal-set* (*G-S*) refers to a body-checking goal-setting period, and *Praise* (*Pse*) refers to a body-checking praise period. In regard to groups, Group S involved talented seniors, Group N involved new players, and Group C involved subjects who played both seasons (Anderson et al., 1988).

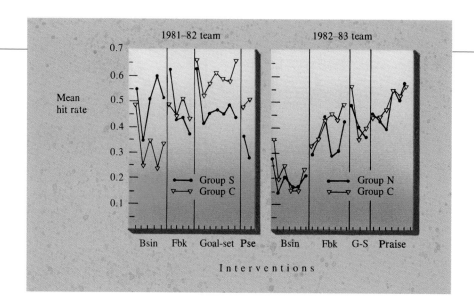

a lesser opponent 10 points in a 21-point game. Similarly, in the 1960s Wilt Chamberlain, perhaps the most physically imposing athlete in history (who once *averaged* 50 points a game for a whole season in the National Basketball Association), developed a fade-away jump shot to show that he could succeed even when giving up his greatest asset, his ability to score from near the basket because of his great strength and height (7 feet, 1 inch tall). By doing so, he made scoring a moderate, rather than easy, challenge for himself—often to the distress of his coach.

As in other areas of life, goal setting is important in sport motivation. A survey of more than 300 male and female intercollegiate athletes found that virtually all of them used goal setting to help enhance their performance and that they generally found it effective (Weinberg et al., 1993). In a study of sit-up performance by children, those who used specific short-term goals improved more than did those who were only told to "do your best" (Hall & Byrne, 1988). A study of the effect of goal setting on the rifle marksmanship of college students found that those who set specific goals improved more than did those who set do-your-best goals (Boyce, 1992). And, as shown in figure 11.11, members of the University of Notre Dame hockey team successfully used goal setting as part of a motivational program to increase their aggressiveness. They increased their rate of legal body checking and, perhaps as a consequence, improved their team record (Anderson et al., 1988). Because of the many factors involved in sport and goal setting, researchers still must determine what kinds of goals are most effective for specific athletes, performing specific tasks, under specific conditions (Weinberg & Weigand, 1993).

Athletes are also more motivated by intrinsic rewards than by extrinsic rewards. A study of youth basketball players found that boys and girls who were high in their intrinsic motivation to play, and low on perceived parental pressure to play, enjoyed playing more than did other children (Brustad, 1988). In a study of college athletes, football players on athletic scholarships reported less intrinsic motivation than did those who were not on scholarships. But among male wrestlers and female athletes, those who were on athletic scholarships reported *more* intrinsic motivation than those who were not. What could account for these findings? Perhaps football coaches use scholarships more as a means of *control*, while wrestling coaches and coaches of female athletes use scholarships more as a means of *informing* athletes about their competence. In terms of the cognitive-evaluation theory, discussed earlier, rewards that are perceived as a means of control may decrease instrinsic motivation, and rewards that are perceived as a means of providing information about competence may increase intrinsic motivation (Ryan, 1980).

The importance of intrinsic motivation in sport was expressed in the response of star shortstop Ozzie Guillen of the Chicago White Sox to the idea of including incentive clauses in his playing contract: "I don't want incentives to play, because I like to play. I don't want to go to the All-Star Game because of money" (Isle, 1988, p. 6). As you can see, motivational factors important in other areas of life are also important in sport. Athletes perform best at an optimal level of arousal, which varies with the individual, the sport, and the task. And athletes are influenced by their achievement motive; their level of motivation is enhanced by their need for achievement, proper use of goal setting, and reliance on intrinsic rewards.

SUMMARY

SOURCES OF MOTIVATION

Motivation is the psychological process that arouses, directs, and maintains behavior. The main sources of motivation include heredity, drives, and incentives. Though William McDougall's instinct theory failed to achieve scientific credibility, interest in the hereditary basis of social behavior remains alive today in the field of sociobiology. Instinct theories gave way to the drive-reduction theory of Clark Hull, which assumes that physiological deprivation causes a need, which induces a state of tension called a drive. Drive reduction aims at restoring a steady state of physiological equilibrium called homeostasis. A drive "pushes" you toward a goal, whereas an incentive is an external stimulus that "pulls" you toward a goal. Abraham Maslow arranged human needs in a hierarchy, with the pursuit of higher needs contingent on the satisfaction of lower ones.

THE HUNGER MOTIVE

Hunger impels you to eat to satisfy your body's need for nutrients. Factors that regulate hunger include taste sensations, stretch and nutrient receptors in the stomach, cholecystokinin secreted by the small intestine, glucose receptors in the liver, and insulin secreted by the pancreas. Areas of the hypothalamus regulate hunger by responding to signals from the blood and internal organs. External food-related cues also influence hunger and eating. The most common eating problem is obesity, which is defined as a body weight more than 20 percent above normal for one's height and body build. Obesity depends on the body's set point, basal metabolic rate, responsiveness to external cues, chronic level of blood insulin, and reaction to stress. Two of the most prevalent eating disorders are anorexia nervosa and bulimia nervosa.

THE SEX MOTIVE

Sex serves as both a drive and an incentive. Sex hormones direct sexual development and sexual behavior. Unlike in other animals, sexual behavior in human adults is controlled more by sociocultural factors than by sex hormones. Formal research on human sexuality began with surveys on male and female sexual behavior conducted by Alfred Kinsey and his colleagues. Later research by William Masters and Virginia Johnson showed that females and males have similar sexual response cycles. Masters and Johnson also developed sex therapy

techniques that have been successful in helping men and women overcome sexual dysfunctions, which are chronic problems at phases in the sexual response cycle. Human beings vary in their gender identity and sexual orientation. Transsexuals feel trapped in a body of the wrong sex and may seek surgery and hormonal treatments to change their appearance. Homosexuals are sexually attracted to members of their own sex.

THE AROUSAL MOTIVE

Arousal is the general level of physiological activation of the brain and body. The Yerkes-Dodson law holds that there is an optimal level of arousal for the performance of a given task, with the optimal level becoming lower as the task becomes more complex. Studies of sensory deprivation by Donald Hebb and his colleagues show that we are motivated to maintain at least a minimal level of sensory stimulation. People also differ in their degree of sensation seeking, which is the motivation to seek high or low levels of sensory stimulation.

THE ACHIEVEMENT MOTIVE

The achievement motive is the desire for mastery, excellence, and accomplishment. Henry Murray and Christiana Morgan introduced the Thematic Apperception Test as a means of assessing the need for achievement. People with a high need for achievement persist at tasks in the face of difficulties, delay gratification in the pursuit of long-term goals, and achieve greater success than do people with a low need for achievement. They also prefer moderately difficult challenges. Your actual achievement behavior in a given situation depends on the strength of your need for achievement, as well as the incentive value of success, your expectancy of success, and the strength of your fear of failure in that situation. Goal setting increases motivation and improves performance by providing incentives. The best goals are specific and challenging, and short-term goals are useful in the pursuit of long-term goals. The intrinsic motivation to engage in an activity can be reduced by extrinsic rewards. Overjustification theory and cognitive-evaluation theory provide different explanations for the detrimental effects of extrinsic rewards.

THINKING ABOUT PSYCHOLOGY: WHAT IS THE RELATIONSHIP BETWEEN MOTIVATION AND SPORT?

Sport psychology is the field that studies the relationship between psychological factors and sport performance, particularly the influence of motivation. In studying motivation and sport, sport psy-chologists are especially interested in the relationship between arousal and performance. To keep from "choking" during competition, athletes must learn to keep from rising above their optimal level of arousal. Athletic performance is also affected by other motivational factors, including the need for achievement, goal setting, and intrinsic motivation.

IMPORTANT CONCEPTS

achievement motive *410*
anorexia nervosa *397*
arousal motive *407*
basal metabolic rate *394*
bulimia nervosa *397*
cognitive-evaluation
     theory *414*
drive *389*
drive-reduction theory *389*
expectancy *412*

extrinsic motivation *414*
fear of failure *412*
gender identity *404*
goal setting *413*
gonads *399*
hierarchy of needs *390*
homeostasis *389*
homosexuality *405*
incentive *390*
incentive value *412*

instinct *388*
intrinsic motivation *414*
motivation *388*
need *389*
obesity *394*
overjustification theory *414*
paraphilia *399*
sensate focusing *404*
sensation seeking *409*

sensory deprivation *408*
set point *393*
sexual dysfunction *403*
sexual orientation *404*
sexual response cycle *401*
sociobiology *389*
sport psychology *415*
transsexualism *404*
Yerkes-Dodson law *407*

MAJOR CONTRIBUTORS

John Atkinson *410*
Walter Cannon *391*
Donald Hebb *407*
Clark Hull *389–390*

Alfred Kinsey *400*
Abraham Maslow *390*
William Masters and
     Virginia Johnson *401*

David McClelland *410*
William McDougall *388*
John Money *407*

Henry Murray and Christiana
     Morgan *411–412*
Judith Rodin *396*
Stanley Schachter *395*

RECOMMENDED READINGS

FOR GENERAL WORKS ON MOTIVATION

Badcock, C. (1991). *Evolution and individual behavior: An introduction to human sociobiology.* New York: Basil Blackwell.

Beck, R. C. (1990). *Motivation: Theories and principles.* (3rd ed.). Englewood Cliffs, NJ: Prentice Hall.

Berman, J. J. (Ed.). (1990). *Nebraska Symposium on Motivation, 1989: Cross-cultural perspectives.* Lincoln: University of Nebraska Press.

Franken, R. E. (1993). *Human motivation* (3rd ed.). Belmont, CA: Brooks/Cole.

Maslow, A. H. (Ed.). (1970). *Motivation and personality.* New York: Harper & Row.

Reeve, J. (1992). *Understanding motivation and emotion.* San Diego: Harcourt Brace Jovanovich.

Senchuk, D. M. (1991). *Against instinct: From biology to philosophical psychology.* Philadelphia: Temple University Press.

FOR MORE ON THE HUNGER MOTIVE

Andersen, A. E. (Ed.). (1990). *Males with eating disorders.* New York: Brunner/Mazel.

Bromberg, J. J. (1988). *Fasting girls: The emergence of anorexia nervosa as a modern disease.* Cambridge, MA: Harvard University Press.

Crowther, J. H., Hobfoll, S. E., Stephens, M. A., & Tennenbaum, D. L. (1992). *The etiology of bulimia nervosa: The individual and familial context.* Bristol, PA: Hemisphere.

Fairburn, C. G., & Wilson, G. T. (Eds.). (1993). *Binge eating: Nature, assessment, and treatment.* New York: Guilford.

Fichter, M. M. (Ed.). (1990). *Bulimia nervosa: Basic research, diagnosis, and therapy.* New York: Wiley.

Gordon, R. A. (1990). *Anorexia and bulimia.* Cambridge, MA: Basil Blackwell.

Hsu, L. K. G. (1990). *Eating disorders.* New York: Guilford.

Logue, A. W. (1991). *The psychology of eating and drinking* (2nd ed.). New York: W. H. Freeman.

Rodin, J. (1992). *Body traps.* New York: Morrow.

Schlundt, D. G., & Johnson, W. G. (1990). *Eating disorders.* Needham Heights, MA: Allyn & Bacon.

Stunkard, A. J., & Wadden, T. A. (1993). *Obesity: Theory and therapy* (2nd ed.). New York: Raven Press.

FOR MORE ON THE SEX MOTIVE

Blair, C. D., & Lanyon, R. I. (1981). Exhibitionism: Etiology and treatment. *Psychological Bulletin, 89,* 439–463.

Bremmer, J. (Ed.). (1989). *From Sappho to de Sade: Moments in the history of sexuality.* New York: Routledge.

Docter, R. F. (1988). *Transvestites and transsexuals: Toward a theory of cross-gender behavior.* New York: Plenum.

Feierman, J. R. (Ed.). (1990). *Pedophilia: Biosocial dimensions.* New York: Springer-Verlag.

Freedman, E., & D'Emilio, J. (1988). *Intimate matters: A history of sexuality in America.* New York: Harper & Row.

Gilman, S. L. (1989). *Sexuality: An illustrated history representing the sexual in medicine and culture from the middle ages to the age of AIDS.* New York: Wiley.

Hyde, J. S. (1993). *Understanding human sexuality* (5th ed.). New York: McGraw-Hill.

Kinsey, A. C., Pomeroy, W. B., & Martin, C. E. (1948). *Sexual behavior in the human male.* Philadelphia: Saunders.

Kinsey, A. C., Pomeroy, W. D., Martin, C. E., & Gebhard, T. H. (1953). *Sexual behavior in the human female.* Philadelphia: Saunders.

Kluft, R. P. (Ed.). (1990). *Incest-related syndromes of adult psychopathology.* Washington, DC: American Psychiatric Press.

Leiblum, S. R., & Rosen, R. C. (1989). (Eds.). *Principles and practice of sex therapy.* New York: Guilford.

Margulis, L., & Sagan, D. (1991). *Mystery dance: On the evolution of human sexuality.* New York: Summit Books.

Masters, W. H., Johnson, V. E., & Kolodny, R. C. (1993). *Biological foundations of human sexuality.* New York: Harper Collins.

McWhirter, D. P., Sanders, S. A., & Reinisch, J. M. (Eds.). (1990). *Homosexuality/heterosexuality: Concepts of sexual orientation.* New York: Oxford University Press.

Money, J. (1994). *Interpreting the unspeakable: Sexual motivation in human behavior.* New York: Continuum.

O'Donohue, W., & Geer, J. H. (Eds.). (1993). *Handbook of sexual dysfunction: Assessment and treatment.* Boston: Allyn & Bacon.

Reinisch, J. M. (1990). *The new Kinsey Institute report on sex.* Newbury Park, CA: Sage Publications.

Rosen, R. C., & Beck, J. G. (1988). *Patterns of sexual arousal: Psychophysiological processes and clinical applications.* New York: Guilford.

Schad-Somers, S. P. (1982). *Sadomasochism: Etiology and treatment.* New York: Human Sciences Press.

Shainberg, L. W., & Byer, C. O. (1994). *Dimensions of human sexuality.* (4th ed.). Dubuque, IA: Wm. C. Brown.

Sipe, A. W. (1990). *A secret world: Sexuality and the search for celibacy.* New York: Brunner/Mazel.

Suggs, D., & Miracle, A. (Eds.). (1993). *Culture and human sexuality.* Belmont, CA: Brooks/Cole.

FOR MORE ON THE AROUSAL MOTIVE

Barabasz, A. F., & Barabasz, M. (Eds.). (1993). *Clinical and experimental restricted environmental stimulation: New developments and perspectives.* New York: Springer-Verlag.

Csikszentmihalyi, M. (1990). *Flow: The psychology of optimal experience.* New York: Harper & Row.

Strelau, J., Eysenck, H. J. (Eds.). (1987). *Personality dimensions and arousal.* New York: Plenum.

Suedfeld, P., Turner, J. W., & Fine, T. H. (Eds.). (1990). *Restricted environmental stimulation: Theoretical and empirical developments in flotation REST.* New York: Springer-Verlag.

Thayer, R. E. (1989). *The biopsychology of mood and arousal.* New York: Oxford University Press.

Zentall, S. S., & Zentall, T. R. (1983). Optimal stimulation: A model of disordered activity and performance in normal and deviant children. *Psychological Bulletin, 94,* 446–471.

Zubek, J. P. (Ed.). (1969). *Sensory deprivation: Fifteen years of research.* New York: Appleton-Century-Crofts.

Zuckerman, M. (1994). *Behavioral expression and biosocial bases of sensation seeking.* New York: Cambridge University Press.

FOR MORE ON THE ACHIEVEMENT MOTIVE

Atkinson, J. W., & Feather, N. T. (Eds.). (1966). *A theory of achievement motivation.* New York: Wiley.

Deci, E. L., & Ryan, R. M. (1985). *Intrinsic motivation and self-determination in human behavior.* New York: Plenum.

Hofstede, G. (1980). *Culture's consequences: International differences in work-related values.* London: Sage Publications.

Locke, E. A., & Latham, G. P. (1990). *A theory of goal setting and task performance.* Englewood Cliffs, NJ: Prentice Hall.

McClelland, D. C. (1980/1993). *Some social consequences of achievement motivation.* New York: Irvington.

Spence, J. T. (Ed.). (1983). *Achievement and achievement motivation.* San Francisco: Freeman.

FOR MORE ON MOTIVATION AND SPORT

Baumeister, R. F. (1985, April). The championship choke. *Psychology Today,* pp. 48–52.

Browne, M. A., & Mahoney, M. J. (1984). Sport psychology. *Annual Review of Psychology, 35,* 605–625.

Cox, R. H. (1993). *Sport psychology* (3rd ed.). Dubuque, IA: Brown & Benchmark.

Cratty, B. J. (1989). *Psychology in contemporary sport.* Englewood Cliffs, NJ: Prentice Hall.

Gill, D. L. (1986). *Psychological dynamics of sport.* Champaign, IL: Human Kinetics.

Locke, E. A., & Latham, G. P. (1985). The application of goal setting to sports. *Journal of Sport Psychology, 7,* 205–222.

Roberts, G. C. (Ed.). (1992). *Motivation in sport and exercise.* Champaign, IL: Human Kinetics.

Snyder, C. W., & Abernethy, B. (Eds.). (1992). *The creative side of experimentation: Personal perspectives from leading researchers in motor control, motor development, and sport psychology.* Champaign, IL: Human Kinetics.

Taylor, J. (1988). Slumpbusting: A systematic analysis of slumps in sports. *Sport Psychologist, 2,* 39–48.

Tutko, T., & Tosi, U. (1990). *Sports psyching.* Los Angeles: Tarcher.

FOR MORE ON CONTRIBUTORS TO THE STUDY OF MOTIVATION

Benison, S., Barger, A. C., & Wolfe, E. L. (1987). *Walter B. Cannon: The life and times of a young scientist.* Cambridge, MA: Belknap/Harvard.

Cohen, I. B. (Ed.). (1980). *The career of William Beaumont and the reception of his discovery.* New York: Arno.

Coleman, E. (Ed.). (1991). *John Money: A tribute.* Binghamton, NY: Haworth.

Douglas, C. (1993). *Translate this darkness: The life of Christiana Morgan.* New York: Simon & Schuster.

Hoffman, E. (1988). *The right to be human: A biography of Abraham Maslow.* Los Angeles: Tarcher.

Jeffrey, F., & Lilly, J. C. (1990). *John Lilly, so far. . . .* Los Angeles: Tarcher.

Pomeroy, W. B. (1982). *Dr. Kinsey and the Institute for Sex Research.* New Haven, CT: Yale University Press.

Robinson, F. G. (1992). *Love's story told: A life of Henry A. Murray.* Cambridge, MA: Harvard University Press.

Robinson, P. (1988). *The modernization of sex: Havelock Ellis, Alfred Kinsey, William Masters, and Virginia Johnson.* Ithaca, NY: Cornell University Press.

Marc Chagall
Green Violinist
1923–24

EMOTION

ow do you feel? Are you *anxious* about an upcoming exam, *depressed* by a recent loss, in *love* with a wonderful person, *angry* at a personal affront, or *happy* about your favorite team's performance? What you are feeling is an *emotion*. The word *emotion* comes from a Latin word meaning "to set in motion," and, like motives, such as sex and hunger, emotions, such as love and anger, motivate behavior that helps us adapt to different situations (Ekman, 1992a). Though it is easy to recognize an emotion, especially one that is a pure, prototypical example (such as extreme anger or intense romantic love), it is difficult to provide a formal definition of the concept itself (Russell, 1991). In fact, one published review of the research literature found 92 separate definitions of emotion (Kleinginna & Kleinginna, 1981). This inability to agree on a single definition of emotion led two emotion researchers to observe, "Everyone knows what an emotion is, until asked to give a definition" (Fehr & Russell, 1984, p. 464).

Despite the difficulty of precisely defining the concept of emotion, most psychologists agree that **emotion** is a motivated state that is marked by physiological arousal, expressive behavior, and mental experience and that varies in its intensity and pleasantness or unpleasantness (Buck, 1985). Consider an angry man. His heart might pound (a sign of physiological arousal), he might grit his teeth (an expressive behavior), and he might feel enraged (an intense, unpleasant mental experience). In trying to explain psychological phenomena, some psychologists prefer to study the biological level (the physiology of emotion), others the behavioral level (the expression of emotion), and still others the mental level (the experience of emotion).

THE PHYSIOLOGY OF EMOTION

What is the physiological basis of emotion? To answer this question, psychologists study the autonomic nervous system, the brain, and neurochemicals.

The Autonomic Nervous System and Emotion

Both your emotional expression and your emotional experience depend on physiological arousal, which reflects activity in your *autonomic nervous system*. The system is called "autonomic" because it functions independently, without the need for conscious, voluntary regulation by the brain. Figure 12.1 illustrates the functions of the two branches of the autonomic nervous system: the *sympathetic nervous system* and the *parasympathetic nervous system*. The interplay of these two systems contributes to the ebb and flow of emotions. The sympathetic nervous system relies on the neurotransmitter *norepinephrine* to regulate its target organs; the parasympathetic nervous system relies on the neurotransmitter *acetylcholine* to regulate its target organs.

Activation of the sympathetic nervous system may stimulate the **fight-or-flight response,** which evolved because it enabled our prehistoric ancestors to meet sudden physical threats (whether from nature, animals, or human beings) by either confronting them or running away from them. After a threat has been met or avoided, the sympathetic nervous system becomes less active and the parasympathetic nervous system becomes more active, calming the body. Yet because the sympathetic nervous system stimulates the secretion of epinephrine and norepinephrine from the adrenal glands into the bloodstream, physiological arousal may last for a while after the threat has disappeared.

emotion
A motivated state marked by physiological arousal, expressive behavior and mental experience.

fight-or-flight response
A state of physiological arousal that enables us to meet sudden threats by either confronting them or running away from them.

FIGURE 12.1

The Autonomic Nervous System
Emotional responses involve the interplay of the two branches of the autonomic nervous system: the sympathetic nervous system, which tends to arouse us, and the parasympathetic nervous system, which tends to return us to a calmer state.

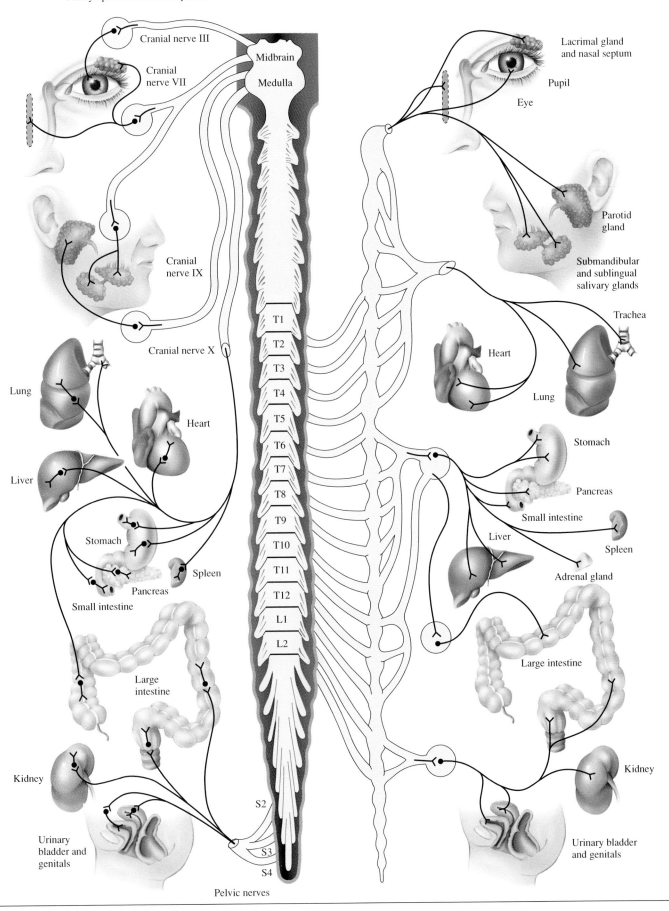

Parasympathetic Nervous System

Cranial nerve III

Cranial nerve VII

Midbrain

Medulla

Cranial nerve IX

Cranial nerve X

Lung

Heart

Liver

Stomach

Spleen

Pancreas

Small intestine

Large intestine

Kidney

Urinary bladder and genitals

Pelvic nerves

Sympathetic Nervous System

Lacrimal gland and nasal septum

Pupil

Eye

Parotid gland

Submandibular and sublingual salivary glands

Trachea

Heart

Lung

Stomach

Pancreas

Small intestine

Spleen

Liver

Adrenal gland

Large intestine

Kidney

Urinary bladder and genitals

T1
T2
T3
T4
T5
T6
T7
T8
T9
T10
T11
T12
L1
L2

S2
S3
S4

FIGURE 12.2

The Limbic System
Our emotional responses are regulated
by activity in the limbic system.

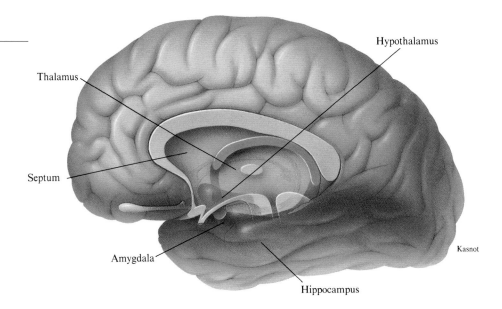

The fight-or-flight response is triggered not only by physical threats but also by psychological threats—such as academic demands that we feel inadequate to meet. To appreciate the role of the autonomic nervous system in the emotional response to a psychological threat, imagine that you are about to give a classroom speech that you did not prepare adequately. As you walk to your class, you experience anxiety associated with physiological arousal induced by your sympathetic nervous system.

As you enter the classroom, you become more alert and energetic as your circulatory system diverts blood rich in oxygen and other nutrients normally destined for your stomach and intestines to your brain and skeletal muscles. Your energy increases as your liver releases sugar into your bloodstream. Your heart pounds rapidly and strongly in response to epinephrine secreted by your adrenal glands. Your bronchioles dilate to permit more oxygen-rich air to enter your lungs, and you breathe more rapidly as your lungs work harder to expel carbon dioxide. A classmate might notice your pupils dilating, which improves your vision by letting more light into your eyes. And you might notice your mouth becoming dry, goose bumps appearing on your arms, and beads of perspiration forming on your forehead. Your dry mouth reflects a marked reduction in salivation. Your goose bumps are caused by hairs standing on end—a remnant of threat displays made by our furry prehistoric ancestors. And your perspiration provides a means of cooling off your aroused body.

Suppose that as you sit in class in this anxious, aroused state, your teacher announces that a surprise guest speaker will lecture for the entire class period. You immediately feel relieved at not having to give your speech and notice your arousal subside—in part because of activity in your autonomic nervous system. Your mind becomes less alert, your muscles less energetic, your heartbeat less noticeable, and your breathing more regular. Your pupils constrict to their normal size, your mouth becomes moist, your goose bumps disappear, and you stop sweating. You might become so profoundly relaxed and relieved that you fall asleep during the guest speaker's lecture.

The Brain and Emotion

Though bodily arousal plays a role in emotionality, the brain is ultimately in control of emotional responses. As discussed in chapter 3, the autonomic nervous system arousal is regulated by the brain structure called the *hypothalamus*, a component of the *limbic system*. The main limbic system structures are illustrated in figure 12.2. Among other things, the hypothalamus helps control changes in breathing and heart output during the fight-or-flight response (Spyer, 1989).

The *amygdala* attaches emotional labels to experiences, enabling us to respond to specific situations in appropriate ways (Sarter & Markowitsch, 1985). Research on rats shows that, by labeling situations as threatening, the amygdala may even prompt other brain structures to induce gastrointestinal changes that contribute to the development of stress-induced ulcers (Henke, 1988b).

The limbic system structure called the *septum* suppresses aversive emotional states. For example, electrical stimulation of the septum in rats reduces their tendency to avoid fear-inducing stimuli (Thomas, 1988). Damage to the septum is associated with hyperemotionality (Poplawsky & Isaacson, 1990), so an animal with a damaged septum will be more fearful than normal. But the inhibition of fear depends on activity in the *lateral* septum. Activity in the *medial* septum might actually increase fear (Thomas, Yadin, & Strickland, 1991).

Though the limbic system is important in the processing of emotions, the *cerebral cortex*, which covers the cerebral hemispheres, is important for our subjective experience of emotion. Research findings suggest that each cerebral hemisphere is specialized for the processing of different emotions, with the left hemisphere more involved in positive emotions and the right hemisphere more involved in negative emotions (Davidson, 1992). But keep in mind that particular emotions are not processed *solely* in one hemisphere or the other.

Much of our knowledge about the role of each hemisphere in emotional experience comes from studies, particularly those conducted by Richard Davidson, that have measured the relative degree of activity in each hemisphere during emotional arousal. For instance, excessive activation of the left hemisphere is associated with euphoria and excessive activation of the right hemisphere is associated with depression (Flor-Henry, 1983). One study measured electrical activity and facial expressions while subjects experienced disgust or happiness. Disgust, a negative emotion, was associated with greater activation of the right hemisphere. Happiness, a positive emotion, was associated with greater activation of the left hemisphere (Davidson et al., 1990). A study that recorded electrical activity from the brains of 10-month-old infants found that hemispheric differences in the processing of emotions appear early in life. Greater activation of the left hemisphere was associated with a pleasant facial expression and a tendency to approach people. In contrast, greater activation of the right hemisphere was associated with an unpleasant facial expression and a tendency to withdraw from people (Fox & Davidson, 1988).

The *Wada test*, which involves selective anesthesia of one cerebral hemisphere to determine hemispheric functions (particularly the site of the speech center), has also provided evidence of the lateralization of emotionality. In the Wada test, the anesthetic sodium amobarbital is injected into the left or right carotid artery of patients who are about to undergo brain surgery. Because the carotid arteries supply blood to the brain, injection of sodium amobarbital into one of them will anesthetize the associated hemisphere. Research using the Wada test shows that laughter and elation (positive emotionality) are more frequent after right-hemisphere anesthesia, while crying (negative emotionality) is more frequent after left-hemisphere anesthesia (Lee et al., 1990).

Further evidence that the left hemisphere is more related to positive emotions and the right hemisphere more related to negative emotions has been provided by studies of brain damage. Because each cerebral hemisphere inhibits the emotional activity of the other, we normally experience neither intensely positive nor intensely negative emotions. But damage to one hemisphere may release the other from its inhibition. Damage to the right hemisphere, releasing the left hemisphere from inhibition, leads to laughing, elation, optimism, and other signs of positive emotion. In contrast, damage to the left hemisphere, releasing the right hemisphere from inhibition, leads to crying, worry, pessimism, and other signs of negative emotion (Leventhal & Tomarken, 1986).

Richard Davidson
"In adults and infants, the experimental arousal of positive, approach-related emotions is associated with selective activation of the left frontal region, while arousal of negative, withdrawal-related emotions is associated with selective activation of the right frontal region."

The Chemistry of Emotion

When we say that there is "good chemistry" or "bad chemistry" between people, we mean that they have positive or negative emotional experiences in response to each other. Research has shown that our emotional responses do, indeed, depend on chemistry—hormones and neurotransmitters that convey emotion-related impulses from one neuron to another or between neurons and body organs (Baum, Grunberg, & Singer, 1992). For example, abnormal levels of the neurotransmitters norepinephrine and serotonin have been implicated in mood disorders, such as severe depression (Curzon, 1982). The role of these neurotransmitters in mood disorders is discussed in chapter 14.

As noted earlier, stressful situations cause the secretion of the hormones epinephrine and norepinephrine, which also serve as neutrotransmitters. In a study of psychologists and physicians, levels of these hormones were measured on a day when the subjects gave a public speech and on a day when they did not. Public speaking was associated with an increase in the level of both epinephrine and norepinephrine. Moreover, there was a rise in blood cholesterol on days when the subjects gave speeches relative to days when they did not. Perhaps stress hormones, by stimulating an increase in low-density lipoproteins (which are implicated in cardiovascular disease), provide one of the mechanisms by which emotional responses to stressful situations contribute to the development of cardiovascular disease (Bolm-Audorff et al., 1989).

The *endorphins*, a class of neurotransmitters discussed in chapters 3 and 5, contribute to emotional experiences by providing pain relief and evoking feelings of euphoria. Even the emotional thrill we experience from a music concert, a motion picture, or a dance performance may depend on endorphin activity. This was demonstrated in a study of college students who listened to a musical passage and then received an injection of either naloxone (a drug that blocks the effects of endorphins) or a placebo (in this case, a saline solution that does not block the effects of endorphins). Neither the subject nor the experimenter knew whether the subject had received naloxone or a placebo (you might recognize this as an application of the *double-blind procedure*, which was described in chapter 2); this prevented subject bias or experimenter bias from affecting the results. After receiving the injection, the subjects again listened to the musical passage. When asked to estimate the intensity of their emotional thrill in response to the music, the subjects who had received naloxone reported a significant decrease in intensity. The subjects who had received a placebo reported no such decrease. Because naloxone blocks the effects of endorphins, but a placebo does not, the findings support the role of endorphins in positive emotional experiences (Goldstein, 1980).

THE EXPRESSION OF EMOTION

How do you know how your fellow students feel? And how do they know how *you* feel? Because our emotional experiences are private, they cannot be directly observed by other people. Instead, emotions are inferred from descriptions of them or from expressive behaviors. Behaviors that express emotions include vocal qualities, body movements, and facial expressions.

Vocal Qualities

When you speak, both your words and your voice convey emotion. The vocal features of speech, other than the words themselves, are called *prosody*. Prosodic features include rate, pitch, and loudness. You can use the same spoken words to express different emotions by simply altering the prosodic features of your speech. Thus, the same statement can sound sincere or sarcastic, depending on its vocal qualities. When you are happy your voice shows an increase in pitch (just recall the last time you heard the voices of two people greeting each other after a long separation). Changes in vocal qualities indicative of changes in emotion tend to be consistent from one person to another and from one culture to another (Frick, 1985). Perhaps these common vocal patterns evolved in our prehistoric, prelanguage ancestors as a universal means of communicating emotional states in everyday social interaction.

Voice quality also affects social relations. In some cases it may cause social rejection, as in a study in which undergraduates rated depressed or nondepressed fellow undergraduates, who differed in how they spoke. Depressed subjects were more likely to be rejected, in part because they spoke in soft, flat voices, with long pauses. This is an important finding, because unappealing prosodic features can create a vicious cycle in which the depressed person alienates others, thereby reducing the likelihood of positive social interactions that might help the person overcome his or her depression (Paddock & Nowicki, 1986).

The prosodic features of speech are regulated primarily by the right cerebral hemisphere, both when we speak (Graves & Landis, 1990) and when we listen to a speaker (Herrero & Hillix, 1990). Evidence for the role of the right hemisphere in prosody comes from studies of stroke victims and patients undergoing the Wada test. Patients with right-hemisphere strokes may retain their ability to speak, but may speak with abnormal emotional tone (Gorelick & Ross, 1987). A study in which the Wada test was given to patients about to undergo brain surgery to relieve their epilepsy found that when the patients received injections of sodium amobarbital in the left carotid artery, they lost their ability to speak. When it was injected in their right carotid artery, they retained their ability to speak but lost the ability to impart emotion to their speech (Ross et al., 1988). In essence, it seems that "the left hemisphere provides the text [words], while the right hemisphere plays the accompaniment [emotional tone]" (Merewether & Alpert, 1990, p. 325).

Body Movements

If you have observed the gestures of impatient drivers in heavy traffic on a hot summer day, you know that body movements can convey emotions. Even movements of the whole body may do so. The performances of ballet dancer Mikhail Baryshnikov or basketball player Michael Jordan are especially appealing because their movements convey emotions.

But how do we know that we are responding to their movements rather than simply to their facial expressions or physical appearances? The importance of body movements in expressing emotion has been demonstrated in studies that have eliminated other nonverbal emotional cues. In one study (Walk & Homan, 1984), college students watched a videotape of people performing dances that portrayed different emotions. To eliminate the influence of facial expressions and physical appearance, the dancers wore lights on their joints and danced in total darkness. Thus, the subjects saw only the

Conveying Emotions through Gestures
Every culture conveys emotions through gestures, though a gesture that has a positive meaning in one culture might have a negative meaning in another (Ekman, Friesen, & Bear, 1984).

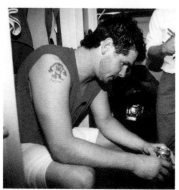

The Thrill of Victory and the Agony of Defeat
Our body movements and postures can convey our positive and negative emotional states in dramatic ways. These photos show outfielder Joe Carter celebrating hitting the home run that won the 1993 World Series for the Toronto Blue Jays, and pitcher Mitch Williams of the Philadelphia Phillies distraught over giving up the home run.

movement of lights. Nonetheless, they accurately identified the emotions represented by the dances. This indicates that the emotional cues provided by body movements are distinct from those provided by facial expressions or physical appearance.

The ability to decode nonverbal behavior is important in social interaction, as exemplified by the following research findings. Females are superior to males in decoding emotional states from body movements (Sogon & Izard, 1987). Elementary school children who are better at decoding nonverbal emotional cues are more popular (Nowicki & Duke, 1992). College roommates rate their relationship more positively when both are high in decoding ability than when one or both are low in it (Hodgins & Zuckerman, 1990). And psychological counselors may be more effective when they are skillful in noting changes in the nonverbal behavior of their clients (Hill & Stephany, 1990).

We seem to prefer an optimal level of nonverbal interaction in everyday social relations. We like people who are neither too nonverbally aloof nor too nonverbally intrusive. In a study that supported this finding, people who were walking on a college campus were asked to respond to a survey. During the brief interaction, they were randomly exposed to one of four conditions related to the interviewer's behavior: (1) eye contact and a momentary touch; (2) eye contact and no touch; (3) no eye contact and a momentary touch; or (4) no eye contact and no touch. At the end of the interaction, the interviewer dropped several folded questionnaires. Subjects in the second or third conditions were more likely to help pick them up than were subjects in the first or fourth conditions. Thus, in agreement with the notion that there is an optimal level of nonverbal communication, the subjects responded more positively to a moderate level of nonverbal interaction (Goldman & Fordyce, 1983).

Facial Expressions

Philip D. Chesterfield, an eighteenth-century British statesman, noted that our faces give away our emotions: "Look in the face of the person to whom you are speaking if you wish to know his real sentiments, for he can command his words more easily than his countenance." Chesterfield's observation may explain, in part, how teachers' expectations create the Pygmalion effect (discussed in chapter 2). Though teachers might believe they are unbiased when speaking to their students, their facial expressions can communicate their true feelings, whether positive or negative, about particular students (Babad, Bernieri, & Rosenthal, 1989).

Research has shown that facial expressions convey both the intensity and the pleasantness of our emotional states. Many cardplayers realize this, leading them to maintain an expressionless poker face to avoid revealing the strength of their hands. But cardplayers should note that any judgment of emotions from a person's facial expression depends, in part, on the facial expressions of other people who are present. For example, an expressionless face will seem sad when presented next to a happy face, but it will seem happy when presented next to a sad face (Russell & Fehr, 1987). So, if everyone else maintains a sad face, the person with a poker face will seem happy—as though she or he has a good hand. And if everyone else maintains a happy face, the person with a poker face will seem sad—as though he or she has a poor hand. As in the recognition of emotions from body movements, females are superior to males in recognizing emotions from facial expressions (Giovannini & Ricci Bitti, 1981).

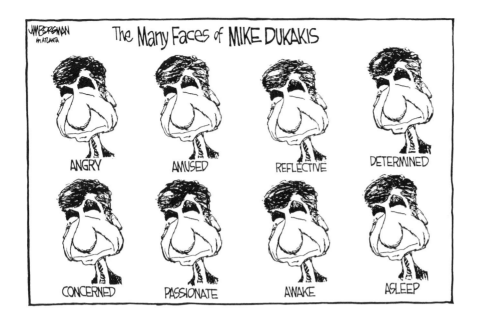

The Many Faces of MIKE DUKAKIS

ANGRY AMUSED REFLECTIVE DETERMINED

CONCERNED PASSIONATE AWAKE ASLEEP

Knowledge of the relationship between facial expressions and emotions has enabled researchers to distinguish honest emotional expressions from fake ones. For example, the face reveals when smiles are sincere or false. Sincere smiles include muscular activity around the eyes, causing the skin to wrinkle, and around the mouth, causing the corners of the lips to rise (Frank & Ekman, 1993). This natural smile is called the *Duchenne smile*. In contrast, when people display insincere smiles, perhaps to hide their negative emotional state, the corners of their lips are drawn downward and their upper lip curls up. In one experiment, subjects were more likely to display the Duchenne smile when they watched a pleasant film than when they watched an unpleasant film. They also reported more positive emotions when they exhibited the Duchenne smile, verifying it as a sign of a pleasant emotional state (Ekman, Davidson, & Friesen, 1990).

Charles Darwin (1872/1965) believed that facial expressions evolved because they promoted survival by communicating emotions and helping individuals distinguish friend from foe. For example, the human facial expression of contempt might be a modification of the snarl found in dogs, apes, and our prehistoric ancestors (Izard & Haynes, 1988). Darwin's belief was supported in an experiment that measured how quickly subjects could detect an angry face or a happy face in a crowd (Hansen & Hansen, 1988). The subjects reported that a single angry face seemed to pop out of the crowd faster than a single happy face. The results supported the subjects' impressions. They were able to detect an angry face faster than a happy face. Why might we have evolved the ability to detect angry faces more quickly than other faces? A possible reason is that it promotes our survival by motivating us to take more-immediate action to confront or to escape from a person displaying an angry face.

Research by Carroll Izard (1990a) and his colleagues supports Darwin's view that facial expressions for basic emotions are inborn and universal. One line of research has found that even people who are blind from birth exhibit facial expressions that represent the basic emotions, including joy, fear, anger, disgust, sadness, and surprise. An early case study involved a 10-year-old girl who had been born deaf and blind. Despite her inability to see normal facial expressions or to receive spoken instructions on how to form them, she displayed appropriate facial expressions for the basic emotions (Goodenough, 1932). Nonetheless, blind infants exhibit a more limited repertoire of facial expressions than do sighted infants (Troster & Brambing, 1992).

A second line of research support for the inborn, universal nature of facial expressions comes from studies showing that young infants produce facial expressions for the basic emotions (Izard et al., 1980). In one study, newborn infants were given solutions of sugar or quinine (which tastes bitter). Despite having no prior experience with those

Carroll Izard
"Certain fundamental emotional expressions [are] reliably identified by samples of individuals in many different cultures, including both literate and preliterate cultures."

FIGURE 12.3

The Universality of Facial Expressions
Support for the inborn, universal nature of facial expressions representing the basic emotions comes from studies showing similar facial expressions in people from different cultures, such as these smiling people from Kenya, Peru, and the United States.

tastes, their facial expressions showed pleasure or displeasure, depending on which solution they had tasted. And the intensity of their facial expressions varied with the strength of the solutions (Ganchrow, Steiner, & Daher, 1983).

Further support for Darwin's evolutionary view of facial expressions comes from studies showing that facial expressions for the basic emotions are universal across cultures, as illustrated in figure 12.3. The subjects in one study were members of the Fore tribe of New Guinea, who had almost no contact with Westerners prior to the study (Ekman & Friesen, 1971). The tribesmen listened to descriptions of a series of emotion-arousing situations representing joy, fear, anger, disgust, sadness, or surprise. The descriptions included situations such as "He is looking at something that smells bad" and "Her friends have come and she is happy." After each description, the tribesmen viewed a set of three photographs of Western faces expressing different emotions, from which they selected the face portraying the emotion of the person in the description they had just heard.

The tribesmen correctly identified expressions portraying joy, anger, sadness, and disgust but failed to distinguish between expressions portraying fear and surprise. Perhaps the tribesmen's expressions for fear and surprise did not differ because similar situations (such as an enemy or a wild animal suddenly appearing from out of the jungle) evoke both fear and surprise in their culture. This study was replicated, with similar results, in a more recent study of people in ten different cultures from around the world (Ekman et al., 1987). In still another study that supported the universality of certain facial expressions, American, Japanese, and Indonesian subjects agreed on the facial expression that represented the emotion of contempt (Ekman & Heider, 1988). The universality of the contempt expression was replicated in a study of Polish, Japanese, Hungarian, and Vietnamese subjects (Matsumoto, 1992).

Regardless of the universality of facial expressions, they play an important role in our everyday lives—and might even influence our political views. In fact, the facial expressions of our favorite television news anchors may affect our preferences for political candidates. A study conducted during the 1984 presidential campaign found that NBC's Tom Brokaw, CBS's Dan Rather, and ABC's Peter Jennings did not show biases in what they said about Ronald Reagan and Walter Mondale. But Jennings showed a bias in his facial expressions. Unlike Brokaw and Rather, Jennings displayed significantly more positive facial expressions when speaking about Reagan than when speaking about Mondale. A telephone survey found that voters who regularly watched Jennings were significantly more likely to vote for Reagan than were those who watched Brokaw or Rather. The researchers concluded that Jennings' biased facial expressions might have made some viewers more favorable toward Reagan. Of course, as stressed in chapter 2, we must be careful to avoid making hasty inferences about causation. Perhaps Jennings' facial expressions did not affect viewers' preferences. The researchers cautioned that, instead, those who already favored Reagan might have preferred to watch Jennings because he smiled more when talking about him (Mullen et al., 1986).

Can a Smile Influence Voters?
During the 1984 presidential campaign, Peter Jennings showed more positive facial expressions when speaking about Ronald Reagan than when speaking about Walter Mondale. Tom Brokaw and Dan Rather showed no such bias. People who watched Jennings were more likely to vote for Reagan than were people who watched Brokaw or Rather (Mullen et al., 1986). Could those voters have been influenced by Jennings' smiles? What other reasons can you think of that might explain this correlation?

Drawing by Ross; © *1983 The New Yorker Magazine, Inc.*

"There's that look again!"

THE EXPERIENCE OF EMOTION

Though we have hundreds of words for emotions, there seem to be only a few basic emotions, from which all others are derived. A recent model of emotion, devised by Robert Plutchik (1980), considers joy, fear, anger, disgust, sadness, surprise, acceptance, and anticipation to be the basic emotions. As illustrated in figure 12.4, more-complex emotions arise from mixtures of these basic ones.

Charles Darwin assumed that the basic emotions evolved because they promoted our survival. For example, disgust (which means "bad taste") might have evolved because it prevented our ancient ancestors from ingesting poisonous substances. This may explain why human beings in all cultures exhibit an early feeling of disgust at the sight and smell of feces—the "universal disgust object" (Rozin & Fallon, 1987). Note that disgust involves each of the major aspects of emotion: physiological change (stomach contractions causing nausea), expressive behavior (a contorted face), and mental experience (a feeling of revulsion). And the facial expression of disgust now has a social meaning as well, expressing revulsion at something that someone has said or done.

Folk wisdom holds that just as certain people are prone to experience unpleasant emotions, certain days—particularly so-called blue Mondays—are more likely to induce unpleasant emotions. A study of the "blue Monday effect" had people who insisted that their moods were lowest on Mondays keep daily diaries of their emotional states (Stone et al., 1985). The results indicated that a given person's emotional states tended to be similar on Monday, Tuesday, Wednesday, and Thursday. But, as you might expect, the person's emotional state on weekend days—Friday, Saturday, and Sunday—tended to be more positive than on weekdays. Evidently our "blue Mondays" owe their "blueness" to a return to our normal weekday emotional state, rather than to something unique about Mondays. In essence, we might have "blue Mondays," but we also have equally blue Tuesdays, Wednesdays, and Thursdays. We simply notice the contrast between "bright Sunday" and "blue Monday" more.

The experience of emotion varies in both its intensity and its pleasantness. People who tend to experience intensely pleasant emotions (such as elation) also tend to experience intensely unpleasant emotions (such as despair). People who tend to experience mildly pleasant emotions (such as gladness) also tend to experience mildly unpleasant emotions (such as disappointment). This might be one reason why our happiness depends more on the frequency, rather than the intensity, of our positive emotional experiences. A second reason is that intensely positive events can make less-intense positive events seem even less positive. And a third reason is that the happier you are

FIGURE 12.4

The Emotion Wheel
According to Robert Plutchik (1980),
there are eight primary emotions,
composed of four pairs of opposites:
joy and sadness, acceptance and
disgust, fear and anger, and surprise
and anticipation. We cannot
experience opposites simultaneously.
Thus, you could not feel joyful and
sad at the same time. The closer
together emotions are on Plutchik's
emotion wheel, the more similar they
are to each other. Mixtures of
adjacent emotions produce other
emotions. For example, the mixture of
joy and acceptance produces love, and
the mixture of anger and disgust
produces contempt.

*REPRINTED WITH SPECIAL PERMIS-
SION FROM PSYCHOLOGY TODAY
MAGAZINE. Copyright © 1980 (Sussex
Publishers, Inc.).*

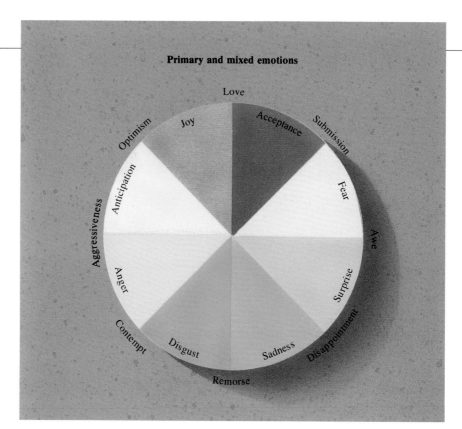

Primary and mixed emotions

Robert Plutchik
"The history of psychology is so
marked with differences as to the
meaning of emotion that some
psychologists have suggested that the
term be eliminated from psychological
writings."

FIGURE 12.5

**Happiness and the Declaration of
Independence**
Thomas Jefferson believed that
happiness is so important that its
pursuit is one of the three unalienable
rights of human beings.

when you succeed at a task, the unhappier you will be when you fail at it (Diener et al.,
1991).

Though emotions help us survive and enrich our lives, they may imperil our health.
Emotions can impair the immune response and, as a result, make us more prone to
illness. For example, depression has an adverse effect on the immune system (O'Leary,
1990), perhaps even impairing its ability to destroy cancer cells (Levenson & Bemis,
1991). The mechanisms by which emotions can stimulate or inhibit the immune system
are discussed in chapter 16.

People tend to view pleasant emotions, such as happiness, as normal and unpleasant emotions, such as depression, as abnormal (Sommers, 1984). Yet, until the past two
decades, psychologists had conducted many more studies of unpleasant emotions. In
fact, *Psychological Abstracts,* the main library research tool of psychologists, first published in the 1920s, did not include the term *happiness* in its index until 1973 (Diener,
1984). Another perusal of *Psychological Abstracts* found that it contained more emotion-
related references under the category of "pathology" than under any other category
(Whissell, 1984). To counter the traditional overemphasis placed on unpleasant emotions, and because unpleasant emotions such as anxiety and depression are discussed in
later chapters, this chapter discusses the topics of happiness and humor.

Happiness

Many philosophers have considered happiness the highest good (Diener, 1984). Thomas Jefferson (pictured in figure 12.5) even made happiness a central issue in the Declaration of Independence. But what factors promote happiness? Our happiness depends
on comparisons we make between ourselves and others and between our current circumstances and our past circumstances (Smith, Diener, & Wedell, 1989). The criteria for
comparison can be as varied as money, job status, academic success, and romantic relationships.

Charles Montesquieu, an eighteenth-century French philosopher, noted: "If one
only wished to be happy, this could be easily accomplished; but we wish to be happier
than other people, and this is always difficult, for we believe others to be happier than

they are." One of the most influential theories of happiness—**social-comparison theory**—shares Montesquieu's assumption about the nature of happiness. The theory considers happiness to be the result of estimating that one's life circumstances are more favorable than those of others, as when you discover that your grade is one of the highest in the class. In one study, college students felt happier about themselves when in the presence of another person who was relatively worse off (Strack et al., 1990). Thus, you can make yourself happier with your own life by purposely comparing it with the lives of those who are less fortunate (Wills, 1981). One factor in social comparison that is less important than commonly believed is wealth. According to happiness researcher Edward Diener (1984), wealthy people are no happier than nonwealthy people, provided that the nonwealthy people have at least the basic necessities of life, such as a job, home, and family. Though this finding holds true in the United States, it does not hold true in all cultures. For example, a study of people in 39 other countries found a stronger relationship between high income and happiness than in the United States (Diener et al., 1993).

According to **adaptation-level theory,** your happiness depends not only on comparing yourself with other people but also on comparing yourself with yourself. Thus, your current happiness depends in part on comparing your present circumstances and your past circumstances. But as your circumstances improve, your standard of happiness becomes higher. This can have surprising emotional consequences for people who gain sudden financial success. Life's small pleasures might no longer make them happy—their standards of happiness might become too high, as revealed by a study of Illinois state lottery winners (Brickman, Coates, & Janoff-Bulman, 1978): Despite winning from $50,000 to $1 million, these winners were no happier than they had been in the past. In fact, they found less pleasure in formerly enjoyable everyday activities, such as watching television, shopping for clothes, or talking with a friend. So, although comparing our circumstances with those of less-fortunate people can make us happier, improvements in our own circumstances might make us adopt increasingly higher standards of happiness—making happiness more and more elusive. Recognizing this, the nineteenth-century clergyman Henry Van Dyke remarked, "It is better to desire the things we have than to have the things we desire."

Humor

Happiness is enhanced by humor, whether offered by friends, funny movies, situation comedies on television, or stand-up comedians in nightclubs. Though philosophers have long argued about the nature of humor, psychologists have only recently begun to study it scientifically. Research findings support the importance of humor in our everyday lives. Humor defuses interpersonal conflicts (McClane & Singer, 1991), contributes to effective teaching (Safford, 1991), promotes the survival of marriages (Schlesinger, 1982), improves social relations in organizations (Duncan & Feisal, 1989), builds rapport during psychological counseling (Warner & Studwell, 1991), helps medical personnel cope with job stresses (Warner, 1991), and even provides a means of confronting the existential reality of death (Thorson, 1985).

One surprising finding has been that humorous people might not feel as extraverted as they act. Consider the class clown, who sees humor in everything. Though that person might be popular, he or she may not be as sociable as you might expect, using humor, instead, as a way to avoid close personal relationships. For example, a study of humorous adolescents found that they often used humor to maintain their social distance from other people (Prasinos & Tittler, 1981). You may have been frustrated at one time or another by such people, who joke about everything, rarely converse in a serious manner, and never disclose their personal feelings. Evidence that some people use humor to maintain their social distance might explain anecdotal reports that many comedians, who might appear socially outgoing in public performances, are socially reclusive in their private lives. Johnny Carson, who retired in 1992 after 30 years as host of the "Tonight Show," was humorous and engaging on stage but relatively somber and socially aloof off stage.

Edward Diener
"Women report more negative affect than men but equal happiness as men. . . . Generally, women's more intense positive emotions balance their higher negative affect."

Money Does Not Necessarily Buy Happiness
If you buy lottery tickets because you believe that winning the jackpot in your state lottery would make you happy, you may be in for a disappointment should you someday win. Lottery winners often are no happier after they win than they were before. In fact, they might no longer gain satisfaction from many of life's little pleasures.

Drawing by Leo Cullum; © 1992 The New Yorker Magazine, Inc.

"Mr. Kendall would like to see one of those flashes of oddball humor."

Granted that humorous people might not be as gregarious as they seem, we are still left with the question: What makes their humor amusing? One factor is the social contexts, such as night clubs, in which humor is expressed. To people who are inebriated, comedians who use blunt, simple humor will seem funnier than comedians who use subtle, complex humor (Weaver et al., 1985). Thus, if you drank a few beers, you would probably find a Three Stooges movie more amusing and a Dennis Miller monologue less amusing.

But what accounts for our responses to humor while in a sober state? The most popular theories are the *disparagement theory*, the *incongruity theory*, and the *release theory* (Berger, 1987). According to C. L. Edson, a twentieth-century American newspaper editor, "We love a joke that hands us a pat on the back while it kicks the other fellow down the stairs." Edson's comment indicates that he favored the **disparagement theory** of humor, first put forth by the seventeenth-century English philosopher Thomas Hobbes. Hobbes claimed that we feel amused when humor makes us feel superior to other people (Nevo, 1985). One study found that humor in which the target is disparaged is perceived as funnier than humor in which the target is uplifted (Mio & Graesser, 1991). Research supporting Hobbes's position has found that we are especially amused when we dislike those to whom we are made to feel superior (Wicker, Barron, & Willis, 1980). Satirists, newspaper columnists, and television commentators take this approach by disparaging certain commonly disliked groups, such as greedy lawyers, crooked politicians, and phony evangelists.

We also like disparaging humor better when we like the person doing the disparaging. Consider David Letterman, host of the Late Show. Why is his disparaging humor perceived as funny? In part because many people find him likable. In a study in which students were presented with examples of Letterman's disparaging humor, those who found him likable rated his humor as funnier (Oppliger & Sherblom, 1992).

In the eighteenth century, the German philosopher Immanuel Kant put forth an alternative theory of humor, the **incongruity theory.** Incongruous humor brings together incompatible ideas in a surprising outcome that violates our expectations (Deckers & Buttram, 1990). The incongruity theory explains why many jokes require timing and may lose something on the second hearing—bad timing or repetition can destroy the incongruity (Kuhlman, 1985). The appreciation of incongruous humor varies with age and conservatism. A study of more than 4,000 subjects aged 14 to 66 found that older people and more-conservative people preferred incongruous humor more, and nonsense humor less, than did younger people and more liberal people (Ruch, McGhee, & Hehl, 1990).

disparagement theory
The theory that humor is amusing when it makes one feel superior to other people.

incongruity theory
The theory that humor is amusing when it brings together incompatible ideas in a surprising outcome that violates one's expectations.

Another theory of humor, **release theory,** is based on Sigmund Freud's claim that humor is a cathartic outlet for anxiety caused by repressed sexual or aggressive energy, as explained in his book *Jokes and Their Relationship to the Unconscious* (Freud, 1905). Humor can raise your level of anxiety—and then suddenly lower it, providing you relief so pleasurable that it can make you laugh (McCauley et al., 1983). Consider a study in which students were told they would be handling or taking blood samples from rats. As they approached the rats, they suddenly discovered they were toys. The students then responded to questionnaires about their reactions to the situation. The more anxious and the more surprised they had been, the funnier they found the situation, thereby supporting the release theory (Shurcliff, 1968). The release theory explains the popularity of humor that plays on our sexual anxieties by weaving a story that ends with a sudden punch line that relieves our tension (Schill & O'Laughlin, 1984).

In a study bearing on the release theory of humor in regard to aggression, high school students were given a frustrating exam. Afterward, they were more likely to respond aggressively to a subsequent frustrating situation. But subjects who were exposed after the exam to a humorous situation that provoked laughter became less likely to respond aggressively to the later frustration. According to the release theory, the subjects' laughter provided a cathartic experience, which released energy that would have provoked later aggression (Ziv, 1987). Despite some research supportive of the release theory, sexual or aggressive humor does not usually reduce the tendency to engage in sex or aggression (Nevo & Nevo, 1983).

The field of humor research is relatively young, and more research is needed to uncover the factors that make people find amusement in one kind of humor but not in another. Such research might explain, for example, why some people (most notably, the French) find Jerry Lewis amusing, while others do not.

THEORIES OF EMOTION

How do we explain emotional experience? Theories of emotion vary in the emphasis they place on physiology, behavior, and cognition.

Physiological Theories of Emotion

Though most theories of emotion recognize the importance of physiological factors, certain theories stress them.

The James-Lange Theory

In the late nineteenth century, the American psychologist William James (1884) claimed that physiological changes precede emotional experiences. Because a Danish physiologist named Carl Lange (1834–1900) made the same claim at about the same time, it became known as the **James-Lange theory.** Note that the theory (illustrated in figure 12.6) violates the commonsense belief that physiological changes are a *consequence* of an emotional experience.

The main implication of the James-Lange theory is that particular emotional events stimulate specific patterns of physiological changes, each evoking a specific emotional experience. According to James (1890/1981, vol. 2, p. 1065):

> • • • Common-sense says, we lose our fortune, are sorry and weep; we meet a bear, are
> frightened and run; we are insulted by a rival, are angry and strike . . . the more
> rational statement is that we feel sorry because we cry, angry because we strike, afraid
> because we tremble.

Your own experience might provide circumstantial evidence in support of this theory. If you have ever barely avoided an automobile accident, you may have noticed your pulse racing and your palms sweating and moments later found yourself overcome by fear.

The James-Lange theory provoked criticism from the American physiologist Walter Cannon (1927). Consider three of his main criticisms. First, Cannon noted that

release theory
The theory that humor is amusing when it relieves one's sexual or aggressive anxiety.

James-Lange theory
The theory that specific patterns of physiological changes evoke specific emotional experiences.

(a)

(b)

(c)

Theories of Humor
Humor researchers have found that humor is based on disparagement, incongruity, or release. (*a*) If you have seen Don Rickles hurl insults at his audience or Joan Rivers make critical remarks about prominent people, you have observed performances that support the disparagement theory of humor. (*b*) The incongruity theory of humor gains support from comedians such as Jay Leno, Carol Leifer, and David Letterman, who play on our sense of the absurd to make us laugh. (*c*) Comedians such as Eddie Murphy and Buddy Hackett, who rely on sexual humor, exemplify the release theory of humor, which assumes that the sudden release of sexual tension induces a feeling of amusement.

FIGURE 12.6

James-Lange Theory of Emotion
According to the James-Lange theory, the perception of an event or object induces a specific pattern of physiological changes, which evokes a specific emotional experience.

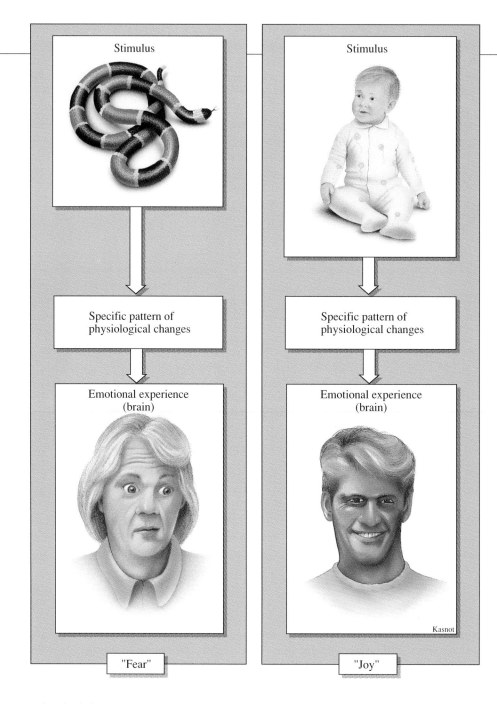

individuals have poor ability to perceive many of the subtle physiological changes induced by the sympathetic nervous system. How could the perception of physiological changes be the basis of emotional experiences when we cannot perceive many of those changes? Second, Cannon noted that different emotions are associated with the same pattern of physiological arousal. How could different emotions be evoked by the same pattern of arousal? And third, Cannon found that physiological changes dependent on the secretion of hormones by the adrenal glands are too slow to be the basis of all emotions. How could a process that takes several seconds account for almost-instantaneous emotional experiences?

In part because of Cannon's criticisms, the James-Lange theory fell into disfavor for several decades. But recent research findings have lent some support to it. In one study, subjects were directed to adopt facial expressions representing fear, anger, disgust, sadness, surprise, and happiness (Ekman, Levenson, & Friesen, 1983). The subjects were

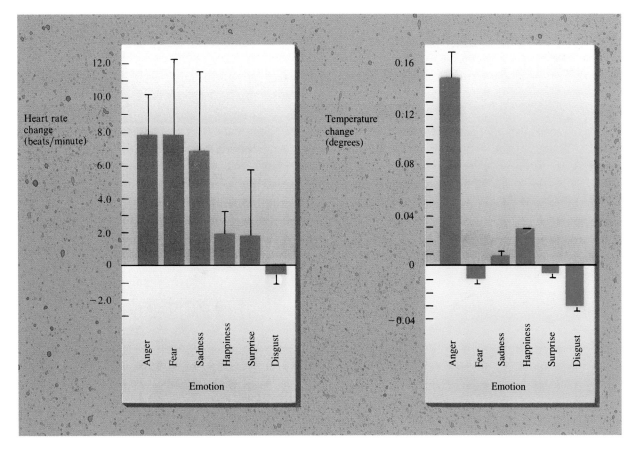

FIGURE 12.7

Specificity of Autonomic Response Patterns
As illustrated in these graphs, heart rate and finger temperature vary between emotions. For example, anger is associated with marked increases in both heart rate and finger temperature, while fear is associated with a marked increase in heart rate and a slight decrease in finger temperature.

told which muscles to contract or relax but were not told which emotions they were expressing. Physiological recordings of heart rate and skin temperature were taken as they maintained the facial expressions. The results showed that the facial expression of fear induced a large increase in heart rate and a slight decrease in finger temperature, while the facial expression of anger induced a large increase in both heart rate and finger temperature. The results are displayed in figure 12.7. (Finger temperature varies with the amount of blood flow through the fingers, with a decrease in blood flow causing a decrease in temperature and an increase in blood flow causing an increase in temperature.) The presence of different patterns of autonomic activity for different emotions has been replicated in non-Western cultures, such as West Sumatra (Levenson et al., 1992).

Note that, in everyday language, when we are afraid, we have "cold feet," and when we are angry, our "blood is boiling." The difference in the patterns of physiological arousal between fear and anger support the assumption of the James-Lange theory that particular emotions are associated with particular patterns of physiological arousal. A more recent study lent further support to the specificity of autonomic nervous system responses in different emotions. Subjects followed muscle-by-muscle instructions for constructing facial expressions associated with particular emotions and imagined past emotional experiences. The subjects' physiological patterns of response distinguished between the emotions (Levenson et al., 1991). Findings from several other studies also support the existence of different physiological patterns for different emotions (Levenson, 1992).

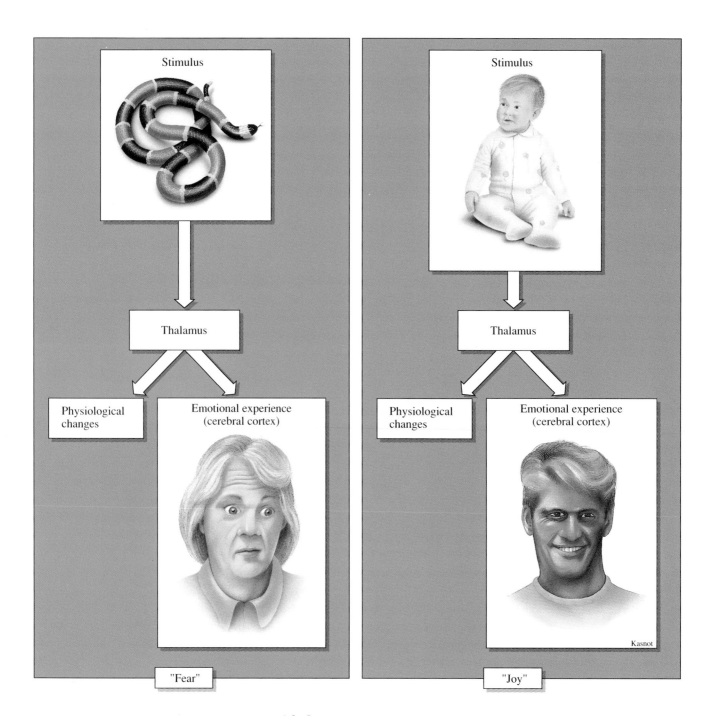

FIGURE 12.8

Cannon-Bard Theory of Emotion
According to the Cannon-Bard theory, when we perceive an event or object, the thalamus activates the skeletal muscles and sympathetic nervous system organs, as well as the cerebral cortex.

The Cannon-Bard Theory

After rejecting the James-Lange theory of emotion, Walter Cannon (1927) and Philip Bard (1934) put forth their own theory, giving equal weight to physiological changes and cognitive processes. The **Cannon-Bard theory** claims that an emotion is produced when an event or object is perceived by the thalamus, the brain structure that conveys this information simultaneously to the cerebral cortex and to the skeletal muscles and sympathetic nervous system. The theory is illustrated in figure 12.8.

Cannon-Bard theory
The theory that an emotion is produced when an event or object is perceived by the thalamus, which conveys this information simultaneously to the cerebral cortex and the skeletal muscles and autonomic nervous system.

The cerebral cortex then uses memories of past experiences to determine the nature of the perceived event or object, providing the subjective experience of emotion. Meanwhile, the muscles and sympathetic nervous system provide the physiological arousal that prepares the individual to take action to adjust to the situation that evoked the emotion. Unlike the James-Lange theory, the Cannon-Bard theory assumes that different emotions are associated with the same state of physiological arousal. The Cannon-Bard theory has failed to gain research support, because the thalamus does not appear to play the role the researchers envisioned. But if the theory is recast in terms of the brain's limbic system instead of the thalamus, the theory *is* supported by research findings. For example, though the thalamus might not directly *cause* emotional responses, it does relay sensory information to the amygdala, which then processes the information. This can occur even when the cerebral cortex is removed; in one study, rats whose visual cortexes had been destroyed still learned to fear visual stimuli associated with pain (LeDoux, Romanski, & Xagoraris, 1989).

Research on victims of spinal cord damage has provided support for the Cannon-Bard theory, while contradicting the James-Lange theory. Studies have found that even people with spinal cord injuries that prevent them from perceiving their bodily arousal experience distinct emotions, often more intensely than before their spinal cord injury (Bermond et al., 1991; Chwalisz, Diener, & Gallagher, 1988). This violates the James-Lange theory's assumption that emotional experience depends on the perception of bodily arousal, while supporting the Cannon-Bard theory's assumption that emotional experience depends on the brain's perception of ongoing events. Of course, as you will learn later, research on victims of spinal cord damage does not rule out sensations from one's own facial expressions as a factor in emotional experience.

The Opponent-Process Theory

In anticipating another theory of emotion, Plato, in the *Phaedo*, states:

⚬ ⚬ ⚬ How strange would appear to be this thing that we call pleasure! And how curiously it is related to what is thought to be its opposite, pain! The two will never be found *together* in a man, and yet if you seek the one and obtain it, you are almost bound always to get the other as well, just as though they were both attached to one and the same head. . . . Wherever the one is found, the other follows up behind. So, in my case, since I had pain in my leg as a result of the fetters, pleasure seems to have come to follow it up.

If Plato were alive today, he might favor the **opponent-process theory of emotion,** which holds that the mammalian brain has evolved mechanisms that counteract strong positive or negative emotions by evoking an opposite emotional response to maintain homeostasis. The theory is illustrated in figure 12.9. According to Richard Solomon (1980), who first put forth the theory, the opposing emotion begins sometime after the onset of the first emotion and lasts longer than the first emotion. If we experience the first emotion on repeated occasions, the opposing emotion grows stronger and the emotion that is experienced becomes a compromise between the two opposing emotional states.

Suppose that you took up skydiving. The first time you parachuted from an airplane you would probably feel terror. After surviving the jump, your feeling of terror would be replaced by a feeling of relief. As you jumped again and again, you would feel anticipation instead of terror as you prepared to jump. And your initial postjump feeling of relief might intensify into a feeling of exhilaration.

The opponent-process theory may explain the depression that often follows the joy of childbirth or the euphoria that often follows the anxiety of final-exams week. It might even explain why some blood donors become seemingly "addicted" to donating blood. When a person first donates blood, she or he might experience fear—but afterward might experience a pleasant feeling known as the "warm glow" effect. If the person repeatedly donates blood, the "warm glow" strengthens, leading the person to donate blood in order to induce that feeling (Piliavin, Callero, & Evans, 1982).

Walter Cannon (1871–1945)
"We do not 'feel sorry because we cry,' as James contended, but we cry because when we are sorry or overjoyed or violently angry or full of tender affections . . . there are nervous discharges by sympathetic channels to various viscera."

opponent-process theory of emotion *The theory that the brain counteracts a strong positive or negative emotion by evoking an opposite emotional response.*

Richard Solomon
"Many hedonic, affective, or emotional states are automatically opposed by central nervous system mechanisms which reduce the intensity of hedonic feelings, both pleasant and aversive."

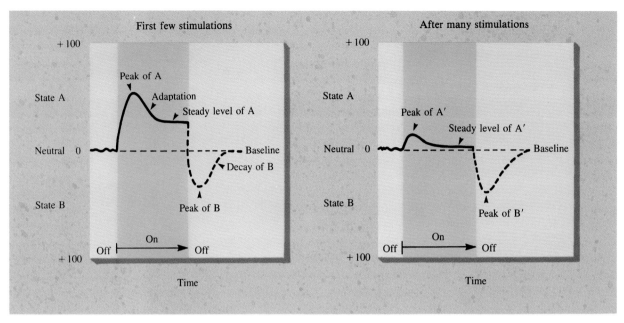

FIGURE 12.9

Opponent-Process Theory of Emotion
According to the opponent-process theory, when we experience an emotion (A), an opposing emotion (B) will counter the first emotion, dampening the experience of that emotion (as indicated by the steady level of A being lower than the peak of A). As we experience the first emotion (A′) on repeated occasions, the opposing emotion (B′) becomes stronger and the first emotion weaker, which leads to an even weaker experience of the first emotion (as indicated by the steady level of A′ being lower than the peak of A′). For example, the first time you drove on a highway you might have experienced fear, followed by a feeling of relief. As you drove on highways on repeated occasions, your feeling of fear eventually gave way to a feeling of mild arousal (Solomon, 1980).

The opponent-process theory implies that our brains are programmed against hedonism, because people who experience intense pleasure are doomed to experience intense displeasure. This provides support for those who favor the "happy medium"—moderation in everything, including emotional experiences.

Behavioral Theories of Emotion: The Facial-Feedback Theory

Benjamin Franklin claimed, "A cheerful face is nearly as good for an invalid as healthy weather." Have you ever received the advice "Put on a happy face" or "Keep a stiff upper lip" from people trying to help you overcome adversity? Both of these bits of advice are commonsense versions of the **facial-feedback theory** of emotion, which holds that our facial expressions affect our emotional experiences. Because it assumes that emotional experience is caused by the perception of physiological changes, the James-Lange theory inspired the facial-feedback theory (Izard, 1990b). As you learned in the discussion of the James-Lange theory, adopting a facial expression characteristic of a particular emotion may induce that emotion (Ekman, Levenson, & Friesen, 1983). But unlike the James-Lange theory, which is primarily concerned with the effects of autonomic nervous system activity on emotion, the facial-feedback theory is limited to the effects of facial expressions.

The facial-feedback theory was put forth in 1907 by the French physician Israel Waynbaum and has recently been restated in various versions. Waynbaum assumed that particular facial expressions alter the flow of blood to particular regions of the brain, thereby evoking particular emotional experiences. For example, smiling might increase the flow of blood to regions of the brain that elevate mood. It remains for research to test Waynbaum's theory, a technically difficult task (Zajonc, 1985).

Contemporary facial-feedback theorists, led by Paul Ekman (1992b), assume that evolution has endowed us with facial expressions that provide different patterns of

facial-feedback theory
The theory that particular facial expressions induce particular emotional experiences.

Fear and Euphoria
According to the opponent-process theory of emotion, the fear this ski jumper experienced when he first learned to jump eventually gave way to a feeling of euphoria.

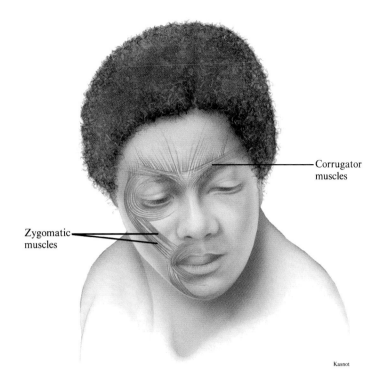

FIGURE 12.10

The Facial-Feedback Theory of Emotion
According to the facial-feedback theory of emotion, particular patterns of sensory feedback from facial expressions evoke particular emotions. Thus, sensory feedback from the corrugator muscles, which are active when we frown, may contribute to unpleasant emotional experiences. Similarly, sensory feedback from the zygomatic muscles, which are active when we smile, may contribute to pleasant emotional experiences.

Corrugator muscles

Zygomatic muscles

Kasnot

sensory feedback of muscle tension levels to the brain, thereby evoking different emotions. The theory is illustrated in figure 12.10. Support for the theory has come from studies that have found that emotional experiences follow facial expressions rather than precede them, and that sensory neurons convey information from facial muscles directly to the hypothalamus, which plays an important role in emotional arousal (Zajonc, 1985).

But the facial-feedback theory has not received unqualified support. Though there is a positive association between particular facial expressions and particular emotional experiences (Adelmann & Zajonc, 1989), the effect of facial feedback on emotional experience tends to be small (Matsumoto, 1987). Some studies also have found that emotional experience depends more on feedback from autonomic nervous system organs than on feedback from facial muscles (Buck, 1980). Apparently, feedback from facial expressions is just one of several factors that govern our emotional experiences.

Though facial expressions might not be the sole cause of emotions, they can contribute to emotional experience. (Try smiling and then frowning, and note the subtle differences they induce in your mood.) In one study, female subjects were asked to imagine three pleasant scenes and three unpleasant scenes (McCanne & Anderson, 1987). The three pleasant scenes were "You get a 4.0 grade point average," "You inherit a million dollars," and "You meet the man of your dreams." The three unpleasant scenes were "Your mother dies," "You lose a really close friendship," and "You lose a limb in an accident."

The subjects imagined each scene three times. The first time they simply imagined the scene. The second time they imagined the scene while maintaining increased muscle tension in one of two muscle groups: either muscles that control smiling or muscles that control frowning. Through the use of biofeedback (discussed in chapter 7), the subjects learned to tense only the target muscles. The third time they imagined the scene, the subjects were instructed to suppress muscle tension in either their smiling muscles or their frowning muscles. The muscles involved are illustrated in figure 12.10. On each occasion, the subjects were asked to report the degree of enjoyment or distress they experienced while imagining the scene. The results provided some support for the facial-feedback theory. Subjects reported less enjoyment when imagining pleasant scenes while suppressing activity in their smiling muscles, and they reported less distress when imagining unpleasant scenes while suppressing activity in their frowning muscles.

Paul Ekman
"Autonomic nervous system activity is not the same for all emotions."

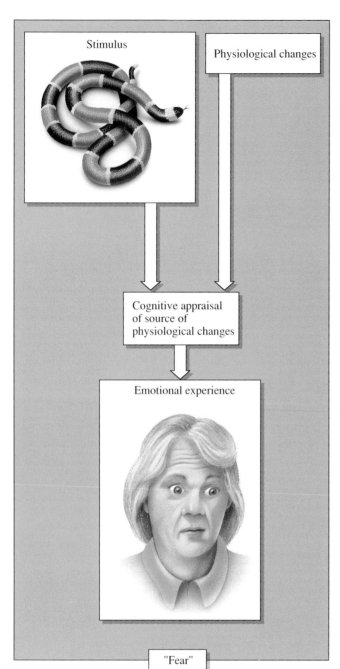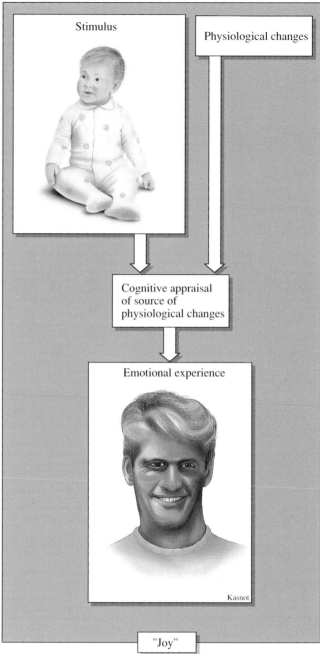

FIGURE 12.11

Two-Factor Theory of Emotion
According to the two-factor theory, when we experience physiological arousal, we seek its source in our immediate situation. The perceived source determines the emotional label we attach to our arousal.

Cognitive Theories of Emotion

More-recent theories of emotion emphasize the importance of cognition (thinking). They assume that our emotional experiences depend on our subjective interpretation of situations in which we find ourselves.

The Two-Factor Theory

Stanley Schachter's **two-factor theory** views emotional experience as the outcome of two factors: physiological arousal and the attribution of a cause for that arousal. The theory is illustrated in figure 12.11.

two-factor theory
The theory that emotional experience is the outcome of physiological arousal and the attribution of a cause for that arousal.

Anatomy of a Classic Research Study:

Do Emotions Depend on the Attribution of a Cause for Our Physiological Arousal?

Rationale

According to Schachter, when you experience physiological arousal, you search for its source. Your attribution of a cause for your arousal determines the emotion that you experience. For example, if you experience intense physiological arousal in the presence of an appealing person, you might attribute your arousal to that person, and, as a result, feel that you are attracted to him or her.

The two-factor theory resembles the James-Lange theory in assuming that emotional experience follows physiological arousal (Winton, 1990). But it is different from the James-Lange theory in holding, as does the Cannon-Bard theory, that all emotions involve similar patterns of physiological arousal. But the Cannon-Bard theory assumes that emotional experience and physiological arousal occur simultaneously; the two-factor theory assumes instead that emotion follows the attribution of a cause for one's physiological arousal.

Method

The original experiment on the two-factor theory provided evidence that when we experience physiological arousal, we seek to identify its source, and that what we identify as the source in turn determines our emotional experience (Schachter & Singer, 1962). Male college students who served as subjects participated one at a time and were told that they were getting an injection of a new vitamin called "Suproxin" to assess its effect on vision. In reality, they received an injection of the hormone epinephrine, which activates the sympathetic nervous system. The epinephrine caused hand tremors, a flushed face, a pounding heart, and rapid breathing. Some subjects (the informed group) were told to expect these changes. Some subjects (the misinformed group) were told to expect itching, numb feet, and headache, and some (the uninformed group) were told nothing about the effects. Other subjects received a placebo injection of a saline solution instead of an injection of epinephrine and were told nothing about its physiological effects.

The subject then waited in a room with the experimenter's accomplice, a male who acted either happy or angry. When acting happy, the accomplice was cheerful and threw paper airplanes, played with a Hula Hoop, and shot wads of paper into a wastebasket. When acting angry, the accomplice was upset, stomped around, and complained about a questionnaire given by the experimenter, which included questions about the bathing habits of the respondent's family and the sex life of his mother. The subject's emotional response to the accomplice was assessed by observing him through a one-way mirror and by having him complete a questionnaire about his feelings.

Results and Discussion

The results showed that the informed subjects were unaffected by the accomplice, while the misinformed subjects and uninformed subjects expressed and experienced emotions similar to those of the accomplice. But the placebo group also expressed and experienced situation-appropriate emotions, despite the lack of drug-induced physiological arousal. Schachter concluded that the informed subjects attributed their arousal to the injection and did not exhibit situation-appropriate emotions. In contrast, the misinformed subjects and the uninformed subjects attributed their physiological arousal to the situation they were in, responding positively when the accomplice acted happy and responding negatively when the accomplice acted angry. Schachter assumed that the placebo subjects became physiologically aroused in response to the emotional display of the accomplice and interpreted their own feelings as congruent with those of the accomplice.

Since the original studies of the two-factor theory in the early 1960s, research has produced inconsistent findings. Consider the theory's assumption that unexplained physiological arousal can just as well provoke feelings of joy as provoke feelings of sadness, depending on the person's interpretation of the source of the arousal. This was contradicted by a study in which subjects received injections of epinephrine without being informed of its true effects. The subjects tended to experience negative emotions, regardless of their immediate social environment. Even those in the presence of a happy person tended to experience unpleasant emotions (Marshall & Zimbardo, 1979). A review of research on Schachter's two-factor theory concluded that the only assumption of the theory that has been consistently supported is that physiological arousal misattributed to an outside source will intensify an emotional experience. There is little evidence that such a misattribution will cause an emotional experience (Reisenzein, 1983).

Stanley Schachter
"Given a state of physiological arousal for which an individual has no immediate explanation, he will label this state and describe his feelings in terms of the cognitions available to him."

FIGURE 12.12

The Cognitive-Appraisal Theory of Emotion
According to the cognitive-appraisal theory, our interpretation of events, rather than the events themselves, determines our emotional experiences. Thus, the same event may evoke different emotions in different people, as in this exhilarated boy and his terrified mother riding on a Ferris wheel.

Richard Lazarus
"Appraisal is a necessary as well as sufficient cause of emotion."

The Cognitive-Appraisal Theory

Though Schachter's two-factor theory has failed to gain strong support, it has stimulated interest in the cognitive basis of emotion. The purest cognitive theory of emotion is the **cognitive-appraisal theory** of Richard Lazarus (1991). The cognitive-appraisal theory, like the two-factor theory, assumes that our emotion at a given time depends on our interpretation of the situation we are in at that time. But, unlike the two-factor theory, the cognitive-appraisal theory downplays the role of physiological arousal. The theory is illustrated in figure 12.12.

This cognitive view of emotion is not new. In *Hamlet,* Shakespeare wrote, "There is nothing either good or bad, but thinking makes it so." Cognitive appraisal can affect your emotions as you prepare for an exam (Abella & Heslin, 1989). For example, you might appraise an impending exam as threatening, while your friend might appraise it as challenging. As a result, the exam might make you feel anxious while making your friend feel eager. People whose jobs make them confront human pain, illness, and death find that the ability to cognitively reappraise situations, perhaps by finding meaning even in the worst disasters, helps them cope emotionally (McCammon et al., 1988).

An early study by Lazarus and his colleagues supported the cognitive-appraisal theory of emotion (Speisman et al., 1964). The subjects watched a film about a tribal ritual in which incisions were made on adolescents' penises. The subjects' level of emotional arousal was measured by recording their heart rate and skin conductance (an increase in the electrical conductivity of the skin, caused by sweating). Subjects all watched the same film but heard different sound tracks. Those in the *silent group* saw the film without a sound track. Those in the *trauma group* were told that the procedure was extremely painful and emotionally distressing. Those in the *intellectualization group* were told about the procedure in a detached, matter-of-fact way, with no mention of feelings. And those in the *denial group* were told that the procedure was not painful and that the boys were overjoyed by the ritual because it signified their entrance into manhood.

Recordings of the subjects' physiological arousal showed that the trauma group experienced greater arousal than the silent group, which in turn experienced greater arousal than the denial and intellectualization groups. The results are displayed in figure 12.13. These findings indicate that subjective appraisal of the situation, rather than the objective situation itself, accounted for the subjects' emotional arousal. Lazarus (1993) has applied his theory of cognitive appraisal in helping individuals cope with stressful situations—a topic discussed in chapter 16.

Though more-recent studies provide additional support for the assumption that your interpretation of a situation affects your emotional state (Smith & Ellsworth, 1985), the cognitive-appraisal theory has been challenged by Robert Zajonc (1984) and others, who insist that cognitive appraisal is not essential to the experience of emotion. For example, you have probably taken an instant liking or disliking to a person without knowing why. And, as noted in chapter 6, research findings show that we can respond emotionally to stimuli we are unaware of (Murphy & Zajonc, 1993). This and other evidence indicates that emotional experience can take place without conscious cognitive appraisal (Izard, 1993).

There is even physiological evidence for this, because of the direct pathways from the thalamus (which relays sensory input to other brain regions) to the limbic system (which plays an important role in emotional processing). These pathways bypass the cerebral cortex, the involvement of which seems required for conscious cognitive appraisal. Thus, we may have emotional reactions to stimuli of which we are unaware (LeDoux, 1986).

What can we conclude from the variety of contradictory theories of emotion? The best we can do is to realize that none of them is sufficient to explain emotion, though each describes a process that contributes to it. Moreover, when considered together, the theories illustrate the importance of the physiological, expressive, and experiential components of emotion.

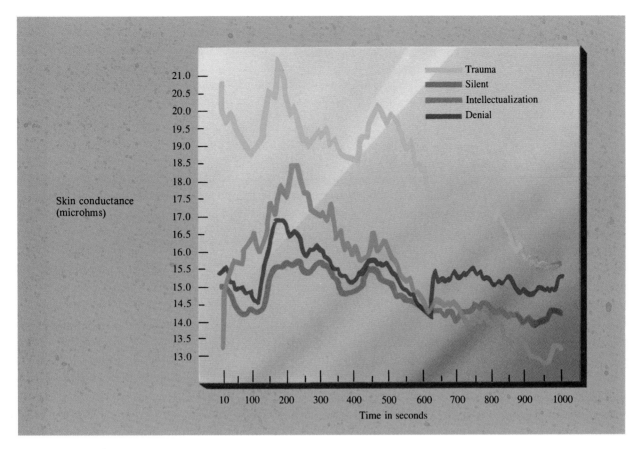

FIGURE 12.13

Cognitive Appraisal and Emotion
The graph shows that the emotional responses of subjects who viewed a film of a ritual in which incisions were made in adolescents' penises depended on the nature of the sound track. Those who heard a sound track that described the procedure as traumatic experienced the greatest emotional arousal (Speisman et al., 1964).

THINKING ABOUT *Psychology*

DO LIE DETECTORS TELL THE TRUTH?

As discussed earlier, in everyday life we may infer a person's emotional state from his or her expressive behavior. We might even infer whether the person is lying. If you have ever detected a phony smile from a salesperson or politician, you probably noted certain cues indicating that the smile was insincere. Perhaps the smile lasted too long—a sign of insincerity. Or perhaps you noticed that the smile was asymmetrical. Phony expressions, including smiles, will usually be more pronounced on the left side of the face than on the right side (Rinn, 1984). Nonetheless, in everyday life most people are poor at detecting deceit from facial expressions. One exception is U.S. Secret Service agents, who learn to attend to nonverbal cues in their efforts to protect the president from attack (Ekman & O'Sullivan, 1991).

The detection of lies from expressive behavior has a long history. The Old Testament describes a case in which King Solomon resolved a dispute between two women who claimed to be the mother of the same infant. Solomon wisely proposed cutting the infant in half, then giving one half to each woman. While one of the women calmly agreed to this, the other pleaded with Solomon to give the infant to her adversary. Solomon reasoned that the pleading woman had to be the real mother, because she was willing to lose the infant rather than see the child killed.

King Solomon inferred lying from expressive behavior, but lie detection has historically been based on the assumption that liars display increased physiological arousal. In the fifteenth century, interrogators for the Inquisition required suspected heretics to swallow pieces of bread and cheese. If the food stuck to the person's palate, he or she was considered guilty. As you will recall, the arousal of the sympathetic nervous system that accompanies emotionality reduces salivation, leading to a dry mouth. A dry mouth would make it more difficult to swallow food. As you can imagine, people brought before the Inquisition would experience increased arousal—whether or not they were heretics—and would be convicted of heresy.

Modern lie detection began in the 1890s with the work of Cesare Lombroso, an Italian criminologist who questioned suspects while recording their heart rate and blood pressure. He assumed that if they showed marked fluctuations in heart rate and blood pressure while responding to questions, they were lying (Kleinmuntz & Szucko, 1984b).

PROCEDURES IN LIE DETECTION

Today the lie detector, or **polygraph test,** typically measures breathing patterns, heart rate, blood pressure, and electrodermal activity. Electrodermal activity reflects the amount of sweating; greater emotionality is associated with more sweating. Though the polygraph test is used to detect lying, no pattern of physiological responses, by itself, indicates lying. Instead, the test detects physiological arousal produced by activation of the sympathetic nervous system. As David Lykken, an expert on lie detection, has said, "The polygraph pens do no special dance when we are lying" (Lykken, 1981, p. 10).

Given that there is no pattern of physiological responses that indicates lying, how is the recording of physiological arousal used to detect lies? The typical polygraph test given to a criminal suspect begins with an explanation of the test and the kinds of questions to be asked. The subject is then asked *control questions,* which are designed to provoke lying about minor transgressions common to almost everyone. For example, the suspect might be asked, "Have you ever stolen anything from an employer?" It is a rare person who has not stolen at least an inexpensive item, yet many people would answer no, creating an increase in physiological arousal; and even suspects who answer yes to a control question would probably experience some increase in physiological arousal in response to that question.

The subject's physiological response to control questions is compared to her or his physiological response to *relevant questions,* which are concerned with facts about the crime, such as, "Did you steal money from the bank safe?" Polygraphers assume that a guilty person will show greater physiological arousal in response to relevant questions and that an innocent person will show greater physiological arousal in response to control questions. Figure 12.14 shows a polygraph printout of differences in arousal in response to the different questions. The typical polygraph test asks about twelve relevant questions, which are repeated three or four times.

ISSUES IN LIE DETECTION

Polygraph testing has provoked controversy because it is far from being a perfect measure of lying. One difficulty is that the accuracy of the polygraph depends, in part, on the subject's physiological reactivity. People with low reactivity exhibit a smaller difference

polygraph test
The "lie detector" test, which assesses lying by measuring changing patterns of physiological arousal in response to particular questions.

The Polygraph Test
The polygraph test assumes that patterns of change in physiological responses, such as heart rate, blood pressure, breathing patterns, and electrodermal activity, will reveal whether a person is lying.

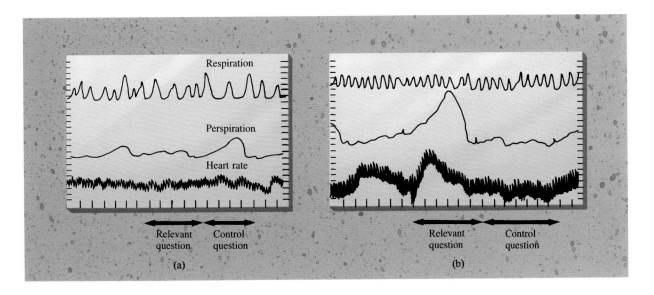

FIGURE 12.14

Relevant Questions versus Control Questions
The polygraph test compares physiological responses to relevant and control questions. (*a*) This is the record of a person who responded less strongly to a question relevant to a crime than to an emotionally arousing control question not relevant to the crime. Such responses indicate to the examiner that the person is telling the truth. (*b*) This is the record of a person who responded more strongly to a question relevant to a crime than to an emotionally arousing control question not relevant to the crime. Responses such as this indicate to the examiner that the person is lying.

between their responses to control questions and their responses to relevant questions than do people with high reactivity. This might cause an unemotional criminal to be declared innocent and an emotional innocent person to be declared guilty (Waid, Wilson, & Orne, 1981). Tranquilizers reduce the detectability of lying by reducing physiological arousal (Waid & Orne, 1982).

Criminals are also aware of countermeasures that can make them appear innocent on a polygraph test. Consider the case of Floyd Fay, an innocent man convicted in 1978 of murdering his best friend and sentenced to life in prison after failing a polygraph test that he had taken voluntarily. Two years later a public defender tracked down the real murderer. While in prison, Fay became an expert on lie detection and taught prisoners how to beat the polygraph test. Of 27 inmates who had admitted their guilt to him, 23 passed their polygraph tests (Kleinmuntz & Szucko, 1984b).

What techniques might fool the polygraph machine? One technique uses the properly timed induction of pain. For example, suppose that during control questions you bite your tongue or step on a tack hidden in your shoe. This would increase your level of physiological arousal in response to control questions, thereby reducing the difference between your physiological responses to control questions and relevant questions (Honts, Hodes, & Raskin, 1985).

Though aware that criminals can fool the polygraph machine, critics of the test are more concerned with the possibility that the polygraph will find innocent people guilty. In the 1980s millions of Americans were subjected to polygraph tests in criminal cases, employment screening, employee honesty checks, and security clearances (Kleinmuntz & Szucko, 1984b). In 1983 President Reagan gave an executive order to use the polygraph test to identify federal employees who reveal classified information. But a report commissioned by Congress found that the polygraph test was invalid in the situations favored by Reagan. The report concluded that the only justifiable use of the polygraph test is in criminal cases (Saxe, Dougherty, & Cross, 1985). Though the test might not be valid, it can elicit confessions from suspects who believe in its effectiveness (Simpson, 1986).

In June of 1988 President Reagan, confronted with overwhelming opposition to the unrestricted use of polygraph tests, signed the Polygraph Protection Act banning

FIGURE 12.15

The Validity of Polygraph Testing
A study by Kleinmuntz and Szucko (1984a) found that the polygraph test is far from foolproof in determining guilt or innocence. About one-third of innocent suspects were judged guilty and about one-quarter of guilty suspects were judged innocent.

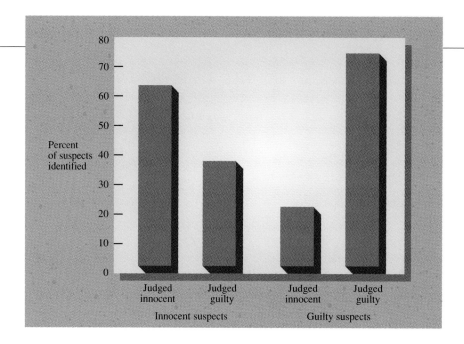

David Lykken
"Since, in the field, most subjects tend to 'fail' the lie test whether they are truthful or deceptive, the method more often detects lying than it does truthful responding."

Guilty Knowledge Test
A method that assesses lying by measuring physiological arousal in response to information that is relevant to a transgression and physiological arousal in response to information that is irrelevant to that transgression.

their use for preemployment screening by private employers. But the law still permitted the use of polygraph tests in ongoing investigations of specific incidents. And drug companies, security services, government agencies, and private companies that have contracts with government intelligence agencies were exempted from the ban on the use of polygraph tests in preemployment screening (Bales, 1988b).

Anatomy of a Classic Research Study: Study:
How Accurate Are Lie Detectors at Judging Guilt and Innocence?

Rationale
What evidence led to the widespread opposition to the unrestricted use of the polygraph? Supporters of the polygraph test claim accuracy rates of 90 percent or better (Raskin & Podlesny, 1979). But research findings indicate that it is much less accurate than that, as revealed by the following study (Kleinmuntz & Szucko, 1984a).

Method
The polygraph printouts of 50 thieves and 50 innocent people were presented to six professional polygraphers from leading lie-detector companies. They were asked questions about real thefts.

Results and Discussion
The results showed that the polygraphers correctly identified 76 percent of the guilty persons and 63 percent of the innocent persons (see figure 12.15). Though their performance was better than chance, this also meant that they incorrectly identified 24 percent of the guilty persons as innocent and 37 percent of the innocent persons as guilty (Kleinmuntz & Szucko, 1984a). The polygraph test's high rate of false positives (that is, identifying innocent persons as guilty) can have tragic consequences for those who are unjustly denied jobs, fired from jobs, or prosecuted for crimes.

THE GUILTY KNOWLEDGE TEST

A promising alternative to the polygraph test is the **Guilty Knowledge Test,** developed by David Lykken (1974). If you have ever played the board game *Clue,* you have some understanding of the test. In contrast to the polygraph test, Lykken's test assesses knowledge about a transgression, rather than alleged anxiety about it. The Guilty Knowledge Test is useful only when details of the transgression are known to the transgressor but not to others who take the test. Consider its use in interrogating suspects in a bank robbery. A suspect would be asked questions about the victim, the site of the crime, and the commission of the crime. Instead of being asked, "Did you steal money from the bank safe?" the suspect would be asked, "Was the money stolen from the _____ ?" This question would be asked several times, each time with different words completing the statement. In this case, the words might be *bank safe, teller's drawer,* and *armored car.*

The Guilty Knowledge Test assumes that a guilty person (who knows details of the crime), but not an innocent person, will show more physiological arousal in response to the relevant words than in response to the irrelevant words. If a person shows greater physiological reactivity to the relevant words in a *series* of statements (a single positive instance would be insufficient), that person would be considered guilty. Of course, examiners should not know any details of the crime. Otherwise, they might affect the suspect's physiological response to relevant words, perhaps by saying those words louder or softer.

A laboratory test in which undergraduates committed mock murders supported the assumption that guilt could be detected by differential physiological responses to relevant and irrelevant stimuli (Timm, 1982). In its first use in a study of real criminals, the Guilty Knowledge Test was given to 50 innocent and 48 guilty subjects. The results supported the effectiveness of the test, particularly its ability to avoid false positives. Judges correctly classified 94 percent of the innocent and 65 percent of the guilty (Elaad, 1990). Research findings indicate that the Guilty Knowledge Test is biased toward false negatives, while control-question tests are biased toward false positives (McCauley & Forman, 1988). So, those more interested in protecting the innocent would favor the Guilty Knowledge Test, while those more interested in ferreting out transgressors would favor the control-question test.

Lykken, recognizing the merits of the Guilty Knowledge Test, urges its widespread adoption (Lykken, 1988). But support for the superiority of the Guilty Knowledge Test has not been universal. One study found no difference in the success of the control-question test and Guilty Knowledge Test in detecting lying (Podlesny & Raskin, 1978). And another study found that subjects with guilty knowledge might still not be detected reliably (Bradley & Warfield, 1984). So even though the Guilty Knowledge Test is more promising than the control-question test, it has not yet gained sufficient research support to merit complete confidence in it. Other researchers are developing a version of the Guilty Knowledge Test that would measure changes in brain-wave patterns to determine when a person has information that he or she is trying to conceal (Bashore & Rapp, 1993).

SUMMARY

THE PHYSIOLOGY OF EMOTION

Emotion is a motivated state marked by physiological arousal, expressive behavior, and mental experience. Emotional arousal depends on activity in the autonomic nervous system and the limbic system. The left cerebral hemisphere plays a greater role in positive emotions; the right cerebral hemisphere plays a greater role in negative emotions. Neurotransmitters, including endorphins, alter our moods by affecting neuronal activity.

THE EXPRESSION OF EMOTION

We express our emotions behaviorally through changes in vocal qualities, body movements, and facial expressions. Charles Darwin believed that facial expressions evolved because they communicate emotions and help individuals distinguish friend from foe. The hereditary basis of facial expressions is supported by research showing cross-cultural consistency in the positive association between particular facial expressions and particular emotions.

THE EXPERIENCE OF EMOTION

Robert Plutchik considers the basic emotions to be joy, fear, anger, disgust, sadness, surprise, acceptance, and anticipation. Emotions vary in their intensity and pleasantness; people who tend to experience intensely pleasant emotions are also likely to experience intensely unpleasant emotions. Psychologists have only recently begun to study pleasant emotions, such as happiness and humor, to the same extent as unpleasant emotions. According to social-comparison theory, happiness is the result of estimating that one's life circumstances are more favorable than those of others. And according to adaptation-level theory, happiness depends on estimating that one's current life circumstances are more favorable than one's past life circumstances. Humor is explained by disparagement theory, incongruity theory, and release theory.

THEORIES OF EMOTION

Psychologists have devised a variety of theories to explain emotional experience. The James-Lange theory assumes that physiological changes precede emotional experiences and that with different patterns of physiological arousal are associated with different emotions. The Cannon-Bard theory claims that the thalamus perceives an event and communicates this information to the cerebral cortex (which provides the subjective experience of emotion) and stimulates the physiological arousal characteristic of emotion. According to the opponent-process theory, the brain has evolved mechanisms that counteract strong positive or negative emotions by evoking an opposite emotional response. If the first emotion is repeated, the opposing emotion gradually strengthens and the first emotion gradually weakens, until a more moderate response becomes habitual.

According to the facial-feedback theory, different emotions are caused by sensory feedback from different facial expressions. The two-factor theory views emotional experience as the consequence of attributing physiological arousal to a particular aspect of one's immediate environment. Cognitive-appraisal theory ignores the role of physiological arousal and considers emotional experience to be solely the result of a person's interpretation of her or his current circumstances.

THINKING ABOUT PSYCHOLOGY: DO LIE DETECTORS TELL THE TRUTH?

The lie detector, or polygraph test, assumes that differences in physiological arousal in response to control questions and relevant questions can be used to determine whether a person is lying. Critics point out that the polygraph can be fooled and that it has poor validity because it finds a large proportion of guilty people innocent and an even larger proportion of innocent people guilty. A promising alternative to the traditional polygraph test is the Guilty Knowledge Test, which depends on the guilty person's physiological arousal to important facts about his or her transgression.

▶▶▶

IMPORTANT CONCEPTS

adaptation-level theory 435
Cannon-Bard theory 440
cognitive-appraisal theory 446
disparagement theory 436

emotion 424
facial-feedback theory 442
fight-or-flight response 424
Guilty Knowledge Test 450

incongruity theory 436
James-Lange theory 437
opponent-process theory of emotion 441

polygraph test 448
release theory 437
social-comparison theory 435
two-factor theory 444

▶▶▶

MAJOR CONTRIBUTORS

Walter Cannon 437, 440–442
Charles Darwin 431, 433
Paul Ekman 442–443

Carroll Izard 431
William James 437
Richard Lazarus 446

David Lykken 450–451
Robert Plutchik 433–434

Stanley Schachter 444–445
Richard Solomon 441–442

▶▶▶

RECOMMENDED READINGS

FOR GENERAL WORKS ON EMOTION

Carlson, J. G., & Hatfield, E. (1992). *Psychology of emotion.* San Diego, CA: Harcourt Brace Jovanovich.

Clark, M. S. (1992). *Emotion and social behavior.* Newbury Park, CA: Sage Publications.

Frijda, N. H. (1987). *The emotions.* New York: Cambridge University Press.

Gardiner, H. N. (1970). *Feeling and emotion: A history of theories.* New York: Greenwood.

Izard, C. E. (1991). *The psychology of emotions.* New York: Plenum.

Lazarus, R. S. (1991). *Emotion and adaptation.* New York: Oxford University Press.

Marcus, H. R., & Kitayama, S. (Eds.). (1994). *Emotion and culture: Empirical studies of mutual influence.* Washington,

DC: American Psychological Association.

Plutchik, R. (1993). *Psychology of emotions.* New York: Harper Collins.

Scherer, K. R., & Ekman, P. (Eds.). (1984). *Approaches to emotion.* Hillsdale, NJ: Erlbaum.

Stein, N., Leventhal, B. L., & Trabasso, T. (Eds.). (1990). *Psychological and biological approaches to emotion.* Hillsdale, NJ: Erlbaum.

Strongman, K. T. (1987). *The psychology of emotion (3rd ed.).* New York: Wiley.

Zajonc, R. B., & McIntosh, D. N. (1992). Emotions research: Some promising questions and some questionable promises. *Psychological Science, 3,* 70–74.

FOR MORE ON THE PHYSIOLOGY OF EMOTION

Blanchard, D. C., & Blanchard, R. J. (1988). Ethoexperimental approaches to the biology of emotion. *Annual Review of Psychology, 39,* 43–68.

Bruyer, R. (Ed.). (1986). *The neuropsychology of face perception and facial expression.* Hillsdale, NJ: Erlbaum.

Cannon, W. B. (1915). *Bodily changes in pain, hunger, fear, and rage.* New York: Appleton.

Heilman, K. M., & Satz, P. (Eds.). (1983). *Neuropsychology of human emotion.* New York: Guilford.

McGeer, P. L., & McGeer, E. G. (1980). Chemistry of mood and emotion. *Annual Review of Psychology, 31,* 273–307.

Miller, L. (1988, February). The emotional brain. *Psychology Today,* pp. 34–42.

Plutchik, R., & Kellerman, H. (Eds.). (1985). *Biological foundations of emotion.* San Diego: Academic Press.

Rinn, W. E. (1984). The neuropsychology of facial expression: A review of the neurological and psychological mechanisms for producing facial expressions. *Psychological Bulletin, 95,* 52–77.

Simonov, P. V. (1986). *The emotional brain.* New York: Plenum.

Thayer, R. E. (1989). *The biopsychology of mood and arousal.* New York: Oxford University Press.

Thompson, J. G. (1988). *The psychobiology of emotions.* New York: Plenum.

Tucker, D. M. (1981). Lateral brain function, emotion, and conceptualization. *Psychological Bulletin, 89,* 19–46.

Vincent, J. D. (1990). *The biology of emotions.* New York: Basil Blackwell.

Wagner, H. L. (1989). *Social psychophysiology and emotion.* New York: Wiley.

FOR MORE ON THE EXPRESSION OF EMOTION

Collier, G. (1985). *Emotional expression.* Hillsdale, NJ: Erlbaum.

Darwin, C. (1872/1965). *The expression of the emotions in man and animals.* Chicago: University of Chicago Press.

Ekman, P. (1973). *Darwin and facial expression: A century of research in review.* San Diego, CA: Academic Press.

Ekman, P. (1980). *The face of man: Expressions of universal emotions in a New Guinea village.* New York: Garland.

Ekman, P. (Ed.). (1983). *Emotion in the human face* (2nd ed.). New York: Cambridge University Press.

Ekman, P. (1985). *Telling lies: Clues to deceit in the marketplace, politics, and marriage.* New York: W. W. Norton.

Ekman, P. (1992). Facial expressions of emotion: New findings, new questions. *Psychological Science, 3,* 34–38.

Goleman, D. (1981, February). The 7,000 faces of Dr. Ekman. *Psychology Today,* pp. 42–49.

Hickson, M. L., & Stacks, D. W. (1993). *Nonverbal communication: Studies and applications* (3rd ed.). Dubuque, IA: Brown & Benchmark.

Izard, C. E. (1971). *The face of emotion.* New York: Irvington.

Poyatos, F. (1988). *Cross-cultural perspectives in nonverbal communication.* Lewiston, NY: Hogrefe & Huber.

Wolfgang, A. (Ed.). (1984). *Nonverbal behavior: Perspective, applications, and intercultural insights.* Lewiston, NY: Hogrefe.

FOR MORE ON THE EXPERIENCE OF EMOTION

Osgood, C., May, W. H., & Miron, M. S. (1975). *Cross-cultural universals of affective meaning.* Urbana: University of Illinois Press.

Plutchik, R. (1991). *The emotions.* Lanham, MD: University Press of America.

Plutchik, R. (1980, February). A language for the emotions. *Psychology Today,* pp. 68–78.

Plutchik, R., & Kellerman, H. (1989). *The measurement of emotions.* San Diego: Academic Press.

Russell, J. A. (1991). Culture and the categorization of emotions.
Psychological Bulletin, 110, 426–450.

Scherer, K. R., Wallbott, H. G., & Summerfield, A. B. (Eds.). (1986). *Experiencing emotion: A cross-cultural study.* New York: Cambridge University Press.

FOR MORE ON HAPPINESS

Argyle, M. (1987). *The psychology of happiness.* New York: Routledge.

Diener, E. (1984). Subjective well-being. *Psychological Bulletin, 95,* 542–575.

Eysenck, M. (1990). *Happiness: Facts and myths.* Hillsdale, NJ: Erlbaum.

Houston, J. (1981). *The pursuit of happiness.* Glenview, IL: Scott, Foresman.

Myers, D. G. (1992). *Searching for joy: Who is happy—and why.* New York: Morrow.

Strack, F., Argyle, M., & Schwarz, N. (Eds.). (1990). *Subjective well-being: An interdisciplinary perspective.* New York: Pergamon.

FOR MORE ON HUMOR

Buckman, E. S. (Ed.). (1993). *The handbook of humor: Clinical applications in psychotherapy.* Melbourne, FL: Krieger.

Fisher, S., & Fisher, R. L. (1981). *Pretend the world is funny and forever: A psychological analysis of comedians, clowns, and actors.* Hillsdale, NJ: Erlbaum.

Freud, S. (1905). Jokes and their relationship to the unconscious. In J. Strachey (Ed.), *The standard edition of the complete psychological works of Sigmund Freud* (Vol. 8). London: Hogarth.

Goldstein, J. H., & McGhee, P. E. (Eds.). (1972). *The psychology of humor: Theoretical perspectives and empirical issues.* San Diego: Academic Press.

Gruner, C. R. (1978). *Understanding laughter: The workings of wit and humor.* Chicago: Nelson-Hall.

Haig, R. A. (1988). *The anatomy of humor: Biopsychosocial and therapeutic perspectives.* Springfield, MA: Charles C Thomas.

Holland, N. N. (1982). *Laughing: A psychology of humor.* Ithaca, NY: Cornell University Press.

Kuhlman, T. L. (1984). *Humor and psychotherapy.* Pacific Grove, CA: Brooks/Cole.

MacHovec, F. J. (1988). *Humor: Theory, history, applications.* Springfield, MA: Charles C Thomas.

McGhee, P. E. (1980). *Humor: Its origin and development.* San Francisco: W. H. Freeman.

McGhee, P. E. (Ed.). (1983). *Handbook of humor research:*
Vol. 1. Basic issues. New York: Springer-Verlag.

McGhee, P. E. (Ed.). (1983). *Handbook of humor research: Vol. 2. Applied studies.* New York: Springer-Verlag.

Mulkay, M. (1988). *On humor.* New York: Basil Blackwell.

Nahemov, L. (Ed.). (1986). *Humor and aging.* San Diego: Academic Press.

Ziv, A. (1984). *National styles of humor.* Westport, CT: Greenwood.

Ziv, A. (1984). *Personality and sense of humor.* New York: Springer.

FOR MORE ON THEORIES OF EMOTION

Adelmann, P. K., & Zajonc, R. B. (1989). Facial efference and the experience of emotion. *Annual Review of Psychology, 40,* 249–289.

Fehr, F. S., & Stern, J. A. (1970). Peripheral physiological variables and emotion: The James-Lange theory revisited. *Psychological Bulletin, 74,* 411–424.

Gardiner, H. M., Metcalf, R. C., & Beebe-Lenter, J. G. (1937). *Feelings and emotion: A history of theories.* New York: American Book.

Izard, C. E., Kagan, J., & Zajonc, R. B. (Eds.). (1988). *Emotions, cognition, and behavior.* New York: Cambridge University Press.

Lazarus, R. (1991). Cognition and motivation in emotion. *American Psychologist, 46,* 352–367.

Lazarus, R. (1991). Progress on a cognitive-motivational-relational theory of emotion. *American Psychologist, 46,* 819–834.

Leventhal, H., & Tomarken, A. J. (1986). Emotion: Today's problems. *Annual Review of Psychology, 37,* 565–610.

Mandler, G. (1990). William James and the construction of emotion. *Psychological Science, 1,* 179–180.

Papanicolaou, A. C. (1989). *Emotion: A reconsideration of the somatic theory.* New York: Gordon & Breach.

Plutchik, R. (1980). *Emotion: A psychoevolutionary synthesis.* New York: Harper & Row.

Plutchik, R., & Kellerman, H. (Ed.). (1980). *Theories of emotion.* San Diego: Academic Press.

Reisenzein, R. (1983). The Schachter theory of emotion: Two decades later. *Psychological Bulletin, 94,* 239–264.

Solomon, R. L. (1980). The opponent-process theory of acquired motivation: The costs of pleasure and the benefits of pain. *American Psychologist, 35,* 691–712.

Stein, N. L., Leventhal, B. L., & Trabasso, T. (Eds.). (1990). *Psychological and biological approaches to emotion.* Hillsdale, NJ: Erlbaum.

Stemmler, G. (1989). The autonomic differentiation of emotions revisited: Convergent and discriminant validation. *Psychological Bulletin, 26,* 617–632.

Zajonc, R. B. (1984). On the primacy of affect. *American Psychologist, 39,* 117–123.

Zajonc, R. B. (1985). Emotion and facial efference: A theory revisited. *Science, 228,* 15–21.

FOR MORE ON LIE DETECTORS

Abrams, S. (1989). *The complete polygraph handbook.* New York: Free Press.

Gale, A. (1988). *The polygraph test: Lies, truth, and science.* Newbury Park, CA: Sage Publications.

Kleinmuntz, B., & Szucko, J. J. (1984). Lie detection in ancient and modern times: A call for contemporary scientific study. *American Psychologist, 39,* 766–776.

Lykken, D. T. (1981). *A tremor in the blood: Uses and abuses of the lie detector.* New York: McGraw-Hill.

Marston, W. M. (1938). *The lie detector test.* New York: Richard R. Smith.

Podlesny, J. A., & Raskin, D. C. (1977). Physiological measures and the detection of deception. *Psychological Bulletin, 84,* 782–799.

Waid, W. M., & Orne, M. T. (1982). The physiological detection of deception. *American Scientist, 70,* 402–409.

FOR MORE ON CONTRIBUTORS TO THE STUDY OF EMOTION

Benison, S., Barger, A. C., & Wolfe, E. L. (1987). *Walter B. Cannon: The life and times of a young scientist.* Cambridge, MA: Harvard University Press.

Darwin, C. (1879/1990). *The autobiography of Charles Darwin.* New York: New York University Press.

Grunberg, N. E., Nisbett, R. E., Rodin, J., & Singer, J. E. (1987). *A distinctive approach to psychological research: The influence of Stanley Schachter.* Hillsdale, NJ: Erlbaum.

Myers, G. E. (1986). *William James: His life and thought.* New Haven, CT: Yale University Press.

CHAPTER 13

Pierre-Auguste Renoir
Monet Painting in His Garden at Argenteuil
1873

PERSONALITY

THINKING ABOUT PSYCHOLOGY

IS PERSONALITY CONSISTENT?

Personality as Inconsistent
Personality as Consistent

Anatomy of a Contemporary Research Study:
In Personality, Are Identical Twins Reared Apart More Like Their Adoptive Parents or Their Biological Parents?

Anatomy of a Classic Research Study:
Is Personality Consistent from One Situation to Another?

personality
An individual's unique, relatively consistent pattern of thinking, feeling, and behaving.

Personality
Comedian Robin Williams epitomizes the notion that one's *personality* involves a unique pattern of thinking, feeling, and behaving.

Y ou have probably categorized your fellow students into those with a "good personality," those with a "bad personality," and even some with "no personality." But exactly what is personality? The word *personality* comes from the Latin word *persona,* meaning "mask." Just as masks distinguished one character from another in ancient Greek and Roman plays, your personality distinguishes you from other people. Your **personality** is your unique, relatively consistent pattern of thinking, feeling, and behaving. To appreciate the uniqueness of each personality, see if you recognize yourself in the following personality description:

> • • • You have a strong need for other people to like and admire you. You have a tendency to be critical of yourself. You have a great deal of unused capacity, which you have not turned to your advantage. . . . Disciplined and controlled on the outside, you tend to be worrisome and insecure inside. . . . At times you are extraverted, affable, and sociable; at other times, you are introverted, wary, and reserved (Ulrich, Stachnik, & Stainton, 1963).

Study after study has shown that when people are given personality tests and then presented with a mock personality description like this one, they tend to accept the description as accurate. They do so because the description *is* accurate. But it is accurate because it contains traits that are shared by almost everyone; it says nothing that distinguishes one person from another. The acceptance of personality descriptions that are true of almost everyone is known as the "Barnum effect" (Meehl, 1956). This reflects P. T. Barnum's saying, "There's a sucker born every minute." We are more likely to succumb to the Barnum effect when the personality description is flattering (Guastello, Guastello, & Craft, 1989).

Astrologers make good use of the Barnum effect (Glick, Gottesman, & Jolton, 1989). In a study of astrological personality descriptions, a researcher placed a newspaper advertisement that offered a free personalized horoscope. Of the 150 persons who responded, 141 (94 percent) said they recognized themselves in the "personalized" description. But each of the respondents had received the same description—the personality profile of a mass murderer from France (Waldrop, 1984b). The description simply contained traits that many persons, whether mass murderers or not, have in common. Thus, the Barnum effect demonstrates that useful personality descriptions must distinguish one person from another. You should no more accept a personality description that fails to recognize your distinctive combination of personal traits than you would accept a physical description that merely states that you have a head, a torso, two eyes, ten toes, and other physical characteristics shared by almost everyone.

Given that each of us has a unique personality, how do we explain our distinctive patterns of thinking, feeling, and behaving? Personality theorists favor several approaches to this question. In reading about them, you will note that the theorists' own life experiences may color their personality theories (Atwood & Tomkins, 1976; Pearce, 1985; Seeman, 1990). The approaches to the study of personality differ on several dimensions, including the importance of biological factors, the influence of unconscious motivation, the extent to which we are molded by the environment, the role of cognitive processes, and the importance of subjective experience.

THE BIOPSYCHOLOGICAL APPROACH

Personality researchers who favor the *biopsychological approach* warn that "any theory that ignores the evidence for the biological underpinnings of human behavior is bound to be an incomplete one" (Kenrick & Dantchik, 1983, p. 302). The biological basis of

personality has been recognized by ancient and modern thinkers alike. The Greek physician-philosopher Hippocrates (460–377 B.C.) presented an early biological view of personality, which was elaborated on by the Greek physician Galen (A.D. 130–200). Hippocrates and Galen claimed that **temperament,** a person's predominant emotional state, reflects the relative levels of body fluids they called *humors.* They associated blood with a cheerful, or *sanguine,* temperament; phlegm with a calm, or *phlegmatic,* temperament; black bile with a depressed, or *melancholic,* temperament; and yellow bile with an irritable, or *choleric,* temperament. Research has failed to find a humoral basis for personality. But as you will read later in this chapter, some modern research supports the existence of the four basic temperaments identified by Hippocrates and Galen (Stelmack & Stalikas, 1991).

temperament
A person's characteristic emotional state, first apparent in early infancy and possibly inborn.

The humoral theory of personality was dominant until the late eighteenth century, when it was joined by phrenology and physiognomy. As described in chapter 3, *phrenology* is the study of the contours of the skull. As illustrated in figure 13.1, phrenologists assumed that specific areas of the brain controlled specific personality characteristics and that the bumps and depressions of the skull indicated the size of those brain areas. Those who believed in *physiognomy,* the study of physical appearance, held that personality was revealed by the features of the face. Physiognomy became so popular that it almost prevented Charles Darwin from embarking on the historic voyage that inspired his theory of evolution. In 1836 the captain of the HMS *Beagle* threatened to reject Darwin as the ship's naturalist because he thought Darwin's nose was the wrong shape for a sailor (Fancher, 1979).

Research failed to support phrenology and physiognomy. Like astrology, they were subject to the Barnum effect. If you felt the contours of a person's head and wrote a personality description that contained flattering generalities, your subject might place unjustified faith in phrenology (Smith, 1986). Phrenologists did, however, spark interest in the study of the biological bases of personality, particularly the role of heredity (Hilts, 1982). The early twentieth century saw biologically inclined personality researchers move from the study of the skull and the face to the study of the relationship between physique and personality.

Physique and Personality

Interest in the relationship between one's physique and one's personality has been with us for centuries. The following passage from Shakespeare's *Julius Caesar* (act 1, scene 2) expresses Caesar's belief that one's physique reveals one's personality:

> Let me have men about me that are fat;
> Sleek-headed men and such as sleep o'nights:
> Yond Cassius has a lean and hungry look;
> He thinks too much: Such men are dangerous.

The scientific study of the relationship between physique and personality began with the work of the German psychiatrist Ernst Kretschmer (1888–1964). Kretschmer (1925) measured the physique of hundreds of mental patients and found a relationship between thin physiques and schizophrenia and between rounded physiques and manic depression. (Both of these disorders are discussed in chapter 14.) But the researcher who did the most to advance the scientific study of the physique-personality relationship was the American physician and psychologist William Sheldon (1898–1977), whose inspiration to become a psychologist came from having William James as his godfather (Hilgard, 1987).

In formulating his *constitutional theory* of personality, Sheldon examined photographs of thousands of young men. He identified three kinds of physiques, which he called **somatotypes.** The *ectomorph* has a thin, frail physique; the *mesomorph* has a muscular, strong physique; and the *endomorph* has a soft, rounded physique. Because Sheldon recognized that few people were pure somatotypes, he rated subjects on a scale of 1 to 7 for each of the three kinds of physiques.

Sheldon also administered personality tests to his subjects. He found that each somatotype was associated with a particular temperament. He called the shy, restrained, and introspective temperament of the ectomorph *cerebrotonia*; the bold, assertive, and energetic temperament of the mesomorph *somatotonia*; and the relaxed, sociable, and easygoing temperament of the endomorph *viscerotonia* (Sheldon & Stevens, 1942).

But how might somatotypes affect personality? Sheldon reasoned that their own somatotypes might affect people's behavior and the behavior of others toward them. For example, a mesomorphic person might be more physically imposing, making the person more self-confident and, as a result, more assertive. Moreover, others might find the mesomorph more attractive, further enhancing her or his self-confidence. Sheldon found that mesomorphs were more common among juvenile delinquents, perhaps because they are stronger and more assertive than ectomorphs or endomorphs. Today, though interest in the study of the relationship between body type and personality remains, psychologists who are interested in the biological bases of personality are more likely to study the effect of heredity on personality development.

Heredity and Personality

A century ago Francis Galton insisted that "nature prevails enormously over nurture" (Holden, 1987b, p. 598). Today those, like Galton, who believe that heredity molds personality assume that evolution has provided us with inborn behavioral tendencies that differ from person to person (Buss, 1990). The field that studies the relationship between heredity and behavior is called *behavioral genetics* (discussed in chapter 4). Research in behavioral genetics has shown that even newborn infants exhibit differences in temperament—some are emotionally placid, others are emotionally reactive (Braungart et al., 1992).

How might these initial differences in temperament contribute to the development of differences in personality? They might affect how infants respond to other people and, in turn, how other people respond to them. For example, a placid infant would be

somatotype
A person's body type, whether ectomorphic (thin), mesomorphic (muscular), or endomorphic (fat).

less responsive to other people. As a consequence, others would be less responsive to the infant. This might predispose the infant to become less sociable later in childhood, laying the groundwork for an introverted adult personality.

Biopsychological Assessment of Personality

In general, the closer the genetic relationship between two persons, the more alike they will be in personality characteristics. Because this relationship may reflect common life experiences, as well as common genetic inheritance, researchers in the biopsychological assessment of personality have resorted to adoption studies to determine the relative contributions of heredity and life experiences.

The Texas Adoption Project, which is discussed in chapter 4, found that, in regard to personality, children tend to resemble their biological parents more than their adoptive parents (Loehlin, Horn, & Willerman, 1990). For example, adopted infants and their biological mothers are more similar in their degree of shyness than are adopted infants and their adoptive mothers (Daniels & Plomin, 1985). Findings such as these indicate that parent-child personality similarity is influenced more by common heredity than by common life experiences, as supported by the following study.

Anatomy of a Contemporary Research Study:

In Personality, Are Identical Twins Reared Apart More Like Their Adoptive Parents or Their Biological Parents?

Rationale

Since 1979, psychologist Thomas Bouchard of the University of Minnesota has conducted the most comprehensive study of identical twins reared apart and then reunited later in life. He has found amazing behavioral similarities between some of the twins. Consider the case of Oskar Stohr and Jack Yufe, who were born in Trinidad to a Jewish father and a Catholic mother. The twins were separated shortly after birth and reared in vastly different life circumstances. While Oskar was reared in Germany as a Nazi by his maternal grandmother, Jack was reared in Trinidad as a Jew by his father. Decades later, when they arrived at the airport in Minneapolis to take part in Bouchard's study, both Jack and Oskar sported mustaches, wire-rimmed glasses, and two-pocket shirts with epaulets. Bouchard found that they both preferred sweet liqueurs, stored rubber bands on their wrists, flushed the toilet before using it, read magazines from back to front, and dipped buttered toast in their coffee (Holden, 1980b). Though there are probably no "flush toilet before using" genes, the men's identical genetic inheritance might have provided them with similar temperaments that predisposed them to develop certain behavioral similarities. In fact, Bouchard and his colleagues have found that the rearing environment has relatively little influence on the development of personality (Bouchard & McGue, 1990).

Studies of identical twins reared apart provide the strongest support for the hereditary basis of personality. Identical twins have 100 percent of their genes in common, while fraternal twins have 50 percent in common. This might explain why identical twins who are adopted and reared by different

Identical Twins Reunited
When reunited at the age of 39 as part of Thomas Bouchard's study, identical twins Jim Lewis and Jim Springer revealed remarkable similarities even though they had been adopted into different homes at 4 weeks of age. Both liked arithmetic but not spelling, drove Chevrolets, had dogs named Toy, chewed their fingernails to the nub, served as deputy sheriffs, enjoyed vacationing in Florida, married women named Linda, and got divorced and then married women named Betty. Both also enjoyed mechanical drawing and carpentry. The photos show them in their basement workshops, where both had built white benches that encircle trees in their backyards.

families are more similar in personality than are fraternal twins who are reared by their biological parents—even three decades after adoption (Tellegen et al., 1988).

Method

The subjects were participants in the Minnesota Twin Study between 1970 and 1984. There were 217 identical twin pairs reared together and 114 fraternal twin pairs reared together. There were 44 identical twin pairs reared apart and 27 fraternal twin pairs reared apart. The twins who had been reared apart had been separated, on the average, more than 30 years. The subjects were given the Multidimensional Personality Questionnaire, which measures basic personality traits.

Results and Discussion

The results indicated that identical twins reared together and identical twins reared apart were highly similar in intelligence. Identical twins reared apart also were more similar than were fraternal twins

Drawing by Chas. Addams; © 1981 The New Yorker Magazine, Inc.

Separated at birth, the Mallifert twins meet accidentally.

reared together. Overall, the heritability of personality was .48. Thus, the subjects' personalities were strongly, though not solely, influenced by heredity. The heritability of personality is the proportion of the variability in personality within a population that is caused by heredity.

Status of the Biopsychological Approach

Research has failed to find the strong relationship between somatotype and personality reported by Sheldon. One of the main problems with Sheldon's research was that *he* rated both the somatotypes and the temperaments of his subjects. This provided room for experimenter bias, perhaps making his ratings support his theory more than they should have. Nonetheless, there is a *modest* relationship between physique and personality. For example, David Lester, one of the few psychologists who still conducts systematic research on somatotypes, found that ectomorphs tend to exhibit the personality traits of cerebrotonia (Lester, 1982). Another study found, as predicted by Sheldon, that mesomorphic males are more extraverted, self-confident, and emotionally stable (Tucker, 1983).

Of course, these relationships do not indicate that physique differences *cause* personality differences. Perhaps, instead, personality differences affect dietary and exercise habits, thereby causing differences in physique. Another possibility is that hereditary factors cause a relationship between physique and personality. For example, David Lester found that newborn ectomorphic infants were more emotionally responsive than infants with other physiques (Lester & Wosnack, 1990). This supported Sheldon's notion that the same genes might determine both physique and temperament (Sheldon & Stevens, 1942).

Putting aside the question of the relationship between physique and personality, how heritable is personality? Estimates of the heritability of personality vary from about 25 percent (Scarr et al., 1981), indicating that environment is more important than heredity, to about 60 percent (Tellegen et al., 1988), indicating that heredity is more important than environment. Surprisingly, the nonshared environment of siblings has a greater influence on their personality development than does their shared environment. That is, experiences they share are less important than experiences they do not share (Plomin & Daniels, 1987).

Thomas Bouchard
"On multiple measures of personality and temperament, occupational and leisure-time interests, and social attitudes, monozygotic twins reared apart seem to be about as similar as monozygotic twins reared together."

David Lester
"The existence of some associations between physique and personality in neonates is consistent with Sheldon's theory."

And what of Bouchard's research on identical twins reared apart? Care must be taken in drawing conclusions from the amazing behavioral similarities in some of the twins he has studied. Imagine that you and a fellow student were both asked thousands of questions (as Bouchard asks his subjects). You would undoubtedly find some surprising similarities between the two of you, even though you were not genetically related. This was demonstrated in a study that found many similarities between pairs of strangers. For example, one pair of women were both Baptists, nursing students, active in tennis and volleyball, fond of English and mathematics, not fond of shorthand, and partial to vacations at historic places (Wyatt et al., 1984). Of course, by comparing twins' performances on formal personality tests, Bouchard does more than simply report selected instances of amazing similarities between certain ones. Given the evidence for both genetic and environmental influences, the best bet is to accept that they both strongly—apparently about equally—affect the development of personality.

THE PSYCHOANALYTIC APPROACH

The *psychoanalytic approach* to personality has its roots in the biopsychological approach. Sigmund Freud, the founder of psychoanalysis, was a physician who hoped to find the biological basis of the psychological processes contained in his psychosexual theory (Knight, 1984).

Psychosexual Theory

Freud (1856–1939) was born in Moravia to Jewish parents, who moved with him to Vienna when he was 4 years old. Though Freud desired a career as a physiology professor, anti-Semitism limited his choice of professions to law, business, or medicine. He chose medicine as a back door into biological research and eventually practiced as a neurologist. Freud became one of the most influential intellectual figures of the twentieth century, yet he refused to capitalize on his fame by taking advantage of commercial opportunities. These included financial enticements to write articles for *Cosmopolitan* magazine and to serve as a Hollywood consultant on movies about famous love affairs (Pervin, 1984). Instead, Freud remained in Vienna until the Nazis began burning his books and threatening his safety. In 1938 he emigrated to England, where he died the following year after suffering for many years from mouth cancer.

Early in his career, Freud became interested in the effects of the mind on physical symptoms. He had studied with the French neurologist Jean Charcot, who demonstrated the power of hypnosis in treating *conversion hysteria*, a disorder characterized by physical symptoms such as deafness, blindness, or paralysis without any physical cause. Charcot used hypnotic suggestion to help his patients regain the use of their lost senses or paralyzed limbs. Freud was also intrigued by a report that psychiatrist Josef Breuer had successfully used a "talking cure" to treat conversion hysteria. Breuer found that by encouraging his patients to talk freely about whatever came to mind, they became aware of the psychological causes of their physical symptoms and, as a result, experienced emotional release, or *catharsis*. This led to the disappearance of the symptoms.

Freud's personality theory reflected his time—the Victorian era of the late nineteenth century. The Victorians valued rationality and self-control of physical drives as characteristics that separated human beings from animals. Freud attributed the symptoms of conversion hysteria to unconscious sexual conflicts, which were symbolized in the symptoms. For example, paralyzed legs might represent a sexual conflict. Freud's claim that sexuality, an animal drive, was an important determinant of human behavior shocked and disgusted many of his contemporaries (Rapp, 1988). Yet, though Freud argued against the extreme sexual inhibitions of his time, he recognized the undesirability of sexual promiscuity (McCarthy, 1981).

Later in his career Freud expanded his theory to include inhibited aggression and inhibited sexuality as important determinants of human behavior. The importance of aggression as a human motive came to him as a result of the carnage of World War I. This led him to claim that we are motivated by both a life instinct, *Eros*, and a death instinct,

Sigmund Freud (1856–1939) and Anna Freud (1895–1982)
After Sigmund Freud's death, his theory was championed by his daughter Anna, who pursued a career as a psychoanalyst.

Drawing by Modell; © 1981 The New Yorker Magazine, Inc.

"And then I say to myself, 'If I really wanted to talk to her, why do I keep forgetting to dial 1 first?' "

Thanatos. Eros and Thanatos, as well as many other terms used by Freud, are Greek words, reflecting his fascination with the culture of ancient Greece. Fittingly, Freud's ashes reside in one of his favorite Greek urns in London (Tourney, 1965).

Levels of Consciousness

As described in chapter 6, Freud divided the mind into three levels. The *conscious mind* is merely the "tip of the iceberg," representing a tiny region of the mind. The contents of the conscious mind are in a constant state of flux as feelings, memories, and perceptions enter and leave. Just below the conscious mind lies the *preconscious mind,* which includes accessible memories—memories that we can recall at will. The *unconscious mind,* the bulk of the mind, lies below both the conscious mind and the preconscious mind. It contains material we cannot recall at will.

Freud claimed that threatening thoughts or feelings are subject to *repression,* the banishment of conscious material into the unconscious. Because Freud assumed that unconscious thoughts and feelings are the most important influences on our behavior, he proclaimed: "The theory of repression is the cornerstone on which the whole structure of psychoanalysis rests" (Freud, 1914/1957, p. 16). The notion of repressed thoughts and feelings led to the concept of *psychic determinism,* which holds that all behavior is influenced by unconscious motives. Thus, even apparently mundane or arbitrary behaviors are meaningful. Psychic determinism is exhibited in *Freudian slips,* unintentional statements that might reveal our repressed feelings. For instance, the slip "I loathe you . . . I mean I love you" might reveal repressed hostility.

The Structure of Personality

As illustrated in figure 13.2, Freud distinguished three structures of personality: the *id,* the *ego,* and the *superego.* The **id** is unconscious and consists of our inborn biological drives. In demanding immediate gratification of drives, most notably sex and aggression, the id obeys the **pleasure principle.** In regard to sex, the id says, "Now!" The word *id* is Latin for "it," reflecting the id's impersonal nature. The classic 1950s science fiction movie *Forbidden Planet* portrays the amoral nature of the id: The id of a mad scientist is transformed into a being of pure energy that runs amok on an alien planet, blindly killing anyone in its path.

Through life experiences we learn that acting on every sexual or aggressive impulse is socially maladaptive. As a consequence, each of us develops an **ego,** Latin for "I." The ego obeys the **reality principle,** directing us to express sexual and aggressive impulses in socially acceptable ways. In regard to sex, the ego says, "Not now, later!" As for aggression, suppose that a teacher refuses to change your grade on an exam that was

id
In Freud's theory, the part of the personality that contains inborn biological drives and that seeks immediate gratification.

pleasure principle
The process by which the id seeks immediate gratification of its impulses.

ego
In Freud's theory, the part of the personality that helps the individual adapt to external reality by making compromises between the id, the superego, and the environment.

reality principle
The process by which the ego directs the individual to express sexual and aggressive impulses in socially acceptable ways.

FIGURE 13.2

The Structure of Personality
Freud divided the personality into the id, ego, and superego. The id is entirely unconscious and demands immediate gratification of its desires. The ego is partly conscious and partly unconscious. This permits it to balance the id's demands with the external demands of social reality and the moralistic demands of the superego, which is also partly conscious and partly unconscious.

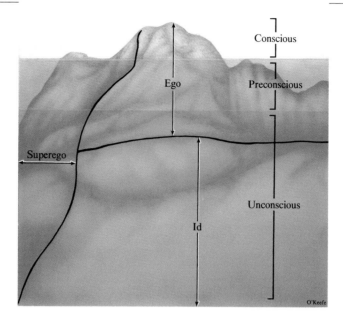

superego
In Freud's theory, the part of the personality that acts as a moral guide telling us what we should and should not do.

defense mechanism
In Freud's theory, a process that distorts reality to prevent the individual from being overwhelmed by anxiety.

graded with an incorrect answer key. Your ego would encourage you to argue with the teacher instead of punching the teacher in the nose.

The **superego** (Latin for "over the I") counteracts the id, which is concerned only with immediate gratification, and the ego, which is concerned only with adapting to reality. The superego acts as our moral guide. It contains the *conscience,* which makes us feel guilty for doing or thinking wrong, and the *ego ideal,* which makes us feel good for doing or thinking right. In regard to sex, the superego says, "Not now, wait until you are married!" Children whose parents do not teach them right from wrong may develop a superego too weak to inhibit aggressive behavior. To Freud, your personality is the outcome of the continual battle for dominance among the id, the ego, and the superego.

Defense Mechanisms

The ego may resort to **defense mechanisms,** which distort reality, to protect itself from the anxiety caused by id impulses, particularly those of sex and aggression. Table 13.1 summarizes the major defense mechanisms. The ego may also use defense mechanisms to relieve the anxiety caused by unpleasant personal experiences and unacceptable personal characteristics. Each of us uses defense mechanisms to varying extents, which contributes to the distinctiveness of each of our personalities. Though defense mechanisms can protect us from experiencing anxiety, they can also prevent us from recognizing and dealing with the true source of the anxiety. As noted in chapter 14, excessive reliance on defense mechanisms characterizes certain psychological disorders (Vaillant, 1992).

Freud considered *repression* to be the main defense mechanism, common to all the others. Because all defense mechanisms involve repression, we are not aware when we are using them. The memory of a traumatic event, such as an auto accident, might be repressed to relieve the anxiety that the memory produces. In recent years, the defense mechanism of repression has become a popular topic in the mass media because of the rise in reports of adults recalling apparently repressed memories of sexual abuse in early childhood. Elizabeth Loftus (Loftus, 1993), whose work on eyewitness testimony is discussed in chapter 8, points out the need for psychologists to find ways to determine the authenticity of such memories. This would help protect the rights of both alleged victims and alleged perpetrators of childhood sexual abuse.

TABLE 13.1	Defense Mechanisms

Repression
The banishment of threatening thoughts, feelings, and memories into the unconscious mind

Denial
The refusal to admit a particular aspect of reality relevant to oneself

Regression
The displaying of immature behaviors that have relieved anxiety in the past

Rationalization
The providing of socially acceptable reasons for one's inappropriate behavior

Intellectualization
The reduction of anxiety by reacting to emotional situations in a detached, unemotional way

Displacement
The expression of feelings toward a person who is less threatening than the true target of those feelings

Projection
The attribution of one's undesirable feelings to others

Reaction Formation
The tendency to act in a manner opposite to one's true feelings

Compensation
The development of a talent as a response to a personal deficiency

Sublimation
The expression of sexual or aggressive impulses through indirect, socially acceptable outlets

We sometimes rely on immature kinds of defense mechanisms. In using *denial*, we simply refuse to admit a particular aspect of reality. A smoker might deny that smoking causes cancer. Terminally ill patients might initially reduce their anxiety by denying they have a fatal disease (Connor, 1986). In resorting to the defense mechanism of *regression*, the individual displays immature behaviors that have relieved anxiety in the past. An adult might respond to job frustrations by crying or throwing temper tantrums.

Other defense mechanisms rely on changing our perception of reality. When we resort to *rationalization*, we provide socially acceptable reasons for our inappropriate behavior. For example, a student whose semester grades include one D and four F's might blame the four F's on studying too much for the course in which he received a D. We might even use rationalization in adjusting to the death of someone we know (Gershuny & Burrows, 1990). People who use *intellectualization* reduce anxiety by reacting to emotional situations in a detached, unemotional way. Instead of reacting to the death of a loved one by crying, they might react by saying, "Everyone must die sometime." Intellectualization is a useful defense mechanism for medical personnel, who must continually deal with death and illness.

In some cases, defense mechanisms direct sexual or aggressive drives in safer directions. A person who fears the consequences of expressing his or her feelings toward a particular person might express them toward someone less threatening. This is known as *displacement*. For example, a worker who hates his boss, but fears criticizing him, might instead constantly criticize his wife. Parents who abuse their children might be displacing their feelings of hostility (Brennan & Andrews, 1990). If we cannot accept our own undesirable feelings, we may resort to *projection*, attributing our undesirable feelings to others. Date rapists might use projection to excuse their behavior by claiming that their victims were sexually provocative.

Shakespeare wrote in *Hamlet*, "The lady doth protest too much, methinks." He was referring to what we now call *reaction formation*—acting in a manner opposite to our innermost feelings. A mother who engages in "smother love" may hide her animosity toward her child by constantly doting on him and hugging him in public. Even Samuel Johnson, the eighteenth-century writer and dictionary editor, reported a classic example of reaction formation. A pair of proper ladies who met him at a literary tea

Displacement
Freud might attribute the angry outbursts of these motorists caught in a traffic jam to the defense mechanism of displacement. Perhaps they have pent up anger against their bosses and are releasing it against each other.

commented, "We see, Dr. Johnson, that you do not have those naughty words in your dictionary." Johnson replied, "And I see, dear ladies, that you have been looking for them" (Morris & Morris, 1985, p. 101).

Defense mechanisms can also affect one's lifestyle. In using *compensation*, a person might react to a personal deficiency by developing another talent. Stevie Wonder may have compensated for his blindness by working to become a great singer and composer. According to Freud, the most successful defense mechanism is *sublimation*, the expression of sexual or aggressive impulses through indirect, socially acceptable outlets. The sex drive can be sublimated through creative activities, such as painting, ballet dancing, or composing music. And the aggressive drive can be sublimated through sports such as football, lacrosse, or field hockey. Support for a relationship between sublimation and creativity came from a recent follow-up study of women, at an average age of 77, from Lewis Terman's longitudinal study of the gifted. (Terman's study, which began in 1921, is discussed in chapter 10.) The follow-up study found that, as Freud would have predicted, sublimation was more common among creative women than among other women (Vaillant & Vaillant, 1990).

Psychosexual Development

Freud assumed that personality development depended on changes in the distribution of sexual energy, which he called **libido,** in regions of the body he called *erogenous zones*. Stimulation of these regions produces pleasure. Thus, he was concerned with stages of *psychosexual development*. Failure to progress smoothly through a particular stage may cause **fixation,** a tendency to continue to engage in behaviors associated with that stage. Freud called the first year of infancy the **oral stage** of development, because the infant gains pleasure from oral activities such as biting, sucking, and chewing. The most important social conflict of this stage is *weaning*. An infant inadequately weaned, because of too much or too little oral gratification, might become fixated at the oral stage. Fixation might lead to an *oral-dependent* personality, marked by passivity, dependency, and gullibility. The person will "swallow anything" and may become a "sucker." Or fixation might lead to an *oral-aggressive* personality, marked by cruelty and sarcastic, "biting" remarks.

At the age of 1 year, the child enters the **anal stage.** He or she now obtains pleasure from defecation and experiences an important conflict regarding toilet training. Freud claimed that inadequate toilet training, either premature or delayed, can lead to fixation at the anal stage. The main characters in the movie and television series "The Odd Couple" represent two kinds of anal fixation. Felix represents the *anal retentive* personality, marked by compulsive cleanliness, orderliness, and fussiness. Oscar represents the *anal expulsive* personality, marked by sloppiness, carelessness, and informality.

Freud claimed that between the ages of 3 and 5, the child passes through the **phallic stage,** in which pleasure is gained from the genitals. This stage is associated with the **Oedipus complex,** in which the child sexually desires the parent of the opposite sex while fearing punishment from the parent of the same sex. Freud noted this conflict in Sophocles's play *Oedipus Rex*, in which Oedipus, abandoned as an infant, later kills his father and marries his mother—without knowing they are his parents.

Freud believed that the Oedipus story reflected a universal truth—the sexual attraction of each child to the opposite-sex parent. Resolution of the conflict leads to identification with the same-sex parent. The boy gives up his desire for his mother because of his *castration anxiety*—his fear that his father will punish him by removing his genitals. The girl, because of *penis envy*, becomes angry at her mother, whom she believes caused the removal of her penis, and becomes attracted to her father. (This is known as the **Electra complex,** after a Greek character who had her mother killed.) But, fearing the loss of maternal love, the girl identifies with her mother, hoping to still attract her father. Through the process of *identification*, boys and girls adopt parental values and develop a superego.

Freud called the period between age 5 and puberty the **latency stage.** He was relatively uninterested in this stage because he believed the child experiences little

libido
Freud's term for the sexual energy of the id.

fixation
In Freud's theory, the failure to mature beyond a particular stage of psychosexual development.

oral stage
In Freud's theory, the stage of personality development, between birth and age 1, during which the infant gains pleasure from oral activities and faces a conflict over weaning.

anal stage
In Freud's theory, the stage of personality development, between ages 1 and 3, during which the child gains pleasure from defecation and faces a conflict over toilet training.

phallic stage
In Freud's theory, the stage of personality development, between ages 3 and 5, during which the child gains pleasure from the genitals and must resolve the Oedipus complex.

Oedipus complex
In Freud's theory, a conflict, during the phallic stage, between the child's sexual desire for the parent of the opposite sex and fear of punishment from the same-sex parent.

Electra complex
A term used by some psychoanalysts, but not by Freud, to refer to the Oedipus complex in females.

latency stage
In Freud's theory, the stage, between age 5 and puberty, during which there is little psychosexual development.

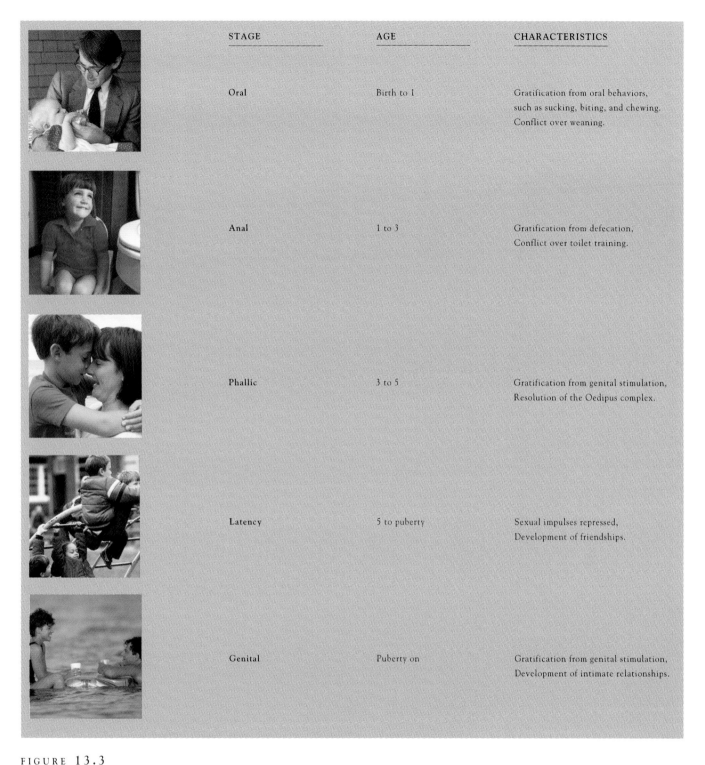

STAGE	AGE	CHARACTERISTICS
Oral	Birth to 1	Gratification from oral behaviors, such as sucking, biting, and chewing. Conflict over weaning.
Anal	1 to 3	Gratification from defecation, Conflict over toilet training.
Phallic	3 to 5	Gratification from genital stimulation, Resolution of the Oedipus complex.
Latency	5 to puberty	Sexual impulses repressed, Development of friendships.
Genital	Puberty on	Gratification from genital stimulation, Development of intimate relationships.

FIGURE 13.3

The Psychosexual Stages of Development

psychosexual development during it. Instead, the child develops social skills and friendships. Finally, during adolescence, the child reaches the **genital stage** and becomes sexually attracted to other people. To Freud, the first three stages are the most important determinants of personality development. He assumed that personality is essentially fixed by the age of 5. Figure 13.3 summarizes these psychosexual stages of development.

genital stage
In Freud's theory, the last stage of personality development, associated with puberty, during which the individual develops erotic attachments to others.

Karen Horney

Harry Stack Sullivan

Erich Fromm

Erik Erikson

FIGURE 13.4

The Neo-Freudians
The neo-Freudians accepted the importance of unconscious motives, but placed greater emphasis on the ego's relationship to society than on the id's demand for gratification.

Karen Horney (1885–1952)
A German immigrant to the United States, she was the first eminent female psychoanalyst. Horney claimed that the personality develops from the child's attempt to seek security by overcoming the *basic anxiety* caused by feeling isolated and helpless in a potentially hostile world. According to Horney (1937), we try to relieve basic anxiety by socially moving toward, against, or away from people. Normally, this means that we become sociable, competitive, or shy. But in extreme cases we exhibit *neurotic trends,* in which we might relieve basic anxiety by being submissive, aggressive, or reclusive. Horney also criticized Freud's view that women feel inferior to men because of penis envy. Instead, she insisted that women envy men's traditionally superior rights and social status.

Harry Stack Sullivan (1892–1949)
One of the pioneers of modern American psychiatry, he lived a lonely and unhappy life, which may partly account for his theory's emphasis on the importance of healthy social relationships. Sullivan (1953) claimed that human beings have a tendency to either accept or reject their experiences as part of themselves. If we reject our unpleasant experiences and, as a consequence, fail to work at improving the inadequate social relations that cause them, we may become divorced from ourselves and develop maladaptive ways of handling anxiety. Sullivan applied his theory to the process of psychiatry and to possible ways of easing international tensions.

Erich Fromm (1900–1980)
A German immigrant, he is best known for his popular book *The Art of Loving* (1956), which applies psychoanalytic concepts to the understanding of love. Fromm based his theory on the individual's conflict between the need for freedom and the anxiety that freedom brings. In capitalistic societies, people may reduce their anxiety by giving up some of their freedom and developing a *marketing orientation,* in which they alter themselves to please others. We may adopt hairstyles, musical interests, and political beliefs simply to advance our standing with other people. In totalitarian countries, people may reduce the anxiety that freedom brings by letting the government control their social, vocational, and political lives. Fromm (1941) discussed this tendency in his book *Escape from Freedom.*

Erik Erikson (1902–1994)
The child of Danish parents, he was reared in Germany and moved to the United States later in his childhood. His father had abandoned his mother before his birth. She remarried soon after Erik's birth, but Erik was not told of his biological father until years later. This may have influenced Erikson's (1968) emphasis on the importance of developing a sense of identity in adolescence and his interest in writing psychobiographies. Psychobiographies apply psychoanalytic principles to understanding the personality development of famous people, including Martin Luther and Mahatma Gandhi.

Individual Psychology

Because Freud's intellectual descendants altered his theory, they became known as *neo-Freudians.* Figure 13.4 presents the views of several of the most renowned of them. One of the most influential of Freud's followers was Alfred Adler (1870–1937). In 1902 Adler, a Viennese physician, joined the regular Wednesday evening group discussions of psychoanalysis at Freud's home and became a devoted disciple. But in 1911 Adler broke with Freud, downplaying the importance of sexual motivation and the unconscious mind. Adler (1927) developed his own theory, which he called *individual psychology.* The popularity of Adler's theory provoked Freud to complain, "I made a pygmy great" (Hergenhahn, 1984, p. 65).

Adler's childhood experiences inspired his theory of personality. He was a sickly child, crippled by rickets and suffering from repeated bouts of pneumonia. He also saw himself as inferior to his stronger and healthier older brother. Adler assumed that because children feel small, weak, and dependent on others, they develop an *inferiority complex.* This motivates them to compensate by *striving for superiority*—that is, developing certain abilities to their maximum extent. For example, Theodore Roosevelt may have compensated for his childhood frailty by becoming a rugged outdoorsman—as Alfred Adler did by becoming an eminent psychoanalyst.

Adler believed that striving for superiority is healthiest when it promotes active concern for the welfare of others, which he called *social interest* (Ferguson, 1989). For example, both a physician and a criminal strive for superiority, but the physician expresses this motive in a socially beneficial way. There is even a positive correlation between social interest and personal happiness (Watkins, 1982). Striving for superiority can lead to *overcompensation,* as in what Adler called *masculine protest.* This means that men (and women) might try to prove themselves by dominating others instead of by developing their own abilities. For example, an Adlerian psychologist might assume that violent "gay bashing" against homosexual men by heterosexual men is an extreme example of masculine protest (Nelson, 1991).

According to Adler, in striving for superiority we develop a *style of life* based on *fictional finalism.* This means that we are motivated by beliefs that might not be objectively true. A person guided by the belief that "nice guys finish last" might exhibit a ruthless, competitive style of life. In contrast, a person guided by the belief that "it is more blessed to give than to receive" might exhibit a helpful, altruistic style of life.

Analytical Psychology

Freud's favorite disciple was Carl Jung (1875–1961). Though Jung, a native of Switzerland, came from a family in which the men traditionally pursued careers as religious pastors, he obeyed a dream that directed him to pursue a career in medicine (Byrne & Kelley, 1981). He later decided to become a psychoanalyst after reading Freud's *The Interpretation of Dreams* (1900/1990). Beginning in 1906, Freud and Jung carried on a lively correspondence, and Freud hoped that Jung would become his successor as head of the psychoanalytic movement. But in 1914 they parted over revisions Jung made in Freud's theory, especially Jung's deemphasis of the sex motive. Jung called his version of psychoanalysis *analytical psychology.*

Though Jung agreed with Freud that we each have our own unconscious mind (the **personal unconscious**), he claimed that we also share a common unconscious mind— the **collective unconscious.** Jung held that the collective unconscious contains inherited memories passed down from generation to generation. He called these memories **archetypes,** which are images that represent important aspects of the accumulated experience of humankind. Jung claimed that archetypes influence our dreams, religious symbols, and artistic creations. As shown in figure 13.5, the characters in the *Star Wars* movies might represent archetypes (Ryback, 1983).

Jung (1959/1969) even connected the archetype of God to reports of flying saucers. Widespread accounts of flying saucer sightings began in the late 1940s, following the horrors of World War II and the advent of the atomic bomb. According to Jung, these sightings stemmed from the desire of people, inspired by the archetype of God, to have a more powerful force than themselves save humankind from self-destruction. Even the round shape of the flying saucer represented the archetypal image of godlike unity and perfection of the archetype of the *self.* Beginning in the 1950s with the movie *The Day the Earth Stood Still* and continuing on with movies such as *Close Encounters of the Third Kind,* science fiction movies have reflected the Jungian theme of powerful aliens arriving in flying saucers to save us from ourselves.

Alfred Adler (1870–1937)
"I began to see clearly in every psychological phenomenon the striving for superiority."

personal unconscious
In Jung's theory, the individual's own unconscious mind, which contains repressed memories.

collective unconscious
In Jung's theory, the unconscious mind that is shared by all human beings and that contains archetypal images passed down from our prehistoric ancestors.

archetypes
In Jung's theory, inherited images that are passed down from our prehistoric ancestors and that reveal themselves as universal symbols in art, dreams, and religion.

FIGURE 13.5

Archetypes
The *Star Wars* "trilogy" has characters that may represent Jungian archetypes. The evil Darth Vader may represent the archetype of the shadow, our animal nature. The elderly Obi-Wan Kenobi may represent the archetype of the wise old man. The adventurer Luke Skywalker may represent the archetype of the hero. And the mysterious Force may represent the archetype of God.

Carl Jung (1875–1961)
"While the personal unconscious is made up essentially of contents which have at one time been conscious but which have disappeared from consciousness through having been forgotten or repressed, the contents of the collective unconscious have never been in consciousness, and therefore have never been individually acquired, but owe their existence exclusively to heredity."

extravert
A person who is socially outgoing and prefers to pay attention to the external environment.

introvert
A person who is socially reserved and prefers to pay attention to his or her private mental experiences.

The archetype of the *mother* is a theme in the novel *Narcissus and Goldmund*, written by Jung's friend Hermann Hesse (1930/1968), whom he also psychoanalyzed. The novel describes how the archetype of the mother guides Goldmund in his constant search for the perfect woman and his fondness for images of the Madonna. A Jungian view claims that the sadness and yearning of nostalgia are caused by being motivated more strongly than normal by the archetype of the mother. This might occur because of insecurity experienced in infancy when the mother fails to attend to the child's emotional needs (Peters, 1985).

The *persona* is another archetype related to the self. While the self is the true, private personality, the persona is the somewhat false social "mask" that we wear in public. *Mandalas*, circular paintings found in cultures throughout the world, represent complete congruence of the self and the persona (Musick, 1976). According to Jung, the persona and self of a psychologically healthy individual are fairly congruent. Incongruence between the self and the persona is the theme of the movie *Zelig*, in which Woody Allen plays a human chameleon who alters his persona—and even his physical appearance—to suit the people he is with. This syndrome, in which people too easily adapt a persona that will appeal to those around them, is often observed by psychotherapists in their clients (Moses, 1989).

Jung also distinguished between the *anima*, the feminine archetype in men, and the *animus*, the masculine archetype in women. According to Jung, a psychologically healthy person, whether female or male, must maintain a balance between masculinity and femininity. A "macho" male who acts tough and rarely expresses tender emotions would be unhealthy, as would a "prissy" female who acts passive and has little control over her emotions.

Jung even contributed to our everyday language by distinguishing between two personality types. **Extraverts** are socially outgoing and pay more attention to the surrounding environment; **introverts** are socially reserved and pay more attention to their private mental experiences. Jung applied this concept in his own life, viewing Freud as an extravert and Adler as an introvert (Monte, 1980).

Psychoanalytic Assessment of Personality

A century ago, Sir Arthur Conan Doyle popularized the use of handwriting analysis, or *graphology*, by having his fictional detective Sherlock Holmes use it to solve crimes. Graphology was an ancestor of psychoanalytic personality tests. Graphologists claim that features of one's handwriting, such as the size, shape, and slant of letters, reveal aspects of one's personality. Graphology is based on the assumption that, because all children in a given culture learn to form written letters and words the same way, any deviations from the original prototypes reflect, in part, one's distinctive personality.

Though raters can match, at a higher-than-chance level, persons they know with graphological reports of those persons (Nevo, 1989), research findings have questioned the practical usefulness of the technique (Peeples, 1990). A major problem with graphology is that it is subject to the Barnum effect, because people will accept vague, generalized graphological descriptions as accurate portrayals of their personalities (McKelvie, 1990). Given the lack of experimental evidence in support of graphology,

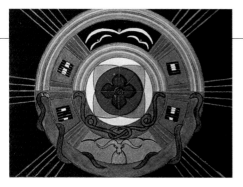 

The Mandala
Balanced, circular paintings such as these have been found in cultures throughout history and throughout the world. Jung claimed that this showed the influence of the archetype of the self, which symbolizes unity and wholeness.

few psychologists today use it to assess personality. Graphology has the same rationale as modern psychoanalytic assessment techniques, which are called **projective tests.** They are based on the assumption that we will "project" our repressed feelings and conflicts onto ambiguous stimuli. Today the most popular projective tests are the *Rorschach test* and the *Thematic Apperception Test*.

projective test
A Freudian personality test based on the assumption that individuals project their unconscious feelings when responding to ambiguous stimuli.

The Rorschach Test

Have you ever seen animal shapes in cloud formations? Have you ever argued about images in abstract paintings? If so, you will have some appreciation for the *Rorschach test*, which asks subjects to report what they see in inkblots. This technique was used centuries ago by Leonardo da Vinci, who evaluated the creativity of young artists by having them create meaningful forms from ambiguous figures (Kaplan & Saccuzzo, 1982). The Rorschach test was introduced in 1921 by the Swiss psychiatrist Hermann Rorschach (1884–1922), who died before he was able to conduct much research with it. The test consists of ten bilaterally symmetrical inkblots. Some of the inkblots are in black and white, and the others include colors.

The Rorschach Test
The basic assumption of the Rorschach test is that what we report seeing in a series of inkblots will reveal our unconscious motives and conflicts.

In responding to the inkblots, the person tells what she or he sees in each one and then reports the features of the inkblot that prompted the response. After scoring each response, based on formal criteria, the examiner uses clinical judgment and one of several available scoring systems to write a profile of the person's motives and conflicts. Such profiles have been used for purposes as diverse as diagnosing psychological disorders (Hilsenroth et al., 1993) and understanding the motivation of clowns, actors, and comedians (Fisher & Fisher, 1981). A published review of studies of the Rorschach test found that it has moderately high validity (Parker, 1983). This makes it an adequate, though not outstanding, personality test.

The Thematic Apperception Test

The *Thematic Apperception Test (TAT)* was created by the American psychoanalyst Henry Murray and his associate Christiana Morgan (Morgan & Murray, 1935). The TAT consists of one blank card and nineteen cards containing black-and-white pictures of people in ambiguous situations. The examiner asks several questions about each one. What is happening in the card? What events led up to that situation? Who are the people in the card? How do they feel? How does the situation turn out? Murray assumed that subjects' responses would reveal their most important needs, such as the need for sex, power, achievement, or affiliation. The TAT is a moderately good predictor of real-life achievement, such as career success (Spangler, 1992). The TAT has also been used to measure changes in the use of defense mechanisms as a result of psychotherapy, as in a study in which 90 subjects responded to TAT cards before and after 15 months of therapy. The results showed an association between a reduction in the use of defense mechanisms as revealed by the TAT and a reduction in psychological symptoms (Cramer & Blatt, 1990). Though the TAT may be too limited to provide general personality profiles, some psychotherapists find that it is useful in eliciting clues about a client's motives and attitudes that might not be elicited in conversations during therapy sessions (Vane, 1981).

Hermann Rorschach (1884–1922)
"The [ink-blot] test often indicates the presence of latent schizophrenia, neuroses which are barely perceptible clinically, and constitutional mood trends."

Salvador Dalí
The surrealistic style of Salvador Dalí, which has a kinship with the psychoanalytic approach to personality, is an attempt to portray images that would normally emerge from the unconscious mind during dreaming.

Status of the Psychoanalytic Approach

Of all the psychoanalytic theories of personality, Freud's has been the most influential, but it has received limited support for its concepts (Fisher & Greenberg, 1985). As described in chapter 6, there is substantial evidence demonstrating the effect of unconscious processes on human behavior (Dixon & Henley, 1991). There is also support for the Freudian view of repression from research showing that people are less likely to recall emotionally unpleasant personal experiences (Hansen & Hansen, 1988).

In contrast, there has been little support for some of Freud's other concepts. Consider his concept of Thanatos, which assumes that we have an unconscious desire to harm ourselves. Though there is evidence that we can harm ourselves by engaging in self-defeating behaviors, there is no evidence that we are motivated by an instinct to engage in deliberate self-destructiveness (Baumeister & Scher, 1988). Research has also failed to support the existence of the Oedipus complex (Daly & Wilson, 1990). In fact, Freud has been criticized for using the Oedipus complex to promote the belief that women are biologically inferior to men and that women have weaker superegos (Hare-Mustin, 1983). Adler and Horney saw the Oedipus complex as rooted in cultural, not biological, reality. Adler believed that women envied men's status and power, not their penises. And Horney even speculated that men share "womb envy," because they cannot give birth to children (Horney, 1926/1967).

Perhaps the greatest weakness of Freudian theory is that many of its terms refer to processes that are neither observable nor measurable. Who has ever seen an id? How can we measure libido? As noted in chapter 2, we cannot conduct experiments on concepts that are not operationally defined.

Despite the limited support for certain psychoanalytic concepts, the psychoanalytic approach has contributed to our understanding of personality. It has revealed that much of our behavior is governed by motives of which we are unaware, as revealed in dreams, and it has stimulated interest in studying sexual behavior and sexual development. It has demonstrated the importance of early childhood experiences, such as infant attachment, it has contributed to the emergence of formal psychological therapies, and it has inspired psychosomatic research, which looks at the effects of psychological factors on illness. It also has influenced the works of artists, writers, and filmmakers. These influences are evident throughout this book.

Adler's theory of personality has influenced cognitive psychology and humanistic psychology through its emphasis on the importance of our subjective experiences of reality. His concept of a style of life that reflects our striving for superiority has an important descendant in the current interest in *Type A behavior*, which is discussed at length in chapter 16 as a possible factor in coronary heart disease. Type A behavior is marked by hostility, competitiveness, and compulsive activity. Research indicates that, in keeping with Adler's theory, a person who exhibits Type A behavior may be combatting feelings of inferiority (Cooney & Zeichner, 1985). In fact, Meyer Friedman, the cardiologist who first identified the Type A behavior pattern in his patients, reported: "About 70 percent of our sample said they received inadequate parental love and then tried to compensate by being aggressive and overcompetitive" ("Type A," 1984, p. 109).

Adler's theory has also influenced the development of the humanistic theory of personality, whose cofounders—including Rollo May, Carl Rogers, and Abraham Maslow—studied with him and gave credit to him for inspiring their own views. Among the Adlerian concepts that impressed humanistic psychologists, the most influential were the concepts of social interest, guiding fiction, and style of life (Ansbacher, 1990).

And what of Jung's theory? Jung's concept of personality types has received research support. One study compared the styles of extraverted painters and introverted painters. Extraverted painters tended to use realistic styles, reflecting their greater attention to the external environment. In contrast, introverted painters tended to use abstract styles, reflecting their greater attention to private mental experience (Loomis & Saltz, 1984). Additional research support for the concepts of introversion and extraversion is discussed later in this chapter.

Jung's concept of the archetype has been criticized because it violates known mechanisms of inheritance in its assumption that memories can be inherited. Nonetheless, research findings support the possibility that something at least akin to archetypes affects human behavior (Rosen et al., 1991). Evidence for this comes from research, explained in chapter 14, showing that we have an inborn predisposition to develop phobias of snakes, heights, and other situations that were dangerous to our prehistoric ancestors. Thus, what Jung called archetypes might be inborn behavioral tendencies rather than inherited memories.

THE DISPOSITIONAL APPROACH

Personality theorists have traditionally assumed that personality is stable over time and consistent across situations. The *dispositional approach* to personality attributes this apparent stability and consistency to relatively enduring personal characteristics called *types* and *traits*.

Type Theories

In his book *Characters*, the Greek philosopher Theophrastus (ca. 372–ca. 287 B.C.) wondered why Greeks differed in personality despite sharing the same culture and geography. He concluded that personality differences arise from inborn predispositions to develop particular personality *types* dominated by a single characteristic. His list of personality types included the Flatterer, the Faultfinder, and the Tasteless Man. Like Theophrastus, some people rely on personality typing when they call certain individuals "nerds" or "jocks." Such people would expect different behavior from a "nerd" than from a "jock."

Today the most influential theory of personality types is Hans Eysenck's *three-factor theory* (Eysenck, 1990). Eysenck (b. 1916), a German psychologist, fled to England after refusing to become a member of Hitler's secret police. Eysenck used the statistical technique of factor analysis (discussed in chapter 10) in identifying three dimensions of personality. By measuring where a person falls on these dimensions, we can determine his or her personality type.

The dimension of *neuroticism* measures a person's level of stability/instability. Stable people are calm, even-tempered, and reliable; unstable people are moody, anxious, and unreliable. The dimension of *psychoticism* measures a person's level of tough-mindedness/tender-mindedness. Tough-minded people are hostile, ruthless, and insensitive, whereas tender-minded people are friendly, empathetic, and cooperative. Juvenile delinquents score high in psychoticism (Furnham & Thompson, 1991).

The dimension of *extraversion* measures a person's level of introversion/extraversion. This dimension, first identified by Jung, has stimulated the most research interest. For example, studies have shown that there are proportionately more introverts among expert chess players than in the general population. Because introverted chess champions may be uncomfortable in social situations, they prefer to avoid victory parties, press conferences, and autograph hounds. They may even feel compelled to leave the chess scene itself. In 1972 the American Bobby Fischer generated unprecedented interest in chess with his brilliant play in winning the World Chess Championship, only to retire into seclusion soon after (Olmo & Stevens, 1984).

Extraversion is associated with happiness. A study of 172 subjects who were asked to record their moods on a number of occasions found that high neuroticism and low extraversion were associated with more-negative, less-stable moods; and low neuroticism and high extraversion were associated with more-positive, more-stable moods (Williams, 1990). Figure 13.6 illustrates the interaction of the dimensions of introversion/extraversion and stability/instability. Note that the interaction of these two dimensions yields four personality types, which are the very ones identified by Hippocrates and Galen many centuries ago (Stelmack & Stalikas, 1991).

There is evidence that the dimensions in Eysenck's theory have a biological basis. For example, research on twins indicates that neuroticism, psychoticism, and extraver-

Hans Eysenck
"Studies of twins demonstrate the strong genetic determination of these [psychoticism, extraversion, and neuroticism] and many other personality factors."

(a)

(b)

(c)

Personality Types
Many movie and television comedies have portrayed the stereotypical personality type known as the "nerd." These include (*a*) Jerry Lewis in several movies, (*b*) Gilda Radner and Bill Murray on "Saturday Night Live," and (*c*) Jaleel White, who plays Urkel on "Family Matters."

trait
A relatively enduring, cross-situationally consistent personality characteristic that is inferred from a person's behavior.

Gordon Allport (1897–1967)
"Important—indeed central—to my theoretical position is my own particular conception of 'trait.'"

Cardinal Traits
Gordon Allport would note that Mother Theresa, who has spent her life helping the poor, exemplifies the cardinal trait of altruism.

sion have a genetic basis. Heredity accounts for half of the variability in these dimensions among people (Eysenck, 1990). Heredity might explain why introverts are more physiologically reactive than extraverts are (Stelmack, 1990). This might, in turn, explain behavioral differences between introverts and extraverts. Because introverts are more physiologically arousable, they may condition easier. This might make introverts more socially inhibited, because they learn more easily to stop performing behaviors that have been punished.

Trait Theories

Instead of describing personality in terms of single types, trait theorists describe personality in terms of distinctive combinations of personal characteristics. A **trait** is a relatively enduring, cross-situationally consistent personality characteristic that is inferred from a person's behavior. Eysenck's theory can be viewed as either a type theory or a trait theory, because the personality types in his theory are products of the interaction of certain trait dimensions. The most influential trait theory has been that of Gordon Allport (1897–1967).

Early in his career, Allport had a brief meeting in Vienna with Sigmund Freud that convinced him that psychoanalysis was not the best approach to the study of personality. Confronted with a silent Freud, Allport broke the silence by describing a boy he had met on a train who had complained of dirty people and whose mother had acted annoyed at his behavior. Freud responded, "And was that little boy you?" Based on this meeting, Allport concluded that psychoanalysis was too concerned with psychic determinism—finding hidden motives for even the most mundane behaviors (Allport, 1967).

Allport began his research by identifying all the English words that refer to personal characteristics. In 1936 Allport and his colleague Henry Odbert, using an unabridged dictionary, counted almost 18,000 such words. By eliminating synonyms and words referring to relatively temporary states (such as "hungry"), they reduced the list to about 4,500 words. Allport then grouped the words into almost 200 clusters of related words, which became the original personality traits in his theory.

Allport distinguished three kinds of traits. *Cardinal traits* are similar to personality types, in that they affect every aspect of the person's life. For example, altruism is a cardinal trait in the personality of Mother Theresa. Because cardinal traits are rare, you probably know few people whose lives are governed by them. *Central traits* affect many aspects of our lives but do not have the pervasive influence of cardinal traits. When you refer to someone as kind, humorous, or conceited, you are usually referring to a central trait. The least important traits are *secondary traits*, because they affect relatively narrow aspects of our lives. Preferences for wearing cuffed pants, reading western novels, or eating chocolate ice cream reflect secondary traits.

Raymond Cattell, a native of England who spent most of his career in the United States, further refined the trait theory of personality. By using factor analysis, Cattell identified sixteen basic traits, which he called *source traits*. These traits became the basis of a widely used personality test that is described later in this chapter.

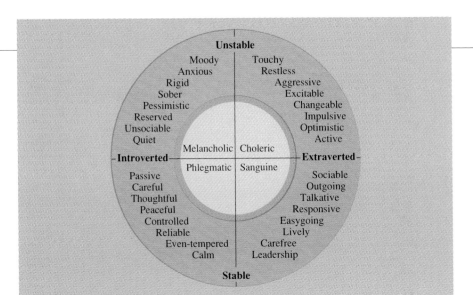

FIGURE 13.6

Eysenck's Primary Personality Dimensions
This drawing shows the interaction of Eysenck's personality dimensions of introversion/extraversion and stability/instability. Note that the four combinations of the dimensions produce the four temperaments identified by Hippocrates more than 2,000 years ago.

Dispositional Assessment of Personality

The dispositional assessment of personality relies on tests of personality types or traits. These are called *objective tests* or *inventories*, because they present subjects with straightforward statements rather than with ambiguous stimuli, as in projective tests. For example, the *Profile of Mood States*, an objective test, has shown that many elite athletes, including wheelchair athletes (Paulsen, French, & Sherrill, 1990), competitive child swimmers (Furst & Hardman, 1988), and professional women tennis players (Wughalter & Gondola, 1991), share a particular personality profile. Figure 13.7 presents an example of this "iceberg" profile.

Tests of Personality Types

One of the most popular objective tests is the *Myers-Briggs Type Indicator* (Briggs & Myers, 1943), which is unusual in that it is a dispositional test based on a psychoanalytic theory. The test assesses, among other personality characteristics, personality types derived from Jung's analytical theory of personality. The subject is presented with pairs of statements and selects the statement in each pair that is closest to how she or he usually acts or feels. A typical item would be, "At parties, do you (a) sometimes get bored or (b) always have fun?" An introvert would be more likely to select (a) and an extravert (b). The test has satisfactory validity (J. B. Murray, 1990) and has been used in a variety of research studies. One study found that teaching styles are related to specific personality profiles on the test (McCutcheon, Schmidt, & Bolden, 1991).

Tests of Personality Traits

The most widely used of all personality tests is the *Minnesota Multiphasic Personality Inventory (MMPI)*, which measures personality traits. The MMPI was developed at the University of Minnesota by psychologist Starke R. Hathaway and psychiatrist John C. McKinley (1943) to diagnose psychological disorders. Hathaway and McKinley used the *empirical method* of test construction, which retains only those questions that discriminate between people who differ on the characteristics of interest. Hathaway and McKinley collected 1,000 statements, which they administered to 700 people, including nonpatients, medical patients, and psychiatric patients. The subjects responded "True," "False," or "Cannot Say" to each statement, depending on whether it was true of them. Hathaway and McKinley kept those statements that tended to be answered the same way by people with particular psychiatric disorders. For example, they included the statement "Nothing in the newspaper interests me except the comics" solely because significantly more depressed people than nondepressed people responded "True" to that statement (Holden, 1986b).

FIGURE 13.7

The "Iceberg Profile"
Studies using the objective personality test called the Profile of Mood States have consistently found that elite athletes share an iceberg-shaped personality profile. They score higher than average on personal vigor, while scoring below average on negative characteristics: tension (anxiety), depression, anger, fatigue, and confusion. Thus, elite athletes appear to be psychologically healthier than the average person. The graph shows the personality profiles of world-class rowers, wrestlers, and runners (milers and marathoners).

REPRINTED WITH PERMISSION FROM PSYCHOLOGY TODAY MAGAZINE. Copyright © 1980 (Sussex Publishers, Inc.).

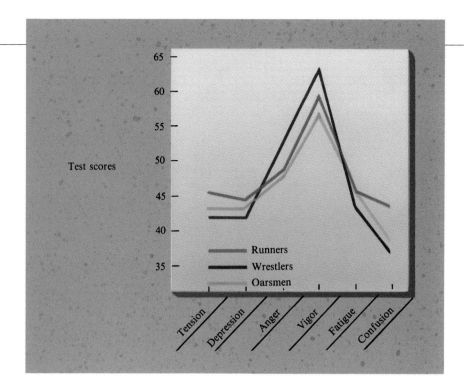

Because trait tests constructed using the empirical method may include some items that seem silly or unrelated to the test's purpose, they have been easy targets for satirical commentary. Art Buchwald, the political columnist-humorist, even created his own personality test with absurd true-false statements such as "I was an imaginary playmate" and "I believe I smell as good as most people" (Vance, 1965). Yet if either of those statements discriminated between persons with a particular psychiatric disorder and persons without it, the statement would be acceptable for inclusion in the MMPI.

As shown in table 13.2, the MMPI has ten clinical scales that measure important personality traits. For example, *hypochondriasis* measures concern with bodily functions and symptoms, and *paranoia* measures suspiciousness and delusions of persecution. The MMPI also has four *validity scales* that test for evasiveness, defensiveness, lying to look good, and faking to look bad. For example, the Lie scale contains statements that describe common human failings to which almost all people respond "True." So, a person who responded "False" to statements such as "I sometimes have violent thoughts" might be lying to create a good impression.

Psychologists commonly use the MMPI to screen applicants for positions in which people with serious psychological disorders might be dangerous, such as police officers or nuclear power plant operators. The MMPI has proved to be a valid means of diagnosing psychological disorders (Parker, Hanson, & Hunsley, 1988). But researchers have found that more recently it has diagnosed a higher proportion of people as psychologically disordered than it did when it was first adopted. Did this mean that more people have psychological disorders now than in the past? Or did it mean that the MMPI's norms were outdated? The latter seemed to be the case. As one critic noted a decade ago, "Whoever takes the MMPI today is being compared with the way a man or woman from Minnesota endorsed those items in the late 1930s and early 1940s" (Herbert 1983a, p. 228).

Because of this, the MMPI was restandardized in the 1980s to avoid comparing people today with the narrow segment of society that served as the standardization group half a century ago—people from farms and small towns with an eighth-grade education

TABLE 13.2	Scales of the MMPI
Scales	**Content**
Clinical Scales	
Hypochondriasis	Items identifying people who are overly concerned with bodily functions and symptoms of physical illness
Depression	Items identifying people who feel hopeless and who experience slowing of thought and action
Hysteria	Items identifying people who avoid problems by developing mental or physical symptoms
Psychopathic deviate	Items identifying people who disregard accepted standards of behavior and have shallow emotional relationships
Masculinity-femininity	Items identifying people with stereotypically male or female interests
Paranoia	Items identifying people with delusions of grandeur or persecution who also exhibit pervasive suspiciousness
Psychasthenia	Items identifying people who feel guilt, worry, and anxiety and who have obsessions and compulsions
Schizophrenia	Items identifying people who exhibit social withdrawal, delusional thoughts, and hallucinations
Hypomania	Items identifying people who are overactive, easily excited, and recklessly impulsive
Social introversion	Items identifying people who are emotionally inhibited and socially shy
Validity Scales	
Cannot say	Items that are not answered, which may indicate evasiveness
Lie	Items indicating an attempt to make a positive impression
Frequency	Items involving responses that are rarely given by normal people, which may indicate an attempt to seem abnormal
Correction	Items revealing a tendency to respond defensively in admitting personal problems or shortcomings

Source: Data from Starke R. Hathaway and John C. McKinley, *Minnesota Multiphasic Personality Inventory* (MMPI), University of Minnesota Press, 1943.

and an average age of 35 years (Adler, 1989). The revised MMPI (the MMPI-2) has added, deleted, or changed many statements. It also has new norms based on a more representative sample of the American population in regard to age, sex, ethnic background, educational level, and region of the country. This makes the MMPI-2, though still imperfect, an improvement over the MMPI (Helmes & Reddon, 1993).

Early critiques of the MMPI-2 show a diversity of opinions, with some experts stressing its weaknesses (Duckworth, 1991) and others its strengths (Graham, 1991). Empirical studies of the MMPI-2 have produced initially favorable findings. Despite the changes in its content, the MMPI-2 produces profiles comparable to those of the MMPI (Ben-Porath & Butcher, 1989; Munley & Zarantonello, 1990).

Another popular test for assessing personality traits is the *16 Personality Factor Questionnaire (16 PF)*, which measures the sixteen source traits identified by Raymond Cattell (1949). Psychologists typically use the 16 PF for general personality testing rather than for diagnosing psychological disorders. The 16 PF contains 187 multiple-choice statements. A typical item would be "I feel mature in most things: (a) True, (b) Uncertain, (c) False." The person's scores on the source traits are plotted on a graph to provide a personality profile, which may be used by employers or career counselors to determine whether the profile is similar to those of people who have been successful in particular professions. The 16 PF has been useful in a variety of applications. For example, it has successfully predicted the likelihood of driving accidents among young adult males in Finland (Hilakivi et al., 1989). Figure 13.8 presents an example of a 16 PF profile.

Status of the Dispositional Approach

Though the dispositional approach to personality has been useful in *describing* personality differences, it is less successful in *explaining* those differences. Suppose that the results of testing with the Myers-Briggs Type Indicator reveal that one of your friends is an "extravert." Someone might ask, "Why is she an extravert?" You might respond,

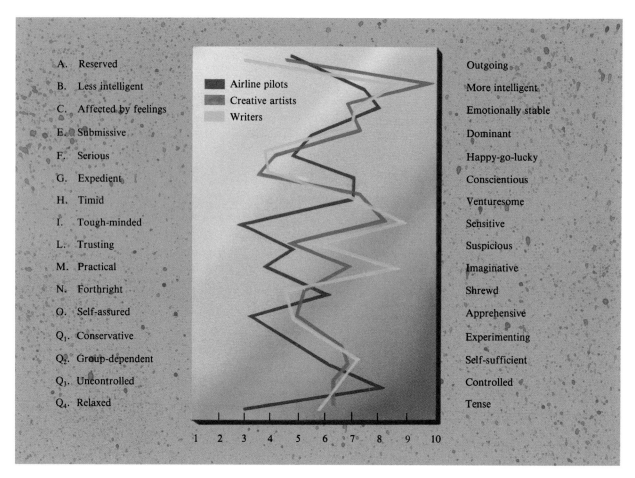

	Airline pilots										
Creative artists											
Writers											

A.	Reserved											Outgoing
B.	Less intelligent											More intelligent
C.	Affected by feelings											Emotionally stable
E.	Submissive											Dominant
F.	Serious											Happy-go-lucky
G.	Expedient											Conscientious
H.	Timid											Venturesome
I.	Tough-minded											Sensitive
L.	Trusting											Suspicious
M.	Practical											Imaginative
N.	Forthright											Shrewd
O.	Self-assured											Apprehensive
Q₁.	Conservative											Experimenting
Q₂.	Group-dependent											Self-sufficient
Q₃.	Uncontrolled											Controlled
Q₄.	Relaxed											Tense

1 2 3 4 5 6 7 8 9 10

FIGURE 13.8

The 16 PF Test

This graph presents personality profiles of writers, creative artists, and airline pilots based on the sixteen personality traits in Cattell's 16 PF Test. The left-hand and right-hand columns present the opposite extremes of each trait. Average scores fall about equidistant between these extremes. Note the differences between the profile of airline pilots and the profiles of the other two groups.

"Because she likes to socialize." The person might then ask, "Why does she like to socialize?" To which you might reply, "Because she is an extravert." This circular reasoning would not explain why your friend is an extravert.

One of the few dispositional theories that tries to explain personality is Eysenck's three-factor theory. The existence of the three personality factors identified by Eysenck has been verified by other researchers (Zuckerman, Kuhlman, & Camac, 1988). The introversion/extraversion dimension has received especially strong research support. One of Eysenck's assumptions is that a person's degree of introversion/extraversion depends on his or her customary level of physiological reactivity. As noted earlier, introverts are more physiologically reactive to stimulation than are extraverts. As explained in chapter 11, we have a tendency to try to adopt a moderate level of arousal. This might explain why introverts avoid stimulation and extraverts seek it. For example, introverted students prefer to work in quieter conditions than do extraverted students. In one study, students were permitted to choose the level of noise they would hear while performing a memory task. Extraverted students chose more intense levels than did introverted students. Moreover, students who were permitted to choose their own noise levels performed better than did students who were assigned noise levels higher or lower than they preferred (Geen, 1984).

In regard to trait theories, research has reduced the number of basic personality traits from Cattell's sixteen to five (Goldberg, 1993). *Extraversion* resembles Eysenck's factor of introversion/extraversion, and *neuroticism* resembles his factor of stability/instability. *Agreeableness* indicates whether a person is warm, good-natured, and cooperative. *Conscientiousness* indicates whether a person is ethical, reliable, and responsible. And *openness to experience* indicates whether a person is curious, imaginative, and interested in intellectual pursuits. Early research on the *five-factor theory* has found that psychological well-being is negatively correlated with neuroticism and positively correlated with extraversion, agreeableness, and conscientiousness. Moreover, we tend to rely on the five factors when we assess people in our everyday lives (McCrae & Costa, 1991), and their validity has been demonstrated across a variety of cultures (McCrae & John, 1992).

THE BEHAVIORAL APPROACH

Those who favor the *behavioral approach* to personality discount biological factors, unconscious influences, and dispositional traits. Instead, they stress the importance of learning and environmental factors.

Operant Conditioning Theory

To B. F. Skinner (1953), whose *operant conditioning theory* is described in chapter 7, there is nothing exceptional about personality. He saw no use for concepts invoking biological predispositions, unconscious motives, personality traits, and the like. What we call *personality*, in Skinner's view, is simply a person's unique pattern of behavior, tied to specific situations (Skinner, 1974). You might say that a fellow student has a "gregarious" personality because you have observed the student engage in behaviors such as initiating conversations, going to parties every weekend, and monopolizing the dormitory telephone.

According to Skinner, we are what we do. And what we do in a particular situation depends on our experiences in that situation and similar situations. We tend to engage in behaviors that have been positively or negatively reinforced and to avoid engaging in behaviors that have been punished or extinguished. Thus, Skinner might assume that a gregarious person has a history of receiving attention or anxiety relief for being socially outgoing in a variety of situations. In contrast, a shy person might have a history of being criticized or ignored in a variety of situations for being socially outgoing.

Social-Cognitive Theory

Social-cognitive theory builds a bridge between Skinner's strict behavioral approach and the cognitive approach to personality, which is discussed later in this chapter. Social-cognitive theory is similar to traditional behavioral theories in stressing the role of reinforcement and punishment in the development of personality. But it is different from traditional behavioral theories in arguing that behavior is affected by cognitive processes. That is, we are more than robotic responders to environmental stimuli—our interpretation of our own personal characteristics and environmental circumstances affects our behavior (Bandura, 1989).

Social-cognitive theory was developed by Albert Bandura (b. 1925), who was reared in Canada and served as president of the American Psychological Association in 1974. Other social-cognitive theories have been developed by Julian Rotter and Walter Mischel. Bandura's theory of personality grew out of his research on observational learning, which is described in chapter 7. According to Bandura, we learn many of our behavioral tendencies by observing other people receiving rewards or punishments for particular behaviors. For example, children learn altruistic behavior from adults who behave in a selfless manner.

Bandura's (1986) theory of personality also stresses the concept of **reciprocal determinism,** which reflects his belief that neither personal dispositions nor environmental factors can by themselves explain behavior. You will note that this differs from environmental determinism, which was favored by Skinner, and psychic determinism,

reciprocal determinism
Bandura's belief that personality traits, environmental factors, and overt behavior affect each other.

FIGURE 13.9

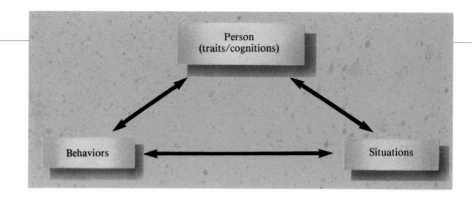

which was favored by Freud. Both of those concepts assume that the person is just a behavioral pawn. Environmental determinism assumes we are pawns controlled by external stimuli, and psychic determinism assumes we are pawns controlled by unconscious motives. Instead, as illustrated in figure 13.9, Bandura assumes that personality traits, environmental factors, and overt behavior affect one another.

Research studies have found that reciprocal determinism can explain many kinds of behaviors, such as those of leaders and followers (Sims & Manz, 1984). Reciprocal determinism even explains why depression is so difficult to overcome (Teichman & Teichman, 1990): A depressed person's negative thoughts and emotions might induce gloomy statements, sad facial expressions, and aloof social behavior. This might make other people avoid or respond negatively toward the depressed person. This social response would then promote continued negative thoughts and emotions in the depressed person, thereby completing a vicious cycle that might be difficult to break.

According to Bandura, one of the most important cognitive factors in reciprocal determinism is **self-efficacy.** This is the extent to which a person believes that she or he can perform behaviors that are necessary to bring about a desired outcome. Self-efficacy determines our choice of activities, our intensity of effort, and our persistence in the face of obstacles and unpleasant experiences, in part by reducing the anxiety that might interfere with engaging in the activity (Bandura, Reese, & Adams, 1982). Self-efficacy helps to explain cessation of smoking (Carey et al., 1989), adherence to physical exercise (Dzewaltowski, Noble, & Shaw, 1990), and students' performance in academic courses (Bandura, 1993). Depressed people tend to have feelings of low self-efficacy, perhaps because they feel a lack of control over the outcomes in their lives (Stanley & Maddux, 1986).

But what determines whether you will have a feeling of self-efficacy in a given situation? The first determinant is *previous success.* You will have a greater feeling of self-efficacy in your psychology course if you have done well in previous courses. The second determinant is *vicarious experience.* You will have a greater feeling of self-efficacy if you know other students who have succeeded in the course. The third determinant is *verbal persuasion.* You will have a greater feeling of self-efficacy if you give yourself pep talks or your advisor convinces you that you have the ability to do well in the course. And the fourth determinant is *physiological arousal.* You will have a greater feeling of self-efficacy if you are at an optimal level of arousal (discussed in chapter 11). If you are too aroused while making a classroom speech and notice your tense muscles, increased heart rate, and irregular breathing pattern, you might become so distracted that you mispronounce words or lose your place.

Behavioral Assessment of Personality

There are two main behavioral approaches to the assessment of personality. One approach examines overt behavior; the other examines cognitions that are closely connected to overt behavior.

self-efficacy
In Bandura's theory, a person's belief that he or she can perform behaviors that are necessary to bring about a desired outcome.

Assessment of Overt Behavior

Theorists who favor the examination of overt behavior believe that we should note what people actually do or say they would do in specific situations rather than simply record their responses to personality tests. During a *situational interview*, the interviewer asks the subject how he or she would act in specific situations. For example, instead of reporting that a potential employee is "conscientious," the interviewer might report that the person would probably not let shoddy products pass on the assembly line. Suppose you are given a situational interview after applying for a job as a summer camp counselor. The interviewer might ask how you would handle homesick campers, campers who refuse to participate in activities, or fellow counselors who use drugs. Research findings indicate that the situational interview is superior to traditional interviews in predicting how an employee will do on the job (Wright, Lichtenfels, & Pursell, 1989).

In *behavioral observation* the subject is observed in real or simulated conditions related to work, school, recreation, or other situations of interest. Behavioral observation is more likely to produce valid findings when it involves several observers who know the person and who on several occasions observe the person in the situation of interest (Moskowitz & Schwarz, 1982). Behavioral observation has been used to assess both children and adults with a variety of characteristics in a variety of circumstances. In regard to children, it has been used to study autism (Freeman & Ritvo, 1982), hyperactivity (Roberts, 1990), and social skills (Gresham, 1981). In regard to adults, it has been used to study consumer responses to humorous advertisements (Scott, Klein, & Bryant, 1990), sex differences in small-group interaction (Anderson & Blanchard, 1982), mental patients in a residential setting (Ward & Naster, 1991), and interactions of people with social anxiety (Glass & Arnkoff, 1989).

Behavioral Observation
Behavioral observation is useful in determining how individuals will behave in real-life situations. The responses of astronauts to isolation, weightlessness, and simulated emergencies help determine whether they will be permitted to take part in space flights.

Another form of behavioral assessment uses the *experience-sampling method*. The subject carries a portable device that beeps at random times, and on hearing the beep the person reports her or his experiences and behaviors at that time. This reveals relationships between specific situations and the person's thoughts, feelings, and behaviors (Hormuth, 1986). Several studies have demonstrated the practical usefulness of experience sampling. A study of elementary school children assessed their mental self-talk while they worked at their seats. Whenever the children heard a buzzer, they recorded their self-talk. The results showed that children who engaged in positive self-talk had higher academic achievement and more-appropriate social behavior, while children who engaged in negative self-talk had poorer academic achievement and less-appropriate social behavior (Manning, 1990). Of course, only experimental research could determine whether self-talk *causes* differences in academic achievement or social behavior.

Cognitive-Behavioral Assessment

As an example of the *cognitive-behavioral assessment* of personality, consider the *Internal-External Locus of Control Scale*, which was developed by Julian Rotter (1966) to measure what he calls the locus of control. Your *locus of control* is the degree to which you expect that you are in control of the outcomes of your behavior or that those outcomes are controlled by factors such as fate, luck, or chance (Rotter, 1990). In the former case you would have an internal locus of control, and in the latter case you would have an external locus of control. Rotter's concept of the locus of control has been so influential that his original study is one of the most frequently cited studies in the recent history of psychology (Sechrest, 1984).

The scale contains 29 pairs of statements, including 6 that serve to disguise the purpose of the test. A typical relevant pair would be similar to the following: "The more effort you expend, the more likely you are to succeed" and "Luck is more important than hard work in job advancement." Your responses would reveal whether you have an internal or an external locus of control. Just as your sense of self-efficacy might affect your behavior in everyday life, your locus of control might determine whether you try to exert control over real-life situations.

Julian Rotter
"Internal versus external control refers to the degree to which persons expect that a reinforcement or an outcome of their behavior is contingent on their own behavior or personal characteristics versus the degree to which persons expect that the reinforcement or outcome is a function of chance, luck, or fate, is under the control of powerful others, or is simply unpredictable."

The locus of control has been used in numerous studies. People with an internal locus of control are less fatalistic, which makes them more likely to seek medical attention for their physical symptoms (Strickland, 1989). An internal locus of control is also associated with better academic achievement, apparently because students with an internal locus of control work harder (Findley & Cooper, 1983). And drivers with an internal locus of control have fewer fatal accidents, perhaps because they are more cautious, attentive, and adept at avoiding dangerous situations (Montag & Comrey, 1987).

Status of the Behavioral Approach

B. F. Skinner's operant conditioning theory of personality has been praised for making psychologists more aware of the influence of learning and environmental factors on personality. But the theory has been criticized by Hans J. Eysenck (1988) for ignoring the influence of heredity on individual differences in personality. Skinner's theory has also been criticized for viewing the person as a passive responder to the environment and for failing to consider the importance of cognitive factors. The social-cognitive theorists have responded by recognizing the importance of cognitive processes, as well as environmental factors.

Bandura's concept of self-efficacy, in particular, has been supported by research findings in a variety of areas in addition to those mentioned earlier. One study found that a person's feeling of self-efficacy in mathematics affected his or her anxiety about mathematics and decision whether to major in it (Hackett, 1985). Another study found that people with feelings of self-efficacy for long-distance running are more likely to enter marathon races, train hard for those races, and continue running despite the pain and fatigue they experience (Okwumabua, 1985). Chapter 16 discusses the relationship of self-efficacy to the maintenance of health.

THE COGNITIVE APPROACH

Like the social-cognitive theory, the *cognitive approach* to personality recognizes the influence of thoughts on behavior. But this approach pays more attention to subjective experience and interpretation, and less attention to objective situations, than does the social-cognitive theory.

Personal-Construct Theory

The most influential cognitive theory of personality is the *personal-construct theory* of George Kelly (1905–1967). Kelly, who spent his childhood on a Kansas farm, was educated in both physics and psychology and worked as an engineer and a psychologist. His background in physics inspired his view of human beings as lay scientists who try to make sense of the world by continually testing and revising hypotheses about social reality. He called these hypotheses **personal constructs** (Kelly, 1963). According to Kelly, your characteristic pattern of personal constructs determines your personality. Thus, instead of being pawns in the hands of heredity, environment, or unconscious motives, we "construe" reality. That is, we actively interpret reality and guide our behavior according to the kind of reality we construe (Cantor, 1990).

Kelly believed that personal constructs are bipolar, meaning that they involve opposite extremes. So, people are rated on categories such as *shy/outgoing*, *safe/dangerous*, or *selfish/generous*. If you hold the personal construct that "strangers are dangerous," you might behave suspiciously toward strangers. Just as scientists retain hypotheses only if they prove accurate, we retain our personal constructs only as long as we believe they are accurate. If you found that elderly strangers are not dangerous, you might revise your personal construct to hold that "young strangers are dangerous." Thus, as a child develops, her or his system of personal constructs becomes increasingly more refined and complex.

Kelly called our ability to apply different personal constructs to a given situation **constructive alternativism**, which he divided into three phases: the *circumspection-preemption-control cycle*. During the *circumspection phase*, we evaluate constructs that

personal construct
A hypothesis about social reality that is held by a person.

constructive alternativism
The process by which a person applies personal constructs to a given situation.

might be relevant to a particular person or situation. During the *preemption phase*, we decide which construct is most relevant to the situation. And during the *control phase*, we follow a course of action based on the chosen construct.

As an example, suppose that someone comes to your door to ask for a contribution to a high school marching band. During the circumspection phase, you would evaluate and choose among several bipolar dimensions to determine which is relevant to the situation. Two might be honest/dishonest and worthy/unworthy. You would consider whether the person seems honest or dishonest and whether the charity seems worthy or unworthy. During the preemption phase, you might determine that the person is honest and that the charity is worthy. During the control phase, these constructs would make you more likely to contribute to the charity.

Personal-construct theory has been useful in research on many psychological topics. These include the study of psychological reactions during mourning (Viney, 1991), changes in the interactions of group members (Neimeyer & Merluzzi, 1982), and recidivism after treatment for a psychological disorder (Smith et al., 1991).

Cognitive Assessment of Personality

The chief technique for the cognitive assessment of personality is the *Role Construct Repertory Test (REP Test)*, which Kelly derived from his personal-construct theory. The REP Test presents the subject with sets of three persons whom the subject knows. The subject must specify a way in which two of the persons are similar to each other and different from the third. A psychologist might present an individual with sets of three persons who play roles of importance to the subject, such as "father," "best friend," and "disliked teacher." The subject then specifies a way in which two of the persons are similar to each other and different from the third. If you were the subject, you might report that your father and your best friend are both sincere, while your most disliked teacher is insincere.

The psychologist repeats this process with several sets of persons. A therapist would take your responses and determine how many constructs you used to distinguish between people. These constructs would be the ones you use to perceive social reality, such as "sincere/insincere." If you relied on too few constructs, you might be inflexible and view people according to stereotypes. In contrast, if you relied on too many constructs, you might be confused and perform poorly in social situations because you would have difficulty predicting people's behavior. In fact, the ability to maintain a relatively stable, yet flexible, set of personal constructs is crucial to psychological well-being (Button, 1983).

The REP Test has been put to good use in studies of personal constructs. It has helped career counselors in vocational planning (Neimeyer, 1989) and has identified the personal constructs we use when making judgments about older adults (Vacc, 1987). The REP Test has also found congruence between the constructs individuals apply to themselves and the constructs applied to them by their friends (Benesch & Page, 1989), and that marital satisfaction is related positively to similarities in the personal-construct systems held by spouses (Neimeyer, 1984). The REP Test has been used in market research to determine the personal constructs that consumers use in evaluating products (Jankowicz, 1987). And the REP Test has even been used to determine the effectiveness of educational programs. One study found that students who participated in a course in cross-cultural counseling developed a more differentiated set of personal constructs regarding members of other cultures (Neimeyer & Fukuyama, 1984).

Status of the Cognitive Approach

George Kelly contributed a method of psychotherapy called **fixed-role therapy,** which encourages clients to adopt roles that promote new, more adaptive constructs. It has been used successfully in treating people with social anxiety or social phobias (Beail & Parker, 1991). After Kelly's death, his theory, which has been called "a classic ahead of its time" (Rorer & Widiger, 1983), has been carried on chiefly by a small group of his

George Kelly (1905–1967)
"[Personal] constructs are used for prediction of things to come, and the world keeps rolling along and revealing these predictions to be either correct or misleading."

fixed-role therapy
A kind of therapy, derived from Kelly's personality theory, that encourages clients to adopt roles that promote new, more adaptive personal constructs.

followers. The theory became popular in Great Britain and Western Europe, and more recently in North America (Landfield, 1984), and stimulated renewed interest in cognitive factors in personality and influenced the development of social-cognitive theory.

The cognitive approach to personality has attracted psychologists who believe that conscious thoughts are more important than unconscious motives or environmental stimuli in determining behavior. But traditional behavioral theorists argue that thoughts do not *cause* behavior. And psychoanalytic theorists criticize cognitive theories for ignoring the irrational, emotional bases of behavior. Nonetheless, there is evidence that we construct our reality by testing hypotheses, observing behaviors related to the hypotheses, and then trying to reduce any incongruence between our hypotheses and the actual behaviors that we observe by revising our personal constructs (Agnew & Brown, 1989).

THE HUMANISTIC APPROACH

In the nineteenth century, the philosopher Jean-Jacques Rousseau praised the "noble savage"—the natural, unspoiled human being, uncorrupted by civilization. Rousseau believed that human beings have an inborn tendency to be good. The *humanistic approach* to personality, which emerged in the 1950s, is a descendant of Rousseau's belief, because most humanistic personality theorists believe that human beings are naturally good. This contrasts with psychoanalytic personality theorists, who believe that human beings are predisposed to be selfish and aggressive, and behavioral personality theorists, who believe that human beings are neither naturally good nor naturally evil.

The humanistic approach also contrasts with the psychoanalytic and behavioral approaches in accepting subjective mental experience as its subject matter. This makes the humanistic approach similar to the cognitive approach, though more concerned with emotional experience. Moreover, the humanistic approach assumes that we have free will, meaning that our actions are not all compelled by id impulses or environmental stimuli.

Self-Actualization Theory

Humanistic theories of personality have some of the flavor of the theories of Jung and Adler in that they view human beings as goal directed and governed by their subjective views of reality. The first humanistic theory of personality was that of Abraham Maslow (1970), whose theory of motivation is discussed in chapter 11. Maslow, reared in Brooklyn, was encouraged by his parents to attend law school. One day he found himself in a course in which he had no interest, and he bolted from the classroom.

Maslow never returned to law school. Instead, against his parents' wishes, he decided to pursue a career in psychology. This willingness to fulfill one's own needs, rather than those of other people, became a hallmark of humanistic theories of personality. As discussed in chapter 11, Maslow believed we have a need for **self-actualization,** the predisposition to try to reach our potentials. The concept of self-actualization is a descendant of Adler's concept of striving for superiority (Crandall, 1980).

But who is self-actualized? Maslow presented several candidates, including President Abraham Lincoln, psychologist William James, and humanitarian Eleanor Roosevelt. Table 13.3 presents a list of characteristics shared by self-actualized people. Maslow decided on these characteristics after testing, interviewing, or reading the works of individuals he considered self-actualized. Our psychological well-being is related, in part, to the extent to which we are self-actualized. For example, one of the reasons why extraverted people tend to be happier than other people is that they are more self-actualized than are more introverted people (Lester, 1990).

Self Theory

Carl Rogers (1902–1987) was born in Oak Park, Illinois, to a devoutly religious family. His religious upbringing led him to enter Union Theological Seminary in New York City. But Rogers left the seminary to pursue a career in psychology, eventually serving

self-actualization
In Maslow's theory, the individual's predisposition to try to fulfill her or his potentials.

"I'm haunted by potential."

Drawing by Cline; © 1992 The New Yorker Magazine, Inc.

as president of the American Psychological Association in 1946. His *self theory* of personality has its roots in the works of William James (Taylor, 1991) and Mary Whiton Calkins (Strunk, 1972).

Rogers pointed out that self-actualization requires acceptance of one's *self*, which is your answer to the question "Who are you?" But each of us experiences some incongruence between the self and personal experience. We may learn to deny our feelings, perhaps claiming that we are not angry, embarrassed, or sexually aroused even when we are. This might make us feel phony or, as Rogers would say, not genuine. This incongruence between the self and experience causes anxiety, which in turn motivates the person to reduce the incongruence by altering the self or reinterpreting the experience.

Note that this battle is similar to that between the id, ego, and superego, with the id seeking free expression of feelings, the superego seeking complete inhibition of them, and the ego trying to achieve a balance. Though complete congruence between the self and experience is impossible and would be maladaptive (we would have no motivation to improve the self if we did not experience some incongruence), people who have a great incongruence between the self and experience may develop psychological disorders. This is discussed in chapter 14.

How does incongruence between the self and experience develop? According to Rogers, children who do not receive *unconditional positive regard*—that is, complete acceptance—from their parents will develop incongruence by denying aspects of their experience. To gain acceptance from parents, a child might express thoughts, feelings, and behaviors that are acceptable to them. For example, a boy whose parents insist that "boys don't cry" may learn to deny his own painful physical and emotional experiences to gain parental approval. Such *conditions of worth* lead children to become rigid and anxious because of a failure to accept their experiences. Instead of becoming self-actualizing, such children may adopt a lifestyle of conformity and ingratiation (Baumeister, 1982).

Psychologically healthy people have congruence between the *actual self* (Rogers's *self*) and the *ideal self* (the person they would like to be). The more self-actualized the person, the less will be the incongruence between the person's actual self and ideal self and, as a result, the greater the person's self-esteem (Moretti & Higgins, 1990). People with a great incongruence between the actual self and the ideal self have more self-

Carl Rogers (1902–1987)
"It has been my experience that persons have a basically positive direction."

- Realistic orientation
- Self-acceptance and acceptance of others and the natural world as they are
- Spontaneity
- Problem-centered rather than self-centered
- Air of detachment and need for privacy
- Autonomous and independent
- Fresh rather than stereotyped appreciation of people and things
- Generally have had profound mystical or spiritual, though not necessarily religious, experiences
- Identification with humankind and a strong social interest
- Tendency to have strong intimate relationships with a few special, loved people rather than superficial relationships with many people
- Democratic values and attitudes
- No confusion of means with ends
- Philosophical rather than hostile sense of humor
- High degree of creativity
- Resistance to cultural conformity
- Transcendence of environment rather than always coping with it

Source: Data from A. H. Maslow, *The Farthest Reaches of Human Nature*, Viking Press, 1971.

The Actual Self and the Ideal Self
Picasso's 1932 painting *Girl before a Mirror* depicts the actual self and the ideal self.

doubts and fewer social skills. In contrast, people with a small incongruence between the actual self and the ideal self are more confident, socially poised, and able to deal with the problems of everyday life (Gough, Fioravanti, & Lazzari, 1983). A study of undergraduates found that as the congruence between their actual and their ideal selves increased, their feelings of happiness increased (Mikulincer & Peer-Goldin, 1991).

One way to protect the actual self is by *self-handicapping,* in which people claim that a task is very difficult or that factors beyond their control might contribute to their less-than-ideal behavior or performance (Leary & Shepperd, 1986). Thus, a student walking into class for a test might remind his classmates that the teacher is known for writing ambiguous questions or that the need to console a friend the night before prevented him from studying enough. Given these excuses, possible failure on the test would be less of a blow to the actual self. And if the student performs well on the test, the actual self would be elevated.

Humanistic Assessment of Personality

How do humanistic psychologists assess personality? Two of the main techniques are the *Personal Orientation Inventory* and the *Q-sort.*

The Personal Orientation Inventory

Psychologists who wish to assess self-actualization commonly use the *Personal Orientation Inventory (POI)* (Shostrom, 1962). The POI determines the degree to which a person's values and attitudes agree with those of Maslow's description of self-actualized people, such as being governed by one's own motives and principles. The inventory contains items that force the person to choose between options, such as (a) "Impressing others is most important" and (b) "Expressing myself is most important." A study of undergraduates found that those who scored higher on the POI were more likely to perform independently on a reasoning task in which others tried to influence their performance (Bordages, 1989).

The Q-Sort

The *Q-sort,* derived from Rogers's self theory, measures the degree of congruence between a person's actual self and her or his ideal self. If you took a Q-sort test, you would be given a pile of cards with a self-descriptive statement on each. A typical statement

Drawing by Modell; © 1985 The New Yorker Magazine, Inc.

"So whether I like you or not isn't what's important. What's important is that *you* like you."

might be "I feel comfortable with strangers." You would put the statements in several piles, ranging from a pile containing statements that are most characteristic of your actual self to a pile containing statements that are least characteristic of your actual self. You would then follow the same procedure for your ideal self, creating a second set of piles. The greater the degree of overlap between the two sets of piles, the greater the congruence between your actual self and your ideal self. Some psychotherapists use the Q-sort method to determine whether therapy has increased the congruence between a client's actual and ideal selves (Leaf et al., 1992).

Status of the Humanistic Approach

Research has produced mixed results in regard to Maslow's concept of self-actualization. There is mixed support for his assumption that self-actualization increases with age. A cross-sectional study (see chapter 4) of women aged 19 to 55 found an increase in their sense of autonomy. That is, the subjects became more motivated by their own feelings than by the influence of other people—a characteristic of self-actualized people (Hyman, 1988). But a cross-sectional study of faculty members aged 30 to 68 found that their self-actualization did not increase with age (Hawkins, Hawkins, & Ryan, 1989).

During the past decade, there has been relatively more research on the self, per se, than on self-actualization. In fact, the decade has seen the sprouting of a variety of "selves." A recent view of the self put forth by E. Tory Higgins (1987) considers the relationship between three selves: the *actual self*, the *ideal self*, and the *ought self*. Incongruence between the actual self (which represents the self in Rogers's theory) and the ideal self will make a person feel depressed. This incongruence is expressed in Woody Allen's remark, "My only regret in life is that I am not someone else." Incongruence between the actual self and the ought self (which is similar to Freud's ego ideal in representing beliefs about one's moral duties) will make a person feel anxious (Straumann & Higgins, 1988). We are motivated to alleviate our personal distress by reducing the incongruence between these selves (Higgins, 1990).

The humanistic approach has been praised for countering psychologists' tendency to study the negative aspects of human experience by encouraging them to study love, creativity, and other positive aspects of human experience. The humanistic approach has also renewed interest in studying conscious mental experience, which was the original subject matter of psychology a century ago (Singer & Kolligian, 1987). Moreover, the humanistic approach might best reflect popular views of personality. A survey of people in everyday life found that most people believe that others would know them best if others knew their private mental experiences rather than their overt behavior (Andersen & Ross, 1984). The humanistic approach has also contributed to the recent interest in self-development, including the emphasis on improving one's physical appearance. For example, improving one's physique through weight training enhances the self-esteem of both men (Tucker, 1982) and women (Trujillo, 1983).

But the humanistic approach has not escaped criticism. Critics accuse it of divorcing the person from both the environment and the unconscious mind and for failing to operationally define and experimentally test abstract concepts such as the concept of self-actualization (Daniels, 1982). And the assumption of the innate goodness of human beings has been called naive by the influential humanistic psychologist Rollo May (1982), who believes that innately good human beings would not have created the evil that the world has known.

Maslow and Rogers have been accused of unintentionally promoting selfishness by stressing the importance of self-actualization without placing an equal emphasis on social responsibility (Geller, 1982). They have even been accused of encouraging the alleged "me generation" of Americans that emerged in the 1980s, many of whose members were supposedly more motivated by self-interest than by an interest in contributing to the well-being of others. But this accusation is countered by research showing that people who have developed a positive self-regard tend to have a *greater* regard for others than do people with a negative self-regard (Epstein & Feist, 1988). Thus, we must be careful not to confuse self-regard with self-centeredness.

Though the humanistic approach to personality has received its share of criticism, Rogers has been widely praised for his contributions to the advancement of psychotherapy, which is discussed in chapter 15. Today, no single approach to personality dominates the others. Each makes a valuable contribution to our understanding of personality.

THINKING ABOUT *Psychology*

IS PERSONALITY CONSISTENT?

Do people behave consistently from one situation to another? Professors who write letters of recommendation for students assume that they do, when they refer to their students as "mature," "friendly," and "conscientious." But will a student who has been mature, friendly, and conscientious in college necessarily exhibit those traits in a job or in graduate school? Since the 1960s, the degree of cross-situational consistency in personality has been one of the most controversial issues in personality research (Siberstein, 1988).

PERSONALITY AS INCONSISTENT

The recent debate over the consistency of personality began in 1968 with the publication of a book by the social-cognitive theorist Walter Mischel. He reported that personality is much less consistent from one situation to another than was commonly believed. Mischel found that the correlation between any two behaviors presumed to represent the same underlying personality trait rarely exceeded a relatively low .30. This means that you could not predict with confidence whether a person who scored high on the trait of generosity would behave in a generous manner in a given situation. For example, a person who scored high on a test measuring generosity might donate to the Salvation Army but might not pick up the check in a restaurant—though both behaviors would presumably reflect the trait of generosity. Based on his review of research findings, Mischel concluded that our behavior is influenced more by the situations in which we find ourselves than by the personality characteristics that we possess.

Though Mischel stimulated the recent debate over the issue of personality consistency, the issue is not new. Forty years before Mischel published his findings, psychologists reported research showing that children's honesty was inconsistent across situations. A child might cheat on a test but not in an athletic event, or lie at school but not at home (Hartshorne & May, 1928).

If personality is inconsistent across situations, why do we perceive it to be consistent in our everyday lives? First, we might confuse the consistency of behavior in a given situation over time with the consistency of that behavior across different situations (Mischel & Peake, 1982). If a fellow student is consistently humorous in your psychology class, you might mistakenly infer that she is humorous at home, at parties, and in the dormitory. Second, we tend to avoid situations that are inconsistent with our personalities (Snyder, 1983). If you view yourself as "even-tempered," you may avoid situations that might make you lose your temper, such as a discussion about the abortion issue.

Third, our first impression of a person can make us discount later behavior that is inconsistent with it (Hayden & Mischel, 1976). If someone is friendly to you the first time you meet but is rude to you the next time you meet, you might say that he was "not himself" today. And fourth, our perception of cross-situational consistency in others might reflect a powerful situational factor—our presence in their environment (Lord, 1982). If others adapt their behavior to our presence, we may erroneously infer that they are consistent across situations.

PERSONALITY AS CONSISTENT

These attacks on cross-situational consistency have provoked responses from those who claim there is more cross-situational consistency than Mischel and his allies believe (Kenrick & Funder, 1988). First, individuals do show consistency on certain traits. But how do we know *which* traits? One way to find out is to ask. People who claim to be consistent on a given trait tend to exhibit behaviors reflecting that trait across situations (Zuckerman et al., 1988). In one study, students were asked to judge how consistent they were on the trait of friendliness. Those who claimed to be friendly across situations were, in fact, more consistently friendly than were students who did not claim to be—as verified by their peers, parents, and other observers (Bem & Allen, 1974).

Second, cross-situational consistency in behavior depends on whether a person is a *high self-monitor* or a *low self-monitor*. High self-monitors are concerned about how people perceive them and adapt their behaviors to fit specific situations, while low self-monitors are less concerned about how people perceive them and do not adapt their behaviors as much to fit specific situations. This means that low self-monitors show greater cross-situational consistency in their behaviors than do high self-monitors (Gangestad & Snyder, 1985).

Third, many of the studies that Mischel reviewed were guaranteed to find low cross-situational consistency, because they either correlated trait test scores with single instances of behaviors or correlated single instances of behaviors with each other. This would be like trying to predict your exact score on your next psychology test from your score on the Scholastic Assessment Test or from your score on a biology test. The prediction would most likely be wrong, because many factors influence your performance on any given academic test. Similarly, many factors other than a given personality trait influence your behavior in a given situation.

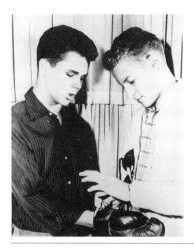

Personality Consistency
Perhaps the most controversial issue in personality research during the past two decades has been the extent to which personality is consistent from one situation to another. If you have watched "Leave It to Beaver," you know that Eddie Haskell is unbearably polite in the presence of Mr. and Mrs. Cleaver, but a wise guy in the presence of Wally and Beaver. Research findings have convinced some personality researchers that our behavior is influenced more by the situation we are in than by the personality characteristics we possess.

Psychologists have achieved greater success in demonstrating cross-situational consistency by using *behavioral aggregation*. In aggregating behaviors, you would observe a person's behavior across several situations. You would then determine how the person *typically*, but not necessarily *always*, behaves—much in the same way that you would find your average on several exams to determine your typical performance in a course. A "humorous" person would be humorous in many, but not all, situations. When we predict how a person will typically behave, instead of how that person will behave in a specific situation, the correlation between traits and behaviors becomes a relatively high .60 or more (Epstein & O'Brien, 1985).

Anatomy of a Classic Research Study:
Is Personality Consistent from One Situation to Another?

Rationale
When behavioral aggregation was applied to the Hartshorne and May (1928) study, the correlation between the trait of honesty and behaviors reflecting honesty rose considerably. Consider a similar study by George Dudycha (1936), which examined personality consistency in regard to punctuality.

Method
Dudycha noted that some people have reputations for always being punctual and others for always being late. He decided to study the phenomenon of punctuality in everyday life, rather than set up artificial situations in which punctuality would be measured. The subjects were 307 male and female undergraduates at Ripon College during the 1934–1935 academic year. Their punctuality was assessed on many occasions in six situations: 8 A.M. classes; dinnertime at a dining hall; conference appointments with professors; extracurricular activities (college band and college singers); church services; and entertainment programs (basketball, plays, and concerts). There were a total of 15,360 observations.

Results and Discussion
When correlations were made between any two of these situations, students were inconsistent. This seemed to indicate that the situation, not personality traits, accounted for punctuality. But, as in the Hartshorne and May (1928) study, when behavioral aggregation was applied to the Dudycha study, college students showed much greater cross-situational consistency in their punctuality. Thus, though personality traits might not predict our behavior in particular situations, they might predict our typical behavior across a variety of related situations.

In the past few years, the cross-situational consistency debate has died down. The trend is for researchers to agree that the best approach is to consider the interaction of the person, the situation, and the behavior in assessing cross-situational consistency (Diener & Larsen, 1984). Even Gordon Allport, the noted trait researcher, viewed human behavior as the product of those factors, with different traits aroused to different degrees by different situations—and not simply as the product of traits themselves (Zuroff, 1986). Of course, some situations (such as being in church) are so powerful that almost all people—regardless of their personalities—will behave the same way in them (Monson, Hesley, & Chernick, 1982).

Walter Mischel
"If human behavior is determined by many interacting variables—both in the person and in the environment—then a focus on any one of them is likely to lead to limited predictions and generalizations."

<hr />

SUMMARY

THE BIOPSYCHOLOGICAL APPROACH

Your personality is your unique, relatively consistent pattern of thoughts, feelings, and behaviors. Closely related to personality is temperament, a person's most characteristic emotional state. Sheldon's constitutional theory holds that different temperaments are associated with different physiques, or somatotypes. Research in behavioral genetics has found evidence of the hereditary basis of temperament and other aspects of personality.

THE PSYCHOANALYTIC APPROACH

Freud's psychosexual theory emphasizes the conflict between biological drives and sociocultural prohibitions in the development of personality. Freud divided the mind into conscious, preconscious, and unconscious levels. He also distinguished between the personality structures called the id, the ego, and the superego. According to Freud, we progress through oral, anal, phallic, latency, and genital stages of development. These stages depend on changes in the distribution of sexual energy. We may use defense mechanisms to protect us from being overwhelmed by anxiety.

Freud's intellectual descendants altered his theory, generally downplaying the importance of sexuality and emphasizing the importance of social relationships. Alfred Adler's theory of individual psychology assumes that personality develops from our attempts to overcome early feelings of inferiority. Carl Jung's theory of analytical psychology assumes that we are influenced by both a personal unconscious and the archetypes in a collective unconscious. Neo-Freudians such as Karen Horney, Erich Fromm, Harry Stack Sullivan, and Erik Erikson have made further changes in Freud's theory. In assessing personality, Freudians may use the Rorschach test and the Thematic Apperception Test to uncover unconscious motives and conflicts.

THE DISPOSITIONAL APPROACH

The dispositional approach to personality attributes the consistency we see in personality to relatively enduring personality attributes. Hans Eysenck's three-factor theory sees personality as dependent on the interaction of three dimensions: stability/instability, tough-minded/tender-minded, and introversion/extraversion. In his trait theory of personality, Gordon Allport distinguished three kinds of traits: cardinal traits, central traits, and secondary traits. Raymond Cattell, in his trait theory, identified sixteen source traits. Personality types are measured by tests such as the Myers-Briggs Type Indicator, and personality traits are measured by tests such as the MMPI or the 16 PF.

THE BEHAVIORAL APPROACH

B. F. Skinner's operant conditioning theory assumes that what we call personality is simply a person's unique pattern of behavior. Albert Bandura's social-cognitive theory argues that cognitive processes influence behavior. His concept of reciprocal determinism points out the mutual influence of personality characteristics, overt behaviors, and environmental factors. One of the most important personality characteristics is self-efficacy, the extent to which a person believes that she or he can perform behaviors that are necessary to bring about a desired outcome. Behavioral assessment is accomplished through behavioral observation, the situational interview, and the experience-sampling method. Julian Rotter's Internal-External Locus of Control Scale is one of the main cognitive-behavioral assessment techniques.

THE COGNITIVE APPROACH

The most influential cognitive theory of personality is George Kelly's personal-construct theory. Kelly assumed that we continually test hypotheses about social reality. These hypotheses are called personal constructs. We alter our personal constructs through the process of constructive alternativism. The person's unique pattern of personal constructs is measured by the Role Construct Repertory Test.

THE HUMANISTIC APPROACH

Abraham Maslow's self-actualization theory is based on his hierarchy of needs. He assumes that we have a need to develop all of our potentials. Maslow identified the characteristics of eminent people whom he believed were self-actualized. Carl Rogers's self theory holds that psychological well-being depends on the congruence between one's self and one's experience. Other researchers point to the importance of congruence between the actual self, the ideal self, and the ought self. Self-actualization is measured by the Personal Orientation Inventory. Congruence between the actual self and the ideal self is measured by using the Q-sort.

THINKING ABOUT PSYCHOLOGY: IS PERSONALITY CONSISTENT?

In 1968 Walter Mischel stimulated controversy by claiming that situations are more important determinants of behavior than are personality traits. He based this conclusion on studies finding that individuals' behavior is not consistent across different situations. Researchers have spent the past two decades debating whether personality is consistent. The conclusion appears to be that personality is neither as inconsistent as Mischel originally claimed nor as consistent as personality theorists had previously claimed. Our behavior is the product of the interaction between personal characteristics and environmental situations. In some cases, powerful personality characteristics dominate environmental situations. In other cases, powerful environmental situations dominate personality characteristics.

IMPORTANT CONCEPTS

RECOMMENDED READINGS

FOR GENERAL WORKS ON PERSONALITY

Craik, K. H., Hogan, R. T., & Wolfe, R. N. (Eds.). (1993). *Fifty years of personality psychology.* New York: Plenum.

Hergenhahn, B. R. (1994). *An introduction to theories of personality* (4th ed.). Englewood Cliffs, NJ: Prentice Hall.

Hogan, R. (1986). What every student should know about personality psychology. In V. P. Makosky (Ed.), *The G. Stanley Hall Lecture Series* (Vol. 6, pp. 39–64). Washington, DC: American Psychological Association.

Kluckhohn, C., Murray, H. A., & Schneider, D. M. (Eds.). (1961). *Personality in nature, society, and culture.* New York: Knopf.

Liebert, R. M., & Spiegler, M. D. (1993). *Personality: Strategies and issues* (7th ed.). Belmont, CA: Brooks/Cole.

Megargee, E. I. (Ed.). (1991). *Personality assessment in America.* Hillsdale, NJ: Erlbaum.

Valsiner, J. (1989). *Human development and culture: The social nature of personality and its study.* New York: Free Press.

FOR MORE ON THE BIOPSYCHOLOGICAL APPROACH

Bates, J. E., & Wachs, T. D. (Eds.). (1994). *Temperament: The individual at the influence of biology and behavior.* Washington, DC: American Psychological Association.

Buss, A. H. (1988). *Personality: Evolutionary heritage and human distinctiveness.* Hillsdale, NJ: Erlbaum.

Eaves, L. J., Eysenck, H. J., & Martin, B. G. (1989). *Genes, culture, and personality.* San Diego: Academic Press.

Holden, C. (1987). The genetics of personality. *Science, 237,* 598–601.

Kagan, J., Snidman, N., Arcus, D., & Reznick, J. S. (1994). *Galen's prophecy: Temperament in human nature.* New York: Basic Books.

Kretschmer, E. (1926/1990). *Physique and character.* Birmingham, AL: Gryphon.

Loehlin, J. C. (1992). *Genes and environment in personality development.* Newbury Park, CA: Sage Publications.

Neubauer, P. B., & Neubauer, A. (1990). *Nature's thumbprint: The new genetics of personality.* Boston: Addison-Wesley.

Sheldon, W. H., & Stevens, S. S. (1942). *The varieties of temperament: A psychology of constitutional differences.* New York: Harper.

Stern, M. B. (1971). *Heads and headlines: The phrenological Fowlers.* Norman: University of Oklahoma Press.

Zuckerman, M. (1991). *Psychobiology of personality.* New York: Cambridge University Press.

FOR MORE ON THE PSYCHOANALYTIC APPROACH

Adler, A. (1956). *The individual psychology of Alfred Adler* (H. L. Ansbacher & R. R. Ansbacher, Eds.). New York: Harper Collins.

Aronow, E., Reznikoff, M., & Moreland, K. (1994). *The Rorschach technique: Content, interpretation, and application.* Boston: Allyn & Bacon.

Erikson, E. H. (1962). *Young man Luther: A study in psychoanalysis and history.* New York: W. W. Norton.

Fine, R. (1990). *The history of psychoanalysis.* New York: Crossroad.

Fisher, S., & Greenberg, R. P. (1985). *Scientific credibility of Freud's theories and therapy.* New York: Columbia University Press.

Freud, A. (1936/1966). *The ego and the mechanisms of defense.* Madison, CT: International Universities Press.

Freud, S. (1940/1969). *An outline of psychoanalysis.* New York: W. W. Norton.

Fromm, E. (1941). *Escape from freedom.* New York: Holt, Rinehart & Winston.

Hentschel, U. (Ed.). (1993). *The concept of defense mechanisms in contemporary psychology.* New York: Springer-Verlag.

Horney, K. (1939). *New ways in psychoanalysis.* New York: W. W. Norton.

Jung, C. G. (1958). *The undiscovered self.* New York: Mentor.

Lester, D. (1981). *The psychological basis of handwriting analysis: The relationship of handwriting to personality psychopathology.* Chicago: Nelson-Hall.

Meisel, M., & Lane, R. C. (Eds.). (1993). *A history of the Division of Psychoanalysis of the American Psychological Association.* Hillsdale, NJ: Erlbaum.

Sullivan, H. S. (1953). *The interpersonal theory of psychiatry.* New York: W. W. Norton.

FOR MORE ON THE DISPOSITIONAL APPROACH

Allport, G. W. (1955). *Becoming: Basic considerations for a psychology of personality.* New Haven, CT: Yale University Press.

Buss, A. H. (1989). Personality as traits. *American Psychologist, 44,* 1378–1388.

Cattell, R. B. (1973, July). Personality pinned down. *Psychology Today,* pp. 40–46.

Eysenck, H. J., & Eysenck, M. W. (1985). *Personality and individual differences.* New York: Plenum.

Graham, J. R. (1990). *MMPI-2: Assessing personality and psychopathology.* New York: Oxford University Press.

McCrae, R. R., & John, O. P. (1992). An introduction to the five-factor model and its applications. *Journal of Personality, 60,* 175–215.

Morgan, W. P. (1980, July). Test of champions: The iceberg profile.

Psychology Today, pp. 92–93, 97–99, 102, 108.

Theophrastus. (1909/1992). *The characters of Theophrastus.* Salem, NH: Ayer.

FOR MORE ON THE BEHAVIORAL APPROACH

Bandura, A. (1986). *Social foundations of thought and action: A social-cognitive theory.* Englewood Cliffs, NJ: Prentice Hall.

Bellack, A. S., & Hersen, M. (Ed.). (1988). *Behavioral assessment: A practical handbook.* New York: Pergamon.

Rotter, J. B. (1990). Internal versus external control of reinforcement: A case history of a variable. *American Psychologist, 45,* 489–493.

Schwarzer, R. (Ed.). (1992). *Self-efficacy: Thought control of action.* New York: Hemisphere.

Skinner, B. F. (1953). *Science and human behavior.* New York: Macmillan.

FOR MORE ON THE COGNITIVE APPROACH

Adams-Webber, J., & Mancuso, J. C. (Eds.). (1983). *Applications of personal construct theory.* New York: Academic Press.

Epting, F. R., & Landfield, A. W. (Eds.). (1985). *Anticipating personal construct psychology.* Lincoln: University of Nebraska Press.

Fransella, F., & Thomas, L. (Eds.). (1988). *Experimenting with personal construct psychology.* New York: Routledge & Kegan Paul.

Kelly, G. A. (1963). *A theory of personality: The psychology of personal constructs.* New York: W. W. Norton.

Neimeyer, R. A. (1985). *The development of personal construct psychology.* Lincoln: University of Nebraska Press.

FOR MORE ON THE HUMANISTIC APPROACH

Baumeister, R. F. (Ed.). (1993). *Self-esteem: The puzzle of low self-regard*. New York: Plenum.

Block, J., & Harrower, M. (Eds.). (1978). *The Q-sort method in personality assessment*. Palo Alto, CA: Consulting Psychologists Press.

Derlega, V. J., Metts, S., Petronio, S., & Margulis, S. T. (1993). *Self-disclosure*. Newbury Park, CA: Sage Publications.

Higgins, R. L., Snyder, C. R., & Berglas, S. (Eds.). (1990). *Self-handicapping: The paradox that isn't*. New York: Plenum.

Levin, J. D. (1992). *Theories of the self*. Bristol, PA: Hemisphere.

Marsella, A. J. (Ed.). (1985). *Culture and self: Asian and Western perspectives*. London: Tavistock.

Rogers, C. R. (1980). *A way of being*. Boston: Houghton Mifflin.

Snyder, M. (1986). *Public appearances—private realities: The psychology of self-monitoring*. New York: W. H. Freeman.

Strunk, O., Jr. (1972). The self-psychology of Mary Whiton Calkins. *Journal of the History of the Behavioral Sciences, 8,* 196–203.

Viney, L. (1969). Self—the history of a concept. *Journal of the History of the Behavioral Sciences, 5,* 349–359.

FOR MORE ON PERSONALITY CONSISTENCY

Epstein, S., & O'Brien, E. J. (1985). The person-situation debate in historical and current perspective. *Psychological Bulletin, 98,* 513–537.

Mischel, W. (1984). Convergences in the search for consistency. *American Psychologist, 39,* 351–364.

Ozer, D. J. (1986). *Consistency in personality*. New York: Springer-Verlag.

FOR MORE ON CONTRIBUTORS TO THE STUDY OF PERSONALITY

Alexander, F., Eisenstein, S., & Grotjahn, M. (Eds.). (1966). *Psychoanalytic pioneers*. New York.

Allport, G. W. (1967). Autobiography. In E. G. Boring & G. Lindzey (Eds.), *A history of psychology in autobiography* (Vol. 5, pp. 1–25). New York: Appleton-Century-Crofts.

Bjork, D. W. (1993). *B. F. Skinner: A life*. New York: Basic Books.

Coles, R. (1970). *Erik Erikson: The growth of his work*. Boston: Atlantic/Little, Brown.

Evans, R. I. (1989). *Albert Bandura: The man and his ideas—a dialogue*. New York: Praeger.

Eysenck, H. J. (1990). *Rebel with a cause: The autobiography of Hans Eysenck*. London: W. H. Allen.

Furumoto, L. (1980). Mary Whiton Calkins (1863–1930). *Psychology of Women Quarterly, 5,* 55–68.

Gay, P. (1988). *Freud: A life for our time*. New York: W. W. Norton.

Hoffman, E. (1988). *The right to be human: A biography of Abraham Maslow*. Los Angeles: Tarcher.

Jankowicz, A. D. (1987). Whatever became of George Kelly? *American Psychologist, 42,* 481–487.

Kirschenbaum, H. (1979). *On becoming Carl Rogers*. New York: Delacorte.

Knapp, G. P. (1989). *The art of living: Erich Fromm's life and works*. New York: Peter Lang.

Perry, H. S. (1982). *Psychiatrist of America: The life of Harry Stack Sullivan*. Cambridge, MA: Harvard University Press.

Quinn, S. (1987). *A mind of her own: The life of Karen Horney*. New York: Summit.

Rattner, J. (1983). *Alfred Adler*. New York: Frederick Ungar.

Stevens, A. (1990). *On Jung*. New York: Routledge.

Young-Bruehl, E. (1988). *Anna Freud*. New York: Summit.

CHAPTER 14

Vincent van Gogh
Self-Portrait Dedicated to Paul Gauguin
1888

PSYCHOLOGICAL DISORDERS

etween 1972 and 1978, a successful, civic-minded Chicago building contractor named John Wayne Gacy murdered 33 boys and young men and buried them under his house. After his capture, Gacy expressed no remorse and, instead, reported that his acts of cold-blooded murder had given him pleasure. Gacy's personal history indicated that he had an *antisocial personality disorder* (Darrach & Norris, 1984).

Following a pregame workout in April 1978, players on the Texas Rangers baseball team were shocked to find pitcher Roger Moret standing immobile, grasping a shower slipper in one hand and staring into his locker. Moret held the pose for almost an hour before being taken to a mental hospital, where he was diagnosed as having a psychological disorder called *catatonic schizophrenia* (Rabun, 1978).

On January 22, 1987, at a televised news conference, Pennsylvania treasurer R. Budd Dwyer committed suicide by putting the barrel of a pistol in his mouth and pulling the trigger. Dwyer had suffered from *major depression* after his conviction on charges of corruption (Cusick, 1987).

THE NATURE OF PSYCHOLOGICAL DISORDERS

Hardly a week goes by without the news media reporting instances of extreme psychological disorders such as these. But how do we determine whether a person has a psychological disorder? What are the causes of psychological disorders? And how are psychological disorders classified? Answers to these questions are provided by psychologists and others in the field of **psychopathology**—the study of psychological disorders.

Criteria for Psychological Disorders

psychopathology
The study of psychological disorders.

In the early 1980s, interviewers from the National Institute of Mental Health went door to door in Baltimore, St. Louis, and New Haven as part of the most ambitious survey ever done on the prevalence of psychological disorders in the United States. Their interviews with more than 10,000 persons found that about 20 percent of adult Americans have one or more psychological disorders (Robins et al., 1984). You probably know people whose patterns of moods, thoughts, and actions make you suspect that they, too, suffer from a psychological disorder. But what are the criteria for determining that a person has such a disorder? The main ones are *abnormality*, *maladaptiveness*, and *personal distress*.

Abnormality

Abnormal behavior deviates from the behavior of the "typical" person—the *norm*. A norm can be qualitative or quantitative. *Qualitatively* abnormal behavior deviates from culturally accepted standards, perhaps even seeming bizarre. A railroad conductor who announces train stops would be normal, while a passenger who announces train stops would be abnormal. *Quantitatively* abnormal behavior deviates from the statistical average. A woman who washes her hands three times a day would be normal, while a woman who washes her hands thirty times a day would be abnormal.

By itself, abnormality is not a sufficient criterion for determining the presence of a psychological disorder. If qualitative abnormality were sufficient, then people who achieve rare accomplishments, such as a Nobel prize winner, an Olympic decathlon champion, and even your student government president, would be considered psychologically disordered. And if quantitative abnormality were sufficient, then even a physician who washes her hands thirty times a day in the course of seeing patients would be considered psychologically disordered. Thus, the context in which "abnormal" behavior occurs must be considered before deciding that it is symptomatic of a psychological disorder.

Still another problem with using abnormality as the sole criterion in diagnosing psychological disorders is the possibility that nonconformists would be considered psychologically disordered solely for opposing the status quo. Should we view all artistic innovators and political dissidents as victims of psychological disorders?

Maladaptiveness

According to the criterion of *maladaptiveness*, you would have a psychological disorder if your behavior seriously disrupted your social, academic, or vocational life. As an example, consider a person with the psychological disorder called *agoraphobia*, characterized by the fear of being in public places. Such a person might be afraid to leave home, and might consequently alienate friends, fail in school, and lose a job. Similarly, a person who uses drugs or alcohol excessively would be considered psychologically disordered, because such behavior would interfere with everyday functioning. But maladaptive behavior is not always a sign of a psychological disorder. Though cramming for exams, failing to eat fruits and vegetables, and driving 90 miles an hour on a busy highway are maladaptive behaviors, they would not necessarily be symptomatic of a psychological disorder.

Personal Distress

The criterion of *personal distress* assumes that our subjective feeling of anxiety, depression, or another unpleasant emotion determines whether we have a psychological disorder. For example, until 1973 the American Psychiatric Association categorized homosexuality as a psychological disorder, primarily because it was considered both abnormal and maladaptive. Then, as the result of lobbying by homosexual rights groups and reconsideration by mental-health professionals (who found no link between homosexuality, per se, and any other psychological disorders), the American Psychiatric Association declared that a homosexual should be considered psychologically disordered only if she or he feels distressed at being a homosexual. This new disorder was called *ego-dystonic homosexuality*. Nonetheless, personal distress might not be a sufficient criterion for determining the presence of a psychological disorder (Widiger & Trull, 1991). Some people, like John Wayne Gacy, may have psychological disorders without feeling distressed by their own behavior.

Behavior that is abnormal, maladaptive, or personally distressing might indicate that a person has a psychological disorder. But there is no single point at which a person moves from being psychologically healthy to being psychologically disordered. Each of us varies on each of the criteria. Thus, there is a degree of subjectivity in even the best answers to the question of how abnormal, maladaptive, or personally distressing a person's behavior must be before we determine that he or she has a psychological disorder.

Viewpoints on Psychological Disorders

Even when psychologists agree on the presence of a particular psychological disorder, they may disagree on its causes. That is, they favor different *viewpoints* regarding the causes of psychological disorders. Since ancient times, people have tried to explain the unusual or distressing behavior patterns that we now call psychological disorders. Many ancient Greek authorities assumed that the gods inflicted psychological disorders on people to punish them for their misdeeds. But the Greek physician Hippocrates (ca. 460–ca. 377 B.C.) argued, instead, that psychological disorders had natural causes. As mentioned in chapter 13, Hippocrates believed that temperament depended on the relative amounts of fluids he called humors, which included blood, phlegm, black bile, and yellow bile. According to Hippocrates, and later the Greek physician Galen (A.D. ca. 130–ca. 200), imbalances in these humors caused psychological disorders. For example, depression was supposedly caused by an excess of "melancholer" (black bile

Does This Man Have a Psychological Disorder?
For three decades, the blind poet and musician "Moondog," whose real name was Louis Thomas Hardin, was a fixture on the streets of midtown Manhattan in New York City. Though Moondog certainly deviated from cultural norms, there was no evidence that his behavior was maladaptive. On the contrary, he made enough money to live on by playing homemade instruments and offering copies of his poetry to passersby. And there was no evidence that his behavior caused him personal distress. In fact, he claimed that truly distressed people were those who tried to adapt themselves to the demands of modern society.

from the spleen) in the brain (Maher & Maher, 1985). To this day, we call depressed people "melancholic."

Despite the efforts of Hippocrates and his followers, supernatural explanations existed alongside naturalistic ones throughout the Middle Ages and the Renaissance. Robert Burton's (1621) *Anatomy of Melancholy*, a classic book on the causes of depression, looked to supernatural causes (including God, the devil, or demons) and natural causes (including the planets, bad marriages, or inadequate diets). Until the nineteenth century, supernatural and natural explanations of psychological disorders vied for dominance.

The sixteenth and seventeenth centuries saw the beginning of opposition to the supernatural view of psychological disorders, which was led by religious authorities. In the late sixteenth century, the Spanish nun Teresa of Avila saved a group of other nuns from being punished as witches. The nuns had inexplicably begun yelling and jumping about with wild abandon, a phenomenon known as *tarantism* or *Saint Vitus's dance*. Teresa convinced the religious authorities that the nuns were not possessed but, rather, were "as if sick." That is, they were suffering from "mental illness."

The sixteenth-century Swiss physician Paracelsus (1493–1541) also rejected the supernatural viewpoint. Instead of attributing unusual behavior to demons, he attributed it to the moon. Paracelsus called the condition *lunacy* and the people who exhibited it *lunatics*. These terms were derived from the Latin word for "moon." Today, half of all college students believe that the full moon can make people behave abnormally. You probably have heard someone say, on an evening when people seem to be acting oddly, "There must be a full moon tonight." But, contrary to popular belief, the moon does not affect the incidence of crime, mental illness, or other abnormal behavior (Rotton & Kelly, 1985).

During the past two centuries, the growth of interest in naturalistic explanations has led scientists to reject supernatural explanations of psychological disorders. Current viewpoints on psychological disorders attribute them to natural factors. As shown in table 14.1, the viewpoints differ in the extent to which they attribute psychological disorders to biological, mental, or environmental factors.

Lunacy
Paracelsus claimed that the moon
could affect behavior, as shown in
this engraving depicting
"moonstruck" women.

The Biopsychological Viewpoint

A century ago, Sigmund Freud remarked, "In view of the intimate connection between things physical and mental, we may look forward to a day when paths of knowledge will be opened up leading from organic biology and chemistry to the field of neurotic phenomena" (Taulbee, 1983, p. 45). As a neurologist, Freud might have approved of the *biopsychological viewpoint*, which favors the study of the biological causes of psychological disorders.

Modern interest in the biological causes of psychological disorders was stimulated in the late nineteenth century when researchers discovered that a disorder called *general paresis*, marked by severe mental deterioration, was caused by infection with syphilis. Researchers in the nineteenth century also found that toxic chemicals, such as mercury, could induce psychological disorders. In fact, the Mad Hatter in *Alice in Wonderland* exhibits psychological symptoms caused by accidental ingestion of the mercury that was used in making felt hats. This was the origin of the phrase *mad as a hatter* (Broad, 1981). Today biopsychological researchers are especially interested in the role of heredity, brain damage, and brain chemistry in the development of psychological disorders.

The Psychoanalytic Viewpoint

The *psychoanalytic viewpoint*, originating in medicine, grew out of the biopsychological viewpoint. But instead of looking for underlying biological causes of psychological disorders, the psychoanalytic viewpoint looks for unconscious causes. As discussed in chapter 13, Sigmund Freud stressed the continual conflict between inborn biological drives, particularly sex, which demand expression, and the norms of society that inhibit their expression. Freud's belief was anticipated more than 2,000 years earlier by Plato, who saw the roots of psychological disorders in the constant battle between passion and reason (Maher & Maher, 1985). According to Freud, conflicts about sex and aggression can be repressed into the unconscious mind, which can lead to feelings of anxiety caused by pent-up sexual or aggressive energy. Freud claimed that we may gain partial relief of this anxiety by resorting to defense mechanisms (discussed in chapter 13). If our defense mechanisms are either inadequate or too rigid, we can develop psychological disorders.

Viewpoint	Causes of Psychological Disorders
Biopsychological	Inherited or acquired brain disorders involving imbalances in neurotransmitters or damage to brain structures
Psychoanalytic	Unconscious conflicts over impulses such as sex and aggression, originating in childhood
Behavioral	Reinforcement of inappropriate behaviors and punishment or extinction of appropriate behaviors
Cognitive	Irrational or maladaptive thinking about one's self, life events, and the world in general
Humanistic	Incongruence between one's actual self and public self as a consequence of trying to live up to the demands of others
Diathesis-Stress	A biological predisposition interacting with stressful life experiences

Both the biopsychological viewpoint and the psychoanalytic viewpoint support the so-called *medical model*, which assumes that disturbing behavior or unpleasant conscious experience is actually a symptom of underlying processes—whether located in the brain or in the unconscious mind. The medical model has contributed a medical vocabulary that is shared by both physicians and many mental-health professionals. This includes terms such as *cure, patient, treatment, diagnosis, mental illness,* and *mental hospital*.

The Behavioral Viewpoint

As discussed in previous chapters, the *behavioral viewpoint* arose in opposition to psychological viewpoints that looked for mental causes of behavior. Those who favor the behavioral viewpoint, such as the late B. F. Skinner, look to the environment and to the learning of maladaptive behaviors for the causes of psychological disorders. A psychological disorder may arise when a person is reinforced for inappropriate behavior or has appropriate behavior punished or extinguished. Social-cognitive theorists, such as Albert Bandura, would add that we may develop a psychological disorder by observing other people's behavior. For example, a person might develop a phobia (an unrealistic fear) of dogs after either being bitten by a dog or observing someone else being bitten by a dog.

Those who favor the behavioral viewpoint, with its emphasis on environmental factors, would also be more likely to consider the negative effects of socioeconomic conditions on psychological well-being. For example, poverty is a predisposing factor in a variety of psychological disorders. The results of a survey of residents of New Haven, Connecticut, found that poverty is associated with a higher risk of almost all psychological disorders. This holds true for young and old, men and women, and blacks and whites (Bruce, Takeuchi, & Leaf, 1991). Perhaps people who grow up in poverty are more likely to experience environments that promote the development of psychological disorders. Of course, this does not rule out the possibility that some people predisposed to develop psychological disorders have poor coping skills, which then leads them to remain in or drift into poverty; that is, their socioeconomic status might be a result of their disorder, not the cause of it.

The Cognitive Viewpoint

The Greek Stoic philosopher Epictetus (A.D. ca. 60–ca. 120) taught that "men are disturbed not by things, but by the views which they take of things." This is the central assumption of the *cognitive viewpoint*, which holds that psychological disorders arise from maladaptive ways of thinking about oneself and the world. George Kelly's personal-construct theory (discussed in chapter 13), the most elaborate cognitive theory of personality, looks to people's personal constructs to determine whether they have psychological disorders. People who fail to maintain a fairly stable, but flexible, set of personal constructs are more likely to suffer from psychological disorders (Button, 1983).

Many cognitive theorists assume that people with psychological disorders hold irrational beliefs that lead to emotional disturbances and maladaptive behaviors. Yet recent studies indicate that people with psychological disorders marked by high levels of anxiety or depression may think *more* rationally and objectively than other people

"Gordon has escaped into optimism."

Drawing by Weber; ©1983 The New Yorker Magazine, Inc.

about themselves and the world (Taylor & Brown, 1988). That is, people without psychological disorders may view the world optimistically, through "rose-colored glasses."

The Humanistic Viewpoint

As described in chapter 13, psychologists who favor the *humanistic viewpoint,* most notably Carl Rogers and Abraham Maslow, stress the importance of self-actualization, which is the fulfillment of one's potentials. Psychological disorders are the result of blocked self-actualization. This occurs when people fail to reach their potential, perhaps because others, especially their parents, discourage them from expressing their true desires, thoughts, and interests. This *conditional positive regard* may lead the person to develop a public self-image that is favorable to others but markedly different from his or her actual, private self. The distress caused by the failure to behave in accordance with one's own desires, thoughts, and interests can lead to the development of a psychological disorder.

The Diathesis-Stress Viewpoint

No single viewpoint provides an adequate explanation of psychological disorders. This has led to the emergence of the **diathesis-stress viewpoint,** which holds that we vary in our biological predispositions to develop psychological disorders (Fowles, 1992). Such a predisposition is called a *diathesis* and is determined, in part, by heredity. A person with a strong predisposition to develop psychological disorders may succumb to even relatively low levels of psychological stress. In contrast, a person with a weak predisposition to develop psychological disorders may resist even extremely high levels of psychological stress. Research findings in support of the diathesis-stress model indicate that social stress interacts with physiological predispositions to produce a variety of psychological disorders. These disorders include obsessive-compulsive disorder (Turner, Beidel, & Nathan, 1985), major depression (Monroe & Simons, 1991), bipolar disorder (Kestenbaum, 1982), and schizophrenia (Fowles, 1992). Each is discussed later in this chapter.

diathesis-stress viewpoint
The assumption that psychological disorders are consequences of the interaction of a biological, inherited predisposition (diathesis) and exposure to stressful life experiences.

Classification of Psychological Disorders

Over the centuries, authorities have distinguished a variety of psychological disorders, each characterized by its own set of symptoms. Hippocrates devised the first system for classifying psychological disorders; it included *mania* (overexcitement), *melancholia* (severe

Emil Kraepelin (1856–1926)
"Manic-depressive insanity . . .
includes on the one hand the whole
domain of so-called *periodic and circular
insanity* [and] on the other hand *simple
mania,* the greater part of the morbid
states termed *melancholia.* . . .
Dementia praecox consists of a series
of states, the common characteristic of
which is a peculiar destruction of the
internal connections of the psychic
personality."

neurosis
*A general category, no longer widely
used, that comprises psychological
disorders associated with maladaptive
attempts to deal with anxiety but with
relatively good contact with reality.*

psychosis
*A general category, no longer widely
used, that comprises severe psychological
disorders associated with thought
disturbances, bizarre behavior, severe
disruption of social relations, and
relatively poor contact with reality.*

depression), and *phrenitis* (disorganized thinking). In 1883 German psychiatrist Emil Kraepelin (1856–1926) devised the first modern classification system, combining Hippocrates' categories of mania and melancholia into a disorder called *manic depression* and renaming phrenitis *dementia praecox.* Today manic depression is called *bipolar disorder* and dementia praecox is called *schizophrenia.*

The DSM-IV

The most widely used system of classification of psychological disorders is the fourth edition of the *Diagnostic and Statistical Manual of Mental Disorders (DSM-IV),* which is published by the American Psychiatric Association. The DSM-IV, which was published in 1994, is a revised version of the DSM-III, which was published in 1980 (and revised in 1987 as the DSM-III-R) and preceded by the DSM-II in 1968 and the DSM-I in 1952. The DSM-IV provides a means of communication among mental-health practitioners, helps practitioners choose the best treatment for particular disorders, and offers a framework for research on the causes of disorders.

The DSM-I and the DSM-II, which were based on psychoanalytic theory, divided disorders into neuroses and psychoses. A **neurosis** involved anxiety, moderate disruption of social relations, and relatively good contact with reality. A **psychosis,** in contrast, involved thought disturbances, bizarre behavior, severe disruption of social relations, and relatively poor contact with reality. The DSM-III and the DSM-IV dropped this psychoanalytic orientation and instead consider the interaction of biological, psychological, and social factors in diagnosing psychological disorders (Linn & Spitzer, 1982).

The DSM-IV provides five axes for diagnosing psychological disorders. Axis I contains sixteen major categories of psychological disorders. Axis II contains personality disorders and mental retardation. Axis III contains medical conditions that might affect the person's psychological disorder. Axis IV contains social and environmental sources of stress the person has been under recently. And Axis V contains an estimate of the person's level of functioning. The Axis I categories are presented in table 14.2.

Because the DSM-IV is relatively new, there has been much more research on the DSM-III. Though the DSM-III was an improvement over previous diagnostic systems, it met with some criticism (McReynolds, 1989). Research found that, overall, the DSM-III diagnostic categories had only modest reliability and validity (Eysenck, Wakefield, & Friedman, 1983), though the reliability and validity of some categories were better than for others (Robins & Helzer, 1986). The *reliability* of a diagnosis refers to the extent to which different raters reach the same diagnosis. For example, will several clinical psychologists independently agree that a given person is schizophrenic? The *validity* of a diagnosis refers to the extent to which a diagnosis is accurate. For example, does a person who has been diagnosed as schizophrenic truly have schizophrenia?

Note that the creation of categories in the DSM is actually an exercise in concept formation. Each category, whether "major depression," "antisocial personality," or "catatonic schizophrenia," is a concept that is defined by certain characteristics. But (as described in chapter 9) *natural concepts,* such as the concepts representing the different psychological disorders, have "fuzzy borders." This means that different disorders might share certain characteristics and that a person might exhibit some but not all of the characteristics of a particular disorder. This makes it difficult to achieve high reliability and validity in diagnosis.

The DSM-III evoked a variety of reactions from professionals. A survey of mental-health professionals in 42 countries other than the United States found general approval of it (Maser, Kaelber, & Weise, 1991). In contrast, most of the respondents in a survey of American psychologists rejected the DSM-III for still being too dependent on the medical model and insufficiently sensitive to interpersonal factors (Smith & Kraft, 1983). This and other issues were considered by mental-health officials at work on the DSM-IV, which has a stronger research base and went through a more critical review process than did earlier versions of the DSM before being published (Widiger & Trull, 1991).

TABLE 14.2   The DSM-IV Axis I Disorders and Multiaxial Evaluation

Axis I Clinical Disorders

1. **Disorders usually first diagnosed in infancy, childhood, or adolescence**   Disorders that appear before adulthood. Examples include stuttering, nocturnal enuresis (bedwetting), attention-deficit/hyperactivity disorder.

2. **Delirium, dementia, and amnestic and other cognitive disorders**   Disorders of the brain caused by drugs, toxins, aging, or diseases. Examples include delirium (extreme mental confusion) and dementia (a marked deterioration of the intellect).

3. **Mental disorders due to a general medical condition**   Disorders due to a medical condition not classified elsewhere. Examples include catatonic disorder due to . . . , personality change due to . . . , and mental disorder due to . . . .

4. **Substance-related disorders**   Disorders that involve dependence on psychoactive drugs to the detriment of everyday functioning. Examples include dependency on cocaine, heroin, alcohol, or marijuana.

5. **Schizophrenia and other psychotic disorders**   Disorders associated with marked disorganization of perception, cognition, emotionality, and behavior. Examples include paranoid schizophrenia, catatonic schizophrenia, and disorganized schizophrenia.

6. **Mood disorders**   Disorders marked by severe emotional disturbances. Examples include major depression and bipolar disorder.

7. **Anxiety disorders**   Disorders associated with extreme anxiety. Examples include phobia, panic disorder, generalized anxiety disorder, obsessive-compulsive disorder, and posttraumatic stress disorder.

8. **Somatoform disorders**   Disorders involving physical symptoms, such as paralysis or sensory loss, without a physical cause. Examples include hypochondriasis and conversion disorder.

9. **Factitious disorders**   Disorders in which the person fakes symptoms of physical or psychological disorders. Examples include lying about symptoms or inducing symptoms.

10. **Dissociative disorders**   Disorders in which conscious awareness is separated from personally relevant thoughts, feelings, and memories. Examples include dissociative amnesia and dissociative fugue.

11. **Sexual and gender identity disorders**   Disorders characterized by sexual dysfunctions, paraphilias (culturally disapproved sexual practices), or confusion about one's gender identity. Examples include male erectile disorder, female orgasmic disorder, exhibitionism, sexual masochism, and transsexualism.

12. **Eating disorders**   Disorders involving maladaptive eating patterns. Examples include anorexia nervosa and bulimia nervosa.

13. **Sleep disorders**   Disorders marked by disruption of the sleep-wake cycle. Examples include insomnia, narcolepsy, hypersomnia, and sleep apnea.

14. **Impulse-control disorders not elsewhere classified**   Disorders associated with an inability to resist the impulse to commit certain maladaptive acts. Examples include kleptomania (compulsive stealing), pyromania (fire starting), and pathological gambling.

15. **Adjustment disorders**   Disorders in which the person fails to adapt adequately to important stressors. Examples include the inability to adapt well to a divorce or to a financial setback.

16. **Other conditions that may be a focus of clinical attention**   Disorders that do not fall within the other categories. Examples include psychological factors affecting medical conditions, relational problems, and problems related to abuse or neglect.

Multiaxial Diagnosis: An Example

Axis I   Alcohol Dependence
Axis II   Antisocial Personality Disorder
Axis III   Alcoholic Cirrhosis of the Liver
Axis IV   Loss of Job, Threatened Eviction, Separation from Spouse
Axis V   Current Level of Functioning: 40
           Highest Level of Functioning in Past Year: 55

Reprinted with permission from the *Diagnostic and Statistical Manual of Mental Disorders*, Fourth Edition. Copyright 1994 American Psychiatric Association.

Criticisms of the Diagnosis of Psychological Disorders

Despite the widespread reliance on the DSM, some researchers criticize the potential negative effects of the diagnosis of psychological disorders. This critical attitude was inspired, in part, by a classic study on the effects of diagnosis.

Anatomy of a Classic Research Study:

Can Sane People Be Recognized in a Mental Hospital?

Rationale

The study was conducted by psychologist David Rosenhan (1973). He wondered whether normal people, complaining of symptoms of schizophrenia, could gain admission to a mental hospital and, once admitted, be discovered by the professional staff.

David Rosenhan
"If sanity and insanity exist, how shall we know them?"

Thomas Szasz
"Mental illness is a myth, whose function it is to disguise and thus render more palatable the bitter pill of moral conflicts in human relations."

anxiety disorder
A psychological disorder marked by persistent anxiety that disrupts everyday functioning.

Method

Rosenhan had eight apparently normal persons, including himself, gain admission to mental hospitals by calling the hospitals for appointments and then complaining of hearing voices that said "empty, hollow, thud." Hearing imaginary voices is a symptom of schizophrenia.

Results and Discussion

The eight "pseudopatients" were admitted to twelve hospitals in five states; their stays ranged from 7 to 52 days. During their stays, the pseudopatients behaved normally, did not complain of hearing voices, and sometimes wrote hundreds of pages of notes about their experiences in the hospitals. Though no staff members discovered they were faking, several real patients accused them of being journalists or professors investigating mental hospitals. Rosenhan concluded that the diagnosis of psychological disorders is influenced more by preconceptions and by the setting in which we find a person than by any objective characteristics of the person, as in the following conversation from Alice in Wonderland:

⚬ ⚬ ⚬ "I don't want to go among mad people," Alice remarked. "Oh, you can't help that," said the Cat: "we're all mad here. I'm mad. You're mad." "How do you know I'm mad?" said Alice. "You must be," said the Cat, "or you wouldn't have come here."

But Rosenhan's study provoked criticism from psychiatrist Robert Spitzer, who helped develop the DSM-III, that he had misinterpreted the results (Spitzer, 1975). First, the admission of the pseudopatients to the mental hospitals was justified, because people who report hearing imaginary voices are exhibiting symptoms of schizophrenia. Second, schizophrenics can go long periods of time without displaying obvious symptoms of schizophrenia. Thus, the staff members who observed the pseudopatients during their stays had no reason to conclude that they were faking. Nonetheless, the power of the label mentally ill to color our judgment of a person was supported by another study. When subjects observed people labeled as mental patients (who actually were not) or similar people not given that label, they were more likely to rate the alleged mental patients as being "unusual" (Piner & Kahle, 1984).

The best-known critic of diagnostic labels is psychiatrist Thomas Szasz (1960), who has gone so far as to call mental illness, including schizophrenia, a "myth." He believes that the behaviors that earn the label of mental illness are "problems in living." According to Szasz, labeling people as mentally ill wrongly blames their maladaptive functioning on an illness. He believes the notion of "mental illness" is a two-edged sword. On the one hand, it may excuse heinous behavior committed by those labeled "mentally ill." On the other hand, it may enable governments to oppress nonconformists by labeling them "mentally ill." As indicated in the following comment, Szasz's claim that mental illness is a myth has provoked hostile responses from other mental-health practitioners:

⚬ ⚬ ⚬ This myth has a seductive appeal for many persons, especially if they do not have to deal clinically with individuals and their families experiencing the anguish, confusion, and terror of schizophrenia. Unfortunately, informing schizophrenics and their relatives that they are having a mythological experience does not seem to be appreciated by them and is not particularly helpful. (Kessler, 1984, p. 380)

The many mental-health professionals who helped create the DSM-IV do not view the psychological disorders it discusses as myths. Among the most important categories of psychological disorders are *anxiety disorders, somatoform disorders, dissociative disorders, mood disorders, schizophrenic disorders,* and *personality disorders.* Figure 14.1 indicates the prevalence of several important psychological disorders.

ANXIETY DISORDERS

You certainly have experienced anxiety when learning to drive, taking an important exam, or going on a first date. *Anxiety* is a feeling of apprehension accompanied by sympathetic nervous system arousal, which produces increases in sweating, heart rate, and breathing rate. Though anxiety is a normal and beneficial part of everyday life, warning us about potential threats, in **anxiety disorders** it becomes intense, chronic, and disruptive of everyday functioning. About 10 to 15 percent of adult Americans

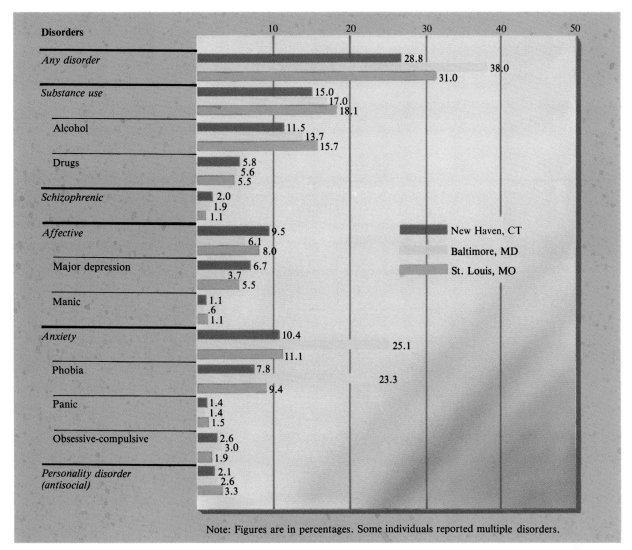

Disorders

Disorder	New Haven, CT	Baltimore, MD	St. Louis, MO
Any disorder	28.8	38.0	31.0
Substance use	15.0	17.0	18.1
Alcohol	11.5	13.7	15.7
Drugs	5.8	5.6	5.5
Schizophrenic	2.0	1.9	1.1
Affective	9.5	6.1	8.0
Major depression	6.7	3.7	5.5
Manic	1.1	.6	1.1
Anxiety	10.4	11.1	25.1
Phobia	7.8	9.4	23.3
Panic	1.4	1.4	1.5
Obsessive-compulsive	2.6	3.0	1.9
Personality disorder (antisocial)	2.1	2.6	3.3

Note: Figures are in percentages. Some individuals reported multiple disorders.

FIGURE 14.1

Prevalence of Some Major Psychological Disorders
A survey of people in three American cities found that about one-third had experienced one or more
DSM-III disorders. Note that the prevalence of certain disorders varied markedly from city to city
(Robins et al., 1984).

suffer from anxiety disorders (Robins et al., 1984), which include *generalized anxiety
disorder, panic disorder, phobias,* and *obsessive-compulsive disorder.*

Generalized Anxiety Disorder

Though we normally experience anxiety in response to stressful situations, the person
with a **generalized anxiety disorder** is in a constant state of anxiety that exists independent of any particular stressful situation. Because the person is constantly anxious, with
no apparent source of the anxiety, the anxiety is said to be "free floating." In essence,
anxiety becomes one of the individual's cardinal personality traits (Rapee, 1991). The
central feature of the generalized anxiety disorder is worry. The person worries constantly about almost everything, including work, school, finances, and social relationships. About 3 percent of the population suffer from generalized anxiety disorder (Reich,
1986).

What accounts for the development of a generalized anxiety disorder?
Biopsychological researchers look to heredity, neurochemistry, and brain arousal for

generalized anxiety disorder
*An anxiety disorder marked by a
persistent state of anxiety that exists
independent of any particular stressful
situation.*

Samuel Turner
"Emerging human and nonhuman primate data suggest that some individuals are likely to be more vulnerable to anxiety than others, and hence are at a greater risk for developing an anxiety disorder."

answers. The children of victims of anxiety disorders are seven times more likely to develop them than are children whose parents are not victims. Samuel Turner, a leading anxiety researcher, notes that though this hints at a possible genetic basis for anxiety disorders, it does not permit us to conclude that anxiety disorders are affected more by common heredity than by common life experiences (Turner, Beidel, & Costello, 1987). Stronger, but also inconclusive, evidence for a hereditary basis of anxiety disorders comes from research that shows a higher concordance rate for identical twins, who share 100 percent of their genes, than for fraternal twins, who typically share 50 percent of their genes (Torgersen, 1983). The *concordance rate* is the likelihood that a person will develop a psychological disorder given that a particular relative has that disorder.

Whether caused more by heredity or by experience, anxiety is associated with a reduction in the activity of neurons dependent on the inhibitory neurotransmitter serotonin (Van Praag, 1991). This might explain why positron emission tomography (PET) indicates that anxiety is associated with increased brain arousal. More specifically, PET scans have shown that when subjects are placed in an anxiety-inducing situation, they show increased arousal in their temporal lobes (Reiman et al., 1989). A contributing factor to the maintenance, though not the onset, of generalized anxiety disorder is the ingestion of caffeine (Bruce et al., 1992).

As for psychological causes of the generalized anxiety disorder, psychoanalysts view it as the consequence of id impulses threatening to overwhelm ego controls. Cognitive-behavioral theorists find that people with a generalized anxiety disorder exaggerate the number of threatening stimuli and their level of threat (Tomarken, Mineka, & Cook, 1989). This places the person in a constant "fight-or-flight" state of arousal. Humanistic psychologists have their own point of view. They believe that anxiety arises from a discrepancy between the actual self and the ought self (Strauman & Higgins, 1988), which are described in chapter 13. This means that we might develop a generalized anxiety disorder when we feel we have failed to live up to desirable standards of behavior.

Panic Disorder

In describing the motivation for his painting *The Scream*, Norwegian artist Edvard Munch (1863–1944) remarked, "I was walking . . . and I felt a loud, unending scream piercing nature" (Blakemore, 1977, p. 155). Both the painting and the statement indicate that Munch may have suffered a *panic attack,* which is a symptom of **panic disorder,** marked by sudden attacks of overwhelming anxiety, accompanied by dizziness, trembling, cold sweats, heart palpitations, shortness of breath, fear of dying, and fear of going crazy. People experiencing panic attacks may also feel detached from their own bodies or feel that other people are not real. Though panic attacks usually last only a few minutes, they are so distressing that more people seek therapy for panic disorder than for any other psychological disorder (Boyd, 1986). About 1.5 percent of Americans experience panic disorder (Weissman, 1990).

Biopsychological and cognitive theorists disagree about the causes of panic disorder (McNally, 1990). Panic disorder runs in families, with a concordance rate among family members of about 20 percent (Crowe, 1990). The concordance rate is higher for identical twins than for fraternal twins (Torgerson, 1989). Again, these findings hint at, but do not guarantee, a genetic predisposition for panic disorder. PET scans have implicated the temporal lobes, because people with panic disorder show higher activity in the right temporal lobe than in the left. This is not found in other people (Reiman et al., 1984).

According to cognitive theorists, panic disorder results from faulty thinking. For example, people prone to panic disorders engage in catastrophic thinking, misattributing physical symptoms of mild arousal caused by factors such as caffeine, exercise, mild stress, or emotional memories, to a serious mental or physical disorder. Separation anxiety evoked by recalling an important person in one's life whom one has lost is especially likely to instigate a panic attack (Free, Winget, & Whitman, 1993). Catastrophic think-

Panic
Edvard Munch's painting *The Scream* (1893) conveys the intense anxiety and terror characteristic of a panic attack.

panic disorder
An anxiety disorder marked by sudden, unexpected attacks of overwhelming anxiety, often associated with the fear of dying or "losing one's mind."

TABLE 14.3	Simple Phobias
Phobia	**Source of Phobia**
Acrophobia	High places
Ailurophobia	Cats
Algophobia	Pain
Aquaphobia	Water
Arachnophobia	Spiders
Astraphobia	Lightning storms
Claustrophobia	Enclosed places
Cynophobia	Dogs
Hematophobia	Blood
Hydrophobia	Water
Monophobia	Being alone
Mysophobia	Dirt
Nyctophobia	Darkness
Ocholophobia	Crowds
Thanatophobia	Death
Triskaidekaphobia	Number 13
Xenophobia	Strangers
Zoophobia	Animals

ing about physical symptoms may induce the overwhelming anxiety that characterizes panic disorder (Agras, 1993). This cognitive explanation of panic has much in common with Schachter's two-factor theory of emotion (discussed in chapter 12), because it assumes that panic occurs when unexplained arousal is attributed to a catastrophic source.

Phobias

The word **phobia** comes from *Phobos*, the name of the Greek god of fear, and refers to the experience of excessive or inappropriate fear. The person realizes that the fear is irrational but cannot control it. The phobia may have maladaptive consequences. For example, patients with *claustrophobia* (the fear of enclosed places) are sometimes too terrified to undergo diagnostic magnetic resonance imaging, which requires them to lie still in a cylinder for up to an hour or more (Kilborn & Labbe, 1990). Phobias are among the most common psychological disorders, afflicting about 6 percent of Americans (Boyd et al., 1990).

The major classes of phobias are *simple phobias*, *social phobias*, and *agoraphobia*. A **simple phobia** is an intense, irrational fear of a specific object or situation, such as a spider or a height. People with simple phobias may go to great lengths to avoid the object or situation they fear. Table 14.3 lists common simple phobias.

People with a **social phobia** fear public scrutiny, perhaps leading them to avoid playing sports, making telephone calls, or performing music in public (Cox & Kenardy, 1993). Social phobia is promoted by increased self-focused attention, which is more likely under conditions of high physiological arousal (Hope, Gansler, & Heimberg, 1989). You have gotten a hint of this experience if you have noticed your mouth becoming dry, your palms sweating, and your heart beating strongly just before making an oral presentation in class.

Agoraphobia is the fear of being in public. The word *agoraphobia* comes from the Greek term for "fear of the marketplace." The word was coined in 1871 to describe the cases of four men who feared being in a city plaza (Boyd & Crump, 1991). Agoraphobics typically have a history of panic attacks. They often avoid public places because they

phobia
An anxiety disorder marked by excessive or inappropriate fear.

simple phobia
A phobia of a specific object or situation.

social phobia
A phobia of situations that involve public scrutiny.

agoraphobia
A phobia associated with fear of being in public, usually because the person fears the embarrassment of a panic attack.

Acrophobia
An acrophobic person might feel anxiety just looking at this photograph of a Dallas window washer hanging in space, let alone contemplating being in his situation.

Fear of Flying
Because of his flying phobia, popular football announcer John Madden travels from city to city in his own bus, often taking days to make trips that would take only hours by airplane.

fear the embarrassment of having witnesses to their panic attacks (Clum & Knowles, 1991). This makes them avoid parties, sporting events, and shopping malls. In extreme cases the person can become a prisoner in her or his own home—terrified to leave for any reason. Because agoraphobia disrupts every aspect of the victim's life, it is the phobia most commonly seen by psychotherapists.

Certain people have a biological, possibly hereditary, predisposition to develop phobias; identical twins have a higher concordance rate than do fraternal twins (Carey, 1990). According to Martin Seligman (1971), evolution has biologically prepared us to develop phobias of potentially dangerous natural objects or situations, such as fire, snakes, and heights. Early human beings who were biologically predisposed to avoid these dangers were more likely to survive long enough to reproduce and, as a result, pass on this predisposition to their offspring in their genes. This might explain why phobias that involve potentially dangerous natural objects, such as snakes, are more persistent than are phobias that involve usually safe natural objects, such as flowers (McNally, 1987). Experiments support this position. When fear is induced by pairing snakes or houses with electric shocks, fear of snakes lasts longer following the experience (Ohman, Erixon, & Lofberg, 1975). The notion that we are genetically predisposed to fear certain things has some commonality with Jung's concept of archetypes (described in chapter 13).

Psychoanalysts believe that phobias are caused by anxiety displaced from a feared object or situation onto another object or situation. By displacing the anxiety, the person keeps the true source unconscious. The classic psychoanalytic case is that of Little Hans, a 5-year-old boy who was afraid to go outside because of his fear of horses. After listening to the background of the case, Sigmund Freud attributed the phobia to inadequate resolution of the Oedipus complex. Freud claimed that Hans had an incestuous desire for his mother and a fear of being punished for it by being castrated by his father. Hans displaced his fear of his father to horses, permitting him to keep his incestuous feelings unconscious.

In contrast, behavioral theorists claim that phobias are learned responses to life situations. Phobias develop because of learning, either through personal experience or through observation of phobic people (Ost, 1985). For example, Little Hans's phobia could have been attributed to a horrifying incident that he witnessed in which horses harnessed to a wagon fell and then struggled to get to their feet (Stafford-Clark, 1965).

Cognitive-behavioral explanations of phobias implicate self-efficacy, which is discussed in chapter 13. Phobic people may believe they lack the ability to cope with stressful situations. Research indicates that a phobic person's feeling of self-efficacy in regard to the feared situation is a more important factor in phobias than is the person's anxiety level or perception of danger (Williams, Turner, & Peer, 1985).

Obsessive-Compulsive Disorder

Have you ever been unable to keep an advertising jingle from continually running through your mind? If so, you have experienced a mild *obsession*, which is a persistent, recurring thought. Obsessions can be self-perpetuating, because the very act of trying to suppress a thought will make it more likely to enter consciousness (Wegner et al., 1987). Have you ever repeatedly checked your alarm clock to make sure it was set the night before an early-morning exam? If so, you have experienced a mild *compulsion*, which is a repetitive action that you feel compelled to perform. People whose obsessions and compulsions interfere with their daily functioning suffer from **obsessive-compulsive disorder.** Obsessive-compulsive disorder is found in about 3 percent of the population (Rasmussen & Eisen, 1990).

There might be a hereditary predisposition in those who develop obsessive-compulsive disorder. This is supported by evidence that obsessive-compulsive disorder runs in families (Lenane et al., 1990). Additional support for a hereditary basis comes from a study of more than 400 pairs of twins, which found that heredity accounted for almost half of the variability in obsessional symptoms from one person to another (Clifford, Murray, & Fulker, 1984).

PET scans have found that obsessive-compulsive persons have abnormally high activity in the frontal lobes (Baxter, 1991). Perhaps compulsive behavior is aimed at reducing this overarousal to more comfortable levels. You might have experienced this, in a milder form, when you felt anxious about school work, spent an hour rearranging your room, and, as a consequence, felt less anxious.

According to psychoanalysts, obsessive-compulsive disorder is caused by fixation at the anal stage, resulting from harsh toilet training. This causes repressed anger directed at the parents. The child defends against the guilt generated by these feelings of anger and later transgressions by repeating certain thoughts and actions over and over. The obsessions and compulsions often have symbolic meaning, as portrayed in Shakespeare's *Macbeth* when Lady Macbeth engages in compulsive handwashing after murdering King Duncan. Behavioral theorists view obsessions and compulsions as ways of avoiding anxiety-

obsessive-compulsive disorder
An anxiety disorder in which the person has recurrent, intrusive thoughts (obsessions) and recurrent urges to perform ritualistic actions (compulsions).

Drawing by Woodman; ©1986 The New Yorker Magazine, Inc.

"But that's what you said yesterday—'Just one more cord'!"

inducing situations. So you might compulsively clean and organize your room to avoid the anxiety of studying for exams and writing term papers.

SOMATOFORM DISORDERS

somatoform disorder
A psychological disorder characterized by physical symptoms in the absence of disease or injury.

Somatoform means "bodylike." A **somatoform disorder** is characterized by physical symptoms in the absence of disease or injury. The symptoms are caused, instead, by psychological factors. Do not confuse somatoform disorders with *malingering*, in which the person purposely invents symptoms in order to be relieved of certain responsibilities. The person with a somatoform disorder truly believes he or she has symptoms of a real physical disorder. Somatoform disorders affect less than 1 percent of the population (Robins et al., 1984). The somatoform disorders include *hypochondriasis* and *conversion disorder*.

Hypochondriasis

hypochondriasis
A somatoform disorder in which the person interprets the slightest physical changes as evidence of a serious illness.

A person with the somatoform disorder known as **hypochondriasis** interprets the slightest physical change in her or his body as evidence of a serious illness. Hypochondriacs may go from physician to physician, searching for the one who will finally diagnose the disease that they are sure is causing their symptoms. Medical students may experience a mild form of hypochondriasis in the so-called medical student syndrome, in which a mere cough might convince them they have lung cancer. As you read about the various psychological disorders, you should beware of developing a similar "psychology student syndrome," in which you interpret your normal variations in mood, thinking, and behavior as symptoms of a psychological disorder. Of course, if your symptoms become distressing, prolonged, or disruptive to your life, you should consider seeking professional counseling.

What accounts for hypochondriasis? Psychoanalysts see it as a defense against becoming aware of feelings of guilt or low self-esteem. Behavioral theorists point to both positive reinforcement, such as being lavished with attention, and negative reinforcement, such as relief from work responsibilities. Cognitivists note that people who develop hypochondriasis fear disease so much that they become overly vigilant about bodily changes, leading them to notice and exaggerate even the slightest ones. A study that compared 60 people with hypochondriasis and 60 people without it found that those with hypochondriasis were more likely to interpret physical symptoms as indicative of disease. They seemed to presume that being healthy means being completely symptom free (Barsky et al., 1993). There is evidence supporting each of these views, but none is clearly superior to the others (Barsky & Klerman, 1983).

Conversion Disorder

conversion disorder
A somatoform disorder in which the person exhibits motor or sensory loss or the alteration of a physiological function without any apparent physical cause.

A person with a **conversion disorder** exhibits loss or alteration of a physical function without any apparent physical cause. In typical cases, the person experiences muscle paralysis, such as difficulty in speaking, or sensory loss, such as an inability to feel an object on the skin. But the apparently lost function is actually intact; a girl who suffered for a year with "paralyzed" legs began using them after simply being given biofeedback that provided her with evidence of activity in her leg muscles (Klonoff & Moore, 1986). Physicians suspect the presence of a conversion disorder when patients display *la belle indifference*—a lack of concern about their symptoms. As illustrated in figure 14.2, a conversion disorder might also be diagnosed by a physician who notices that a patient's symptoms are anatomically impossible.

Theories explaining conversion disorder have a long, and sometimes bizarre, history. An Egyptian papyrus dating from 1900 B.C. attributed the disorder, which was believed to be limited to women, to a wandering uterus (Jones, 1980). Hippocrates accepted this explanation and called the disorder *hysteria*, from the Greek word for "uterus." Because Hippocrates believed that the uterus wandered when a woman was

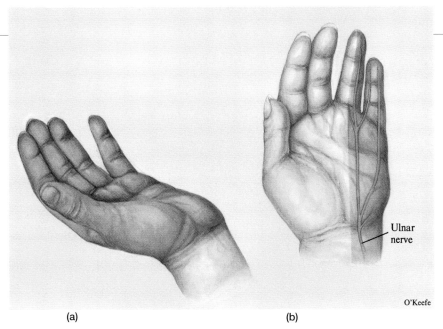

FIGURE 14.2

Conversion Disorder
(a) A person with "glove anesthesia" will complain of numbness in the hand from the wrist to the tips of the fingers. This is easily diagnosed as a conversion disorder because damage to the sensory nerves of the hand will not produce this pattern of sensory loss. Different areas of the hand are served by the ulnar, radial, and median nerves. If a given nerve is injured, there will be numbness in only a portion of the hand. For example, (b) damage to the ulnar nerve produces numbness along the outer edge of the hand.

Ulnar nerve

O'Keefe

(a)   (b)

sexually frustrated, he prescribed marriage as a cure. The wandering-womb view lost credibility in the face of nineteenth-century science.

Modern biopsychological researchers have found that somatoform disorders run in families. The concordance rate for identical twins is three times greater than for fraternal twins (about 30 percent versus about 10 percent). But it is unclear whether the higher concordance rate for identical twins simply reflects greater genetic similarity or greater similarity in their life experiences (Torgersen, 1986).

In the late nineteenth century, Sigmund Freud claimed that hysteria resulted from anxiety generated by repressed sexual impulses. The anxiety was converted into symbolic physical symptoms, such as paralyzed legs, that enabled a woman to avoid acting on her sexual impulses. Freud called such disorders *conversion hysteria*. Today, to avoid the implication that the disorder is strictly a female problem, it is called *conversion disorder*. There is evidence that severe psychological trauma, such as sexual abuse, might induce a conversion disorder (Rothbaum & Foa, 1991).

Behavioral theorists assume that somatoform disorders occur because they are reinforced by increased attention or a reduction in responsibilities. Children may be prone to somatoform disorders after they observe other members of their family being reinforced for their physical symptoms (Mullins & Olson, 1990). Explanations consistent with humanistic psychology see somatoform disorders as ways to protect the self through *self-handicapping*. One piece of evidence for the self-handicapping explanation is that unemployed Appalachian coal miners show an increased incidence of conversion disorder. Perhaps this helps them save face for being out of work. (Jones, 1980). Moreover, people with hypochondriasis are more likely to complain of symptoms when they know they are going to be evaluated (Smith, Snyder, & Perkins, 1983). For example, a person who complains of a sore throat before a threatening speaking engagement might not be blamed for a poor performance.

DISSOCIATIVE DISORDERS

In a **dissociative disorder,** the person's conscious mind loses access to certain of his or her thoughts, feelings, and memories. The dissociative disorders include *psychogenic amnesia, psychogenic fugue,* and *multiple personality*. Early trauma, such as sexual, physical, or emotional abuse, may predispose a person to develop a dissociative disorder (Kluft, 1987).

dissociative disorder
A psychological disorder in which thoughts, feelings, and memories become separated from conscious awareness.

Psychogenic Amnesia

While being interrogated about his assassination of Robert F. Kennedy in 1968, Sirhan Sirhan was unable to recall the incident (Bower, 1981). He apparently suffered from **psychogenic amnesia,** the inability to recall personally significant memories (Coons & Milstein, 1992). The lost memories are usually related to a traumatic event, such as witnessing a catastrophe. Victims of psychogenic amnesia typically regain the lost memories after a period of hours or days. The psychoanalytic viewpoint assumes that the repression of painful memories causes psychogenic amnesia. This was supported by a study in which people who viewed slides of normal and disfigured faces accompanied by verbal descriptions had poorer recall of the descriptions associated with the disfigured faces (Christianson & Nilsson, 1984).

Psychogenic Fugue

In September 1980, a young woman was found wandering in Birch State Park, Florida. She could not recall who she was or where she was from. After a nationally televised appearance on a morning television show, she was reunited with her family in Illinois. She suffered from **psychogenic fugue,** which is marked by the memory loss characteristic of psychogenic amnesia, the loss of one's identity, and fleeing from one's home. (The word *fugue* comes from the Latin word meaning "to flee.") The person may adopt a new identity, only to emerge from the fugue state days, months, or years later, recalling nothing that had happened during the intervening period. In one case a 15-year-old girl assumed a new identity, spoke a foreign language she had learned in school, adopted new dress and grooming habits, and showed new skills, interests, and personality traits for 6 days (Venn, 1984).

Multiple Personality

In 1812 Benjamin Rush, the founder of American psychiatry, reported the following summary of his case study of a minister's wife:

> ° ° ° In her paroxysms of madness she resumed her gay habits, spoke French, and ridiculed the tenets and practices of the sect to which she belonged. In the intervals of her fits she renounced her gay habits, became zealously devoted to the religious principles and ceremonies of the Methodists, and forgot everything she did and said during the fits of her insanity. (Carlson, 1981, p. 668)

This was one of the first well-documented cases of **multiple personality,** in which a person has two or more distinct personalities that alternate with one another, as in the story of Dr. Jekyll and Mr. Hyde (Garcia, 1990). The multiple personalities may include males and females, children and adults, and moral and immoral persons. A quiet, retiring middle-aged woman might alternate with a flamboyant, promiscuous young woman. Each personality might have its own way of walking, writing, and speaking, and some might even be animals (Hendrickson, McCarty, & Goodwin, 1990).

You are probably familiar with two cases of multiple personality that were made into movies based on best-selling books: the story of Chris Sizemore, portrayed by Joanne Woodward in *The Three Faces of Eve*, and the story of Sybil Dorsett, portrayed by Sally Field in *Sybil*. At the height of her disorder, Sizemore had 22 distinct personalities. Her personalities were finally integrated in 1975, and she went on speaking tours to discuss her experiences (Sizemore & Huber, 1988).

People who develop multiple personalities almost always have had traumatic childhood experiences. As a child, Chris Sizemore witnessed a man drown, observed the bloody body parts of a man who had been cut to pieces in a sawmill, and was forced to kiss her grandfather's corpse. A study of 71 patients with multiple personality disorder in the Netherlands found that 94.4 percent had a history of childhood physical and sexual abuse (Boon & Draijer, 1993). Sybil Dorsett's mother locked her in closets and sexually tortured her.

psychogenic amnesia
A dissociative disorder marked by the inability to recall personally significant memories.

psychogenic fugue
A dissociative disorder marked by the memory loss characteristic of psychogenic amnesia, the loss of one's identity, and fleeing from one's home.

Psychogenic Fugue
In September 1980, this young woman was found naked and starving in Birch State Park in Florida. She could not recall who she was or where she was from—a case of psychogenic fugue. Those who took care of her called her "Jane Doe." Even after being reunited with an Illinois couple who claimed to be her parents, she was unable to recall her identity or her past.

multiple personality
A dissociative disorder in which the person has two or more distinct personalities that alternate with one another.

(a)

(b)

(c)

(d)

Multiple Personality
In the 1957 film *The Three Faces of Eve*, Joanne Woodward portrayed a woman with 3 different personalities. (*a*) The personality named Eve White was prim and proper; (*b*) the personality named Eve Black was sexually promiscuous; and (*c*) the personality named Jane was a balanced compromise between the other two. (*d*) More than two decades later, a woman named Chris Sizemore revealed that she was the woman portrayed by Joanne Woodward. After years of therapy she was finally able to maintain a single, integrated personality—instead of the 22 she displayed at one point in her life.

Because of a marked increase in reported cases of multiple personality in the 1980s, some researchers believe multiple personalities are being overdiagnosed and are simply the product of role playing, just as the "hidden observer" in hypnosis (discussed in chapter 6) might be a case of role playing. This possibility was demonstrated in a study in which students were hypnotized and asked to reveal the hidden personality of an accused multiple murderer called Harry or Betty Hodgins. Eighty percent did so. This indicates that at least some reputed cases of multiple personality disorder may be no more than role playing, whether intentional or not (Spanos, Weekes, & Bertrand, 1985).

MOOD DISORDERS

We all experience periodic fluctuations in our emotions, such as becoming briefly depressed after failing an exam or briefly elated after getting an A. But people with **mood disorders** experience prolonged periods of extreme depression or elation, often unrelated to their current circumstances, that disrupt their everyday functioning.

Major Depression

We normally feel depressed after personal losses or failures; the frequency and intensity of depressive episodes varies from person to person. Winston Churchill was so hounded by depression that he called it the "black dog" that followed him around. Since World War II, depression has become ten times more common among Americans (Seligman,

mood disorder
A psychological disorder marked by prolonged periods of extreme depression or elation, often unrelated to the person's current situation.

Seasonal Affective Disorder
Some people experience seasonal bouts of severe depression, typically in the winter. Research shows that such victims of seasonal affective disorder may gain relief if their day is artificially extended by exposing them to extra light before dawn or after sunset.

Norman Rosenthal
"There is agreement among clinical researchers that seasonal affective disorder is a common condition and that in a large percentage of cases the symptoms of winter depression respond well to treatment with bright environmental light."

1989) and is considered the common cold of psychological disorders. Depression is so prevalent and distressing that, when advice columnist Ann Landers offered a pamphlet on depression to her readers, 250,000 persons wrote for it (Holden, 1986a).

People with **major depression** experience extreme distress that disrupts their lives for weeks or months at a time. They may express despondency, helplessness, and loss of self-esteem. Their depression is usually worse in the morning (Graw et al., 1991). They may also suffer from an inability to fall asleep or to stay asleep, lose their appetite or overeat, feel constantly fatigued, abandon good grooming habits, withdraw from social relations, lose interest in sex, find it difficult to concentrate, and fail to perform up to their normal academic and vocational standards. About 2 to 3 percent of men and about 5 to 9 percent of women suffer from major depression (American Psychiatric Association, 1994).

Norman Rosenthal and his colleagues have identified a form of depression called **seasonal affective disorder** (Rosenthal, 1993). Victims suffer from extreme depression during certain seasons. Though seasonal affective disorder is usually associated with winter depression, it can also occur in the summer. Seasonal affective disorder may be caused by an inability to adjust physiologically to seasonal changes in light levels (Wehr & Rosenthal, 1989). Winter seasonal affective disorder is treated by extending the day by exposing victims to artificial bright light before sunrise or after sunset. Though its exact mechanism is unknown, this treatment has antidepressant effects (Wehr et al., 1986).

People who suffer from major depression are more susceptible to suicide (Petronis et al., 1990). Though some suicides are done for honor, as in the Japanese ritual of hara-kiri, or to escape intolerable pain, as in some cases of terminal cancer, most are associated with major depression. There are more than 200,000 suicide attempts each year in the United States, with more than 25,000 fatalities. Though most people who commit suicide first give warnings, the vast majority do not leave notes that explain why they killed themselves (Heim & Lester, 1990).

Who commits suicide? Sex, race, and age are factors. Three times more females than males attempt suicide, but three times more males than females succeed; this is because males tend to use more-lethal means, such as gunshots to the head, while females tend to use less-lethal means, such as overdoses of depressant drugs (Cross & Hirschfield, 1986). Whites and Native Americans commit suicide more often than blacks do (Ellis & Range, 1989). People over 65 years old commit suicide more often than do members of younger age groups (McIntosh, 1991). Though suicide rates are lower for high school and college students than for older people, suicide is one of the most common causes of death for the 15- to 24-year-old age group. Adolescent suicide is often associated with a dysfunctional family (Husain, 1990) and drug or alcohol use (Rivinus, 1990). Because even children commit suicide, parents and school personnel should be aware of the possibility in depressed, withdrawn children (Fasko & Fasko, 1990–1991).

During your lifetime, you will probably know people you suspect are contemplating suicide. According to Edwin Shneidman (1987), a leading expert, about 80 percent of people who attempt suicide give warnings before their attempts. This makes it important to take threats seriously and to take appropriate actions to prevent suicide attempts. A study of high school students found that few had knowledge of major warning signs and appropriate responses to suicidal threats by their peers (Norton, Durlak, & Richards, 1989). Major warning signs include changes in moods and habits associated with severe depression, such as emotional apathy, social withdrawal, poor grooming habits, loss of interest in recreational activities, tying up loose ends in their lives, and outright threats of suicide (Shaughnessy & Nystul, 1985).

One of the main factors that keep suicidal people from attempting suicide is social support, which may reduce the effect of negative events on the suicidal person (Slater & Depue, 1981). To prevent suicides, professionals have devised formal suicide awareness programs. In some programs, college resident assistants are trained to recognize verbal, behavioral, and situational warning signs of suicide. They are also taught how

TABLE 14.4	Suicide Prevention

1. Because suicide attempts are, indeed, usually cries for help, the simple act of providing an empathetic response may reduce the immediate likelihood of an actual attempt. Just talking about a problem may reduce its apparent dreadfulness and help the person realize possible solutions other than suicide.

2. Broaden the suicidal person's options to more than a choice between death and a hopeless, helpless life. You might have the person make a list of options and then rank them in order of preference. Suicide may no longer rank first.

3. An immediate goal should be to relieve the psychological pain of the person by intervening, if possible, with those who might be contributing to the pain, whether friends, lovers, teachers, or family members.

4. Encourage the person to seek professional help, even if you have to make the appointment for the person and accompany him or her to it. Many cities have 24-hour suicide hotlines or walk-in centers to provide emergency counseling.

to respond to suicide threats, how to make referrals to professional counselors, and how to support those who seek therapy (Grosz, 1990). Though there is no guaranteed way to prevent suicide, table 14.4 presents several steps suggested by Edwin Shneidman that might dissuade a suicidal person.

Bipolar Disorder

A biblical story describes how King Saul stripped off his clothes in public, exhibited alternating bouts of elation and severe depression, and eventually committed suicide. Though the story attributes his behavior to evil spirits, psychologists might attribute it to a bipolar disorder. **Bipolar disorder,** formerly called *manic depression*, is characterized by days or weeks of mania alternating with longer periods of major depression, typically separated by days or weeks of normal moods.

Mania (from the Greek term for "madness") is characterized by euphoria, hyperactivity, grandiose ideas, incoherent talkativeness, unrealistic optimism, and inflated self-esteem. Manic people are sexually, physically, and financially reckless. They may also overestimate their own abilities, perhaps leading them to make rash business deals or to leave a sedentary job to train for the Olympics. At some time in their lives, about 1 percent of adults have bipolar disorder, which is equally common in males and females (American Psychiatric Association, 1994).

Causes of Mood Disorders

What accounts for mood disorders? Each of the major viewpoints offers its own explanations.

The Biopsychological Viewpoint

Mood disorders have a biological basis, apparently influenced by heredity. Identical twins have higher concordance rates for major depression (Allen, 1976) and bipolar disorder (Bertelsen, Harvald, & Hauge, 1977) than do fraternal twins. Because identical twins have the same genetic inheritance, while fraternal twins are no more genetically alike than ordinary siblings, this provides evidence of a hereditary predisposition to develop mood disorders. The following study found a possible chromosomal basis for bipolar disorder.

Edwin Shneidman
"Working with suicidal persons borrows from the goals of crisis intervention: not to take on and ameliorate the individual's personality structure and cure all neuroses but simply to keep the person alive."

bipolar disorder
A mood disorder marked by periods of mania alternating with longer periods of major depression.

mania
A mood disorder marked by euphoria, hyperactivity, grandiose ideas, annoying talkativeness, unrealistic optimism, and inflated self-esteem.

⌐ Anatomy of a Contemporary Research Study:
Is There a Hereditary Basis for Bipolar Disorder?

Rationale
Evidence supportive of a hereditary basis for bipolar disorder was provided by a study of the Amish community in Lancaster County, Pennsylvania. Because the Amish have an isolated community that includes descendants from only 30 ancestors in the eighteenth century, only marrying among themselves, they provide an excellent opportunity to study the influence of heredity on psychological disorders. The study was conducted by Janice Egeland and her colleagues (1987).

(a)

(b)

(c)

(d)

Mood Disorders
Celebrities, as well as everyday people, may face lives dominated by a mood disorder. Among the best known have been (*a*) author Anne Sexton, (*b*) actress Patty Duke, (*c*) talk-show host Dick Cavett, and (*d*) "60 Minutes" reporter Mike Wallace.

Heredity and Bipolar Disorder
The Amish community in Lancaster County, Pennsylvania, has provided the opportunity for determining the hereditary basis of bipolar disorder. The Amish keep good genealogical records and rarely marry anyone from outside their community. Janice Egeland and her colleagues (1987) found that bipolar disorder was linked to a specific genetic defect in an extended family in the Amish community.

Method
Egeland studied the families of people with bipolar disorder. She used blood tests to examine their chromosome structures.

Results and Discussion
Egeland found that Amish people who suffer from bipolar disorder share a defective gene on the 11th chromosome. But because only 63 percent of those with this defect develop the disorder, perhaps differences in life experience also play a role. Note that this observation also supports the diathesis-stress view of psychological disorders.

But similar studies of families in which bipolar disorder follows a hereditary pattern have failed to find a genetic marker on the 11th chromosome. These include a study of three other North American families (Detera-Wadleigh et al., 1987), three Icelandic families (Hodgkinson et al., 1987), and two Australian families (Mitchell et al., 1991). Even the original Amish study has been called into question. The addition of more family members with bipolar disorder and a reevaluation of the data indicate that the genetic marker for bipolar disorder in the Amish is either not on the 11th chromosome or is on both the 11th chromosome and another chromosome (Barinaga, 1989). This reinforces the importance of research replication, which was stressed in chapter 2. Of course, it is possible that some cases of bipolar disorder are linked to the 11th chromosome while others are not (Faraone, Kremen, & Tsuang, 1990). Another possibility is that relatives of persons with bipolar disorder who are diagnosed with major depression actually have bipolar disorder; this misdiagnosis would result in an underestimation of the linkage of bipolar disorder to a specific gene (Blacker & Tsuang, 1993).

The hereditary predisposition to develop mood disorders may manifest itself by its effect on neurotransmitters. Major depression is related to abnormally low levels of *serotonin* or *norepinephrine* in the brain (McNeal & Cimbolic, 1986). One study measured levels of a chemical by-product of serotonin in the cerebrospinal fluid of depressed people who had tried suicide. Of those with above-average levels, none subsequently committed suicide. Of those with below-average levels, 20 percent subsequently did (Traskman et al., 1981). Antidepressant drugs, often prescribed for suicidal people, act by increasing the levels of serotonin (Willner, 1985) and norepinephrine (Simson et al., 1986).

Serotonin seems to moderate norepinephrine's relationship to both mania and major depression. Depression is associated with a combination of low levels of both serotonin and norepinephrine, while mania is associated with a combination of low

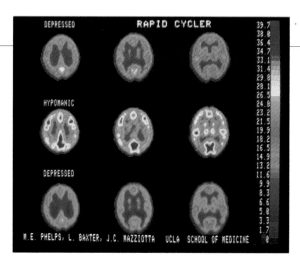

FIGURE 14.3

Brain Activity in Bipolar Disorder
These PET scans show the brain activity of a rapid-cycling bipolar patient. The patient cycled between mania and depression every 24 to 48 hours. The top and bottom sets of scans were obtained during periods when the patient was depressed. The middle set of scans was obtained during a manic period. Note that the red areas indicate significantly higher brain activity during the manic period (Phelps & Mazziotta, 1985).

levels of serotonin and high levels of norepinephrine. Figure 14.3 shows that mania is also associated with unusually high levels of brain arousal, perhaps related to these neurotransmitter levels. Moreover, studies using the PET scan have found that victims of major depression tend to have relatively less left-hemisphere activity than right-hemisphere activity (Martinot et al., 1990).

The Psychoanalytic Viewpoint

The traditional psychoanalytic view holds that the loss of a parent or rejection by a parent early in childhood predisposes the person to experience depression whenever she or he suffers a personal loss, such as a job or a lover, later in life. Because such children feel it is unacceptable to express anger at the lost or rejecting parent, they learn to turn their anger on themselves, creating feelings of guilt and self-loathing (Freud, 1917/1963). But research studies have found that this cannot explain all cases of depression. For example, both depressed and nondepressed adults are equally likely to have suffered the loss of a parent in childhood (Crook & Eliot, 1980).

The Behavioral Viewpoint

Behavioral explanations of depression stress the role of learning and environmental factors. One of the most influential behavioral theories of depression is Peter Lewinsohn's *reinforcement theory*, which assumes that depressed people lack the social skills needed to gain normal social reinforcement from others and might instead provoke negative reactions from them. For example, depressed people stimulate less smiling, fewer statements of support, more unpleasant facial expressions, and more negative remarks from others than do nondepressed people (Gotlib & Robinson, 1982). Lewinsohn points out that the depressed person is caught in a vicious cycle in which reduced social reinforcement leads to depression and depressed behavior further reduces social reinforcement (Youngren & Lewinsohn, 1980).

An influential cognitive-behavioral theory of depression is based on Martin Seligman's notion of *learned helplessness*, which results from experiences that indicate one has little control over the events in one's life. Because perceived lack of control does not always lead to depression, Seligman and his followers, in a reformulated version of his theory, now explain depression in terms of the attributions we make for events in our lives. Depressed people attribute negative events in their lives to stable, global, and internal factors (Abramson, Seligman, & Teasdale, 1978). A *stable factor* is unlikely to change. A *global factor* affects almost all areas of one's life. And an *internal factor* is a characteristic of one's self rather than of the environment. Research on learned helplessness and depression has tended to find that, as predicted, depressed people make internal, stable, and global attributions for negative events in their lives (Sweeney, Anderson, & Bailey, 1986). For example, college freshmen who attribute their poor academic performance

Janice Egeland
"An analysis . . . localized a dominant gene conferring a strong predisposition to manic-depressive disease to the tip of the short arm of chromosome 11."

Peter Lewinsohn
"Depressed persons, as a group, are less socially skillful than nondepressed individuals."

to internal, stable, and global factors—such as intelligence—become more depressed than do those who attribute their own poor academic performance to external, unstable, and specific factors—such as being assigned difficult teachers (Peterson & Barrett, 1987). The reformulated learned-helplessness hypothesis for depression has also been supported in non–North American cultures, such as Turkey (Aydin & Aydin, 1992).

A 5-year longitudinal study identified the development of this pessimistic explanatory style in children who became prone to depression. Early in the study, children's depression was predicted by negative events, and not by their explanatory style. Later both negative events and a pessimistic explanatory style predicted children's depression. Eventually children who had developed pessimistic explanatory styles maintained them even after their depression had subsided. This made them more susceptible to future bouts of depression (Nolen-Hoeksema, Girgus, & Seligman, 1992).

The Cognitive Viewpoint

Research inspired by George Kelly's personal construct theory has found that depressed people hold more-negative personal constructs about themselves than do nondepressed people (Neimeyer, 1983). But the most influential cognitive view of depression is Aaron Beck's (1967) *cognitive theory*. Beck has found that depressed people exhibit what he calls a *cognitive triad:* They have a negative view of themselves, their current circumstances, and their future possibilities. The cognitive triad is common among depressed psychiatric patients, but it is not common among other psychiatric patients. This indicates that the triad is specific to depression (Giles & Shaw, 1987). The cognitive triad is maintained by the tendency of depressed people to overgeneralize from negative events. For example, depressed people tend to assume that a single failure means they are incompetent (Carver & Ganellen, 1983).

As mentioned earlier in the chapter, people with psychological disorders may have more-objective beliefs about themselves and the world than do people without such disorders. Depression researcher Lauren Alloy and her colleagues have found that this is especially true of depressed people. Nondepressed people, but not depressed people, overestimate the likelihood that positive events, and underestimate the likelihood that negative events, will happen to them (Crocker, Alloy, & Kayne, 1988). This leads to the surprising conclusion that if you are not depressed, it might mean that you have an unrealistically positive view of yourself and the world. Depressed people, in contrast, are painfully accurate in their view of their reality.

One problem with cognitive theories of depression is the difficulty in determining whether the patterns of thought that characterize depressed people are the *cause* of their depression or the *result* of their depression. To determine this requires prospective studies, which follow people over a period of time, to determine whether depressed thinking styles precede, accompany, or follow the onset of depression. Because there is more evidence that depressed thinking styles accompany or follow the onset of depression, they might not be its cause (Brewin, 1985).

This conclusion was supported by an experiment in which groups of depressed people received either daily doses of antidepressant drugs or twice-weekly psychotherapy sessions. Both groups showed decreases in depression and more-positive views of themselves and the world. Because even those who received only drugs showed cognitive improvement, perhaps nondepressed styles of thinking are simply a consequence of feeling good and depressed styles of thinking are simply a consequence of feeling bad (Simons, Garfield, & Murphy, 1984).

The Humanistic Viewpoint

Those who favor the humanistic viewpoint attribute depression to the frustration of self-actualization. More specifically, depressed people suffer from incongruence between their actual self and their ideal self (Strauman & Higgins, 1988). The actual self is the person's subjective appraisal of his or her own qualities. The ideal self is the person's subjective judgment of the person he or she would like to become. If the actual self has qualities that are too distinct from those of the ideal self, the person becomes depressed.

Lauren Alloy
"Whereas nondepressives exhibit a self-enhancing bias in which they underestimate their probability of failure relative to that of similar others, depressives do not succumb to either positive or negative social comparison biases in prediction."

SCHIZOPHRENIA

In middle age, Edvard Munch, the founder of modern expressionist painting (and whose painting *The Scream* is shown earlier in the chapter), began acting in odd ways. He became a social recluse, believed his paintings were his children, and claimed they were too jealous to be exhibited with other paintings (Wilson, 1967). Munch's actions were symptoms of **schizophrenia,** a severe psychological disorder characterized by impaired social, emotional, cognitive, and perceptual functioning.

The modern classification of schizophrenia began in 1860 when the Belgian psychiatrist Benedict Morel used the Latin term *demence precoce* (meaning "premature mental deterioration") to describe the behavior of a brilliant, outgoing 13-year-old boy who gradually withdrew socially and deteriorated intellectually. The term was popularized by German psychiatrist Emil Kraepelin in his diagnostic system as *dementia praecox*. In 1911 the Swiss psychiatrist Eugen Bleuler (1857–1939) coined the term *schizophrenia* (from the Greek terms for "split mind") to refer to the disorder. This reflected his belief that schizophrenia involved a splitting apart of the normally integrated functions of perceiving, feeling, and thinking. About 1 percent of the population are victims of schizophrenia, which is equally prevalent among males and females. Schizophrenic patients occupy half of the beds in mental hospitals and cost the American economy billions of dollars each year.

schizophrenia
A class of psychological disorders characterized by grossly impaired social, emotional, cognitive, and perceptual functioning.

Characteristics of Schizophrenia

To be diagnosed as schizophrenic, a person must display symptoms for at least 6 months (American Psychiatric Association, 1994). People with schizophrenia typically experience *hallucinations*, which are perceptual experiences in the absence of sensory stimulation. The great Spanish painter Francisco Goya (1746–1828) had visual hallucinations that drove him to paint pictures of ghosts, witches, and vampires on the walls of his home (Wilson, 1967). But schizophrenic hallucinations are usually auditory, typically voices that may ridicule the person or order the person to commit antisocial acts. Hallucinations seem to result from the failure of the cognitive mechanism that normally lets us distinguish between experiences generated by the mind and experiences evoked by external stimuli (Bentall, 1990).

Schizophrenia is also characterized by cognitive disturbances. Schizophrenic people are easily distracted by irrelevant stimuli. This inability to focus attention may account for the cognitive fragmentation that is a hallmark of schizophrenia (Gjerde, 1983). Because this fragmentation is also evident in schizophrenic language, you might find it frustrating to converse with someone who is schizophrenic. A schizophrenic person's speech might include invented words called *neologisms*, as in "The children have to have this 'accentuative' law so they don't go into the 'mortite' law of the church" (Vetter, 1969, p. 189). The schizophrenic person's speech may also include a meaningless jumble of words called a *word salad*, such as "The house burnt the cow horrendously always" (Vetter, 1969, p. 147).

Among the most distinctive cognitive disturbances in schizophrenia are delusions. A *delusion* is a belief that is held despite compelling evidence to the contrary, such as Edvard Munch's belief that his paintings were his children and were jealous of other paintings. The most common delusions are delusions of influence, such as the belief that one's thoughts are being beamed to all parts of the universe (*thought broadcasting*). Less common are *delusions of grandeur*, in which the person believes that she or he is a famous or powerful person. The fascinating book *The Three Christs of Ypsilanti* (Rokeach, 1964/ 1981) describes the cases of three men in a mental hospital who had the same delusion of grandeur—each claimed to be Jesus Christ. The workings of the schizophrenic mind are vividly illustrated when they meet and each man tries to explain why he is Jesus and the others merely impostors.

Schizophrenic people typically have flat or inappropriate emotionality. Emotional flatness is shown by an unchanging facial expression, a lack of expressive gestures, and an absence of vocal inflections. Emotional inappropriateness is shown by bizarre

The Paintings of Louis Wain
Wain (1860–1939) was a British artist who gained acclaim for his paintings of cats in human situations. But, after developing schizophrenia, he no longer painted with a sense of humor. Instead, his paintings revealed his mental deterioration, becoming progressively more fragmented and bizarre.

outbursts, such as laughing when someone is seriously injured. Schizophrenia is also associated with unusual motor behavior, such as tracing patterns in the air or holding poses for hours. And, as in the case of Edvard Munch, schizophrenic people are usually socially withdrawn, with few, if any, friends. This may first appear in childhood. Mark David Chapman, who murdered John Lennon, was a reclusive child who lived in a world of imaginary little people who he claimed inhabited the walls of his living room and looked up to him as their king (Huyghe, 1982).

Kinds of Schizophrenia

Diagnosticians distinguish several kinds of schizophrenic disorders. Cases that do not fall neatly into any one of the major categories of schizophrenia are commonly lumped into a category called **undifferentiated schizophrenia**. People with **disorganized schizophrenia** show personality deterioration, speak gibberish, dress outlandishly, perform ritualized movements, and engage in obscene behavior. Odd, inappropriate laughter is a hallmark of the disorder (Black, 1982). The bizarreness of their behavior and the incoherence of their speech can make it impossible for them to maintain normal social relationships.

undifferentiated schizophrenia
A catchall category for cases that do not fall neatly into any single kind of schizophrenia.

disorganized schizophrenia
A type of schizophrenia marked by severe personality deterioration and extremely bizarre behavior.

Catatonic schizophrenia is characterized by unusual motor behavior, often alternating between catatonic excitement and catatonic stupor. In *catatonic excitement* the person paces frantically, speaks incoherently, and engages in stereotyped movements. In *catatonic stupor* the person may become mute and barely move, possibly freezing in positions for hours or days. The person may even exhibit "waxy flexibility," in which he or she can be moved from one frozen pose to another. Nonetheless, even when in a catatonic stupor, the individual typically remains aware of what is happening in the immediate environment (Ratner et al., 1981).

Paranoid schizophrenia is characterized by hallucinations, delusions, suspiciousness, and argumentativeness. This disorder was portrayed in the World War II movie *The Caine Mutiny*, in which Captain Queeg (played by Humphrey Bogart) developed paranoid delusions in the face of wartime stress. He accused his crew of conspiring against him, and even conducted a full-scale investigation to determine who stole strawberries from the ship's kitchen. In more extreme cases, paranoid schizophrenic persons may feel so threatened that they become violent.

Causes of Schizophrenia

No single viewpoint can explain all cases of schizophrenia or why some people with certain risk factors develop schizophrenia and others do not. Note that even when a risk factor is identified it may be unclear whether the factor causes schizophrenia, whether schizophrenia causes the factor, or whether other factors cause both the apparent risk factor and schizophrenia.

The Biopsychological Viewpoint

Biopsychological theories of schizophrenia emphasize genetic, biochemical, and neurological causes. There are several biological factors, but no single one is specific for schizophrenia (Szymanski, Kane, & Lieberman, 1991).   It seems that schizophrenia is best explained by the diathesis-stress viewpoint, which sees it as the outcome of the interaction between a genetic predisposition and stressful life experiences (Gottesman, McGuffin, & Farmer, 1987). For example, children who have both a genetic predisposition to become schizophrenic and the stress of losing their father are more likely to develop schizophrenia than are children with only one of those factors (Walker et al., 1981).

Schizophrenia runs in families—the closer the genetic relationship to a schizophrenic, the more likely a person is to become schizophrenic. Figure 14.4 shows that the concordance rates for schizophrenia appear to have a strong hereditary basis (Faraone & Tsuang, 1985). A recent study found a concordance rate of 48 percent for identical twins and only 4 percent for fraternal twins (Onstad et al., 1991). Yet the higher concordance rate for identical twins than for fraternal twins might be caused by the more similar treatment that identical twins receive, rather than by their identical genetic endowment.

To assess the relative contributions of heredity and experience, researchers have turned to adoption studies. Many of these studies have been conducted in Denmark, where the government maintains excellent birth and adoption records. The studies support the genetic basis of schizophrenia. For example, schizophrenia is more common in the biological relatives of schizophrenic adoptees than among their adoptive relatives; children adopted from schizophrenic parents have a greater risk of schizophrenia than do children adopted from normal parents; and children of normal parents adopted by schizophrenic parents do not show an increased risk of schizophrenia (Buchsbaum & Haier, 1983).

Given the apparent hereditary basis of schizophrenia, what biological differences might exist between people who develop schizophrenia and those who do not? Studies have found a relationship between schizophrenia and brain chemistry, most notably high levels of activity at synapses that use the neurotransmitter *dopamine*. What evidence is there of a dopamine basis for schizophrenia? First, drugs that are used to treat schizophrenia work by blocking dopamine receptors. Second, drugs such as amphetamines, which increase dopamine levels in the brain, can induce schizophrenic

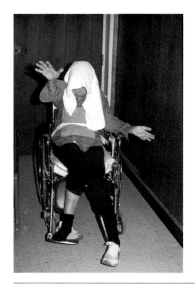

Catatonic Schizophrenia
A person with catatonic schizophrenia may maintain bizarre postures.

catatonic schizophrenia
A type of schizophrenia marked by unusual motor behavior, such as bizarre actions, extreme agitation, or immobile stupor.

paranoid schizophrenia
A type of schizophrenia marked by hallucinations, delusions, suspiciousness, and argumentativeness.

FIGURE 14.4

Heredity and the Risk of
Schizophrenia
The concordance rates for schizophrenia between people become higher as
their genetic similarity becomes
greater. This provides evidence
supportive of the hereditary basis of
schizophrenia, but cannot by itself
rule out the influence of the degree of
similarity in life experiences
(Gottesman & Shields, 1982).

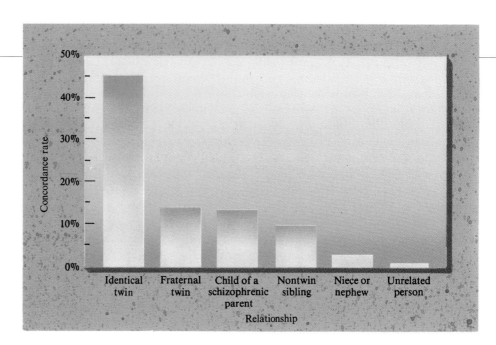

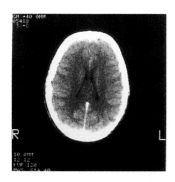

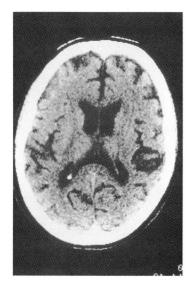

FIGURE 14.5

Schizophrenia and Neurological
Dysfunctions
CAT scans of the brains of people
with schizophrenia often show atrophy
and enlarged ventricles. Notice that
the ventricles (the dark areas) in the
schizophrenic brain (below) are much
larger than those in the normal brain
(above).

symptoms in normal people. Third, L-dopa, a drug used to treat Parkinson's disease
because it increases dopamine levels in the brain, can induce schizophrenic symptoms
in Parkinson's victims (Nicol & Gottesman, 1983).

Another promising area of research on the causes of schizophrenia involves the
study of neurological dysfunctions. PET scans have shown that schizophrenia is often
associated with unusual brain activity. Schizophrenics tend to have lower activity
in their frontal lobes when performing cognitive tasks than do other people (Buchsbaum
et al., 1990). As discussed in chapter 3, the frontal lobes are important in thinking,
planning, attention, and problem solving, each of which is often deficient in
schizophrenia.

As illustrated in figure 14.5, some schizophrenics have atrophy of brain tissue,
creating enlargement of the cerebral ventricles, the fluid-filled chambers inside the
brain (Raz & Raz, 1990). Enlarged ventricles are less common in other serious psychological disorders. For example, they are significantly more common in schizophrenia
than in major depression (Rossi et al., 1989) and bipolar disorder (Swayze et al., 1990).
Because the cerebral ventricles of schizophrenics continue to enlarge as the disorder
progresses, the enlargement might be governed by some yet unknown degenerative process
(Woods & Wolf, 1983).

Particular kinds of neurological disorders may be associated with particular sets of
schizophrenic symptoms. According to schizophrenia researcher Nancy Andreasen, there
are two kinds of schizophrenic syndromes, characterized by either positive symptoms or
negative symptoms (Andreasen & Flaum, 1991). *Positive symptoms* are active symptoms
that include hallucinations, delusions, thought disorders, and bizarre behaviors. People
with positive symptoms experience acute episodes, show progressively worsening symptoms, respond well to drug treatment, have increased numbers of dopamine receptors,
and reveal no brain structure pathology. In contrast, *negative symptoms* are passive symptoms that include mutism, apathy, flat affect, social withdrawal, intellectual impairment, poverty of speech, and inability to experience pleasure. People with negative
symptoms experience chronic disorders, respond poorly to drug treatment, do not show
dopamine hyperactivity, and often have enlarged brain ventricles and atrophy of the
cerebral cortex (Seidman, 1983).

More recently, Andreasen and her associates have reported that negative symptoms are not consistently associated with ventricular enlargement (Andreasen et al.,

1990). Moreover, it might be premature to divide schizophrenia into just two categories containing either positive or negative symptoms; the positive symptom cluster may be split into more than one cluster (Arndt, Alliger, & Andreasen, 1991).

The Psychoanalytic Viewpoint

According to the psychoanalytic viewpoint, people who become schizophrenic fail to overcome their dependence on their mothers and, as a result, become fixated at the oral stage. This gives them a weak ego that may fail to defend them against the anxiety caused by unconscious id impulses and external stressors. Instead, they cope with anxiety by resorting to behaviors characteristic of the oral stage, including fantasy, silly actions, incoherent speech, and irrational thinking.

Recent research, in the spirit of the psychoanalytic viewpoint, has found that parents high in what is known as *expressed emotion* may contribute to the maintenance or relapse of schizophrenia in their child. Parents who are high in expressed emotion criticize their child and become emotionally overprotective. Because of the impact of expressed emotion, schizophrenic children who avoid contact with their families tend to exhibit better psychological adjustment than do schizophrenic children who maintain contact with them (Cole & Kazarian, 1993).

The Behavioral Viewpoint

Behavioral theories of schizophrenia, which stress the role of learning, assume that schizophrenics are rewarded for behaving in bizarre ways (Ullmann & Krasner, 1975). This was portrayed in the 1974 movie *A Woman under the Influence*, in which a woman (played by Gena Rowlands) makes bizarre sounds to be rewarded with attention from her boorish husband (played by Peter Falk). Even on her return from a mental hospital her husband urges her to make the same sounds—in front of a houseful of people at a welcome-home party. Behavioral theorists also assume that a person who engages in bizarre behavior provokes social rejection from others, which in turn contributes to the suspiciousness and social withdrawal characteristic of schizophrenia.

The Cognitive Viewpoint

Proponents of the cognitive viewpoint emphasize disturbances of attention and thinking as the main factors in schizophrenia. As the noted schizophrenia researcher Eugen Bleuler observed earlier in this century, people with schizophrenia seem "incapable of holding the train of thought in the proper channel" (Baribeau-Braun, Picton, & Gosselin, 1983). Children exposed to parents who communicate in confusing, irrational ways are predisposed to develop the disturbed cognitive activity of schizophrenia (Doane et al., 1981). And research inspired by personal-construct theory has found that the disordered thinking that characterizes schizophrenia is found in people who use either too few or too many personal-construct dimensions in perceiving social reality. People with an optimal number of personal-construct dimensions would respond to interpersonal events in a more flexible, appropriate way than schizophrenic people do (Phillips, 1981).

The Humanistic Viewpoint

According to the humanistic viewpoint, schizophrenia is caused by extreme incongruence between the public self and the actual self. R. D. Laing (1967) claimed that schizophrenia results when a person develops a false public self to confront an intolerable life situation. This retreat from reality permits the person to experience her or his actual self. The schizophrenic person's bizarre thinking, language, and behavior are indicative of this retreat from reality. In contrast to other humanistic psychologists, Laing recommended that family, friends, and professionals permit the schizophrenic person to go on what he called a "voyage of self-discovery" into his or her actual self, rather than interfering with that process through the administration of drugs or commitment to a mental hospital.

Nancy Andreasen
"Patients with ventricular enlargement tend to have a preponderance of negative symptoms, while patients without ventricular enlargement tend to have a preponderance of positive symptoms."

Laing's critics claim that he romanticized schizophrenia, in the same way that nineteenth-century poets romanticized tuberculosis, by implying that it is somehow noble to have a serious psychological disorder. One of Laing's chief critics is Mark Vonnegut, son of novelist Kurt Vonnegut. Mark had been a follower of Laing's until he suffered several episodes of schizophrenia, as described in his autobiography *The Eden Express* (Vonnegut, 1975). When Mark recovered, he did not describe a voyage of self-discovery. Instead, he related a horrifying experience that he would have been better off without. Mark's disillusionment with Laing's view of schizophrenia led him to write a commentary for *Harper's* magazine entitled "Why I Want to Bite R. D. Laing" (Vonnegut, 1974).

PERSONALITY DISORDERS

Axis II of the DSM-IV includes the **personality disorders,** which are long-standing, inflexible, maladaptive patterns of behavior. People with personality disorders exhibit certain personality traits to an unusual, inappropriate extreme. Personality disorders are negative examples of what Alfred Adler called a style of life (discussed in chapter 13). Professionals have found it difficult to make differential diagnoses of many of the personality disorders, because one personality disorder may share symptoms with another (Morey, 1988). Table 14.5 summarizes the personality disorders. Because of its harmful effects on society, the personality disorder that has inspired particular interest is the *antisocial personality disorder*.

The Antisocial Personality Disorder

The antisocial personality disorder is found in about 3 percent of American males and less than 1 percent of American females. In the nineteenth century it was called *moral insanity*, and for most of this century it was called *psychopathy* or *sociopathy*. The **antisocial personality disorder** is characterized by maladaptive behavior beginning in childhood. This includes lying, stealing, truancy, vandalism, fighting, drug abuse, physical cruelty, academic failure, and early sexual activity. Adults with an antisocial personality might not conform to social norms. They might fail to hold a job, to honor financial obligations, or to fulfill parental responsibilities.

Because people with an antisocial personality can be charming, lie with a straight face, and talk their way out of trouble, they may pursue careers as shyster lawyers, crooked politicians, or phoney evangelists. Two hallmarks of the antisocial personality are impulsive behavior, such as reckless driving or promiscuous sexual relations, and a remarkable lack of guilt for the pain and suffering they inflict on others.

In extreme cases, people with an antisocial personality engage in criminal activities, yet fail to change their behavior even after being punished for it. Criminals with an antisocial personality violate the conditions of their release more than do comparable prisoners without an antisocial personality (Hart, Knapp, & Hare, 1988). Robert Hare, a noted researcher on the antisocial personality disorder, has found that, fortunately for society, criminals with an antisocial personality tend to "burn out" after age 40 and commit fewer crimes than do other criminals (Hare, McPherson, & Forth, 1988).

Causes of the Antisocial Personality Disorder

The antisocial personality disorder has been subjected to more research than other personality disorders, and studies have provided evidence of a physiological predisposition. Thomas Bouchard's University of Minnesota study of identical twins who were separated in infancy and then reunited years later (discussed in chapter 13) indicates that the antisocial personality has a genetic basis (Grove et al., 1990). Heredity provides people who develop an antisocial personality with an unusually low level of physiological reactivity to stress (Ogloff & Wong, 1990). As discussed in chapter 11, we try to maintain an optimal level of physiological arousal. Perhaps the unusually low level of arousal of people with an antisocial personality motivates them to engage in behaviors that increase their level of arousal (L. Ellis, 1987). While some people seek to increase

The Antisocial Personality
Charles Manson was born to a teenage prostitute, raised first by her, then by an aunt and uncle, and again by her. He left home at 14, repeatedly ran afoul of the law, and escaped from numerous juvenile detention centers. In the late 1960s he used his charismatic personality to develop a cult following in California. In August 1969, he convinced his followers to invade an exclusive area of Los Angeles and murder and mutilate pregnant actress Sharon Tate and five other persons. Since his imprisonment, Manson has expressed no remorse for his crime. He is an extreme example of a person with an antisocial personality disorder. He behaved impulsively, failed to learn from punishment, enjoyed harming other people, and expressed no guilt concerning his actions.

personality disorder
A psychological disorder characterized by enduring, inflexible, maladaptive patterns of behavior.

Robert Hare
"Psychopaths seldom commit violent crimes colored by intense emotional arousal."

Disorders	Symptoms
Disorders Characterized by Odd or Eccentric Behavior	
Paranoid personality disorder	Unrealistic mistrust and suspiciousness of people
Schizoid personality disorder	Problems in forming emotional relationships with others
Schizotypal personality disorder	Oddities of thinking, perception, communication, and behavior not severe enough to be diagnosed as schizophrenia
Disorders Characterized by Dramatic, Emotional, or Erratic Behavior	
Antisocial personality disorder	Continually violating the rights of others, being prone to impulsive behavior, and feeling no guilt for the harm done to others
Borderline personality disorder	Instable in mood, behavior, self-image, and social relationships
Histrionic personality disorder	Overly dramatic behavior, self-centered, and craving attention
Narcissistic personality disorder	Grandiose sense of self-importance, insists on being the center of attention, and lacks empathy for others
Disorders Characterized by Anxious or Fearful Behavior	
Avoidant personality disorder	Hypersensitive to potential rejection by others, causing social withdrawal despite a desire for social relationships
Dependent personality disorder	Fails to take responsibility for own life, instead relying on others to make decisions
Obsessive-compulsive personality disorder	Preoccupied with rules, schedules, organization, and trivial details, and unable to express emotional warmth

their arousal by engaging in auto racing and similar socially acceptable activities, others learn to do so by committing bank robberies and similar antisocial activities.

But what makes one person with a low level of physiological arousal seek thrills through auto racing and another seek thrills through robbing banks? In explaining the antisocial personality disorder, psychoanalysts stress the influence of abusive parents or physically absent parents, who make the child feel rejected. Because such children have no emotional ties to their parents, they fail to develop an adequate superego, including a conscience. Behaviorists believe that the antisocial personality disorder is caused by parents who reward, or fail to punish, their children for engaging in antisocial behaviors such as lying, stealing, or aggression. There is some evidence that people with antisocial personalities, perhaps because of their low physiological reactivity, are less likely to learn from punishment for misdeeds. They do not show the normal increase in anxiety when exposed to punishment (Eysenck, 1982).

antisocial personality disorder
A personality disorder marked by impulsive, manipulative, often criminal behavior, without any feelings of guilt in the perpetrator.

THINKING ABOUT *Psychology*

SHOULD WE RETAIN THE INSANITY DEFENSE?

More than 2,000 years ago, Plato noted that "someone may commit an act when mad or afflicted with disease . . . let him pay simply for the damage; and let him be exempt from other punishment" (quoted in Carson & Butcher, 1992, p. 32). Today, Plato would

The Insanity Defense
The successful use of the insanity defense by John Hinckley, Jr., following his assassination attempt on President Ronald Reagan stimulated debate on the use of that defense in criminal cases.

insanity
A legal term attesting that a person is not responsible for his or her own actions, including criminal behavior.

face opposition from those who argue against the insanity defense. Spurred by the successful insanity plea of John Hinckley, Jr., following his attempted assassination of President Ronald Reagan, many people have criticized the insanity defense as a miscarriage of justice.

Hinckley claimed that he had been motivated by his desire to impress actress Jodie Foster. After being declared legally insane and committed to St. Elizabeth's Hospital in Washington, D.C., he wrote a letter that was published in *Newsweek* in which he claimed, "Sending a John Hinckley to a mental hospital instead of prison is the American way" (Hinckley, 1982). In criticizing Hinckley's successful use of the insanity defense, columnist William F. Buckley wrote that "realism [concerning the decision] begins by sticking out our tongues at the judge and jurors who went along with the expensive charade" (Buckley, 1982, p. 917).

THE NATURE OF THE INSANITY DEFENSE

Both supporters and opponents of the insanity defense may misunderstand it. **Insanity** is a legal, not a psychological or psychiatric, term attesting that a person is not responsible for his or her own actions. In criminal cases, this is usually determined by a jury. The insanity defense was formalized in 1843 in the case of Daniel M'Naghten, a paranoid schizophrenic man who had tried to murder the English prime minister Robert Peel, who he believed was persecuting him. But M'Naghten killed Peel's secretary Edward Drummond by mistake. After a controversial trial, M'Naghten was ruled not guilty by reason of insanity and was committed to a mental hospital.

Queen Victoria was so upset by this verdict that she asked the House of Lords to review the case. It upheld the decision, and the M'Naghten rule became a guiding principle in English law. The rule states that a person is not guilty if, at the time of a crime, the person did not know what she or he was doing or that it was wrong. The M'Naghten verdict led an Englishman named Thomas Campbell to write the following poem, which was widely distributed (Perr, 1983, p. 873):

> *Ye people of England: exult and be glad*
> *For ye're now at the will of the merciless mad.*
> *[The insane are] A privileg'd class, whom no statute controls*
> *And their murderous charter exists in their souls.*
> *Do they wish to spill blood—they have only to play*
> *A few pranks—get asylum'd a month and a day*
> *Then heigh! to escape from the mad-doctor's keys,*
> *And to pistol or stab whomsoever they please.*

Today the most widely used standard for determining insanity in the United States is that of the American Law Institute. The standard comprises two rules. The *cognitive rule*, similar to the M'Naghten rule, says that a person was insane at the time of a crime if the person did not know what he or she did or did not know that it was wrong. The *volitional rule*, which presumes the reality of free will, says that a person was insane at the time of a crime if the person was not in voluntary control of her or his behavior. As described in chapter 3, an autopsy performed on Charles Whitman, the so-called Texas Tower killer, revealed that he had a brain tumor of the limbic system, a region of the brain that helps control aggression. Had Whitman gone to trial, he might have used the volitional rule as his defense, claiming that the tumor made him unable to control his behavior.

CONTROVERSY CONCERNING THE INSANITY DEFENSE

Dissatisfaction with the insanity defense in American courts did not begin with the case of John Hinckley. An earlier case that created a controversy was that of Ezra Pound, a renowned American poet who broadcast propaganda for Italy against the Allies during

Historical Concern about the Insanity Defense
An 1881 cartoon ridicules the insanity defense of Charles Guiteau, assassin of President James Garfield. Guiteau, in jester's outfit, chuckles beneath Garfield's coffin while gentlemen in the background howl over law books. A jury found Guiteau guilty.

Source: Harper's Weekly, December 10, 1881.

World War II. After the war he was accused of treason, but escaped punishment by successfully pleading insanity. Pound was committed to St. Elizabeth's Hospital, where he was treated as a celebrity and given special privileges. Critics of the insanity verdict in Pound's case claimed that the hospital supervisor led a conspiracy that encouraged Pound to fake symptoms of paranoid schizophrenia so he would be declared insane (Torrey, 1981).

Recent Controversial Cases

In recent decades, several cases involving the insanity defense, including that of John Hinckley, Jr., have provoked controversy. In 1979, in a widely publicized case, former San Francisco city supervisor Dan White murdered popular mayor George Moscone and city supervisor Harvey Milk, the first openly homosexual person to hold that post. White's lawyer claimed that White had been insane at the time of the killings because eating junk food had so raised his blood-sugar level that it made him lose voluntary control over his behavior. This became known as the "Twinkie defense." A compromise verdict was reached, and White was sentenced to 7 years for manslaughter. After his early release, White committed suicide. White's use of the insanity defense was considered an injustice by critics of the "not guilty by reason of insanity" plea, including Thomas Szasz (1980).

Despite outrage over alleged abuses of the insanity defense, it is used in less than 1 percent of felony crimes and is rarely successful (Holden, 1983). In a noteworthy case, Kenneth Bianchi, the so-called Hillside Strangler, who raped and murdered at least ten women in California in 1977, pleaded insanity. His defense lawyer claimed that Bianchi had a multiple personality disorder, and that another personality, of whom he was unaware, had committed the murders. In a 1984 Public Broadcasting System documentary,

Martin Orne

"The content, boundaries, and number of [Kenneth Bianchi's] personalities changed in response to cues about how to make the conditions more believable, and his response to hypnosis appeared to reflect conscious role playing."

psychiatrists debated whether Bianchi truly had multiple personalities. Some of those who examined Bianchi under hypnosis found that a personality known as "Steve" admitted to the killings (Watkins, 1984).

Those who believed that Bianchi was faking his disorder noted that he had a collection of psychology textbooks that contained descriptions of cases of multiple personality. Moreover, his personal history and pattern of behavior provided no evidence that he had suffered from inexplicable changes in identity and behavior. Psychiatrist Martin Orne contradicted Bianchi's diagnosis and successfully argued that Bianchi was, instead, a clever person with an antisocial personality disorder (Orne, Dinges, & Orne, 1984). When it appeared that his insanity plea would fail, Bianchi agreed to a plea bargain and was sentenced to life in prison (Fisher, 1984). Though there has been a recent trend for more defendants to use the multiple personality disorder as an insanity defense, few have been successful (Radwin, 1991).

Proposed Alternatives

The notoriety of cases such as those of John Hinckley, Dan White, and Kenneth Bianchi prompted a reevaluation of the insanity defense by state legislatures and professional organizations. Some states have abandoned the insanity defense entirely, while others have adopted a rule of *guilty but mentally ill*. This requires that an insane person who committed a crime be placed in a mental hospital until she or he is no longer mentally ill, at which time the person would serve the remainder of the sentence in prison. There is also a trend toward placing the burden on the defendant to prove that she or he was insane at the time of the crime, rather than placing it on the prosecutor to prove that the defendant was sane.

The American Psychiatric Association, the American Psychological Association, and the American Bar Association have their own positions regarding the insanity defense. The American Psychiatric Association was so embarrassed by the contradictory testimony of psychiatrists in the Hinckley trial that it published its first statement ever on the insanity defense. The statement says that the insanity defense is a legal and moral question, not a psychiatric one, and that psychiatrists should testify only about a defendant's mental status and motivation—not about a defendant's responsibility for a crime (Herbert, 1983b).

The American Psychological Association has taken a more cautious approach, calling for research on the effects of the insanity defense before deciding to eliminate it or replace it with a plea of guilty but mentally ill (Mervis, 1984). The past few years have, in fact, seen several studies on the insanity defense. An archival research study found that legislation passed in 1982 in California to make it more difficult to invoke the insanity defense produced no change in the rate of insanity pleas or acquittals over the next 3 years (McGreevy, Steadman, & Callahan, 1991). In an experiment on the effect of the guilty-but-mentally-ill verdict option, undergraduates participated as jurors in a mock trial. They then answered questions about the case. Subjects who were given the guilty-but-mentally-ill verdict option showed a two-thirds reduction in the verdicts of either guilty or not guilty by reason of insanity when compared to subjects not given that option (Poulson, 1990). These findings were supported by a study in which undergraduates and community residents responded to mock crimes; again, the availability of a guilty-but-mentally-ill verdict reduced the likelihood of verdicts of guilty or not guilty by reason of insanity (Roberts & Golding, 1991).

The American Bar Association would retain the cognitive rule, but would eliminate the volitional (that is, free will) rule, in the insanity defense. A person who did not know what he or she was doing could still use the insanity defense. As the American Bar Association explains:

> Someone who knowingly stole a radio, for example, would be legally responsible even if he believed it was issuing instructions to him from Mars. Mental illness would only be a defense if a person were so psychotic that he thought he was squeezing an orange when he was strangling a child. (Holden, 1983, p. 994)

The volitional rule has come under especially strong attack because it may be impossible to determine whether a person has acted from free will or from an irresistible impulse. It remains to be seen whether legislatures will completely overturn our long tradition of not holding people with severe psychological disorders responsible for criminal actions. Both science and politics will determine the outcome of this issue, reflecting the battle between empiricism and emotionalism in regard to the insanity defense (Rogers, 1987).

SUMMARY

THE NATURE OF PSYCHOLOGICAL DISORDERS

Researchers in the field of psychopathology study psychological disorders. The criteria for determining the presence of a psychological disorder include abnormality, maladaptiveness, and personal distress. The major viewpoints on the causes of psychological disorders include the biopsychological, psychoanalytic, behavioral, cognitive, and humanistic viewpoints. The more recent diathesis-stress viewpoint sees psychological disorders as products of the interaction between a biological predisposition and stressful life experiences.

The *Diagnostic and Statistical Manual of Mental Disorders* (DSM-IV), published by the American Psychiatric Association, is the accepted standard for classifying psychological disorders. But the reliability and validity of the DSM have been questioned. Some authorities, such as psychiatrist Thomas Szasz and psychologist David Rosenhan, have criticized the wisdom of using any kind of classification system at all.

ANXIETY DISORDERS

Anxiety disorders are associated with anxiety that is intense and disruptive of everyday functioning. A generalized anxiety disorder is a constant state of anxiety that exists independently of any particular stressful situation. A panic disorder is marked by sudden attacks of overwhelming anxiety, accompanied by dizziness, trembling, cold sweats, heart palpitations, shortness of breath, fear of dying, and fear of going crazy.

Phobias are excessive or inappropriate fears. A simple phobia involves a specific object or situation. A social phobia involves fear of public scrutiny. And agoraphobia involves fear of being in public, usually because the person fears being embarrassed by having a panic attack. People whose obsessions and compulsions interfere with their daily functioning suffer from an obsessive-compulsive disorder. An obsession is a persistent, recurring thought, and a compulsion is a repetitive action that one feels compelled to perform.

SOMATOFORM DISORDERS

The somatoform disorders are characterized by physical symptoms in the absence of disease or injury. The symptoms are caused, instead, by psychological factors. A person with hypochondriasis interprets the slightest physical changes in his or her body as evidence of a serious illness. A person with a conversion disorder exhibits loss or alteration of a physical function without any apparent physical cause.

DISSOCIATIVE DISORDERS

In dissociative disorders, the person's conscious awareness becomes separated from certain of her or his thoughts, feelings, and memories. A person with psychogenic amnesia is unable to recall personally significant memories. A person with psychogenic fugue suffers from psychogenic amnesia and loss of identity and flees from home. And a person with a multiple personality disorder has two or more distinct personalities that vie for dominance.

MOOD DISORDERS

Mood disorders involve prolonged periods of extreme depression or elation, often unrelated to objective circumstances. People with major depression experience depression that is so intense and prolonged that it causes severe distress and disrupts their lives. In such cases, suicide is always a concern. People who attempt suicide usually give warnings, so suicidal threats should be taken seriously. In bipolar disorder, the person alternates between periods of mania and major depression. Mania is characterized by euphoria, hyperactivity, grandiose ideas, annoying talkativeness, unrealistic optimism, and inflated self-esteem.

SCHIZOPHRENIA

Schizophrenia is characterized by a severe disruption of perception, cognition, emotionality, behavior, and social relationships. The most serious kind of schizophrenia is disorganized schizophrenia, marked by a complete collapse of the personality and the intellect. Catatonic schizophrenia is marked by unusual motor behavior. Paranoid schizophrenia is marked by hallucinations, delusions, suspiciousness, and argumentativeness.

PERSONALITY DISORDERS

Personality disorders are long-standing, inflexible, maladaptive patterns of behavior. Of greatest concern is the antisocial personality disorder, associated with lying, stealing, fighting, drug abuse, physical cruelty, and lack of responsibility. Persons suffering from this disorder also behave impulsively, fail to learn from punishment, and express no remorse for the pain and suffering they inflict on others.

THINKING ABOUT PSYCHOLOGY: SHOULD WE RETAIN THE INSANITY DEFENSE?

Insanity is a legal term attesting that a person is not responsible for his or her own actions. The insanity defense was first used in 1843 in the case of Daniel M'Naghten. Today the insanity defense is based on two rules. The cognitive rule says that a person was insane at the time of a crime if the person did not know what she or he did or that it was wrong. The volitional rule says that a person was insane at the time of a crime if the person was not in voluntary control of his or her behavior. The successful use of the insanity defense by John Hinckley, Jr., the would-be assassin of President Ronald Reagan, has sparked debate over the merits of the insanity defense. Despite this controversy, the insanity defense is rarely used and is even more rarely successful.

IMPORTANT CONCEPTS

agoraphobia 507
antisocial personality
  disorder 524
anxiety disorder 504
bipolar disorder 515
catatonic schizophrenia 521
conversion disorder 510
diathesis-stress viewpoint 501
disorganized schizophrenia 520

dissociative disorder 511
generalized anxiety disorder 505
hypochondriasis 510
insanity 526
major depression 514
mania 515
mood disorder 513
multiple personality 512
neurosis 502

obsessive-compulsive
  disorder 509
panic disorder 506
paranoid schizophrenia 521
personality disorder 524
phobia 507
psychogenic amnesia 512
psychogenic fugue 512
psychopathology 496

psychosis 502
schizophrenia 519
seasonal affective disorder 514
simple phobia 507
social phobia 507
somatoform disorder 510
undifferentiated
  schizophrenia 520

MAJOR CONTRIBUTORS

Lauren Alloy 518
Nancy Andreasen 522
Aaron Beck 518
Janice Egeland 515
Sigmund Freud 499, 511

Robert Hare 524
Emil Kraepelin 502
R. D. Laing 523
Peter Lewinsohn 517
Abraham Maslow 501

Martin Orne 528
Carl Rogers 501
David Rosenhan 503
Norman Rosenthal 514
Martin Seligman 508

Edwin Shneidman 514
Robert Spitzer 504
Thomas Szasz 504

RECOMMENDED READINGS

FOR GENERAL WORKS ON
PSYCHOLOGICAL DISORDERS

Carson, R. C., & Butcher, J. N.
  (1992). *Abnormal psychology*
  (9th ed.). New York:
  HarperCollins.
Porter, R. (1989). *A social history of
  madness*. New York: New
  American Library.
Schwartz, S. (1993). *Classic studies
  in abnormal psychology*.
  Mountain View, CA: Mayfield.
Weckowicz, T. E., & Liebel-
  Weckowicz, H. (1990). *A history
  of great ideas in abnormal
  psychology*. New York: Elsevier.

FOR MORE ON THE VIEW-
POINTS ON PSYCHOLOGICAL
DISORDERS

Andreasen, N. C. (1984). *The
  broken brain: The biological
  revolution in psychiatry*. New
  York: Harper & Row.
Gaw, A. C. (Ed.). (1992). *Culture,
  ethnicity, and mental illness*.
  Washington, DC: American
  Psychiatric Press.
Hollandsworth, J. G., Jr. (1990).
  *The physiology of psychological
  disorders*. New York: Plenum.

Leff, J. (1988). *Psychiatry around the
  globe: A transcultural view*.
  Washington, DC: American
  Psychiatric Press.
Masling, J. M., & Bornstein, R. F.
  (Eds.). (1993). *Psychoanalytic
  perspectives in psychopathology*.
  Washington, DC: American
  Psychological Association.
Mezzich, J., & Berganza, C. (1984).
  Culture and psychopathology.
  New York: Columbia University
  Press.
Nemiah, J. C. (1984). The
  unconscious in psychopathol-
  ogy. In K. S. Bowers &
  D. Meichenbaum (Eds.), *The
  unconscious reconsidered* (pp.
  49–87). New York: Wiley.
Szasz, T. S. (1984). *The myth of
  mental illness*. New York: Harper
  & Row.
Taylor, S. E. (1989). *Positive
  illusions: Creative self-deception
  and the healthy mind*. New York:
  Basic Books.
Triandis, H. C., & Draguns, J. G.
  (Eds.). (1980). *Handbook of
  cross-cultural psychology: Vol 6.
  Psychopathology*. Boston: Allyn
  & Bacon.

Ward, C. A. (Ed.). (1989). *Altered
  states of consciousness and mental
  health: A cross-cultural
  perspective*. Newbury Park, CA:
  Sage Publcations.

FOR MORE ON CLASSIFICA-
TION OF PSYCHOLOGICAL
DISORDERS

Amchin, J. (1990). *Psychiatric
  diagnosis: A biopsychosocial
  approach using DSM-III-R*.
  Washington, DC: American
  Psychiatric Press.
American Psychiatric Association.
  (1994). *Diagnostic and statistical
  manual of mental disorders-IV*.
  Washington, DC: American
  Psychiatric Press.
Cooper, B. (Ed.). (1987). *The
  epidemiology of psychiatric
  disorders*. Baltimore: The Johns
  Hopkins University Press.
Dohrenwald, B. P., Dohrenwald,
  B. S., Gould, M. S., Link, B.,
  Neugebauer, R., & Wunsch-
  Hitzig, R. (1980). *Mental illness
  in the United States: Epidemiologi-
  cal estimates*. New York: Praeger.
Robins, L., & Regier, D. A. (Eds.).
  (1991). *Psychiatric disorders in
  America*. New York: Free Press.

Spitzer, R. L., Williams, J. B. W., &
  Skodol, A. E. (Eds.). (1983).
  *International perspectives on
  DSM-III*. Washington, DC:
  American Psychiatric Press.
Vice, J. (1992). *From patients to
  persons: The psychiatric critiques
  of Thomas Szasz, Peter Sedgwick
  and R. D. Laing*. New York:
  Peter Lang.
Weissman, M., Myers, J., & Ross,
  C. (Eds.). (1986). *Community
  surveys of psychiatric disorders*.
  New Brunswick, NJ: Rutgers
  University Press.

FOR MORE ON ANXIETY
DISORDERS

Baker, R. (1992). *Panic disorder:
  Theory, research, and therapy*.
  New York: Wiley.
Barlow, D. H. (1988). *Anxiety and
  its disorders: The nature and
  treatment of anxiety and panic*.
  New York: Guilford.
De Silva, P., & Rachman, S.
  (1992). *Obsessive-compulsive
  disorder: The facts*. New York:
  Oxford University Press.
Gournay, K. (1989). *Agoraphobia:
  Current perspectives on theory and
  treatment*. New York: Routledge.

Hollander, E. (Ed.). (1992). *Obsessive-compulsive related disorders*. Washington, DC: American Psychiatric Press.

Knapp, T. J., & Schumacher, M. T. (1988). *Westphal's "Die agoraphobie": The beginnings of agoraphobia*. Lanham, MD: University Press of America.

Nardo, D. (1992). *Anxiety and phobias*. New York: Chelsea House.

Rapee, R. M., & Barlow, D. H. (Eds.). (1991). *Chronic anxiety: Generalized anxiety disorder and mixed anxiety-depression*. New York: Guilford.

Taylor, C. B., & Arnow, B. (1988). *The nature and treatment of anxiety disorders*. New York: Free Press.

Wegner, D. (1989). *White bears and other unwanted thoughts*. New York: Viking Penguin.

Zal, H. M. (1990). *Panic disorder: The great pretender*. New York: Plenum.

FOR MORE ON SOMATOFORM DISORDERS

Baur, S. (1988). *Hypochondria: Woeful imaginings*. Berkeley: University of California Press.

Breuer, J., & Freud, S. (1895/1982). *Studies on hysteria*. New York: Basic Books.

Kellner, R. (1985). *Somatization and hypochondriasis*. New York: Greenwood.

Slavney, P. R. (1990). *Perspectives on hysteria*. Baltimore: The Johns Hopkins University Press.

Veith, I. (1965). *Hysteria: The history of a disease*. Chicago: University of Chicago Press.

FOR MORE ON DISSOCIATIVE DISORDERS

Baldwin, L. (1984). *Oneselves: Multiple personalities, 1811–1981*. Jefferson, NC: McFarland.

Confer, W. N., & Ables, B. S. (1983). *Multiple personality: Etiology, diagnosis, and treatment*. New York: Human Sciences Press.

Klein, R., & Doane, B. (Eds.). (1992). *Psychological concepts and dissociative disorders*. Hillsdale, NJ: Erlbaum.

Kluft, R. P., & Fine, C. G. (Eds.). (1993). *Clinical perspectives on multiple personality disorder*. Washington, DC: American Psychiatric Press.

Prince, M. (1906/1969). *Dissociation of a personality: A biographical study in abnormal psychology*. Westport, CT: Greenwood.

Putnam, F. W. (1989). *Diagnosis and treatment of multiple personality disorder*. New York: Guilford.

Ross, C. A. (1989). *Multiple personality disorder: Diagnosis, clinical features, and treatment*. New York: Wiley.

Schreiber, F. (1974). *Sybil*. New York: Warner.

Sizemore, C. C., & Pitillo, E. S. (1977). *I'm Eve*. New York: Jove/Harcourt Brace Jovanovich.

Thigpen, C. H., & Cleckley, H. M. (1957). *The three faces of Eve*. New York: McGraw-Hill.

FOR MORE ON MOOD DISORDERS

Burton, R. (1621/1988). *The anatomy of melancholy*. Birmingham, AL: Gryphon.

Endler, N. S. (1982). *Holiday of darkness: A psychologist's personal journey out of his depression*. New York: Wiley.

Goodwin, F. K., & Jamison, K. R. (1990). *Manic-depressive illness*. New York: Oxford University Press.

Jackson, S. W. (1986). *Melancholia and depression: From Hippocratic times to modern times*. New Haven, CT: Yale University Press.

Kleinman, A., & Good, B. (Eds.). (1985). *Culture and depression: Studies in anthropology and cross-cultural psychiatry of affective disorders*. Berkeley: University of California Press.

Lester, D. (1992). *Why people kill themselves: A 1990s summary of research findings on suicidal behavior*. Springfield, IL: Charles C Thomas.

Paykel. E. S. (Ed.). (1992). *Handbook of affective disorders*. New York: Guilford.

Rosenthal, N. E. (1993). *Winter blues: Seasonal affective disorder—What it is and how to overcome it*. New York: Guilford.

Seligman, M. E. P. (1989). Research in clinical psychology: Why is there so much depression today? In I. S. Cohen (Ed.), *G. Stanley Hall Lecture Series* (Vol. 9, pp. 75–96). Washington, DC: American Psychological Association.

Shneidman, E. (1993). *Suicide as psychache: A clinical approach to suicidal behavior*. Northvale, NJ: Aronson.

Styron, W. (1990). *Darkness visible: A memoir of madness*. New York: Random House.

Tsuang, M. T., & Faraone, S. V. (1990). *The genetics of mood disorders*. Baltimore: The Johns Hopkins University Press.

Wolpert, E. A. (Ed.). (1977). *Manic-depressive illness: History of a syndrome*. New York: International Universities Press.

FOR MORE ON SCHIZOPHRENIA

Arieti, S. (1974). *Interpretation of schizophrenia*. New York: Basic Books.

Gottesman, I. I. (1991). *Schizophrenia genesis: The origins of madness*. New York: W. H. Freeman.

Howells, J. G. (1991). *The concept of schizophrenia: Historical perspectives*. Washington, DC: American Psychiatric Press.

Kay, S. R. (1991). *Positive and negative syndromes in schizophrenia*. New York: Brunner/Mazel.

Leff, J., & Vaughn, C. (1985). *Expressed emotion in families: Its significance for mental illness*. New York: Guilford.

Rochester, S., & Martin, J. R. (1979). *Crazy talk: A study of the discourse of schizophrenic speakers*. New York: Plenum.

Rokeach, M. (1964/1981). *The three Christs of Ypsilanti*. New York: Columbia University Press.

Siegel, R. K. (1992). *Fire in the brain: Clinical tales of hallucination*. New York: Dutton.

FOR MORE ON PERSONALITY DISORDERS

Bornstein, R. F. (1993). *The dependent personality*. New York: Guilford.

Cauwels, J. M. (1992). *Imbroglio: Rising to the challenges of borderline personality disorder*. New York: W. W. Norton.

Cleckley, H. (1976). *The mask of sanity: An attempt to clarify some issues about the so-called psychopathic personality*. St. Louis: Mosby.

Costa, P. T., Jr., & Widiger, T. A. (Eds.). (1993). *Personality disorders and the five-factor model of personality*. Washington, DC: American Psychological Association.

Horowitz, M. J. (1991). *Hysterical personality style and the histrionic personality disorder*. Northvale, NJ: Aronson.

Kantor, M. (1993). *Distancing: A guide to avoidance and avoidant personality disorder*. Westport, CT: Greenwood.

Masterson, J. F. (1981). *The narcissistic and borderline disorders: An integrated developmental approach*. New York: Brunner-Mazel.

Parsons, R. D., & Wicks, R. J. (Eds.). (1983). *Passive-aggressiveness: Theory and practice*. New York: Brunner/Mazel.

Turkat, I. D. (1990). *The personality disorders*. New York: Pergamon.

FOR MORE ON THE INSANITY DEFENSE

Caplan, L. (1984). *The insanity defense and the trial of John W. Hinckley, Jr.* Boston: Godine.

Finkel, N. J. (1988). *Insanity on trial*. New York: Plenum.

Hermann, D. H. (1983). *The insanity defense: Philosophical, historical, and legal perspectives*. Springfield, IL: Charles C Thomas.

Maeder, T. (1985). *Crime and madness: The origins and evolution of the insanity defense*. New York: Harper & Row.

Moran, R. (1981). *Knowing right from wrong: The insanity defense of Daniel McNaughtan*. New York: Free Press.

Rosenberg, C. E. (1968). *The trial of the assassin Guiteau*. Chicago: University of Chicago Press.

Simon, R. J., & Aronson, D. E. (1988). *The insanity defense: A critical assessment of law and policy in the post-Hinckley era*. Westport, CT: Praeger.

Steadman, H. J., McGreevy, M. A., Morrissey, J. P., Callahan, L. A., Robbins, P. C., & Cirincione, C. (1993). *Before and after Hinckley: Evaluating insanity defense reform*. New York: Guilford.

Torrey, E. F. (1984). *The roots of treason: Ezra Pound and the secrets of St. Elizabeth's*. London: Sidgwick & Jackson.

West, D. J., & Walk, A. (Ed.). (1977). *Daniel McNaughton: His trial and the aftermath*. Kent, England: Gaskell Books.

FOR MORE ON CONTRIBUTORS TO THE STUDY OF PSYCHOLOGICAL DISORDERS

Gay, P. (1988). *Freud: A life for our time*. New York: W. W. Norton.

Hirschmuller, A. (1978). *The life and work of Josef Breuer: Physiology and psychoanalysis*. New York: New York University Press.

Hoffman, E. (1988). *The right to be human: A biography of Abraham Maslow*. Los Angeles: Tarcher.

Kirschenbaum, H. (1979). *On becoming Carl Rogers*. New York: Delacorte.

Laing, R. D. (1985). *Wisdom, madness, and folly: The making of a psychiatrist*. New York: McGraw-Hill.

Vatz, R. E., & Weinberg, L. S. (Eds.). *Thomas Szasz: Primary values and major contentions*. Buffalo, NY: Prometheus.

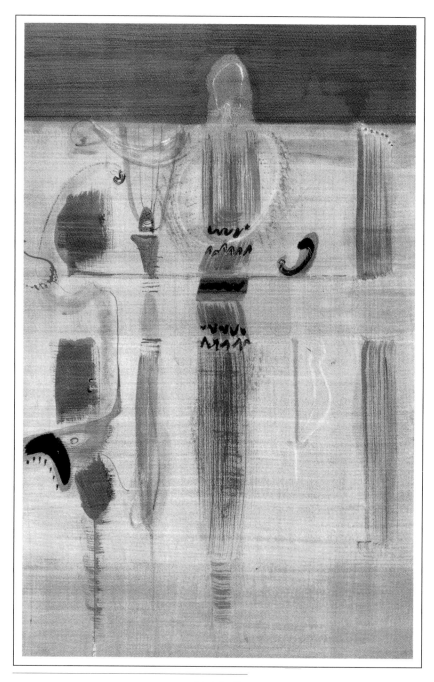

Mark Rothko
Vessels of Magic
1946

THERAPY

I n everyday life, when we feel anxious or depressed, or behave in a maladaptive way, we can usually rely on our own resources to carry us through. We may analyze the causes of our distress or our ineffective behavior and try to change our environment, our thinking, or our behavior. By doing so, we might relieve our distress and function better. Occasionally we might seek the advice of friends, relatives, or acquaintances to help us overcome our problems. We may also receive advice from informal counselors, such as bartenders and hairdressers. There are even special training programs to make hairdressers better informal counselors (Cowen, 1982). Despite the help you may receive from friends, relatives, and acquaintances, at some time in your life you might become so distressed or behave so maladaptively that you develop a psychological disorder that leads you to seek professional help. The treatment of psychological disorders has come a long way since its ancient origins.

THE HISTORY OF THERAPY

If you visit the Smithsonian Institute in Washington, D.C., you will encounter a display of Stone Age skulls with holes cut in them. The holes were produced by **trephining:** Sharp stones were used to chip holes in the skull. Some authorities believe this was done to let out demons that supposedly caused abnormal behavior. Of course, without written records there is no way to know if this was the true reason (Maher & Maher, 1985). Perhaps trephining was performed for some unknown medical purpose. If trephining was in fact performed to banish demons, it followed logically from the presumed cause of the abnormal behavior. From ancient times until today, the kinds of therapy used in the treatment of psychological disorders have been based on the presumed causes of those disorders.

The Greek philosopher Hippocrates (460–377 B.C.) turned away from the supernatural explanation of psychological disorders, which attributed them to demons or punishment from the gods, in favor of a naturalistic explanation. As discussed in chapter 14, Hippocrates believed that many psychological disorders were caused by imbalances in fluids that he called humors, which included blood, phlegm, black bile, and yellow bile. This led him to recommend treatments aimed at restoring their balance. For example, because Hippocrates believed an excess of blood caused the agitated state of mania, he treated mania with bloodletting. As you would expect, people weakened by the loss of blood became less agitated.

During the early Christian era, such naturalistic treatments existed side by side with supernatural ones—such as, as described in the New Testament, Jesus' curing a madman by casting demons out of him and into a herd of pigs. Until the Middle Ages, treatments for psychological disorders were generally humane, at worst involving mild forms of exorcism that might hurl insults at the devil. But by the late Middle Ages, treatments increasingly involved physical punishment—literally attempts to "beat the devil out of" a person.

This inhumane treatment continued into the Renaissance, which also saw the advent of *insane asylums*. Though some of these institutions were pleasant communities in which residents received humane treatment, most were no better than prisons in which inmates lived under deplorable conditions. The most humane asylum was the town of Geel in Belgium, where people with mental disorders lived in the homes of townspeople, moved about freely, and worked to support themselves. Geel continues today to provide humane care for 800 individuals who live with 600 families (Godemont, 1992).

trephining
An ancient technique that used sharp stones to chip holes in the skull, possibly to let out evil spirits that supposedly caused abnormal behavior.

Trephining
These skulls show the effect of trephining, in which sharp rocks were used to chip holes in the skull. Some authorities believe this was to let out evil spirits that supposedly caused bizarre thinking and behavior. The growth of new bone around the holes in some trephined skulls indicates that many people survived the surgery.

Bedlam
This engraving by William Hogarth (1697–1764) depicts the asylum of St. Mary's of Bethlehem (better known as "Bedlam") in London, notorious for the inhumane treatment of its residents. Even Shakespeare referred to the bedlam of Bedlam in *King Lear* (act 2, scene 3):

The country gives me proof and precedent
Of Bedlam beggars, who, with roaring voices,
Strike in their numb'd and mortified bare arms
Pins, wooden pricks, nails, sprigs of rosemary;
And . . .
Sometimes with lunatic bans, sometimes with prayers, Enforce their charity.

Few Renaissance asylums were as pleasant as Geel. The most notorious one was St. Mary's of Bethlehem in London. This was a nightmarish place where inmates were treated like animals in a zoo. On weekends, families would go on outings to the asylum, pay a small admission fee, and be entertained by the antics of the inmates. Visitors called the male inmates of St. Mary's "Tom Fools," contributing the word *tomfoolery* to our language (Morris & Morris, 1985). And the asylum became known as "Bedlam," reflecting the cockney pronunciation of Bethlehem. The word *bedlam* came to mean any confused, uproarious scene.

In 1792 inhumane conditions in French insane asylums and the positive model of Geel spurred the physician Philippe Pinel (1745–1826) to institute what he called **moral therapy** at the Bicetre asylum in Paris (Weiner, 1992). Moral therapy was based on the premise that humane treatment, honest work, and pleasant recreation would promote mental well-being. Though Pinel implemented the reforms, they were suggested to him by Jean-Baptiste Pussin, who supervised the inmates at Bicetre (Weiner, 1979). Pinel had the inmates unchained, provided with good food, and treated with kindness. He even instituted the revolutionary technique of speaking with them about their problems. The first inmate released was a powerful man who had been chained in a dark cell for 40 years after killing a guard with a blow from his manacles. Onlookers were surprised (and relieved) when he simply strolled outside, gazed up at the sky, and exclaimed, "Ah, how beautiful" (Bromberg, 1954, p. 83).

Pinel's moral therapy spread throughout Europe. It was introduced to the United States by Benjamin Rush (1745–1813), a slavery abolitionist, a signer of the Declaration of Independence, and the founder of American psychiatry. As part of moral therapy, which was congruent with his religious beliefs (Thielman & Larson, 1984), Rush prescribed work, travel, and reading. He also prescribed physical treatments that with hindsight we might view as barbaric, but he believed that they had therapeutic value. For example, because Rush assumed that depressed people had too little blood in their brains, he whirled them around in special chairs to force blood from their bodies into their heads. Figure 15.1 shows several treatment devices that were popular in the nineteenth century.

In the 1840s Dorothea Dix (1802–1887), a Massachusetts schoolteacher, shocked the U.S. Congress with reports of the brutal treatment of the inmates of insane asylums. Due to her efforts, many state mental hospitals were built throughout the United States,

moral therapy
An approach to therapy, developed by Philippe Pinel, that provided mental patients with humane treatment.

Pinel Unchaining the Inmates of an Asylum
Philippe Pinel shocked and frightened many of his fellow French citizens by freeing the inmates of insane asylums and providing them with humane treatment. When opponents asked, "Citizen, are not you yourself crazy, that you would free these beasts?" Pinel replied, "I am convinced that these *people* are not incurable if they can have air and liberty" (Bromberg, 1954, p. 83).

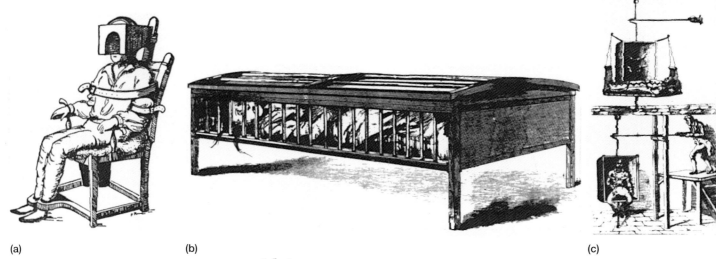

(a)   (b)   (c)

FIGURE 15.1

Nineteenth-Century Treatment Devices
Benjamin Rush invented (*a*) the "tranquilizing chair" to calm manic patients. Other devices that were popular in the nineteenth century included (*b*) the "crib," which was used to restrain violent patients, and (*c*) the "circulating swing," which was used to restore balance to allegedly out-of-balance body fluids.

Benjamin Rush (1745–1813)
"Madness has been exclusively in the mind. I object to this opinion . . . because the mind is incapable of any operations independently of impressions communicated to it through the medium of the body."

psychotherapy
The treatment of psychological disorders through psychological, as opposed to biomedical, means, generally involving verbal interaction with a professional therapist.

often in rural settings, that provided good food, social activities, and employment on farms. Dix also had influence in Canada, including the establishment of the first mental hospital in Nova Scotia (Goldman, 1990). Unfortunately, over time many of these mental hospitals became human warehouses, providing custodial care and little else. This contradicted the humane treatment Dix had envisioned (Viney & Bartsch, 1984).

In the early twentieth century, public concern about the deplorable conditions in state mental hospitals grew after the publication of *A Mind That Found Itself* by a Yale University graduate named Clifford Beers (Beers, 1908/1970). The book described the physical abuse he suffered during his 3 years in the Connecticut State Hospital. Beers (1876–1943) founded the mental-health movement, which promotes the humane treatment of people with mental disorders. The mental-health movement has seen mental hospitals joined by group homes, private practices, and counseling centers as alternative treatment sites for psychological disorders.

Today, specially trained professionals offer therapy for psychological disorders. Psychological therapy, or **psychotherapy,** involves the therapeutic interaction of a professional therapist with one or more persons suffering from a psychological disorder. Though there are many orientations toward psychotherapy, most psychotherapists favor an *eclectic orientation*, in which they select techniques from different orientations that they believe will help particular clients (Smith, 1982). This indicates that the practice of therapy is as much an art as it is a science. The first therapeutic orientation was the psychoanalytic.

THE PSYCHOANALYTIC ORIENTATION

From 1880 to 1882 the Austrian physician Joseph Breuer (1842–1925) treated a young woman he called Anna O., who had symptoms of conversion hysteria (described in chapter 13). She suffered from impaired vision, paralyzed legs, and difficulty swallowing, without any physical causes. Breuer found that when Anna O. spoke freely about her condition, her symptoms disappeared. She called this her "talking cure" or "chimney sweeping." As she spoke freely, she often recalled distressing childhood experiences. By talking about them, she obtained emotional release, followed by a reduction in her physical symptoms.

The Mental Hospital
Many of the mental hospitals built through the efforts of Dorothea Dix are still used today.

Dorothea Dix (1802–1887)
"Were I to recount the one hundreth part of the shocking scenes of sorrow, suffering, abuse, and degradation to which I have been witness—searched out in jails, in poorhouses, in pens and block-houses, in caves, in cages and cells, in dungeons and cellars; men and women in chains, frantic, bruised, lacerated, and debased, your souls would grow sick at the horrid recital."

Breuer called this process of emotional release **catharsis.** In 1882 Breuer abruptly broke off therapy with Anna O. after finding that she had become sexually and emotionally attached to him—even claiming to be pregnant with his child. Later, after recovering, Anna O., under her real name of Bertha Pappenheim (1859–1936), became a philanthropist, a founder of the social work profession, and a leader in the women's rights movement. Breuer's treatment of her marked the beginning of modern psychotherapy (Hollender, 1980).

The Nature of Psychoanalysis

After Breuer related the case of Anna O. to him and after observing similar conditions in some of his patients, Sigmund Freud turned from medicine to the study of psychological disorders. Freud found that childhood emotional conflicts repressed into the unconscious mind instigate the use of defense mechanisms. The excessive or inadequate use of defense mechanisms causes the symptoms of psychological disorders, including conversion hysteria. Freud's aim was to make the person gain insight into his or her repressed conflicts, thereby inducing catharsis and relieving the underlying conflict. This led Freud to develop the form of therapy known as **psychoanalysis.**

Clifford Beers (1876–1943)
"Is it not, then, an atrocious anomaly that the treatment often meted out to insane persons is the very treatment which would deprive some sane persons of their reason?"

catharsis
In psychoanalysis, the release of repressed emotional energy as a consequence of insight into the unconscious causes of one's psychological problems.

psychoanalysis
A type of psychotherapy, developed by Sigmund Freud, aimed at uncovering the unconscious causes of psychological disorders.

Traditional Freudian psychoanalysis takes place with the client reclining on a couch and the therapist sitting nearby, just out of sight. Freud claimed that this arrangement relaxes the client, thereby reducing inhibitions about discussing emotional topics. He also believed that the arrangement allows the therapist to focus on what the client is saying. Some authorities argue that, instead, Freud preferred this arrangement because he was shy and disliked making eye contact with his clients (Corsini, 1984).

Freud usually saw clients for less than a year, and he reportedly cured the composer Gustav Mahler of impotence in one 4-hour session that provided Mahler with insight into the cause of his problem (Goleman, 1981). Today, traditional Freudian psychoanalysts might see clients three to five times a week for years. Though Freudian psychoanalysis does not always take years, at $100 or more a session it is beyond the financial reach of most people.

Joseph Breuer (1842–1925)
"In 1880 I had observed a patient suffering from a severe hysteria, who in the course of her illness displayed such peculiar symptoms as to convince me that here a glimpse was being offered into deeper layers of psychopathological processes."

Psychoanalysis Today
Though most psychotherapists now favor seated, face-to-face interaction with their clients, some psychoanalytic psychotherapists still sit out of sight of the client, who reclines on a couch.

analysis of free associations
In psychoanalysis, the process by which the therapist interprets the underlying meaning of the client's uncensored reports of anything that comes to mind.

analysis of resistances
In psychoanalysis, the process by which the therapist interprets client behaviors that interfere with therapeutic progress toward uncovering unconscious conflicts.

analysis of dreams
In psychoanalysis, the process by which the therapist interprets the symbolic, manifest content of dreams to reveal their true, latent content to the client.

analysis of transference
In psychoanalysis, the process by which the therapist interprets the feelings expressed by the client toward the therapist as being indicative of the feelings typically expressed by the client toward important people in his or her personal life.

Techniques in Psychoanalysis

An important goal of psychoanalytic techniques is to make the client's unconscious conflicts conscious. To accomplish this, the therapist actively *interprets* the significance of what the client says, thereby acting as more than a cold mirror that simply reflects back exactly what the client says. The process by which clients use a therapist's interpretations of what they say to gain insight into the unconscious conflicts that are causing their problems is called *working through*. The therapist's interpretations are based on the analysis of *free associations, resistances, dreams,* and *transference*.

The main technique of psychoanalysis is the **analysis of free associations,** which has much in common with Anna O.'s "talking cure." In free association, the client is urged to report any thoughts or feelings that come to mind—no matter how trivial, bizarre, or embarrassing they seem. Freud assumed, based on the principle of psychic determinism (discussed in chapters 1 and 13), that free association would unlock meaningful information. This assumption was not new, because free association was used as long ago as ancient Greece. In Aristophanes' play *The Clouds,* Socrates uses free association to help a man gain self-knowledge.

In the **analysis of resistances,** the psychoanalyst notes behaviors that interfere with therapeutic progress. Signs of resistance include arriving late, missing sessions, acting belligerent, talking about insignificant topics, or bringing up important matters just before the end of a session. The client holds on dearly to resistances to block awareness of painful memories or conflicts. By interpreting the meaning of the client's resistances, the therapist helps the client uncover the unconscious conflicts that provoke them. Suppose a client changes the topic whenever the therapist asks him about his father. The therapist might interpret this as a sign that the client has unconscious emotional conflicts about his father.

As explained in chapter 6, Freud believed that the **analysis of dreams** was the "royal road to the unconscious." He claimed that dreams symbolized unconscious sexual and aggressive conflicts. Freud relied on his own dreams, as well as those of his clients, to illustrate his theory (Mautner, 1991). Having the client free-associate about the content of a series of dreams allows the psychoanalyst to interpret the symbolic, or *manifest,* content of the client's dreams to reveal the true, or *latent,* content—their true meaning.

The key to a psychoanalytic cure is the **analysis of transference** (Miller, 1983). Transference is the tendency of the client to act toward the therapist in the way she or he acts toward important people in everyday life, such as a boss, spouse, parent, or teacher. Transference can be positive or negative. In *positive transference* the client expresses feelings of approval and affection toward the therapist—as Anna O. expressed toward Breuer. In *negative transference* the client expresses feelings of disapproval and rejection toward the therapist—such as criticizing the therapist's skill. By interpreting transference, the therapist helps the client gain insight into the social origins of his or her current emotional problems.

Traditional Freudian psychoanalysis inspired many offshoots. Freud's students Carl Jung and Alfred Adler broke with him and developed their own versions of psychoanalysis. During succeeding decades, neo-Freudians such as Karen Horney, Melanie Klein, Erich Fromm, Harry Stack Sullivan, Jacques Lacan, and Heinz Kohut developed their own versions. Nonetheless, psychoanalysis, in its various forms, went from being the choice of most therapists in the 1950s to being the choice of about 15 percent in the 1980s (Smith, 1982). One of the main reasons for this declining trend is that other, less costly and less lengthy, therapies are at least as effective as psychoanalysis (Fisher & Greenberg, 1985). Today few therapists are strict Freudians. Instead, many practice what is called *psychodynamic therapy,* which employs aspects of psychoanalysis in face-to-face, once-a-week therapy lasting months instead of years. Psychodynamic therapists also rely more on discussions of past and present social relationships than on trying to uncover hidden conflicts. Psychodynamic therapy has proved effective in the treatment of a variety of psychological disorders (Goldfried, Greenberg, & Marmar, 1990).

Drawing by Shanahan; © 1989 The New Yorker Magazine, Inc.

THE BEHAVIORAL ORIENTATION

In 1952 British psychologist Hans Eysenck coined the term **behavior therapy** to refer to treatments that favor changing maladaptive behaviors rather than providing insight into unconscious conflicts. According to Eysenck, simply knowing why you are depressed and experiencing catharsis will not necessarily make you less depressed. Unlike traditional psychoanalysts, behavior therapists ignore unconscious conflicts, emphasize present behavior, and assume that therapy can be accomplished in weeks or months rather than in years. To behavior therapists, abnormal behavior, like normal behavior, is learned and therefore can be unlearned.

Psychoanalytic therapists responded to the challenge of this new form of therapy by insisting that the elimination of maladaptive behaviors without dealing with the supposed underlying, unconscious causes would produce *symptom substitution*—the replacement of one maladaptive behavior with another. But studies have shown that directly changing maladaptive behaviors is not followed by the substitution of other maladaptive behaviors (Kazdin, 1982a). Behavior therapists change maladaptive behaviors by applying the principles of classical conditioning, operant conditioning, and social-learning theory.

behavior therapy
The therapeutic application of the principles of learning to change maladaptive behaviors.

Classical-Conditioning Therapies

As explained in chapter 7, in classical conditioning, a stimulus associated with another stimulus that elicits a response may itself come to elicit that response. Therapies based on classical conditioning stress the importance of stimuli in controlling behavior. The goal of these therapies is the removal of the stimuli that control maladaptive behaviors or the promotion of more-adaptive responses to those stimuli.

Counterconditioning

The technique of **counterconditioning** replaces unpleasant emotional responses to stimuli with pleasant ones. The procedure is based on the assumption that we cannot simultaneously experience an unpleasant feeling, such as anxiety, and a pleasant feeling, such as relaxation. Counterconditioning was used in the following classic study by Mary Cover Jones.

counterconditioning
A behavior therapy technique that applies the principles of classical conditioning to replace unpleasant emotional responses to stimuli with more pleasant ones.

Pioneers of Behavior Therapy
Joseph Wolpe (1988), who developed systematic desensitization, called Mary Cover Jones "the founding mother of behavior therapy" for introducing the use of counterconditioning in treating phobias.

● Anatomy of a Classic Research Study:
Can Phobias Be Eliminated by Counterconditioning?

Rationale

Therapeutic counterconditioning was introduced by John B. Watson's student Mary Cover Jones (1896–1987). As described in chapter 7, Watson had conditioned a boy he called Little Albert to fear a white rat by pairing the rat with a loud sound. Watson proposed that the fear could be eliminated by pairing the rat with a pleasant stimulus, such as pleasurable stroking (Watson & Rayner, 1920).

Method

While working at Columbia University, Jones (1924) took Watson's suggestion and, under his advisement, tried to rid a 3-year-old boy named Peter of a rabbit phobia he had developed. (The origin of his phobia was unknown.) This was part of a larger project that tried to help institutionalized children overcome their phobias through a variety of techniques. Jones used what she called "direct conditioning," which is now known as counterconditioning. Jones presented Peter with candy and then brought a caged rabbit closer and closer to him. This was done twice a day for 2 months.

Results and Discussion

At first Peter cried when the rabbit was within 20 feet of him. Over the course of the study, he became less and less fearful of it. On the last day he asked for the rabbit, petted it, tried to pick it up, and finally played with it on a windowsill. Evidently, the pleasant feelings that Peter experienced in response to the candy gradually became associated with the rabbit. This reduced his fear of the rabbit. Jones cautioned, however, that this was a delicate procedure. If performed too rapidly, it could produce the opposite effect—fear of the candy.

systematic desensitization
A form of counterconditioning that trains the client to maintain a state of relaxation in the presence of imagined anxiety-inducing stimuli.

Today the most widely used form of counterconditioning is **systematic desensitization,** developed by Joseph Wolpe (1958) for treating phobias. Systematic desensitization involves three steps. The first step is for the client to practice *progressive relaxation,* a technique developed in the 1930s by Edmund Jacobson to relieve anxiety. To learn progressive relaxation, clients sit in a comfortable chair and practice successively tensing and relaxing each of the major muscle groups—including those of the head, arms, body, and legs—until they gain the ability to relax their entire body.

The second step is the construction of an *anxiety hierarchy,* consisting of a series of anxiety-inducing scenes related to the person's phobia. The client lists 10 to 20 scenes, rating them on a 100-point scale from least to most anxiety inducing. A rating of zero would mean that the scene induces no anxiety; a rating of 100 would mean that the scene induces abject terror. Suppose that you have *arachnophobia*—a spider phobia. You might rate a photo of a spider a 5, a spider on your arm a 60, and a spider on your face an 85. Table 15.1 presents an example of an anxiety hierarchy.

Systematic desensitization has been successful in treating a wide variety of phobias. These include fear of blood (Elmore, Wildman, & Westefeld, 1980), dentists (Klepac, 1986), hypodermic needles (Rainwater et al., 1988), public speaking (Rossi & Seiler, 1989–1990), and magnetic resonance imaging chambers (Klonoff, Janata, & Kaufman, 1986).

TABLE 15.1	A Test-Anxiety Hierarchy

Initial Rating of Distress	Fear-Inducing Scene
0	Registering for next semester's courses
5	Going over the course outline in class
20	Hearing the instructor announce that the midterm exam will take place in three weeks
30	Discussing the difficulty of the exam with fellow students
45	Reviewing your notes one week before the exam
50	Attending a review session three days before the exam
60	Listening to the professor explain what to expect on the exam the day before it
65	Studying alone the day before the exam
70	Studying with a group of students the night before the exam
75	Overhearing superior students expressing their self-doubts about the exam
80	Realizing that you are running out of study time at 1:00 A.M. the night before the exam
90	Entering the class before the exam and having the professor remind you that one-third of your final grade depends on it
95	Reading the exam questions and discovering that you do not recognize several of them
100	Answering the exam questions while hearing other students hyperventilating and muttering about them

Given the success of systematic desensitization in treating phobias, what accounts for its effectiveness? Is relaxation a necessary component? Perhaps not. In some cases, systematic desensitization is successful when it simply presents successive items on the anxiety hierarchy to clients who have not engaged in progressive relaxation. This means that systematic desensitization may accomplish its effects through extinction rather than through counterconditioning, because the client experiences the imagined situations without experiencing the expected adverse consequences (Levin & Gross, 1985). The following study assessed the possible role of endorphins in systematic desensitization.

Anatomy of a Contemporary Research Study:
Do Endorphins Mediate the Effect of Systematic Desensitization on Phobias?

Rationale
A study of systematic desensitization indicated that, whatever the reason for its effectiveness, it might exert its effects through the actions of endorphins (Egan et al., 1988). As discussed in chapter 3, endorphins are the brain's own opiatelike chemicals, capable of inducing feelings of pleasure.

Method
The subjects all suffered from simple phobias (see chapter 14), such as fear of heights, fear of dogs, and fear of elevators. The subjects were randomly assigned into two groups. Prior to sessions of systematic desensitization, 6 subjects (the experimental group) received intravenous infusions of naloxone, a drug that blocks the effect of endorphins, and 5 subjects (the control group) received intravenous infusions of a placebo, a saline solution with no specific effects. Because the study used the double-blind procedure, neither the subjects nor the experimenter knew which subjects received naloxone and which received the placebo. This controlled for any subject or experimenter biases. The subjects received eight sessions over a period of 4 weeks.

Results and Discussion
The results indicated that the subjects who received the placebo experienced a significant decrease in the severity of their phobias, while those who received naloxone did not. Because naloxone blocks the effects of the endorphins, the results support the possible role of endorphins in the effects of systematic desensitization. The pleasant feelings produced by the endorphins may become conditioned to the formerly fear-inducing stimuli.

Therapy 541

In Vivo Desensitization
A phobia sufferer may gain relief through in vivo desensitization, which involves gradual exposure to more and more anxiety-inducing situations related to the phobia. This man, suffering from a fear of heights (acrophobia), may have begun therapy by simply looking out of a first-floor window. He has progressed to the point that he is able to walk onto the roof of a tall building. But note that he still holds tightly to the ledge. He should eventually be able to peer over the ledge without having to grasp it.

Of course, the ultimate test of systematic desensitization is the ability to face the actual source of your phobia (Foa & Kozak, 1986). One way of assuring such success is to use **in vivo desensitization,** which physically exposes the client to successive situations on the client's anxiety hierarchy. In vivo desensitization has been successful in treating claustrophobia (Fabian & Haley, 1991), school phobia (Houlihan & Jones, 1989), and many other kinds of phobias. In one case, a woman who had chronic nightmares about snakes was relieved of them by an in vivo procedure that had her gradually approach a live, harmless snake (Eccles, Wilde, & Marshall, 1988).

Aversion Therapy

In a sense, **aversion therapy** is the opposite of systematic desensitization. The goal of aversion therapy is to make a formerly pleasurable, but maladaptive, behavior unpleasant. In aversion therapy, a stimulus that normally elicits a maladaptive response is paired with an unpleasant stimulus, leading to a reduction in the maladaptive response. Aversion therapy was introduced in the 1930s to treat alcoholism by administering painful electric shocks to alcoholic patients in the presence of the sight, smell, and taste of alcohol. Today aversion therapy for alcoholism uses drugs that make the individual feel deathly ill after drinking alcohol. The drugs interfere with the metabolism of alcohol, leading to the buildup of a toxic chemical that induces nausea and dizziness.

A study of 685 alcoholics treated with aversion therapy using illness-inducing drugs found that two-thirds were abstinent 1 year later and one-third were abstinent 3 years later (Wiens & Menustik, 1983). In treating alcoholism, aversion therapy with drugs is superior to aversion therapy with electric shocks (Cannon & Baker, 1981). This supports the concept of *behavioral preparedness*, discussed in chapters 7 and 14. We seem to have an inborn tendency to associate stomach distress with tastes such as alcohol rather than with external sources of pain such as electric shocks. Aversion therapy has also been used to treat a variety of other behavioral problems, including smoking, bedwetting, overeating, and sexual abuse of children.

Operant-Conditioning Therapies

Treatments based on operant conditioning change maladaptive behaviors by controlling their consequences. This is known as **behavior modification** and is based on the work of learning theorist B. F. Skinner. Popular forms of behavior modification rely on the behavioral contingencies of positive reinforcement and punishment.

Positive Reinforcement

One of the most important uses of positive reinforcement has been in treating patients in mental hospitals. Residents of mental hospitals have traditionally relied on the staff to take care of all their needs. This often leads to passivity, a decrease in self-care, and a general decline in dignified behavior. But "talking therapies," such as psychoanalytic therapy, have been ineffective in improving the behavior of hospitalized patients suffering from schizophrenia or mood disorders.

The development of the "token economy" provided a way to overcome this problem (Ayllon & Azrin, 1968). The **token economy** provides tokens (often plastic poker chips) as positive reinforcement for desirable behaviors, such as making beds, taking showers, or wearing appropriate clothing. The patients use the tokens to purchase items such as books or candy and privileges such as television or passes to leave the hospital grounds. The use of the token economy has proved successful in mental hospitals and other settings (Glynn, 1990), including classrooms and community residences for the mentally retarded (Kazdin, 1982b). In one study, a token economy helped mentally retarded subjects maintain an aerobic exercise program, which provided them with improved physical fitness (Croce, 1990).

FIGURE 15.2

Punishment and Autism
This autistic child wears a device developed at Johns Hopkins University called the Self-Injurious Behavior Inhibiting System, which delivers a mild electric shock to his leg whenever he bangs his head. This and similar devices have been used with success to reduce self-injurious behavior by autistic children. As you can imagine, the use of such devices has sparked controversy (Landers, 1987).

Punishment

Though less desirable than positive reinforcement, punishment can also be effective in changing maladaptive behaviors. In fact, it may sometimes be the only way to prevent inappropriate, or even dangerous, behavior. In using punishment, the therapist provides aversive consequences for maladaptive behavior. A controversial application of punishment has been the use of mild electric shocks to reduce self-biting, head banging, and other self-destructive behaviors in autistic children, who do not respond to talking therapies. One technique is illustrated in figure 15.2. Before using punishments such as mild electric shock, therapists must first present their rationale and gain approval from parents and fellow professionals. Once the self-injurious behavior has stopped, the therapist uses positive reinforcement to promote more-appropriate behaviors. The combination of punishment and positive reinforcement has been effective in improving the behavior of autistic children, though it does not make them behave completely like normal children (Lovass, 1987).

Extinction

If a person is not reinforced for a behavior, whether adaptive or maladaptive, it will become extinguished. The technique of *flooding* takes advantage of this in the elimination of intense fears and phobias. While systematic desensitization trains the client to relax and experience a graded series of anxiety-inducing situations, **flooding** exposes the client to a situation that evokes intense anxiety. In *imaginal flooding*, the client is asked to hold in mind an image of the feared situation; in *in vivo flooding*, the client is placed in the actual feared situation. As clients experience the situation mentally or in reality, their anxiety diminishes because they are prevented from escaping and thereby negatively reinforcing their flight behavior through fear reduction. Of course, care must be taken to protect the client from being overwhelmed by fear. A study that used flooding with 20 social-phobic clients demonstrated a significant decrease in their anxiety levels and heart rate, indicating extinction of their phobias (Turner et al., 1992). Flooding also has helped clients overcome anxiety disorders such as agoraphobia (Jansson & Ost, 1982) and panic disorder (Fava et al., 1991). Imaginal flooding and in vivo flooding are equally effective in extinguishing fears (James, 1986).

flooding
An extinction procedure in which a phobic client is exposed to a stimulus that evokes intense anxiety.

FIGURE 15.3

Modeling and Phobias
People may learn to overcome their phobias by observing other people either handle objects they are afraid to handle or perform in situations in which they are afraid to perform. The graph shows the results of a study comparing the effectiveness of three kinds of therapy for snake phobia. The control group received no therapy. As you can see, all three therapies produced more approaches to the snakes than did the control condition. But participant modeling produced more improvement than did symbolic modeling (in which subjects watched models on film) or systematic desensitization (Bandura, Blanchard, & Ritter, 1969).

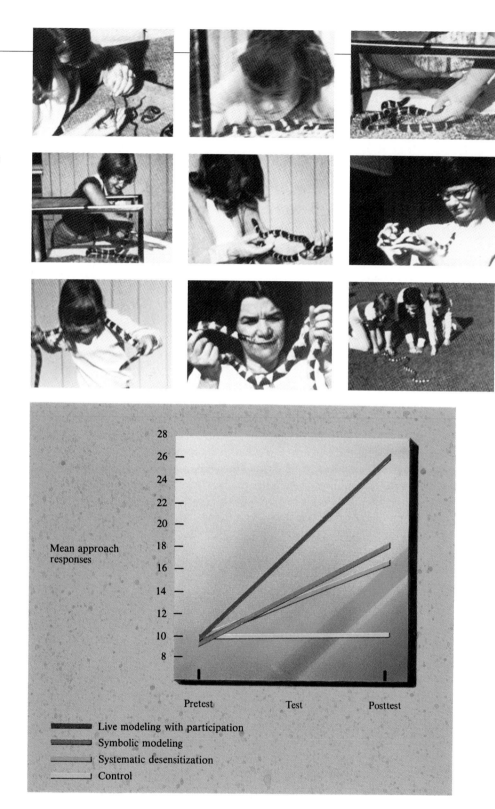

Mean approach responses

■■■ Live modeling with participation
■■■ Symbolic modeling
── Systematic desensitization
── Control

Social-Learning Therapies

In treating Peter's rabbit phobia, Mary Cover Jones (1924) sometimes let Peter observe children playing with a rabbit. By doing so, Jones made use of social learning, which was discussed in chapter 7 in regard to Albert Bandura's theory of observational learning. Therapists who use social learning have their clients watch other people model adaptive behaviors either in person or on videotape. As shown in figure 15.3, clients learn to

TABLE 15.2	Common Irrational Beliefs

1. It is a dire necessity for an adult to be loved or approved by virtually every other significant person in his or her community.

2. One should be thoroughly competent, adequate, and achieving in all possible respects if one is to consider oneself worthwhile.

3. Certain people are bad, wicked, or villainous and should be severely blamed and punished for their villainy.

4. It is awful and catastrophic when things are not the way one would very much like them to be.

5. Human unhappiness is externally caused and people have little or no ability to control their sorrows and disturbances.

6. If something is or may be dangerous or fearsome one should be terribly concerned about it and should keep dwelling on the possibility of its occurring.

7. It is easier to avoid than to face certain life difficulties and self-responsibilities.

8. One should be dependent on others and need someone stronger than oneself on whom to rely.

9. One's past history is an all-important determiner of one's present behavior, and because something once strongly affected one's life, it should indefinitely have a similar effect.

10. One should become quite upset over other people's problems and disturbances.

11. There is invariably a right, precise, and perfect solution to human problems and it is catastrophic if this perfect solution is not found.

From A. Ellis, *Reason and Emotion in Psychotherapy*. Copyright © 1962 Lyle Stuart, Inc., Secaucus, NJ. Reprinted with permission.

acquire social skills or to overcome phobias by performing the behavior that is being modeled. Therapists may also use **participant modeling,** in which the therapist models the desired behavior while the client watches. The client then tries to perform the behavior. Participant modeling has been successful in helping individuals overcome their fears, including fears of surgery (Faust, Olson, & Rodriguez, 1991), harmless snakes (Hughes, 1990), performing gymnastics (McAuley, 1985), and dogs and cats (Ladouceur, 1983).

participant modeling
A form of social-learning therapy in which the client learns to perform more-adaptive behaviors by first observing the therapist model the desired behaviors.

THE COGNITIVE ORIENTATION

The Greek Stoic philosopher Epictetus (A.D. ca. 60–ca. 120) noted that irrational people tend to become emotionally upset. This indicates the kinship between Stoic philosophy and the cognitive orientation to therapy (Montgomery, 1993). Cognitive therapists believe that events in themselves do not cause maladaptive emotions and behaviors. Instead, it is our interpretation of events that does so. Given this assumption, cognitive therapists believe that changes in thinking can produce changes in maladaptive emotions or behaviors. Because cognitive therapies can include aspects of behavior therapy, they are commonly called *cognitive-behavior therapies*. They have been effective in treating many kinds of anxiety disorders, including phobias (Heimberg, 1989), generalized anxiety disorder (Marks, 1989), and panic disorder (Mattick et al., 1990).

Rational-Emotive Therapy

The former psychoanalytic psychotherapist Albert Ellis developed the first cognitive therapy, which he called **rational-emotive therapy (R-E-T).** A survey of therapists found that in recent decades Ellis has been second only to Carl Rogers in his influence on the field of psychotherapy (Smith, 1982). Ellis's therapy is based on his *A-B-C theory of emotion,* in which A is an activating event, B is an irrational belief, and C is an emotional consequence. Ellis (1962) points out that most of us believe that A causes C, when, in fact, B causes C. Imagine that you fail an exam (A) and experience depression (C). Ellis would attribute your depression not to your failure but to an irrational belief, such as the belief (B) that you must be perfect. Thus, your irrational belief, not your failure, causes your depression. Table 15.2 lists common irrational beliefs that Ellis claims guide many of our lives.

Though therapists who use R-E-T may develop warm, empathetic relationships with their clients, Ellis himself is more interested in demolishing, sometimes harshly,

rational-emotive therapy (R-E-T)
A type of cognitive therapy, developed by Albert Ellis, that treats psychological disorders by forcing the client to give up irrational beliefs.

TABLE 15.3   Rational-Emotive Therapy

This transcript illustrates how the rational-emotive therapist (T) challenges the client (C) to change irrational beliefs. The client is a 23-year-old young woman experiencing intense feelings of guilt for not living up to her parents' strict standards.

C: Well, this is the way it was in school, if I didn't do well in one particular thing, or even on a particular test—and little crises that came up—if I didn't do as well as I had wanted to do.

T: Right. You beat yourself over the head.

C: Yes.

T: But why? What's the point? Are you supposed to be perfect? Why the hell shouldn't human beings make mistakes, be imperfect?

C: Maybe you always expect yourself to be perfect.

T: Yes. But is that *sane?*

C: No.

T: Why do it? Why not give up that unrealistic expectation?

C: But then I can't accept myself.

T: But you're saying, "It's shameful to make mistakes." *Why* is it shameful? Why can't you go to somebody else when you make a mistake and say, "Yes, I made a mistake"? Why is that so awful? . . .

C: It might all go back to, as you said, the need for approval. If I don't make mistakes, then people will look up to me. If I do it all perfectly—

T: Yes, that's part of it. That, is the erroneous belief; that if you never make mistakes everybody will love you and that it is necessary they do. That's right. That's a big part of it. But is it true, incidentally? Suppose you never did make mistakes—*would* people love you? They'd sometimes hate your guts, wouldn't they?

Reprinted by permission, Science & Behavior Books, Inc., Palo Alto, California, 1971.

Albert Ellis

"It is my contention . . . that all effective psychotherapists, whether or not they realize what they are doing, teach or induce their patients to reperceive or rethink their life events and philosophies and thereby to change their unrealistic and illogical thought, emotion, and behavior."

cognitive therapy
A type of therapy, developed by Aaron Beck, that aims at eliminating exaggerated negative beliefs about oneself, the world, or the future.

the irrational ideas of his clients. After identifying a client's irrational beliefs, Ellis challenges the client to provide evidence supporting them. Ellis then contradicts any irrational evidence, almost demanding that the client agree with him. Table 15.3 presents a verbatim transcript illustrating the use of R-E-T.

R-E-T is effective (Silverman, McCarthy, & McGovern, 1992). It has helped social phobics (Mersch, Emmelkamp, & Lips, 1991), obsessive-compulsives (Emmelkamp & Beens, 1991), and people suffering from a variety of other disorders. Research has found that changes in irrational beliefs produced by R-E-T are, indeed, the factors responsible for the emotional relief gained by R-E-T clients (T. W. Smith, 1983).

Cognitive Therapy

As discussed in chapter 14, psychiatrist Aaron Beck assumes that depression is caused by negative beliefs about oneself, the world, and the future (Beck et al., 1979). Thus, depressed people tend to blame themselves rather than their circumstances for misfortunes, attend more to negative events than to positive events, and have a pessimistic view of the future. Depressed people also overgeneralize from rare or minor negative events in their lives. The goal of Beck's **cognitive therapy** is to change such exaggerated beliefs in treating psychological disorders, most notably depression.

Beck is less directive in his approach than Ellis is. Beck employs a Socratic technique, in which he asks clients questions that lead them to recognize their irrational beliefs. Beck has clients keep a daily record of their thoughts and urges them to note irrational beliefs and replace them with rational ones. A client who claims, "I am an awful student and will never amount to anything," might be encouraged to think, instead, "I am doing poorly in school because I do not study enough. If I change my study habits, I will graduate and pursue a desirable career." To promote positive experiences, Beck might begin by giving the client homework assignments that guarantee success, such as having a client who feels socially incompetent speak to a close friend on the telephone. Cognitive therapy has been especially successful in treating depression, which was its original purpose (Whisman, 1993).

Stress-Inoculation Training

Donald Meichenbaum goes beyond Ellis and Beck in his emphasis on the promotion of positive thinking in his clients. Meichenbaum has received support from recent studies, discussed in chapter 14, showing that people with psychological disorders tend to be objective and rational in their beliefs. People without such disorders tend to hold unrealistically positive beliefs about themselves and the world.

In applying **stress-inoculation training,** Meichenbaum (1985) helps clients change their pessimistic thinking into optimistic thinking when in stressful situations. The therapist first explores the client's characteristic ways of thinking and responding in particular situations that create distress. A baseball player who fears making an error might be trained to say, "I hope they hit the ball to me. If they do, I'll make the play because I make the play in practice." The therapist might model more-appropriate thought patterns and behaviors for the client to consider. The client then rehearses the thought patterns by saying them out loud and, if feasible, rehearses the behaviors. The client next proceeds to test the new thought patterns and behaviors in real-life situations and reports back to the therapist on their effectiveness. Stress-inoculation training has helped patients face cardiac catheterization (Kendall et al., 1979), pianists overcome performance anxiety (Kendrick et al., 1982), college students reduce their fear of public speaking (Altmaier et al., 1985), and elementary school teachers adjust to anxiety-inducing situations (Cecil & Forman, 1990).

Meichenbaum's technique has even been used to treat writing anxiety. In one study, subjects were assigned to one of three conditions. The first condition combined stress-inoculation training with writing instruction; the second condition combined writing instruction with interpersonal attention; and the third condition (the control group) involved no treatment. Subjects in the first two groups reported reductions in their anxiety levels that were greater than those reported by subjects in the control group, but only the combination of stress-inoculation training and writing instruction improved writing quality—and significantly more of those in that group were able to pass a college freshman English equivalency examination (Salovey & Haar, 1990).

THE HUMANISTIC ORIENTATION

About 10 percent of psychotherapists practice some form of *humanistic therapy*, making it one of the most popular approaches to therapy (Smith, 1982). Unlike the psychoanalytic orientation, the humanistic orientation stresses the present rather than the past, and conscious, rather than unconscious, experience. Unlike the behavioral orientation, the humanistic orientation stresses the importance of subjective mental experience rather than objective environmental circumstances. And, unlike the cognitive orientation, the humanistic orientation encourages the expression of emotion rather than its control.

Person-Centered Therapy

The most popular kind of humanistic therapy is **person-centered therapy,** originally called *client-centered therapy*. It was developed in the 1950s by Carl Rogers (1902–1987), a former psychoanalytic psychotherapist, as one of the first alternatives to psychoanalysis. As noted earlier, a survey of therapists found that Rogers has been the most influential of all contemporary psychotherapists (Smith, 1982). Whereas the rational-emotive therapist is *directive* in challenging the irrational beliefs of clients, the person-centered therapist is *nondirective* in permitting clients to find their own answers to their problems and thereby proceed toward self-actualization (Bozarth & Brodley, 1991). This is in keeping with the humanistic concept of self-actualization (Rogers, 1951) and reminiscent of the Socratic method of self-discovery favored by Plato.

Since person-centered therapists give no advice, how do they help their clients? Their goal is to facilitate the pursuit of self-actualization, not by offering expertise but by providing a social climate in which clients feel comfortable being themselves (Bozarth

Aaron Beck
"The depressed person has a global negative view of himself, the outside world, and the future."

Donald Meichenbaum
"Analogous to medical inoculation, stress-inoculation training is designed to build 'psychological antibodies,' or coping skills, and to enhance resistance through exposure to stimuli that are strong enough to arouse defenses without being so powerful as to overcome them."

stress-inoculation training
A type of cognitive therapy, developed by Donald Meichenbaum, that helps clients change their pessimistic thinking into more positive thinking when in stressful situations.

person-centered therapy
A type of humanistic therapy, developed by Carl Rogers, that helps clients find their own answers to their problems.

& Brodley, 1991). They do so by promoting self-acceptance. As discussed in chapter 14, humanistic psychologists assume that psychological disorders arise from an incongruence between a person's public self and her or his actual self. This makes the person distort reality or deny feelings, trying to avoid the anxiety caused by failing to act in accordance with those feelings. The goal of person-centered therapy is to help individuals reduce this incongruence by expressing and accepting their true feelings. Perhaps cathartic experiences generated in psychoanalysis work, not because they release pent-up emotions, but because, as humanistic therapists insist, they put individuals in touch with their true feelings (Nichols & Efran, 1985).

The person-centered therapist promotes self-actualization through reflection of feelings, genuineness, accurate empathy, and unconditional positive regard (Rogers, 1957). Note that a close friend or relative whom you consider a "good listener" and valued counselor probably exhibits these characteristics, too. *Reflection of feelings* is the main technique of person-centered therapy. The therapist is an active listener who serves as a therapeutic mirror, attending to the emotional content of what the client says and restating it to the client. This helps clients recognize their true feelings. By being *genuine* the therapist acts in a concerned, open, and sincere manner rather than in a detached, closed, and phony manner. This makes clients more willing to disclose their true feelings. During his career, Rogers increasingly stressed the importance of genuineness (Bozarth, 1990).

The client also becomes more willing to share feelings when the therapist shows *accurate empathy*, which means that the therapist's words and actions indicate a true understanding of how the client feels (Strupp, 1989). Because accurate empathy is important even in everyday informal counseling, psychologists have tried to train people to be more empathetic. In one study, undergraduates were assigned to special empathy training groups or to a no-training control group. The program lasted 4 weeks. The subjects were then observed on videotape as they discussed common student problems with their peers. Students who had received training were more empathetic in their responses than were students who had not. These findings held even when the trainees were reassessed a year later (Kremer & Dietzen, 1991).

Perhaps the most difficult task for the person-centered therapist is the maintenance of *unconditional positive regard*—acting in a personally warm and accepting manner. The therapist must remain nonjudgmental no matter how distasteful she or he finds the client's thoughts, feelings, and actions to be. This encourages clients to freely express and deal with even the most distressing aspects of themselves. It does not, however, mean that the therapist must approve of the client's behavior, only that the therapist must accept the client's personal experiences.

The personal warmth conveyed by unconditional positive regard is a key aspect of therapy. A study of clients at a university counseling center found that the therapist's personal warmth was one of the most important factors in their willingness to stay in therapy (Hynan, 1990). And a survey of more than 500 therapists found that even they considered personal warmth to be one of the most important factors in selecting their own therapists (Norcross, Strausser, & Faltus, 1988). Table 15.4 presents a verbatim transcript that illustrates the use of person-centered therapy.

Though Rogers urged therapists to be nondirective, even he was unable to fulfill that ideal perfectly. A study of films and audio recordings of therapy sessions involving Rogers showed that he was nondirective as long as the client was expressing insight into his or her problems. He became less so when the client failed to express insight. At times, Rogers even became directive (Truax, 1966), which is more characteristic of practitioners of the form of humanistic therapy called *Gestalt therapy*.

Gestalt Therapy

Imagine a therapy that combines aspects of psychoanalysis, R-E-T, and client-centered therapy, and you might conceive of **Gestalt therapy.** Fritz Perls (1893–1970), a former psychoanalytic psychotherapist and the founder of Gestalt therapy, claimed, "The idea of Gestalt therapy is to change paper people to real people" (Perls, 1973, p. 120). To

TABLE 15.4	Person-Centered Therapy

This transcript illustrates how the person-centered therapist (T) acts as a psychological mirror, reflecting back the feelings expressed in statements by the client (C). The client feels anxious about taking responsibility for her life. Notice how the therapist is less directive than the one in the transcript of rational-emotive therapy in table 15.3.

C: Um-hum. That's why I say . . . (*slowly and very thoughtfully*) well, with that sort of foundation, well, it's really up to me. I mean, it seems to be really apparent to me that I can't depend on someone else giving me an education. (*very softly*) I'll really have to get it myself.

T: It really begins to come home—there's only one person that can educate you—a realization that perhaps nobody else can give you an education.

C: Um-hum. (long pause—while she sits thinking) I have all the symptoms of fright (*laughs softly*).

T: Fright: That this is a scary thing, is that what you mean?

C: Um-hum. (*very long pause—obviously struggling with feelings in herself*)

T: Do you want to say any more about what you mean by that? That it really does give you the symptoms of fright?

C: (*laughs*) I, uh . . . I don't know whether I quite know. I mean . . . Well, it really seems like I'm cut loose (*pause*), and it seems that I'm very—I don't know—in a vulnerable position, but I, uh, I brought this up and it, uh, somehow it almost came out without saying it. It seems to be . . . it's something I let out.

T: Hardly a part of you.

C: Well, I felt surprised.

T: As though, "Well for goodness sake, did I say that?" (*both chuckle*).

Rogers, Carl R., *On Becoming a Person*. Copyright © 1961 by Houghton Mifflin Company. Reprinted by permission.

Perls, paper people were those out of touch with their true feelings, making them live "inauthentic lives." Like psychoanalysis, Gestalt therapy seeks to bring unconscious feelings into conscious awareness. Like person-centered therapy, Gestalt therapy tries to increase the client's emotional expressiveness. And like rational-emotive therapy, Gestalt therapy may be confrontational in forcing clients to change maladaptive ways of thinking and behaving.

Despite its name, Gestalt therapy is not derived from Gestalt psychology (Henle, 1978a), which is discussed in chapter 1, except in stressing the need to achieve wholeness of the personality—meaning that one's emotions, language, and actions should be congruent with one another (Crose, 1990). Gestalt therapists insist that clients take responsibility for their own behavior, rather than blame other people or events for their problems, and that clients live in the here and now, rather than being concerned about events occurring at other places and times. Gestalt therapists also assume that people who are aware of their feelings can exert greater control over their reactions to events. The Gestalt therapist notes any signs that the client is not being brutally honest about his or her feelings, at times by observing the client's nonverbal communication—posture, gestures, facial expressions, and tone of voice. For example, a client who denies feeling anxious while tightly clenching his fists would be accused of lying about his emotions.

One way that Gestalt therapists help clients develop emotional awareness is through a variety of psychological exercises. In the *two-chair exercise*, the client alternately sits in one chair and then another, with each chair representing an aspect of herself, such as the extravert and the introvert. The client proceeds to carry on a dialogue between the two aspects. The two-chair exercise has proved effective in relieving emotional distress (Greenberg & Dompierre, 1981) and in making important decisions (Clarke & Greenberg, 1986).

But Perls has been criticized for promoting self-centeredness and emotional callousness, as in his "Gestalt prayer" (Perls, 1972, p. 70): "I do my thing and you do your thing. I am not in this world to live up to your expectations. And you are not in this world to live up to mine. You are you and I am I. And if by chance we find each other, it's beautiful. If not, then it can't be helped." This outlook has been accused of endangering the fabric of society by promoting self-centeredness, social aloofness, and indifference to the well-being of others (Cadwallader, 1984).

Fritz Perls (1893–1970)
Fritz Perls, the founder of Gestalt therapy, was a refugee from Nazi Germany. Loyal followers were attracted to his center at Esalen Institute in Big Sur, California, in the 1960s in the hope of becoming "authentic people." Perls was a charismatic person who thought as highly of himself as did his followers, claiming, "I believe I am the best therapist for any type of neurosis in the States, maybe in the world" (Prochaska, 1984, p. 128).

Irvin Yalom
"Existential psychotherapy is a dynamic approach to therapy which focuses on concerns that are rooted in the individual's existence. . . : death, freedom, isolation, and meaninglessness."

Victor Frankl
"Life holds a potential meaning under any conditions, even the most miserable ones."

existential psychotherapy
A type of humanistic therapy that helps the client overcome emotional or behavioral problems by dealing with major philosophical issues in life, including death, freedom, isolation, and meaning.

logotherapy
A form of existential therapy, developed by Victor Frankl, that helps the client find meaning in life.

psychodrama
A form of psychoanalytic group therapy, developed by Jacob Moreno, that aims at achieving insight and catharsis through acting out real-life situations.

Existential Therapy

Another kind of humanistic therapy, **existential psychotherapy,** takes a more philosophical approach than either person-centered therapy or Gestalt therapy. Existential therapists assume that emotional and behavioral problems are symptoms of an inability to come to grips with the ultimate issues of life. Irvin Yalom (1980), a leading existential therapist, points to four issues that each of us must face: the inevitability of death, the responsibility for our own choices, the isolation of each person from all others, and the need to find meaning in life. For example, a person who has not developed an adequate philosophy of death might, in a sense, anesthetize herself or himself against facing this issue through excessive use of drugs, promiscuous sexual behavior, or working relentlessly without taking a day off.

A form of existential psychotherapy called **logotherapy** is especially concerned with helping clients find meaning in their lives. Victor Frankl, the psychiatrist who created logotherapy, used it successfully during World War II in one of the most stressful situations imaginable—Nazi concentration camps. Frankl prevented many of his fellow inmates from collapsing emotionally by helping them find meaning in their suffering. He did so by convincing them that meaning could be found in maintaining their human dignity no matter what was done to them (Frankl, 1961).

Today, logotherapists continue to believe that one of the most important goals of their practice is to help their clients find meaning in their lives. For example, suppose that a man who finds meaning in his life only through his work loses his job. He may become particularly vulnerable to anxiety or depression. In such a case, the logotherapist would try to help him find new meaning in his life (Greenlee, 1990). Logotherapy can also improve self-esteem, as in a study in which former prison inmates who had participated in logotherapy sessions saw themselves less as passive victims of unfortunate circumstances and more as survivors who could still take control of their lives (Henrion, 1989).

THE SOCIAL-RELATIONS ORIENTATION

The therapeutic orientations that have been discussed so far involve a therapist and a client. In contrast, the *social-relations orientation* assumes that, because many psychological problems involve interpersonal relationships, additional people must be brought into the therapy process.

Group Therapy

In 1905 Joseph Pratt, a Boston physician, found that his tuberculosis patients gained relief from emotional distress by meeting in groups to discuss their feelings. This marked the beginning of group therapy (Allen, 1990). But group therapy did not become an important form of therapy until World War II, when a limited number of therapists found themselves faced with more people in need of therapy than they could see individually (Hersen, Kazdin, & Bellack, 1983). Because group therapy allows a therapist to see more people (usually six to twelve in a group) in less time, more people can receive help at less cost per person. Group therapy provides participants with a range of role models, encouragement from others with similar problems, feedback about their own behavior, assurance that their problems are not unique, and the opportunity to try out new behaviors. Group therapy has been used effectively to improve the emotional well-being of people as varied as alcoholics (Solomon, 1982), schizophrenics (Kanas, 1986), cancer victims (Harman, 1991), and bereaved relatives (Zimpfer, 1991).

Psychoanalytic Group Therapies

Group therapies derived from psychoanalysis emphasize insight and emotional catharsis. In 1910 Jacob Moreno (1892–1974), a Romanian psychiatrist, introduced the psychoanalytic group therapy called *psychodrama*, and in 1931 he coined the term *group therapy*. **Psychodrama** aims at achieving insight and catharsis through acting out real-life situations, which may lead to changes in thought, emotion, and behavior. The

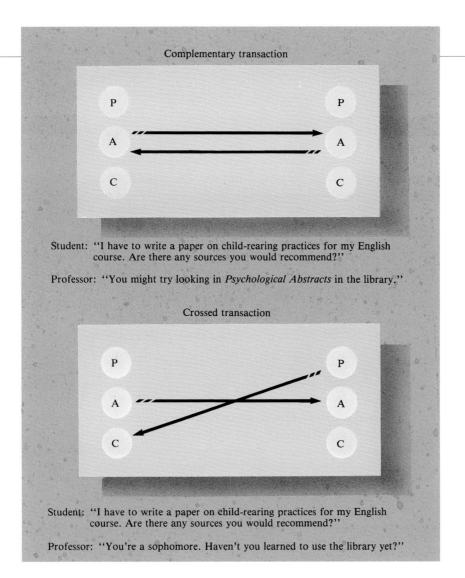

Complementary transaction

Student: "I have to write a paper on child-rearing practices for my English course. Are there any sources you would recommend?"

Professor: "You might try looking in *Psychological Abstracts* in the library."

Crossed transaction

Student: "I have to write a paper on child-rearing practices for my English course. Are there any sources you would recommend?"

Professor: "You're a sophomore. Haven't you learned to use the library yet?"

FIGURE 15.4

Transactional Analysis
According to Eric Berne (1964), our social relationships involve transactions in which we act as parent, adult, or child. In a complementary transaction, two persons act according to the same role. In a crossed transaction, two persons act according to different roles.

therapist functions as a director, making observations and offering suggestions. One technique of psychodrama is *role reversal,* in which a participant plays the role of a family member or other important person. This provides insight into the other person's motives and empathy for that person's feelings. Psychodrama is about as effective as other kinds of group therapy (Garfield, 1983).

A more recent form of group therapy inspired by psychoanalysis is **transactional analysis (TA),** popularized in the 1960s by psychiatrist Eric Berne (1910–1970) in his best-selling book *Games People Play* (1964). Berne claimed that we act according to one of three roles: child, parent, or adult. These resemble the Freudian personality structures of id, superego, and ego, respectively. The *child,* like the id, acts impulsively and demands immediate gratification. The *parent,* like the superego, is authoritarian and guides moral behavior. And the *adult,* like the ego, promotes rational and responsible behavior.

Each role is adaptive in certain situations and maladaptive in others. For example, acting childish is appropriate at parties but not at job interviews. According to Berne, our relationships involve *transactions*—social interactions between these roles. *Complementary transactions,* in which both individuals act according to the same role, are usually best. *Crossed transactions,* as when one person acts as a child and the other acts as an adult, are maladaptive. Figure 15.4 presents examples of complementary and crossed transactions.

The goal of TA is to analyze transactions between group members. These are the "games" that people play, which reflect our *life scripts*—the pervasive themes that we

Psychodrama
Psychodrama emphasizes the importance of emotional expression and emotional insight.

transactional analysis (TA)
A form of psychoanalytic group therapy, developed by Eric Berne, that helps clients change their immature or inappropriate ways of relating to other people.

Eric Berne (1910–1970)
"At any given moment each individual in a social aggregation will exhibit a Parental, Adult, or Child ego state and . . . individuals can shift with varying degrees of readiness from one ego state to another."

social-skills training
A form of behavioral group therapy that improves the client's social relationships by improving her or his interpersonal skills.

assertiveness training
A form of social-skills training that teaches clients to express their feelings directly, instead of passively or aggressively.

Assertiveness Training
People who have trouble saying no to other people's requests, participating in classroom discussions, or returning bad food in a restaurant may benefit from assertiveness training. But note that *aggressiveness*, which is marked by hostility, is not the same as *assertiveness*, which is marked by the constructive expression of one's feelings.

encounter group
A derivative of humanistic group therapy in which group members learn to be themselves by openly expressing their true feelings to one another.

follow in our social relations. For example, a person might have a life script that supports her or his feelings of worthlessness and continually play games that provoke responses from others that support that script. The available empirical studies have found both successful (Lammers, 1990) and unsuccessful (Olson et al., 1981) outcomes of TA.

Behavioral Group Therapies

Psychologists who favor behavioral group therapies assume that changes in overt behavior will bring relief of emotional distress. A popular form of behavioral group therapy, also used in individual therapy, is **social-skills training** (la Greca, 1993). Its goal is to improve social relationships by improving social skills, such as cultivating friendships or carrying on conversations. Participants are encouraged to rehearse new behaviors in the group setting. Members of the group may model more effective behaviors. And shaping (see chapter 7) may be used to gradually develop more effective behaviors. Social-skills training has helped children overcome shyness (Van Hasselt et al., 1984), adolescents overcome social anxiety (Blair & Fretz, 1980), and adults overcome depression (Thase et al., 1984).

A form of social-skills training called **assertiveness training** (Salter, 1949) helps people learn to express their feelings constructively in social situations. Many people experience poor social relations because they are unassertive. They are unable to ask for favors, to say no to requests, or to complain about poor service. By learning to express their feelings, formerly unassertive people relieve their anxiety and have more-rewarding social relations.

Members of assertiveness-training groups try out assertive behaviors in the group situation. The therapist typically models assertive behaviors, aggressive behaviors, and passive behaviors to permit group members to distinguish between them. *Assertive* people express their feelings directly and constructively. *Aggressive* people express their feelings directly but with a hostile edge. And *passive* people express their feelings indirectly, as in pouting.

One assertiveness-training technique is the *broken record,* in which those who have trouble saying "no" practice repeating brief statements that reject requests. The therapist and group members critique each participant's attempts at assertive behaviors. Assertiveness training has improved the communication skills and self-esteem of people as diverse as athletes (Connelly, 1988), working women (Stake & Pearlman, 1980), college students (Wolff & Desiderato, 1980), and physically disabled adults (Glueckauf & Quittner, 1992).

Humanistic Group Therapies

The humanistic group therapies encourage awareness and acceptance of emotional experiences. In the late 1940s, studies of small-group relationships carried out at the National Training Laboratories in Bethel, Maine, led to the development of sensitivity training groups. The early sensitivity groups, called *training groups* (or *T-groups*), helped business people improve their relationships with workers and colleagues. Today sensitivity groups are also popular with the clergy, police, educators, and other professionals.

Sensitivity groups have twelve to twenty members. Participants explore their own feelings and become aware of how their actions affect the feelings of others. They learn to rely on reason and cooperation instead of coercion and manipulation. A study of the effectiveness of sensitivity groups found that social-skills training was superior to sensitivity training in improving social skills and reducing social anxiety (Monti et al., 1980).

A relative of sensitivity training is the **encounter group,** an offshoot of the *human potential movement* that arose in the 1950s and declined in the early 1970s (Finkelstein, Wenegrat, & Yalom, 1982). Encounter groups may involve people who have had little or no prior contact with one another. The groups meet for hours or days. Compared with sensitivity groups, encounter groups are more concerned with the open expression of emotions than with improving social relationships. Encounter groups promote crying, cursing, and verbal abuse. They might also encourage physical touching as a means of

Encounter Groups
Encounter group therapy promotes
the expression and acceptance of
strong emotions, whether positive or
negative. The growth of encounter
groups in the 1960s prompted Carl
Rogers to claim: "The Encounter
Group is perhaps the most significant
social invention of this century. The
demand for it is utterly beyond belief.
It is one of the most rapidly growing
social phenomena in the United
States. It has permeated industry, is
coming into education, is reaching
families, professionals in the helping
fields, and many other individuals"
(Rogers, 1968, p. 3).

overcoming social isolation. One study found that drug abusers who participated in an encounter group session that lasted 16 hours had an improved self-image compared to those who did not (Page, Richmond, & de la Serna, 1987). Encounter groups have even been used to resolve conflicts among college faculty members (Herrick, Kvale, & Goodykoontz, 1991).

But studies of encounter groups indicate that their slight beneficial effects can be temporary (Kilmann & Sotile, 1976) and that they may attract people ill-suited for intense emotional confrontations. Some participants are even emotionally harmed by their experiences (Hartley, Roback, & Abramowitz, 1976). This is especially true of encounter groups in which the leader tries to break down individual selves, hoping to cause the participants to subject themselves to the group—similar to initiations into certain cults (Cushman, 1989). The potential danger of encounter group participation is made even greater by the fact that people who join the groups tend to be more distressed than their peers who do not (Klar et al., 1990).

The encounter group movement did lead to the emergence of typically less confrontational *self-help groups* for drug abusers, widowed people, and others with specific shared problems. The groups are conducted by people who have experienced those problems. For example, self-help groups for phobia sufferers would be run by former phobics (Ross, 1980), and self-help groups for divorced persons would be run by divorced people (Byrne, 1990).

Family Therapy

Group therapy usually brings together unrelated people; **family therapy** brings together members of the same family. The basic assumption of family therapy is that a family member with problems related to her or his family life cannot be treated apart from the family. The main goals of family therapy are the constructive expression of feelings and the establishment of rules that family members agree to follow. In family therapy, one of the family members—known as the *identified patient*—is assumed to bear the brunt of the family's problems. Typically, the family is brought together for family therapy after that person has entered individual psychotherapy.

Family therapy tries to improve communications and relationships among family members, who learn to provide feedback and to accept feedback from each other. The therapist helps family members establish an atmosphere in which no individual is blamed

Family Therapy
In family therapy, family members
gain insight into their maladaptive
patterns of interaction and learn to
change them into healthier ones.

family therapy
*A form of group therapy that encourages
the constructive expression of feelings
and the establishment of rules that family
members agree to follow.*

"You wait here. I'll talk to him."

Virginia Satir (1916–1988)
"Any individual's behavior is a response to the complex set of regular and predictable 'rules' governing his family group, though these rules may not be consciously known to him or the family."

for all the family's problems. A popular form of family therapy is *structural family therapy*, developed by Salvadore Minuchin (1974). Minuchin emphasizes the emotional "boundaries" between family members. Boundaries that are too rigid create inadequate emotional contact between family members, and boundaries that are too diffuse create intrusive familiarity between family members. What is needed is to establish a flexible family that can shift boundaries to manage different types of stress (Kassop, 1987).

The structural family therapist assesses the structure of the family members' interactions, perhaps even observing the family at home. Family therapists, such as the late Virginia Satir, may then have family members draw diagrams of these relationships and discuss how certain of the relationships are maladaptive (Satir, Bitter, & Krestensen, 1988). Perhaps the family is too child-oriented, or perhaps a parent and child are allied against the other parent. The goal of the therapist is to have the family replace these maladaptive relationships with more-effective ones.

Family therapy is about as effective as individual therapy. A review of family therapy studies found that people who have been in family therapy are better off than 76 percent of those who have received no treatment or an alternative treatment other than individual therapy (Markus, Lange, & Pettigrew, 1990). And family therapy improves both the relationships among family members and the well-being of individual family members (Hazelrigg, Cooper, & Borduin, 1987).

THE BIOPSYCHOLOGICAL ORIENTATION

Though Sigmund Freud practiced psychoanalysis, he predicted that, as science progressed, therapies for psychological disorders would become more and more biological (Trotter, 1981). During the past few decades, the *biopsychological orientation* has, indeed, become an important approach to therapy. It is based on the assumption that psychological disorders are associated with brain dysfunctions and consequently will respond to treatments that alter brain activity. Biopsychological treatments, because they involve medical procedures, can be offered only by psychiatrists and other physicians. The biopsychological treatments include *psychosurgery, electroconvulsive therapy,* and *drug therapy*.

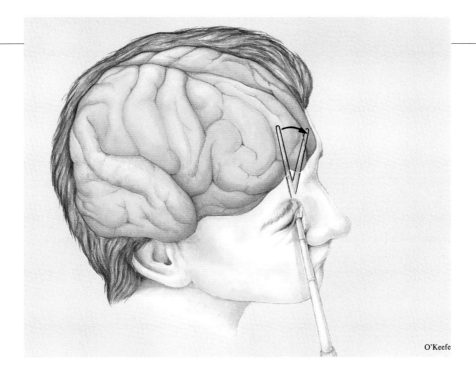

FIGURE 15.5

Transorbital Leucotomy
In the form of psychosurgery called transorbital leucotomy, a surgeon uses a mallet to drive a surgical pick through the thin bone of the eye socket into the brain. The surgeon then levers the pick back and forth, severing portions of the frontal lobes from the rest of the brain.

O'Keefe

Psychosurgery

While attending a professional meeting in 1935, Portuguese psychiatrist Egas Moniz was impressed by a report that agitated chimpanzees became calmer after undergoing brain surgery that separated their frontal lobes from the rest of their brain. Moniz wondered whether such **psychosurgery** might also benefit agitated mental patients. Psychosurgery had first been used in the late nineteenth century in Great Britain in unsuccessful attempts to treat mental illness (Berrios, 1990). Moniz convinced neurosurgeon Almeida Lima to perform *prefrontal lobotomies* on anesthetized patients. Lima drilled holes in the patient's temples, inserted a scalpel through the holes, and cut away portions of the frontal lobes. Moniz reported many successes in calming agitated patients. He won a Nobel prize in 1949 for inventing psychosurgery, which was considered a humane alternative to locking agitated patients in padded rooms or restraining them in straitjackets (Valenstein, 1980).

Psychosurgery was introduced to the United States in 1936 by neurosurgeon Walter Freeman and psychiatrist James Watts. They favored a technique called *transorbital leucotomy*, which is illustrated in figure 15.5. The patient's eyesocket, which is called the orbit, is anesthetized (the brain itself is insensitive to pain), and a mallet is used to drive a surgical pick into the frontal lobe. The pick is then levered back and forth to separate portions of the lobe from the rest of the brain.

By 1979, psychosurgery had been performed on about 35,000 mental patients in the United States. But the use of psychosurgery has declined markedly. One reason is its unpredictable effects—some patients improve, others become apathetic or violent. A second reason for its decline was the advent of drug therapies in the 1950s and 1960s, which provided safer, more effective, and more humane treatment. And a third reason was public opposition to what seemed to be a barbaric means of behavior control. Today, psychosurgery is rarely used in the United States; when it is used, it more often involves the use of electrodes inserted into the brain's limbic system. A direct current is sent through the electrodes, heating and thereby destroying small amounts of tissue in precise areas of the limbic system. This technique has achieved some success in treating obsessive-compulsive disorder (Rappaport, 1992).

psychosurgery
The treatment of psychological disorders by destroying brain tissue.

FIGURE 15.6

Electroconvulsive Therapy
In electroconvulsive therapy, the patient receives a series of treatments in which a brief electric current is passed through the brain, inducing a brain seizure that relieves the person's depression through mechanisms that are still unclear.

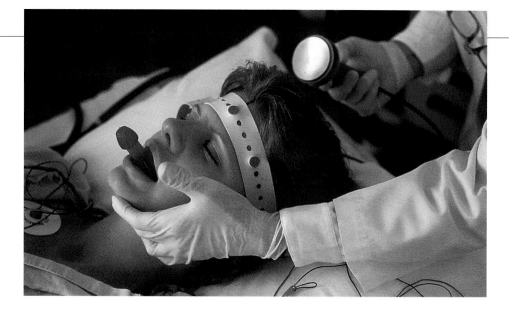

Electroconvulsive Therapy

In the early nineteenth century, Benjamin Rush employed "shock therapy" in treating depressed patients. With a dirty surgical instrument he made an incision in the patient's neck, and the resulting infection produced a large boil. Rush then shocked the patient by unexpectedly popping open the boil with a needle. He reported that many patients showed a decrease in their symptoms after such treatments. Of course, the objectivity of his reports can be questioned.

Modern "shock therapy" began in 1935 with almost simultaneous reports of its use by the Hungarian psychiatrist Ladislas von Meduna and the Austrian physician Manfred Sakel (Fink, 1984). Sakel found that schizophrenic patients showed improvement following convulsions induced by insulin overdoses. Von Meduna noted that schizophrenia and epilepsy rarely occurred in the same person. He inferred that the induction of brain seizures might relieve the symptoms of schizophrenia. Von Meduna used the drug camphor to induce seizures, but he found that, though the treatments relieved some patients' symptoms, they harmed or even killed other patients.

In 1938, on a visit to a slaughterhouse, Italian psychiatrist Ugo Cerletti watched pigs being rendered unconscious by electric shocks. Cerletti reasoned that electric shock might be a safe alternative to drug-induced shock therapy in calming agitated schizophrenic patients. This led Cerletti and his fellow psychiatrist Lucio Bini to introduce **electroconvulsive therapy (ECT)** (Endler, 1988). ECT uses a brief electrical current to induce brain seizures. Though ECT was originally used for treating agitated patients, it proved more successful in elevating the mood of severely depressed patients who had failed to respond to drug therapy. A major published review of the research literature found that it is unclear, overall, whether either ECT or antidepressant drugs are superior to the other in the treatment of major depression (Piper, 1993).

As shown in figure 15.6, a psychiatrist administers ECT by attaching electrodes to one or both temples of a patient who is under general anesthesia and who has been given a muscle relaxant. The muscle relaxant prevents injuries that might otherwise be caused by violent contractions of the muscles. A burst of electricity of 70 to 150 volts is passed through the brain for about half a second. This induces a brain seizure, which is followed by a period of unconsciousness lasting up to 30 minutes. The patient typically receives three treatments a week for several weeks (Scovern & Kilmann, 1980).

ECT can be more effective than antidepressant drugs for treating severe depression. Because ECT produces more-rapid improvement than antidepressant drugs, which can take several weeks, it is the treatment of choice for depressed people in imminent danger of committing suicide (Persad, 1990). But ECT's mechanism of action is unclear.

electroconvulsive therapy (ECT)
A biomedical therapy that uses brief electric currents to induce brain seizures in victims of major depression.

As explained in chapter 14, depression is associated with low levels of norepinephrine. A logical, though unconfirmed, explanation is that ECT stimulates an increase in the level of norepinephrine in the brain (Masserano, Takimoto, & Weiner, 1981). Other studies, using animals, have found that ECT might work by increasing the level of endorphins in the brain, thereby lifting the depressed person's mood (Alexopoulos et al., 1983). This has yet to be demonstrated in human beings (Jackson & Nutt, 1990).

In recent years there has been controversy about ECT's safety and effectiveness. In the past, the violence of the convulsions induced by ECT often broke bones and tore muscles. Today, muscle relaxants prevent such damage. But ECT still causes *retrograde amnesia*—the forgetting of events that occurred from minutes to days prior to the treatment. In 1982 the potential side effects of ECT and fears that ECT could be used to control people against their will led Berkeley, California, to ban its use. But citizens who argued that this violated the rights of those who might benefit from ECT convinced a California superior court judge to remove the ban (Cunningham, 1983).

A published review of research on ECT found no evidence that it caused detectable brain damage, though it can induce subtle damage. The review concluded that ECT merits continued use because it can relieve severe depression and prevent suicide (Weiner, 1984). Those who favor the availability of ECT were heartened by a report from the National Institutes of Health stating that ECT is rarely fatal and rarely produces long-lasting memory losses (Holden, 1985). The debate about the desirability of using ECT remains as much emotional and political as scientific.

Drug Therapy

Since its introduction in the 1950s, drug therapy has become the most widely used form of biomedical therapy. It has been responsible for freeing patients from restraints and padded rooms and permitting many more to live outside of mental hospitals. As discussed in chapter 14, some psychological disorders are associated with abnormal levels of neurotransmitters in the brain. Drug therapies generally work by restoring neurotransmitter activity to more-normal levels. But a common criticism of drug therapies is that they may relieve symptoms without changing the person's ability to adjust to everyday stressors. This means that concurrent psychotherapy is desirable to help clients learn more-adaptive ways of thinking and behaving.

Antianxiety Drugs

Because of their calming effect, the **antianxiety drugs** were originally called *tranquilizers*. Today the most widely prescribed are the *benzodiazepines*, such as Xanax, Valium, and Librium. In fact, the prevalence of anxiety disorders has made the antianxiety drugs the most widely prescribed psychoactive drugs. Antianxiety drugs are effective in treating panic disorder. In a double-blind study, subjects received either Xanax or a placebo. Those who received Xanax showed a significantly greater reduction in their panic attacks than did those who received a placebo (Alexander, 1993). The benzodiazepines work by stimulating special receptors in the brain that enhance the effects of the neurotransmitter GABA (Greenblatt, Shader, & Abernethy, 1983), which inhibits brain activity. The benzodiazepines can also produce side effects, including drowsiness, depression, and dependence.

antianxiety drugs
Psychoactive drugs, commonly known as minor tranquilizers, that are used to treat anxiety disorders.

Antidepressant Drugs

The first **antidepressant drugs** were the MAO *inhibitors*, such as Nardil. Originally used to treat tuberculosis, they were prescribed as antidepressants after physicians noted that they induced euphoria in tuberculosis patients. The MAO inhibitors work by blocking enzymes that normally break down the neurotransmitters serotonin and norepinephrine. This increases the levels of those neurotransmitters in the brain, elevating the patient's mood.

But the MAO inhibitors fell into disfavor because they can cause dangerously high blood pressure in patients who eat foods (such as cheeses) or drink beverages (such as beer) that contain the amino acid tyramine. The MAO inhibitors have largely been

antidepressant drugs
Psychoactive drugs that are used to treat major depression.

replaced by the *tricyclic antidepressants*, such as Elavil and Tofranil. The tricyclics increase the levels of serotonin and norepinephrine in the brain by preventing their reuptake by brain neurons that release them. Though the tricyclics are effective in treating depression (Task Force on the Use of Laboratory Tests in Psychiatry, 1985), they take 2 to 4 weeks to have an effect. This means that suicidal patients given antidepressants must be watched carefully during that period. Though there were early reports that Prozac might, in some cases, increase suicidal thinking and, perhaps, suicidal behavior (Teicher, Glod, & Cole, 1990), there is little scientific evidence to support that concern (Crundell, 1993). Psychotherapy is usually superior to antidepressant drugs in producing lasting improvement in depressed people (Steinbrueck, Maxwell, & Howard, 1983).

Antimania Drugs

antimania drugs
Psychoactive drugs, most notably lithium carbonate, that are used to treat a bipolar disorder.

In the 1940s, Australian physician John Cade observed that the chemical lithium calmed agitated guinea pigs. Contrary to his belief, the lithium apparently did so because it made them feel sick, not because of any effect on the brain. Cade then tried lithium on patients and found that it calmed those suffering from mania—apparently, in that case, because of its effect on the brain. Psychiatrists now prescribe the **antimania drug** *lithium carbonate* to prevent the extreme mood swings of bipolar disorder (Keck & McElroy, 1993). Lithium seems to work by normalizing the flow of ions across the membranes of brain neurons (Tosteson, 1981). Psychiatrists must vigilantly monitor patients taking lithium because it can produce dangerous side effects, including seizures, brain damage, and irregular heart rhythms (Honchar, Olney, & Sherman, 1983).

Antipsychotic Drugs

antipsychotic drugs
Psychoactive drugs, commonly known as major tranquilizers, that are used to treat schizophrenia.

For centuries, physicians in India prescribed the snakeroot plant for calming agitated patients. Beginning in the 1940s, a chemical derivative of the plant *reserpine* was used to reduce symptoms of mania and schizophrenia. But reserpine fell into disfavor because of its tendency to cause depression and low blood pressure. The 1950s saw the development of safer **antipsychotic drugs** called *phenothiazines*, such as Thorazine, for treating people with schizophrenia. French physicians had noted that the drug, used to sedate patients before surgery, calmed psychotic patients.

The phenothiazines relieve the positive symptoms of schizophrenia, but not the negative ones (Killian et al., 1984). As discussed in chapter 14, positive symptoms include hallucinations, disordered thinking, and bizarre behavior, while negative symptoms include emotional apathy and social withdrawal. The phenothiazines work by blocking brain receptor sites for the neurotransmitter dopamine (Sternberg et al., 1982). Unfortunately, long-term use of antipsychotic drugs can cause the bizarre motor side effects that characterize *tardive dyskinesia*, which include grimacing, lip smacking, and limb flailing (Gardos et al., 1987).

COMMUNITY MENTAL HEALTH

deinstitutionalization
The movement toward treating people with psychological disorders in community settings instead of mental hospitals.

As discussed earlier, for most of the nineteenth and twentieth centuries, state mental hospitals served as the primary sites of treatment for people with serious psychological disorders. But since the 1950s there has been a movement toward **deinstitutionalization,** which promotes the treatment of people in community settings instead of in mental hospitals. As shown in figure 15.7, the number of patients in mental hospitals declined from a high of 559,000 in 1955 to fewer than 140,000 in the early 1980s (Bassuk, 1984).

What accounts for this trend? First, the introduction of drug treatments made it more feasible for mental patients to function in the outside world. Second, mental hospitals had become underfunded, understaffed, and overcrowded. Many were little more than human warehouses, full of patients wasting away their lives with no hope of improvement. Community-based treatment seemed to be a cheaper, superior alternative. Third, increasing concern for the legal rights of mental patients made it more difficult to have people committed to mental hospitals and to keep them there. And fourth, the Community Mental Health Centers Act of 1963, sponsored by President

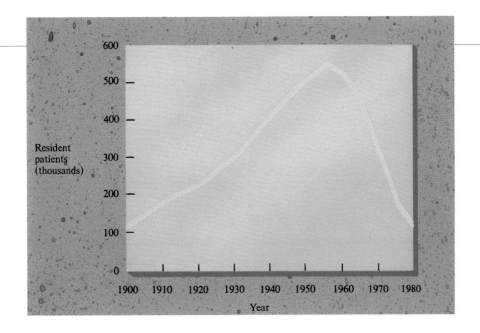

FIGURE 15.7

Deinstitutionalization
As a result of deinstitutionalization, the number of patients in state mental hospitals in 1980 was less than one-fourth the number in 1955.

From "The Homelessness Problem" by E. L. Bassuk. Copyright © 1984 by Scientific American, Inc. All rights reserved.

John F. Kennedy, mandated the establishment of federally funded centers in every community in the United States. These centers were to provide services to prevent and treat psychological disorders, further reducing the need for mental hospitals.

Community mental-health centers provide a variety of services. Outpatient counseling permits people to receive therapy while living and working in the community. Short-term inpatient treatment allows a person experiencing major depression to spend a brief period of time in a local center, receiving drug therapy, counseling, and practical assistance, instead of being committed to a state hospital possibly hours from home. The 24-hour emergency care services might include a suicide hotline, a refuge for battered wives, and a shelter for runaways. Consultation and education are provided to courts, police, and public welfare agencies; for example, a trained counselor might present a program on drug-abuse prevention to schoolchildren.

Community mental-health centers have three main goals in the prevention of psychological disorders. *Primary prevention* helps prevent psychological disorders by fostering social support systems, eliminating sources of stress, and strengthening individuals' ability to deal with stressors (Gesten & Jason, 1987). This might be promoted by reducing unemployment and making available low-cost housing. *Secondary prevention* provides early treatment for people at immediate risk of developing psychological disorders, sometimes through *crisis intervention*. Community mental-health centers often go into action following disasters in which people are killed or communities are ravaged. In 1985, when a Philadelphia neighborhood was destroyed by fire after a bomb was dropped on a house occupied by members of the radical organization MOVE, community mental-health centers provided counseling for children who had been trapped in their nearby schools and terrified by the fire and gunshots. *Tertiary prevention* helps people who have full-blown psychological disorders to keep them from getting worse and to prevent relapses. Among the main community approaches to tertiary prevention are community residences, or *halfway houses,* that provide homelike, structured environments in which former mental hospital patients readjust to independent living.

Primary, secondary, and tertiary prevention have been applied to the prevention of problems such as mental retardation (Scott & Carran, 1987), developmental abnormalities in infants (Simeonsson, 1991), sexual violence on college campuses (Roark, 1989), and alcohol abuse among college students (Kinney & Peltier, 1986). Consider primary, secondary, and tertiary prevention of anorexia nervosa on a college campus: Primary prevention would be aimed at those at risk in the college community. Secondary prevention would provide treatment for those who have developed symptoms. And

The Crisis Intervention Center
The community mental-health system is aided by crisis intervention centers. These centers handle emergencies such as rape cases, physical abuse, suicide threats, or other problems that require immediate help. This photograph shows an emergency telephone for use by those who contemplate jumping from a bridge that has been the site of many suicides.

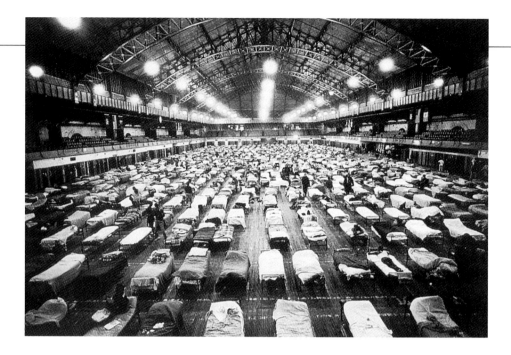

The Homeless Mentally Ill
The deinstitutionalization movement, the lack of community mental-health services, and the lack of low-cost housing have contributed to the homelessness problem. This photograph shows homeless people in an armory shelter in New York City.

tertiary prevention would involve the treatment of advanced cases and the prevention of relapses (Crisp, 1986).

Despite its noble intentions, deinstitutionalization has worked better in theory than in practice (Lamb, 1993). Communities too often provide inadequate aftercare for discharged mental patients (Dennis et al., 1991). Even when funding is available for treatment facilities, such as halfway houses, homeowners often oppose the placement of such facilities in their neighborhoods (Turkington, 1984). And the policies of private and government insurance programs regarding reimbursement for the treatment of psychological disorders encourage hospitalization instead of less-costly and more-effective community-based treatments. For example, insurance programs that fully reimburse patients for hospital stays might require partial payment for outpatient treatment (Kiesler, 1982).

As a consequence, former mental-hospital patients who lack family support might have little choice but to live on the street. About 30 percent of the homeless people on the streets of major cities and, increasingly, on the streets of smaller ones are former residents of mental hospitals (Searight & Searight, 1988). And regardless of whether they are former residents of mental hospitals, many homeless people have symptoms of psychological disorders, which could be either causes or effects of their homelessness (Fischer & Breakey, 1991). Though this has produced a need for more residential facilities, the main response of governmental agencies has been to open short-term emergency shelters.

The potential benefits of adequate support for deinstitutionalization are evident in the results of a study that compared community care for former mental hospital patients in the comparable cities of Portland, Oregon, and Vancouver, British Columbia. At the time of the study, Portland provided few community mental-health services, while Vancouver provided many private and public services. One year after their discharge, formerly hospitalized schizophrenics in Vancouver were less likely than those in Portland to have been readmitted and more likely to be employed and to report a greater sense of psychological well-being. Because the two groups were initially equivalent, the greater progress of the Vancouver group was attributed to community services rather than to preexisting differences between the groups (Beiser et al., 1985).

The inadequacies of deinstitutionalization have provoked legal actions. Homeless mental patients in Denver, New York, and Los Angeles have sued to receive housing, treatment, and supervision to enable them to remain in the community. In other cases, people who have been judged ready for discharge but who have not been discharged

Johnny M.
After a traumatic childhood, "Johnny M." became emotionally disturbed and was committed to a mental hospital. As part of deinstitutionalization, he was discharged from the hospital and lived for a while in a single room. After his building was converted into condominiums, he was left destitute to live on the streets.

because of inadequate housing and community services have sued to receive community housing, treatment, and supervision (Cunningham, 1984). But some critics, frustrated by the inadequacy of services for former mental-hospital patients, urge more-limited deinstitutionalization, reasoning that people would be better off confined in mental hospitals than living in subway tunnels, cardboard boxes, or store entrances (Thomas, 1981).

THE RIGHTS OF THE THERAPY CLIENT

Does a resident of a mental hospital have the right to refuse treatment? Does a resident of a mental hospital have the right to receive treatment? Is what a client reveals to a therapist privileged information? These questions have generated heated debate during the past three decades.

The Rights of Hospitalized Patients

People who are committed to mental hospitals lose many of their rights, including their rights to vote, to marry, to divorce, and to sign contracts. Revelations about past psychiatric practices in the former Soviet Union show the extent to which the commitment process can be abused. Soviet psychiatrists used unusual diagnoses, such as "reformist delusions" and "schizophrenia with religious delirium," to commit political or religious dissidents to mental hospitals (Faraone, 1982).

Ideally, only people who are judged to be dangerous to themselves or others can be involuntarily committed to mental hospitals. The need to demonstrate that people are dangerous before they can be committed was formalized by the United States Supreme Court in 1979 in *Addington v. Texas* (Hays, 1989). Commitment usually requires that two psychiatrists document that the person is dangerous. During the commitment process, the person has the right to a lawyer, to call witnesses, and to a hearing or a jury trial. The final decision on commitment is made by a judge or jury, not a psychiatrist.

Court decisions have also ruled that people committed to mental hospitals have a right to receive treatment. In 1975, in the widely publicized case *Donaldson v. O'Connor*, the United States Supreme Court ruled that mental patients have a right to more than custodial care. If they are not given treatment, are not dangerous, and can survive in the community, they must be released. The case was brought by Kenneth Donaldson, who had been confined for 15 years in a Florida mental hospital without treatment. But the court ruling in his case may be difficult to put into practice in particular cases. For example, what one judge considers treatment, another might not. Moreover, it is difficult to predict whether a person will be dangerous if released from custodial care (Bernard, 1977). Legal decisions such as this contributed to the deinstitutionalization movement by making it more difficult to keep mental patients hospitalized against their will. If treatment for a patient is unavailable in the hospital, the patient has the right to be released.

In 1983, in *Rogers v. Commissioner of Mental Health,* the Massachusetts Supreme Court ruled that mental patients also have a right to *refuse* treatment, unless a court judges them to be incompetent to make their own decisions (Hermann, 1990). A person committed to a mental hospital is not automatically considered incompetent. When the Rogers case was first presented, critics claimed that such a ruling would merely give mental patients the right to "rot with their rights on" (Appelbaum & Gutheil, 1980). In reality, the decision appears to have had little influence. A Massachusetts study found that few cases of involuntary treatment were reviewed in court, and the ones that were reviewed were usually decided in favor of those who had prescribed treatment for a patient who had refused it (Veliz & James, 1987). Thomas Szasz (1991), the noted critic of psychiatry, has ridiculed legislators for passing laws that help commit people to institutions, letting them become comfortable in them as though they were their homes, and then making laws that push them out onto the street without providing proper resources in the communities to help them make their transition back to independent living.

The Right to Confidentiality

But what of the rights of individuals receiving therapy? One of the most important is the right to confidentiality. In general, therapists are ethically, but not always legally, bound to keep confidential the information revealed by their clients. The extent to which this information is privileged varies from state to state. In recent decades, the most significant legal decision concerning confidentiality was the *Tarasoff* decision, a ruling by the California Supreme Court that a therapist who believes that a client might harm a particular person must protect or warn that person. The ruling came in the case of Prosenjit Poddar, who murdered his former girlfriend, Tatiana Tarasoff.

In 1969 Poddar had informed his therapist at the counseling center of the University of California at Berkeley that he intended to kill Tarasoff. The therapist reported the threat to the campus police, who ordered Poddar to stay away from Tarasoff. Two months later Poddar murdered her, leading her parents to sue the therapist, the police, and the university. In 1976 the court ruled in favor of the parents; the therapist should have directly warned Tarasoff about Poddar's threat (Everstine et al., 1980). The duty to warn has also become an issue in other countries, including Canada (Birch, 1992) and Australia (McMahon, 1992).

This decision upholding the *duty to warn* influenced similar decisions in other states and has provoked concern among therapists for several reasons. First, no therapist can reliably predict whether a threat made by a client is a serious one (Rubin & Mills, 1983). If a student in a moment of anger about an unfair exam says to a therapist, "I could just *kill* my psychology professor," should the therapist immediately warn the professor?

Second, it can be impractical to warn potential victims. In one case, a client threatened to kill "rich people." He then murdered a wealthy couple. Considering the duty to warn, this prompted a therapist to ask whether a sign should have been posted reading, "All rich people watch out!" (Fisher, 1985). The spread of AIDS has exacerbated the conflict between confidentiality and the duty to warn (Totten, Lamb, & Reeder, 1990). Should a therapist warn the potential sex partners of clients who have the AIDS virus (Knapp & VandeCreek, 1992)? Critics of the duty to warn also wonder why therapists should be required to reveal confidential information when the same legal jurisdiction might not require laypersons to do so (Wallace, 1988).

Third, given the duty to warn, a therapist and a client might feel inhibited about discussing the client's hostility toward certain people, thereby failing to defuse the hostility and possibly making the client even more likely to commit an act of violence. This possibility was the basis of a 1988 ruling by the Court of Appeals in North Carolina in the case of *Currie v. United States.* The court ruled that psychiatrists did not have a duty

TABLE 15.5	Kinds of Therapists
Clinical Psychologist	A clinical psychologist has earned a doctoral degree in clinical psychology, including training in both research and clinical skills, and has served a one-year clinical internship. Clinical psychologists typically work in private practice, counseling centers, or mental hospitals.
Counseling Psychologist	A counseling psychologist has either a master's degree or a doctoral degree in counseling psychology. Counseling psychologists tend to have less training in research skills and tend to treat less severe or more narrow problems than do clinical psychologists. Thus, counseling psychologists might limit their counseling to families, married couples, or college students. Counseling psychologists typically work in private practice, mental-health centers, or college counseling centers. In fact, college counselors are more likely to be counseling psychologists, while hospital psychologists are more likely to be clinical psychologists (Watkins et al., 1986).
Pastoral Counselor	A pastoral counselor is a layperson or a member of the clergy who has earned a master's degree in pastoral counseling. Pastoral counselors combine spiritual and psychological counseling in their work in settings such as prisons, churches, hospitals, or counseling centers. Some people prefer seeing a pastoral counselor, because they find it less stigmatizing than seeing a clinical or counseling psychologist (Bales, 1986).
Psychiatrist	A psychiatrist is a physician who has served a three- or four-year residency in a mental hospital or a psychiatric ward of a general hospital. Though psychiatrists often rely on biomedical therapies, particularly drug therapy, some restrict their practices to psychotherapy. Psychiatrists usually work in private practice, psychiatric wards, or mental hospitals. A psychoanalyst is a psychiatrist (or, sometimes a psychologist) with special training in psychoanalytic psychotherapy. Psychoanalysts receive their training at psychoanalytic institutes and almost always work in private practice.
Psychiatric Nurse	A psychiatric nurse is a registered nurse who has a master's degree (M.S.N.) in nursing and specialized training in psychiatric care. Psychiatric nurses usually work under the supervision of psychiatrists in psychiatric wards or mental hospitals.
Psychiatric Social Worker	A psychiatric social worker has a master's degree (M.S.W.) in social work and training in the counseling of individuals and families. Psychiatric social workers work in hospitals, private practice, human service agencies, and mental-health centers.
Paraprofessional	A paraprofessional may lack an advanced degree—or anything more than a high school diploma—but has special training in counseling people with certain problems, such as obesity, drug abuse, or criminal conduct. Paraprofessionals are often people who have overcome the problem that they treat and who work under professional supervision in mental-health centers or in self-help groups.

to commit people to mental hospitals for threatening acts of violence. The case concerned a 1982 murder in which a man, who was under the care of Veterans Administration psychiatrists, shot a fellow IBM employee after making threats against IBM. The victim's relatives sued, claiming that the psychiatrists should have committed the man after he made threats against IBM. The court ruled that such a duty would prevent psychiatrists and clients from discussing hostile feelings, perhaps *increasing* the probability of violence (Bales, 1988a). The implications of the *Tarasoff* decision continue to perplex therapists, who must balance the need to serve their clients while protecting themselves from potential lawsuits if third parties are harmed by their clients (Monahan, 1993).

THE SELECTION OF A THERAPIST

At times in your life, you or someone you know may face psychological problems that require more than friendly advice. When personal problems disrupt your social, academic, or vocational life, or when you experience severe and prolonged emotional distress, you might be wise to seek the help of a therapist. You could receive therapy from a psychologist, a psychiatrist, or a variety of other kinds of therapists (listed in table 15.5).

Just as there is no single way to find a physician, there is no single way to find a therapist. As you will read later in this chapter, in general the personal qualities of the therapist matter more than the kind of therapy she or he practices. You should remember that most therapists are eclectic (Jensen, Bergin, & Greaves, 1990), selecting their techniques from a variety of approaches to therapy. Perhaps the best-known eclectic therapy is Arnold Lazarus's *multimodal therapy* (Lazarus & Lazarus, 1986). Lazarus

© by Sidney Harris.

"I utilize the best from Freud, the best from Jung and the best from my Uncle Marty, a very smart fellow."

believes that the therapist should be free to combine techniques related to what he calls "BASIC ID." The letters of this acronym stand for *behavior, affect, sensation, imagery, cognition, interpersonal,* and *drugs.* But critics of the eclectic approach argue that it is illogical to combine techniques that are based on different views of human nature and different outlooks on the causes of psychological disorders (Patterson, 1989).

How might you find a therapist, eclectic or otherwise? Your college counseling center might be a good place to start. You may have a friend, relative, or professor who can recommend a therapist or counseling center to you. Other potential sources of help or referral include community mental-health centers, psychological associations, and mental-health associations. You can find many of these organizations, as well as private practitioners, listed in the Yellow Pages.

After finding a therapist, try to assess her or his credentials, reputation, therapeutic approach, and interpersonal manner as best you can. Does the therapist have legitimate academic and clinical training? Do you know anyone who will vouch for the therapist's competence? Does the therapist's approach make sense for your problem? Do you feel comfortable talking with the therapist? The therapist should be warm, open, concerned, and empathetic. If you find that you lack confidence in the therapist, feel free to seek help elsewhere. Once you are in therapy, do not expect instant miracles; but if you make little progress after a reasonable length of time, feel free to end the relationship.

THINKING ABOUT *Psychology*

IS PSYCHOTHERAPY EFFECTIVE?

In 1952 Hans Eysenck published an article that sparked a debate on the effectiveness of psychotherapy that has continued to this day. Based on his review of twenty-four studies of psychotherapy with neurotics (people suffering from disorders involving moderate anxiety or depression), Eysenck concluded that about two-thirds of those who received psychotherapy improved. This would have provided strong evidence in support of the effectiveness of psychoanalysis (then the dominant kind of psychotherapy), had Eysenck not also found that about two-thirds of control subjects who had received *no* therapy also improved. He called improvement without therapy **spontaneous remission** and attributed it to beneficial factors that occurred in the person's everyday life. Because those who received no therapy were as likely to improve as those who received therapy, Eysenck concluded that psychotherapy is ineffective.

Eysenck's article provoked criticisms of its methodological shortcomings. One shortcoming was that many of the untreated people were under the care of physicians who prescribed drugs for them and provided informal counseling. Another shortcoming was that the treated groups and untreated groups were not equivalent, differing in educational level, socioeconomic status, and motivation to improve. This meant that the control group might have had a better initial prognosis than the treatment group had. Still another shortcoming was that Eysenck overestimated the rate of spontaneous remission, which other researchers have found is closer to 40 percent than to 65 percent (Bergin & Lambert, 1978).

spontaneous remission
The improvement of some persons with psychological disorders without their undergoing formal therapy.

EVALUATION OF PSYCHOTHERAPY

During the decades since Eysenck's article, hundreds of studies have assessed the effectiveness of psychotherapy. But this is a difficult scientific endeavor. For one thing, the definition of "effective" varies with the aim of therapy. Recall the criteria for psychological disorders discussed in chapter 14. Should therapy aim to restore normality? change maladaptive behavior? relieve personal distress?

The aims will also vary with the orientation to therapy. A psychoanalytic therapist might look for insight into unconscious conflicts that originate in childhood and result in cathartic release of repressed emotions. A behavioral therapist might look for changes in maladaptive behaviors. A rational-emotive therapist might look for sound changes in thinking. And a person-centered therapist might look for greater acceptance of oneself, personal warts and all.

Moreover, who is to judge whether these changes have occurred? A survey of client satisfaction with psychotherapy found that about three-quarters of those who responded said that they were "satisfied" (Lebow, 1982). But clients, as well as therapists, can be biased in favor of reporting improvement. To avoid bias, friends, family members, teachers, or employers might also be asked for their assessment of the client. This provides cross-validation of client and therapist assessments of improvement.

What has the admittedly imperfect research on the effectiveness of psychotherapy found? The general conclusion drawn from research conducted since Eysenck issued his challenge is that both psychotherapy and placebo therapy are more effective than no therapy and that psychotherapy is superior to placebo therapy. Placebo effects in psychotherapy are caused by factors such as the client's faith in the therapist's ability and the client's expectation of success (Critelli & Neumann, 1984).

Mary Lee Smith and her colleagues (1980) published a comprehensive review that summarized the results of 475 studies on the effectiveness of psychotherapy. They found that, on the average, the typical psychotherapy client is better off than 80 percent of untreated persons. And, as indicated in figure 15.8, there is little overall difference in the effectiveness of the various approaches to therapy. So, psychotherapy does work, but no single kind stands out as clearly more effective than the others (Stiles, Shapiro, & Elliott, 1986).

More recently, results of an ambitious $10 million study sponsored by the National Institute of Mental Health have lent further support to the effectiveness of psychotherapy. The study randomly assigned 239 severely depressed subjects into four groups. The psychotherapy treatments were offered at the University of Pittsburgh, the University of Oklahoma, and George Washington University. One group received Beck's cognitive therapy. A second group received interpersonal psychotherapy (a form of psychoanalytic therapy). A third group received the antidepressant drug imipramine. And a fourth group received a placebo treatment that involved a placebo pill and a minimal amount of social support from a therapist.

FIGURE 15.8

The Effectiveness of Psychotherapy
Research has found that psychotherapy is effective, but that no
approach is consistently better than
any other approach. This graph shows
the effectiveness of different kinds of
therapy relative to no treatment.
Overall, people given psychotherapy
show, on the average, significantly
greater improvement than about 80
percent of untreated people (Smith,
Glass, & Miller, 1980).

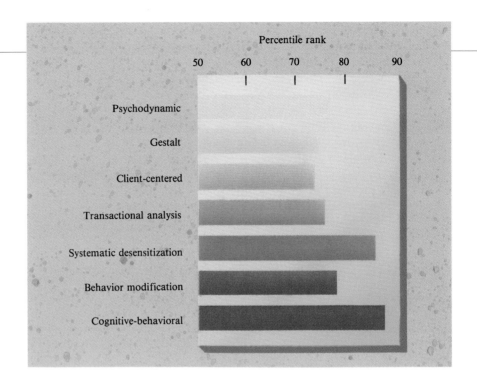

The participants were assessed after 16 weeks of therapy and again at a follow-up
18 months later. As expected, all of the groups improved; the three forms of active
therapy eliminated depression in 50 to 60 percent of the subjects, and the placebo
therapy eliminated depression in about 30 percent of the subjects. There were no
differences in effectiveness between the three active forms of therapy. Though drug
therapy relieved symptoms more quickly, the two psychotherapies eventually caught up
(Mervis, 1986).

FACTORS IN THE EFFECTIVENESS OF PSYCHOTHERAPY

Given the consensus that psychotherapy is effective and that no approach is significantly more effective than any other approach, researchers are faced with the question,
What factors account for the effectiveness of psychotherapy? In trying to answer this
question, researchers study therapy characteristics, client characteristics, and therapist
characteristics.

Therapy Characteristics

A review by Lester Luborsky and his colleagues (1971) of therapy, client, and therapist
factors found that the poorest predictor of success in therapy was the nature of the
therapy itself. The only important therapy characteristic was the number of therapy
sessions—the more sessions, the greater the improvement. As shown in figure 15.9, a
more recent review of fifteen studies of psychotherapy using more than 2,400 clients
found that 50 percent of clients improved by the end of 8 weekly sessions and 75 percent
improved by the end of 26 weekly sessions. Additional sessions added little to the therapeutic outcome, indicating that most clients gain maximum benefit from relatively brief
psychotherapy (Howard et al., 1986). Brief psychotherapy, sometimes with a time limit
put in a contract between the therapist and the client, has grown in popularity. Depending on the agreement between the therapist and the client, brief therapy will last less
than 6 months. Arnold Lazarus (1989) believes that brief psychotherapy will become
increasingly popular as more and more people who seek therapy lack the funds to pay
for lengthy therapy.

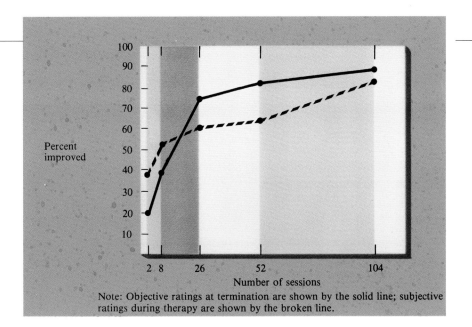

FIGURE 15.9

The Length of Therapy and Therapy Effectiveness
As the number of therapy sessions increases, the percentage of clients who improve increases. But after the 26th session, additional sessions help relatively few clients. Note the slight difference between objective ratings of improvement given by therapists and subjective ratings given by the clients themselves, though the general trend is similar for both (Howard et al., 1986).

Percent improved

Number of sessions

Note: Objective ratings at termination are shown by the solid line; subjective ratings during therapy are shown by the broken line.

Client Characteristics

The review by Luborsky and his colleagues (1971) found that therapeutic success was related to client characteristics. Clients were more likely to improve if they were higher in education, intelligence, and socioeconomic status. Improvement was also greatest in those with less severe disorders and disorders of recent onset. Other factors that promoted therapeutic success were a more adequate personality and greater motivation to change. Unfortunately, no client characteristics have been documented that can serve as a basis for the selection of a particular treatment (Dance & Neufeld, 1988).

Therapist Characteristics

Therapy is an intense, intimate, vulnerable relationship between human beings. The common factor in all effective therapies is the quality of the therapeutic relationship between the client and therapist (Patterson, 1984). The kind of therapy is generally less important than the qualities of the therapist (Lambert, 1989). Though it might be logical to assume that therapy would be best when the client and therapist are similar, there is little evidence that similarity in their sex (Mogul, 1982), race (Atkinson, 1983), or personality (Rinaldi, 1987) has a consistent impact on therapeutic outcomes.

Just what therapist characteristics *are* important, then? The client's perception of therapist empathy has been consistently identified as an important factor in the effectiveness of psychotherapy (Free et al., 1985). The importance of accurate empathy was first noted by Carl Rogers. In fact, Rogers began the formal study of the therapy process by taping his therapy sessions and analyzing his interactions with clients (Gendlin, 1988). As noted earlier, though personal warmth and genuineness cannot be taught, empathy can (Ju, 1982). Perhaps students who intend to become therapists should have their degree of personal warmth and genuineness, in addition to their academic credentials, assessed as part of the application process for admission to graduate school.

Empathy is so important in the practice of psychotherapy that empathetic people are sometimes as effective as trained psychotherapists. In one study, Vanderbilt University students with anxiety disorders were treated by either professional psychotherapists or empathetic professors. The results showed that the psychotherapists and the professors were equally effective in helping the students (Strupp & Hadley, 1979). Additional support for the importance of personal, as well as professional, skills came from a published review of research on the effectiveness of paraprofessionals, people who usually have less training and experience than professionals do, but who help in the treatment

Lester Luborsky
"Researchers have reached the consensus opinion that the evidence strongly supports the positive conclusion that most patients *will* benefit from psychotherapy."

of specific problems. The review found that paraprofessionals are sometimes as effective as professionals are (Hattie, Sharpley, & Rogers, 1984). This indicates that certain personal characteristics of therapists, rather than their training and experience, may determine their effectiveness. Nonetheless, studies have found that professional training does usually add something to the therapeutic process, making well-trained therapists more effective than less-trained "caring people." For example, professional therapists are more effective than paraprofessionals in reducing the emotional distress of chemotherapy patients (Carey & Burish, 1987).

Researchers are refining their methods to study the more precise question: What kind of therapy, offered by what kind of therapist, is helpful for what kind of client, experiencing what kind of problem, in what kind of circumstances? We must wait for future studies testing interactions among these factors to determine the most effective combinations. Currently, the best we can do is determine the effectiveness of two factors at a time, such as the therapist and the client (Talley, Strupp, & Morey, 1990). In some cases, particular kinds of therapies are best for particular kinds of problems. For example, behavior therapy is superior to other therapies in the treatment of phobias (Goisman, 1983). We can only look forward to the day when we can make more-precise declarations, such as: "Systematic desensitization offered by an empathetic psychologist will prove superior for a middle-aged college student with a public-speaking phobia when addressing strangers."

SUMMARY

THE HISTORY OF THERAPY

People with psychological disorders may seek professional therapy. Modern therapy has come a long way since ancient times. In trephining, holes were cut in the skull, possibly to release evil spirits that were alleged to cause abnormal behavior. Hippocrates introduced a more naturalistic form of treatment, including procedures to restore the balance of body humors. The Renaissance saw the appearance of insane asylums; some, such as Bedlam, were awful places, but others, such as Geel, provided humane treatment. Near the end of the eighteenth century, Philippe Pinel released asylum inmates and championed moral therapy. Moral therapy was introduced to America by Benjamin Rush, who also used unusual devices for treating certain disorders. Through the efforts of Dorothea Dix, state mental hospitals were built throughout the United States. But they became crowded and deteriorated into mere human warehouses. In the early twentieth century, a book by Clifford Beers, describing his horrible experiences in a mental hospital, led to the founding of the mental-health movement, which promotes the prevention and humane treatment of psychological disorders.

THE PSYCHOANALYTIC ORIENTATION

After hearing Joseph Breuer's report of the benefits of catharsis in the case of Anna O., Sigmund Freud developed psychoanalysis. Psychoanalysis principally involves the analysis of free associations, dreams, resistances, and transference. The goal of these analyses is to have the client gain insight into unconscious conflicts and experience catharsis.

THE BEHAVIORAL ORIENTATION

The behavioral orientation emphasizes the importance of learning and environmental influences. Two of the main kinds of behavioral therapy based on classical conditioning are systematic desensitization, which is useful in treating phobias, and aversion therapy, which

makes formerly pleasurable, but maladaptive, behavior unpleasant. One of the main applications of the operant conditioning principle of positive reinforcement is the use of a token economy in institutional settings. The operant conditioning principle of punishment is useful in eliminating behaviors, such as self-injurious behavior in autistic children. Albert Bandura's social-learning theory has contributed participant modeling as a way to overcome phobias.

THE COGNITIVE ORIENTATION

The cognitive orientation assumes that thoughts about events, rather than events themselves, cause psychological disorders. In Albert Ellis's rational-emotive therapy, the client learns to change irrational thinking. Aaron Beck developed cognitive therapy to help depressed people think less negatively about themselves, the world, and the future. And Donald Meichenbaum uses stress-inoculation training to help people be more optimistic when in stressful situations.

THE HUMANISTIC ORIENTATION

The humanistic orientation emphasizes the importance of being aware of one's emotions and feeling free to express them. Carl Rogers's person-centered therapy, a form of nondirective therapy, helps clients find their own solutions to their problems. In contrast, Fritz Perls's Gestalt therapy is more directive in making clients face their true feelings and act on them. Existential therapy aims at providing the client with a personal philosophy that can address the basic issues of life.

THE SOCIAL-RELATIONS ORIENTATION

The social-relations orientation assumes that people cannot be treated as isolated individuals. In group therapy, people, usually strangers, are brought together for therapy. Group therapy derived from the psychoanalytic approach includes psychodrama and transactional analysis. Group therapy derived from the behavioral approach includes social-skills training and assertiveness training. And group therapy derived from the humanistic approach includes sensitivity groups and encounter groups. In family therapy, family members gain insight into their unhealthy patterns of interaction and learn to change them.

THE BIOPSYCHOLOGICAL ORIENTATION

The biomedical orientation uses medical procedures to treat psychological disorders. The main procedures include psychosurgery (rarely used today), electroconvulsive therapy for depression, and drug therapy. Psychiatrists may prescribe antianxiety drugs, antidepressant drugs, antimania drugs and antipsychotic drugs.

COMMUNITY MENTAL HEALTH

The community mental-health movement was stimulated by deinstitutionalization, the treatment of people in community settings instead of in mental hospitals. Community mental-health centers aid in both prevention and treatment of psychological disorders. The failure to provide adequate housing and services for former mental-hospital patients has contributed to the growing homelessness problem.

THE RIGHTS OF THE THERAPY CLIENT

Laws require that formal procedures be followed before a person is committed to a mental hospital. Once in a mental hospital, patients have the right to refuse treatment and the right to receive treatment. What clients reveal in therapy sessions is normally confidential, but legal cases have led to the concept of the duty to warn.

THE SELECTION OF A THERAPIST

There are many kinds of therapists, including both professionals and paraprofessionals. Most professional therapists are eclectic. You should be as careful in selecting a therapist as you are in selecting a physician.

THINKING ABOUT PSYCHOLOGY: IS PSYCHOTHERAPY EFFECTIVE?

In 1952 Hans Eysenck challenged psychotherapists by claiming that people who received psychotherapy improved no more than did people who received no therapy. Subsequent research has shown that psychotherapy is better than no therapy and better than placebo therapy. But no single kind of therapy stands out as clearly superior to the rest. More-sophisticated research is required to determine the ideal combinations of therapy, therapist, and client factors for treating specific disorders.

IMPORTANT CONCEPTS

MAJOR CONTRIBUTORS

RECOMMENDED READINGS

FOR GENERAL WORKS ON THERAPY
Aftel, M., Lakoff, R. T., & Coleman, L. (1986). When talk is not cheap: Or, how to find the right therapist when you don't know where to begin. New York: Warner.

Basch, M. F. (1990). Understanding psychotherapy: The science behind the art. New York: Basic Books.
Corsini, R. J., & Wedding, D. (Eds.). (1989). Current psychotherapies (4th ed.). Itasca, IL: F. E. Peacock.

Mahoney, M. J. (1991). Human change processes: The scientific foundations of psychotherapy. New York: Basic Books.
Patterson, C. H. (1990). Theories of counseling and psychotherapy (4th ed.). New York: Harper & Row.

Sue, D. W., & Sue, D. (1990). Counseling the culturally different. New York: Wiley.
Yalom, I. D. (1989). Love's executioner and other tales of psychotherapy. New York: Basic Books.

Zeig, J. K., & Munion, W. M. (Eds.). (1990). *What is psychotherapy?* San Francisco: Jossey-Bass.

FOR MORE ON THE HISTORY OF THERAPY

Alexander, F. G., & Selesnick, S. T. (1966). *The history of psychiatry.* New York: Harper & Row.

Barton, W. E. (1987). *The history and influence of the American Psychiatric Association.* Washington, DC: American Psychiatric Press.

Bromberg, W. (1954). *Man above humanity: A history of psychotherapy.* Philadelphia: Lippincott.

Reisman, J. M. (1976). *A history of clinical psychology.* New York: Irvington.

Roccatagliata, G. (1986). *A history of ancient psychiatry.* Westport, CT: Greenwood.

Walker, C. E. (Ed.). (1991). *Clinical psychology: Historical and research foundations.* New York: Plenum.

Warsh, C. K. (1990). *Moments of unreason: The practice of Canadian psychiatry and the Homewood Retreat, 1883–1923.* Toronto: University of Toronto Press.

Whiteley, J. M. (Ed.). (1980). *The history of counseling psychology.* Pacific Grove, CA: Brooks/Cole.

Zeig, J. K. (Ed.). (1987). *The evolution of psychotherapy.* New York: Brunner/Mazel.

Zeig, J. K. (Ed.). (1992). *The evolution of psychotherapy: The second conference.* New York: Brunner/Mazel.

Zilboorg, G., & Henry, G. W. (1941). *A history of medical psychology.* New York: W. W. Norton.

FOR MORE ON THE PSYCHOANALYTIC ORIENTATION

Carotenuto, A. (1991). *Kant's dove: The history of transference in psychoanalysis.* Wilmette, IL: Chiron.

Fisher, S., & Greenberg, R. P. (1985). *The scientific credibility of Freud's theories and therapy.* New York: Columbia University Press.

Kris, A. O. (1987). *Free association.* New Haven, CT: Yale University Press.

Luborsky, L., & Crits-Christoph, P. (1990). *Understanding transference.* New York: Basic Books.

Rapaport, D. (1974). *The history of the concept of the association of ideas.* Madison, CT: International Universities Press.

Reik, T. (1952). *Listening with the third ear: The inner experience of a psychoanalyst.* New York: Farrar, Straus.

Strean, H. S. (1990). *Resolving resistances in psychotherapy.* New York: Brunner/Mazel.

Weiss, J., Sampson, H., & the Mount Zion Psychotherapy Research Group. (1986). *The psychoanalytic process: Theory, clinical observations, and empirical research.* New York: Guilford.

FOR MORE ON THE BEHAVIORAL ORIENTATION

Boudewyns, P. A., & Shipley, R. H. (Eds.). (1983). *Flooding and implosive therapy: Direct therapeutic exposure in clinical practice.* New York: Plenum.

Cautela, J. R., & Kearney, A. J. (1986). *The covert conditioning handbook.* New York: Springer.

Hadley, N. H. (1985). *Foundations of aversion therapy.* New York: Luce.

Kazdin, A. E. (1978). *History of behavior modification.* Baltimore: University Park Press.

Kazdin, A. E. (1977). *The token economy: A review and evaluation.* New York: Plenum.

Wolpe, J. (1991). *The practice of behavior therapy* (4th ed.). Boston: Allyn & Bacon.

FOR MORE ON THE COGNITIVE ORIENTATION

Dalton, P., & Dunnett, G. (1992). *A psychology for living: Personal construct theory for professionals and clients.* New York: Wiley.

Ellis, A. (1988). *Rational-emotive therapy.* Boston: Allyn & Bacon.

Meichenbaum, D. (1985). *Stress-inoculation training.* New York: Pergamon.

Safran, J. D., & Segal, Z. V. (1990). *The process of cognitive therapy.* New York: Basic Books.

FOR MORE ON THE HUMANISTIC ORIENTATION

Frankl, V. E. (1959/1992). *Man's search for meaning: An introduction to logotherapy.* Boston: Beacon Press.

Harman, R. L. (1990). *Gestalt therapy: Discussions with the masters.* Springfield, MA: Charles C Thomas.

Mearns, D., & Thorne, B. (1988). *Person-centered counseling in action.* Newbury Park, CA: Sage Publications.

Rogers, C. R. (1951). *Client-centered therapy.* Boston: Houghton Mifflin.

Yalom, I. D. (1980). *Existential psychotherapy.* New York: Basic Books.

FOR MORE ON THE SOCIAL-RELATIONS ORIENTATION

Blatner, A., & Blatner, A. (1988). *Foundations of psychodrama: History, theory, and practice.* New York: Springer.

Bornstein, P. H., & Bornstein, M. T. (1986). *Marital therapy: A behavioral communications approach.* New York: Pergamon.

Clarkson, P. (1991). *Transactional analysis psychotherapy: An integrated approach.* New York: Routledge.

Minuchin, S., & Nichols, M. P. (1992). *Family healing: Tales of hope and renewal from family therapy.* New York: Free Press.

Rakos, R. F. (1990). *Assertive behavior.* New York: Routledge.

Yalom, I. D. (1985). *The theory and practice of group psychotherapy.* New York: Basic Books.

FOR MORE ON THE BIOPSYCHOLOGICAL ORIENTATION

Abrams, R. (1992). *Electroconvulsive therapy* (2nd ed.). New York: Oxford University Press.

Fisher, S., & Greenberg, R. P. (Eds.). (1989). *The limits of biological treatments for psychological distress.* Hillsdale, NJ: Erlbaum.

Silverstone, T., & Turner, P. (1988). *Drug treatment in psychiatry.* New York: Routledge.

Valenstein, E. S. (1986). *Great and desperate cures: The rise and decline of psychosurgery and other radical treatments for mental illness.* New York: Basic Books.

Zigun, J. R. (1991). *Biological psychiatry.* Baltimore: Williams & Wilkins.

FOR MORE ON COMMUNITY MENTAL HEALTH

Bassuk, E. L. (1984, July). The homelessness problem. *Scientific American*, pp. 40–45.

Dear, M. J., & Wolch, J. R. (1992). *Landscapes of despair: From deinstitutionalization to homelessness.* Princeton, NJ: Princeton University Press.

Isaac, R. J., & Armat, V. C. (1990). *Madness in the streets: How psychiatry and the law abandoned the mentally ill.* New York: Free Press.

Johnson, A. B. (1990). *Out of bedlam: The truth about deinstitutionalization.* New York: Basic Books.

Jones, J. M., Levine, I. S., & Rosenberg, A. A. (Eds.). (1991). Homelessness [Special issue]. *American Psychologist, 46*(11).

Levine, M. (1981). *The history and politics of community mental health.* New York: Oxford University Press.

Mosher, L., & Burt, L. (1994). *Community mental health: A practical guide.* New York: W. W. Norton.

FOR MORE ON THE RIGHTS OF THE THERAPY CLIENT

Appelbaum, P. S., Lidz, C. W., & Meisel, A. (1987). *Informed consent: Legal theory and clinical practice.* New York: Oxford University Press.

Beck, J. C. (Ed.). (1990). *Confidentiality versus the duty to protect: Foreseeable harm in the practice of psychiatry.* Washington, DC: American Psychiatric Press.

Donaldson, K. (1976). *Insanity inside and out: The personal story behind the landmark Supreme Court decision.* New York: Crown.

Felthous, A. R. (1989). *The psychotherapist's duty to warn or protect.* Springfield, IL: Charles C Thomas.

Jones, R., & Parlour, R. R. (Eds.). (1981). *Wyatt v. Stickney: Retrospect and prospect.* Orlando: Grune & Stratton.

Lakin, M. (1988). *Ethical issues in the psychotherapies.* New York: Oxford University Press.

Simon, C. (1988, June). Boundaries of confidence. *Psychology Today*, pp. 23–26.

VandeCreek, L., & Knapp, S. (1993). *Tarasoff and beyond: Legal and clinical considerations in the treatment of life-endangering patients.* Sarasota, FL: Professional Resource Press.

FOR MORE ON THE EFFECTIVENESS OF PSYCHOTHERAPY

Garfield, S. L., & Bergin, A. E. (Eds.). (1986). *Handbook of psychotherapy and behavior change.* New York: Wiley.

Lambert, M. J., Christensen, E. R., & Dejulio, S. S. (1989). *The assessment of psychotherapy outcome.* New York: Wiley.

Luborsky, L., Crits-Christoph, P., Mintz, J., & Auerbach, A. (1988). *Who will benefit from psychotherapy? Predicting therapeutic outcomes.* New York: Basic Books.

Smith, M. L., Glass, G. V., & Miller, T. I. (1980). *The benefits of psychotherapy.* Baltimore: The Johns Hopkins University Press.

van Kalmthout, M. A., Wojciechowski, F. L., & Schaap, C. (Eds.). (1985). *Common factors in psychotherapy*. New York: Taylor & Francis.

FOR MORE ON CONTRIBUTORS TO THE STUDY OF THERAPY

Burston. D. (1991). *The legacy of Erich Fromm*. Cambridge. MA: Harvard University Press.

Clarkson, P., & Mackewn, J. (1993). *Fritz Perls*. Newbury Park, CA: Sage Publications.

Dain, N. (1980). *Clifford Beers: Advocate for the insane*. Pittsburgh: University of Pittsburgh Press.

Evans, R. I. (1989). *Albert Bandura: The man and his ideas—a dialogue*. Westport, CT: Praeger.

Gay, P. (1988). *Freud: A life for our time*. New York: W. W. Norton.

Gollaher, D. (1994). *A voice for the mad: The life of Dorothea Dix*. New York: Free Press.

Grosskurth, P. (1986). *Melanie Klein: Her world and her work*. New York: Knopf.

Hawke, D. F. (1971). *Benjamin Rush: Revolutionary gadfly*. New York: Irvington.

Hirschmuller, A. (1978). *The life and work of Josef Breuer: Physiology and psychoanalysis*. New York: New York University Press.

Jorgensen, E. W., & Jorgensen, H. I. (1984). *Eric Berne: Master gamesman—a transactional biography*. New York: Grove-Weidenfeld.

Kirschenbaum, H. (1979). *On becoming Carl Rogers*. New York: Delacorte.

Perry, H. S. (1982). *Psychiatrist of America: The life of Harry Stack Sullivan*. Cambridge, MA: Harvard University Press.

Quinn, S. (1987). *A mind of her own: The life of Karen Horney*. New York: Summit.

Rattner, J. (1983). *Alfred Adler*. New York: Frederick Ungar.

Sayers, J. (1991). *Mothers of psychoanalysis: Helene Deutsch, Karen Horney, Anna Freud, and Melanie Klein*. New York: W. W. Norton.

Stevens, A. (1990). *On Jung*. New York: Routledge.

Walker, C. E. (1991). *The history of clinical psychology in autobiography* (Vol. 1). Pacific Grove, CA: Brooks/Cole.

Walker, C. E. (1992). *The history of clinical psychology in autobiography* (Vol. 2). Pacific Grove, CA: Brooks/Cole.

Weishaar, M. (1992). *Aaron Beck*. Newbury Park, CA: Sage Publications.

Wiener, D. N. (1988). *Albert Ellis: Passionate skeptic*. Westport, CT: Praeger.

Young-Bruehl, E. (1988). *Anna Freud*. New York: Summit.

CHAPTER 16

Miriam Schapiro
Conservatory: Portrait of Frida Kahlo
1988

PSYCHOLOGY AND HEALTH

D

o you overeat, smoke cigarettes, drive recklessly, exercise rarely, drink excessive amounts of alcohol, fail to follow your physician's medical recommendations, or respond inefficiently to stressful situations? If you engage in any of these maladaptive behaviors, which are among the leading causes of death in the United States, you may be reducing your life span. In fact, according to the National Academy of Sciences, half of the mortality from the ten leading causes of death in the United States is strongly influenced by personal lifestyle (Hamburg, 1982).

This statement would not have been true at the turn of the century, when most North Americans died from infectious diseases such as influenza, pneumonia, or tuberculosis. But the development of vaccines and antibiotics, as well as improved hygiene and public sanitation practices, led to a decline in the importance of infectious diseases in illness and mortality. This was accompanied by a surge in the relative importance of noninfectious diseases, especially those caused by dangerous or unhealthy behaviors. A century ago, cancer and cardiovascular disease, which are promoted by unhealthy lifestyles pursued over a span of decades, were relatively uncommon causes of death among Americans. Today they are the two most common causes. We now are more likely to become ill or die because of our own actions than because of viruses or bacteria that invade our bodies. Thus, you are more likely to hear of a smoker who has died from lung cancer than of a person struck down by polio—an all too common event until the development of the Salk vaccine in the 1950s. The role of psychological factors in the onset and prevention of cancer, cardiovascular disease, and other illnesses that are affected by lifestyle is one of the main problems studied by psychologists in the field of *health psychology.*

Health psychology is the field that studies the role of psychological factors in the promotion of health and the prevention of illness. Health psychology has grown so rapidly that even clinical psychologists, traditionally concerned with the treatment of psychological disorders, now conduct more research in health psychology than in any other area (Sayette & Mayne, 1990). Health psychologists favor a *biopsychosocial model* of health and illness, which emphasizes the interaction of biological, psychological, and social factors. In contrast, the traditional *biomedical model* emphasizes biological factors and neglects psychological and social ones. The chief topics of interest to health psychologists are the relationship between stress and illness, the modification of health-impairing habits, and the promotion of adaptive reactions to illness (Krantz, Grunberg, & Baum, 1985).

STRESS AND ILLNESS

In the 1960s, undergraduates at Penn State University, recognizing their isolation in rural, peaceful State College, Pennsylvania, dubbed the town and its surroundings "Happy Valley." The students were vindicated in 1988, when California psychologist Robert Levine reported the results of his survey of living conditions in the United States. He concluded that State College had the distinction of being the least stressful place to live in America (Rossi, 1988).

But what is *stress?* According to Canadian endocrinologist Hans Selye (1907–1982), the founder of modern stress research, **stress** is the physiological response of the body to physical and psychological demands. Such demands are known as **stressors.** Though stress has been implicated as a factor in illness, some degree of stress is normal, necessary, and unavoidable. As Selye noted, "complete freedom from stress is death" (Selye, 1980, p. 128). Stress acts as a motivator to make us adjust our behavior to meet

---

health psychology
The field that applies psychological principles to the prevention and treatment of physical illness.

Behavioral Causes of Illness and Death
Half of the mortality from the leading causes of death in the United States is influenced by unhealthy or dangerous behaviors, such as overeating, failing to exercise, and overexposing oneself to the sun.

stress
The physiological response of the body to physical and psychological demands.

stressor
A physical or psychological demand that induces physiological adjustment.

Stress
The physical and psychological demands on this worker will induce what Hans Selye called "stress."

changing demands, as when we study for an upcoming exam, wear a sweater in cold weather, or seek companionship when lonely. Stress can even be pleasurable, as when we attend a party, play a game of Scrabble, or shoot river rapids on a raft. Selye called unpleasant stress *distress* and pleasant stress *eustress* (from the Greek for "good stress").

Sources of Stress

Researchers look at stressors from two points of view. Some categorize stressors by their psychological effects. Others categorize them by the kinds of life events they represent.

Psychological Stressors

There are three general categories of psychological stressors: *frustration, pressure,* and *conflict.* You experience **frustration** when you are blocked from reaching a goal. Minor frustrations include waiting in line at a movie theater or performing poorly on an exam. Major frustrations include losing one's job or flunking out of school. Our jobs can also be sources of chronic frustration. A study of professional word processors found that those who worked on computer systems with slow response times felt more frustrated and experienced more physical discomfort than did those who worked on faster systems (Schleifer & Amick, 1989). Because differences in physiological reactivity to frustration exist in early infancy, your degree of physiological reactivity to frustrating situations may be affected by heredity (Fox, 1989).

frustration
The emotional state induced when one is blocked from reaching a goal.

You experience **pressure** when you must fulfill responsibilities that tax your abilities, such as writing a research paper or working to pay for your tuition. Even great athletes experience pressure during competition. Pressure might explain why, contrary to popular belief, the home team in the deciding game of a professional baseball or basketball championship series is more likely to *lose*. This was discovered by an archival study of baseball World Series records from 1924 through 1982 and National Basketball Association championship records from 1967 through 1982 (Baumeister & Steinhilber, 1984). In contrast, in nondeciding games, the home team retains a home-field advantage. Evidently, there is a home-field *disadvantage* only in deciding games.

pressure
The emotional state induced when one is confronted by personal responsibilities that tax one's abilities.

Pressure and the Home-Field Disadvantage
In deciding games of the World Series, the pressure of playing before home fans can interfere with the home team's performance. The players can become so self-conscious that they attend to normally automatic, unconscious movements. As a result, they may lose their optimal timing and coordination, hampering their performance. Of course, home teams sometimes win deciding games, as in the 1991 World Series, in which Kirby Puckett and his fellow Minnesota Twins won the seventh game.

conflict
The emotional state induced when one is torn between two or more potential courses of action.

approach-approach conflict
A conflict in which one must choose between two desirable courses of action.

avoidance-avoidance conflict
A conflict in which one must choose between two undesirable courses of action.

approach-avoidance conflict
A conflict in which one is faced by a course of action that has both desirable and undesirable qualities.

What could explain the difference in home-team performance between early games and deciding games? The researchers attributed this to the increased *pressure* of playing important games before home fans. This pressure makes home-team players more self-conscious. As a result, they pay attention to the performance of skilled movements that they normally perform automatically with little or no conscious awareness. The home-team players become less fluid in their movements and more prone to perform below their normal level of ability. For example, in the World Series, the home team makes significantly more errors in seventh games than in earlier games. And in NBA championships, the home team's shooting percentage is significantly lower in seventh games than in earlier games. Evidently, the pressure of performing before wildly cheering home fans can make members of the home team "choke."

You experience a **conflict** when you are torn between two or more potential courses of action. Gestalt psychologist Kurt Lewin (1935) identified three kinds of conflicts: *approach-approach*, *avoidance-avoidance*, and *approach-avoidance*. In an **approach-approach conflict,** you are torn between two desirable courses of action. This might occur when one friend invites you to attend a party, another invites you to attend a concert, and you can't do both because they're at the same time. This is usually the least stressful kind of conflict, because both options are desirable. But the pursuit of two desirable, yet conflicting, options can induce intense distress—as is experienced by many adults, especially women, who pursue both a career and parenthood (Lewis & Cooper, 1983). Job demands may lead to neglect of parental duties; caring for a sick child may lead to neglect of job responsibilities. Both scenarios would induce stress. Some people avoid the conflicting demands of work and parenthood by pursuing only one or the other, while others find that remaining in the conflict is more desirable. And, more and more, neither parent has a choice—they must both work in order to support themselves and their children.

In an **avoidance-avoidance conflict,** you are forced to choose between two unpleasant courses of action, such as going to the dentist or suffering with a toothache. Though you might delay making a choice for as long as possible, the conflict is resolved when one option forces you to choose it as the lesser of two evils. An unbearable toothache would eventually make you go to the dentist. But some people caught in an avoidance-avoidance conflict find both courses of action intolerable. This may lead them to seek the artificial solace of drugs or alcohol. Even animal research provides support for this. Moderate doses of alcohol weaken avoidance-avoidance conflicts in laboratory rats (Mansfield, 1979). Perhaps human beings who use alcohol to relieve their stress, at times, do so to weaken their own avoidance-avoidance conflicts.

In an **approach-avoidance conflict,** you are simultaneously drawn to and repelled by the same goal. College seniors may experience this when they consider their upcoming graduation, which has both desirable and undesirable aspects. Dieters might be attracted by a luscious dessert and repulsed by the thought of added body fat. The approach-avoidance conflict is also at the heart of Freudian theory. For example, the Freudian interpretation of conversion disorder (see chapter 14), in which a person experiences motor or sensory loss without any physical cause, views it as the outcome of a conflict between the desire to approach sex and the desire to avoid guilt for engaging in it (O'Neill & Kempler, 1969).

As first noted by psychologist Neal Miller, a person in an approach-avoidance conflict (such as a conflict over sexual behavior) vacillates, sometimes moving toward the goal and at other times moving away from it (Dollard & Miller, 1950). When you are far from the goal, both your approach tendency and your avoidance tendency are relatively weak, with your approach tendency typically being stronger than your avoidance tendency. This motivates you to approach the goal. As you move toward the goal, both your approach tendency and your avoidance tendency intensify. But your avoidance tendency increases faster than your approach tendency. If the avoidance tendency eventually surpasses the approach tendency, you may fail to reach the goal. This is illustrated in figure 16.1.

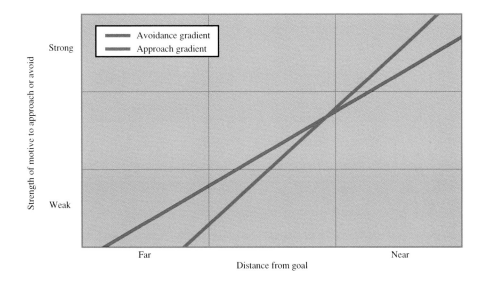

FIGURE 16.1

Approach-Avoidance Conflict
In an approach-avoidance conflict, the approach and avoidance tendencies both increase in strength the closer you get to a goal. But the avoidance tendency increases more rapidly. Vacillation between approach and avoidance will be greatest at the point where the two tendencies are of about equal strength. In the graph, this is the point where the approach and avoidance gradients cross.

Legend:
- Avoidance gradient
- Approach gradient

Y-axis: Strength of motive to approach or avoid — Strong / Weak
X-axis: Far / Near — Distance from goal

Drawing by Eric Teitelbaum; © *1990 The New Yorker Magazine, Inc.*

"You take all the time you need, Larry—this certainly is a big decision."

Consider engaged couples, who commonly experience an approach-avoidance conflict. When they get engaged, their approach tendency is much stronger than their avoidance tendency. But as they get closer to the wedding day, they might develop "cold feet" as they think more about the negative aspects of marriage. In extreme cases, the avoidance tendency can become so strong that the bride or groom fails to appear at the wedding ceremony. Given the many approach-avoidance conflicts we experience in our everyday lives, people who are flexible in selecting an approach or avoidance strategy will be more successful in coping with stress than will people who rely too much on one strategy (Roth & Cohen, 1986).

Life Events

Frustration, pressure, and conflict are often the results of life events. These include both major *life changes* and everyday *hassles*. Throughout life each of us must adjust to life changes, both pleasant ones (such as graduation from college) and unpleasant ones (such as the death of a loved one). Interest in the relationship between life changes and illness began when Thomas Holmes and Richard Rahe (1967) developed the *Social Readjustment Rating Scale*. Holmes and Rahe asked medical patients to report positive and negative life changes that had occurred during the months before they became ill. This generated the list of 43 kinds of life changes in table 16.1.

TABLE 16.1 Social Readjustment Rating Scale

Life Event	Mean Value	Life Event	Mean Value
Death of spouse	100	Son or daughter leaving home	29
Divorce	73	Trouble with in-laws	29
Marital separation	65	Outstanding personal achievement	28
Jail term	63	Spouse begins or stops work	26
Death of close family member	63	Begin or end school	26
Personal injury or illness	53	Change in living conditions	25
Marriage	50	Revision of personal habits	24
Fired at work	47	Trouble with boss	23
Marital reconciliation	45	Change in work hours or conditions	20
Retirement	45	Change in residence	20
Change in health of family member	44	Change in schools	20
Pregnancy	40	Change in recreation	19
Sex difficulties	39	Change in church activities	19
Gain of new family member	39	Change in social activities	18
Business readjustment	39	Mortgage or loan for lesser purchase (car, TV, etc.)	17
Change in financial state	38	Change in sleeping habits	16
Death of close friend	37	Change in number of family get-togethers	15
Change to different line of work	36	Change in eating habits	15
Change in number of arguments with spouse	35	Vacation	13
Mortgage or loan for major purchase (home, etc.)	31	Christmas	12
Foreclosure on mortgage or loan	30	Minor violations of the law	11
Change in responsibilities at work	29		

Reprinted with permission from *Journal of Psychosomatic Research*, 11: 213–218, T. H. Holmes and R. H. Rahe, "The Social Readjustment Rating Scale," 1967, Elsevier Science Ltd., Pergamon Imprint, Oxford, England.

Richard Rahe
"By use of a life chart, which chronologically documents a person's major life events and concomitant health status over his or her life span, a fuller understanding can be reached regarding why an individual becomes ill at a particular time."

Members of another sample were then asked to rate, on a 100-point scale, the degree of life change, or *adjustment*, required by each of the 43. Each kind of life change was rated relative to getting married, which Holmes and Rahe gave the arbitrary value of 50. Note that the death of a spouse has the highest rating—100 points. Minor violations of the law have the lowest rating—11 points. Also note that the scale includes both negative events, such as the foreclosure of a mortgage or loan, and positive events, such as Christmas.

Your *life change score* is the sum of the scores for your life changes that occurred in a given period of time, generally the past year. Holmes and Rahe found that people who had a total life-change score of more than 300 points in the preceding year were more than twice as likely to become ill as people who had a total of less than 300 points. People who suffer from diseases or disorders as varied as breast cancer (Forsen, 1991) and migraine headaches (de Benedittis, Lorenzetti, & Pieri, 1990) tend to report that they experienced more life changes than normal before the onset of their afflictions. Richard Rahe (1992) even discovered this relationship in the life of Vincent van Gogh, who experienced clusters of stressful life events close to the times when he suffered from serious physical illnesses.

Note, however, that a positive correlation between life changes and illness indicates only that there *might* be a causal relationship between the two (Cooper, Cooper, & Faragher, 1986). In fact, one of the greatest weaknesses of the Social Readjustment Rating Scale is that its very content might overestimate the relationship between life changes and illness. The scale contains some life changes that may be either causes *or* effects of illness (Zimmerman, 1983). The most obvious examples are "change in eating habits," "change in sleeping habits," and "personal injury or illness." Moreover, though Holmes and Rahe assumed that adjustment to changes brought about by life events— whether positive or negative—induced stress, subsequent research has shown that it is the nature of the events, rather than change itself, that induces stress. Negative life changes tend to induce stress more than neutral or positive life changes do (Monroe, 1982). This agrees with Selye's distinction between distress and eustress.

Posttraumatic Stress Disorder
In September 1992, Hurricane Andrew struck Florida and became the most costly storm in U.S. history. Survivors of disasters like this commonly experience posttraumatic stress disorder.

Traumatic events, such as wars or disasters, are often associated with a syndrome known as **posttraumatic stress disorder,** which can appear months or years after the event. The disorder is marked by a variety of symptoms. Emotional symptoms include anxiety, emotional apathy, and survivor guilt. Cognitive symptoms include hypervigilance, difficulty concentrating, and flashbacks of the event. Behavioral symptoms include insomnia and social detachment. Posttraumatic stress disorder is especially common among victims of rape. They initially experience intense anxiety and depression, which tend to diminish gradually over the first year. Nonetheless, 20 percent of rape victims have long-lasting emotional scars (Hanson, 1990).

posttraumatic stress disorder
A syndrome of physical and psychological symptoms that appears as a delayed response after exposure to an extremely emotionally distressing event.

Though posttraumatic stress disorder may occur following any of a variety of traumas, including rapes, earthquakes, kidnappings, and airplane crashes, it has been most widely publicized in regard to Vietnam War veterans who developed it years after returning to the United States. In Vietnam veterans, posttraumatic stress disorder is as much a delayed grief reaction as it is a delayed stress reaction. The disorder typically erupts when years of emotional repression give way to memories of tragic human losses (Widdison & Salisbury, 1989–1990).

At least 15 percent of American veterans of the Vietnam War developed posttraumatic stress disorder (McGuire, 1990). The rate among Canadian veterans of the Vietnam War is even higher, in part because of differences in social support available to the two groups. Canadian veterans have tended to be more isolated from other veterans, to receive even less recognition for their service, and to have fewer options for obtaining professional help to relieve their distress (Stretch, 1991).

Posttraumatic stress disorder is also associated with an increased risk of physical illness. For example, in 1980 a natural disaster struck the state of Washington—the eruption of the Mount Saint Helens volcano in the Cascade Mountains. Though more than 100 miles from the volcano, the town of Othello was covered by volcanic ash. Residents of that farming community suffered the distress of their fields' being covered with ash, the fear of the effects of the ash on their health, and the dread that the volcano would erupt again. During the 6 months that followed the disaster, a local medical clinic reported an almost 200 percent increase in stress-related illnesses among the residents of Othello. There also was an almost 20 percent increase in the local death rate (Adams & Adams, 1984).

Catastrophes such as the Mount Saint Helens eruption have demonstrated the need to have trained disaster teams ready to go into action to prevent emotional, as well as physical, problems (Mangelsdorff, 1985). For those who develop posttraumatic stress disorder, behavior therapy aimed at reducing the anxiety associated with memories of the traumatic event has been effective in relieving personal distress (Foa & Rothbaum, 1989).

Though major life changes are important stress-inducing events, they are not the sole ones. A decade ago Richard Lazarus and his colleagues found other important, though less dramatic, stress-inducing events: the *hassles* of everyday life (Kanner et al., 1981). A typical day can be filled with dozens of hassles, such as forgetting one's keys, being stuck in traffic, or dealing with a rude salesperson. People who experience many daily hassles are more likely to suffer from health problems, including headaches, sore throats, and influenza (DeLongis, Folkman, & Lazarus, 1988).

Life changes can promote illness indirectly by increasing daily hassles. Studies have found that there is a stronger association between hassles and illness than between life changes and illness (Ivancevich, 1986). Why might this be? Consider a person who gets divorced—a major life change. The stress she or he experiences might be a product not only of the divorce process itself but also of the need to cope with new daily hassles. Perhaps the person must now fulfill all the responsibilities that had been shared during the marriage, including grocery shopping, meal preparation, house cleaning, and child care. The person's adrenal glands might respond by increasing their secretion of the hormones cortisol, epinephrine, and norepinephrine (Brantley et al., 1988). Though these hormones help us adapt to stressors, they also impair the immune system's ability to protect us from illness (Marx, 1985).

Most research on the relationship between daily hassles and illnesses makes it difficult to determine whether they are just correlated with each other or whether hassles actually promote illness. This is because few *prospective* studies have been conducted on the relationship between hassles and health. A prospective study would investigate whether a person's current level of hassles is predictive of his or her future health. This contrasts with *retrospective* studies, which simply find that people who are ill report more hassles in their recent past.

One of the few prospective studies of the effects of daily hassles found that hassles do, in fact, promote illness. On two occasions, adolescent girls who served as subjects in the study were asked to indicate, for each of twenty commonly experienced circumstances, whether it had occurred in their lives and whether they rated its occurrence as positive or negative. They also completed an illness symptoms checklist and a personality test measuring depression. The results indicated that negative circumstances were associated with depression and poor health. But this was true only when the girls also reported low levels of positive circumstances, or *uplifts*. Apparently, uplifts can buffer the effects of hassles, making them have fewer negative effects (Siegel & Brown, 1988). This, again, is in keeping with Selye's distinction between distress (such as hassles) and eustress (such as uplifts). In fact, research indicates that the immune system response may be stronger during periods of eustress than during periods of distress (Snyder, Roghmann, & Sigal, 1993). During times of maximum hassles, such as the last few weeks of a semester, students might do well to seek compensatory uplifts, such as attending a movie, going to a party, or visiting a friend.

Effects of Stress

Whether it is caused by life changes or daily hassles, stress is marked by physiological arousal and, in some cases, reduced resistance to disease. In the nineteenth century, English physician Daniel Hack Tuke wrote one of the first books on the physiological effects of psychological stressors, *Illustrations of the Influence of the Mind on the Body* (Weiss, 1972). Today, Tuke's intellectual descendants study the effects of both physical and psychological stressors on physiological arousal. As explained in chapter 12, physical and psychological stressors evoke the *fight-or-flight response*, first described by physiologist Walter Cannon (1915/1989). The fight-or-flight response involves activation of the sympathetic nervous system and secretion of stress hormones (cortisol, epinephrine, and norepinephrine) by the adrenal glands.

Cannon's work influenced that of Hans Selye. Selye (1936) hoped to discover a new sex hormone. As part of his research, he injected rats with extracts of ovarian tissue. He found that the rats developed stomach ulcerations, enlarged adrenal glands, and atrophied spleens, lymph nodes, and thymus glands. Selye later observed that rats displayed this same response to a variety of stressors, including heat, cold, injuries, and infections. This indicated that his initial findings were not necessarily caused by a sex hormone.

Selye also found that animals and people, in reacting to stressors, go through three stages, which he called the **general adaptation syndrome.** During the first stage, the *alarm reaction*, the body prepares to cope with the stressor by increasing activity in the sympathetic nervous system and adrenal glands (the fight-or-flight response). Selye noted that during the alarm stage different stressors produced similar symptoms, such as fatigue, fever, headache, and loss of appetite.

If the body continues to be exposed to the stressor, it enters the *stage of resistance*, during which it becomes more resistant to the stressor. The stage of resistance is like the second wind you may experience while playing a sport or studying for a final exam. During a second wind, your initial fatigue gives way to a feeling of renewed energy and well-being. Yet your resistance to disease may decline. During final-exams week you might be able to cope well enough to study for all your exams despite a decrease in sleep, exercise, recreation, and normal meals, but soon after finals are over you might come down with the flu. Selye called stress-induced illnesses "diseases of adaptation."

If you succumb to disease, you may have entered the *stage of exhaustion*. At this point, the person's resistance to disease collapses; in extreme cases, death can follow. Though Selye believed that all stressors produce similar patterns of physiological responses, more-recent research indicates that different stressors may produce different patterns (Krantz & Manuck, 1984). Your physiological response to rush-hour traffic might be different from your physiological response to a job interview. This shows the importance of your subjective *cognitive appraisal* of the stressor, which is discussed later in this chapter.

Stress and Noninfectious Diseases

As noted in chapter 12, the fight-or-flight response evolved because it helped animals and human beings cope with periodic stressors, such as wildfires or animal attacks. Unfortunately, in twentieth-century industrialized countries, we are subjected to continual, rather than periodic, stressors. The infrequent saber-toothed-tiger attack has been replaced by rush-hour traffic jams, three exams on one day, and threats of muggers on city streets. The repeated activation of the fight-or-flight response takes its toll on the body, possibly causing or aggravating diseases, including noninfectious ones. These stress-affected noninfectious diseases include asthma (Moran, 1991), headaches (Andrasik, 1990), diabetes (Fisher et al., 1982), gastric ulcers (Young et al., 1987), rheumatoid arthritis (Lerman, 1987), ulcerative colitis (Schwarz & Blanchard, 1990), and essential hypertension (McCaffrey & Blanchard, 1985). Such diseases have traditionally been called *psychosomatic illnesses*, based on the assumption that they are caused or worsened by emotional factors, such as unconscious conflicts.

Of all the diseases that might be affected by stress, coronary heart disease has received the most attention from health psychologists. Coronary heart disease is caused by **atherosclerosis,** which is promoted by cholesterol deposits in the coronary arteries. Even the stress of everyday college life may affect the level of cholesterol in your blood. In fact, college students who merely anticipate an upcoming exam show significant increases in their levels of blood cholesterol (Van Doornen & van Blokland, 1987). Stress can also promote coronary heart disease by stimulating the elevation of heart rate and blood pressure, as well as the repeated release of stress hormones. This can damage the walls of the coronary arteries by increasing blood turbulence and levels of stress hormones in the blood, making the walls of the coronary arteries more susceptible to the buildup of cholesterol plaques (Krantz & Manuck, 1984). Figure 16.2 illustrates the effect of atherosclerosis on the coronary arteries. In people with coronary heart disease, sudden, intense stress may even induce fatal heart attacks (Kamarck & Jennings, 1991).

general adaptation syndrome
As first identified by Hans Selye, the body's stress response, which includes the stages of alarm, resistance, and exhaustion.

Hans Selye (1907–1982)
"Even prehistoric man must have recognized a common element in the sense of exhaustion that overcame him in conjunction with hard labor, agonizing fear, lengthy exposure to cold or heat, starvation, loss of blood, or any kind of disease."

atherosclerosis
The narrowing of arteries caused by the accumulation of cholesterol deposits.

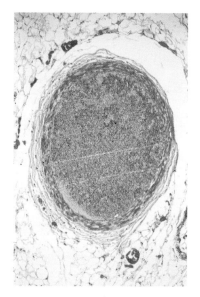

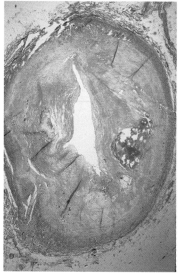

FIGURE 16.2

Atherosclerosis
Diets high in cholesterol contribute to atherosclerosis, which narrows coronary arteries and predisposes the person to heart attacks. The top photograph shows a cross section of a healthy artery, and the bottom photograph shows a cross section of an atherosclerotic artery.

psychoneuroimmunology
The interdisciplinary field that studies the relationship between psychological factors and physical illness.

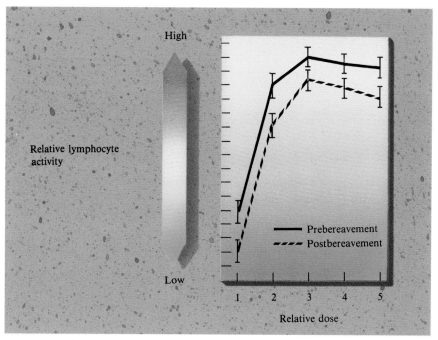

FIGURE 16.3

Bereavement and the Immune Response
During the first 2 months after the death of their wives, widowers show a decrease in the proliferation of lymphocytes in response to doses of antigens (Schleifer et al., 1983).

Stress and Infectious Diseases

In 1884 a physician reported in a British medical journal that the depression experienced by mourners at funerals predisposed them to develop illnesses (Baker, 1987). A century later, a research study provided a scientific basis for this observation. As shown in figure 16.3, the study found that men whose wives had died of breast cancer showed impaired functioning of their immune systems during the first 2 months of their bereavement (Schleifer et al., 1983). This agrees with research showing that depression is associated with suppression of the immune system (O'Leary, 1990).

The realization that stressful events, such as the death of a loved one, can impair the immune system led to the emergence of **psychoneuroimmunology,** the interdisciplinary field that studies the relationship between psychological factors and illness, especially the effects of stress on the immune system (Ader & Cohen, 1993). This field recognizes that stress affects the immune system through the mediation of the brain and the endocrine system (Ader, Felten, & Cohen, 1990). Though many of the mechanisms by which stress suppresses the immune system remain to be determined, one mechanism is well established. This is illustrated in figure 16.4. Stress prompts the hypothalamus to secrete a hormone that stimulates the pituitary gland to secrete adrenocorticotropic hormone (ACTH), which then stimulates the adrenal cortex to secrete corticosteroids. The hypothalamus also increases activity in the sympathetic nervous system, which stimulates the adrenal medulla to secrete the hormones epinephrine and norepinephrine. As noted earlier, though adrenal hormones might make us more resistant to stressors, they can also impair our immune systems (Boneau et al., 1993).

The cells chiefly responsible for the immunological response to infections are white blood cells called B-lymphocytes and T-lymphocytes. *B-lymphocytes* attack invading bacteria, and *T-lymphocytes* attack viruses, cancer cells, and foreign tissues. The immunosuppressive effects of stress hormones might explain why Apollo astronauts, after returning to Earth from stressful trips to the moon, had impaired immune responses (Jemmott & Locke, 1984). But you do not have to go to the moon to experience stress-induced suppression of your immune response, as revealed in a study of dental students.

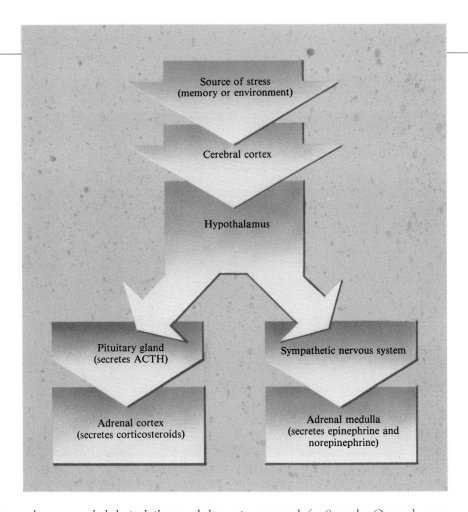

FIGURE 16.4

Stress Pathways
When the cerebral cortex processes stressful memories or stressful input from the immediate environment, it stimulates a physiological response by way of the endocrine system and the sympathetic nervous system. Both pathways involve the hypothalamus. The hypothalamus signals the pituitary gland, which secretes adrenocorticotropic hormone (ACTH). ACTH, in turn, stimulates the adrenal cortex to secrete corticosteroid hormones, which mobilize the body's energy stores, reduce tissue inflammation, and inhibit the immune response. The hypothalamus also sends signals through the sympathetic nervous system to the adrenal medulla, which in turn stimulates the release of epinephrine and norepinephrine. These hormones contribute to the physiological arousal characteristic of the "fight or flight" response.

The students recorded their daily mood three times a week for 8 weeks. On each occasion a sample of their saliva was taken and mixed with an *antigen* (a substance that induces an immune response). The results showed that their B-lymphocyte response to the antigen was stronger on days when they were in a good mood (eustress) than on days when they were in a bad mood (distress) (Stone et al., 1987).

There is also evidence that the immune response might be subject to classical conditioning, meaning that normally neutral stimuli may come to enhance it or to suppress it. A leading researcher in this area has been psychologist Robert Ader. In a study that demonstrated conditioned suppression of the immune response, Ader and his colleague Nicholas Cohen (1982) let mice taste saccharin-flavored water and then injected them with the drug cyclophosphamide, which induces nausea. As expected, the mice developed an aversion to sweet-tasting water. But when some of the them were later forced to drink sweet-tasting water, several developed illnesses and died. Ader and Cohen attributed this to another effect of cyclophosphamide—the suppression of the immune response. They apparently had conditioned suppression of the mice's immune response, with the sweet-tasting water serving as the conditioned stimulus. This process is diagrammed in figure 16.5. Animal research indicates that conditioned immunosuppression might be mediated by the actions of epinephrine and norepinephrine (Lysle, Cunnick, & Maslonek, 1991).

Perhaps classical conditioning will one day be applied clinically to enhance immune responses in people who have low resistance to infections, such as those at risk for *acquired immune deficiency syndrome* (*AIDS*), which is caused by the *human immunodeficiency virus* (*HIV*). AIDS victims experience stress induced by both their illness and hostile social reactions to them. Such stress might further impair the functioning of their immune systems, making them even more vulnerable to infections that may prove fatal (Kiecolt-Glaser & Glaser, 1988).

FIGURE 16.5

Conditioned Immunosuppression
When Ader and Cohen (1982) paired saccharin-sweetened water with cyclophosphamide, a drug that suppresses the immune response, they found that the sweet-tasting water itself came to elicit immunosuppression. (See chapter 7 for a discussion of the relationship between the UCS, UCR, CS, and CR.)

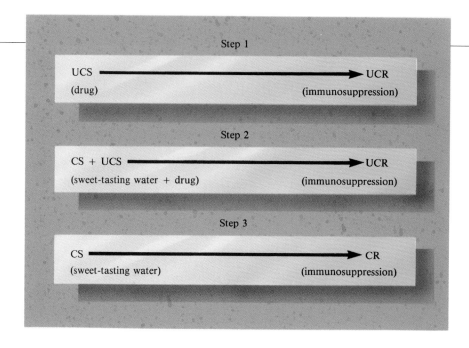

Robert Ader
"Immune responses, like other physiological processes, can be modified by classical conditioning."

Classical conditioning might also be used to suppress undesirable immune responses, such as those that occur in *autoimmune diseases,* in which the immune system attacks a person's own body tissues as though they were foreign. One candidate for such treatment might be rheumatoid arthritis, which is affected by stress (McFarlane & Brooks, 1990). Preliminary research indicates that another beneficial application of conditioned immunosuppression might be in preventing the rejection of transplanted tissues and organs. In one study, skin grafts in rats were less likely to be rejected when the rats had been conditioned to suppress their immune response (Gorczynski, 1990). Though routine conditioning of the immune system is not yet feasible, hypothetically it will be possible in the future.

Stress and Cancer

In the second century, the Greek physician Galen noted that depressed women were more likely to develop cancer than were happy women. But modern research has produced inconsistent findings concerning this apparent relationship between emotions and cancer. Consider a study of medical students who had been given personality tests in medical school and were assessed 30 years later: Of those who had been emotionally expressive, less than 1 percent had developed cancer. Those who had been loners, and presumably more emotionally controlled, were 16 times more likely to develop cancer than were those who were emotionally expressive (Shaffer et al., 1987). But research linking emotion and cancer has been countered by research failing to find such an association. A study of almost 7,000 people followed from 1965 to 1982 in Alameda County, California, found a relationship between depression and death from causes other than cancer, but no relationship between depression and cancer incidence or mortality (Kaplan & Reynolds, 1988).

Assuming that our emotions can, at least under certain circumstances, affect the progress of cancer, what mechanisms might account for this? Stress might indirectly promote cancer by encouraging cancer-inducing behaviors, such as smoking tobacco, eating high-fat foods, and drinking too much alcohol; stress might also directly interfere with the immune system's ability to defend against cancer. In fact, during periods when they are under intense academic pressure, medical students exhibit a reduction in the activity of *natural killer cells,* the lymphocytes responsible for detecting and destroying cancer cells. This appears to be the result of a decrease in the production of *interferon,* a chemical needed for the proper functioning of natural killer cells (Glaser et al., 1986).

In reflecting on the link between psychological factors and cancer, note that though stress can impair the immune system's ability to destroy cancerous cells, there is little evidence that stress can *cause* normal cells to become cancerous (Levenson & Bemis, 1991).

Scientific support for psychological effects on resistance to cancer has come from animal research that has demonstrated both conditioned suppression and conditioned enhancement of natural killer cell activity. In one study, mice were classically conditioned by pairing saccharin-flavored water as the conditioned stimulus with an injection of either an immunosuppressing drug or an immunoenhancing drug as the unconditioned stimulus. Conditioning occurred in one pairing of the saccharin flavor and the drug. Subsequent exposure to the saccharin led to either enhancement or suppression of natural killer cell activity, depending on the drug that had been used as the unconditioned stimulus (Hiramoto et al., 1987).

Mediation of Stress

More than 2,000 years ago, Hippocrates recognized the relationship between individual factors and physiological responses when he observed that it is more important to know what sort of person has a disease than to know what sort of disease a person has (Rees, 1983). Because of variability among individuals, a given stressor will not evoke the same physiological response in every person. Our reactions to stress are mediated by a variety of factors. These include *physiological reactivity, cognitive appraisal, explanatory style, feeling of control, psychological hardiness, sense of humor,* and *social support.*

Physiological Reactivity

People differ in their physiological reactivity to stressors. *Physiological reactivity* refers to increases in heart rate, blood pressure, and stress hormone secretion in response to stressors. In one study, men with mild hypertension played a video game while their heart rate and blood pressure were measured. Those who displayed high heart-rate acceleration while playing the game also displayed greater increases in blood pressure. Blood tests showed that high accelerators had higher levels of blood cholesterol than did low accelerators. This may explain the higher risk of atherosclerosis in people with greater physiological reactivity (Jorgensen et al., 1988).

Reactivity, in turn, depends on other factors. Differences in cardiovascular reactivity between females and males indicate that sex is a factor. For example, males show greater increases in both cardiovascular activity and secretion of stress hormones in response to stressors. This might contribute to the greater vulnerability of males to coronary heart disease (Stoney, Davis, & Matthews, 1987). Physiological reactivity is also related to physical fitness. Physically fit people show less physiological reactivity to stressors than do unfit people. For example, physically fit people respond to stressors with smaller increases in the secretion of adrenal stress hormones (Sothmann et al., 1987). Thus, if you wish to reduce the toll that stress takes on your cardiovascular system, you might be wise to maintain a high level of physical fitness. You also might be wise to limit your intake of caffeine, because it increases physiological reactivity in response to stressors (Pincomb et al., 1987). This might make you wary of drinking cup after cup of coffee during final-exams week.

Cognitive Appraisal

Richard Lazarus believes that one of the reasons the same stressor, such as a minor daily hassle or major life change, can induce high stress in one person and little or no stress in another is that the two interpret the stressor differently. This is known as **cognitive appraisal** (Lazarus, 1993b). In *primary appraisal* you judge whether a particular situation is a positive or negative stressor that requires an adaptive coping response. When you judge that a situation is stressful, you would then engage in *secondary appraisal* by determining whether you have the ability to cope with the stressor. The role of cognitive appraisal in affecting our physiological response to stress was demonstrated in a

cognitive appraisal
The subjective interpretation of the severity of a stressor.

replication of a study that had been conducted by Lazarus and his colleagues on reactions to a stressful film (Lazarus et al., 1985), which was discussed in chapter 12. In the replication, two groups of college students viewed a film depicting three factory accidents. Before viewing the film, one group heard a statement that simply told them the content of the film, and the other group heard a statement that urged them to adopt a detached, analytical attitude while watching the film. The latter group, which used intellectualization as a means of cognitive appraisal, showed less physiological arousal than did the former group (Dandoy & Goldstein, 1990). Consider final exams. Students who perceive them to be highly demanding and who lack confidence in their ability to perform well on them will experience greater stress than will students who perceive their upcoming exams as moderately demanding and are confident of their ability to perform well. This view has been supported by research finding lower levels of physiological reactivity to stressors in people who are high in *self-efficacy* (Bandura, 1982b), a concept (discussed in chapter 13) that has much in common with the notion of secondary appraisal.

Explanatory Style

As discussed in chapter 14, depressed people tend to have a pessimistic explanatory style. They attribute unpleasant events to *stable, global,* and *internal* characteristics of themselves. In other words, depressed people attribute unpleasant events to their own unchanging, pervasive, personal characteristics—such as a lack of intelligence. The possible role of a pessimistic explanatory style in the promotion of illness was supported by a follow-up study of 99 graduates of the Harvard University classes of 1942 through 1944. Graduates who had pessimistic explanatory styles at the age of 25 (based on questionnaires they had completed at that time in their lives) became less healthy between the ages of 45 and 60—even though all of the graduates had been healthy at age 25 (Peterson, Seligman, & Vaillant, 1988). The researchers hypothesized that this pessimistic style might make people less likely to curb negative life events, leading to more-numerous and more-severe negative life events. A pessimistic explanatory style might also lead to poor health habits, suppression of the immune system, or withdrawal from sources of social support. Each of these factors can promote illness.

Feeling of Control

Research findings have converged on personal feelings of control over stressors as one of the most important factors mediating the relationship between stress and illness. For example, people who work at demanding jobs with little control over job stressors are more likely to develop coronary heart disease (Krantz et al., 1988). A lack of on-the-job control can even adversely affect the well-being of astronauts. When the Apollo astronauts returned to Earth after their trip to the moon, they displayed impaired immune responses. This might have been a consequence of their being forced to remain passive during their highly stressful journey of almost half a million miles. In *The Right Stuff,* Tom Wolfe points out the importance of a feeling of control for test pilots and the problems it caused in the recruitment of test pilots to become astronauts:

* * * The pilot's, particularly the hot pilot's, main psychological bulwark under stress was his knowledge that he controlled the ship and could always do something. . . . This obsession with active control, it was argued, would only tend to cause problems on Mercury [space] flights. What was required was a man whose main talent was for doing nothing under stress. (Wolfe, 1979, p. 151)

People in all walks of life benefit from a sense of control over the stressors that affect them. Residents of retirement homes who are given greater responsibility for self-care and everyday activities live longer and healthier lives than do residents whose lives are controlled by staff members, in part because residents who feel greater control over their daily lives maintain stronger immune responses. People who feel a lack of control tend to secrete greater amounts of stress hormones in response to stress, which in turn can impair their immune system (Rodin, 1986).

Consider the "good patient" in the hospital, who adopts a passive, compliant role—leaving his or her recovery up to nurses and physicians. The poorer recuperative powers of such patients are associated with **learned helplessness**—the feeling that one has little control over events in one's life. Learned helplessness is even more stressful when the person attributes it to her or his own shortcomings rather than to external circumstances (Raps et al., 1982). In a best-selling book describing his recovery from a massive heart attack, Norman Cousins, former editor of the *Saturday Review*, claimed that his insistence on taking personal responsibility for his recovery—including devising his own rehabilitation program—helped him regain his health. In contrast, as Cousins noted in his book, "good patients" discover that "a weak body becomes weaker in a mood of total surrender" (Cousins, 1983, p. 223).

Psychological Hardiness

In studying executives working under high stress, psychologist Suzanne Kobasa and her colleagues found that some were more likely than others to succumb to illness. After giving a group of executives a battery of personality tests and following them for a period of 5 years, she found that those who were illness resistant tended to share a constellation of personality characteristics that made them hardier than those who were illness prone (Kobasa, Maddi, & Kahn, 1982). People high in **psychological hardiness** are more resistant to stressors and consequently are less susceptible to stress-related illness. A study of suburban police officers found that those who scored high in psychological hardiness had lower absenteeism rates than those who scored low in psychological hardiness (Tang & Hammontree, 1992).

What characteristics are shared by people high in hardiness? Hardy people face stressors with a sense of commitment, challenge, and control. People who feel a sense of *commitment* are actively involved in practical activities and social relationships, rather than being alienated from them. Hardy students are committed to their course work rather than being alienated from it. People who feel a sense of *challenge* view life's stressors as opportunities for personal growth rather than as burdens to be endured. Hardy students view term papers as chances to improve in their knowledge, thinking, and writing, rather than as just unpleasant demands on their time. And people who feel a sense of *control* believe they have the personal resources to cope with stressors, rather than being helpless in the face of them. Hardy students believe that their abilities and efforts will lead to academic success, rather than believing that nothing they do will make a difference. Note that research on psychological hardiness provides further support for the importance of a feeling of control in adapting to stressors. Figure 16.6 presents examples of the three components of hardiness.

But how does hardiness reduce susceptibility to illness? One way is by making hardy individuals less physiologically reactive to stressors (Wiebe, 1991). Another way is by affecting health habits. People high in personal hardiness, compared to people low in it, are more likely to maintain good health habits in the face of stress (Wiebe & McCallum, 1986). Perhaps hardy students are more resistant to illness because they are more likely to eat well, take vitamins, exercise more, and seek medical attention for minor ailments even when confronted by social, financial, and academic stressors.

Sense of Humor

As Norman Cousins (1983) pointed out, people have long recognized the beneficial effect of a sense of humor on health. The seventeenth-century physician Thomas Sydenham noted that "the arrival of a good clown exercises more beneficial influence upon the health of a town than 20 asses laded with drugs." When Cousins (1979) found himself suffering from a rare, often incurable neuromuscular disease, he sped his recovery by watching Marx Brothers movies and episodes of the television show "Candid Camera." Research has supported Cousins' anecdotal report, showing that people with a sense of humor experience less stress and better health (Anderson & Arnoult, 1989). Nonetheless, not all kinds of humor are beneficial. People who use hostile, derogatory humor tend to experience poorer health (Carroll, 1990).

learned helplessness
A feeling of futility caused by the belief that one has little or no control over events in one's life, which can make one stop trying and become depressed.

Norman Cousins (1915–1992)
"In general, anything that restores a sense of control to a patient can be a profound aid to a physician in treating serious illness. That sense of control is more than a mood or attitude, and may be a vital pathway between the brain, the endocrine system, and the immune system."

psychological hardiness
A personality characteristic—marked by feelings of commitment, challenge, and control—that promotes resistance to stress.

Suzanne Kobasa
"Hardiness has an active emphasis in that it predisposes persons to interact more intensely with stressful events in order to transform them into less stressful forms."

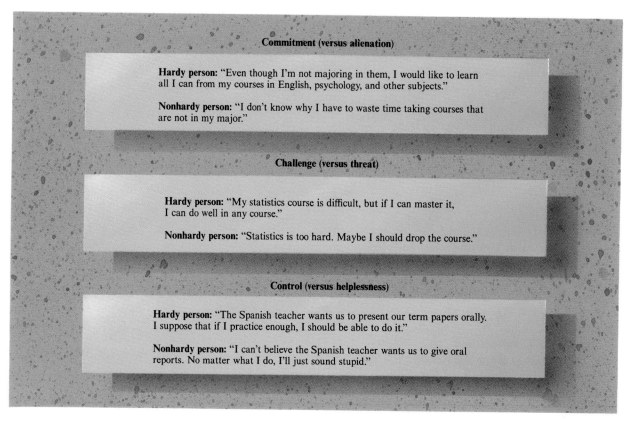

Commitment (versus alienation)

Hardy person: "Even though I'm not majoring in them, I would like to learn all I can from my courses in English, psychology, and other subjects."

Nonhardy person: "I don't know why I have to waste time taking courses that are not in my major."

Challenge (versus threat)

Hardy person: "My statistics course is difficult, but if I can master it, I can do well in any course."

Nonhardy person: "Statistics is too hard. Maybe I should drop the course."

Control (versus helplessness)

Hardy person: "The Spanish teacher wants us to present our term papers orally. I suppose that if I practice enough, I should be able to do it."

Nonhardy person: "I can't believe the Spanish teacher wants us to give oral reports. No matter what I do, I'll just sound stupid."

FIGURE **16.6**

Psychological Hardiness
People who score high in psychological hardiness have a feeling of commitment, challenge, and control instead of a feeling of alienation, threat, and helplessness.

Humor and Health
Norman Cousins relied on Marx Brothers movies to help him recover from a rare neuromuscular disease. Research has shown that a sense of humor reduces our response to stressors and may help us maintain our health or recover from illness.

Stress and Social Support
People with adequate social support are less likely to develop stress-related illnesses

Humor relieves stress by inducing laughter, making stressors seem less negative, and evoking social support from other people (Nezu, Nezu, & Blissett, 1988). Moreover, people who use humor to cope with stress tend to be high in psychological hardiness. And the use of humor is even associated with a more effective immune response. For example, a study of women who had recently given birth found that those who used humor to cope with stress had fewer upper respiratory tract infections. Even their infants had fewer such infections, perhaps because they received more antibodies in their mother's milk (Dillon & Totten, 1989).

Social Support

Misery may indeed love company. People who are socially isolated and who are introverted or lack social skills are at increased risk for illness (Cohen & Williamson, 1991). People with social support are less likely to suffer illness. In fact, social support is the most important psychological factor in buffering recently widowed people against illness (Windholz, Marmar, & Horowitz, 1985). Social support can be tangible, in the form of money or practical help, or intangible, in the form of advice or encouragement about how to remove or tolerate the stressor. Social support helps by reducing the effects of stressful life events, promoting recovery from illness, and increasing adherence to medical regimens (Heitzmann & Kaplan, 1988). Even social support provided by the presence of a pet animal can reduce physiological reactivity to stressors (Allen et al., 1991).

People with genital herpes, a viral disease that causes recurrent painful sores on the genitals, who receive social support have fewer recurrences. The opportunity to talk about, rather than having to hide, their illness seems to be especially important in relieving distress and reducing recurrences (Vander Plate, Aral, & Magder, 1988). And AIDS patients who have recently been diagnosed as being HIV-positive experience less distress when they have social support (Blaney et al., 1991). This is especially important in the case of AIDS, because social support seems to reduce the immunosuppressive effects of stress (Kennedy, Kiecolt-Glaser, & Glaser, 1988).

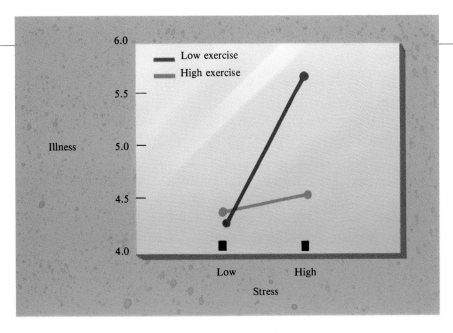

FIGURE 16.7

Exercise and Illness
A study of the relationship between exercise and illness found that adolescents who exercised little and adolescents who exercised regularly did not differ in their incidence of illness when under low levels of stress. In contrast, when under high levels of stress, those who exercised regularly had a significantly lower incidence of illness than did those who exercised little (Brown & Siegel, 1988).

What experimental evidence is there that social support boosts the immune response? In one study, samples of saliva were taken from healthy college students 5 days before their first final exam, during the final-exams period, and 14 days after their last final exam. The samples were analyzed for the level of immunoglobulin A, an antibody that provides immunity against infections of the upper respiratory tract, gastrointestinal tract, and urogenital system. Salivary concentrations of immunoglobulin A after the final-exams period were lower than before it. But students who reported more-adequate social support during the pre-exam period had consistently higher immunoglobulin A concentrations than did their peers who reported less-adequate social support (Jemmott & Magloire, 1988).

Coping with Stress

Coping with stress has much in common with St. Francis of Assisi's "Serenity Prayer," which asks God for the wisdom to know the difference between what one can change and what one cannot. Some methods of coping involve an attempt to confront the stressor or avoid the source of stress; others involve reducing its impact. For example, suppose you are having difficulty in a course. You might confront the stressor by studying more hours or avoid the stressor by dropping the course. Or, instead, you might reduce the impact of the stressor by reappraising its severity, practicing a relaxation technique, or participating in regular aerobic exercise. Some people enroll in formal stress-management programs, which may combine several methods of coping. In fact, research has demonstrated that exercise, relaxation, and stress-management programs are each effective in reducing the physiological arousal that accompanies stress (Bruning & Frew, 1987).

Exercise

Three decades ago, President John F. Kennedy, a physical fitness proponent, noted, "The Greeks knew that intelligence and skill can only function at the peak of their capacity when the body is healthy and strong—that hearty spirits and tough minds usually inhabit sound bodies" (Silva & Weinberg, 1984, p. 416). Kennedy would approve of the recent trend toward greater concern with personal fitness among adults. The only way to achieve fitness is to maintain a program that includes regular aerobic exercise (exercise that markedly raises heart rate for at least 20 minutes). The beneficial effect of exercise was demonstrated in a longitudinal study that found that adolescents under high levels of stress who exercised regularly had a significantly lower incidence of illness than did adolescents who exercised little (Brown & Siegel, 1988). The results are presented in figure 16.7. People who exercise benefit because they become less physiologically reactive to stressors (Rejeski et al., 1991) and more confident in their

FIGURE 16.8

Relaxation and Blood Pressure
This graph shows the results of a study in which a subject practiced relaxation. Relaxation practice was associated with lower systolic and diastolic blood pressure readings. When relaxation practice was withdrawn, blood pressure rose (Hoelscher, 1987).

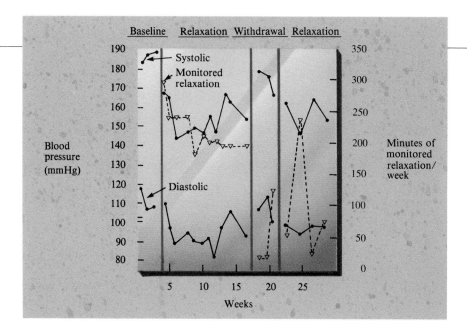

Relaxation

Stress is associated with physiological arousal, so health psychologists emphasize the importance of relaxation training. Several techniques have proved effective in reducing physiological arousal. These include hypnosis (Wadden & Anderton, 1982), meditation (Barr & Benson, 1984), biofeedback (McGrady et al., 1987), slow, rhythmic breathing (Fried, 1987), and restricted environmental stimulation, or REST (Suedfeld, Roy, & Landon, 1982). Hypnosis and meditation are discussed in chapter 6, biofeedback in chapter 7, and REST in chapter 11.

The most basic relaxation technique is **progressive relaxation,** which was developed decades ago by Edmund Jacobson (1929/1974). To practice progressive relaxation, successively tense and relax each of the major muscle groups of your body. By doing so, you learn to distinguish muscle tension from relaxation and, eventually, to relieve anxiety by immediately relaxing your muscles. This will reduce activity in your sympathetic nervous system, as well. As illustrated in figure 16.8, progressive relaxation has been effective in reducing symptoms of physiological arousal, including high blood pressure (Hoelscher, 1987).

Progressive relaxation can even enhance the immunological response (Van Rood et al., 1993). Consider the following experiment that involved medical students. Blood samples were taken from students 1 month before midterm exams and then on the day of the exams. Half of the students were randomly assigned to participate in regular relaxation practice during the month between the two measurement days. The students who were not assigned to practice relaxation, compared to the students who were, displayed a significantly greater decrease in natural killer cell activity between the first and second measurements (Kiecolt-Glaser et al., 1986). You will recall that natural killer cells are one of the body's main defenses against cancer cells.

Stress-Management Programs

The past decade has seen an increase in stress-management programs, which typically involve regular exercise, relaxation training, and cognitive-behavioral therapy. Stress-management programs have been effective in reducing physiological arousal and anxiety in participants, including college students facing the pressure of final-exams week

progressive relaxation
A stress-reducing procedure that involves the successive tensing and relaxing of each of the major muscle groups of the body.

Edmund Jacobson (1888–1983)
"To be excited and to be fully relaxed are physiological opposites. Both states cannot exist . . . at the same time."

ability to control them (Plante & Rodin, 1990). Because high physical fitness is associated with lower absenteeism (Tucker, Aldana, & Friedman, 1990), employers have increasingly promoted programs that help their employees maintain their physical fitness.

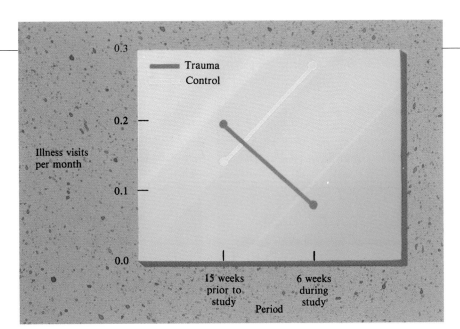

FIGURE 16.9

Writing and Illness
College students who wrote about their emotionally distressing (traumatic) experiences made fewer visits to their college health center than did comparable students who did not write about their experiences (Pennebaker, Kiecolt-Glaser, & Glaser 1988).

(Hudesman, Beck, & Smith, 1987), adolescents experiencing stress caused by diabetes (Boardway et al., 1993), and athletes afraid of criticism of their performances (Anshel, Gregory, & Kaczmarek, 1990). Even stress-management programs consisting of writing about one's problems can help relieve stress, as in the following study.

Anatomy of a Classic Research Study:
Can Writing about Our Problems Make Us More Healthy?

Rationale
Even relatively simple stress-management techniques have proved effective, as in a study of college students by James Pennebaker, Janice Kiecolt-Glaser, and Ronald Glaser (1988). The study was inspired by the belief that the failure to express one's problems promotes stress and, in the long run, illness. It replicated a study (Pennebaker & Beall, 1986) that found that writing about traumatic personal experiences led to fewer visits to the student health center for illness. The question in this study was, Why?

Method
Fifty healthy undergraduates participated in the study and were randomly assigned to two groups. One group was told to write about traumatic experiences, and the other group was told to write about superficial topics; they were to write on these topics for 20 minutes a day for 4 consecutive days. T-lymphocyte activity against antigens was measured from blood samples taken the day before writing began, the last day of writing, and 6 weeks after writing. The health center kept records of the number of visits of each student for illness for the 15 weeks prior to the study and for the 6 weeks of the study.

Results and Discussion
The procedure of writing about traumatic events was not simply cathartic, because the subjects' moods and physical symptoms were temporarily worse after writing. Yet, later those who wrote about their traumatic experiences had lower physiological arousal and better functioning of their immune systems. As indicated in figure 16.9, those who wrote about their traumatic experiences also made fewer visits to the college health center. Thus, emotionally confronting traumatic events can relieve stress and improve immune function.

HEALTH-IMPAIRING HABITS

Habits as varied as smoking, overeating, avoiding exercise, and failing to wear seat belts sharply increase the chances of illness, injury, or death. Yet a study found that college students tended to have an "it can't happen to me" attitude. Their estimate of the

(a)   (b)

(c)   (d)

probability that their own risky behaviors would lead to illness or injury underestimated the actual probability. Because of our inability to estimate the true riskiness of our behaviors, programs aimed at changing health-impairing habits must not only point out risky behaviors but make participants realize that those habits make them more susceptible to unhealthy consequences than they might believe (Weinstein, 1984). An ambitious community program in New Zealand called Superhealth Basic used brief group sessions to help participants improve their behaviors related to sleep, stress, weight, smoking, drinking, exercise, and nutrition. Participants showed significant improvements in their health (Abbott & Raeburn, 1989).

One of the most important factors that determines whether people are motivated to engage in health-promoting behavior is their feeling of self-efficacy (Kelly, Zyzanski, & Alemagno, 1991). This agrees with research, mentioned earlier, that has converged on a sense of control as an important factor in moderating stress. People high in self-efficacy feel that their actions will be effective. People with a high sense of self-efficacy in regard to health-promoting behaviors are more likely to see their benefits and to downplay barriers to performing them (Alexy, 1991). Feelings of self-efficacy are positively related to important health-promoting behaviors, including maintenance of smoking cessation, control of diet and body weight, and adherence to preventive health behaviors (O'Leary, 1985). Among the most important health-impairing habits are unsafe sexual practices, lack of exercise, smoking tobacco, and poor nutrition.

AIDS and Unsafe Sexual Practices

Today many health psychologists have turned their attention to unsafe behaviors related to the spread of AIDS. AIDS kills its victims by impairing their immune systems, making them eventually succumb to cancer or opportunistic infections. Since 1981, when it was first identified, AIDS has spread through much of the world with alarming rapidity. No group is safe from it today. AIDS afflicts people of all ages, sexes, races, and sexual orientations.

The AIDS virus is spread by blood or semen (Catania et al., 1990). Some victims, most notably hemophiliacs, have acquired the virus in transfusions of contaminated blood. Heroin addicts can acquire it by sharing hypodermic needles with infected addicts. The virus can also be transmitted through sexual activity, including anal sex and vaginal sex. Even infants born to mothers with AIDS are at high risk of developing the disease. Transmission of the virus from infected dental or medical personnel to their patients, or from infected patients to dental or medical personnel, is much less likely. There is no evidence that the virus is spread by kissing, simple touching, food handling, or other casual kinds of contact.

Because AIDS is, so far, inevitably fatal, its prevention is crucial. One of the primary means of prevention is educating people to avoid risky behaviors. Foremost among the suggestions has been to practice "safe sex" (or at least "safer sex"). In regard to AIDS, the safest sex is abstinence or limiting oneself to an uninfected partner. Many people choose not to abstain, however, and may have a series of partners, so the next-best suggestions are to use condoms and reduce the number of one's sex partners.

Efforts to reduce risky behaviors have achieved some success. Though elsewhere in the world AIDS is more prevalent among heterosexuals, in North America it has been more prevalent among homosexual men. This has been attributed to the common practice of unprotected anal sex. The 10 percent of heterosexuals who practice anal sex are also at increased risk of contracting AIDS (Voeller, 1991). Because it has so ravaged the North American homosexual community, the earliest anti-AIDS programs have been aimed at homosexuals. Cities with large homosexual populations have instituted workshops on AIDS prevention for homosexual and bisexual men. Such programs have been effective. For example, a survey of homosexual men in San Francisco, where there is a high level of AIDS education, found a significant increase in their use of condoms (Catania et al., 1991).

Lack of Exercise

People who exercise regularly are healthier and live longer than those who do not. Exercise promotes health and longer life, in part by boosting the immune system. For example, subjects who had tested positive for the AIDS virus showed enhanced immunological responses after participating in an aerobic exercise program (Antoni et al., 1991). One way aerobic exercise boosts the immune response is by raising the level of a chemical factor that helps immune system cells fight infections (Cannon & Kluger, 1983).

There is stronger evidence for the effectiveness of exercise in preventing obesity and cardiovascular disease. Aerobic exercise (such as running, swimming, bicycling, brisk walking, or cross-country skiing) combats obesity by burning calories, raising the basal metabolic rate, and inhibiting the appetite. Aerobic exercise also reduces the cardiovascular risk factors of high blood cholesterol and high blood pressure (Martin & Dubbert, 1985).

The health risks of physical inactivity and the health benefits of exercise have led many sedentary people to start exercising. Even employers, who see the benefits of having a healthy workforce, have instituted employee fitness programs. Early findings indicate that these are successful in reducing absenteeism, turnover, and health-care costs (Gebhardt & Crump, 1990). Unfortunately, of those who begin formal exercise programs, about 50 percent will drop out within 6 months. According to Rod Dishman, an authority on exercise adherence, people who are obese or who have symptoms of cardiovascular disease—the very people who might benefit most from exercise—are less likely to exercise (Dishman & Gettman, 1980). Among the most common reasons for failing to adhere to exercise programs are a lack of time and a lack of motivation (McAuley et al., 1990).

The failure of both healthy and unhealthy people to maintain programs of exercise has prompted health psychologists to study ways of increasing exercise adherence. In one study, groups of people engaged in jogging, aerobic dancing, or pre-ski training for 10 weeks. Some of the participants in each of the three groups also took part in a special program to increase their motivation to exercise. The program made participants more aware of obstacles to exercise and taught them how to cope with periodic exercise lapses, instead of having an all-or-none attitude. Rather than giving up after exercise lapses, exercisers were urged to return immediately to their exercise programs. The results showed that those who participated in the adherence program, compared to those who did not, were indeed more likely to adhere to their exercise programs (Belisle, Roskies, & Levesque, 1987).

Exercise
People who exercise are more stress resistant and disease resistant than people who do not. The well-publicized benefits of exercise account for the popularity of exercise "gurus" such as Jane Fonda, Jack LaLanne, and Richard Simmons.

Smoking Tobacco

Perhaps the worst single health-impairing habit is smoking tobacco (Velicer et al., 1992).

Effects of Smoking

Smokers become addicted to the nicotine in tobacco. Though smokers claim they smoke to relieve anxiety or to make them more alert, they actually smoke to avoid the unpleasant symptoms of nicotine withdrawal, which include irritability, hand tremors, heart palpitations, and difficulty concentrating. Thus, addicted smokers smoke to regulate the level of nicotine in their bodies (Leventhal & Cleary, 1980). Under stressful circumstances smokers report that smoking reduces their anxiety (Gilbert & Spielberger, 1987), perhaps because stress makes their body crave higher levels of nicotine. Smoking is especially difficult to resist because it can become a conditioned response to many everyday situations, as in the case of smokers who light a cigarette when answering the telephone, after eating a meal, or upon leaving a class.

Smoking produces harmful side effects through the actions of tars and other substances in cigarette smoke. Smoking causes fatigue by reducing the blood's ability to carry oxygen, making smoking an especially bad habit for athletes. But, more important, smoking contributes to the deaths of more than 300,000 Americans each year from stroke, cancer, emphysema, and heart disease. Because both smoking and cholesterol contribute to coronary heart disease, smokers who have high cholesterol levels reduce their life span even more than smokers with low cholesterol levels (Perkins, 1985). Despite the harmful effects of smoking, governments permit it—and even profit from it. In 1565 King James I of England, though viewing smoking as a despicable habit, chose to tax cigarettes rather than ban them, a practice governments still follow today (Whitlock, 1987).

Prevention and Treatment of Smoking

The ill effects of smoking make imperative programs to prevent the onset of smoking and to help smokers quit. Children are more likely to start smoking if their parents and peers smoke. Many smoking-prevention programs are based in schools and provide information about the immediate and long-term social and physical consequences of smoking. Students learn that, in the short run, smoking causes bad breath, yellow teeth and fingers, and weakened stamina. They also learn that, in the long run, smoking causes cancer, emphysema, and cardiovascular disease. But simply providing children with information about the ill effects of smoking is not enough to prevent them from starting. Smoking-prevention programs must also teach students how to resist peer pressure and advertisements that encourage them to begin smoking. Overall, smoking-prevention programs have been effective, reducing the number of new smokers among participants by 50 percent (Flay, 1985b).

Though programs to prevent the onset of smoking are important, programs to help people stop smoking are also necessary. Health psychologists use a variety of techniques to help people stop. Subjects are taught to expect certain symptoms of nicotine withdrawal, which typically last 4 weeks. But certain consequences of quitting, including hunger, weight gain, and nicotine craving, may persist for 6 months or more (Hughes et al., 1991). Nicotine prevents weight gain by reducing hunger and increasing metabolism (Winders & Grunberg, 1989). Because more harm is caused by tars and other chemicals in tobacco than by the nicotine, some treatments aim at preventing smoking by providing subjects with nicotine through safer routes. These nicotine-replacement techniques prevent some of the relapse caused by nicotine craving or the desire to avoid weight gain.

The chief nicotine-replacement technique has been the use of *nicotine chewing gum* (Basler et al., 1992). A technique growing in popularity is the use of a *nicotine patch*, which provides nicotine through the skin (Hartman, Jarvik, & Wilkins, 1989). Nicotine replacement has proved successful. One study compared the effectiveness of nicotine gum and the effectiveness of placebo gum (which did not contain nicotine). During the first 10 weeks after they quit smoking, those who chewed nicotine gum experienced

Mark Twain (1835–1910)
"To cease smoking is the easiest thing I ever did; I ought to know because I've done it a thousand times."

less-intense withdrawal symptoms than those who chewed placebo gum (Gross & Stitzer, 1989). Not only does nicotine gum reduce withdrawal symptoms; people who quit smoking by using nicotine gum later had longer abstinence than people who quit without using nicotine gum (Killen et al., 1990). Another advantage of nicotine gum is that it may increase the motivation of weight-conscious smokers to abstain from smoking. A study of more than a thousand participants in a smoking relapse prevention program found that those who chewed nicotine gum gained significantly less weight than those who did not (Killen, Fortmann, & Newman, 1990).

Of course, nicotine gum does not help smokers overcome their *addiction* to nicotine. Those who wish to overcome their addiction do better if they are high in two of the factors that appear repeatedly as health promoters: a feeling of self-efficacy (Nicki, Remington, & MacDonald, 1984) and the presence of social support (Carey et al., 1989). For those who are motivated to overcome their addiction, *nicotine fading* is useful. This technique gradually weans smokers off nicotine by having them use cigarettes with lower and lower nicotine content until it has been reduced to virtually zero (McGovern & Lando, 1991).

A more extreme technique is *rapid smoking*, a form of aversion therapy in which the smoker is forced to take a puff every 6 to 8 seconds for several minutes. This induces feelings of nausea and dizziness, and after several sessions the person may develop an aversion to smoking. Like nicotine fading, rapid smoking has proved effective (Tiffany, Martin, & Baker, 1986). But rapid smoking, which floods the bloodstream with nicotine, can induce heartbeat irregularities—a result that might be dangerous for smokers with cardiac problems. Nonetheless, a study that compared the benefits of quitting to the risks of rapid smoking concluded that smokers with mild or moderate heart disease would be less likely to be harmed by rapid smoking than by continuing to be smokers (Hall et al., 1984).

Another approach to smoking cessation involves *self-management programs*, which use behavior modification to promote smoking cessation. The programs encourage smokers to avoid stimuli that act as cues for smoking, such as coffee breaks, alcoholic beverages, and other smokers. Still another way of promoting smoking cessation is to train physicians in how to help their patients stop. One study included 83 family physicians with nearly 2,000 patients who smoked. Physicians who had received special training in smoking cessation had more patients who quit smoking and abstained longer than did physicians who had not received training (Lindsay et al., 1989). If all family physicians received such training, they might help thousands more patients quit smoking.

Poor Nutrition

The relationship between diet and health has been known since biblical days. In the book of Daniel in the Old Testament, the Babylonian king Nebuchadnezzar orders that captured Judean boys of noble descent be given food and wine from his royal table. Daniel, one of the captured boys, begs the chief eunuch not to make the boys violate religious dietary laws by forcing them to eat "unclean" foods and drink "unclean" beverages from the table:

• • • But he [the eunuch] warned Daniel, "I am afraid of my lord the king: he has assigned you food and drink, and if he sees you looking thinner in the face than the other boys of your age, my head will be in danger with the king because of you." At this Daniel turned to the guard whom the chief eunuch had assigned to Daniel, Hananiah, Mishael, and Azariah. He said, "Please allow your servants a ten-day trial, during which we are given only vegetables to eat and water to drink. You can then compare our looks with those of the boys who eat the king's food; go by what you see, and treat your servants accordingly." The man agreed to do what they asked and put them on ten days' trial. When the ten days were over they looked and were in better health than any of the boys who had eaten their allowance from the royal table; so the guard withdrew their allowance of food and the wine they were to drink, and gave them vegetables. (Daniel, 1:3–17)

FIGURE 16.10

The Ideal Female Figure
In Western cultures the ideal female figure has changed over time. The ideal has at times been represented by the plump Rubenesque nude of the early seventeenth century, the voluptuous actress Marilyn Monroe of the 1950s, and the muscular athlete Florence Griffith-Joyner of the 1980s.

Kelly Brownell
"Body weight is regulated by an interaction of biological, behavioral, and cultural factors."

This passage demonstrates Daniel's realization that diet affects physical well-being. It also demonstrates a bit of scientific sophistication, because he recommended using an "experimental group," which would eat a vegetarian diet, and a "control group," which would eat a normal diet. Today health psychologists, too, recognize the importance of diet in health and illness.

Health psychologists are especially concerned with the relationship between diet and cardiovascular disease. A high-fat diet is one of the main risk factors in cardiovascular disease. High-fat diets contribute to high blood pressure and high levels of cholesterol in the blood, which promote atherosclerosis by the buildup of plaque deposits that narrow the arteries. The narrowing of cerebral arteries and coronary arteries reduces blood flow, promoting strokes and heart attacks. Health psychologists have developed programs that combine nutritional education and behavior modification to help people reduce their risks of cardiovascular disease by adopting healthier eating habits. For example, programs that reduce fat intake produce significant reductions in blood pressure in participants with elevated blood pressure (Jacob, Wing, & Shapiro, 1987). Though these programs are effective in improving eating habits, their long-term effectiveness has yet to be demonstrated (Jeffery, 1988).

A high-fat diet also contributes to obesity—an important risk factor in illness for both men and women. Yet, in Western cultures, a leaner figure has been stylish for women only since the early twentieth century, and a muscularly toned figure only in the past decade or two. For the preceding 600 years, cultural standards favored a more rounded figure (Bennett & Gurin, 1982). You have probably seen this in Renaissance paintings that depict the ideal woman as being plump. Figure 16.10 depicts changes in cultural views concerning the ideal female figure. Even today some cultures favor rotund women. Thus, body weight is regulated by cultural, as well as biological and behavioral, factors (Brownell & Wadden, 1991).

But current Western standards of beauty, and concern with the health-impairing effects of obesity, make weight loss a major North American preoccupation. Weight reduction seems deceptively easy: You simply make sure that you burn more calories than you ingest. Yet, as noted by obesity researcher Kelly Brownell (1982), less than 5 percent of obese people maintain their weight loss long enough to be considered "cured." Some obesity researchers argue that this pessimistic figure represents only people who have been in formal weight-loss programs. In contrast, almost two-thirds of people who try to lose weight on their own succeed. Perhaps those who seek treatment for obesity are a select group of people who are the least likely to succeed (Schachter, 1982).

Because of the great cultural variability in perceptions of ideal body types and the difficulty that obese people have in maintaining weight loss, some critics favor acceptance of one's body type. There are even group counseling programs that encourage fat acceptance instead of fat rejection. Participants discuss ways of maintaining social relationships despite being fat in a culture that frowns on fat people (Tenzer, 1989).

Though some people adjust well to being obese, many others would prefer to lose weight for aesthetic, social, or medical reasons. How can people control their weight?

Culture and Obesity
Hawaiian-born Konishiki, the first non-Japanese sumo champion, weighs well over 500 pounds. His obesity is valued, rather than frowned on, in sumo culture.

A common but ineffective approach is dieting. People who diet may drastically reduce their caloric intake for weeks or months. Unfortunately, as dieters lose weight, their basal metabolic rate slows (Foreyt, 1987), forcing them to diet indefinitely to maintain their lower level of weight—an impossible feat. Because dieting cannot last for a lifetime, dieters eventually return to the same eating habits that contributed to their obesity. Moreover, dieting is unhealthy; 25 percent of diet-induced weight loss consists of lean body tissue, including skeletal muscle (Brownell, 1982).

Failing to change their eating habits, obese people often resort to diet pills, usually amphetamines, which produce weight loss by their effects on the hypothalamus, though the exact mechanism is unknown (Paul, Hulihan-Giblin, & Skolnick, 1982). Amphetamines, however, eventually lose their effectiveness and can cause insomnia, high blood pressure, and symptoms of paranoid schizophrenia.

Formal psychological approaches to weight loss rely on behavior therapy in conjunction with aerobic exercise. In behavior therapy programs, participants monitor their eating behaviors, change maladaptive eating habits, and correct misconceptions about eating. Aerobic exercise promotes weight loss not only by burning calories during the exercise but by raising the metabolic rate for hours afterward. This counters diet-induced decreases in the basal metabolic rate. Weight loss through aerobic exercise is also healthier than weight loss through dieting alone, because only 5 percent of weight loss will be lean tissue (Brownell, 1982). Despite the effectiveness of aerobic exercise in weight control, half of those who enroll in formal exercise programs drop out within a few months (McMinn, 1984). As with other health-related behaviors of participants in behavior therapy programs for weight loss, those who complete the programs report initially higher self-efficacy than do those who drop out (Mitchell & Stuart, 1984). Programs that emphasize gradual, rather than abrupt, changes in diet and exercise are more successful in achieving adherence and weight loss (Epstein & Wing, 1980).

Morbid Obesity
People who are more than 100 percent above their normal weight are considered morbidly obese. Some cases of morbid obesity are astounding. In a widely publicized case, comedian and nutritionist Dick Gregory helped the late Walter Hudson, a man weighing more than 1,000 pounds, lose several hundred pounds. Gregory learned of him when he heard news reports describing how Hudson had become wedged in a doorway and had escaped only after having the doorway cut from around him. In some cases of extreme obesity, the person spends his or her entire life trapped indoors, barely able to walk and possibly unable to fit through doorways.

REACTIONS TO ILLNESS

Despite your best efforts to adapt to stress and to live a healthy lifestyle, you will periodically suffer from illness. Health psychologists study ways to encourage people to seek treatment for symptoms of illness, to reduce patient distress, and to increase patient adherence to medical regimens.

Losing the Weight Is the Easy Part
Talk-show host Oprah Winfrey has gained attention for her repeated efforts to lose weight and keep it off. Her difficulty in doing so is shared by millions of people.

Seeking Treatment

What do you do when you experience a headache, nausea, diarrhea, dizziness, constipation, or nasal congestion? Your reaction would depend on your interpretation of the symptoms. This would depend, in turn, on your past experience with these symptoms, information you have received about them, their intensity, and their duration. Some people inappropriately seek medical attention for the most minor symptoms. However, many others deny, ignore, or misinterpret their symptoms, which might make them fail to seek help; as a consequence, many people let minor ailments become serious, or delay treatment of serious ailments that might be cured by early treatment.

The importance of seeking appropriate medical treatment has inspired health psychologists to study factors that motivate people to seek treatment. An important factor is social support. People with social support may be encouraged to seek treatment, may be referred to appropriate medical personnel, and may feel less anxious about seeking treatment (Roberts, 1988). Even one's explanatory style can affect the decision to seek medical treatment. A study of undergraduates found that those with a pessimistic explanatory style (discussed earlier) were less likely than optimistic students to seek medical treatment. Thus, the finding that pessimistic people are usually less healthy than optimistic ones might be caused by their greater passivity in the face of disease. Pessimistic people do not believe their actions will produce desirable outcomes (Lin & Peterson, 1990), such as good health. This indicates that a sense of control over stressors can affect health by influencing one's response to illness as well as by altering the immune response or health-promoting behaviors.

Patient Distress

Illness, especially chronic illness or illness that requires surgery or painful procedures, induces distress in patients. Patients differ in their ability to cope with illness or stressful medical procedures. Once again, an important factor is self-efficacy. For example, people who suffer from chronic pain cope more effectively if they are confident of their ability to do so (Jensen, Turner, & Romano, 1991). Some patients can also benefit from formal techniques that encourage effective coping with pain or stressful procedures. These patients include cancer sufferers (Telch & Telch, 1985), children who undergo prolonged or repeated hospitalizations (Yap, 1988), and burn victims who must undergo excruciatingly painful skin debridement and grafts (Wisely, Masur, & Morgan, 1983).

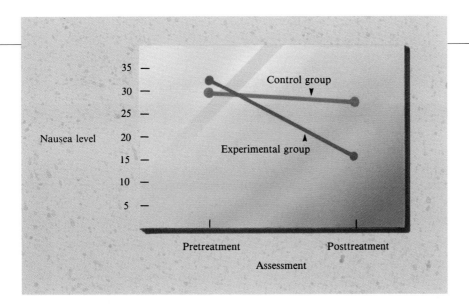

FIGURE 16.11

Controlling Patient Distress
Children who played video games while undergoing cancer chemotherapy (the experimental group) showed a marked reduction in nausea. In contrast, children who did not play video games while undergoing cancer chemotherapy (the control group) showed little change in nausea (Redd et al., 1987).

In some cases, relatively simple procedures can reduce illness-related distress. In a study of children undergoing chemotherapy for cancer, the experimental group played video games during their chemotherapy and a control group did not. As shown in figure 16.11, children in the experimental group reported less anxiety and nausea. The children who played video games were apparently distracted from the unpleasant sensations caused by the chemotherapy (Redd et al., 1987).

The most effective means of preparing patients for stressful medical procedures include informing them of the procedures they will undergo, forewarning them of the sensations they will experience, instructing them on how to cope with the procedure, and modeling—letting them observe someone who has successfully undergone the procedure (Schultheis, Peterson, & Selby, 1987). Modeling has been an especially effective technique for reducing patient distress during unpleasant medical procedures (Ludwick-Rosenthal & Neufeld, 1988).

Observing a patient who has undergone successful surgery can be beneficial to a patient about to undergo surgery. Patients waiting to undergo coronary bypass surgery who have a hospital roommate who has just undergone successful surgery of any kind are less anxious before surgery, walk more after surgery, and go home sooner than are similar patients who have a roommate who is about to undergo surgery. Apparently, simply observing a person who has survived surgery has a calming effect on patients anticipating surgery. Moreover, people who have undergone surgery can reduce the distress of patients about to undergo surgery by letting them know what to expect and suggesting ways to cope with the situation (Kulik & Mahler, 1987).

More-elaborate techniques, including stress-inoculation training (see chapter 15), have also proved effective in reducing the distress of surgery patients. In one study, surgery patients received either stress-inoculation training or standard hospital instructions. Those who received stress-inoculation training experienced less anxiety, used less pain medication, and recovered in fewer days than did the other patients (Wells et al., 1986).

Adherence to Medical Regimens

Recovery from illness often depends on following a medical regimen recommended by a physician. This might include a prescription drug, a restricted diet, or an exercise program. Adherence is important in medical regimens aimed at controlling diabetes (Bradley, 1989), relieving arthritis pain (Freund et al., 1991), lowering high blood pressure (Dunbar-Jacob, Dwyer, & Dunning, 1991), reducing blood cholesterol levels (Carmody,

Patient-Physician Relationship
Physicians who are empathetic have patients who are more satisfied and more cooperative than do physicians who are matter-of-fact in their relationships with patients.

Matarazzo, & Istvan, 1987), and aiding kidney dialysis through proper diet (Finn & Alcorn, 1986). But patients might fail to follow a treatment regimen because they do not understand the physician's instructions (Glen & Anderson, 1989).

The relationship between the patient and the physician plays a key role in patient adherence. Patients are more likely to adhere to regimens prescribed by physicians they like. One of the most important factors determining whether a patient will be satisfied with a physician is the physician's emotional warmth during consultations. (Recall the importance of the psychotherapist's warmth, as discussed in chapter 15.) A physician who acts more like an automobile mechanic fixing a car than a human service provider helping a client will evoke negative reactions from patients. A study in which other physicians rated videotaped physician-patient interaction supported this. The results indicated that the most important determinant of patient satisfaction with the consultation was the emotional expressiveness of the physician (Bensing, 1991).

Sometimes patients abandon their medical regimens prematurely because they no longer notice any symptoms. Consider a patient with essential hypertension (chronic high blood pressure) who must take medication, watch her diet, and follow an exercise program. Because we have, at best, a slight ability to sense the level of our blood pressure (Pennebaker & Watson, 1988), the patient might assume, incorrectly, that because she does not feel like she has high blood pressure, she actually does not have high blood pressure—and abandon her prescribed medical regimen. This again points to the importance of adequate communication between the physician and the patient.

As you have just read, health psychologists have demonstrated that we play an active role in maintaining our health, succumbing to disease, and recovering from illness. Though some diseases and injuries are unavoidable, we can no longer view ourselves as simply the passive victims of viruses, bacteria, or carcinogens. By learning to adapt effectively to stressors, to eliminate risky behaviors, and to adopt health-promoting behaviors, we can greatly reduce our chances of illness, injury, and death. For example, the way in which you adapt to everyday stressors may affect your risk of developing coronary heart disease, as exemplified by research on Type A behavior.

THINKING ABOUT *Psychology*

DOES TYPE A BEHAVIOR PROMOTE CORONARY HEART DISEASE?

On November 2, 1988, "Iron Mike" Ditka, the tough head coach of the Chicago Bears football team and former star tight end, was hospitalized with a mild heart attack. In a televised interview on ESPN, Ditka's physician reported that Ditka had none of the common physical risk factors for coronary heart disease, such as smoking, obesity, or lack of exercise. His only risk factor was a psychological one: *Type A behavior*. A published review of research on Type A behavior in middle-aged men (such as Mike Ditka) found that Type A behavior was prevalent in 70 percent of those with coronary heart disease, and in only 46 percent of those who were healthy (Miller et al., 1991).

CHARACTERISTICS OF TYPE A BEHAVIOR

What are the characteristics of Type A behavior? They were first described in the following classic research study.

Anatomy of a Classic Research Study:
Is There a Relationship between Behavior and Heart Disease?

Rationale

In the late 1950s, San Francisco cardiologist Meyer Friedman noticed that his waiting room chairs were worn along the front edges. He interpreted this as a sign of the impatience of his patients, who spoke rapidly and interrupted frequently during conversations. The patients were also easily angered, highly competitive, and driven to do more and more in less and less time. Friedman, with his colleague Ray Rosenman, called this syndrome of behaviors **Type A behavior.** *In contrast, Type B behavior is characterized by patience, an even temper, and willingness to do a limited number of things in a reasonable amount of time. The Type A person might also show* time urgency *by changing lanes to advance a single car length,* chronic activation *by staying busy most of every day, and* multiphasic activity *by reading, eating, and watching television at the same time (Wright, 1988). This lifestyle means that the Type A person is in a constant state of fight or flight. Would this lifestyle be associated with a greater risk of heart disease? Let's look at an early study by Friedman and Rosenman (1959) to answer this question.*

Method

Friedman and Rosenman asked managers and supervisors of large companies to identify colleagues who fit the description of the Type A and Type B behavior patterns. They identified 83 men, including many executives, who fit each pattern. No women were included because at the time there were relatively few women in executive positions. The subjects were interviewed about their medical history and behavioral tendencies, such as being driven to succeed, feeling highly competitive, and feeling under chronic time pressure. They were observed for body movements, tone of voice, teeth clenching, and any observable signs of impatience. Based on the interview, 69 of the men were labeled pure Type A and 58 of the men were labeled pure Type B. The subjects also kept diaries of their food and alcohol intake for 1 week, and their blood cholesterol levels were measured.

Results and Discussion

Friedman and Rosenman found that the Type A subjects had significantly higher levels of blood cholesterol than did the Type B subjects. More important, 28 percent of the Type A subjects had symptoms of coronary heart disease, whereas only 4 percent of the Type B subjects had such symptoms. Before leaping to the conclusion that the study demonstrated that Type A behavior promotes heart disease, note two other findings. First, the Type A subjects smoked much more than Type B did. Today we know that smoking is a major risk factor in heart disease. Second, the Type A subjects' parents had a higher incidence of coronary heart disease than did the Type B subjects' parents. Perhaps the Type A subjects inherited a genetic tendency to develop heart disease. Of course, there could just as well be a genetic tendency toward Type A behavior, which in turn might promote heart disease. In any case, Friedman and Rosenman contributed one of the first formal studies demonstrating a possible link between behavior and heart disease.

Later, based on their subsequent research findings, Friedman and Rosenman boldly concluded:

• • • *In the absence of Type A Behavior Pattern, coronary heart disease almost never occurs before 70 years of age, regardless of the fatty foods eaten, the cigarettes smoked or the lack of exercise. But when this behavior pattern is present, coronary heart disease can easily erupt in one's thirties or forties. (Friedman & Rosenman, 1974, p. xi)*

In 1975 Friedman, Rosenman, and their colleagues (Rosenman et al., 1975) reported the results of a study on coronary heart disease that began in 1960 and lasted 9 years—the Western Collaborative Group Study. They studied more than 3,000 middle-aged men who were free of heart disease at the beginning of the study. Each of the men

Mike Ditka and Type A Behavior
When Mike Ditka, the intense, aggressive former head coach of the Chicago Bears, suffered a heart attack during the 1988 football season, his only risk factor was a Type A behavior pattern.

Type A behavior
A syndrome—marked by impatience, hostility, and extreme competitiveness—that may be associated with the development of coronary heart disease.

Multiphasic Activity
The Type A behavior pattern is associated with multiphasic activity, in which the person engages in several activities at once as part of a continual effort to do more and more in less and less time.

Ray Rosenman
"The Type A behavior pattern has been studied since the 1950s, and its status as an independent risk factor for coronary heart disease is well established."

Hostility and Coronary Heart Disease
Research studies have converged on antagonistic hostility as the component of the Type A behavior pattern that is most strongly associated with the development of coronary heart disease.

was categorized as Type A or Type B, based on an interview. The subjects answered questions related to Type A behavior, and the examiner noted behavioral manifestations of Type A behavior during the interview, such as rapid speech, hostile comments, or interrupting the examiner. The results indicated that during the period of the study, the men classified as Type A were more than twice as likely to develop coronary heart disease as were the men classified as Type B (Rosenman et al., 1975). The pattern of behavior shown by Type A's indicates that they are overconcerned with control of their environment. This leads to repeated physiological arousal when other people, time constraints, or personal responsibilities threaten their sense of control (Houston, 1983).

Type A behavior is not just a style of responding to the environment; it can induce the very environmental situations that evoke it. This was demonstrated in a study that compared Type A and Type B police radio dispatchers during work shifts. Type A's generated more job pressures by initiating extra work tasks for themselves and attending to multiple tasks at the same time. Moreover, perhaps following the adage "If you want something done, give it to a busy person," their coworkers and supervisors looked to them when there were additional tasks to be performed. So, Type A people can help create the very work conditions that promote a driven, time-urgent, impatient behavioral style (Kirmeyer & Biggers, 1988). A Type A student might take a course overload, work a full-time job, serve on several student committees, and participate in intramural sports at the same time. Research shows that Type A students report both more daily hassles and more daily uplifts than do Type B's (Margiotta, Davilla, & Hicks, 1990).

But the strength of the relationship between Type A behavior and coronary heart disease was brought into question by the results of a 22-year follow-up of participants in the Western Collaborative Group Study, which found no relationship between Type A behavior and coronary heart disease mortality. In fact, Type A's who had suffered a heart attack had a somewhat *lower* risk of a second heart attack. Of course, this might have been a result of other factors, such as greater medical attention given to Type A than to Type B heart-attack victims (Ragland & Brand, 1988). And though these results indicate that the *overall* pattern of Type A behavior is unrelated to coronary heart disease, research findings have been converging on a specific component of the Type A behavior pattern, *antagonistic hostility*, as the factor most related to coronary heart disease (Diamond, 1982; Linden, 1987). Research indicates that people with antagonistic hostility are more physiologically reactive to stressors, such as competitive tasks (Felsten & Leitten, 1993) or social interactions in which they reveal personal information (Christensen & Smith, 1993).

This was supported in another follow-up of participants in the Western Collaborative Group Study, which found that hostility was the only component of Type A behavior that remained a significant risk factor for coronary heart disease (Hecker et al., 1988). Antagonistic hostility is characterized less by outbursts of anger and more by acting in a rude, cynical, condescending, and uncooperative manner (Dembroski & Costa, 1988). Antagonistic hostility might affect cardiovascular health by inducing repeated physiological arousal, interpersonal conflict, and lack of social support (Smith & Pope, 1990).

EFFECTS OF TYPE A BEHAVIOR

Regardless of whether antagonistic hostility or some other aspect of Type A behavior, rather than the overall pattern of Type A behavior, promotes coronary heart disease, how might it do so? One way might be through the effects of stress hormones. Redford Williams and his colleagues (1982) had Type A and Type B male college students perform the stressful task of counting aloud backward by 17s from 7,683. The first to finish would win a prize. The results indicated that the Type A's displayed a significantly greater increase in levels of the adrenal gland stress hormones cortisol, epinephrine, and norepinephrine. These stress hormones promote the buildup of cholesterol plaques on the walls of arteries, narrowing them and increasing the risk of heart attacks due to atherosclerosis (Fava, Littman, & Halperin, 1987). Perhaps, in everyday life, Type A's induce similar physiological responses in themselves by their eagerness to subject themselves to stressful competitive situations.

Another possible factor mediating the effect of Type A behavior on coronary heart disease is the tendency of Type A people to ignore symptoms of illness. Before being hospitalized with his heart attack, Mike Ditka had ignored pain earlier in the week; at a team workout shortly before the heart attack, his assistant coaches forced him to seek medical attention. His job meant more to him than his health. This tendency of Type A's to discount illness first appears in childhood. Type A children are less likely to complain of symptoms of illness, and Type A children who have surgery miss fewer days of school than do Type B's (Leikin, Firestone, & McGrath, 1988).

DEVELOPMENT OF TYPE A BEHAVIOR

Once researchers identified the characteristics of Type A behavior and its harmful effects, they became interested in studying how Type A behavior develops. Though there is only weak evidence of a hereditary basis for Type A behavior, there is strong evidence that the pattern runs in families. In a study of male and female adolescents, those who scored high on the hostility component of Type A behavior and also had a parent suffering from essential hypertension showed a greater elevation in blood pressure in response to stressful tasks than did subjects who had a parent suffering from essential hypertension but who did not score high on hostility (McCann & Matthews, 1988).

Karen Matthews, a leading researcher on Type A behavior, points to child-rearing practices as the primary origin of Type A behavior. Parents of Type A children encourage them to try harder even when they do well and offer them few spontaneous positive comments. Type A children might be given no standards except "Do better," which makes it difficult for them to develop internal standards of achievement. They may then seek to compare their academic performance with the best in their class. This might contribute to the development of the hard-driving component of the Type A behavior pattern (Matthews & Woodall, 1988). You probably know fellow students who want not only an A on an exam but the highest grade in the class.

MODIFICATION OF TYPE A BEHAVIOR

Because of the possible association between Type A behavior and coronary heart disease, its modification might be wise. But a paradox of Type A behavior is that Type A persons are not necessarily disturbed by their behavior. Why change a behavior pattern that is rewarded in competitive Western society? Programs to modify the Type A behavior of those who are willing to participate try to alter specific components of the Type A behavior pattern, particularly impatience, hostility, and competitiveness.

One such program has been successful in reducing Type A behavior in people who are especially prone to it—college teachers. Teachers received cognitive behavior modification and assertiveness training in eight 2-hour group sessions. The participants learned to modify their maladaptive beliefs and attitudes related to anger, impatience, hostility, and competitive drive. They also learned to express themselves assertively, rather than passively or aggressively. A follow-up found that the participants displayed less impatience and less hostility a year later (Thurman, 1985).

As you can see, though the worn edges of Friedman's waiting room chairs have inspired much research, many questions about Type A behavior as a risk factor in coronary heart disease remain to be answered. Which aspects of the Type A behavior pattern promote coronary heart disease? What physiological mechanisms account for the relationship between Type A behavior and coronary heart disease? Why do some people adopt the Type A behavior pattern while others adopt the Type B pattern? What protects certain Type A people from coronary heart disease? How can we best modify the Type A behavior pattern?

Redford Williams
"Research evaluating the relationship between hostility and coronary heart disease suggests that higher levels of anger toward others coupled with difficulty in expressing that anger form a key neurotic conflict in the predisposition to coronary heart disease."

Karen Matthews
"Type A children's awareness of high standards . . . may maintain their struggle to strive after everescalating goals."

SUMMARY

STRESS AND ILLNESS

Health psychology is the field that studies the role of psychological factors in the promotion of health and the prevention of illness and injury. One of the main topics of interest to health psychologists is stress, the physiological response of the body to physical and psychological demands. The main psychological kinds of stress are frustration, pressure, and conflict. They are associated with life changes and daily hassles.

Hans Selye identified a pattern of physiological response to stress that he called the general adaptation syndrome, which includes the alarm reaction, the stage of resistance, and the stage of exhaustion. Stress has been linked to noninfectious disease, infectious disease, and cancer. The field that studies the relationship between psychological factors and illness is called psychoneuroimmunology.

The relationship between stress and illness is mediated by a variety of factors. These include physiological reactivity, cognitive appraisal, explanatory style, feelings of control, personal hardiness, sense of humor, and social support. Formal methods of coping with stress include relaxation, exercise, and stress-management programs.

HEALTH-IMPAIRING HABITS

Most deaths in the United States are associated with unhealthy habits, including unsafe sexual practices, lack of exercise, smoking tobacco, and poor nutrition. Programs aimed at changing these habits hold promise for reducing the incidence of illness and death.

REACTIONS TO ILLNESS

Health psychologists study aspects of how people cope with illness, including seeking treatment, patient distress, and adherence to medical regimens. The patient-practitioner relationship is an important factor in adherence.

THINKING ABOUT PSYCHOLOGY: DOES TYPE A BEHAVIOR PROMOTE CORONARY HEART DISEASE?

People who display Type A behavior are easily angered, highly competitive, and driven to do more and more in less and less time. They also show time urgency, chronic activation, and multiphasic activity. Research indicates that at least some components of the Type A behavior pattern, particularly antagonistic hostility, are related to the development of coronary heart disease.

Type A behavior may increase the risk of coronary heart disease by increasing blood pressure and levels of stress hormones such as cortisol, epinephrine, and norepinephrine. Type A behavior originates in childhood and is associated with parents who constantly encourage their children to improve without providing clear standards of achievement. Programs aimed at reducing the risk of coronary heart disease by altering the Type A behavior pattern show promise, but their effect on the incidence of coronary heart disease remains to be determined.

IMPORTANT CONCEPTS

MAJOR CONTRIBUTORS

RECOMMENDED READINGS

FOR GENERAL WORKS ON HEALTH PSYCHOLOGY
Bernard, L., & Krupat, E. (1993). *Health psychology.* San Diego: Harcourt Brace Jovanovich.
Dasen, P. R., Berry, J. W., & Sartorius, N. (Eds.). (1988). *Health and cross-cultural psychology.* Newbury Park, CA: Sage Publications.
Sarafino, E. P. (1994). *Health psychology: Biopsychosocial interaction.* New York: Wiley.
Taylor, S. E. (1991). *Health psychology* (2nd ed.). New York: McGraw-Hill.

FOR MORE ON STRESS AND ILLNESS
Ader, R., Felten, D. L., & Cohen, N. (Eds.). (1991). *Psychoneuroimmunology.* San Diego: Academic Press.

Brown, G. W., & Harris, T. O. (Eds.). (1989). *Life events and illness.* New York: Guilford.
Buchanan, G., & Seligman, M. E. (Eds.). (1994). *Explanatory style.* Hillsdale, NJ: Erlbaum.

Cohen, S., & Syme, S. L. (Eds.). (1985). *Social support and health*. San Diego: Academic Press.

Cooper, C. L., & Watson, M. (Eds.). (1991). *Cancer and stress*. New York: Wiley.

Cousins, N. (1989). *Head first: The biology of hope*. New York: Dutton.

Dohrenwald, B. S., & Dohrenwald, B. P. (Eds.). (1987). *Stressful life events*. New York: Wiley.

Fisher, S. (1984). *Stress and the perception of control*. Hillsdale, NJ: Erlbaum.

Fried, R. (1990). *The breath connection*. New York: Human Sciences Press.

Goldberger, L., & Breznitz, S. (Eds.). (1993). *Handbook of stress: Theoretical and clinical aspects*. New York: Free Press.

Gordon, J. (1990). *Stress management*. New York: Chelsea House.

Greenberg, J. S. (1993). *Comprehensive stress management* (4th ed.). Dubuque, IA: Brown & Benchmark.

Holmes, T. H., & David, E. M. (Eds.). (1989). *Life change, life events, and illness: Selected papers*. Westport, CT: Praeger.

Jacobson, E. (1929/1974). *Progressive relaxation*. Chicago: University of Chicago Press.

Kasl, S. V., & Cooper, C. L. (1987). *Stress and health*. New York: Wiley.

Lazarus, R. S. (1991). *Stress and coping* (3rd ed.). New York: Columbia University Press.

Lefcourt, H. M., & Martin, R. A. (1986). *Humor and life stress*. New York: Springer-Verlag.

Lipton, M. I. (1994). *Posttraumatic stress disorder*. Springfield, IL: Charles C Thomas.

Maddi, S. R., & Kobasa, S. (1984). *Hardy executive: Health under stress*. Belmont, CA: Brooks/Cole.

McCabe, P. M., Schneiderman, N., Field, T., & Skyler, J. (Eds.). (1991). *Stress, coping, and disease*. Hillsdale, NJ: Erlbaum.

Pennebaker, J. (1990). *Opening up: The healing power of confiding in others*. New York: Morrow.

Peterson, C., Maier, S.F., & Seligman, M. E. P. (1993). *Learned helplessness: A theory for the age of personal control*. New York: Oxford University Press.

Pines, A., & Aronson, E. (1988). *Career burnout: Causes and cures*. New York: Free Press.

Rice, P. L. (1992). *Stress and health* (2nd ed.). Belmont, CA: Brooks/Cole.

Saigh, P. A. (1990). *Posttraumatic stress disorder*. New York: Pergamon.

Sarason, B. R., Sarason, I., & Pierce, G. R. (Eds.). (1990). *Social support: An international view*. New York: Wiley.

Schiraldi, G. R. (1994). *Stress management strategies* (2nd ed.). Dubuque, IA: Wm. C. Brown.

Schneiderman, N., McCabe, P., & Baum, A. (Eds.). (1992). *Stress and disease processes: Perspectives in behavioral medicine*. Hillsdale, NJ: Erlbaum.

Seligman, M. E. (Ed.). *Learned optimism*. New York: Random House.

Selye, H. (1956). *The stress of life*. New York: McGraw-Hill.

Shorter, E. (1992). *From paralysis to fatigue: A history of psychosomatic illness in the modern era*. New York: Free Press.

Taylor, S. E. (1989). *Positive illusions: Creative self-deception and the healthy mind*. New York: Basic Books.

FOR MORE ON HEALTH-RELATED BEHAVIORS

Blacker, R. S. (1987). *The psychological experience of surgery*. New York: Wiley.

Cramer, J. A., & Spilker, B. (1991). *Patient compliance in medical practice and clinical trials*. New York: Raven Press.

Dishman, R. K. (1994). *Advances in exercise adherence*. Champaign, IL: Human Kinetics.

Ferrence, R. G. (1990). *Deadly fashion: The rise and fall of cigarette smoking in North America*. New York: Garland.

Fisher, S., & Todd, A. D. (1992). *The social organization of doctor-patient communication*. Norwood, NJ: Ablex.

Friedman, H. S. (1991). *The self-healing personality: Why some people achieve health and others succumb to illness*. New York: Henry Holt.

Gregg, C. H., Robertus, J. L., & Stone, J. B. (1989). *The psychological aspects of chronic illness*. Springfield, MA: Charles C Thomas.

Manning, W. G., Keeler, E. B., Newhouse, J. P., Sloss, E. M., & Wasserman, J. (1991). *The costs of poor health habits*. Cambridge, MA: Harvard University Press.

Mermelstein, R. J. (1990). *Smoking cessation: A biopsychosocial approach*. New York: Pergamon.

Phillips, E. L. (1988). *Patient compliance: New light on health delivery systems in medicine and psychotherapy*. Lewiston, NY: Hans Huber.

Polivy, J., & Herman, C. P. (1983). *Breaking the diet habit: The natural weight alternative*. New York: Basic Books.

Sachs, M. L., & Buffone, G. W. (Eds.). (1984). *Running as therapy: An integrated approach*. Lincoln: University of Nebraska Press.

Seraganian, P. (Ed.). (1992). *Exercise psychology: The influence of physical exercise on psychological processes*. New York: Wiley.

Temoshok, L., & Baum, A. (Eds.). (1990). *Psychosocial perspectives on AIDS*. Hillsdale, NJ: Erlbaum.

Willis, J. D., & Campbell, L. F. (1992). *Exercise psychology*. Champaign, IL: Human Kinetics.

FOR MORE ON TYPE A BEHAVIOR

Friedman, M., & Ulmer, D. (1984). *Treating Type A behavior and your heart*. New York: Knopf.

Houston, B. K., & Snyder, C. R. (Eds.). (1988). *Type A behavior pattern: Research, theory, and intervention*. New York: Wiley.

Roskies, E. (1987). *Stress management for the healthy Type A: Theory and practice*. New York: Guilford.

Siegman, A. W., & Smith, T. W. (Eds.). (1993). *Anger, hostility, and the heart*. Hillsdale, NJ: Erlbaum.

Williams, R. (1989). *The trusting heart: Great news about Type A behavior*. New York: Random House.

FOR MORE ON CONTRIBUTORS TO THE STUDY OF PSYCHOLOGY AND HEALTH

Benison, S., Barger, A. C., & Wolfe, E. L. (1987). *Walter B. Cannon: The life and times of a young scientist*. Cambridge, MA: Belknap/Harvard.

Selye, H. (1979). *The stress of my life: A scientist's memoirs*. New York: Van Nostrand Reinhold.

CHAPTER 17

Claude Monet
Boulevard des Capucines
1873

SOCIAL BEHAVIOR

n the 1890s, bicycle racing was a major spectator sport in North America. As mentioned in chapter 11, Norman Triplett (1898) noted that those who raced against other riders rode faster than those who raced against time. He decided to study this phenomenon experimentally by having boys spin fishing reels as fast as they could while competing either against time or against another boy. He found that those who competed against another boy performed faster. This was one of the first experiments in **social psychology,** the field that studies behavior in its interpersonal context—that is, how people affect one another's thoughts, feelings, and behaviors. Though social-psychological studies were conducted before the turn of the century and the first social-psychology textbooks were published in 1908 (Pepitone, 1981), social psychology did not become a major field of study until after World War II, when many psychologists became interested in the formal study of social behavior. The major topics of interest to social psychologists include *social cognition, social attraction, social attitudes, group processes, prosocial behavior,* and *aggression.*

SOCIAL COGNITION

Psychologists who study **social cognition** are concerned with how we perceive, interpret, and predict social behavior. As you will read, though social cognition is usually accurate (Jussim, 1991), biases and subjectivity can distort it. Two of the main topics in social cognition are *social attribution* and *impression formation.*

Social Attribution

As first noted in the 1940s by social psychologist Fritz Heider (1944), when we engage in **social attribution** we determine the extent to which a person's behavior (whether our own or someone else's) is caused by the person or by the person's circumstances. When you decide that the person is primarily responsible for his or her behavior, you are making a *dispositional attribution.* When you decide that circumstances are primarily responsible for a person's behavior, you are making a *situational attribution.* Consider the Los Angeles riots of April 1992. Citizens, politicians, and commentators were quick to place blame on either the rioters or their circumstances. Those who believed the rioters were motivated by immorality and a personal inclination toward violence made dispositional attributions. In contrast, those who believed the rioters were responding to racism and grinding poverty made situational attributions.

Kelley's Attributional Principles

There were so many studies of social attribution in the 1970s that it became known as "the decade of attribution theory in social psychology" (Weiner, 1985b, p. 74). The most influential attribution theorist of that decade was Harold Kelley; he identified factors that determine when we make dispositional attributions or situational attributions. Kelley (1973) found that social attributions depend on *consistency, distinctiveness,* and *consensus.* **Consistency** is the extent to which a person behaves in the same way in a given situation on different occasions. **Distinctiveness** is the extent to which a person behaves in the same way across different situations. And **consensus** is the extent to which, in a given situation, other people behave the same as the person being observed.

These factors played a role in a study of college students who were manipulated into either cheating or not cheating during an experiment. When asked to explain their behavior, those who had cheated made situational attributions for their actions and those who had not cheated made dispositional attributions. Cheaters noted the high

---

social psychology
The field that studies how people affect one another's thoughts, feelings, and behaviors.

social cognition
The process of perceiving, interpreting, and predicting social behavior.

social attribution
The cognitive process by which we infer the causes of both our own and other people's social behavior.

Harold Kelley
"Individuals, in making attributions for behavior, expect to encounter information patterns indicating . . . person or circumstance causation. Each of these patterns is characterized by certain levels of consensus, distinctiveness, and consistency."

consistency
The extent to which a person behaves in the same way in a given situation on different occasions.

distinctiveness
The extent to which a person behaves in the same way across different situations.

consensus
The extent to which, in a given situation, other people behave in the same way as the person being observed.

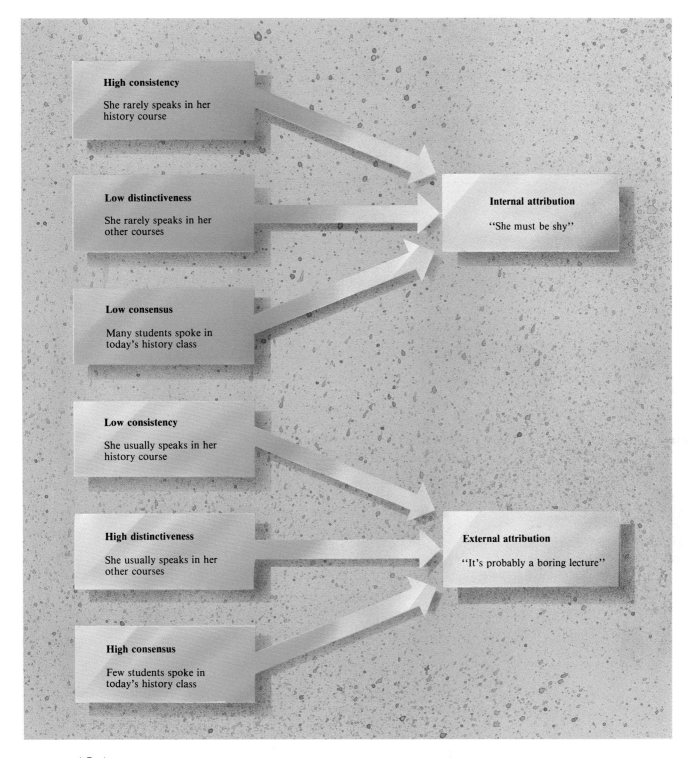

FIGURE 17.1

Dispositional and Situational Attribution
In deciding why a student did not speak today in a history class, Kelley (1973) would have us consider the factors of consistency, distinctiveness, and consensus. These are only two of the many possible combinations of the three factors.

distinctiveness, high consensus, and low consistency of their actions. Noncheaters noted the low distinctiveness, low consensus, and high consistency of their actions. The cheaters' attributions helped them maintain a positive self-image, and the noncheaters' attributions helped them enhance their self-image (Forsyth, Pope, & McMillan, 1985). Figure 17.1 illustrates these two patterns of social attribution.

FIGURE 17.2

Dimensions of Social Attribution
According to Bernard Weiner, we may explain our successes and failures by attributing them to internal or external causes that are either stable or unstable.

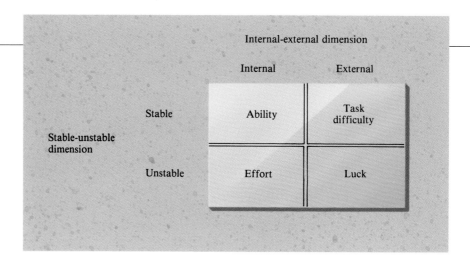

Bernard Weiner
"A variety of sources of information are used to reach causal inferences in achievement-related contexts. The primary perceived causes of success and failure are ability and effort."

fundamental attribution error
The bias to attribute other people's behavior to dispositional factors.

Weiner's Attributional Dimensions

Kelley's theory of attribution was soon joined by one devised by Bernard Weiner (1985a) to explain our successes and failures. Weiner and his colleagues found that estimating the relative impact of dispositional and situational factors is important but cannot by itself explain all social attributions. Weiner identified three dimensions that govern social attribution. The *internal-external dimension* is akin to Kelley's distinction between dispositional and situational attribution. The *stable-unstable dimension* refers to the degree to which we attribute a behavior to a factor that is stable or unstable. And the *controllable-uncontrollable dimension* indicates the extent to which we attribute a behavior to a factor that is controllable or uncontrollable.

You may on occasion have intuitively used these dimensions in making excuses that both maintain your self-esteem and prevent other people from becoming angry with you (Weiner, Figueroa-Munoz, & Kakihara, 1991). Suppose you submit a term paper late. Your excuse would be more effective if you attribute your behavior to external, unstable, and uncontrollable factors, such as a family emergency, than if you attribute it to internal, stable, and controllable factors, such as a difficulty in budgeting your time effectively. Weiner has found that people in a variety of cultures around the world use these dimensions in making attributions for success and failure (Schuster, Forsterling, & Weiner, 1989). Figure 17.2 illustrates the interaction of Weiner's stable-unstable dimension and internal-external dimension.

College counselors have used Weiner's attributional dimensions to help freshmen adjust to college. In one study, counselors made use of the stable-unstable dimension in a program to help college freshmen who were doing poorly become more optimistic. The program tried to convince freshmen that their low grades were caused by unstable, instead of stable, factors. Freshmen were given data indicating that students tend to improve their grades after the freshman year. They were also shown videotapes of juniors and seniors who reported that their grade point averages had increased since their freshman year. Freshmen who were exposed to this information were significantly less likely to leave college and had significantly greater increases in grade point average during their sophomore year than did those who were not exposed to it (Wilson & Linville, 1982).

Biases in Social Attribution

If human beings were as rational and objective as Mr. Spock in "Star Trek," the social attribution process would be a straightforward affair. But, being somewhat irrational and subjective, we exhibit biases in the social attributions we make. One bias is the tendency to attribute other people's behavior to dispositional factors. This is known as the **fundamental attribution error** (Nisbett & Ross, 1980). For example, a study of elementary school teachers found that they tended to overestimate the importance of dispositional factors in making attributions for their students' success or failure (Burger, Cooper, & Good, 1982).

In contrast, we tend to attribute our own behavior to situational factors. A survey of advice columns, including "Dear Abby" and "Ann Landers," found that people who write for advice tend to attribute their own problems to situational factors but tend to attribute other people's problems to dispositional factors (Schoeneman & Rubanowitz, 1985). Thus, in explaining why other people are on unemployment compensation, we might attribute it to their laziness. Yet, if we find ourselves on unemployment compensation, we might attribute it to a bad economy. This tendency for observers to make dispositional attributions for the behavior of others but situational attributions for their own behavior is called the **actor-observer bias.**

Why are we subject to the actor-observer bias? One explanation is that we usually have greater knowledge of the circumstances that influence our own behavior than of those that influence other people's behavior. As an example, suppose that a student is consistently absent from her introductory psychology course. Her professor might attribute the absences to her unreliable nature. In contrast, the student might attribute her absences to dull lectures. Thus, the greater awareness that the student has of the circumstances affecting her behavior might lead her to make a situational attribution for her absences. In contrast, the professor, being aware of only the student's behavior, might be biased in favor of making a dispositional attribution for her absences (Eisen, 1979).

We are also subject to a **self-serving bias,** which is the tendency to make dispositional attributions for our own positive behaviors and situational attributions for our own negative behaviors. A study of college students found that those who received high grades (A's or B's) tended to make dispositional attributions for their own performance, attributing their success to their own efforts and abilities. In contrast, students who received lower grades (C's, D's, or F's) tended to make situational attributions, attributing their lack of success to bad luck and difficult tests (Bernstein, Stephan, & Davis, 1979). The self-serving bias is in keeping with evidence (discussed in chapter 13) that positive mental health is associated with the maintenance of a somewhat unrealistically positive view of oneself (Taylor & Brown, 1988).

Impression Formation

In addition to making attributions about the causes of behavior, we spend a great deal of our time making judgments about the personal characteristics of people. This is known as **impression formation.** Consider victims of rape. An experiment found that the ways in which women testify about their attacks can create markedly different impressions. Subjects viewed films of an actress who played the role of a rape victim. Those who saw a film in which she discussed her rape in an emotional manner held her less responsible for the rape than did those who saw a film in which she spoke as if she were emotionally numbed by her experience (Winkel & Koppelaar, 1991).

The deliberate attempt to control the impressions that others form of us is called **impression management** (Leary & Kowalski, 1990). For example, workers may engage in impression management when speaking to clients on the telephone (Witt, 1991) or when trying to influence the behavior of their supervisors (Deluga, 1991). Psychologists have found that, in addition to using impression management to influence others, we also use it to make our public self congruent with our ideal self (Baumeister, 1982).

As discussed in chapter 13, a common technique that we use in impression management is self-handicapping. When we self-handicap, we let others know that we are performing under a handicap. If we then do well, we look good to others. If we then do poorly, others will attribute our poor performance to our "handicap." Consider a student who announces that he did not study enough for an exam. Success on the exam would reflect well on his ability; failure on the exam could be attributed to inadequate study time rather than to lack of ability—thereby protecting his self-esteem (Tice & Baumeister, 1990).

The Actor-Observer Bias
If you were the driver of the red car, which struck the car on the right, you would probably blame the accident on situational factors, such as a bad road. Yet if you saw someone else have the accident, you would probably blame it on dispositional factors, such as carelessness.

actor-observer bias
The tendency of observers to make dispositional attributions for the behavior of others but to make situational attributions for their own behavior.

self-serving bias
The tendency to make dispositional attributions for one's successes and situational attributions for one's failures.

The Self-Serving Bias
The winners of this game would probably attribute their success to their effort and ability. In contrast, the losers would probably attribute their failure to poor officiating or the harsh weather conditions.

impression formation
The process of making judgments about the personal characteristics of others.

impression management
The deliberate attempt to control the impression that others form of us.

Drawing by Handelsman; © 1984 The New Yorker Magazine, Inc.

"The basis of our defense will be that a man of your standing in the community, whatever else he may be, is certainly no thief."

social schema
A cognitive structure comprising the presumed characteristics of a role, an event, a person, or a group.

Social Schemas
Would you think differently about someone who was called "Frank Sinatra's mouthpiece" as opposed to "Frank Sinatra's spokesperson"?

stereotype
A social schema that incorporates characteristics, which may be positive or negative, supposedly shared by almost all members of a group.

Social Schemas

College professor. Rock concert. Bill Cosby. Eskimo. Each of these involves a **social schema,** which comprises the presumed characteristics of a role, event, person, or group. Social schemas bring order to what might otherwise be a chaotic social world by permitting us to interpret and predict the behavior of others. A social schema can have powerful effects on our social perception. Think of the labels *spokesperson* and *mouthpiece.* Would you expect different behaviors from individuals described by these terms? The social schema for *mouthpiece* includes negative characteristics that the social schema for *spokesperson* does not. The possible negative impression created by the label *mouthpiece* was the basis of a lawsuit on behalf of Frank Sinatra's attorney against *Barron's Business and Financial Weekly,* which referred to the attorney as "Sinatra's mouthpiece." The results of a survey sponsored by Sinatra's attorney showed that the term *mouthpiece* created a negative impression in the minds of readers. This was introduced as evidence in court. Though the judge accepted the validity of this evidence, *Barron's* won the case on the grounds of freedom of the press (Kramer et al., 1985).

Social Stereotypes

If you believe that virtually all members of any social group—men, women, blacks, whites, Jews, Christians, and so on—share a set of characteristics that is unique to that group, you are guilty of stereotyping. A **stereotype** is a social schema that incorporates characteristics, which can be positive or negative, that supposedly belong to almost all members of a group. Thus, stereotypes are based, in part, on our tendency to view members of our own group (our *in-group*) as more variable than members of another group (an *out-group*). For example, a study of college sororities found that members judged their own members as more dissimilar than members of another sorority (Park & Rothbart, 1982).

Stereotypes are used to make predictions about the behavior of group members. We are likely to rely on stereotypes in making decisions about others' behavior when we have little else but their group memberships on which to base our decisions. Of course, few people who hold stereotypes assume that *all* members of an out-group share the same characteristics. Thus, when confronted with someone who violates a stereotype, they simply assimilate that person into their out-group schema as an exception to the rule (Hewstone, Johnston, & Aird, 1992).

Our stereotypic expectations can affect our interactions with others. In one experiment, undergraduates were given the opportunity to get acquainted with a person who was described as either another student or a psychotherapy client. During their meetings, those who believed that their partners were psychotherapy clients treated the person more negatively than did those who believed that their partners were fellow students. In turn, when the student believed that the partner was a psychotherapy client, the partner behaved in a less socially desirable way (Sibicky & Dovidio, 1986).

First Impressions

When we first meet a person, we might have little information about the individual other than her or his sex, race, apparent age, and physical appearance. Each of these characteristics might activate a particular social schema, which in turn will create a first impression of that person. A first impression functions as a social schema to guide our predictions of a person's behavior and our desire to interact with that person. First impressions are important in many situations, such as in determining whether college roommates will become friends (Berg, 1984).

First impressions can be based on as little as a person's facial features, as shown by a study in which subjects were asked to match photographs of faces to a list of occupations. Certain faces were consistently matched with "honest occupation" such as engineer, physician, or clergy, while certain other faces were consistently matched with "dishonest occupations" such as rapist, armed robber, or mass murderer (Goldstein, Chance, & Gilbert, 1984). Even one's hair—or lack of hair—can affect other people's first impressions. A study that compared subjects' first impressions of balding and nonbalding men found that their first impressions of balding men were less favorable. The balding men were considered not only less attractive but also less likely to have appealing personal qualities and interpersonal skills (Cash, 1990). If this type of bias is shared by people in general, we might unfairly favor or disfavor particular people because of the social schemas evoked by their faces, baldness, or other superficial characteristics. You can appreciate how undesirable this would be in certain situations, such as jury trials or job interviews. This is even more important in light of research findings that negative information has an even stronger influence on our first impressions than does positive information (Klein, 1991).

A classic experiment by Harold Kelley (1950) demonstrated the importance of a first impression on our evaluation of a stranger. Undergraduates were given a written description of a guest lecturer as "a rather warm person, industrious, critical, practical, and determined" or the same description with the word *warm* replaced by the word *cold*. After the lecture, which provided the opportunity for questions and discussion, the students were asked for their impressions of the lecturer. Students who had been told that the lecturer was warm rated him as more informal, sociable, and humorous than did those who were told he was cold. Those who had been told the lecturer was warm also asked more questions and participated in more discussions with him. This indicated that the students assimilated the lecturer's behavior into the schema they had been given. This study was successfully replicated 30 years later using a similar methodology (Widmeyer & Loy, 1988).

Self-Fulfilling Prophecy

One of the important effects of first impressions is the **self-fulfilling prophecy,** which is the tendency for one person's expectations to make a second person behave in accordance with them. This occurs because the social schema we have of the other person will make us act a certain way toward that person, which in turn will make the person respond in accordance with our expectations (Darley & Fazio, 1980). A classic experiment, which showed how first impressions can create self-fulfilling prophecies,

First Impressions
Do these women bring different thoughts and feelings to mind? Your first impressions of them might determine how you initially act toward them.

self-fulfilling prophecy
The tendency for one person's expectations to influence another person to behave in accordance with them.

Proximity and Social Attraction
Proximity provides an opportunity for friendships to develop. For example, a study found that recruits at the Maryland State Police Academy whose last names began with letters near one another in the alphabet were more likely to become friends. The reason was proximity: The recruits were assigned to their barracks rooms and classroom seats in alphabetical order (Segal, 1974).

investigated the influence of teachers' expectations on the performance of school-children. The teachers were told that a new intelligence test indicated that certain students were "late bloomers" and would show a marked increase in intelligence by the end of the school year. The label *late bloomer* was actually assigned randomly to about 20 percent of the students. Yet, at the end of the school year, the "late bloomers" showed a significantly greater increase in IQ scores than did the students who were not given that label. Apparently, the teachers' expectations led them to treat the "late bloomers" differently than they treated the other students, thereby creating a self-fulfilling prophecy (Rosenthal & Jacobson, 1968).

SOCIAL ATTRACTION

While forming impressions of other people, we also develop *social attraction* toward some of them. By this point in the semester, you have probably become friendly with certain students; you might even have developed a romantic relationship with someone in particular. Social psychologists interested in social attraction seek answers to questions like these: Why do we like certain people more than others? What is the nature of romantic love?

Liking

Think of the students you have met this semester. Who do you like? Who do you not like? Among the factors that determine which ones you like are *proximity*, *familiarity*, *physical attractiveness*, *similarity*, and *self-disclosure*.

Proximity

Research has consistently supported the importance of proximity in the development of friendships, as in a classic study of the residents of apartments in a housing project for married students at the Massachusetts Institute of Technology. The closer students lived to one another, the more likely they were to become friends. In fact, 41 percent of the students reported that their best friends lived next door. Because the students had been randomly assigned to apartments, their initial degree of liking for one another could not explain the findings (Festinger, Schachter, & Back, 1950). These findings were replicated in a study of friendship networks among residents of a city housing project. The closer they lived to one another, the more likely they were to become friends (Nahemow & Lawton, 1975).

Familiarity

Proximity makes us more familiar with certain people. But contrary to the popular saying, familiarity tends to breed liking, not contempt. As explained in chapter 6, the more familiar we become with a stimulus, whether a car, a painting, or a professor, the more we will like it. So, in general, the more we interact with particular people, the more we tend to like them (Moreland & Zajonc, 1982). Of course, this *mere exposure effect* holds only when the people do not behave in negative ways. The effect of familiarity on liking is not lost on politicians, who enhance their popularity by making repeated television appearances. The more familiar we are with public figures (assuming they do nothing scandalous), the more we tend to like them (Harrison, 1969).

The mere exposure effect was supported by a clever experiment that used female college students as subjects. For each subject, two photographs of the subject were presented to the subject and to a friend. One photograph was a direct image of the subject; the second was a mirror image—what the subject would see when looking at herself in a mirror. Mirror images and normal photographic images differ because our faces are not perfectly symmetrical—the left and right sides look different. Subjects and friends were asked to choose which of the two photographs was preferable. Friends were more likely to choose the direct image, while subjects were more likely to choose the mirror image. This was evidence for the mere exposure effect, because the friends were more familiar with the direct image, while the subjects were more familiar with their own mirror image (Mita, Dermer, & Knight, 1977). This link between facial familiarity and liking might even explain why people tend to marry individuals who look somewhat like them. Because we are more familiar with our own face and those of relatives who look like us, we come to prefer faces that look like ours (Hinsz, 1989).

Physical Attractiveness

Proximity not only lets us become familiar with people, but also lets us note their appearance. We tend to like physically attractive people more than physically unattractive ones. This can have practical benefits for attractive people. For example, physically attractive people are perceived as more mentally healthy (Feingold, 1992) and socially competent (Eagly et al., 1991), and they tend to have more-successful careers (Dickey-Bryant et al., 1986). In an early experiment on physical attractiveness, freshmen at the University of Minnesota took part in a computer dating study. They completed

personality and aptitude tests and were told that they would be paired based on their responses. In reality, they were paired randomly. Independent judges rated the physical attractiveness of each student. The couples then attended a dance that lasted several hours and rated their partners on a questionnaire. The results showed that physical attractiveness was the most important factor in determining whether subjects liked their partners and whether they desired to date them again (Walster et al., 1966). Though we prefer highly attractive people, social sorting usually leads us to have friends (Cash & Derlega, 1978) and romantic partners (Folkes, 1982) who are similar to us in physical attractiveness.

Similarity

Do opposites attract? Or do birds of a feather flock together? You may recall the experiment discussed in chapter 2 that showed we are more attracted to people whose attitudes are similar to our own (Byrne, Ervin, & Lamberth, 1970). This has been replicated in other studies (Gonzales et al., 1983; Neimeyer & Mitchell, 1988). But this interpretation has been challenged by research showing that we are likely to associate with people who hold similar attitudes simply by default, because we are *repulsed* by those who have dissimilar ones. Life's circumstances simply put us in religious, political, recreational, and educational settings where we are likely to associate with people who share our attitudes (Rosenbaum, 1986). Other research indicates that we like people who share our activity preferences even more than we like people who share our attitudes (Lydon, Jamieson, & Zanna, 1988). Thus, you might enjoy playing sports or going to music concerts even with someone whose sexual, religious, and political values differ from yours.

Self-Disclosure

To determine whether we share similar attitudes and interests with someone else, we must engage in *self-disclosure*, in which we reveal our beliefs, feelings, and experiences. People who engage in mutual self-disclosure have more satisfactory social relationships than people who do not (Franzoi, Davis, & Young, 1985). Relationships are promoted both by the reciprocation of self-disclosure and by gradual increases in it. When people disclose highly personal information to us too early in a relationship, we may become uneasy, suspicious, and less attracted to them (Huston & Levinger, 1978). If someone you have just met has ever regaled you with his or her whole life story, including intimate details, you might have felt uncomfortable and uninterested in pursuing the relationship.

Romantic Love

Love might make the world go round, but there were few scientific studies of romantic love until the 1970s. Some people believe that the scientific study of romantic love either is doomed to failure or invades an area of life that is better left as an everlasting mystery. In fact, William Proxmire, former senator from Wisconsin, gave his first Golden Fleece Award to a study of romantic love that was supported by an $84,000 grant from the National Science Foundation. Proxmire regularly gave the award to studies that *he* believed were the greatest waste of taxpayers' money. In bestowing his first award, Proxmire claimed, "Right at the top of the things we don't want to know is why a man falls in love with a woman" (Adler & Carey, 1980, p. 89).

Unimpressed by Proxmire's criticism, social psychologists have continued to conduct research on romantic love. Unlike Proxmire, they realize that the findings of such research have been used to help prevent and relieve the emotional and physical suffering that is produced by unhappy romantic relationships, including spouse abuse, child abuse, and divorce. What have researchers discovered about the nature of romantic love? For one thing, the concept of love has "fuzzy boundaries" (discussed in chapter 9). That is, we know love when we see it or experience it, but we cannot define it by a single set of features without finding that there are exceptions to any definition we put forth (Fehr & Russell, 1991).

Theories of Love

Elaine Hatfield, undaunted by earning the first Golden Fleece Award for research she conducted with her colleague, Ellen Berscheid, distinguishes between passionate love and companionate love (Hatfield, 1988). **Passionate love,** commonly known as sexual love, involves intense emotional arousal, including sexual feelings. **Companionate love** involves feelings of affection and commitment to the relationship. Over time, romantic relationships tend to decline in passionate love and increase in companionate love.

More research has been conducted on passionate love than on companionate love. According to Berscheid and Hatfield, passionate love depends on three factors. First, the culture must promote the notion of passionate love. Passionate love has been important in Western cultures only since the Middle Ages, and even today some cultures have no concept of it. Second, the person must experience a state of intense emotional arousal. Third, the emotional arousal must be associated with a romantic partner (Berscheid & Walster, 1974).

Berscheid and Hatfield's theory of romantic love incorporates aspects of Stanley Schachter's two-factor theory of emotion. As explained in chapter 12, Schachter's theory assumes that you will experience a particular emotion when you perceive that you are physiologically aroused and attribute that arousal to an emotionally relevant aspect of the situation in which you find yourself. The two-factor theory assumes that romantic love is the result of being physiologically aroused in a situation that promotes the labeling of that arousal as romantic love.

The two-factor theory of romantic love was supported by a clever experiment that took place on two bridges in Vancouver, British Columbia (Dutton & Aron, 1974). One, the Capilano River Bridge, was 5 feet wide, 450 feet long, and 230 feet above rocky rapids. It had low handrails and was constructed of wooden boards attached to wire cables, which made it prone to wobble back and forth, inducing fear-related physiological arousal in those who walked across it. The other bridge, over a tiny tributary of the Capilano River, was wide, solid, immobile, and only 10 feet above the water. These characteristics made that bridge less likely to induce arousal in those who walked across it.

Whenever a man walked across one of the bridges, he was met by an attractive woman who was the experimenter's accomplice. The woman asked each man to participate in a psychology course project about the effects of scenic attractions on creativity. Each man was shown a picture of a man and a woman in an ambiguous situation and was asked to write a brief dramatic story about the picture. The woman then gave the man her telephone number in case he wanted to ask her any questions about the study. The results showed that, compared with the men on the other bridge, the men who were on the bridge that induced physiological arousal wrote stories with more sexual content and were more likely to call the woman later.

According to the two-factor theory of romantic love, the men on the bridge that induced arousal had attributed their arousal to the presence of the attractive woman, leading them to experience romantic feelings toward her. But this interpretation of the

Ellen Berscheid (above) and Elaine Hatfield
The evidence suggests that most individuals docilely accept the prescription that beauty and sexual and romantic passion are inexorably linked.

passionate love
Love characterized by intense emotional arousal and sexual feelings.

companionate love
Love characterized by feelings of affection and commitment to a relationship with another person.

Companionate Love
For romantic love to last after passionate love has waned, romantic partners must maintain the deep affection that characterizes companionate love.

FIGURE **17.3**

Love and Arousal
Physiological arousal in the presence of an appropriate person can intensify feelings of romantic love.

attitude
An evaluation, containing cognitive, emotional, and behavioral components, of an idea, event, object, or person.

results has been rejected by some researchers, who offer an alternative interpretation that assumes that the presence of the woman reduced the men's fear of the bridge, which, as a consequence, conditioned them to find her more attractive (Riordan & Tedeschi, 1983).

Nonetheless, results of studies similar to the Capilano River study have supported the two-factor theory of romantic love. In one such study, men who were physiologically aroused by exercise while in the presence of an attractive woman were more attracted to that woman than were men who were not physiologically aroused (White, Fishbein, & Rutstein, 1981). Based on the two-factor theory of romantic love, why would you expect the exhilaration experienced by the couple in figure 17.3 to increase their romantic feelings toward each other?

Promoting Romantic Love

What factors promote romantic love? As with liking someone, similarity is an important factor. We tend to date and to marry people who are similar to us in attractiveness (Murstein, 1972), as well as in age, race, religion, ethnic background, and educational level (Buss, 1985). A survey found that when males and females were asked to rate the factors that would make someone attractive as a romantic partner, a sense of humor was the most important one (Buss, 1988). We also prefer romantic partners who are similar to us in sensation seeking (which is discussed in chapter 11). Thus, couples, whether dating or married, in which one member is a "homebody" and the other is a "party animal" are less likely to be satisfied (Schroth, 1991).

Self-disclosure plays an even stronger role in romantic love than in interpersonal liking (Critelli & Dupre, 1978). A study of 18-year-old dating couples found that those who engaged in mutual self-disclosure early in the relationship were more likely to be together 4 months later (Berg & McQuinn, 1986). In keeping with Erich Fromm's notion of the *marketing orientation* in social relations (see figure 13.4), there is evidence that people seeking romantic relationships may engage in premeditated self-disclosure to make favorable impressions on those they seek to attract. Thus, some "open" people may not be as spontaneous as they seem (Wintrob, 1987).

Another important factor in romantic relationships is equity, the belief that each partner is contributing equally to the relationship, which promotes contentment and commitment (Winn, Crawford, & Fischer, 1991). The most successful marriages are ones marked by equal contributions by the husband and wife, in which neither one dominates the relationship (Gray-Little & Burks, 1983). Even the mere promise of equity might be important in promoting romantic relationships. This has been shown in archival research on personal advertisements. A survey of 800 advertisements placed by individuals seeking romantic partners found that the advertisers tended to seek equitable relationships. But women and men differed in complementary ways in the rewards they sought and offered. Men tended to seek attractive women, while offering financial security in return. In contrast, women tended to seek financially secure men, while offering physical attractiveness in return (Harrison, 1977). These findings have been replicated in more-recent archival research (Koestner & Wheeler, 1988; Rajecki, Bledsoe, & Rasmussen, 1991; Sitton & Rippee, 1986) and in a laboratory experiment (Sprecher, 1989). This indicates that the movement for equality between women and men has yet to replace traditional sources of equity in romantic relationships with ones that are the same for males and females—at least for those who advertise for romance.

SOCIAL ATTITUDES

What are your feelings about the insanity defense? Surprise parties? Abstract art? Sorority members? Your answers to these questions would reveal your attitudes. **Attitudes** are evaluations of ideas (such as the insanity defense), events (such as surprise parties), objects (such as abstract art), or people (such as sorority members). In the 1930s, the noted psychologist Gordon Allport claimed that the concept of attitude was the single most important concept in social psychology. It no longer maintains such a lofty position, but it is still one of the most widely studied concepts in social psychology.

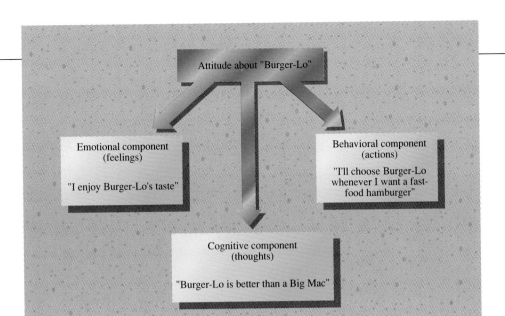

FIGURE 17.4

The Components of Attitudes
Attitudes have emotional, cognitive, and behavioral components.

As shown in figure 17.4, attitudes have emotional, cognitive, and behavioral components (Breckler, 1984). To appreciate this, imagine that you have been asked to participate in a market research survey of attitudes toward a new low-cholesterol, fast-food hamburger called "Burger-Lo." The market researcher would determine your attitude toward Burger-Lo by measuring one or more of the three components of your attitude. Your *emotional* response might be measured by a questionnaire asking you to rate your feelings about Burger-Lo's taste, aroma, texture, and appearance. Your *cognitive* response might be measured by asking you to describe the thoughts that Burger-Lo brings to mind, such as "It's better than a Big Mac." And your *behavioral* response might be measured by observing whether you choose Burger-Lo over several other fast-food hamburgers in a blind taste test.

The Formation of Attitudes

How are our attitudes formed? Some are learned through *classical conditioning* (see chapter 7) by the pairing of something desirable or undesirable with the object of the attitude (Cacioppo et al., 1992). If Burger-Lo tastes good, you will associate that experience with Burger-Lo and develop a positive attitude toward it. Research indicates that our food preferences are, in fact, influenced by classical conditioning (Rozin & Zellner, 1985). Advertisers of foods and other products take advantage of classical conditioning by pairing them with stimuli that are already desirable (Allen & Janiszewski, 1989).

Attitudes can also be formed through *operant conditioning*, as in an experiment conducted at the University of Hawaii (Insko, 1965). Undergraduates, contacted by telephone, were asked whether they agreed or disagreed with statements that favored or opposed a proposed "Springtime Aloha Week." The caller positively reinforced certain statements by saying "good." For half of the telephone calls, the caller said "good" whenever the student agreed with a statement favoring the proposal. For the other half, the caller said "good" whenever the student agreed with a statement opposing the proposal. One week later the students were given a "local issues questionnaire." Among the items in the questionnaire was a question asking whether they favored or opposed the proposed Springtime Aloha Week. The responses to that question showed that students who earlier had been reinforced for making statements that favored the Springtime Aloha Week were more likely to favor it, while students who earlier had been reinforced for making statements that opposed it were more likely to oppose it.

According to *social-learning theory*, many of our attitudes are learned through observing others, particularly our parents, our peers, and characters on television shows, being

The Power of Persuasion
We are continually exposed to persuasive messages in everyday life.

punished or positively reinforced for expressing particular behaviors (Kanekar, 1976). Suppose that a child repeatedly observes her parents responding positively to her older sister for expressing certain political or religious attitudes. Because she would want to receive the same positive responses from her parents, she might adopt similar attitudes.

The Art of Persuasion

In 1956, Edward Schein published an article that described the results of his interviews with United Nations soldiers who, as prisoners during the Korean War, had been subjected to so-called brainwashing. Publicity about brainwashing, and fears that it could be used by totalitarian governments to control citizens, stimulated further interest in studying factors that affect persuasion and resistance to it. **Persuasion** is the attempt to influence the attitudes of other people. Today researchers have less interest in studying brainwashing than in studying the use of persuasion in everyday life, whether by friends, relatives, advertisers, or politicians.

According to Richard Petty and John Cacioppo (1981), persuasive messages may take a *central route* or a *peripheral route*. A message that takes a central route relies on clear, explicit arguments about the issue at hand. This encourages active consideration of the merits of the arguments. In contrast, a message that takes a peripheral route relies on factors other than the merits of the arguments, such as characteristics of the source or the situational context. The central and peripheral routes are related to the main factors in persuasion: the *source*, the *message*, and the *audience*. These three factors were first studied more than 2,000 years ago by Aristotle. He found that persuasion was most effective when the source had good character, the message was supported by strong evidence, and the audience was in a receptive frame of mind (Jones, 1985).

The Source

One of the important peripheral factors in persuasion is the source of the message. The greater the *credibility* of the source, the greater the persuasiveness of the message. Politicians realize this and gain votes by having credible supporters praise their merits and criticize their opponents' faults (Calantone & Warshaw, 1985). But what determines a source's credibility? Two of the most important factors are the source's expertise and trustworthiness. We perceive sources as especially *trustworthy* when their message is not an obvious attempt at persuasion, as when the message is contrary to the source's ex-

Richard Petty and John Cacioppo
"There are only two fundamentally different 'routes' to changing a person's attitudes. One route, which we call the *central route*, emphasizes the information a person has about the person, object, or issue under consideration; and the other route, which we call the *peripheral route*, emphasizes just about anything else."

pected position (Wood & Eagly, 1981). For example, as noted in chapter 10, Sir Cyril Burt's biographer concluded that Burt had fabricated data supporting a strong genetic basis for intelligence. The author of an article that discussed Burt's biography claimed, "The conclusion carries more weight because the author of the biography, Professor Leslie Hearnshaw, began his task as an admirer" (Hawkes, 1979, p. 673). If Hearnshaw had been a critic of Burt's work, his conclusion would have been less credible.

Sources that are *attractive*, because they are likable or physically appealing, are also more persuasive. Advertisers take advantage of this by having attractive actors appear in their commercials (Kahle & Homer, 1985). Even the appeal of politicians is affected by their attractiveness. Richard Nixon's unattractive appearance during a debate with John F. Kennedy may have cost him the 1960 presidential election. Nixon's five-o'clock shadow and tendency to perspire made him less attractive to voters who watched the debate on television. Surveys found that those who watched the debate on television rated Kennedy the winner, while those who listened to it on the radio rated Nixon the winner (Weisman, 1988). Having learned from Nixon's mistake, today's politicians make sure that they appear as attractive as possible on television.

We are also more likely to be persuaded by sources who are *similar* to us in ways that are relevant to the object of the message. For example, high school students respond more favorably to nutrition information from sources similar to them (Feldman, 1984), and viewers respond more positively to television advertisements with actors of their own race (Whittler, 1991).

The Message

It might surprise you to learn that it is not always desirable to present arguments that support only your position. Acknowledging the other side of an issue, while strongly supporting your own, is at times more effective (Allen et al., 1990). This was discovered by social psychologist Carl Hovland and his colleagues in the waning days of World War II, following the surrender of Germany (Hovland, Lumsdaine, & Sheffield, 1949). The military asked Hovland for advice on how to convince soldiers that the war against Japan would take a long time to win. The researchers presented soldiers with a 15-minute talk that presented either one-sided or two-sided arguments. In the one-sided argument, they presented only arguments about why the war would not be over soon, such as the fighting spirit of the Japanese. In the two-sided argument, they presented both that argument *and* arguments explaining why the war might end earlier, such as Allied air superiority. Before and after the message, the subjects were given surveys that included questions about how long they believed the war would last.

The results showed that those who originally believed the war would take a long time to win were more influenced by the one-sided argument and became more extreme

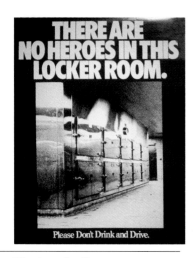

The Appeal to Fear
Persuasive appeals that rely on fear can be effective if the supposed threat is severe, its likelihood is high, and we can do something to prevent or eliminate it.

in their attitudes. But those who originally believed there would be an early end to the war were more influenced by the two-sided argument. As you can see, if the listener already favors your position or has no counterarguments handy, arguments that favor your position alone will be more persuasive. But if the listener opposes your position, arguments that acknowledge both sides of the issue will be more persuasive. Two-sided messages are superior to one-sided ones in persuasive appeals as diverse as selling deodorants and promoting mass transit systems (Golden & Alpert, 1987). Two-sided arguments are effective because they enhance the credibility of the source and decrease counterarguing by the listener (Kamins & Assael, 1987).

The Audience

Persuasion depends on the audience, as well as the source and the message. An important audience factor is intelligence, because it determines whether a message will be more effective using the central or the peripheral route. People of relatively high intelligence are more likely to be influenced by messages supported by rational arguments—the central route. People of relatively low intelligence are more likely to be influenced by messages supported by factors other than rational arguments—the peripheral route. Relatively intelligent people are more likely to attend to rational arguments because they are better able to comprehend them (Eagly & Warren, 1976). Overall, people of lower intelligence are more easily influenced than people of higher intelligence (Rhodes & Wood, 1992).

Another important factor is whether the audience finds the message personally relevant. A message's relevance for a particular audience determines whether the central route or the peripheral route will be more effective (Petty & Cacioppo, 1990). When a message has high relevance to an audience, the central route will be more effective. When a message has low relevance, the peripheral route will be more effective. This was the finding of a study that measured student attitudes toward recommended policy changes at a university. The changes would be instituted either the following year (high relevance) or in 10 years (low relevance). Students who were asked to respond to arguments about policy changes of high relevance were influenced more by the quality of the arguments (central route) than by the expertise of the source (peripheral route). In contrast, students who were asked to respond to arguments about policy changes of low relevance were influenced more by the expertise of the source than by the quality of the arguments (Petty, Cacioppo, & Goldman, 1981).

Attitudes and Behavior

Common sense tells us that if we know a person's attitudes, we can accurately predict her or his behavior. But research has shown that the relationship is not that simple. For one thing, our behavior might not always agree with our attitudes. Perhaps more surprisingly, our behavior can sometimes affect our attitudes.

The Influence of Attitudes on Behavior

Until the late 1960s, most social psychologists accepted the commonsense notion that our behavior is consistent with our attitudes. But researchers began to find that this was not always so (Cooper & Croyle, 1984). You have seen this exhibited dramatically by television evangelists who preach sexual denial while themselves engaging in a variety of extramarital sexual relations.

Though widespread interest in the inconsistency between attitudes and behaviors is only two decades old, evidence supporting the inconsistency between attitudes and behaviors appeared as early as the 1930s, when sociologist Richard LaPiere (1934) traveled with a young Chinese couple for 10,000 miles throughout the United States. They ate at 184 restaurants and stayed at 66 hotels, motels, and other places. Though anti-Chinese feelings were strong at that time, only 1 of the 250 establishments refused them service. Six months after the journey, LaPiere wrote to each of the establishments, asking whether they would serve Chinese people. Of the 128 that replied, 118

(92 percent) said they would not. LaPiere concluded that this showed that our behaviors do not always agree with our attitudes. But the study had a major flaw. The people who served them (waiters and desk clerks) may not have been the same people who responded to LaPiere's letter (owners and managers). Nonetheless, LaPiere's study stimulated interest in research on the ability of attitude questionnaires to predict real-life behavior (Dockery & Bedeian, 1989).

But what determines whether our attitudes and behaviors will be consistent? Attitude-behavior consistency is affected by *self-monitoring*. As discussed in chapter 13, high self-monitors adapt their behaviors to fit different situations and low self-monitors behave in a relatively consistent manner across situations. Low self-monitors show greater consistency between their attitudes and their behaviors than do high self-monitors (Ajzen, Timko, & White, 1982). For example, low self-monitors show a more consistent relationship between their religious attitudes and their religious behaviors. This means that low self-monitors tend to behave in accordance with their religious attitudes regardless of the situation they are in (Zanna, Olson, & Fazio, 1980).

Another factor in attitude-behavior consistency is the specificity of the attitude and the behavior. Your attitudes and behaviors are more consistent with one another when they are at similar levels of specificity (Weigel, Vernon, & Tognacci, 1974). For example, your attitude toward safe driving might not predict whether you will obey the speed limit tomorrow morning, but it will predict your general tendency, over time, to engage in safe driving behaviors, such as checking your tire pressure, using turn signals, and obeying the speed limit. And your attitude toward the environmentalist Sierra Club (a specific attitude) would be a better predictor of your active participation in Sierra Club activities (a set of specific behaviors related to that attitude) than would be your attitude toward the environment (a general attitude).

The Influence of Behavior on Attitudes

In the mid-1950s, Leon Festinger and his colleagues (Festinger, Riecken, & Schachter, 1956) were intrigued by a sect whose members believed they would be saved by aliens in flying saucers at midnight prior to the day of a prophesized worldwide flood. But neither the aliens nor the flood ever arrived. Did the members lose their faith? Some did, but many reported that their faith was strengthened. They simply concluded that the aliens had rewarded their faith by saving the world from the flood. These members simply changed their belief in order to justify their action.

The ability of the sect's members to relieve the emotional distress they experienced when the prophecy failed to come true stimulated Festinger's interest in attitude change and his development of the **cognitive dissonance theory.** Cognitive dissonance is an unpleasant state of tension associated with high physiological arousal (Elkin & Leippe, 1986; Etgen & Rosen, 1993), which is caused by the realization that one has cognitions that are inconsistent with each other. This would occur in people who believe that smoking is dangerous yet find themselves to be smokers. We are motivated to reduce the unpleasant arousal associated with cognitive dissonance by making our cognitions consistent. Thus, a smoker might stop smoking, simply discount reports that link smoking to disease, or estimate that the risk is lower in his or her own case (Lee, 1989).

The theory of cognitive dissonance has practical applications in promoting positive behaviors, such as water conservation. One study aroused cognitive dissonance in female swimmers who used their campus swimming pool by making them feel hypocritical about their showering habits. This was done by getting some of the subjects to recall times when they wasted water while showering, make a public commitment to conserve water, and urge others to take shorter showers. This inconsistency between their beliefs and their behavior was expected to arouse cognitive dissonance and, as a consequence, make them change their behavior. The results supported this, because subjects in the hypocrisy condition took significantly shorter showers than subjects not in that condition. Subjects who only were reminded that they had wasted water or who only made the public proconservation statement did not reduce the amount of water they used

cognitive dissonance theory
Leon Festinger's theory that attitude change is motivated by the desire to relieve the unpleasant state of tension caused when one holds cognitions that are inconsistent with each other.

FIGURE 17.5

Cognitive Dissonance
Subjects who were paid $1 for telling other people that a boring task was interesting later rated the task as more enjoyable than did subjects who were paid $20 for telling the same white lie (Festinger & Carlsmith, 1959).

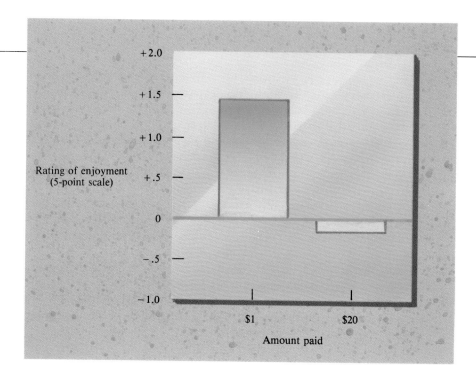

Leon Festinger (1919–1989)
"The human organism tries to establish internal harmony, consistency, or congruity among his opinions, attitudes, knowledge, and values."

self-perception theory
Daryl Bem's theory that when we are unsure of our attitudes we infer them from our own behavior.

when showering (Dickerson et al., 1992). According to cognitive dissonance theory, the subjects in the hypocrisy condition reduced their distress by changing their behavior.

The more we feel responsible for the inconsistencies between our cognitions, the stronger will be our feelings of cognitive dissonance and the more motivated we will be to change them. This was the finding of the first experimental study of cognitive dissonance (Festinger & Carlsmith, 1959). Students were asked to perform boring tasks, one of which was to arrange small spools on a tray, dump the tray, and arrange the spools again and again for half an hour. Each student was paid either $1 or $20 to tell the next student that the task was enjoyable. After the experiment was over, the students were asked to express their attitude toward the task. Their responses violated what common sense predicted. As shown in figure 17.5, those who were paid less ($1) tended to rate the task as interesting, while those who were paid more ($20) tended to rate the task as boring.

What could account for this finding? According to the theory of cognitive dissonance, the students experienced unpleasant arousal because their claim that the task was interesting did not agree with their belief that the task was boring. But those who were paid $20 to lie about the task experienced weaker cognitive dissonance because they could justify their lies by attributing them to the large payment they received. In contrast, those who were paid only $1 to lie experienced stronger cognitive dissonance because they could not attribute their lies to such a paltry sum. Consequently, those who were paid only $1 reduced the dissonance between their cognitions by changing their attitudes toward the task, rating it as more interesting than it actually was.

The cognitive dissonance interpretation of attitude change has been challenged by a theory put forth by Daryl Bem (1967). According to his **self-perception theory,** attitude change is not motivated by our need to reduce cognitive dissonance. Instead, we infer our attitudes from our behavior in the same way that we infer other people's attitudes from their behavior. When we observe people behaving under no apparent external constraints, we use the behavior to make inferences about their attitudes. Likewise, when the situation we are in does not place strong constraints on our behavior, we might infer our attitudes from our behavior. Perhaps self-perception theory explains why we tend to favor our home sports teams. Because of our proximity to them, we are more likely to attend our home teams' games, watch our home teams on television, and read about them in the newspaper. Because we perceive ourselves engaging in these behaviors, we may infer that we like our home teams.

But how does self-perception theory explain why students who were paid $1 for lying showed greater attitude change than students who were paid $20? According to Bem, the students did not experience cognitive dissonance. Instead, they determined whether their behavior was attributable to themselves or to the situation. The students who were paid $20 attributed their behavior to being paid a relatively large sum of money. They had no reason to attribute their behavior to their attitude. In contrast, the students who were paid $1 could not attribute their behavior to such a small sum of money. Consequently, those students attributed their behavior to their attitude, perhaps saying to themselves, "If I told another student that the task was interesting and I was not induced to do so by a large amount of money, then the task must have been interesting to me."

Neither cognitive dissonance theory nor self-perception theory has emerged as the clearly superior explanation of the effect of behavior on attitudes. But each seems to be superior in certain circumstances. While cognitive dissonance theory seems to be better at explaining the effect of behavior on well-defined attitudes, self-perception theory seems to be better at explaining the effect of behavior on poorly defined attitudes (Chaiken & Baldwin, 1981).

Social Prejudice

Two decades ago, third-grade teacher Jane Elliott of Riceville, Iowa, gained national attention for a demonstration she gave of the devastating psychological effects of a particular kind of attitude: social prejudice. She divided her students, who all were white, into a blue-eyed group and a brown-eyed group. On the first day of the demonstration, Elliott declared that blue-eyed people were superior to brown-eyed people. The next day, she declared that brown-eyed people were superior to blue-eyed people.

Members of the superior group were given privileges, such as sitting where they wanted to in class, going to lunch early, and staying late at recess. Members of the inferior group were made to wear identification collars and were not permitted to play with members of the superior group. Elliott reported that during the two-day demonstration, students who were made to feel inferior became depressed and performed poorly on classwork (Leonard, 1970). If prejudice could have this effect in an artificial, temporary situation, imagine the effect that prejudice has on children who are its targets in everyday life.

Prejudice is a positive or negative attitude toward a person based on her or his membership in a particular group. The behavioral component of prejudice is *discrimination*, which involves treating persons differently, whether positively or negatively, based only on their group membership. For example, a study found that students who evaluated the applications of males and females favored females for jobs that required warmth and submission and males for jobs that required shrewdness and leadership. The jobs for which males were favored were also those for which high-achieving applicants were favored. This suggests that female applicants are more apt to be discriminated against when applying for higher-status jobs (Zebrowitz, Tenenbaum, & Goldstein, 1991).

prejudice
An attitude, usually negative, toward others, based on their membership in particular groups.

Factors That Promote Prejudice

What factors account for the origin and maintenance of prejudice? As with all attitudes, learning plays an important role. Parents, peers, and the media all provide input, informing us of the supposed characteristics of particular groups. Research has been especially concerned with factors that promote prejudice. The horrors of Nazism in the 1930s and 1940s led to a major research program at the University of California at Berkeley aimed at identifying the personality characteristics associated with fascist tendencies (Adorno et al., 1950). Based on the results of tests and interviews with adult Californians, the researchers discovered what they called the *authoritarian personality*. People with an

Prejudice and Social Learning
Adult models play a powerful role in determining whether children will become prejudiced against members of other groups.

authoritarian personality tend to be obedient toward their superiors and domineering toward subordinates (*authoritarianism*), prejudiced in favor of their own groups and against other groups (*ethnocentrism*), and unwilling to accept their own faults but willing to place them on members of other groups (*projection*). Authoritarians tend to be prejudiced against other racial and religious groups, as well as other out-groups, such as AIDS victims (Cunningham et al., 1991).

Researchers have identified factors that predispose people to develop authoritarian personalities. Such people tend to have parents who gave them little affection, relied on physical punishment, and refused to accept any back talk. This pattern of child rearing induces frustration, which leads to feelings of anger. Afraid to direct this anger against their parents, children may displace it onto members of other groups, who become the targets of prejudice and serve as scapegoats. Such painful upbringings can induce low self-esteem, which is found more often in those who practice discrimination (Hogg & Sunderland, 1991). You might recognize this as a Freudian interpretation of the development of the authoritarian personality.

You may recall from earlier in the chapter that one of the most important factors in interpersonal attraction is attitude similarity. Prejudiced people perceive stereotyped groups as having attitudes that are different from those of their own groups. In fact, when there is little or no pressure to discriminate, race or ethnicity is less important than attitude similarity in determining racial or ethnic discrimination (Insko, Nacoste, & Moe, 1983). In a study of this phenomenon, subjects were asked to choose a work partner. When they were given information about another's race and attitudes, their choices were influenced more by their similarity in attitudes than by their similarity in race (Rokeach & Mezei, 1966).

Factors That Reduce Prejudice

Social psychologists are also concerned with finding ways to reduce prejudice. But this is difficult, because we are hesitant to revise our judgments that are based on stereotypes. We modify our stereotypes gradually through individual experiences and by creating subtypes to accommodate instances that we cannot easily assimilate. The latter occurs when a person says, "Some of my best friends are . . . ," which might only mean that the speaker believes there are some exceptions to the stereotypes he or she holds. As mentioned earlier, we do not necessarily revise our stereotypes after experiencing a few dramatic exceptions to them (Weber & Crocker, 1983).

In the 1950s, Gordon Allport (1954) insisted that prejudice could be reduced by increasing social contact between members of different social groups. At about the same time, in 1954, in the landmark case of *Brown v. Board of Education of Topeka*, the United States Supreme Court ruled that "separate but equal" schools did not provide black children with the same benefits as white children received. The Court's decision was influenced by research showing that segregated schools hurt the self-esteem of black children, increased racial prejudice, and encouraged whites to view blacks as inferior.

Equal-Status Contact
Contact between members of different groups will be more likely to reduce prejudice if the people have equal educational, organizational, or socioeconomic status.

For example, a study by Kenneth Clark and Mamie Phipps Clark found that black children believed white dolls were better than black ones and preferred to play with white ones (Clark & Clark, 1947). A published review of studies of self-concept in black children revealed that research findings differ according to whether the research was conducted before or after the civil rights movement of the 1960s. Earlier studies reported that blacks had lower self-esteem than whites; studies conducted after the civil rights movement have found that this is no longer true (Spurlock, 1986).

Events during the past three decades have shown that social contact alone might not produce the effects predicted by Allport and the Supreme Court. For contact between groups to reduce prejudice, the contact must be between group members of equal status (Spangenberg & Nel, 1983). If the contact is between group members of unequal status, then prejudice may actually increase. The effectiveness of equal-status contact in reducing racial prejudice was supported by a study of black children and white children who spent a week at a summer camp. The children were between 8 and 12 years old and were of equally low socioeconomic status. At the end of the week, children of both races had more positive attitudes toward children of the other race (Clore et al., 1978). Under such equal-status conditions, black children are more likely to experience enhanced self-esteem, to improve their academic performance, and to experience less discrimination from white children (Cook, 1985).

Another way to reduce prejudice is to promote intergroup cooperation (Desforges et al., 1991), a suggestion put forth earlier by Gordon Allport (1954). One approach is the **jigsaw method,** devised by Elliot Aronson. Aronson assigned elementary school children of different ethnic groups into mixed groups and gave each group different lessons to learn, which they had to combine later to solve problems. Those who participated in this study became more friendly with and less prejudiced against one another (Aronson & Bridgeman, 1979). Several studies have demonstrated the effectiveness of the jigsaw method in increasing fondness between members of different ethnic groups when compared to classrooms that did not use it (Aronson, 1987).

Unfortunately, cooperative efforts, including the jigsaw method (Moskowitz et al., 1985), do not always increase liking. If cooperative efforts fail, members of one group may attribute responsibility for this to members of the other group. And if cooperative efforts succeed, members of one group will attribute responsibility for the success to a favorable situation, rather than giving any credit to members of the other group (Brewer & Kramer, 1985). Thus, in certain situations, members of a cooperating group will be caught in a no-win, "Catch-22" situation. As you can see, though prejudice can be overcome, it is difficult to do so.

GROUP PROCESSES

In everyday life we refer to any collection of people as a "group." But social psychologists favor a narrower definition of a **group** as a collection of two or more persons who interact and have mutual influence. Examples of groups include a sorority, a softball team, and the board of trustees of your school. In the late 1940s, hoping to understand the social factors that contributed to the Great Depression, the rise of European dictatorships, and World War II, social psychologists became more interested in studying the factors that affect relationships between members of groups (Zander, 1979). This remains an important area of research in social psychology, and includes the topics of *group decision making, group performance,* and *group influence.*

Group Decision Making

As members of groups, we are often called upon to make group decisions. A family must decide which new house to buy, college administrators must decide which proposed new academic majors to approve, and government officials must decide on air pollution standards. Decisions made by groups are not simply the outcome of rational give-and-take, with the wisest decision automatically emerging. They are affected by other factors as well.

Mamie Phipps Clark and Kenneth B. Clark
Through their research, Kenneth B. Clark and Mamie Phipps Clark demonstrated the harmful effects of racial segregation. The U.S. Supreme Court cited their work in support of the landmark 1954 decision, *Brown v. Board of Education of Topeka, Kansas,* which outlawed segregation in public schools (Guthrie, 1976).

jigsaw method
Elliott Aronson's approach to reducing prejudice by having members of different groups contribute to the solution of a problem.

Elliott Aronson
"Children in the interdependent, jigsaw classrooms grow to like each other better, develop a greater liking for school, and develop greater self-esteem than children in traditional classrooms."

group
A collection of two or more persons who interact and have mutual influence on each other.

Group Polarization
One of the most important situations in which group polarization is desirable is in jury deliberations. We expect the members of juries to start with neutral positions concerning the defendant and then, after deliberation, to move to a more extreme position—deciding that the defendant is either guilty or innocent.

Group Polarization

In the 1950s, social critic William H. Whyte (1956) claimed that groups, notably those within business and government organizations, tended to make safe, compromise decisions instead of risky, extreme decisions. Whyte assumed that this tendency explained why organizations failed to be as creative and innovative as individuals. In the 1960s, his view was challenged by studies that found a tendency for group decisions to be *riskier* than decisions made by individuals who composed those groups (Stoner, 1961). This tendency became known as the *risky shift* (Wallach, Kogan, & Bem, 1962).

But later research found that groups tend to make decisions in either a risky *or* a cautious direction, rather than in only a risky direction. The tendency for groups to make more-extreme decisions than their individual members would make is called **group polarization.** For example, when groups of high school students either high or low in racial prejudice discussed racial issues, groups that were low in prejudice became even less prejudiced and groups that were high in prejudice became even more prejudiced (Myers & Bishop, 1970).

What accounts for group polarization? *Persuasive-argumentation theory* assumes that group members who initially hold a moderate position about an issue will move in the direction of the most persuasive arguments, which will eventually move the group toward either a risky or a cautious decision (Mongeau & Garlick, 1988).

group polarization
The tendency for groups to make more-extreme decisions than their members would make as individuals.

Minority Influence

Does the majority always determine the outcome of group decision making? In general, the answer is yes. This tendency becomes stronger as the size of the majority increases relative to the size of the minority (Maass & Clark, 1984). The majority has the power to convince group members to go along with its decision, in part because of its ability to criticize and socially ostracize those who dissent. Yet, under certain circumstances, minorities may influence group decisions.

If you are part of a minority and wish to influence group decisions, you should follow several well-established principles. First, you must present rational, rather than emotional, reasons for your position. This means that you must take the central, rather than peripheral, route of persuasion to make the majority consider your position. Second, you must appear absolutely confident in your position, with no wavering at all. If you are unsure of your position, majority members will discount it. Third, you must be consistent in your position over time. Again, if you are inconsistent, your opponents will

discredit you. Fourth, try to bring at least one other person over to your side. A minority of two is much more credible and influential than a minority of one. Fifth, you must be patient. Though majorities may initially dismiss minority positions, the passage of time might make them privately ponder the evidence you have provided and gradually change their positions (Nemeth, 1986). This shift may occur even among group members who continue to declare their allegiance to the majority position (Maass & Clark, 1984).

Groupthink

On January 28, 1986, the space shuttle *Challenger* exploded shortly after taking off from Cape Canaveral, killing all of the crew members and shocking the millions of television viewers excited by the presence of the first teacher-astronaut, Christa McAuliffe. The committee that investigated this tragedy reported that the explosion was caused by a faulty joint seal in one of the rocket boosters. The decision to launch the shuttle had been made despite warnings from engineers that the joint might fail in cold weather. This ill-fated decision has been attributed to *groupthink,* which in this case put safety second to currying favor with the public and Congress (Esser & Lindoerfer, 1989; Moorhead, Ference, & Neck, 1991).

The term **groupthink,** coined by psychologist Irving Janis (1918–1990), refers to a decision-making process in small, cohesive groups that places unanimity ahead of critical thinking and aims at premature consensus (McCauley, 1989). Groupthink is promoted by several factors: a charismatic leader, feelings of invulnerability, discrediting of contrary evidence, fear of criticism for disagreeing, the desire to maintain group harmony, isolation from outside influences, and disparaging outsiders as incompetent. In criticizing the decision to launch the *Challenger*, Senator John Glenn of Ohio, the first American to orbit Earth, referred to feelings of invulnerability among the officials who made the decision: "The mindset of a few people in key positions at NASA had changed from an optimistic and supersafety conscious 'can do' attitude, when I was in the program, to an arrogant 'can't fail' attitude" (Zaldivar, 1986, p. 12-A).

Janis (1983) found that groupthink has affected many momentous decisions by presidents, including President Roosevelt's failure to anticipate the attack on Pearl Harbor, President Johnson's escalation of the Vietnam War, and President Nixon's complicity in the Watergate cover-up. Janis believes that groupthink also explains the ill-fated 1961 Bay of Pigs invasion, in which Cuban exiles who had been trained by the CIA landed at the Bay of Pigs in an unsuccessful attempt to overthrow Fidel Castro.

Irving Janis (1918–1990)
"I use the term *groupthink* as a quick and easy way to refer to a mode of thinking that people engage in when they are deeply involved in a cohesive in-group, when the members' strivings for unanimity override their motivation to realistically appraise alternative courses of action."

groupthink
The tendency of small, cohesive groups to place unanimity ahead of critical thinking in making decisions.

In meetings with his advisors to decide whether to invade, President John F. Kennedy, a strong leader, had played an active role in the group discussions, the group had failed to seek outside opinions, and the group had ignored contrary information about the expected strength of Cuban resistance to the invasion.

Janis's concept of groupthink has received support from experimental studies on group decision making. Groups with directive leaders consider fewer alternatives than do groups with leaders who encourage member participation, especially if the leader expresses her or his opinion early in deliberation (Leana, 1985). Moreover, members of highly cohesive groups show little disagreement and express a high level of confidence in their decisions, yet make poorer decisions than less-cohesive groups do (Callaway & Esser, 1984). Nonetheless, the groupthink phenomenon does not always occur during group decision making and, when it does occur, it does not always produce negative outcomes (Aldag & Fuller, 1993).

Group Performance

One of the first topics to be studied by social psychologists was the influence of groups on the task performances of their members. Social psychologists have been especially interested in studying the effects of *social facilitation* and *social loafing* on performance.

Social Facilitation

social facilitation
The improvement in a person's task performance when in the presence of other people.

As mentioned earlier in the chapter, a century ago Norman Triplett (1898) observed that people performed faster when competing against other people than when competing against a clock. Two decades later psychologist Floyd Allport (1920) found that people performed a variety of tasks better when working in the same room than when working in separate rooms. Allport called the improvement in performance caused by the presence of other people **social facilitation.**

But later studies found that the presence of others may sometimes *impair* performance, a process called *social inhibition*. A review of 241 studies involving almost 24,000 subjects found that the presence of other people improves performance on simple or well-learned tasks and impairs performance on complex or poorly learned tasks (Bond & Titus, 1983). For example, in one study, children tried to balance on a teeterboard for as long as possible. Children who were highly skilled performed better in the presence of others; children who were poorly skilled performed better when alone (MacCracken & Stadulis, 1985). Even college students learning to use computers may perform better when working alone than when working in the presence of an instructor (Schneider & Shugar, 1990).

What would account for these findings? The most influential explanation for both social facilitation and social inhibition is the *drive theory* of Robert Zajonc (1965), which was derived from a motivational theory put forth by Clark Hull (1943). According to Zajonc the presence of other people increases physiological arousal, which energizes the performer's most well-learned responses to a task. For those who are good at a task, the most well-learned responses will be effective ones. Consequently, those people will perform *better* in the presence of others. In contrast, for those who are not good at a task, the most well-learned responses will be ineffective ones. Consequently, those people will perform *worse* in the presence of others. This has practical implications. When you are learning to perform a new task, whether playing golf or playing the piano, you should practice as much as possible alone before seeking to play in the presence of others.

Our drive level may increase in the presence of others because of *evaluation apprehension*. Consider a field study in which male and female runners were timed (without their being aware of it) as they ran along a 90-yard segment of a footpath. One-third of the subjects ran alone, one-third encountered a female facing them at the halfway point, and one-third encountered a female seated with her back to them at the halfway point. Only the group that encountered a female facing them (putting her in position to evaluate them) showed a significant acceleration between the first and second halves of the segment (Worringham & Messick, 1983).

Social Facilitation and Social Inhibition
Because of social facilitation, a professional bicycle racer may perform better in the presence of other people. In contrast, because of social inhibition, a child learning to ride a bicycle may perform better when practicing alone.

Social Loafing

Social facilitation is concerned with the effects of others on individual performance. But what of the effect of others on individuals performing a task with a common goal? In the 1880s, a French agricultural engineer named Max Ringelmann found that people exerted less effort when working in groups than when working alone. He had men pull on a rope attached to a meter that measured the strength of their pull. As the number of men pulling increased from one to eight, the average strength of each man's pull decreased. Ringelmann attributed this to a loss of coordination when working with other people, a phenomenon that became known as the *Ringelmann effect* (Kravitz & Martin, 1986). His study was successfully replicated almost a century later (Ingham et al., 1974).

More recently, the Ringelmann effect has been attributed to a decrease in the effort exerted by individuals when working together, a phenomenon known as **social loafing.** This supports the old saying, "Many hands make light the work." Social loafing has been demonstrated in many studies. In one experiment, high school cheerleaders cheered either alone or in pairs. Sound-level recordings found that individual cheerleaders cheered louder when alone than when cheering with a partner (Hardy & Latané, 1988).

According to the concept of *diffusion of responsibility,* social loafing occurs when group members feel anonymous; believing that their individual performances are dispensable, they are less motivated to exert their maximum effort. Because of this, committees are often inefficient in accomplishing their goals, each member expecting someone else to do the work. A good way to reduce social loafing is to convince group members that their individual efforts will be evaluated or that they will be held accountable (Weldon & Gargano, 1988). For example, when swimmers are identified, they swim faster in relays than individually; but when they are not identified, they swim faster individually than in relays (Williams et al., 1989). Because football linemen are relatively anonymous, they can be especially subject to social loafing. Years ago, legendary Ohio State University football coach Woody Hayes reduced social loafing by making his linemen less anonymous. He videotaped every play, rated each lineman's performance, and held weekly press conferences to announce the lineman of the week and to present special helmet decals to linemen for outstanding performances (Williams, Harkins, & Latané, 1981).

Social Influence

The groups we belong to influence our behavior in ways that range from subtle prodding to direct demands. We are influenced by police, bosses, clergy, parents, spouses, teachers, physicians, advertisers, politicians, salespersons, and a host of other people. Among the most important kinds of group influence are *conformity, compliance,* and *obedience.*

Conformity

Do you dress the way you do because your friends dress that way? Do you hold certain religious beliefs because your parents hold them? If you answered yes to these questions, you would be exhibiting **conformity,** which means behaving in accordance with real or imagined group pressure.

The power of conformity was demonstrated in a classic series of experiments conducted by psychologist Solomon Asch in the 1950s. In a typical experiment, a male college student who had volunteered to be a research subject was told that he would be taking part in a study of visual perception. He was seated at a table with six other "subjects," who were actually the experimenter's confederates. As illustrated in figure 17.6, the experimenter presented a series of trials in which he displayed two large white cards. One card contained three vertical lines of different lengths. The second card contained a single vertical line clearly equal in length to one of the three lines on the first card. On each of 18 trials, the participants were asked, one person at a time, to choose the line on the first card that was the same length as the line on the second card. The lengths of the lines varied from trial to trial. On the first 2 trials each confederate

Social Loafing
Because of social loafing, these people will probably exert less individual effort than they would if they pulled by themselves.

social loafing
A decrease in the individual effort exerted by group members when working together on a task.

Conformity
Our tendency to conform, whether in dress or in other ways, knows no boundaries of age.

conformity
Behaving in accordance with group expectations with little or no overt pressure to do so.

(a)

(b)

FIGURE 17.6

The Asch Study
Subjects (*a*) in one of Solomon Asch's studies (*c*) had to decide which of three lines was equal in length to another line. The photograph (*b*) shows the confusion of subject number 6 when other subjects chose the wrong line.

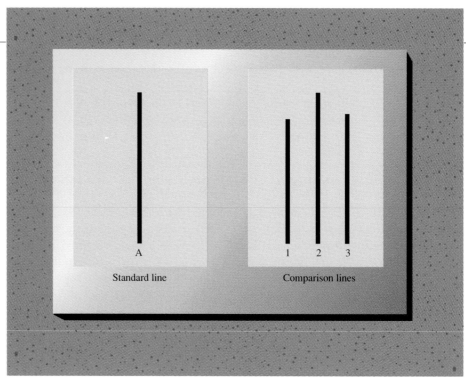

Standard line   Comparison lines

(c)

chose the correct line. But on the third trial, and on 11 of the succeeding trials, the confederates chose a line that was clearly *not* the same length as the single line. On the first few bogus trials, the subject appeared uncomfortable but usually chose the correct line. But over the course of the 12 bogus trials, the subject sometimes conformed to the erroneous choices made by the confederates.

The results indicated that, overall, the subjects conformed on 37 percent of the bogus trials. Three-quarters of the subjects conformed on at least one bogus trial. In replications of the experiment, Asch varied the number of confederates from one to fifteen persons. As illustrated in figure 17.7, he found that the subjects' tendency to conform increased dramatically until there were three confederates, with additional confederates inducing smaller increases in conformity (Asch, 1955). Though some attempts to replicate Asch's study have failed (Lalancette & Standing, 1990), his research has been successfully replicated with American (Larsen, 1990), Dutch (Vlaander & Van Rooijen, 1985), Kuwaiti (Amir, 1984), and British (Nicholson, Cole, & Rocklin, 1985) subjects.

In Asch's study, why did the subjects conform to the obviously erroneous judgments of strangers? Some claimed they really saw the lines as equal, and others assumed that the confederates knew something they did not. But their main reason for

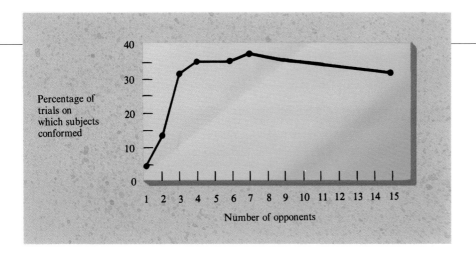

FIGURE 17.7

Conformity and Group Size
Asch (1955) found that conformity increased dramatically as the number of opponents increased to three. Adding more than three opponents did little to increase conformity.

From "Opinions and Social Pressure" by Solomon Asch. Copyright © 1955 by Scientific American, Inc. All rights reserved.

conforming was their need for social approval—they feared social rejection. The subjects found, as do many people, that it is difficult to be the lone dissenter in a group. In variations of the experiment in which one of the confederates joined the subject in dissenting, the subjects conformed on less than one-tenth, rather than on one-third, of the bogus trials (Asch, 1955). Thus, dissent is more likely when we have fellow dissenters.

Compliance

We are continually bombarded with requests. A friend might want to borrow your car. A professor might ask you to help move laboratory equipment. An advertiser might urge you to purchase a particular deodorant. The process by which a person agrees to a request that is backed by little or no threat of punishment is called **compliance.**

Years ago, it was common for salespersons to go door-to-door trying to sell encyclopedias, vacuum cleaners, or other products. Every salesperson knew that a person who complied with the small request to be permitted inside to discuss or demonstrate a product would then be more likely to comply with the larger request to purchase the product. This became known as the **foot-in-the-door technique** (Dillard, 1991).

This technique can produce extraordinary degrees of compliance. In one study, women were surveyed by telephone to ask them questions about the brand of soap they used. Three days later they were called again, as were a group of similar women who had not received the first call. This time the caller asked each woman for permission to send a team of men who would rummage through her cabinets to record the household items that she used. Of those who had complied with the first (small) request, 53 percent agreed to permit a team to visit their home. Of those who received only the second (large) request, just 22 percent agreed to permit a team to visit their home (Freedman & Fraser, 1966). The foot-in-the-door technique has proved so effective that it has even been used to promote organ donations (Carducci et al., 1989).

Why is the foot-in-the-door technique effective? Self-perception theory, which assumes that we infer our attitudes from observing our own behavior, provides an answer (Eisenberg et al., 1987). If you freely comply with a small, worthwhile request, you will view yourself as a person who has a positive attitude toward worthwhile requests. Because you wish to be consistent with your self-perception, you will be more likely to comply with other requests. Support for this explanation has been mixed (Dillard, 1990; Kilbourne, 1989).

Salespeople also know that those who refuse to purchase a particular item will be more likely to comply with a request to purchase a less expensive item. Fostering compliance by presenting a smaller request after a larger request has been denied is called the **door-in-the-face technique** (Dillard, 1991). We resort to this technique in our everyday lives in situations such as negotiating salaries (perhaps asking for several

Solomon Asch
"How, and to what extent, do social forces constrain peoples' opinions and attitudes?"

compliance
Behaving in accordance with a request that is backed by little or no threat of punishment.

foot-in-the-door technique
Increasing the likelihood that someone will comply with a request by first getting them to comply with a smaller one.

door-in-the-face technique
Increasing the likelihood that someone will comply with a request by first getting them to reject a larger one.

thousand dollars more than we expect), selling our homes (typically asking for 20 percent more than we will accept), or convincing professors to give us extra time to complete term papers (boldly asking for an extra week when we would gladly settle for two extra days). Even charities use the technique. In one study, potential volunteers were asked to commit themselves to serve as a Big Brother or Big Sister at a juvenile detention center for 2 hours a week for 2 years. After they rejected this large request, they were subjected to a much smaller request—to chaperon a group of low-income children on a single 2-hour visit to a zoo. The subjects were more likely to comply with this request than were those who had not been asked earlier to serve as a Big Brother or Big Sister (Cialdini et al., 1975).

The door-in-the-face technique depends on social norms that require that concessions offered by one negotiating party be met by concessions from the other party. The willingness of one person to reduce the size of an initial request would be a concession, imposing social pressure on the person who had refused the first request to comply with the second one (Cann, Sherman, & Elkes, 1975). The foot-in-the door technique is generally more effective than the door-in-the-face technique (Fern, Monroe, & Avila, 1986).

The Foot-in-the-Door Technique
If you have ever been in a major city or large airport, you have probably observed panhandlers use the foot-in-the-door technique. A panhandler might ask a passerby for a quarter to call home. If the person complies, the panhandler might then ask for a dollar for busfare home. A person who complies with the smaller request will be more likely to comply with the larger request than will one who is subjected only to the larger request.

Obedience

Would you assist in the cold-blooded murder of innocent people if your superior ordered you to? This question deals with the limits of **obedience**—the following of orders given by an authority. The limits of obedience were at the heart of the Nuremberg war crime trials held after World War II. The defendants were Nazis accused of crimes against humanity for their complicity in the executions of millions of innocent people during World War II, most notably the genocide of 6 million Jews. The defendants claimed that they were only following orders.

A more recent example of the dangers of blind obedience occurred in 1978. To avoid a government investigation of his practices, the Reverend Jim Jones fled California with members of his "People's Temple" cult and established "Jonestown" in Guyana. The group's norms included blind obedience to Jones. When a team led by Congressman Leo Ryan visited to investigate the cult, Jones had Ryan gunned down and then ordered cult members to commit suicide by drinking from a large bowl of Kool-Aid laced with cyanide. Those who disobeyed were shot by loyal followers, who then killed themselves. Jones killed himself with a gunshot to his head. More than 900 people, including infants and children, died in the bloodbath (Matthews et al., 1978). The suprising extent to which people will obey orders to harm others was demonstrated in the following classic study.

The Jonestown Massacre
Obedience to Jim Jones led to the murder or suicide of more than 900 members of his "People's Temple."

obedience
Following orders given by an authority.

Anatomy of a Classic Research Study:
Would You Harm Someone Just Because an Authority Figure Ordered You To?

Rationale

Are people who obey orders to hurt innocent people unusually cruel, or are most human beings susceptible to obeying such orders? This question led psychologist Stanley Milgram (1963) of Yale University to conduct one of the most famous—and controversial—of all psychology experiments.

Method

Milgram's subjects were adult men who had responded to an advertisement for volunteers to participate in a study of the effects of punishment on learning. On arriving at the laboratory, each subject was introduced to a pleasant, middle-aged man who would also participate in the experiment. In reality, the man was a confederate of the experimenter. The experimenter asked both men to draw a slip of paper out of a hat to determine who would be the "teacher" and who would be the "learner." The drawing was rigged so that the subject was always the teacher.

As shown in figure 17.8, the subject communicated with the learner over an intercom as the learner performed a memory task while strapped to an electrified chair in another room. The subject sat at a control panel with a series of switches with labels ranging from "Slight Shock" (15 volts) to

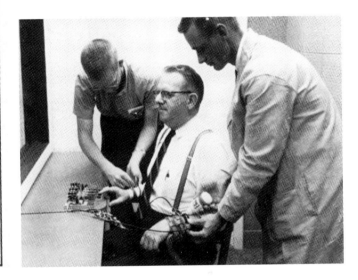

FIGURE 17.8

Milgram's Study of Obedience
Stanley Milgram advertised for people who would be willing to take part in a study of memory. The photographs show the "shock generator" that he used and a subject helping the experimenter attach electrodes to the learner's arm.

"Danger: Severe Shock" (450 volts) in 15-volt increments. The experimenter instructed the subject to administer an increasingly strong electric shock to the learner's hand whenever he made an error. At higher shock levels, the learner cried out in pain or begged the teacher to stop. Many subjects responded to the learner's distress with sweating, trembling, and stuttering. If the subject hesitated to administer a shock, the experimenter might say, "You have no other choice, you must go on," and remind the teacher that he, the experimenter, was responsible for any ill effects. Note the similarity between this incremental approach and the foot-in-the-door technique (Gilbert, 1981). This approach is also used in the training of professional torturers or "brainwashers" (Gibson, 1991; Haritos-Fatouros, 1988).

Results and Discussion

How far do you think you would have gone as the teacher in Milgram's study? Surveys of psychiatrists and Yale students had predicted that less than 2 percent of the subjects would reach the maximum level. To Milgram's surprise, two-thirds of the subjects reached the maximum level of shock, and none stopped before reaching 300 volts—the point at which the learner frantically banged on the wall and stopped answering questions. (By the way, the learner never received a shock. In fact, his responses were played on a tape recorder.)

Could the prestige of Yale University and the apparent legitimacy of a laboratory study have affected the subjects? Milgram replicated the study in a run-down office building. He did not wear a

FIGURE 17.9

Proximity and Obedience
Subjects in Milgram's studies were more willing to give maximum shocks when the subject and learner were in separate rooms. They were less willing when they sat near the learner. And they were the least willing when they had to force the learner's hand onto a shock grid.

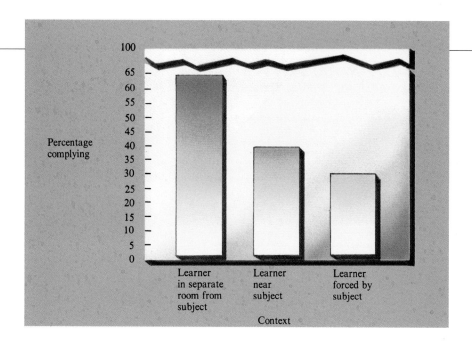

Stanley Milgram (1933–1984)
"A substantial proportion of people do what they are told to do, irrespective of the content of the act and without limitations of conscience, so long as they perceive that the command comes from a legitimate authority."

laboratory coat, and he made no reference to Yale. He obtained impressive results nonetheless. Of those who participated, 48 percent reached the maximum level of shock. Would physically separating the subject and the learner have an effect? Somewhat. Figure 17.9 shows that when the subject sat near the learner, 40 percent reached the maximum. Even when the subject had to force the learner's hand onto a shock grid, 30 percent still reached the maximum (Milgram, 1974). Milgram's original experiment has also been successfully replicated in other countries, which indicates that extreme obedience to authority is common across cultures (Shanab & Yahya, 1977).

Milgram's research has disturbing implications. The line that separates both Nazi war criminals and followers of Jim Jones from us may be thinner than we would like to believe. Many of us, given orders by someone we consider to be a legitimate authority who we assume will be responsible for our actions, might be willing to harm an innocent person. Despite the insight it provided into the nature of obedience, Milgram's research provoked criticism, most notably from Diana Baumrind (1964). She claimed that Milgram's use of deception increased distrust of psychological researchers and that his subjects' self-esteem was damaged by the realization that they might harm an innocent person simply because an authority figure ordered them to.

In response to these criticisms, Milgram reported that 84 percent of the subjects in his study were glad they had participated, that there was no evidence that any of them developed long-term emotional distress, and that the importance of the findings made the use of deception worthwhile (Milgram, 1964). Given today's increased concern with the rights of research subjects, partly in response to studies like Milgram's, it is unlikely that any researchers would replicate his studies.

PROSOCIAL BEHAVIOR

On a spring day in 1986, 1-year-old Jennifer Kroll, of West Chicago, Illinois, fell into her family's swimming pool. Jennifer's mother, after pulling Jennifer out of the pool and discovering that she was not breathing, ran outside and began screaming for help. Her screams were heard by James Patridge, who had been confined to a wheelchair since losing his legs in a land-mine explosion during the Vietnam War. Patridge responded by rolling his wheelchair toward the pool, until he encountered heavy brush, forcing him to crawl the final 20 yards. Patridge revived Jennifer by using cardiopulmonary resuscitation ("God's Hand," 1986). Patridge's heroic act led to offers of financial rewards, which he declined to accept, saying that saving Jennifer's life was reward enough.

Altruism

Patridge's act is an example of **prosocial behavior**—helping others in need. His behavior also might be an example of **altruism**—helping others without the expectation of a reward in return. But are altruistic acts ever truly selfless? Perhaps people who engage in apparently altruistic behaviors do receive some kind of immaterial rewards. The most famous person to make this claim was Abraham Lincoln. During a train trip, Lincoln looked out his window and saw several piglets drowning. He ordered the train to stop so they could be saved. When praised for his action, Lincoln discounted altruism as his motive, claiming, instead, that his act was motivated by the selfish desire to avoid a guilty conscience (Batson et al., 1986).

Social psychologists interested in the study of altruism have been especially concerned with *empathy*, the ability to feel the emotions that someone else feels. Some researchers have found that prosocial behavior associated with feelings of empathy is truly altruistic (Batson & Shaw, 1991), while prosocial behavior associated with the desire to relieve one's own distress is not (Schroeder et al., 1988). But what of people whose prosocial behavior is associated with feelings of both distress and empathy? In an experiment, subjects were empathetically aroused and led to anticipate an imminent mood-enhancing experience. The experimenters reasoned that if the motivation to help were directed toward the goal of negative-state relief, then empathetically aroused individuals who anticipate mood-enhancement should help less than those who do not. The rate of helping among high-empathy subjects was no lower when they anticipated mood enhancement than when they did not. Regardless of anticipated mood enhancement, high-empathy subjects helped more than low-empathy subjects did. The results supported the empathy-altruism hypothesis (Batson et al., 1989).

This question was also the concern of a study whose results contradicted the study just described. After completing a questionnaire that measured their level of sadness and their level of empathy for a person in need, the subjects were given the opportunity to help the person. The results indicated that the subjects' willingness to help was related more to their sadness score than to their empathy score, indicating that they acted more out of a desire to reduce their own distress than out of a desire to reduce the distress of the other person. In fact, when the subjects were given a "mood fixing" placebo that allegedly made it impossible for them to alter their moods, fewer subjects were willing

prosocial behavior
Behavior that helps others in need.

altruism
The helping of others without the expectation of a reward.

Robert Cialdini
"An observer's heightened empathy for a sufferer brings with it increased personal sadness in the observer and . . . it is the egoistic desire to relieve the sadness, rather than the selfless desire to relieve the sufferer, that motivates helping."

FIGURE 17.10

The Murder of Kitty Genovese
On returning home from work, Kitty Genovese (*1*) drove into a parking lot, noticed a man, and walked toward a police call box (*2*) but was attacked by the man. He left twice but returned to attack her again (*3*) and again (*4*). None of the 38 neighbors who reported hearing her screams intervened to save her.

negative state relief theory
The theory that we engage in prosocial behavior to relieve our own state of emotional distress at another's plight.

bystander intervention
The act of helping someone who is in immediate need of aid.

to help, even when they had high empathy scores (Cialdini et al., 1987). This study provided scientific support for the **negative state relief theory** of prosocial behavior of Robert Cialdini (Schaller & Cialdini, 1988).

Published reviews of relevant research have produced inconsistent findings in regard to the existence of altruistic helping (Carlson & Miller, 1987; Cialdini & Fultz, 1990). So it is still unclear whether our prosocial behavior is motivated more by our empathy for others or by the desire to relieve our own negative emotional states.

Bystander Intervention

Regardless of his motivation, James Patridge's rescue of Jennifer was an example of **bystander intervention,** the act of helping someone who is in immediate need of aid. Interest in the study of bystander intervention was stimulated by a widely publicized tragedy in which bystanders failed to help save a woman's life. At 3:20 A.M. on March 13, 1964, a 28-year-old woman named Kitty Genovese was returning home from her job as a bar manager. As she walked to her apartment building in the New York City borough of Queens, she was attacked by a mugger who repeatedly stabbed her. Figure 17.10 shows the site of her attack. Thirty-eight of her neighbors reported that they had been awakened by her screams and had rushed to look out their windows. The assailant left twice, returning each time to continue his attack until, finally, Kitty Genovese died.

How would you have responded had you been one of her neighbors? The neighbors' responses might surprise you. At no time during these three separate attacks, which took a half hour to complete, did any of the 38 persons who saw or heard them try to help Kitty Genovese or even call the police. When questioned by police and reporters, the witnesses gave a variety of explanations for why they had not called the police. Their reasons included feeling tired, assuming it was a lovers' quarrel, and believing that "it can't happen here" (Gansberg, 1964). The murder of Kitty Genovese gained national attention, and the apparent apathy of her neighbors was taken as a sign of the callous, impersonal nature of the residents of big cities.

But, appalled by the tragedy, social psychologists John Darley and Bibb Latané rejected this commonsense explanation as too simplistic. Instead, they conducted a series of research studies to determine the factors that affect the willingness of bystanders to intervene in emergencies. Darley and Latané found that bystander intervention involves a series of steps, which are presented in figure 17.11. The intervention process may continue through each of these steps or be halted at any one.

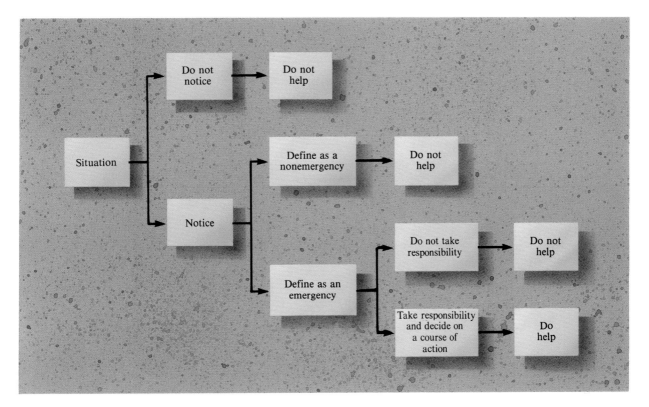

FIGURE 17.11

Steps in Bystander Intervention
According to Bibb Latané and John Darley (1968), bystanders go through certain steps before
intervening in emergencies. The possibility of intervening can be inhibited at any of these steps.

Noticing the Victim

To intervene in an emergency, you must first notice the event or the victim. James
Patridge heard the screams of Jennifer Kroll's mother, and neighbors heard the screams
of Kitty Genovese.

Interpreting the Situation as an Emergency

The same event may be interpreted as an emergency or as a nonemergency. James Patridge
was confronted by an unambiguous situation. He interpreted the screams of Jennifer's
mother as a sign that there was an emergency. In contrast, there was some ambiguity in
Kitty Genovese's situation. In fact, when there is an apparent confrontation between a
man and a woman, bystanders tend to assume that it is a lovers' quarrel rather than a true
emergency (Shotland & Straw, 1976). Because almost all of Kitty Genovese's neighbors
interpreted the situation as a nonemergency, at that point there was little likelihood
that she would be helped.

Taking Personal Responsibility

After interpreting the situation as an emergency, Patridge took responsibility for intervening. But not even those who may have interpreted Kitty Genovese's situation as an
emergency took responsibility for helping her. Darley and Latané discovered a surprising
reason for this. Contrary to what you might expect, as the number of bystanders *increases*, the likelihood of a bystander's intervening *decreases*. Note that this is true only
in situations involving strangers. In emergencies involving highly cohesive groups of
people, the probability of intervention will increase as the number of bystanders increases (Rutkowski, Gruder, & Romer, 1983).

Noticing the Victim
Two Indianapolis firefighters are
comforted by a third after one of them
broke his arm trying to catch the
other, who had fallen from a height of
30 feet from a blazing building. Both
of the injured men survived.

FIGURE 17.12

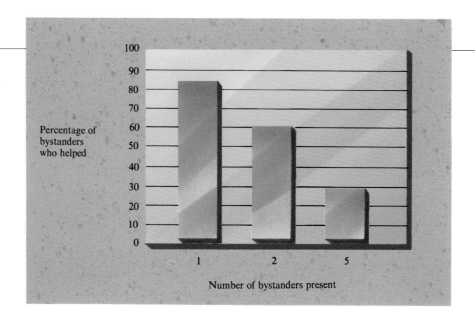

Diffusion of Responsibility
Darley and Latané (1968) found that
as the number of bystanders increased,
the likelihood of any of them going to
the aid of a woman apparently having
an epileptic seizure decreased.

Bibb Latané
"Even when bystanders to an
emergency cannot see or be
influenced by each other, the more
bystanders who are present, the less
likely any one bystander will be to
intervene and provide aid."

The influence of the number of bystanders on bystander intervention was demonstrated in an early study by Darley and Latané (1968). They had college students meet to discuss the problems they faced in attending school in New York City. Each student was led to a room and told to communicate with other students over an intercom. The students were told that there were two, three, or six students taking part in the discussion, but all of the other students were the experimenter's confederates; in fact, the remarks of the other students were tape recordings. Early in the session the subject (the nonconfederate) heard another student apparently having an epileptic seizure and crying out for help.

Figure 17.12 shows that of those subjects who believed they were a lone bystander, 85 percent sought help for the stricken person. Of those who believed they were one of two bystanders, 62 percent sought help. And of those who believed they were one of five bystanders, only 31 percent sought help. One reason for this is the diffusion of responsibility: As the number of bystanders increases, the responsibility felt by each one decreases. So, the students who were exposed to a mock epileptic seizure felt less responsibility for helping the victim when they believed other bystanders were present. In contrast to Kitty Genovese's neighbors, who assumed that other neighbors had been awakened, Patridge may have assumed that no one else could intervene, leaving him with the responsibility.

Deciding on a Course of Action

The decision to intervene depends, in part, on whether the bystander feels competent to meet the demands of the situation (Clark & Word, 1974). Patridge decided to wheel himself toward the pool and then crawl to it. Because Patridge had training in cardiopulmonary resuscitation, while Jennifer Kroll's mother did not, he felt more competent to try to revive Jennifer. Though none did so until after Kitty Genovese was dead, her neighbors might have at least considered calling the police when they heard her screams. A study that interviewed people who had intervened in violent crimes, such as muggings and armed robberies, found that they were usually larger and stronger than those who did not. Moreover, they typically were better trained to cope with crimes and emergencies, having had significantly more police training and emergency medical training. Thus, they felt more competent to help (Huston et al., 1981).

Expertise and Bystander Intervention
In dangerous situations, bystanders will be more likely to intervene when they feel competent to do so. A person specially trained to rescue people trapped by floodwater, such as this park ranger, will be more likely to intervene than will someone who is not.

Taking Action

Patridge propelled himself to Jennifer's side and revived her. Kitty Genovese's neighbors could have yelled, helped her, or called police. Patridge believed the potential benefits of intervention outweighed the potential costs. As discussed in chapter 11, Abraham Maslow assumed that people are more motivated by the need for safety than by the need for self-esteem. This might explain why bystanders who believe that intervening in an emergency would place them in danger (as some may have believed in the case of Kitty Genovese) are less likely to intervene, even if failure to do so would lower their self-esteem. In fact, people who are more motivated by the need for safety are less likely to intervene in dangerous emergencies, such as explosions, than those more motivated by the need for self-esteem (Wilson & Petruska, 1984).

The characteristics of the victim also influence bystander intervention. One of the most important characteristics is the degree to which the victim appears responsible for his or her predicament. You might recognize this as an example of social attribution. If we make dispositional attributions for a person's predicament, we will be less likely to help than if we make situational attributions for it (Weiner, 1980). We are more likely to help people in need when we perceive their situation to be the result of uncontrollable factors, such as a sudden illness, than when we perceive it to be the result of controllable factors, such as personal recklessness (Schmidt & Weiner, 1988).

As you can now appreciate, bystander intervention is not simply the product of a particular personality type. Instead, it is a complex process that depends on the interaction between characteristics of the victim, the bystander, and the situation.

Raoul Wallenberg (1912–?)
During World War II, Raoul Wallenberg, a Christian Swedish diplomat, risked his life to help thousands of Jews escape from Hungary and avoid being murdered by Nazis. He took personal responsibility for rescuing them, had the skill to do so, and dared to take action. After the war, he was captured by the Soviet Union. He is presumed to have died in custody.

AGGRESSION

As much as human beings are capable of prosocial behavior, they are, unfortunately, just as capable of antisocial behavior. The most extreme form of antisocial behavior is **aggression,** which is behavior aimed at causing harm to another person. American society is marked by frequent acts of extreme aggression. A survey found that, in the United States, a person is murdered about every half hour (Siegel, 1983). What accounts for the prevalence of such violent acts?

aggression
Behavior aimed at causing harm to another person.

Aggressive Rituals
According to Konrad Lorenz, human beings lack the inborn ritualistic forms of aggression that generally prevent animals from trying to injure or kill members of their own species.

Catharsis and Violence
According to Freud, both the participants and the spectators at this wrestling match should show a decrease in their tendencies toward violence as the result of catharsis. But research has found that, on the contrary, watching or taking part in violence will increase one's tendency to engage in it.

Konrad Lorenz (1903–1989)
"Real beasts of prey, such as lions and wolves, that live in packs, have developed inhibitions because of their natural weapons. These inhibitions prevent their using these instruments of death against their own kind. . . . Mankind is different."

Theories of Aggression

One class of theories views aggression as the product of physiology. A second class of theories views aggression as the product of experience.

Aggression as the Product of Physiology

The earliest theories of aggression claimed that it was instinctive. An *instinct* is an inborn tendency, unaffected by learning, to engage in a relatively complex behavior that characterizes members of a species—such as nest building in birds. After observing the extraordinary violence of World War I, Sigmund Freud concluded that human aggression is caused by an instinct that he called *Thanatos* (Greek for "death"). According to Freud, Thanatos causes a buildup of aggressive energy, which must be released periodically through a process called *catharsis*. This would prevent outbursts of extreme violence. You might experience catharsis by playing football, field hockey, or another aggressive sport.

Nobel prize-winning ethologist Konrad Lorenz (1966) agreed with Freud that we have an instinct for aggression. He claimed that all animals have a powerful aggressive drive that, like the sex drive, promotes the survival of their species. But because animals have evolved natural weapons such as fangs and claws that can kill, they have also evolved ritualistic behaviors to inhibit aggression and prevent unnecessary injuries and deaths. In contrast, because human beings have not evolved natural weapons that can kill, they have not evolved ritualistic behaviors to inhibit aggression against their own species. As a consequence, human beings are less inhibited in using artificial weapons such as clubs, spears, guns, and missiles against one another. Lorenz, like Freud, believed that outbursts of aggression could be avoided only by providing outlets for the cathartic release of aggressive energy through means such as sports (Leakey & Lewin, 1977). But research has failed to support the belief that aggression can be reduced through catharsis. In fact, people who engage in aggression usually become *more* likely to engage in it (Geen, Stonner, & Shope, 1975).

The relatively new field called *sociobiology* (discussed in chapter 11) assumes there is a strong hereditary basis for aggression and other social behaviors (Wilson, 1975). Studies of twins have provided evidence supporting this. Psychologists who study twins might compare the aggressiveness of identical twins reared together to the aggressiveness of fraternal twins reared together. These researchers assume that if heredity plays a role in aggression, identical twins (who are genetically identical) will be more similar in aggressiveness than will fraternal twins (who are no more alike genetically than ordinary siblings). Twin studies have, indeed, found this, providing evidence for the hereditary basis of aggressiveness (Rushton et al., 1986). Of course, this does not rule out the possibility that identical twins are more similar in aggressiveness because they are treated more alike than fraternal twins are.

What might be the physiological means by which heredity affects aggression? Several brain structures play important roles, particularly structures of the limbic system, including the amygdala and the hypothalamus (Weiger & Bear, 1988). Another factor is the sex hormone testosterone. Violent criminals have higher levels of testosterone than do nonviolent criminals (Rubin, Reinisch, & Haskett, 1981). Levels of anger in elderly men correlate positively with their testosterone levels (Gray, Jackson, & McKinlay, 1991). Athletes who use anabolic steroids, which are synthetic derivatives of testosterone, become more aggressive (Gregg & Rejeski, 1990). Castration of male sex offenders lowers testosterone levels and reduces sex drive and sex-crime recidivism (Bradford, 1988). And male and female children whose mothers received a synthetic form of testosterone during pregnancy are more aggressive than are their same-sex siblings who were not exposed to the synthetic hormone prenatally (Reinisch, 1981).

Aggression as the Product of Experience

While some researchers look to hereditary factors, most look to life experiences as the main determinants of aggression. In the late 1930s, a team of behaviorists concluded that aggression is caused by frustration (Dollard et al., 1939). This became known as the **frustration-aggression hypothesis.** As noted in chapter 16, we experience frustration when we are blocked from reaching a goal. But the frustration-aggression hypothesis is an inadequate explanation of aggression, because experiences other than frustration can cause aggression, and frustration does not always lead to it.

The inadequacies of the frustration-aggression hypothesis led psychologist Leonard Berkowitz to develop the *revised frustration-aggression hypothesis.* According to Berkowitz (1974), frustration does not directly provoke aggression. Instead, it directly provokes anger or another unpleasant emotion, such as anxiety or depression. The unpleasant emotion, in turn, will provoke aggression—particularly when stimuli (such as guns) that have been associated with aggression are present. Berkowitz demonstrated this in a study in which male college students gave electric shocks to other students to induce feelings of anger in the shock recipients. When students who had received shocks were given the opportunity to give shocks to those who had shocked them, they gave more shocks when an aggressive stimulus such as a revolver, rather than a neutral stimulus such as a badminton racket, was left on the table (Berkowitz & LePage, 1967). Though some studies have failed to support the revised frustration-aggression hypothesis (Buss, Booker, & Buss, 1972), many have found that anger in the presence of aggressive stimuli does tend to provoke aggression (Rule & Nesdale, 1976). Moreover, unexpected frustrations, because they evoke stronger unpleasant emotions, will be more likely to provoke aggression than will expected frustrations (Berkowitz, 1989).

As described in chapter 7, much of our behavior is the product of social learning—learning by observing the behavior of others. Aggression is no exception to this. We may learn to be aggressive by observing people who act aggressively. In a classic experiment by Albert Bandura, children in a nursery school who observed an adult punching an inflated "Bobo doll" were more likely to engage in similar aggression against the Bobo doll than were children who had not observed the aggressive model (Bandura, Ross, & Ross, 1963). This is illustrated in figure 17.13. The observational learning of aggression is promoted by observing models who are rewarded for aggression and is inhibited by observing models who are punished for aggression. Today social-learning theory is a widely studied and widely accepted theory of aggression.

Television and Aggression

As you might expect, social-learning theory predicts that televised violence will promote real-life violence. An early study of the effects of televised violence presented excerpts of the violent television show "The Untouchables" or nonviolent track-and-field events to children between 5 and 9 years old. Children who viewed the violent scenes were more likely to act aggressively toward another child and for a longer time (Liebert & Baron, 1972). In a more recent study, second- and third-grade boys who watched a violent television program were later more violent during a game of floor hockey than were boys who had watched a nonviolent television program (Josephson, 1987). Because children as young as 4 years old typically watch 4 hours of television a day (Singer, 1983), findings such as these have provoked concern.

Concern about the effects of televised violence on aggression is not new. It has existed ever since television became a popular medium in the 1950s (Carpenter, 1955).

frustration-aggression hypothesis
The assumption that frustration causes aggression.

Leonard Berkowitz
"Frustrations generate aggressive inclinations to the degree that they arouse negative affect."

FIGURE 17.13

Observational Learning of Aggression
Bandura, Ross, and Ross (1963) found that children exposed to an aggressive adult model acted more aggressively themselves.

Television and Aggression
Researchers have yet to reach a consensus on the extent of the effects of televised violence on real-life aggression.

The first congressional report on the effects of television was a 1954 report on its impact on juvenile delinquency. Since then, reports on the social effects of television have appeared every few years. Major reports, sponsored by the National Institute of Mental Health, on the social effects of television appeared in 1972 and 1982. Both reports found that violence on television led to aggressive behavior by children and adolescents and recommended a decrease in televised violence (Walsh, 1983). But critics of these reports claimed that the results of laboratory experiments on the effects of televised violence might not generalize to real life and that field studies on the effects of televised violence failed to control all of the other variables that might encourage violence (Fisher, 1983).

Psychologists themselves have not reached a consensus on the effects of televised violence. One published review found only a weak relationship between televised violence and aggression (Freedman, 1986). Another finding is that the relationship between televised violence and real-life aggression is bidirectional. This means that televised violence makes people more aggressive *and* that people who are aggressive choose to watch more televised violence (Wiegman, Kuttschreuter, & Baarda, 1992). Still another possibility is that both television watching and aggressiveness are influenced by a third factor—heredity. Though there is no "television-watching gene," the number of hours of television watched by children aged 3, 4, and 5 years has a hereditary basis (Plomin et al., 1990). Perhaps an inherited tendency to seek stimulation accounts for the positive correlation between television watching and aggressiveness. Of course, without additional evidence, this remains just a hypothesis.

Group Violence

In the year A.D. 59, opposing fans rioted at the Pompeii amphitheater during a gladiatorial contest, prompting the Roman Senate to ban such contests in Pompeii for 10 years. The twentieth century has also seen its share of riots instigated by athletic events.

Group Violence
Rival British and Italian soccer fans
rioted at a 1985 game in Brussels,
leaving dozens dead and hundreds
injured. Knowing the factors that
promote group violence may help us
prevent incidents like this in the
future.

In 1985 a riot at a soccer game in Brussels killed 38 people and injured more than 400 (Bredemeier & Shields, 1985).

What makes normally peaceful individuals become violent when they are in groups? We are usually aware of our own thoughts, feelings, and perceptions and are concerned about being socially evaluated. But, when in groups, we may become less aware of ourselves and less concerned about being socially evaluated. Leon Festinger named this process **deindividuation** (Festinger, Pepitone, & Newcomb, 1952). As the result of deindividuation, our behavior might no longer be governed by our social norms, which in turn can lead to the loss of normal restraints against undesirable behavior, making us more likely to participate in group violence. Moreover, the anonymity provided by group membership can make us less concerned with the impression we make on other people, because we feel less accountable for our own actions (Prentice-Dunn & Rogers, 1982).

Deindividuation is more likely when the group is large and when the group members feel anonymous and are emotionally aroused. This means that large groups of people, wearing masks, uniforms, or disguises and aroused by drugs, dancing, chanting, or oratory, will be more likely to engage in violence. These factors account for the use of hooded uniforms and frenzied meetings by members of the Ku Klux Klan.

deindividuation
The process by which group members become less aware of themselves as individuals and less concerned about being socially evaluated.

THINKING ABOUT *Psychology*

DOES PORNOGRAPHY CAUSE SEXUAL AGGRESSION?

One of the most distressing social statistics concerning aggression is that one American woman in eight is raped during her lifetime, usually before the age of 18 ("Survey Finds Most Rape Victims Are Minors," 1992). Women in colleges and universities are not

Former Surgeon General C. Everett Koop
"Pornography that portrays sexual aggression as pleasurable for the victim increases the acceptance of the use of coercion in sexual relations."

pornography
Sexually explicit material intended to incite sexual arousal.

immune to sexual aggression, including date rape. A sample of 6,159 male and female college students found that 27.5 percent of the women reported being raped or sexually assaulted and 7.7 percent of the men reported committing or attempting rape (Koss, Gidycz, & Wisniewski, 1987). This high incidence of sexual aggression has prompted researchers to study the factors that might promote it. One of the most controversial and extensively studied of these factors is **pornography,** which is sexually explicit material intended to incite sexual arousal.

GOVERNMENT REPORTS ON PORNOGRAPHY AND AGGRESSION

In 1970, the President's Commission on Obscenity and Pornography concluded that exposure to pornography does not make men likely to commit sexual aggression. More recently, in ceremonies associated with the signing of the Child Protection Act of 1984, President Reagan announced his intention to sponsor a study of the effects of pornography. In 1985, he appointed an eleven-member commission headed by Attorney General Edwin Meese—the Attorney General's Commission on Pornography.

The commission's report, published in 1986, concluded that exposure to either violent or nonviolent pornography may cause aggression against women. Two members of the commission, Ellen Levine, editor of *Woman's Day*, and Judith Becker, a Columbia University psychologist, wrote a dissenting opinion in which they claimed that the report incorrectly characterized the correlational evidence as supportive of a *causal* link between pornography and sexual aggression (Wilcox, 1987). You will recall that it is important to distinguish between causation and correlation when interpreting research findings. It is conceivable that pornography causes sexual aggression, that men who commit sexual aggression may be more likely to seek pornography, or that some men may have personal characteristics that make them enjoy pornography *and* commit sexual aggression.

The results of a 1986 conference sponsored by Surgeon General C. Everett Koop, "Report of the Surgeon General's Workshop on Pornography and Public Health" (Koop, 1987), were published several months after the attorney general's report. Unlike Meese, Koop, who also was morally appalled by pornography (but committed to objective scientific discourse), relied on testimony from some of the most eminent researchers in the field. The workshop met with opposition from both ends of the political spectrum.

Liberals attacked the workshop as a threat to civil liberties; conservatives attacked it as a threat to the nation's moral fiber.

Based on the data presented at the workshop, Koop concluded that children and adolescents who participate in the production of pornography experience adverse, enduring effects, such as eventual involvement in child prostitution. He also concluded that rape portraying sexual aggression as pleasurable for the victim increases the acceptance of coercion in sexual relations and *might* increase the incidence of rape by promoting the view that women enjoy being forced to have sex. Koop's report, unlike Meese's, did not conclude that nonviolent pornography *causes* aggression against women.

EMPIRICAL RESEARCH ON PORNOGRAPHY AND AGGRESSION

What kinds of research studies served as the bases for the Meese and Koop reports? Many have been conducted by Neil Malamuth, Edward Donnerstein, and their colleagues. In one experiment, male and female college students read erotic passages that portrayed either consenting sex or rape. The rape victim was portrayed either as being distressed or as enjoying herself and having an orgasm. The subjects reported that they were more sexually aroused by the portrayal of consenting sex than by the portrayal of rape. But when the rape victim was portrayed as having an orgasm, the subjects reported that they were as sexually aroused as they were by the portrayal of consenting sex. Females were more aroused when the victim experienced orgasm and no pain; males were more aroused when the victim experienced orgasm and pain. These results indicate that portrayals of violent sexual attacks might condition people, especially males, to associate sex with aggression. This association might promote sexual attacks (Malamuth, Heim, & Feshbach, 1980) as indicated by the following research study.

Neil Malamuth
"The mass media can contribute to a cultural climate that is more accepting of aggression against women."

Anatomy of a Contemporary Research Study:
Do Pornographic Films Promote Aggression against Women?

Rationale

Another experiment examined several factors related to violence against women induced by erotic films (Donnerstein & Berkowitz, 1981). The study considered whether the films were violent or not and whether the victim enjoyed being raped.

Method

Eighty male undergraduates were randomly assigned to one of four conditions in which they watched one of four films: a talk-show interview (neutral film); a young couple making love (erotic film); a woman enjoying being raped by two men (positive aggressive film); and a woman suffering during a rape by two men (negative aggressive film). Half of the men in each group were also insulted and angered by women confederates of the experimenter who pretended to be subjects in the study, and half were not. The men were given the opportunity to retaliate against the confederates by giving them electric shocks when they made mistakes on a memory task. The intensity of the shock was used as a measure of aggression.

Results and Discussion

As shown in figure 17.14, the results indicated that men who had seen the neutral or nonviolent erotic film displayed relatively little aggression. Both angered and nonangered men who had seen the film of the rape in which the woman enjoyed it displayed higher levels of aggression. And, of the men who had seen the rape during which the woman suffered, those who had been angered behaved more aggressively than those who had not. These results might also hold outside of the laboratory, because men who are sexually aroused by portrayals of sexual aggression against women are more likely to report that they would attack women (Malamuth, 1986).

Some research findings support the conclusions of the attorney general's commission (Page, 1990), but most findings are more consistent with those of the surgeon general's commission. There is little evidence that nonviolent pornography causes sexual aggression against women. There is somewhat

FIGURE 17.14

Pornography and Aggression
The results of the study by Donnerstein and Berkowitz (1981) showed that men who had been provoked and then watched an aggressive erotic film in which a woman acted as though she enjoyed being raped behaved the most aggressively toward women.

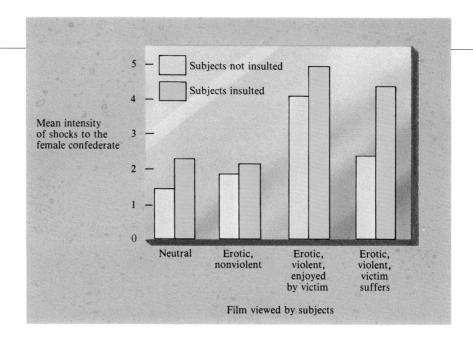

stronger evidence that violent pornography, especially when it supports the myth that women enjoy being raped, causes aggression against women (Donnerstein & Linz, 1986). But this conclusion is based mainly on the results of laboratory experiments that have considered only short-term effects of violent pornography and that might not generalize outside of the laboratory. Of course, whether violent erotic movies, such as the "teenage slasher" movies of the past decade, cause aggression against women is a scientific question. Whether such films are harmful in other ways is a legal, moral, social, and political dilemma.

SUMMARY

SOCIAL COGNITION

Social psychology is the field that studies social relationships. The process by which we determine the causes of social behavior is called social attribution. When you decide that a person is responsible for her or his own behavior, you are making a dispositional attribution. And when you decide that circumstances are responsible for a person's behavior, you are making a situational attribution.

Harold Kelley identified three factors that interact in determining whether we make dispositional or situational attributions: consistency, distinctiveness, and consensus. Bernard Weiner's more ambitious theory of attribution looks at the interaction of the internal-external, stable-unstable, and controllable-uncontrollable dimensions. Major biases in social attribution include the fundamental attribution error, the actor-observer bias, and the self-serving bias.

Impression formation is the process by which we make judgments about the personal characteristics of people. This often depends on social schemas, which comprise the presumed characteristics of a role, an event, a person, or a group. Changes in our schemas depend on the interaction of accommodation and assimilation. Our first impressions play an important role in impression formation, in some cases creating a self-fulfilling prophecy.

SOCIAL ATTRACTION

Psychologists interested in studying social attraction are concerned with the factors that make us like or love other people. Liking depends on the factors of proximity, familiarity, physical attractiveness, similarity, and self-disclosure. Researchers who study love distinguish between passionate love and companionate love. According to Ellen Bersheid and Elaine Hatfield, romantic love depends on cultural support for the concept of romantic love, a state of physiological arousal, and the presence of an appropriate person to love. Among the most important factors in promoting love are similarity, self-disclosure, and equity.

SOCIAL ATTITUDES

Attitudes are evaluations of ideas, events, objects, or people. Attitudes have emotional, cognitive, and behavioral components. Classical conditioning, operant conditioning, and social-learning theory explain how attitudes are learned. We are often subjected to persuasive messages aimed at getting us to change our attitudes. Persuasive messages can take a central route or a peripheral route. Persuasiveness depends on the message, the source, and the audience.

Sources that are more credible and attractive are more persuasive. Under certain circumstances, two-sided messages will be more effective than one-sided messages. The intelligence level of the receiver and the relevance of the message also determine the effectiveness of persuasive messages. But our attitudes might not always accurately predict our behavior. Moreover, our behavior can sometimes affect our attitudes, a phenomenon that is explained by cognitive dissonance theory and self-perception theory.

Prejudice is a positive or negative attitude toward others based on their membership in particular groups. The behavioral component of prejudice is discrimination. Among the important factors promoting prejudice are stereotypes and the authoritarian personality. Prejudice can be reduced when there is equal-status contact and intergroup cooperation.

GROUP PROCESSES

Psychologists interested in social influence study the effects of social relationships on thinking, feeling, and behaving. Decision making in groups can be affected by group polarization, which is the tendency for groups to make more-extreme decisions than their members would make as individuals. Group decisions are also characterized by groupthink, in which group members place greater emphasis on unanimity than on critical thinking. Minorities can affect group decisions by being rational, confident, consistent, and patient.

Groups can affect task performance through social facilitation, which is the improvement of performance caused by the presence of other people, and social inhibition, which is the impairment of performance caused by the presence of other people. Our performance can also be affected by social loafing, which is the tendency of individuals to exert less effort when performing in groups.

Human relationships are characterized by conformity, compliance, and obedience. Conformity is behaving in accordance with group norms with little or no overt pressure to do so. Compliance is agreeing to a request that is backed by little or no threat of punishment. Two of the chief techniques for inducing compliance are the foot-in-the-door technique and the door-in-the-face technique. Obedience is following orders given by an authority. Stanley Milgram found that most people are all too willing to harm other people when ordered to do so by a legitimate authority figure.

PROSOCIAL BEHAVIOR

Prosocial behavior involves helping others in need. Altruism is helping others without the expectation of a reward in return. Some researchers have found that true altruism occurs only when prosocial behavior is done out of empathy, rather than out of a desire to reduce one's own distress at the plight of another person. Other researchers have found, instead, that prosocial behavior is never truly altruistic—it always depends on the desire to reduce our own distress. Psychologists who study prosocial behavior are especially concerned with bystander intervention, the act of helping someone who is in immediate need of aid. Bystander intervention depends on noticing the victim, interpreting the situation as an emergency, taking personal responsibility, deciding on a course of action, and taking action to help.

AGGRESSION

Aggression is behavior aimed at causing harm to someone else. Some theories view aggression as inborn. Sigmund Freud and Konrad Lorenz believed that aggression is instinctive, meaning that we have no choice but to engage in it periodically. Today most researchers reject the instinct theory of aggression but still study hereditary influences on it. Most researchers look to life experiences as the main determinants of aggression. According to the frustration-aggression hypothesis, aggression becomes more likely after we have been blocked from reaching a goal. According to social-learning theory, we may learn to be aggressive by observing people who act aggressively. Group violence is promoted by deindividuation, which is the loss of self-awareness and the feeling of anonymity that comes from being part of a group. The past two decades have seen a yet-unresolved controversy about the effects of televised violence on real-life aggression.

THINKING ABOUT PSYCHOLOGY: DOES PORNOGRAPHY CAUSE SEXUAL AGGRESSION?

Pornography is sexually explicit material intended to provoke sexual arousal. Reports by the attorney general and the surgeon general of the United States published in 1986 and 1987 disagree about the effects of pornography on sexual aggression. Perhaps the only generally accepted finding is that violent pornography is more likely than nonviolent pornography to affect sexual aggression.

IMPORTANT CONCEPTS

RECOMMENDED READINGS

FOR GENERAL WORKS ON SOCIAL BEHAVIOR

Aron, A., & Aron, E. N. (1985). *The heart of social psychology.* Lexington, MA: Lexington Books.

Aronson, E. (1992). *The social animal.* (6th ed.). New York: W. H. Freeman.

Aronson, E., Ellsworth, P., Carlsmith, J. M., & Gonzalez, M. (1990). *Methods of research in social psychology.* New York: McGraw-Hill.

Bond, M. H. (Ed.). (1988). *The cross-cultural challenge to social psychology.* Newbury Park, CA: Sage Publications.

Deaux, K., Dane, F., & Wrightsman, L. (1993). *Social psychology in the nineties.* Belmont, CA: Brooks/Cole.

Festinger, L. (Ed.). (1980). *Retrospective on social psychology.* New York: Oxford University Press.

Gergen, K. J., & Gergen, M. M. (Eds.). (1984). *Historical social psychology.* Hillsdale, NJ: Erlbaum.

Gilmour, R., & Duck, S. (Eds.). (1980). *The development of social psychology.* London: Academic Press.

Jackson, J. M. (1988). *Social psychology, past and present.* Hillsdale, NJ: Erlbaum.

Leary, M. R. (Ed.). (1989). *The state of social psychology: Issues, themes, and controversies.* Newbury Park, CA: Sage Publications.

Lippa, R. A. (1994). *Introduction to social psychology* (2nd ed.). Pacific Grove, CA: Brooks/Cole.

Moghaddam, F. M., Taylor, D. M., & Wright, S. C. (1992). *Social psychology in cross-cultural perspective.* New York: W. H. Freeman.

Patnoe, S. (1988). *A narrative history of experimental social psychology: The Lewin tradition.* New York: Springer.

Triandis, H. C. (1994). *Social behavior and culture.* New York: McGraw-Hill.

FOR MORE ON SOCIAL COGNITION

Fiske, S. T., & Taylor, S. E. (1991). *Social cognition.* New York: McGraw-Hill.

Goffman, E. (1959). *The presentation of self in everyday life.* Garden City, NY: Doubleday.

Graham, S., & Folkes, V. S. (Eds.). (1990). *Attribution theory: Applications to achievement, mental health, and interpersonal conflict.* Hillsdale, NJ: Erlbaum.

Harvey, J. H., Orbuch, T. L., & Weber, A. L. (Eds.). (1991). *Attributions, accounts, and close relationships.* New York: Springer-Verlag.

Hewstone, M. (1989). *Causal attribution: From cognitive processes to collective beliefs.* New York: Basil Blackwell.

Higgins, R. L., Snyder, C. R., & Berglas, S. (1990). *Self-handicapping.* New York: Plenum.

Hinton, P. (1993). *The psychology of interpersonal perception.* New York: Routledge.

Jones, E. E. (1990). *Interpersonal perception.* New York: W. H. Freeman.

Jones, R. A. (1977). *Self-fulfilling prophecies: Social, psychological, and physiological effects of expectancies.* Hillsdale, NJ: Erlbaum.

Schlenker, B. S., & Weigold, M. F. (1980). *Impression management: The self-concept.* Melbourne, FL: Krieger.

Snyder, M. (1987). *Public appearances/private realities: The psychology of self-monitoring.* New York: W. H. Freeman.

Weary, G., & Harvey, J. H. (1989). *Attribution.* New York: Springer-Verlag.

Weiner, B. (1986). *An attributional theory of motivation and emotion.* New York: Springer-Verlag.

Zebrowitz, L. A. (1990). *Social perception.* Pacific Grove, CA: Brooks/Cole.

FOR MORE ON SOCIAL ATTRACTION

Brehm, S. S. (1992). *Intimate relationships.* New York: McGraw-Hill.

Derlega, V. J., Metts, S., Petronio, S., & Margulis, S. T. (1993). *Self-disclosure.* Newbury Park, CA: Sage Publications.

Fromm, E. (1956). *The art of loving.* New York: Harper & Row.

Hatfield, E., & Rapson, R. L. (1993). *Love, sex, and intimacy: Their psychology, biology, and history.* New York: HarperCollins.

Hatfield, E., & Sprecher, S. (1986). *Mirror, mirror: The importance of looks in everyday life.* Albany: State University of New York Press.

Hatfield, E., & Walster, G. W. (1985). *A new look at love.* Lanham, MD: University Press of America.

Hendrick, S. S., & Hendrick, C. (1992). *Liking, loving, and relating.* Pacific Grove, CA: Brooks/Cole.

Hendrick, S. S., & Hendrick, C. (1992). *Romantic love.* Newbury Park, CA: Sage Publications.

Sternberg, R. J. (1988). *The triangle of love: Intimacy, passion, commitment.* New York: Basic Books.

FOR MORE ON SOCIAL ATTITUDES

Adorno, T. W., Frenkel-Brunswik, E., Levinson, D. J., & Sanford, R. N. (1950/1982). *The authoritarian personality.* New York: W. W. Norton.

Ajzen, I. (1989). *Attitudes, personality, and behavior.* Chicago: Dorsey.

Aronson, E. (1987). Teaching students what they think they already know about prejudice and desegregation. In V. P. Makosky (Ed.), *The G. Stanley Hall Lecture Series* (Vol. 7, pp. 69–84). Washington, DC: American Psychological Association.

Aronson, E. (1991). *The age of propaganda: The everyday use and abuse of persuasion.* New York: W. H. Freeman.

Bar-Tal, D., Grauman, C. T., Kruglanski, A. W., & Stroebe, W. (1989). *Stereotyping and prejudice.* New York: Springer-Verlag.

Bethlehem, D. (1985). *A social psychology of prejudice.* New York: St. Martin's Press.

Cialdini, R. B. (1994). *Influence: The new psychology of modern persuasion.* New York: Morrow.

Cushman, D. P., & McPhee, R. D. (1980). *Message-attitude-behavior relationship: Theory, methodology and application.* San Diego: Academic Press.

Dovidio, J. F., & Gaertner, S. L. (Eds.). (1986). *Prejudice, discrimination, and racism.* San Diego: Academic Press.

Duckitt, J. (1992). *The social psychology of prejudice.* Westport, CT: Greenwood.

Eagly, A., Chaiken, S., & Youngblood, D. (Eds.). (1992). *The psychology of attitudes.* San Diego: Harcourt Brace Jovanovich.

Festinger, L. (1957). *A theory of cognitive dissonance.* Stanford, CA: Stanford University Press.

Festinger, L., Riecken, H. W., & Schachter, S. (1956). *When prophecy fails: A social and psychological study of a modern group that predicted the destruction of the world.* New York: Harper & Row.

Jowett, G. S., & O'Donnell, V. (1986). *Propaganda and persuasion.* Newbury Park, CA: Sage Publications.

O'Keefe, D. J. (1990). *Persuasion: Theory and research.* Newbury Park, CA: Sage Publications.

Oskamp, S. (1991). *Attitudes and opinions.* Englewood Cliffs, NJ: Prentice Hall.

Petty, R. E., & Cacioppo, J. T. (1981). *Attitudes and persuasion: Classic and contemporary approaches.* Dubuque, IA: Wm. C. Brown.

Reardon, K. K. (1991). *Persuasion in practice*. Newbury Park, CA: Sage Publications.

Williams, J. E., & Best, D. L. (1990). *Measuring sex stereotypes: A thirty-nation study*. Newbury Park, CA: Sage Publications.

Yuker, H. E. (1988). *Attitudes toward persons with disabilities*. New York: Springer.

Zanna, M. P., & Olson, J. M. (Eds.). (1994). *The psychology of prejudice*. Hillsdale, NJ: Erlbaum.

FOR MORE ON GROUP PROCESSES

Brown, R. (1988). *Group processes*. Cambridge, MA: Basil Blackwell.

Cialdini, R. B. (1988). *Influence: Science and practice*. Glenview, IL: Scott, Foresman.

Fisher, B. A. (1990). *Small group decision making*. New York: McGraw-Hill.

Forsyth, D. R. (1990). *Group dynamics*. Monterey, CA: Brooks/Cole.

Galanter, M. (1989). *Cults: Faith, healing, and coercion*. New York: Oxford University Press.

Guerin, B. (1993). *Social facilitation*. New York: Cambridge University Press.

Hart, P. (1990). *Groupthink in government*. New York: Taylor & Francis.

Hendrick, C. (Ed.). (1987). *Group processes and intergroup relations*. Newbury Park, CA: Sage Publications.

Janis, I. L. (1982). *Groupthink: Psychological studies of policy decisions and fiascoes* (2nd ed.). Boston: Houghton Mifflin.

Kelman, H. C., & Hamilton, V. L. (1989). *Crimes of obedience: Toward a social psychology of authority and responsibility*. New Haven, CT: Yale University Press.

Milgram, S. (1974). *Obedience to authority*. New York: Harper & Row.

Miller, A. G. (1986). *The obedience experiments: A case study of controversy in social science*. Westport, CT: Praeger.

Mugny, G., & Perez, J. A. (1991). *The social psychology of minority influence*. New York: Cambridge University Press.

Paicheler, G. (1988). *The psychology of social influence*. New York: Cambridge University Press.

Paulus, P. B. (1989). *Psychology of group influence*. Hillsdale, NJ: Erlbaum.

Suedfeld, P. (1990). *Psychology and torture*. New York: Hemisphere.

Thibaut, J. W., & Kelley, H. H. (1986). *The social psychology of groups*. New Brunswick, NJ: Transaction.

Trenholm, S. (1989). *Persuasion and social influence*. Englewood Cliffs, NJ: Prentice Hall.

Turner, J. C. (1991). *Social influence*. Belmont, CA: Brooks/Cole.

FOR MORE ON PROSOCIAL BEHAVIOR

Badcock, C. R. (1986). *The problem of altruism: Freudian-Darwinian solutions*. New York: Basil Blackwell.

Batson, C. D. (1991). *The altruism question: Toward a social-psychological answer*. Hillsdale, NJ: Erlbaum.

Clark, M. S. (Ed.). (1991). *Prosocial behavior*. Newbury Park, CA: Sage Publications.

Eisenberg, N., & Mussen, P. (Eds.). (1989). *The roots of prosocial behavior in children*. New York: Cambridge University Press.

Kohn, A. (1990). *The brighter side of human nature: Altruism and empathy in everyday life*. New York: Basic Books.

Latané, B., & Darley, J. M. (1970). *The unresponsive bystander: Why doesn't he help?* Englewood Cliffs, NJ: Prentice Hall.

Oliner, S. P., & Oliner, P. M. (1988). *The altruistic personality: Rescuers of Jews in Nazi Europe*. New York: Free Press.

Piliavin, J. A., & Callero, P. L. (1991). *Giving blood: The development of an altruistic identity*. Baltimore: The Johns Hopkins University Press.

Piliavin, J. A., Dovidio, J. F., Gaertner, S. L., & Clark, R. D. (1981). *Emergency intervention*. New York: Academic Press.

FOR MORE ON AGGRESSION

Berkowitz, L. (1993). *Aggression: Its causes, consequences, and control*. New York: McGraw-Hill.

Browne, K. D., & Archer, J. (Ed.). (1989). *Human aggression: Naturalistic approaches*. New York: Routledge.

Dollard, J. D., Doob, L. W., Miller, N. E., Mowrer, O. H., & Sears, R. R. (1939/1980). *Frustration and aggression*. New York: Greenwood.

Ellis, L. (1989). *Theories of rape: Inquiries into the causes of sexual aggression*. New York: Taylor & Francis.

Geen, R. G. (1990). *Human aggression*. Monterey, CA: Brooks/Cole.

Goldstein, A. P., & Segall, M. H. (1983). *Aggression in global perspective*. New York: Pergamon.

Liebert, R. M., & Sprafkin, J. (1988). *The early window: Effects of television on children and youth*. New York: Pergamon.

Potegal, M., & Knutson, J. (1994). *Dynamics of aggression: Biological and social processes*. Hillsdale, NJ: Erlbaum.

Prentky, R. A., & Quinsey, V. L. (1988). *Human sexual aggression*. New York: New York Academy of Sciences.

Van der Dennen, J. M., & Falger, V. S. (Eds.). (1990). *Sociobiology and conflict*. New York: Routledge.

FOR MORE ON PORNOGRAPHY AND AGGRESSION

Donnerstein, E., Linz, D., & Penrod, S. (1986). *The question of pornography: Research findings and policy implications*. New York: Free Press.

Koop, C. E. (1987). Report of the Surgeon General's Workshop on Pornography and Public Health. *American Psychologist, 42*, 944–945.

Linz, D., Donnerstein, E., & Penrod, S. (1987). The findings and recommendations of the attorney general's commission on pornography. *American Psychologist, 42*, 946–953.

Malamuth, N. M., & Donnerstein, E. (Eds.). (1984). *Pornography and sexual aggression*. San Diego: Academic Press.

Yaffe, M., & Nelson, E. (1983). *The influence of pornography on behaviour*. San Diego: Academic Press.

Zillmann, D., & Bryant, J. (Eds.). (1989). *Pornography: Research advances and policy considerations*. Hillsdale, NJ: Erlbaum.

FOR MORE ON CONTRIBUTORS TO THE STUDY OF SOCIAL BEHAVIOR

Evans, R. I. (1989). *Albert Bandura: The man and his ideas: A dialogue*. New York: Praeger.

Gay, P. (1988). *Freud: A life for our time*. New York: W. W. Norton.

Heider, F. (1983). *The life of a psychologist: An autobiography*. Lawrence: University of Kansas Press.

Rock, I. (Ed.). (1990). *The legacy of Solomon Asch: Essays in cognition and social psychology*. Hillsdale, NJ: Erlbaum.

Now that you know what psychologists do and some of the fields in which they special-ize, you might be interested in pursuing a career in psychology. Table A.1 lists the many divisions of the American Psychological Association, providing further evidence of the diversity of pursuits available to budding psychologists. A career as a psychologist would potentially permit you to combine teaching, research, and practice in any of a wide variety of fields.

A major in psychology is particularly attractive because it is intrinsically interest-ing, provides marketable skills, and prepares students for further education or for em-ployment (Lunneborg, 1978). No undergraduate major enhances one's ability to under-stand human and animal behavior more than psychology does. A major in psychology is also attractive because it does more than provide training in a narrow discipline aimed primarily at getting a first job. It improves personal and practical skills that make stu-dents more adaptable to many career opportunities. Students who major in psychology improve their abilities in writing, speaking, and problem solving. These students also learn to be open-minded skeptics capable of objectively evaluating claims made by scientists, advertisers, politicians, and people in everyday life. Most undergraduate psy-chology programs also provide experience in using statistics and computers.

BECOMING A PSYCHOLOGIST

If you decide to major in psychology as preparation for a career as a psychologist, you need to realize that the bachelor's degree is not adequate preparation; you must pursue graduate studies. Though psychologists may have a bachelor's degree in a field other than psychology, they usually have a bachelor's degree (B.A. or B.S.) in psychology. You would need 1 to 2 years of study beyond the bachelor's level to earn a master's degree (M.A., M.S., or M.Ed.). A master's degree usually requires advanced courses in psychol-ogy related to a field of specialization and completion of a written thesis or original research study. The most popular fields of specialization for those with a master's degree are clinical psychology, counseling psychology, and school psychology.

You would need 4 to 6 more years of study beyond the bachelor's level to earn a doctoral degree (Ph.D., Psy.D., or Ed.D.). The Ph.D. requires advanced courses in re-search methods, statistics, and a specialized field of study. It also requires completion of an ambitious original research project, which is then described in a written doctoral dissertation. The Psy.D. requires advanced courses in a particular field of study, usually clinical or counseling psychology, and an internship in an applied setting, such as a community mental health center. The Ph.D. indicates expertise in conducting research; the Psy.D. indicates expertise in providing therapy. But note that many psychologists who practice clinical or counseling psychology have a Ph.D., which means that they, too, are experts in providing therapy and have served an internship in an applied setting. Almost all states require that a person earn a doctoral degree, serve an internship, and pass a licensing exam to be licensed as a psychologist. The Ed.D. is normally offered by an education department and usually signifies expertise in relating psychology to edu-cation or counseling.

If you are considering a career in psychology, you should be aware of ways to make yourself more attractive to prospective graduate programs:

1. You must earn high grades—at least a B average for desirable graduate programs, and a B+ or A− average for the most competitive ones.

2. You must perform well on the Graduate Record Examination (GRE), which is analogous to the SAT or ACT exam that you probably took for

1.	General psychology	26.	History of psychology
2.	Teaching of psychology	27.	Society for community research and action
3.	Experimental psychology	28.	Psychopharmacology and substance abuse
4.	Unassigned	29.	Psychotherapy
5.	Evaluation, measurement, and statistics	30.	Psychological hypnosis
6.	Physiological and comparative psychology	31.	State psychological association affairs
7.	Developmental psychology	32.	Humanistic psychology
8.	Personality and social psychology	33.	Mental retardation and developmental disabilities
9.	Society for the psychological study of social issues	34.	Population and environmental psychology
10.	Psychology and the arts	35.	Psychology of women
11.	Unassigned	36.	Psychologists interested in religious issues
12.	Clinical psychology	37.	Child, youth, and family services
13.	Consulting psychology	38.	Health psychology
14.	Society for industrial and organizational psychology	39.	Psychoanalysis
15.	Educational psychology	40.	Clinical neuropsychology
16.	School psychology	41.	American psychology-law society
17.	Counseling psychology	42.	Psychologists in independent practice
18.	Psychologists in public service	43.	Family psychology
19.	Military psychology	44.	Society for the psychological study of lesbian and gay issues
20.	Adult development and aging	45.	Society for the psychological study of ethnic-minority issues
21.	Applied experimental and engineering psychology	46.	Media psychology
22.	Rehabilitation psychology	47.	Exercise and sport psychology
23.	Consumer psychology	48.	Peace psychology
24.	Theoretical and philosophical psychology	49.	Group psychology and group psychotherapy
25.	Experimental analysis of behavior	50.	Psychology of addictive behaviors

entrance into your undergraduate school. The GRE includes three subtests that measure verbal ability, mathematical ability, and reasoning ability, and an advanced test of general knowledge of psychology.

3. You might also be required to take the Miller Analogies Test, which assesses the ability to reason through the use of analogies.

4. You should perform research under faculty supervision and, preferably, present your findings at one of the many undergraduate psychology research conferences each spring. These conferences are announced in the *APA Monitor*, the *American Psychologist*, and *The Teaching of Psychology*, one or more of which should be available in your library or from a psychology faculty member.

5. You should serve an undergraduate internship in a setting geared to your career goals. You might even be able to serve a teaching internship under faculty supervision or a peer counseling internship sponsored by your campus counseling center.

6. You should get to know several psychology faculty members so that they provide advice and, eventually, write letters of recommendation for you. It is impossible for professors to write sterling letters for students they hardly know.

7. You should be active in your psychology club or Psi Chi (the national psychology honor society) chapter.

8. You should do summer work or volunteer work related to your career goals.

9. You should broaden yourself by taking courses in disciplines other than psychology. These might include courses in logic, writing, public speaking, and computer science.

10. You should discuss your career goals and graduate programs of interest with your faculty advisor. If you intend to proceed immediately to graduate school, you should begin considering graduate schools no later than your junior year.

You can get information about psychology and graduate training from psychological associations. These include the American Psychological Association, the American Psychological Society, the Canadian Psychological Association, regional associations, state associations, and local associations.

OTHER CAREER OPTIONS

Individuals who major in psychology may also choose to pursue graduate study in disciplines other than psychology. Many psychology majors pursue graduate study in law, medicine, computer science, or business administration. Of course, to pursue any of these careers, you should take courses that will prepare you for graduate study in your discipline of interest. For example, psychology majors who plan to attend medical school must also take courses in biology, chemistry, physics, and mathematics.

With proper course work and student teaching experience, you can become a high school teacher. The combination of a bachelor's degree in psychology, appropriate elective courses, and experience in a relevant setting can make a graduate attractive to prospective employers. If you major in psychology, it is advisable to minor in a discipline related to your career interests.

With a proper background, psychology majors can even compete with business majors. Business firms consider the following attributes for entry-level employees: first, technical skills such as accounting and interviewing skills; second, conceptual skills such as problem-solving ability and the ability to fit into the organization; third, social skills such as understanding human behavior; and fourth, communication skills such as writing, speaking, and listening (Carducci & Wheat, 1984). If you intend to enter the business world with a degree in psychology, you should consider taking courses in accounting, management, marketing, and other related areas. You might even serve as an undergraduate intern in a local business or industry and seek part-time and summer employment in a relevant setting.

Psychology majors are especially attractive to employers of all kinds because the psychology curriculum enhances their social, communication, and problem-solving skills. American Telephone and Telegraph (AT&T) has found that students with bachelor's degrees in liberal arts majors that provide a broad background, such as psychology, philosophy, history, and English, progress more rapidly in management than do business or engineering majors (Candland, 1982).

RECOMMENDED READINGS AND SOURCES OF INFORMATION

FOR MORE ON CAREERS IN PSYCHOLOGY

American Psychological Association. (Revised annually). *Graduate study in psychology*. Washington, DC: Author.

American Psychological Association. (1986). *Careers in psychology*. Washington, DC: Author.

Fretz, B. R., & Stang, D. J. (1980). *Not for seniors only!* Washington, DC: American Psychological Association.

Keith-Spiegel, P. (1990). *The complete guide to graduate school admission: Psychology*. Hillsdale, NJ: Erlbaum.

Kilburg, R. R. (1991). *How to manage your career in psychology*. Washington, DC: American Psychological Association.

Mayne, T., & Sayette, M. (1990). *Insider's guide to graduate programs in clinical psychology*. New York: Guilford.

Poe, R. E. (1990). Psychology careers material: Selected resources. *Teaching of Psychology, 17*, 175–178.

Woods, P. (Ed.). (1986). *The psychology major*. Washington, DC: American Psychological Association.

Woods, P. J., & Wilkinson, C. S. (Eds.). (1987). *Is psychology the major for you?* Washington, DC: American Psychological Association.

FOR MORE INFORMATION ON ANY ASPECT OF PSYCHOLOGY

American Psychological Association
750 1st St. NE
Washington, DC 20002

American Psychological Society
1511 K Street, NW
Washington, DC 20005

Canadian Psychological Association
Chemin Vincent Road
Old Chelsea Quebec
Canada J0X 2N0

Scales of Measurement
    Nominal Scales
    Ordinal Scales
    Interval Scales
    Ratio Scales

Representation of Data
    Frequency Distributions
    Graphs
        Pie Graph
        Frequency Histogram
        Frequency Polygon
        Line Graph

Descriptive Statistics
    Measures of Central Tendency
        Mode
        Median
        Mean

    Measures of Variability
        Range
        Variance
        Standard Deviation
    The Normal Curve
        Standard Scores
        Percentiles

Correlational Statistics
    Scatter Plots
    Pearson's Product-Moment
        Correlation

Inferential Statistics
    Hypothesis Testing
    Statistical Significance

> To understand God's thoughts we must study statistics; for these are the measure of his purpose. (Florence Nightingale, 1820–1910)

Most psychological research involves measurement, whether from a *case study* of a person with multiple personalities, a *naturalistic observational study* of chimpanzee parental behavior in the wild, a *survey study* of consumer product preferences, a *correlational study* of the relationship between aerobic exercise and well-being, or an *experimental study* on the effects of mood on memory. In each case, measurement yields a set of numbers, which are the findings, or *data,* produced by the research study. Though a simple perusal of a set of data may provide an appreciation of the gist of the research findings, such an approach to data analysis is too imprecise for science. The use of *statistics* provides a more precise approach. As discussed in chapter 2, psychologists and other scientists use statistics to summarize data, find relationships between sets of data, and determine whether experimental manipulations have had a statistically significant effect.

    The word **statistics** has two meanings: (1) the field that applies mathematical techniques to the organizing, summarizing, and interpreting of data, and (2) the actual mathematical techniques themselves. Knowledge of statistics has many practical benefits. Even a rudimentary knowledge of statistics will make you better able to evaluate statistical claims made by science reporters, weather forecasters, television advertisers, political candidates, government officials, and other persons who may use statistics in the information or arguments they present.

statistics
Mathematical techniques used to summarize research data or to determine whether the data support the researcher's hypothesis.

SCALES OF MEASUREMENT

Measurements are made on a variety of scales: *nominal scales, ordinal scales, interval scales,* and *ratio scales.* As one proceeds from the first to the last of these scales, their degree of precision increases; that is, they convey more and more information about what is being measured. Scales of measurement are important because they determine the kind of statistic that is appropriate to use with a particular kind of data.

Nominal Scales

A **nominal scale** of measurement is the simplest kind. It places objects, individuals, or characteristics into categories. Examples of nominal scales include telephone numbers, street address numbers, license plate numbers, team uniform numbers, and student identification numbers. Note that these numbers do not indicate magnitude. In fact, categorization by names instead of numbers also qualifies as nominal data. (The word *nominal* comes from the Latin word for "name.") For example, a developmental psychologist studying social changes during the undergraduate years might identify each class by its name (freshman, sophomore, junior, senior) or by a number (1 = freshman; 2 = sophomore; 3 = junior; 4 = senior). Similarly, consider the *DSM-IV*, which (as explained in chapter 14) categorizes psychological disorders by both name and code number. For example, the code numbers for paranoid schizophrenia and agoraphobia (which are discussed in chapter 14) are 295.30 and 300.22, respectively. Again, the numbers are just labels; they do not indicate the relative severity of the disorders.

nominal scale
A scale of measurement that places objects, individuals, or characteristics into categories.

Ordinal Scales

An **ordinal scale** indicates the relative magnitude of scores. The relative heights of your family members, the order in which runners finish in a race, and the daily major league baseball standings are ordinal data. They indicate rank position, but they do not tell how far apart one position is from another. Because ordinal data only represent ranks, equal differences between scores on an ordinal scale do not necessarily indicate equal differences in what they represent. For example, the difference in time between the second-place finisher and the fifth-place finisher in a race is not necessarily the same as the difference in time between the sixth-place finisher and the ninth-place finisher, even though in each case the racers finish three positions apart.

ordinal scale
A scale of measurement that indicates the relative, but not exact, magnitude of scores.

Interval Scales

An **interval scale,** like an ordinal scale, indicates relative magnitude. Unlike numbers on an ordinal scale, numbers on an interval scale indicate the exact magnitude of what they represent. Moreover, equal distances between numbers on an interval scale represent equal differences in magnitude. Consider temperature measured in degrees Fahrenheit or Centigrade. On either scale, the difference between 80 and 85 degrees is equivalent to the difference between 65 and 70 degrees. But interval scales have an arbitrary zero point. Though the zero point on the Centigrade scale is the point at which water freezes, it is not the lowest possible temperature. And the zero point on the Fahrenheit scale is just another point along the scale. Because interval scales lack a true zero point, it is meaningless to refer to ratios between scores on such scales. For example, 40 degrees Fahrenheit is not twice as hot as 20 degrees Fahrenheit. Because the lack of a true zero point is only a minor limitation, many statistics make use of interval data.

interval scale
A scale of measurement that indicates the exact magnitude of scores, but not their ratio to one another.

Ratio Scales

A **ratio scale** has all the characteristics of an interval scale, as well as a true zero point. This permits statements about the ratio of one score to another. For example, because weight loss falls on a ratio scale, it would be meaningful to say that a person who lost 8 pounds lost twice as much as a person who lost 4 pounds. Other variables that fall on ratio scales include time, height, and distance. Because it has a true zero point, the Kelvin scale of absolute temperature is also on a ratio scale. The same statistics are used with interval data and ratio data.

ratio scale
A scale of measurement that indicates the ratio of scores to one another.

REPRESENTATION OF DATA

Because a list of raw data may be difficult to interpret, psychologists prefer to represent their data in an organized way. Two of the most common ways are *frequency distributions* and *graphs*.

TABLE B.1		Frequency Distributions of Exam Scores		

Exam Scores

83	81	90	82	83
89	81	80	90	80
88	90	88	92	88
90	93	89	84	94

Ungrouped Data		Grouped Data	
Score	Frequency	Score	Frequency
94	1	90–94	7
93	1	85–89	5
92	1	80–84	8
91	0		N = 20
90	4		
89	2		
88	3		
87	0		
86	0		
85	0		
84	1		
83	2		
82	1		
81	2		
80	2		
	N = 20		

Frequency Distributions

frequency distribution
A list of the frequency of each score or group of scores in a set of scores.

Suppose that you had a set of 20 scores from a 100-point psychology exam. You might arrange them in a **frequency distribution,** which lists the frequency of each score or group of scores in a set of scores. Using the set of scores in table B.1, you would set up a column that included the highest and lowest scores, as well as the possible scores in between. In this case, the highest score is 94 and the lowest is 80. You would then count the frequency of each score and list it in a separate column. The total of the frequencies in the distribution is symbolized by the letter N.

The frequency distribution might show a pattern in the set of scores that is not apparent when simply examining the individual scores. In this example (presented in table B.1), the exam scores do not bunch up toward the lower, middle, or upper portions of the distribution. In some cases, when you have a relatively large number of scores, you might prefer to use a *grouped* frequency distribution. The scores would be grouped into intervals, and the frequency of scores in each interval would be listed in a separate column. The intervals can be of any size, but, for ease of construction, the lowest number in each interval should be a multiple of the interval size (with an interval size of 5 or 10 units most convenient to use). A grouped frequency distribution provides less-precise information than does an ungrouped one, because the individual scores are lost.

Graphs

If a picture is worth a thousand words, then a graph is worth several paragraphs in a research report. Because it provides a pictorial representation of the distribution of scores, a graph can be an even more effective representation of research data than is a frequency distribution. Among the most common kinds of graphs are *pie graphs, frequency histograms, frequency polygons,* and *line graphs.*

Pie Graph

pie graph
A graph that represents data as percentages of a pie.

A simple, but visually effective, way of representing frequency data is the **pie graph.** It represents data as percentages of a pie-shaped graph. The total of the slices of the pie must add up to 100 percent. Note that pie graphs are used in figure 1.1 in chapter 1 to

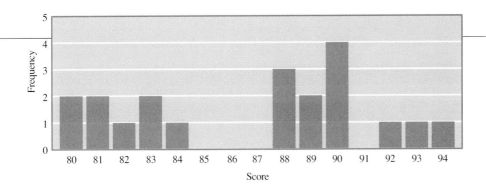

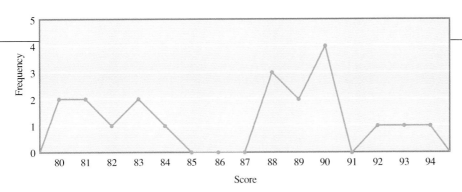

represent the percentage of psychologists in major fields of psychology and particular employment settings. The pie graph is especially useful with nominal data.

Frequency Histogram

Another approach to representing frequency data is the **frequency histogram,** which graphs frequencies as bars. In general, the scores are plotted on the *abscissa* (the horizontal axis) and the frequencies on the *ordinate* (the vertical axis). The width of the bars represents the intervals, and the height of the bars represents the frequency of scores in each interval. Figure B.1 is a frequency histogram of the exam scores in the ungrouped frequency distribution presented in table B.1.

frequency histogram
A graph that displays the frequency of scores as bars.

Frequency Polygon

A **frequency polygon** serves the same purpose as a frequency histogram. As shown in figure B.2, the frequency polygon is drawn by connecting the points, representing frequencies, located above the scores. Note that the polygon is completed by extending it to the abscissa one score below the lowest score and one score above the highest score in the distribution.

An advantage of the frequency polygon over the frequency histogram is that it permits the plotting of more than one distribution on the same set of axes. Plotting more than one frequency histogram on a set of axes would create a confusing graph. If more than one frequency polygon is plotted on a set of axes, they should be distinguished from one another. This can be done by drawing a different kind of line for each polygon (perhaps a solid line for one and a broken line for the other), drawing the lines in different colors (perhaps red for one polygon and blue for the other), or representing the points above the scores with geometric shapes (perhaps a circle for one polygon and a triangle for the other).

A graph in which scores bunch up toward either end of the abscissa (as shown in figure B.3) is said to be *skewed*. The skewness of a graph is in the direction of its "tail." If the scores bunch up toward the high end, the graph has a **negative skew.** This might occur on an unusually easy exam. If the scores bunch up toward the low end, the graph has a **positive skew.** This might occur on an unusually difficult exam.

frequency polygon
A graph that displays the frequency of scores by connecting points representing them above each score.

negative skew
A graph that has scores bunching up toward the positive end of the abscissa.

positive skew
A graph that has scores bunching up toward the negative end of the abscissa.

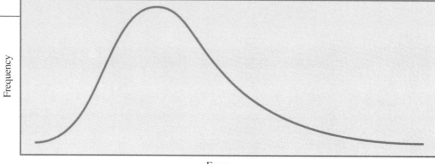

Exam scores

A positively skewed distribution

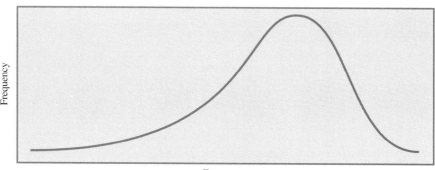

Exam scores

A negatively skewed distribution

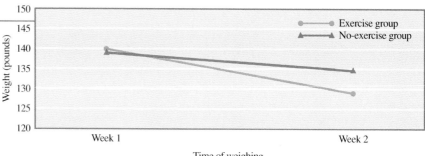

Line Graph

While pie graphs, frequency histograms, and frequency polygons are useful for plotting frequency data, a **line graph** is useful for plotting data generated by experiments. It uses lines to represent the relationship between independent and dependent variables. If you skim through this textbook, you will see several examples of line graphs. The graph shown in figure B.4 represents the data from the experiment on exercise and weight loss discussed in chapter 2.

line graph
A graph used to plot data showing the relationship between independent and dependent variables in an experiment.

DESCRIPTIVE STATISTICS

Suppose you gained access to the hundreds, or thousands, of high school grade point averages of all of the freshmen at your college or university. What is the most typical score? How similar are the scores? Simply scanning the scores would provide, at best, gross approximations of the answers to these questions. To obtain precise answers, psychologists use **descriptive statistics,** which include *measures of central tendency* and *measures of variability*.

descriptive statistics
Statistics that summarize research data.

Measures of Central Tendency

A measure of central tendency is a score that best represents a distribution of scores. The kind of measure that is appropriate depends on the scale of measurement that is used. The measures of central tendency include the *mode*, the *median*, and the *mean*.

Mode

The **mode** is the most frequently occurring score in a set of scores. In the frequency distribution of exam scores discussed above, the mode is 90. If two scores occur equally often, the distribution is *bimodal*. Any distribution that has two or more scores that occur equally often is called *multimodal*. The mode can be used with any scale of measurement, but it is the only measure of central tendency that can be used with nominal data. For example, the mode would be the only acceptable measure of central tendency for determining the most common academic major at your school. The winner of a presidential primary election in which there are several candidates would represent the mode—the person selected by more voters than any other.

The mode can also have practical benefits. Imagine a car dealership given the option of carrying a particular model, but limited to selecting just one color. The dealership owner would be wise to choose the mode—the color preferred by more people than any other.

mode
The score that occurs most frequently in a set of scores.

Median

The **median** is the middle score in a distribution of scores that have been ranked in numerical order. If the median is located between two scores, it is assigned the value of the midpoint between them (for example, the median of 23, 34, 55, and 68 would equal 44.5). The median requires at least ordinal data; it would be impossible to find the median of data on a nominal scale. For example, since academic majors do not differ in magnitude, it would make no sense to ask what the median major is at a college. The median is the best measure of central tendency for skewed distributions, because it is unaffected by extreme scores. Note that in the example below the median is the same in both sets of exam scores, even though the second set contains an extreme score.

median
The middle score in a set of scores that have been ordered from lowest to highest.

| Exam A | 23, | 25, | **63,** | 64, | 67 |
| Exam B | 23, | 25, | **63,** | 64, | 98 |

Mean

The **mean** is the arithmetic average, or simply the average, of a set of scores. You are probably more familiar with it than with the mode or the median. You encounter the mean in everyday life whenever you calculate your exam average, batting average, gas mileage average, or a host of other averages. The mean requires interval or ratio data.

The mean of a sample is calculated by adding all the scores and dividing by the number of scores. Unlike the median, the mean is affected by extreme scores. As shown below, one extreme score will pull the mean in its direction—especially if there are few scores in the set of scores. Thus, the mean may be a misleading statistic when used with a skewed distribution. For example, while the mean of the five exam scores below is 79, the median would be 93—a more satisfying estimate of the student's typical performance. In a symmetrical distribution the measures of central tendency are identical.

mean
The arithmetic average of a set of scores.

Exam Scores: 19,   92,   93,   94,   97

$$\overline{X} = \frac{\Sigma X}{N} = \frac{19 + 92 + 93 + 94 + 97}{5} = 79$$

When Disraeli pointed out the ease of lying with statistics, he might have been referring, in particular, to measures of central tendency. Suppose a baseball general manager is negotiating with an agent about a salary for a baseball catcher of average ability. Both might use a measure of central tendency to prove his own point, perhaps based on the

TABLE B.2	Baseball Salaries for Catchers

Player	Salary
A	$200,000
B	$250,000
C	$290,000
D	$340,000
E	$550,000
F	$670,000
G	$4,000,000

salaries of the top seven catchers, as shown in table B.2. The general manager might claim that a salary of $340,000 (the median) would provide the player with what he deserves—an average salary. The agent might counter that a salary of $900,000 (the mean) would provide the player with what he deserves—an average salary. Note that neither would technically be lying—they would simply be using statistics that favored their position. As the Scottish writer Andrew Lang (1844–1912) warned, beware of anyone who "uses statistics as a drunken man uses lampposts—for support rather than for illumination."

Measures of Variability

A distribution of scores that contained scores that were all the same would have no variability. This is rare. Almost all distributions have variability; that is, they contain scores that differ from one another. Consider the members of your psychology class. They would vary on a host of measures, including height, weight, and grade point average. Measures of variability include the *range*, the *variance*, and the *standard deviation*.

Range

range
A statistic representing the difference between the highest and lowest scores in a set of scores.

The **range,** which requires at least ordinal data, is the difference between the highest and lowest scores in a distribution. This provides limited information, because distributions in which scores bunch up toward the beginning, middle, or end of the distribution might have the same range. Of course the range is useful as a rough estimate of how a score compares with the highest and lowest in a distribution. For example, a student might find it useful to know whether he or she did near the best or the worst on an exam. The range of scores in the distribution of 20 grades in the earlier example in table B.1 would be the difference between 94 and 80, or 14.

Variance

variance
A measure of variability indicating the average of the squared deviations from the mean.

A more informative measure of variability is the **variance,** which represents the variability of scores around their group mean. Unlike the range, the variance takes into account every score in the distribution. Technically, the variance is the average of the squared deviations from the mean. The variance requires either interval or ratio data.

Suppose you wanted to calculate the variance for both of the sets of 10-point quiz scores on the next page. First, find the group mean. Second, find the deviation of each score from the group mean. Note that deviation scores will be negative for scores that are below the mean. As a check on your calculations, the sum of the deviation scores should equal zero. Third, square the deviation scores. By squaring the scores, negative scores are made positive and extreme scores are given relatively more weight. Fourth, find the sum of the squared deviation scores. Fifth, divide the sum by the number of scores. This yields the variance. Note that the variance for quiz A is larger than that for quiz B, indicating that students were more varied in their performances on quiz A.

Quiz A		
1, 2, 6, 8, 9		

$$\overline{X} = \frac{\Sigma X}{N} = \frac{1 + 2 + 6 + 8 + 9}{5} = \frac{26}{5} = 5.2$$

Score	Deviation	Deviation²
1	−4.2	17.64
2	−3.2	10.24
6	.8	.64
8	2.8	7.84
9	3.8	14.44

$$\Sigma \text{Deviation}^2 = 50.80$$

$$\text{Variance} = \frac{\Sigma \text{Deviation}^2}{N} = \frac{50.80}{5} = 10.16$$

Quiz B		
4, 5, 6, 7, 8		

$$\overline{Y} = \frac{\Sigma Y}{N} = \frac{4 + 5 + 6 + 7 + 8}{5} = \frac{30}{5} = 6$$

Score	Deviation	Deviation²
4	−2	4
5	−1	1
6	0	0
7	1	1
8	2	4

$$\Sigma \text{Deviation}^2 = 10$$

$$\text{Variance} = \frac{\Sigma \text{Deviation}^2}{N} = \frac{10}{5} = 2$$

Standard Deviation

The **standard deviation,** or S, is the square root of the variance. The standard deviation of quiz A above would be

$$S = \sqrt{S^2} = \sqrt{10.16} = 3.19.$$

standard deviation
A statistic representing the degree of dispersion of a set of scores around their mean.

The standard deviation of quiz B above would be

$$S = \sqrt{S^2} = \sqrt{2} = 1.414.$$

Why not simply use the variance? One reason is that, unlike the variance, the standard deviation is in the same units as the raw scores. This makes the standard deviation more meaningful. Thus, it would make more sense to discuss the variability of a set of IQ scores in IQ points than in squared IQ points. The standard deviation is used in the calculation of many other statistics.

The Normal Curve

As illustrated in figure B.5, the **normal curve** is a bell-shaped graph that represents a hypothetical frequency distribution in which the frequency of scores is greatest near the mean and progressively decreases toward the extremes. In essence, the normal curve is a smooth frequency polygon based on an infinite number of scores. The mean, median, and mode of a normal curve are the same. Many physical or psychological characteristics, such as height, weight, and intelligence, fall on a normal curve.

normal curve
A bell-shaped graph representing a hypothetical frequency distribution for a given characteristic.

One useful characteristic of a normal curve is that certain percentages of scores fall at certain distances (measured in standard deviation units) from its mean. A special statistical table makes it a simple matter to determine the percentage of scores that fall above or below a particular score or between two scores on the curve. For example, about 68 percent of scores fall between plus and minus one standard deviation from the mean; about 95 percent fall between plus and minus two standard deviations from the mean; and about 99 percent fall between plus and minus three standard deviations from the mean.

For example, consider an IQ test, with a mean of 100 and a standard deviation of 15. What percentage of people score above 130? Because intelligence scores fall on a normal curve, about 95 percent of the scores fall within two standard deviations of the mean. Thus, about 5 percent fall more than two standard deviations from the mean. Because the normal curve is symmetrical, 2.5 percent of the people would score above 130 (mentally gifted) and about 2.5 percent below 70 (mentally retarded).

**Normal Distribution, or
Bell-Shaped Curve**
This graph shows the normal
distribution of IQ scores as measured
by the Wechsler Adult Intelligence
Scale. The normal distribution is a
type of bell-shaped frequency polygon
in which most of the scores are
clustered around the mean. The scores
become less frequent the farther they
appear above or below the mean.

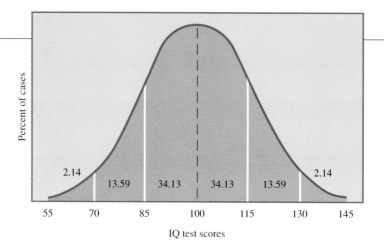

Standard Scores

Scores on a normal curve may be expressed in terms of their distance from the mean of the distribution in standard deviation units. These transformed scores are called standard scores, or *z scores*. One of the main advantages of *z* scores is that they permit scores on different distributions to be compared to each other. For example, which would be superior, a 73 on your biology exam or a 58 on your English exam? It would depend on the mean and standard deviation of each distribution of scores. The formula for a *z* score is

$$Z = \frac{X - \overline{X}}{S}$$

In the formula, X is a raw score, $\overline{X}$ is the mean of the set of scores containing the raw score, and S is the standard deviation of that set of scores. Suppose the mean for the biology score was 83 and the standard deviation was 5, while the mean for the English exam was 52 and the standard deviation was 3. The *z* score for your biology exam score would be

$$Z = \frac{73 - 83}{5} = -2$$

and the *z* score for your English exam score would be

$$Z = \frac{58 - 52}{3} = 2$$

Thus, the apparently inferior score of 58, being two standard deviations above its group mean, is actually superior to the score of 73, which is two standard deviations below its group mean.

If you took the SAT, a test that was designed to have a mean of 500 and a standard deviation of 100, you would be able to tell how well you performed relative to others. A score of 600 would yield a *z* score of 1. Because about 68 percent of the scores on a normal curve fall within 1 standard deviation of the mean, and the normal curve is symmetrical, about 34 percent of the scores fall between the mean and one standard deviation above the mean. Thus, about 84 percent (that is, 50 percent plus 34 percent) fall below a *z* score of 1.

Percentiles

percentile
The score at or below which a particular percentage of scores fall.

Scores along the abscissa of the normal curve also represent **percentiles**—the scores at or below which particular percentages of scores fall. For example, the mode, median, and mean fall at the 50th percentile. While a *z* score of 1 would be equal to the 84th percentile, a *z* score of −1 would be equal to the 16th percentile.

CORRELATIONAL STATISTICS

So far, you have been reading about statistics that describe sets of data. In many research studies, psychologists rely on **correlational statistics,** which determine the relationship between two variables. Correlational statistics yield a number called the **coefficient of correlation.** The coefficient may vary from 0.00 to 1.00 or −1.00. In a positive correlation, scores on two different distributions increase and decrease together. For example, there is a positive correlation between high school average and freshmen grade point average in college. In a negative correlation, as scores increase on one distribution they decrease on the other. For example, there is a negative correlation between absenteeism and course performance. The strength of a correlation depends on its size, not its sign. For example, a correlation of −.72 is stronger than a correlation of .53.

correlational statistics
Statistics that determine the relationship between two variables.

coefficient of correlation
A number that represents the direction and strength of a correlation.

Correlational statistics are important because they permit us to determine the strength and direction of the relationship between different sets of data or to predict scores on one distribution based on our knowledge of scores on another. If the correlation between two sets of data were a perfect 1.00, we could predict one score from another with complete accuracy. But because correlations are almost always less than perfect, we predict one score from another only with a particular *probability* of being correct—the higher the correlation, the higher the probability.

It cannot be stressed strongly enough that correlation does not mean causation. For example, years ago, authorities presumed that autistic children, who have poor social and communication skills, were caused by "refrigerator mothers." Mothers of autistic children were aloof from them. This was taken as a sign that the children suffered from mothers who were emotionally cold. Knowing that this is simply a correlation, you might wonder whether causality was in the opposite direction. Perhaps autistic children, who do not respond to their mothers, cause their mothers to become aloof from them. Moreover, why would a mother have several normal children, then an autistic child, and then several more normal ones? It would be difficult to believe she was a warm parent to all but one. Today, evidence indicates that autism is a neurological problem that has nothing to do with the mother's emotionality.

As another example, though there is a positive correlation between smoking and cancer in human beings, this is not scientifically acceptable evidence that smoking *causes* cancer. Perhaps another factor (such as a level of stress tolerance) might make someone prone to both smoking and cancer, without smoking's necessarily causing cancer. Of course, correlation does not imply the *absence* of causation. For example, there may, indeed, be a causal relationship between smoking and cancer. The prudent thing would be to assume that there is.

Scatter Plots

Correlational data is graphed using a **scatter plot,** also known as a *scattergram* or *scatter diagram*. In a scatter plot, one variable is plotted on the abscissa and the other on the ordinate. Each subject's scores on both variables is indicated by a dot placed at the junction between those scores on the graph. This produces one dot for each subject. The pattern of the dots gives a rough impression of the size and direction of the correlation. In fact, a line drawn through the dots, or *line of best fit,* helps estimate this. The closer the dots lie to a straight line, the stronger the correlation. Figure B.6 illustrates several kinds of correlation.

scatter plot
A graph of a correlational relationship.

Pearson's Product-Moment Correlation

The most commonly used correlational statistic is the **Pearson's product-moment correlation (Pearson's r),** named for the English statistician Karl Pearson. Pearson's *r* is used with interval or ratio data. One formula for calculating it is presented in figure B.7. The example assesses the relationship between home runs and stolen bases by five baseball players during one month of a season.

Pearson's product-moment correlation
Perhaps the most commonly used correlational statistic.

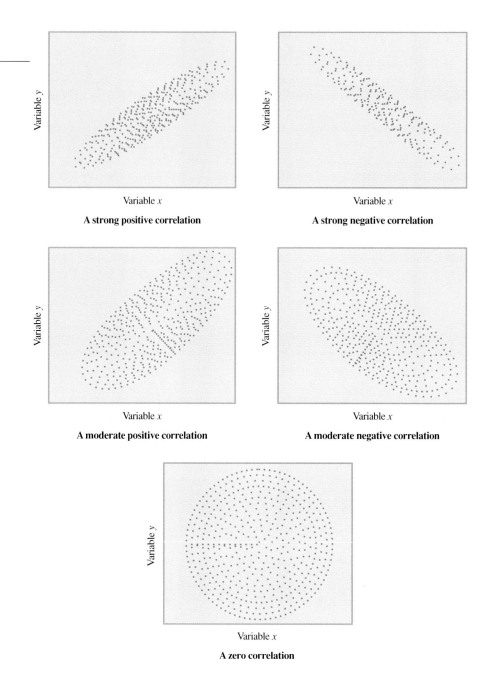

A strong positive correlation

A strong negative correlation

A moderate positive correlation

A moderate negative correlation

A zero correlation

INFERENTIAL STATISTICS

inferential statistics
Statistics used to determine whether changes in a dependent variable are caused by an independent variable.

Inferential statistics help us determine whether the difference we find between our experimental and control groups is caused by the manipulation of the independent variable or by chance variation in the performances of the groups. If the difference has a low probability of being caused by chance variation, we can feel confident in the inferences we make from our samples to the populations they represent.

Hypothesis Testing

null hypothesis
The prediction that the independent variable will have no effect on the dependent variable in an experiment.

In experiments, psychologists use inferential statistics to test the **null hypothesis.** This hypothesis states that the independent variable has no effect on the dependent variable. Consider an experimental study of the effect of overlearning on memory in college

Player	Home Runs (X)	Stolen Bases (Y)
A	8	3
B	2	6
C	1	2
D	5	1
E	6	3
	$\sum X = 22$	$\sum Y = 15$

$$r = \frac{\sum(\text{deviation from } \bar{X})(\text{deviation from } \bar{Y})}{N(S_X)(S_Y)}$$

Pearson's Product-Moment Correlation
This is a small negative correlation. It indicates that there is a slight tendency for stolen bases to decrease as home runs increase; that is, home-run hitters are somewhat less likely to steal bases.

Step 1: Calculate the means ($\bar{X}$ and $\bar{Y}$, respectively) of the two groups

$$\bar{X} = \frac{\sum X}{N} = \frac{22}{5} = 4.4 \qquad \bar{Y} = \frac{\sum Y}{N} = \frac{15}{5} = 3$$

Step 2: Find the deviation of each score from its mean

Deviation from $\bar{X}$	Deviation from $\bar{Y}$
$8 - 4.4 = 3.6$	$3 - 3 = 0$
$2 - 4.4 = -2.4$	$6 - 3 = 3$
$1 - 4.4 = -3.4$	$2 - 3 = -1$
$5 - 4.4 = 0.6$	$1 - 3 = -2$
$6 - 4.4 = 1.6$	$3 - 3 = 0$

Step 3: Multiply the paired deviation scores

(Deviation from $\bar{X}$)(Deviation from $\bar{Y}$)

$$
\begin{aligned}
(3.6)(0) &= 0.0 \\
(-2.4)(3) &= -7.2 \\
(-3.4)(-1) &= 3.4 \\
(0.6)(-2) &= -1.2 \\
(1.6)(0) &= 0.0 \\
\sum &= -5.0
\end{aligned}
$$

Step 4: Calculate the standard deviations for both groups

$$S_X = \sqrt{\frac{\sum \text{Deviation}^2}{N}} \qquad S_Y = \sqrt{\frac{\sum \text{Deviation}^2}{N}}$$

1) Square the deviation scores

(Deviation from $\bar{X}$)^2	(Deviation from $\bar{Y}$)^2
$(3.6)^2 = 12.96$	$0^2 = 0$
$(-2.4)^2 = 5.76$	$3^2 = 9$
$(-3.4)^2 = 11.56$	$-1^2 = 1$
$(0.6)^2 = 0.36$	$-2^2 = 4$
$(1.6)^2 = 2.56$	$0^2 = 0$
$\sum(\text{Deviation from } \bar{X})^2 = 33.20$	$\sum(\text{Deviation from } \bar{Y})^2 = 14$

2) Substitute in the formula and calculate

$$S_X = \sqrt{\frac{33.20}{5}} \qquad S_Y = \sqrt{\frac{14}{5}}$$

$$S_X = 2.58 \qquad S_Y = 1.67$$

Step 5: Substitute in the correlation formula and calculate

$$r = \frac{-5}{5(2.58)(1.67)}$$

$$r = -0.23$$

students. As discussed in chapter 8, when we use overlearning, we study material until we know it perfectly—and then continue to study it some more. At the beginning of the experiment, the subjects would be selected from the same population (college students) and randomly assigned to either the experimental group (overlearning) or the control group (normal studying). Thus, the independent variable would be the method of studying (overlearning versus normal studying). The dependent variable might be a 100-point exam on the material studied.

If the experimental manipulation has no effect, the experimental and control groups would not differ significantly in their performance on the exam. In that case, we would fail to reject the null hypothesis. If the experimental manipulation has an effect, the two groups would differ significantly in their performance on the exam. In that case, we would reject the null hypothesis. This would indirectly support the *research hypothesis*, which would predict that overlearning improves exam performance. But how large must a difference be between groups for it to be significant? To determine whether the difference between groups is large enough to minimize chance variation as an alternative explanation of the results, we must determine the *statistical significance* of the difference between them.

Statistical Significance

The characteristics of samples drawn from the population they represent will almost always vary somewhat from those of the true population. This is known as *sampling error*. Thus, a sample of five students taken from your psychology class (the population) would vary somewhat from the class means in age, height, weight, intelligence, grade point average, and other characteristics.

If we repeatedly took random samples of five students, we would continue to find that they differ from the population. But what of the difference between the means of two samples, presumably representing different populations, such as a population of students who practice overlearning and a population of students who practice normal study habits? How large would the differences have to be before we attributed them to the independent variable rather than to chance? In this example, how much difference in the performance of the experimental group and the control group would be needed before we could confidently attribute the difference to the practice of overlearning?

The larger the difference between the means of two samples, the less likely it would be attributable to chance. Psychologists typically accept a difference between sample means as statistically significant if it has a probability of less than 5 percent of occurring by chance. This is known as the .05 level of statistical significance. In regard to the example, if the difference between the experimental group and the control group has less than a 5 percent probability of occurring by chance, we would reject the null hypothesis. Our research hypothesis would be supported: overlearning is effective; the sample means of the experimental and control groups represent different populations (that is, the population that would be exposed to overlearning and the population that would not be exposed to it). Scientists who wish to use a stricter standard employ the .01 level of statistical significance. This means that a difference would be statistically significant if it had a probability of less than 1 percent of being obtained by chance alone.

The difference between the means of two groups will more likely be statistically significant under the following conditions:

1. When the samples are large.

2. When the difference between the means is large.

3. When the variability within the groups is small.

statistical significance
A low probability (usually less than 5 percent) that the results of a research study are due to chance factors rather than to the independent variable.

Note that **statistical significance** is a statement of probability. We can never be certain that what is true of our samples is true of the populations they represent. This is one of the reasons why, as stressed in chapter 2, all scientific findings are tentative. Moreover, *statistical* significance does not indicate *practical* significance. A statistically significant effect may be too small or be produced at too great a cost of time or money to be useful. What if those who practice overlearning must study an extra hour each day to improve their exam performance by a statistically significant, yet relatively small, 3 points. Knowing this, students might choose to spend their time in another way. As the American statesman Henry Clay (1777–1852) noted, in determining the importance of research findings, by themselves "statistics are no substitute for judgment."

When psychologists test the difference between the means of two sets of scores that are on interval or ratio scales, they often use a technique called the **t test.** When they wish to test the differences between the means of three or more such groups, they often use **analysis of variance.** The calculation of those statistics is covered in advanced courses in statistics and research methods.

t test
A statistical technique used to determine whether the difference between two sets of scores is statistically significant.

analysis of variance
A statistical technique used to determine whether the difference between three or more sets of scores is statistically significant.

SUMMARY

SCALES OF MEASUREMENT

Research data falls on one of four kinds of measurement scales. Nominal scales (such as the diagnoses of psychological disorders) classify data, but do not indicate magnitude. Ordinal scales (such as finishing positions in a race) rank data, but do not indicate exact magnitudes. Interval scales (such as temperature in degrees Fahrenheit) indicate exact magnitudes, but do not permit statements about the ratio of one score to another. Ratio scales (such as scores on an exam) permit statements about the ratio of one score to another.

REPRESENTATION OF DATA

Data is often represented in frequency distributions, which indicate the frequency of each score in a set of scores. Psychologists also use graphs to represent data. These include pie graphs, frequency histograms, frequency polygons, and line graphs. Line graphs are important in representing the results of experiments, because they are used to illustrate the relationship between independent and dependent variables.

DESCRIPTIVE STATISTICS

Descriptive statistics summarize and organize research data. Measures of central tendency represent the typical score in a set of scores. The mode is the most frequently occurring score, the median is the middle score, and the mean is the arithmetic average of the set of scores. Measures of variability represent the degree of dispersion of scores. The range is the difference between the highest and lowest scores. The variance is the average of the squared deviations from the mean of the set of scores. And the standard deviation is the square root of the variance.

Many kinds of measurements fall on a normal, or bell-shaped, curve. A certain percentage of scores fall below each point on the abscissa of the normal curve. Standard scores, such as the z score, represent points along the abscissa in standard deviation units. Percentiles identify the percentage of scores that fall below a particular score.

CORRELATIONAL STATISTICS

Correlational statistics assess the relationship between two or more sets of scores. A correlation may be positive or negative and vary from 0.00 to plus or minus 1.00. The existence of a correlation does not necessarily mean that one of the correlated variables causes changes in the other. Nor does the existence of a correlation preclude that possibility. Correlations are commonly graphed on scatter plots. Perhaps the most common correlational technique is the Pearson's product-moment correlation.

INFERENTIAL STATISTICS

Inferential statistics permit experimenters to determine whether their findings can be generalized from their samples to the populations they represent. Consider a simple experiment in which an experimental group that is exposed to a condition is compared to a control group that is not. For the difference between the means of the two groups to be statistically significant, the difference must have a low probability (usually less than 5 percent) of occurring by normal random variation. When psychologists assess the difference between the two groups, they often use a statistic called the t test. When they assess the differences between more than two groups, they often uses a statistic called analysis of variance.

IMPORTANT CONCEPTS

RECOMMENDED READINGS

Cohen, J. (1990). Things I have learned so far. *American Psychologist, 45*, 1304–1312.

Comrey, A., Bott, P., & Lee, H. (1989). *Elementary statistics: A problem-solving approach.* Dubuque, IA: Wm. C. Brown.

Cowles, M. (1989). *Statistics in psychology: An historical perspective.* Hillsdale, NJ: Erlbaum.

Holmes, C. B. (1990). *The honest truth about lying with statistics.* Springfield, IL: Charles C Thomas.

Huff, C. (1954/1982). *How to lie with statistics.* New York: W.W. Norton.

Kimble, G. A. (1978). *How to use (and misuse) statistics.* Englewood Cliffs, NJ: Prentice Hall.

Stigler, S. M. (1986). *The history of statistics.* Cambridge, MA: Harvard University Press.

Tankard, J. W., Jr. (1984). *The statistical pioneers.* Cambridge, MA: Schenkman.

Yaremko, R. M., Harari, H., Harrison, R. C., & Lynn, E. (1982). *Reference handbook of research and statistical methods.* New York: Harper & Row.

absolute threshold The minimum amount of stimulation that an individual can detect through a given sense *163*

accommodation 1. The cognitive process that revises existing schemas to incorporate new information. 2. The process by which the thickness of the lens in the eye changes to focus images of objects located at different distances from the eye. *127, 168*

achievement motive The desire for mastery, excellence, and accomplishment. *410*

achievement test A test that measures knowledge of a particular subject. *358*

acronym A mnemonic device that involves forming a term from the first letters of a series of words that are to be recalled. *308*

action potential A series of changes in the electrical charge across the axonal membrane that occurs after the axon has reached its firing threshold. *75*

activation-synthesis theory The theory that dreams are the by-products of the mind's attempt to make sense of the spontaneous changes in physiological activity generated by the pons during REM sleep. *226*

actor-observer bias The tendency of observers to make dispositional attributions for the behavior of others but to make situational attributions for their own behavior. *611*

acupuncture A pain-relieving technique that relies on the insertion of fine needles into various sites on the body. *198*

adaptation-level theory The theory that happiness depends on comparing one's present circumstances with one's past circumstances. *435*

adolescence The transition period lasting from the onset of puberty to the beginning of adulthood. *140*

adrenal glands Endocrine glands that secrete hormones that regulate the excretion of minerals and the body's response to stress. *84*

adulthood The period beginning when the individual assumes responsibility for her or his own life. *145*

afterimage A visual image that persists after the removal of a stimulus. *175*

age regression A hypnotic state in which the individual apparently behaves as she or he did as a child. *232*

aggression Behavior aimed at causing harm to another person. *641*

agoraphobia A phobia associated with fear of being in public, usually because the person fears the embarrassment of a panic attack. *507*

algorithm A problem-solving rule or procedure that, when followed step by step, assures that a correct solution will be found. *327*

all-or-none law The principle that once a neuron reaches its firing threshold, a neural impulse travels at full strength along the entire length of its axon. *75*

altruism The helping of others without the expectation of a reward. *637*

Alzheimer's disease A brain disorder characterized by difficulty in forming new memories and by general mental deterioration. *79*

amphetamines Stimulants used to maintain alertness and wakefulness. *239*

amygdala A limbic system structure that evaluates information from the immediate environment, contributing to feelings of fear, anger, or relief. *89*

anal stage In Freud's theory, the stage of personality development, between ages 1 and 3, during which the child gains pleasure from defecation and faces a conflict over toilet training. *466*

analysis of dreams In psychoanalysis, the process by which the therapist interprets the symbolic, manifest content of dreams to reveal their true, latent content to the client. *538*

analysis of free associations In psychoanalysis, the process by which the therapist interprets the underlying meaning of the client's uncensored reports of anything that comes to mind. *538*

analysis of resistances In psychoanalysis, the process by which the therapist interprets client behaviors that interfere with therapeutic progress toward uncovering unconscious conflicts. *538*

analysis of transference In psychoanalysis, the process by which the therapist interprets the feelings expressed by the client toward the therapist as being indicative of the feelings typically expressed by the client toward important people in his or her personal life. *538*

analysis of variance A statistical technique used to determine whether the difference between three or more sets of scores is statistically significant. *A–17*

analytic introspection A research method in which highly trained subjects report the contents of their conscious mental experiences. *10*

anorexia nervosa An eating disorder marked by self-starvation. *397*

antianxiety drugs Psychoactive drugs, commonly known as minor tranquilizers, that are used to treat anxiety disorders. *557*

antidepressant drugs Psychoactive drugs that are used to treat major depression. *557*

antimania drugs Psychoactive drugs, most notably lithium carbonate, that are used to treat a bipolar disorder. *558*

antipsychotic drugs Psychoactive drugs, commonly known as major tranquilizers, that are used to treat schizophrenia. *558*

antisocial personality disorder A personality disorder marked by impulsive, manipulative, often criminal behavior, without any feelings of guilt in the perpetrator. *524*

anxiety disorder A psychological disorder marked by persistent anxiety that disrupts everyday functioning. *504*

applied research Research aimed at improving the quality of life and solving practical problems. *21*

approach-approach conflict A conflict in which one must choose between two desirable courses of action. *576*

approach-avoidance conflict A conflict in which one is faced by a course of action that has both desirable and undesirable qualities. *576*

aptitude test A test designed to predict a person's potential to benefit from instruction in a particular academic or vocational setting. *359*

archetypes In Jung's theory, inherited images that are passed down from our prehistoric ancestors and that reveal themselves as universal symbols in art, dreams, and religion. *469*

archival research The systematic examination of collections of letters, manuscripts, tape recordings, video recordings, or other materials. *47*

arousal motive The motive to maintain an optimal level of physiological activation. *407*

artificial intelligence (AI) The field that integrates computer science and cognitive psychology in studying information processing through the design of computer programs that appear to exhibit intelligence. *336*

assertiveness training A form of social-skills training that teaches clients to express their feelings directly, instead of passively or aggressively. *552*

assimilation The cognitive process that interprets new information in light of existing schemas. *127*

association areas Regions of the cerebral cortex that integrate information from the primary cortical areas and other brain areas. *92*

atherosclerosis The narrowing of arteries caused by the accumulation of cholesterol deposits. *581*

attention The process by which the individual focuses awareness on certain contents of consciousness while ignoring others. 212

attitude An evaluation, containing cognitive, emotional, and behavioral components, of an idea, event, object, or person. 618

audition The sense of hearing. 187

auditory cortex The area of the temporal lobes that processes sounds. 94, 189

auditory nerve The nerve that conducts impulses from the cochlea to the brain. 189

authoritarian personality A personality type marked by the tendency to obey superiors while dominating subordinates, to favor one's own group while being prejudiced against other groups, and to be unwilling to admit one's own faults while projecting them onto members of other groups. 626

authoritative parenting An effective style of parenting, in which the parent is warm and loving, yet sets well-defined limits that he or she enforces in an appropriate manner. 133

automatic processing Information processing that requires less conscious awareness and mental effort, and that does not interfere with the performance of other ongoing activities. 244

autonomic nervous system The division of the peripheral nervous system that controls automatic, involuntary physiological processes. 70

autonomy versus shame and doubt Erikson's developmental stage in which success is achieved by gaining a degree of independence from one's parents. 132

availability heuristic In decision making, the tendency to estimate the probability of an event by how easily relevant instances of it come to mind. 335

aversion therapy A form of behavior therapy that inhibits maladaptive behavior by pairing a stimulus that normally elicits a maladaptive response with an unpleasant stimulus. 542

avoidance-avoidance conflict A conflict in which one must choose between two undesirable courses of action. 576

avoidance learning Learning to prevent the occurrence of an aversive stimulus by giving an appropriate response to a warning stimulus. 268

axon The relatively long fiber of the neuron that conducts neural impulses. 73

axonal conduction The transmission of a neural impulse along the length of an axon. 74

barbiturates Depressants used to induce sleep or anesthesia. 237

basal ganglia A set of forebrain structures that promote smooth voluntary movements. 88

basal metabolic rate The rate at which the body burns calories just to keep itself alive. 394

basic research Research aimed at finding answers to questions out of theoretical interest or intellectual curiosity. 21

basilar membrane A membrane running the length of the cochlea that contains the auditory receptor (hair) cells. 189

behavioral contingencies Relationships between behaviors and their consequences, such as positive reinforcement, negative reinforcement, extinction, and punishment. 263

behavioral genetics The study of the relationship between heredity and behavior. 115

behavioral perspective The psychological viewpoint, descended from behaviorism, that emphasizes the importance of studying environmental influences on overt behavior, yet in some cases permits the study of mental processes. 17

behavioral preparedness The degree to which members of a species are innately prepared to learn particular behaviors. 274

behaviorism The early school of psychology that rejected the study of mental processes in favor of the study of overt behavior. 13

behavior modification The application of the principles of operant conditioning to change maladaptive behaviors. 542

behavior therapy The therapeutic application of the principles of learning to change maladaptive behaviors. 539

binocular cues Depth perception cues that require input from the two eyes. 180

biofeedback A form of operant conditioning that enables an individual either to learn to control a normally involuntary physiological process or to gain better control of a normally voluntary one when provided with visual or auditory feedback of the state of that process. 279

biopsychological perspective The psychological viewpoint that stresses the importance of physiological factors in behavior and mental processes. 20

biopsychology The field that studies the relationship between physiological and psychological processes. 22, 70

bipolar disorder A mood disorder marked by periods of mania alternating with longer periods of major depression. 515

blocking The process by which a neutral stimulus paired with a conditioned stimulus that already elicits a conditioned response fails to become a conditioned stimulus. 275

brain The portion of the central nervous system that is located in the skull and plays important roles in sensation, movement, and information processing. 70

brightness constancy The perceptual process that makes an object maintain a particular level of brightness despite changes in the amount of light reflected from it. 183

Broca's area The area of the frontal lobe responsible for the production of speech. 96

bulimia nervosa An eating disorder marked by bingeing and purging. 397

bystander intervention The act of helping someone who is in immediate need of aid. 638

caffeine A stimulant used to increase mental alertness. 239

cannabis sativa A hallucinogen derived from the hemp plant and ingested in the form of marijuana or hashish. 242

Cannon-Bard theory The theory that an emotion is produced when an event or object is perceived by the thalamus, which conveys this information simultaneously to the cerebral cortex and the skeletal muscles and autonomic nervous system. 440

case study An in-depth study of an individual. 43

catatonic schizophrenia A type of schizophrenia marked by unusual motor behavior, such as bizarre actions, extreme agitation, or immobile stupor. 521

catharsis In psychoanalysis, the release of repressed emotional energy as a consequence of insight into the unconscious causes of one's psychological problems. 537

causation The demonstration of an effect of one or more variables on another variable. 48

central nervous system The division of the nervous system consisting of the brain and the spinal cord. 70

cerebellum A hindbrain structure that controls the timing of well-learned movements. 87

cerebral cortex The outer covering of the forebrain. 91

cerebral hemispheres The left and right halves of the cerebrum. 92

cerebral palsy A movement disorder caused by brain damage and that is sometimes accompanied by mental retardation. 367

chaining An operant conditioning procedure used to establish a desired sequence of behaviors by positively reinforcing each behavior in the sequence. 266

childhood The period that extends from birth until the onset of puberty. 122

circadian rhythms Twenty-four-hour cycles of psychological and physiological changes, most notably the sleep-wake cycle. 213

clairvoyance The ability to perceive objects or events without any sensory contact with them. 202

classical conditioning A form of learning in which a neutral stimulus comes to elicit a response after being associated with a stimulus that already elicits that response. 256

clinical psychology The field that applies psychological principles to the prevention, diagnosis, and treatment of psychological disorders. 23

cocaine A stimulant used to induce mental alertness and euphoria. 240

cochlea The spiral, fluid-filled structure of the inner ear that contains the receptor cells for hearing. 189

coefficient of correlation 1. A statistic that assesses the degree of association between two or more variables. 2. A number that represents the direction and strength of a correlation. 59, A–13

cognitive appraisal The subjective interpretation of the severity of a stressor. 585

cognitive-appraisal theory The theory that one's emotion at a given time depends on one's interpretation of the situation one is in. 446

cognitive-developmental theory A theory of gender-role development that assumes the child must first understand the concept of gender before adopting behaviors that are gender related. 137

cognitive dissonance theory Leon Festinger's theory that attitude change is motivated by the desire to relieve the unpleasant state of tension caused when one holds cognitions that are inconsistent with each other. 623

cognitive-evaluation theory The theory that a person's intrinsic motivation will increase when a reward is perceived as a source of information but will decrease when a reward is perceived as an attempt to exert control. 414

cognitive perspective The psychological viewpoint that favors the study of how the mind organizes perceptions, processes information, and interprets experiences. 19

cognitive psychology The field of psychology that studies how the mind organizes perceptions, processes information, and interprets experiences. 322

cognitive therapy A type of therapy, developed by Aaron Beck, that aims at eliminating exaggerated negative beliefs about oneself, the world, or the future. 546

cohort A group of people of the same age. *119*

cohort-sequential research Research that begins as a cross-sectional study of different cohorts and then follows the cohorts longitudinally. *120*

collective unconscious In Jung's theory, the unconscious mind that is shared by all human beings and that contains archetypal images passed down from our prehistoric ancestors. *469*

color blindness The inability to distinguish between certain colors, most often red and green. *176*

companionate love Love characterized by feelings of affection and commitment to a relationship with another person. *617*

comparative psychology The field that studies similarities and differences in the physiology, behaviors, and abilities of animals, including human beings. *22*

compliance Behaving in accordance with a request that is backed by little or no threat of punishment. *633*

computed tomography (CT) A brain-scanning technique that relies on X rays to construct computer-generated images of the brain or body. *95*

computer-assisted instruction The use of computers to provide programmed instruction. *272*

concept A category of objects, events, qualities, or relations that share certain features. *323*

concrete operational stage The Piagetian stage, extending from 7 to 12 years of age, during which the child learns to reason logically about objects that are physically present. *129*

conditioned response (CR) In classical conditioning, the learned response given to a particular conditioned stimulus. *256*

conditioned stimulus (CS) In classical conditioning, a neutral stimulus that comes to elicit a particular conditioned response after being paired with a particular unconditioned stimulus that already elicits that response. *256*

conditioned taste aversion A taste aversion induced by pairing a taste with gastrointestinal distress. *260*

conduction deafness Hearing loss usually caused by blockage of the auditory canal, damage to the eardrum, or deterioration of the ossicles of the middle ear. *192*

cones Receptor cells of the retina that play an important role in daylight vision and color vision. *169*

conflict The emotional state induced when one is torn between two or more potential courses of action. *576*

confluence model The view that each child is born into an intellectual environment that is dependent on the intelligence levels of her or his parents and siblings, with the number of children and the interval between births affecting the intelligence of each successive child. *380*

conformity Behaving in accordance with group expectations with little or no overt pressure to do so. *631*

confounding variable A variable whose unwanted effect on the dependent variable might be confused with that of the independent variable. *51*

conscious mind The level of consciousness that includes the mental experiences that we are aware of at a given moment. *247*

consciousness The awareness of one's own mental activity, including thoughts, feelings, and sensations. *210*

consensus The extent to which, in a given situation, other people behave in the same way as the person being observed. *608*

conservation The realization that changing the form of a substance does not change its amount. *129*

consistency The extent to which a person behaves in the same way in a given situation on different occasions. *608*

constructive alternativism The process by which a person applies personal constructs to a given situation. *482*

constructive recall The distortion of memories by adding, dropping, or changing details to fit a schema. *298*

context-dependent memory The tendency for recall to be best when the environmental context present during the encoding of a memory is also present during attempts at retrieving it. *303*

continuous schedule of reinforcement A schedule of reinforcement that provides reinforcement for each instance of a desired response. *266*

control group The subjects in an experiment who are not exposed to the experimental condition of interest. *50*

controlled processing Information processing that involves conscious awareness and mental effort, and that interferes with the performance of other ongoing activities. *244*

conventional level In Kohlberg's theory, the level of moral reasoning characterized by concern with upholding laws and conventional values and by favoring obedience to authority. *154*

convergent thinking The cognitive process that focuses on finding conventional solutions to problems. *333*

conversion disorder A somatoform disorder in which the person exhibits motor or sensory loss or the alteration of a physiological function without any apparent physical cause. *510*

cornea The round, transparent area at the front of the sclera that allows light to enter the eye. *167*

corpus callosum A thick bundle of axons that provides a means of communication between the cerebral hemispheres, which is severed in so-called split-brain surgery. *105*

correlation The degree of relationship between two or more variables. *48*

correlational research Research that studies the degree of relationship between two or more variables. *48*

correlational statistics Statistics that determine the relationship between two variables. *A–13*

counseling psychology The field that applies psychological principles to help individuals deal with problems of daily living, generally less severe ones than those treated by clinical psychologists. *23*

counterconditioning A behavior therapy technique that applies the principles of classical conditioning to replace unpleasant emotional responses to stimuli with more pleasant ones. *539*

creativity A form of problem solving that generates novel, socially valued solutions to problems. *331*

critical period A period in childhood when experience with language produces optimal language acquisition. *344*

cross-sectional research A research design in which groups of subjects of different ages are compared at the same point in time. *119*

crystallized intelligence The form of intelligence that reflects knowledge acquired through schooling and in everyday life. *147, 372*

cultural-familial retardation Mental retardation apparently caused by social or cultural deprivation. *366*

dark adaptation The process by which the eyes become more sensitive to light when under low illumination. *174*

daydreaming A state of consciousness that involves shifting attention from external stimuli to self-generated thoughts and images. *211*

debriefing A procedure, after the completion of a research study, that informs subjects of the purpose of the study and aims to remove any physical or psychological distress caused by participation. *62*

decay theory The theory that forgetting occurs because memories naturally fade over time. *300*

decision making A form of problem solving in which one tries to make the best choice from among alternative judgments or courses of action. *334*

declarative memory The long-term memory system that contains memories of facts. *293*

deep structure The underlying meaning of a statement. *341*

defense mechanism In Freud's theory, a process that distorts reality to prevent the individual from being overwhelmed by anxiety. *464*

deindividuation The process by which group members become less aware of themselves as individuals and less concerned about being socially evaluated. *645*

deinstitutionalization The movement toward treating people with psychological disorders in community settings instead of mental hospitals. *558*

deja vu The feeling that one has experienced a present experience sometime in the past. *202*

dendrites The branchlike structures of the neuron that receive neural impulses. *73*

dependent variable A variable showing the effect of the independent variable. *50*

depressants Psychoactive drugs that inhibit activity in the central nervous system. *235*

depth perception The perception of the relative distance of objects. *180*

descriptive research Research that involves the recording of behaviors that have been observed systematically. *41*

descriptive statistics Statistics that summarize research data. *57, A–8*

determinism The assumption that every event has physical, potentially measurable, causes. *36*

developmental psychology The field that studies physical, cognitive, and psychosocial changes across the life span. *23, 114*

diathesis-stress viewpoint The assumption that psychological disorders are consequences of the interaction of a biological, inherited predisposition (diathesis) and exposure to stressful life experiences. *501*

difference threshold The minimum amount of change in stimulation that can be detected. *165*

differential psychology The field of psychology that studies individual differences in intellectual, personality, and physical characteristics. *9, 360*

discriminative stimulus In operant conditioning, a stimulus that indicates the likelihood that a particular response will be reinforced. *264*

disorganized schizophrenia A type of schizophrenia marked by severe personality deterioration and extremely bizarre behavior. *520*

disparagement theory The theory that humor is amusing when it makes one feel superior to other people. *436*

displacement The characteristic of language marked by the ability to refer to objects and events that are not present. *338*

dissociation A state in which the mind is split into two or more independent streams of consciousness. *231*

dissociative disorder A psychological disorder in which thoughts, feelings, and memories become separated from conscious awareness. *511*

distinctiveness The extent to which a person behaves in the same way across different situations. *608*

distributed practice Spreading out the memorization of information or the learning of a motor skill over several sessions. *306*

divergent thinking The cognitive process by which an individual freely considers a variety of potential solutions to artistic, literary, scientific, or practical problems. *333*

door-in-the-face technique Increasing the likelihood that someone will comply with a request by first getting them to reject a larger one. *633*

double-blind technique A procedure that controls experimenter bias and subject bias by preventing experimenters and subjects from knowing which subjects have been assigned to particular conditions. *55*

Down syndrome A form of mental retardation, associated with certain physical deformities, that is caused by an extra, third chromosome on the 21st pair. *367*

dream A storylike sequence of visual images, usually occurring during REM sleep. *222*

drive A state of psychological tension induced by a need. *389*

drive-reduction theory The theory that behavior is motivated by the need to reduce drives such as sex or hunger. *389*

echoic memory Auditory sensory memory, which lasts up to 4 or more seconds. *289*

educational psychology The field that applies psychological principles to improving curriculum, teaching methods, and administrative procedures. *24*

ego In Freud's theory, the part of the personality that helps the individual adapt to external reality by making compromises between the id, the superego, and the environment. *463*

egocentrism The inability to perceive physical reality from the perspective of another person. *129*

elaborative rehearsal Actively organizing new information to make it more meaningful, and integrating it with information already stored in long-term memory. *292*

Electra complex A term used by some psychoanalysts, but not by Freud, to refer to the Oedipus complex in females. *466*

electroconvulsive therapy (ECT) A biomedical therapy that uses brief electric currents to induce brain seizures in victims of major depression. *556*

electroencephalograph (EEG) A device used to record patterns of electrical activity produced by neuronal activity in the brain. *85*

embryonic stage The prenatal period that lasts from the end of the second week through the eighth week. *120*

emotion A motivated state marked by physiological arousal, expressive behavior, and mental experience. *424*

empiricism The philosophical position that true knowledge comes through the senses. *6*

encoding The conversion of information into a form that can be stored in memory. *287*

encoding specificity The principle that recall will be best when cues that were associated with the encoding of a memory are also present during attempts at retrieving it. *303*

encounter group A derivative of humanistic group therapy in which group members learn to be themselves by openly expressing their true feelings to one another. *552*

endocrine system Glands that secrete hormones into the bloodstream. *81*

endorphins Neurotransmitters that play a role in pleasure, pain relief, and other functions. *80*

engineering psychology The field that applies psychological principles to the design of equipment and instruments. *24*

engram A memory trace in the brain. *310*

environmental psychology The field that applies psychological principles to improving the physical environment, including the design of buildings and the reduction of noise. *24*

episodic memory The subsystem of declarative memory that contains memories of personal experiences tied to particular times and places. *294*

escape learning Learning to perform a behavior that terminates an aversive stimulus, as in negative reinforcement. *268*

ethology The study of animal behavior in the natural environment. *43*

ethyl alcohol A depressant found in beverages and commonly used to reduce social inhibitions. *235*

eugenics The practice of encouraging supposedly superior people to reproduce, while preventing supposedly inferior people from reproducing. *376*

existential psychology A form of humanistic psychology that emphasizes subjective mental experience and human free will. *19*

existential psychotherapy A type of humanistic therapy that helps the client overcome emotional or behavioral problems by dealing with major philosophical issues in life, including death, freedom, isolation, and meaning. *550*

expectancy In achievement situations, the perceived probability of success in a particular area. *412*

experimental group The subjects in an experiment who are exposed to the experimental condition of interest. *50*

experimental method Research that manipulates one or more variables, while controlling others, to determine the effects on one or more other variables. *49*

experimental psychology The field primarily concerned with laboratory research on basic psychological processes, including perception, learning, memory, thinking, language, motivation, and emotion. *22*

experimenter bias effect The tendency of experimenters to let their expectancies alter the way they treat their subjects. *54*

expert system A computer program that displays expertise in a specific domain of knowledge. *336*

explicit memory The process by which we intentionally recall past events or information of which we are consciously aware. *248*

external validity The extent to which the results of a research study can be generalized to other people, animals, or settings. *56*

extinction 1. In classical conditioning, the gradual disappearance of the conditioned response when the conditioned stimulus is repeatedly presented without being paired with the unconditioned stimulus. 2. In operant conditioning, the gradual disappearance of a response that is no longer followed by a reinforcer. *258, 268*

extrasensory perception (ESP) The ability to perceive events without the use of sensory receptors. *201*

extravert A person who is socially outgoing and prefers to pay attention to the external environment. *470*

extrinsic motivation The desire to perform a behavior to obtain an external reward, such as praise, grades, or money. *414*

facial-feedback theory The theory that particular facial expressions induce particular emotional experiences. *442*

factor analysis A statistical technique that determines the degree of correlation between performances on various tasks to determine the extent to which they reflect particular underlying characteristics, which are known as factors. *371*

family therapy A form of group therapy that encourages the constructive expression of feelings and the establishment of rules that family members agree to follow. *553*

fear of failure The motivation to avoid achievement situations that might bring failure. *412*

feature-detector theory The view that we construct our perceptions from neurons of the brain that are sensitive to specific features of stimuli. *178*

fetal alcohol syndrome A disorder, marked by physical defects and mental retardation, that can afflict the offspring of women who drink alcohol during pregnancy. *122*

fetal stage The prenatal period that lasts from the end of the eighth week through birth. *121*

fight-or-flight response A state of physiological arousal that enables us to meet sudden threats by either confronting them or running away from them. *424*

figure-ground perception The distinguishing of an object (the figure) from its surroundings (the ground). *178*

fixation In Freud's theory, the failure to mature beyond a particular stage of psychosexual development. *466*

fixed-interval schedule of reinforcement A partial schedule of reinforcement that provides reinforcement for the first desired response made after a set length of time. *268*

fixed-ratio schedule of reinforcement A partial schedule of reinforcement that provides reinforcement after a set number of desired responses. *267*

fixed-role therapy A kind of therapy, derived from Kelly's personality theory, that encourages clients to adopt roles that promote new, more adaptive personal constructs. *483*

flashbulb memory A vivid, long-lasting memory of a surprising, important, emotionally arousing event. *286*

flooding An extinction procedure in which a phobic client is exposed to a stimulus that evokes intense anxiety. *543*

fluid intelligence The form of intelligence that reflects reasoning ability, memory capacity, and speed of information processing. *147, 372*

foot-in-the-door technique Increasing the likelihood that someone will comply with a request by first getting them to comply with a smaller one. *633*

forensic psychology The field that applies psychological principles to improve the legal system, including the work of police and juries. *24*

forgetting The failure to retrieve information from memory. *288*

forgetting curve A graph showing that forgetting is initially rapid and then slows. *300*

formal operational stage The Piagetian stage, beginning at about age 12, marked by the ability to use abstract reasoning and to solve problems by testing hypotheses. *143*

fovea A small area at the center of the retina that contains only cones and provides the most acute vision. *170*

framing effect In decision making, biases introduced into the decision-making process by presenting an issue or situation in a certain manner. *336*

frequency distribution A list of the frequency of each score or group of scores in a set of scores. *A–6*

frequency histogram A graph that displays the frequency of scores as bars. *A–7*

frequency polygon A graph that displays the frequency of scores by connecting points representing them above each score. *A–7*

frequency theory The theory of pitch perception that assumes that the basilar membrane vibrates as a whole in direct proportion to the frequency of the sound waves striking the eardrum. *190*

frontal lobe A lobe of the cerebral cortex responsible for motor control and higher mental processes. *92*

frustration The emotional state induced when one is blocked from reaching a goal. *575*

frustration-aggression hypothesis The assumption that frustration causes aggression. *643*

functional fixedness The inability to realize that a problem can be solved by using a familiar object in an unusual way. *329*

functionalism The early school of psychology that studied how the conscious mind helps the individual adapt to the environment. *11*

fundamental attribution error The bias to attribute other people's behavior to dispositional factors. *610*

gate-control theory The theory that pain impulses can be blocked by the closing of a neuronal gate in the spinal cord. *198*

gender identity A person's self-perceived sex. *404*

gender roles The behaviors that are considered appropriate for females or males in a given culture. *136*

gender-schema theory A theory of gender-role development that combines aspects of social learning theory and cognitive-developmental theory. *137*

general adaptation syndrome As first identified by Hans Selye, the body's stress response, which includes the stages of alarm, resistance, and exhaustion. *581*

generalized anxiety disorder An anxiety disorder marked by a persistent state of anxiety that exists independent of any particular stressful situation. *505*

generativity The characteristic of language marked by the ability to combine words in novel, meaningful ways. *338*

generativity versus stagnation Erikson's developmental stage in which success is achieved by becoming less self-absorbed and more concerned with the well-being of others. *150*

genital stage In Freud's theory, the last stage of personality development, associated with puberty, during which the individual develops erotic attachments to others. *467*

genotype An individual's genetic inheritance. *116*

germinal stage The prenatal period that lasts from conception through the second week. *120*

Gestalt psychology The early school of psychology that claimed that we perceive and think about wholes rather than simply about combinations of separate elements. *14*

Gestalt therapy A type of humanistic therapy, developed by Fritz Perls, that encourages clients to become aware of their true feelings and to take responsibility for their own actions. *548*

glial cell A kind of cell that provides a physical support structure for the neurons, supplies them with nutrition, removes neuronal metabolic waste materials, facilitates the transmission of messages by neurons, and helps regenerate damaged neurons in the peripheral nervous system. *72*

goal setting The establishment of a particular level of performance to achieve in the future. *413*

gonads The male and female sex glands, the testes and the ovaries. *399*

grammar The set of rules that governs the proper use and combination of language symbols. *340*

group A collection of two or more persons who interact and have mutual influence on each other. *627*

group polarization The tendency for groups to make more-extreme decisions than their members would make as individuals. *628*

groupthink The tendency of small, cohesive groups to place unanimity ahead of critical thinking in making decisions. *629*

Guilty Knowledge Test A method that assesses lying by measuring physiological arousal in response to information that is relevant to a transgression and physiological arousal in response to information that is irrelevant to that transgression. *450*

gustation The sense of taste, which detects molecules dissolved in the saliva. *195*

hallucinogens Psychoactive drugs that induce extreme alterations in consciousness, including visual hallucinations, a sense of timelessness, and feelings of depersonalization. *240*

health psychology The field that applies psychological principles to the prevention and treatment of physical illness. *24, 574*

heritability The extent to which variability in a characteristic within a group can be attributed to heredity. *117, 377*

heuristic A general principle or "rule of thumb" that guides problem solving, though it does not guarantee a correct solution. *328*

hidden observer Ernest Hilgard's term for the part of the hypnotized person's consciousness that is not under the control of the hypnotist. *231*

hierarchy of needs Abraham Maslow's arrangement of needs in the order of their motivational priority, ranging from physiological needs to the needs for self-actualization and transcendence. *390*

higher-order conditioning In classical conditioning, the establishment of a conditioned response to a neutral stimulus that has been paired with an existing conditioned stimulus. *256*

hippocampus A limbic system structure that contributes to the formation of memories. *89*

historicism An approach to history that studies the past for its own sake, in the context of beliefs and knowledge that characterized the period being studied. *4*

holophrastic speech The use of single words to represent whole phrases or sentences. *342*

homeostasis A steady state of physiological equilibrium. *389*

homosexuality A consistent preference for sexual relations with members of one's own sex. *405*

hormones Chemicals, secreted by endocrine glands, that play a role in a variety of functions, including synaptic transmission. *81*

hospice movement The movement to provide care for the terminally ill in settings that are as close as possible to everyday life, and that emphasizes the need to reduce pain and suffering. *152*

humanistic perspective The psychological viewpoint that holds that the proper subject matter of psychology is the individual's subjective experience of the world. *18*

hypermnesia The hypnotic enhancement of recall. *230*

hyperopia Visual farsightedness, which is caused by a shortened eyeball. *168*

hypnosis An induced state of consciousness in which one person responds to suggestions by another person for alterations in perception, thinking, and behavior. *226*

hypochondriasis A somatoform disorder in which the person interprets the slightest physical changes as evidence of a serious illness. *510*

hypothalamus A forebrain structure that helps to regulate aspects of motivation and emotion, including eating, drinking, sexual behavior, body temperature, and stress responses, through its effects on the pituitary gland and the autonomic nervous system. *89*

hypothesis A testable prediction about the relationship between two or more events or characteristics. *37*

iconic memory Visual sensory memory, which lasts up to about a second. *288*

id In Freud's theory, the part of the personality that contains inborn biological drives and that seeks immediate gratification. *463*

identity versus role confusion Erikson's developmental stage in which success is achieved by establishing a sense of personal identity. *144*

illusory contours The perception of edges that do not actually exist, as though they were the outlines of real objects. *180*

implicit memory The process by which a past event or information stored in memory can influence our present behavior without our conscious recollection of the event or information. *248*

impression formation The process of making judgments about the personal characteristics of others. *611*

impression management The deliberate attempt to control the impression that others form of us. *611*

incentive An external stimulus that pulls an individual toward a goal. *390*

incentive value The perceived rewards that accompany success in a particular area. *412*

incongruity theory The theory that humor is amusing when it brings together incompatible ideas in a surprising outcome that violates one's expectations. *437*

independent variable A variable manipulated by the experimenter to determine its effect on another, dependent, variable. 49

industrial/organizational psychology The field that applies psychological principles to improve productivity in businesses, industries, and government agencies. 24

industry versus inferiority Erikson's developmental stage in which success is achieved by developing a sense of competency. 133

infancy The period that extends from birth through 2 years of age. 122

inferential statistics Statistics used to determine whether changes in a dependent variable are caused by an independent variable. 59, A–14

information-processing model The view that the processing of memories involves encoding, storage, and retrieval. 288

inhalants Depressants that are inhaled to induce altered states of consciousness. 237

initiative versus guilt Erikson's developmental stage in which success is achieved by behaving in a spontaneous but socially appropriate way. 132

insanity A legal term attesting that a person is not responsible for his or her own actions, including criminal behavior. 526

insight An approach to problem solving that depends on mental manipulation of information rather than overt trial and error, and produces sudden solutions to problems. 327

insomnia Chronic difficulty in either falling asleep or staying asleep. 221

instinct A relatively complex, inherited behavior pattern characteristic of a species. 388

instinctive drift The reversion of animals to behaviors characteristic of their species even when being reinforced for performing other behaviors. 274

instrumental conditioning A form of learning in which a behavior becomes more or less probable, depending on its consequences. 263

integrity versus despair Erikson's developmental stage in which success is achieved by reflecting back on a meaningful life. 151

intelligence The global capacity to act purposefully, to think rationally, and to deal effectively with the environment. 358

intelligence quotient (IQ) 1. Originally, the ratio of mental age to chronological age; that is, MA/CA × 100. 2. Today, the score on an intelligence test, calculated by comparing a person's performance to norms for her or his age group. 361

intelligence test A test that assesses overall mental ability. 359

interference theory The theory that forgetting results from some memories' interfering with the ability to remember other memories. 301

internal validity The extent to which changes in a dependent variable can be attributed to one or more independent variables rather than to a confounding variable. 51

interneuron A neuron that conveys messages between neurons in the brain or spinal cord. 72

interval scale A scale of measurement that indicates the exact magnitude of scores, but not their ratio to one another. A–5

intimacy versus isolation Erikson's developmental stage in which success is achieved by establishing a relationship with a strong sense of emotional attachment and personal commitment. 148

intrinsic motivation The desire to perform a behavior for its own sake. 414

introvert A person who is socially reserved and prefers to pay attention to his or her private mental experiences. 470

in vivo desensitization A form of counterconditioning that trains the client to maintain a state of relaxation in the presence of anxiety-inducing stimuli. 542

iris The donut-shaped band of muscles behind the cornea that gives the eye its color and controls the size of the pupil. 167

James-Lange theory The theory that specific patterns of physiological changes evoke specific emotional experiences. 437

jigsaw method Elliott Aronson's approach to reducing prejudice by having members of different groups contribute to the solution of a problem. 627

just noticeable difference (jnd) Weber and Fechner's term for the difference threshold. 165

kinesthetic sense The sense that provides information about the position of the joints, the degree of tension in the muscles, and the movement of the arms and legs. 199

language A formal system of communication involving symbols—whether spoken, written, or gestured—and rules for combining them. 338

latency stage In Freud's theory, the stage, between age 5 and puberty, during which there is little psychosexual development. 466

latent content Sigmund Freud's term for the true, though disguised, meaning of a dream. 225

latent learning Learning that occurs without the reinforcement of overt behavior. 276

law of effect Edward Thorndike's principle that a behavior followed by a satisfying state of affairs is strengthened and a behavior followed by an annoying state of affairs is weakened. 263

learned helplessness A feeling of futility caused by the belief that one has little or no control over events in one's life, which can make one stop trying and become depressed. 273, 587

learning A relatively permanent change in knowledge or behavior resulting from experience. 254

lens The transparent structure behind the pupil that focuses light onto the retina. 168

levels of processing theory The theory that the "depth" at which we process information determines how well it is encoded, stored, and retrieved. 293

libido Freud's term for the sexual energy of the id. 466

limbic system A group of forebrain structures that promote the survival of the individual and, as a result, the continuation of the species by their influence on emotion, motivation, and memory. 89

line graph A graph used to plot data showing the relationship between independent and dependent variables in an experiment. A–8

linguistic relativity hypothesis The assumption that one's perception of the world is molded by one's language. 346

link method A mnemonic device that involves connecting, in sequence, images of items to be memorized, to make them easier to recall. 308

logical concept A concept formed by identifying the specific features possessed by all things to which concept applies. 323

logotherapy A form of existential therapy, developed by Victor Frankl, that helps the client find meaning in life. 550

longitudinal research A research design in which the same group of subjects is tested or observed repeatedly over a period of time. 119

long-term memory The stage of memory that can store a virtually unlimited amount of information relatively permanently. 287

loudness perception The subjective experience of the intensity of a sound, which corresponds most closely to the amplitude of the sound waves composing it. 191

LSD A hallucinogen derived from a fungus that grows on rye grain. 241

lucid dreaming The ability to be aware that one is dreaming and to direct one's dreams. 224

magnetic resonance imaging (MRI) A brain-scanning technique that relies on strong magnetic fields to construct computer-generated images of the brain or body. 95

maintenance rehearsal Repeating information to oneself to keep it in short-term memory. 292

major depression A mood disorder marked by depression so intense and prolonged that the person may be unable to function in everyday life. 514

mania A mood disorder marked by euphoria, hyperactivity, grandiose ideas, annoying talkativeness, unrealistic optimism, and inflated self-esteem. 515

manifest content Sigmund Freud's term for the verbally reported dream. 225

massed practice Cramming the memorization of information or the learning of a motor skill into one session. 306

maturation The sequential unfolding of inherited predispositions in physical and motor development. 114

mean The arithmetic average of a set of scores. 57, A–9

mean length of utterance (MLU) The average length of spoken statements, used as a measure of language development in children. 343

measurement The use of numbers to represent events or characteristics. 40

measure of central tendency A statistic that represents the "typical" score in a set of scores. 57

measure of variability A statistic describing the degree of dispersion in a set of scores. 58

median The middle score in a set of scores that have been ordered from lowest to highest. 57, A–9

meditation A procedure that uses mental exercises to achieve a highly focused state of consciousness. 233

medulla oblongata A hindbrain structure that regulates breathing, heart rate, blood pressure, and other life functions. 86

memory The process by which information is acquired, stored in the brain, and later retrieved. 286

menarche The beginning of menstruation, usually occurring between the ages of 11 and 13. 141

mental giftedness Intellectual superiority marked by an IQ above 130 and exceptionally high scores on achievement tests in specific subjects, such as mathematics. 369

mental retardation Intellectual deficiency marked by an IQ below 70 and difficulties performing in everyday life. 365

mental set A tendency to use a particular problem-solving strategy that has succeeded in the past but that may interfere with solving a problem requiring a new strategy. 329

mental telepathy The ability to perceive the thoughts of others without any sensory contact with them. *202*

method of loci A mnemonic device in which items to be recalled are associated with landmarks in a familiar place and then recalled during a mental walk from one landmark to another. *307*

method of savings The assessment of memory by comparing the number of trials needed to memorize a given amount of information and the number of trials needed to memorize it again at a later time. *299*

mnemonic device A technique for organizing information to be memorized to make it easier to remember. *308*

mode The score that occurs most frequently in a set of scores. *57, A-9*

monocular cues Depth perception cues that require input from only one eye. *181*

mood disorder A psychological disorder marked by prolonged periods of extreme depression or elation, often unrelated to the person's current situation. *513*

moon illusion The misperception that the moon is larger when it is at the horizon than when it is overhead. *183*

moral therapy An approach to therapy, developed by Philippe Pinel, that provided mental patients with humane treatment. *535*

morpheme The smallest meaningful unit of language. *340*

motivation The psychological processes that arouse, direct, and maintain behavior toward a goal. *388*

motor cortex The area of the frontal lobes that controls specific voluntary body movements. *92*

motor neuron A neuron that sends messages from the central nervous system to smooth muscles, cardiac muscle, or skeletal muscles. *72*

multiple personality A dissociative disorder in which the person has two or more distinct personalities that alternate with one another. *512*

myelin A white fatty substance that forms sheaths around certain axons and increases the speed of neural impulses. *76*

myopia Visual nearsightedness, which is caused by an elongated eyeball. *168*

narcolepsy A condition in which an awake person suffers from repeated, sudden, and irresistible REM sleep attacks. *222*

natural concept A concept, typically formed through everyday experience, whose members possess some, but not all, of a common set of features. *324*

naturalistic observation The recording of the behavior of subjects in their natural environments, with little or no intervention by the researcher. *42*

need A motivated state caused by physiological deprivation, such as a lack of food or water. *389*

negative correlation A correlation between two variables in which the variables tend to change in opposite directions. *48*

negative reinforcement In operant conditioning, an increase in the probability of a behavior that is followed by the removal of an aversive stimulus. *268*

negative skew A graph that has scores bunching up toward the positive end of the abscissa. *A-7*

negative state relief theory The theory that we engage in prosocial behavior to relieve our own state of emotional distress at another's plight. *638*

neglect syndrome A disorder, caused by damage to a parietal lobe, in which the individual acts as though the side of her or his world opposite from the damaged lobe does not exist. *104*

neodissociation theory The theory that hypnosis induces a dissociated state of consciousness. *231*

nerve A bundle of axons that conveys information to or from the central nervous system. *70*

nerve deafness Hearing loss caused by damage to the hair cells of the basilar membrane or the axons of the auditory nerve. *192*

nervous system The chief means of communication in the body, which transmits messages along neurons. *70*

neural grafting The transplantation of brain tissue or, in some cases, adrenal gland tissue into a brain to restore functions lost because of brain damage. *100*

neuron A cell specialized for the transmission of information in the nervous system. *70*

neurosis A general category, no longer widely used, that comprises psychological disorders associated with maladaptive attempts to deal with anxiety but with relatively good contact with reality. *502*

neurotransmitters Chemicals secreted by neurons that provide the means of synaptic transmission. *77*

nicotine A stimulant used to regulate physical and mental arousal. *239*

nightmare A frightening REM dream. *223*

night terror A frightening NREM experience, common in childhood, in which the individual may suddenly sit up, let out a bloodcurdling scream, speak incoherently, and quickly fall back to sleep, yet usually fails to recall it on awakening. *223*

nominal scale A scale of measurement that places objects, individuals, or characteristics into categories. *A-5*

norm A score, based on the test performances of large numbers of subjects, that is used as a standard for assessing the performances of test takers. *47*

normal curve A bell-shaped graph representing a hypothetical frequency distribution for a given characteristic. *A-11*

NREM sleep The stages of sleep not associated with rapid eye movements and marked by relatively little dreaming. *216*

null hypothesis The prediction that the independent variable will have no effect on the dependent variable in an experiment. *A-14*

obedience Following orders given by an authority. *634*

obesity A body weight more than 20 percent above the norm for one's height and build. *394*

object permanence The realization that objects exist even when they are no longer visible. *342*

observational learning Learning a behavior by observing the consequences that others receive for performing it. *276*

obsessive-compulsive disorder An anxiety disorder in which the person has recurrent, intrusive thoughts (obsessions) and recurrent urges to perform ritualistic actions (compulsions). *509*

occipital lobe A lobe of the cerebral cortex responsible for processing vision. *94*

Oedipus complex In Freud's theory, a conflict, during the phallic stage, between the child's sexual desire for the parent of the opposite sex and fear of punishment from the same-sex parent. *466*

olfaction The sense of smell, which detects molecules carried in the air. *194*

operant conditioning B. F. Skinner's term for instrumental conditioning. *263*

operational definition The definition of behaviors or qualities in terms of the procedures used to measure them. *40*

opiates Depressant drugs, derived from opium, used to relieve pain or to induce a euphoric state of consciousness. *238*

opponent-process theory The theory that color vision depends on red-green, blue-yellow, and black-white opponent processes in the brain. *175*

opponent-process theory of emotion The theory that the brain counteracts a strong positive or negative emotion by evoking an opposite emotional response. *441*

optic chiasm The point under the frontal lobes at which some axons from each of the optic nerves cross over to the opposite side of the brain. *171*

optic nerve The nerve formed from the axons of ganglion cells that carries visual impulses from the retina to the brain. *170*

oral stage In Freud's theory, the stage of personality development, between birth and age 1, during which the infant gains pleasure from oral activities and faces a conflict over weaning. *466*

ordinal scale A scale of measurement that indicates the relative, but not exact, magnitude of scores. *A-5*

otolith organs The vestibular organs that detect horizontal or vertical linear movement of the head. *199*

ovaries The female gonads, which secrete hormones that regulate the development of the female reproductive system and secondary sex characteristics. *82*

overextension The tendency to apply a word to more objects or actions than it actually represents. *342*

overjustification theory The theory that an extrinsic reward will decrease intrinsic motivation when a person attributes her or his performance to that reward. *414*

overlearning Studying material beyond the point of initial mastery. *306*

overregularization The application of a grammatical rule without making necessary exceptions to it. *343*

pancreas An endocrine gland that secretes hormones that regulate the level of blood sugar. *84*

panic disorder An anxiety disorder marked by sudden, unexpected attacks of overwhelming anxiety, often associated with the fear of dying or "losing one's mind." *506*

parallel processing The processing of different information simultaneously. *337*

paranoid schizophrenia A type of schizophrenia marked by hallucinations, delusions, suspiciousness, and argumentativeness. *521*

paraphilia A way of obtaining sexual gratification that violates legal or cultural norms concerning proper sex objects and sexual practices. *399*

parapsychology The study of extrasensory perception, psychokinesis, and related phenomena. *201*

parasympathetic nervous system The division of the autonomic nervous system that calms the body and serves maintenance functions. *70*

parietal lobe A lobe of the cerebral cortex responsible for processing body sensations and perceiving spatial relations. *93*

Parkinson's disease A degenerative disease of the dopamine pathway from the substantia nigra, which causes marked disturbances in motor behavior. *87*

partial schedule of reinforcement A schedule of reinforcement that reinforces some, but not all, instances of a desired response. *267*

participant modeling A form of social-learning therapy in which the client learns to perform more-adaptive behaviors by first observing the therapist model the desired behaviors. *545*

passionate love Love characterized by intense emotional arousal and sexual feelings. *617*

Pearson's product-moment correlation Perhaps the most commonly used correlational statistic. *A–13*

pegword method A mnemonic device that involves associating items to be recalled with objects that rhyme with the numbers *1, 2, 3,* and so on, to make the items easier to recall. *308*

percentile The score at or below which a particular percentage of scores fall. *A–12*

perception The process that organizes sensations into meaningful patterns. *162*

perception without awareness The unconscious perception of stimuli that normally exceed the absolute threshold but fall outside our focus of attention. *243*

peripheral nervous system The division of the nervous system, composed of the nerves, that conveys sensory information to the central nervous system and motor commands from the central nervous system to the skeletal muscles and internal organs. *70*

personal construct A hypothesis about social reality that is held by a person. *482*

personality An individual's unique, relatively consistent pattern of thinking, feeling, and behaving. *456*

personality disorder A psychological disorder characterized by enduring, inflexible, maladaptive patterns of behavior. *524*

personality psychology The field that focuses on factors accounting for the differences in behavior and enduring personal characteristics among individuals. *23*

personal unconscious In Jung's theory, the individual's own unconscious mind, which contains repressed memories. *469*

person-centered therapy A type of humanistic therapy, developed by Carl Rogers, that helps clients find their own answers to their problems. *547*

persuasion The attempt to influence the attitudes of other people. *620*

phallic stage In Freud's theory, the stage of personality development, between ages 3 and 5, during which the child gains pleasure from the genitals and must resolve the Oedipus complex. *466*

phase advance Shortening the sleep-wake cycle, as occurs when traveling from west to east. *214*

phase delay Lengthening the sleep-wake cycle, as occurs when traveling from east to west. *214*

phenotype The overt expression of an individual's inheritance, which may also show the influence of the environment. *116*

phenylketonuria (PKU) A hereditary enzyme deficiency that, if left untreated in the infant, causes mental retardation. *367*

pheromones Odorous chemicals secreted by an animal that affect the behavior of other animals. *195*

phi phenomenon Apparent motion caused by the presentation of different stimuli in rapid succession. *14*

phobia An anxiety disorder marked by excessive or inappropriate fear. *507*

phoneme The smallest unit of sound in a language. *340*

phonology The study of the sounds that compose languages. *340*

photopigments Chemicals, including rhodopsin and iodopsin, that enable the rods and cones to generate neural impulses. *173*

phrenology A discredited technique for determining intellectual abilities and personality traits by examining the bumps and depressions of the skull. *98*

pie graph A graph that represents data as percentages of a pie. *A–6*

pineal gland An endocrine gland that secretes a hormone that has a general tranquilizing effect on the body and that helps regulate biological rhythms. *84, 213*

pitch perception The subjective experience of the highness or lowness of a sound, which corresponds most closely to the frequency of the sound waves that compose it. *190*

pituitary gland An endocrine gland that regulates many of the other endocrine glands by secreting hormones that affect those glands. *81*

placebo An inactive substance that may induce some of the effects of the drug for which it has been substituted. *198*

place theory The theory of pitch perception that assumes that hair cells at particular points on the basilar membrane are maximally responsive to sound waves of particular frequencies. *190*

plasticity The ability of the brain to alter its neuronal pathways. *99*

pleasure principle The process by which the id seeks immediate gratification of its impulses. *463*

polygraph test The "lie detector" test, which assesses lying by measuring changing patterns of physiological arousal in response to particular questions. *448*

pons A hindbrain structure that regulates the sleep-wake cycle. *87*

population A group of individuals who share certain characteristics. *45*

pornography Sexually explicit material intended to incite sexual arousal. *646*

positive correlation A correlation in which variables tend to change in the same direction. *48*

positive reinforcement In operant conditioning, an increase in the probability of a behavior that is followed by a desirable stimulus. *263*

positive skew A graph that has scores bunching up toward the negative end of the abscissa. *A–7*

positron-emission tomography (PET) A brain-scanning technique that produces color-coded pictures showing the relative activity of different brain areas. *94*

postconventional level In Kohlberg's theory, the level of moral reasoning characterized by concern with obeying mutually agreed upon laws and by the need to uphold human dignity. *154*

posthypnotic suggestions Suggestions directing subjects to carry out particular behaviors or to have particular experiences after leaving hypnosis. *230*

posttraumatic stress disorder A syndrome of physical and psychological symptoms that appears as a delayed response after exposure to an extremely emotionally distressing event. *579*

pragmatics The relationship between language and its social context. *341*

precognition The ability to perceive events in the future. *202*

preconscious mind The level of consciousness that contains feelings and memories that we are unaware of at the moment but can become aware of at will. *247*

preconventional level In Kohlberg's theory, the level of moral reasoning characterized by concern with the consequences that behavior has to oneself. *154*

prejudice An attitude, usually negative, toward others, based on their membership in particular groups. *625*

Premack principle The principle that a more probable behavior can be used as a reinforcer for a less probable one. *263*

preoperational stage The Piagetian stage, extending from 2 to 7 years of age, during which the child's use of language becomes more sophisticated but the child has difficulty with the logical mental manipulation of information. *128*

presentism An approach to history that studies the past in the context of present beliefs and knowledge. *4*

pressure The emotional state induced when one is confronted by personal responsibilities that tax one's abilities. *575*

primary cortical areas Regions of the cerebral cortex that serve motor or sensory functions. *92*

primary reinforcer In operant conditioning, an unlearned reinforcer, which satisfies a biological need such as air, food, or water. *264*

proactive interference The process by which old memories interfere with the ability to remember new memories. *301*

problem solving The thought process by which an individual overcomes obstacles to reach a goal. *325*

procedural memory The long-term memory system that contains memories of how to perform particular actions or skills. *293*

programmed instruction A step-by-step approach, based on operant conditioning, in which the learner proceeds at his or her own pace through more and more difficult material and receives immediate knowledge of the results of each response. *272*

progressive relaxation A stress-reducing procedure that involves the successive tensing and relaxing of each of the major muscle groups of the body. *590*

projective test A Freudian personality test based on the assumption that individuals project their unconscious feelings when responding to ambiguous stimuli. *471*

prosocial behavior Behavior that helps others in need. *637*

prosopagnosia The inability to recognize familiar faces, which is typically caused by damage to the occipital lobes. *96*

prototype The best representative of a concept. *324*

psychiatry The field of medicine that diagnoses and treats psychological disorders by using medical or psychological forms of therapy. *24*

psychic determinism The Freudian assumption that all behaviors are influenced by unconscious motives. *15*

psychoactive drugs Chemicals that induce changes in mood, thinking, perception, and behavior by affecting neuronal activity in the brain. *235*

psychoanalysis 1. The early school of psychology that emphasized the importance of unconscious causes of behavior. 2. A type of psychotherapy, developed by Sigmund Freud, aimed at uncovering the unconscious causes of psychological disorders. *15, 537*

psychoanalytic perspective The psychological viewpoint, descended from psychoanalysis, that places less emphasis on biological motives and more emphasis on the importance of interpersonal relationships. *18*

psychodrama A form of psychoanalytic group therapy, developed by Jacob Moreno, that aims at achieving insight and catharsis through acting out real-life situations. *550*

psychogenic amnesia A dissociative disorder marked by the inability to recall personally significant memories. *512*

psychogenic fugue A dissociative disorder marked by the memory loss characteristic of psychogenic amnesia, the loss of one's identity, and fleeing from one's home. *512*

psychokinesis (PK) The ability to control objects with the mind alone. *202*

psychological hardiness A personality characteristic—marked by feelings of commitment, challenge, and control—that promotes resistance to stress. *587*

psychological test A formal sample of a person's behavior, whether written or performed. *46*

psychology The science of behavior and mental processes. *4*

psychoneuroimmunology The interdisciplinary field that studies the relationship between psychological factors and physical illness. *582*

psychopathology The study of psychological disorders. *496*

psychophysics The study of the relationship between the physical characteristics of stimuli and the conscious psychological experiences they produce. *8, 162*

psychosis A general category, no longer widely used, that comprises severe psychological disorders associated with thought disturbances, bizarre behavior, severe disruption of social relations, and relatively poor contact with reality. *502*

psychosurgery The treatment of psychological disorders by destroying of brain tissue. *555*

psychotherapy The treatment of psychological disorders through psychological, as opposed to biomedical, means, generally involving verbal interaction with a professional therapist. *536*

puberty The period of rapid physical change that occurs during adolescence, including the development of the ability to reproduce sexually. *141*

punishment In operant conditioning, the process by which an aversive stimulus decreases the probability of a response that precedes it. *269*

pupil The opening at the center of the iris that controls how much light enters the eye. *167*

quasi-experimental research The use of experimental research methods in situations in which the researcher might not be able to randomly assign subjects to the experimental and control conditions. *50*

random assignment The assignment of subjects to experimental and control conditions so that each subject is as likely to be assigned to one condition as to another. *53*

random sampling The selection of a sample from a population so that each member of the population has an equal chance of being included. *46*

range A statistic representing the difference between the highest and lowest scores in a set of scores. *58, A–10*

rational-emotive therapy (R-E-T) A type of cognitive therapy, developed by Albert Ellis, that treats psychological disorders by forcing the client to give up irrational beliefs. *545*

rationalism The philosophical position that true knowledge comes through correct reasoning. *5*

ratio scale A scale of measurement that indicates the ratio of scores to one another. *A–5*

reality principle The process by which the ego directs the individual to express sexual and aggressive impulses in socially acceptable ways. *463*

reciprocal determinism Bandura's belief that personality traits, environmental factors, and overt behavior affect each other. *479*

reflex An automatic, involuntary motor response to sensory stimulation. *72*

relaxation response A variation of transcendental meditation in which the individual may repeat a sound other than a mantra. *234*

release theory The theory that humor is amusing when it relieves one's sexual or aggressive anxiety. *437*

reliability The extent to which a test gives consistent results. *47*

REM sleep The stage of sleep associated with rapid eye movements, an active brain-wave pattern, and vivid dreams. *216*

replication The repetition of a research study, usually with some alterations in its subjects, methods, or setting, to determine whether the principles derived from that study hold up under similar circumstances. *37*

representativeness heuristic In decision making, the assumption that characteristics of a small sample are representative of its population. *335*

repression The process by which emotionally threatening experiences are banished from the conscious mind to the unconscious mind. *302*

resting potential The electrical charge of a neuron when it is not firing a neural impulse. *74*

reticular formation A diffuse network of neurons, extending from the hindbrain through the midbrain and into the forebrain, that helps maintain vigilance and an optimal level of brain arousal. *87*

retina The light-sensitive inner membrane of the eye that contains the receptor cells for vision. *168*

retrieval The recovery of information from memory. *287*

retroactive interference The process by which new memories interfere with the ability to remember old memories. *301*

rods Receptor cells of the retina that play an important role in night vision and peripheral vision. *169*

saccadic movements Continuous small darting movements of the eyes that bring new portions of scenes into focus on the foveae. *171*

sample A group of subjects selected from a population. *45*

scatter plot A graph of a correlational relationship. *A–13*

schema A mental model incorporating the characteristics of particular persons, objects, events, or situations. *127*

schema theory The theory that long-term memories are stored as parts of schemas, which are cognitive structures that organize knowledge about events or objects. *296*

schizophrenia A class of psychological disorders characterized by grossly impaired social, emotional, cognitive, and perceptual functioning. *519*

school psychology The field that applies psychological principles to improving the academic performance and social behavior of students in elementary, junior high, and high schools. *24*

scientific method A source of knowledge based on the assumption that knowledge comes from the objective, systematic observation and measurement of particular variables and the events they affect. *37*

scientific paradigm A model that determines the appropriate goals, methods, and subject matter of a science. *17*

sclera The tough, white outer membrane of the eye. *167*

seasonal affective disorder A mood disorder in which severe depression arises during a particular season, usually the winter. *514*

secondary reinforcer In operant conditioning, a neutral stimulus that becomes reinforcing after being associated with a primary reinforcer. *264*

self-actualization In Maslow's theory, the individual's predisposition to try to fulfill her or his potentials. *484*

self-efficacy In Bandura's theory, a person's belief that he or she can perform behaviors that are necessary to bring about a desired outcome. *480*

self-fulfilling prophecy The tendency for one person's expectations to influence another person to behave in accordance with them. *613*

self-perception theory Daryl Bem's theory that when we are unsure of our attitudes we infer them from our own behavior. *624*

self-serving bias The tendency to make dispositional attributions for one's successes and situational attributions for one's failures. *611*

semanticity The characteristic of language marked by the use of symbols to convey thoughts in a meaningful way. *338*

semantic memory The subsystem of declarative memory that contains general information about the world. *293*

semantic network theory The theory that memories are stored as nodes interconnected by links that represent their relationships. *295*

semantics The study of how language conveys meaning. *341*

semicircular canals The curved vestibular organs of the inner ear that detect movements of the head in any direction. *199*

sensate focusing A sex therapy technique that at first involves nongenital caressing and gradually progresses to sexual intercourse. *404*

sensation The process that detects stimuli from the body or surroundings. *162*

sensation seeking The extent to which an individual seeks sensory stimulation. *409*

sensorimotor stage The Piagetian stage, from birth through the second year, during which the infant learns to coordinate sensory experiences and motor behavior. *127*

sensory adaptation The tendency of the sensory receptors to respond less and less to a constant stimulus. *165*

sensory deprivation The prolonged withdrawal of normal levels of external stimulation. *408*

sensory memory The stage of memory that briefly, for at most a few seconds, stores exact replicas of sensations. *287*

sensory neuron A neuron that sends messages from sensory receptors to the central nervous system. *72*

sensory receptors Specialized cells that detect stimuli and convert their energy into neural impulses. *162*

sensory transduction The process by which sensory receptors convert stimuli into neural impulses. *162*

serial-position effect The superiority of immediate recall for items at the beginning and end of a list. *298*

serial processing The processing of information one step at a time. *337*

set point A specific body weight that the brain tries to maintain through the regulation of diet, activity, and metabolism. *393*

sexual dysfunction A chronic problem at one or more phases of the sexual response cycle. *403*

sexual orientation One's sexual attraction toward members of either one's own sex or the opposite sex. *404*

sexual response cycle During sexual activity, the phases of excitement, plateau, orgasm, and resolution. *401*

shape constancy The perceptual process that makes an object appear to maintain its normal shape regardless of the angle from which it is viewed. *182*

shaping An operant conditioning procedure that involves the positive reinforcement of successive approximations of an initially improbable behavior to eventually bring about that behavior. *265*

short-term memory The stage of memory that can store a few items of unrehearsed information for up to about 20 seconds. *287*

signal-detection theory The theory holding that the detection of a stimulus depends on both the intensity of the stimulus and the physical and psychological state of the individual. *163*

simple phobia A phobia of a specific object or situation. *507*

size constancy The perceptual process that makes an object appear to remain the same size despite changes in the size of the image it casts on the retina. *182*

skepticism An attitude that doubts all claims not supported by solid research evidence. *36*

Skinner box An enclosure that contains a bar or key that can be pressed to obtain food or water, which is used to study operant conditioning in rats, pigeons, or other small animals. *263*

skin senses The senses of touch, temperature, and pain. *196*

sleep apnea A condition in which a person awakens repeatedly in order to breathe. *221*

smooth pursuit movements Eye movements that track objects. *170*

social attachment A strong emotional relationship between an infant and a caregiver. *130*

social attribution The cognitive process by which we infer the causes of both our own and other people's social behavior. *608*

social clock The major events that typically occur at certain times in the typical life cycle in a given culture. *140*

social cognition The process of perceiving, interpreting, and predicting social behavior. *608*

social-comparison theory The theory that happiness is the result of estimating that one's life circumstances are more favorable than those of others. *435*

social facilitation The improvement in a person's task performance when in the presence of other people. *630*

social learning theory A theory of gender-role development that assumes that people learn social behaviors mainly through observation and mental processing of information. *136, 277*

social loafing A decrease in the individual effort exerted by group members when working together on a task. *631*

social phobia A phobia of situations that involve public scrutiny. *507*

social psychology The field that studies how people affect one another's thoughts, feelings, and behaviors. *23, 608*

social schema A cognitive structure comprising the presumed characteristics of a role, an event, a person, or a group. *612*

social-skills training A form of behavioral group therapy that improves the client's social relationships by improving her or his interpersonal skills. *552*

sociobiology The study of the hereditary basis of human and animal social behavior. *389*

soma The cell body, which serves as the neuron's control center. *72*

somatic nervous system The division of the peripheral nervous system that sends messages from the sensory organs to the central nervous system and messages from the central nervous system to the skeletal muscles. *70*

somatoform disorder A psychological disorder characterized by physical symptoms in the absence of disease or injury. *510*

somatosensory cortex The area of the parietal lobes that processes information from sensory receptors in the skin. *93, 197*

somatotype A person's body type, whether ectomorphic (thin), mesomorphic (muscular), or endomorphic (fat). *458*

sound localization The process by which the individual determines the location of a sound. *193*

spatial frequency filter theory The theory that visual perception depends on the detection and analysis of variations in patterns of light and dark. *180*

spinal cord The portion of the central nervous system that is located in the spine and plays a role in body reflexes and in communicating information between the brain and the peripheral nervous system. *70*

split-brain research Research on hemispheric specialization that studies individuals in whom the corpus callosum has been severed. *105*

spontaneous recovery 1. In classical conditioning, the reappearance after a period of time of a conditioned response that has been subjected to extinction. 2. In operant conditioning, the reappearance after a period of time of a behavior that has been subjected to extinction. *258, 269*

spontaneous remission The improvement of some persons with psychological disorders without their undergoing formal therapy. *565*

sport psychology The field that applies psychological principles to help amateur and professional athletes improve their performance. *24, 415*

SQ3R method A study technique in which the student surveys, questions, reads, recites, and reviews course material. *306*

standard deviation A statistic representing the degree of dispersion of a set of scores around their mean. *58, A–11*

standardization 1. A procedure assuring that a test is administered and scored in a consistent manner. 2. A procedure for establishing test norms by giving a test to large samples of people who are representative of those for whom the test is designed. *47*

state-dependent memory The tendency for recall to be best when one's emotional or physiological state is the same during the recall of a memory as it was during the encoding of that memory. *304*

statistical significance A low probability (usually less than 5 percent) that the results of a research study are due to chance factors rather than to the independent variable. *59, A–16*

statistics Mathematical techniques used to summarize research data or to determine whether the data support the researcher's hypothesis. *37, A–4*

stereochemical theory The theory of olfaction and gustation that assumes that receptors are stimulated by molecules of particular sizes and shapes. *194*

stereotype A social schema that incorporates characteristics, which may be positive or negative, supposedly shared by almost all members of a group. *612*

stimulants Psychoactive drugs that increase central nervous system activity. *238*

stimulus discrimination In classical conditioning, giving a conditioned response to the conditioned stimulus but not to stimuli similar to it. *258*

stimulus generalization In classical conditioning, giving a conditioned response to stimuli similar to the conditioned stimulus. *257*

storage The retention of information in memory. *287*

stress The physiological response of the body to physical and psychological demands. *574*

stress-inoculation training A type of cognitive therapy, developed by Donald Meichenbaum, that helps clients change their pessimistic thinking into more positive thinking when in stressful situations. *547*

stressor A physical or psychological demand that induces physiological adjustment. *574*

structuralism The early school of psychology that sought to identify the components of the conscious mind. *10*

subject bias The tendency of people who know they are subjects in a study to behave in a way other than they normally would. *53*

subliminal perception The unconscious perception of stimuli that are too weak to exceed the absolute threshold for detection. *244*

subliminal psychodynamic activation The use of subliminal messages to stimulate unconscious fantasies. *247*

substantia nigra A midbrain structure that promotes smooth voluntary body movements. *87*

superego In Freud's theory, the part of the personality that acts as a moral guide telling us what we should and should not do. *464*

surface structure The word arrangements used to express thoughts. *341*

survey A set of questions related to a particular topic of interest administered through an interview or questionnaire. *45*

sympathetic nervous system The division of the autonomic nervous system that arouses the body to prepare it for action. *70*

synapse The junction between a neuron and another neuron, a gland, a muscle, or a sensory organ. *77*

synaptic transmission The conveying of a neural impulse between a neuron and another neuron or a gland, muscle, or sensory organ. *76*

synesthesia The process in which an individual experiences sensations in one sensory modality that are characteristic of another. *241*

syntax The rules that govern the acceptable arrangement of words in phrases and sentences. *340*

systematic desensitization A form of counterconditioning that trains the client to maintain a state of relaxation in the presence of imagined anxiety-inducing stimuli. *540*

taste buds Structures lining the grooves of the tongue that contain the taste receptor cells. *195*

tectum A midbrain structure that mediates reflexive responses to visual and auditory stimuli. *87*

telegraphic speech Speech marked by reliance on nouns and verbs, while omitting other parts of speech, including articles and prepositions. *342*

temperament A person's characteristic emotional state, first apparent in early infancy and possibly inborn. *457*

temporal lobe A lobe of the cerebral cortex responsible for processing hearing. *94*

teratogen A noxious substance, such as a virus or drug, that can cause prenatal defects. *121*

testes The male gonads, which secrete hormones that regulate the development of the male reproductive system and secondary sex characteristics. *82*

thalamus A forebrain structure that acts as a sensory relay station for taste, body, visual, and auditory sensations. *88*

theory An integrated set of statements that summarizes and explains research findings, and from which research hypotheses may be derived. *40*

theory of multiple intelligences Howard Gardner's theory of intelligence, which assumes that the brain has evolved separate systems for seven kinds of intelligence. *373*

thinking The mental manipulation of words and images, as in concept formation, problem solving, and decision making. *322*

thyroid gland An endocrine gland that secretes hormones needed for normal metabolism, physical growth, and brain development. *81*

timbre The subjective experience that identifies a particular sound and corresponds most closely to the mixture of sound waves composing it. *192*

tip-of-the-tongue phenomenon The inability to recall information that one knows has been stored in long-term memory. *303*

token economy An operant conditioning procedure that uses tokens as positive reinforcers in programs designed to promote desirable behaviors, with the tokens later used to purchase desired items or privileges. *272, 542*

trait A relatively enduring, cross-situationally consistent personality characteristic that is inferred from a person's behavior. *474*

transactional analysis (TA) A form of psychoanalytic group therapy, developed by Eric Berne, that helps clients change their immature or inappropriate ways of relating to other people. *551*

transcendental meditation (TM) A form of meditation in which the individual relaxes and repeats a sound called a mantra for two 20-minute periods a day. *234*

transcutaneous electrical nerve stimulation (TENS) The use of electrical stimulation of sites on the body to provide pain relief, apparently by stimulating the release of endorphins. *198*

transformational grammar The rules by which languages generate surface structures from deep structures, and deep structures from surface structures. *341*

transitive inference The application of previously learned relationships to infer new relationships. *129*

transsexualism A condition in which a genetic male or female has the gender identity of the opposite sex. *404*

trephining An ancient technique that used sharp stones to chip holes in the skull, possibly to let out evil spirits that supposedly caused abnormal behavior. *534*

trial and error An approach to problem solving in which the individual tries one possible solution after another until one works. *326*

triarchic theory of intelligence Robert Sternberg's theory of intelligence, which assumes that there are three main kinds of intelligence: componential, experiential, and contextual. *373*

trichromatic theory The theory that color vision depends on the relative degree of stimulation of red, green, and blue receptors. *175*

trust versus mistrust Erikson's developmental stage in which success is achieved by having a secure social attachment with a caregiver. *130*

t test A statistical technique used to determine whether the difference between two sets of scores is statistically significant. *A-17*

two-factor theory The theory that emotional experience is the outcome of physiological arousal and the attribution of a cause for that arousal. *444*

tympanic membrane The eardrum; a membrane separating the outer and middle ears that vibrates in response to sound waves that strike it. *188*

Type A behavior A syndrome—marked by impatience, hostility, and extreme competitiveness—that may be associated with the development of coronary heart disease. *601*

unconditioned response (UCR) In classical conditioning, an unlearned, automatic response to a particular unconditioned stimulus. *256*

unconditioned stimulus (UCS) In classical conditioning, a stimulus that automatically elicits a particular unconditioned response. *256*

unconscious mind The level of consciousness that contains thoughts, feelings, and memories that influence us without our awareness and that we cannot become aware of at will. *247*

underextension The tendency to apply a word to fewer objects or actions than it actually represents. *342*

undifferentiated schizophrenia A catchall category for cases that do not fall neatly into any single kind of schizophrenia. *520*

validity The extent to which a test measures what it is supposed to measure. *47*

variable An event, behavior, or characteristic that has two or more values. *48*

variable-interval schedule of reinforcement A partial schedule of reinforcement that provides reinforcement for the first desired response made after varying, unpredictable lengths of time. *268*

variable-ratio schedule of reinforcement A partial schedule of reinforcement that provides reinforcement after varying, unpredictable numbers of desired responses. *267*

variance A measure of variability indicating the average of the squared deviations from the mean. *A-10*

vestibular sense The sense that provides information about one's position in space and helps in the maintenance of balance. *199*

visible spectrum The portion of the electromagnetic spectrum that we commonly call light. *165*

vision The sense that detects objects by the light reflected from them into the eyes. *165*

visual cortex The area of the occipital lobes that processes visual input. *94, 171*

visual illusion A misperception of physical reality usually caused by the misapplication of visual cues. *183*

volley theory The theory of pitch perception that assumes that sound waves of particular frequencies induce auditory neurons to fire in volleys, with one volley following another. *190*

Wada test A technique in which a cerebral hemisphere is anesthetized to assess hemispheric specialization. *103*

Weber's law The principle that the amount of change in stimulation needed to produce a just noticeable difference is a constant proportion of the original stimulus. *165*

Wernicke's area The area of the temporal lobe responsible for the comprehension of speech. *96*

Yerkes-Dodson law The principle that the relationship between arousal and performance is best represented by an inverted U-shaped curve. *407*

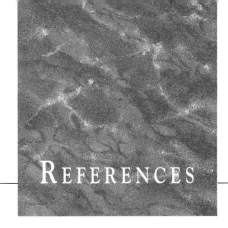

REFERENCES

Aarons, L. (1976). Sleep-assisted instruction. *Psychological Bulletin, 83*, 1–40.

Abbott, M. W., & Raeburn, J. M. (1989). Superhealth: A community-based health promotion programme. *Mental Health in Australia, 2*, 25–35.

Abella, R., & Heslin, R. (1989). Appraisal processes, coping, and the regulation of stress-related emotions in a college examination. *Basic and Applied Social Psychology, 10*, 311–327.

Abelson, R. P. (1981). Psychological status of the script concept. *American Psychologist, 36*, 715–729.

Abernethy, E. M. (1940). The effect of changed environmental conditions upon the results of college examinations. *Journal of Psychology, 10*, 293–301.

Abramowitz, S. I. (1986). Psychosocial outcomes of sex reassignment surgery. *Journal of Consulting and Clinical Psychology, 54*, 183–189.

Abramson, L. Y., Seligman, M. E. P., & Teasdale, J. D. (1978). Learned helplessness in humans: Critique and reformulation. *Journal of Abnormal Psychology, 87*, 49–74.

Adams, P. R., & Adams, G. R. (1984). Mount Saint Helen's ashfall: Evidence for a disaster stress reaction. *American Psychologist, 39*, 252–260.

Adams, W. L., Garry, P. J., Rhyne, R., & Hunt, W. C. (1990). Alcohol intake in the healthy elderly: Changes with age in a cross-sectional and longitudinal study. *Journal of the American Geriatrics Society, 38*, 211–216.

Adelmann, P. K., & Zajonc, R. B. (1989). Facial efference and the experience of emotion. *Annual Review of Psychology, 40*, 249–289.

Adelson, B. (1984). When novices surpass experts: The difficulty of a task may increase with expertise. *Journal of Experimental Psychology: Learning, Memory, and Cognition, 10*, 483–495.

Ader, R., & Cohen, N. (1982). Behaviorally conditioned immunosuppression and murine systemic lupus erythematosus. *Science, 215*, 1534–1536.

Ader, R., & Cohen, N. (1993). Psychoneuroimmunology: Conditioning and stress. *Annual Review of Psychology, 44*, 53–85.

Ader, R., Felten, D., & Cohen, N. (1990). Interactions between the brain and the immune system. *Annual Review of Pharmacology and Toxicology, 30*, 561–602.

Adler, A. (1927). *Understanding human nature.* New York: Greenberg.

Adler, J., & Carey, J. (1980, February 25). The science of love. *Newsweek*, pp. 89–90.

Adler, T. (1989, November). Revision brings test "to the twenty-first century." *APA Monitor*, pp. 1, 6.

Adorno, T. W., Frenkel-Brunswik, E., Levinson, D. J., & Sanford, R. N. (1950). *The authoritarian personality.* New York: Harper & Row.

Afnan, S. M. (1958/1980). *Avicenna: His life and works.* Westport, CT: Greenwood.

Agmo, A., & Berendfeld, R. (1990). Reinforcing properties of ejaculation in the male rat: Role of opioids and dopamine. *Behavioral Neuroscience, 104*, 177–182.

Agnew, N. M., & Brown, J. L. (1989). Foundations for a model of knowing: I. Constructing reality. *Canadian Psychology, 30*, 152–167.

Agras, W. S. (1993). The diagnosis and treatment of panic disorder. *Annual Review of Medicine, 44*, 39–51.

Aiken, L. R. (1982). *Psychological testing and assessment.* Boston: Allyn & Bacon.

Ainsworth, M. D. S. (1979). Infant-mother attachment. *American Psychologist, 34*, 932–937.

Ainsworth, M. S. (1993). Attachment as related to mother-infant interaction. *Advances in Infant Research, 8*, 1–50.

Aisner, R., & Terkel, J. (1992). Ontogeny of pine cone opening behavior in the black rat, Rattus rattus. *Animal Behaviour, 44*, 327–336.

Ajzen, I., Timko, C., & White, J. B. (1982). Self-monitoring and the attitude-behavior relation. *Journal of Personality and Social Psychology, 42*, 426–435.

Akande, A. (1991). Perception of visual illusions in a sample of Nigerian children. *Perceptual and Motor Skills, 72*, 25–26.

Akerstedt, T. (1988). Sleepiness as a consequence of shift work. *Sleep, 11*, 17–34.

Alba, J. W., & Hasher, L. (1983). Is memory schematic? *Psychological Bulletin, 93*, 203–231.

Aldag, R. J., & Fuller, S. R. (1993). Beyond fiasco: A reappraisal of the groupthink phenomenon and a new model of group decision processes. *Psychological Bulletin, 113*, 533–552.

Aldrich, M. S. (1992). Narcolepsy. *Neurology, 42*, 34–43.

Alexander, G. E., & Crutcher, M. D. (1990). Preparation for movement: Neural representations of intended direction in three motor areas of the monkey. *Journal of Neurophysiology, 64*, 133–150.

Alexander, P. E. (1993). Alprazolam-XR in the treatment of panic disorder: Results of a randomized, double-blind, fixed-dose, placebo-controlled multicenter study. *Psychiatric Annals, 23*, 14–18.

Alexopoulos, G. S., Inturrisi, C. E., Lipman, R., Frances, R., Haycox, J., Dougherty, J. H., & Rossier, J. (1983). Plasma immunoreactive beta-endorphin levels in depression: Effect of electroconvulsive therapy. *Archives of General Psychiatry, 40*, 181–183.

Alexy, B. B. (1991). Factors associated with participation or nonparticipation in a workplace wellness center. *Research in Nursing and Health, 14*, 33–40.

Allen, C. T., & Janiszewski, C. A. (1989). Assessing the role of contingency awareness in attitudinal conditioning with implications for advertising research. *Journal of Marketing Research, 26*, 30–43.

Allen, K. M., Blascovich, J., Tomaka, J., & Kelsey, R. M. (1991). Presence of human friends and pet dogs as moderators of autonomic responses to stress in women. *Journal of Personality and Social Psychology, 61*, 582–589.

Allen, M., Hale, J., Mongeau, P., & Berkowitz-Stafford, S. (1990). Testing a model of message sidedness: Three replications. *Communication Monographs, 57*, 275–291.

Allen, M. G. (1976). Twin studies of affective illness. *Archives of General Psychiatry, 33*, 1476–1478.

Allen, M. G. (1990). Group psychotherapy: Past, present, and future. *Psychiatric Annals, 20*, 358–361.

Allison, P. D., & Furstenberg, F. F., Jr. (1989). How marital dissolution affects children: Variation by age and sex. *Developmental Psychology, 25*, 540–549.

Allport, F. H. (1920). The influence of the group upon association and thought. *Journal of Experimental Psychology, 3*, 159–182.

Allport, G. W. (1954). *The nature of prejudice.* Reading, MA: Addison-Wesley.

Allport, G. W. (1967). Autobiography. In E. G. Boring & G. Lindzey (Eds.), A history of psychology in autobiography (Vol. 5). New York: Appleton-Century-Crofts.

Altmaier, E. M., Leary, M. R., Halpern, S., & Sellers, J. E. (1985). Effects of stress inoculation and participant modeling on confidence and anxiety: Testing predictions of self-efficacy theory. *Journal of Social and Clinical Psychology, 3*, 500–505.

Alzate, H. (1985). Vaginal eroticism and female orgasm: A current appraisal. *Journal of Sex and Marital Therapy, 11*, 271–284.

Amabile, T. M. (1985). Motivation and creativity effects of motivational orientation on creative writers. *Journal of Personality and Social Psychology, 48*, 393–399.

Amabile, T. M. (1989). *Growing up creative*. New York: Random House.

Amabile, T. M., Goldfarb, P., & Brackfield, S. C. (1990). Social influences on creativity: Evaluation, coaction, and surveillance. *Creativity Research Journal, 3*, 6–21.

Amato, P. R., & Keith, B. (1991). Parental divorce and the well-being of children: A meta-analysis. *Psychological Bulletin, 110*, 26–46.

Amemori, T., Ermakova, I. V., Buresova, O., & Zigova, T. (1989). Brain transplants enhance rather than reduce the impairment of spatial memory and olfaction in bulbectomized rats. *Behavioral Neuroscience, 103*, 61–70.

American Psychiatric Association. (1994). *Diagnostic and statistical manual of mental disorders* (4th ed.). Washington, DC: American Psychological Association.

Amir, T. (1984). The Asch conformity effect: A study in Kuwait. *Social Behavior and Personality, 12*, 187–190.

Amoore, J. E. (1963). Stereochemical theory of olfaction. *Nature, 198*, 271–277.

Anand, B. K., & Brobeck, J. R. (1951). Hypothalamic control of food intake in rats and cats. *Yale Journal of Biology and Medicine, 24*, 123–140.

Anastasi, A. (1958). Heredity, environment, and the question "How?" *American Psychologist, 65*, 197–208.

Anastasi, A. (1985). Psychological testing: Basic concepts and common misconceptions. In A. M. Rogers & C. J. Scheirer (Eds.), *The G. Stanley Hall Lecture Series* (Vol. 5, pp. 87–120. Washington, DC: American Psychological Association.

Anastasi, A. (1986). Evolutionary concepts of test validation. *Annual Review of Psychology, 37*, 1–15.

Andersen, A. E., & DiDomenico, L. (1992). Diet vs. shape content of popular male and female magazines: A dose-response relationship to the incidence of eating disorders? *International Journal of Eating Disorders, 11*, 283–287.

Andersen, A. E., Woodward, P. J., Spalder, A., & Koss, M. (1993). Body size and shape characteristics of personal ("in search of") ads. *International Journal of Eating Disorders, 14*, 111–115.

Andersen, S. M., & Ross, L. (1984). Self-knowledge and social inference: I. The impact of cognitive/affective and behavioral data. *Journal of Personality and Social Psychology, 46*, 280–293.

Anderson, C. A., & Arnoult, L. H. (1989). An examination of perceived control, humor, irrational beliefs, and positive stress as moderators of the relation between negative stress and health. *Basic and Applied Social Psychology, 10*, 101–117.

Anderson, D. C., Crowell, C. R., Doman, M., & Howard, G. S. (1988). Performance posting, goal setting, and activity-contingent praise as applied to a university hockey team. *Journal of Applied Psychology, 73*, 87–95.

Anderson, J. R. (1983). Retrieval of information from long-term memory. *Science, 220*, 25–30.

Anderson, K. J., Revelle, W., & Lynch, M. J. (1989). Caffeine, impulsivity, and memory scanning: A comparison of two explanations for the Yerkes-Dodson effect. *Motivation and Emotion, 13*, 1–20.

Anderson, L. R., & Blanchard, P. N. (1982). Sex differences in task and social-emotional behavior. *Basic and Applied Social Psychology, 3*, 109–139.

Anderson, R. A., Baron, R. S., & Logan, H. (1991). Distraction, control, and dental stress. *Journal of Applied Social Psychology, 21*, 156–171.

Andrasik, F. (1990). Psychologic and behavioral aspects of chronic headache. *Neurologic Clinics, 8*, 961–976.

Andre, T. (1979). Does answering higher-level questions while reading facilitate productive learning? *Review of Educational Research, 49*, 280–318.

Andreasen, N. C., & Flaum, M. (1991). Schizophrenia: The characteristic symptoms. *Schizophrenia Bulletin, 17*, 27–49.

Andreasen, N. C., Flaum, M., Swayze, V. W., & Tyrrell, G. (1990). Positive and negative symptoms in schizophrenia: A critical reappraisal. *Archives of General Psychiatry, 47*, 615–621.

Andreassen, P. B. (1988). Explaining the price-volume relationship: The difference between price changes and changing prices. *Organizational Behavior and Human Decision Processes, 41*, 371–389.

Angus, R. G., Heslegrave, R. J., & Myles, W. S. (1985). Effects of prolonged sleep deprivation, with and without chronic physical exercise, on mood and performance. *Psychophysiology, 22*, 276–282.

Ansbacher, H. L. (1990). Alfred Adler's influence on the three leading cofounders of humanistic psychology. *Journal of Humanistic Psychology, 30*, 45–53.

Anschutz, L., Camp, C. J., Markley, R. P., & Kramer, J. J. (1985). Maintenance and generalization of mnemonics for grocery shopping by older adults. *Experimental Aging Research, 11*, 157–160.

Anshel, M. H., Gregory, W. L., & Kaczmarek, M. (1990). The effectiveness of a stress training program in coping with criticism in sport: A test of the COPE model. *Journal of Sport Behavior, 13*, 194–217.

Antoni, M. H., LaPerriere, A., Schneiderman, N., & Fletcher, M. A. (1991). Stress and immunity in individuals at risk for AIDS. *Stress Medicine, 7*, 35–44.

Antunano, M. J., & Hernandez, J. M. (1989). Incidence of airsickness among military parachutists. *Aviation, Space, and Environmental Medicine, 60*, 792–797.

Ape language. (1981). *Science, 211*, 86–88.

Appelbaum, P. S., & Gutheil, T. G. (1980). The Boston State Hospital case: "Involuntary mind control," the Constitution, and the "right to rot." *American Journal of Psychiatry, 137*, 720–723.

Ardila, A., Montanes, P., & Gempeler, J. (1986). Echoic memory and language perception. *Brain and Language, 29*, 134–140.

Arehart-Treichel, J. (1981). Beta-endorphins in the placenta. *Science News, 120*, 89.

Arndt, S., Alliger, R. J., & Andreasen, N. C. (1991). The distinction of positive and negative symptoms: The failure of a two-dimensional model. *British Journal of Psychiatry, 158*, 317–322.

Aronson, E. (1987). Teaching students what they think they already know about prejudice and desegregation. In V. P. Makosky (Ed.), *The G. Stanley Hall Lecture Series* (Vol. 7., pp. 69–84). Washington, DC: American Psychological Association.

Aronson, E., & Bridgeman, D. (1979). Jigsaw groups and the desegregated classroom: In pursuit of common goals. *Personality and Social Psychology Bulletin, 5*, 438–446.

Arterberry, M., Yonas, A., & Benson, A. S. (1989). Self-produced locomotion and the development of responsiveness to linear perspective and texture gradients. *Developmental Psychology, 25*, 976–982.

Asch, S. E. (1955, November). Opinions and social pressure. *Scientific American*, pp. 31–35.

Aserinsky, E., & Kleitman, N. (1953). Regularly occurring periods of eye motility and concomitant phenomena during sleep. *Science, 118*, 273–274.

Aserinsky, E., Lynch, J. A., Mack, M. E., Tzankoff, S. P., & Hurn, E. (1985). Comparison of eye motion in wakefulness and REM sleep. *Psychophysiology, 22*, 1–10.

Ash, D. W., & Holding, D. H. (1990). Backward versus forward chaining in the acquisition of a keyboard skill. *Human Factors, 32*, 139–146.

Aslin, R. N., & Smith, L. B. (1988). Perceptual development. *Annual Review of Psychology, 39*, 435–474.

Asscheman, H., & Gorren, L. J. (1992). Hormone treatment in transsexuals. *Journal of Psychology and Human Sexuality, 5*, 39–54.

Astin, G. R., & Garber, H. (1982). *The rise and fall of national test scores*. New York: Academic Press.

Atkinson, D. R. (1983). Ethnic similarity in counseling psychology: A review of research. *Counseling Psychologist, 11*, 79–92.

Atkinson, J. W. (1981). Studying personality in the context of an advanced motivational psychology. *American Psychologist, 36*, 117–128.

Atkinson, J. W., & Litwin, G. H. (1960). Achievement motive and test anxiety concerned as motive to approach success and motive to avoid failure. *Journal of Abnormal and Social Psychology, 60*, 52–63.

Attie, I., & Brooks-Gunn, J. (1989). Development of eating problems in adolescent girls: A longitudinal study. *Developmental Psychology, 25*, 70–79.

Atwood, G. E., & Tomkins, S. S. (1976). On the subjectivity of personality theory. *Journal of the History of the Behavioral Sciences, 12*, 166–177.

Aydin, G., & Aydin, O. (1992). Learned helplessness and explanatory style in Turkish samples. *Journal of Social Psychology, 132*, 117–119.

Ayllon, T., & Azrin, N. H. (1968). *The token economy: A motivational system for therapy and rehabilitation*. New York: Appleton-Century-Crofts.

Babad, E., Bernieri, F., & Rosenthal, R. (1989). When less information is more informative: Diagnosing teacher expectations from brief samples of behavior. *British Journal of Educational Psychology, 59*, 281–295.

Bach-y-Rita, P. (1990). Brain plasticity as a basis for recovery of function in humans. *Neuropsychologia, 28*, 547–554.

Baddeley, A. D. (1982). Domains of recollection. *Psychological Review, 89*, 708–729.

Bahill, A. T., & LaRitz, T. (1984). Why can't batters keep their eyes on the ball? *American Scientist, 72*, 249–253.

Bahrick, H. P. (1984). Semantic memory content in permastore: Fifty years of memory for Spanish learned in school. *Journal of Experimental Psychology: General, 113*, 1–29.

Bahrick, H. P., Bahrick, P. O., & Wittlinger, R. P. (1975). Fifty years of memory for names and faces: A cross-sectional approach. *Journal of Experimental Psychology: General, 104*, 54–75.

Bailey, J. M., Pillard, R. C., Neale, M. C., & Agyei, Y. (1993). Heritable factors influence sexual orientation in women. *Archives of General Psychiatry, 50*, 217–223.

Baillargeon, R., & DeVos, J. (1991). Object permanence in young infants: Further evidence. *Child Development, 62*, 1227–1246.

Baird, J. C., & Wagner, M. (1982). The moon illusion: I. How high is the sky? *Journal of Experimental Psychology: General, 111*, 296–303.

Baird, J. C., Wagner, M., & Fuld, K. (1990). A simple but powerful theory of the moon illusion. *Journal of Experimental Psychology: Human Perception and Performance, 16*, 675–677.

Baker, G. H. B. (1987). Psychological factors and immunity. *Journal of Psychosomatic Research, 31*, 1–10.

Baker, T. B., & Tiffany, S. T. (1985). Morphine tolerance as habituation. *Psychological Review, 92*, 78–108.

Balanovski, E., & Taylor, J. G. (1978). Can electromagnetism account for extra sensory phenomena? *Nature, 276*, 64–67.

Baldwin, B. A., de la Riva, C., & Ebenezer, I. S. (1990). Effects of intracerebroventricular injection of dynorphin, leumorphin, and a neoendorphin on operant feeding in pigs. *Physiology and Behavior, 48*, 821–824.

Baldwin, E. (1993). The case for animal research in psychology. *Journal of Social Issues, 49*, 121–131.

Baldwin, M. W. (1954). Subjective measurements in television. *American Psychologist, 9*, 231–234.

Bales, J. (1986, September). Pastoral counseling. *APA Monitor*, p. 16.

Bales, J. (1988a, March). Court rules no duty to commit in N.C. *APA Monitor*, p. 20.

Bales, J. (1988b, August). Pre-work polygraph ban signed by Reagan. *APA Monitor*, p. 5.

Bandura, A. (1965). Influence of model's reinforcement contingencies on the acquisition of imitative responses. *Journal of Personality and Social Psychology, 1*, 589–595.

Bandura, A. (1977). *Social learning theory*. Englewood Cliffs, NJ: Prentice Hall.

Bandura, A. (1978). On distinguishing between logical and empirical verification: A comment on Smedslund. *Scandinavian Journal of Psychology, 19*, 97–99.

Bandura, A. (1982a). The psychology of chance encounters and life paths. *American Psychologist, 37*, 747–755.

Bandura, A. (1982b). Self-efficacy mechanism in human agency. *American Psychologist, 37*, 122–147.

Bandura, A. (1986). *Social foundations of thought and action: A social-cognitive theory*. Englewood Cliffs, NJ: Prentice Hall.

Bandura, A. (1989). Human agency in social cognitive theory. *American Psychologist, 44*, 1175–1184.

Bandura, A. (1993). Perceived self-efficacy in cognitive development and functioning. *Educational Psychologist, 28*, 117–148.

Bandura, A., Blanchard, E. B., & Ritter, B. (1969). The relative efficacy of desensitization and modeling approaches for inducing behavioral, affective, and attitudinal changes. *Journal of Personality and Social Psychology, 13*, 173–199.

Bandura, A., Reese, L., & Adams, N. E. (1982). Microanalysis of action and fear arousal as a function of differential levels of perceived self-efficacy. *Journal of Personality and Social Psychology, 43*, 5–21.

Bandura, A., Ross, D., & Ross, S. A. (1963). Imitation of film-mediated aggressive models. *Journal of Abnormal and Social Psychology, 66*, 3–11.

Bandura, A., & Schunk, D. H. (1981). Cultivating competence, self-efficacy, and intrinsic interest through proximal self-motivation. *Journal of Personality and Social Psychology, 41*, 586–598.

Barabasz, A. F., & Barabasz, M. (1989). Effects of restricted environmental stimulation: Enhancement of hypnotizability for experimental and chronic pain control. *International Journal of Clinical and Experimental Hypnosis, 37*, 217–231.

Barabasz, A. F., Barabasz, M., & Bauman, J. (1993). Restricted environmental stimulation technique improves human performance: Rifle marksmanship. *Perceptual and Motor Skills, 76*, 867–873.

Barbut, M. (1993). Comments on a pseudo-mathematical model in social psychology. *European Journal of Social Psychology, 23*, 203–210.

Barchas, P. R., & Perlaki, K. M. (1986). Processing of preconsciously acquired information measured by hemispheric asymmetry and selection accuracy. *Behavioral Neuroscience, 100*, 343–349.

Bard, P. (1934). On emotional experience after decortication with some remarks on theoretical views. *Psychological Review, 41*, 309–329.

Baribeau-Braun, J., Picton, T. W., & Gosselin, J. Y. (1983). Schizophrenia: A neuro-psychological evaluation of abnormal information processing. *Science, 219*, 874–876.

Barinaga, M. (1989). Manic-depression gene put in limbo. *Science, 246*, 886–887.

Barlow, D. H. (1986). Causes of sexual dysfunction: The role of anxiety and cognitive interference. *Journal of Consulting and Clinical Psychology, 54*, 140–148.

Barnes, D. M. (1987). Hippocampus studied for learning mechanisms. *Science, 236*, 1628–1629.

Barnes, M. L., & Rosenthal, R. (1985). Interpersonal effects of experimenter attractiveness, attire, and gender. *Journal of Personality & Social Psychology, 48*, 435–446.

Barnett, S. K. (1984). The mentor role: A task of generativity. *Journal of Human Behavior and Learning, 1*, 15–18.

Baron, R. (1983). "Sweet smell of success?" The impact of pleasant artificial scents on evaluations of job applicants. *Journal of Applied Psychology, 68*, 709–713.

Baron, R. A., & Ransberger, V. M. (1978). Ambient temperature and the occurrence of collective violence: The "long, hot summer" revisited. *Journal of Personality and Social Psychology, 36*, 351–360.

Barr, B. P., & Benson, H. (1984). The relaxation response and cardiovascular disorders. *Behavioral Medicine Update, 6(4)*, 28–30.

Barrett, P. T., Daum, I., & Eysenck, H. J. (1990). Sensory nerve conduction and intelligence: A methodological study. *Journal of Psychophysiology, 4*, 1–13.

Barron, F., & Harrington, D. M. (1981). Creativity, intelligence, and personality. *Annual Review of Psychology, 32*, 439–476.

Barsky, A. J., Coeytaux, R. R., Sarnie, M. K., & Cleary, P. D. (1993). Hypochondriacal patients' beliefs about good health. *American Journal of Psychiatry, 150*, 1085–1089.

Barsky, A. J., & Klerman, G. L. (1983). Overview: Hypochondriasis, bodily complaints, and somatic styles. *American Journal of Psychiatry, 140*, 273–283.

Bartlett, F. C. (1932). *Remembering: A study in experimental and social psychology*. Cambridge, England: Cambridge University Press.

Bartoshuk, L. M., Cain, W. S., & Pfaffmann, C. (1985). Taste and olfaction. In G. A. Kimble & K. Schlesinger (Eds.), *Topics in the history of psychology* (pp. 221–260). Hillsdale, NJ: Erlbaum.

Bartus, R. T., Dean, R. L., III, Beer, B., & Lippa, A. S. (1982). The cholinergic hypothesis of geriatric memory application. *Science, 217*, 408–409.

Bartusiak, M. (1980, November). Beeper man. *Discover*, p. 57.

Basadur, M. S., Wakabayashi, M., & Takai, J. (1992). Training effects on the divergent thinking attitudes of Japanese managers. *International Journal of Intercultural Relations, 16*, 329–345.

Bashore, T. R., & Rapp, P. E. (1993). Are there alternatives to traditional polygraph procedures? *Psychological Bulletin, 113*, 3–22.

Baskett, L. M. (1984). Ordinal position differences in children's family interactions. *Developmental Psychology, 20*, 1026–1031.

Baskin, Y. (1983, August). Interview with Roger Sperry. *Omni*, pp. 68–73, 98–100.

Basler, H. D., Brinkmeier, U., Buser, K., & Gluth, G. (1992). Nicotine gum assisted group therapy in smokers with an increased risk of coronary disease: Evaluation in a primary care setting format. *Health Education Research, 7*, 87–95.

Basmajian, J. V. (1963). Control and training of individual motor units. *Science, 141*, 440–441.

Basmajian, J. V. (1988). Research foundations of EMG biofeedback in rehabilitation. *Biofeedback and Self-Regulation, 13*, 275–298.

Bassuk, E. L. (1984, July). The homelessness problem. *Scientific American*, pp. 40–45.

Basu, A. K. (1982). Comparison of four intelligence tests with culturally disadvantaged children. *International Newsletter—Educational Evaluation and Research, 21*, 18–19.

Bateman, T. S., Karwan, K. R., & Kazee, T. A. (1983). Getting a fresh start: A natural quasi-experimental test of the performance effects of moving to a new job. *Journal of Applied Psychology, 68*, 517–524.

Batson, C. D., Batson, J. G., Griffitt, C. A., Barrientos, S., Brandt, J. R., Sprengelmeyer, P., & Bayly, M. J. (1989). Negative-state relief and the empathy-altruism hypothesis. *Journal of Personality and Social Psychology, 56*, 922–933.

Batson, C. D., Bolen, M. H., Cross, J. A., & Neuringer-Benefiel, H. E. (1986). Where is the altruism in the altruistic personality? *Journal of Personality and Social Psychology, 50*, 212–220.

Batson, C. D., & Shaw, L. L. (1991). Evidence for altruism: Toward a pluralism of prosocial motives. *Psychological Inquiry, 2*, 107–122.

Baucom, D. H., Besch, P. J., & Callahan, S. (1985). Relation between testosterone concentration, sex role identity, and personality among females. *Journal of Personality and Social Psychology, 48*, 1218–1226.

Baum, A., Grunberg, N. E., & Singer, J. E. (1992). Biochemical measurements in the study of emotion. *Psychological Science, 3*, 56–60.

Baumeister, R. F. (1982). A self-presentational view of social phenomena. *Psychological Bulletin, 91*, 3–26.

Baumeister, R. F. (1984). Choking under pressure: Self-consciousness and paradoxical effects of incentives on skillful performance. *Journal of Personality and Social Psychology, 46*, 610–620.

Baumeister, R. F. (1988). Should we stop studying sex differences altogether? *American Psychologist, 43*, 1092–1095.

Baumeister, R. F., & Scher, S. J. (1988). Self-defeating behavior patterns among normal individuals: Review and analysis of common self-destructive tendencies. *Psychological Bulletin, 104*, 3–22.

Baumeister, R. F., & Steinhilber, A. (1984). Paradoxical effects of supportive audiences on performance under pressure: The home field disadvantage in sports championships. *Journal of Personality and Social Psychology, 47*, 85–93.

Baumrind, D. (1964). Some thoughts on ethics of research: After reading Milgram's "Behavioral Study of Obedience." *American Psychologist, 19*, 421–423.

Baumrind, D. (1983). Rejoinder to Lewis's reinterpretation of parental firm control effects: Are authoritative families really harmonious? *Psychological Bulletin, 94*, 132–142.

Baumrind, D. (1985). Research using intentional deception: Ethical issues revisited. *American Psychologist, 40*, 165–174.

Baumrind, D. (1991). The influence of parenting style on adolescent competence and substance use. *Journal of Early Adolescence, 11*, 56–95.

Baxter, L. R. (1991). PET studies of cerebral function in major depression and obsessive-compulsive disorder: The emerging prefrontal cortex concensus. *Annals of Clinical Psychiatry, 3*, 103–109.

Bayley, N. (1933). Mental growth during the first three years: A developmental study of sixty-one children by repeated tests. *Genetic Psychology Monographs, 14*, 1–92.

Bayley, N. (1955). On the growth of intelligence. *American Psychologist, 10*, 805–818.

Bayton, J. A. (1975). Francis Sumner, Max Meenes, and the training of black psychologists. *American Psychologist, 30*, 185–186.

Beail, N., & Parker, S. (1991). Group fixed-role therapy: A clinical application. *International Journal of Personal Construct Psychology, 4*, 85–95.

Beatty, J. (1982). Task-evoked pupillary responses, processing load, and the structure of processing resources. *Psychological Bulletin, 91*, 276–292.

Beatty, W. W. (1984). Discriminating drunkenness: A replication. *Bulletin of the Psychonomic Society, 22*, 431–432.

Beaumont, W. (1833/1988). *Experiments and observations on the gastric juice, and the physiology of digestion.* Wayne, NJ: Lederle.

Beck, A. T. (1967). *Depression: Clinical, experimental and theoretical aspects.* New York: Harper & Row.

Beck, A. T., Rush, A. J., Shaw, B. F., & Emery, G. (1979). *Cognitive therapy of depression.* New York: Guilford Press.

Becker, J. B., Curran, E. J., & Freed, W. J. (1990). Adrenal medulla graft induced recovery of function in an animal model of Parkinson's disease: Possible mechanisms of action. *Canadian Journal of Psychology, 44*, 293–310.

Beckham, J. C., Keefe, F. J., Caldwell, D. S., & Brown, C. J. (1991). Biofeedback as a means to alter electromyographic activity in a total knee replacement patient. *Biofeedback and Self-Regulation, 16*, 23–35.

Beeghley, L., & Sellers, C. (1986). Adolescents and sex: A structural theory of premarital sex in the United States. *Deviant Behavior, 7*, 313–336.

Beers, C. W. (1908/1970). *A mind that found itself.* New York: Doubleday.

Behrend, D. A. (1988). Overextensions in early language comprehension: Evidence from a signal detection approach. *Journal of Child Language, 15*, 63–75.

Beiser, M., Shore, J. H., Peters, R., & Tatum, W. (1985). Does community care for the mentally ill make a difference? A tale of two cities. *American Journal of Psychiatry, 142*, 1047–1052.

Bekoff, M., Gruen, L., Townsend, S.E., & Rollin, B. E. (1992). Animals in science: Some areas revisited. *Animal Behaviour, 44*, 473–484.

Belisle, M., Roskies, E., & Levesque, J. M. (1987). Improving adherence to physical activity. *Health Psychology, 6*, 159–172.

Bell, A. P., Weinberg, M. S., & Hammersmith, S. J. (1981). *Sexual preference: Its development in men and women.* Bloomington: Indiana University Press.

Bell, J. E., & Eisenberg, N. (1985). Life satisfaction in midlife childless and empty-nest men and women. *Lifestyles, 7*, 146–155.

Bellas, D. N., Novelly, R. A., Eskenazi, B., & Wasserstein, J. (1988). Unilateral displacement in the olfactory sense: A manifestation of the unilateral neglect syndrome. *Cortex, 24*, 267–275.

Belmont, L., & Marolla, F. A. (1973). Birth order, family size, and intelligence. *Science, 182*, 1096–1101.

Belsky, J. (1988). The "effects" of infant day care reconsidered. *Early Childhood Research Quarterly, 3*, 235–272.

Belsky, J., & Pensky, E. (1988). Marital change across the transition to parenthood. *Marriage and Family Review, 12*, 133–156.

Bem, D. J. (1967). Self-perception: An alternative interpretation of cognitive dissonance phenomena. *Psychological Review, 74*, 183–200.

Bem, D. J., & Allen, A. (1974). On predicting some of the people some of the time: The search for cross-situational consistencies in behavior. *Psychological Review, 81*, 506–520.

Bem, S. L. (1981). Gender schema theory: A cognitive account of sex typing. *Psychological Review, 88*, 354–364.

Bemis, K. M. (1978). Current approaches to the etiology and treatment of anorexia nervosa. *Psychological Bulletin, 85*, 593–617.

Benbow, C. P. (1988). Sex differences in mathematical reasoning ability in intellectually talented preadolescents: Their nature, effect, and possible causes. *Behavioral and Brain Sciences, 11*, 169–232.

Benbow, C. P., Arjmand, O., & Walberg, H. J. (1991). Educational productivity predictors among mathematically talented students. *Journal of Educational Research, 84*, 215–223.

Benbow, C. P., & Stanley, J. C. (1983). Sex differences in mathematical reasoning ability: More facts. *Science, 222*, 1029–1031.

Benesch, K. F., & Page, M. M. (1989). Self-construct systems and interpersonal congruence. *Journal of Personality, 57*, 139–173.

Benjamin, L. T., Jr. (1988). A history of teaching machines. *American Psychologist, 43*, 703–712.

Bennett, W., & Gurin, J. (1982). *The dieter's dilemma.* New York: Basic Books.

Ben-Porath, Y. S., & Butcher, J. N. (1989). The comparability of MMPI and MMPI-2 scales and profiles. *Psychological Assessment, 1*, 345–347.

Bensing, J. (1991). Doctor-patient communication and the quality of care. *Social Science and Medicine, 32*, 1301–1310.

Benson, H., & Friedman, R. (1985). A rebuttal to the conclusions of David S. Holme's article: "Meditation and somatic arousal reduction." *American Psychologist, 40*, 725–728.

Bentall, R. P. (1990). The illusion of reality: A review and integration of psychological research on hallucinations. *Psychological Bulletin, 107*, 82–95.

Benton, D., & Sargent, J. (1992). Breakfast, blood glucose and memory. *Biological Psychology, 33*, 207–210.

Berg, J. H. (1984). Development of friendship between roommates. *Journal of Personality and Social Psychology, 46*, 346–356.

Berg, J. H., & McQuinn, R. D. (1986). Attraction and exchange in continuing and noncontinuing dating relationships. *Journal of Personality and Social Psychology, 50*, 942–952.

Bergeman, C. S., Plomin, R., McClearn, G. E., & Pedersen, N. L. (1988). Genotype-environment interaction in personality development: Identical twins reared apart. *Psychology and Aging, 3*, 399–406.

Berger, A. A. (1987). Humor: An introduction. *American Behavioral Scientist, 30*, 6–15.

Bergin, A. E., & Lambert, E. (1978). The evaluation of therapeutic outcome. In S. L. Garfield & A. E. Bergin (Eds.), *Handbook of psychotherapy and behavior change* (pp. 139–189). New York: Wiley.

Berko, J. (1958). The child's learning of English morphology. *Word, 14*, 150–177.

Berkowitz, L. (1974). Some determinants of impulsive aggression. *Psychological Review, 81*, 165–176.

Berkowitz, L. (1989). Frustration-aggression hypothesis: Examination and reformulation. *Psychological Bulletin, 106*, 59–73.

Berkowitz, L., & LePage, A. (1967). Weapons as aggression-eliciting stimuli. *Journal of Personality and Social Psychology, 7*, 202–207.

Berkowitz, M. W., Mueller, C. W., Schnell, S. V., & Padberg, U. (1986). Moral reasoning and judgments of aggression. *Journal of Personality and Social Psychology, 51*, 885–891.

Berlin, R. M., & Qayyum, U. (1986). Sleepwalking: Diagnosis and treatment through the life cycle. *Psychosomatics, 27*, 755–760.

Bermond, B., Fasotti, L., Nieuwenhuyse, B., & Schuerman, J. (1991). Spinal cord lesions, peripheral feedback, and intensities of emotional feelings. *Cognition and Emotion, 5*, 201–220.

Bernard, J. (1981). The good-provider role: Its rise and fall. *American Psychologist, 36*, 1–12.

Bernard, J. L. (1977). The significance for psychology of *O'Connor v. Donaldson. American Psychologist, 32*, 1085–1088.

Berndt, T. J., & Hoyle, S. G. (1985). Stability and change in childhood and adolescent friendships. *Developmental Psychology, 21*, 1007–1015.

Berndt, T. J., & Zigler, E. F. (1985). Developmental psychology. In G. A. Kimble & K. Schlesinger (Eds.), *Topics in the history of psychology* (Vol. 2, pp. 115–150). Hillsdale, NJ: Erlbaum.

Berne, E. (1964). *Games people play.* New York: Grove Press.

Bernier, D., & Gaston, L. (1989). Stress management: A review. *Canada's Mental Health, 37*, 15–19.

Berninger, V. W. (1988). Development of operational thought without a normal sensorimotor stage. *Intelligence, 12*, 219–230.

Bernstein, I. L. (1978). Learned taste aversions in children receiving chemotherapy. *Science, 200*, 1302–1303.

Bernstein, I. L. (1991). Aversion conditioning in response to cancer and cancer treatment. *Clinical Psychology Review, 11*, 185–191.

Bernstein, J. J., & Goldberg, W. J. (1989). Graft derived reafferentation of host spinal cord is not necessary for amelioration of lesion-induced deficits: Possible role of migrating grafted astrocytes. *Brain Research Bulletin, 22*, 139–146.

Bernstein, W. M., Stephan, W. G., & Davis, M. H. (1979). Explaining attributions for achievement: A path-analytic approach. *Journal of Personality and Social Psychology, 37*, 1810–1821.

Berquier, A., & Ashton, R. (1992). Characteristics of the frequent nightmare sufferer. *Journal of Abnormal Psychology, 101*, 246–250.

Berrios, G. E. (1990). A British contribution to the history of functional brain surgery. *Journal of Psychopharmacology, 4*, 140–144.

Berscheid, E., & Walster, E. (1974). A little bit about love. In T. L. Houston (Ed.), *Foundations of interpersonal attraction.* New York: Academic Press.

Bertelsen, A., Harvald, B., & Hauge, M. (1977). A Danish twin study of manic-depressive disorders. *British Journal of Psychiatry, 130*, 330–351.

Bexton, W. H., Heron, W., & Scott, T. H. (1954). Effects of decreased variation in the sensory environment. *Canadian Journal of Psychology, 8*, 70–76.

Billings, R. S., & Schaalman, M. L. (1980). Administrators' estimations of the probability of outcomes of school desegregation: A field test of the availability heuristic. *Organizational Behavior and Human Performance, 26*, 97–114.

Binik, Y. M., Westbury, C. F., & Servan-Schreiber, D. (1989). Interaction with a "sex-expert" system enhances attitudes towards computerized sex therapy. *Behaviour Research and Therapy, 27*, 303–306.

Birch, D. E. (1992). Duty to protect: Update and Canadian perspective. *Canadian Psychology, 33*, 94–104.

Bjork, D. W. (1988). *William James: The center of his vision.* New York: Columbia University Press.

Bjork, E. L., & Cummings, E. M. (1984). Infant search errors: Stage of concept development or stage of memory development. *Memory and Cognition, 12*, 1–19.

Bjorklund, D. F., & Buchanan, J. J. (1989). Developmental and knowledge-base differences in the acquisition and extension of a memory strategy. *Journal of Experimental Child Psychology, 48*, 451–471.

Black, D. W. (1982). Pathological laughter: A review of the literature. *Journal of Nervous and Mental Disease, 170*, 67–71.

Black, J. E., Isaacs, K. R., & Greenough, W. T. (1991). Usual vs. successful aging: Some notes on experiential factors. *Neurobiology of Aging, 12*, 325–328.

Blacker, D., & Tsuang, M. T. (1993). Unipolar relatives in bipolar pedigrees: Are they bipolar? *Psychiatric Genetics, 3*, 5–16.

Blair, M. C., & Fretz, B. R. (1980). Interpersonal skills training for premedical students. *Journal of Counseling Psychology, 27*, 380–384.

Blair, M. E., & Shimp, T. A. (1992). Consequences of an unpleasant experience with music: A second-order negative conditioning perspective. *Journal of Advertising, 21*, 35–43.

Blakemore, C. (1977). *Mechanics of the mind.* New York: Cambridge University Press.

Blakemore, C., & Cooper, G. F. (1970). Development of the brain depends on the visual environment. *Nature, 228*, 477–478.

Blaney, N. T., Goodkin, K., Morgan, R. O., & Feaster, D. (1991). A stress-moderator model of distress in early HIV–1 infection: Concurrent analysis of life events, hardiness and social support. *Journal of Psychosomatic Research, 35*, 297–305.

Blankfield, R. P. (1991). Suggestion, relaxation, and hypnosis as adjuncts in the care of surgery patients: A review of the literature. *American Journal of Clinical Hypnosis, 33*, 172–186.

Blasi, A. (1980). Bridging moral cognition and moral action: A critical review of the literature. *Psychological Bulletin, 88*, 1–45.

Blechman, E. A., Tinsley, B., Carella, E. T., & McEnroe, M. J. (1985). Childhood competence and behavior problems. *Journal of Abnormal Psychology, 94*, 70–77.

Bliss, T. V. (1990). Maintenance is presynaptic. *Nature, 346*, 698–699.

Bliss, T. V., & Collingridge, G. L. (1993). A synaptic model of memory: Long-term potentiation in the hippocampus. *Nature, 361*, 31–39.

Bloomquist, D. W. (1985). Teaching sensation and perception: Its ambiguous and subliminal aspects. In A. M. Rogers & C. J. Scheirer (Eds.), *The G. Stanley Hall Lecture Series* (Vol. 5, pp. 157–203). Washington, DC: American Psychological Association.

Boardway, R. H., Delamater, A. M., Tomakowsky, J., & Gutai, J. P. (1993). Stress management training for adolescents with diabetes. *Journal of Pediatric Psychology, 18*, 29–45.

Bohan, J. S. (1990). Contextual history: A framework for re-placing women in the history of psychology. *Psychology of Women Quarterly, 14*, 213–227.

Bohannon, J. N., III, & Stanowicz, L. (1988). The issue of negative evidence: Adult responses to children's language errors. *Developmental Psychology, 24*, 684–689.

Boice, R. (1983). Observations skill. *Psychological Bulletin, 93*, 3–29.

Bolhuis, J. J., & Van Kampen, H. S. (1988). Serial-position curves in spatial memory of rats: Primary and recency effects. *Quarterly Journal of Experimental Psychology: Comparative and Physiological Psychology, 40*, 135–149.

Bolles, R. C. (1979). *Learning theory.* New York: Holt, Rinehart & Winston.

Bolm-Audorff, U., Schwammle, J., Ehlenz, K., & Kaffarnik, H. (1989). Plasma level of catecholamines and lipids when speaking before an audience. *Work and Stress, 3*, 249–253.

Bond, C. F., Jr., Pitre, U., & Van Leeuwen, M. D. (1991). Encoding operations and the next-in-line effect. *Personality and Social Psychology Bulletin, 17*, 435–441.

Bond, C. F., Jr., & Titus, L. J. (1983). Social facilitation: A meta-analysis of 241 studies. *Psychological Bulletin, 94*, 265–292.

Bonds, D. R., & Crosby, L. O. (1986). "An adoption study of human obesity": Comment. *New England Journal of Medicine, 315*, 128.

Boneau, C. A. (1974). Paradigm regained?: Cognitive behaviorism revisited. *American Psychologist, 29*, 297–309.

Boneau, R. H., Sheridan, J. F., Feng, N., & Glaser, R. (1993). Stress-induced modulation of the primary cellular immune response to herpes simplex virus infection is mediated by both adrenal-dependent and independent mechanisms. *Journal of Neuroimmunology, 42*, 167–176.

Boon, S., & Draijer, N. (1993). Multiple personality disorder in the Netherlands: A clinical investigation of 71 patients. *American Journal of Psychiatry, 150*, 489–494.

Bordage, G. (1987). The curriculum: Overloaded and too general? *Medical Education, 21*, 183–188.

Bordages, J. W. (1989). Self-actualization and personal autonomy. *Psychological Reports, 64*, 1263–1266.

Boring, E. G. (1943). The moon illusion. *American Journal of Physics, 11*, 55–60.

Boring, E. G. (1950). *A history of experimental psychology: Original sources and contemporary research.* New York: Appleton-Century-Crofts.

Bornstein, R. F. (1989). Subliminal techniques as propaganda tools: Review and critique. *Journal of Mind and Behavior, 10*, 231–262.

Bornstein, R. F. (1993). Implicit perception, implicit memory, and the recovery of unconscious material in psychotherapy. *Journal of Nervous and Mental Disease, 181*, 337–344.

Bornstein, R. F., & D'Agostino, P. R. (1992). Stimulus recognition and the mere exposure effect. *Journal of Personality and Social Psychology, 63*, 545–552.

Bornstein, R. F., Leone, D. R., & Galley, D. J. (1987). The generalizability of subliminal mere exposure effects: Influence of stimuli perceived without awareness on social behavior. *Journal of Personality and Social Psychology, 53*, 1070–1079.

Botman, H. I., & Crovitz, H. F. (1989–1990). Dream reports and autobiographical memory. *Imagination, Cognition, and Personality, 9*, 213–224.

Bouchard, T. J., Jr., Lykken, D. T., McGue, M., Segal, N. L., & Tellegen, A. (1990). Sources of human psychological differences: The Minnesota Study of Twins Reared Apart. *Science, 250*, 223–228.

Bouchard, T. J., Jr., & McGue, M. (1981). Familial studies of intelligence: A review. *Science, 212*, 1055–1059.

Bouchard, T. J., Jr., & McGue, M. (1990). Genetic and rearing environmental influences on adult personality: An analysis of adopted twins reared apart. *Journal of Personality, 58*, 263–292.

Boudreau, R. A., Killip, S. M., MacInnis, S. C., Milloy, D. G., & Rogers, T. B. (1983). An evaluation of Graduate Record Examinations as predictors of graduate success in a Canadian context. *Canadian Psychology, 24*, 191–199.

Bouton, M. E., & Swartzentruber, D. (1991). Sources of relapse after extinction in Pavlovian and instrumental learning. *Clinical Psychology Review, 11*, 123–140.

Bouzid, N., & Crawshaw, C. M. (1987). Massed versus distributed word processor training. *Applied Ergonomics, 18*, 220–222.

Bowd, A. D. (1990). A decade of debate on animal research on research in psychology: Room for consensus? *Canadian Psychologist, 31*, 74–82.

Bower, G. H. (1970). Analysis of a mnemonic device. *American Scientist, 58*, 496–510.

Bower, G. H. (1981). Mood and memory. *American Psychologist, 36*, 129–148.

Bower, G. H., & Clark, M. C. (1969). Narrative stories as mediators for serial learning. *Psychonomic Science, 14*, 181–182.

Bowers, L. B. (1990). Traumas precipitating female delinquency: Implications for assessment, practice, and policy. *Child and Adolescent Social Work Journal, 7*, 389–402.

Bowlby, J. (1988). *A secure base: Parent-child attachment and healthy human development.* New York: Basic Books.

Bowman, M. L. (1989). Testing individual differences in ancient China. *American Psychologist, 44*, 576–578.

Boyce, B. A. (1992). The effects of goal proximity on skill acquisition and retention of a shooting task in a field-based setting. *Journal of Sport and Exercise Psychology, 14*, 298–308.

Boyd, J. H. (1990). Use of mental health services for the treatment of panic disorder. *American Journal of Psychiatry, 143*, 1569–1574.

Boyd, J. H., & Crump, T. (1991). Westphal's agoraphobia. *Journal of Anxiety Disorders, 5*, 77–86.

Boyd, J. H., Rae, D. S., Thompson, J. W., & Burns, B. J. (1990). Phobia: Prevalence and risk factors. *Social Psychiatry and Psychiatric Epidemiology, 25*, 314–323.

Boylin, W., Gordon, S. K., & Nehrke, M. F. (1976). Reminiscing and ego integrity in institutionalized elderly males. *Gerontologist, 16*, 118–124.

Boynton, R. M. (1988). Color vision. *Annual Review of Psychology, 39*, 69–100.

Bozarth, J. D. (1990). The evolution of Carl Rogers as a therapist. *Person-Centered Review, 5*, 387–393.

Bozarth, J. D., & Brodley, B. T. (1991). Actualization: A functional concept in client-centered therapy. *Journal of Social Behavior & Personality, 6*, 45–59.

Brackbill, Y., & Nichols, P. L. (1982). A test of the confluence model of intellectual development. *Developmental Psychology, 18*, 192–198.

Bradbury, T. N., & Fincham, F. D. (1990). Attributions in marriage: Review and critique. *Psychological Bulletin, 107*, 3–33.

Bradford, J. M. (1988). Organic treatment of the male sexual offender. *Annals of the New York Academy of Sciences, 528*, 193–202.

Bradley, L. A. (1989). Adherence with treatment regimens among adult rheumatoid arthritis patients: Current status and future directions. *Arthritis Care and Research, 2*, S33–S39.

Bradley, M. T., & Warfield, J. F. (1984). Innocence, information, and the Guilty Knowledge Test in the detection of deception. *Psychophysiology, 21*, 683–689.

Brady, D. R., & Mufson, E. J. (1990). Amygdaloid pathology in Alzheimer's disease: Qualitative and quantitative analysis. *Dementia, 1*, 5–17.

Brantley, P. J., Dietz, L. S., McKnight, G. T., Jones, G. N., & Tulley, R. (1988). Convergence between the Daily Stress Inventory and endocrine measures of stress. *Journal of Consulting and Clinical Psychology, 56*, 549–551.

Brashear, D. B., & Munsick, R. A. (1991). Hymenal dyspareunia. *Journal of Sex Education and Therapy, 17*, 27–31.

Braungart, J. M., Plomin, R., DeFries, J. C., & Fulker, D. W. (1992). Genetic influence on tester-rated infant temperament as assessed by Bayley's Infant Behavior Record: Nonadoptive and adoptive siblings and twins. *Developmental Psychology, 28*, 40–47.

Breathnach, C. S. (1989). Validation of language localization by computer-assisted tomographic and topographic techniques. *Irish Journal of Psychological Medicine, 6*, 11–18.

Breathnach, C. S. (1992). Eduard Hitzig, neurophysiologist and psychiatrist. *History of Psychiatry, 3*, 329–338.

Brecher, E. M. (1972). *Licit and illicit drugs.* Boston: Little, Brown.

Breckler, S. J. (1984). Empirical validation of affect, behavior, and cognition as distinct components of attitude. *Journal of Personality and Social Psychology, 47*, 1191–1205.

Bredemeier, B. J., & Shields, D. L. (1985, October). Values and violence in sports today. *Psychology Today*, pp. 22–32.

Breier, A., & Paul, S. M. (1990). The GABA-sub(A)/benzodiazepine receptor: Implications for the molecular basis of anxiety. *Journal of Psychiatric Research, 24*, 91–104.

Breland, K., & Breland, M. (1961). The misbehavior of organisms. *American Psychologist, 16*, 681–684.

Brennan, J. L., & Andrews, G. (1990). An examination of defense style in parents who abuse children. *Journal of Nervous and Mental Disease, 178*, 592–595.

Brentar, J., & Lynn, S. J. (1989). "Negative" effects and hypnosis: A critical examination. *British Journal of Experimental and Clinical Hypnosis, 6*, 75–84.

Brewer, M. B., & Kramer, R. M. (1985). The psychology of intergroup attitudes and behavior. *Annual Review of Psychology, 36*, 219–243.

Brewin, C. R. (1985). Depression and causal attributions: What is their relation? *Psychological Bulletin, 98*, 297–309.

Brickman, P., Coates, D., & Janoff-Bulman, R. (1978). Lottery winners and accident victims: Is happiness relative? *Journal of Personality and Social Psychology, 36*, 917–927.

Briggs, K. C., & Myers, I. B. (1943). *Myers-Briggs type indicator.* Palo Alto, CA: Consulting Psychologists Press.

Brigham, C. C. (1923). *A study of American intelligence.* Princeton, NJ: Princeton University Press.

Brigham, C. C. (1930). Intelligence tests of immigrant groups. *Psychological Review, 37*, 158–165.

Brigham, T. A. (1989). On the importance of reorganizing the difference between experiments and correlational studies. *American Psychologist, 44*, 1077–1078.

Bringmann, M. W., Tyler, K. E., McAhren, P. E., Bringmann, W. G. (1989). A successful and unsuccessful replication of William Stern's eyewitness research. *Perceptual and Motor Skills, 69*, 619–625.

Bringmann, W., & Tweney, R. D. (1980). *Wundt studies.* Toronto: Hogrefe.

Broad, W. J. (1981). Sir Isaac Newton: Mad as a hatter. *Science, 213*, 1341–1344.

Broberg, D. J., & Bernstein, I. L. (1987). Candy as a scapegoat in the prevention of food aversions in children receiving chemotherapy. *Cancer, 60*, 2344–2347.

Brody, L. R. (1985). Gender differences in emotional development: A review of theories and research. *Journal of Personality, 53*, 102–149.

Bromberg, W. (1954). *Man above humanity: A history of psychotherapy.* Philadelphia: Lippincott.

Bronstein, P. (1984). Differences in mothers' and fathers' behaviors toward children: A cross-cultural comparison. *Developmental Psychology, 20,* 995–1003.

Brooks, K., & Siegel, M. (1991). Children as eyewitnesses: Memory, suggestibilty, and credibility. *Australian Psychologist, 26,* 84–88.

Brooks-Gunn, J., & Furstenberg, F. F., Jr. (1989). Adolescent sexual behavior. *American Psychologist, 44,* 249–257.

Brooks-Gunn, J., & Warren, M. P. (1989). Biological and social contributions to negative affect in young adolescent girls. *Child Development, 60,* 40–55.

Broughton, R. (1990). The prototype concept in personality assessment. *Canadian Psychology, 31,* 26–37.

Brown, A. S. (1991). A review of the tip-of-the-tongue experience. *Psychological Bulletin, 109,* 204–223.

Brown, D. M., Fuqua, J. W., & Otts, D. A. (1986). Helping reluctant readers "stick" to it. *Academic Therapy, 21,* 599–604.

Brown, J. D., & Siegel, J. M. (1988). Exercise as a buffer of life stress: A prospective study of adolescent health. *Health Psychology, 7,* 341–353.

Brown, R. (1973). *A first language: The early stages.* Cambridge, MA: Harvard University Press.

Brown, R., & Kulik, J. (1977). Flashbulb memories. *Cognition, 5,* 73–99.

Brownell, K. D. (1982). Obesity: Understanding and treating a serious, prevalent and refractory disorder. *Journal of Consulting and Clinical Psychology, 50,* 820–840.

Brownell, K. D., & Wadden, T. A. (1991). The heterogeneity of obesity: Fitting treatments to individuals. *Behavior Therapy, 22,* 153–177.

Bruce, M., Scott, N., Shine, P., & Lader, M. (1992). Anxiogenic effects of caffeine in patients with anxiety disorders. *Archives of General Psychiatry, 49,* 867–869.

Bruce, M. L., Takeuchi, D. T., & Leaf, P. J. (1991). Poverty and psychiatric status: Longitudinal evidence from the New Haven Epidemiologic Catchment Area study. *Archives of General Psychiatry, 48,* 470–474.

Bruner, J. S. (1956). Freud and the image of man. *American Psychologist, 11,* 463–466.

Bruning, N. S., & Frew, D. R. (1987). Effects of exercise, relaxation, and management skills training on physiological stress indicators: A field experiment. *Journal of Applied Psychology, 72,* 515–521.

Brustad, R. J. (1988). Affective outcomes in competitive youth sport: The influence of intrapersonal and socialization factors. *Journal of Sport and Exercise Psychology, 10,* 307–321.

Buchsbaum, M. S., & Haier, R. J. (1983). Psychopathology: Biological approaches. *Annual Review of Psychology, 34,* 401–430.

Buck, R. (1980). Nonverbal behavior and the theory of emotion: The facial-feedback hypothesis. *Journal of Personality and Social Psychology, 38,* 811–824.

Buck, R. (1985). Prime theory: An integrated view of motivation and emotion. *Psychological Review, 92,* 389–413.

Buckley, K. W. (1982). The selling of a psychologist: John Broadus Watson and the application of behavioral techniques to advertising. *Journal of the History of the Behavioral Sciences, 18,* 207–221.

Buckley, K. W. (1989). *Mechanical man: John Broadus Watson and the beginnings of behaviorism.* New York: Guilford.

Buckley, W. F. (1982). The Hinckley mess. *National Review, 34,* 916–917.

Buhrmester, D. (1990). Intimacy of friendship, interpersonal competence, and adjustment during preadolescence and adolescence. *Child Development, 61,* 1101–1111.

Burchinal, M. R., Bryant, D. M., Lee, M. W., & Ramey, C. T. (1992). Early day care, infant-mother attachment, and maternal responsiveness in the infant's first year. *Early Childhood Research Quarterly, 3,* 383–396.

Burger, J. M., Cooper, H. M., & Good, T. L. (1982). Teacher attributions of student performance: Effects of outcome. *Personality and Social Psychology Bulletin, 8,* 685–690.

Burnette, M. M., & Adams, H. E. (1987). Detection of noncontingent feedback in EMG biofeedback. *Biofeedback and Self-Regulation, 12,* 281–293.

Burns, M., & Moskowitz, H. (1989–1990). Two experiments on alcohol-caffeine interaction. *Alcohol, Drugs, and Driving, 5/6,* 303–315.

Burton, D. (1988). Do anxious swimmers swim slower? Reexamining the elusive anxiety-performance relationship. *Journal of Sport and Exercise Psychology, 10,* 45–61.

Burton, R., (1621/1988). *The anatomy of melancholy.* Birmingham, AL: Gryphon.

Buss, A., Booker, A., & Buss, E. (1972). Firing a weapon and aggression. *Journal of Personality and Social Psychology, 22,* 296–302.

Buss, A. R. (1976). Galton and the birth of differential psychology and eugenics: Social, political, and economic forces. *Journal of the History of the Behavioral Sciences, 12,* 47–58.

Buss, D. M. (1985). Human mate selection. *American Scientist, 73,* 47–51.

Buss, D. M. (1988). The evolution of human intrasexual competition. *Journal of Personality and Social Psychology, 54,* 616–628.

Buss, D. M. (1990). Toward a biologically informed psychology of personality. *Journal of Personality, 58,* 1–16.

Buss, D. M., & Barnes, M. (1986). Preferences in human mate selection. *Journal of Personality and Social Psychology, 50,* 559–570.

Bussey, K., & Bandura, A. (1984). Influence of gender constancy and social power on sex-linked modeling. *Journal of Personality and Social Psychology, 47,* 1292–1302.

Button, E. (1983). Personal construct theory and psychological well-being. *British Journal of Medical Psychology, 56,* 313–321.

Buyer, L. S. (1988). Creative problem solving: A comparison of performance under different instructions. *Journal of Creative Behavior, 22,* 55–61.

Byers, P. H. (1986). Infant crying during aircraft descent. *Nursing Research, 35,* 260–262.

Byrne, D., Ervin, C. R., & Lamberth, J. (1970). Continuity between the experimental study of attraction and real-life computer dating. *Journal of Personality and Social Psychology, 16,* 157–165.

Byrne, D., & Kelley, K. C. (1981). *An introduction to personality.* Englewood Cliffs, NJ: Prentice Hall.

Byrne, R. C. (1990). The effectiveness of the Beginning Experience Workshop: A paraprofessional group marathon workshop for divorce adjustment. *Journal of Divorce, 13,* 101–120.

Byrne, W., Bleier, R., & Houston, L. (1988). Variations in human corpus callosum do not predict gender: A study using magnetic resonance imaging. *Behavioral Neuroscience, 102,* 222–227.

Cacioppo, J. T., Marshall-Goodell, B. S., Tassinary, L. G., & Petty, R. E. (1992). Rudimentary determinants of attitudes: Classical conditioning is more effective when prior knowledge about the attitude stimulus is low than high. *Journal of Experimental Social Psychology, 28,* 207–233.

Cadwallader, E. H. (1984). Values in Fritz Perls' Gestalt Therapy: On the dangers of half-truths. *Counseling and Values, 28,* 192–201.

Cain, D. P., & Vanderwolf, C. H. (1990). A critique of Rushton on race, brain size and intelligence. *Personality and Individual Differences, 11,* 777–784.

Calantone, R. J., & Warshaw, P. R. (1985). Negating the effects of fear appraisals in election campaigns. *Journal of Applied Psychology, 70,* 627–633.

Calkins, M. W. (1893). Statistics of dreams. *American Journal of Psychology, 5,* 311–343.

Calkins, M. W. (1901). *An introduction to psychology.* New York: Macmillan.

Calkins, M. W. (1913). Psychology and the behaviorist. *Psychological Bulletin, 10,* 288–291.

Calkins, M. W. (1930). Mary Whiton Calkins. In C. Murchison (Ed.). *A history of psychology in autobiography* (Vol. 1., pp. 31–62). New York: Russell & Russell.

Callaway, M. R., & Esser, J. K. (1984). Groupthink: Effects of cohesiveness and problem-solving procedures on group decision making. *Social Behavior and Personality, 12,* 157–164.

Camel, J. E., Withers, G. S., & Greenough, W. T. (1986). Persistence of visual cortex dendritic alterations induced by postweaning exposure to a "superenriched" environment in rats. *Behavioral Neuroscience, 100,* 810–813.

Cameron, M. J., & Cappello, M. J. (1993). "We'll cross that hurdle when we get to it": Teaching athletic performance within adaptive physical education. *Behavior Modification, 17,* 136–147.

Campbell, J. B., Tyrrell, D. J., & Zingaro, M. (1993). Sensation seeking among whitewater canoe and kayak paddlers. *Personality and Individual Differences, 14,* 489–491.

Campione, J. E., & Brown, A. L. (1979). Toward a theory of intelligence: Contributions from research with retarded children. *Intelligence, 2,* 279–304.

Candland, D. K. (1982). Selective pressure and the teaching of psychology: The fox and the hedgehog. *Teaching of Psychology, 9,* 20–23.

Cann, A., Sherman, S. J., & Elkes, R. (1975). Effects of initial request size and timing of a second request on compliance: The foot in the door and the door in the face. *Journal of Personality and Social Psychology, 32,* 774–782.

Cannon, D. S., & Baker, T. B. (1981). Emetic and electric shock alcohol aversion therapy: Assessment of conditioning. *Journal of Consulting and Clinical Psychology, 49,* 20–33.

Cannon, J. G., & Kluger, M. J. (1983). Endogenous pyrogen activity in human plasma after exercise. *Science, 220,* 617–619.

Cannon, W. B. (1915/1989). *Bodily changes in pain, hunger, fear, and rage.* Birmingham, AL: Gryphon.

Cannon, W. B. (1927). The James-Lange theory of emotions: A critical examination and an alternative. *American Journal of Psychology, 39,* 106–124.

Cannon, W. B., & Washburn, A. L. (1912). An explanation of hunger. *American Journal of Physiology, 29,* 444–454.

Cantor, N. (1990). From thought to behavior: "Having" and "doing" in the study of personality and cognition. *American Psychologist, 45,* 735–750.

Caplan, L. J., & Barr, R. A. (1989). On the relationship between category intensions and extensions in children. *Journal of Experimental Child Psychology, 47,* 413–429.

Caplan, P. J., MacPherson, G. M., & Tobin, P. (1985). Do sex-related differences in spatial abilities exist?: A multilevel critique with new data. *American Psychologist, 40,* 786–799.

Carducci, B. J., Deuser, P. S., Bauer, A., & Large, M. (1989). An application of the foot-in-the-door technique to organ donation. *Journal of Business and Psychology, 4,* 245–249.

Carducci, B. J., & Wheat, J. E. (1984, September). Business: An open door for psych majors. *APA Monitor,* p. 20.

Carey, G. (1990). Genes, fears, phobias, and phobic disorders. *Journal of Counseling and Development, 68,* 628–632.

Carey, M. P., & Burish, T. G. (1987). Providing relaxation training to cancer chemotherapy patients: A comparison of three delivery techniques. *Journal of Consulting and Clinical Psychology, 55,* 732–737.

Carey, M. P., Snel, D. L., Carey, K. B., & Richards, C. S. (1989). Self-initiated smoking cessation: A review of the empirical literature from a stress and coping perspective. *Cognitive Therapy and Research, 13,* 323–341.

Carlat, D. J., & Camargo, C. A. (1991). Review of bulimia nervosa in males. *American Journal of Psychiatry, 148,* 831–843.

Carlberg, C., & Kavale, K. (1980). The efficacy of special versus regular class placement for exceptional children: A meta-analysis. *Journal of Special Education, 14,* 295–309.

Carlson, C. R., White, D. K., & Turkat, I. D. (1982). Night terrors: A clinical and empirical review. *Clinical Psychology Review, 2,* 455–468.

Carlson, E. T. (1981). The history of multiple personality in the United States: I. The beginnings. *American Journal of Psychiatry, 138,* 666–668.

Carlson, M., & Miller, N. (1987). Explanation of the relation between negative mood and helping. *Psychological Bulletin, 102,* 91–108.

Carlsson, A. (1988). The current status of the dopamine hypothesis of schizophrenia. *Neuropsycho-pharmacology, 1,* 179–186.

Carmichael, L., Hogan, H. P., & Walter, A. (1932). An experimental study of the effect of language on the reproduction of visually perceived form. *Journal of Experimental Psychology, 15,* 73–86.

Carmody, T. P., Matarazzo, J. D., & Istvan, J. A. (1987). Promoting adherence to heart-healthy diets: A review of the literature. *Journal of Compliance in Health Care, 2,* 105–124.

Carpenter, C. R. (1955). Psychological research using television. *American Psychologist, 10,* 606–610.

Carroll, J. L. (1990). The relationship between humor appreciation and perceived physical health. *Psychology: A Journal of Human Behavior, 27,* 34–37.

Carskadon, M. A., & Dement, W. C. (1981). Cumulative effect of sleep deprivation on daytime sleepiness. *Psychophysiology, 18,* 107–113.

Carson, R. C., & Butcher, J. N. (1992). *Abnormal psychology* (9th ed.). New York: HarperCollins.

Cartwright, R. D. (1978). *A primer on sleep and dreaming.* Reading, MA: Addison-Wesley.

Cartwright, R. D. (1991). Dreams that work: The relation of dream incorporation to adaptation to stressful events. *Dreaming: Journal of the Association for the Study of Dreams, 1,* 3–9.

Carver, C. S., & Ganellen, R. J. (1983). Depression and components of self-punitiveness: High standards, self-criticism, and overgeneralization. *Journal of Abnormal Psychology, 92,* 330–337.

Cash, T. F. (1990). Losing hair, losing points? The effects of male pattern baldness on social impression formation. *Journal of Applied Social Psychology, 20,* 154–167.

Cash, T. F., & Derlega, V. J. (1978). The matching hypothesis: Physical attractiveness among same-sexed friends. *Personality and Social Psychology Bulletin, 4,* 240–243.

Cassone, V. M. (1990). Effects of melatonin on vertebrate circadian systems. *Trends in Neurosciences, 13,* 457–464.

Catania, J. A., Coates, T. J., Stall, R., & Bye, L. (1991). Changes in condom use among homosexual men in San Francisco. *Health Psychology, 10,* 190–199.

Catania, J. A., Gibson, D. R., Chitwood, D. D., & Coates, T. J. (1990). Methodological problems in AIDS behavioral research: Influences on measurement error and participation bias in studies of sexual behavior. *Psychological Bulletin, 108,* 339–362.

Cattell, J. M. (1890). Mental tests and measurements. *Mind, 15,* 373–381.

Cattell, R. B. (1940). A culture free intelligence test: I. *Journal of Educational Psychology, 31,* 161–179.

Cattell, R. B. (1949). *Sixteen personality factor questionnaire.* Champaign, IL: Institute for Personality and Ability Testing.

Ceci, S. J., & Bruck, M. (1993). Suggestibility of the child witness: A historical review and synthesis. *Psychological Bulletin, 113,* 403–439.

Ceci, S. J., & Liker, J. J. (1986). A day at the races: A study of IQ, expertise, and cognitive complexity. *Journal of Experimental Psychology: General, 115,* 255–266.

Ceci, S. J., Ross, D. F., & Toglia, M. P. (1987). Suggestibility of children's memory: Psychological implications. *Journal of Experimental Psychology: General, 116,* 38–49.

Cecil, M. A., & Forman, S. G. (1990). Effects of stress inoculation training and coworker support groups on teachers' stress. *Journal of School Psychology, 28,* 105–118.

Chadwick, H. (1986). *Augustine.* New York: Oxford University Press.

Chaiken, S., & Baldwin, M. W. (1981). Affective-cognitive consistency and the effect of salient behavioral information on the self-perception of attitudes. *Journal of Personality and Social Psychology, 41,* 1–12.

Chapman, R. K., Elkins, G. R., & Carter, B. D. (1982). Childhood hypnotic susceptibility: A review. *Journal of the American Society of Psychosomatic Dentistry and Medicine, 29,* 54–63.

Charlesworth, W. R. (1992). Darwin and developmental psychology: Past and present. *Developmental Psychology, 28,* 5–16.

Charness, N. (1992). The impact of chess research on cognitive science. *Psychological Research, 54,* 4–9.

Chase, W. G., & Simon, H. A. (1973). Perception in chess. *Cognitive Psychology, 4,* 55–81.

Chen, D. M., Collins, J. S., & Goldsmith, T. H. (1984). The ultraviolet receptor of bird retinas. *Science, 225,* 337–340.

Cherry, E. C. (1953). Some experiments on the recognition of speech with one and two ears. *Journal of the Acoustical Society of America, 25,* 975–979.

Chi, M. T. H., & Koeske, R. D. (1983). Network representation of a child's dinosaur knowledge. *Developmental Psychology, 19,* 29–39.

Child, I. L. (1985). Psychology and anomalous observations: The question of ESP in dreams. *American Psychologist, 40,* 1219–1230.

Chipuer, H. M., Rovine, M. J., & Plomin, R. (1990). LISREL modeling: Genetic and environmental influences on IQ revisited. *Intelligence, 14,* 11–29.

Chomsky, N. (1986). *Knowledge of language: Its nature, origin, and use.* New York: Praeger.

Chrisler, J. C. (1988). Conditioning the instructor's behavior: A class project in psychology of learning. *Teaching of Psychology, 15,* 135–137.

Christensen, A. J., & Smith, T. W. (1993). Cynical hostility and cardiovascular reactivity during self-disclosure. *Psychosomatic Medicine, 55,* 193–202.

Christensen, L. (1988). Deception in psychological research: When is its use justified? *Personality and Social Psychology Bulletin, 14,* 664–675.

Christianson, S. A., & Loftus, E. F. (1987). Memory for traumatic events. *Applied Cognitive Psychology, 1,* 225–239.

Christianson, S. A., & Nilsson, L. (1984). Functional amnesia as induced by a psychological trauma. *Memory and Cognition, 12,* 142–155.

Christopher, F. S., & Cate, R. M. (1985). Anticipated influences on sexual decision making for first intercourse. *Family Relations: Journal of Applied Family and Child Studies, 34,* 265–270.

Chwalisz, K., Diener, E., & Gallagher, D. (1988). Autonomic arousal feedback and emotional experience: Evidence from the spinal cord injured. *Journal of Personality and Social Psychology, 54,* 820–828.

Cialdini, R. B., & Fultz, J. (1990). Interpreting the negative mood-helping literature via "mega"-analysis: A contrary view. *Psychological Bulletin, 107,* 210–214.

Cialdini, R. B., Schaller, M., Houlihan, D., Arps, K., Fultz, J., & Beaman, A. L. (1987). Empathy-based helping: Is it selflessly motivated? *Journal of Personality and Social Psychology, 52,* 749–758.

Cialdini, R. B., Vincent, J. E., Lewis, S. J., Catalan, J., Wheeler, D., & Darley, B. L. (1975). Reciprocal concessions procedure for inducing compliance: The door-in-the-face technique. *Journal of Personality and Social Psychology, 31,* 206–215.

Cicerone, C. M., & Hayhoe, M. M. (1990). The size of the pool for bleaching in human rod vision. *Vision Research, 30,* 693–697.

Cicerone, C. M., & Nerger, J. L. (1989). The density of cones in the fovea centralis of the human dichromat. *Vision Research, 29,* 1587–1595.

Clark, K. B., & Clark, M. P. (1947). Racial identification and preference in Negro children. In T. M. Newcomb & E. L. Hartley (Eds.), *Readings in social psychology* (pp. 169–178). New York: Holt.

Clark, M. E., & Hirschman, R. (1990). Effects of paced respiration on anxiety reduction in a clinical population. *Biofeedback and Self-Regulation, 15,* 273–284.

Clark, R. D., & Maass, A. (1990). The effects of majority size on minority influence. *European Journal of Social Psychology, 20,* 99–117.

Clark, R. D., & Word, L. E. (1974). Where is the apathetic bystander? Situational characteristics of the emergency. *Journal of Personality and Social Psychology, 29,* 279–287.

Clarke, J. T., Gates, R. D., Hogan, S. E., & Barrett, M. (1987). Neuropsychological studies on adolescents with phenylketonuria returned to phenylalanine-restricted diets. *American Journal on Mental Retardation, 92,* 255–262.

Clarke, K. M., & Greenberg, L. S. (1986). Differential effects of the Gestalt two-chair intervention and problem solving in resolving decisional conflict. *Journal of Counseling Psychology, 33,* 11–15.

Clarke, M. J. (1985). Suicides by opium and its derivatives in England and Wales, 1850–1950. *Psychological Medicine, 15,* 327–342.

Clements, D. H. (1987). Computers and young children: A review of research. *Young Children, 43,* 34–44.

Cliffe, M. J. (1991). Behaviour modification by successive approximation: Saxon age examples from Bede. *British Journal of Clinical Psychology, 30,* 367–369.

Clifford, C. A., Murray, R. M., & Fulker, D. W. (1984). Genetic and environmental influences on obsessional traits and symptoms. *Psychological Medicine, 14,* 791–800.

Clore, G. L., Bray, R. M., Itkin, S. M., & Murphy, P. (1978). Interracial attitudes and behavior at a summer camp. *Journal of Personality and Social Psychology, 36,* 107–116.

Clum, G. A., & Knowles, S. L. (1991). Why do some people with panic disorders become avoidant? A review. *Clinical Psychology Review, 11,* 295–313.

Cofer, C. N. (1985). Drives and motives. In G. A. Kimble & K. Schlesinger (Eds.), *Topics in the history of psychology* (Vol. 2, pp. 151–190). Hillsdale, NJ: Erlbaum.

Cogan, D., & Cogan, R. (1984). Classical salivary conditioning: An easy demonstration. *Teaching of Psychology, 11,* 170–171.

Cohen, D. B. (1979). *Sleep and dreaming: Origins, nature and functions.* New York: Pergamon.

Cohen, M. R., Pickar, D., & DuBois, M. (1983). The role of the endogenous opioid system in the human stress response. *Psychiatric Clinics of North America, 6,* 457–471.

Cohen, N. J., & Squire, L. R. (1980). Preserved learning and retention of pattern-analyzing skill in amnesia: Dissociation of knowing how and knowing that. *Science, 210,* 207–210.

Cohen, S., & Williamson, G. M. (1991). Stress and infectious disease in humans. *Psychological Bulletin, 109,* 5–24.

Coile, D. C., & Miller, N. E. (1984). How radical animal activists try to mislead humane people. *American Psychologist, 39,* 700–701.

Coke-Pepsi slugfest. (1976, July 26). *Time,* pp. 64–65.

Cole, J. D., & Kazarian, S. S. (1993). Predictive validity of the Level of Expressed Emotion (LEE) Scale: Readmission follow-up data for 1, 2, and 5-year periods. *Journal of Clinical Psychology, 49,* 216–218.

Colegrove, F. W. (1899). Individual memories. *American Journal of Psychology, 10,* 228–255.

Coles, R. (1970). *Erik Erikson: The growth of his work.* Boston: Atlantic/Little, Brown.

Collins, A. M., & Loftus, E. F. (1975). A spreading-activation theory of semantic processing. *Psychological Review, 82,* 407–428.

Collins, R. L., & Marlatt, G. A. (1981). Social modeling as a determinant of drinking behavior: Implications for prevention and treatment. *Addictive Behaviors, 6,* 233–239.

Comrey, A. L., Michael, W. B., & Fruchter, B. (1988). J. P. Guilford (1897–1987). *American Psychologist, 43,* 1086–1087.

Connelly, D. (1988). Increasing intensity of play of nonassertive athletes. *Sport Psychologist, 2,* 255–265.

Connor, S. R. (1986). Measurement of denial in the terminally ill: A critical review. *Hospice Journal, 2,* 51–68.

Conrad, R. (1962). An association between memory errors and errors due to acoustic masking of speech. *Nature, 193,* 1314–1315.

Constantinople, A. (1969). An Eriksonian measure of personality development in college students. *Developmental Psychology, 1,* 357–372.

Conway, M., & Ross, M. (1984). Getting what you want by revising what you had. *Journal of Personality and Social Psychology, 47,* 738–748.

Cook, M., & Mineka, S. (1989). Observational conditioning of fear to fear-relevant versus fear-irrelevant stimuli in rhesus monkeys. *Journal of Abnormal Psychology, 98,* 448–459.

Cook, S. W. (1985). Experimenting on social issues: The case of school desegregation. *American Psychologist, 40,* 452–460.

Coon, D. J. (1982). Eponymy, obscurity, Twitmyer, and Pavlov. *Journal of the History of the Behavioral Sciences, 18,* 255–262.

Coon, H., Fulker, D. W., DeFries, J. C., & Plomin, R. (1990). Home environment and cognitive ability of seven-year-old children in the Colorado Adoption Project: Genetic and environmental etiologies. *Developmental Psychology, 26,* 459–468.

Cooney, J. L., & Zeichner, A. (1985). Selective attention to negative feedback in Type A and Type B individuals. *Journal of Abnormal Psychology, 94,* 110–112.

Coons, P. M., & Milstein, V. (1992). Psychogenic amnesia: A clinical investigation of 25 cases. *Dissociation: Progress in the Dissociative Disorders, 5,* 73–79.

Cooper, C. L., Cooper, R. D., & Faragher, B. (1986). Psychosocial stress as a precursor to breast cancer: A review. *Current Psychological Research and Reviews, 5,* 268–280.

Cooper, G. D., Adams, H. B., & Scott, J. C. (1988). Studies in REST: I. Reduced Environmental Stimulation Therapy (REST) and reduced alcohol consumption. *Journal of Substance Abuse Treatment, 5,* 61–68.

Cooper, J., & Croyle, R. T. (1984). Attitudes and attitude change. *Annual Review of Psychology, 35,* 395–426.

Coren, S., & Aks, D. J. (1990). Moon illusion in pictures: A multimechanism approach. *Journal of Experimental Psychology: Human Perception and Performance, 16,* 365–380.

Cornell-Bell, A. H., Finkbeiner, M., Cooper, M. S., & Smith, S. J. (1990). Glutamate induces calcium waves in cultured astrocytes: Long-range glial signaling. *Science, 247,* 470–473.

Corr, C. A. (1993). Coping with dying: Lessons that we should and should not learn from the work of Elisabeth Kübler-Ross. *Death Studies, 17,* 69–83.

Corsini, R. J. (1984). *Current psychotherapies.* Itasca, IL: F. E. Peacock.

Corter, J. E., & Gluck, M. A. (1992). Explaining basic categories: Feature predictability and information. *Psychological Bulletin, 111,* 291–303.

Cotman, C. W., Monaghan, D. T., & Ganong, A. H. (1988). Excitatory amino acid neurotransmission: NMDA receptors and Hebb-type synaptic plasticity. *Annual Review of Neuroscience, 11,* 61–80.

Cousins, N. (1979). *Anatomy of an illness as perceived by the patient.* New York: W. W. Norton.

Cousins, N. (1983). *The healing heart: Antidotes to panic and helplessness.* New York: W. W. Norton.

Cowan, N. (1984). On short and long auditory stories. *Psychological Bulletin, 96,* 341–370.

Cowan, N. (1988). Evolving conceptions of memory storage, selective attention, and their mutual constraints within the human information-processing systems. *Psychological Bulletin, 104,* 163–191.

Cowart, B. J. (1981). Development of taste perception in humans: Sensitivity and preference through the life span. *Psychological Bulletin, 90,* 43–73.

Cowen, E. L. (1982). Help is where you find it: Four informal helping groups. *American Psychologist, 37,* 385–395.

Cowles, M. (1989). *Statistics in psychology: An historical perspective.* Hillsdale, NJ: Erlbaum.

Cox, G. L., & Merkel, W. T. (1989). A qualitative review of psychosocial treatments for bulimia. *Journal of Nervous and Mental Disease, 177,* 77–84.

Cox, W. J., & Kenardy, J. (1993). Performance anxiety, social phobia, and setting effects in instrumental music students. *Journal of Anxiety Disorders, 7,* 49–60.

Craft, S., Zallen, G., & Baker, L. D. (1992). Glucose and memory in mild senile dementia of the Alzheimer type. *Journal of Clinical and Experimental Neuropsychology, 14,* 253–267.

Craig, J. C., & Evans, P. M. (1987). Vibrotactile masking and the persistence of tactual features. *Perception and Psychophysics, 42,* 309–317.

Craik, F. I. M., & Lockhart, R. S. (1972). Levels of processing: A framework for memory research. *Journal of Verbal Learning and Verbal Behavior, 11,* 671–684.

Craik, F. I. M., & Tulving, E. (1975). Depth of processing and the retention of words in episodic memory. *Journal of Experimental Psychology: General, 104,* 268–294.

Cramer, P., & Blatt, S. J. (1990). Use of the TAT to measure change in defense mechanisms following intensive psychotherapy. *Journal of Personality Assessment, 54,* 236–251.

Crandall, J. E. (1980). Adler's concept of social interest: Theory, measurement, and implications for adjustment. *Journal of Personality and Social Psychology, 39,* 481–495.

Cravens, H. (1992). A scientific project locked in time: The Terman Genetic Studies of Genius, 1920s–1950s. *American Psychologist, 47,* 183–189.

Crisp, A. H. (1986). The integration of "self-help" and "help" in the prevention of anorexia nervosa. *British Review of Bulimia and Anorexia Nervosa, 1,* 27–39.

Critelli, J. W., & Dupre, K. M. (1978). Self-disclosure and romantic attraction. *Journal of Social Psychology, 106,* 127–128.

Critelli, J. W., & Neumann, K. F. (1984). The placebo: Conceptual analysis of a construct in transition. *American Psychologist, 39,* 32–39.

Croce, R. V. (1986). The effects of EMG biofeedback on strength acquisition. *Biofeedback and Self-Regulation, 11,* 299–310.

Croce, R. V. (1990). Effects of exercise and diet on body composition and cardiovascular fitness in adults with severe mental retardation. *Education & Training in Mental Retardation, 25,* 176–187.

Crocker, J., Alloy, L. B., & Kayne, N. T. (1988). Attributional style, depression, and perceptions of consensus for events. *Journal of Personality and Social Psychology, 54,* 840–846.

Crockett, D. J., Foreman, M. E., Alden, L., & Blasberg, B. (1986). A comparison of treatment modes in the management of myofascial pain dysfunction syndrome. *Biofeedback and Self-Regulation, 11,* 279–291.

Crook, T., & Eliot, J. (1980). Parental death during childhood and adult depression: A critical review of the literature. *Psychological Bulletin, 87,* 252–259.

Crose, R. (1990). Reviewing the past in the here and now: Using Gestalt therapy techniques with life review. *Journal of Mental Health Counseling, 12,* 279–287.

Cross, C. K., & Hirschfield, R. M. A. (1986). Psychosocial factors and suicidal behavior. *Annals of the New York Academy of Science, 487,* 77–89.

Crowe, R. R. (1990). Panic disorder: Genetic considerations. *Journal of Psychiatric Research, 24,* 129–134.

Crundell, J. K. (1993). Fluoxetine and suicidal ideation: A review of the literature. *International Journal of Neuroscience, 68,* 73–84.

Culebras, A., & Moore, J. T. (1989). Magnetic resonance findings in REM sleep behavior disorder. *Neurology, 39,* 1519–1523.

Cummings, J. L., & Victoroff, J. I. (1990). Noncognitive neuropsychiatric syndromes in Alzheimer's disease. *Neuropsychiatry, Neuropsychology, and Behavioral Neurology, 3,* 140–158.

Cunningham, J. A., Dollinger, S. J., Satz, M., & Rotter, N. S. (1991). Personality correlates of prejudice against AIDS victims. *Bulletin of the Psychonomic Society, 29,* 165–167.

Cunningham, S. (1983, March). Superior court restarts electroshock in Berkeley. *APA Monitor,* p. 17.

Cunningham, S. (1984, August). Chronic patients sue for community housing. *APA Monitor,* p. 21.

Cunningham, S. (1985, July). Chimps use sign language to talk to each other. *APA Monitor,* p. 11.

Curcio, C. A., Sloan, K. R., Jr., Packer, O., Hendrickson, A. E., & Kalina, R. E. (1987). Distribution of cones in human and monkey retina: Individual variability and radial asymmetry. *Science, 236,* 579–582.

Curzon, G. (1982). Transmitter amines in depression. *Psychological Medicine, 12,* 465–470.

Cushman, P. (1989). Iron fists/velvet gloves: A study of a mass marathon psychology training. *Psychotherapy, 26,* 23–39.

Cusick, F. (1987, January 23). No one saw signs until it was over. *Philadelphia Inquirer,* p. 1-A.

Cutting, J. E. (1987). Perception and information. *Annual Review of Psychology, 38,* 61–90.

Cytowic, R. E. (1989). Synesthesia and mapping of subjective sensory dimensions. *Neurology, 39,* 849–850.

Czeisler, C. A., Moore-Ede, M. C., & Coleman, R. M. (1982). Rotating shift work schedules that disrupt sleep are improved by applying circadian principles. *Science, 217,* 460–463.

Daly, M., & Wilson, M. (1990). Is parent-offspring conflict sex-linked? Freudian and Darwinian models. *Journal of Personality, 58,* 163–189.

Dance, K. A., & Neufeld, R. W. J. (1988). Aptitude-treatment interaction research in the clinical setting: A review of attempts to dispel the "patient uniformity" myth. *Psychological Bulletin, 104,* 192–213.

Dandoy, A. C., & Goldstein, A. G. (1990). The use of cognitive appraisal to reduce stress reactions: A replication. *Journal of Social Behavior and Personality, 5,* 275–285.

Danenberg, M. A., Loos-Cosgrove, M., & LoVerde, M. (1987). Temporary hearing loss and rock music. *Language, Speech, and Hearing Services in Schools, 18,* 267–274.

Daniels, D., & Plomin, R. (1985). Origins of individual differences in infant shyness. *Developmental Psychology, 21,* 118–121.

Daniels, M. (1982). The development of the concept of self-actualization in the writings of Abraham Maslow. *Current Psychological Reviews, 2,* 61–75.

Danziger, K. (1990). *Constructing the subject: Historical origins of psychological research.* New York: Cambridge University Press.

Darch, C. B., Carnine, D. W., & Kameenui, E. J. (1986). The role of graphic organizers and social structure in content area instruction. *Journal of Reading Behavior, 18,* 275–295.

Darian-Smith, I. (1982). Touch in primates. *Annual Review of Psychology, 33,* 155–194.

Darley, J. M., & Fazio, R. H. (1980). Expectancy confirmation processes arising in the social interaction sequence. *American Psychologist, 35,* 867–881.

Darley, J. M., & Latané, B. (1968). Bystander intervention in emergencies: Diffusion of responsibilities. *Journal of Personality and Social Psychology, 8,* 377–383.

Darling, C. A., Davidson, J. K., & Cox, R. P. (1991). Female sexual response and the timing of partner orgasm. *Journal of Sex and Marital Therapy, 17,* 3–21.

Darrach, B., & Norris, J. (1984, August). An American tragedy. *Life,* pp. 58–74.

Darwin, C. (1859/1975). *The origin of species.* New York: W. W. Norton.

Darwin, C. (1872/1965). *The expression of the emotions in man and animals.* Chicago: University of Chicago Press.

Darwin, C. (1877/1977). A biographical sketch of an infant. In P. H. Barrett (Ed.), *The collected papers of Charles Darwin* (pp. 191–200). Chicago: University of Chicago Press.

Davidson, R. J. (1992). Emotion and affective style: Hemispheric substrates. *Psychological Science, 3,* 39–43.

Davidson, R. J., Ekman, P., Saron, C. D., Senulis, J. A., & Friesen, W. V. (1990). Approach-withdrawal and cerebral asymmetry: Emotion expression and brain physiology: I. *Journal of Personality and Social Psychology, 58,* 330–341.

Davis, A., & Eels, K. (1953). *Davis-Eels games.* Yonkers, NY: World Book.

Davis, H., & Memmott, J. (1982). Counting behavior in animals: A critical evaluation. *Psychological Bulletin, 92,* 547–571.

Davis, H. P., Rosenzweig, M. R., Becker, L. A., & Sather, K. J. (1988). Biological psychology's relationships to psychology and neuroscience. *American Psychologist, 43,* 359–371.

Davis, J., Schiffman, H. R., & Greist-Bousquet, S. (1990). Semantic context and figure-ground organization. *Psychological Research, 52,* 306–309.

Davis, J. M., Sargent, R. G., Brayboy, T. D., & Bartoli, W. P. (1992). Thermogenic effects of pre-prandial and post-prandial exercise in obese females. *Addictive Behaviors, 17,* 185–190.

Davis, J. O. (1988). Strategies for managing athlete's jet lag. *Sport Psychologist, 2,* 154–160.

Davis, R. (1986). Knowledge-based systems. *Science, 231,* 957–963.

Davis, S. F., Thomas, R. L., & Weaver, M. S. (1982). Psychology's contemporary and all-time notables: Student, faculty, and chairperson viewpoints. *Bulletin of the Psychonomic Society, 20,* 3–6.

Deahl, M. (1991). Cannabis and memory loss. *British Journal of Addiction, 86,* 249–252.

DeAngelis, G. C., Ohzawa, I., & Freeman, R. D. (1991). Depth is encoded in the visual cortex by a specialized receptive field structure. *Nature, 352,* 156–159.

Deaux, K. (1985). Sex and gender. *Annual Review of Psychology, 36,* 49–81.

de Benedittis, G., Lorenzetti, A., & Pieri, A. (1990). The role of stressful life events in the onset of chronic primary headache. *Pain, 40*, 65–75.

DeCarli, C., Kaye, J. A., Horwitz, B., & Rapoport, S. I. (1990). Critical analysis of the use of computer-assisted transverse axial tomography to study human brain in aging and dementia of the Alzheimer type. *Neurology, 40*, 872–883.

DeCasper, A. J., & Spence, M. J. (1986). Prenatal maternal speech influences newborns' perception of speech sounds. *Infant Behavior and Development, 9*, 133–150.

de Castro, J. M. (1993). Genetic influences on daily intake and meal patterns of humans. *Physiology and Behavior, 53*, 777–782.

DeCharms, R., & Moeller, G. H. (1962). Values expressed in American children's readers: 1800–1950. *Journal of Abnormal and Social Psychology, 64*, 136–142.

Deci, E. L., Nezlek, J., & Sheinman, L. (1981). Characteristics of the rewarder and intrinsic motivation of the rewardee. *Journal of Personality and Social Psychology, 40*, 1–10.

Deckers, L., & Buttram, R. T. (1990). Humor as a response to incongruities within or between schemata. *Humor: International Journal of Humor Research, 3*, 53–64.

DeLacoste-Utamsing, C., & Holloway, R. L. (1982). Sexual dimorphism in the human corpus callosum. *Science, 216*, 1431–1432.

Delmonte, M. M. (1984). Physiological responses during meditation and rest. *Biofeedback and Self-Regulation, 9*, 181–200.

DeLongis, A., Folkman, S., & Lazarus, R. S. (1988). The impact of daily stress on health and mood: Psychological and social resources as mediators. *Journal of Personality and Social Psychology, 54*, 486–495.

Deluga, R. J. (1991). The relationship of upward-influencing behavior with subordinate-impression management characteristics. *Journal of Applied Social Psychology, 21*, 1145–1160.

de Manaceine, M. (1899). *Sleep: Its physiology, pathology, hygiene, and psychology.* New York: Charles Scribner's Sons.

Dember, W. N., & Bagwell, M. (1985). A history of perception. In G. A. Kimble & K. Schlesinger (Eds.), *Topics in the history of psychology* (pp. 261–304). Hillsdale, NJ: Erlbaum.

Dembroski, T. M., & Costa, P. T., Jr. (1988). Assessment of coronary-prone behavior: A current overview. *Annals of Behavioral Medicine, 10*, 60–63.

Dement, W. C. (1960). The effect of dream deprivation. *Science, 131*, 1705–1707.

Dement, W. C. (1976). *Some must watch while some must sleep.* San Francisco: W. H. Freeman.

Dement, W. C., & Wolpert, E. (1958). The relation of eye movements, body motility, and external stimuli to dream content. *Journal of Experimental Psychology, 53*, 543–553.

Dempster, F. N. (1985). Proactive interference in sentence recall: Topic similarity effects and individual differences. *Memory and Cognition, 13*, 81–89.

Dempster, F. N., & Farris, R. (1990). The spacing effect: Research and practice. *Journal of Research and Development in Education, 23*, 97–101.

Denmark, F. L. (1980). Psyche: From rocking the cradle to rocking the boat. *American Psychologist, 35*, 1057–1065.

Denney, N. W., Field, J. K., & Quadagno, D. (1984). Sex differences in sexual needs and desires. *Archives of Sexual Behavior, 13*, 233–245.

Dennis, D. L., Buckner, J. C., Lipton, F. R., & Levine, I. S. (1991). A decade of research and services for homeless mentally ill persons: Where do we stand? *American Psychologist, 46*, 1129–1138.

Desforges, D. M., Lord, C. G., Ramsey, S. L., Manson, J. A., van Leeuwen, M. D., West, S. C., & Lepper, M. R. (1991). Effects of structured cooperative contact on changing negative attitudes toward stigmatized social groups. *Journal of Personality and Social Psychology, 60*, 531–544.

Detera-Wadleigh, S. D., Berrettini, W. H., Goldin, L. R., Boorman, D., Anderson, S., & Gershon, E. S. (1987). Close linkage of c-Harvey-ras-I and the insulin gene to affective disorder is ruled out in three North American pedigrees. *Nature, 325*, 806–808.

de Valois, R. L., Abramov, I., & Jacobs, G. H. (1966). Analysis of response patterns of LGN cells. *Journal of the Optical Society of America, 56*, 966–977.

de Valois, R. L., & de Valois, K. K. (1980). Spatial vision. *Annual Review of Psychology, 31*, 309–341.

Devine, D. P., & Spanos, N. P. (1990). Effectiveness of maximally different cognitive strategies and expectancy in attenuation of reported pain. *Journal of Personality and Social Psychology, 58*, 672–678.

Devins, G. M., & Seland, T. P. (1987). Emotional impact of multiple sclerosis: Recent findings and suggestions for future research. *Psychological Bulletin, 101*, 363–375.

Dewsbury, D. A. (1990). Early interactions between animal psychologists and animal activists and the founding of the APA Committee on Precautions in Animal Experimentation. *American Psychologist, 45*, 315–327.

Diaconis, P. (1978). Statistical problems in ESP research. *Science, 201*, 131–136.

Diamond, E. L. (1982). The role of anger and hostility in essential hypertension and coronary heart disease. *Psychological Bulletin, 92*, 410–433.

Diamond, M. C. (1988). *Enriching heredity: The impact of the environment on the anatomy of the brain.* New York: Free Press.

Diaz Soto, L. (1989). Relationship between home environment and intrinsic versus extrinsic orientation of higher achieving and lower achieving Puerto Rican children. *Educational Research Quarterly, 13*, 22–36.

Dickerson, C. A., Thibodeau, R., Aronson, E., & Miller, D. (1992). Using cognitive dissonance to encourage water conservation. *Journal of Applied Social Psychology, 22*, 841–854.

Dickey-Bryant, L., Lautenschlager, G. J., Mendoza, J. L., & Abrahams, N. (1986). Facial attractiveness and its relation to occupational success. *Journal of Applied Psychology, 71*, 16–19.

Dickson, D. (1984). Edinburgh sets up parapsychology chair. *Science, 223*, 1274.

Diener, E. (1984). Subjective well-being. *Psychological Bulletin, 95*, 542–575.

Diener, E., Colvin, C. R., Pavot, W. G., & Allman, A. (1991). The psychic costs of intense positive affect. *Journal of Personality and Social Psychology, 61*, 492–503.

Diener, E., & Larsen, R. J. (1984). Temporal stability and cross-situational consistency of affective, behavioral, and cognitive responses. *Journal of Personality and Social Psychology, 47*, 871–883.

Diener, E., Sandvik, E., Seidlitz, L., & Diener, M. (1993). The relationship between income and subjective well-being: Relative or absolute? *Social Indicators Research, 28*, 195–223.

Diers, C. J. (1974). Historical trends in the age of menarche and menopause. *Psychological Reports, 34*, 931–937.

Dillard, J. P. (1990). Self-inference and the foot-in-the-door technique: Quantity of behavior and attitudinal mediation. *Human Communication Research, 16*, 422–447.

Dillard, J. P. (1991). The current status of research on sequential-request compliance techniques. *Personality and Social Psychology Bulletin, 17*, 283–288.

Dillon, K. M., & Totten, M. C. (1989). Psychological factors, immunocompetence, and health of breast-feeding mothers and their infants. *Journal of Genetic Psychology, 150*, 155–162.

Dishman, R. J., & Gettman, L. R. (1980). Psychobiologic influences on exercise adherence. *Journal of Sport Psychology, 2*, 295–310.

Dixon, N. F., & Henley, S. H. (1991). Unconscious perception: Possible implications of data from academic research for clinical practice. *Journal of Nervous and Mental Disease, 179*, 243–252.

Doane, J. A., West, K. L., Goldstein, M. J., Rodnick, E. H., & Jones, J. E. (1981). Parental communication deviance and affective style: Predictors of subsequent schizophrenia spectrum disorders in vulnerable adolescents. *Archives of General Psychiatry, 38*, 679–685.

Dobelle, W. H., Maldejovsky, M. G., Evans, J. R., Roberts, T. S., & Girvin, J. P. (1976). "Braille" reading by a blind volunteer by visual cortex stimulation. *Nature, 259*, 111–112.

Dockery, T. M., & Bedeian, A. G. (1989). "Attitudes versus actions": LaPiere's (1934) classic study revisited. *Social Behavior and Personality, 17*, 9–16.

Dohrn, C. S., Lichtor, J. L., Coalson, D. W., & Uitvlugt, A. (1993). Reinforcing effects of extended inhalation of nitrous oxide in humans. *Drug and Alcohol Dependence, 31*, 265–280.

Dolce, J. J., & Raczynski, J. M. (1985). Neuromuscular activity and electromyography in painful backs: Psychological and biomechanical models in assessment and treatment. *Psychological Bulletin, 97*, 502–520.

Dollard, J., Doob, I. W., Miller, N. E., Mowrer, O. H., & Sears, R. R. (1939). *Frustration and aggression.* New York: McGraw-Hill.

Dollard, J., & Miller, N. E. (1950). *Personality and psychotherapy.* New York: McGraw-Hill.

Donnerstein, E. I., & Berkowitz, L. (1981). Victim reactions in aggressive erotic films as a factor in violence against women. *Journal of Personality and Social Psychology, 41*, 710–724.

Donnerstein, E. I., & Linz, D. G. (1986). Mass media sexual violence and male viewers: Current theory and research. *American Behavioral Scientist, 29*, 601–618.

Dover, A. (1983). Computers and the gifted: Past, present, and future. *Gifted Child Quarterly, 27*, 81–85.

Doyle, A. C. (1930). *The complete Sherlock Holmes.* Garden City, NY: Doubleday.

Doyle, J. (1989). *The male experience.* Dubuque, IA: Wm. C. Brown.

Doyle, M. C. (1984). Enhancing dream pleasure with Senoi strategy. *Journal of Clinical Psychology, 40*, 467–474.

Driskell, J. E., Willis, R. P., & Copper, C. (1992). Effect of overlearning on retention. *Journal of Applied Psychology, 77*, 615–622.

Dronkers, N. F., & Knight, R. T. (1989). Right-sided neglect in a left-hander: Evidence for reversed hemispheric specialization of attention capacity. *Neuropsychologia, 27*, 729–735.

Droste, C., Greenlee, M. W., Schreck, M., & Roskamm, H. (1991). Experimental pain thresholds and plasma beta-endorphin levels during exercise. *Medicine and Science in Sports and Exercise, 23*, 334–342.

Dubner, R., & Bennett, G. J. (1983). Spinal and trigeminal mechanisms of nociception. *Annual Review of Neuroscience, 6*, 381–418.

Duckro, P. N. (1991). Biofeedback in the management of headache: II. *Headache Quarterly, 2*, 17–22.

Duckworth, J. C. (1991). The Minnesota Multiphasic Personality Inventory-2: A review. *Journal of Counseling and Development, 69*, 564–567.

Dudycha, G. J. (1936). An objective study of punctuality in relation to personality and achievement. *Archives of Psychology, 29*, 1–53.

Dunbar-Jacob, J., Dwyer, K., & Dunning, E. J. (1991). Compliance with antihypertensive regimen: A review of the research in the 1980s. *Annals of Behavioral Medicine, 13*, 31–39.

Duncan, W. J., & Feisal, J. P. (1989). No laughing matter: Patterns of humor in the workplace. *Organizational Dynamics, 17*, 18–30.

Dunnett, S. B. (1991). Neural transplants as a treatment for Alzheimer's disease? *Psychological Medicine, 21*, 825–830.

Durbin, D. L., Darling, N., Steinberg, L., & Brown, B. B. (1993). Parenting style and peer group membership among European-American adolescents. *Journal of Research on Adolescence, 3*, 87–100.

Dussault, J. H., & Ruel, J. (1987). Thyroid hormones and brain development. *Annual Review of Physiology, 49*, 321–334.

Dutton, D. G., & Aron, A. P. (1974). Some evidence for heightened sexual attraction under conditions of high anxiety. *Journal of Personality and Social Psychology, 30*, 510–517.

Duyme, M. (1988). School success and social class: An adoption study. *Developmental Psychology, 24*, 203–209.

Dworkin, B. R., & Miller, N. E. (1986). Failure to replicate visceral learning in the acute curarized rat preparation. *Behavioral Neuroscience, 100*, 299–314.

Dwyer, T. (1986, June 15). How the will to win drove an athlete to the edge. *Philadelphia Inquirer*, pp. 1-A, 8-A.

Dzewaltowski, D. A., Noble, J. M., & Shaw, J. M. (1990). Physical activity participation: Social cognitive theory versus the theories of reasoned action and planned behavior. *Journal of Sport and Exercise Psychology, 12*, 388–405.

Eagly, A. H. (1984). Gender and social influence: A social psychological analysis. *American Psychologist, 38*, 971–981.

Eagly, A. H., Ashmore, R. D., Makhijani, M. G., & Longo, L. C. (1991). What is beautiful is good, but . . . : A meta-analytic review of research of the physical attractiveness stereotype. *Psychological Bulletin, 110*, 109–128.

Eagly, A. H., & Steffen, V. J. (1986). Gender and aggressive behavior: A meta-analytic review of the social psychological literature. *Psychological Bulletin, 100*, 309–330.

Eagly, A. H., & Warren, R. (1976). Intelligence, comprehension, and opinion change. *Journal of Personality and Social Psychology, 44*, 226–242.

Ebbeck, V., & Weiss, M. R. (1988). The arousal-performance relationship: Task characteristics and performance measures in track and field athletics. *Sport Psychologist, 2*, 13–27.

Ebbinghaus, H. (1885/1913). *Memory: A contribution to experimental psychology.* New York: Columbia University Press.

Eccles, A., Wilde, A., & Marshall, W. L. (1988). In vivo desensitization in the treatment of recurrent nightmares. *Journal of Behavior Therapy and Experimental Psychiatry, 19*, 285–288.

Ecenbarger, W. (1987, June 4). The forgotten sense. *Philadelphia Inquirer Magazine*, pp. 24–26, 34–35.

Eckerman, C. O., Davis, C. C., & Didow, S. M. (1989). Toddlers' emerging ways of achieving social coordinations with a peer. *Child Development, 60*, 440–453.

Eckert, E. D., Bouchard, T. J., Bohlen, J., & Heston, L. L. (1986). Homosexuality in monozygotic twins reared apart. *British Journal of Psychiatry, 148*, 421–425.

Edeline, J. M., & Weinberger, N. M. (1991). Subcortical adaptive filtering in the auditory system: Associative receptive field plasticity in the dorsal medial geniculate body. *Behavioral Neuroscience, 105*, 154–175.

Edelman, G. M (1984, April). Cell adhesion molecules: A molecular basis for animal form. *Scientific American*, pp. 118–129.

Edelmann, R. J., & Golombok, S. (1989). Stress and reproductive failure. *Journal of Reproductive and Infant Psychology, 7*, 79–86.

Edinger, J. D., Marsh, G. R., McCall, W. V., & Erwin, C. W. (1990). Daytime functioning and nighttime sleep before, during, and after a 146-hour tennis match. *Sleep*, 526–532.

Egan, K. J., Carr, J. E., Hunt, D. D., & Adamson, R. (1988). Endogenous opiate system and systematic desensitization. *Journal of Consulting and Clinical Psychology, 56*, 287–291.

Egeland, J. A., Gerhard, D. S., Pauls, D. L., Sussex, J. N., Kidd, K. K., Allen, C. R., Hostetter, A. M., & Housman, D. E. (1987). Bipolar affective disorders linked to DNA markers on chromosome 11. *Nature, 325*, 783–787.

Egeth, H. (1992). Dichotic listening: Long-lived echoes of Broadbent's early studies. *Journal of Experimental Psychology: General, 121*, 124.

Ehara, T. H. (1980, December). On the electronic chess circuit. *Science 80*, pp. 78, 80.

Ehrlichman, H., & Halpern, J. N. (1988). Affect and memory: Effects of pleasant and unpleasant odors on retrieval of happy and unhappy memories. *Journal of Personality and Social Psychology, 55*, 769–779.

Eich, J. E. (1980). The cue-dependent nature of state-dependent retrieval. *Memory and Cognition, 8*, 157–173.

Eich, J. E., Weingartner, H., Stillman, R. C., & Gillin, J. C. (1975). State-dependent accessibility of retrieval cues in the retention of a categorized list. *Journal of Verbal Learning and Verbal Behavior, 14*, 408–417.

Eichhorn, S. K. (1982). Congenital cytomegalovirus infection: A significant cause of deafness and mental deficiency. *American Annals of the Deaf, 127*, 838–843.

Eisdorfer, C. (1983). Conceptual models of aging: The challenge of a new frontier. *American Psychologist, 38*, 197–202.

Eisen, S. V. (1979). Actor-observer differences in information inference and casual attribution. *Journal of Personality and Social Psychology, 37*, 261–272.

Eisenberg, N., Cialdini, R. B., McCreath, H., & Shell, R. (1987). Consistency-based compliance: When and why do children become vulnerable? *Journal of Personality and Social Psychology, 52*, 1174–1181.

Eisenberg, N., & Lennon, R. (1983). Sex differences in empathy and related capacities. *Psychological Bulletin, 94*, 100–131.

Ekman, P. (1992a). An argument for basic emotions. *Cognition and Emotion, 6*, 169–200.

Ekman, P. (1992b). Facial expressions of emotion: New findings, new questions. *Psychological Science, 3*, 34–38.

Ekman, P., Davidson, R. J., & Friesen, W. V. (1990). The Duchenne smile: Emotional expression and brain physiology: 2. *Journal of Personality and Social Psychology, 58*, 342–353.

Ekman, P., & Friesen, W. V. (1971). Constants across cultures in the face and emotion. *Journal of Personality and Social Psychology, 17*, 124–129.

Ekman, P., Friesen, W. V., & Bear, J. (1984, May). The international language of gestures. *Psychology Today*, pp. 64–69.

Ekman, P., Friesen, W. V., O'Sullivan, M., Chan, A., Diacoyanni-Tarlatzis, I., Heider, K., Krause, R., LeCompte, W. A., Pitcairn, T., Ricci-Bitti, P. E., Scherer, K., Tomita, M., & Tzavaras, A. (1987). Universals and cultural differences in the judgments of facial expressions of emotion. *Journal of Personality and Social Psychology, 53*, 712–717.

Ekman, P., & Heider, K. G. (1988). The universality of a contempt expression: A replication. *Motivation and Emotion, 12*, 303–308.

Ekman, P., Levenson, R. W., & Friesen, W. V. (1983). Autonomic nervous system activity distinguishes among emotions. *Science, 221*, 1208–1210.

Ekman, P., & O'Sullivan, M. (1991). Who can catch a liar? *American Psychologist, 46*, 913–920.

Elaad, E. (1990). Detection of guilty knowledge in real-life criminal investigations. *Journal of Applied Psychology, 75,* 521–529.

Elkin, R. A., & Leippe, M. R. (1986). Physiological arousal, dissonance, and attitude change: Evidence for a dissonance-arousal link and a "don't remind me" effect. *Journal of Personality and Social Psychology, 51,* 55–65.

Elkins, R. L. (1987). An experimenter effect on place avoidance learning of selectively-bred taste-aversion prone and resistant rats. *Medical Science Research: Psychology & Psychiatry, 15,* 1181–1182.

Ellenberger, H. F. (1970). *The discovery of the unconscious: The history and evolution of dynamic psychiatry.* New York: Basic Books.

Elliott, R. (1988). Tests, abilities, race, and conflict. *Intelligence, 12,* 333–350.

Ellis, A. (1962). *Reason and emotion in psychotherapy.* New York: Lyle Stuart.

Ellis, H. C. (1987). Recent developments in human memory. In V. P. Makosy (Ed.), *The G. Stanley Hall Lecture Series* (Vol. 7, pp. 161–206). Washington, DC: American Psychological Association.

Ellis, J. B., & Range, L. M. (1989). Characteristics of suicidal individuals: A review. *Death Studies, 13,* 485–500.

Ellis, L. (1987). Relationships of criminality and psychopathy with eight other apparent behavioral manifestations of sub-optimal arousal. *Personality and Individual Differences, 8,* 905–925.

Ellis, L., & Ames, M. A. (1987). Neurohormonal functioning and sexual orientation: A theory of homosexuality-heterosexuality. *Psychological Bulletin, 101,* 233–258.

Ellison, W. J. (1987). State execution of juveniles: Defining "youth" as a mitigating factor for imposing a sentence of less than death. *Law and Psychology Review, 11,* 1–38.

Elmore, R. T., Jr., Wildman, R. W., II, & Westefeld, J. S. (1980). The use of systematic desensitization in the treatment of blood phobia. *Journal of Behavior Therapy and Experimental Psychiatry, 11,* 277–279.

Emmelkamp, P. M., & Beens, H. (1991). Cognitive therapy with obsessive-compulsive disorder: A comparative evaluation. *Behaviour Research & Therapy, 29,* 293–300.

Endler, N. S. (1988). The origins of electroconvulsive therapy (ECT). *Convulsive Therapy, 4,* 5–23.

Engle, M. J., & Volpe, J. J. (1990). Glutamine synthetase activity of developing astrocytes is inhibited in vitro by very low concentrations of lead. *Developmental Brain Research, 55,* 283–287.

Epstein, L. H., & Cluess, P. A. (1986). Behavioral genetics of childhood obesity. *Behavior Therapy, 17,* 324–334.

Epstein, L. H., & Wing, R. R. (1980). Aerobic exercise and weight. *Addictive Behaviors, 5,* 371–388.

Epstein, R. (1991). Skinner, creativity, and the problem of spontaneous behavior. *Psychological Science, 2,* 362–370.

Epstein, R., Kirshnit, C. E., Lanza, R. P., & Rubin, L. C. (1984). "Insight" in the pigeon: Antecedents and determinants of an intelligent performance. *Nature, 308,* 61–62.

Epstein, S., & Feist, G. J. (1988). Relation between self- and other-acceptance and its moderation by identification. *Journal of Personality and Social Psychology, 54,* 309–315.

Epstein, S., & O'Brien, E. J. (1985). The person-situation debate in historical and current perspective. *Psychological Bulletin, 98,* 513–537.

Erbaugh, S. J. (1986). Effects of aquatic training on swimming skill development of preschool children. *Perceptual and Motor Skills, 62,* 439–446.

Ericsson, K. A., & Crutcher, R. J. (1991). Introspection and verbal reports on cognitive processes—two approaches to the study of thinking: A response to Howe. *New Ideas in Psychology, 9,* 57–71.

Ericsson, K. A., & Polson, P. G. (1988). An experimental analysis of the mechanisms of a memory skill. *Journal of Experimental Psychology: Learning, Memory, and Cognition, 14,* 305–316.

Erikson, E. (1963). *Childhood and society.* New York: W. W. Norton.

Erikson, E. (1968). *Identity: Youth and crisis.* New York: W. W. Norton.

Erzinger, S. (1991). Communication between Spanish-speaking patients and their doctors in medical encounters. *Culture, Medicine and Psychiatry, 15,* 91–110.

Eslinger, P. J., Damasio, A. R., & Van Hoesen, G. W. (1982). Olfactory dysfunction in man: Anatomical and behavioral aspects. *Brain and Cognition, 1,* 259–285.

Esser, J. K., & Lindoerfer, J. S. (1989). Groupthink and the space shuttle Challenger accident: Toward a quantitative case analysis. *Journal of Behavioral Decision Making, 2,* 167–177.

Etaugh, C. (1980). Effects of nonmaternal care on children: Research evidence and popular views. *American Psychologist, 35,* 309–319.

Etgen, M. P., & Rosen, E. F. (1993). Cognitive dissonance: Physiological arousal in the performance expectancy paradigm. *Bulletin of the Psychonomic Society, 31,* 229–231.

Everstine, L., Everstine, D. S., Heymann, G. M., True, R. H., Frey, D. H., Johnson, H. G., & Seiden, R. H. (1980). Privacy and confidentiality in psychotherapy. *American Psychologist, 35,* 828–840.

Ewert, J., Levin, H. S., Watson, M. G., & Kalisky, Z. (1989). Procedural memory during posttraumatic amnesia in survivors of severe closed head injury: Implications for rehabilitation. *Archives of Neurology, 46,* 911–916.

Eysenck, H. J. (1952). The effects of psychotherapy: An evaluation. *Journal of Consulting Psychology, 16,* 319–324.

Eysenck, H. J. (1982). *Personality, genetics, and behavior: Selected papers.* New York: Praeger.

Eysenck, H. J. (1988). Skinner, Skinnerism, and the Skinnerian in psychology. *Counseling Psychology Quarterly, 1,* 299–301.

Eysenck, H. J. (1990). Genetic and environmental contributions to individual differences: The three major dimensions of personality. *Journal of Personality, 58,* 245–261.

Eysenck, H. J., Wakefield, J. A., Jr., & Friedman, A. F. (1983). Diagnosis and clinical assessment: The DSM-III. *Annual Review of Psychology, 34,* 167–193.

Fabian, L. J., & Haley, W. E. (1991). Behavioral treatment of claustrophobia in a geriatric patient: A case study. *Clinical Gerontologist, 10,* 15–22.

Fagot, B. I., Leinbach, M. D., & Hagan, R. (1986). Gender labeling and the adoption of sex-typed behaviors. *Developmental Psychology, 22,* 440–443.

Faiman, C. P., de Erausquin, G. A., & Baratti, C. M. (1988). Vasopressin modulates the activity of nicotinic cholinergic mechanisms during memory retrieval in mice. *Behavioral and Neural Biology, 50,* 112–119.

Falbo, T., & Polit, D. F. (1986). Quantitative review of the only-child literature: Research evidence and theory development. *Psychological Bulletin, 100,* 176–189.

Fallon, A. E., & Rozin, P. (1985). Sex differences in perceptions of desirable body shape. *Journal of Abnormal Psychology, 94,* 102–105.

Fancher, R. E. (1979). *Pioneers of psychology.* New York: W. W. Norton.

Fancher, R. E. (1984). Not Conley, but Burt and others: A reply. *Journal of the History of the Behavioral Sciences, 20,* 186.

Fancher, R. E. (1987). Henry Goddard and the Kallikak Family photographs: "Conscious skulduggery" or "Whig history"? *American Psychologist, 42,* 585–590.

Fancher, R. E. (1990). *Pioneers of psychology.* New York: W. W. Norton.

Faraone, S. V. (1982). Psychiatry and political repression in the Soviet Union. *American Psychologist, 37,* 1105–1112.

Faraone, S. V., Kremen, W. S., & Tsuang, M. T. (1990). Genetic transmission of major affective disorders: Quantitative models and linkage analyses. *Psychological Bulletin, 108,* 109–127.

Faraone, S. V., & Tsuang, M. T. (1985). Quantitative models of the genetic transmission of schizophrenia. *Psychological Bulletin, 98,* 41–46.

Farrimond, T. (1990). Effect of alcohol on visual constancy values and possible relation to driving performance. *Perceptual and Motor Skills, 70,* 291–295.

Farthing, G. W., Venturino, M., & Brown, S. W. (1984). Suggestion and distraction in the control of pain: Test of two hypotheses. *Journal of Abnormal Psychology, 93,* 266–276.

Fasko, S. N., & Fasko, D. (1990–1991). Suicidal behavior in children. *Psychology: A Journal of Human Behavior, 27,* 10–16.

Faust, J., Olson, R., & Rodriguez, H. (1991). Same-day surgery preparation: Reduction of pediatric patient arousal and distress through participant modeling. *Journal of Consulting and Clinical Psychology, 59,* 475–478.

Fava, G. A., Grandi, S., Canestrari, R., & Grasso, P. (1991). Mechanisms of change of panic attacks with exposure treatment of agoraphobia. *Journal of Affective Disorders, 22,* 65–71.

Fava, M., Littman, A., & Halperin, P. (1987). Neuroendocrine correlates of the Type A behavior pattern: A review and new hypotheses. *International Journal of Psychiatry in Medicine, 17,* 289–307.

Feder, H. H. (1984). Hormones and sexual behavior. *Annual Review of Psychology, 35,* 165–200.

Fehr, B., & Russell, J. A. (1984). Concept of emotion viewed from a prototypic perspective. *Journal of Experimental Psychology: General, 113,* 464–486.

Fehr, B., & Russell, J. A. (1991). The concept of love viewed from a prototype perspective. *Journal of Personality and Social Psychology, 60,* 425–438.

Feingold, A. (1992). Good-looking people are not what we think. *Psychological Bulletin, 111,* 304–341.

Feldman, R. H. (1984). The influence of communicator characteristics on the nutrition attitudes and behavior of high school students. *Journal of School Health, 54,* 149–151.

Fellman, B. (1985, May). A clockwork gland. *Science 85,* pp. 76–81.

Felsten, G., & Leitten, C. L. (1993). Expressive, but not neurotic hostility is related to cardiovascular reactivity during a hostile competitive task. *Personality and Individual Differences, 14,* 805–813.

Ferguson, E. D. (1989). Adler's motivational theory: An historical perspective on belonging and the fundamental human striving. *Individual Psychology: Journal of Adlerian Theory, Research, and Practice, 45,* 354–361.

Fern, E. F., Monroe, K. B., & Avila, R. A. (1986). Effectiveness of multiple request strategies: A synthesis of research results. *Journal of Marketing Research, 23,* 144–152.

Ferris, A. M., & Duffy, V. B. (1989). Effect of olfactory deficits on nutritional status: Does age predict persons at risk? *Annals of the New York Academy of Sciences, 561,* 113–123.

Festinger, L., & Carlsmith, J. M. (1959). Cognitive consequences of forced compliance. *Journal of Abnormal and Social Psychology, 58,* 203–210.

Festinger, L., Pepitone, A., & Newcomb, T. (1952). Some consequences of deindividuation in a group. *Journal of Abnormal and Social Psychology, 47,* 382–389.

Festinger, L., Riecken, H. W., & Schachter, S. (1956). *When prophecy fails.* New York: Harper & Row.

Festinger, L., Schachter, S., & Back, K. (1950). *Social pressures in informal groups: A study of a housing community.* Stanford, CA: Stanford University Press.

Field, T. M. (1991). Quality infant day-care and grade school behavior and performance. *Child Development, 62,* 863–870.

Field, T. M., Woodson, R., Greenberg, R., & Cohen, D. (1982). Discrimination and imitation of facial expressions by neonates. *Science, 218,* 179–181.

Filsinger, E. E., Braun, J. J., Monte, W. C., & Linder, D. E. (1984). Human (*Homo sapiens*) responses to the pig (*Sus scrofa*) sex pheromone 5 alpha-androst-16-en-3-one. *Journal of Comparative Psychology, 98,* 219–222.

Findley, M. J., & Cooper, H. M. (1983). Locus of control and academic achievement: A literature review. *Journal of Personality and Social Psychology, 44,* 419–427.

Fine, A., Meldrum, B. S., & Patel, S. (1990). Modulation of experimentally induced epilepsy by intracerebral grafts of fetal GABAergic neurons. *Neuropsychologia, 28,* 627–634.

Fink, M. (1984). Meduna and the origins of convulsive therapy. *American Journal of Psychiatry, 141,* 1034–1041.

Finkelstein, P., Wenegrat, B., & Yalom, I. (1982). Large group awareness training. *Annual Review of Psychology, 33,* 515–539.

Finn, P. E., & Alcorn, J. D. (1986). Noncompliance to hemodialysis dietary regimens: Literature review and treatment recommendations. *Rehabilitation Psychology, 31,* 67–78.

Fischer, K. W., & Silvern, L. (1985). Stages and individual differences in cognitive development. *Annual Review of Psychology, 36,* 613–648.

Fischer, P. J., & Breakey, W. R. (1991). The epidemiology of alcohol, drug, and mental disorders among homeless persons. *American Psychologist, 46,* 1115–1128.

Fisher, E. B., Delamater, A. M., Bertelson, A. D., & Kirkley, B. G. (1982). Psychological factors in diabetes and its treatment. *Journal of Consulting and Clinical Psychology, 50,* 993–1003.

Fisher, K. (1983, February). TV violence. *APA Monitor,* pp. 7, 9.

Fisher, K. (1984, April). Strangler's mind becomes a trap for psychologists. *APA Monitor,* pp. 10–11, 13.

Fisher, K. (1985, November). Duty to warn: Where does it end? *APA Monitor,* pp. 24–25.

Fisher, K. (1986, March). Animal research: Few alternatives seen for behavioral studies. *APA Monitor,* pp. 16–17.

Fisher, S., & Fisher, R. L. (1981). *Pretend the world is funny and forever: A psychological analysis of comedians, clowns, and actors.* Hillsdale, NJ: Erlbaum.

Fisher, S., & Greenberg, R. P. (1985). *The scientific credibility of Freud's theories and therapy.* New York: Columbia University Press.

Fisher, S. K., & Ciuffreda, K. J. (1989). The effect of accommodative hysteresis on apparent distance. *Ophthalamic and Physiological Optics, 9,* 184–190.

Fiske, D. W., Conley, J. J., & Goldberg, L. R. (1987). E. Lowell Kelly (1905–1986). *American Psychologist, 42,* 511–512.

Flannagan, D. A., & Blick, K. A. (1989). Levels of processing and the retention of word meanings. *Perceptual and Motor Skills, 68,* 1123–1128.

Flavell, J. H., Shipstead, S. G., & Croft, K. (1980). What young children think you see when their eyes are closed. *Cognition, 8,* 369–387.

Flay, B. R. (1985a). Adolescent smoking: Onset and prevention. *Annals of Behavioral Medicine, 7,* 9–13.

Flay, B. R. (1985b). Psychosocial approaches to smoking prevention: A review of findings. *Health Psychology, 4,* 449–488.

Fletcher, G. J. (1984). Psychology and common sense. *American Psychologist, 39,* 203–213.

Fletcher, R. (1990). *The Cyril Burt scandal: Case for the defence.* New York: Macmillan.

Flor-Henry, P. (1983). Mood, the right hemisphere and the implications of spatial information-perceiving systems. *Research Communications in Psychology, Psychiatry, and Behavior, 8,* 143–170.

Flynn, J. R. (1987). Massive IQ gains in 14 nations: What IQ tests really measure. *Psychological Bulletin, 101,* 171–191.

Foa, E. B., & Kozak, M. J. (1986). Emotional processing of fear: Exposure to corrective information. *Psychological Bulletin, 99,* 20–35.

Foa, E. B., & Rothbaum, B. O. (1989). Behavioural psychotherapy for post-traumatic stress disorder. *International Review of Psychiatry, 1,* 219–226.

Foerstl, J. (1989). Early interest in the idiot savant. *American Journal of Psychiatry, 146,* 566.

Foley, J. M. (1988). Experiments on human pattern vision. *Hiroshima Forum for Psychology, 13,* 51–61.

Folkes, V. S. (1982). Forming relationships and the matching hypothesis. *Personality and Social Psychology Bulletin, 8,* 631–636.

Folkes, V. S. (1988). The availability heuristic and perceived risk. *Journal of Consumer Research, 15,* 13–23.

Ford, M. R., & Lowery, C. R. (1986). Gender differences in moral reasoning: A comparison of the use of justice and care orientations. *Journal of Personality and Social Psychology, 50,* 777–783.

Foreyt, J. P. (1987). Issues in the assessment and treatment of obesity. *Journal of Consulting and Clinical Psychology, 55,* 677–684.

Forsen, A. (1991). Psychosocial stress as a risk for breast cancer. *Psychotherapy and Psychosomatics, 55,* 176–185.

Forsyth, D. R., Pope, W. R., & McMillan, J. H. (1985). Students' reactions after cheating: An attributional analysis. *Contemporary Educational Psychology, 10,* 72–82.

Fowles, D. C. (1992). Schizophrenia: Diathesis-stress revisited. *Annual Review of Psychology, 43,* 303–336.

Fox, D. K., Hopkins, B. L., & Anger, W. K. (1987). The long-term effects of a token economy on safety performance in open-pit mining. *Journal of Applied Behavior Analysis, 20,* 215–224.

Fox, J. L. (1984). The brain's dynamic way of keeping in touch. *Science, 225,* 820–821.

Fox, L. H. (1981). Identification of the academically gifted. *American Psychologist, 36,* 1103–1111.

Fox, N. A. (1989). Infant response to frustrating and mildly stressful events: A positive look at anger in the first year. *New Directions for Child Development, 45,* 47–64.

Fox, N. A., & Davidson, R. J. (1988). Patterns of brain electrical activity during facial signs of emotion in 10-month-old infants. *Developmental Psychology, 24,* 230–236.

Frank, M. G., & Ekman, P. (1993). Not all smiles are created equal: The differences between enjoyment and nonenjoyment smiles. *Humor: International Journal of Humor Research, 6,* 9–26.

Frankl, V. E. (1961). Logotherapy and the challenge of suffering. *Review of Existential Psychology and Psychiatry, 1,* 3–7.

Franzoi, S. L., Davis, M. H., & Young, R. D. (1985). The effects of private self-consciousness and perspective talking in close relationships. *Journal of Personality and Social Psychology, 48,* 1584–1594.

Frederiksen, N. (1986). Toward a broader conception of human intelligence. *American Psychologist, 41,* 445–452.

Free, N. K., Green, B. L., Grace, M. C., Chernus, L. A., & Whitman, R. M. (1985). Empathy and outcome in brief focal dynamic therapy. *American Journal of Psychiatry, 142,* 917–921.

Free, N. K., Winget, C. N., & Whitman, R. M. (1993). Separation anxiety in panic disorder. *American Journal of Psychiatry, 150,* 595–599.

Freedman, J. L. (1984). Effect of television violence on aggressiveness. *Psychological Bulletin, 96,* 227–246.

Freedman, J. L. (1986). Television violence and aggression: A rejoinder. *Psychological Bulletin, 100,* 372–378.

Freedman, J. L., & Fraser, S. C. (1966). Compliance without pressure. *Journal of Personality and Social Psychology, 4,* 195–202.

Freeman, B. J., & Ritvo, E. R. (1982). The syndrome of autism: A critical review of diagnostic systems, follow-up studies, and the theoretical background of the behavioral observation scale. *Advances in Child Behavioral Analysis and Therapy, 2,* 1–39.

Freud, S. (1900/1990). *The interpretation of dreams.* New York: Basic Books.

Freud, S. (1901/1965). *Psychopathology of everyday life.* New York: W. W. Norton.

Freud, S. (1901/1990). *The psychopathology of everyday life.* New York: W. W. Norton.

Freud, S. (1905). *Jokes and their relationship to the unconscious.* London: Hogarth Press.

Freud, S. (1914/1957). On the history of the psychoanalytic movement. In J. Strachey (Ed.), *The standard edition of the complete psychological works of Sigmund Freud* (Vol. 14, pp. 7–66). London: Hogarth Press.

Freud, S. (1917/1963). Mourning and melancholia. In J. Strachey (Ed.), *The standard edition of the complete psychological works of Sigmund Freud* (Vol. 14, pp. 243–258). London: Hogarth Press.

Freud, S. (1974). *Cocaine papers* (R. Byck, Ed.). New York: Stonehill.

Freund, A., Johnson, S. B., Silverstein, J., & Thomas, J. (1991). Assessing daily management of childhood diabetes using 24-hour recall interviews: Reliability and stability. *Health Psychology, 10,* 200–208.

Frezza, M., di Padova, C., Pozzato, G., Terpin, M., Baraona, E., & Lieber, C. S. (1990). High blood alcohol levels in women: The role of decreased gastric alcohol dehydrogenase activity and first-pass metabolism. *New England Journal of Medicine, 322,* 95–99.

Frick, R. W. (1985). Communicating emotion: The role of prosodic features. *Psychological Bulletin, 97,* 412–429.

Fried, P. A., & Watkinson, B. (1990). Thirty-six and forty-eight-month neurobehavioral follow-up of children prenatally exposed to marijuana, cigarettes, and alcohol. *Journal of Developmental and Behavioral Pediatrics, 11,* 49–58.

Fried, R. (1987). Relaxation with biofeedback-assisted guided imagery: The importance of breathing rate as an index of hypoarousal. *Biofeedback and Self-Control, 12,* 273–279.

Friedman, M., & Rosenman, R. H. (1959). Association of specific overt behavior pattern with blood and cardiovascular findings. *Journal of the American Medical Association, 169,* 1286–1296.

Friedman, M., & Rosenman, R. H. (1974). *Type A behavior and your heart.* New York: Knopf.

Friedman, M. P., & Wilson, R. W. (1975). Application of unobtrusive measures to the study of textbook usage by college students. *Journal of Applied Psychology, 60,* 659–662.

Friedman, R. C., & Downey, J. (1993). Neurobiology and sexual orientation: Current relationships. *Journal of Neuropsychiatry and Clinical Neurosciences, 5,* 131–153.

Fritsch, G., & Hitzig, E. (1870/1960). On the electrical excitability of the cerebrum. Springfield, IL: Charles C Thomas.

Fromm, E. (1941). *Escape from freedom.* New York: Holt, Rinehart & Winston.

Fromm, E. (1956). *The art of loving.* New York: Harper & Row.

Fudin, R., & Nicastro, R. (1988). Can caffeine antagonize alcohol-induced performance decrements in humans? *Perceptual and Motor Skills, 67,* 375–391.

Fukuda, T., Kanada, K., & Saito, S. (1990). An ergonomic evaluation of lens accommodation related to visual circumstances. *Ergonomics, 33,* 811–831.

Fulker, D. W., DeFries, J. C., & Plomin, R. (1988). Genetic influence on general mental ability increases between infancy and middle childhood. *Nature, 336,* 767–769.

Furedy, J. J. (1987). Specific versus placebo effects in biofeedback training: A critical perspective. *Biofeedback and Self-Regulation, 12,* 169–184.

Furnham, A., & Thompson, J. (1991). Personality and self-reported delinquency. *Personality and Individual Differences, 12,* 585–593.

Furst, D. M., & Hardman, J. S. (1988). The iceberg profile and young competitive swimmers. *Perceptual and Motor Skills, 67,* 478.

Furumoto, L. (1980). Mary Whiton Calkins (1863–1930). *Psychology of Women Quarterly, 5,* 55–68.

Furumoto, L. (1988). Shared knowledge: The experimentalists, 1904–1929. In J. G. Morawski (Ed.), *The rise of experimentation in American psychology* (pp. 94–113). New Haven, CT: Yale University Press.

Furumoto, L. (1992). Joining separate spheres: Christine Ladd-Franklin, woman-scientist (1847–1930). *American Psychologist, 47,* 175–182.

Galanter, E. (1962). *New directions in psychology.* New York: Holt, Rinehart & Winston.

Galef, B. G., Jr. (1980). Diving for food: Analysis of a possible case of social learning in wild rats (*Rattus norvegicus*). *Journal of Comparative and Physiological Psychology, 94,* 416–425.

Galef, B. G., Jr. (1986). Social identification of toxic diets by Norway rats (*Rattus norvegicus*). *Journal of Comparative Psychology, 100,* 331–334.

Gallup, G. G., Jr., & Suarez, S. D. (1985). Alternatives to the use of animals in psychological research. *American Psychologist, 40,* 1104–1111.

Galton, F. (1869). *Hereditary genius.* London: Macmillan.

Ganchrow, J. R., Steiner, J. E., & Daher, M. (1983). Neonatal facial expressions in response to different qualities and intensities of gustatory stimuli. *Infant Behavior and Development, 6,* 189–200.

Gander, P. H., Nguyen, D., Rosekind, M. R., & Connell, L. J. (1993). Age, circadian rhythms, and sleep loss in flight crews. *Aviation, Space, and Environmental Medicine, 64,* 189–195.

Gangestad, S., & Snyder, M. (1985). "To carve nature at its joints": On the existence of discrete classes in personality. *Psychological Review, 92,* 317–349.

Ganley, R. M. (1989). Emotion and eating in obesity: A review of the literature. *International Journal of Eating Disorders, 8,* 343–361.

Gansberg, M. (1964, March 27). Thirty-seven who saw murder didn't call the police. *New York Times,* pp. 1, 38.

Garcia, E. E. (1990). A brief note on "Jekyll and Hyde" and MPD. *Dissociation: Progress in the Dissociative Disorders, 3,* 165–166.

Garcia, J. (1981). Tilting at the paper mills of academe. *American Psychologist, 36,* 149–158.

Garcia, J., Kimeldorf, D. J., Hunt, E. L., & Davies, B. P. (1956). Food and water consumption of rats during exposure to gamma radiation. *Radiation Research, 4,* 33–41.

Garcia, J., & Koelling, R. A. (1966). The relation of cue to consequence in avoidance learning. *Psychonomic Science, 4,* 123–124.

Gardner, B. T. (1992, July 28). Personal communication.

Gardner, D. G. (1986). Activation theory and task design: An empirical test of several new predictions. *Journal of Applied Psychology, 71,* 411–418.

Gardner, H. (1983). *Frames of mind: The theory of multiple intelligences.* New York: Basic Books.

Gardner, H. (1985). *The mind's new science: A history of the cognitive revolution.* New York: Basic Books.

Gardner, R. A., & Gardner, B. T. (1969). Teaching sign language to a chimpanzee. *Science, 165,* 664–672.

Gardos, G., Cole, J. O., Salomon, M., & Schniebolk, S. (1987). Clinical forms of severe tardive dyskinesia. *American Journal of Psychiatry, 144,* 895–902.

Garfield, S. L. (1983). Effectiveness of psychotherapy: The perennial controversy. *Professional Psychology, 14,* 35–43.

Garfield, S. L. (1992). Comments on "Retrospect: Psychology as a profession" by J. McKeen Cattell (1937). *Journal of Consulting and Clinical Psychology, 60,* 9–15.

Garonzik, R. (1989). Hand dominance and implications for left-handed operation of controls. *Ergonomics, 32,* 1185–1192.

Gash, D. M., & Sladek, J. R. (1984). Functional and nonfunctional transplants: Studies with grafted hypothalamic and preoptic neurons. *Trends in Neurosciences, 7,* 391–394.

Gastil, J. (1990). Generic pronouns and sexist language: The oxymoronic character of masculine generics. *Sex Roles, 23,* 629–643.

Gathercole, S. E., & Conway, M. A. (1988). Exploring long-term modality effects: Vocalization leads to best retention. *Memory and Cognition, 16,* 110–119.

Gauld, A. O. (1990). The early history of hypnotic skin marking and blistering. *British Journal of Experimental and Clinical Hypnosis, 7,* 139–152.

Gawin, F. H. (1991). Cocaine addiction: Psychology and neurophysiology. *Science, 251,* 1580–1586.

Gay, P. (1988). *Freud: A life for our time.* New York: W. W. Norton.

Gay, V. (1986). Augustine: The reader as self-object. *Journal for the Scientific Study of Religion, 25,* 64–76.

Gazzaniga, M. S. (1967, August). The split brain in man. *Scientific American,* pp. 24–29.

Gazzaniga, M. S. (1983). Right hemisphere language following brain bisection: A 20-year perspective. *American Psychologist, 38,* 525–537.

Gebhardt, D. L., & Crump, C. E. (1990). Employee fitness and wellness programs in the workplace. *American Psychologist, 45,* 262–272.

Geen, R. G. (1984). Preferred stimulation levels in introverts and extraverts: Effects on arousal and performance. *Journal of Personality and Social Psychology, 46,* 1303–1312.

Geen, R. G., Stonner, D., & Shope, G. L. (1975). The facilitation of aggression by aggression: Evidence against the catharsis hypothesis. *Journal of Personality and Social Psychology, 31,* 721–726.

Geer, J. H., & Quartaaro, J. D. (1976). Vaginal blood volume responses during masturbation. *Archives of Sexual Behavior, 5,* 403–413.

Geffen, G., & Quinn, K. (1984). Hemispheric specialization and ear advantages in processing speech. *Psychological Bulletin, 96,* 273–291.

Gelb, S. A. (1986). Henry H. Goddard and the immigrants, 1910–1917: The studies and their social context. *Journal of the History of the Behavioral Sciences, 22,* 324–332.

Geller, L. (1982, Spring). The failure of self-actualization theory: A critique of Carl Rogers and Abraham Maslow. *Journal of Humanistic Psychology, 22,* 56–73.

Gendlin, E. T. (1988). Obituary: Carl Rogers (1902–1987). *American Psychologist, 43,* 127–128.

George, W. H., & Marlatt, G. A. (1986). The effects of alcohol and anger on interest in violence, erotica, and deviance. *Journal of Abnormal Psychology, 95,* 150–158.

Geracioti, T. D., & Liddle, R. A. (1988). Impaired cholecystokinin secretion in bulimia nervosa. *New England Journal of Medicine, 319,* 683–688.

Gerrard, M. (1987). Sex, sex guilt, and contraceptive use revisited: The 1980s. *Journal of Personality and Social Psychology, 52,* 975–980.

Geschwind, N. (1979, September). Specializations of the human brain. *Scientific American,* pp. 180–199.

Gershuny, B. S., & Burrows, D. (1990). The use of rationalization and denial to reduce accident-related and illness-related death anxiety. *Bulletin of the Psychonomic Society, 28,* 161–163.

Gesten, E. L., & Jason, L. A. (1987). Social and community interventions. *Annual Review of Psychology, 38,* 427–460.

Gibbons, B. (1986). The intimate sense of smell. *National Geographic, 170,* 324–361.

Gibbs, E. D., Teti, D. M., & Bond, L. A. (1987). Infant-sibling communication: Relationships to birth-spacing and cognitive and linguistic development. *Infant Behavior and Development, 10,* 307–323.

Gibson, E. J., & Walk, R. D. (1960, April). The visual cliff. *Scientific American,* pp. 67–71.

Gibson, J. J. (1979). *The ecological approach to visual perception.* Boston: Houghton Mifflin.

Gibson, J. T. (1991). Training people to inflict pain: State terror and social learning. *Journal of Humanistic Psychology, 31,* 72–87.

Gilbert, D. G., & Hagen, R. L. (1980). Taste in underweight, overweight, and normal-weight subjects before, during, and after sucrose ingestion. *Addictive Behaviors, 5,* 137–142.

Gilbert, D. G., & Spielberger, C. D. (1987). Effects of smoking on heart rate, anxiety, and feelings of success during social interaction. *Journal of Behavioral Medicine, 10,* 629–638.

Gilbert, S. J. (1981). Another look at the Milgram obedience studies: The role of the graduated series of shocks. *Personality and Social Psychology Bulletin, 7,* 690–695.

Giles, D. E., & Shaw, B. F. (1987). Beck's cognitive theory of depression: Convergence of constructs. *Comprehensive Psychiatry, 28,* 416–427.

Gill, D. (1980). *Quest: The life of Elisabeth Kübler-Ross.* New York: Harper & Row.

Gillam, B. (1980, January). Geometrical illusions. *Scientific American,* pp. 102–111.

Gillette, M. U. (1986). The suprachiasmatic nuclei: Circadian phase-shifts induced at the time of hypothalamic slice preparation are preserved in vitro. *Brain Research, 379,* 176–181.

Gilligan, C. (1982). *In a different voice: Psychological theory and women's development.* Cambridge, MA: Harvard University Press.

Gilliland, K., & Andress, D. (1981). Ad lib caffeine consumption, symptoms of caffeinism, and academic performance. *American Journal of Psychiatry, 138,* 512–514.

Gillman, M. A. (1986). Analgesic (subanesthetic) nitrous oxide interacts with the endogenous opioid system: A review of the evidence. *Life Sciences, 39,* 1209–1221.

Gilmartin, B., Gray, L. S., & Winn, B. (1991). The amelioration of myopia using biofeedback of accommodation: A review. *Ophthalmic and Physiological Optics, 11,* 304–313.

Gilovich, T., Vallone, R., & Tversky, A. (1985). The hot hand in basketball: On misperception of random sequences. *Cognitive Psychology, 17,* 295–314.

Gingerich, W. J. (1990). Expert systems: New tools for professional decision-making. *Computers in Human Services, 6,* 219–230.

Giovannini, D., & Ricci Bitti, P. E. (1981). Culture and sex effect in recognizing emotions by facial and gestural cues. *Italian Journal of Psychology, 8,* 95–102.

Gisiner, R., & Schusterman, R. J. (1992). Sequence, syntax, and semantics: Responses of a language-trained sea lion (*Zalophus californianus*) to novel sign combinations. *Journal of Comparative, 106,* 78–91.

Gjerde, P. F. (1983). Attentional capacity dysfunction and arousal in schizophrenia. *Psychological Bulletin, 93,* 57–72.

Gladue, B. A., Green, R., & Hellman, R. E. (1984). Neuroendocrine response to estrogen and sexual orientation. *Science, 225,* 1496–1499.

Glaser, R., Rice, J., Speicher, C. E., Stout, J. C., & Kiecolt-Glaser, J. K. (1986). Stress depresses interferon production by leukocytes concomitant with a decrease in natural killer cell activity. *Behavioral Neuroscience, 100,* 675–678.

Glass, A. L., & Waterman, D. (1988). Predictions of movie entertainment value and the representativeness heuristic. *Applied Cognitive Psychology, 2,* 173–179.

Glass, C. R., & Arnkoff, D. B. (1989). Behavioral assessment of social anxiety and social phobia. *Clinical Psychology Review, 9,* 75–90.

Glen, L., & Anderson, J. A. (1989). Medication and the elderly: A review. *Journal of Geriatric Drug Therapy, 4,* 59–89.

Glenn, S. S., & Ellis, J. (1988). Do the Kallikaks look "menacing" or "retarded"? *American Psychologist, 43,* 742–743.

Glick, P., Gottesman, D., & Jolton, J. (1989). The fault is not in the stars: Susceptibility of skeptics and believers in astrology to the Barnum effect. *Personality and Social Psychology Bulletin, 15,* 572–583.

Gliedman, J. (1983, November). Interview with Noam Chomsky. *Omni,* pp. 112–118, 171–174.

Glucksberg, S., & Danks, J. H. (1968). Effects of discriminative labels and of nonsense labels upon availability of novel functions. *Journal of Verbal Learning and Verbal Behavior, 7,* 72–76.

Glueckauf, R. L., & Quittner, A. L. (1992). Assertiveness training for disabled adults in wheelchairs: Self-report, role-play, and activity pattern outcomes. *Journal of Consulting and Clinical Psychology, 60,* 419–425.

Glynn, S. M. (1990). Token economy approaches for psychiatric patients: Progress and pitfalls over 25 years. *Behavior Modification, 14,* 387–407.

Goddard, H. H. (1912). *The Kallikak family: A study in the heredity of feeblemindedness.* New York: Macmillan.

Goddard, H. H. (1917). Mental tests and the immigrant. *Journal of Delinquency, 2,* 243–277.

Godden, D. R., & Baddeley, A. D. (1975). Context-dependent memory in two natural environments: On land and under water. *British Journal of Psychology, 66,* 325–331.

Godemont, M. (1992). Six hundred years of family care in Geel, Belgium: 600 years of familiarity with madness in town life. *Community Alternatives: International Journal of Family Care, 4,* 155–168.

"God's hand": Legless veteran crawls to save life of a baby. (1986, June 6). *Philadelphia Inquirer,* pp. 1-A, 24-A.

Goebel, B. L., & Boeck, B. E. (1987). Ego integrity and fear of death: A comparison of institutionalized and independently living older adults. *Death Studies, 11,* 193–204.

Goebel, B. L., & Brown, D. R. (1981). Age differences in motivation related to Maslow's need hierarchy. *Developmental Psychology, 17,* 809–815.

Goisman, R. M. (1983). Therapeutic approaches to phobia: A comparison. *American Journal of Psychotherapy, 37,* 227–234.

Gold, M. S., Pottash, A. L. C., Sweeney, D. R., Martin, D. M., & Davies, R. K. (1980). Further evidence of hypothalamic-pituitary dysfunction in anorexia nervosa. *American Journal of Psychiatry, 137,* 101–102.

Goldberg, L. R. (1993). The structure of phenotypic personality traits. *American Psychologist, 48,* 26–34.

Goldbloom, D. S., & Garfinkel, P. E. (1990). The serotonin hypothesis of bulimia nervosa: Theory and evidence. *Canadian Journal of Psychiatry, 35,* 741–744.

Golden, L. L., & Alpert, M. I. (1987). Comparative analysis of the relative effectiveness of one- and two-sided communication for contrasting products. *Journal of Advertising, 16,* 18–25, 68.

Goldfried, M. R., Greenberg, L. S., & Marmar, C. (1990). Individual psychotherapy: Process and outcome. *Annual Review of Psychology, 41,* 659–688.

Goldin-Meadow, S., & Mylander, C. (1983). Gestural communication in deaf children: Noneffect of parental input on language development. *Science, 221,* 372–373.

Goldman, D. L. (1990). Dorothea Dix and her two missions of mercy in Nova Scotia. *Canadian Journal of Psychiatry, 35,* 139–143.

Goldman, M., & Fordyce, J. (1983). Prosocial behavior as affected by eye contact, touch, and voice expression. *Journal of Social Psychology, 121*, 125–129.

Goldsmith, H. H., & Alansky, J. A. (1987). Maternal and infant temperamental predictors of attachment: A meta-analytic review. *Journal of Consulting and Clinical Psychology, 55*, 805–816.

Goldstein, A. (1980). Thrills in response to music and other stimuli. *Physiological Psychology, 8*, 126–129.

Goldstein, A. G., Chance, J. E., & Gilbert, B. (1984). Facial stereotypes of good guys and bad guys: A replication and extension. *Bulletin of the Psychonomic Society, 22*, 549–552.

Goldstein, S. R., & Hall, D. (1990). Variable ratio control of the spitting response in the archer fish (*Toxotes jaculator*). *Journal of Comparative Psychology, 104*, 373–376.

Goleman, D. (1981, August). Deadlines for change: Therapy in the age of Reaganomics. *Psychology Today*, pp. 60–69.

Gonzales, M. H., Davis, J. M., Loney, G. L., Lukens, C. K., & Junghans, C. M. (1983). Interactional approach to interpersonal attraction. *Journal of Personality and Social Psychology, 44*, 1192–1197.

Gonzalez, R. (1989). Ministering intelligence: A Venezuelan experience in the promotion of cognitive abilities. *International Journal of Mental Health, 18*, 5–18.

Goodall, J. (1990). *Through a window: My thirty years with the chimpanzees of Gombe.* Boston: Houghton Mifflin.

Goodenough, F. L. (1932). Expression of the emotions in a blind-deaf child. *Journal of Abnormal and Social Psychology, 27*, 328–333.

Goodman, C. S., & Bastiani, M. J. (1984, December). How embryonic nerve cells recognize one another. *Scientific American*, pp. 58–66.

Goodman, E. S. (1980). Margaret F. Washburn (1871–1939): First woman Ph.D. in psychology. *Psychology of Women Quarterly, 5*, 69–80.

Goodwin, C. J. (1985). On the origins of Titchener's experimentalists. *Journal of the History of the Behavioral Sciences, 21*, 383–389.

Goodwin, C. J. (1987). In Hall's shadow: Edmund Clark Sanford (1859–1924). *Journal of the History of the Behavioral Sciences, 23*, 153–168.

Gorassini, D., Sowerby, D., Creighton, A., & Fry, G. (1991). Hypnotic suggestibility enhancement through brief cognitive skill training. *Journal of Personality & Social Psychology, 61*, 289–297.

Gorczynski, R. M. (1990). Conditioned enhancement of skin allografts in mice. *Brain, Behavior and Immunity, 4*, 85–92.

Gordon, D. E. (1990). Formal operational thinking: The role of cognitive-developmental processes in adolescent decision making about pregnancy and contraception. *American Journal of Orthopsychiatry, 60*, 346–356.

Gordon, I. E., & Earle, D. C. (1992). Visual illusions: A short review. *Australian Journal of Psychology, 44*, 153–156.

Gorelick, P. B., & Ross, E. D. (1987). The aprosodias: Further functional-anatomical evidence for the organization of affective language in the right hemisphere. *Journal of Neurology, Neurosurgery, and Psychiatry, 50*, 553–560.

Gorman, J. (1985, February). My fair software. *Discover*, pp. 64–65.

Gosnell, B. A., & Hsiao, S. (1984). Effects of cholecystokinin on taste preference and sensitivity in rats. *Behavioral Neuroscience, 98*, 452–460.

Gotlib, I. H., & Robinson, L. A. (1982). Responses to depressed individuals: Discrepancies between self-report and observer-rated behavior. *Journal of Abnormal Psychology, 91*, 231–240.

Gottesman, I. I., McGuffin, P., & Farmer, A. E. (1987). Clinical genetics as clues to the "real" genetics of schizophrenia: A decade of modest gains while playing for time. *Schizophrenia Bulletin, 13*, 23–47.

Gottesman, I. L., & Shields, J. (1982). *Schizophrenia: The epigenetic puzzle.* Cambridge, MA: Cambridge University Press.

Gough, H. G., Fioravanti, M., & Lazzari, R. (1983). Some implications of self versus ideal-self congruence on the revised Adjective Check List. *Journal of Personality and Social Psychology, 44*, 1214–1220.

Gould, S. J. (1978). Morton's ranking of races by cranial capacity: Unconscious manipulation of data may be a scientific norm. *Science, 200*, 503–509.

Gould, S. J. (1981). *The mismeasure of man.* New York: W. W. Norton.

Graham, J. R. (1991). Comments on Duckworth's review of the Minnesota Multiphasic Personality Inventory–2. *Journal of Counseling and Development, 69*, 570–571.

Graham-Clay, S. (1983). Fetal alcohol syndrome: A review of the current human research. *Canada's Mental Health, 31*, 2–5.

Graves, R., & Landis, T. (1990). Asymmetry in mouth opening during different speech tasks. *International Journal of Psychology, 25*, 179–189.

Graw, P., Krauchi, K., Wirz-Justice, A., & Poldinger, W. (1991). Diurnal variation of symptoms in seasonal affective disorder. *Psychiatry Research, 37*, 105–111.

Gray, A., Jackson, D. N., & McKinlay, J. B. (1991). The relation between dominance, anger, and hormones in normally aging men: Results from the Massachusetts Male Aging Study. *Psychosomatic Medicine, 53*, 375–385.

Gray, P. H. (1980). Behaviorism: Some truths that need telling, some errors that need correcting. *Bulletin of the Psychonomic Society, 15*, 357–360.

Gray-Little, B., & Burks, N. (1983). Power and satisfaction in marriage: A review and critique. *Psychological Bulletin, 93*, 513–538.

Green, A. J., & Gilhooly, K. J. (1990). Individual differences and effective learning procedures: The case of statistical computing. *International Journal of Man Machine Studies, 33*, 97–119.

Green, J. A., & Shellenberger, R. D. (1986). Biofeedback research and the ghost in the box: A reply to Roberts. *American Psychologist, 41*, 1003–1005.

Greenberg, L. S., & Dompierre, L. M. (1981). Specific effects of Gestalt two-chair dialogue on intrapsychic conflict in counseling. *Journal of Counseling Psychology, 28*, 288–294.

Greenblatt, D. J., Shader, R. I., & Abernethy, D. R. (1983). Drug therapy: Current status of benzodiazepines. *New England Journal of Medicine, 309*, 354–358.

Greendale, G. A., & Judd, H. L. (1993). The menopause: Health implications and clinical management. *Journal of the American Geriatrics Society, 41*, 426–436.

Greene, E., Flynn, M. S., & Loftus, E. F. (1982). Inducing resistance to misleading information. *Journal of Verbal Learning and Verbal Behavior, 21*, 207–219.

Greene, R. L. (1987). Effects of maintenance rehearsal on human memory. *Psychological Bulletin, 102*, 403–413.

Greenlee, R. W. (1990). The unemployed Appalachian coal miner's search for meaning. *International Forum for Logotherapy, 13*, 71–75.

Greeno, J. G. (1980). Psychology of learning, 1960–1980: One participant's observations. *American Psychologist, 35*, 713–728.

Gregg, E., & Rejeski, W. J. (1990). Social psychobiologic dysfunction associated with anabolic steroid abuse: A review. *Sport Psychologist, 4*, 275–284.

Gregg, R. H. (1983). Biofeedback and biophysical monitoring during pregnancy and labor. In J. V. Basmajian (Ed.), *Biofeedback: Principles and practice for clinicians* (pp. 282–288). Baltimore: Williams & Wilkins.

Gregory, R. L. (1987). *The Oxford companion to the mind.* New York: Oxford University Press.

Gregory, R. L. (1991). Putting illusions in their place. *Perception, 20*, 1–4.

Gresham, F. M. (1981). Assessment of children's social skills. *Journal of School Psychology, 19*, 120–133.

Grieser, D., & Kuhl, P. (1988). Maternal speech to infants in a tonal language: Support for universal prosodic features in motherese. *Developmental Psychology, 24*, 14–20.

Grilo, C. M., & Pogue-Geile, M. F. (1991). The nature of environmental influences on weight and obesity: A behavior genetic analysis. *Psychological Bulletin, 110*, 520–537.

Gross, J., & Stitzer, M. L. (1989). Nicotine replacement: Ten-week effects on tobacco withdrawal symptoms. *Psychopharmacology, 98*, 334–341.

Grossberg, I. N., & Cornell, D. G. (1988). The relationship between personality adjustment and high intelligence: Terman versus Hollingworth. *Exceptional Children, 55*, 266–272.

Grosz, R. D. (1990). Suicide: Training the resident assistant as an interventionist. *Journal of College Student Psychotherapy, 4*, 179–194.

Grove, W. M., Eckert, E. D., Heston, L., & Bouchard, T. J. (1990). Heritability of substance abuse and antisocial behavior: A study of monozygotic twins reared apart. *Biological Psychiatry, 27*, 1293–1304.

Grych, J. H., & Fincham, R. J. (1990). Marital conflict and children's adjustment: A cognitive-contextual framework. *Psychological Bulletin, 108*, 267–290.

Guastello, S. J., Guastello, D. D., & Craft, L. L. (1989). Assessment of the Barnum effect in computer-based test interpretations. *Journal of Psychology, 123*, 477–484.

Guilford, J. P. (1950). Creativity. *American Psychologist, 5*, 444–454.

Guilford, J. P. (1959). Three faces of intellect. *American Psychologist, 14*, 469–479.

Guilford, J. P. (1980). Fluid and crystallized intelligences: Two fanciful concepts. *Psychological Bulletin, 88*, 406–412.

Guilford, J. P. (1984). Varieties of divergent production. *Journal of Creative Behavior, 18*, 1–10.

Guilford, J. P. (1985). The structure of intellect model. In B. B. Wolman (Ed.), *Handbook of Intelligence* (pp. 225–266). New York: Wiley.

Gulevich, G., Dement, W., & Johnson, L. (1966). Psychiatric and EEG observations on a case of prolonged (264 hours) wakefulness. *Archives of General Psychiatry, 15*, 29–35.

Gusella, J. L., & Fried, P. A. (1984). Effects of maternal social drinking and smoking on offspring at 13 months. *Neurobehavioral Toxicology and Teratology, 6*, 13–17.

Gustafson, R., & Kallmen, H. (1990). Subliminal stimulation and cognitive and motor performance. *Perceptual and Motor Skills, 71*, 87–96.

Gustavson, C. R., Garcia, J., Hawkins, W. G., & Rusiniak, K. W. (1974). Coyote predation control by aversive conditioning. *Science, 184*, 581–583.

Guthrie, E. V. (1976). *Even the rat was white: A historical view of psychology.* New York: Harper & Row.

Haber, R. N. (1979). Twenty years of haunting eidetic imagery: Where's the ghost? *Behavioral and Brain Sciences, 2*, 583–629.

Haber, R. N. (1980). How we perceive depth from flat pictures. *American Scientist, 68*, 370–380.

Hackett, G. (1985). Role of mathematics self-efficacy in the choice of math-related majors of college women and men: A path analysis. *Journal of Counseling Psychology, 32*, 47–56.

Hale, M., Jr. (1980). *Hugo Münsterberg: The origins of applied psychology.* Philadelphia: Temple University Press.

Hall, C. S. (1966). *The meaning of dreams.* New York: McGraw-Hill.

Hall, C. S. (1984). "A ubiquitous sex difference in dreams" revisited. *Journal of Personality and Social Psychology, 46*, 1109–1117.

Hall, G. S. (1904). *Adolescence.* New York: Appleton.

Hall, H. K., & Byrne, A. T. J. (1988). Goal setting in sport: Clarifying recent anomalies. *Journal of Sport and Exercise Psychology, 10*, 184–198.

Hall, J. B. (1986). The cardiopulmonary failure of sleep-disordered breathing. *Journal of the American Medical Association, 255*, 930–933.

Hall, R. G., Sachs, D. P., Hall, S. M., & Benowitz, N. L. (1984). Two-year efficacy and safety of rapid smoking therapy in patients with cardiac and pulmonary disease. *Journal of Consulting and Clinical Psychology, 52*, 574–581.

Halpern, L., Blake, R., & Hillerbrand, J. (1986). Psychoacoustics of a chilling sound. *Perception and Psychophysics, 39*, 77–80.

Hama, A. T., & Sagen, J. (1993). Reduced pain-related behavior by adrenal medullary transplants in rats with experimental painful peripheral neuropathy. *Pain, 52*, 223–231.

Hamburg, D. A. (1982). Health and behavior. *Science, 217*, 399.

Hamer, D. H., Hu, S., Magnuson, V. L., & Hu, N. (1993). A linkage between DNA markers on the X chromosome and male sexual orientation. *Science, 261*, 321–327.

Hamill, R., Decamp Wilson, T., & Nisbett, R. E. (1980). Insensitivity to sample bias: Generalizing from atypical cases. *Journal of Personality and Social Psychology, 39*, 578–589.

Hamilton, M. C. (1988). Using masculine generics: Does generic *he* increase male bias in the user's imagery? *Sex Roles, 19*, 785–799.

Hamlett, K. W., & Curry, J. F. (1990). Anorexia nervosa in adolescent males: A review and case study. *Child Psychiatry and Human Development, 21*, 79–94.

Handelmann, G. E., Nevins, M. E., Mueller, L. L., & Arnolde, M. (1989). Milacemide, a glycine prodrug, enhances performance of learning tasks in normal and amnestic rodents. *Pharmacology, Biochemistry, and Behavior, 34*, 823–828.

Hansen, C. H., & Hansen, R. D. (1988). Finding the face in the crowd: An anger superiority effect. *Journal of Personality and Social Psychology, 54*, 917–924.

Hanson, R. K. (1990). The psychological impact of sexual assault on women and children: A review. *Annals of Sex Research, 3*, 187–232.

Harbin, G., Durst, L., & Harbin, D. (1989). Evaluation of oculomotor response in relationship to sports performance. *Medicine and Science in Sports and Exercise, 21*, 258–262.

Hardaway, R. A. (1990). Subliminally activated symbiotic fantasies: Fact and artifacts. *Psychological Bulletin, 107*, 177–195.

Hardy, C. J., & Latané, B. (1988). Social loafing in cheerleaders: Effects of team membership and competition. *Journal of Sport and Exercise Psychology, 10*, 109–114.

Hardyck, C., & Petrinovich, L. F. (1977). Left-handedness. *Psychological Bulletin, 84*, 385–404.

Hare, R. D., McPherson, L. M., & Forth, A. E. (1988). Male psychopaths and their criminal careers. *Journal of Consulting and Clinical Psychology, 56*, 710–714.

Hare-Mustin, R. T. (1983). An appraisal of the relationship between women and psychotherapy: 80 years after the case of Dora. *American Psychologist, 38*, 593–601.

Haritos-Fatouros, M. (1988). The official torturer: A learning model for obedience to the authority of violence. *Journal of Applied Social Psychology, 18*, 1107–1120.

Harlow, H. F., & Zimmerman, R. R. (1959). Affectional responses in the infant monkey. *Science, 130*, 421–432.

Harman, M. J. (1991). The use of group psychotherapy with cancer patients: A review of recent literature. *Journal for Specialists in Group Work, 16*, 56–61.

Harrington, D. M., Block, J. H., & Block, J. (1987). Testing aspects of Carl Rogers' theory of creative environments: Child-rearing antecedents of creative potential in young adolescents. *Journal of Personality and Social Psychology, 52*, 851–856.

Harris, B. (1979). Whatever happened to Little Albert? *American Psychologist, 34*, 151–160.

Harris, M. J., & Rosenthal, R. (1985). Mediation of interpersonal expectancy effects: Thirty-one meta-analyses. *Psychological Bulletin, 97*, 363–386.

Harris, R. L., Ellicott, A. M., & Holmes, D. S. (1986). The timing of psychosocial transitions and changes in women's lives: An examination of women aged 45 to 60. *Journal of Personality and Social Psychology, 51*, 409–416.

Harrison, A. A. (1969). Exposure and popularity. *Journal of Personality, 37*, 359–377.

Harrison, A. A. (1977). Let's make a deal: An analysis of revelations and stipulations in lonely hearts advertisements. *Journal of Personality and Social Psychology, 35*, 257–264.

Harrison, D. W., Gavin, M. R., & Isaac, W. (1988). A portable biofeedback device for autonomic responses. *Journal of Psychopathology and Behavioral Assessment, 10*, 217–224.

Hart, J. D., & Cichanski, K. A. (1981). A comparison of frontal EMG biofeedback in the treatment of muscle-contraction headache. *Biofeedback and Self-Regulation, 6*, 63–74.

Hart, S. D., Knapp, P. R., & Hare, R. D. (1988). Performance of male psychopaths following conditional release from prison. *Journal of Consulting and Clinical Psychology, 56*, 227–232.

Hartley, D., Roback, H. B., & Abramowitz, S. I. (1976). Deterioration effects in encounter groups. *American Psychologist, 31*, 247–255.

Hartley, J., & Homa, D. (1981). Abstraction of stylistic concepts. *Journal of Experimental Psychology: Human Learning and Memory, 7*, 33–46.

Hartman, N., Jarvik, M. E., & Wilkins, J. N. (1989). Reduction of cigarette smoking by use of a nicotine patch. *Archives of General Psychiatry, 46*, 289.

Hartshorne, H., & May, M. A. (1928). *Studies in deceit.* New York: Macmillan.

Hartup, W. W. (1989). Social relationships and their developmental significance. *American Psychologist, 44*, 120–126.

Haskell, R. E. (1986–1987). Social cognition, language, and the non-conscious expression of racial ideology. *Imagination, Cognition, and Personality, 6*, 75–97.

Hassett, J. (1978). *A primer of psychophysiology.* San Francisco: Freeman.

Hatfield, E. (1988). Passionate and companionate love. In R. J. Sternberg & M. L. Barnes (Eds.), *The psychology of love.* New Haven, CT: Yale University Press.

Hathaway, S. R., & McKinley, J. C. (1943). *Minnesota Multiphasic Personality Inventory.* New York: Psychological Corporation.

Hattie, J. A., Sharpley, C. F., & Rogers, H. J. (1984). Comparative effectiveness of professional and paraprofessional helpers. *Psychological Bulletin, 95*, 534–541.

Hawkes, N. (1979). Tracing Burt's descent to scientific fraud. *Science, 205*, 673–675.

Hawkins, M. J., Hawkins, W. E., & Ryan, E. R. (1989). Self-actualization as related to age of faculty members at a large midwestern university. *Psychological Reports, 65*, 1120–1122.

Hawton, K., & Catalan, J. (1990). Sex therapy for vaginismus: Characteristics of couples and treatment outcome. *Sexual and Marital Therapy, 5*, 39–48.

Hawton, K., Catalan, J., Martin, P., & Fagg, J. (1986). Long-term outcome of sex therapy. *Behaviour Research and Therapy, 24*, 665–675.

Hayden, T., & Mischel, W. (1976). Maintaining trait consistency in the resolution of behavioral inconsistency: The wolf in sheep's clothing? *Journal of Personality, 44*, 109–132.

Hayes, C. (1951). *The ape in our house.* New York: Harper & Row.

Hayes, D. S., Chemelski, B. E., & Palmer, M. (1982). Nursery rhymes and prose passages: Preschoolers' liking and short-term retention of story events. *Developmental Psychology, 18*, 49–56.

Hayes, R. L., Pechura, C. M., Katayama, Y., Povlishuck, J. T., Giebel, M. L., & Becker, D. P. (1984). Activation of pontine cholinergic sites implicated in unconsciousness following cerebral concussions in the cat. *Science, 223,* 301–303.

Hayflick, L. (1980, January). The cell biology of human aging. *Scientific American,* pp. 58–65.

Hays, J. R. (1989). The role of *Addington v. Texas* on involuntary civil commitment. *Psychological Reports, 65,* 1211–1215.

Hayslip, B., Jr., & Leon, J. (1992). *Hospice care.* Newbury Park, CA: Sage Publications.

Haywood, H. C., Meyers, C. E., & Switzky, H. N. (1982). Mental retardation. *Annual Review of Psychology, 33,* 309–342.

Hazelrigg, M. D., Cooper, H. M., & Borduin, C. M. (1987). Evaluating the effectiveness of family therapies: An integrative review and analysis. *Psychological Bulletin, 101,* 428–442.

Hazelrigg, P. J., Cooper, H., & Strathman, A. J. (1991). Personality moderators of the experimenter expectancy effect: A reexamination of five hypotheses. *Personality and Social Psychology Bulletin, 17,* 569–579.

Hearne, K. M. (1989). A nationwide mass dream-telepathy experiment. *Journal of the Society for Psychical Research, 55,* 271–274.

Hearnshaw, L. S. (1979). *Cyril Burt: Psychologist.* Ithaca: Cornell University Press.

Hearnshaw, L. S. (1985). Francis Bacon: Harbinger of scientific psychology. *Revista de Historia de la Psicologia, 6,* 5–14.

Heath, A. C., Kendler, K. S., Eaves, L. J., & Martin, N. G. (1990). Evidence for genetic influences on sleep disturbance and sleep pattern in twins. *Sleep, 13,* 318–335.

Heath, R. G., Martens, S., Leach, B. E., Cohen, M., & Feigley, L. A. (1958). Behavioral changes in nonpsychotic volunteers following administration of taraxein, a substance obtained from serum of schizophrenic patients. *American Journal of Psychiatry, 11,* 917–920.

Heatherton, T. F., Polivy, J., & Herman, C. P. (1989). Restraint and internal responsiveness: Effects of placebo manipulation of hunger state on eating. *Journal of Abnormal Psychology, 98,* 89–92.

Heatherton, T. F., Polivy, J., & Herman, C. P. (1990). Dietary restraint: Some current findings and speculations. *Psychology of Addictive Behaviors, 4,* 100–106.

Hebb, D. O. (1955). Drives and the C.N.S. (conceptual nervous system). *Psychological Review, 62,* 243–254.

Hebb, D. O. (1958). The motivating effects of exteroceptive stimulation. *American Psychologist, 13,* 109–113.

Hechinger, N. (1981, March). Seeing without eyes. *Science 81,* pp. 38–43.

Hecker, M. H., Chesney, M. A., Black, G. W., & Frautschi, N. (1988). Coronary-prone behaviors in the Western Collaborative Group Study. *Psychosomatic Medicine, 50,* 153–164.

Hedges, L. V. (1987). How hard is hard science, how soft is soft science? The empirical cumulativeness of research. *American Psychologist, 42,* 443–455.

Heffner, H. E. (1983). Hearing in large and small dogs: Absolute thresholds and size of the tympanic membrane. *Behavioral Neuroscience, 97,* 310–318.

Heider, F. (1944). Social perception and phenomenal causality. *Psychological Review, 51,* 358–374.

Heim, N., & Lester, D. (1990). Do suicides who write notes differ from those who do not? A study of suicides in West Berlin. *Acta Psychiatrica Scandinavica, 82,* 372–373.

Heimberg, R. G. (1989). Cognitive and behavioral treatments for social phobia: A critical analysis. *Clinical Psychology Review, 9,* 107–128.

Heitzmann, C. A., & Kaplan, M. (1988). Assessment of methods for measuring social support. *Health Psychology, 7,* 75–109.

Hellige, J. B. (1990). Hemispheric asymmetry. *Annual Review of Psychology, 41,* 55–80.

Helmes, E., & Reddon, J. R. (1993). A perspective on developments in assessing psychopathology: A critical review of the MMPI and MMPI-2. *Psychological Bulletin, 113,* 453–471.

Helmholtz, H. von (1866/1962). *Treatise on physiological optics* (3 vols.). New York: Dover.

Helmreich, R. L., Spence, J. T., Beane, W. E., Lucker, G. W., & Matthews, K. A. (1980). Making it in academic psychology: Demographic and personality correlates of attainment. *Journal of Personality and Social Psychology, 39,* 896–908.

Hendrick, C. (1990). Replications, strict replications, and conceptual replications: Are they important? *Journal of Social Behavior and Personality, 5,* 41–49.

Hendrick, S., Hendrick, C., Slapion-Foote, M., & Foote, F. (1985). Gender differences in sexual attitudes. *Journal of Personality and Social Psychology, 48,* 1630–1642.

Hendrickson, K. M., McCarty, T., & Goodwin, J. M. (1990). Animal alters: Case reports. *Dissociation: Progress in the Dissociative Disorders, 3,* 218–221.

Hendrixson, L. L. (1989). Care versus justice: Two moral perspectives in the Baby "M" surrogacy case. *Journal of Sex Education and Therapy, 15,* 247–256.

Henke, P. G. (1988a). Electrophysiological activity in the central nucleus of the amygdala: Emotionality and stress ulcers in rats. *Behavioral Neuroscience, 102,* 77–83.

Henke, P. G. (1988b). Recent studies of the central nucleus of the amygdala and stress ulcers. *Neuroscience and Biobehavioral Reviews, 12,* 143–150.

Henle, M. (1978a). Gestalt psychology and gestalt therapy. *Journal of the History of the Behavioral Sciences, 14,* 23–32.

Henle, M. (1978b). One man against the Nazis: Wolfgang Kohler. *American Psychologist, 33,* 939–944.

Hennessey, B. A., & Zbikowski, S. M. (1993). Immunizing children against the negative effects of reward: A further examination of intrinsic motivation training techniques. *Creativity Research Journal, 6,* 297–307.

Henrion, R. (1989). Logotherapy for former prisoners. *International Forum for Logotherapy, 12,* 95–96.

Henry, J. L. (1982). Possible involvement of endorphins in altered states of consciousness. *Ethos, 10,* 394–408.

Herbert, W. (1983a). MMPI: Redefining normality for modern times. *Science News, 134,* 228.

Herbert, W. (1983b). Remembrance of things partly. *Science News, 124,* 378–381.

Hergenhahn, B. R. (1984). *An introduction to theories of personality.* Englewood Cliffs, NJ: Prentice Hall.

Herkenhahn, M., Lynn, A. B., deCosta, B. R., & Richfield, E. K. (1991). Neuronal localization of cannabinoid receptors in the basal ganglia of the rat. *Brain Research, 547,* 267–274.

Herman, C. P., Olmsted, M. P., & Polivy, J. (1983). Obesity, externality, and susceptibility to social influence: An integrated analysis. *Journal of Personality and Social Psychology, 45,* 926–934.

Herman, L. M., Morrel-Samuels, P., & Pack, A. A. (1990). Bottlenosed dolphin and human recognition of veridical and degraded video displays of an artificial gestural language. *Journal of Experimental Psychology: General, 119,* 215–230.

Hermann, D. H. (1990). Autonomy, self determination, the right of involuntarily committed persons to refuse treatment, and the use of substituted judgment in medication decisions involving incompetent persons. *International Journal of Law and Psychiatry, 4,* 361–385.

Herning, R. I. (1985). Cocaine increases EEG beta: A replication of Hans Berger's historic experiments. *Electroencephalography and Clinical Neurophysiology, 60,* 470–477.

Herod, J. W., & Smith, J. (1982). A review of Senoi dream principles: Adaptation to hypnoanalysis. *Medical Hypnoanalysis, 3,* 96–107.

Herrero, J. V., & Hillix, W. A. (1990). Hemispheric performance in detecting prosody: A competitive dichotic listening task. *Perceptual and Motor Skills, 71,* 479–486.

Herrick, C., Kvale, J. K., & Goodykoontz, L. G. (1991). Resolving faculty conflict: Application of a psychotherapeutic model in an encounter group process. *Journal for Specialists in Group Work, 16,* 32–39.

Herrnstein, R. J., Nickerson, R. S., de Sanchez, M., & Swets, J. A. (1986). Teaching thinking skills. *American Psychologist, 41,* 1279–1289.

Hersen, M., Kazdin, A. E., & Bellack, A. S. (Eds.). (1983). *The clinical psychology handbook.* New York: Pergamon.

Hess, E. H. (1975, November). The role of pupil size in communication. *Scientific American,* pp. 110–112, 116–119.

Hesse, H. (1930/1968). *Narcissus and Goldmund.* New York: Farrar, Straus & Giroux.

Hetherington, A. W., & Ranson, S. W. (1942). The spontaneous activity and food intake of rats with hypothalamic lesions. *American Journal of Physiology, 136,* 609–617.

Heyes, C. M., Dawson, G. R., & Nokes, T. (1992). Imitation in rats: Initial responding and transfer evidence. *Quarterly Journal of Experimental Psychology Comparative and Physiological Psychology, 45B,* 229–240.

Hewstone, M., Johnston, L., & Aird, P. (1992). Cognitive models of stereotype change: II. Perceptions of homogeneous and heterogenous groups. *European Journal of Social Psychology, 22,* 235–249.

Hiatt, S. W., Campos, J. J., & Emde, R. N. (1980). Facial patterning and infant emotional expression: Happiness, surprise, and fear. *Annual Progress in Child Psychiatry and Child Development,* 95–121.

Hicks, R. A., Johnson, C., & Pellegrini, R. J. (1992). Changes in the self-reported consistency of normal habitual sleep duration of college students (1978 and 1992). *Perceptual and Motor Skills, 75,* 1168–1170.

Higgins, E. T. (1987). Self-discrepancy: A theory relating self and affect. *Psychological Review, 94,* 319–340.

Higgins, E. T. (1990). Self-state representations: Patterns of interconnected beliefs with specific holistic meanings and importance. *Bulletin of the Psychonomic Society, 28,* 248–253.

Hilakivi, I., Veilahti, J., Asplund, P., & Sinivuo, J. (1989). A sixteen-factor personality test for predicting automobile driving accidents of young drivers. *Accident Analysis and Prevention, 21,* 413–418.

Hilgard, E. R. (1973). A neodissociative interpretation of pain reduction in hypnosis. *Psychological Review, 80,* 403–419.

Hilgard, E. R. (1978, January). Hypnosis and consciousness. *Human Nature,* pp. 42–49.

Hilgard, E. R. (1982). Hypnotic susceptibility and implications for measurement. *International Journal of Clinical and Experimental Hypnosis, 30,* 394–403.

Hilgard, E. R. (1987). *Psychology in America: A historical survey.* San Diego: Harcourt Brace Jovanovich.

Hill, C. E., & Stephany, A. (1990). Relation of nonverbal behavior to client reactions. *Journal of Counseling Psychology, 37,* 22–26.

Hill, R. D., Allen, A. C., & McWhorter, P. (1991). Stories as a mnemonic aid for older learners. *Psychology and Aging, 6,* 484–486.

Hill, T. W. (1990). Peyotism and the control of heavy drinking: The Nebraska Winnebago in the early 1900s. *Human Organization, 49,* 255–265.

Hilsenroth, M. J., Hibbard, S. R., Nash, M. R., & Handler, L. (1993). A Rorschach study of narcissism, defense, and aggression in borderline, narcissistic, and Cluster C personality disorders. *Journal of Personality Assessment, 60,* 346–361.

Hilts, V. L. (1982). Obeying the laws of hereditary descent: Phrenological views on inheritance and eugenics. *Journal of the History of the Behavioral Sciences, 18,* 62–77.

Hinckley, J. W. (1982, September 20). The insanity defense and me. *Newsweek,* p. 30.

Hindeland, M. J. (1971). Edward Bradford Titchener: A pioneer in perception. *Journal of the History of the Behavioral Sciences, 7,* 23–28.

Hinsz, V. B. (1989). Facial resemblance in engaged and married couples. *Journal of Social and Personal Relationships, 6,* 223–229.

Hiramoto, R. N., Hiramoto, N. S., Solvason, H. B., & Ghanta, V. K. (1987). Regulation of natural immunity (NK activity) by conditioning. *Annals of the New York Academy of Sciences, 496,* 545–552.

Hirsch, H. V. B., & Spinelli, D. N. (1970). Visual experience modifies distribution of horizontally and vertically oriented receptive fields in cats. *Science, 168,* 869–871.

Hobson, J. A. (1985, November/December). Can psychoanalysis be saved? *Sciences,* pp. 52–58.

Hobson, J. A. (1988). *The dreaming brain.* New York: Basic Books.

Hobson, J. A., & McCarley, R. W. (1977). The brain as a dream state generator: An activation-synthesis hypothesis of the dream process. *American Journal of Psychiatry, 134,* 1335–1348.

Hodgins, H. S., & Zuckerman, M. (1990). The effect of nonverbal sensitivity on social interaction. *Journal of Nonverbal Behavior, 14,* 155–170.

Hodgkinson, S., Sherrington, R., Gurling, H., & Marchbanks, R. (1987). Molecular genetic evidence for heterogeneity in manic-depression. *Nature, 325,* 805–806.

Hoelscher, T. J. (1987). Maintenance of relaxation-induced blood pressure reductions: The importance of continued relaxation practice. *Biofeedback and Self-Regulation, 12,* 3–12.

Hoff-Ginsberg, E. (1986). Function and structure in maternal speech: Their relation to the child's development of syntax. *Developmental Psychology, 22,* 155–163.

Hoffman, C., Lau, I., & Johnson, D. R. (1986). The linguistic relativity of person cognition: An English-Chinese comparison. *Journal of Personality and Social Psychology, 51,* 1097–1105.

Hoffman, L. W. (1989). Effects of maternal employment in the two-parent family. *American Psychologist, 44,* 283–292.

Hoffman, L. W. (1991). The influence of the family environment on personality: Accounting for sibling differences. *Psychological Bulletin, 110,* 187–203.

Hofmann, A. (1983). *LSD: My problem child.* Los Angeles: Tarcher.

Hofsten, C. (1983). Eye-hand coordination in the newborn. *Developmental Psychology, 18,* 450–461.

Hogg, M. A., & Sunderland, J. (1991). Self-esteem and intergroup discrimination in the minimal group paradigm. *British Journal of Social Psychology, 30,* 51–62.

Holden, C. (1980a). Identical twins reared apart. *Science, 207,* 1323–1328.

Holden, C. (1980b, November). Twins reunited: More than the faces are familiar. *Science 80,* pp. 55–59.

Holden, C. (1983). Insanity defense reexamined. *Science, 222,* 994–995.

Holden, C. (1985). A guarded endorsement for shock therapy. *Science, 228,* 1510–1511.

Holden, C. (1986a). Depression research advances, treatment lags. *Science, 233,* 723–726.

Holden, C. (1986b). Researchers grapple with problems of updating classic psychological test. *Science, 233,* 1249–1251.

Holden, C. (1987a). Animal regulations: So far, so good. *Science, 238,* 880–882.

Holden, C. (1987b). The genetics of personality. *Science, 237,* 598–601.

Hollender, M. H. (1980). The case of Anna O.: A reformulation. *American Journal of Psychiatry, 137,* 797–800.

Hollender, M. H. (1983). The 51st landmark article. *Journal of the American Medical Association, 250,* 228–229.

Hollins, M., Delemos, K. A., & Goble, A. K. (1991). Vibrotactile adaptation on the face. *Perception and Psychophysics, 49,* 21–30.

Holmes, D. S. (1974). Investigations of repression: Differential recall of material experimentally or naturally associated with ego threat. *Psychology Bulletin, 81,* 632–653.

Holmes, D. S. (1984). Meditation and somatic arousal reduction: A review of the experimental evidence. *American Psychologist, 39,* 1–10.

Holmes, M. (1986, August 3). 20 years ago, the Texas tower massacre. *Philadelphia Inquirer,* p. 3-E.

Holmes, T. H., & Rahe, R. H. (1967). The Social Readjustment Rating Scale. *Journal of Psychosomatic Research, 11,* 213–218.

Holtgraves, T., & Skeel, J. (1992). Cognitive biases in playing the lottery: Estimating the odds and choosing the numbers. *Journal of Applied Social Psychology, 22,* 934–952.

Homa, D. (1983). An assessment of two extraordinary speed-readers. *Bulletin of the Psychonomic Society, 21,* 123–126.

Homant, R. J., Kennedy, D. B., & Howton, J. D. (1993). Sensation seeking as a factor in police pursuit. *Criminal Justice and Behavior, 20,* 293–305.

Honchar, M. P., Olney, J. W., & Sherman, W. R. (1983). Systematic cholinergic agents induce seizures and brain damage in lithium-treated rats. *Science, 220,* 323–325.

Honorton, C., & Ferrari, D. C. (1989). "Future telling": A meta-analysis of forced-choice precognition experiments, 1935–1987. *Journal of Parapsychology, 53,* 281–308.

Honts, C. R., Hodes, R. L., & Raskin, D. C. (1985). Effects of physical countermeasures on the physiological detection of deception. *Journal of Applied Psychology, 70,* 177–187.

Hope, D. A., Gansler, D. A., & Heimberg, R. G. (1989). Attentional focus and causal attributions in social phobia: Implications from social psychology. *Clinical Psychology Review, 9,* 49–60.

Hoppe, R. B. (1988). In search of a phenomenon: Research in parapsychology [Review of *Foundations of parapsychology*]. *Contemporary Psychology, 33,* 129–130.

Hormuth, S. E. (1986). The sampling of experiences *in situ. Journal of Personality, 54,* 262–293.

Horn, J. L., & Cattell, R. C. (1966). Refinement and test of the theory of fluid and crystallized general intelligences. *Journal of Educational Psychology, 57,* 253–270.

Horn, J. L., & Donaldson, G. (1976). On the myth of individual decline in adulthood. *American Psychologist, 31,* 701–719.

Horn, J. M. (1983). The Texas Adoption Project: Adopted children and their intellectual resemblance to biological and adoptive parents. *Child Development, 54,* 268–275.

Horne, J. A. (1988). Sleep loss and "divergent" thinking ability. *Sleep, 11,* 528–536.

Horner, M. D. (1990). Psychobiological evidence for the distinction between episodic and semantic memory. *Neuropsychology Review, 1,* 281–321.

Horney, K. (1926/1967). The flight from womanhood. In K. Horney, *Feminine psychology* [H. Kelman, Ed.] (pp. 54–70). New York: W. W. Norton.

Horney, K. (1937). *The neurotic personality of our time.* New York: W. W. Norton.

Horowitz, F. D. (1992). John B. Watson's legacy: Learning and environment. *Developmental Psychology, 28,* 360–367.

Houlihan, D. D., & Jones, R. N. (1989). Treatment of a boy's school phobia with in vivo systematic desensitization. *Professional School Psychology, 4,* 285–293.

Houston, B. K. (1983). Psychophysiological responsivity and the Type A behavior pattern. *Journal of Research in Personality, 17,* 22–39.

Hovland, C. I., Lumsdaine, A., & Sheffield, F. (1949). *Experiments on mass communication.* Princeton, NJ: Princeton University Press.

Howard, C., & D'Orban, P. T. (1987). Violence in sleep: Medico-legal issues and two case reports. *Psychological Medicine, 17,* 915–925.

Howard, K. I., Kopta, S. M., Krausse, M. S., & Orlinsky, D. E. (1986). The dose-effect relationship in psychotherapy. *American Psychologist, 41,* 159–164.

Howe, M. J., & Smith, J. (1988). Calendar calculating in "idiot savants": How do they do it? *British Journal of Psychology, 79,* 371–386.

Hsu, F. H., Anantharaman, R., Campbell, M., & Nowatzyk, A. (1990, October). A grandmaster chess machine. *Scientific American,* pp. 44–50.

Hsu, L. G., Chester B. E., & Santhouse, R. (1990). Bulimia nervosa in eleven sets of twins: A clinical report. *International Journal of Eating Disorders, 9,* 275–282.

Hsu, L. G., & Sobkiewicz, T. A. (1991). Body image disturbance: Time to abandon the concept for eating disorders? *International Journal of Eating Disorders, 10,* 15–30.

Hubel, D. H., & Wiesel, T. N. (1979, September). Brain mechanisms of vision. *Scientific American,* pp. 130–144.

Huber, H. P., & Gramer, M. (1990). Psychophysiological response patterns in relaxation processes. *German Journal of Psychology, 14,* 98–106.

Huber, S. J., Shulman, H. G., Paulson, G. W., & Shuttleworth, E. C. (1989). Dose-dependent memory impairment in Parkinson's disease. *Neurology, 39,* 438–440.

Hudesman, J., Beck, P., & Smith, C. M. (1987). The use of stress reduction training in a college curriculum for health science students. *Psychology: A Quarterly Journal of Human Behavior, 24,* 55–59.

Hughes, D. (1990). Participant modeling as a classroom activity. *Teaching of Psychology, 7,* 238–240.

Hughes, J., Smith, T. W., Kosterlitz, H. W., Fothergill, L. A., Morgan, B. A., & Morris, H. R. (1975). Identification of two related pentapeptides from the brain with potent opiate agonistic activity. *Nature, 258,* 577–579.

Hughes, J. R., Gust, S. W., Skoog, K., & Keenan, R. (1991). Symptoms of tobacco withdrawal: A replication and extension. *Archives of General Psychiatry, 48,* 52–59.

Hughes, J. R., Higgins, S. T., Bickel, W. K., Hunt, W. K., Fenwick, J. W., Gulliver, S. B., & Mireault, G. C. (1991). Caffeine self-administration, withdrawal, and adverse effects among coffee drinkers. *Archives of General Psychiatry, 48,* 611–617.

Hull, C. L. (1943). *Principles of behavior.* New York: Appleton-Century-Crofts.

Hull, J. G., & Bond, C. F., Jr. (1986). Social and behavioral consequences of alcohol consumption and expectancy: A meta-analysis. *Psychological Bulletin, 99,* 347–360.

Humphreys, M. S., & Revelle, W. (1984). Personality, motivation, and performance: A theory of the relationship between individual differences and information processing. *Psychological Review, 91,* 153–184.

Hunt, E., & Agnoli, F. (1991). The Whorfian hypothesis: A cognitive psychology perspective. *Psychological Review, 98,* 377–389.

Hunt, J. M. (1979). Psychological development: Early experience. *Annual Review of Psychology, 30,* 103–143.

Hurford, J. R. (1991). The evolution of the critical period for language acquisition. *Cognition, 40,* 159–201.

Hurst, L. C., & Mulhall, D. J. (1988). Another calendar savant. *British Journal of Psychiatry, 152,* 274–277.

Husain, S. A. (1990). Current perspective on the role of psychosocial factors in adolescent suicide. *Psychiatric Annals, 20,* 122–127.

Huston, A. C., Watkins, B. A., & Kunkel, E. (1989). Public policy and children's television. *American Psychologist, 44,* 424–433.

Huston, T. L., & Levinger, G. (1978). Interpersonal attraction and relationships. *Annual Review of Psychology, 29,* 115–156.

Huston, T. L., Ruggiero, M., Conner, R., & Geis, G. (1981). Bystander intervention into crime: A study based on naturally-occurring episodes. *Social Psychology Quarterly, 44,* 14–23.

Hutchins, C. M. (1981, October). The acoustics of violin plates. *Scientific American,* pp. 170–174, 177–180, 182–186.

Huttenlocher, P. R. (1990). Morphometric study of human cerebral cortex development. *Neuropsychologia, 28,* 517–527.

Huxley, A. (1932). *Brave new world.* New York: Harper & Row.

Huxley, A. (1954). *The doors of perception.* New York: Harper & Row.

Huyghe, P. (1982, July). Imaginary friends. *Omni,* pp. 22, 121.

Hyde, J. S. (1984). Children's understanding of sexist language. *Developmental Psychology, 20,* 697–706.

Hyde, J. S., & Linn, M. C. (1988). Gender differences in verbal ability: A meta-analysis. *Psychological Bulletin, 104,* 53–69.

Hyman, R. B. (1988). Four stages of adulthood: An exploratory study of growth patterns of inner-direction and time-competence in women. *Journal of Research in Personality, 22,* 117–127.

Hynan, D. J. (1990). Client reasons and experiences in treatment that influence termination of psychotherapy. *Journal of Clinical Psychology, 46,* 891–895.

Immergluck, L. (1964). Determinism-freedom in contemporary psychology: An ancient problem revisited. *American Psychologist, 19,* 270–281.

Ingelfinger, F. J. (1944). The late effects of total and subtotal gastrectomy. *New England Journal of Medicine, 231,* 321–327.

Ingham, A. G., Levinger, G., Graves, J., & Peckham, V. (1974). The Ringelmann effect: Studies of group size and group performance. *Journal of Experimental Social Psychology, 10,* 371–384.

Inglis, A., & Greenglass, E. R. (1989). Motivation for marriage among women and men. *Psychological Reports, 65,* 1035–1042.

Inoki, R., Hayashi, T., Kudo, T., & Matsumoto, K. (1978). Effects of aspirin and morphine on the release of a bradykinin-like substance into the subcutaneous perfusate of the rat paw. *Pain, 5,* 53–63.

Insko, C. A. (1965). Verbal reinforcement of attitude. *Journal of Personality and Social Psychology, 2,* 621–623.

Insko, C. A., Nacoste, R. W., & Moe, J. L. (1983). Belief congruence and racial discrimination: Review of the evidence and critical evaluation. *European Journal of Social Psychology, 13,* 153–174.

Isen, A. M., Daubman, K. A., & Nowicki, G. P. (1987). Positive affect facilitates creative problem solving. *Journal of Personality and Social Psychology, 52,* 1122–1131.

Isle, S. (1988, September 12). Color Braves blue for second-class feeling. *Sporting News,* p. 6.

Ispa, J. M., Thornburg, K. R., & Gray, M. M. (1990). Relations between early childhood care arrangements and college students' psychosocial development and academic performance. *Adolescence, 25,* 529–542.

Ivancevich, J. M. (1986). Life events and hassles as predictors of health symptoms, job performance and absenteeism. *Journal of Occupational Behaviour, 7,* 39–51.

Iversen, I. H. (1992). Skinner's early research: From reflexology to operant conditioning. *American Psychologist, 47,* 1318–1328.

Iyer, P. (1986, October). A mysterious sect gives its name to political murder. *Smithsonian,* pp. 145–162.

Izard, C. E. (1990a). Facial expressions and the regulation of emotions. *Journal of Personality and Social Psychology, 58,* 487–498.

Izard, C. E. (1990b). The substrates and functions of emotion feelings: William James and current emotion theory. *Personality and Social Psychology Bulletin, 16,* 626–635.

Izard, C. E. (1993). Four systems for emotion activation: Cognitive and noncognitive processes. *Psychological Review, 100,* 68–90.

Izard, C. E., & Haynes, O. M. (1988). On the form and universality of the contempt expression: A challenge to Ekman and Friesen's claim of discovery. *Motivation and Emotion, 12,* 1–16.

Izard, C. E., Huebner, R. R., Risser, D., McGinnes, G. C., & Dougherty, L. M. (1980). The young infant's ability to produce discrete emotion expressions. *Developmental Psychology, 16,* 132–140.

Jacklin, C. N. (1989). Female and male: Issues of gender. *American Psychologist, 44,* 127–133.

Jackson, H. C., & Nutt, D. J. (1990). Does electroconvulsive shock therapy work through opioid mechanisms? *Human Psychopharmacology Clinical and Experimental, 5,* 3–23.

Jacob, R. G., Wing, R. R., & Shapiro, A. P. (1987). The behavioral treatment of hypertension: Long-term effects. *Behavior Therapy, 18,* 325–352.

Jacobson, E. (1929/1974). *Progressive relaxation.* Chicago: University of Chicago Press.

Jacobson, E. (1979, September/ October). I was there. *APA Monitor*, p. 13.

James, J. E. (1986). Review of the relative efficacy of imaginal and in vivo flooding in the treatment of clinical fear. *Behavioural Psychotherapy, 14*, 183–191.

James, W. (1882). Subjective effects of nitrous oxide. *Mind, 7*, 186–208.

James, W. (1884). What is an emotion? *Mind, 9*, 188–205.

James, W. (1890/1950). *The principles of psychology*. New York: Dover.

James, W. (1890/1981). *The principles of psychology* (2 vols.). Cambridge, MA: Harvard University Press.

James, W. (1902/1992). *The varieties of religious experience*. New York: Gryphon.

James, W. (1904). Does consciousness exist? *Journal of Philosophy, Psychology, and Scientific Methods, 1*, 477–491.

Jamieson, D. G., & Morosan, D. E. (1986). Training non-native speech contrasts in adults: Acquisition of the English O-O contrast by Francophones. *Perception and Psychophysics, 40*, 205–215.

Janis, I. L. (1983). *Groupthink: Psychological studies of policy decisions and fiascoes*. Boston: Houghton Mifflin.

Jankowicz, A. D. (1987). Whatever became of George Kelly? Applications and implications. *American Psychologist, 42*, 481–487.

Jansson, L., & Ost, L. G. (1982). Behavioral treatments for agoraphobia: An evaluative review. *Clinical Psychology Review, 2*, 311–336.

Jeffery, R. W. (1988). Dietary risk factors and their modification in cardiovascular disease. *Journal of Consulting and Clinical Psychology, 56*, 350–357.

Jemmott, J. B., & Locke, S. E. (1984). Psychosocial factors, immunologic mediation, and human susceptibility to infectious diseases: How much do we know? *Psychological Bulletin, 95*, 78–108.

Jemmott, J. B., & Magloire, K. (1988). Academic stress, social support, and secretory immunoglobulin A. *Journal of Personality and Social Psychology, 55*, 803–810.

Jenkins, J. G., & Dallenbach, K. M. (1924). Obliviscence during sleep and waking. *American Journal of Psychology, 35*, 605–612.

Jensen, A. J. (1969). How much can we boost IQ and scholastic achievement? *Harvard Educational Review, 39*, 1–123.

Jensen, A. R. (1980). *Bias in mental testing*. New York: Free Press.

Jensen, J. P., Bergin, A. E., & Greaves, D. W. (1990). The meaning of eclecticism: New survey and analysis of components. *Professional Psychology: Research and Practice, 21*, 124–130.

Jensen, M. P., Turner, J. A., & Romano, J. M. (1991). Self-efficacy and outcome expectancies: Relationship to chronic pain coping strategies and adjustment. *Pain, 44*, 263–269.

Jernigan, T. L., Salmon, D. P., Butters, N., & Hesselink, J. R. (1991). Cerebral structure on MRI: 2. Specific changes in Alzheimer's and Huntington's diseases. *Biological Psychiatry, 29*, 68–81.

Joag, S. G., Mowen, J. C., & Gentry, J. W. (1990). Risk perception in a simulated industrial purchasing task: The effects of single versus multi-play decisions. *Journal of Behavioral Decision Making, 3*, 91–108.

Johnson, C., & Flach, A. (1985). Family characteristics of 105 patients with bulimia. *American Journal of Psychiatry, 142*, 1321–1324.

Johnson, J. S., & Newport, E. L. (1989). Critical period effects in second language learning: The influence of maturational state on the acquisition of English as a second language. *Cognitive Psychology, 21*, 60–99.

Johnson, L. M., & Morris, E. K. (1987). Public information on research with nonhumans. *American Psychologist, 42*, 103–104.

Johnson, R. C., McClearn, G. E., Yuen, S., Nagoshi, C. T., Ahern, F. M., & Cole, R. E. (1985). Galton's data a century later. *American Psychologist, 40*, 875–892.

Johnston, M. W., Griffeth, R. W., Burton, S., & Carson, P. P. (1993). An exploratory investigation into the relationships between promotion and turnover: A quasi-experimental longitudinal study. *Journal of Management, 19*, 33–49.

Jonas, G. (1972). *Visceral learning: Toward a science of self-control*. New York: Viking.

Jones, E. E. (1985). History of social psychology. In G. A. Kimble & K. Schlesinger (Eds.), *Topics in the history of psychology* (Vol. 2, pp. 371–407). Hillsdale, NJ: Erlbaum.

Jones, L. (1900). Education during sleep. *Suggestive Therapeutics, 8*, 283–285.

Jones, L. A. (1986). Perception of force and weight: Theory and research. *Psychological Bulletin, 100*, 29–42.

Jones, L. V. (1984). White-black achievement differences: The narrowing gap. *American Psychologist, 39*, 1207–1213.

Jones, M. C. (1924). The elimination of children's fears. *Journal of Experimental Psychology, 7*, 383–390.

Jones, M. C. (1965). Psychological correlates of somatic development. *Child Development, 36*, 899–911.

Jones, M. M. (1980). Conversion disorder: Anachronism or evolutionary form? A review of the neurologic, behavioral, and psychoanalytic literature. *Psychological Bulletin, 87*, 427–441.

Jorgensen, R. S., Nash, J. K., Lasser, N. L., Hymowitz, N., & Langer, A. W. (1988). Heart rate acceleration and its relationship to total serum cholesterol, triglycerides, and blood pressure. *Psychophysiology, 25*, 39–44.

Josephson, W. L. (1987). Television violence and children's aggression: Testing the priming, social script, and disinhibition predictions. *Journal of Personality and Social Psychology, 53*, 882–890.

Joubert, P. H., & Van Os, B. E. (1989). The effect of hypnosis, placebo, paracetamol, and naloxone on the response to dental pulp stimulation. *Current Therapeutic Research, 46*, 774–781.

Joyce, J. (1916/1967). *A portrait of the artist as a young man*. New York: Viking.

Ju, J. J. (1982). Counselor variables and rehabilitation outcomes: A literature overview. *Journal of Applied Rehabilitation Counseling, 13*, 28–31, 43.

Judge, S. J., & Cumming, B. G. (1986). Neurons in the monkey mibrain with activity related to vergence eye movement and accommodation. *Journal of Neurophysiology, 55*, 915–930.

Julien, R. M. (1981). *A primer of drug action*. San Francisco: Freeman.

Jung, C. G. (1959/1969). *Flying saucers: A modern myth of things seen in the sky*. New York: Signet.

Jussim, L. (1991). Social perception and social reality: A reflection-construction model. *Psychological Review, 98*, 54–73.

Kaas, J. H. (1987). The organization of neocortex in mammals: Implications for theories of brain function. *Annual Review of Psychology, 38*, 129–151.

Kahle, L. R., & Homer, P. M. (1985). Physical attractiveness of the celebrity endorser: A social adaptation perspective. *Journal of Consumer Research, 11*, 954–961.

Kahn, T. J. (1990). The adolescent transsexual in a juvenile corrections institution: A case study. *Child and Youth Care Quarterly, 19*, 21–29.

Kahneman, D. (1991). Judgment and decision making: A personal view. *Psychological Science, 2*, 142–145.

Kahneman, D., & Tversky, A. (1973). On the psychology of prediction. *Psychological Review, 80*, 237–251.

Kahneman, D., & Tversky, A. (1982, January). The psychology of preferences. *Scientific American*, pp. 160–173.

Kalmun, A. J. (1982). Electric and magnetic field detection in elasmobranch fishes. *Science, 218*, 916–918.

Kamarck, T. W., & Jennings, J. R. (1991). Biobehavioral factors in sudden cardiac death. *Psychological Bulletin, 109*, 42–75.

Kamin, L. (1969). Predictability, surprise, attention, and conditioning. In B. Campbell & R. Church (Eds.), *Punishment and aversive behavior*. New York: Appleton-Century-Crofts.

Kamin, L. J. (1974). *The science and politics of IQ*. New York: Wiley.

Kamins, M. A., & Assael, H. (1987). Two-sided versus one-sided appeals: A cognitive perspective on argumentation, source derogation, and the effect of disconfirming trial on belief change. *Journal of Marketing Research, 24*, 29–39.

Kamiya, J. (1969). Operant control of the EEG alpha rhythm and some of its reported effects on consciousness. In C. Tart (Ed.), *Altered states of consciousness* (pp. 489–501). New York: Wiley.

Kanas, N. (1986). Group therapy with schizophrenics: A review of controlled studies. *International Journal of Group Psychotherapy, 36*, 339–351.

Kandel, E., & Freed, D. (1989). Frontal-lobe dysfunction and antisocial behavior: A review. *Journal of Clinical Psychology, 45*, 404–413.

Kandel, E., Mednick, S. A., Kirkegaard-Sorensen, L., Hutchings, B., Knop, J., Rosenberg, R., & Schulsinger, R. (1988). IQ as a protective factor for subjects at high risk for antisocial behavior. *Journal of Consulting and Clinical Psychology, 56*, 224–226.

Kandel, E. R., & Schwartz, J. H. (1982). Molecular biology of learning: Modulation of transmitter release. *Science, 218*, 433–443.

Kanekar, S. (1976). Observational learning of attitudes: A behavioral analysis. *European Journal of Social Psychology, 6*, 5–24.

Kanner, A. D., Coyne, J. C., Schaefer, C., & Lazarus, R. S. (1981). Comparisons of two modes of stress measurement: Daily hassles and uplifts versus major life events. *Journal of Behavioral Medicine, 4,* 1–39.

Kanzer, M. (1988). Early reviews of *The Interpretation of Dreams. Psychoanalytic Study of the Child, 43,* 33–48.

Kao, E. C., Ngan, P. W., Wilson, S., & Kunovich, R. (1990). Wire-bending test as a predictor of preclinical performance by dental students. *Perceptual and Motor Skills, 71,* 667–673.

Kaplan, G. A., & Reynolds, P. (1988). Depression and cancer mortality and morbidity: Prospective evidence from the Alameda county study. *Journal of Behavioral Medicine, 11,* 1–13.

Kaplan, R. M., & Saccuzzo, D. P. (1982). *Psychological testing: Principles, applications, and issues.* Belmont, CA: Brooks/Cole.

Kassop, M. (1987). Salvador Minuchin: A sociological analysis of his family therapy theory. *Clinical Sociology Review, 5,* 158–167.

Katz, J. (1984). Symptom prescription: A review of the clinical outcome literature. *Clinical Psychology Review, 4,* 703–717.

Kaufman, J., & Cicchetti, D. (1989). Effects of maltreatment on school-age children's socioemotional development: Assessments in a day-camp setting. *Developmental Psychology, 25,* 516–524.

Kaufman, J., & Zigler, E. (1987). Do abused children become abusive parents? *American Journal of Orthopsychiatry, 57,* 186–192.

Kaufman, L., & Rock, I. (1962, July). The moon illusion. *Scientific American,* pp. 120–130.

Kawai, M. (1991). Developmental change of adjustment behavior in reaching: A cross-sectional study from 9 to 36 months of age. *Japanese Psychological Research, 33,* 153–159.

Kazdin, A. E. (1982a). Symptom substitution, generalization, and response covariation: Implications for psychotherapy outcome. *Psychological Bulletin, 91,* 349–365.

Kazdin, A. E. (1982b). The token economy: A decade later. *Journal of Applied Behavior Analysis, 15,* 431–445.

Keck, P. E., & McElroy, S. L. (1993). Current perspectives on treatment of bipolar disorder with lithium. *Psychiatric Annals, 23,* 64–69.

Keesey, R. E., & Powley, T. L. (1986). The regulation of body weight. *Annual Review of Psychology, 37,* 109–133.

Keith, J. R., & McVety, K. M. (1988). Latent place learning in a novel environment and the influences of prior training in rats. *Psychobiology, 16,* 146–151.

Keller, F. S. (1991). Burrhus Frederic Skinner (1904–1990). *Journal of the History of the Behavioral Sciences, 27,* 3–6.

Kelley, H. H. (1950). The warm-cold variable in first impressions of personality. *Journal of Personality, 18,* 431–439.

Kelley, H. H. (1973). The processes of causal attributions. *American Psychologist, 28,* 107–128.

Kellogg, W. N., & Kellogg, L. A. (1933). *The ape and the child.* New York: McGraw-Hill.

Kelly, G. A. (1963). *A theory of personality: The psychology of personal constructs.* New York: W. W. Norton.

Kelly, J. A. (1986). Psychological research and the rights of animals: Disagreement with Miller. *American Psychologist, 41,* 839–841.

Kelly, M. P., Strassberg, D. S., & Kircher, J. R. (1990). Attitudinal and experiential correlates of anorgasmia. *Archives of Sexual Behavior, 19,* 165–177.

Kelly, R. B., Zyzanski, S. J., & Alemagno, S. A. (1991). Prediction of motivation and behavior change following health promotion: Role of health beliefs, social support, and self-efficacy. *Social Science and Medicine, 32,* 311–320.

Kendall, P. C., Williams, L., Pechacek, T. F., Graham, T. F., Shisslak, C., & Horzoff, N. (1979). Cognitive-behavioral and patient education interventions in cardiac catheterization procedures. *Journal of Consulting and Clinical Psychology, 47,* 49–58.

Kendrick, K. M., & Baldwin, B. A. (1987). Cells in temporal cortex of conscious sheep can respond preferentially to the sight of faces. *Science, 236,* 448–450.

Kendrick, M. J., Craig, K. D., Lawson, D. M., & Davidson, P. O. (1982). Cognitive behavioral therapy for musical performance anxiety. *Journal of Consulting and Clinical Psychology, 50,* 353–362.

Kennedy, S., Kiecolt-Glaser, J. K., & Glaser, R. (1988). Immunological consequences of acute and chronic stressors: Mediating role of interpersonal relationships. *British Journal of Medical Psychology, 1,* 77–85.

Kenrick, D. T., & Dantchik, A. (1983). Interactionism, idiographics, and the social psychological invasion of personality. *Journal of Personality, 51,* 286–307.

Kenrick, D. T., & Funder, D. C. (1988). Profiting from controversy: Lessons from the person-situation debate. *American Psychologist, 43,* 23–34.

Kershner, J. R., & Ledger, G. (1985). Effect of sex, intelligence, and style of thinking on creativity: A comparison of gifted and average IQ children. *Journal of Personality and Social Psychology, 48,* 1033–1040.

Keshaven, M. S., Reynolds, C. F., & Kupfer, D. J. (1990). Electroencephalographic sleep in schizophrenia: A critical review. *Comprehensive Psychiatry, 31,* 34–47.

Kessler, S. (1984). The myth of mythical disease [Review of *Schizophrenia: Medical diagnosis or moral verdict?*]. *Contemporary Psychology, 29,* 380–381.

Kestenbaum, C. J. (1982). Children and adolescents at risk for manic-depressive illness: Introduction and overview. *Adolescent Psychiatry, 10,* 245–255.

Keys, A., Brozek, J., Henschel, A., Mickelson, O., & Taylor, H. L. (1950). *The biology of human starvation.* Minneapolis: University of Minnesota Press.

Kiecolt-Glaser, J. K., & Glaser, R. (1988). Psychological influences on immunity: Implications for AIDS. *American Psychologist, 43,* 892–898.

Kiecolt-Glaser, J. K., Glaser, R., Strain, E. C., Stout, J. C., Tarr, K. L., Holliday, J. E., & Speicher, C. E. (1986). Modulation of cellular immunity in medical students. *Journal of Behavioral Medicine, 9,* 5–21.

Kiesler, C. A. (1982). Mental hospitals and alternative care: Noninstitutionalization as potential public policy for mental patients. *American Psychologist, 37,* 349–360.

Kihlstrom, J. F. (1987). The cognitive unconscious. *Science, 237,* 1445–1452.

Kihlstrom, J. F., & McConkey, K. M. (1990). William James and hypnosis: A centennial reflection. *Psychological Science, 1,* 174–178.

Kilborn, L. C., & Labbe, E. E. (1990). Magnetic resonance imaging scanning procedures: Development of phobic response during scan and at one-month follow-up. *Journal of Behavioral Medicine, 13,* 391–401.

Kilbourne, B. K. (1989). A cross-cultural investigation of the foot-in-the-door compliance induction procedure. *Journal of Cross-Cultural Psychology, 20,* 3–38.

Killackey, H. P. (1990). Neocortical expansion: An attempt toward relating phylogeny and ontogeny. *Journal of Cognitive Neuroscience, 2,* 1–17.

Killen, J. D., Fortmann, S. P., & Newman, B. (1990). Weight change among participants in a large sample minimal contact smoking relapse prevention trial. *Addictive Behaviors, 15,* 323–332.

Killen, J. D., Fortmann, S. P., Newman, B., & Varady, A. (1990). Evaluation of a treatment approach combining nicotine gum with self-guided behavioral treatments for smoking relapse prevention. *Journal of Consulting and Clinical Psychology, 58,* 85–92.

Killian, G. A., Holzman, P. S., Davis, J. M., & Gibbons, R. (1984). Effects of psychotropic medication on selected cognitive and perceptual measures. *Journal of Abnormal Psychology, 93,* 58–70.

Kilmann, P. R., Boland, J. P., Norton, S. P., & Davidson, E. (1986). Perspectives of sex therapy outcome: A survey of AASECT providers. *Journal of Sex and Marital Therapy, 12,* 116–138.

Kilmann, P. R., & Sotile, W. M. (1976). The marathon encounter group: A review of the outcome literature. *Psychological Bulletin, 83,* 827–850.

Kim, J. J., DeCola, J. P., Landeira-Fernandez, J., & Fanselow, M. S. (1991). N-methyl-D-aspartate receptor antagonist APV blocks acquisition but not expression of fear conditioning. *Behavioral Neuroscience, 105,* 126–133.

Kimball, M. M. (1989). A new perspective on women's math achievement. *Psychological Bulletin, 105,* 198–214.

Kimble, D. P. (1990). Functional effects of neural grafting in the mammalian central nervous system. *Psychological Bulletin, 108,* 462–479.

Kimble, G. A. (1981). Biological and cognitive constraints on learning. In L. T. Benjamin, Jr. (Ed.), *The G. Stanley Hall Lecture Series* (Vol. 1, pp. 11–60). Washington, DC: American Psychological Association.

Kimble, G. A. (1989). Psychology from the standpoint of a generalist. *American Psychologist, 44,* 491–499.

Kimmel, A. J. (1991). Predictable biases in ethical decision making of American psychologists. *American Psychologist, 46,* 786–788.

Kinney, J., & Peltier, D. (1986). A model alcohol program for the college health service. *Journal of American College Health, 34,* 229–233.

Kinsey, A. C., Pomeroy, W. D., & Martin, C. E. (1948). *Sexual behavior in the human male.* Philadelphia: Saunders.

Kinsey, A. C., Pomeroy, W. D., Martin, C. E., & Gebhard, T. H. (1953). *Sexual behavior in the human female.* Philadelphia: Saunders.

Kirmeyer, S. L., & Biggers, K. (1988). Environmental demand and demand engineering behavior: An observational analysis of the Type A patterns. *Journal of Personality and Social Psychology, 54,* 997–1005.

Klar, Y., Mendola, R., Fisher, J. D., & Silver, R. C. (1990). Characteristics of participants in a large group awareness training. *Journal of Consulting and Clinical Psychology 58,* 99–108.

Klein, J. G. (1991). Negativity effects in impression formation: A test in the political arena. *Personality and Social Psychology Bulletin, 17,* 412–418.

Klein, S. B. (1982). *Motivation: Biosocial approaches.* New York: McGraw-Hill.

Kleinginna, P. R., & Kleinginna, A. M. (1981). A categorized list of emotion definitions, with suggestions for a consensual definition. *Motivation and Emotion, 5,* 345–379.

Kleinmuntz, B., & Szucko, J. J. (1984a). A field study of the fallibility of polygraph lie detection. *Nature, 308,* 449–450.

Kleinmuntz, B., & Szucko, J. J. (1984b). Lie detection in ancient and modern times: A call for contemporary scientific study. *American Psychologist, 39,* 766–776.

Klepac, R. K. (1986). Fear and avoidance of dental treatment in adults. *Annals of Behavioral Medicine, 8,* 17–22.

Klonoff, E. A., Janata, J. W., & Kaufman, B. (1986). The use of systematic desensitization to overcome resistance to magnetic resonance imaging (MRI) scanning. *Journal of Behavior Therapy and Experimental Psychiatry, 17,* 189–192.

Klonoff, E. A., & Moore, D. J. (1986). "Conversion reactions" in adolescents: A biofeedback-based operant approach. *Journal of Behavior Therapy and Experimental Psychiatry, 17,* 179–184.

Klosterhalfen, W., & Klosterhalfen, S. (1983). A critical analysis of the animal experiments cited in support of learned helplessness. *Psychologische Beitrage, 25,* 436–458.

Kluft, R. P. (1987). An update on multiple personality disorder. *Hospital and Community Psychiatry, 38,* 363–373.

Kluger, M. A., Jamner, L. D., & Tursky, B. (1985). Comparison of the effectiveness of biofeedback and relaxation training on handwarming. *Psychophysiology, 22,* 162–166.

Klüver, H., & Bucy, P. C. (1937). "Psychic blindness" and other symptoms following bilateral temporal lobectomy in rhesus monkeys. *American Journal of Physiology, 119,* 352–353.

Knapp, S., & VandeCreek, L. (1992). Public policy issues in applying the "duty to protect" to HIV-positive patients. *Psychotherapy in Private Practice, 10,* 53–61.

Knapp, T. J., & Shodahl, S. A. (1974). Ben Franklin as a behavior modifier: A note. *Behavior Therapy, 5,* 656–660.

Knight, I. F. (1984). Freud's "Project": A theory for studies on hysteria. *Journal of the History of the Behavioral Sciences, 20,* 340–358.

Knudsen, E. I. (1981, December). The hearing of the barn owl. *Scientific American,* pp. 112–113, 115–116, 118–125.

Kobasa, S. C., Maddi, S. R., & Kahn, S. (1982). Hardiness and health: A prospective study. *Journal of Personality and Social Psychology, 42,* 168–177.

Koch, C., & Poggio, T. (1983). Electrical properties of dendritic spines. *Trends in Neurosciences, 6,* 80–83.

Koenigsberger, L. (1906/1965). *Hermann von Helmholtz.* New York: Dover.

Koestner, R., & Wheeler, L. (1988). Self-presentation in personal advertisements: The influence of implicit notions of attraction and role expectations. *Journal of Social and Personal Relationships, 5,* 149–160.

Kohlberg, L. (1966a). A cognitive-developmental analysis of children's sex-role concepts and attitudes. In E. E. Maccoby (Ed.), *The development of sex differences.* Stanford, CA: Stanford University Press.

Kohlberg, L. (1966b). *Essays on moral development: The psychology of moral development.* San Francisco: Harper & Row.

Kohlberg, L. (1981). *Essays on moral development.* New York: Harper & Row.

Kohler, W. (1925). *The mentality of apes.* New York: Harcourt Brace Jovanovich.

Kohler, W. (1959). Gestalt psychology today. *American Psychologist, 14,* 727–734.

Kohnken, G., & Maass, A. (1988). Eyewitness testimony: False alarms on biased instructions. *Journal of Applied Psychology, 73,* 363–370.

Kokkinidis, L., & Anisman, H. (1980). Amphetamine models of paranoid schizophrenia: An overview and elaboration of animal experimentation. *Psychological Bulletin, 88,* 551–579.

Kolata, G. (1985). Why do people get fat? *Science, 227,* 1327–1328.

Kolata, G. (1986). New drug counters alcohol intoxication. *Science, 234,* 1198–1199.

Kolata, G. (1987). Associations or rules in learning language? *Science, 237,* 133–134.

Kolb, B. (1989). Brain development, plasticity, and behavior. *American Psychologist, 44,* 1203–1212.

Koop, C. E. (1987). Report of the Surgeon General's Workshop on Pornography and Public Health. *American Psychologist, 42,* 944–945.

Kopelman, M. D. (1986). The cholinergic neurotransmitter system in human memory and dementia: A review. *Quarterly Journal of Experimental Psychology: Human Experimental Psychology, 38,* 535–573.

Koppe, S. (1983). The psychology of the neuron: Freud, Cajal, and Golgi. *Scandinavian Journal of Psychology, 24,* 1–12.

Korn, J. H., Davis, R., & Davis, S. F. (1991). Historians and chairpersons' judgments of eminence among psychologists. *American Psychologist, 46,* 789–792.

Koss, M. P., Gidycz, C. A., & Wisniewski, N. (1987). The scope of rape: Incidence and prevalence of sexual aggression and victimization in a national sample of higher education students. *Journal of Consulting and Clinical Psychology, 55,* 162–170.

Kosslyn, S. M. (1988). Aspects of a cognitive neuroscience of mental imagery. *Science, 240,* 1621–1626.

Kothera, L., Fudin, R., & Nicastro, R. (1990). Effects of subliminal psychodynamic activation on dart-throwing performance: Another nonreplication. *Perceptual and Motor Skills, 71,* 1015–1022.

Kotze, H. F., & Moller, A. T. (1990). Effect of auditory subliminal stimulation on GSR. *Psychological Reports, 67,* 931–934.

Krafka, C., & Penrod, S. (1985). Reinstatement of context in a field experiment on eyewitness identification. *Journal of Personality and Social Psychology, 49,* 58–69.

Kraizer, S., Witte, S., Fryer, G. E., & Miyoshi, T. (1990). Children in self-care: A new perspective. *Child Welfare, 69,* 571–581.

Kramer, D. E., & Bayern, C. D. (1984). The effects of behavioral strategies on creativity training. *Journal of Creative Behavior, 18,* 23–24.

Kramer, T. H., Buckhout, R., Eugenio, P., & Cohen, R. (1985). Presence of malice: Scientific evaluation of reader response to innuendo. *Bulletin of the Psychonomic Society, 23,* 61–63.

Krantz, D. S., Contrada, R. J., Hill, D. R., & Friedler, E. (1988). Environmental stress and biobehavioral antecedents of coronary heart disease. *Journal of Consulting and Clinical Psychology, 56,* 333–341.

Krantz, D. S., Grunberg, N. E., & Baum, A. (1985). Health psychology. *Annual Review of Psychology, 36,* 349–383.

Krantz, D. S., & Manuck, S. B. (1984). Acute psychophysiologic reactivity and risk of cardiovascular disease: A review and methodologic critique. *Psychological Bulletin, 96,* 4 35–464.

Kravitz, D. A., & Martin, B. (1986). Ringelmann rediscovered: The original article. *Journal of Personality and Social Psychology, 50,* 936–941.

Krech, D. (1968). Titchener on experimental psychology. *American Psychologist, 23,* 367–368.

Krechevsky, M., & Gardner, H. (1990). Approaching school intelligently: An infusion approach. *Contributions to Human Development, 21,* 79–94.

Kremer, J. F., & Dietzen, L. L. (1991). Two approaches to teaching accurate empathy to undergraduates: Teacher-intensive and self-directed. *Journal of College Student Development, 32,* 69–75.

Kreppner, K. (1992). William L. Stern, 1871–1938: A neglected founder of developmental psychology. *Developmental Psychology, 28,* 539–547.

Kretschmer, E. (1925). *Physique and character.* New York: Harcourt, Brace.

Kreshel, P. J. (1990). John B. Watson at J. Walter Thompson: The legitimation of "science" in advertising. *Journal of Advertising, 19,* 49–59.

Kromer, L. F. (1987). Nerve growth factor treatment after brain injury prevents neuronal death. *Science, 235,* 214–216.

Krupa, D. J., Thompson, J. K., & Thompson, R. F. (1993). Localization of a memory trace in the mammalian brain. *Science, 260,* 989–991.

Kübler-Ross, E. (1969). *On death and dying.* New York: Macmillan.

Kübler-Ross, E. (1974). *Questions and answers on death and dying.* New York: Macmillan.

Kuhlman, T. L. (1985). A study of salience and motivational theories of humor. *Journal of Personality and Social Psychology, 49,* 281–286.

Kuhn, T. S. (1970). *The structure of scientific revolutions.* Chicago: University of Chicago Press.

Kukla, A. (1989). Nonempirical issues in psychology. *American Psychologist, 44,* 785–794.

Kulik, J. A., & Mahler, H. I. M. (1987). Effects of preoperative roommate assignment and preoperative anxiety and recovery from coronary-bypass surgery. *Health Psychology, 6,* 525–543.

Kunda, Z., & Schwartz, S. H. (1983). Undermining intrinsic moral motivation: External reward and self-presentation. *Journal of Personality and Social Psychology, 45,* 763–771.

Kunzendorf, R. G. (1989). After-images of eidetic images: A developmental study. *Journal of Mental Imagery, 13,* 55–62.

Kurdek, L. A. (1993). Predicting marital dissolution: A 5-year prospective longitudinal study of newlywed couples. *Journal of Personality and Social Psychology, 64,* 221–242.

Kurz, A., Romero, B., & Lauter, H. (1990). The onset of Alzheimer's disease: A longitudinal case study and a trial of new diagnostic criteria. *Psychiatry, 53,* 53–61.

Kurzweil, R. (1985). What is artificial intelligence anyway? *American Scientist, 73,* 258–264.

Kusnecov, A., King, M. G., & Husband, A. J. (1989). Immunomodulation by behavioral conditioning. *Biological Psychology, 28,* 25–39.

LaBerge, S. (1985). *Lucid dreaming: The power of being awake and aware in your dreams.* Los Angeles: Tarcher.

Lackner, J. R., & DiZio, P. (1991). Decreased susceptibility to motion sickness during exposure to visual inversion in microgravity. *Aviation, Space, and Environmental Medicine, 62,* 206–211.

Ladd-Franklin, C. (1929). *Colour and colour theories.* New York: Harcourt, Brace & Company.

Ladouceur, R. (1983). Participant modeling with or without cognitive treatment for phobias. *Journal of Consulting and Clinical Psychology, 51,* 942–944.

Ladouceur, R., & Gros-Louis, Y. (1986). Paradoxical intention versus stimulus control in the treatment of severe insomnia. *Journal of Behavior Therapy and Experimental Psychiatry, 17,* 267–269.

LaFreniere, P. J., & Sroufe, L. A. (1985). Profiles of peer competence in the preschool: Interrelations between measures, influence of social ecology, and relation to attachment history. *Developmental Psychology, 21,* 56–69.

la Greca, A. M. (1993). Social skills training with children: Where do we go from here? *Journal of Clinical Child Psychology, 22,* 288–298.

Laing, R. D. (1967). *The politics of experience.* New York: Ballantine Books.

Lalancette, M. F., & Standing, L. G. (1990). Asch fails again. *Social Behavior and Personality, 18,* 7–12.

Lamb, H. R. (1989). Lessons learned from deinstitutionalization in the U.S. *British Journal of Psychiatry, 162,* 587–592.

Lamb, M. E., & Sternberg, K. J. (1990). Some thoughts about infant daycare. *Research and Clinical Center for Child Development,* March (No. 12), 71–77.

Lambert, M. J. (1989). The individual therapist's contribution to psychotherapy process and outcome. *Clinical Psychology Review, 9,* 469–485.

Lambert, N. M. (1981). Psychological evidence in Larry P. v. Wilson Riles. *American Psychologist, 36,* 937–952.

Lammers, W. (1990). From cure to care: Transactional analysis treatment of adult asthma. *Transactional Analysis Journal, 20,* 245–252.

Landers, S. (1987, December). Aversive device sparks controversy. *APA Monitor,* p. 15.

Landesman, S., & Butterfield, E. C. (1987). Normalization and deinstitutionalization of mentally retarded individuals: Controversy and facts. *American Psychologist, 42,* 809–816.

Landesman, S., & Ramey, C. (1989). Developmental psychology and mental retardation: Integrating scientific principles with treatment practices. *American Psychologist, 44,* 409–415.

Landfield, A. W. (1984). Personal construct psychology: A developmental perspective. *Journal of Social and Clinical Psychology, 2,* 97–107.

Landy, F. J. (1992). Hugo Munsterberg: Victim or visionary? *Journal of Applied Psychology, 77,* 787–802.

Lang, W., Goldenberg, G., Podreka, I., & Cheyne, D. (1990). Parkinsonism as a disturbance of movement initiation. *Journal of Psychophysiology, 4,* 123–136.

Langenbucher, J. W., & Nathan, P. E. (1983). Psychology, public policy, and the evidence for alcohol intoxication. *American Psychologist, 38,* 1070–1077.

Langone, J. (1983, September). B. F. Skinner: Beyond reward and punishment. *Discover,* pp. 38–46.

LaPiere, R. T. (1934). Attitudes versus action. *Social Forces, 13,* 230–237.

La Pointe, F. H. (1970). Origin and evolution of the term "psychology." *American Psychologist, 25,* 640–646.

Larsen, K. S. (1990). The Asch conformity experiment: Replication and transhistorical comparisons. *Journal of Social Behavior and Personality, 5,* 163–168.

Larson, G. E., & Saccuzzo, D. P. (1989). Cognitive correlates of general intelligence: Toward a process theory of g. *Intelligence, 13,* 5–31.

Lashley, K. S. (1950). In search of the engram. In *Symposium of the Society for Experimental Biology* (Vol. 4, pp. 454–482). New York: Cambridge University Press.

Latané, B., & Darley, J. M. (1968). Group inhibition of bystander intervention in emergencies. *Journal of Personality and Social Psychology, 10,* 215–221.

Lauer, C., Riemann, D., Lund, R., & Berger, M. (1987). Shortened REM latency: A consequence of psychological strain? *Psychophysiology, 24,* 263–271.

Laurence, J. R., & Perry, C. (1983). Hypnotically created memory among highly hypnotizable subjects. *Science, 222,* 523–524.

Laver, A. B. (1972). Precursors of psychology in ancient Egypt. *Journal of the History of the Behavioral Sciences, 8,* 181–195.

Lavie, P., & Hobson, J. A. (1986). Origin of dreams: Anticipation of modern theories in the philosophy and physiology of the 18th and 19th centuries. *Psychological Bulletin, 100,* 229–240.

Lavoie, D. R., & Good, R. (1988). The nature and use of prediction skills in a biological computer simulation. *Journal of Research in Science Teaching, 25,* 335–360.

Lazarus, A. A. (1989). Brief psychotherapy: The multimodal model. *Professional Psychology, 26,* 6–10.

Lazarus, A. A., & Lazarus, C. N. (1986). Reactions from a multimodal perspective. *International Journal of Eclectic Psychotherapy, 5,* 328–330.

Lazarus, J. C., & Todor, J. I. (1987). Age differences in the magnitude of associated movement. *Developmental Medicine and Child Neurology, 29,* 726–733.

Lazarus, R. S. (1991). Progress on a cognitive-motivational-relational theory of emotion. *American Psychologist, 46,* 819–834.

Lazarus, R. S. (1993a). Coping theory and research: Past, present, and future. *Psychosomatic Medicine, 55,* 234–247.

Lazarus, R. S. (1993b). From psychological stress to the emotions: A history of changing outlooks. *Annual Review of Psychology, 44,* 1–21.

Lazarus, R. S., DeLongis, A., Folkman, S., & Gruen, R. (1985). Stress and adaptational outcomes: The problem of confounded measures. *American Psychologist, 40,* 770–779.

Leaf, R. C., Krauss, D. H., Dantzig, S. A., & Alington, D. E. (1992). Educational equivalents of psychotherapy: Positive and negative mental health benefits after group therapy exercises by college students. *Journal of Rational Emotive and Cognitive Behavior Therapy, 10,* 189–206.

Leak, G. K. (1981). Debriefing and gratuitous procedures. *American Psychologist, 36,* 317.

Leakey, R. E., & Lewin, R. (1977, November). Is it our culture, not our genes, that makes us killers? *Smithsonian,* pp. 56–64.

Leana, C. R. (1985). A partial test of Janis' groupthink model: Effects of group cohesiveness and leader behavior on defective decision making. *Journal of Management, 11,* 5–17.

Learman, L. A., Avorn, J., Everitt, D. E., & Rosenthal, R. (1990). Pygmalion in the nursing home: The effects of caregiver expectations on patient outcomes. *Journal of the American Geriatrics Society, 38,* 797–803.

Leary, M. R., & Kowalski, R. M. (1990). Impression management: A literature review and two-component model. *Psychological Bulletin, 107,* 34–47.

Leary, M. R., & Shepperd, J. A. (1986). Behavioral self-handicaps versus self-reported handicaps: A conceptual note. *Journal of Personality and Social Psychology, 51,* 1265–1268.

Lebow, J. (1982). Consumer satisfaction with mental health treatment. *Psychological Bulletin, 91,* 244–259.

LeDoux, J. E. (1986). Sensory systems and emotion: A model of affective processing. *Integrative Psychiatry, 4,* 237–243.

LeDoux, J. E., Romanski, L., & Xagoraris, A. (1989). Indelibility of subcortical emotional memories. *Journal of Cognitive Neuroscience, 1,* 238–243.

Lee, C. (1989). Perceptions of immunity to disease in adult smokers. *Journal of Behavioral Medicine, 12,* 267–277.

Lee, G. P., Loring, D. W., Meader, K. J., & Brooks, B. B. (1990). Hemispheric specialization for emotional expression: A reexamination of results from intracarotid administration of sodium amobarbital. *Brain and Cognition, 12,* 267–280.

Lee, V. E., Brooks-Gunn, J., Schnur, E., & Liaw, F.-R. (1990). Are Head Start effects sustained? A longitudinal follow-up comparison of disadvantaged children attending Head Start, no preschool, and other preschool programs. *Child Development, 61,* 495–507.

Leibowitz, H. W., & Pick, H. A., Jr. (1972). Cross-cultural and educational aspects of the Ponzo perspective illusion. *Perception and Psychophysics, 12,* 430–432.

Leibowitz, S. F. (1988). Hypothalamic paraventricular nucleus: Interaction between a sub-noradrenergic system and circulating hormones and nutrients in relation to energy balance. *Neuroscience and Biobehavioral Reviews, 12,* 101–109.

Leikin, L., Firestone, P., & McGrath, P. (1988). Physical symptom reporting in Type A and Type B children. *Journal of Consulting and Clinical Psychology, 56,* 721–726.

Leitenberg, H., Rosen, J. C., Gross, J., Nudelman, S., & Vara, L. S. (1988). Exposure plus response-prevention treatment of bulimia nervosa. *Journal of Consulting and Clinical Psychology, 56,* 535–541.

Leonard, J. (1970, May 8). Ghetto for blue eyes in the classroom. *Life,* p. 16.

Lepper, M. R., Greene, D., & Nisbett, R. E. (1973). Undermining children's intrinsic interest with extrinsic reward: A test of the "overjustification" hypothesis. *Journal of Personality and Social Psychology, 28,* 129–137.

Lerman, C. E. (1987). Rheumatoid arthritis: Psychological factors in the etiology, course, and treatment. *Clinical Psychology Review, 7,* 413–425.

Lescaudron, L., & Stein, D. G. (1990). Functional recovery following transplants of embryonic brain tissue in rats with lesions of visual, frontal and motor cortex: Problems and prospects for future research. *Neuropsychologia, 28,* 585–599.

Leserman, J., Stuart, E. M., Mamish, M. E., & Benson, H. (1989). The efficacy of the relaxation response in preparing for cardiac surgery. *Behavioral Medicine, 15,* 111–117.

Lester, D. (1982). Ectomorphy and personality. *Psychological Reports, 51,* 1182.

Lester, D. (1990). Maslow's hierarchy of needs and personality. *Personality and Individual Differences, 11,* 1187–1188.

Lester, D., & Wosnack, K. (1990). An exploratory test of Sheldon's theory of personality in neonates. *Perceptual and Motor Skills, 71,* 1282.

Levenson, J. L., & Bemis, C. (1991). The role of psychological factors in cancer onset and progression. *Psychosomatics, 32,* 124–132.

Levenson, R. W. (1992). Autonomic nervous system differences among emotions. *Psychological Science, 3,* 23–27.

Levenson, R. W., Carstensen, L. L., Friesen, W. V., & Ekman, P. (1991). Emotion, physiology, and expression in old age. *Psychology and Aging, 6,* 28–35.

Levenson, R. W., Ekman, P., Heider, K., & Friesen, W. V. (1992). Emotion and autonomic nervous system activity in the Minangkabau of West Sumatra. *Journal of Personality and Social Psychology, 62,* 972–988.

Leventhal, H., & Cleary, P. D. (1980). The smoking problem: A review of the research and theory in behavioral risk modification. *Psychological Bulletin, 88,* 370–405.

Leventhal, H., & Tomarken, A. J. (1986). Emotion: Today's problems. *Annual Review of Psychology, 37,* 565–610.

Levin, I. P., & Gaeth, J. (1988). How consumers are affected by the framing of attribute information before and after consuming the product. *Journal of Consumer Research, 15,* 374–378.

Levin, I. P., Schnittjer, S. K., & Thee, S. L. (1988). Information framing effects in social and personal decisions. *Journal of Experimental Social Psychology, 24,* 520–529.

Levin, R. B., & Gross, A. M. (1985). The role of relaxation in systematic desensitization. *Behaviour Research and Therapy, 23,* 187–196.

Levine, J. D., Clark, R., Devor, M., Helms, C., Moskowitz, M. A., & Basbaum, A. I. (1984). Interneuronal substance P contributes to the severity of experimental arthritis. *Science, 226,* 547–549.

Levine, J. S., & MacNichol, E. F., Jr. (1982, February). Color vision in fishes. *Scientific American,* pp. 140–149.

Levine, M. (1976). The academic achievement test: Its historical context and social functions. *American Psychologist, 31,* 228–238.

Levine, S. B., Risen, C. B., & Althof, S. E. (1990). Essay on the diagnosis and nature of paraphilia. *Journal of Sex and Marital Therapy, 16,* 89–102.

LeVine, W. R., & Irvine, J. J. (1984). In vivo EMG biofeedback in violin and viola pedagogy. *Biofeedback and Self-Regulation, 9,* 161–168.

Levinson, D. J. (1978). *The seasons of a man's life.* New York: Knopf.

Levinson, D. J. (1986). A conception of adult development. *American Psychologist, 41,* 3–13.

Levinson, S. E., & Liberman, M. Y. (1981, April). Speech recognition by computer. *Scientific American,* pp. 64–76.

Levinthal, C. F. (1988). *Messengers of paradise.* New York: Anchor/ Doubleday.

Levitan, A. A., & Ronan, W. J. (1988). Problems in the treatment of obesity and eating disorders. *Medical Hypnoanalysis Journal, 3,* 131–136.

Levitt, E. E. (1983). Estimating the duration of sexual behavior: A laboratory analog study. *Archives of Sexual Behavior, 12,* 329–335.

Levitt, M. J., Weber, R. A., & Clark, M. C. (1986). Social network relationships as sources of maternal support and well-being. *Developmental Psychology, 22,* 310–316.

Levitz-Jones, E. M., & Orlofsky, J. L. (1985). Separation-individuation and intimacy capacity in college women. *Journal of Personality and Social Psychology, 49,* 156–169.

Levy, J. (1983). Language, cognition, and the right hemisphere: A response to Gazzaniga. *American Psychologist, 38,* 538–541.

Levy, J. (1985, May). Right brain, left brain: Fact and fiction. *Psychology Today,* pp. 38–39.

Lewicki, P. (1985). Nonconscious biasing effects of single instances on subsequent judgments. *Journal of Personality and Social Psychology, 48,* 563–574.

Lewin, K. (1935). *A dynamic theory of personality.* New York: McGraw-Hill.

Lewin, R. (1986). How unusual are unusual events? *Science, 233,* 1385.

Lewin, R. (1988). Cloud over Parkinson's therapy. *Science, 240,* 390–392.

Lewis, D. (1899/1983). The gynecologic consideration of the sexual act. *Journal of the American Medical Association, 250,* 222–227.

Lewis, J. (1981). *Something hidden: A biography of Wilder Penfield.* New York: Doubleday.

Lewis, S., & Cooper, C. L. (1983). The stress of combining occupational and parental roles: A review of the literature. *Bulletin of the British Psychological Society, 36,* 341–345.

Ley, P. (1982). Satisfaction, compliance and communication. *British Journal of Clinical Psychology, 21,* 241–254.

Li, D., Wu, Z., Shao, D., & Liu, S. (1991). The relationship of sleep to learning and memory. *International Journal of Mental Health, 20,* 41–47.

Libo, L. M., & Arnold, G. E. (1983). Relaxation practice after biofeedback therapy: A long-term follow-up study of utilization and effectiveness. *Biofeedback and Self-Regulation, 8,* 217–227.

Lieber, J., & Semmel, M. I. (1985). Effectiveness of computer application to instruction with mildly handicapped learners: A review. *RASE: Remedial and Special Education, 6,* 5–12.

Lieberman, D. A. (1979). Behaviorism and the mind: A (limited) call for a return to introspection. *American Psychologist, 34,* 319–333.

Liebert, R. M., & Baron, R. A. (1972). Some immediate effects of television violence on children's behavior. *Developmental Psychology, 6,* 469–475.

Lief, H. I., & Hubschman, L. (1993). Orgasm in the postoperative transsexual. *Archives of Sexual Behavior, 22,* 145–155.

Liegois, M. J. (1899). The relation of hypnotism to crime. *Suggestive Therapeutics, 6,* 18–21.

Lin, E. H., & Peterson, C. (1990). Pessimistic explanatory style and response to illness. *Behaviour Research and Therapy, 28,* 243–248.

Lindberg, D. C. (1983). *Roger Bacon's philosophy of nature.* New York: Oxford University Press.

Linden, W. (1987). On the impending death of the Type A construct: Or is there a phoenix rising from the ashes? *Canadian Journal of Behavioural Science, 19,* 177–190.

Lindsay, E. A., Wilson, D. M., Best, J. A., & Williams, D. G. (1989). A randomized trial of physician training for smoking cessation. *American Journal of Health Promotion, 3*, 11–18.

Lindsay, R. C., & Adair, J. G. (1990). Do ethically recommended research procedures influence the perceived ethicality of social psychological research? *Canadian Journal of Behavioural Science, 22*, 282–294.

Lindsay, R. C., & Holden, R. R. (1987). The introductory psychology subject pool in Canadian universities. *Canadian Psychology, 28*, 45–52.

Lindvall, O., Brundin, P., Widner, H., Rehncrona, S., Gustavii, B., Frackowiak, R., Leenders, K. L., Sawle, G., Rothweel, J. C., Marsden, C. D., & Bjorklund, A. (1990). Grafts of fetal dopamine neurons survive and improve motor function in Parkinson's disease. *Science, 247*, 574–577.

Linn, L., & Spitzer, R. L. (1982). DSM-III: Implications for liaison psychiatry and psychosomatic medicine. *Journal of the American Medical Association, 247*, 3207–3209.

Linn, R. L. (1982). Admissions testing on trial. *American Psychologist, 37*, 279–291.

Lipman, J. J., Miller, B. E., Mays, K. S., & Miller, M. N. (1990). Peak B endorphin concentration in cerebrospinal fluid: Reduced in chronic pain patients and increased during the placebo response. *Psychopharmacology, 102*, 112–116.

Lisberger, S. G., Morris, E. J., & Tychsen, L. (1987). Visual motion processing and sensory-motor integration for smooth pursuit eye movements. *Annual Review of Neuroscience, 10*, 97–129.

Liuzzi, F. J., & Lasek, R. J. (1987). Astrocytes block axonal regeneration in mammals by activating the physiological stop pathway. *Science, 237*, 642–645.

Livingstone, M., & Hubel, D. (1988). Segregation of form, color, movement, and depth: Anatomy, physiology, and perception. *Science, 240*, 740–749.

Lloyd, J., & Barenblatt, L. (1984). Intrinsic intellectuality: Its relations to social class, intelligence, and achievement. *Journal of Personality and Social Psychology, 46*, 646–654.

Lloyd, M. A., & Appel, J. B. (1976). Signal detection theory and the psychophysics of pain: An introduction and review. *Psychosomatic Medicine, 38*, 79–94.

LoBello, S. G., & Gulgoz, S. (1991). Factor analysis of the Wechsler Preschool and Primary Scale of Intelligence—Revised. *Psychological Assessment, 3*, 130–132.

Lockart, R. S., & Craik, F. I. (1990). Levels of processing: A retrospective commentary on a framework for memory research. *Canadian Journal of Psychology, 44*, 87–112.

Locke, E. A., & Latham, G. P. (1985). The application of goal setting to sports. *Journal of Sport Psychology, 7*, 205–222.

Locke, J. (1690/1956). *An essay concerning human understanding.* New York: Oxford University Press.

Locke, J. (1690/1959). *An essay concerning human understanding.* New York: Dover.

Locurto, C. (1990). The malleability of IQ as judged from adoption studies. *Intelligence, 14*, 275–292.

Locurto, C. (1991). Beyond IQ in preschool programs? *Intelligence, 15*, 295–312.

Loeb, G. E. (1985, February). The functional replacement of the ear. *Scientific American*, pp. 104–111.

Loeber, R., & Dishion, T. (1983). Early predictors of male delinquency: A review. *Psychological Bulletin, 94*, 68–99.

Loehlin, J. C., Horn, J. M., & Willerman, L. (1989). Modeling IQ change: Evidence from the Texas Adoption Project. *Child Development, 60*, 993–1004.

Loehlin, J. C., Horn, J. M., & Willerman, L. (1990). Heredity, environment, and personality change: Evidence from the Texas Adoption Project. *Journal of Personality, 58*, 221–243.

Loftus, E. F. (1982). Memory and its distortions. In A. M. Rogers and C. J. Scheirer (Eds.), *The G. Stanley Hall Lecture Series* (Vol. 2, pp. 119–154). Washington, DC: American Psychological Association.

Loftus, E. F. (1993). The reality of repressed memories. *American Psychologist, 48*, 518–537.

Loftus, E. F., & Burns, T. E. (1982). Mental shock can produce retrograde amnesia. *Memory and Learning, 10*, 318–323.

Loftus, E. F., & Hoffman, H. G. (1989). Misinformation and memory: The creation of new memories. *Journal of Experimental Psychology: General, 118*, 100–104.

Loftus, E. F., & Palmer, J. C. (1974). Reconstruction of automobile destruction: An example of the interaction between language and memory. *Journal of Verbal Learning and Verbal Behavior, 13*, 585–589.

Loftus, G. R., Duncan, J., & Gehrig, P. (1992). On the time course of perceptual information that results from a brief visual presentation. *Journal of Experimental Psychology: Human Perception and Performance, 18*, 530–549.

Long, G. M., & Beaton, R. J. (1982). The case for peripheral persistence: Effects of target and background luminance on a partial-report task. *Journal of Experimental Psychology: Human Perception and Performance, 8*, 383–391.

Loomis, A. L., Harvey, E. N., & Hobart, G. A. (1937). Electrical potentials of the human brain. *Journal of Experimental Psychology, 21*, 127–144.

Loomis, M., & Saltz, E. (1984). Cognitive styles as predictors of artistic styles. *Journal of Personality, 52*, 22–35.

Lopes, L. L. (1981). Decision making in the short run. *Journal of Experimental Psychology: Human Learning and Memory, 7*, 377–385.

LoPiccolo, J., & Stock, W. E. (1986). Treatment of sexual dysfunction. *Journal of Consulting and Clinical Psychology, 54*, 158–167.

Lord, C. G. (1982). Predicting behavioral consistency from an individual's perception of situational similarities. *Journal of Personality and Social Psychology, 42*, 1076–1088.

Lorenz, K. Z. (1966). *On aggression.* New York: Harcourt Brace Jovanovich.

Lorig, T. S., Herman, K. B., Schwartz, G. E., & Cain, W. S. (1990). EEG activity during administration of low-concentration odors. *Bulletin of the Psychonomic Society, 28*, 405–408.

Loring, D. W., Meador, K. J., Lee, G. P., & King, D. W. (Eds.). (1991). *Amobarbitol effects and lateralized brain function: The Wada test.* New York: Springer-Verlag.

Loring, D. W., & Sheer, D. E. (1984). Laterality of 40 Hz EEG and EMG during cognitive performance. *Psychophysiology, 21*, 34–38.

Lovass, O. I. (1987). Behavioral treatment and normal educational and intellectual functioning in young autistic children. *Journal of Consulting and Clinical Psychology, 55*, 3–9.

Lovko, A. M., & Ullman, D. G. (1989). Research on the adjustment of latchkey children: Role of background/demographic and latchkey situation variables. *Journal of Clinical Child Psychology, 18*, 16–24.

Lowe, G. (1982). Alcohol-induced state-dependent learning: Differentiating stimulus and storage hypotheses. *Current Psychological Research, 2*, 215–222.

Lowery, C. R., & Settle, S. A. (1985). Effects of divorce on children: Differential impact of custody and visitation patterns. *Family Relations: Journal of Applied Family and Child Studies, 34*, 455–463.

Lu, Z. L., Williamson, S. J., & Kaufman, L. (1992). Behavioral lifetime of human auditory sensory memory predicted by physiological measures. *Science, 258*, 1668–1670.

Lubar, J. F. (1991). Discourse on the development of EEG diagnostics and biofeedback for attention-deficit/hyperactivity disorders. *Biofeedback and Self-Regulation, 16*, 201–225.

Luborsky, L., Chandler, M., Auerbach, A. H., Cohen, J., & Bachrach, H. M. (1971). Factors influencing the outcome of psychotherapy: A review of quantitative research. *Psychological Bulletin, 75*, 145–185.

Luchins, A. (1946). Classroom experiments on mental sets. *American Journal of Psychology, 59*, 295–298.

Luck, S. J., Hillyard, S. A., Mangun, G. R., & Gazzaniga, M. S. (1989). Independent hemispheric attentional systems mediate visual search in split-brain patients. *Nature, 342*, 543–545.

Ludwick-Rosenthal, R., & Neufeld, R. W. (1988). Stress management during noxious medical procedures: An evaluative review of outcome studies. *Psychological Bulletin, 104*, 326–342.

Lundstrom, B., Pauly, I. B., & Walinder, J. (1984). Outcome of sex reassignment surgery. *Acta Psychiatrica Scandinavica, 70*, 289–294.

Lunneborg, P. W. (1978). *Why study psychology?* Monterey, CA: Brooks/Cole.

Lydon, J. E., Jamieson, D., & Zanna, M. P. (1988). Interpersonal similarity and the social and intellectual dimensions of first impressions. *Social Cognition, 6*, 269–286.

Lykken, D. T. (1974). Psychology and the lie detector industry. *American Psychologist, 29*, 725–739.

Lykken, D. T. (1981). *A tremor in the blood: Uses and abuses of the lie detector.* New York: McGraw-Hill.

Lykken, D. T. (1982). Research with twins: The concept of emergenesis. *Psychophysiology, 19*, 361–373.

Lykken, D. T. (1988). Detection of guilty knowledge: A comment on Forman and McCauley. *Journal of Applied Psychology, 73*, 303–304.

Lykken, D. T., Bouchard, T. J., Jr., McGue, M., & Tellegen, A. (1993). Heritability of Interests: A twin study. *Journal of Applied Psychology, 78*, 649–661.

Lynn, M. (1988). The effects of alcohol consumption on restaurant tipping. *Personality and Social Psychology Bulletin, 14,* 87–91.

Lynn, R. (1982). IQ in Japan and the United States shows a growing disparity. *Nature, 297,* 222–223.

Lynn, R., & Wilson, R. G. (1990). Reaction times, movement times and intelligence among Irish nine-year-olds. *Irish Journal of Psychology, 11,* 329–341.

Lynn, S. J., & Rhue, J. W. (1988). Fantasy proneness: Hypnosis, developmental antecedents, and psychopathology. *American Psychologist, 43,* 35–44.

Lysle, D. T., Cunnick, J. E., & Maslonek, K. A. (1991). Pharmacological manipulation of immune alterations induced by an aversive conditioned stimulus: Evidence for a-adrenergic receptor-mediated Pavlovian conditioning process. *Behavioral Neuroscience, 105,* 443–449.

Lytton, H., & Romney, D. M. (1991). Parents' differential socialization of boys and girls: A meta-analysis. *Psychological Bulletin, 109,* 267–296.

Maass, A., & Clark, R. D. (1984). Hidden impact of minorities: Fifteen years of minority influence research. *Psychological Bulletin, 95,* 428–450.

Maccoby, E. E., & Jacklin, C. N. (1974). *The psychology of sex differences* (2 vols.). Stanford, CA: Stanford University Press.

MacCracken, M. J., & Stadulis, R. E. (1985). Social facilitation of young children's dynamic balance performance. *Journal of Sport Psychology, 7,* 150–165.

MacFarlane, J. G., Cleghorn, J. M., Brown, G. M., & Streiner, D. L. (1991). The effects of exogenous melatonin on the total sleep time and daytime alertness of chronic insomniacs: A preliminary study. *Biological Psychiatry, 30,* 371–376.

Mack, A., Heuer, F., Villardi, K., & Chambers, D. (1985). The dissociation of position and extent in Muller-Lyer figures. *Perception and Psychophysics, 37,* 335–344.

Mack, S. (1981). Novel help for the handicapped. *Science, 212,* 26–27.

Mackenzie, B. (1984). Explaining race differences in IQ: The logic, the methodology, and the evidence. *American Psychologist, 39,* 1214–1233.

MacLean, H. N. (1993). *Once upon a time: A true story of memory, murder, and the law.* New York: HarperCollins.

MacLeod, C. M. (1988). Forgotten but not gone: Savings for pictures and words in long-term memory. *Journal of Experimental Psychology: Learning, Memory, and Cognition, 14,* 195–212.

MacTurk, R. H., McCarthy, M. E., Vietze, P. M., & Yarrow, L. J. (1987). Sequential analysis of mastery behavior in 6- and 12-month-old infants. *Developmental Psychology, 23,* 199–203.

Madigan, M. W., & O'Hara, R. (1992). Short-term memory at the turn of the century: Mary Whiton Calkins's memory research. *American Psychologist, 47,* 170–174.

Madrazo, I., Drucker-Colin, R., Diaz, V., Martinez-Mata, J., Torres, C., & Becerril, J. J. (1987). Open microsurgical autograft of adrenal medulla to the right caudate nucleus in two patients with intractable Parkinson's disease. *New England Journal of Medicine, 316,* 831–834.

Maher, W. B., & Maher, B. A. (1985). Psychopathology: 1. From ancient times to the 18th century. In G. A. Kimble & K. Schlesinger (Eds.), *Topics in the history of psychology* (Vol. 2, pp. 251–294). Hillsdale, NJ: Erlbaum.

Mahowald, M. B. (1989). Neural fetal tissue transplantation: Should we do what we can do? *Neurologic Clinics, 7,* 745–757.

Maier, N. R. (1931). Reasoning in humans. *Journal of Comparative Psychology, 12,* 181–194.

Main, M., & George, C. (1985). Responses of abused and disadvantaged toddlers to distress in agemates: A study in the day-care setting. *Developmental Psychology, 21,* 407–412.

Malamuth, N. M. (1986). Predictors of naturalistic sexual aggression. *Journal of Personality and Social Psychology, 50,* 953–962.

Malamuth, N. M., Heim, M., & Feshbach, S. (1980). Sexual responsiveness of college students to rape depictions: Inhibitory and disinhibitory effects. *Journal of Personality and Social Psychology, 38,* 399–408.

Malinowski, C. I., & Smith, C. P. (1985). Moral reasoning and moral conduct: An investigation prompted by Kohlberg's theory. *Journal of Personality and Social Psychology, 49,* 1016–1027.

Mamberg, A. B., & Yaksh, T. L. (1992). Hyperalgesia mediated by spinal glutamate or substance P receptor blocked by spinal cyclooxygenase inhibition. *Science, 257,* 1276–1279.

Mandai, O., Guerrien, A., Sockeel, P., & Dujardin, K. (1989). REM sleep modifications following a Morse code learning session in humans. *Physiology and Behavior, 46,* 639–642.

Mandl, G. (1985). Responses of visual cells in cat superior colliculus to relative pattern movement. *Vision Research, 25,* 267–281.

Mangelsdorff, A. D. (1985). Lessons learned and forgotten: The need for prevention and mental health interventions in disaster preparedness. *Journal of Community Psychology, 13,* 239–257.

Manicas, P. T., & Secord, P. F. (1983). Implications for psychology of the new philosophy of science. *American Psychologist, 38,* 399–413.

Manning, B. H. (1990). A categorical analysis of children's self-talk during independent school assignments. *Journal of Instructional Psychology, 17,* 208–217.

Manning, C. A., Parsons, M. W., & Gold, P. E. (1992). Anterograde and retrograde enhancement of 24-hour memory by glucose in elderly humans. *Behavioral and Neural Biology, 58,* 125–130.

Mansfield, J. G. (1979). Dose-related effects of ethanol on avoidance-avoidance conflict behavior in the rat. *Psychopharmacology, 66,* 67–71.

Maragos, W. F., Greenamyre, J. T., Penney, J. B., & Young, A. B. (1987). Glutamate dysfunction in Alzheimer's disease: A hypothesis. *Trends in Neuroscience, 10,* 65–68.

Maranto, G. (1984, December). Aging: Can we slow the inevitable? *Discover,* pp. 17–21.

Marcus, G. F., Pinker, S., Ullman, M., Hollander, M., Rosen, T. J., & Ku, F. (1992). *Overregularization in language acquisition.* Chicago: University of Chicago Press.

Margiotta, E. W., Davilla, D. A., & Hicks, R. A. (1990). Type A-B behavior and the self-report of daily hassles and uplifts. *Perceptual and Motor Skills, 70,* 777–778.

Margolis, R. B., & Mynatt, C. R. (1986). The effects of external and self-administered reward on high base rate behavior. *Cognitive Therapy and Research, 10,* 109–122.

Marken, R. S., & Powers, W. T. (1989). Random-walk chemotaxis: Trial and error as a control process. *Behavioral Neuroscience, 103,* 1348–1355.

Marks, M. (1989). Behavioural psychotherapy for generalized anxiety disorder. *International Review of Psychiatry, 1,* 235–244.

Markus, E., Lange, A., & Pettigrew, T. F. (1990). Effectiveness of family therapy: A meta-analysis. *Journal of Family Therapy, 12,* 205–221.

Marsden, C. D. (1982). The mysterious motor function of the basal ganglia. *Neurology, 32,* 514–539.

Marshall, G. D., & Zimbardo, P. G. (1979). Affective consequences of inadequately explained physiological arousal. *Journal of Personality and Social Psychology, 37,* 970–988.

Marshall, J. C., & Halligan, P. W. (1988). Blindsight and insight in visuo-spatial neglect. *Nature, 336,* 766–767.

Marshall, M. E. (1969). Gustav Fechner, Dr. Mises, and the comparative anatomy of angels. *Journal of the History of the Behavioral Sciences, 5,* 39–58.

Martin, J. E., & Dubbert, P. M. (1985). Exercise in hypertension. *Annals of Behavioral Medicine, 7*(1), 13–18.

Martin, M. A. (1985). Students' applications of self-questioning study techniques: An investigation of their efficacy. *Reading Psychology, 6,* 69–83.

Martinot, J. L., Hardy, P., Feline, A., & Huret, J. D. (1990). Left prefrontal glucose hypometabolism in the depressed state: A confirmation. *American Journal of Psychiatry, 147,* 1313–1317.

Marx, J. L. (1980). Ape-language controversy flares up. *Science, 207,* 1330–1332.

Marx, J. L. (1982). Autoimmunity in left-handers. *Science, 217,* 141–144.

Marx, M. H., & Cronan-Hillix, W. A. (1987). *Systems and theories in psychology.* New York: McGraw-Hill.

Maser, J. D., Kaelber, C., & Weise, R. E. (1991). International use and attitudes toward DSM-III and DSM-III-R: Growing consensus in psychiatric classification. *Journal of Abnormal Psychology, 100,* 271–279.

Maslow, A. H. (1970). *Motivation and personality.* New York: Harper & Row.

Massaro, D. W. (1991). Psychology as a cognitive science. *Psychological Science, 2,* 302–307.

Masserano, J. M., Takimoto, G. S., & Weiner, N. (1981). Electroconvulsive shock increases tyrosine hydroxylase activity via the brain and adrenal gland of the rat. *Science, 214,* 662–665.

Masters, K. S. (1992). Hypnotic susceptibility, cognitive dissociation, and runner's high in a sample of marathon runners. *American Journal of Clinical Hypnosis, 34,* 193–201.

Masters, W. H., & Johnson, V. E. (1966). *Human sexual response.* Boston: Little, Brown.

Masters, W. H., & Johnson, V. E. (1970). *Human sexual inadequacy.* Boston: Little, Brown.

Matson, J. L., DiLorenzo, T. M., & Esveldt-Dawson, K. (1981). Independence training as a method of enhancing self-help skills acquisition of the mentally retarded. *Behaviour Research and Therapy, 19,* 399–405.

Matsumoto, D. (1987). The role of facial response in the experience of emotion: More methodological problems and a meta-analysis. *Journal of Personality and Social Psychology, 52,* 769–774.

Matsumoto, D. (1992). More evidence for the universality of a contempt expression. *Motivation and Emotion, 16,* 363–368.

Matt, G. E., Vazquez, C., & Campbell, W. K. (1992). Mood-congruent recall of affectively toned stimuli: A meta-analytic review. *Clinical Psychology Review, 12,* 227–255.

Matthews, K. A., & Woodall, K. L. (1988). Childhood origins of overt Type A behaviors and cardiovascular reactivity to behavioral stressors. *Annals of Behavioral Medicine, 10,* 71–77.

Matthews, T., Harper, C. J., Fuller, T., Nater, T., & Lubenow, C. G. (1978, December 4). The cult of death. *Newsweek,* pp. 38–53.

Mattick, R. P., Andrews, G., Hadzi-Pavlovic, D., & Christensen, H. (1990). Treatment of panic and agoraphobia: An integrative review. *Journal of Nervous and Mental Disease, 178,* 567–576.

Maugh, T. (1982a). The scent makes sense. *Science, 215,* 1224.

Maugh, T. (1982b). Sleep-promoting factor isolated. *Science, 216,* 1400.

Mauskopf, S., & McVaugh, M. (1981). Joseph Banks Rhine (1895–1980). *American Psychologist, 36,* 310–311.

Mautner, B. (1991). Freud's Irma dream: A psychoanalytic interpretation. *International Journal of Psycho-Analysis, 72,* 275–286.

May, R. (1982, Summer). The problem of evil: An open letter to Carl Rogers. *Journal of Humanistic Psychology,* pp. 10–21.

Mayberry, J. S., & Eichen, E. B. (1991). The long-lasting advantage of learning sign language in childhood: Another look at the critical period for language acquisition. *Journal of Memory and Language, 30,* 486–512.

Mayer, D. J. (1983). Biobehavioral modulation of pain transmission. *National Institute on Drug Abuse: Research Monograph Series, 45,* 46–69.

Mayer, S. J., & Russell, J. S. (1987). Behavior modeling training in organizations: Concerns and conclusions. *Journal of Management, 13,* 21–40.

McAdams, D. P., de St. Aubin, E., & Logan, R. L. (1993). Generativity among youth, midlife, and older adults. *Psychology and Aging, 8,* 221–230.

McAleney, P. J., Barabasz, A., & Barabasz, M. (1990). Effects of flotation restricted environmental stimulation on intercollegiate tennis performance. *Perceptual and Motor Skills, 71,* 1023–1028.

McAuley, E. (1985). Modeling and self-efficacy: A test of Bandura's model. *Journal of Sport Psychology, 7,* 283–295.

McAuley, E., Poag, K., Gleason, A., & Wraith, S. (1990). Attrition from exercise programs: Attributional and affective perspectives. *Journal of Social Behavior and Personality, 5,* 591–602.

McCaffrey, R. J., & Blanchard, E. B. (1985). Stress management approaches to the treatment of essential hypertension. *Annals of Behavioral Medicine, 7,* 5–12.

McCammon, S., Durham, T. W., Allison, E. J., & Williamson, J. E. (1988). Emergency workers' cognitive appraisal and coping with traumatic events. *Journal of Traumatic Stress, 1,* 353–372.

McCann, B. S., & Matthews, K. A. (1988). Influences of potential for hostility, Type A behavior, and parental history of hypertension on adolescents' cardiovascular responses during stress. *Psychophysiology, 25,* 503–511.

McCanne, T. R., & Anderson, J. A. (1987). Emotional responding following experimental manipulation of facial electromyographic activity. *Journal of Personality and Social Psychology, 52,* 759–768.

McCarthy, T. (1981). Freud and the problem of sexuality. *Journal of the History of the Behavioral Sciences, 17,* 332–339.

McCaul, K. D., & Malott, J. M. (1984). Distraction and coping with pain. *Psychological Bulletin, 95,* 516–533.

McCauley, C. (1989). The nature of social influence in groupthink: Compliance and internalization. *Journal of Personality and Social Psychology, 57,* 250–260.

McCauley, C., Durham, M., Copley, J. B., & Johnson, J. P. (1985). Patients' perceptions of treatment for kidney failure: The impact of personal experience on population predictions. *Journal of Experimental Social Psychology, 21,* 138–148.

McCauley, C., & Forman, R. F. (1988). A review of the Office of Technology Assessment report on polygraph validity. *Basic and Applied Social Psychology, 9,* 73–84.

McCauley, C., Woods, K., Coolidge, C., & Kulick, W. (1983). More aggressive cartoons are funnier. *Journal of Personality and Social Psychology, 44,* 817–823.

McClane, W. E., & Singer, D. D. (1991). The effective use of humor in organizational development. *Organization Development Journal, 9,* 67–72.

McClelland, D. C. (1985). How motives, skills, and values determine what people do. *American Psychologist, 40,* 812–825.

McCloskey, M., & Egeth, H. E. (1983). Eyewitness identification: What can a psychologist tell a jury? *American Psychologist, 38,* 550–563.

McCloskey, M., Wible, C. G., & Cohen, N. J. (1988). Is there a special flashbulb-memory mechanism? *Journal of Experimental Psychology: General, 117,* 171–181.

McConaghy, N., & Blaszcynski, A. (1991). Initial stages of validation by penile volume assessment that sexual orientation is distributed dimensionally. *Comprehensive Psychiatry, 32,* 52–58.

McConnell, J. V., Cutter, R. L., & McNeil, E. B. (1958). Subliminal stimulation: An overview. *American Psychologist, 13,* 229–242.

McConnell, J. V., Jacobson, A. L., & Kimble, D. P. (1959). The effects of regeneration upon retention of a conditioned response in the planarian. *Journal of Comparative and Physiological Psychology, 52,* 1–5.

McCormick, N. B., & Jones, A. J. (1989). Gender differences in flirtation. *Journal of Sex Education and Therapy, 15,* 271–282.

McCoy, R. W. (1985). Phrenology and popular gullibility. *Skeptical Inquirer, 9,* 261–268.

McCrae, R. R., & Costa, P. T. (1991). Adding Liebe and Arbeit: The full five-factor model and well-being. *Personality and Social Psychology Bulletin, 17,* 227–232.

McCrae, R. R., & John, O. P. (1992). An introduction to the five-factor model and its applications. *Journal of Personality, 60,* 175–215.

McCutcheon, J. W., Schmidt, C. P., & Bolden, S. H. (1991). Relationships among selected personality variables, academic achievement and student teaching behavior. *Journal of Research and Development in Education, 24,* 38–44.

McDougall, W. (1908). *Social psychology.* New York: G. Putnam & Sons.

McFadden, D., & Wightman, F. L. (1983). Audition: Some relations between normal and pathological hearing. *Annual Review of Psychology, 34,* 94–128.

McFarlane, A. C., & Brooks, P. M. (1990). Psychoimmunology and rheumatoid arthritis: Concepts and methodologies. *International Journal of Psychiatry in Medicine, 20,* 307–322.

McGee, R. A., & Wolfe, D. A. (1991). Psychological maltreatment: Toward an operational definition. *Development and Psychopathology, 3,* 3–18.

McGovern, P. G., & Lando, H. A. (1991). Reduced nicotine exposure and abstinence outcome in two nicotine fading methods. *Addictive Behaviors, 16,* 11–20.

McGrady, A., Turner, J. W., Fine, T. H., & Higgins, J. T. (1987). Effects of biobehaviorally assisted relaxation training on blood pressure, plasma renin, cortisol, and aldosterone levels in borderline essential hypertension. *Clinical Biofeedback and Health, 10,* 16–25.

McGrady, A., Woerner, M., Bernal, G. A. A., & Higgins, J. T., Jr. (1987). Effect of biofeedback-assisted relaxation on blood pressure and cortisol levels in normotensives and hypertensives. *Journal of Behavioral Medicine, 10,* 301–310.

McGreevy, M. A., Steadman, H. J., & Callahan, L. A. (1991). The negligible effects of California's 1982 reform of the insanity defense test. *American Journal of Psychiatry, 148,* 744–750.

McGue, M., Gottesman, I. I., & Rao, D. C. (1986). The analysis of schizophrenia family data. *Behavioral Genetics, 16,* 75–87.

McGuigan, F. J. (1970). Covert oral behavior during the silent performance of language tasks. *Psychological Bulletin, 74,* 309–326.

McGuinness, T. P. (1984). Hypnosis in the treatment of phobias: A review of the literature. *American Journal of Clinical Hypnosis, 26,* 261–272.

McGuire, B. (1990). Post-traumatic stress disorder: A review. *Irish Journal of Psychology, 11,* 1–23.

McGuire, T. M. (1982). Ancient Mayan mushroom connections: A transcendental interaction model. *Journal of Psychoactive Drugs, 14,* 221–238.

McIntosh, J. L. (1991). Middle-age suicide: A literature review and epidemiological study. *Death Studies, 15,* 21–37.

McKelvie, S. J. (1990). Student acceptance of a generalized personality description: Forer's graphologist revisited. *Journal of Social Behavior and Personality, 5,* 91–95.

McKinney, M., & Richelson, E. (1984). The coupling of the neuronal muscarinic receptor to responses. *Annual Review of Pharmacology and Toxicology, 24,* 121–146.

McMahon, M. (1992). Dangerousness, confidentiality, and the duty to protect. *Australian Psychologist, 27,* 12–16.

McMinn, M. R. (1984). Mechanisms of energy balance in obesity. *Behavioral Neuroscience, 98,* 375–393.

McNally, R. J. (1987). Preparedness and phobias: A review. *Psychological Bulletin, 101,* 283–303.

McNally, R. J. (1990). Psychological approaches to panic disorder: A review. *Psychological Bulletin, 108,* 403–419.

McNeal, E. T., & Cimbolic, P. (1986). Antidepressants and biochemical theories of depression. *Psychological Bulletin, 99,* 361–374.

McPherson, K. S. (1985). On intelligence testing and immigration legislation. *American Psychologist, 40,* 242–243.

McReynolds, P. (1989). Diagnosis and clinical assessment: Current status and major issues. *Annual Review of Psychology, 40,* 83–108.

McWilliams, R., Nietupski, J., & Hamre-Nietupski, S. (1990). Teaching complex activities to students with moderate handicaps through the forward chaining of shorter total cycle response sequences. *Education and Training in Mental Retardation, 25,* 292–298.

McWilliams, S. A., & Tuttle, R. J. (1973). Long-term psychological effects of LSD. *Psychological Bulletin, 79,* 341–351.

Medin, D. L. (1989). Concepts and conceptual structure. *American Psychologist, 44,* 1469–1481.

Mednick, S. A. (1962). The associative basis of the creative process. *Psychological Review, 69,* 220–232.

Mednick, S. A., Gabrielli, W. F., & Hutchings, B. (1984). Genetic influences in criminal convictions: Evidence from an adoption cohort. *Science, 224,* 891–894.

Meehl, P. E. (1956). Wanted: A good cookbook. *American Psychologist, 11,* 263–272.

Meeker, W. B., & Barber, T. X. (1971). Toward an explanation of stage hypnosis. *Journal of Abnormal Psychology, 77,* 61–70.

Meichenbaum, D. (1985). *Stress-inoculation training.* New York: Pergamon Press.

Meichenbaum, D. H., Bowers, K. S., & Ross, R. R. (1969). A behavioral analysis of teacher expectancy effect. *Journal of Personality & Social Psychology, 13,* 306–316.

Melanoma risk and socio-economic class. (1983). *Science News, 124,* 232.

Melton, G. B., & Grey, J. N. (1988). Ethical dilemmas in AIDS research: Individual privacy and public health. *American Psychologist, 43,* 60–64.

Melzack, R., & Wall, P. D. (1965). Pain mechanisms: A new theory. *Science, 150,* 971–979.

Memory transfer. (1966). *Science, 153,* 658–659.

Mendelson, W. B., Maczaj, M., & Holt, J. (1991). Buspirone administration to sleep apnea patients. *Journal of Clinical Psychopharmacology, 11,* 71–72.

Merewether, F. C., & Alpert, M. (1990). The components and neuroanatomical bases of prosody. *Journal of Communication Disorders, 23,* 325–336.

Merikle, P. M. (1992). Perception without awareness: Critical issues. *American Psychologist, 47,* 792–795.

Mersch, P. P., Emmelkamp, P. M., & Lips, C. (1991). Social phobia: Individual response patterns and the long-term effects of behavioral and cognitive interventions. A follow-up study. *Behaviour Research and Therapy, 29,* 357–362.

Mervis, J. (1984, March). Council ends forums trial, opens way for new divisions. *APA Monitor,* pp. 10–11.

Mervis, J. (1986, July). NIMH data point way to effective treatment. *APA Monitor,* pp. 1, 13.

Messer, S. C., Wuensch, K. L., & Diamond, J. M. (1989). Former latchkey children: Personality and academic correlates. *Journal of Genetic Psychology, 150,* 301–309.

Messer, W. S., & Griggs, R. A. (1989). Student belief and involvement in the paranormal and performance in introductory psychology. *Teaching of Psychology, 16,* 187–191.

Messick, S., & Jungeblut, A. (1981). Time and method in coaching for the SAT. *Psychological Bulletin, 89,* 191–196.

Messier, C., Durkin, T., Mrabet, O., & Destrade, C. (1990). Memory-improving action of glucose: Indirect evidence for a facilitation of hippocampal acetylcholine synthesis. *Behavioural Brain Research, 39,* 135–143.

Metcalfe, J., & Wiebe, D. (1987). Intuition in insight and noninsight problem solving. *Memory and Cognition, 15,* 238–246.

Mewaldt, S. P., Ghoneim, M. M., Choi, W. W., & Korttila, K. (1988). Nitrous oxide and human state-dependent memory. *Pharmacology, Biochemistry, and Behavior, 30,* 83–87.

Meyer, D. R., Gurklis, J. A., & Cloud, M. D. (1985). An equipotential function of the cerebral cortex. *Physiological Psychology, 13,* 48–50.

Meyer-Bahlburg, H. F. (1990–1991). Will prenatal hormone treatment prevent homosexuality? *Journal of Child and Adolescent Psychopharmacology, 1,* 279–283.

Michaels, R. R., Huber, M. J., & McCann, D. S. (1976). Evaluation of transcendental meditation as a method of reducing stress. *Science, 192,* 1242–1244.

Miczek, K. A., Thompson, M. L., & Shuster, L. (1982). Opioid-like analgesia in defeated mice. *Science, 215,* 1520–1523.

Middlebrooks, J. C., & Green, D. M. (1991). Sound localization by human listeners. *Annual Review of Psychology, 42,* 135–159.

Mikulincer, M., & Peer-Goldin, I. (1991). Self-congruence and the experience of happiness. *British Journal of Social Psychology, 30,* 21–35.

Milan, R. J., Kilmann, P. R., & Boland, J. P. (1988). Treatment outcome of secondary orgasmic dysfunction: A two- to six-year follow-up. *Archives of Sexual Behavior, 17,* 463–480.

Milgram, S. (1963). Behavioral study of obedience. *Journal of Abnormal and Social Psychology, 67,* 371–378.

Milgram, S. (1964). Issues in the study of obedience: A reply to Baumrind. *American Psychologist, 19,* 848–852.

Milgram, S. (1974). *Obedience to authority.* New York: Harper & Row.

Miller, B., & Marshall, J. C. (1987). Coercive sex on the university campus. *Journal of College Student Personnel, 28,* 38–47.

Miller, G. A. (1956). The magical number seven, plus or minus two: Some limits on our capacity for processing information. *Psychological Review, 63,* 81–97.

Miller, G. A. (1990). The place of language in a scientific psychology. *Psychological Science, 1,* 7–14.

Miller, H. L., Chaplin, W. F., & Coombs, D. W. (1990). Cause and correlation: One more time. *Psychological Reports, 66,* 1293–1294.

Miller, I. J., & Reedy, F. E. (1990). Variations in human taste bud density and taste intensity perception. *Physiology and Behavior, 47,* 1213–1219.

Miller, J. (1983). Three constructions of transference in Freud, 1895–1915. *Journal of the History of the Behavioral Sciences, 19,* 153–172.

Miller, J. A. (1984). Sexual ambiguity: Getting down to the gene. *Science News, 125,* 230.

Miller, L. L., & Branconnier, R. J. (1983). Cannabis: Effects on memory and the cholinergic limbic system. *Psychological Bulletin, 93,* 441–456.

Miller, M. G. (1984). Oral somatosensory factors in dietary self-selection in rats. *Behavioral Neuroscience, 98,* 416–423.

Miller, N. E. (1985). The value of behavioral research on animals. *American Psychologist, 40,* 423–440.

Miller, N. S., & Gold, M. S. (1990). Organic solvents and aerosols: An overview of abuse and dependence. *Annals of Clinical Psychiatry, 2,* 85–92.

Miller, P. C., Lefcourt, H. M., Holmes, J. G., Ware, E. E., & Saleh, W. E. (1986). Marital locus of control and marital problem solving. *Journal of Personality and Social Psychology, 51,* 161–169.

Miller, R. J., Pigion, R. G., & Martin, K. D. (1985). The effects of ingested alcohol on accommodation. *Perception and Psychophysics, 37,* 407–414.

Miller, T. Q., Turner, C. W., Tindale, R. S., Posavac, E. J., & Dugoni, B. L. (1991). Reasons for the trend toward null findings in research on Type A behavior. *Psychological Bulletin, 110,* 469–485.

Miller-Jones, D. (1989). Culture and testing. *American Psychologist, 44,* 360–366.

Mineka, S., & Cook, M. (1993). Mechanisms involved in the observational conditioning of fear. *Journal of Experimental Psychology General, 122,* 23–38.

Minuchin, S. (1974). *Families and family therapy.* Cambridge, MA: Harvard University Press.

Mio, J. S., & Graesser, A. C. (1991). Humor, language, and metaphor. *Metaphor and Symbolic Activity, 6,* 87–102.

Mischel, W. (1968). *Personality and assessment.* New York: Wiley.

Mischel, W., & Peake, P. J. (1982). Beyond deja vu in the search for cross-situational consistency. *Psychological Review, 89,* 730–755.

Miserandino, M. (1991). Memory and the seven dwarfs. *Teaching of Psychology, 18,* 169–171.

Mita, T. H., Dermer, M., & Knight, J. (1977). Reversed facial images and the mere-exposure hypothesis. *Journal of Personality and Social Psychology, 35,* 597–601.

Mitchell, C., & Stuart, R. B. (1984). Effect of self-efficacy on dropout from obesity treatment. *Journal of Consulting and Clinical Psychology, 52,* 1100–1101.

Mitchell, J. E., & Eckert, E. D. (1987). Scope and significance of eating disorders. *Journal of Consulting and Clinical Psychology, 55,* 628–634.

Mitchell, J. E., Laine, D. E., Morley, J. E., & Levine, A. S. (1986). Naloxone but not CCK-8 may attenuate binge-eating behavior in patients with bulimia syndrome. *Biological Psychiatry, 21,* 1399–1406.

Mitchell, P., Waters, B., Morrison, N., & Shine, J. (1991). Close linkage of bipolar disorder to chromosome 11 markers is excluded in two large Australian pedigrees. *Journal of Affective Disorders, 21,* 23–32.

Mitler, M. M., Hajdukovic, R., & Erman, M. K. (1993). Treatment of narcolepsy with methamphetamine. *Sleep, 16,* 306–317.

Miyazaki, K. (1990). The speed of musical pitch identification by absolute-pitch possessors. *Music Perception, 8,* 177–188.

Mogul, K. M. (1982). Overview: The sex of the therapist. *American Journal of Psychiatry, 139,* 1–11.

Mollon, J. D. (1982). Color vision. *Annual Review of Psychology, 33,* 41–85.

Monahan, J. (1993). Limiting therapist exposure to Tarasoff liability: Guidelines for risk containment. *American Psychologist, 48,* 242–250.

Money, J. (1986). *Venuses penuses: Sexology, sexosophy, and exigency theory.* Buffalo, NY: Prometheus.

Money, J. (1987). Sin, sickness, or status? Homosexual gender identity and psychoneuroendocrinology. *American Psychologist, 42,* 384–399.

Mongeau, P. A., & Garlick, R. (1988). Social comparison and persuasive arguments as determinants of group polarization. *Communication Research Reports, 5,* 120–125.

Monroe, S. M. (1982). Life events and disorder: Event-symptom associations and the course of disorder. *Journal of Abnormal Psychology, 91,* 14–24.

Monroe, S. M., & Simons, A. D. (1991). Diathesis-stress theories in the context of life stress research: Implications for the depressive disorders. *Psychological Bulletin, 110,* 406–425.

Monson, T. C., Hesley, J. W., & Chernick, L. (1982). Specifying when personality traits can and cannot predict behavior: An alternative to abandoning the attempt to predict single-act criteria. *Journal of Personality and Social Psychology, 43,* 385–399.

Montag, I., & Comrey, A. L. (1987). Internality and externality as correlates of involvement in fatal driving accidents. *Journal of Applied Psychology, 72,* 339–343.

Monte, C. F. (1980). *Beneath the mask: An introduction to theories of personality.* New York: Holt, Rinehart & Winston.

Montgomery, R. W. (1993). The ancient origins of cognitive therapy: The reemergence of stoicism. *Journal of Cognitive Psychotherapy, 7,* 5–19.

Monti, P. M., Curran, J. P., Corriveau, D. P., DeLancey, A. L., & Hagerman, S. M. (1980). Effects of social skills training groups and sensitivity training groups with psychiatric patients. *Journal of Consulting and Clinical Psychology, 48,* 241–248.

Montour, K. (1977). William James Sidis: The broken twig. *American Psychologist, 32,* 265–279.

Montplaisir, J., Bedard, M. A., Richer, F., & Rouleau, I. (1992). Neurobehavioral manifestations in obstructive sleep apnea syndrome before and after treatment with continuous positive airway pressure. *Sleep, 15,* S17–S19.

Moore, M. (1984). Sex and acknowledgments: A nonreactive study. *Sex Roles, 10,* 1021–1031.

Moorhead, G., Ference, R., & Neck, C. P. (1991). Group decision fiascoes continue: Space shuttle Challenger and a revised groupthink framework. *Human Relations, 44,* 539–550.

Moran, M. G. (1991). Psychological factors affecting pulmonary and rheumatologic diseases: A review. *Psychosomatics, 32,* 14–23.

Morawski, J. G. (1982). Assessing psychology's moral heritage through our neglected utopias. *American Psychologist, 37,* 1082–1095.

Moray, N. (1959). Attention in dichotic listening: Affective cues and the influence of instructions. *Quarterly Journal of Experimental Psychology, 11,* 56–60.

Mordkoff, J. T., Yantis, S., & Egeth, H. E. (1990). Detecting conjunctions of color and form in parallel. *Perception and Psychophysics, 48,* 157–168.

Moreland, R. L., & Zajonc, R. B. (1982). Exposure effects in person perception: Familiarity, similarity, and attraction. *Journal of Experimental Social Psychology, 18,* 395–415.

Moretti, M. M., & Higgins, E. T. (1990). Relating self-discrepancy to self-esteem: The contribution of discrepancy beyond actual-self ratings. *Journal of Experimental Social Psychology, 26,* 108–123.

Morey, L. C. (1988). Personality disorders in DSM-III and DSM-III-R: Convergence, coverage, and internal consistency. *American Journal of Psychiatry, 145,* 573–577.

Morgan, C., & Murray, H. A. (1935). A method of investigating fantasies. *Archives of Neurology and Psychiatry, 4,* 310–329.

Morley, J. E., & Levine, A. S. (1980). Stress-induced eating is mediated through endogenous opiates. *Science, 209,* 1259–1261.

Moroff, S. V. (1986). Qualitative and ethical issues in quantitative clinical decision making. *New York Journal of Medicine, 86,* 250–253.

Morris, S. (1980, April). Interview: James Randi. *Omni,* pp. 76–78, 104, 106, 108.

Morris, W., & Morris, M. (1985). *Harper dictionary of contemporary usage.* New York: Harper & Row.

Morrison, A. R. (1983, April). A window on the sleeping brain. *Scientific American,* pp. 94–102.

Morrongiello, B. A., Fenwick, K. D., & Chance, G. (1990). "Sound localization acuity in very young infants: An observer-based testing procedure": Correction. *Developmental Psychology, 26,* 1003.

Mortimer, R. G., & Fell, J. C. (1989). Older drivers: Their night fatal crash involvement and risk. *Accident Analysis and Prevention, 21,* 273–282.

Moruzzi, G., & Magoun, H. W. (1949). Brain stem reticular formation and activation of the EEG. *Electroencephalography and Clinical Neurophysiology, 1,* 455–473.

Moses, L. N. (1989). The Zelig Syndrome. *Issues in Ego Psychology, 12,* 117–126.

Moskowitz, D. S., & Schwarz, J. C. (1982). Validity comparison of behavior counts and ratings by knowledgeable informants. *Journal of Personality and Social Psychology, 42,* 518–528.

Moskowitz, H. (1985). Marihuana and driving. *Accident Analysis and Prevention, 17,* 323–345.

Moskowitz, J. M., Malvin, J. H., Schaeffer, G. A., & Schaps, E. (1985). Evaluation of jigsaw, a cooperative learning technique. *Contemporary Educational Psychology, 10,* 104–112.

Moskowitz, M. J. (1977). Hugo Münsterberg: A study in the history of applied psychology. *American Psychologist, 32,* 824–842.

Mowrer, O. H. (1947). On the dual nature of learning—A reinterpretation of "conditioning" and "problem solving." *Harvard Educational Review, 17,* 102–148.

Mowrer, O. H., & Mowrer, W. M. (1938). Enuresis: A method for its study and treatment. *American Journal of Orthopsychiatry, 8,* 436–559.

Mudd, S., Conway, C. G., & Schindler, D. E. (1990). The eye as music critic: Pupil response and verbal preferences. *Studia Psychologica, 32,* 23–30.

Muehlenhard, C. L., & Cook, S. W. (1988). Men's self-reports of unwanted sexual activity. *Journal of Sex Research, 24,* 58–72.

Mueller, C. G. (1979). Some origins of psychology as a science. *Annual Review of Psychology, 30,* 9–29.

Mullen, B., Futrell, D., Stairs, D., Tice, D. M., Baumeister, R. F., Dawson, K. E., Radloff, C. E., Goethals, G. R., Kennedy, J. G., & Rosenfeld, P. (1986). Newscasters' facial expressions and voting behavior of viewers: Can a smile elect a president? *Journal of Personality and Social Psychology, 51,* 291–295.

Mullington, J., & Broughton, R. (1993). Scheduled naps in the management of daytime sleepiness in narcolepsy-cataplexy. *Sleep, 16,* 444–456.

Mullins, L. L., & Olson, R. A. (1990). Familial factors in the etiology, maintenance, and treatment of somatoform disorders in children. *Family Systems Medicine, 8,* 159–175.

Mumford, M. D., & Gustafson, S. B. (1988). Creativity syndrome: Integration, application, and innovation. *Psychological Bulletin, 103,* 27–43.

Munley, P. H., & Zarantonello, M. M. (1990). A comparison of MMPI profile types with corresponding estimated MMPI–2 profiles. *Journal of Clinical Psychology, 46,* 803–811.

Münsterberg, H. (1908). *On the witness stand.* New York: Doubleday.

Murphy, G. L., & Medin, D. L. (1985). The role of theories in conceptual coherence. *Psychological Review, 92,* 289–316.

Murphy, S. T., & Zajonc, R. B. (1993). Affect, cognition, and awareness: Affective priming with optimal and suboptimal stimulus exposures. *Journal of Personality and Social Psychology, 64,* 723–739.

Murray, D. J. (1976). Research on human memory in the 19th century. *Canadian Journal of Psychology, 30,* 201–220.

Murray, D. J. (1990). Fechner's later psychophysics. *Canadian Psychology, 31,* 54–60.

Murray, H. A. (1938). *Explorations in personality.* New York: Oxford University Press.

Murray, J. B. (1990). Review of research on the Myers-Briggs Type Indicator. *Perceptual and Motor Skills, 70,* 1187–1202.

Murstein, B. (1972). Physical attractiveness and marital choice. *Journal of Personality and Social Psychology, 22,* 8–12.

Musick, P. L. (1976). Primitive percepts and collective creativity. *Art Psychotherapy, 3,* 43–50.

Mustillo, P. (1985). Binocular mechanisms mediating crossed and uncrossed stereopsis. *Psychological Bulletin, 97,* 187–201.

Mwamwenda, T. S. (1993). Formal operations and academic achievement. *Journal of Psychology, 127,* 99–103.

Myers, D. G., & Bishop, G. D. (1970). Discussion effects on racial attitudes. *Science, 169,* 778–779.

Myerscough, R., & Taylor, S. (1985). The effects of marijuana on human physical aggression. *Journal of Personality and Social Psychology, 49,* 1541–1546.

Nahai, F., & Brown, D. M. (1983). Further applications of electromyographic muscle reeducation. In J. V. Basmajian (Ed.), *Biofeedback: Principles and practice for clinicians* (pp. 107–110). Baltimore: Williams & Wilkins.

Nahemow, L., & Lawton, M. P. (1975). Similarity and propinquity in friendship formation. *Journal of Personality and Social Psychology, 32,* 205–213.

Narens, L., & Mausfeld, R. (1992). On the relationship of the psychological and the physical in psychophysics. *Psychological Review, 99,* 467–479.

NAS calls tests fair but limited. (1982, April). *APA Monitor,* p. 2.

Nash, M. (1987). What, if anything, is regressed about hypnotic age regression? A review of the empirical literature. *Psychological Bulletin, 102,* 42–52.

Navon, D. (1974). Forest before trees: The precedence of global features in visual perception. *Cognitive Psychology, 9,* 353–383.

Neimeyer, G. J. (1984). Cognitive complexity and marital satisfaction. *Journal of Social and Clinical Psychology, 2,* 258–263.

Neimeyer, G. J. (1989). Applications of repertory grid technique to vocational assessment. *Journal of Counseling and Development, 67,* 585–589.

Neimeyer, G. J., & Fukuyama, M. (1984). Exploring the content and structure of cross-cultural attitudes. *Counselor Education and Supervision, 23,* 214–224.

Neimeyer, G. J., & Merluzzi, T. V. (1982). Group structure and group process: Personal construct theory and group development. *Small Group Behavior, 13,* 150–164.

Neimeyer, R. A. (1983). Toward a personal construct conceptualization of depression and suicide. *Death Education, 7,* 127–173.

Neimeyer, R. A., & Mitchell, K. A. (1988). Similarity and attraction: A longitudinal study. *Journal of Social and Personal Relationships, 5,* 131–148.

Neisser, U. (1981). John Dean's memory: A case study. *Cognition, 9,* 1–22.

Neisser, U. (1984). Interpreting Harry Bahrick's discovery: What confers immunity against forgetting? *Journal of Experimental Psychology: General, 113,* 32–35.

Neisser, U., & Becklen, R. (1975). Selective looking: Attending to visually specified events. *Cognitive Psychology, 7,* 480–494.

Nelson, K. E. (1977). Facilitating children's syntax acquisition. *Developmental Psychology, 18,* 101–107.

Nelson, M. O. (1991). Another look at masculine protest. *Individual Psychology: Journal of Adlerian Theory, Research, and Practice, 47,* 490–497.

Nelson, T. O., Leonesio, R. J., Shimamura, A. P., Landwehr, R. F., & Narens, L. (1982). Overlearning and the feeling of knowing. *Journal of Experimental Psychology: Learning, Memory, and Cognition, 8,* 279–288.

Nemeth, C. J. (1986). Differential contributions of majority and minority influence. *Psychological Review, 93,* 23–32.

Nenty, H. J. (1986). Cross-culture bias analysis of Cattell Culture-Fair Intelligence Test. *Perspectives in Psychological Researches, 9,* 1–16.

Nevo, B. (1989). Validation of graphology through use of a matching method based on ranking. *Perceptual and Motor Skills, 69,* 1331–1336.

Nevo, O. (1985). Does one ever really laugh at one's own expense? *Journal of Personality and Social Psychology, 49,* 799–807.

Nevo, O., & Nevo, B. (1983). What do you do when asked to answer humorously? *Journal of Personality and Social Psychology, 44,* 188–194.

Newcomb, M. D., & Bentler, P. M. (1989). Substance use and abuse among children and teenagers. *American Psychologist, 44,* 242–248.

Newcomb, M. D., & Harlow, L. L. (1986). Life events and substance use among adolescents: Mediating effects of perceived loss of control and meaningfulness in life. *Journal of Personality and Social Psychology, 51,* 564–577.

Newcomer, S. F., & Udry, J. R. (1985). Oral sex in an adolescent population. *Archives of Sexual Behavior, 14,* 41–46.

Newell, A., & Simon, H. (1972). *Human problem solving.* Englewood Cliffs, NJ: Prentice Hall.

Newman, E. A., & Hartline, P. H. (1982, March). The infrared "vision" of snakes. *Scientific American,* pp. 116–124, 127.

Newman, J., & Layton, B. D. (1984). Overjustification: A self-perception perspective. *Personality and Social Psychology Bulletin, 10,* 419–425.

Nezu, A. M., Nezu, C. M., & Blissett, S. E. (1988). Sense of humor as a moderator of the relation between stressful events and psychological distress: A prospective analysis. *Journal of Personality and Social Psychology, 54,* 520–525.

Nicholls, J. G. (1972). Creativity in the person who will never produce anything original or useful: The concept of creativity as a normally distributed trait. *American Psychologist, 27,* 717–727.

Nicholls, J. G. (1984). Achievement motivation: Conceptions of ability, subjective experience, task choice, and performance. *Psychological Review, 91,* 328–346.

Nichols, M. P., & Efran, J. S. (1985). Catharsis in psychotherapy: A new perspective. *Psychotherapy, 22,* 46–58.

Nicholson, N., Cole, S. G., & Rocklin, T. (1985). Conformity in the Asch situation: A comparison between contemporary British and U.S. university students. *British Journal of Social Psychology, 24,* 59–63.

Nickerson, R. S., & Adams, M. J. (1979). Long-term memory for a common object. *Cognitive Psychology, 11,* 287–307.

Nicki, R. M., Remington, R. E., & MacDonald, G. A. (1984). Self-efficacy, nicotine-fading/self-monitoring and cigarette-smoking behaviour. *Behaviour Research and Therapy, 22,* 477–485.

Nicol, S. E., & Gottesman, I. I. (1983). Clues to the genetics and neurobiology of schizophrenia. *American Scientist, 71,* 398–404.

Nicoll, R. A., & Madison, D. V. (1982). General anesthetics hyperpolarize neurons in the vertebrate nervous system. *Science, 217,* 1055–1057.

Niedenthal, P. M. (1990). Implicit perception of affective information. *Journal of Experimental Social Psychology, 26,* 505–527.

Nielsen, T. A. (1993). Changes in the kinesthetic content of dreams following somatosensory stimulation of leg muscles during REM sleep. *Dreaming: Journal of the Association for the Study of Dreams, 3,* 99–113.

Niemiec, R., & Walberg, H. J. (1987). Comparative effects of computer-assisted instruction: A synthesis of reviews. *Journal of Educational Computing Research, 3,* 19–37.

Niles, L. P., & Peace, C. H. (1990). Allosteric modulation of t-(-sup-3-sup-5S) butylbicyclophosphorothionate binding in rat brain by melatonin. *Brain Research Bulletin, 24,* 635–638.

Nisbett, R. E., & Ross, L. (1980). *Human inference: Strategies and shortcomings of social judgment.* Englewood Cliffs, NJ: Prentice Hall.

Nissen, M. J., Knopman, D. S., & Schachter, D. L. (1987). Neurochemical dissociation of memory systems. *Neurology, 37,* 789–794.

Noel, P. S., & Carlson, E. T. (1970). Origins of the word "phrenology." *American Journal of Psychiatry, 127,* 694–697.

Nolen-Hoeksema, S., Girgus, J. S., & Seligman, M. E. (1992). Predictors and consequences of childhood depressive symptoms: A 5-year longitudinal study. *Journal of Abnormal Psychology, 101,* 405–422.

Nonneman, A. J., & Corwin, J. V. (1981). Differential effects of prefrontal cortex ablation in neonatal, juvenile, and young adult rats. *Journal of Comparative and Physiological Psychology, 95,* 588–602.

Norcross, J. C., Strausser, D. J., & Faltus, F. J. (1988). The therapist's therapist. *American Journal of Psychotherapy, 42,* 53–66.

Nordstrom, R., Lorenzi, P., & Hall, R. V. (1990). A review of public posting of performance feedback in work settings. *Journal of Organizational Behavior Management, 11,* 101–123.

Norris, N. P. (1978). Fragile subjects. *American Psychologist, 33,* 962–963.

Norton, E. M., Durlak, J. A., & Richards, M. H. (1989). Peer knowledge of and reactions to adolescent suicide. *Journal of Youth and Adolescence, 18,* 427–437.

Nosofsky, R. M. (1991). Relation between the rational model and the context model of categorization. *Psychological Science, 2,* 416–421.

Notz, W. W. (1975). Work motivation and the negative effects of extrinsic rewards: A review with implications for theory and practice. *American Psychologist, 30,* 884–891.

Nowicki, S., & Duke, M. P. (1992). The association of children's nonverbal decoding abilities with their popularity, locus of control, and academic achievement. *Journal of Genetic Psychology, 153,* 385–393.

Ochse, R., & Van Lill, B. (1990). A critical appraisal of the theoretical validity of the Mednick remote association test. *South African Journal of Psychology, 20,* 195–199.

O'Connell, A. N., & Russo, N. F. (Eds.). (1990). *Women in psychology: A bio-bibliographic sourcebook.* New York: Greenwood.

O'Connor, K. P. (1981). The intentional paradigm and cognitive psychophysiology. *Psychophysiology, 18,* 121–128.

O'Connor, N., & Hermelin, B. (1992). Do young calendrical calculators improve with age? *Journal of Child Psychology and Psychiatry and Allied Disciplines, 33,* 907–912.

Oden, G. C. (1984). Dependence, independence, and emergence of word features. *Journal of Experimental Psychology: Human Perception and Performance, 10,* 394–405.

Oden, M. H. (1968). The fulfillment of promise: 40-year followup of the Terman gifted group. *Genetic Psychology Monographs, 77,* 3–93.

Offer, D., & Sabshin, M. (Eds.). (1984). *Normality and the life cycle.* New York: Basic Books.

Ogden, J. A. (1989). Visuospatial and other "right-hemispheric" functions after long recovery periods in left-hemispherectomized subjects. *Neuropsychologia, 27,* 765–776.

Ogilvie, R. D., McDonagh, D. M., Stone, S. N., & Wilkinson, R. T. (1988). Eye movements and the detection of sleep onset. *Psychophysiology, 25,* 81–91.

Ogloff, J. R., & Wong, S. (1990). Electrodermal and cardiovascular evidence of a coping response in psychopaths. *Criminal Justice and Behavior, 17,* 231–245.

Ohman, A., Erixon, G., & Lofberg, I. (1975). Phobias and preparedness: Phobic versus neutral pictures as conditioned stimuli for human autonomic responses. *Journal of Abnormal Psychology, 84,* 41–45.

Okagaki, L., & Sternberg, R. J. (1993). Parental beliefs and children's school performance. *Child Development, 64,* 36–56.

Okwumabua, T. M. (1985). Psychological and physical contributions to marathon performance: An exploratory investigation. *Journal of Sport Behavior, 8,* 163–171.

Olds, J. (1956, October). Pleasure centers in the brain. *Scientific American,* pp. 105–116.

Olds, J., & Milner, P. (1954). Positive reinforcement produced by electrical stimulations of septal area and other regions of rat brain. *Journal of Comparative and Physiological Psychology, 47,* 419–427.

O'Leary, A. (1985). Self-efficacy and health. *Behaviour Research and Therapy, 23,* 437–451.

O'Leary, A. (1990). Stress, emotion, and human immune function. *Psychological Bulletin, 108,* 363–382.

O'Leary, K. D., & Smith, D. A. (1991). Marital interactions. *Annual Review of Psychology, 42,* 191–212.

Oller, D. K., & Eilers, R. E. (1988). The role of audition in infant babbling. *Child Development, 59,* 441–449.

Olmo, R. J., & Stevens, G. L. (1984, August). Chess champs: Introverts at play. *Psychology Today,* pp. 72, 74.

Olson, R. P., Ganley, R., Devine, V. T., & Dorsey, G. C., Jr. (1981). Long-term effects of behavioral versus insight-oriented therapy with inpatient alcoholics. *Journal of Consulting and Clinical Psychology, 49,* 866–877.

O'Neill, M., & Kempler, B. (1969). Approach and avoidance responses of the hysterical personality to sexual stimuli. *Journal of Abnormal Psychology, 74,* 300–305.

Onstad, S., Skre, I., Torgersen, S., & Kringlen, E. (1991). Twin concordance for DSM-III-R schizophrenia. *Acta Psychiatrica Scandinavica, 83,* 395–401.

Oosterveld, W. J. (1987). The combined effect of Cinnarizine and domperidone on vestibular susceptibility. *Aviation, Space, and Environmental Medicine, 58,* 218–223.

Oppliger, P. A., & Sherblom, J. C. (1992). Humor: Incongruity, disparagement, and David Letterman. *Communication Research Reports, 9,* 99–108.

Orne, M. T. (1951). The mechanisms of hypnotic age regression: An experimental study. *Journal of Abnormal and Social Psychology, 46,* 213–225.

Orne, M. T., Dinges, D. F., & Orne, E. C. (1984). On the differential diagnosis of multiple personality in the forensic context. *International Journal of Clinical and Experimental Hypnosis, 32,* 118–169.

Orne, M. T., & Evans, F. J. (1965). Social control in the psychological experiment: Antisocial behavior and hypnosis. *Journal of Personality and Social Psychology, 1,* 189–200.

Orwell, G. (1949). *1984.* New York: Harcourt Brace Jovanovich.

Ost, L. G. (1985). Ways of acquiring phobias and outcome of behavioral treatments. *Behaviour Research and Therapy, 23,* 683–689.

Paddock, J. R., & Nowicki, S. (1986). Paralanguage and the interpersonal impact of dysphoria: It's not what you say but how you say it. *Social Behavior and Personality, 14,* 29–44.

Page, R. C., Richmond, B. O., & de la Serna, M. (1987). Marathon group counseling with illicit drug abusers: Effects on self-perceptions. *Small Group Behavior, 18,* 483–497.

Page, S. (1990). The turnaround on pornography research: Some implications for psychology and women. *Canadian Psychology, 31,* 359–367.

Paikoff, R. L., and Brooks-Gunn, J. (1991). Do parent-child relationships change during puberty? *Psychological Bulletin, 110,* 47–66.

Parham, K., & Willott, J. F. (1990). Effects of inferior colliculus lesions on the acoustic startle response. *Behavioral Neuroscience, 104,* 831–840.

Parisi, T. (1987). Why Freud failed: Some implications for neurophysiology and sociobiology. *American Psychologist, 42,* 235–245.

Park, B., & Rothbart, M. (1982). Perception of out-group homogeneity and levels of social categorization: Memory for the subordinate attributes of in-group and out-group members. *Journal of Personality and Social Psychology, 42,* 1051–1068.

Park, D. C., Smith, A. D., & Cavanaugh, J. C. (1990). Metamemories of memory researchers. *Memory and Cognition, 18,* 321–327.

Parker, K. (1983). A meta-analysis of the reliability and validity of the Rorschach. *Journal of Personality Assessment, 47,* 227–231.

Parker, K. C. H., Hanson, R. K., & Hunsley, J. (1988). MMPI, Rorschach, and WAIS: A meta-analytic comparison of reliability, stability, and validity. *Psychological Bulletin, 103,* 367–373.

Parker, S. (1990). A note on the growth of the use of statistical tests in *Perception and Psychophysics. Bulletin of the Psychonomic Society, 28,* 565–566.

Parsons, M. W., & Gold, P. E. (1992). Glucose enhancement of memory in elderly humans: An inverted-U dose-response curve. *Neurobiology of Aging, 13,* 401–404.

Parten, M. B. (1932). Social participation among pre-school children. *Journal of Abnormal and Social Psychology, 27,* 243–269.

Patterson, C. H. (1984). Empathy, warmth, and genuineness in psychotherapy: A review of reviews. *Psychotherapy, 21,* 431–438.

Patterson, C. H. (1989). Eclecticism in psychotherapy: Is integration possible? *Psychotherapy, 26,* 157–161.

Patterson, D. R., Everett, J. J., Burns, G. L., & Marvin, J. A. (1992). Hypnosis for the treatment of burn pain. *Journal of Consulting and Clinical Psychology, 60,* 713–717.

Patterson, F. G., Patterson, L. H., & Brentari, D. K. (1987). Language in child, chimp, and gorilla. *American Psychologist, 42,* 270–272.

Patton, J. E., Routh, D. K., & Stinard, T. A. (1986). Where do children study? Behavioral observations. *Bulletin of the Psychonomic Society, 24,* 439–440.

Paul, S. M., Hulihan-Giblin, B., & Skolnick, P. (1982). (+)-amphetamine binding to rat hypothalamus: Relation to anorexic potency of phenylethylamines. *Science, 218,* 487–490.

Paulsen, F. (1899/1963). *Immanuel Kant: His life and doctrine.* New York: Ungar.

Paulsen, P., French, R., & Sherrill, C. (1990). Comparison of wheelchair athletes and nonathletes on selected mood states. *Perceptual and Motor Skills, 71,* 1160–1162.

Pavlov, I. P. (1928). *Lectures on conditioned reflexes.* New York: Liveright.

Pearce, J. (1985). Harry Stack Sullivan: Theory and practice. *American Journal of Social Psychiatry, 5,* 5–13.

Pears, R., & Bryant, P. E. (1990). Transitive inferences by young children about spatial position. *British Journal of Psychology, 81,* 497–510.

Pearson, J., Brandeis, L., & Cuello, A. C. (1982). Depletion of substance P-containing axons in substantia gelatinosa of patients with diminished pain sensitivity. *Nature, 295,* 61–63.

Peeples, E. E. (1990). Training, certification, and experience of handwriting analysts. *Perceptual and Motor Skills, 70,* 1219–1226.

Penfield, W. (1975). *The mystery of the mind.* Princeton, NJ: Princeton University Press.

Pennebaker, J. W., & Beall, S. K. (1986). Confronting a traumatic event: Toward an understanding of inhibition and disease. *Journal of Abnormal Psychology, 95,* 274–281.

Pennebaker, J. W., Kiecolt-Glaser, J. K., & Glaser, R. (1988). Disclosure of traumas and immune function: Health implications for psychotherapy. *Journal of Consulting and Clinical Psychology, 56,* 239–245.

Pennebaker, J. W., & Watson, D. (1988). Blood pressure estimation and beliefs among normotensives and hypertensives. *Health Psychology, 7,* 309–328.

Pepitone, A. (1981). Lessons from the history of social psychology. *American Psychologist, 36,* 972–985.

Perkins, K. A. (1985). The synergestic effect of smoking and serum cholesterol on coronary heart disease. *Health Psychology, 4,* 337–360.

Perlow, M. J., Freed, W. J., Hoffer, B. J., Seiger, A., Olson, L., & Wyatt, R. J. (1979). Brain grafts reduce motor abnormalities produced by destruction of nigrostriatal dopamine system. *Science, 204,* 643–647.

Perls, F. (1972). Interview with Frederick Perls. In A. Bry (Ed.), *Inside psychotherapy* (pp. 58–70). New York: Basic Books.

Perls, F. (1973). *The Gestalt approach and eyewitness to therapy.* Palo Alto, CA: Science & Behavior Books.

Perr, I. N. (1983). The insanity defense: A tale of two cities. *American Journal of Psychiatry, 140,* 873–874.

Persad, E. (1990). Electroconvulsive therapy in depression. *Canadian Journal of Psychiatry, 35,* 175–182.

Pert, C. B., & Snyder, S. H. (1973). Opiate receptor: Demonstration in nervous tissue. *Science, 179,* 1031–1034.

Pervin, L. A. (1984). *Personality: Theory and research.* New York: Wiley.

Peters, R., & McGee, R. (1982). Cigarette smoking and state-dependent memory. *Psychopharmacology, 76,* 232–235.

Peters, R. M. (1985). Reflections on the origin and aim of nostalgia. *Journal of Analytical Psychology, 30,* 135–148.

Petersen, A. C. (1988). Adolescent development. *Annual Review of Psychology, 39,* 583–607.

Peterson, C., & Barrett, L. C. (1987). Explanatory style and academic performance among university freshmen. *Journal of Personality and Social Psychology, 53,* 603–607.

Peterson, C., Seligman, M. E. P., & Vaillant, G. E. (1988). Pessimistic explanatory style is a risk factor for physical illness: A 35-year longitudinal study. *Journal of Personality and Social Psychology, 55,* 23–27.

Peterson, I. (1983). Playing chess bit by bit. *Science News, 124,* 236–237.

Peterson, L. (1989). Latchkey children's preparation for self-care: Overestimated, under-rehearsed, and unsafe. *Journal of Clinical Child Psychology, 18,* 36–43.

Peterson, L. R., & Peterson, M. (1959). Short-term retention of individual verbal items. *Journal of Experimental Psychology, 58,* 193–198.

Petronis, K. R., Samuels, J. F., Moscicki, E. K., & Anthony, J. C. (1990). An epidemiologic investigation of potential risk factors for suicide attempts. *Social Psychiatry and Psychiatric Epidemiology, 25,* 193–199.

Pettersen, L., Yonas, A., & Fisch, R. O. (1980). The development of blinking in response to impending collision in preterm, full-term, and postterm infants. *Infant Behavior and Development, 3,* 155–165.

Petty, R. E., & Cacioppo, J. T. (1990). Involvement and persuasion: Tradition versus integration. *Psychological Bulletin, 107,* 367–374.

Petty, R. E., Cacioppo, J. T., & Goldman, R. (1981). Personal involvement as a determinant of argument-based persuasion. *Journal of Personality and Social Psychology, 41,* 847–855.

Phelps, M. E., & Mazziotta, J. C. (1985). Positron-emission tomography: Human brain function and biochemistry. *Science, 228,* 799–809.

Philipp, E., Pirke, K. M., Kellner, M. B., & Krieg, J. C. (1991). Disturbed cholecystokinin secretion in patients with eating disorders. *Life Sciences, 48,* 2443–2450.

Phillips, D. P., & Brugge, J. F. (1985). Progress in neurophysiology of sound localization. *Annual Review of Psychology, 36,* 245–274.

Phillips, R. D., Wagner, S. H., Fells, C. A., & Lynch, M. (1990). Do infants recognize emotion in facial expressions? Categorical and "metaphorical" evidence. *Infant Behavior and Development, 13,* 71–84.

Phillips, W. M. (1981). The minimax problem of personal construct organization and schizophrenic thought disorder. *Journal of Clinical Psychology, 37,* 692–698.

Phinney, V. G., Jensen, L. C., Olsen, J. A., & Cundick, B. (1990). The relationship between early development and psychosexual behaviors in adolescent females. *Adolescence, 25,* 321–332.

Piaget, J. (1932). *The moral judgment of the child.* New York: Harcourt, Brace & World.

Piaget, J. (1952). *The origins of intelligence in children.* New York: International Universities Press.

Pierce, P. A., & Peroutka, S. J. (1990). Antagonist properties of d-LSD at 5-hydroxytryptamine sub-2 receptors. *Neuropsychopharmacology, 3,* 503–508.

Piliavin, J. A., Callero, P. L., & Evans, E. E. (1982). Addiction to altruism: Opponent-process theory and habitual blood donation. *Journal of Personality and Social Psychology, 43,* 1200–1213.

Pillard, R. C., Poumadere, J., & Carretta, A. (1981). Is homosexuality familial? A review, some data, and a suggestion. *Archives of Sexual Behavior, 10,* 465–475.

Pillemer, D. B., Koff, E., Rhinehart, E. D., & Rierdan, J. (1987). Flashbulb memories of menarche and adult menstrual distress. *Journal of Adolescence, 10,* 187–199.

Pincomb, G. A., Lovallo, W. R., Passey, R. B., Brackett, D. J., & Wilson, M. F. (1987). Caffeine enhances the physiological response to occupational stress in medical students. *Health Psychology, 6,* 101–112.

Piner, K. E., & Kahle, L. R. (1984). Adapting to the stigmatizing label of mental illness: Foregone but not forgotten. *Journal of Personality and Social Psychology, 47,* 805–811.

Pines, M. (1981, September). The civilizing of Genie. *Psychology Today,* pp. 28–34.

Piper, A. (1993). Tricyclic antidepressants versus electroconvulsive therapy: A review of the evidence for efficacy in depression. *Annals of Clinical Psychiatry, 5,* 13–23.

Pitsikas, N., Carli, M., Fidecka, S., & Algeri, S. (1990). Effect of life-long hypocaloric diet on age-related changes in motor and cognitive behavior in a rat population. *Neurobiology of Aging, 11,* 417–423.

Plante, T. G., & Rodin, J. (1990). Physical fitness and enhanced psychological health. *Current Psychology: Research and Reviews 9,* 3–24.

Plass, J. A., & Hill, K. T. (1986). Children's achievement strategies and test performance: The role of time pressure, evaluation, anxiety, and sex. *Developmental Psychology, 22,* 31–36.

Plomin, R., Corley, R., DeFries, J. C., & Fulker, D. W. (1990). Individual differences in television viewing in early childhood: Nature as well as nurture. *Psychological Science, 1,* 371–377.

Plomin, R., & Daniels, D. (1987). Why are children in the same family so different from each other? *Behavioral and Brain Sciences, 10,* 1–16.

Plomin, R., Loehlin, J. C., & DeFries, J. C. (1985). Genetic and environmental components of "environmental" influences. *Developmental Psychology, 21,* 391–402.

Plomin, R., & Rende, R. (1991). Human behavioral genetics. *Annual Review of Psychology, 42,* 161–190.

Plotkin, W. B. (1979). The alpha experience revisited: Biofeedback in the transformation of psychological state. *Psychological Bulletin, 86,* 1132–1148.

Plous, S. (1991) An attitude survey of animal rights activists. *Psychological Science, 2,* 192–196.

Plutchik, R. (1980, February). A language for the emotions. *Psychology Today,* pp. 68–78.

Podlesny, J. A., & Raskin, D. C. (1978). Effectiveness of techniques and physiological measures in the detection of deception. *Psychophysiology, 15,* 344–359.

Poffenberger, A. T. (Ed.). (1947/1973). *James McKeen Cattell: Man of Science. Vol. 1: Psychological Research.* New York: Arno.

Poincaré, H. (1948, August). Mathematical creation. *Scientific American,* pp. 14–17.

Pollak, G. D., Wenstrup, J. J., & Fuzessey, Z. M. (1986). Auditory processing in the mustache bat's inferior colliculus. *Trends in Neurosciences, 9,* 556–561.

Pollard, T. G. (1990). Relative addiction potential of major centrally-active drugs and drug classes: Inhalants and anesthetics. *Advances in Alcohol & Substance Abuse, 9,* 149–165.

Pomerleau, C. S., & Pomerleau, O. F. (1987). The effects of a psychological stressor on cigarette smoking and subsequent behavioral and physiological responses. *Psychophysiology, 24,* 278–285.

Poplawsky, A., & Isaacson, R. L. (1990). Nimodipine accelerates recovery from the hyperemotionality produced by septal lesions. *Behavioral and Neural Biology, 53*, 133–139.

Popplestone, J. A., & McPherson, M. W. (1976). Ten years at the Archives of the History of American Psychology. *American Psychologist, 31*, 533–534.

Posner, M. I., Inhoff, A. W., Friedrich, F. J., & Cohen, A. (1987). Isolating attentional systems: A cognitive-anatomical analysis. *Psychobiology, 15*, 107–121.

Postman, L. (1985). Human learning and memory. In G. A. Kimble & K. Schlesinger (Eds.), *Topics in the history of psychology* (Vol. 1, pp. 69–134). Hillsdale, NJ: Erlbaum.

Potgieter, J., & Bisschoff, F. (1990). Sensation seeking among medium- and low-risk sports participants. *Perceptual and Motor Skills, 71*, 1203–1206.

Poulos, C. X., & Cappell, H. (1991). Homeostatic theory of drug tolerance: A general model of physiological adaptation. *Psychological Review, 98*, 390–408.

Poulson, R. L. (1990). Mock juror attribution of criminal responsibility: Effects of race and the guilty but mentally ill (GBMI) verdict option. *Journal of Applied Social Psychology, 20*, 1596–1611.

Powell, D. J., & Fuller, R. W. (1983). Marijuana and sex: Strange bedpartners. *Journal of Psychoactive Drugs, 15*, 269–280.

Prager, K. J. (1989). Intimacy status and couple communication. *Journal of Social and Personal Relationships, 6*, 435–449.

Prasinos, S., & Tittler, B. I. (1981). The family relationships of humor-oriented adolescents. *Journal of Personality, 47*, 295–305.

Pratt, K. J. (1962). Motivation and learning in medieval writings. *American Psychologist, 17*, 496–500.

Premack, D. (1965). Reinforcement theory. In D. Levine (Ed.), *Nebraska symposium on motivation* (pp. 123–188). Lincoln: University of Nebraska Press.

Premack, D. (1971). Language in chimpanzee? *Science, 172*, 808–822.

Prentice-Dunn, S., & Rogers, R. W. (1982). Effects of public and private self-awareness on deindividuation and aggression. *Journal of Personality and Social Psychology, 3*, 503–513.

Preyer, W. (1882/1973). *The mind of the child*. Salem, NH: Ayer.

Pribram, K. H. (1985, September). "Holism" could close cognition era. *APA Monitor*, pp. 5–6.

Price, R. A., & Gottesman, I. I. (1991). Body fat in identical twins reared apart: Roles for genes and environment. *Behavior Genetics, 21*, 1–7.

Price-Williams, E., Gordon, W., & Ramirez, M. (1969). Skill and conservation: A study of pottery-making children. *Developmental Psychology, 1*, 769.

Prochaska, J. O. (1984). *Systems of psychotherapy: A transtheoretical approach*. Homewood, IL: Dorsey.

Proefrock, D. W. (1981). Adolescence: Social fact and psychological concept. *Adolescence, 16*, 851–858.

Program power. (1981, April). *Scientific American*, pp. 83–85.

Pryde, N. A. (1989). Sex therapy in context. *Sexual and Marital Therapy, 4*, 215–227.

Psychic Abscam. (1983, March). *Discover*, pp. 10, 13.

A psychic Watergate. (1981, June). *Discover*, p. 8.

Puccio, G. J. (1991). William Duff's eighteenth century examination of original genius and its relationship to contemporary creativity research. *Journal of Creative Behavior, 25*, 1–10.

Pullum, G. K. (1991). *The great Eskimo vocabulary hoax*. Chicago: University of Chicago Press.

Purifoy, F. E., Grodsky, A., & Giambra, L. M. (1992). The relationship of sexual daydreaming to sexual activity, sexual drive, and sexual attitudes for women across the life-span. *Archives of Sexual Behavior, 21*, 369–385.

Pyryt, M. C. (1993). The fulfillment of promise revisited: A discriminant analysis of factors predicting success in the Terman study. *Roeper Review, 15*, 178–179.

Quinton, A. (1980). *Francis Bacon*. New York: Hill & Wang.

Rabinowitz, F. M. (1984). The heredity-environment controversy: A Victorian legacy. *Canadian Psychology, 25*, 159–166.

Rabun, M. (1978, April). Frightening sight greets Rangers in dressing room. *Altoona Mirror*.

Rachal, J. R. (1984). The computer in the ABE and GED classroom: A review of the literature. *Adult Education Quarterly, 35*, 86–95.

Rachman, S. (1991). Neo-conditioning and the classical theory of fear acquisition. *Clinical Psychology Review, 11*, 155–173.

Radwin, J. O. (1991). The multiple personality disorder: Has this trendy alibi lost its way? *Law and Psychology Review, 15*, 351–373.

Ragland, D. R., & Brand, R. J. (1988). Type A behavior and mortality from coronary heart disease. *New England Journal of Medicine, 318*, 65–69.

Raglin, J. S., & Turner, P. E. (1993). Anxiety and performance in track and field athletes: A comparison of the inverted-U hypothesis with Zone of Optimal Function theory. *Personality and Individual Differences, 14*, 163–171.

Rahe, R. H. (1992). Van Gogh and the life chart. *Integrative Physiological and Behavioral Science, 27*, 323–335.

Rainwater, N., Sweet, A. A., Elliott, L., & Bowers, M. (1988). Systematic desensitization in the treatment of needle phobias for children with diabetes. *Child and Family Behavior Therapy, 10*, 19–31.

Rajecki, D. W., Bledsoe, S. B., & Rasmussen, J. L. (1991). Successful personal ads: Gender differences and similarities in offers, stipulations, and outcomes. *Basic and Applied Social Psychology, 12*, 457–469.

Raloff, J. (1982). Noise can be hazardous to your health. *Science News, 121*, 377–381.

Rambo, L. R. (1980). Ethics, evolution, and the psychology of William James. *Journal of the History of the Behavioral Sciences, 16*, 50–57.

Ramón y Cajal, S. (1937/1966). *Recollections of my life*. Cambridge, MA: MIT Press.

Rapee, R. M. (1991). Generalized anxiety disorder: A review of clinical features and theoretical concepts. *Clinical Psychology Review, 11*, 419–440.

Rapp, B. C., & Caramazza, A. (1989). General or specific access to word meaning; A claim re-examined. *Cognitive Neuropsychology, 6*, 251–272.

Rapp, D. (1988). The reception of Freud by the British press: General interest and literary magazines, 1920–1925. *Journal of the History of the Behavioral Sciences, 24*, 191–201.

Rappaport, Z. H. (1992). Psychosurgery in the modern era: Therapeutic and ethical aspects. *Medicine and Law, 11*, 449–453.

Raps, C. S., Peterson, C., Jonas, M., & Seligman, M. E. P. (1982). Patient behavior in hospitals: Helplessness, reactance, or both? *Journal of Personality and Social Psychology, 42*, 1036–1041.

Raskin, D. C., & Podlesny, J. A. (1979). Truth and deception: A reply to Lykken. *Psychological Bulletin, 86*, 54–59.

Rasmussen, S. A., & Eisen, J. L. (1990). Epidemiology of obsessive-compulsive disorder. *Journal of Clinical Psychiatry, 51*, 10–13.

Ratner, H. H., Schell, D. A., Crimmins, A., Mittelman, D., & Baldinelli, L. (1987). Changes in adults' prose recall: Aging or cognitive demands? *Developmental Psychology, 23*, 521–525.

Ratner, S. C., Karon, B. P., VandenBos, G. R., & Denny, M. R. (1981). The adaptive significance of the catatonic stupor in humans and animals from an evolutionary perspective. *Academic Psychology Bulletin, 3*, 273–279.

Ravelli, G. P., Stein, Z. A., & Susser, M. W. (1976). Obesity in young men after famine exposure in utero in early infancy. *New England Journal of Medicine, 295*, 349–353.

Ray, O. (1983). *Drugs, society, and human behavior*. St. Louis: Mosby.

Rayner, K., Slowiaczek, M. L., Clifton, C., Jr., & Bertera, J. H. (1983). Latency of sequential eye movements: Implications for reading. *Journal of Experimental Psychology: Human Perception and Performance, 9*, 912–922.

Raz, S., & Raz, N. (1990). Structural brain abnormalities in the major psychoses: A quantitative review of the evidence from computerized imaging. *Psychological Bulletin, 108*, 93–108.

Read, M. S. (1982). Malnutrition and behavior. *Applied Research in Mental Retardation, 3*, 279–291.

Read, P. P. (1974). *Alive: The story of the Andes survivors*. Philadelphia: Lippincott.

Redd, W. H., Jacobsen, P. B., Die-Trill, M., Dermatis, H., McEvoy, M., & Holland, J. C. (1987). Cognitive/attentional distraction in the control of conditioned nausea in pediatric cancer patients receiving chemotherapy. *Journal of Consulting and Clinical Psychology, 55*, 391–395.

Reddy, A. V., & Reddy, P. B. (1983). Creativity and intelligence. *Psychological Studies, 28*, 20–24.

Reeder, K., & Shapiro, J. (1993). Relationships between early literate experience and knowledge and children's linguistic pragmatic strategies. *Journal of Pragmatics, 19*, 1–22.

Rees, L. (1983). The development of psychosomatic medicine during the past 25 years. *Journal of Psychosomatic Medicine, 27*, 157–164.

Reese, E. P. (1986). Learning about teaching from teaching about learning: Presenting behavioral analysis in an introductory survey course. In V. P. Makosky (Ed.), *The G. Stanley Hall Lecture Series* (Vol. 6, pp. 65–127). Washington, DC: American Psychological Association.

Reese, H. W., & Fremouw, W. J. (1984). Normal and normative ethics in behavioral sciences. *American Psychologist, 39,* 863–876.

Reich, J. H. (1986). The epidemiology of anxiety. *Journal of Nervous and Mental Disease, 174,* 129–136.

Reilly, R. R., & Chao, G. R. (1982). Validity and fairness of some alternative employee selection procedures. *Personnel Psychology, 35,* 1–62.

Reiman, E. M., Fusselman, M. J., Fox, P. T., & Raichle, M. E. (1989). Neuroanatomical correlates of anticipatory anxiety. *Science, 243,* 1071–1074.

Reiman, E. M., Raichle, M. E., Butler, F. K., Herscovitch, P., & Robins, E. (1984). A focal brain abnormality in panic disorder, a severe form of anxiety. *Nature, 310,* 683–685.

Reinisch, J. M. (1981). Prenatal exposure to synthetic progestins increases potential for aggression in humans. *Science, 211,* 1171–1173.

Reis, S. (1989). Reflections on policy affecting the education of gifted and talented students: Past and future perspectives. *American Psychologist, 44,* 399–408.

Reisenzein, R. (1983). The Schachter theory of emotion: Two decades later. *Psychological Bulletin, 94,* 239–264.

Reitman, J. S. (1974). Without surreptitious rehearsal, information in short-term memory decays. *Journal of Verbal Learning and Verbal Behavior, 13,* 365–377.

Rejeski, J., Gregg, E., Thompson, A., & Berry, M. (1991). The effects of varying doses of acute aerobic exercise on psychophysiological stress responses in highly trained cyclists. *Journal of Sport and Exercise Psychology, 13,* 188–199.

Relinger, H. (1984). Hypnotic hypermnesia: A critical review. *American Journal of Clinical Hypnosis, 26,* 212–225.

Renner, J. W., Abraham, M. R., Grzybowski, E. B., & Marek, E. A. (1990). Understandings and misunderstandings of eighth graders of four physics concepts found in textbooks. *Journal of Research in Science Teaching, 27,* 35–54.

Rescorla, R. A. (1968). Probability of shock in the presence and absence of CS in fear conditioning. *Journal of Comparative and Physiological Psychology, 66,* 1–5.

Rescorla, R. A. (1988). Pavlovian conditioning: It's not what you think it is. *American Psychologist, 43,* 151–160.

Rescorla, R. A., & Holland, P. C. (1982). Behavioral studies of associative learning in animals. *Annual Review of Psychology, 33,* 265–308.

Restle, F. (1970). Moon illusion explained on the basis of relative size. *Science, 167,* 1092–1096.

Rheingold, H. L., & Adams, J. L. (1980). The significance of speech to newborns. *Developmental Psychology, 16,* 397–403.

Rhodes, N., & Wood, W. (1992). Self-esteem and intelligence affect influenceability: The mediating role of message reception. *Psychological Bulletin, 111,* 156–171.

Ricci, L. C., & Wellman, M. M. (1990). Monoamines: Biochemical markers of suicide? *Journal of Clinical Psychology, 46,* 106–116.

Rice, M. L. (1989). Children's language acquisition. *American Psychologist, 44,* 149–156.

Richardson, J. T. E., & Zucco, G. M. (1989). Cognition and olfaction: A review. *Psychological Bulletin, 105,* 352–360.

Rieber, R. W. (Ed.). (1980). *Wilhelm Wundt and the making of a scientific psychology.* New York: Plenum.

Rierdan, J., & Koff, E. (1990). Premenarcheal predictors of the experience of menarche: A prospective study. *Journal of Adolescent Health Care, 11,* 404–407.

Riggs, L. A. (1985). Sensory processes: Vision. In G. A. Kimble & K. Schlesinger (Eds.), *Topics in the history of psychology* (Vol. 1, pp. 165–220). Hillsdale, NJ: Erlbaum.

Rinaldi, R. C. (1987). Patient-therapist personality similarity and the therapeutic relationship. *Psychotherapy in Private Practice, 5,* 11–29.

Rinn, W. E. (1984). The neuropsychology of facial expression: A review of the neurological and psychological mechanisms for producing facial expressions. *Psychological Bulletin, 95,* 52–77.

Riordan, C. A., & Tedeschi, J. T. (1983). Attraction in aversive environments: Some evidence for classical conditioning and negative reinforcement. *Journal of Personality and Social Psychology, 44,* 683–692.

Risse, G. B. (1976). Vocational guidance during the Depression: Phrenology versus applied psychology. *Journal of the History of the Behavioral Sciences, 12,* 130–140.

Rivera-Tovar, L. A., & Jones, R. T. (1990). Effect of elaboration on the acquisition and maintenance of cardiopulmonary resuscitation. *Journal of Pediatric Psychology, 15,* 123–138.

Rivinus, T. M. (1990). The deadly embrace: The suicidal impulse and substance use and abuse in the college student. *Journal of College Student Psychotherapy, 4,* 45–77.

Roark, M. L. (1989). Sexual violence. *New Directions for Student Services, 47,* 41–52.

Roberts, A. H. (1985). Biofeedback: Research, training, and clinical roles. *American Psychologist, 40,* 938–941.

Roberts, C. F., & Golding, S. L. (1991). The social construction of criminal responsibility and insanity. *Law and Human Behavior, 15,* 349–376.

Roberts, J. E., & Schuele, C. M. (1990). Otitis media and later academic performance: The linkage and implications for intervention. *Topics in Language Disorders, 11,* 43–62.

Roberts, M. A. (1990). A behavioral observation method for differentiating hyperactive and aggressive boys. *Journal of Abnormal Child Psychology, 18,* 131–142.

Roberts, M. C., & Fanurik, D. (1986). Rewarding elementary school children for their use of safety belts. *Health Psychology, 5,* 185–196.

Roberts, P., & Newton, P. M. (1987). Levinsonian studies of women's adult development. *Psychology and Aging, 2,* 154–163.

Roberts, S. J. (1988). Social support and help seeking: Review of the literature. *Advances in Nursing Science, 10,* 1–11.

Robins, L. N., & Helzer, J. E. (1986). Diagnosis and clinical assessment: The current state of psychiatric diagnosis. *Annual Review of Psychology, 37,* 409–432.

Robins, L. N., Helzer, J. E., Weissman, M. M., Orvaschel, H., Gruenberg, E., Burke, J. D., Jr., & Regier, D. A. (1984). Lifetime prevalence of specific psychiatric disorders in three sites. *Archives of General Psychiatry, 41,* 949–958.

Robinson, D. (1982). Cerebral plurality and the unity of the self. *American Psychologist, 37,* 904–910.

Robinson, F. P. (1970). *Effective study.* New York: Harper & Row.

Rockwell, T. (1979). Pseudoscience or pseudocriticism? *Journal of Parapsychology, 43,* 221–231.

Rodgers, J. E. (1982, June). The malleable memory of eyewitnesses. *Science, 82,* pp. 32–35.

Rodgers, J. L. (1988). Birth order, SAT, and confluence: Spurious correlations and no causality. *American Psychologist, 43,* 476–477.

Rodgers, R., & Hunter, J. E. (1991). Impact of management by objectives on organizational productivity. *Journal of Applied Psychology, 76,* 322–336.

Rodin, J. (1981). Current status of the internal-external hypothesis for obesity: What went wrong? *American Psychologist, 36,* 361–372.

Rodin, J. (1985). Insulin levels, hunger, and food intake: An example of feedback loops in body weight regulation. *Health Psychology, 4,* 1–24.

Rodin, J. (1986). Aging and health: Effects of the sense of control. *Science, 233,* 1271–1276.

Rodman, H., Pratto, D. J., & Nelson, R. S. (1985). Child-care arrangements and children's functioning: A comparison of self-care adult-care children. *Developmental Psychology, 21,* 413–418.

Rogers, C. R. (1951). *Client-centered therapy.* Boston: Houghton Mifflin.

Rogers, C. R. (1957). The necessary and sufficient conditions of therapeutic personality change. *Journal of Consulting Psychology, 21,* 95–103.

Rogers, C. R. (1961). *On becoming a person: A therapist's view of psychotherapy.* Boston: Houghton Mifflin.

Rogers, C. R. (1968). Interpersonal relationships. *Journal of Applied Behavioral Science, 4,* 1–12.

Rogers, C. R. (1985). Toward a more human science of the person. *Journal of Humanistic Psychology, 25,* 7–24.

Rogers, R. (1987). APA's position on the insanity defense: Empiricism versus emotionalism. *American Psychologist, 42,* 840–848.

Rogers, R. C. (1985). The chemical senses. *Science, 229,* 374–375.

Rogers, R. L., Meyer, J. S., & Mortel, K. F. (1990). After reaching retirement age physical activity sustains cerebral perfusion and cognition. *Journal of the American Geriatrics Society, 38,* 123–128.

Rokeach, M. (1964/1981). *The three Christs of Ypsilanti.* New York: Columbia University Press.

Rokeach, M., & Mezei, L. (1966). Race and shared belief as factors in social choice. *Science, 151,* 167–172.

Rolnick, A., & Bles, W. (1989). Performance and well-being under tilting conditions: The effects of visual reference and artificial horizon. *Aviation, Space, and Environmental Medicine, 60,* 779–785.

Rolnick, A., & Lubow, R. E. (1991). Why is the driver rarely motion sick? The role of controllability in motion sickness. *Ergonomics, 34,* 867–879.

Rorer, L. G., & Widiger, T. A. (1983). Personality structure and assessment. *Annual Review of Psychology, 34,* 431–463.

Rosch, E. (1975). Cognitive representations of semantic categories. *Journal of Experimental Psychology: General, 104,* 192–233.

Rose, J. E., & Fantino, E. (1978). Conditioned reinforcement and discrimination in second-order schedules. *Journal of the Experimental Analysis of Behavior, 29,* 393–418.

Rosen, D. H., Smith, S. M., Huston, H. L., & Gonzalez, G. (1991). Empirical study of associations between symbols and their meanings: Evidence of collective unconscious (archetypal) memory. *Journal of Analytical Psychology, 36,* 211–228.

Rosenbaum, M. E. (1986). The repulsion hypothesis: On the nondevelopment of relationships. *Journal of Personality and Social Psychology, 51,* 1156–1166.

Rosenhan, D. L. (1973). On being sane in insane places. *Science, 179,* 250–258.

Rosenman, R. H., Brand, R. J., Jenkins, D., Friedman, M., Straus, R., & Wurm, M. (1975). Coronary heart disease in the Western Collaborative Group Study: Final follow-up experience of 8 1/2 years. *Journal of the American Psychological Association, 233,* 872–877.

Rosenthal, N. E. (1993). *Winter blues: Seasonal affective disorder—what it is and how to overcome it.* New York: Guilford.

Rosenthal, R., & Fode, K. L. (1963). The effect of experimenter bias on the performance of the albino rat. *Behavioral Science, 8,* 183–189.

Rosenthal, R., & Jacobson, L. (1968). *Pygmalion in the classroom.* New York: Holt, Rinehart & Winston.

Rosenzweig, M. R. (1984). Experience, memory, and the brain. *American Psychologist, 39,* 365–376.

Ross, D. (1972). *G. Stanley Hall: The psychologist as prophet.* Chicago: University of Chicago Press.

Ross, E. D., Edmondson, J. A., Seibert, G. B., & Homan, R. W. (1988). Acoustic analysis of affective prosody during right-sided Wada test: A within-subjects verification of the right hemisphere's role in language. *Brain and Language, 33,* 128–145.

Ross, H. E., & Ross, G. M. (1976). Did Ptolemy understand the moon illusion? *Perception, 5,* 377–385.

Ross, J. (1980). The use of former phobics in the treatment of phobias. *American Journal of Psychiatry, 137,* 715–717.

Rossi, A., Stratta, P., di Michele, V., & Bolino, F. (1989). A computerized tomographic study in patients with depressive disorder: A comparison with schizophrenic patients and controls. *Acta Psychiatrica Belgica, 89,* 56–61.

Rossi, A. M., & Seiler, W. J. (1989–1990). The comparative effectiveness of systematic desensitization and an integrative approach in treating public speaking anxiety: A literature review and a preliminary investigation. *Imagination, Cognition, and Personality, 9,* 49–66.

Rossi, F. (1988, November 8). Stress test. *Philadelphia Inquirer,* pp. 1-E, 10-E.

Roth, S., & Cohen, L. J. (1986). Approach, avoidance, and coping with stress. *American Psychologist, 41,* 813–819.

Roth, T., & Roehrs, T. (1988). Sleepiness and motor vehicle accidents. *International Clinical Psychopharmacology, 3,* 111–116.

Rothbaum, B. O., & Foa, E. B. (1991). Exposure treatment of PTSD concomitant with conversion mutism: A case study. *Behavior Therapy, 22,* 449–456.

Rothblum, E. D. (1990). Psychological factors in the Antarctic. *Journal of Psychology, 124,* 253–273.

Rotter, J. B. (1966). Generalized expectancies for internal versus external control of reinforcement. *Psychological Monographs, 80.*

Rotter, J. B. (1990). Internal versus external control of reinforcement: Case history of a variable. *American Psychologist, 45,* 489–493.

Rotton, J., & Kelly, I. W. (1985). Much ado about the full moon: A meta-analysis of lunar-lunacy research. *Psychological Bulletin, 97,* 286–306.

Roug, L., Landberg, I., & Lundberg, L. J. (1989). Phonetic development in early infancy: A study of four Swedish children during the first eighteen months of life. *Journal of Child Language, 16,* 19–40.

Routh, D. K. (1969). Conditioning of vocal response differentiation in infants. *Developmental Psychology, 1,* 219–226.

Rowsell, H. C. (1988). The status of animal experimentation in Canada. *International Journal of Psychology, 23,* 377–381.

Roy-Byrne, P. P., Uhde, T. W., Holcomb, H. H., & Thompson, K. (1987). Effects of diazepam on cognitive processes in normal subjects. *Psychopharmacology, 91,* 30–33.

Rozin, P., & Fallon, A. E. (1987). A perspective on disgust. *Psychological Review, 94,* 23–41.

Rozin, P., & Zellner, D. (1985). The role of Pavlovian conditioning in the acquisition of food likes and dislikes. *Annals of the New York Academy of Sciences, 443,* 189–202.

Rubin, J. R., Provenzano, F. J., & Luria, Z. (1974). The eye of the beholder: Parents' views on sex of newborns. *American Journal of Orthopsychiatry, 44,* 512–519.

Rubin, L. C., & Mills, M. J. (1983). Behavioral precipitants to civil commitment. *American Journal of Psychiatry, 140,* 603–606.

Rubin, R. T., Reinisch, J. M., & Haskett, R. F. (1981). Postnatal gonadal steroid effects on human behavior. *Science, 211,* 1318–1324.

Rubin, Z. (1985). Deceiving ourselves about deception: Comment on Smith and Richardson's "Amelioration of deception and harm in psychological research." *Journal of Personality and Social Psychology, 48,* 252–253.

Ruch, W., McGhee, P. E., & Hehl, F. J. (1990). Age differences in the enjoyment of incongruity-resolution and nonsense humor during adulthood. *Psychology and Aging, 5,* 348–355.

Ruda, M. A. (1982). Opiates and pain pathways: Demonstration of enkephalin synapses on dorsal horn projection neurons. *Science, 215,* 1523–1525.

Ruffman, T. K., & Olson, D. R. (1989). Children's ascriptions of knowledge to others. *Developmental Psychology, 25,* 601–606.

Rule, B. G., & Nesdale, A. R. (1976). Emotional arousal and aggressive behavior. *Psychological Bulletin, 83,* 851–863.

Rumbaugh, D. M., Gill, T. V., & von Glasersfeld, E. C. (1973). Reading and sentence completion by a chimpanzee (*Pan*). *Science, 182,* 731–733.

Rummel, A., & Feinberg, R. (1988). Cognitive Evaluation Theory: A meta-analytic review of the literature. *Social Behavior and Personality, 16,* 147–164.

Rury, J. L. (1988). Race, region, and education: An analysis of Black and White scores on the 1917 Army Alpha Intelligence Test. *Journal of Negro Education, 57,* 51–65.

Rushton, J. P. (1990a). Creativity, intelligence, and psychoticism. *Personality and Individual Differences, 11,* 1291–1298.

Rushton, J. P. (1990b). Race, brain size and intelligence: A rejoinder to Cain and Vanderwolf. *Personality and Individual Differences, 11,* 785–794.

Rushton, J. P., Fulker, D. W., Neale, M. C., Nias, D. K. B., & Eysenck, H. J. (1986). Altruism and aggression: The heritability of individual differences. *Journal of Personality and Social Psychology, 50,* 1192–1198.

Russell, J. A. (1991). In defense of a prototype approach to emotion concepts. *Journal of Personality and Social Psychology, 60,* 37–47.

Russell, J. A., & Fehr, B. (1987). Relativity in the perception of emotion in facial expressions. *Journal of Experimental Psychology: General, 116,* 223–237.

Russell, M. J. (1976). Human olfactory communication. *Nature, 260,* 520–522.

Russell, T. G., Rowe, W., & Smouse, A. D. (1991). Subliminal self-help tapes and academic achievement: An evaluation. *Journal of Counseling and Development, 69,* 359–362.

Russo, N. F., & Denmark, F. L. (1987). Contributions of women to psychology. *Annual Review of Psychology, 38,* 279–298.

Rust, J., Golombok, S., & Collier, J. (1988). Marital problems and sexual dysfunction: How are they related? *British Journal of Psychiatry, 152,* 629–631.

Rutkowski, G. K., Gruder, C. L., & Romer, D. (1983). Group cohesiveness, social norms, and bystander intervention. *Journal of Personality and Social Psychology, 44,* 545–552.

Ryan, E. D. (1980). Attribution, intrinsic motivation, and athletics: A replication and extension. In C. H. Nadeau, W. R. Halliwell, K. M. Newell, & G. C. Roberts (Eds.), *Psychology of motor behavior and sport—1979* (pp. 19–26). Champaign, IL: Human Kinetics.

Ryan, R. H., & Geiselman, R. E. (1991). Effects of biased information on the relationship between eyewitness confidence and accuracy. *Bulletin of the Psychonomic Society, 29,* 7–9.

Ryback, D. (1983). Jedi and Jungian forces. *Psychological Perspectives, 14,* 238–244.

Rychlak, J. F. (1988). *The psychology of rigorous humanism.* New York: New York University Press.

Saal, F. E., Johnson, C. B., & Weber, N. (1989). Friendly or sexy? It may depend on whom you ask. *Psychology of Women Quarterly, 13,* 263–276.

Safford, F. (1991). Humor as an aid in gerontological education. *Gerontology and Geriatrics Education, 11,* 27–37.

Sacks, O. (1985). *The man who mistook his wife for a hat and other clinical tales*. New York: Summit.

Sagen, J., Pappas, G. D., & Perlow, M. J. (1986). Adrenal medullary tissue transplants in the rat spinal cord reduce pain sensitivity. *Brain Research, 384*, 189–194.

Sagen, J., Sortwell, C. E., & Pappas, G. D. (1990). Monoaminergic neural transplants prevent learned helplessness in a rat depression model. *Biological Psychiatry, 28*, 1037–1048.

Salovey, P., & Haar, M. D. (1990). The efficacy of cognitive-behavior therapy and writing process training for alleviating writing anxiety. *Cognitive Therapy and Research, 14*, 513–526.

Salter, A. (1949). *Conditioned reflex therapy*. New York: Creative Age Press.

Salthouse, T. A. (1990). Working memory as a processing resource in cognitive aging. *Developmental Review, 10*, 101–124.

Salthouse, T. A. (1991). Mediation of adult age differences in cognition by reductions in working memory and speed of processing. *Psychological Science, 2*, 179–183.

Samelson, F. (1981). Struggle for scientific authority: The reception of Watson's behaviorism, 1913–1920. *Journal of the History of the Behavioral Sciences, 17*, 399–425.

Sanberg, P. R., Moran, T. H., Kubos, K. L., & Coyle, J. T. (1984). Automated measurement of stereotypic behavior in rats. *Behavioral Neuroscience, 97*, 830–832.

Sandford, D. A., Elzinga, R. H., & Grainger, W. (1987). Evaluation of a residential behavioral program for behaviorally disturbed, mentally retarded young adults. *American Journal of Mental Deficiency, 91*, 431–434.

Santee, J. L., Keister, M. E., & Kleinman, K. M. (1980). Incentives to enhance the effects of electromyographic feedback training in stroke patients. *Biofeedback and Self-Regulation, 5*, 51–56.

Sappington, A. A. (1990). Recent psychological approaches to the free will versus determinism issue. *Psychological Bulletin, 108*, 19–29.

Sarason, S. (1984). If it can be studied or developed, should it be? *American Psychologist, 39*, 477–485.

Sarter, M., & Markowitsch, H. J. (1985). Involvement of the amygdala in learning and memory: A critical review, with emphasis on anatomical relations. *Behavioral Neuroscience, 99*, 342–380.

Satir, V., Bitter, J. R., & Krestensen, K. K. (1988). Family reconstruction: The family within—a group experience. *Journal for Specialists in Group Work, 13*, 200–208.

Saunders, D. M., Fisher, W. A., Hewitt, E. C., & Clayton, J. P. (1985). A method for empirically assessing volunteer selection effects: Recruitment procedures and responses to erotica. *Journal of Personality and Social Psychology, 49*, 1703–1712.

Savage-Rumbaugh, E. S. (1987). Communication, symbolic communication, and language: Reply to Seidenberg and Petitto. *Journal of Experimental Psychology: General, 116*, 288–292.

Savage-Rumbaugh, E. S. (1990). Language acquisition in a nonhuman species: Implications for the innateness debate. *Developmental Psychobiology, 23*, 599–620.

Savage-Rumbaugh, E. S., Rumbaugh, D. M., Smith, S. T., & Lawson, J. (1980). Reference: The linguistic essential. *Science, 210*, 922–925.

Savage-Rumbaugh, E. S., McDonald, K., Sevcik, R. A., Hopkins, W. D., & Rupert, E. (1986). Spontaneous symbol acquisition and communicative use by pygmy chimpanzees (*Pan paniscus*). *Journal of Experimental Psychology: General, 115*, 211–235.

Saxe, L., Dougherty, D., & Cross, T. (1985). The validity of polygraph testing: Scientific analysis and public controversy. *American Psychologist, 40*, 355–366.

Sayette, M. A., & Mayne, T. J. (1990). Survey of current clinical and research trends in clinical psychology. *American Psychologist, 45*, 1263–1266.

Scarborough, E., & Furumoto, L. (1987). *Untold lives: The first generation of American women psychologists*. New York: Columbia University Press.

Scarborough, H. S., Rescorla, L., Tager-Flusberg, H., & Fowler, A. E. (1991). The relation of utterance length to grammatical complexity in normal and language-disordered groups. *Applied Psycholinguistics, 12*, 23–45.

Scarr, S. (1985). Constructing psychology: Making facts and fables for our times. *American Psychologist, 40*, 499–512.

Scarr, S. (1988). Race and gender as psychological variables: Social and ethical issues. *American Psychologist, 43*, 56–59.

Scarr, S., & Carter-Saltzman, L. (1979). Twin method: Defense of a critical assumption. *Behavior Genetics, 9*, 527–542.

Scarr, S., Webber, P. L., Weinberg, R. A., & Wittig, M. A. (1981). Personality resemblance among adolescents and their parents in biologically related and adoptive families. *Journal of Personality and Social Psychology, 40*, 885–898.

Scarr, S., & Weinberg, R. A. (1976). IQ test performance of black children adopted by white families. *American Psychologist, 31*, 726–739.

Scarr, S., & Weinberg, R. A. (1983). The Minnesota Adoption Studies: Genetic differences and malleability. *Child Development, 54*, 260–267.

Schaal, B. (1988). Olfaction in infants and children: Developmental and functional perspectives. *Chemical Senses, 13*, 145–190.

Schab, F. R. (1991). Odor memory: Taking stock. *Psychological Bulletin, 109*, 242–251.

Schachter, D. L. (1976). The hypnagogic state: A critical review of the literature. *Psychological Bulletin, 83*, 452–481.

Schachter, D. L. (1983). Amnesia observed: Remembering and forgetting in a natural environment. *Journal of Abnormal Psychology, 92*, 236–242.

Schachter, D. L. (1992). Understanding implicit memory: A cognitive neuroscience approach. *American Psychologist, 47*, 559–569.

Schachter, D. L., Chiu, C.-Y. P., & Ochsner, K. N. (1993). Implicit memory: A selective review. *Annual Review of Neuroscience, 16*, 159–182.

Schachter, S. (1971). Some extraordinary facts about obese humans and rats. *American Psychologist, 26*, 129–144.

Schachter, S. (1982). Recidivism and self-cure of smoking and obesity. *American Psychologist, 37*, 436–444.

Schachter, S., & Singer, J. E. (1962). Cognitive, social and physiological determinants of emotional state. *Psychological Review, 69*, 379–399.

Schaie, K. W. (1989). Perceptual speed in adulthood: Cross-sectional and longitudinal studies. *Psychology and Aging, 4*, 443–453.

Schaie, K. W., & Hertzog, C. (1983). Fourteen-year cohort-sequential analyses of adult intellectual development. *Developmental Psychology, 19*, 531–543.

Schaie, K. W., Labouvie, G. V., & Barrett, T. J. (1973). Selective attrition effects in a 14-year study of adult intelligence. *Journal of Gerontology, 28*, 328–334.

Schaller, M., & Cialdini, R. B. (1988). The economics of empathic helping: Support for a mood management motive. *Journal of Experimental Social Psychology, 24*, 163–181.

Schein, E. (1956). The Chinese indoctrination program for prisoners of war: A study of attempted "brainwashing." *Psychiatry, 19*, 149–172.

Schiff, M., Duyme, M., Dumaret, A., & Tomkiewicz, S. (1982). How much could we boost scholastic achievement and IQ scores? A direct answer from a French adoption study. *Cognition, 12*, 165–196.

Schill, T., & O'Laughlin, M. S. (1984). Humor preference and coping with stress. *Psychological Reports, 55*, 309–310.

Schiller, F. (1979). *Paul Broca: Founder of French anthropology, explorer of the brain*. Berkeley: University of California Press.

Schilling, R. F., & Weaver, G. E. (1983). Effects of extraneous verbal information on memory for telephone numbers. *Journal of Applied Psychology, 68*, 559–564.

Schleifer, L. M., & Amick, B. C. (1989). System response time and method of pay: Stress effects in computer-based tasks. *International Journal of Human-Computer Interaction, 1*, 23–39.

Schleifer, S. J., Keller, S. E., Camerino, M., Thornton, J. C., & Stein, M. (1983). Suppression of lymphocytic stimulation following bereavement. *Journal of the American Medical Association, 250*, 374–377.

Schlesinger, B. (1982). Lasting marriages in the 1980s. *Conciliation Courts Review, 20*, 43–49.

Schlesinger, K. (1985). Behavioral genetics and the nature-nurture question. In G. A. Kimble & K. Schlesinger (Eds.), *Topics in the history of psychology* (Vol. 2, pp. 19–62). Hillsdale, NJ: Erlbaum.

Schmeidler, G. R. (1985). Belief and disbelief in psi. *Parapsychology Review, 16*, 1–4.

Schmidt, G., & Weiner, B. (1988). A attribution-affect-action theory of behavior: Replications of judgments of help-giving. *Personality and Social Psychology Bulletin, 14*, 610–621.

Schmidt, S. R., & Bohannon, J. N. (1988). In defense of the flashbulb-memory hypothesis: A comment on McCloskey, Wible, and Cohen (1988). *Journal of Experimental Psychology: General, 117*, 332–335.

Schnaiberg, A., & Goldenberg, S. (1989). From empty nest to crowded nest: The dynamics of incompletely launched young adults. *Social Problems, 36*, 251–269.

Schneider, B., Trehub, S. E., & Bull, D. (1980). High frequency hearing in infants. *Science, 207*, 1003–1004.

Schneider, C. J. (1987). Cost effectiveness of biofeedback and behavioral medicine treatments: A review of the literature. *Biofeedback and Self-Regulation, 12*, 71–92.

Schneider, H. G., & Shugar, G. J. (1990). Audience and feedback effects in computer learning. *Computers in Human Behavior, 6*, 315–321.

Schneider, W., & Shiffrin, R. M. (1977). Controlled and automatic human information processing: I. Detection, search, and attention. *Psychological Review, 84*, 1–66.

Schneider, W. H. (1992). After Binet: French intelligence testing, 1900–1950. *Journal of the History of the Behavioral Sciences, 28*, 111–132.

Schneider-Helmert, D., & Spinweber, C. L. (1986). Evaluation of l-tryptophan for treatment of insomnia: A review. *Psychopharmacology, 89*, 1–7.

Schoeneman, T. J., & Rubanowitz, D. E. (1985). Attributions in the advice columns: Actors and observers, causes and reasons. *Personality and Social Psychology Bulletin, 11*, 315–325.

Schroeder, D. A., Dovidio, J. F., Sibicky, M. E., Matthews, L. L., & Allen, J. L. (1988). Empathic concern and helping behavior: Egoism or altruism? *Journal of Experimental Social Psychology, 24*, 333–353.

Schroth, M. L. (1991). Dyadic adjustment and sensation seeking compatibility. *Personality and Individual Differences, 12*, 467–471.

Schull, W. J., Norton, S., & Jensh, R. P. (1990). Ionizing radiation and the developing brain. *Neurotoxicology and Teratology, 12*, 249–260.

Schultheis, K., Peterson, L., & Selby, V. (1987). Preparation for stressful medical procedures and person-by-treatment interactions. *Clinical Psychology Review, 7*, 329–352.

Schulz, R., & Curnow, C. (1988). Peak performance and age among superathletes: Track and field, swimming, baseball, tennis, and golf. *Journal of Gerontology, 43*, 113–120.

Schumacher, M., Coirini, H., Pfaff, D. W., & McEwen, B. S. (1990). Light-dark differences in behavioral sensitivity to oxytocin. *Behavioral Neuroscience, 105*, 487–492.

Schuster, B., Forsterling, F., & Weiner, B. (1989). Perceiving the causes of success and failure: A cross-cultural examination of attributional concepts. *Journal of Cross-Cultural Psychology, 20*, 191–213.

Schwarz, S. P., & Blanchard, E. B. (1990). Inflammatory bowel disease: A review of the psychological assessment and treatment literature. *Annals of Behavioral Medicine, 12*, 95–105.

Schweitzer, P. K., Muehlbach, M. J., & Walsh, J. K. (1992). Countermeasures for night work performance deficits: The effect of napping or caffeine on continuous performance at night. *Work and Stress, 6*, 355–365.

Schwolow, R., Wilckens, E., & Roth, N. (1988). Effect of transcutaneous nerve stimulation (TENS) on dental pain: Comparison of psychophysical and neurophysiological data and application in dentistry. *Activitas Nervosa Superior, 30*, 129–130.

Scott, C., Klein, D. M., & Bryant, J. (1990). Consumer response to humor in advertising: A series of field studies using behavioral observation. *Journal of Consumer Research, 16*, 498–501.

Scott, K. G., & Carran, D. T. (1987). The epidemiology and prevention of mental retardation. *American Psychologist, 42*, 801–804.

Scovern, A. W., & Kilmann, P. R. (1980). Status of electroconvulsive therapy: Review of the outcome literature. *Psychological Bulletin, 87*, 260–303.

Scoville, W. B., & Milner, B. (1957). Loss of recent memory after bilateral hippocampal lesions. *Journal of Neurology, Neurosurgery, and Psychiatry, 20*, 11–21.

Searight, H. R., & Searight, P. R. (1988). The homeless mentally ill: Overview, policy implications, and adult foster care as a neglected resource. *Adult Foster Care Journal, 2*, 235–259.

Sears, D. O. (1986). College sophomores in the laboratory: Influences of a narrow data base on social psychology's view of human nature. *Journal of Personality and Social Psychology, 51*, 515–530.

Sears, R. R. (1977). Source of life satisfaction of the Terman gifted men. *American Psychologist, 32*, 119–128.

Sebel, P., Bonke, B., & Winograd, E. (1993). *Memory and awareness in anesthesia.* Englewood Cliffs, NJ: Prentice Hall.

Sechrest, L. (1984). Review of *The development and application of social language theory: Selected papers. Journal of the History of the Behavioral Sciences, 20*, 228–230.

Seeman, J. (1990). Theory as autobiography: The development of Carl Rogers. *Person-Centered Review, 5*, 373–386.

Segal, J., & Luce, G. G. (1966). *Sleep.* New York: Arena Books.

Segal, M. W. (1974). Alphabet and attaction: An unobtrusive measure of the effect of propinquity in a field setting. *Journal of Personality and Social Psychology, 30*, 654–657.

Segall, M. H., Dasen, P. R., Berry, J. W., & Poortinga, Y. H. (1990). *Human behavior in global perspective: An introduction to cross-cultural psychology.* New York: Pergamon.

Seidman, L. J. (1983). Schizophrenia and brain dysfunction: An integration of recent neurodiagnostic findings. *Psychological Bulletin, 94*, 195–238.

Seligman, M. E. P. (1970). On the generality of the laws of learning. *Psychocortical Review, 77*, 406–418.

Seligman, M. E. P. (1971). Phobias and preparedness. *Behavior Therapy, 2*, 307–320.

Seligman, M. E. P. (1989). Research in clinical psychology: Why is there so much depression today? In I. S. Cohen (Ed.), *The G. Stanley Hall Lecture Series* (Vol. 9, pp. 75–96). Washington, DC: American Psychological Association.

Seligman, M. E. P., & Maier, S. F. (1967). Failure to escape traumatic shock. *Journal of Experimental Psychology, 74*, 1–9.

Selye, H. (1936). A syndrome produced by diverse nocuous agents. *Nature, 138*, 32.

Selye, H. (1980). The stress concept today. In I. L. Kutash, L. B. Schlesinger, & Associates (Eds.), *Handbook on stress and anxiety* (pp. 127–143). San Francisco: Jossey-Bass.

Serebriakoff, V. (1985). *Mensa: The society for the highly intelligent.* New York: Stein & Day.

Sergent, J., & Signoret, J.-L. (1992). Implicit access to knowledge derived from unrecognized faces in prosopagnosia. *Cerebral Cortex, 2*, 389–400.

Seyfarth, R. M., Cheney, D. L., & Marler, P. (1980). Monkey responses to three different alarm calls: Evidence of predator classification and semantic communication. *Science, 210*, 801–803.

Shaffer, J. W., Graves, P. L., Swank, R. T., & Pearson, T. A. (1987). Clustering of personality traits in youth and the subsequent development of cancer among physicians. *Journal of Behavioral Medicine, 10*, 441–447.

Shah, M., & Jeffery, R. W. (1991). Is obesity due to overeating and inactivity, or to a defective metabolic rate? A review. *Annals of Behavioral Medicine, 13*, 73–81.

Shaham, Y., Singer, J. E., & Schaeffer, M. H. (1992). Stability/instability of cognitive strategies across tasks determine whether stress will affect judgmental processes. *Journal of Applied Social Psychology, 22*, 691–713.

Shanab, M. E., & Yahya, K. A. (1977). A behavioral study of obedience in children. *Journal of Personality and Social Psychology, 35*, 530–536.

Shapiro, C. M., Bortz, R., Mitchell, D., Bartel, P., & Jooste, P. (1981). Slow-wave sleep: A recovery period after exercise. *Science, 214*, 1253–1254.

Shapley, R. (1990). Visual sensitivity and parallel retinocortical channels. *Annual Review of Psychology, 41*, 635–658.

Sharp, C. W., & Freeman, C. P. (1993). The medical complications of anorexia nervosa. *British Journal of Psychiatry, 162*, 452–462.

Sharpsteen, D. J. (1993). Romantic jealousy as an emotion concept: A prototype analysis. *Journal of Social and Personal Relationships, 10*, 69–82.

Shattuck, R. (1980). *The forbidden experiment: The story of the wild boy of Aveyron.* New York: Washington Square Press.

Shaughnessy, M. F., & Nystul, M. S. (1985). Preventing the greatest loss—suicide. *Creative Child and Adult Quarterly, 10*, 164–169.

Shearn, D. W. (1962). Operant conditioning of heart rate. *Science, 137*, 530–531.

Sheehan, P. W., Green, V., & Truesdale, P. (1992). Influence of rapport on hypnotically induced pseudomemory. *Journal of Abnormal Psychology, 101*, 690–700.

Sheehan, P. W., & Tilden, J. (1983). Effects of suggestibility and hypnosis on accurate and distorted retrieval from memory. *Journal of Experimental Psychology: Learning, Memory, and Cognition, 9*, 283–293.

Sheldon, W. H., & Stevens, S. S. (1942). *The varieties of temperament: A psychology of constitutional differences.* New York: Harper.

Shepard, R. N. (1984). Ecological constraints on internal representation: Resonant kinematics of perceiving, imagining, and dreaming. *Psychological Review, 91*, 417–447.

Sherwin, R., & Corbett, S. (1985). Campus sexual norms and dating relationships: A trend analysis. *Journal of Sex Research, 21*, 258–274.

Shettleworth, S. J., & Juergensen, M. R. (1980). Reinforcement of the organization of behavior in golden hamsters: Brain stimulation reinforcement for seven action patterns. *Journal of Experimental Psychology: Animal Behavior Processes, 6*, 352–375.

Shevrin, H., & Dickman, S. (1980). The psychological unconscious: A necessary assumption for all psychological theory? *American Psychologist, 35*, 421–434.

Shields, S. A. (1975). Functionalism, Darwinism, and the psychology of women: A study in social myth. *American Psychologist, 30*, 739–754.

Shiffrin, R. M., & Atkinson, R. C. (1969). Storage and retrieval processes in long-term memory. *Psychological Review, 76*, 179–193.

Shiraishi, T. (1990). CCK as a central satiety factor: Behavioral and electrophysiological evidence. *Physiology and Behavior, 48*, 879–885.

Shneidman, E. (1987, March). At the point of no return. *Psychology Today*, pp. 54–58.

Shockley, W. (1972). Dysgenics, geneticity, raceology: A challenge to the intellectual responsibility of educators. *Phi Delta Kappan, 53*, 297–307.

Shor, R. E., & Orne, E. C. (1962). *Harvard Group Scale of Hypnotic Susceptibility, Form A*. Palo Alto, CA: Consulting Psychologists Press.

Shostrom, E. L. (1962). *Personal orientation inventory*. San Diego: EDITS.

Shotland, R. L., & Straw, M. J. (1976). Bystander response to an assault: When a man attacks a woman. *Journal of Personality and Social Psychology, 34*, 990–999.

Shurcliff, A. (1968). Judged humor, arousal, and the relief theory. *Journal of Personality and Social Psychology, 8*, 360–363.

Siberstein, A. (1988). An Aristotelan resolution of the idiographic versus nomothetic tension. *American Psychologist, 43*, 425–430.

Sibicky, M., & Dovidio, J. F. (1986). Stigma of psychological therapy: Stereotypes, interpersonal reactions, and the self-fulfilling prophecy. *Journal of Counseling Psychology, 33*, 148–154.

Siegel, J. M., & Brown, J. D. (1988). A prospective study of stressful circumstances, illness symptoms, and depressed mood among adolescents. *Developmental Psychology, 24*, 715–721.

Siegel, M. (1983). Crime and violence in America: The victims. *American Psychologist, 38*, 1267–1273.

Siegel, S., Hinson, R., Krank, M. D., & McCully, J. (1982). Heroin overdose death: Contribution of drug-associated environmental cues. *Science, 216*, 436–437.

Silinsky, E. M. (1989). Adenosine derivatives and neuronal function. *Seminars in the Neurosciences, 1*, 155–165.

Silva, J. M., III, & Weinberg, R. S. (1984). *Psychological foundations of sport*. Champaign, IL: Human Kinetics.

Silverman, L. H., & Lachmann, F. M. (1985). The therapeutic properties of unconscious oneness fantasies: Evidence and treatment implications. *Contemporary Psychoanalysis, 21*, 91–115.

Silverman, M. S., McCarthy, M., & McGovern, T. (1992). A review of outcome studies of rational-emotive therapy from 1982–1989. *Journal of Rational-Emotive and Cognitive Behavior Therapy, 10*, 111–186.

Silverstein, L. B. (1991). Transforming the debate about child care and maternal employment. *American Psychologist, 46*, 1025–1032.

Simeonsson, R. J. (1991). Primary, secondary, and tertiary prevention in early intervention. *Journal of Early Intervention, 15*, 124–134.

Simon, N. (1979). Kaspar Hauser's recovery and autopsy: A perspective on neurological and sociological requirements for language development. *Annual Progress in Child Psychiatry and Child Development*, 215–224.

Simons, A. D., Garfield, S. L., & Murphy, G. E. (1984). The process of change in cognitive therapy and pharmacotherapy for depression. *Archives of General Psychiatry, 41*, 45–51.

Simonton, D. K. (1988). Age and outstanding achievement: What do we know after a century of research? *Psychological Bulletin, 104*, 251–267.

Simpson, B. A. (1986). The polygraph: Concept, usage, and validity. *Psychology: A Quarterly Journal of Human Behavior, 23*, 42–45.

Sims, H. P., & Manz, C. C. (1984). Observing leader behavior: Toward reciprocal determinism in leadership theory. *Journal of Applied Psychology, 69*, 222–232.

Simson, P. G., Weiss, J. M., Ambrose, M. J., & Webster, A. (1986). Infusion of a monoamine oxidase inhibitor into the locus coeruleus can prevent stress-induced behavioral depression. *Biological Psychiatry, 21*, 724–734.

Singer, A. G., & Macrides, F. (1990). Aphrodisin: Pheromone or transducer? *Chemical Senses, 15*, 199–203.

Singer, D. G. (1983). A time to reexamine the role of television in our lives. *American Psychologist, 38*, 815–816.

Singer, J. L. (1975). Navigating the stream of consciousness. *American Psychologist, 30*, 727–738.

Singer, J. L., & Kolligian, J., Jr. (1987). Personality: Developments in the study of private experience. *Annual Review of Psychology, 38*, 533–574.

Sitton, S., & Rippee, E. T. (1986). Women still want marriage: Sex differences in lonely hearts advertisements. *Psychological Reports, 58*, 257–258.

Sizemore, C. C., & Huber, R. J. (1988). The 22 faces of Eve. *Individual Psychology: Journal of Adlerian Theory, Research, and Practice, 44*, 53–62.

Skinner, B. F. (1945, October). Baby in a box. *Ladies' Home Journal*, pp. 30–31.

Skinner, B. F. (1948). *Walden Two*. New York: Macmillan.

Skinner, B. F. (1953). *Science and human behavior*. New York: Macmillan.

Skinner, B. F. (1956). A case history in scientific method. *American Psychologist, 11*, 221–233.

Skinner, B. F. (1957). *Verbal behavior*. New York: Appleton-Century-Crofts.

Skinner, B. F. (1960). Pigeons in a pelican. *American Psychologist, 15*, 28–37.

Skinner, B. F. (1971). *Beyond freedom and dignity*. New York: Knopf.

Skinner, B. F. (1974). *About behaviorism*. New York: Knopf.

Skinner, B. F. (1984). The shame of American education. *American Psychologist, 39*, 947–954.

Skinner, B. F. (1986). What is wrong with daily life in the Western World? *American Psychologist, 41*, 220–222.

Skinner, B. F. (1989). Teaching machines. *Science, 243*, 1535.

Skinner, N. F. (1983). Switching answers on multiple-choice questions: Shrewdness or shibboleth? *Teaching of Psychology, 10*, 220–222.

Slater, J., & Depue, R. A. (1981). The contribution of environmental events and social support to serious suicide attempts in primary depressive disorder. *Journal of Abnormal Psychology, 90*, 275–285.

Smith, B. M., Schumaker, J. B., Schaeffer, J., & Sherman, J. A. (1982). Increasing participation and improving the quality of discussion in seventh-grade social studies classes. *Journal of Applied Behavior Analysis, 15*, 97–110.

Smith, C. A., & Ellsworth, P. C. (1985). Patterns of cognitive appraisal in emotion. *Journal of Personality and Social Psychology, 48*, 813–838.

Smith, D. (1982). Trends in counseling and psychotherapy. *American Psychologist, 37*, 802–809.

Smith, D., & Kraft, W. A. (1983). DSM-III: Do psychologists really want an alternative? *American Psychologist, 38*, 777–785.

Smith, D. G., Standing, L., & de Man, A. (1992). Verbal memory elicited by ambient odor. *Perceptual and Motor Skills, 74*, 339–343.

Smith, H. V. (1992). Is there a magical number 7+–2? The role of exposure duration and information content in immediate recall. *Irish Journal of Psychology, 13*, 85–97.

Smith, J. D. (1988). Fancher on Gould, Goddard, and historical interpretation: A reply. *American Psychologist, 43*, 744–745.

Smith, J. E., Stefan, C., Kovaleski, M., & Johnson, G. (1991). Recidivism and dependency in a psychiatric population: An investigation with Kelly's Dependency Grid. *International Journal of Personal Construct Psychology, 4*, 157–173.

Smith, L. T. (1974). The interanimal transfer phenomenon: A review. *Psychological Bulletin, 81*, 1078–1095.

Smith, M. B. (1986). The plausible assessment report: A phrenological example. *Professional Psychology: Research and Practice, 17*, 294–295.

Smith, M. C. (1983). Hypnotic memory enhancement of witnesses: Does it work? *Psychological Bulletin, 94*, 387–407.

Smith, M. L., Glass, G. V., & Miller, T. I. (1980). *The benefits of psychotherapy*. Baltimore: The Johns Hopkins University Press.

Smith, P. B. (1975). Controlled studies of the outcome of sensitivity training. *Psychological Bulletin, 82*, 597–622.

Smith, P. F., & Curthoys, I. S. (1989). Mechanisms of recovery following unilateral labyrinthectomy: A review. *Brain Research Reviews, 14*, 155–180.

Smith, R. H., Diener, E., & Wedell, D. H. (1989). Intrapersonal and social comparison determinants of happiness: A range-frequency analysis. *Journal of Personality and Social Psychology, 56*, 317–325.

Smith, S. M. (1984). A comparison of two techniques for reducing context-dependent forgetting. *Memory and Cognition, 12*, 477–482.

Smith, S. M. (1985). Environmental context and recognition memory reconsidered. *Bulletin of the Psychonomic Society, 23*, 173–176.

Smith, S. M., Brown, H. O., Toman, J. E. P., & Goodman, L. S. (1947). The lack of cerebral effects of d-tubercurarine. *Anesthesiology, 8*, 1–14.

Smith, S. S., & Richardson, D. (1983). Amelioration of deception and harm in psychological research: The important role of debriefing. *Journal of Personality and Social Psychology, 44*, 1075–1082.

Smith, T., Snyder, C. R., & Perkins, S. C. (1983). The self-serving function of hypochondriacal complaints: Physical symptoms as self-handicapping strategies. *Journal of Personality and Social Psychology, 44*, 787–797.

Smith, T. W. (1983). Change in irrational beliefs and the outcome of rational-emotive psychotherapy. *Journal of Consulting and Clinical Psychology, 51*, 156–157.

Smith, T. W., & Pope, M. K. (1990). Cynical hostility as a health risk: Current status and future directions. *Journal of Social Behavior and Personality, 5*, 77–88.

Snarey, J., Son, L., Kuehne, V. S., Hauser, S., & Vaillant, G. (1987). The role of parenting in men's psychosocial development: A longitudinal study of early adulthood infertility and midlife generativity. *Developmental Psychology, 23*, 593–603.

Snarey, J. R., Reimer, J., & Kohlberg, L. (1985). Development of social-moral reasoning among kibbutz adolescents: A longitudinal cross-cultural study. *Developmental Psychology, 21*, 3–17.

Sno, H. N., Schalken, H. F., & de Jonghe, F. (1992). Empirical research on deja vu experiences: A review. *Behavioural-Neurology, 5*, 155–160.

Snow, C. E. (1981). The uses of imitation. *Journal of Child Language, 8*, 205–212.

Snyder, B. K., Roghmann, K. J., & Sigal, L. H. (1993). Stress and psychosocial factors: Effects on primary cellular immune response. *Journal of Behavioral Medicine, 16*, 143–161.

Snyder, M. (1983). The influence of individuals on situations: Implications for understanding the links between personality and social behavior. *Journal of Personality, 51*, 497–516.

Snyderman, M., & Herrnstein, R. J. (1983). Intelligence tests and the Immigration Act of 1924. *American Psychologist, 38*, 986–995.

Sobrian, S. K., Burton, L. E., Robinson, N. L., & Ashe, W. K. (1990). Neurobehavioral and immunological effects of prenatal cocaine exposure in rats. *Pharmacology, Biochemistry, and Behavior, 35*, 617–629.

Sogon, S., & Izard, C. E. (1987). Sex differences in emotion recognition by observing body movements: A case of American students. *Japanese Psychological Research, 29*, 89–93.

Sokolov, E. N., & Izmailov, C. A. (1988). Three-stage model of color vision. *Sensory Systems, 2*, 314–320.

Solomon, P. R., & Morse, D. L. (1981). Teaching the principles of operant conditioning through laboratory experience: The rat olympics. *Teaching Psychology, 8*, 111–112.

Solomon, R. L. (1980). The opponent-process theory of acquired motivation: The costs of pleasure and the benefits of pain. *American Psychologist, 35*, 691–712.

Solomon, S., & Guglielmo, K. M. (1985). Treatment of headache by transcutaneous electrical stimulation. *Headache, 25*, 12–15.

Solomon, S. D. (1982). Individual versus group therapy: Current status in the treatment of alcoholism. *Advances in Alcohol and Substance Abuse, 2*, 69–86.

Sommers, S. (1984). Reported emotions and conventions of emotionality among college students. *Journal of Personality and Social Psychology, 46*, 207–215.

Sondhaus, E., & Finger, S. (1988). Aphasia and the CNS from Imhotep to Broca. *Neuropsychology, 2*, 87–110.

Sonstroem, R. J., & Bernardo, P. (1982). Intraindividual pregame state anxiety and basketball performance: A re-examination of the inverted-U curve. *Journal of Sport Psychology, 4*, 235–245.

Sothmann, M. S., Horn, T. S., Hart, B. A., & Gustafson, A. B. (1987). Comparison of discrete cardiovascular fitness groups on plasma, catecholamine and selected behavioral responses to psychological stress. *Psychophysiology, 24*, 47–54.

Spangenberg, J., & Nel, E. M. (1983). The effect of equal-status contact on ethnic attitudes. *Journal of Social Psychology, 121*, 173–180.

Spangler, W. D. (1992). Validity of questionnaire and TAT measures of need for achievement: Two meta-analyses. *Psychological Bulletin, 112*, 140–154.

Spanos, N. P., & Hewitt, E. C. (1980). The hidden observer in hypnotic analgesia: Discovery or experimental creation? *Journal of Personality and Social Psychology, 49*, 1201–1214.

Spanos, N. P., McNeil, C., & Stam, H. J. (1982). Hypnotically "reliving" a prior burn: Effects on blister formation and localized skin temperature. *Journal of Abnormal Psychology, 91*, 303–305.

Spanos, N. P., Weekes, J. R., & Bertrand, L. D. (1985). Multiple personality: A social psychological perspective. *Journal of Abnormal Psychology, 94*, 362–376.

Spearman, C. (1927). *The abilities of man.* London: Macmillan.

Spector, I. P., & Carey, M. P. (1990). Incidence and prevalence of the sexual dysfunctions: A critical review of the empirical literature. *Archives of Sexual Behavior, 19*, 389–408.

Speisman, J. C., Lazarus, R. S., Mordkoff, A., & Davison, L. (1964). Experimental reduction of stress based on ego-defense theory. *Journal of Abnormal and Social Psychology, 68*, 367–380.

Sperling, G. (1960). The information available in brief visual presentations. *Psychological Monographs, 74* (498).

Sperry, R. (1982). Some effects of disconnecting the cerebral hemispheres. *Science, 217*, 1223–1226.

Spetch, M. L., Wilkie, D. M., & Pinel, J. P. J. (1981). Backward conditioning: A reevaluation of the empirical evidence. *Psychological Bulletin, 89*, 163–175.

Spiegel, D., Cutcomb, S., Ren, C., & Pribram, K. (1985). Hypnotic hallucination alters evoked potentials. *Journal of Abnormal Psychology, 94*, 249–255.

Spiess, W. F., Geer, J. H., & O'Donohue, W. T. (1984). Premature ejaculation: Investigation of factors in ejaculatory latency. *Journal of Abnormal Psychology, 93*, 242–245.

Spitzer, R. L. (1975). On pseudoscience in science, logic in remission, and psychiatric diagnosis: A critique of Rosenhan's "On being sane in insane places." *Journal of Abnormal Psychology, 84*, 442–452.

Sprecher, S. (1989). The importance to males and females of physical attractiveness, earning potential, and expressiveness in initial attraction. *Sex Roles, 21*, 591–607.

Spring, B., Chiodo, J., & Bowen, D. J. (1987). Carbohydrates, tryptophan, and behavior: A methodological review. *Psychological Bulletin, 102*, 234–256.

Springer, S. P., & Deutsch, G. (1989). *Left brain, right brain.* San Francisco: Freeman.

Springer, S. P., & Deutsch, G. (1993). *Left brain, right brain* (4th ed.). New York: W. H. Freeman.

Spurgeon, A., & Harrington, J. M. (1989). Work performance and health of junior hospital doctors: A review of the literature. *Work and Stress, 3*, 117–128.

Spurlock, J. (1986). Development of self-concept in Afro-American children. *Hospital and Community Psychiatry, 37*, 66–70.

Spyer, K. M. (1989). Neural mechanisms involved in cardiovascular control during affective behavior. *Trends in Neurosciences, 12*, 506–513.

Squire, L. R. (1992). Declarative and nondeclarative memory: Multiple brain systems supporting learning and memory. *Journal of Cognitive Neuroscience, 4*, 232–243.

Stafford-Clark, D. (1965). *What Freud really said.* New York: Schocken Books.

Stairs, A. (1992). Self-image, world-image: Speculations on identity from experiences with Inuit. *Ethos, 20*, 116–126.

Stake, J. E., & Pearlman, J. (1980). Assertiveness training as an intervention technique for low performance self-esteem women. *Journal of Counseling Psychology, 27*, 276–281.

Stankov, L., & Chen, K. (1988). Can we boost fluid and crystallized intelligence? A structural modelling approach. *Australian Journal of Psychology, 40*, 363–376.

Stanley, M. A., & Maddux, J. E. (1986). Self-efficacy theory: Potential contributions to understanding cognitions in depression. *Journal of Social and Clinical Psychology, 4*, 268–278.

Stapleton, J. M., Guthrie, S., & Linnoila, M. (1986). Effects of alcohol and other psychotropic drugs on eye movements: Relevance to traffic safety. *Journal of Studies on Alcohol, 47*, 426–432.

Stapp, J., Tucker, A. M., & VandenBos, G. R. (1985). Census of psychological personnel: 1983. *American Psychologist, 40*, 1317–1351.

Stark, E. (1981, September). Pigeon patrol. *Science, 81*, pp. 85–86.

Steele, C. M., Critchlow, B., & Liu, T. J. (1985). Alcohol and social behavior: 2. The helpful drunkard. *Journal of Personality and Social Psychology, 48*, 35–46.

Stehouwer, D. J. (1987). Effect of tectotomy and decerebration on spontaneous and elicited behavior of tadpoles and juvenile frogs. *Behavioral Neuroscience, 101*, 378–384.

Steinberg, L., Fegley, S., & Dornbusch, S. M. (1993). Negative impact of part-time work on adolescent adjustment: Evidence from a longitudinal study. *Developmental Psychology, 29*, 171–180.

Steinberg, L., Lamborn, S. D., Dornbusch, S. M., & Darling, N. (1992). Impact of parenting practices on adolescent achievement: Authoritative parenting, school achievement, and encouragement to succeed. *Child Development, 63*, 1266–1281.

Steinbrueck, S. M., Maxwell, S. E., & Howard, G. S. (1983). A meta-analysis of psychotherapy and drug therapy in the treatment of unipolar depression with adults. *Journal of Consulting and Clinical Psychology, 51*, 856–863.

Steiner, S. S., & Dince, W. M. (1981). Biofeedback efficacy studies: A critique of critiques. *Biofeedback and Self-Regulation, 6*, 275–288.

Stelmack, R. M. (1990). Biological bases of extraversion: Psychophysiological evidence. *Journal of Personality, 58*, 293–311.

Stelmack, R. M., & Stalikas, A. (1991). Galen and the humour theory of temperament. *Personality and Individual Differences, 12*, 255–263.

Stemmer, N. (1990). Skinner's *Verbal Behavior*, Chomsky's review, and mentalism. *Journal of the Experimental Analysis of Behavior, 54*, 307–315.

Sternberg, D. E., Van Kammen, D. P., Lerner, P., & Bunney, W. E. (1982). Schizophrenia: Dopamine beta-hydroxylase activity and treatment response. *Science, 216*, 1423–1425.

Sternberg, R. J. (1984). *Beyond IQ: A triarchic theory of intelligence*. New York: Cambridge University Press.

Sternberg, R. J., Conway, B. E., Ketron, J. L., & Bernstein, M. (1981). People's conceptions of intelligence. *Journal of Personality and Social Psychology, 41*, 37–55.

Sternberg, R. J., & Wagner, R. K. (1993). The g-ocentric view of intelligence and job performance is wrong. *Current Directions in Psychological Science, 2*, 1–5.

Sternberg, S. (1966). High speed scanning in human memory. *Science, 153*, 652–654.

Stevens, J. C. (1989). Food quality reports from noninstitutionalized aged. *Annals of the New York Academy of Sciences, 561*, 87–93.

Stiles, W. B., Shapiro, D. A., & Elliott, R. (1986). Are all psychotherapies equivalent? *American Psychologist, 41*, 165–180.

St. Lawrence, J. S., & Madakasira, S. (1992). Evaluation and treatment of premature ejaculation: A critical review. *International Journal of Psychiatry in Medicine, 22*, 77–97.

Stocking, G. W., Jr. (1965). On the limits of "presentism" and "historicism" in the historiography of the behavioral sciences. *Journal of the History of the Behavioral Sciences 1*, 211–218.

Stone, A. A., Cox, D. S., Valdimarsdottir, H., Jandorf, L., & Neale, J. M. (1987). Evidence that secretory IgA antibody is associated with daily mood. *Journal of Personality and Social Psychology, 52*, 988–993.

Stone, A. A., Hedges, S. M., Neale, J. M., & Satin, M. S. (1985). Prospective and cross-sectional mood reports offer no evidence of a "blue Monday" phenomenon. *Journal of Personality and Social Psychology, 49*, 129–134.

Stone, W. S., Rudd, R. J., & Gold, P. E. (1990). Amphetamine, epinephrine, and glucose enhancement of memory retrieval. *Psychology, 18*, 227–230.

Stoner, J. A. F. (1961). *A comparison of individual and group decisions involving risk*. Unpublished master's thesis, Massachusetts Institute of Technology.

Storms, M. D. (1981). A theory of erotic orientation development. *Psychological Review, 88*, 340–353.

Strack, F., Schwarz, N., Chassein, B., & Kern, D. (1990). Salience of comparison standards and the activation of social norms: Consequences for judgements of happiness and their communication. *British Journal of Social Psychology, 29*, 303–314.

Strange, W., & Dittmann, S. (1984). Effects of discrimination training on the perception of r-l by Japanese adults learning English. *Perception and Psychophysics, 36*, 131–145.

Strassman, R. J. (1984). Adverse reactions to psychedelic drugs: A review of the literature. *Journal of Nervous and Mental Disease, 172*, 577–595.

Stratton, G. M. (1917). The mnemonic feat of the "Shass Pollak." *Psychological Review, 24*, 244–247.

Straub, W. F. (1982). Sensation seeking among high- and low-risk male athletes. *Journal of Sport Psychology, 4*, 246–253.

Strauman, T. J., & Higgins, E. T. (1988). Self-discrepancies as predictors of vulnerability to distinct syndromes of chronic emotional distress. *Journal of Personality, 56*, 685–707.

Streissguth, A. P., Randels, S. P., & Smith, D. F. (1991). A test-retest study of intelligence in patients with fetal alcohol syndrome: Implications for care. *Journal of the American Academy of Child and Adolescent Psychiatry, 30*, 584–587.

Stretch, R. H. (1991). Psychosocial readjustment of Canadian Vietnam veterans. *Journal of Consulting and Clinical Psychology, 59*, 188–189.

Strichartz, A. F., & Burton, R. V. (1990). Lies and truth: A study of the development of the concept. *Child Development, 61*, 211–220.

Stricker, E. M., & McCann, M. J. (1985). Visceral factors in the control of food intake. *Brain Research Bulletin, 14*, 687–692.

Stricker, E. M., & Verbalis, J. G. (1987). Biological bases of hunger and satiety. *Annals of Behavioral Medicine, 9*, 3–8.

Strickland, B. R. (1989). Internal-external control expectancies: From contingency to creativity. *American Psychologist, 44*, 1–12.

Striegel-Moore, R. H., Silberstein, L. R., & Rodin, J. (1986). Toward an understanding of risk factors in bulimia. *American Psychologist, 41*, 246–263.

Strober, M., & Humphrey, L. L. (1987). Familial contributions to the etiology and course of anorexia nervosa and bulimia. *Journal of Consulting and Clinical Psychology, 55*, 654–659.

Stroebe, M. S., & Stroebe, W. (1983). Who suffers more? Sex differences in health risks of the widowed. *Psychological Bulletin, 93*, 279–301.

Strunk, O. (1972). The self-psychology of Mary Whiton Calkins. *Journal of the History of the Behavioral Sciences, 8*, 196–203.

Strupp, H. H. (1989). Psychotherapy: Can the practitioner learn from the researcher? *American Psychologist, 44*, 717–724.

Strupp, H. H., & Hadley, S. W. (1979). Specific versus nonspecific factors in psychotherapy: A controlled study of outcome. *Archives of General Psychiatry, 36*, 1125–1136.

Stunkard, A. J., Sorensen, T., Hanis, C., Teasdale, T. W., Chakraborty, R., Schull, W. J., & Schulsinger, F. (1986). An adoption study of human obesity. *New England Journal of Medicine, 314*, 193–198.

Stunkard, A. J., Stinnett, J. L., & Smoller, J. W. (1986). Psychological and social aspects of the surgical treatment of obesity. *American Journal of Psychiatry, 143*, 417–429.

Sturgeon, R. S., Cooper, L. M., & Howell, R. J. (1989). Pupil response: A psychophysiological measure of fear during analogue desensitization. *Perceptual and Motor Skills, 69*, 1351–1367.

Stuss, D. T., & Benson, D. F. (1984). Neuropsychological studies of the frontal lobes. *Psychological Bulletin, 95*, 3–28.

Sue, S., & Okazaki, S. (1990). Asian-American educational achievements: A phenomenon in search of an explanation. *American Psychologist, 45*, 913–920.

Suedfeld, P. (1990). Restricted environmental stimulation and smoking cessation: A 15-year progress report. *International Journal of the Addictions, 25*, 861–888.

Suedfeld, P., & Bruno, T. (1990). Flotation REST and imagery in the improvement of athletic performance. *Journal of Exercise and Exercise Psychology, 12*, 82–85.

Suedfeld, P., Collier, D. E., & Hartnett, B. D. (1993). Enhancing perceptual-motor accuracy through flotation REST. *Sport Psychologist, 7*, 151–159.

Suedfeld, P., & Coren, S. (1989). Perceptual isolation, sensory deprivation, and REST: Moving introductory psychology texts out of the 1950s. *Canadian Psychology, 30*, 17–29.

Suedfeld, P., Metcalfe, J., & Bluck, S. (1987). Enhancement of scientific creativity by flotation REST (restricted environmental stimulation technique). *Journal of Environmental Psychology, 7*, 219–231.

Suedfeld, P., Roy, C., & Landon, P. B. (1982). Restricted environmental stimulation therapy in the treatment of essential hypertension. *Behaviour Research and Therapy, 20*, 553–559.

Suler, J. R. (1980). Primary process thinking and creativity. *Psychological Bulletin, 88*, 144–165.

Sulin, R. A., & Dooling, D. J. (1974). Intrusion of a thematic idea in retention of prose. *Journal of Experimental Psychology, 103*, 255–262.

Sullivan, H. S. (1953). *An interpersonal theory of psychiatry*. New York: W. W. Norton.

Sulloway, F. J. (1979). *Freud: Biologist of the mind*. New York: Basic Books.

Sumino, R., & Dubner, R. (1981). Response characteristics of specific thermoreceptive afferents innervating monkey facial skin and their relationship to human thermal sensitivity. *Brain Research Reviews, 3*, 105–122.

Superkids?: A sperm bank for Nobelists. (1980, March 10). *Time*, p. 49.

Survey finds most rape victims are minors: Many are under 10. (1992, April 26). *Philadelphia Inquirer*, p. A–6.

Sussan, T. A. (1990). How to handle due process litigation effectively under the Education for All Handicapped Children Act of 1975. *Journal of Reading, Writing, and Learning Disabilities International, 6,* 63–70.

Swaab, D. F., & Hofman, M. A. (1990). An enlarged suprachiasmatic nucleus in homosexual men. *Brain Research, 537,* 141–148.

Swaim, R. C., Oetting, E. R., Edwards, R. W., & Beauvais, F. (1989). Links from emotional distress to adolescent drug use: A path model. *Journal of Consulting and Clinical Psychology, 57,* 227–231.

Swain, J. J., Allard, G. B., & Holborn, S. W. (1982). The good toothbrushing game: A school-based dental hygiene program for increasing the toothbrushing effectiveness of children. *Journal of Applied Behavior Analysis, 15,* 171–176.

Swain, R. B. (1984, August). Message from a heaving deck. *Discover,* pp. 60–62, 64.

Swayze, V. W., Andreasen, N. C., Alliger, R. J., & Ehrhardt, J. C. (1990). Structural brain abnormalities in bipolar affective disorder: Ventricular enlargement and focal signal hyperintensities. *Archives of General Psychiatry, 47,* 1054–1059.

Sweeney, P. D., Anderson, K., & Bailey, S. (1986). Attributional style in depression: A meta-analytic review. *Journal of Personality and Social Psychology, 50,* 974–991.

Swenson, R. S., Danielsen, E. H., Klausen, B. S., & Erlich, E. (1989). Deficits in beam-walking after neonatal motor cortical lesions are not spared by fetal cortical transplants in rats. *Journal of Neural Transplantation, 1,* 129–133.

Swiezy, N. B., Matson, J. L., & Box, P. (1992). The Good Behavior Game: A token reinforcement system for preschoolers. *Child and Family Behavior Therapy, 14,* 21–32.

Swindale, N. V. (1982). The development of columnar systems in the mammalian visual cortex: The role of innate and environmental factors. *Trends in Neurosciences, 5,* 235–241.

Szasz, T. (1960). The myth of mental illness. *American Psychologist, 15,* 113–118.

Szasz, T. (1980). "J'Accuse": Psychiatry and the diminished American capacity for justice. *Journal of Mind and Behavior, 1,* 111–120.

Szasz, T. (1991). Noncoercive psychiatry: An oxymoron: Reflections on Law, Liberty, and Psychiatry. *Journal of Humanistic Psychology, 31,* 117–125.

Szymanski, S., Kane, J. M., & Lieberman, J. A. (1991). A selective review of biological markers in schizophrenia. *Schizophrenia Bulletin, 17,* 99–111.

Takagi, M., Toda, H., Yoshizawa, T., & Hara, N. (1992). Ocular convergence-related neuronal responses in the lateral suprasylvian area of alert cats. *Neuroscience Research, 15,* 229–234.

Takahata, Y., Hasegawa, T., & Nishida, T. (1984). Chimpanzee predation in the Mahale Mountains from August 1979 to May 1982. *International Journal of Primatology, 5,* 213–233.

Takeshige, C. (1985). Differentiation between acupuncture and non-acupuncture points by association with analgesia inhibitory system. *Acupuncture and Electro-Therapeutics Research, 10,* 195–202.

Talley, P. F., Strupp, H. H., & Morey, L. C. (1990). Matchmaking in psychotherapy: Patient-therapist dimensions and their impact on outcome. *Journal of Consulting and Clinical Psychology, 58,* 182–188.

Tang, T. L., & Hammontree, M. L. (1992). The effects of hardiness, police stress, and life stress on police officers' illness and absenteeism. *Public Personnel Management, 21,* 493–510.

Tankard, J. W. (1984). *The statistical pioneers.* Cambridge, MA: Schenkman.

Tarchanoff, J. R. (1885). Uber die willkurliche acceleration der herzschlage beim menschen (Voluntary acceleration of the heart beat in man). *Pflugers Archives, 35,* 109–135. Reprinted in D. Shapiro et al. (Eds.), *Biofeedback and Self-Control, 1972* (pp. 3–20), Chicago: Aldine-Atherton (1973).

Task Force on the Use of Laboratory Tests in Psychiatry. (1985). Tricyclic antidepressants—blood level measurements and clinical outcome: An APA task force report. *American Journal of Psychiatry, 142,* 155–162.

Taulbee, P. (1983). Solving the mystery of anxiety. *Science News, 124,* 45.

Taylor, E. (1991). William James and the humanistic tradition. *Journal of Humanistic Psychology, 31,* 56–74.

Taylor, R. L. (1990). The Larry P. decision a decade later: Problems and future directions. *Mental Retardation, 28,* iii–vi.

Taylor, S. E., & Brown, J. D. (1988). Illusion and well-being: A social psychological perspective on mental health. *Psychological Bulletin, 103,* 193–210.

Teaching a machine the shades of gray. (1981). *Science News, 119,* 38–39.

Teicher, M. H., Glod, C., & Cole, J. O. (1990). Emergence of intense suicide preoccupation during fluoxetine treatment. *American Journal of Psychiatry, 147,* 207–210.

Teichman, Y., & Teichman, M. (1990). Interpersonal view of depression: Review and integration. *Journal of Family Psychology, 3,* 349–367.

Teigen, K. H. (1984). A note on the origin of the term "nature and nurture": Not Shakespeare and Galton, but Mulcaster. *Journal of the History of the Behavioral Sciences, 20,* 363–364.

Telch, C. F., & Telch, M. J. (1985). Psychological approaches for enhancing coping among cancer patients: A review. *Clinical Psychology Review, 5,* 325–344.

Tellegen, A., Lykken, D. T., Bouchard, T. J., Jr., Wilcox, K. J., Segal, N. L., & Rich, S. (1988). Personality similarity in twins reared apart and together. *Journal of Personality and Social Psychology, 54,* 1031–1039.

Tenzer, S. (1989). Fat acceptance therapy (F.A.T.): A non-dieting group approach to physical wellness, insight and self-acceptance. *Women and Therapy, 8,* 39–47.

Terman, L. M. (1917). The intelligence quotient of Francis Galton in childhood. *American Journal of Psychology, 28,* 209–215.

Terrace, H. S. (1985). In the beginning was the "name." *American Psychologist, 40,* 1011–1028.

Terrace, H. S., Petitto, L. A., Sanders, R. J., & Bever, T. G. (1979). Can an ape create a sentence? *Science, 206,* 891–902.

Terry, R. L., & Stanley, J. W. (1974). Manipulations of consumer directional responses. *Psychology, 11,* 17–20.

Thase, M. E., Hersen, M., Bellack, A. S., Himmelhoch, J. M., Kornblith, S. J., & Greenwald, D. P. (1984). Social skills training and endogenous depression. *Journal of Behavior Therapy and Experimental Psychiatry, 15,* 101–108.

Thielman, S. B., & Larson, D. B. (1984). Christianity and early American care for the insane: The work of doctor Benjamin Rush. *Journal of Psychology & Christianity, 3,* 27–34.

Thomas, E. (1988). Forebrain mechanisms in the relief of fear: The role of the lateral septum. *Psychobiology, 16,* 36–44.

Thomas, E., Yadin, E., & Strickland, C. E. (1991). Septal unit activity during classical conditioning: A regional comparison. *Brain Research, 547,* 303–308.

Thomas, H. (1993). A theory explaining sex differences in high mathematical ability has been around for some time. *Behavioral and Brain Sciences, 16,* 187–189.

Thomas, J. R., & French, K. E. (1985). Gender differences across age in motor performance: A meta-analysis. *Psychological Bulletin, 98,* 260–282.

Thomas, L. (1981, December). On the need for asylums. *Discover,* pp. 68, 71.

Thomas, R. E., Vaidya, S. C., Herrick, R. T., & Congleton, J. (1993). The effects of biofeedback on carpal tunnel syndrome. *Ergonomics, 36,* 353–361.

Thompson, J. P., Anglin, M. D., Emboden, W., & Fisher, D. G. (1985). Mushroom use by college students. *Journal of Drug Education, 15,* 111–124.

Thorndike, E. L. (1898). Animal intelligence: An experimental study of the associative processes in animals. *Psychological Review Monograph Supplement, 2* (No. 8).

Thorndike, E. L. (1961). Edward Lee Thorndike. In C. Murchison (Ed.), *A history of psychology in autobiography* (Vol. 3, pp. 263–270). New York: Russell & Russell.

Thorson, J. A. (1985). A funny thing happened on the way to the morgue: Some thoughts on humor and death, and a taxonomy of the humor associated with death. *Death Studies, 9,* 201–216.

Thurman, C. W. (1985). Effectiveness of cognitive-behavioral treatments in reducing Type A behavior among university faculty one year later. *Journal of Counseling Psychology, 32,* 445–448.

Thurstone, L. L. (1938). *Primary mental abilities.* Chicago: University of Chicago Press.

Tice, D. M., & Baumeister, R. F. (1990). Self-esteem, self-handicapping, and self-presentation: The strategy of inadequate practice. *Journal of Personality, 58,* 443–464.

Tiffany, S. T., Martin, E. M., & Baker, T. B. (1986). Treatments for cigarette smoking: An evaluation of the contributions of aversion and counseling procedures. *Behaviour Research and Therapy, 24,* 437–452.

Tilley, A. J., & Empson, J. A. (1978). REM sleep and memory consolidation. *Biological Psychology, 6,* 293–300.

Timberlake, W., & Farmer-Dougan, V. A. (1991). Reinforcement in applied settings: Figuring out ahead of time what will work. *Psychological Bulletin, 110,* 379–391.

Timberlake, W., & Melcer, T. (1988). Effects of poisoning on predatory and ingestive behavior toward artificial prey in rats (*Rattus norvegicus*). *Journal of Comparative Psychology, 102,* 182–187.

Timm, H. W. (1982). Effect of altered outcome expectancies stemming from placebo and feedback treatments on the validity of the guilty knowledge technique. *Journal of Applied Psychology, 67,* 391–400.

Tolman, E. C. (1932). *Purposive behavior in animals and man.* New York: Appleton-Century-Crofts.

Tolman, E. C., & Honzik, C. H. (1930). Introduction and removal of reward, and maze performance in rats. *University of California Publications in Psychology, 4,* 257–275.

Tomarken, A. J., Mineka, S., & Cook, M. (1989). Fear-relevant selective associations and covariation bias. *Journal of Abnormal Psychology, 98,* 381–394.

Tomizuka, C., & Tobias, S. (1981). Mathematical ability: Is sex a factor? *Science, 212,* 114.

Tordoff, M. G., Novin, D., & Russek, M. (1982). Effects of hepatic denervation of the anorexic response to epinephrine, amphetamine, and lithium chloride: A behavioral identification of glucostatic afferents. *Journal of Comparative and Physiological Psychology, 96,* 361–375.

Torgersen, S. (1983). Genetic factors in anxiety disorders. *Archives of General Psychiatry, 40,* 1085–1089.

Torgersen, S. (1986). Genetics of somatoform disorders. *Archives of General Psychiatry, 43,* 502–505.

Torgersen, S. (1989). Genetics of panic disorder. *Psychiatria Fennica,* (Supplement), 29–34.

Torrance, E. P. (1993). The beyonders in a 30-year longitudinal study of creative achievement. *Roeper Review, 15,* 131–135.

Torrey, E. F. (1981, November). The protection of Ezra Pound. *Psychology Today,* pp. 57–66.

Tosteson, D. C. (1981, April). Lithium and mania. *Scientific American,* pp. 164–174.

Totten, G., Lamb, D. H., & Reeder, G. D. (1990). Tarasoff and confidentiality in AIDS-related psychotherapy. *Professional Psychology: Research and Practice, 21,* 155–160.

Tourney, G. (1965). Freud and the Greeks: A study of the influence of classical Greek mythology and philosophy upon the development of Freudian thought. *Journal of the History of the Behavioral Sciences, 1,* 67–87.

Towbin, A. (1978). Cerebral dysfunctions related to perinatal organic damage: Clinical-neuropathologic correlations. *Journal of Abnormal Psychology, 87,* 617–635.

Towell, A., Muscat, R., & Willner, P. (1989). Noradrenergic receptor interactions in feeding elicited by stimulation of the paraventricular hypothalamus. *Pharmacology, Biochemistry, and Behavior, 32,* 133–139.

Tranel, D., & Damasio, A. R. (1985). Knowledge without our awareness: An automatic index of facial recognition by prosopagnosics. *Science, 228,* 1453–1454.

Traskman, L., Asberg, M., Bertilsson, L., & Sjostrand, L. (1981). Monoamine metabolites in CSF and suicidal behavior. *Archives of General Psychiatry, 38,* 631–636.

Treisman, M. (1977). Motion sickness: An evolutionary hypothesis. *Science, 197,* 493–495.

Trepper, T. S. (1990). In celebration of the case study. *Journal of Family Psychotherapy, 1,* 5–13.

Trice, A. D., & Ogden, E. P. (1987). Informed consent: 9. Effects of the withdrawal clause in longitudinal research. *Perceptual and Motor Skills, 65,* 135–138.

Triplet, R. G. (1992). Discriminatory biases in the perception of illness: The application of availability and representativeness heuristics to the AIDS crisis. *Basic and Applied Social Psychology, 13,* 303–322.

Triplett, N. (1898). The dynamogenic factors in pacemaking and competition. *American Journal of Psychology, 9,* 507–553.

Troster, H., & Bambring, M. (1992). Early social-emotional development in blind infants. *Child Care, Health and Development, 18,* 207–227.

Trotter, K., Dallas, K., & Verdone, P. (1988). Olfactory stimuli and their effects on REM dreams. *Psychiatric Journal of the University of Ottawa, 13,* 94–96.

Trotter, R. J. (1981). Psychiatry for the 80's. *Science News, 119,* 348–349.

Trotter, R. J. (1986, August). Three heads are better than one. *Psychology Today,* pp. 56–62.

Truax, C. B. (1966). Reinforcement and nonreinforcement in Rogerian psychotherapy. *Journal of Abnormal Psychology, 71,* 1–9.

Trujillo, C. M. (1983). The effect of weight training and running exercise intervention programs on the self-esteem of college women. *International Journal of Sport Psychology, 14,* 162–173.

Tucker, L. A. (1982). Effect of a weight training program on the self-concept of college males. *Perceptual and Motor Skills, 54,* 1055–1061.

Tucker, L. A. (1983). Muscular strength: A predictor of personality in males. *Journal of Sports Medicine and Physical Fitness, 23,* 213–220.

Tucker, L. A., Aldana, S. G., & Friedman, G. M. (1990). Cardiovascular fitness and absenteeism in 8,301 employed adults. *American Journal of Health Promotion, 5,* 140–145.

Tulsky, F. N. (1986, March 28). $988,000 is awarded in suit over lost psychic power. *Philadelphia Inquirer,* p. 1-A.

Tulving, E. (1985). How many memory systems are there? *American Psychologist, 40,* 385–398.

Tulving, E., Schachter, D. L., McLachlan, D. R., & Moscovitch, M. (1988). Priming of semantic autobiographical knowledge: A case study of retrograde amnesia. *Brain and Cognition, 8,* 3–20.

Tulving, E., & Thomson, D. M. (1973). Encoding specificity and retrieval processes in episodic memory. *Psychological Review, 80,* 352–373.

Turkheimer, E. (1991). Individual and group differences in adoption studies of IQ. *Psychological Bulletin, 110,* 392–405.

Turkington, C. (1984, August). Supportive homes few, barriers many. *APA Monitor,* pp. 20, 22.

Turnbull, C. M. (1961). Some observations regarding the experiences of the Bambuti Pygmies. *American Journal of Psychology, 74,* 304–308.

Turner, S. M., & Beidel, D. C. (1989). Social phobia: Clinical syndrome, diagnosis, and comorbidity. *Clinical Psychology Review, 9,* 3–18.

Turner, S. M., Beidel, D. C., & Costello, A. (1987). Psychopathology in the offspring of anxiety disorder patients. *Journal of Consulting and Clinical Psychology, 55,* 229–235.

Turner, S. M., Beidel, D. C., Long, P. J., & Greenhouse, J. (1992). Reduction of fear in social phobics: An examination of extinction patterns. *Behavior Therapy, 23,* 389–403.

Turner, S. M., Beidel, D. C., & Nathan, R. S. (1985). Biological factors in obsessive-compulsive disorders. *Psychological Bulletin, 97,* 430–450.

Tversky, A., & Kahneman, D. (1973). Availability: A heuristic for judging frequency and probability. *Cognitive Psychology, 5,* 207–232.

Tyler, R. S., Opie, J. M., Fryauf-Bertschy, H., & Gantz, B. J. (1992). Future directions for cochlear implants. *Journal of Speech, Language Pathology, and Audiology, 16,* 151–164.

Type A: A change of heart and mind. (1984). *Science News, 126,* 109.

Tyrrell, R. A., & Leibowitz, H. W. (1990). The relation of vergence effort to reports of visual fatigue following prolonged near work. *Human Factors, 32,* 341–357.

Uliano, K. C., & Carey, J. R. (1984). MBERT: A BASIC program to alleviate experimenter effect in biofeedback research. *Perceptual & Motor Skills, 58,* 206.

Ullman, M., Krippner, S., & Vaughan, A. (1973). *Dream telepathy.* New York: Macmillan.

Ullmann, L. P., & Krasner, L. (1975). *Psychological approaches to abnormal behavior.* Englewood Cliffs, NJ: Prentice Hall.

Ulrich, R. E., Stachnik, T. J., & Stainton, N. R. (1963). Student acceptance of generalized personality interpretations. *Psychological Reports, 13,* 831–834.

Unger, G., Desiderio, D. M., & Parr, W. (1972). Isolation, identification and synthesis of a specific-behavior-inducing brain peptide. *Nature, 238,* 198–202.

Ungs, T. J., & Sangal, S. P. (1990). Perception of near-earth altitudes by pilots: Ascending versus descending over both a land and water surface. *Aviation, Space, and Environmental Medicine, 61,* 1098–1101.

Vacc, N. A. (1987). Gerontological Counseling Grid: Making judgments about older adults. *Counselor Education and Supervision, 26,* 310–316.

Vaillant, G. E. (1992). The historical origins and future potential of Sigmund Freud's concept of the mechanisms of defense. *International Review of Psychoanalysis, 19,* 35–50.

Vaillant, G. E., & Milofsky, E. (1980). Natural history of male psychological health: 9. Empirical evidence for Erikson's model of the life cycle. *American Journal of Psychiatry, 137,* 1348–1359.

Vaillant, G. E., & Vaillant, C. O. (1990). Determinants and consequences of creativity in a cohort of gifted women. *Psychology of Women Quarterly, 14,* 607–616.

Valenstein, E. S. (1980). *The psychosurgery debate.* San Francisco: Freeman.

Valentine, C. W. (1930). The innate bases of fear. *Journal of Genetic Psychology, 37,* 485–497.

Vance, E. B., & Wagner, N. N. (1976). Written descriptions of orgasm: A study of sex differences. *Archives of Sexual Behavior, 5,* 87–98.

Vance, F. L. (1965). I was an imaginary playmate. *American Psychologist, 20,* 990.

Van Denburg, E. J., & Kurtz, R. M. (1989). Changes in body attitude as a function of posthypnotic suggestions. *International Journal of Clinical and Experimental Hypnosis, 37,* 15–30.

Vanden Pol, R. A., Iwata, B. A., Ivancic, M. T., Page, T. J., Neef, N. A., & Whitley, F. P. (1981). Teaching the handicapped to eat in public places: Acquisition, generalization, and maintenance of restaurant skills. *Journal of Applied Behavior Analysis, 14,* 64–69.

Vander Mey, B. J. (1988). The sexual victimization of male children: A review of previous research. *Child Abuse and Neglect, 12,* 61–72.

Vander Plate, C., Aral, S. O., & Magder, L. (1988). The relationship among genital herpes simplex virus, stress, and social support. *Health Psychology, 7,* 159–168.

Van Doorren, L. J. P., & van Blokland, R. (1987). Serum-cholesterol: Sex specific psychological correlates during rest and stress. *Journal of Psychosomatic Research, 31,* 239–249.

Vane, J. R. (1981). The Thematic Apperception Test: A review. *Clinical Psychology Review, 1,* 319–336.

Van Hasselt, V. B., Griest, D. L., Kazdin, A. E., Esveldt-Dawson, K., & Unis, A. S. (1984). Poor peer interactions and social isolation: A case report of successful *in vivo* social skills training on a child psychiatric inpatient unit. *Journal of Behavior Therapy and Experimental Psychiatry, 15,* 271–276.

Van Praag, H. M. (1991). Serotonergic dysfunction and aggression control. *Psychological Medicine, 21,* 15–19.

Van Rood, Y. R., Bogaards, M., Goulmy, E., & Van Houwelingen, H. C. (1993). The effects of stress and relaxation on the in vitro immune response in man: A meta-analytic study. *Journal of Behavioral Medicine, 16,* 163–181.

Vein, A. M., Sidorov, A. A., Martazaev, M. S., & Karlov, A. V. (1991). Physical exercise and nocturnal sleep in healthy humans. *Human Physiology, 17,* 391–397.

Vela-Bueno, A., Soldatos, C. R., & Julius, D. A. (1987). Parasomnias: Sleepwalking, night terrors, and nightmares. *Psychiatric Annals, 17,* 465–469.

Velicer, W. F., Prochaska, J. O., Rossi, J. S., & Snow, M. G. (1992). Assessing outcome in smoking cessation studies. *Psychological Bulletin, 111,* 23–41.

Veliz, J., & James, W. S. (1987). Medicine court: Rogers in practice. *American Journal of Psychiatry, 144,* 62–67.

Venn, J. (1984). Family etiology and remission in a case of psychogenic fugue. *Family Process, 23,* 429–435.

Veroff, J., Depner, C., Kulka, R., & Douvan, E. (1980). Comparison of American motives: 1957 versus 1976. *Journal of Personality and Social Psychology, 39,* 1249–1262.

Vetter, H. J. (1969). *Language behavior and psychopathology.* Chicago: Rand McNally.

Vicente, K. J., & Brewer, W. F. (1993). Reconstructive remembering of the scientific literature. *Cognition, 46,* 101–128.

Vickers, J. N. (1992). Gaze control in putting. *Perception, 21,* 117–132.

Vidal, F., Buscaglia, M., & Voneche, J. J. (1983). Darwinism and developmental psychology. *Journal of the History of the Behavioral Sciences, 19,* 81–94.

Vincent, K. R. (1991). Black/white IQ differences: Does age make the difference? *Journal of Clinical Psychology, 47,* 266–270.

Viney, L. L. (1991). The personal construct theory of death and loss: Toward a more individually oriented grief therapy. *Death Studies, 15,* 139–155.

Viney, W. (1989). The cyclops and the twelve-eyed toad: William James and the unity-disunity problem in psychology. *American Psychologist, 44,* 1261–1265.

Viney, W. (1990). The tempering effect of determinism in the legal system: A response to Rychlak and Rychlak. *New Ideas in Psychology, 8,* 31–42.

Viney, W., & Bartsch, K. (1984). Dorothea Lynde Dix: Positive or negative influence on the development of treatment for the mentally ill. *Social Science Journal, 21,* 71–82.

Vlaander, G. P., & Van Rooijen, L. (1985). Independence and conformity in Holland: Asch's experiment three decades later. *Gedrag: Tijdschrift voor Psychologie, 13,* 49–55.

Voeller, B. (1991). AIDS and heterosexual anal intercourse. *Archives of Sexual Behavior, 20,* 233–276.

Vokey, J. R., & Read, J. D. (1985). Subliminal messages: Between the devil and the media. *American Psychologist, 40,* 1231–1239.

von Békésy, G. (1957, August). The ear. *Scientific American,* pp. 66–78.

von der Heydt, R., Peterhans, E., & Baumgartner, G. (1984). Illusory contours and cortical neuron responses. *Science, 224,* 1260–1262.

von Frisch, K. (1974). Decoding the language of a bee. *Science, 185,* 663–668.

von Mayrhauser, R. T. (1989). Making intelligence functional: Walter Dill Scott and applied psychological testing in World War I. *Journal of the History of the Behavioral Sciences, 25,* 60–72.

von Senden, M. (1932/1960). *Space and sight.* Glencoe, IL: Free Press.

Vonnegut, M. (1974, April). Why I want to bite R. D. Laing. *Harper's Magazine,* pp. 90–92.

Vonnegut, M. (1975). *The Eden express.* New York: Bantam Books.

Vrooman, J. R. (1970). *Rene' Descartes: A biography.* New York: Putnam.

Wadden, T. A., & Anderton, C. H. (1982). The clinical use of hypnosis. *Psychological Bulletin, 91,* 215–243.

Wagaman, J. D., Barabasz, A. F., & Barabasz, M. (1991). Flotation REST and imagery in the improvement of collegiate basketball performance. *Perceptual and Motor Skills, 72,* 119–122.

Wagstaff, G. F., Vella, M., & Perfect, T. (1992). The effect of hypnotically elicited testimony on jurors' judgments of guilt and innocence. *Journal of Social Psychology, 132,* 591–595.

Waid, W. M., & Orne, M. T. (1982). The physiological detection of deception. *American Scientist, 70,* 402–409.

Waid, W. M., Wilson, S. K., & Orne, M. T. (1981). Cross-modal physiological effects of electrodermal ability in the detection of deception. *Journal of Personality and Social Psychology, 40,* 1118–1125.

Wald, G. (1964). The receptors of human color vision. *Science, 145,* 1007–1017.

Waldhauser, F., Saletu, B., & Trinchard-Lugan, I. (1990). Sleep laboratory investigations on hypnotic properties of melatonin. *Psychopharmacology, 100,* 222–226.

Waldrop, M. M. (1984a). Artificial intelligence in parallel. *Science, 225,* 608–610.

Waldrop, M. M. (1984b, June). Astrology's off target. *Science 84,* pp. 80, 82.

Walk, R. D., & Homan, C. P. (1984). Emotion and dance in dynamic light displays. *Bulletin of the Psychonomic Society, 22,* 437–440.

Walker, E., Hoppes, E., Emory, E., Mednick, S., & Schulsinger, F. (1981). Environmental factors related to schizophrenia in psychophysiologically labile high-risk males. *Journal of Abnormal Psychology, 90,* 313–320.

Walker, L. J. (1984). Sex differences in the development of moral reasoning: A critical review. *Child Development, 55,* 677–691.

Walker, L. J. (1986). Experiential and cognitive sources of moral development in adulthood. *Human Development, 29,* 113–124.

Walker, L. J. (1989). A longitudinal study of moral reasoning. *Child Development, 60,* 157–166.

Wallabaum, A. B., Rzewnicki, R., Steele, H., & Suedfeld, P. (1991). Progressive muscle relaxation and restricted environmental stimulation therapy for chronic tension headache: A pilot study. *International Journal of Psychosomatics, 38,* 33–39.

Wallace, A. (1986). *The prodigy.* New York: Dutton.

Wallace, R. E. (1988). Abolish the duty to protect: It's time to release the scapegoats. *Psychotherapy in Private Practice, 6,* 55–63.

Wallace, R. K., & Benson, H. (1972, February). The physiology of meditation. *Scientific American,* pp. 84–90.

Wallach, H., & Marshall, F. J. (1986). Shape constancy in pictorial representation. *Perception and Psychophysics, 39,* 233–235.

Wallach, M. A., Kogan, N., & Bem, D. J. (1962). Group influence on individual risk taking. *Journal of Abnormal and Social Psychology, 65,* 75–86.

Waller, N. G., Kojetin, B. A., Bouchard, T. J., & Lykken, D. T. (1990). Genetic and environmental influences on religious interests, attitudes, and values: A study of twins reared apart and together. *Psychological Science, 1,* 138–142.

Wallis, C. (1984, June 11). Unlocking pain's secrets. *Time,* pp. 58–66.

Walsh, J. (1981). A plenipotentiary for human intelligence. *Science, 214,* 640–641.

Walsh, J. (1983). Wide world of reports. *Science, 214,* 640–641.

Walster, E., Aronson, V., Abrahams, D., & Rottman, L. (1966). Importance of physical attractiveness in dating behavior. *Journal of Personality and Social Psychology, 4,* 508–516.

Walters, G. C., & Grusec, J. E. (1977). *Punishment.* San Francisco: Freeman.

Waltz, D. L. (1982, October). Artificial intelligence. *Scientific American,* pp. 118–133.

Wang, J. J., & Kaufman, A. S. (1993). Changes in fluid and crystallized intelligence across the 20- to 90-year age range in the K-BIT. *Journal of Psycheducational Assessment, 11,* 29–37.

Warburton, D. M., & Wesnes, K. (1984). Drugs as research tools in psychology: Cholinergic drugs and information processing. *Neuropsychobiology, 11,* 121–132.

Ward, J. C., & Naster, B. J. (1991). Reliability of an observational system used to monitor behavior in a mental health residential treatment unit. *Journal of Mental Health Administration, 18,* 64–68.

Warner, M. J., & Studwell, R. W. (1991). Humor: A powerful counseling tool. *Journal of College Student Psychotherapy, 5,* 59–69.

Warner, S. L. (1991). Humor: A coping response for student nurses. *Archives of Psychiatric Nursing, 5,* 10–16.

Washburn, M. F. (1916). *Movement and mental imagery.* Boston: Houghton Mifflin.

Waters, R. S., Samulack, D. D., Dykes, R. W., & McKinley, P. A. (1990). Topographic organization of baboon primary motor cortex: Face, hand, forelimb, and shoulder representation. *Somatosensory and Motor Research, 7,* 485–514.

Watkins, C. E., Jr. (1982). A decade of research in support of Adlerian psychological theory. *Individual Psychology: Journal of Adlerian Theory, Research, and Practice, 38,* 90–99.

Watkins, C. E., Jr., Lopez, F. G., Campbell, V. L., & Himmell, C. D. (1986). Counseling psychology and clinical psychology: Some preliminary comparative data. *American Psychologist, 41,* 581–584.

Watkins, J. G. (1984). The Bianchi (L.A. Hillside Strangler) case: Sociopath or multiple personality? *International Journal of Clinical and Experimental Hypnosis, 32,* 67–101.

Watkins, J. G. (1989). Hypnotic hypermnesia and forensic hypnosis: A cross-examination. *American Journal of Clinical Hypnosis, 32,* 71–83.

Watson, J. B. (1913). Psychology as the behaviorist views it. *Psychological Review, 20,* 158–177.

Watson, J. B. (1930). *Behaviorism.* New York: W. W. Norton.

Watson, J. B. (1961). John Broadus Watson. In C. Murchison (Ed.), *A history of psychology in autobiography* (Vol. 3, pp. 271–281). New York: Russell & Russell.

Watson, J. B., & Rayner, R. (1920). Conditioned emotional reactions. *Journal of Experimental Psychology, 3,* 1–14.

Watts, B. L. (1982). Individual differences in circadian activity rhythms and their effects on roommate relationships. *Journal of Personality, 50,* 374–384.

Weaver, C. A. (1993). Do you need a "flash" to form a flashbulb memory? *Journal of Experimental Psychology: General, 122,* 39–46.

Weaver, J. B., Masland, J. L., Kharazmi, S., & Zillman, D. (1985). Effect of alcoholic intoxication on the appreciation of different types of humor. *Journal of Personality and Social Psychology, 49,* 781–787.

Webb, C. (1977). The use of myoelectric facial feedback in teaching facial expression to the blind. *Biofeedback and Self-Regulation, 2,* 147–160.

Webb, E. J., Campbell, D. T., Schwartz, R. D., & Sechrest, L. (1966). *Unobtrusive measures: Nonreactive research in the social sciences.* Chicago: Rand McNally.

Webb, W. B. (1975). *Sleep: The gentle tyrant.* Englewood Cliffs, NJ: Prentice Hall.

Webb, W. B. (1981). An essay on consciousness. *Teaching of Psychology, 8,* 15–19.

Webb, W. B. (1985). Sleep and dreaming. In G. A. Kimble & K. Schlesinger (Eds.), *Topics in the history of psychology* (Vol. 2, pp. 191–217). Hillsdale, NJ: Erlbaum.

Webb, W. B. (1987). The proximal effects of two- and four-hour naps within extended performance without sleep. *Psychophysiology, 24,* 426–429.

Webb, W. B., & Agnew, H. W., Jr. (1975). Are we chronically sleep deprived? *Bulletin of the Psychonomic Society, 6,* 47–48.

Weber, J. M., Klesges, R. C., & Klesges, L. M. (1988). Dietary restraint and obesity: Their effects on dietary intake. *Journal of Behavioral Medicine, 11,* 185–199.

Weber, R., & Crocker, J. (1983). Cognitive processes in the revision of stereotype beliefs. *Journal of Personality and Social Psychology, 45,* 961–977.

Webster, S., & Coleman, S. R. (1992). The reception of Clark L. Hull's behavior theory, 1943–1960. *Psychological Reports, 70,* 1063–1071.

Wechsler, D. (1958). *Measurement and appraisal of adult intelligence.* Baltimore: Williams & Wilkins.

Weekes, J. R., Lynn, S. J., Green, J. P., & Brentar, J. T. (1992). Pseudomemory in hypnotized and task-motivated subjects. *Journal of Abnormal Psychology, 101,* 356–360.

Wegner, D. M., Schneider, D. J., Carter, S. R., III, & White, T. L. (1987). Paradoxical effects of thought suppression. *Journal of Personality and Social Psychology, 53,* 5–13.

Wehr, T. A., Jacobsen, F. M., Sack, D. A., Arendt, J., Tamarkin, L., & Rosenthal, N. E. (1986). Phototherapy of seasonal affective disorder. *Archives of General Psychiatry, 43,* 870–875.

Wehr, T. A., & Rosenthal, N. E. (1989). Seasonality and affective illness. *American Journal of Psychiatry, 146,* 829–839.

Weigel, R. H., Vernon, D. T. A., & Tognacci, L. N. (1974). Specificity of the attitude as a determinant of attitude-behavior congruence. *Journal of Personality and Social Psychology, 30,* 724–728.

Weiger, W. A., & Bear, D. M. (1988). An approach to the neurology of aggression. *Journal of Psychiatric Research, 22,* 85–98.

Wiegman, O., Kuttschreuter, M., & Baarda, B. (1992). A longitudinal study of the effects of television viewing on aggressive and prosocial behaviours. *British Journal of Social Psychology, 31,* 147–164.

Weinberg, R., Burton, D., Yukelson, D., & Weigand, D. (1993). Goal setting in competitive sport: An exploratory investigation of practices of collegiate athletes. *Sport Psychologist, 7,* 275–289.

Weinberg, R. A. (1989). Intelligence and IQ: Landmark issues and great debates. *American Psychologist, 44,* 98–104.

Weinberg, R. A., Scarr, S., & Waldman, I. D. (1992). The Minnesota Transracial Adoption Study: A follow-up of IQ test performance at adolescence. *Intelligence, 16,* 117–135.

Weinberg, R. S., & Weigand, D. (1993). Goal setting in sport and exercise: A reaction to Locke. *Journal of Sport and Exercise Psychology, 15,* 88–96.

Weinberger, J., & Silverman, L. H. (1990). Testability and empirical verification of psychoanalytic dynamic propositions through subliminal psychodynamic activation. *Psychoanalytic Psychology, 7,* 299–339.

Weiner, B. (1980). A cognitive (attribution)-emotion-action model of motivated behavior: An analysis of judgments of help-giving. *Journal of Personality and Social Psychology, 39,* 186–200.

Weiner, B. (1985a). An attributional theory of achievement motivation and emotion. *Psychological Review, 92,* 548–573.

Weiner, B. (1985b). "Spontaneous" causal thinking. *Psychological Bulletin, 97,* 74–84.

Weiner, B., Figueroa-Munoz, A., & Kakihara, C. (1991). The goals of excuses and communication strategies related to causal perceptions. *Personality and Social Psychology Bulletin, 17,* 4–13.

Weiner, D. B. (1979). The apprenticeship of Philippe Pinel: A new document, "Observations of Citizen Pussin on the insane." *American Journal of Psychiatry, 136,* 1128–1134.

Weiner, D. B. (1992). Philippe Pinel's "Memoir on Madness" of December 11, 1794: A fundamental text of modern psychiatry. *American Journal of Psychiatry, 149,* 725–732.

Weiner, R. D. (1984). Convulsive therapy: 50 years later. *American Journal of Psychiatry, 141,* 1078–1079.

Weinstein, L., & Almaguer, L. L. (1987). "I'm bored!" *Bulletin of the Psychonomic Society, 25,* 389–390.

Weinstein, N. D. (1984). Reducing unrealistic optimism about illness susceptibility. *Health Psychology, 3,* 431–457.

Weir, P. (1990). Hypnosis and the treatment of burned patients: A review of the literature. *Australian Journal of Clinical Hypnotherapy and Hypnosis, 11,* 11–15.

Weisberg, R. W. (1992). Metacognition and insight during problem solving: Comment on Metcalfe. *Journal of Experimental Psychology: Learning, Memory, and Cognition, 18,* 426–431.

Weisburd, S. (1984). Whales and dolphins use magnetic "roads." *Science News, 126,* 391.

Weisman, J. (1988, November 19–25). Remembering JFK: Our first TV president. *TV Guide,* pp. 2–4, 6–8.

Weiss, J. M. (1972, June). Psychological factors in stress and disease. *Scientific American,* pp. 104–113.

Weissman, M. M. (1990). The hidden patient: Unrecognized panic disorder. *Journal of Clinical Psychiatry, 51,* 5–8.

Weitzenhoffer, A. M., & Hilgard, E. R. (1962). *Stanford Scale of Hypnotic Susceptibility, Form C.* Palo Alto, CA: Consulting Psychologists Press.

Weldon, E., & Gargano, G. M. (1988). Cognitive loafing: The effects of accountability and shared responsibility on cognitive effort. *Personality and Social Psychology Bulletin, 14,* 159–171.

Wells, G. L., & Lindsay, R. C. L. (1985). Methodological notes on the accuracy-confidence relation in eyewitness identification. *Journal of Applied Psychology, 70,* 413–419.

Wells, J. K., Howard, G. S., Nowlin, W. F., & Vargas, M. J. (1986). Presurgical anxiety and postsurgical pain and adjustment: Effects of a stress inoculation procedure. *Journal of Consulting and Clinical Psychology, 54,* 831–835.

Welsh, D. H., Bernstein, D. J., & Luthans, F. (1992). Application of the Premack principle of reinforcement to the quality performance of service employees. *Journal of Organizational Behavior-Management, 13,* 9–32.

Werker, J. F., & McLeod, P. J. (1989). Infant preference for both male and female infant-directed talk: A developmental study of attentional and affective responsiveness. *Canadian Journal of Psychology, 43,* 230–246.

Werner, W. E., Schauble, P. G., & Knudson, M. S. (1982). An argument for revival of hypnosis in obstetrics. *American Journal of Clinical Hypnosis, 24,* 149–171.

Wertheimer, M. (1978). Humanistic psychology and the humane but tough-minded psychologist. *American Psychologist, 33,* 739–745.

Wever, E. G., & Bray, C. W. (1937). The perception of low tones and the resonance volley theory. *Journal of Psychology, 3,* 101–114.

Whishaw, I. Q. (1991). Latent learning in a swimming pool place task by rats: Evidence for the use of associative and not cognitive mapping processes. *Quarterly Journal of Experimental Psychology: Comparative and Physiological Psychology, 43,* 83–103.

Whisman, M. A. (1993). Mediators and moderators of change in cognitive therapy of depression. *Psychological Bulletin, 114,* 248–265.

Whissell, C. M. (1984). Emotion: A classification of current literature. *Perceptual and Motor Skills, 59,* 599–609.

Whitbourne, S. K., & Hulicka, I. M. (1990). Ageism in undergraduate psychology texts. *American Psychologist, 45,* 1127–1136.

White, G. L., Fishbein, S., & Rutstein, J. (1981). Passionate love and the misattribution of arousal. *Journal of Personality, 41,* 56–62.

White, S. H. (1990). Child study at Clark University. *Journal of the History of the Behavioral Sciences, 26,* 131–150.

Whitehurst, G. J., Falco, F. L., Lonigan, C. J., Fischel, J. E., DeBaryshe, B. D., Valdez-Menchaca, M. C., & Caulfield, M. (1988). Accelerating language development through picture book reading. *Developmental Psychology, 24,* 552–559.

Whitlock, F. A. (1987). Addiction. In R. L. Gregory (Ed.), *Oxford companion to the mind* (pp. 3–5). New York: Oxford University Press.

Whittler, T. E. (1991). The effects of actors' race in commercial advertising: Review and extension. *Journal of Advertising, 20,* 54–60.

Whorf, B. L. (1956). Science and linguistics. In J. B. Carroll (Ed.), *Language, thought, and reality: Selected writings of Benjamin Lee Whorf* (pp. 207–219). Cambridge, MA: MIT Press.

Whyte, W. H. (1956). *The organization man.* New York: Simon & Schuster.

Widdison, H. A., & Salisbury, H. G. (1989–1990). The Delayed Stress Syndrome: A pathological delayed grief reaction? *Omega: Journal of Death and Dying, 20,* 293–306.

Wideman, M. V., & Singer, J. E. (1984). The role of psychological mechanisms in preparation for childbirth. *American Psychologist, 39,* 1357–1371.

Widiger, T. A., & Trull, T. J. (1991). Diagnosis and clinical assessment. *Annual Review of Psychology, 42,* 109–133.

Widmeyer, W. N., & Loy, J. W. (1988). When you're hot, you're hot: Warm-cold effects in first impressions of persons and teaching effectiveness. *Journal of Educational Psychology, 80,* 118–121.

Wiebe, D. J. (1991). Hardiness and stress moderation: A test of proposed mechanisms. *Journal of Personality and Social Psychology, 60,* 89–99.

Wiebe, D. J., & McCallum, D. M. (1986). Health practices and hardiness as mediators in the stress-illness relationship. *Health Psychology, 5,* 425–438.

Wiens, A. N., & Menustik, C. E. (1983). Treatment outcome and patient characteristics in an aversion therapy program for alcoholism. *American Psychologist, 38,* 1089–1096.

Wightman, D. C., & Lintern, G. (1984, August). Part-task training of tracking in manual control. *NAVTRAEQUIPCEN* (Technical Report 81-C-0105–2).

Wilcox, B. L. (1987). Pornography, social science, and politics: When research and ideology collide. *American Psychologist, 42,* 941–943.

Wilcox, J. A. (1990). Fluoxetine and bulimia. *Journal of Psychoactive Drugs, 22,* 81–82.

Wilding, J., Rashid, W., Gilmore, D., & Valentine, E. (1986). A comparison of two mnemonic methods in learning medical information. *Human Learning: Journal of Practical Research and Applications, 5,* 211–217.

Williams, C. D. (1959). The elimination of tantrum behavior by extinction procedures. *Journal of Abnormal and Social Psychology, 59,* 269.

Williams, D. G. (1990). Effects of psychoticism, extraversion, and neuroticism in current mood: A statistical review of six studies. *Personality and Individual Differences, 11,* 615–630.

Williams, J., Merritt, J., Rittenhouse, C., & Hobson, J. A. (1992). Bizarreness in dreams and fantasies: Implications for the activation-synthesis hypothesis. *Consciousness and Cognition: An International Journal, 1,* 172–185.

Williams, K., Harkins, S., & Latané, R. (1981). Identifiability as a determinant of social loafing: Two cheering experiments. *Journal of Personality and Social Psychology, 40,* 303–311.

Williams, K. D., Nida, S. A., Baca, L. D., & Latané, B. (1989). Social loafing and swimming: Effects of identifiability on individual and relay performance of intercollegiate swimmers. *Basic and Applied Social Psychology, 10,* 73–81.

Williams, R. B., Jr., Kuhn, C. M., Melosh, W., White, A. D., & Schonberg, S. M. (1982). Type A behavior and elevated physiological and neuroendocrine responses to cognitive tasks. *Science, 218,* 483–485.

Williams, R. M. (1984). Field observations and surveys in combat zones. *Social Psychology Quarterly, 47,* 186–192.

Williams, S. L., & Kinney, P. J. (1991). Performance and nonperformance strategies for coping with acute pain: The role of perceived self-efficacy, expected outcomes, and attention. *Cognitive Therapy and Research, 15,* 1–19.

Williams, S. L., Turner, S. M., & Peer, D. F. (1985). Guided mastery and performance desensitization treatments for severe acrophobia. *Journal of Consulting and Clinical Psychology, 53,* 237–247.

Willner, P. (1985). Antidepressants and serotonergic neurotransmission: An integrative review. *Psychopharmacology, 85,* 387–404.

Wills, T. A. (1981). Downward comparison principles in social psychology. *Psychological Bulletin, 90,* 245–271.

Wilson, E. O. (1975). *Sociobiology: The new synthesis.* Cambridge, MA: Harvard University Press.

Wilson, G. D. (1987). Male-female differences in sexual activity, enjoyment, and fantasies. *Personality and Individual Differences, 8,* 125–127.

Wilson, J. P., & Petruska, R. (1984). Motivation, model attributes, and prosocial behavior. *Journal of Personality and Social Psychology, 46,* 458–468.

Wilson, J. R. (1967). *The mind.* New York: Time.

Wilson, T. D., & Linville, P. W. (1982). Improving the academic performance of college freshmen: Attribution therapy revisited. *Journal of Personality and Social Psychology, 42,* 367–376.

Wilson, V. E., & Bird, E. I. (1981). Effects of relaxation and/or biofeedback training upon hip flexion in gymnasts. *Biofeedback and Self-Regulation, 6,* 25–34.

Winders, S. E., & Grunberg, N. E. (1989). Nicotine, tobacco smoke, and body weight: A review of the animal literature. *Annals of Behavioral Medicine, 11,* 125–133.

Windholz, G. (1992). Pavlov's conceptualization of learning. *American Journal of Psychology, 105,* 459–469.

Windholz, M. J., Marmar, C. R., & Horowitz, M. J. (1985). A review of the research on conjugal bereavement: Impact on health and efficacy of intervention. *Comprehensive Psychiatry, 26,* 433–447.

Winefield, A. H. (1982). Methodological difficulties in demonstrating learned helplessness in humans. *Journal of General Psychology, 107,* 255–266.

Wing, L. L., Tapson, G. S., & Geyer, M. A. (1990). 5-HT–2 mediation of acute behavioral effects of hallucinogens in rats. *Psychopharmacology, 100,* 417–425.

Winkel, F. W., & Koppelaar, L. (1991). Rape victims' style of self-presentation and secondary victimization by the environment: An experiment. *Journal of Interpersonal Violence, 6,* 29–40.

Winn, K. I., Crawford, D. W., & Fischer, J. L. (1991). Equity and commitment in romance versus friendship. *Journal of Social Behavior and Personality, 6,* 301–314.

Winton, W. M. (1990). Jamesian aspects of misattribution research. *Personality and Social Psychology Bulletin, 16,* 652–664.

Wintrob, H. L. (1987). Self-disclosure as a marketable commodity. *Journal of Social Behavior and Personality, 2,* 77–88.

Wise, R. A., & Rompre, P. P. (1989). Brain dopamine and reward. *Annual Review of Psychology, 40,* 191–225.

Wisely, D. W., Masur, F. T., & Morgan, S. B. (1983). Psychological aspects of severe burn injuries in children. *Health Psychology, 2,* 45–72.

Witt, L. A. (1991). Person-situation effects on self-presentation on the telephone at work. *Journal of Social Psychology, 131,* 213–218.

Wittig, M. A. (1985). Metatheoretical dilemmas in the psychology of gender. *American Psychologist, 40,* 400–411.

Wixted, J. T. (1991). Conditions and consequences of maintenance rehearsal. *Journal of Experimental Psychology: Learning, Memory, and Cognition, 17,* 963–973.

Wixted, J. T., & Ebbesen, E. B. (1991). On the form of forgetting. *Psychological Science, 2,* 409–415.

Wojcikiewicz, A., & Orlick, T. (1987). The effects of post-hypnotic suggestion and relaxation with suggestion on competitive fencing anxiety and performance. *International Journal of Sport Psychology, 18,* 303–313.

Wolfe, D. A., Mendes, M. G., & Factor, D. (1984). A parent-administered program to reduce children's television viewing. *Journal of Applied Behavior Analysis, 17,* 267–272.

Wolfe, J. (1936). Effectiveness of token rewards for chimpanzees. *Comparative Psychology Monographs, 12* (No. 5).

Wolfe, T. (1979). *The right stuff.* New York: Bantam.

Wolfensberger, W. (1972). *Normalization.* Toronto: National Institute on Mental Retardation.

Wolff, J., & Desiderato, O. (1980). Transfer of assertion-training effects to roommates of program participants. *Journal of Counseling Psychology, 27,* 484–491.

Wolkowitz, O. M., Gertz, B., Weingartner, H., & Beccaria, L. (1990). Hunger in humans induced by MK-329, a specific peripheral-type cholecystokinin receptor antagonist. *Biological Psychiatry, 28,* 169–173.

Wollen, K. A., Weber, A., & Lowry, D. H. (1972). Bizarreness versus interaction of mental images as determinants of learning. *Cognitive Psychology, 3,* 518–523.

Wolpe, J. (1958). *Psychotherapy by reciprocal inhibition.* Stanford, CA: Stanford University Press.

Wolpe, J. (1988). Obituary: Mary Cover Jones 1896–1987. *Journal of Behavior Therapy and Experimental Psychiatry, 19,* 34.

Wolpin, M., Marston, A., Randolph, C., & Clothier, A. (1992). Individual difference correlates of reported lucid dreaming frequency and control. *Journal of Mental Imagery, 16,* 231–236.

Wood, J. M., Bootzin, R. R., Rosenhan, D., Nolen-Hoeksema, S., & Jourden, F. (1992). Effects of the 1989 San Francisco earthquake on frequency and content of nightmares. *Journal of Abnormal Psychology, 101,* 219–224.

Wood, W., & Eagly, A. H. (1981). Stages in the analysis of persuasive messages: The role of causal attributions and message comprehension. *Journal of Experimental and Social Psychology, 40,* 246–259.

Woods, B. T., & Wolf, J. (1983). A reconsideration of the relation of ventricular enlargement to duration of illness in schizophrenia. *American Journal of Psychiatry, 140,* 1564–1570.

Woods, P. A., Higson, P. J., & Tannahill, M. M. (1984). Token-economy progresses with chronic psychotic patients: The importance of direct measurement and objective evaluation for long-term maintenance. *Behavior Research and Therapy, 22,* 41–51.

Worringham, C. J., & Messick, D. M. (1983). Social facilitation of running: An unobtrusive study. *Journal of Social Psychology, 121,* 23–29.

Wright, A. A., Cook, R. G., Rivera, J. J., & Shyan, M. R. (1990). Naming, rehearsal, and interstimulus interval effects in memory processing. *Journal of Experimental Psychology: Learning, Memory, and Cognition, 16,* 1043–1059.

Wright, L. (1988). The Type A behavior pattern and coronary artery disease. *American Psychologist, 43,* 2–14.

Wright, P. M., Lichtenfels, P. A., & Pursell, E. D. (1989). The structured interview: Additional studies and a meta-analysis. *Journal of Occupational Psychology, 62,* 191–199.

Wu, J. C., & Bunney, W. E. (1990). The biological basis of an antidepressant response to sleep deprivation and relapse. *American Journal of Psychiatry, 147,* 14–21.

Wughalter, E. H., & Gondola, J. C. (1991). Mood states of professional female tennis players. *Perceptual and Motor Skills, 73,* 187–190.

Wundt, W. (1874). *Grundzüge der physiologische Psychologie* [Principles of physiological psychology]. Leipzig: Engelmann.

Wurtz, R. H., Goldberg, M. E., & Robinson, D. L. (1982, June). Brain mechanisms of visual attention. *Scientific American,* pp. 124–135.

Wyatt, G. E., Peters, S. D., & Guthrie, D. (1988). Kinsey revisited: I. Comparisons of the sexual socialization and sexual behavior of white women over 33 years. *Archives of Sexual Behavior, 17,* 201–239.

Wyatt, J. W., Posey, A., Welker, W., & Seamonds, C. (1984). Natural levels of similarities between identical twins and between unrelated people. *Skeptical Inquirer, 9,* 62–66.

Yalom, I. D. (1980). *Existential psychotherapy.* New York: Basic Books.

Yap, J. N. (1988). The effects of hospitalization and surgery on children: A critical review. *Journal of Applied Developmental Psychology, 9,* 349–358.

Yarmey, A. D. (1973). I recognize your face but I can't remember your name: Further evidence on the tip-of-the-tongue phenomenon. *Memory and Cognition, 1,* 287–290.

Yates, J. (1985). The content of awareness is a model of the world. *Psychological Review, 92,* 249–284.

Yerkes, R. M., & Dodson, J. D. (1908). The relation of strength of stimulus to rapidity of habit-formation. *Journal of Comparative Neurology and Psychology, 18,* 459–482.

Young, A. W., & Ellis, H. D. (1989). Childhood prosopagnosia. *Brain and Cognition, 9,* 16–47.

Young, L. D., Richter, J. E., Bradley, L. A., & Anderson, K. O. (1987). Disorders of the upper gastrointestinal system: An overview. *Annals of Behavioral Medicine, 9* (3), 7–12.

Youngren, M. A., & Lewinsohn, P. M. (1980). The functional relation between depression and problematic interpersonal behavior. *Journal of Abnormal Psychology, 89,* 333–341.

Yu, S., & Ho, I. K. (1990). Effects of acute barbiturate administration, tolerance, and dependence on brain GABA system: Comparison to alcohol and benzodiazepines. *Alcohol, 7,* 261–272.

Zadra, A. L., Donderi, D. C., & Pihl, R. O. (1992). Efficacy of lucid dream induction for lucid and non-lucid dreamers. *Dreaming: Journal of the Association for the Study of Dreams, 2,* 85–97.

Zajonc, R. B. (1965). Social facilitation. *Science, 149,* 269–274.

Zajonc, R. B. (1976). Family configuration and intelligence. *Science, 192,* 227–236.

Zajonc, R. B. (1984). On the primacy of affect. *American Psychologist, 39,* 117–123.

Zajonc, R. B. (1985). Emotion and facial efference: A theory revisited. *Science, 228,* 15–21.

Zajonc, R. B. (1986). The decline and rise of scholastic aptitude scores: A prediction derived from the confluence model. *American Psychologist, 41,* 862–867.

Zajonc, R. B. (1993). The confluence model: Differential or difference equation. *European Journal of Social Psychology, 23,* 211–215.

Zaldivar, R. A. (1986, June 10). Panel faults NASA on shuttle. *Philadelphia Inquirer,* pp. 1–A, 12–A.

Zander, A. (1979). The psychology of group processes. *Annual Review of Psychology, 30,* 417–451.

Zanna, M. P., Olson, J. M., & Fazio, R. H. (1980). Attitude-behavior consistency: An individual difference perspective. *Journal of Personality and Social Psychology, 38,* 432–440.

Zatorre, R. J. (1984). Musical perception and cerebral function: A critical review. *Music Perception, 2,* 196–221.

Zebrowitz, L. A., Tenenbaum, D. R., & Goldstein, L. H. (1991). The impact of job applicants' facial maturity, gender, and academic achievement on hiring recommendations. *Journal of Applied Social Psychology, 21,* 525–548.

Zigler, E., Abelson, W. D., Trickett, P. K., & Seitz, V. (1982). Is an intervention program necessary in order to improve economically disadvantaged children's IQ scores? *Child Development, 33,* 340–348.

Zimmerman, M. (1983). Methodological issues in the assessment of life events: A review of issues and research. *Clinical Psychology Review, 3,* 339–370.

Zimpfer, D. G. (1991). Groups for grief and survivorship after bereavement: A review. *Journal for Specialists in Group Work, 16,* 46–55.

Ziporyn, T. (1982). Taste and smell: The neglected senses. *Journal of the American Medical Association, 247,* 277–285.

Ziv, A. (1987). The effect of humor on aggression catharsis in the classroom. *Journal of Psychology, 121,* 359–364.

Zola-Morgan, S. M., & Squire, L. R. (1990). The primate hipppocampal formation: Evidence for a time-limited role in memory storage. *Science, 250,* 288–290.

Zuckerman, M. (1979). *Sensation seeking: Beyond the optimal level of arousal.* Hillside, NJ: Erlbaum.

Zuckerman, M. (1990). The psychophysiology of sensation seeking. *Journal of Personality, 58,* 313–345.

Zuckerman, M., Buchsbaum, M. S., & Murphy, D. L. (1980). Sensation seeking and its biological correlates. *Psychological Bulletin, 88,* 187–214.

Zuckerman, M., Koestner, R., DeBoy, T., Garcia, T., Maresca, B. C., & Sartoris, J. M. (1988). To predict some of the people some of the time: A reexamination of the moderator variable approach in personality theory. *Journal of Personality and Social Psychology, 54,* 1006–1019.

Zuckerman, M., Kuhlman, D. M., & Camac, C. (1988). What lies beyond E and N? Factor analyses of scales believed to measure basic dimensions of personality. *Journal of Personality and Social Psychology, 54,* 96–107.

Zuroff, D. C. (1986). Was Gordon Allport a trait theorist? *Journal of Personality and Social Psychology, 51,* 983–1000.

Zweigenhaft, R. L. (1977). The empirical study of signature size. *Social Behavior & Personality, 5,* 177–185.

Zwislocki, J. J. (1981). Sound analysis in the ear: A history of discoveries. *American Scientist, 69,* 184–192.

Photographs

Chapter 1

Opener: Charles Olson, *Recognition*, 1993. Acrylic/Canvas 84″ × 60″ Collection of the Artist; **p. 5:** © Daniel Wray/The Image Works; **p. 7(top & bottom), p. 8(top):** © The Granger Collection; **p. 8(bottom):** Bettmann Archive; **p. 9(top):** National Library of Medicine; **p. 9(bottom):** © Archives of the History of American Psychology, University of Akron, OH; **p. 10:** Archives of the History of American Psychology, Anna Berliner Memoirs; **p. 11(top):** Dictionary of American Portraits, Dover Publications, Inc.; **p. 11(bottom):** National Library of Medicine; **p. 12(top):** © Archives of the History of American Psychology, University of Akron, OH; **p. 12 (bottom):** Courtesy Howard University; **p. 13:** Culver Pictures; **p. 15:** Archives of the History of American Psychology, Mary Henle Papers; **p. 16:** Archives of the History of American Psychology, Seymour Wapner Gift, Permission Clark University Archives; **p. 18(top):** © Christopher Johnson/Stock Boston; **p. 18(bottom):** The Wellcome Institute Library, London; **p. 19:** Bettmann Archive; **p. 20(top):** Courtesy Herbert A. Simon; **p. 20(bottom):** Courtesy Roger Sperry; **p. 22(left & right):** © Lawrence Migdale/Photo Researchers, Inc.; **1.2a:** © Vandystadt/Photo Researchers, Inc.; **1.2b:** © John Eastcott/The Image Works; **1.2c:** © Bill Auth/Uniphoto; **p. 25:** Courtesy of Florence L. Denmark/Photo by Robert Wesner; **p. 26:** Courtesy Laurel Furumoto; **p. 27:** Archives of the History of American Psychology Photographic Collection, Courtesy Evan Calkins.

Chapter 2

Opener: Vasily Kandinsky, *Composition 8*, July 1923, Oil on Canvas, 55 ⅛ × 79 ⅛″ Solomon R. Guggenheim Museum, New York, gift, Solomon R. Guggenheim, 1937. Photo: David Heald © The Solomon R. Guggenheim Foundation, New York, FN37.262. © 1994 Artists Rights Society (ARS), New York/ ADAGP, Paris; **p. 34:** © Jean Higgins/Unicorn Stock Photo;

p. 35(top): © Toni Michaels; **p. 35(middle):** National Library of Medicine; **p. 35(bottom):** The Granger Collection; **p. 38:** © Bob Daemmrich/ Stock Boston; **p. 39:** © Mark Antman/ The Image Works; **p. 43:** © Penelope Breese/Liaison; **p. 44:** Photofest; **p. 46:** © Laura Dwight; **p. 47:** Bettmann Archive; **p. 48:** Courtesy John Popplestone; **p. 49:** © Lorraine Rorke/ The Image Works; **p. 52:** Wide World Photos, Inc.; **p. 54:** Courtesy Robert Rosenthal; **p. 59:** © Science Photo Library/Photo Researchers; **p. 62:** Courtesy Diana Baumrind; **p. 63(top):** © Paul Conklin; **p. 63(bottom):** Courtesy of Bernard Rollin, photo by Steve Suther, *Beef Today*; **p. 64:** © Matt Meadows/Peter Arnold, Inc.

Chapter 3

Opener: *Radiator Building-Night*, New York. 1927. Georgia O'Keefe. Stieglitz Collection, Carl Van Vechten Museum and Gallery of Art–Fisk University, Nashville, Tennessee. © 1994 The Georgia O'Keeffe Foundation/ Artists Rights Society (ARS), New York; **p. 70:** The Granger Collection; **p. 71:** AP/Wide World Photos; **p. 72:** © Fred McConnaughey/Photo Researchers; **3.3b:** © Biophoto Associates/Photo Researchers, Inc.; **p. 76:** Historical Pictures/Stock Montage; **p. 77:** Mary Evans Picture Library; **p. 79:** © Dan Goode/Photo Researchers, Inc.; **p. 80:** © Jules Asher; **p. 81:** Bettmann Archive; **p. 82(left):** Personality Photos; **p. 82(right):** © Charlie Newman/Sygma; **p. 85:** © A. Glauberman/Photo Researchers, Inc.; **3.7:** © Larry Mulvehill/Photo Researchers, Inc.; **3.8b:** WCB Communications, Inc./Karl Rubin Photographer; **p. 88:** National Library of Medicine; **p. 90(top & bottom):** Wide World Photos, Inc.; **p. 93:** Bettmann Archive; **p. 94:** Wilder Penfield Papers/Montreal Neurological Institute; **3.12:** Courtesy Drs. Michael Phelps and John Mazziotta, UCLA School of Medicine; **p. 96:** Dr. Francis Schiller; **p. 100:** Courtesy Jacqueline Sagen; **3.16:** Courtesy Drs. John Mazziotta and Michael Phelps, UCLA School of Medicine; **3.17:** Wurtz,

Scientific American, June 1982; **3.18a:** © Fred Hossler/Visuals Unlimited; **p. 107:** Courtesy Jerre Levy.

Chapter 4

Opener: Edward Potthast, *Children At Shore*. Dr. Spencer H. Gross, Pamela G. Fisher, and Lawrence E. Gross; **p. 114:** © Archives of the History of American Psychology, University of Akron, OH; **p. 118:** Courtesy Robert Plomin; **p. 119:** Archives of the History of American Psychology; **4.1a, b, c & d:** Petit Format/ Photo Researchers; **4.2:** School of Medicine/University of Washington; **p. 122:** © Sharon L. Fox/ The Picture Cube; **p. 123(left & right):** © Scala/Art Resource, NY; **4.4 & 125 (bottom right):** Courtesy Tiffany Field; **4.5a & b:** © Enrico Ferorelli; **p. 127:** © Yves De Braine/ Black Star; **4.6a & b:** © D. Goodman/ Monkmeyer Press; **4.7a, b & c:** © Laura Dwight/Peter Arnold, Inc.; **4.8:** Harlow Primate Laboratory, University of Wisconsin; **p. 130:** Archives of the History of American Psychology; **p. 131(bottom):** © Daniel Grogan; **p. 134, p. 135 (left & right):** © Laura Dwight; **p. 136:** Courtesy of Eleanor Maccoby; **p. 137:** © David Strickler/The Picture Cube; **p. 138:** © Frank Siteman/The Picture Cube; **p. 139(top):** Courtesy Camilla Benbow; **p. 139(bottom):** Courtesy Julian Stanley; **p. 141(top left):** Personality Photos; **p. 141(top right):** Bettmann Archive; **p. 141(middle left):** Personality Photos; **p. 141(middle right & bottom left):** Bettmann Archive; **p. 141(bottom right):** © Wesly Bocxe/Photo Researchers; **p. 143:** © Estate of Sybil Shelton/Peter Arnold, Inc.; **p. 144(bottom left):** The Bettmann Archive; **p. 144(top left):** © Lisa Law/ The Image Works; **p. 144(top right):** © Topham/The Image Works; **p. 146:** Wide World Photos, Inc.; **p. 147(top):** Courtesy Gregg Amore; **p. 147(middle left):** © Jaye R. Phillips/The Picture Cube; **p. 147(middle right):** © Mark Antman/The Image Works; **p. 147(bottom right):** Courtesy Warner Schaie; **p. 148:** © Toni Michaels; **p. 149:** © Arni Katz/Unicorn Stock Photos; **p. 151(top):** © Bob

Daemmrich/The Image Works; **p. 151(middle left & middle right):** Bettmann Archive; **p. 152:** Courtesy Dame Cicely Saunders, OM, DBE, FRCP, Physician & Founder of St. Christopher's Hospice; **p. 153(top left):** © A. Rodham/Unicorn Stock Photos; **p. 153(top right):** © SIU/ Science Source/Photo Researchers; **p. 153(middle right):** Bettmann Archive; **p. 155(bottom right):** Harvard University Archives; **p. 155(top right):** Wide World Photos, Inc.; **p. 155(top left):** Bettmann Archive; **p. 156:** © Keith Carter Photography.

Chapter 5

Opener: *Fall Plowing*, From the John Deere & Co. Art Collection. © 1995 Estate of Grant Wood/VAGA, New York; **p. 162:** Personality Photos; **5.1:** From Dallenbach, K.M. (1951). A Puzzle Picture with a New Principle of Concealment. *American Journal of Psychology*, 54, 431–433; **p. 166:** © David Grossman/Photo Researchers; **p. 170:** Wide World Photos, Inc.; **p. 175(top right):** © Villafuerto/ Texastock; **p. 175(bottom right):** © Explorer/Photo Researchers; **5.12a & b:** Fritz Goreau/*Life* Magazine © 1944 Time Inc.; **p. 177(top):** Art Institute of Chicago, Helen Birch Bartlett Memorial Collection; **p. 177(bottom right) & p. 178(top left):** Archives of the History of American Psychology, University of Akron, OH; **5.15:** Kaiser-Porcelain Ltd.; **p. 180(bottom left):** © Ira Wyman/Sygma; **5.19:** The Granger Collection; **5.20a:** © Thomas Kitchin/ Tom Stack and Associates; **5.20b:** Uniphoto; **5.20c:** © Greg Vaughn/Tom Stack and Associates; **5.20d:** © Harold Chapman/The Image Works; **5.20e & f:** © Jean Claude Lejeune; **5.21a & b:** © Mark Antman/The Image Works; **p. 184:** Bettmann Archive; **5.22a:** Copyright Arthur Sirdofsky; **5.24b:** © Van Bucher/Photo Researchers; **p. 189 & p. 190:** Wide World Photos, Inc.; **p. 192:** © T. Orban/Sygma; **p. 193:** © Alan Hinerfeld; **p. 194(top left & bottom left):** © Louis Psihoyos/ Contact Press Images; **p. 196:** © J. P. Ferrero/Explorer/Photo Researchers,

Line Art, Excerpts

Chapter 1

Figure 1.1: Source: Data from Joy Stapp, et al., "Census of Psychological Personnel: 1983" in *American Psychologist*, 40:1317–1351, American Psychological Association, 1985.

Chapter 3

Figure 3.4: From Kurt Schlesinger and Philip M. Groves, *Psychology: A Dynamic Science*. Copyright © 1976 Wm. C. Brown Communications, Inc., Dubuque, Iowa. Reprinted by permission of the author.
Figure 3.14: From John W. Santrock, *Psychology*, 3d ed. Copyright © 1991 Wm. C. Brown Communications, Inc., Dubuque, Iowa. All Rights Reserved. Reprinted by permission.

Chapter 4

Figure 4.9: From J. M. Tanner, et al., "Standards from Birth to Maturity for Height, Weight, Height Velocity, and Weight Velocity" in *Archives of Diseases in Childhood*. Copyright © 1966 British Medical Association, London, England. Reprinted by permission.
Figure 4.10: Source: Data from D. K. Simonton, "Age and Outstanding Achievement: What Do We Know after a Century of Research?" in *Psychological Bulletin*, 104:251–267, American Psychological Association, 1988.

Chapter 5

Figure 5.2: Source: Data from Eugene Galanter, p. 97, 1962.
Figure 5.3: From John W. Santrock, *Psychology: The Science of Mind and Behavior*, 3d ed. Copyright © 1991 Wm. C. Brown Communications, Inc., Dubuque, Iowa. All Rights Reserved. Reprinted by permission.
Figure 5.4: From John W. Hole, Jr., *Human Anatomy and Physiology*, 6th ed. Copyright © 1993 Wm. C. Brown Communications, Inc., Dubuque, Iowa. All Rights Reserved. Reprinted by permission.
Figure 5.9: From G. A. Kimble and K. Schlesinger (eds.), *Topics in the History of Psychology*, Vol. 1:173. Copyright © 1985 Lawrence Erlbaum Associates, Inc., Hillsdale, NJ. Reprinted by permission.
Figure 5.10: Figure from *Visual Perception* by Tom N. Cornsweet, copyright © 1970 by Harcourt Brace & Company, reproduced by permission of the publisher.
Figure 5.11: From G. Wald and P. K. Brown, "Human Color Vision and Color Blindness" in *Cold Spring Harbor Laboratory Symposia on Quantitative Biology*, 30:351. Copyright © 1965 Cold Spring Harbor. Reprinted by permission.
Figure 5.13: From John W. Santrock, *Psychology: The Science of Mind and Behavior*, 2d ed. Copyright © 1988 Wm. C. Brown Communications, Inc., Dubuque, Iowa. All Rights Reserved. Reprinted by permission.
Figure 5.16: Figure from *Fundamentals of Child Development*, Second Edition, by Harry Munsinger, copyright © 1975 by Holt, Rinehart and Winston, Inc.
Figure 5.18: From Bradley and Petry, "Organizational Determinants of Subjective Contour" in *American Journal of Psychology*, 90:253–262. Copyright © 1977 The University of Illinois Press. Reprinted by permission.
Poem, p. 183: From *When Found, Make a Verse Of* (Simon & Schuster). © 1949 Helen Bevington. Originally in *The New Yorker*.
Figure 5.22: From Benjamin B. Lahey, *Psychology: An Introduction*, 3d ed. Copyright © 1989 Wm. C. Brown Communications, Inc., Dubuque, Iowa. All Rights Reserved. Reprinted by permission.
Figure 5.24a: From John W. Santrock, *Psychology: The Science of Mind and Behavior*, 3d ed. Copyright © 1991 Wm. C. Brown Communications, Inc., Dubuque, Iowa. All Rights Reserved. Reprinted by permission.
Figure 5.26: From John W. Santrock, *Psychology: The Science of Mind and Behavior*, 3d ed. Copyright © 1991 Wm. C. Brown Communications, Inc., Dubuque, Iowa. All Rights Reserved. Reprinted by permission.

Chapter 6

Figure 6.1: From W. B. Webb and H. W. Agnew, Jr., "Sleeping and Waking In a Time-Free Environment" in *Aerospace Medicine*, 45:617–622. Copyright © 1974 Aerospace Medical Association, Washington, DC. Reprinted by permission.
Figure 6.3: From R. D. Cartwright, *A Primer on Sleep and Dreaming*. Copyright © 1978 Addison-Wesley Publishing Company, Reading, MA. Reprinted by permission of the author.
Figure 6.6: From Spanos and Hewitt, *Journal of Personality and Social Psychology*, 39:1209. Copyright 1980 by the American Psychological Association. Reprinted by permission.

Chapter 7

Figure 7.1: From Benjamin B. Lahey, *Psychology: An Introduction*, 3d ed. Copyright © 1989 Wm. C. Brown Communications, Inc., Dubuque, Iowa. All Rights Reserved. Reprinted by permission.
Figure 7.4: Source: Data from Ilene L. Bernstein, "Learned Taste Aversions in Children Receiving Chemotherapy" in *Science*, 200:1302–1303, American Association for the Advancement of Science, 1978.
Line art, p. 263: From William N. Dember, et al., *General Psychology*, 2d ed. Copyright © 1984 Lawrence Erlbaum Associates, Inc., Hillsdale, NJ. Reprinted by permission.
Figure 7.8: From M. C. Roberts and D. Fanurick, "Rewarding Elementary Schoolchildren for their Use of Safety Belts" in *Health Psychology*, 5:192. Copyright © 1986 Lawrence Erlbaum Associates, Inc., Hillsdale, NJ. Reprinted by permission.
Figure 7.10: From E. C. Tolman and C. H. Honzik, "Introduction and Removal of the Reward and Maze Performance in Rats" in *University of California Publications in Psychology*, 4:257–275. Copyright © 1930 University of California Press, Berkeley, CA. Reprinted by permission.

Chapter 8

Figure 8.2: Source: G. Sperling, *Psychological Monographs*, 74 (whole no. 498), 1960.
Figure 8.3: Source: L. R. Peterson and M. J. Peterson, "Short-Term Retention of Individual Items" in *Journal of Experimental Psychology*, 58:193–198, 1959.
Figure 8.4: From R. S. Nickerson and M. J. Adams, *Cognitive Psychology*, 11:297. Copyright © 1979 Academic Press. Reprinted by permission.
Figure 8.5: Source: Data from F. I. M. Craik and E. Tulving, *Journal of Experimental Psychology: General*, 104:268–294, American Psychological Association, 1975.

Figure 8.6: From A. M. Collins and E. F. Loftus, "A Spreading Activation Theory of Semantic Processing" in *Psychological Review*, 82:407–428. Copyright 1975 by the American Psychological Association. Reprinted by permission.
Figure 8.8: (top): Source (top): Hermann Ebbinghaus, *Uber das Cedachnis (On Memory)*, 1885.
Figure 8.8 (bottom): From H. P. Bahrick, "Semantic Memory Content in Permastore: Fifty Years of Memory for Spanish Learned in School" in *Journal of Experimental Psychology: General*, 113:1–19. Copyright © 1984 by the American Psychological Association. Reprinted by permission.
Figure 8.9: Source: J. G. Jenkins and K. M. Dallenbach, "Obliviscence During Sleeping and Waking" in *American Journal of Psychology*, 35:605–612, 1924.
Figure 8.10: Adapted from D. R. Godden and A. D. Baddeley, "Context-Dependent Memory in Two Natural Environments: On Land and Under Water" in *British Journal of Psychology*, 66:325–331. Copyright © 1975 British Psychological Society, Leicester, England. Reprinted by permission.
Figure 8.13: From G. H. Bower and M. C. Clark, "Narrative Stories as Mediators for Serial Learning" in *Psychonomic Science*, 14:181–182. Copyright © 1969 The Psychonomic Society, Inc. Reprinted by permission of The Psychonomic Society, Inc.
Figure 8.16: Source: Data from E. F. Loftus and J. C. Palmer, "Reconstruction of Automobile Destruction: An Example of the Interaction Between Language and Memory" in *Journal of Verbal Learning and Verbal Behavior*, 13:585–589, American Psychological Association, 1974.

Chapter 9

Figure 9.1: From Benjamin B. Lahey, *Psychology: An Introduction*, 3d ed. Copyright © 1989 Wm. C. Brown Communications, Inc., Dubuque, Iowa. All Rights Reserved. Reprinted by permission.
Figure 9.5: Source: Abraham S. Luchins, "Mechanization in Problem-Solving: The Effect of Einstellung" in *Psychological Monographs 6* (whole no. 248), 1942.
Figure 9.10: Source: Data from S. A. Mednick, "The Associative Basis of the Creative Process" in *Psychological Review*, 69:220–232, American Psychological Association, 1962.
Figure 9.11: Source: Data from The Nobel Foundation, 1974.
Figure 9.12: From Roger Brown, et al., "The Child's Grammar from I-III" in *Minnesota Symposium on Child Psychology*, Vol. 2, John P. Hill (ed.). Copyright © 1969 University of Minnesota Press, Minneapolis, MN. Reprinted by permission.

Figure 9.13: Source: L. Carmichael, et al., "An Experimental Study of the Effect of Language on the Reproduction of Visually Perceived Form in *Journal of Experimental Psychology*, 15:73–86, 1932.

Chapter 10
Figure 10.2: A5 taken from the Raven *Standard Progressive Matrices*. Reprinted by permission of J. C. Raven Limited.
Figure 10.3: Source: J. P. Guilford, "Three Faces of Intellect" in *American Psychologist*, 14:469–479, 1959.
Figure 10.4: From J. L. Horn and G. Donaldson, "On the Myth of Intellectual Decline in Adulthood" in *American Psychologist*, 31:701–719. Copyright 1976 by the American Psychological Association. Reprinted by permission.
Figure 10.5: From T. J. Bouchard, et al., "Familial Studies of Intelligence: A Review" in *Science,* 212:1055–1059. Copyright 1981 by the AAAS. Reprinted by permission.
Figure 10.6: From R. B. Zajonc, "The Decline and Rise of Scholastic Aptitude Scores: A Prediction Derived from the Confluence Model" in *American Psychologist*, 41:862–867. Copyright by the American Psychological Association. Reprinted by permission.

Chapter 11
Figure 11.2: This diagram was taken from *Foundations of Experimental Psychology* (C. Murchison, ed.), 1929, and is reprinted by permission of Clark University Press.
Figure 11.4: Source: Data from *New England Journal of Medicine*, 314:193–198, Massachusetts Medical Society, 1986.
Figure 11.5: From A. J. Stunkard, et al., "Use of the Danish Adoption Register for the Study of Obesity and Thinness" in *The Genetics of Neurological and Psychiatric Disorders*, S. Kety (ed.). Copyright © 1983 Raven Press, New York, NY. Reprinted by permission.
Figure 11.6: Copyright © Masters and Johnson Institute. Reprinted by permission.
Figure 11.9: Source: Data from R. de Charms and G. H. Moeller, "Values Expressed in American Children's Readers: 1800–1950" in *Journal of Abnormal and Social Psychology*, 64:136–142, American Psychological Association, 1962.

Figure 11.11: From D. C. Anderson, et al., "Performance Posing, Goal Setting, and Activity-Contingent Praise as Applied to a University Hockey Team" in *Journal of Applied Psychology*, 73: 87–95. Copyright 1988 by the American Psychological Association. Reprinted by permission.

Chapter 12
Figure 12.7: From P. Ekman, et al., "Autonomic Nervous System Activity Distinguishers Among Emotions" in *Science*, 221:1208–1210. Copyright 1983 by the AAAS. Reprinted by permission.
Figure 12.9: From R. L. Solomon, "The Opponent-Process Theory of Acquired Motivation: The Costs of Pleasure and the Benefits of Pain" in *American Psychologist*, 35:691–712. Copyright 1980 by the American Psychological Association. Reprinted by permission.
Figure 12.13: From J. C. Speisman, et al., "Experimental Reduction of Stress Based on Ego-Defense Theory" in *Journal of Abnormal and Social Psychology*, 68:367–380. Copyright 1964 by the American Psychological Association. Reprinted by permission.
Figure 12.15: Source: Data from B. Kleinmuntz and J. Szucko, "A Field Study of the Fallibility of Polygraph Lie Detection" in *Nature*, 308:449–450, Macmillan Magazine Ltd., 1984.

Chapter 13
Figure 13.6: Copyright © Hans J. Eysenck.
Figure 13.8: Adapted from R. B. Cattell, "Personality Pinned Down" in *Psychology Today*. Copyright © 1973 Institute for Personality and Ability Testing, Inc., Champaign, IL. Reprinted by permission of the author.

Chapter 14
Figure 14.1: Source: Data from L. N. Robins, et al., "Lifetime Prevalence of Specific Psychiatric Disorders in Three Sites" in *Archives of General Psychiatry*, 41:949–958, American Medical Association, 1984.
Figure 14.4: Source: Data from I. I. Gottesman and J. Shields, *Schizophrenia: The Epigenetic Puzzle*, Cambridge University Press, 1982.
Line art, p. 527: Source: *Harper's Weekly*, December 10, 1881.

Chapter 15
Figure 15.3(bottom): From A. Bandura, et al., "The Relative Efficacy of Desensitization and Modeling Approaches for Inducing Behavioral, Affective, and Attitudinal Changes" in *Journal of Personality and Social Psychology*, 13:173–199. Copyright 1969 by the American Psychological Association. Reprinted by permission.
Figure 15.8: Smith, Mary Lee, Gene V. Glass, Thomas I. Miller: *The Benefits of Psychotherapy*. The Johns Hopkins University Press, Baltimore/London, 1981, p. 89.
Figure 15.9: From K. I. Howard, et al., "The Dose-Effect Relationship in Psychotherapy" in *American Psychologist*, p. 160. Copyright by the American Psychological Association. Reprinted by permission.

Chapter 16
Figure 16.1: From Benjamin B. Lahey, *Psychology: An Introduction*, 4th ed. Copyright © 1992 Wm. C. Brown Communications, Inc., Dubuque, Iowa. All Rights Reserved. Reprinted by permission.
Figure 16.3: From S. J. Schleifer, et al., *Journal of the American Medical Association*, 250:374–377. Copyright 1983, American Medical Association. Reprinted by permission.
Figure 16.7: From J. D. Browne and J. M. Siegel, "Exercise As a Buffer of Life Stress: A Prospective Study of Adolescent Health" in *Health Psychology*, 7:342–353. Copyright © 1988 Lawrence Erlbaum Associates, Inc., Hillsdale, NJ. Reprinted by permission.
Figure 16.8: From T. J. Hoelscher, "Maintenance of Relaxation-Induced Blood Pressure Reductions: The Importance of Continued Relaxation Practices" in *Biofeedback and Self-Regulation*, 12:3–12. Copyright © 1987 Plenum Publishing Corporation, New York, NY. Reprinted by permission.
Figure 16.9: From J. W. Pennebaker, et al., "Disclosure of Traumas and Immune Function" in *Journal of Consulting and Clinical Psychology*, 56:239–245. Copyright 1988 by the American Psychological Association. Reprinted by permission.

Figure 16.11: Source: Data from W. H. Redd, et al., "Cognitive/Attentional Distraction in the Control of Conditional Nausea in Pediatric Cancer Patients Receiving Chemotherapy" in *Journal of Consulting and Clinical Psychology*, 55:391–395, American Psychological Association, 1987.

Chapter 17
Figure 17.5: Source: Data from L. Festinger and J. M. Carlsmith, "Cognitive Consequences of Forced Compliance" in *Journal of Abnormal and Social Psychology*, 58, American Psychological Association, 1959.
Figure 17.6: Source (line art): Solomon E. Asch, "Studies of Independence and Conformity: A Minority of One Against a Unanimous Majority" in *Psychological Monographs* 90 (whole no. 416), 1956.
Figure 17.8: "PUBLIC ANNOUNCEMENT" figure from *Obedience to Authority* by STANLEY MILGRAM. Copyright © 1974 by Stanley Milgram. Reprinted by permission of HarperCollins Publishers, Inc.
Figure 17.9: Source: Data from Stanley Milgram, "Some Conditions of Obedience and Disobedience to Authority" in *Human Relations*, Vol. 18, No. 1, 1965, pp. 57–75; and Stanley Milgram, *Obedience to Authority* Harper & Row, Publishers, 1974, p. 35.
Figure 17.11: Source: Data from Bibb Latane and John M. Darley, "Group Inhibition of Bystander Intervention in Emergencies" in *Journal of Personality and Social Psychology*, 10:215–221, American Psychological Association, 1968.
Figure 17.12: From J. M. Darley and B. Latane, "Bystander Intervention in Emergencies: Diffusion of Responsibility" in *Journal of Personality and Social Psychology*, 8:377–383. Copyright 1968 by the American Psychological Association. Reprinted by permission.
Figure 17.14: From E. Donnerstein and L. Berkowitz, "Victim Reactions in Aggressive Erotic Films as a Factor in Violence Against Women" in *Journal of Personality and Social Psychology*, 41:710–724. Copyright 1981 by the American Psychological Association. Reprinted by permission.

INDEX

N a m e

Aarons, L., 243
Abbott, M. W., 592
Abella, R., 446
Abelson, R. P., 336
Abernethy, D. R., 557
Abernethy, E. M., 303
Abramowitz, S. I., 404, 553
Abramson, L. Y., 517
Adair, J. G., 62
Adams, G. R., 579
Adams, H. B., 409
Adams, H. E., 280
Adams, J. L., 343
Adams, M. J., 292
Adams, N. E., 480
Adams, P. R., 579
Adams, W. L., 120
Adelmann, P. K., 443
Adelson, B., 329
Ader, R., 582, 583, 584
Adler, A., 468
Adler, J., 617
Adler, T., 477
Adorno, T. W., 625
Afnan, S. M., 6
Agmo, A., 402
Agnew, H. W., Jr., 218
Agnew, N. M., 484
Agnoli, F., 349
Agras, W. S., 507
Aiken, L. R., 363
Ainsworth, M. S., 131
Aird, P., 613
Aisner, R., 277
Ajzen, I., 623
Akande, A., 186
Akerstedt, T., 214
Aks, D. J., 185
Alansky, J. A., 131
Alba, J. W., 296–297
Alcorn, J. D., 600
Aldag, R. J., 630
Aldana, S. G., 590
Aldrich, M. S., 222
Alemagno, S. A., 592
Alexander, G. E., 92
Alexander, P. E., 557
Alexopoulos, G. S., 557
Alexy, B. B., 592
Allard, G. B., 271
Allen, A., 489
Allen, A. C., 309
Allen, C. T., 619
Allen, K. M., 588
Allen, M., 621
Allen, M. G., 515, 550
Alliger, R. J., 523

Allison, P. D., 135
Alloy, L. B., 518
Allport, F. H., 630
Allport, G. W., 474, 626, 627
Almaguer, L. L., 409
Alpert, M. I., 429, 622
Althof, S. E., 399
Altmaier, E. M., 547
Alzate, H., 402
Amabile, T. M., 333
Amato, P. R., 135
Amemori, T., 101
American Psychiatric Association, 366,
    514, 515, 519
Ames, M. A., 405, 406
Amick, B. C., 575
Amir, T., 632
Amoore, J. E., 194
Anand, B. K., 393
Anastasi, A., 46, 47, 383
Andersen, A. E., 397
Andersen, S. M., 488
Anderson, C. A., 587
Anderson, D. C., 418
Anderson, J. A., 443, 600
Anderson, J. R., 297
Anderson, K. J., 407, 517
Anderson, L. R., 481
Anderson, R. A., 199
Anderton, C. H., 590
Andrasik, F., 581
Andre, T., 306
Andreasen, N. C., 522–523
Andreassen, P. B., 335
Andress, D., 239
Andrews, G., 465
Anger, W. K., 272
Angus, R. G., 219
Anisman, H., 239
Ansbacher, H. L., 472
Anschutz, L., 307
Anshel, M. H., 591
Antoni, M. H., 593
Antunano, M. J., 200
Appel, J. B., 165
Appelbaum, P. S., 562
Aral, S. O., 588
Ardila, A., 289
Arehart-Treichel, J., 81
Arjmand, O., 370
Arndt, S., 523
Arnkoff, D. B., 481
Arnold, G. E., 281
Arnoult, L. H., 587
Aron, A. P., 617
Aronson, E., 627
Arterberry, M., 182

Asch, S. E., 632, 633
Aserinsky, E., 217
Ash, D. W., 266
Ashton, R., 223
Aslin, R. N., 125, 126
Assael, H., 622
Asscheman, H., 404
Astin, G. R., 381
Atkinson, D. R., 567
Atkinson, J. W., 388, 412, 417
Atkinson, R. C., 287
Attie, I., 397
Atwood, G. E., 456
Avila, R. A., 634
Aydin, G., 518
Aydin, O., 518
Ayllon, T., 542
Azrin, N. H., 542

Baarda, B., 644
Babad, E., 430
Bach-y-Rita, P., 99
Back, K., 614
Baddeley, A. D., 303, 304
Bagwell, M., 186
Bahill, A. T., 170
Bahrick, H. P., 306
Bahrick, P. O., 306
Bailey, J. M., 405
Bailey, S., 517
Baillargeon, R., 128
Baird, J. C., 183, 185
Baker, G. H. B., 582
Baker, L. D., 314
Baker, T. B., 259, 542, 595
Balanovski, E., 204
Baldwin, B. A., 96, 180, 396
Baldwin, E., 64
Baldwin, M. W., 8, 625
Bales, J., 450, 563
Bambring, M., 431
Bandura, A., 35, 137, 148, 277, 278,
    345, 413, 479, 480, 544, 586, 643,
    644
Barabasz, A. F., 409, 416
Barabasz, M., 409, 416
Baratti, C. M., 81
Barber, T. X., 230
Barbut, M., 381
Barchas, P. R., 107
Bard, P., 440
Barenblatt, L., 414
Baribeau-Braun, J., 523
Barinaga, M., 516
Barlow, D. H., 403
Barnes, D. M., 89
Barnes, M. L., 54, 148

Barnett, S. K., 150
Baron, R. A., 194, 643
Baron, R. S., 199
Barr, B. P., 590
Barr, R. A., 342
Barrett, L. C., 518
Barrett, P. T., 360
Barrett, T. J., 119
Barron, F., 331
Barsky, A. J., 510
Bartlett, F. C., 296
Bartoshuk, L. M., 194, 195
Bartsch, K., 536
Bartus, R. T., 313
Bartusiak, M., 211
Basadur, M. S., 334
Bashore, T. R., 451
Baskett, L. M., 136
Baskin, Y., 108
Basler, H. D., 594
Basmajian, J. V., 279, 280
Bassuk, E. L., 558
Bastiani, M. J., 85
Basu, A. K., 364
Bateman, T. S., 51
Batson, C. D., 637
Baucom, D. H., 139
Baum, A., 428, 574
Bauman, J., 416
Baumeister, R. F., 48, 140, 415, 472,
    485, 575, 611
Baumgartner, G., 180
Baumrind, D., 62, 133, 636
Baxter, L. R., 509
Bayern, C. D., 325
Bayley, N., 125, 363
Bayton, J. A., 12
Beail, N., 483
Beall, S. K., 591
Bear, D. M., 642
Beaton, R. J., 289
Beatty, J., 167
Beatty, W. W., 39
Beaumont, W., 391
Beck, A. T., 518, 546
Beck, P., 591
Becker, J. B., 101
Beckham, J. C., 280
Becklen, R., 212
Bedeian, A. G., 623
Beeghley, L., 401
Beens, H., 546
Beers, C. W., 536
Behrend, D. A., 342
Beidel, D. C., 501, 506
Beiser, M., 560
Bekoff, M., 63

Belisle, M., 593
Bell, A. P., 406
Bell, J. E., 149
Bellack, A. S., 550
Bellas, D. N., 104
Belmont, L., 380
Belsky, J., 134, 149
Bem, D. J., 489, 624, 628
Bem, S. L., 137
Bemis, C., 434, 585
Bemis, K. M., 397
Benbow, C. P., 138, 139, 370
Benesch, K. F., 483
Benjamin, L. T., Jr., 272
Bennett, G. J., 198
Bennett, W., 596
Ben-Porath, Y. S., 477
Bensing, J., 600
Benson, A. S., 182
Benson, D. F., 96
Benson, H., 234, 590
Bentall, R. P., 519
Bentler, P. M., 145
Benton, D., 314
Berenfeld, R., 402
Berg, J. H., 613, 618
Bergeman, C. S., 118
Berger, A. A., 436
Bergin, A. E., 563, 565
Berko, J., 343
Berkowitz, L., 643, 647, 648
Berkowitz, M. W., 153
Berlin, R. M., 216
Bermond, B., 441
Bernard, J. L., 136, 562
Bernardo, P., 415
Berndt, T. J., 114, 135
Berne, E., 551
Bernieri, F., 430
Berninger, V. W., 127
Bernquier, A., 223
Bernstein, D. J., 264
Bernstein, I. L., 261, 262
Bernstein, J. J., 101
Bernstein, W. M., 611
Berrios, G. E., 555
Berscheid, E., 617
Bertelsen, A., 515
Bertrand, L. D., 513
Besch, P. J., 139
Bexton, W. H., 409
Biggers, K., 602
Billings, R. S., 335
Binik, Y. M., 337
Birch, D. E., 562
Bird, E. I., 280
Bishop, G. D., 628
Bisschoff, F., 415
Bitter, J. R., 554
Bjork, D. W., 11, 12, 36, 70
Bjork, E. L., 128
Bjorklund, D. F., 294
Black, D. W., 520
Black, J. E., 146
Blacker, D., 516
Blair, M. C., 552
Blair, M. E., 256
Blake, R., 192
Blakemore, C., 88, 186, 506
Blanchard, E. B., 544, 581
Blanchard, P. N., 481
Blaney, N. T., 588
Blankfield, R. P., 230

Blasi, A., 155
Blaszcynski, A., 406
Blatt, S. J., 471
Blechman, E. A., 133
Bledsoe, S. B., 618
Bleier, R., 139
Bles, W., 201
Blick, K. A., 306
Bliss, T. V., 311, 313
Blissett, S. E., 588
Block, J. H., 334
Bloomquist, D. W., 162
Bluck, S., 409
Boardway, R. H., 591
Boeck, B. E., 152
Bohan, J. S., 25
Bohannon, J. N., III, 286, 346
Boice, R., 39
Boland, J. P., 404
Bolden, S. H., 475
Bolhuis, J. J., 298
Bolles, R. C., 254
Bolm-Audorff, U., 428
Bond, C. F., Jr., 237, 293, 630
Bond, L. A., 380
Bonds, D. R., 395
Boneau, C. A., 274
Boneau, R. H., 582
Bonke, B., 243
Booker, A., 643
Boon, S., 512
Bordage, G., 325
Bordages, J. W., 486
Borduin, C. M., 554
Boring, E. G., 9, 13, 183
Bornstein, R. F., 244, 245, 246, 248
Botman, H. I., 223
Bouchard, T. J., Jr., 117, 118, 379, 459
Boudreau, R. A., 48
Bouton, M. E., 258
Bouzid, N., 307
Bowd, A. D., 64
Bowen, D. J., 221
Bower, G. H., 304, 307, 309, 512
Bowers, K. S., 56
Bowers, L. B., 133
Bowlby, J., 130
Bowman, M. L., 359
Box, P., 272
Boyce, B. A., 418
Boyd, J. H., 506, 507
Boylin, W., 151
Boynton, R. M., 178
Bozarth, J. D., 547–548
Brackbill, Y., 381
Brackfield, S. C., 333
Bradbury, T. N., 149
Bradford, J. M., 643
Bradley, L. A., 599
Bradley, M. T., 451
Brady, D. R., 312
Branconnier, R. J., 79, 242
Brand, R. J., 602
Brandeis, L., 198
Brantley, P. J., 580
Brashear, D. B., 403
Braungart, J. M., 458
Bray, C. W., 190
Breakey, W. R., 560
Breathnach, C. S., 92, 96
Brecher, E. M., 237, 238
Breckler, S. J., 619
Bredemeier, B. J., 645

Breier, A., 79
Breland, K., 274
Breland, M., 274
Brennan, J. L., 465
Brentar, J., 230
Brewer, M. B., 627
Brewer, W. F., 298
Brewin, C. R., 518
Brickman, P., 435
Bridgeman, D., 627
Briggs, K. C., 475
Brigham, C. C., 376
Brigham, T. A., 48
Bringmann, M. W., 9, 315
Broad, W. J., 499
Brobeck, J. R., 393
Broberg, D. J., 262
Brodley, B. T., 547–548
Bromberg, W., 535
Bronstein, P., 131
Brooks, K., 315
Brooks, P. M., 584
Brooks-Gunn, J., 142, 145, 397
Broughton, R., 222, 324
Brown, A. L., 368
Brown, A. S., 303
Brown, D. M., 272, 280
Brown, D. R., 390
Brown, J. D., 501, 580, 589, 611
Brown, J. L., 484
Brown, R., 286, 343
Brown, S. W., 229
Brownell, K. D., 596, 597
Bruce, M. L., 500, 506
Bruck, M., 315
Brugge, J. F., 193
Bruner, J. S., 16
Bruning, N. S., 589
Bruno, T., 416
Brustad, R. J., 418
Bryant, J., 481
Bryant, P. E., 129
Buchanan, J. J., 294
Buchsbaum, M. S., 409, 521
Buck, R., 424, 443
Buckley, K. W., 13, 14, 16, 526
Bucy, P. C., 89
Buhrmester, D., 135
Bull, D., 191
Bunney, W. E., 219
Burchinal, M. R., 134
Burger, J. M., 611
Burish, T. G., 568
Burks, N., 618
Burnette, M. M., 280
Burns, M., 170
Burns, T. E., 302
Burrows, D., 465
Burton, D., 417
Burton, R., 498
Burton, R. V., 324
Buscaglia, M., 115
Buss, A., 643
Buss, A. R., 9, 137
Buss, D. M., 148, 458, 618
Buss, E., 643
Bussey, K., 137
Butcher, J. N., 477, 525
Butterfield, E. C., 369
Button, E., 483, 500
Buttram, R. T., 436
Buyer, L. S., 333
Byers, P. H., 189
Byrne, A. T. J., 418

Byrne, D., 38, 40, 62, 469, 616
Byrne, R. C., 553
Byrne, W., 139

Cacioppo, J. T., 619, 620, 622
Cadwallader, E. H., 549
Cain, D. P., 55
Cain, W. S., 194, 195
Calantone, R. J., 620
Calkins, M. W., 26, 27, 222, 223
Callahan, L. A., 528
Callahan, S., 139
Callaway, M. R., 630
Callero, P. L., 441
Camac, C., 478
Camel, J. E., 123
Cameron, M. J., 265
Campbell, J. B., 415
Campbell, W. K., 305
Campione, J. E., 368
Campos, J. J., 131
Candland, D. K., 655
Cann, A., 634
Cannon, D. S., 542
Cannon, J. G., 593
Cannon, W. B., 391, 392, 437, 440, 580
Cantor, N., 482
Caplan, L. J., 342
Caplan, P. J., 138
Cappell, H., 235
Cappello, M. J., 265
Caramazza, A., 297
Carducci, B. J., 633, 655
Carey, G., 508
Carey, J., 617
Carey, J. R., 55
Carey, M. P., 403, 480, 568, 595
Carlat, D. J., 398
Carlberg, C., 34
Carlsmith, J. M., 624
Carlson, C. R., 223
Carlson, E. T., 98, 512
Carlson, M., 638
Carlsson, A., 79
Carmargo, C. A., 398
Carmichael, L., 347
Carmody, T. P., 599–600
Carnine, D. W., 306
Carran, D. T., 366, 559
Carretta, A., 405
Carroll, J. L., 587
Carskadon, M. A., 218
Carson, R. C., 525
Carter, B. D., 228
Carter-Saltzman, L., 379
Cartwright, R. D., 225, 226
Carver, C. S., 518
Cash, T. F., 613, 616
Cassone, V. M., 84
Catalan, J., 403
Catania, J. A., 592, 593
Cate, R. M., 401
Cattell, J. M., 360
Cattell, R. B., 364, 477
Cattell, R. C., 372
Cavanaugh, J. C., 310
Ceci, S. J., 315, 371
Cecil, M. A., 547
Chadwick, H., 324
Chaiken, S., 625
Chance, G., 126
Chance, J. E., 613

Chao, G. R., 364
Chaplin, W. F., 49
Chapman, R. K., 228
Charness, N., 336
Chase, W. G., 291
Chemelski, B. E., 308
Chen, D. M., 166
Chen, K., 372
Cheney, D. L., 339
Chernick, L., 490
Cherry, E. C., 244
Chester, B. E., 398
Chi, M. T. H., 295
Child, I. L., 204
Chiodo, J., 221
Chipuer, H. M., 117
Chiu, C. Y. P., 248
Chomsky, N., 346
Chrisler, J. C., 265
Christensen, A. J., 602
Christensen, L., 62
Christianson, S. A., 302, 512
Christopher, F. S., 401
Chwalisz, K., 441
Cialdini, R. B., 634, 638
Cicchetti, D., 133
Cicerone, C. M., 170, 176
Cichanski, K. A., 280
Cimbolic, P., 516
Ciuffreda, K. J., 181
Clark, K. B., 627
Clark, M. C., 149, 309
Clark, M. E., 280
Clark, M. P., 627
Clark, R. D., 628, 629, 640
Clarke, J. T., 367
Clarke, K. M., 549
Clarke, M. J., 238
Cleary, P. D., 594
Clements, D. H., 272
Cliffe, M. J., 265
Clifford, C. A., 509
Clore, G. L., 627
Cloud, M. D., 99
Cluess, P. A., 115
Clum, G. A., 508
Coates, D., 435
Cofer, C. N., 388
Cogan, D., 256
Cogan, R., 256
Cohen, D. B., 220
Cohen, L. J., 577
Cohen, M. R., 81
Cohen, N., 582, 583, 584
Cohen, N. J., 286, 312
Cohen, S., 588
Coile, D. C., 65
Coke-Pepsi slugfest, 53
Cole, J. D., 523
Cole, J. O., 558
Cole, S. G., 632
Colegrove, F. W., 286
Coleman, R. M., 214
Coleman, S. R., 389
Coles, R., 130
Collier, D. E., 416
Collier, J., 403
Collingridge, G. L., 313
Collins, A. M., 295, 296
Collins, J. S., 166
Collins, R. L., 277
Comrey, A. L., 372, 482
Conley, J. J., 181

Connelly, D., 552
Connor, S. R., 465
Conrad, R., 290
Constantinople, A., 144
Conway, C. G., 168
Conway, M. A., 302, 306
Cook, M., 277, 506
Cook, S. W., 401, 627
Coon, D. J., 255
Coon, H., 379
Cooney, J. L., 472
Coons, P. M., 512
Cooper, C. L., 576, 578
Cooper, G. D., 409
Cooper, G. F., 186
Cooper, H. M., 55, 482, 554, 611
Cooper, J., 622
Cooper, L. M., 168
Cooper, R. D., 578
Copper, C., 306
Corbett, S., 401
Coren, S., 185, 409
Cornell, D. G., 369
Cornell-Bell, A. H., 72
Corr, C. A., 152
Corsini, R. J., 537
Corter, J. E., 323
Corwin, J. V., 100
Costa, P. T., Jr., 479, 602
Costello, A., 506
Cotman, C. W., 80
Cousins, N., 587
Cowan, N., 288, 289
Cowart, B. J., 195
Cowen, E. L., 534
Cowles, M., 40, 41, 57
Cox, G. L., 398
Cox, R. P., 403
Cox, W. J., 507
Craft, L. L., 456
Craft, S., 314
Craig, J. C., 290
Craik, F. I. M., 293, 295
Cramer, P., 471
Crandall, J. E., 484
Cravens, H., 369
Crawford, D. W., 618
Crawshaw, C. M., 307
Crisp, A. H., 560
Critchlow, B., 235
Critelli, J. W., 565, 618
Croce, R. V., 280, 542
Crocker, J., 518, 626
Crockett, D. J., 198
Croft, K., 129
Cronan-Hillix, W. A., 11
Crook, T., 517
Crosby, L. O., 395
Crose, R., 549
Cross, C. K., 514
Cross, T., 449
Crovitz, H. F., 223
Crowe, R. R., 506
Croyle, R. T., 622
Crump, C. E., 593
Crump, T., 507
Crundell, J. K., 558
Crutcher, M. D., 92
Crutcher, R. J., 11
Cuello, A. C., 198
Culebras, A., 87
Cumming, B. G., 181
Cummings, E. M., 128
Cummings, J. L., 91

Cunnick, J. E., 583
Cunningham, J. A., 626
Cunningham, S., 350, 557, 561
Curcio, C. A., 170
Curnow, C., 146
Curran, E. J., 101
Curry, J. F., 44
Curthoys, I. S., 200
Curzon, G., 428
Cushman, P., 553
Cusick, F., 496
Cutter, R. L., 245
Cutting, J. E., 178
Cytowic, R. E., 241
Czeisler, C. A., 214

D'Agostino, P. R., 245
Dallas, K., 224
Dallenbach, K. M., 300, 301
Daly, M., 472
Damasio, A. R., 194, 244
Dance, K. A., 567
Dandoy, A. C., 586
Danenberg, M. A., 192
Daniels, D., 459, 461
Daniels, M., 488
Danks, J. H., 331
Dantchik, A., 456
Danziger, K., 37, 56
Darch, C. B., 306
Darian-Smith, I., 197
Darley, J. M., 613, 639, 640
Darling, C. A., 403
Darrach, B., 496
Darwin, C., 8, 70, 114, 431
Daubman, K. A., 334
Daum, I., 360
Davidson, J. K., 403
Davidson, R. J., 427, 431
Davilla, D. A., 602
Davis, A., 364
Davis, C. C., 136
Davis, H., 349
Davis, H. P., 70
Davis, J., 178
Davis, J. M., 394
Davis, J. O., 214
Davis, M. H., 611, 616
Davis, R., 17, 337
Davis, S. F., 16, 17
Dawson, G. R., 277
Deahl, M., 242
DeAngelis, G. C., 181
Deaux, K., 139, 140
de Benedittis, G., 578
DeCarli, C., 95
DeCasper, A. J., 122
de Castro, J. M., 394
DeCharms, R., 410, 411
Deci, E. L., 414
Deckers, L., 436
DeFries, J. C., 118, 379
DeLacoste-Utamsing, C., 139
de la Riva, C., 396
de la Serna, M., 553
Delemos, K. A., 165
Delmonte, M. M., 234
DeLongis, A., 580
Deluga, R. J., 611
de Man, A., 303
Dember, W. N., 186
Dement, W., 219

Dement, W. C., 218, 224
Dempster, F. N., 301, 306
Denmark, F. L., 24, 27
Denney, N. W., 402
Dennis, D. L., 560
Depue, R. A., 514
Derlega, V. F., 616
Dermer, M., 615
Desforges, D. M., 627
Desiderato, O., 552
Desiderio, D. M., 312
de St. Aubin, E., 150
Detera-Wadleigh, S. D., 516
Deutsch, G., 102, 105, 107–108
de Valois, K. K., 180
de Valois, R. L., 176, 180
Devine, D. P., 198
Devins, G. M., 76
DeVos, J., 128
Dewsbury, D. A., 63
Diaconis, P., 203, 204
Diamond, E. L., 602
Diamond, J. M., 134
Diamond, M. C., 123
Diaz Soto, L., 414
Dickerson, C. A., 624
Dickey-Bryant, L., 615
Dickman, S., 18
Dickson, D., 202
DiDomenico, L., 397
Didow, S. M., 136
Diener, E., 434, 435, 441, 490
Diers, C. J., 142
Dietzen, L. L., 548
Dillard, J. P., 633
Dillon, K. M., 588
DiLorenzo, T. M., 368
Dince, W. M., 281
Dinges, D. F., 528
Dishion, T., 145
Dishman, R. J., 593
Dittmann, S., 340
Dixon, N. F., 472
DiZio, P., 200
Doane, J. A., 523
Dobelle, W. H., 173
Dockery, T. M., 623
Dodson, J. D., 407
Dohrn, C. S., 237
Dolce, J. J., 198
Dollard, J., 576, 643
Donaldson, G., 373
Donderi, D. C., 224
Donnerstein, E., 647, 648
Dooling, D. J., 297
D'Orban, P. T., 217
Dornbusch, S. M., 119
Dougherty, D., 449
Dover, A., 272
Dovidio, J. F., 613
Downey, J., 407
Doyle, A. C., 40
Doyle, J., 146
Doyle, M. C., 224
Draijer, N., 512
Driskell, J. E., 306
Dronkers, N. F., 104
Droste, C., 81
Dubbert, P. M., 593
Dubner, R., 197, 198
DuBois, M., 81
Duckro, P. N., 281
Duckworth, J. C., 477

Gershuny, B. S., 465
Geschwind, N., 96, 97
Gesten, E. L., 559
Gettman, L. R., 593
Geyer, M. A., 240
Giambra, L. M., 211
Gibbons, B., 194, 195
Gibbs, E. D., 380
Gibson, E. J., 125, 126
Gibson, J. J., 178
Gidycz, C. A., 646
Gilbert, B., 613
Gilbert, D. G., 395, 594
Gilbert, S. J., 635
Giles, D. E., 518
Gilhooly, K. J., 326
Gill, D., 152, 341
Gill, T. V., 350
Gillam, B., 185
Gillette, M. U., 214
Gilligan, C., 144, 155
Gilliland, K., 239
Gillman, M. A., 237
Gilmartin, B., 280
Gilovich, T., 335
Gingerich, W. J., 337
Giovannini, D., 430
Girgus, J. S., 518
Gisiner, R., 349
Gjerde, P. F., 519
Gladue, B. A., 405
Glaser, R., 583, 584, 588
Glass, A. L., 335
Glass, C. R., 481
Glass, G. V., 566
Glen, L., 600
Glenn, S. S., 366
Glick, P., 456
Gliedman, J., 341
Glod, C., 558
Gluck, M. A., 323
Glucksberg, S., 331
Glueckauf, R. L., 552
Glynn, S. M., 542
Goble, A. K., 165
Goddard, H. H., 366, 376
Godden, D. R., 303, 304
Godemont, M., 534
Goebel, B. L., 152, 390
Goisman, R. M., 568
Gold, M. S., 237, 397
Gold, P. E., 84, 314
Goldberg, L. R., 181, 478
Goldberg, M. E., 105
Goldberg, W. J., 101
Goldbloom, D. S., 398
Golden, L. L., 622
Goldenberg, S., 150
Goldfarb, P., 333
Goldfried, M. R., 538
Golding, S. L., 528
Goldin-Meadow, S., 346
Goldman, D. L., 536
Goldman, M., 430
Goldsmith, H. H., 131
Goldsmith, T. H., 166
Goldstein, A. G., 428, 586, 613
Goldstein, L. H., 625
Goldstein, S. R., 267
Goleman, D., 537
Golombok, S., 83, 403
Gondola, J. C., 475
Gonzales, M. H., 616

Gonzalez, R., 382
Good, R., 143
Good, T. L., 611
Goodall, J., 43
Goodenough, F. L., 431
Goodman, C. S., 85
Goodman, E. S., 25
Goodwin, C. J., 12, 25
Goodwin, J. M., 512
Goodykoontz, L. G., 553
Gorassini, D., 228
Gorczynski, R. M., 584
Gordon, D. E., 145
Gordon, I. E., 183
Gordon, S. K., 151
Gordon, W., 130
Gorelick, P. B., 429
Gorman, J., 341
Gorren, L. J., 404
Gosnell, B. A., 392
Gosselin, J. Y., 523
Gotlib, I. H., 517
Gottesman, D., 456
Gottesman, I. I., 115, 118, 394, 521,
   522
Gough, H. G., 486
Gould, S. J., 55, 368, 376, 377
Graesser, A. C., 436
Graham, J. R., 477
Graham-Clay, S., 367
Grainger, W., 272
Gramer, M., 235
Graves, R., 429
Graw, P., 514
Gray, A., 643
Gray, L. S., 280
Gray, M. M., 134
Gray, P. H., 13
Gray-Little, B., 618
Greaves, D. W., 563
Green, A. J., 326
Green, D. M., 193
Green, J. A., 281
Green, R., 405
Green, V., 230
Greenberg, L. S., 538, 549
Greenberg, R. P., 225, 472, 538
Greenblatt, D. J., 557
Greendale, G. A., 146
Greene, D., 414
Greene, E., 317
Greene, R. L., 293
Greenglass, E. R., 148
Greenlee, R. W., 550
Greeno, J. G., 276
Greenough, W. T., 123, 146
Gregg, E., 643
Gregg, R. H., 280
Gregory, R. L., 74, 183
Gregory, W. L., 591
Greist-Bousquet, S., 178
Gresham, F. M., 481
Grey, J. N., 62
Grieser, D., 126
Griggs, R. A., 201
Grilo, C. M., 395
Grodsky, A., 211
Gros-Louis, Y., 221
Gross, A. M., 541
Gross, J., 595
Grossberg, I. N., 369
Grosz, R. D., 515
Grove, W. M., 524

Gruder, C. L., 639
Grunberg, N. E., 428, 574, 594
Grych, J. H., 135
Guastello, D. D., 456
Guastello, S. J., 456
Guglielmo, K. M., 199
Guilford, J. P., 333, 371, 372
Gulevich, G., 219
Gulgoz, S., 362
Gurin, J., 596
Gurklis, J. A., 99
Gusella, J. L., 122
Gustafson, R., 247
Gustafson, S. B., 331
Gustavson, C. R., 260
Gutheil, T. G., 562
Guthrie, D., 401
Guthrie, E. V., 627
Guthrie, S., 181

Haar, M. D., 547
Haber, R. N., 181, 291
Hackett, G., 482
Hadley, S. W., 567
Hagan, R., 137
Hagen, R. L., 395
Haier, R. J., 521
Hajdukovic, R., 222
Hale, M., Jr., 12, 222
Haley, W. E., 542
Hall, C. S., 223
Hall, D., 267
Hall, G. S., 140
Hall, H. K., 418
Hall, J. B., 221
Hall, R. G., 595
Hall, R. V., 413
Halligan, P. W., 244
Halperin, P., 603
Halpern, J. N., 305
Halpern, L., 192
Hama, A. T., 101
Hamburg, D. A., 574
Hamer, D. H., 405
Hamill, R., 335
Hamilton, M. C., 349
Hamlett, K. W., 44
Hammersmith, S. J., 406
Hammontree, M. L., 587
Hamre-Nietupski, S., 266
Handelmann, G. E., 80
Hansen, C. H., 431, 472
Hansen, R. D., 431, 472
Hanson, R. K., 476, 579
Harbin, D., 170
Harbin, G., 170
Hardaway, R. A., 248
Hardman, J. S., 475
Hardy, C. J., 631
Hardyck, C., 103
Hare, R. D., 524
Hare-Mustin, R. T., 472
Haritos-Fatouros, M., 635
Harkins, S., 631
Harlow, H. F., 131
Harlow, L. L., 145
Harman, M. J., 550
Harrington, D. M., 331, 334
Harrington, J. M., 219
Harris, M. J., 54
Harris, R. L., 150
Harrison, A. A., 615, 618
Harrison, D. W., 281

Hart, J. D., 280
Hart, S. D., 524
Hartley, D., 553
Hartley, J., 325
Hartline, P. H., 166
Hartman, N., 594
Hartnett, B. D., 416
Hartshorne, H., 489, 490
Hartup, W. W., 135
Harvald, B., 515
Harvey, E. N., 215
Hasegawa, T., 43
Hasher, L., 296–297
Haskell, R. E., 42
Haskett, R. F., 642
Hassett, J., 74
Hatfield, E., 617
Hathaway, S. R., 475
Hattie, J. A., 568
Hauge, M., 515
Hawkes, N., 621
Hawkins, M. J., 487
Hawkins, W. E., 487
Hawton, K., 403, 404
Hayden, T., 489
Hayes, C., 350
Hayes, D. S., 308
Hayes, R. L., 87
Hayflick, L., 146
Hayhoe, M. M., 170
Haynes, O. M., 431
Hays, J. R., 561
Hayslip, B., Jr., 152
Haywood, H. C., 365
Hazelrigg, M. D., 554
Hazelrigg, P. J., 55
Hearne, K. M., 202
Hearnshaw, L. S., 7, 378
Heath, A. C., 217
Heatherton, T. F., 398
Hebb, D. O., 407, 408
Hechinger, N., 197
Hecker, M. H., 602
Hedges, L. V., 40
Heffner, H. E., 190
Hehl, F. J., 436
Heider, F., 608
Heider, K. G., 432
Heim, M., 647
Heim, N., 514
Heimberg, R. G., 507, 545
Heitzmann, C. A., 588
Hellige, J. B., 102
Hellman, R. E., 405
Helmes, E., 477
Helmholtz, H. von, 175
Helmreich, R. L., 412
Helzer, J. E., 502
Hendrick, C., 57
Hendrick, S., 145
Hendrickson, K. M., 512
Hendrixson, L. L., 156
Henke, P. G., 89, 427
Henle, M., 15, 549
Henley, S. H., 472
Hennessey, B. A., 414
Henrion, R., 550
Henry, J. L., 81
Herbert, W., 312, 476, 528
Hergenhahn, B. R., 469
Herkenhahn, M., 242
Herman, C. P., 395, 398
Herman, L. M., 349
Hermann, D. H., 562

Hermelin, B., 358
Hernandez, J. M., 200
Herning, R. I., 86
Hernstein, R. J., 377
Herod, J. W., 224
Heron, W., 409
Herrero, J. V., 429
Herrick, C., 553
Herrnstein, R. J., 382
Hersen, M., 550
Hertzog, C., 147
Heslegrave, R. J., 219
Hesley, J. W., 490
Heslin, R., 446
Hess, E. H., 168
Hesse, H., 470
Hetherington, A. W., 393
Hewitt, E. C., 232
Hewstone, M., 613
Heyes, C. M., 277
Hiatt, S. W., 131
Hicks, R. A., 218, 602
Higgins, E. T., 485, 487, 506, 518
Higson, P. J., 273
Hilakivi, I., 477
Hilgard, E. R., 9, 226, 228, 231, 241,
    330, 458
Hill, C. E., 430
Hill, K. T., 407
Hill, R. D., 309
Hill, T. W., 240
Hillerbrand, J., 192
Hillix, W. A., 429
Hilsenroth, M. J., 471
Hilts, V. L., 457
Hinckley, J. W., 526
Hindeland, M. J., 10
Hinsz, V. B., 615
Hiramoto, R. N., 585
Hirsch, H. V. B., 186
Hirschfield, R. M. A., 514
Hirschman, R., 280
Hitzig, E., 92
Ho, I. K., 237
Hobart, G. A., 215
Hobson, J. A., 16, 226
Hodes, R. L., 449
Hodgins, H. S., 430
Hodgkinson, S., 516
Hoelscher, T. J., 590
Hoff-Ginsberg, E., 343
Hoffman, C., 348
Hoffman, H. G., 317
Hoffman, L. W., 118
Hofman, M. A., 406
Hofmann, A., 241
Hofsten, C., 127
Hogan, H. P., 347
Hogg, M. A., 626
Holborn, S. W., 271
Holden, C., 64, 458, 459, 475, 514,
    527, 528, 557
Holden, R. R., 62
Holding, D. H., 266
Holland, P. C., 256
Hollender, M. H., 400, 537
Hollins, M., 165
Holmes, D. S., 150, 234, 302
Holmes, M., 89
Holmes, T. H., 577, 578
Holt, J., 221
Holtgraves, T., 335
Homa, D., 171, 325

Homan, C. P., 429
Homant, R. J., 410
Homer, P. M., 621
Honchar, M. P., 558
Honorton, C., 204
Honts, C. R., 449
Honzik, C. H., 276, 277
Hope, D. A., 507
Hopkins, B. L., 272
Hoppe, R. B., 204
Hormuth, S. E., 481
Horn, J. L., 372, 373
Horn, J. M., 115, 379, 459
Horne, J. A., 334
Horner, M. D., 294
Horney, K., 468, 472
Horowitz, F. D., 14
Horowitz, M. J., 588
Houlihan, D. D., 542
Houston, B. K., 602
Houston, L., 139
Hovland, C. I., 621
Howard, C., 217
Howard, G. S., 558
Howard, K. I., 566, 567
Howe, M. J., 358
Howell, R. J., 168
Howton, J. D., 410
Hoyle, S. G., 135
Hsiao, S., 392
Hsu, L. G., 337, 396, 398
Hubel, D. H., 173, 178
Huber, H. P., 235
Huber, M. J., 234
Huber, R. J., 512
Huber, S. J., 304
Hubschman, L., 404
Hudesman, J., 591
Hughes, D., 545
Hughes, J., 80
Hughes, J. R., 239, 594
Hulicka, I. M., 151
Hulihan-Giblin, B., 597
Hull, C. L., 389, 630
Hull, J. G., 237
Humphrey, L. L., 397
Humphreys, M. S., 412
Hunsley, J., 476
Hunt, E., 349
Hunt, J. M., 152
Hunter, J. E., 413
Hurford, J. R., 344
Hurst, L. C., 358
Husain, S. A., 514
Husband, A. J., 258
Huston, A. C., 278
Huston, T. L., 616, 640
Hutchings, B., 115
Hutchins, C. M., 193
Huttenlocher, P. R., 99, 123
Huxley, A., 240, 258
Huyghe, P., 520
Hyde, J. S., 138, 349
Hyman, R. B., 487
Hynan, D. J., 548

Immergluck, L., 36
Ingelfinger, F. J., 392
Ingham, A. G., 631
Inglis, A., 148
Inoki, R., 198
Insko, C. A., 619, 626
Irvine, J. J., 280

Isaac, W., 281
Isaacs, K. R., 146
Isaacson, R. L., 427
Isen, A. M., 334
Isle, S., 419
Ispa, J. M., 134
Istvan, J. A., 599–600
Ivancevich, J. M., 580
Iversen, I. H., 263
Iyer, P., 242
Izard, C. E., 430, 431, 442, 446
Izmailov, C. A., 176

Jacklin, C. N., 139
Jackson, D. N., 643
Jackson, H. C., 557
Jacob, R. G., 596
Jacobson, A. L., 312
Jacobson, E., 11, 590
Jacobson, L., 54, 614
James, J. E., 543
James, W., 4, 16, 45, 70, 125, 210, 212,
    213, 237, 242, 287, 292, 297, 298,
    303, 305, 307, 388, 437, 562
Jamieson, D., 616
Jamieson, D. G., 340
Jamner, L. D., 281
Janata, J. W., 540
Janis, I. L., 629
Janiszewski, C., 619
Jankowicz, A. D., 483
Janoff-Bulman, R., 435
Jansson, L., 543
Jarvik, M. E., 594
Jason, L. A., 559
Jeffery, R. W., 394, 596
Jemmott, J. B., 582, 589
Jenkins, J. G., 300, 301
Jennings, J. R., 581
Jensen, A. J., 381
Jensen, A. R., 364
Jensen, J. P., 563
Jensen, M. P., 598
Jensh, R. P., 121, 367
Jernigan, T. L., 95
Joag, S. G., 334
John, O. P., 479
Johnson, C., 218, 398, 401
Johnson, D. R., 348
Johnson, J. S., 344, 345
Johnson, L., 219
Johnson, L. M., 65
Johnson, R. C., 359
Johnson, V. E., 401, 403, 404
Johnston, L., 613
Johnston, M. W., 51
Jolton, J., 456
Jonas, G., 334
Jones, A. J., 42
Jones, E. E., 620
Jones, L., 243
Jones, L. A., 199
Jones, L. V., 381
Jones, M. C., 142, 259, 540, 544
Jones, M. M., 510, 511
Jones, R. N., 542
Jones, R. T., 293
Jorgensen, R. S., 585
Josephson, W. L., 643
Joubert, P. H., 199
Joyce, J., 211
Ju, J. J., 567
Judd, H. L., 146

Judge, S. J., 181
Juergensen, M. R., 274
Julien, R. M., 241, 242
Julius, D. A., 216
Jung, C. G., 469
Jungeblut, A., 363
Jussim, L., 608

Kaas, J. H., 99
Kaczmarek, M., 591
Kaelber, C., 502
Kahle, L. R., 504, 621
Kahn, S., 587
Kahn, T. J., 44
Kahneman, D., 335, 336
Kakihara, C., 610
Kallmen, H., 247
Kalmun, A. J., 162
Kamarck, T. W., 581
Kameenui, E. J., 306
Kamin, L., 275
Kamin, L. J., 378
Kamins, M. A., 622
Kamiya, J., 279
Kanada, K., 168
Kanas, N., 550
Kandel, E., 88, 358
Kandel, E. R., 311
Kane, J. M., 521
Kanekar, S., 620
Kanzer, M., 225
Kao, E. C., 359
Kaplan, G. A., 584
Kaplan, M., 588
Kaplan, R. M., 471
Karwan, K. R., 51
Kassop, M., 554
Katz, J., 221
Kaufman, A. S., 147, 372
Kaufman, B., 540
Kaufman, J., 133
Kaufman, L., 183, 290
Kavale, K., 34
Kawai, M., 119
Kayne, N. T., 518
Kazarian, S. S., 523
Kazdin, A. E., 539, 542, 550
Kazee, T. A., 51
Keck, P. E., 558
Keesey, R. E., 393
Keister, M. F., 280
Keith, B., 135
Keith, J. R., 276
Keller, F. S., 17
Kelley, H. H., 608, 609, 613
Kelley, K. C., 469
Kellogg, L. A., 349
Kellogg, W. N., 349
Kelly, G. A., 482
Kelly, I. W., 498
Kelly, J. A., 65
Kelly, M. P., 403
Kelly, R. B., 592
Kempler, B., 576
Kenardy, J., 507
Kendall, P. C., 547
Kendrick, K. M., 96, 180
Kendrick, M. J., 547
Kennedy, D. B., 410
Kennedy, S., 588
Kenrick, D. T., 456, 489
Kershner, J. R., 331
Keshaven, M. S., 224

Loring, D. W., 103
Lovass, O. I., 543
LoVerde, M., 192
Lovko, A. M., 134
Lowe, G., 304
Lowery, C. R., 135, 156
Lowry, D. H., 308
Loy, J. W., 613
Lu, Z. L., 290
Lubar, J. F., 280
Luborsky, L., 566, 567
Lubow, R. E., 200
Luce, G. G., 456
Luchins, A., 329
Luck, S. J., 108
Ludwick-Rosenthal, R., 599
Lumsdaine, A., 621
Lundberg, L. J., 342
Lundstrom, B., 404
Lunneborg, P. W., 653
Luria, Z., 136
Luthans, F., 264
Lydon, J. E., 616
Lykken, D. T., 118, 378, 448, 450, 451
Lynch, M. J., 407
Lynn, M., 235
Lynn, R., 360, 382
Lynn, S. J., 228, 230
Lysle, D. T., 583
Lytton, H., 136

Maass, A., 316, 628, 629
Maccoby, E. E., 136, 138
MacCracken, M. J., 630
MacDonald, G. A., 595
MacFarlane, J. G., 214
Mack, A., 185
Mack, S., 271
Mackenzie, B., 363–364
MacLean, H. N., 302
MacLeod, C. M., 299
MacNichol, E. F., Jr., 175
MacPherson, G. M., 138
Macrides, F., 195
MacTurk, R. H., 127
Maczaj, M., 221
Madakasira, S., 404
Maddi, S. R., 587
Maddux, J. E., 480
Madigan, M. W., 298
Madison, D. V., 75
Madrazo, I., 102
Magder, L., 588
Magloire, K., 589
Magoun, H. W., 87
Maher, B. A., 498, 499, 534
Maher, W. B., 498, 499, 534
Mahler, H. I. M., 599
Mahowald, M. B., 101
Maier, N. R., 330, 331
Maier, S. F., 273
Main, M., 133
Malamuth, N. M., 647
Malinowski, C. I., 155
Malott, J. M., 199
Mamberg, A. B., 80
Mandai, O., 220
Mandl, G., 181
Mangelsdorff, A. D., 580
Manicas, P. T., 40
Manning, B. H., 481
Manning, C. A., 314
Mansfield, J. G., 576

Manuck, S. B., 581
Manz, C. C., 480
Maragos, W. F., 313
Maranto, G., 146
Marcus, G. F., 343
Margiotta, E. W., 602
Margolis, R. B., 414
Marken, R. S., 326
Markowitsch, H. J., 427
Marks, M., 545
Markus, E., 554
Marlatt, G. A., 56, 277
Marmar, C., 538, 588
Marolla, F. A., 380
Marsden, C. D., 88
Marshall, F. J., 183
Marshall, G. D., 445
Marshall, J. C., 244, 401
Marshall, M. E., 8
Marshall, W. L., 542
Martin, B., 631
Martin, C. E., 400
Martin, E. M., 595
Martin, J. E., 593
Martin, K. D., 168
Martin, M. A., 306
Martinot, J. L., 517
Marx, J. L., 352, 580
Marx, M. H., 11
Maser, J. D., 502
Maslonek, K. A., 583
Maslow, A. H., 390, 484
Massaro, D. W., 322
Masserano, J. M., 557
Masters, K. S., 231
Masters, W. H., 401, 403, 404
Masur, F. T., 598
Matarazzo, J. D., 599–600
Matson, J. L., 272, 368
Matsumoto, D., 432, 443
Matt, G. E., 305
Matthews, K. A., 603
Matthews, T., 634
Mattick, R. P., 545
Maugh, T., 195, 221
Mausfeld, R., 8
Mauskopf, S., 202
Mautner, B., 538
Maxwell, S. E., 558
May, M. A., 489, 490
May, R., 488
Mayberry, J. S., 344
Mayer, D. J., 199
Mayer, S. J., 277
Mazziotta, J. C., 95, 104, 517
McAdams, D. P., 150
McAleney, P. J., 416
McAuley, E., 545, 593
McCaffrey, R. J., 581
McCallum, D. M., 587
McCammon, S., 446
McCann, B. S., 603
McCann, D. S., 234
McCann, M. J., 392
McCanne, T. R., 443
McCarley, R. W., 226
McCarthy, M., 546
McCarthy, T., 81, 462
McCarty, T., 512
McCaul, K. D., 199
McCauley, C., 335, 437, 451, 629
McClane, W. E., 435
McClelland, D. C., 411, 412

McCloskey, M., 286, 317
McConaghy, N., 406
McConkey, K. M., 233
McConnell, J. V., 245
McConnell, J. W., 312
McCormick, N. B., 42
McCoy, R. W., 98
McCrae, R. R., 479
McCutcheon, J. W., 475
McDougall, W., 388
McElroy, S. L., 558
McFadden, D., 190
McFarlane, A. C., 584
McGee, R., 304
McGee, R. A., 40
McGhee, P. E., 436
McGovern, P. G., 595
McGovern, T., 546
McGrady, A., 409, 590
McGrath, P., 603
McGreevy, M. A., 528
McGue, M., 115, 379, 459
McGuffin, P., 521
McGuigan, F. J., 322
McGuinness, T. P., 230
McGuire, B., 579
McGuire, T. M., 240
McIntosh, J. L., 514
McKelvie, S. J., 470
McKinlay, J. B., 643
McKinley, J. C., 475
McKinney, M., 313
McLeod, P. J., 132
McMahon, M., 562
McMillan, J. H., 609
McMinn, M. R., 597
McNally, R. J., 262, 506, 508
McNeal, E. T., 516
McNeil, C., 229
McNeil, E. B., 245
McPherson, K. S., 377
McPherson, L. M., 524
McPherson, M. W., 47
McQuinn, R. D., 618
McReynolds, P., 502
McVaugh, M., 202
McVety, K. M., 276
McWhorter, P., 309
McWilliams, R., 266
McWilliams, S. A., 241
Medin, D. L., 323, 324
Mednick, S. A., 115, 333, 334
Meehl, P. E., 456
Meeker, W. B., 230
Meichenbaum, D., 56, 547
Melcer, T., 260
Meldrum, B. S., 101
Melton, G. B., 62
Melzack, R., 198
Memmott, J., 349
Mendelson, W. B., 221
Mendes, M. G., 272
Menustik, C. E., 542
Merewether, F. C., 429
Merikle, P. M., 243
Merkel, W. T., 398
Merluzzi, T. V., 483
Mersch, P. P., 546
Mervis, J., 528, 566
Messer, S. C., 134
Messer, W. S., 201
Messick, D. M., 630
Messick, S., 363

Messier, C., 314
Metcalfe, J., 327, 409
Mewaldt, S. P., 304
Meyer, D. R., 99
Meyer, J. S., 146
Meyer-Bahlburg, H. F., 405
Meyers, C. E., 365
Mezei, L., 626
Michael, W. B., 372
Michaels, R. R., 234
Micze, K. A., 81
Middlebrooks, J. C., 193
Mikulincer, M., 486
Milan, R. J., 404
Milgram, S., 634, 636
Miller, B., 401
Miller, G. A., 290, 346
Miller, H. L., 49
Miller, I. J., 195
Miller, J., 538
Miller, J. A., 121
Miller, L. L., 79, 242
Miller, M. G., 391
Miller, N., 638
Miller, N. E., 64, 65, 279, 576
Miller, N. S., 237
Miller, P. C., 149
Miller, R. J., 168
Miller, T. I., 566
Miller, T. Q., 600
Miller-Jones, D., 364
Mills, M. J., 562
Milner, P., 89
Milofsky, E., 130
Milstein, V., 512
Mineka, S., 277, 506
Minuchin, S., 554
Mio, J. S., 436
Mischel, W., 489
Miserandino, M., 303
Mita, T. H., 615
Mitchell, C., 597
Mitchell, J. E., 396, 397
Mitchell, K. A., 616
Mitchell, P., 516
Mitler, M. M., 222
Miyazaki, K., 190
Moe, J. L., 626
Moeller, G. H., 410, 411
Mogul, K. M., 567
Moller, A. T., 244
Mollon, J. D., 177
Monaghan, D. T., 80
Monahan, J., 563
Money, J., 400, 407
Mongeau, P. A., 628
Monroe, K. B., 634
Monroe, S. M., 501, 578
Monson, T. C., 490
Montanes, P., 289
Monte, C. F., 470
Montgomery, R. W., 545
Monti, P. M., 552
Montnag, I., 482
Montour, K., 369
Montplaisir, J., 222
Moore, D. J., 510
Moore, J. T., 87
Moore, M., 48
Moore-Ede, M. C., 214
Moorhead, G., 629
Moran, M. G., 581
Morawski, J. G., 14

Moray, N., 212
Mordkoff, J. T., 338
Moreland, R. L., 615
Moretti, M. M., 485
Morey, L. C., 524, 568
Morgan, C., 411, 471
Morgan, S. B., 598
Morley, J. E., 396
Moroff, S. V., 334
Morosan, D. E., 340
Morrel-Samuels, P., 349
Morris, E. J., 87
Morris, E. K., 65
Morris, M., 466, 535
Morris, S., 203
Morris, W., 466, 535
Morrison, A. R., 220
Morrongiello, B. A., 126
Morse, D. L., 267
Mortel, K. F., 146
Mortimer, R. G., 174
Moruzzi, G., 87
Moses, L. N., 470
Moskowitz, D. S., 481
Moskowitz, H., 170, 242
Moskowitz, J. M., 627
Moskowitz, M. J., 12
Mowen, J. C., 334
Mowrer, O. H., 256, 268
Mowrer, W. M., 256
Mudd, S., 168
Muehlbach, M. J., 218
Muehlenhard, C. L., 401
Mueller, C. G., 14
Mufson, E. J., 312
Mulhall, D. J., 358
Mullen, B., 432
Mullington, J., 222
Mullins, L. L., 511
Mumford, M. D., 331
Munley, P. H., 477
Munsick, R. A., 403
Münsterberg, H., 314
Murphy, D. L., 409
Murphy, G. E., 518
Murphy, G. L., 323
Murphy, S. T., 446
Murray, D. J., 163
Murray, H. A., 410, 411, 471
Murray, J. B., 475
Murray, R. M., 509
Murstein, B., 618
Muscat, R., 393
Musick, P. L., 470
Mwamwenda, T. S., 143
Myers, D. G., 628
Myers, I. B., 475
Myerscough, R., 242
Mylander, C., 346
Myles, W. S., 219
Mynatt, C. R., 414

Nacoste, R. W., 626
Nahai, F., 280
Nahemow, L., 614
Narens, L., 8
Nash, M., 232
Naster, B. J., 481
Nathan, P. E., 38
Nathan, R. S., 501
Navon, D., 178
Neck, C. P., 629
Nehrke, M. F., 151

Neimeyer, G. J., 483
Neimeyer, R. A., 518, 616
Neisser, U., 212, 297
Nel, E. M., 627
Nelson, K. E., 345
Nelson, M. O., 469
Nelson, R. S., 134
Nelson, T. O., 306
Nemeth, C. J., 629
Nenty, H. J., 364
Nerger, J. L., 176
Nesdale, A. R., 643
Neufeld, R. W. J., 567, 599
Neumann, K. F., 565
Nevo, B., 437, 470
Nevo, O., 436, 437
Newcomb, M. D., 145
Newcomb, T., 645
Newcomer, S. F., 401
Newell, A., 327
Newman, B., 595
Newman, E. A., 166
Newman, J., 414
Newport, E. L., 344, 345
Newton, P. M., 150
Nezlek, J., 414
Nezu, A. M., 588
Nezu, C. M., 588
Nicastro, R., 239, 248
Nicholls, J. G., 331, 417
Nichols, M. P., 548
Nichols, P. L., 381
Nicholson, N., 632
Nickerson, R. S., 292
Nicki, R. M., 595
Nicol, S. E., 522
Nicoll, R. A., 75
Niedenthal, P. M., 245
Nielsen, T. A., 224
Niemiec, R., 272
Nietupski, J., 266
Niles, L. P., 84
Nilsson, L., 512
Nisbett, R. E., 414, 610
Nishida, T., 43
Nissen, M. J., 313
Noble, J. M., 480
Noel, P. S., 98
Nokes, T., 277
Nolen-Hoeksema, S., 518
Nonneman, A. J., 100
Norcross, J. C., 548
Nordstrom, R., 413
Norris, J., 496
Norris, N. P., 62
Norton, E. M., 514
Norton, S., 121, 367
Nosofsky, R. M., 324
Notz, W. W., 414
Novin, D., 392
Nowicki, G. P., 334
Nowicki, S., 429, 430
Nutt, D. J., 557
Nystul, M. S., 514

O'Brien, E. J., 490
Ochse, R., 334
O'Connell, A. N., 26
O'Connor, K. P., 19
O'Connor, N., 358
Oden, G. C., 178
Oden, M. H., 370
O'Donohue, W. T., 403

Offer, D., 145
Ogden, E. P., 62
Ogden, J. A., 100
Ogilvie, R. D., 216
Ogloff, J. R., 524
O'Hara, R., 298
Ohman, A., 508
Ohzawa, I., 181
Okagaki, L., 373
Okazaki, S., 383
Okwumabua, T. M., 482
O'Laughlin, M. S., 437
Olds, J., 89
O'Leary, A., 434, 582, 592
O'Leary, K. D., 149
Oller, D. K., 342
Olmo, R. J., 473
Olmsted, M. P., 395
Olney, J. W., 558
Olson, D. R., 129
Olson, J. M., 623
Olson, R. A., 511, 545
Olson, R. P., 552
O'Neill, M., 576
Onstad, S., 521
Oosterveld, W. J., 200
Oppliger, P. A., 436
Orlick, T., 230
Orlofsky, J. L., 148
Orne, E. C., 228, 528
Orne, M. T., 230, 232, 449, 528
Orwell, G., 346
Ost, L. G., 508, 543
O'Sullivan, M., 448
Otts, D. A., 272

Pack, A. A., 349
Paddock, J. R., 429
Page, M. M., 483
Page, R. C., 553
Page, S., 647
Paikoff, R. L., 142, 145
Palmer, J. C., 316, 317
Palmer, M., 308
Pappas, G. D., 101
Parham, K., 87
Parisi, T., 226
Park, B., 612
Park, D. C., 310
Parker, K. C. H., 471, 476
Parker, S., 57, 483
Parr, W., 312
Parsons, M. W., 314
Parten, M. B., 135
Patel, S., 101
Patterson, C. H., 564, 567
Patterson, D. R., 229
Patterson, F. G., 351
Patterson, L. H., 351
Patton, J. E., 407
Paul, S. M., 79, 597
Paulsen, F., 7
Paulsen, P., 475
Pauly, I. B., 404
Pavlov, I. P., 262
Peace, C. H., 84
Peake, P. J., 489
Pearce, J., 456
Pearlman, J., 552
Pears, R., 129
Pearson, J., 198
Peeples, E. E., 470
Peer, D. F., 509

Peer-Goldin, I., 486
Pellegrini, R. J., 218
Peltier, D., 559
Penfield, W., 84, 108
Pennebaker, J. W., 591, 600
Penrod, S., 317
Pensky, E., 149
Pepitone, A., 608, 645
Perfect, T., 230
Perkins, K. A., 594
Perkins, S. C., 511
Perlaki, K. M., 107
Perlow, M. J., 101
Perls, F., 548, 549
Peroutka, S. J., 241
Perr, I. N., 526
Perry, C., 230
Persad, E., 556
Pert, C. B., 80
Pervin, L. A., 462
Peterhans, E., 180
Peters, R., 304
Peters, R. M., 470
Peters, S. D., 401
Petersen, A. C., 140, 142
Peterson, C., 518, 586, 598
Peterson, I., 337
Peterson, L., 134, 599
Peterson, L. R., 291, 292
Peterson, M., 291, 292
Petrinovich, L. F., 103
Petronis, K. R., 514
Petruska, R., 641
Pettersen, L., 121
Pettigrew, T. F., 554
Petty, R. E., 620, 622
Pfaffmann, C., 194, 195
Phelps, M. E., 95, 104, 517
Philipp, E., 397
Phillips, D. P., 193
Phillips, R. D., 126
Phillips, W. M., 523
Phinney, V. G., 142
Piaget, J., 127, 153
Pick, H. A., Jr., 187
Pickar, D., 81
Picton, T. W., 523
Pierce, P. A., 241
Pieri, A., 578
Pigion, R. G., 168
Pihl, R. O., 224
Piliavin, J. A., 441
Pillard, R. C., 405
Pillemer, D. B., 286
Pincomb, G. A., 585
Pinel, J. P. J., 257
Piner, K. E., 504
Pines, M., 344, 345
Piper, A., 556
Pitre, U., 293
Pitsikas, N., 146
Plante, T. G., 590
Plass, J. A., 407
Plomin, R., 117, 118, 378, 379, 459,
    461, 644
Plotkin, W. B., 280
Plous, S., 63
Plutchik, R., 433, 434
Podlesny, J. A., 450, 451
Poffenberger, A. T., 9
Poggio, T., 73
Pogue-Geile, M. F., 395
Poincaré, H., 331

Polit, D. F., 136
Polivy, J., 395, 398
Pollak, G. D., 87
Pollard, T. G., 237
Polson, P. G., 294
Pomerleau, C. S., 239
Pomerleau, O. F., 239
Pomeroy, W. D., 400
Pope, M. K., 602
Pope, W. R., 609
Poplawsky, A., 427
Popplestone, J. A., 47
Posner, M. I., 104
Postman, L., 291, 298, 315
Potgieter, J., 415
Poulos, C. X., 235
Poulson, R. L., 528
Poumadere, J., 405
Powell, D. J., 242
Powers, W. T., 326
Powley, T. L., 393
Prager, K. J., 149
Prasinos, S., 435
Pratt, K. J., 6
Pratto, D. J., 134
Premack, D., 263, 350
Prentice-Dunn, S., 645
Preyer, W., 114
Pribram, K. H., 323
Price, R. A., 118, 394
Price-Williams, E., 130
Prochaska, J. O., 549
Proefrock, D. W., 140
Provenzano, F. J., 136
Pryde, N. A., 404
Puccio, G. J., 333
Pullum, G. K., 347
Purifoy, F. E., 211
Pyryt, M. C., 119

Qayyum, U., 216
Quadagno, D., 402
Quartaaro, J. D., 402
Quinn, K., 94
Quinton, A., 7
Quittner, A. L., 552

Rabinowitz, F. M., 115, 376
Rabun, M., 496
Rachal, J. R., 272
Rachman, S., 277
Raczynski, J. M., 198
Radwin, J. O., 528
Raeburn, J. M., 592
Ragland, D. R., 602
Raglin, J. S., 416
Rahe, R. H., 577, 578
Rainwater, N., 540
Rajecki, D. W., 618
Raloff, J., 192
Rambo, L. R., 11
Ramey, C., 365
Ramirez, M., 130
Ramón y Cajal, S., 76
Randels, S. P., 122
Range, L. M., 514
Ranson, S. W., 393
Rao, D. C., 115
Rapee, R. M., 505
Rapp, B. C., 297
Rapp, D., 16, 462
Rapp, P. E., 451
Rappaport, Z. H., 55

Raps, C. S., 587
Raskin, D. C., 449, 450, 451
Rasmussen, J. L., 618
Rasmussen, S. A., 509
Ratner, H. H., 148
Ratner, S. C., 521
Ravelli, G. P., 395
Ray, O., 239
Rayner, K., 171
Rayner, R., 259, 540
Raz, N., 522
Raz, S., 522
Read, J. D., 246
Read, M. S., 367
Read, P. P., 388
Redd, W. H., 599
Reddon, J. R., 477
Reddy, A. V., 333
Reddy, P. B., 333
Reeder, G. D., 562
Reeder, K., 341
Reedy, F. E., 195
Rees, L., 585
Reese, E. P., 260, 268
Reese, H. W., 61
Reese, L., 480
Reich, J. H., 505
Reilly, R. R., 364
Reiman, E. M., 506
Reimer, J., 155
Reinisch, J. M., 642, 643
Reis, S., 369
Reisenzein, R., 445
Reitman, J. S., 291
Rejeski, W. J., 589, 643
Relinger, H., 230
Remington, R. E., 595
Rende, R., 378
Renner, J. W., 143
Rescorla, R. A., 256, 275
Restle, F., 184
Revelle, W., 407, 412
Reynolds, C. F., 224
Reynolds, P., 584
Rheingold, H. L., 343
Rhodes, N., 622
Rhue, J. W., 228
Ricci, L. C., 79
Ricci Bitti, P. E., 430
Rice, M. L., 342
Richards, M. H., 514
Richardson, D., 62, 63
Richardson, J. T. E., 194
Richelson, E., 313
Richmond, B. O., 553
Rieber, R. W., 211
Riecken, H. W., 623
Rierdan, J., 142
Riggs, L. A., 166, 168, 169, 171, 173, 184
Rinaldi, R. C., 567
Rinn, W. E., 447
Riordan, C. A., 618
Rippee, E. T., 618
Risen, C. B., 399
Risse, G. B., 98
Ritter, B., 544
Ritvo, E. R., 481
Rivera-Tovar, L. A., 293
Rivinus, T. M., 514
Roark, M. L., 559
Roback, H. B., 553
Roberts, A. H., 280

Roberts, C. F., 528
Roberts, J. E., 188
Roberts, M. A., 481
Roberts, M. C., 270
Roberts, P., 150
Roberts, S. J., 598
Robins, L. N., 496, 502, 505, 510
Robinson, D. L., 105, 108
Robinson, F. P., 306
Robinson, L. A., 517
Rock, I., 183
Rocklin, T., 632
Rockwell, T., 204
Rodgers, J. E., 314
Rodgers, J. L., 381
Rodgers, R., 413
Rodin, J., 84, 392, 394, 396, 586, 590
Rodman, H., 134
Rodriguez, H., 545
Roehrs, T., 220
Rogers, C. R., 19, 195, 547, 548, 553
Rogers, H. J., 568
Rogers, R., 529
Rogers, R. L., 146
Rogers, R. W., 645
Roghmann, K. J., 580
Rokeach, M., 519, 626
Rolnick, A., 200, 201
Romano, J. M., 598
Romanski, L., 441
Romer, D., 639
Romero, A., 44
Romney, D. M., 136
Rompre, P. P., 79
Rorer, L. G., 483
Rosch, E., 324
Rose, J. E., 275
Rosen, R. H., 473
Rosen, E. F., 623
Rosenbaum, M. E., 616
Rosenhan, D. L., 503
Rosenman, R. H., 601, 602
Rosenthal, N. E., 514
Rosenthal, R., 54, 430, 614
Rosenzweig, M. R., 123
Roskies, E., 593
Ross, D., 203, 315, 643, 644
Ross, E. D., 429
Ross, G. M., 184
Ross, H. E., 184
Ross, J., 553
Ross, L., 488, 610
Ross, M., 302
Ross, R. R., 56
Ross, S. A., 643, 644
Rossi, A. M., 522, 540
Rossi, F., 574
Roth, N., 198
Roth, S., 577
Roth, T., 220
Rothbart, M., 612
Rothbaum, B. O., 511, 580
Rothblum, E. D., 408
Rotter, J. B., 481
Rotton, J., 498
Roug, L., 342
Routh, D. K., 345, 407
Rovine, M. J., 117
Rowe, W., 246
Rowsell, H. C., 64
Roy, C., 590
Roy-Byrne, P. P., 304
Rozin, P., 396, 397, 433, 619

Rubanowitz, D. E., 611
Rubin, J. R., 136
Rubin, L. C., 562
Rubin, R. T., 642
Rubin, Z., 62, 63
Ruch, W., 436
Ruda, M. A., 198
Rudd, R. J., 84
Ruel, J., 82
Ruffman, T. K., 129
Rule, B. G., 643
Rumbaugh, D. M., 350
Rummel, A., 414
Rury, J. L., 377
Rushton, J. P., 55, 331, 642
Russek, M., 392
Russell, J. A., 324, 325, 424, 430, 617
Russell, J. S., 277
Russell, M. J., 194
Russell, T. G., 246
Russo, N. F., 26, 27
Rust, J., 403
Rutkowski, G. K., 639
Rutstein, J., 618
Ryan, E. D., 418
Ryan, E. R., 487
Ryan, R. H., 316
Ryback, D., 469
Rychlak, J. F., 19

Saal, F. E., 401
Sabshin, M., 145
Saccuzzo, D. P., 371, 471
Sacks, O., 162, 199
Safford, F., 435
Sagen, J., 101
Saito, S., 168
Saletu, B., 84
Salisbury, H. G., 579
Salovey, P., 547
Salter, A., 552
Salthouse, T. A., 147, 290
Saltz, E., 472
Samelson, F., 27
Sanberg, P. R., 55
Sandford, D. A., 272
Sangal, S. P., 180
Santee, J. L., 280
Santhouse, R., 398
Sappington, A. A., 36
Sarason, S., 383
Sargent, J., 314
Sarter, M., 427
Satir, V., 554
Saunders, D. M., 56
Savage-Rumbaugh, E. S., 352
Saxe, L., 449
Sayette, M. A., 574
Scarborough, E., 26, 27
Scarborough, H. S., 343
Scarr, S., 36, 140, 379, 380, 461
Schaal, B., 193
Schaalman, M. L., 335
Schab, F. R., 194
Schachter, D. L., 211, 248, 293, 294, 313
Schachter, S., 395, 445, 596, 614, 623
Schaeffer, M. H., 335
Schaie, K. W., 119, 147
Schalken, H. F., 202
Schaller, M., 638
Schauble, P. G., 199
Schein, E., 620

Wegner, D. M., 509
Wehr, T. A., 514
Weigand, D., 418
Weigel, R. H., 623
Weiger, W. A., 642
Weinberg, M. S., 406
Weinberg, R., 418
Weinberg, R. A., 365, 380
Weinberg, R. S., 418, 589
Weinberger, J., 247
Weinberger, N. M., 189
Weiner, B., 608, 610, 641
Weiner, D. B., 535
Weiner, N., 557
Weiner, R. D., 557
Weinstein, L., 409
Weinstein, N. D., 592
Weir, P., 199
Weisberg, R. W., 327
Weisburd, S., 162
Weise, R. E., 502
Weisman, J., 621
Weiss, J. M., 580
Weiss, M. R., 407
Weissman, M. M., 506
Weitzenhoffer, A. M., 228
Weldon, E., 631
Wellman, M. M., 79
Wells, G. L., 316
Wells, J. K., 599
Welsh, D. H., 264
Wenegrat, B., 552
Wenstrup, J. J., 87
Werker, J. F., 132
Werner, W. E., 199
Wertheimer, M., 19
Wesnes, K., 239
Westbury, C. F., 337
Westefeld, J. S., 540
Wever, E. G., 190
Wheat, J. E., 655
Wheeler, L., 618
Whishaw, I. Q., 276
Whisman, M. A., 546
Whissell, C. M., 434
Whitbourne, S. K., 151
White, D. K., 223
White, G. L., 618
White, J. B., 623

White, S. H., 114
Whitehurst, G. J., 345
Whitlock, F. A., 235, 238, 594
Whitman, R. M., 506
Whittler, T. E., 621
Whorf, B. L., 346
Whyte, W. H., 628
Wible, C. G., 286
Widdison, H. A., 579
Wideman, M. V., 122
Widiger, T. A., 483, 497, 502
Widmeyer, W. N., 613
Wiebe, D. J., 327, 587
Wiegman, O., 644
Wiens, A. N., 542
Wiesel, T. N., 178
Wightman, D. C., 266
Wightman, F. L., 190
Wilckens, E., 198
Wilcox, B. L., 646
Wilcox, J. A., 398
Wilde, A., 542
Wilding, J., 308
Wildman, R. W., II, 540
Wilkie, D. M., 257
Wilkins, J. N., 594
Willerman, L., 379, 459
Williams, C. D., 272
Williams, D. G., 473
Williams, J., 226
Williams, K., 631
Williams, K. D., 631
Williams, R. B., Jr., 602
Williams, R. M., 42
Williams, S. L., 199, 509
Williamson, G. M., 588
Williamson, S. J., 290
Willis, R. P., 306
Willner, P., 393, 516
Willott, J. F., 87
Wills, T. A., 435
Wilson, E. O., 389, 642
Wilson, G. D., 401
Wilson, J. P., 641
Wilson, J. R., 74, 519
Wilson, M., 472
Wilson, R. G., 360
Wilson, R. W., 42
Wilson, S. K., 449

Wilson, T. D., 610
Wilson, V. E., 280
Winders, S. E., 594
Windholz, G., 326
Windholz, M. J., 588
Winefield, A. H., 273
Wing, L. L., 240
Wing, R. R., 596, 597
Winget, C. N., 506
Winkel, F. W., 611
Winn, B., 280
Winn, K. I., 618
Winograd, E., 243
Winton, W. M., 445
Wintrob, H. L., 618
Wise, R. A., 79
Wisely, D. W., 598
Wisniewski, N., 646
Withers, G. S., 123
Witt, L. A., 611
Wittig, M. A., 138
Wittlinger, R. P., 306
Wixted, J. T., 293, 300
Wojcikiewicz, A., 230
Wolf, J., 522
Wolfe, D. A., 40, 272
Wolfe, J., 264
Wolfe, T., 586
Wolfensberger, W., 368
Wolff, J., 552
Wolkowitz, O. M., 392
Wollen, K. A., 308
Wolpe, J., 540
Wolpin, M., 224
Wood, J. M., 223
Wood, W., 621, 622
Woodall, K. L., 603
Woods, B. T., 522
Woods, P. A., 273
Word, L. E., 640
Worringham, C. J., 630
Wosnack, K., 461
Wright, A. A., 298
Wright, L., 601
Wright, P. M., 481
Wu, J. C., 219
Wuensch, K. L., 134
Wughalter, E. H., 475
Wurtz, R. H., 105

Wyatt, G. E., 401
Wyatt, J. W., 118, 462

Xagoraris, A., 441

Yadin, E., 427
Yahya, K. A., 636
Yaksh, T. L., 80
Yalom, I. D., 550, 552
Yantis, S., 338
Yap, J. N., 598
Yarmey, A. D., 303
Yates, J., 211
Yerkes, R. M., 407
Yonas, A., 121, 182
Young, L. D., 581
Young, R. D., 616
Youngren, M. A., 517
Yu, S., 237

Zadra, A. L., 224
Zajonc, R. B., 380, 381, 442, 443, 446,
    615, 630
Zaldivar, R. A., 629
Zallen, G., 314
Zander, A., 627
Zanna, M. P., 616, 623
Zarantonello, M. M., 477
Zatorre, R. J., 103, 104
Zbikowski, S. M., 414
Zebrowitz, L. A., 625
Zeichner, A., 472
Zellner, D., 619
Zigler, E., 133, 381
Zigler, E. F., 114
Zimbardo, P. G., 445
Zimmerman, M., 578
Zimmerman, R. R., 131
Zimpfer, D. G., 550
Zingaro, M., 415
Ziporyn, T., 196
Ziv, A., 437
Zola-Morgan, S. M., 311
Zucco, G. M., 194
Zuckerman, M., 409, 415, 430, 478, 489
Zuroff, D. C., 490
Zweigenhaft, R. L., 47
Zwislocki, J. J., 190
Zyzanski, S. J., 592

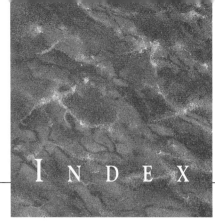

Autonomic nervous system, 70, 71, 72
    emotion and, 424–425, 426
Autonomy versus shame and doubt,
    130, 132
Availability heuristic, 335, 336
Average, arithmetic, 57, A-9–A-10
Average intellectual environment, 380
Aversion therapy, 542
Avoidance-avoidance conflict, 576
Avoidance learning, 268
Awareness, perception without,
    243–244
Axonal conduction, 74
Axons, 73–74

Backward chaining, 266
Backward conditioning, 257
Bacon, Francis, 7, 40
Bacon, Roger, 6
Bandura, Albert, 479
Barbiturates, 237
Barnum effect, 456
Basal ganglia, 88
Basal metabolic rate, 394–395
Basic research, 21
Basilar membrane, 189
Bedwetting, 256
Beers, Clifford, 536, 537
Behavior
    attitudes and, 619
    hypnosis and, 230
    influence of attitudes on, 622–623
    influence on attitudes, 623–625
    prosocial. See Prosocial behavior
    sexual. See Sexual behavior
    social. See Social behavior
    Type A. See Type A personality
Behavioral aggregation, 490
Behavioral approach to personality,
    479–482
    assessment and, 480–482
    operant conditioning and, 479
    social-cognitive theory and,
        479–480
    status of, 482
Behavioral contingencies, 263
Behavioral genetics, 115–117
    personality and, 458–459
Behavioral group therapy, 552
Behavioral observation, 481
Behavioral perspective, 17–18,
    521–523
    on causes of mood disorders,
        517–518
    on psychological disorders, 500
Behavioral preparedness, 274, 542
Behaviorism, 13–14, 17
    cognitive, 18
Behavior modification, 273. See also
    Operant-conditioning therapies
Behavior therapy, 539–545
    classical conditioning in, 539–542
    operant conditioning in, 542–543
    social-learning, 544–545
Belongingness, operant conditioning
    and, 273–274
Belongingness needs, 390, 391
Benzedrine, 239
Benzodiazepines, 557
Beta rhythm, 86
Beta waves, 215
Bias
    actor-observer, 611
    experimenter, 54–55

in intelligence testing, 363–364
response, 163
self-serving, 611
in social attribution, 610–611
subject, 53
Biased samples, 46
Bimodal distribution, A-9
Binet, Alfred, 360
Binocular cues, 180–181
Biofeedback, 278–281
    applications of, 279–280
    historical background of, 279
    nature of, 279
    research on, evaluation of, 280–281
Biological constraints
    on classical conditioning, 262
    on operant conditioning, 273–274
Biological rhythms, 84
Biomedical model. See also Medical
    model
    of health and illness, 574
Biopsychological approach to
    personality, 456–462
    assessment and, 459–461
    heredity and, 458–459
    physique and, 458
    status of, 461–462
Biopsychological perspective, 20
    on causes of mood disorders,
        515–517
    on causes of schizophrenia,
        521–523
    on psychological disorders, 499
    therapy and, 554–558
Biopsychological processes, 69–109
Biopsychology, 5, 22, 70. See also Brain;
    Endocrine system; Hormones;
    Nervous system
Biopsychosocial model of health and
    illness, 574
Bipolar cells, retinal, 169, 170
Bipolar disorder, 515
Bleuler, Eugen, 519
Blindness, color, 176–177
Blind spot, 171, 172
Blocking, 275, 276
"Blue Monday effect," 433
B-lymphocytes, 582, 583
Bodily-kinesthetic intelligence, 374
Body movements, emotional expression
    and, 429–430
Body senses, 199–201
Bottom-up perception, 178–180
Bradykinin, 198
Braid, James, 228
Brain, 70, 84–108
    adaptation and, 71
    development of, 123
    emotion and, 426–427
    evolution of, 91
    functions of, 85–97
    gray matter of, 76
    hemispheric specialization of, 102–
        108, 427
    hunger and, 392–393
    imaging of, 94–95
    integration of areas of, 96–97
    localization of functions in, 97–98
    mapping and, 93–94
    memory and, 310–312
    mood disorders and, 516–517
    opiate receptors in, 80–81
    plasticity of, 99–100

schizophrenia and, 522
sexual orientation and, 406
split-brain research and, 105–108
storage and, 294
vision and, 166, 171–173
white matter of, 76
Brain damage
    mental retardation and, 366
    recovery of functions after, 99–100
Brainstem, 88
Brightness constancy, vision and, 183
Brightness of light, 166
Broca, Paul, 8
Broca's aphasia, 96
Broca's area, 96, 97
Broken record, 552
Bulimia nervosa, 397–398
Bystander intervention, 638–641

Caffeine, 239
Caffeinism, 239
Calkins, Mary Whiton, 12, 25–27
Camphoraceous odors, 194
Cancer, stress and, 584–585
Cannabis sativa, 242
Cannon-Bard theory of emotion,
    440–441
Cardinal traits, 474
Careers in psychology, 21–25,
    A-1–A-3
Case studies, 43–45, A-4
Castration anxiety, 466
Cataplexy, 222
Catatonic excitement, 521
Catatonic schizophrenia, 496, 521
Catatonic stupor, 521
Cattell, James McKeen, 9
Causation, correlation and, 48–49
Cell-adhesion molecule, 120
Cell body of neuron, 72–73
Central nervous system, 70. See also Brain
Central route, persuasive messages
    and, 620
Central tendency, measures of, 57–58,
    A-9–A-10
Central traits, 474
Cerebellum, 87
    memory and, 310–311
    vestibular sense and, 200
Cerebral cortex, 91–94
    emotion and, 427
Cerebral palsy, 367
Cerebrotonia, 458
Cerebrum, 91
C fibers, 198
Chaining, 266
Chemical senses, 193–196
Child abuse, 133
Childbirth, natural, 122
Child development, 122
    cognitive, 128–130, 381–383
    of language, 342–343, 345–346
    physical, 124
    psychosexual, 466–467
    psychosocial, 132–140
Child psychology, 114
Child rearing, 133
    operant conditioning for, 271–272
Chloride, resting potential and, 74
Chloroform, 237
Cholecystokinin, hunger and, 392
Choline, memory and, 313
Chromosomes, 116, 120
Chunk, 291

Cigarette smoking. See Smoking
Circadian rhythms, 213–214
Circumspection-preemption-control
    cycle, 482–483
Clairvoyance, 202
Classical conditioning, 254–262
    acquisition of conditioned response
        in, 256–257
    applications of, 258–262
    attitude formation and, 619
    backward, 257
    biological constraints on, 262
    cognitive explanations of, 275
    delayed, 256
    extinction and spontaneous
        recovery in, 258
    higher-order, 256
    simultaneous, 257
    stimulus generalization and
        stimulus discrimination in,
        257–258
    trade, 256–257
Classical-conditioning therapies,
    539–542
    aversion therapy, 542
    counterconditioning, 539–542
    immune response and, 583, 584
Claustrophobia, 507
Client-centered therapy, 19, 547–548
Clinical psychologist, 563
Clinical psychology, 23
Closure, form perception and, 178, 179
Cocaine, 240
Cochlea, 189
Cochlear implants, 192, 193
Cocktail party phenomenon, 212
Cognition. See also Intelligence;
    Thinking
    attitudes and, 619
    disturbances of, in schizophrenia, 519
    hypnosis and, 229–230
    sex differences in, 138–139
    social, 608–614
Cognitive appraisal, of stressors, 581,
    585–586
Cognitive-appraisal theory of emotion,
    446, 447
Cognitive approach to personality,
    482–484
    assessment and, 483
    personal-construct theory and,
        482–483
    status of, 483–484
Cognitive behaviorism, 18
Cognitive-behavior therapies, 545–547
    cognitive, 546
    rational-emotive therapy, 545–546
    stress-inoculation training, 547
Cognitive development, 126–130. See
    also Intelligence; Thinking
    in adolescence, 142–143
    in adulthood, 147–148
    in childhood, 128–130, 381–383
    in infancy, 126–128
Cognitive-developmental theory of
    gender-role development, 137
Cognitive dissonance theory, 623–624
Cognitive-evaluation theory, 414–415
Cognitive learning, 274–278
    associative, 274–275, 276
    latent, 276, 277
    observational, 276–278
"Cognitive maps," 276

Dying, 152, 153
Dyspareunia, 403

Ear, 188–189
    vestibular sense and, 199–200
Eardrum, 188
Early-morning awakening, 221
Eating disorders, 396–398
Ebbinghaus, Hermann, 9, 298
Echoic memory, 289–290
Eclectic orientation, 536
Ecological theory of visual
        perception, 178
ECT. See Electroconvulsive therapy
        (ECT)
Ectomorph, 458
Education
    enrichment programs and, 381–383
    of mentally retarded persons,
        368–369
    operant conditioning for, 272
    of psychologists, A-1–A-3
Educational psychology, 23
EEG. See Electroencephalography
        (EEG)
Egg, 120
Ego, 463–464
Egocentrism, 129
Ego-dystonic homosexuality, 497
Ego ideal, 464
Eidetic memory, 291
Ejaculation
    premature, 403, 404
    retarded, 403
Elaborative rehearsal, 292–293
Elavil, 558
Electra complex, 466
Electroconvulsive therapy (ECT),
        556–557
Electrodes, 85
Electroencephalography (EEG), 85–86
    during sleep, 215–216, 217
Electromagnetic spectrum, 165–166
Elevation as cue for depth perception,
        182
"Emanation hypothesis," 166
Embryonic stage, 120–121
Emotion, 423–452
    attitudes and, 619
    autonomic nervous system and,
        424–425, 426
    brain and, 426–427
    chemistry of, 428
    cognitive theories of, 444–446
    experience of, 433–437
    expressed, in schizophrenia, 523
    expression of, 428–432
    facial-feedback theory of, 442–443
    lie detectors and, 447–451
    physiological theories of, 437–442
Emotional development. See
        Psychosocial development
Empathy
    altruism and, 637
    in person-centered therapy, 548
    sex differences in, 139
    of therapist, 567–568
Empiricism, 6
"Empty nest syndrome," 150
Encoding, 287
    long-term memory and, 292–293,
        294, 295
Encoding specificity, 303
Encounter groups, 552–553

Endocrine system, 81–84. See also
        Hormones
    components of, 81, 82
Endomorph, 458
Endorphins, 80–81
    counterconditioning and, 541
    emotion and, 428
Engineering psychology, 23
Engram, 310–311
Enuresis, nocturnal, 256
Environmental factors. See also
        Experience; Nature-nurture
        issue
    hunger and, 393–394
Environmental psychology, 23
Enzymes, 77
Epictetus, 500, 545
Epinephrine, 83, 84
    emotion and, 428
Episodic memory, 294
Equipotentiality, 99–100
Erectile dysfunction, 403
Ergotism, 241
Erikson, Erik, 130, 144, 468
Erogenous zones, 466
Escape learning, 268
ESP. See Extrasensory perception (ESP)
Esteem needs, 390, 391
Estrogens, 82, 83
    adolescent physical development
        and, 141–142
    sexual behavior and, 399
    sexual orientation and, 405
Ether, 237
Ethereal odors, 194
Ethics of research, 61–65
Ethnocentrism, prejudice and, 626
Ethology, 43
Ethyl alcohol. See Alcohol
Eugenics, 376
Eustachian tubes, 188–189
Eustress, 575
Evaluation apprehension, 630
Excitatory neurotransmitters, 77
Excitement phase of sexual response
        cycle, 401–402
Exercise
    lack of, 593
    for stress management, 589–590
Exhaustion stage in general adaptation
        syndrome, 581
Existential psychology, 19
Existential therapy, 550
Exocrine glands, 81
Expectation, consciousness and, 212
Experience
    aggression and, 643, 644
    brain development and, 123
    openness to, 479
    perception and, 186–187
Experience-sampling method, 481
Experiential intelligence, 373
Experiment, field, 38
Experimental group, 50, 51
Experimental method, 49–51, 52
Experimental psychology, 22
Experimental research, 49–57, A-4
    experimental method in, 49–51, 52
    external validity and, 56–57
    internal validity and, 51, 53–56
Experimenter bias effect, 54–55
Experimenter effects, 53–56
Expert systems, 336–337, 338

Explanation as research goal, 41
Explanatory style, health and, 586
Explicit memory, 248
Explicit-memory tests, 299
External auditory canal, 188
External validity, 56–57
Extinction
    in classical conditioning, 257–258
    in operant conditioning, 268–269
    in operant-conditioning therapies,
        543
Extracellular fluid, 74
Extrasensory perception (ESP),
        201–204
    alleged abilities and, 201–202
    research on, 202–204
Extraversion, 18, 470, 473, 478–479
Extrinsic motivation, 414
Eye, 167–171, 172
    movements of, 170–171
Eyewitness testimony, 314–317

Facial expressions, 430–432
    infant imitation of, 125
Facial-feedback theory of emotion,
        442–443
Facilitation, social, 630
Factor-analytic theories of intelligence,
        371–372
Fallopian tubes, 120
False alarm, 163
Familial retardation, 366
Familiarity, liking and, 615
Family studies, 117–118. See also
        Adoption studies; Twin studies
    of intelligence, 378–383
Family therapy, 553–554
Farsightedness, 168–169
Feature-detector theory of form
        perception, 178, 180
Fechner, Gustav, 8, 162–163
Feelings. See also Emotion
    reflection of, in person-centered
        therapy, 548
Festinger, Leon, 624
Fetal alcohol syndrome, 122, 367
Fetal stage, 121–122
Fetishism, 400
Fictional finalism, 469
Field experiment, 38
Fight-or-flight response, 424, 426,
        580, 581
Figure-ground perception, 178–180
Firing threshold, 75, 76
First impressions, 613
Fisher, Ronald, 59, 61
Five-factor theory of personality, 479
Fixation, 466
Fixed-interval schedule of reinforce-
        ment, 268
Fixed-ratio schedule of reinforcement, 267
Fixed-role therapy, 483
Flashbulb memories, 286
Flat emotionality in schizophrenia,
        519–520
Floatation REST, 409, 416
Flooding, 543
Floral odors, 194
Flourens, Pierre, 8
Fluid intelligence, 147, 372
Foot-in-the-door technique, 633, 634
Forebrain, functions of, 88–97
Forensic psychology, 23

Forgetting, 298–305
    cue-dependence theory of, 303–304
    decay theory of, 300–301
    interference theory of, 301
    motivation theory of, 301–303
Forgetting curve, 300
Formal operational stage, 127, 143
Form perception, 178–180
Forward chaining, 266
Fovea, 170
Framing effects, 335–336
Fraternal twins, 118
Free association, analysis of, 538
Free nerve endings, 198
Frequency distributions, A-6
Frequency histogram, A-7
Frequency of sound waves, 188
Frequency polygon, A-7, A-8
Frequency theory of pitch perception,
        190
Freud, Anna, 18, 462
Freud, Sigmund, 15–16, 462
Freudian slips, 16, 463
Fromm, Erich, 18, 468
Frontal lobe, 92–93
Frustration, 575
Frustration-aggression hypothesis, 643
Fugue, psychogenic, 512
Functional fixedness, 329–331
Functionalism, 11–12, 17
Fundamental attribution error, 610–611
Furumoto, Laurel, 26

GABA. See Gamma aminobutyric acid
        (GABA)
Gage, Phineas, 88
Galen, 497–498
Gall, Franz Joseph, 97–98
Galton, Francis, 8–9, 359–360
Galvani, Luigi, 74
Gambling, schedules of reinforcement
        and, 268
Gamma aminobutyric acid
        (GABA), 79
    alcohol and, 235
Ganglion cells, retinal, 169, 170
Gate-control theory of pain, 198
Gays, 405
Gender identity, 404, 405
Gender roles, development of, 136–137
Gender-schema theory of gender-role
        development, 137
General adaptation syndrome, 581
General intelligence factor, 371–372
Generalization, stimulus, 257–258
Generalized anxiety disorder, 505–506
Generativity, language and, 338, 340
Generativity versus stagnation, 130,
        150, 151
Genetic factors
    behavioral genetics and, 115–117,
        458–459
    family studies and, 117–118. See
        also Adoption studies; Twin
        studies
    in giftedness, 369–370
    motivation and, 388–389
    personality and, 458–459
    in schizophrenia, 521
Genie, 344, 345
Genital stage, 467
Genius. See Mental giftedness
Genotype, 116

German measles
    fetal development and, 121–122
    mental retardation and, 367
Germinal stage, 120
Gesell, Arnold, 119
Gestalt psychology, 14–15, 17
    form perception and, 178, 179
Gestalt therapy, 548–549
Giantism, 81, 82
Gibson, James J., 178
Giftedness. See Mental giftedness
Glial cells, 72
Global factors, 517
"Glove anesthesia," 511
Glucose
    hunger and, 392
    memory and, 314
Glucose receptors, hunger and, 392
Glycine, 79–80
Glycogen, hunger and, 392
Goal setting, 413
Goddard, Henry, 361, 376
Golgi, Camillo, 76–77
Gonadotropic hormones, 82, 83
Gonads, 399
    hormones of, 82, 83
Good boy-nice girl orientation, 154
Gosset, William Sealy, 60–61
Goya, Francisco, 519
Grammar, transformational, 341
Graphology, 470–471
Graphs, A-6–A-8
Gray matter, 76
Ground, figure-ground perception
    and, 178
Group decision making, 627–630
    groupthink and, 629–630
    minority influence and, 628–629
    polarization and, 628
Group polarization, 628
Group therapy, 550–553
    behavioral, 552
    humanistic, 552–553
    psychoanalytic, 550–552
Groupthink, 629–630
Group violence, 644–645
Growth hormone, 81, 82, 83
Guilford, J.P., 371–372
Guilty but mentally ill rule, 528
Guilty Knowledge Test, 450–451
Gustation, 195–196

Habits, health-impairing, 591–597
Halfway houses, 559
Hall, G. Stanley, 12, 114
Hallucinations, 519, 521
Hallucinogens, 236, 240–242
Hammer (bone), 188
Happiness, 434–435
Hashish, 242
Head Start program, 381
Health, 573–604. See also Illness
    habits impairing, 591–597
    stress and. See Stress
Health psychologists, 5
Health psychology, 23, 574
Hearing, 187–193
    auditory perception and, 190–193
    auditory system and, 188–189
    sound localization and, 193
Helmholtz, Hermann von, 7–8, 175
Helping behavior. See Prosocial
    behavior

Hemispherectomy, 100
Hemispheric specialization, 102–108
    damaged brain and, 104, 105
    emotion and, 427
    intact brain and, 103–104
    split-brain research and, 105–108
Heredity. See Genetic factors; Nature-
    nurture issue
Hering, Ewald, 175
Heritability, 117
    of intelligence, 377–378
Heroin, 238, 260
Herpes virus infections, mental
    retardation and, 367
Hertz (Hz), 188
Heuristics
    decision making and, 335, 336
    problem solving and, 328
Hidden observer, 231, 232
Hierarchy of needs, 390, 391
Higher-order conditioning, 256
Hindbrain, functions of, 86–87
Hippocampus, 89–91
    memory and, 311–312
Hippocrates, 84–85, 497, 501–502,
    510–511, 534
Historicism, 4
HIV. See Human immunodeficiency
    virus (HIV)
Holophrastic speech, 342
Homelessness, 560
Homeostasis, 389
Homosexuality, 405–407, 497
Hormones
    adolescent physical development
        and, 141–142
    hunger and, 392
    pituitary, 81–84
    sex determination and, 120–121
    sex differences in social behavior
        and, 139
    sexual behavior and, 399
    sexual orientation and, 405
Horney, Karen, 18, 468
Hospice movement, 152, 153
Hospitalization, commitment and, 561
Hull, Clark, 389, 390
Human immunodeficiency virus
    (HIV), 583
Humanistic approach to personality,
    484–488
    assessment and, 486–487
    self-actualization and, 484, 486
    self theory and, 484–486
    status of, 487–488
Humanistic perspective, 18–19
    on causes of mood disorders, 518
    on causes of schizophrenia,
        523–524
    on psychological disorders, 501
Humanistic therapy, 547–560
    existential, 550
    Gestalt, 548–549
    group, 552–553
    person-centered, 547–548
Human potential movement, 552
Human subjects, ethical treatment of,
    61–63
Humor, 435–437
    health and, 587–588
Humors, 457
Hunger, 391–398
    bodily factors regulating, 391–392
    brain factors regulating, 392–393

eating disorders and, 396–398
environmental factor regulating,
    393–394
obesity and, 394–396
Hypermnesia, 230
Hyperopia, 168–169
Hypnagogic state, 211
Hypnosis, 226–233
    effects of, 229–230
    hypnotic induction and, 228–229
    nature of, 231–233
Hypochondriasis, 510
Hypochondriasis scale, 476
Hypothalamus, 81, 89
    drives and, 389
    emotion and, 426–427
    hormones of, 83
    hunger and, 393
    sexual orientation and, 406
Hypothesis, 37
    testing, A-14–A-16
Hypoxia, mental retardation and, 367
Hysteria, conversion, 15, 511

"Iceberg profile," 476
Iconic memory, 288–289
Id, 463
Ideal self, 485–486
Identical twins, 118
Identification, 466
Identified patient, 553
Identity versus role confusion, 130, 144
Illness
    autoimmune, 584
    cancer, 584–585
    personality and, 600–603
    psychoneuroimmunology and,
        582–584
    psychosomatic, 581, 582
    reactions to, 597–600
    stress and. See Stress
Illusions, visual, 183–185
Illusory contours, 180
Imaginal flooding, 543
Immune system, stress and, 582–584
Implicit memory, 248
Implicit-memory tests, 299–300
Impression formation, 611–614
    first impressions and, 613
    self-fulfilling prophecy and,
        613–614
    social schemas and, 612
    social stereotypes and, 612–613
Impression management, 611
Incentives, 390
Incongruity theory of humor, 436, 437
Incus, 188
Independent variable, 49–50
Individual psychology, 468–469
Industrial/organizational psychology, 23
Industry versus inferiority, 130, 133
Infant development, 122
    cognitive, in infancy, 126–128
    of language, 342, 345
    perceptual, 125–126
    physical, 123–124
    psychosexual, 466
    psychosocial, 130–132
Inferences
    transitive, 129
    unconscious, 178
Inferential statistics, 59–61,
    A-14–A-17

hypothesis testing and, A-14–A-16
statistical significance and, 59–60,
    A-16–A-17
Inferiority complex, 469
Influence, 631–636
    compliance and, 633–634
    conformity and, 631–633
    obedience and, 634–636
    social, 631–636
Information processing, memory and,
    287–288
In-group, 612
Inhalants, 237
Inhibition, social, 630
Inhibitory neurotransmitters, 77
Initiative versus guilt, 130, 132–133
Inner ear, 189
Insane asylums, 534–535
Insanity defense, 525–529
Insecurely attached infants, 131
Insight, problem solving and, 327, 328
Insomnia, 221
Instinctive drift, 274
Instincts, 254
Instrumental conditioning. See Operant
    conditioning
Insulin, 83, 84
    hunger and, 392
Integrity versus despair, 130, 151
Intellectual enrichment programs,
    381–383
Intellectualization, 465
Intelligence, 357–384
    artificial, 322, 336–338
    crystallized, 147
    factor-analytic theories of, 371–372
    fluid, 147
    fluid and crystallized, 372
    giftedness and, 369–370
    mental retardation and, 365–369
    multiple, theory of, 373–375
    nature-nurture issue and, 375–383
    triarchic theory of, 373–375
Intelligence quotient (IQ), 361–362
    enrichment programs and, 381–383
    mental retardation and, 365–366
Intelligence testing, 358–365
    bias in, 363–364
    historical background of, 359–362
    issues in, 362–365
Interference theory, 301
Interferon, 584
Internal-external dimension,
    attribution and, 610
Internal factors, 517
Internal Locus of Control Scale, 481
Internal validity, 51, 53–56
Interneurons, 72
Interpersonal intelligence, 374
Interposition as cue for depth
    perception, 181, 182
Interval scales, A-5
Interval schedule of reinforcement, 268
Interviews
    situational, 481
    in survey research, 45
Intimacy versus isolation, 130, 148–149
Intracellular fluid, 74
Intrapersonal intelligence, 374
Intrinsic motivation, achievement
    motivation and, 413–415
Introversion, 18
Introverts, 470
In vivo desensitization, 542

In vivo flooding, 543
Iodopsin, 173
Ion channels, 75
IQ. See Intelligence quotient (IQ)
Iris, 167

Jacobson, Edmund, 590
James, William, 11–12, 45
James-Lange theory of emotion, 437–439
Jigsaw method, 627
Jung, Carl, 18, 469, 470
Just noticeable difference (jnd), 165

Kant, Immanuel, 7
Keller, Helen, 162
Kelly, George, 19–20, 482
Kidneys, hormones of, 83
Kinesthetic sense, 199
Kinsey, Alfred, 401
Klein, Melanie, 18
Knowledge, sources of, 34–36
Koffka, Kurt, 15
Kohler, Wolfgang, 15, 327
Kraeplin, Emil, 501

La belle indifference, 510
Ladd-Franklin, Christine, 25, 177
Lamaze method, 122
Language, 338–349
   apes and, 349–352
   sexist, 348–349
   structure of, 340–342
   thinking and, 346–349
Language acquisition, 342–346
   critical period for, 344–345
   stages in, 342–343
   theories of, 345–346
Latchkey children, 134–135
Latency stage, 466–467
Latent content of dreams, 225, 538
Latent learning, cognitive factors in, 276, 277
Lateral hypothalamus (LH), hunger and, 393
Laudanum, 238
Law of effect, 263
L-dopa, 88
   schizophrenia and, 522
Learned helplessness
   health and, 587
   mood disorders and, 517–518
Learning, 253–282. See also Classical conditioning; Operant conditioning
   associative, 274–275, 276
   avoidance, 268
   biofeedback and, 278–281
   cognitive, 274–278
   escape, 268
   latent, 276, 277
   observational. See Observational learning
   overlearning and, 306, 307
Lens (of eye), 168–169
Lesbians, 405
Levels of processing theory, 293
Lewin, Kurt, 15
LH. See Lateral hypothalamus (LH)
Libido, 466
Librium, 557
Lie detectors, 447–451
   Guilty Knowledge Test and, 450–451

issues concerning, 448–450
procedures for, 448, 449
Life, style of, 469
Life change score, 578
Life events as stressors, 577–580
Light, 165–166
   mixing, 175, 176
Liking, 614–616
   familiarity and, 615
   physical attractiveness and, 615–616
   proximity and, 614
   self-disclosure and, 616
   similarity and, 616
Limbic system, 89–91
   emotion and, 426–427
Limb-withdrawal reflex, 72, 73
Limen, 162–165
Linear perspective, 181, 182
Line graphs, A-8
Linguistic intelligence, 374
Linguistic relativity hypothesis, 346–349
   sexist language and, 348–349
Link, semantic network theory and, 295, 296
Link method, 308–309
Listening, dichotic, 243–244
Lithium carbonate, 558
Liver, hunger and, 392
Loafing, social, 631
Lobes of brain, 92–94
Loci, method of, 307–308
Locke, John, 7, 35
Locus of control, 481–482
Loewi, Otto, 77
Logical concepts, 323–324
Logical-mathematic intelligence, 374
Longitudinal research, 119
Long-term memory, 287, 291–305
   eidetic memory, 291
   encoding and, 292–293, 294, 295
   forgetting and, 298–305
   retrieval and, 297–298
   storage and, 293–297
Long-term potentiation, 311
Lorenz, Konrad, 642
Loudness perception, 191–192, 193
Love. See Romantic love
Love needs, 390, 391
LSD. See Lysergic acid diethylamide (LSD)
Lucid dreaming, 224
Lunatics, 498
Lysergic acid diethylamide (LSD), 241

Magnetic resonance imaging (MRI), 95
Mainstreaming, 368
Maintenance rehearsal, 291, 292
Major depression, 496, 513–515
Major tranquilizers, 235
Maladaptiveness, psychological disorders and, 497
Malleus, 188
Malnutrition, mental retardation and, 367
Management by objectives, 413
Mania, 515
Manic depression, 515
Manifest content of dreams, 225, 538
MAO inhibitors, 557–558
Marijuana, 242

Marriage, 148–149. See also Divorce; Romantic love
   death of spouse and, 151–152
Masculine protest, 469
Maslow, Abraham, 18–19
Massed practice, 306–307
Mathematical abilities
   in precocious youth, 370
   sex differences in, 138–139
Maturation, 114
   of adolescents, 142
   learning and, 254
McDougall, William, 388
Mean, 57, A-9–A-10
Mean length of utterance (MLU), 343
Measurement, 40
Measurement scales, A-4–A-5
Measures of central tendency, 57–58, A-9–A-10
Measures of variability, 58, A-10–A-11
Median, 57, A-9
Medical model, 500. See also Biomedical model
Medical treatment
   adherence to regimens and, 599–600
   seeking, 598
Meditation, 233–235
   effects of, 234–235
   techniques for, 233–234
Medulla oblongata, 86
Melatonin, 83, 84
   circadian rhythms and, 213–214
Memory, 285–318
   anatomy of, 310–312
   chemistry of, 312–314
   explicit, 248
   eyewitness testimony and, 314–317
   flashbulb, 286
   implicit, 248
   improving, 305–310
   information processing and, 287–288
   long-term. See Long-term memory
   prenatal formation of, 122
   REM sleep and, 220
   sensory, 287, 288–290
   short-term, 287, 290–291
Memory trace, 310–311
Menopause, 146
Mental age, 360–361
Mental giftedness, 369–370
   genetic studies of, 369–370
   mathematic ability and, 370
Mental retardation, 365–369
   causes of, 366–368
   classification of, 365–366
   education and, 368–369
   intelligence quotient (IQ) and, 365–366
Mental set, 329
Mental telepathy, 85, 202. See also Extrasensory perception (ESP)
Mental tests, 360
Mere exposure effect, 615
Mescaline, 240–241
Mesmer, Anton, 227
Mesmerism, 227, 228
Mesomorph, 458
Message, persuasive, 621–622
Methedrine, 239
Method of loci, 307–308
Method of savings, 299

Midbrain, functions of, 87–88
Middle ear, 188
Mild mental retardation, 368
Mild retardation, 366
Milgram, Stanley, 636
Mind of the Child, The (Preyer), 114
Minnesota Multiphasic Personality Inventory (MMPI), 475–477
Minority influence, 628–629
MLU. See Mean length of utterance (MLU)
M'Naughten rule, 526
Mnemonic devices, 305, 307–310
Mode, 57, A-9
Modeling. See Observational learning
Moderate mental retardation, 368
Moderate retardation, 366
Monochromats, 177
Monocular cues, 181–182
Monozygotic twins, 118
Montreal procedure, 93–94
Mood-congruent memory, 305
Mood-dependent memory, 304
Mood disorders, 496, 513–518
   bipolar, 515
   causes of, 515–518
   major depression, 513–515
Mood swings, adolescent, causes of, 142
Moon illusion, 183–184
Moral development, 152–156
   basis of, 152
   Kohlberg's theory of, 153–156
Moral insanity, 524
Moral therapy, 535
Morbid obesity, 596
Morphemes, 340
Morphine, 238
Motion parallax, 181
Motion sickness, 200–201
Motivation, 387–420
   achievement motive and, 410–415, 417–419
   arousal motive and, 407–410, 415–417
   consciousness and, 212
   creativity and, 333
   extrinsic, 414
   forgetting and, 302
   hunger motive and, 391–398
   intrinsic, 413–415
   sex motive and, 398–407
   sources of, 388–390
   sport and, 415–419
Motivation research, 5
Motivation theory of forgetting, 301–303
Motor cortex, 92–93
Motor development in infancy, 123, 124
Motor homunculus, 93–94
Motor neurons, 72
MRI. See Magnetic resonance imaging (MRI)
Müller-Lyer illusion, 185
Multimodal distribution, A-9
Multimodal therapy, 563–564
Multiple intelligences, theory of, 373–375
Multiple personality, 44–45, 512–513
Multiple sclerosis, 76
Münsterberg, Hugo, 12
Musical intelligence, 374
Musky odors, 194
Myelin, 76

Phase delay, 214
Phenothiazines, 558
Phenotype, 116
Phenylketonuria (PKU), 367
Pheromones, 195
Phi phenomenon, 14–15
Phobias, 497, 507–509
    classical conditioning and, 259
    counterconditioning for, 540–542
    observational learning for
        treatment of, 540–542
Phonemes, 340
Phonology, 340
Phosphenes, 173
"Photographic memory," 291
Photopigments, 173
Photoreceptors, 169, 173–174
Phrenitis, 502
Phrenology, 97–99, 457
Physical attractiveness
    liking and, 615–616
    of source of persuasive message, 621
Physical dependence on drugs, 235
Physical development
    in adolescence, 141–142
    in adulthood, 146
    in infancy, 123–124
Physiognomy, 457
Physiological needs, 390, 391
Physiological reactivity to stressors, 585
Piaget, Jean, 19, 126–127
"Pickwickian syndrome," 221
Pictorial cues, 181–182
Pie graphs, A-6–A-7
Pigment mixing, 175, 176
Pineal gland
    circadian rhythms and, 213–214
    hormones of, 83, 84
Pinel, Philippe, 535
Pinna, 188, 189
Pitch perception, 190
Pituitary gland, 81
    hormones of, 81–84
PK. See Psychokinesis (PK)
PKU. See Phenylketonuria (PKU)
Placebos, 198, 199
Placenta, 120
Place theory of pitch perception, 190
Plasticity, 99–102
    neural transplantation and,
        100–102
    recovery of functions after brain
        damage and, 99–100
Plateau phase of sexual response
    cycle, 402
Plato, 5–6
Play, psychosocial development and,
    135–136
Pleasure principle, 463
Polygenic traits, 116–117
Polygraph test. See Lie detectors
Pons, 87
Ponzo illusion, 187
Population, 45–46
Pornography, sexual aggression and,
    645–649
Positive correlation, 48, 59, 60
Positive reinforcement
    in operant conditioning, 263–268
    in operant-conditioning therapies,
        542
    seat-belt use and, 270
Positive skew, A-7
Positive symptoms in schizophrenia, 522

Positive transference, 538
Positron emission tomography (PET),
    94–95
Postconventional level of moral
    development, 153, 154–155
Posterior pituitary gland, hormones of,
    81, 83
Posttraumatic stress disorder, 579–580
Potassium ions, 74
Practice, distributed and massed,
    306–307
Pragmatics, 341
Precociousness. See Mental giftedness
Precognition, 202
Preconscious mind, 247, 463
Preconventional level of moral
    development, 153, 154
Prediction as research goal, 40–41
Predictive validity, 47, 363
Preemption phase of circumspection-
    preemption-control cycle, 483
Preexperimental research, 50, 52
Prefrontal lobotomies, 555
Pregnancy. See Prenatal development
Prejudice, 625–627
    factors promoting, 625–626
    factors reducing, 626–627
Premack principle, 263–264
Premature ejaculation, 403, 404
Prenatal development, 120–122
    causes of mental retardation during,
        366–367
    embryonic stage of, 120–121
    fetal stage of, 121–122
    germinal stage of, 120
Preoperational stage, 127, 128–129
Presentational thought, 128
Presentism, 4
Pressure, 575–576
Prevention
    of psychological disorders, 559–560
    of smoking, 594
Primacy effect, 298
Primary appraisal of stressors, 585
Primary cortical areas, 92
Primary memory, 287
Primary mental abilities, 371
Primary prevention, 559
Primary reinforcer, 264
Primary sex characteristics, 141
Proactive interference, 301
Problem solving, 325–331
    algorithms and, 327–328
    dreams and, 227
    heuristics and, 328
    impediments to, 328–331, 332
    insight and, 327, 328
    by trial and error, 326
Procedural memory, 293
Processing
    automatic, 244
    controlled, 244
    serial and parallel, 337–338
Products, intelligence and, 372
Profile of Mood States, 475
Profound retardation, 366
Progesterone, 82, 83
Program evaluation, 50–51
Programmed instruction, 272
Progressive relaxation for stress
    management, 590
Projection, 465
    prejudice and, 626

Projective tests, 471
Prolactin, 83
Prosocial behavior, 636–641
    altruism, 637–638
    bystander intervention, 638–641
Prosody, emotional expression and,
    428–429
Prosopagnosia, 96, 162, 244
Proteins, resting potential and, 74
Prototypes, 324–325
Proximal stimulus, depth perception
    and, 180
Proximity
    form perception and, 178, 179
    liking and, 614
Psilocybin, 240
Psychiatric nurse, 563
Psychiatric social worker, 563
Psychiatrist, 563
Psychiatry, 23
Psychic determinism, 15–16, 247, 463
Psychoactive drugs, 235–242
    addiction to, 235, 595
    classical conditioning and, 259–260
    depressants, 122, 235–238
    fetal development and, 122
    hallucinogens, 236, 240–242
    mental retardation and, 366–367
    schizophrenia and, 521–522
    stimulants, 236, 238–240
    use during adolescence, 145
Psychoanalysis, 15–17, 536–538
    techniques in, 538
Psychoanalytic approach to personality,
    462–473
    analytical psychology and, 469–470
    assessment and, 470–471
    individual psychology and,
        468–469
    psychosexual theory and, 462–468
    status of, 472–473
Psychoanalytic group therapy, 550–552
Psychoanalytic perspective, 18
    on causes of mood disorders, 517
    on causes of schizophrenia,
        521–523
    on psychological disorders, 499–
        500
    on unconscious, 246–248
Psychodrama, 550–551
Psychodynamic activation, subliminal,
    247–248
Psychodynamic therapy, 538
Psychogenic amnesia, 512
Psychogenic fugue, 512
Psychokinesis (PK), 202
Psychological dependence on drugs, 235
Psychological disorders, 493–530
    anxiety, 504–510
    causes of, 498, 500
    classification of, 501–504
    criteria for, 496–497
    dissociative, 511–513
    insanity defense and, 525–526
    mood, 496, 513–518
    operant conditioning and, 273
    personality, 496, 524–525
    perspectives on, 497–501
    prevention of, 559–560
    research on diagnosis of, 503–504
    schizophrenia, 496, 502, 519–524
    somatoform, 510–511
    spontaneous remission and, 565
    treatment of. See Therapy

Psychological hardiness, 587, 588
Psychological stressors, 575–577
Psychological tests, 46–47
Psychologists, training of, A-1–A-3
Psychology
    careers in, 21–25, A-1–A-3
    contemporary perspectives of,
        17–20
    definition of, 4
    growth of, 9–17, 24–25
    philosophical roots of, 5–7
    as science, 33–66
    scientific roots of, 7–9
    women in, 24–27
Psychoneuroimmunology, 582–584
Psychopathology, 496
Psychopathy, 524
Psychophysics, 8, 162–165
Psychosexual development
    in childhood, 466–467
    in infancy, 466
Psychosexual theory, 462–467
    consciousness levels and, 463
    defense mechanisms and, 464–466
    development and, 466–467
    personality structure and, 463–464
Psychosis, 502
Psychosocial development, 130–140
    in adolescence, 143–145
    in childhood, 132–140
    child-rearing practices and, 133
    day care and, 133–135
    in early adulthood, 148–149
    gender-role development, 136–137
    in infancy, 130–132
    in late adulthood, 151–152
    in middle adulthood, 149–150, 151
    parental relationships and, 135
    peer interaction and, 135–136
    sex differences in, 137–140
Psychosomatic diseases, 581, 582
Psychosurgery, 555
Psychotherapy. See Therapy
Psychoticism, 473
Puberty, 141
Pungent odors, 194
Punishment, 269
    in operant-conditioning therapies,
        543
Pupil, 167–168
Pupillometry, 168
Purity of light, 166
Putrid odors, 194
Pygmalion effect, 54

Q-Sort, 486–487
Quasi-experimental research, 50–51, 52
Questionnaires in survey research, 45
Questions
    eyewitness testimony and, 316–317
    lie detectors and, 448, 449

Ramón y Cajal, Santiago, 76–77
Random assignment, 53
Random sampling, 46
Range, 58, A-10
Rapid eye movement sleep. See REM
    sleep
Rapid smoking, 595
Rational-emotive therapy (R-E-T),
    545–546
Rationalism, 5–6
Rationalization, 465
Ratio scales, A-5

Ratio schedule of reinforcement, 267–268
Reaction formation, 465–466
Reality principle, 463–464
Reasoning, 35
Recall
    constructive, 298
    distortion of, 302–303
Recency effect, 298
Receptors
    glucose, 392
    N-methyl-D-aspartate, memory and, 313
    sensory, 162
Recessive genes, 116
Reciprocal determinism, 479–480
Recognition test, 299
Reflection of feelings in person-centered therapy, 548
Reflexes, 72, 254
    vestibulo-ocular, 200
Refractory period of sexual response cycle, 403
Regression, 465
Rehearsal
    elaborative, 292–293
    maintenance, 291, 292
Reinforcement
    negative, 268
    positive, 263–268, 270
Reinforcement schedules, 266–268
Reinforcement theory of mood disorders, 517
Reinforcers, 263–265
Reinterpretation, 198
Relative size as cue for depth perception, 181
Relative-size hypothesis, moon illusion and, 184
Relaxation for stress management, 590
Relaxation response, meditation and, 234
Relearning, 299
Release theory of humor, 437
Reliability
    in research, 47
    of tests, 362–363
REM-rebound effect, 224
REM sleep, 216–217
    as adaptive inactivity, 220
    deprivation of, 218–219
    dreams and, 217, 223, 226
    memory and, 220
    REM-rebound effect and, 224
Replication, 37–38
Repolarization, 75, 76
Representativeness heuristic, 335
Repression, 302, 464, 465
Research, 21–22, 39–65
    applied, 21
    basic, 21
    on biofeedback, evaluation of, 280–281
    cohort-sequential, 120
    control as goal of, 41
    correlational, 48–49
    cross-sectional, 119–120
    description as goal of, 39–40
    descriptive, 41–48
    in developmental psychology, 117–120
    on diagnosis of psychological disorders, 503–504
    on emotion, 428

ethics of, 61–65
experimental, 49–57, 52
explanation as goal of, 41
on extrasensory perception, 202–204
family studies and, 117–118. See also Adoption studies; Twin studies
on heritability of intelligence, 377–378
longitudinal, 119
on pornography and aggression, 647–648
prediction as goal of, 40–41
preexperimental, 50, 52
quasi-experimental, 50–51, 52
scientific method and, 36–39
on sexual behavior, 400–403
statistical analysis of. See Statistics
Research hypothesis, 37
    testing, A-14–A-16
Resistance, stage of, in general adaptation syndrome, 581
Resistances, analysis of, 538
Resolution phase of sexual response cycle, 403
Response
    conditioned, 256, 257, 258, 275
    unconditioned, 256, 257, 259, 262
Response bias, 163
Responsibility
    bystander intervention and, 639–640
    diffusion, 631
Resting potentials, 74–75, 76
Restricted environmental stimulation (REST), 409, 416
R-E-T. See Rational-emotive therapy (R-E-T)
Retarded ejaculation, 403
Reticular formation, 87
Retina, 168
    cells of, 169
Retinal disparity, 181
Retrieval from long-term memory, 287–288, 297–298
Retroactive interference, 301
Re-uptake, 77
Revised frustration-aggression hypothesis, 643
Rhodopsin, 173
Ribonucleic acid (RNA), 116
Rights. See Patient rights
Risky shift, 628
RNA. See Ribonucleic acid (RNA)
Rods, 169, 173–174
Rogers, Carl, 19, 484–485, 547
Role Construct Repertory Test (REP Test), 483
Romantic love, 616–618
    promoting, 618
    theories of, 617–618
Rorschach, Hermann, 471
Rorschach Test, 471
Rubella (German measles)
    fetal development and, 121–122
    mental retardation and, 367
Rubin, Edgar, 178
Rush, Benjamin, 535, 536
Rutherford, Ernest, 190

Saccadic movements, 170, 171
Sadomasochism, 400
Safe sex, 592–593
Safety needs, 390, 391

Saint Augustine, 6
Saint Vitus' dance, 498
Sample, 45–46
Satiation, 264–265
Satir, Virginia, 554
Saturation of light, 166
Savants, autistic, 358
Savings, method of, 299
Scatter plots (scatter diagrams; scattergrams), A-13, A-14
Schedules of reinforcement, 266–268
Schemas, 127
    of conservation, 129–130
    social, 612
Schema theory, 296–297
Schizophrenia, 496, 502, 519–524
    causes of, 521–524
    characteristics of, 519–520
    types of, 520–521
Scholastic Assessment Test (SAT), predictive validity of, 363
School psychology, 23
Scientific method, 4, 36–39
    steps in, 37–39
Scientific paradigm, 17
Sclera, 167
Scotophobin, 312
Seasonal affective disorder, 514
Seat-belt use, positive reinforcement and, 270
Secondary appraisal of stressors, 585
Secondary memory, 287
Secondary prevention, 559
Secondary reinforcer, 264
Secondary sex characteristics, 141
Secondary traits, 474
Securely attached infants, 131
Security needs, 390, 391
Selective permeability of neuronal membrane, 74–75
Self, actual and ideal, 485–486
Self-actualization, 19
    need for, 390, 391
    in person-centered therapy, 548
Self-actualization theory of personality, 484, 486
Self-disclosure, liking and, 616
Self-efficacy, 480
Self-fulfilling prophecy, 54, 613–614
Self-handicapping, 486, 511
Self-help groups, 553
Self-management programs for smoking cessation, 595
Self-monitoring
    of attitudes and behavior, 623
    personality consistency and, 489
Self-perception theory, 624–625
Self-serving bias, 611
Self theory of personality, 484–486
Selye, Hans, 581
Semanticity, 338, 339–340
Semantic memory, 293–294
Semantic network theory, 295, 296
Semantics, 341–342
Semen, 402
Semicircular canals, 199–200
Sensate focusing in sex therapy, 404
Sensation, 162–165. See also specific senses
    visual, 173–178
Sensation seeking, 409–410
Sensitivity to pain, 165
Sensorimotor stage, 127–128

Sensory adaptation, 165, 166. See also Just noticeable difference (jnd)
Sensory deprivation, 408–409
Sensory homunculus, 93–94
Sensory memory, 287, 288–290
Sensory neurons, 72
Sensory receptors, 162
Sensory registers, 287
Sensory thresholds, 162–165
    absolute, 163–165
    difference, 165
Sensory transduction, 162
Septum, emotion and, 427
Serial-position effect, 298
Serial processing, 337–338
Serotonin, 79
    bulimia nervosa and, 398
    mood disorders and, 516–517
Set point
    hunger and, 393
    obesity and, 394–395
Severe retardation, 366
Sex determination, 120–121
Sex differences in psychosocial development, 137–140
Sexist language, 348–349
Sex therapy, 403–404
Sexual behavior, 398–407
    in adolescence, 145
    in adulthood, 146
    aggressive, pornography and, 645–649
    AIDS and, 401
    gender identity and, 404, 405
    Kinsey's surveys of, 400–401
    Masters and Johnson's research on sexual response cycle and, 401–403
    physiological factors affecting, 399
    sexual dysfunctions and, 403–404
    sexual orientation and, 405–407
    sociocultural factors affecting, 399–400
    unsafe sex and AIDS and, 592–593
Sexual orientation, 404, 405–407
Sexual response cycle, 401–403
Shading patterns as cue for depth perception, 182
Shape constancy, vision and, 182–183
Shaping, 265–266
Sheldon, William, 458
Sherrington, Charles, 77
Shift work, 214, 215
Short-term memory, 287, 290–291
    capacity of, 290–291, 292
Siblings, psychosocial development and, 136
Signal-detection theory, 163, 165
Significance, statistical, 59–60, A-16–A-17
Sign language, 322
Similarity
    form perception and, 178, 179
    liking and, 616
Simon, Theodore, 360
Simple phobia, 507
Simultaneous conditioning, 257
Sina, Abu Ibn, 6
Situational attribution, 608
Situational interview, 481
16 Personality factor Questionnaire (16 PF), 477, 478
16 PF. See 16 Personality factor Questionnaire (16 PF)

Theta waves, 215
Thinking, 322–338. *See also* Cognition
    artificial intelligence and, 322,
        336–338
    concept formation and, 323–325
    convergent and divergent, 333–334
    creativity and, 331, 333–334
    critical, 36–37
    decision making and, 334–336
    language and, 346–349
    panic disorder and, 506–507
    presentational, 128
    problem solving and, 325–331, 332
Thorazine, 558
Thorndike, Edward, 262–263
Thought broadcasting, 519
Three-factor theory of personality,
    473, 478
Thresholds, sensory. *See* Sensory
    thresholds
Thurstone, Louis, 371
Thyroid gland, hormones of, 81–82, 83
Thyroid-stimulating hormone, 81–82, 83
Thyroxin, 81–82, 83
Timbre perception, 192–193
Tip-of-the-tongue phenomenon, 303
Titchener, Edward, 10–11
T-lymphocytes, 582
Tobacco use. *See* Smoking
Tofranil, 558
Token economy, 272, 542
Tolerance to drugs, 235, 259
Tolman, Edward, 276
Top-down processing, 178–180
Touch sense, 197
Trace conditioning, 256–257
Training groups, 552
Trait theories of personality, 474,
    478–479
Tranquilizers, 235, 557
Transactional analysis (TA), 551–552
Transcendence needs, 390, 391
Transcendental meditation (TM), 234
Transcutaneous electrical nerve
    stimulation (TENS), 198–199
Transduction, sensory, 162
Transference, analysis of, 538
Transformational grammar, 341
Transitive inferences, 129
Transorbital leucotomy, 555
Transsexualism, 404, 405
Transvestitism, 400
Treatment. *See* Medical treatment;
    Therapy
Trephining, 534

Trial and error, 326
Triarchic theory of intelligence,
    373–375
Trichromatic theory of color vision,
    175, 178
Trichromats, 176
Tricyclic antidepressants, 558
Trigrams, 291
Trust versus mistrust, 130
Tryptophan, 79
t test, 60–61, A-17
Twain, Mark, 594
Twin studies, 118
    of intelligence, 379
Two-chair exercise, 549
Two-factor theory of emotion, 444–445
Two-factor theory of romantic love,
    617–618
Tympanic membrane, 188
Type A personality, 39–40, 472
    coronary heart disease and, 600–
        603
    development of, 603
    modification of behavior and, 603
Type B personality, 601–603
Type theories of personality, 473–474

UCR. *See* Unconditioned response
    (UCR)
UCS. *See* Unconditioned stimulus
    (UCS)
Ultraviolet light, 166
Unconditional positive regard, 485
    in person-centered therapy, 548
Unconditioned response (UCR), 256,
    257, 259, 262
Unconditioned stimulus (UCS),
    256–257, 258, 259, 262, 275
Unconscious
    collective, 469
    personal, 469
Unconscious inferences, 178
Unconscious mind, 242–248, 463
    Freudian view of, 246–248
    perception without awareness and,
        243–244
    subliminal perception and,
        244–246
Underextension, 342
Undifferentiated schizophrenia, 520
Universal ethical principle
    orientation, 155

Vaginismus, 403
Vagus nerve, 77
    hunger and, 392

Validity
    in research, 51, 53–57
    of tests, 47, 363–365
Validity scales, 476
Valium, 557
Variability, measures of, 58,
    A-10–A-11
Variable, 48
    confounding, 51, 53
    dependent, 50
    independent, 49–50
Variable-interval schedule of
    reinforcement, 268
Variable-ratio schedule of reinforce-
    ment, 267–268
Variance, A-10–A-11
Vasopressin, 81, 82
Ventromedial hypothalamus (VMH),
    hunger and, 393
Vestibular sense, 199–201
Vestibulo-ocular reflex, 200
Viscerotonia, 458
Visible spectrum, 165–166, 167
Vision, 165–187. *See also* Visual
    perception; Visual sensation
    brain and, 171–173
    eye and, 167–171, 172
Visual acuity, 168
Visual cliff, 125–126
Visual cortex, 94, 171, 173
Visual illusions, 183–185
Visual pathway, 171, 172
Visual pathways, 173
    experience and, 186
Visual perception, 178–187
    of depth, 180–182
    experience and, 186–187
    of forms, 178–180
    illusions and, 183–185
    perceptual constancies and, 182–183
Visual sensation, 173–178
    color vision and, 175–178
    dark adaptation and, 174
Visual sensory memory, 288–289
VMH. *See* Ventromedial hypothalamus
    (VMH)
Vocal qualities, emotional expression
    and, 428–429
Volitional rule, insanity defense and,
    526, 529
Volley theory of pitch perception, 190
von Békésy, Georg, 190
Voyeurism, 400

Wada test, 103–104, 427
Wain, Louis, 520
WAIS. *See* Wechsler Adult Intelli-
    gence Scale (WAIS)
Waldeyer, William, 70
Warn, duty to, 562–563
Washburn, Margaret Floy, 25
Watson, John B., 12–13
Wavelength of light, 165–166
Weaning, 466
Weber, Ernst, 8, 162
Weber's law. *See* Just noticeable
    difference (jnd)
Wechsler, David, 358
Wechsler Adult Intelligence Scale
    (WAIS), 362
Wechsler-Bellevue Intelligence
    Scale, 362
Wechsler Intelligence Scale for
    Children (WISC), 362
Wechsler Preschool and Primary Scale
    of Intelligence (WPPSI), 362
Weight loss, 596–597
Wernicke's aphasia, 96–97
Wernicke's area, 96, 97
Wertheimer, Max, 14–15
White matter, 76
Whorf, Benjamin Lee, 346
Wild Boy of Aveyron, 344, 345
WISC. *See* Wechsler Intelligence Scale
    for Children (WISC)
Wish fulfillment, dreams and, 227
Withdrawal symptoms, drugs and, 235
Women in psychology, 24–27
Working memory, 287, 290–291
    capacity of, 290–291
Working through, 538
WPPSI. *See* Wechsler Preschool and
    Primary Scale of Intelligence
    (WPPSI)
Wundt, Wilhelm, 9, 10

Xanax, 557
X rays, mental retardation and, 367

Yerkes, Robert, 376
Yerkes-Dodson law, 407, 416–417
Young-Helmholtz theory of color
    vision, 175

Zero correlation, 59, 60
z scores, A-12
Zygote, 120